Java™ Swing

THE JAVA™ SERIES

Exploring Java™

Java™ Threads

Java™ Network Programming

Java™ Virtual Machine

Java™ AWT Reference

Java™ Language Reference

Java™ Fundamental Classes Reference

Database Programming with JDBC™ and Java™

Java™ Distributed Computing

Developing Java Beans™

Java™ Security

Java™ Cryptography

Java™ Swing

Also from O'Reilly

Java™ in a Nutshell

Java™ in a Nutshell, Deluxe Edition

Java™ Examples in a Nutshell

Java™ Swing

Robert Eckstein, Marc Loy, and Dave Wood

O'REILLY®

Beijing · Cambridge · Farnham · Köln · Paris · Sebastopol · Taipei · Tokyo

Java™ Swing

by Robert Eckstein, Marc Loy, and Dave Wood

Copyright © 1998 O'Reilly & Associates, Inc. All rights reserved.
Printed in the United States of America.

Published by O'Reilly & Associates, Inc., 101 Morris Street, Sebastopol, CA 95472.

Editor: Mike Loukides

Production Editor: David Futato

Printing History:

September 1998:	First Edition
December 1998:	Package names changed to match FCS; other minor corrections

This book is printed on acid-free paper with 85% recycled content, 15% post-consumer waste. O'Reilly & Associates is committed to using paper with the highest recycled content available consistent with high quality.

ISBN: 1-56592-455-X   [5/99]

Table of Contents

Preface

Since Java was first released, its user interface facilities have been a significant weakness. The Abstract Window Toolkit (AWT) was part of the JDK from the beginning, but it really wasn't sufficient to support a complex user interface. It supported everything you could do in an HTML form, and provided free-standing frames, menus, and a few other objects, but you'd be hard-pressed to implement an application as complex as Quicken or Lotus Notes. AWT also had its share of portability problems; it relied heavily on the runtime platform's native user interface components, and it wasn't always possible to hide differences in the way these components behaved.

JDK 1.1 fixed a number of problems—most notably, it introduced a new event model that was much more efficient and easier to use—but it didn't make any major additions to the basic components. We got a `ScrollPane` and a `PopupMenu`, but that was about it. Furthermore, AWT still relied on the native components, and therefore continued to have portability problems.

In April of 1997, JavaSoft announced the Java Foundation Classes, or JFC, which supersedes (and includes) AWT. A major part of the JFC is a new set of user interface components that is much more complete, flexible, and portable. These new components are called "Swing." (The JFC also includes a comprehensive facility for 2D graphics, printing, and "drag-and-drop.") With Swing, you can design interfaces with tree components, tables, tabbed dialogs, tooltips, and many other features that computer users have grown accustomed to.

In addition to the new components, Swing makes three major improvements on the AWT. First, it doesn't rely on the runtime platform's native components. It's written entirely in Java, and creates its own components. This new approach should solve the portability problem, since components don't inherit the weird behaviors from the runtime environment. Second, because Swing is in complete control of the components, it's in control of the way components look on the screen, and gives you more control of how your applications look. You can choose between several pre-built "look-and-feels," or you can create your own if you want your software to show your personal style. This feature is called "Pluggable Look-and-Feel" or PLAF. Third, Swing makes a very clear distinction between the data a component displays (the "model") and the actual display (the "view"). While the fine points of this distinction are appreciated mostly by computer scientists, it has important implications for all developers. This separation means that components are extremely flexible. It's easy to adapt components to display new kinds of data that their original design didn't anticipate, or to change the way a component looks without getting tangled up in assumptions about the data it represents.

The first official release of Swing, for use with JDK 1.1, took place in the spring of 1998. Swing (and the rest of JFC) is a part of JDK 1.2, and is currently revolutionizing Java user interface development. This book shows you how to join the revolution.

What This Book Covers

This book gives a complete introduction to the entire Swing component set. Of course, it shows you how to use all of the components: how to display them on the screen, register for events, and get information from them. You'd expect that in any Swing book. This book goes much further. It goes into detail about the model-delegate architecture behind the components, and discusses all of the data models. Understanding the models is essential when you're working on an application that requires something significantly different from the components' default behavior: for example, if you need a component that displays a different data type, or one that structures data in some non-standard way, you'll need to work with the data models. This book also discusses how to create your own look-and-feel, and how to write "accessible" user interfaces.

There are a few topics that this book doesn't cover, and assumes you already know. First, we assume you know the Java language. For Swing, it's particularly important to have a good grasp of inner classes (both named and anonymous), which are used by Swing itself and in our examples. We assume that you understand the JDK 1.1 event model, Java's mechanism for communicating between asynchronous threads. Swing introduces many new event types, all of which are discussed in this book, but we only provide an overview of the event mechanism as a whole. We also assume that you understand the older AWT components, particularly the Component and Container classes, which are superclasses of the new Swing JComponent. We assume that you understand the AWT layout managers, all of which are usable within Swing applications. If you are new to Java, or would like a review, you can find a complete discussion of these topics in *Java AWT* by John Zukowski, or a solid introduction in *Exploring Java* by Pat Niemeyer and Joshua Peck (both published by O'Reilly). We do not assume that you know anything about other JFC topics, like Java 2D; all the drawing and font manipulation in this book can be done with the older (JDK 1.1) AWT. (We do cover the JFC's Accessibility API, which is supported by every Swing component.)

We were hoping to say that this book was based on JDK 1.2. Unfortunately, nothing is ever quite that simple. As this book goes to press, the most recent release of JDK is 1.2 beta 4, which incorporates Swing 1.1 beta. The most recent version of Swing that has been "blessed" as an officially released product is Swing 1.0.3. The differences between these versions are minor, and we've tried to point them out, but we do feel like we're swimming in version number soup.

One significant problem we've faced is Sun's waffling on the Swing package names. Swing was first released in the com.sun.java.swing package hierarchy, which was supposed to be a temporary resting place. With JDK 1.2, Swing was supposed to move into the java.awt.swing hierarchy. For some reason, Sun backed off, and kept Swing in the com.sun hierarchy for beta 4. They then moved it to javax.swing for the first official release of JDK 1.2—except for a few oddball platform-specific packages (like the Windows look-and-feel) that remain in com.sun. We've been at our wit's end trying to fix the package names, both in the book and in the online source files. At any rate, for JDK 1.2 and Swing 1.1 (for use with JDK 1.1), the major Swing classes are in the following packages:*

javax.accessibility

> Classes to support accessibility for people who have difficulty using standard user interfaces. Covered in Chapter 25, *Programming with Accessibility*.

javax.swing

> The bulk of the Swing components. Covered in Chapters 3 through 14, and 27 and 28.

javax.swing.border

> Classes for drawing fancy borders around components. Covered in Chapter 13, *Borders*.

javax.swing.colorchooser

> Classes providing suport for the JColorChooser component (Chapter 12).

javax.swing.event

> Swing events. Covered throughout the book.

javax.swing.filechooser

> Classes providing support for the JFileChooser comonent (Chapter 12).

---

* The latest rumor is that Sun will rechristen JDK 1.2 when the final official release occurs—it will probably be called Java 2.

javax.swing.pending

A home for components that aren't ready for prime time; these components aren't discussed in this book, though we'll add them to future editions when they graduate from the pending package.

javax.swing.plaf

Classes supporting "pluggable look and feel," including classes that implement the Metal and Multi look-and-feels. (Implementations of the Windows and Motif L&Fs are packaged under com.sun.java.swing.plaf.) Covered in Chapter 26, *Look & Feel.*

javax.swing.table

Classes providing support for the JTable component (JTable itself is in javax.swing). Covered in Chapter 15, *Tables*, and Chapter 16, *Advanced Table Examples.*

javax.swing.text

Classes providing support for the text components (JTextField, etc.; the components themselves are in the javax.swing package). Covered in Chapters 19 through 24. The text.html package has a subpackage, parser, that includes tools for parsing HTML. We expect significant upgrades to the HTMLEditorKit; when there's news, we'll make an update to this chapter available online. Check O'Reilly's web site for the latest information.

javax.swing.text.html and *javax.swing.text.rtf*

"Editor kits" for working with HTML and Microsoft RTF documents. Covered in Chapter 24, *EditorKits and TextActions.*

javax.swing.tree

Classes providing support for the JTree component (JTree itself is in javax.swing). Covered in Chapter 17, *Trees.*

javax.swing.undo

Classes that implement undoable operations. Covered in Chapter 18, *Undo.*

About the Source Code

All the examples for this book are available via anonymous FTP from *ftp://ftp.oreilly.com/pub/examples/java/swing/*. The examples are available as a JAR file, a ZIP archive, and as a compressed TAR archive. The files named swing-old use the old (com.sun) package hierarchy, and have been tested against JDK 1.2 beta 4. The files named swing have been converted to the new (javax) package hierarchy, and have been tested against the JDK 1.2 Release Candidate 1.

Conventions

The following font conventions are followed throughout this book:

Italic

> is used for filenames, file extensions, URLs, application names, and emphasis.

`Constant width`

> is used for Java class names, functions, variables, components, properties, data types, events, and snippets of code that appear in text.

We use tables throughout the book to present lists of properties (as defined by the JavaBeans specification). Here's an example from the hypothetical `JFoo` class that shows how we use these tables:

Table 1: Properties of the Fictional JFoo Class

Property	Data Type	get	is	set	bound	Default Value
`opaque*`	`boolean`	•	•	•	•	`true`

See also properties from the JComponent class (Table 3-5).

This table indicates that a `JFoo` object has a read/write bound property named `opaque`, with the data type `boolean`. This property has accessor methods with the signatures:

```
public boolean getOpaque();
public boolean isOpaque();
public void setOpaque( boolean opaque );
```

These methods aren't listed separately when we discuss the class's other methods. Because this is a bound property, changing its value generates a `PropertyChangeEvent`. `JFoo` has also inherited properties from the `JComponent` class; see the discussion of that class for these properties. The asterisk after the property name indicates that the `opaque` property is also inherited; it is listed here because the `JFoo` class has changed the behavior of the property in some way— either by adding accessor methods or changing the default value.

We've listed default values for properties wherever applicable. To save space, we abuse Java's syntax slightly and omit the `new` operator in these tables.

The Swing group has introduced some confusion into the notion of a "bound property" by adding a new lightweight event, `ChangeEvent`, that is a stateless version of the `PropertyChangeEvent`. In these tables, we adhere strictly to the JavaBeans definition of a bound property: modifying a bound property generates a `PropertyChangeEvent`. Properties that generate a `ChangeEvent` are noted in the "Events" sections.

In some of the property tables, we've separated out some special properties that are particularly important in terms of the model-view-controller architecture. These properties are UI, UIClassID, and model properties, such as model and document.

The class diagrams that appear throughout the book are similar to the ones used in *Java in a Nutshell* and other Java Series books from O'Reilly. Solid lines indicate inheritance relationships; dotted lines indicate interface relationships. In the following figure, ClassA extends AbstractClass, which implements InterfaceX. There are two interface relationships that we don't show in this way. All Swing classes implement Serializable, and showing this relationship explicitly would clutter the diagram; just assume that any Swing class implements Serializable, unless stated otherwise in the text. Many Swing classes implement the Accessible interface; rather than cluttering the diagrams, we show that a class implements Accessible by putting an A in the upper-right corner of a box.

We also use the class diagrams to show information about relations between classes. In the figure, the long-dashed arrow indicates that ClassA uses ClassB. The label on the arrow indicates the nature of the relationship; other common relations are "contains" and "creates". *1..* * indicates the multiplicity of the relationship. Here, an instance of ClassA uses one or more instances of ClassB. Other multiplicities are *1* (exactly one instance), *0..* * (any number of instances), and *0..1* (zero or one instance).

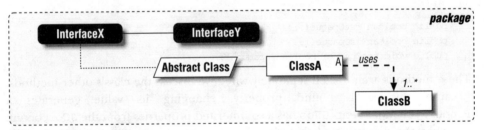

Figure 1: Class diagram notation

Acknowledgments

We're particularly indebted to our technical reviewers. Eric Brower, Dave Geoghegan, Jeff Johnson, Jonathan Knudsen, and Enrique Kortright all read the entire book (or most of it) and provided excellent feedback. The following members of the Swing development team contributed their time by providing specific comments on individual chapters: Philip Milne, Ray Ryan, Georges Saab, Scott Violet, and William Walker. Their feedback was invaluable. Finally, Dave Flanagan was looking at a draft to get up to speed on Swing for his own writing, and made some useful suggestions.

Dave Wood

I'd like to personally thank all the members of the Swing team who found time in their very busy schedules to review parts of the book—your comments were extremely valuable. Specifically, thanks to Ray Ryan for the detailed review of the Undo chapter. I'd also like to thank Jonathan Knudsen for providing great feedback on several chapters in very little time. A great big thanks to Bob (who I finally met in person at JavaOne) and Marc (who I hope to meet in real life *some day*) for being great to work with and to our editor, Mike Loukides, for somehow managing to keep track of this constantly evolving technology and three authors who were travelling all around the world writing about it. I'd also like to thank Stu Stern and Mark Bauhaus for giving me an opportunity to work and learn as a Java-guy at the Sun Java Center. Thanks, too, to my family for all your encouragement. Most importantly, I thank my wife, Shannon, for putting up with a husband who spent most of the last eight months either out of the country or in front of the computer (or both!). You truly are the best thing. Lastly, thanks to my cats, Pussin and Toast, for being there.

Robert Eckstein

I'd first like to thank my co-authors: Dave Wood, for his precise reviews of my chapters, and Marc Loy, for his humorous email that kept me sane for just a little while longer. I'd also like to thank the members of the Swing team that took the time the look over this book: specifically, Georges Saab for his treatment of menus and Willie Walker for offering wonderful insight into accessibility. In the words of David Flanagan: "Any errors that remain are of course my own." I'm also deeply indebted to Mike and Barbara Finn for emergency hardware support, as well as Jay Moore, John Hendricks, and Pat Mondoy at Motorola for letting me construct a project in Swing while working on this book, and of course Bill Rosenblatt for getting me this gig in the first place. A huge thanks goes out to my wife Michelle, who put up with a husband on six hours of sleep (or less) each night and still provided an endless amount of love and patience. Finally, an ocean of gratitude to Mike Loukides, editor and friend, who took sentences composed solely of caffeine and stale wit and (somehow) transformed them into chapters worthy of an O'Reilly book.

Marc Loy

I want to thank my cohorts Dave, Bob and Mike for making this rather large project fun to do—and believe me, with this many pages, that's a non-trivial task. Thanks to Jonathan Knudsen for his emergency reviews. And thanks, too, to the folks on the Swing team who made this a better book through vigilant reviews as well as giving us the components to write about in the first place. (Really! I'm still having a lot of fun with this!) I am continually indebted to my colleagues Tom Berry, Damian Moshak and Brian Cole for their support and input throughout this project. Though highly cliché, I also want to thank Mom and Dad for all the gifts (and genes) they have given me. My biggest thanks go to my partner Ron Becker for living with me in "book mode" yet again and making dinner when it really counted.

We all want to thank the many members of O'Reilly's production department, who put in lots of work under a tight schedule and integrated many last minute changes. Producing a book about a moving target is difficult work, to say the least. Rob Romano did all the illustrations and screen dumps (literally hundreds of them); David Futato was the production editor, and kept everything on track, as well as proofread the entire volume; and Colleen Miceli copyedited the manuscript. Seth Maislin wrote the index; Hanna Dyer designed the cover; Nancy Priest designed the interior; Nancy Wolfe Kotary and Mike Sierra provided tool support; Ellie Fountain Maden and Clairemarie Fisher O'Leary gave quality assurance; and Sheryl Avruch oversaw production management.

1

Introducing Swing

Welcome to Swing! By now, you're probably wondering what Swing is, and how you can use it to spice up your Java applications. Or perhaps you're curious as to how the Swing components fit into the overall Java strategy. Then again, maybe you just want to see what all the hype is about. Well, you've come to the right place; this book is all about Swing and its components. So let's dive right in and answer the first question that you're probably asking right now, which is...

What Is Swing?

If you poke around the Java home page *(http://java.sun.com/)*, you'll find Swing advertised as a set of customizable graphical components whose look-and-feel can be dictated at runtime. In reality, however, Swing is much more than this. Swing is the next-generation GUI toolkit that Sun Microsystems is developing to enable enterprise development in Java. By *enterprise development*, we mean that programmers can use Swing to create large-scale Java applications with a wide array of powerful components. In addition, you can easily extend or modify these components to control their appearance and behavior.

Swing is not an acronym. The name represents the collaborative choice of its designers when the project was kicked off in late 1996. Swing is actually part of a larger family of Java products known as the Java Foundation Classes (JFC), which incorporate many of the features of Netscape's Internet Foundation Classes (IFC), as well as design aspects from IBM's Taligent division and Lighthouse Design. Swing has been in active development since the beta period of the Java Development Kit (JDK) 1.1, circa spring of 1997. The Swing APIs entered beta in the latter half of 1997 and their initial release was in March of 1998. When released, the Swing 1.0 libraries contained nearly 250 classes and 80 interfaces.

Although Swing was developed separately from the core Java Development Kit, it does require at least JDK 1.1.5 to run. Swing builds on the event model introduced in the 1.1 series of JDKs; you cannot use the Swing libraries with the older JDK 1.0.2. In addition, you must have a Java 1.1–enabled browser to support Swing applets.

What Are the Java Foundation Classes (JFC)?

The Java Foundation Classes (JFC) are a suite of libraries designed to assist programmers in creating enterprise applications with Java. The Swing API is only one of five libraries that make up the JFC. The Java Foundation Classes also consist of the Abstract Window Toolkit (AWT), the Accessibility API, the 2D API, and enhanced support for drag-and-drop capabilities. While the Swing API is the primary focus of this book, here is a brief introduction to the other elements in the JFC:

AWT

The Abstract Window Toolkit is the basic GUI toolkit shipped with all versions of the Java Development Kit. While Swing does not reuse any of the older AWT components, it does build off of the lightweight component facilities introduced in AWT 1.1.

Accessibility

The accessibility package provides assistance to users who have trouble with traditional user interfaces. Accessibility tools can be used in conjunction with devices such as audible text readers or braille keyboards to allow direct access to the Swing components. Accessibility is split into two parts: the Accessibility API, which is shipped with the Swing distribution, and the Accessibility Utilities API, distributed separately. All Swing components contain support for accessibility, so this book dedicates an entire chapter (Chapter 24, *EditorKits and TextActions*) to accessibility design and use.

2D API

The 2D API contains classes for implementing various painting styles, complex shapes, fonts, and colors. This Java package is loosely based on APIs that were licensed from IBM's Taligent division. The 2D API classes are not part of Swing, so they will not be covered in this book.

Drag and Drop

Drag and drop is one of the more common metaphors used in graphical interfaces today. The user is allowed to click and "hold" a GUI object, moving it to another window or frame in the desktop with predictable results. The Drag and Drop API allows users to implement droppable elements that transfer information between Java applications and native applications. Drag and Drop is also not part of Swing, so we will not discuss it here.

Figure 1-1 enumerates the various components of the Java Foundation Classes. Because part of the Accessibility API is shipped with the Swing distribution, we show it overlapping Swing.

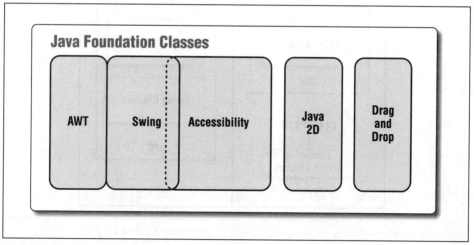

Figure 1-1. The five APIs of the Java Foundation Classes

Is Swing a Replacement for AWT?

No. Swing is actually built on top of the core 1.1 and 1.2 AWT libraries. Because Swing does not contain any platform-specific (native) code, you can deploy the Swing distribution on any platform that implements the Java 1.1.5 virtual machine or above. In fact, if you have JDK 1.2 on your platform, then the Swing classes will already be available and there's nothing further to download. If you do not have JDK 1.2, you can download the entire set of Swing libraries as a set of Java Archive (JAR) files from the Swing home page: *http://java.sun.com/products/jfc*. In either case, it is generally a good idea to visit this URL for any extra packages or look-and-feels that may be distributed separately from the core Swing libraries.

Figure 1-2 shows the relationship between Swing, AWT, and the Java Development Kit in both the 1.1 and 1.2 JDKs. In JDK 1.1, the Swing classes must be down-loaded separately and included as an archive file on the classpath (*swingall.jar*).[*] JDK 1.2 comes with a Swing distribution, although the relationship between Swing

---

[*] The standalone Swing distributions contain several other JAR files. *swingall.jar* is everything (except the contents of *multi.jar*) wrapped into one lump, and is all you normally need to know about. For complete-ness, the other JAR files are: *swing.jar*, which contains everthing but the individual look-and-feel packages; *motif.jar*, which contains the Motif (Unix) look-and-feel; *windows.jar*, which contains the Windows look-and-feel; *multi.jar*, which contains a special look-and-feel that allows additional (often non-visual) L&Fs to be used in conjunction with the primary L&F; and *beaninfo.jar*, which contains special classes used by GUI development tools.

and the rest of the JDK has shifted during the beta process. Nevertheless, if you have installed JDK 1.2, you should have Swing.

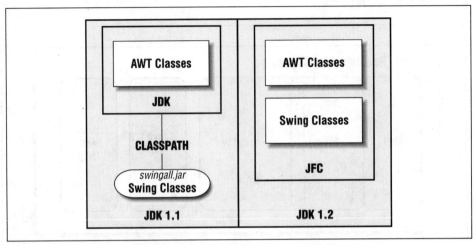

Figure 1-2. Relationships between Swing, AWT, and the JDK in the 1.1 and 1.2 JDKs

Swing contains nearly twice the number of graphical components as its immediate predecessor, AWT 1.1. Many are components that have been scribbled on programmer wish-lists since Java first debuted—including tables, trees, internal frames, and a plethora of advanced text components. In addition, Swing contains many design advances over AWT. For example, Swing introduces a new `Action` class that makes it easier to coordinate GUI components with the functionality they perform. You'll also find that a much cleaner design prevails throughout Swing; this cuts down on the number of unexpected surprises that you're likely to face while coding.

Swing depends extensively on the event handling mechanism of AWT 1.1, although it does not define a comparatively large amount of events for itself. Each Swing component also contains a variable number of exportable properties. This combination of properties and events in the design was no accident. Each of the Swing components, like the AWT 1.1 components before them, adhere to the popular JavaBeans specification. As you might have guessed, this means that you can import all of the Swing components into various GUI-builder tools—useful for powerful visual programming.[*]

---

[*] Currently, most of the IDEs are struggling to fully support Swing. However, we expect this to improve rapidly over time.

Rethinking the AWT

To understand why Swing exists, it helps to understand the market forces that drive Java as a whole. The Java Programming Language was developed in 1993 and 1994, largely under the guidance of James Gosling and Bill Joy at Sun Microsystems, Inc. When Sun released the Java Development Kit on the Internet, it ignited a firestorm of excitement that swept through the computing industry. At first, developers primarily experimented with Java for *applets*: mini-programs that were embedded in client-side web browsers. However, as Java matured over the course of the next two years, many developers began using Java to develop full-scale applications.

Or at least they tried. As developers ported Java to more and more platforms, its weak points started to show. The language was robust and scalable, extremely powerful as a networking tool, and served well as an easy-to-learn successor to the more established C++. The primary criticism, however, was that it was an interpreted language, which means that by definition it executed code slower than its native, compiled equivalents. Consequently, many developers flocked to *just-in-time* (JIT) compilers—highly optimized interpreters—to speed up their large-scale applications. This solved many problems. Throughout it all, however, one weak point that continually received scathing criticism was the graphical widgets that Java was built on: the Abstract Window Toolkit (AWT). The primary issue here was that AWT provided only the minimal amount of functionality necessary to create a windowing application. For enterprise applications, it quickly became clear that programmers needed something bigger.

After nearly a year of intense scrutiny, the AWT classes were ready for a change. From Java 1.0 to Java 1.1, the AWT reimplemented its event model from a "chain" design to an "event subscriber" design. This meant that instead of propagating events up a predefined hierarchy of components, interested classes simply registered with other components to receive noteworthy events. Because events typically involve only the sender and receiver, this eliminated much of the overhead in propagating them. When component events were triggered, an event object was passed only to those classes interested in receiving them.

JavaSoft developers also began to see that relying on native widgets for the AWT components was proving to be troublesome. Similar components looked and behaved differently on many platforms, and coding for the ever-expanding differences of each platform became a maintenance nightmare. In addition, reusing the component widgets for each platform limited the abilities of the components and proved expensive on system memory.

Clearly, JavaSoft knew that AWT wasn't enough. It wasn't that the AWT classes didn't work; they simply didn't provide the functionality necessary for full scale enterprise applications. At the 1997 JavaOne Conference in San Francisco, Java-Soft announced the Java Foundation Classes. Key to the design of the JFC was that the new Swing components would be written entirely in Java and have a consistent look-and-feel across platforms. This allowed Swing and the JFC to be used on any platform that supported Java 1.1 or later; all the user had to do was to include the appropriate JAR files on the CLASSPATH, and each of the components were available for use.

JFC vs. AFC

At about the same time that Sun Microsystems, Inc. announced the JFC, their chief competitor, Microsoft, announced a similar framework under the name Application Foundation Classes (AFC). The AFC libraries consist of two major packages: UI and FX.

UI

> A graphical toolkit that is similar in scope to the Swing classes.

FX

> Complimentary classes that allow the user better control over various graphics functions, including colors and fonts.

The AFC classes are similar to JFC in many respects, and although the event mechanisms are different, the goals are the same. The most visible difference to programmers is in the operating environment: JFC requires the services of JDK 1.1, while the AFC can co-exist with the more browser-friendly JDK 1.0.2. In addition, AFC does not reuse any of the AWT 1.1 classes, but instead defines its own lightweight hierarchy of graphics components.

Which development library is better? Of course, Microsoft would have you believe that AFC far exceeds JFC, while Sun would have you believe the opposite. Putting aside the marketing hype and any religious issues, the choice largely depends on personal preference. Both JFC and AFC contain enough classes to build a very robust enterprise application, and each side has its own pros and cons.

NOTE   Since that time, the AFC has been slightly changed and is now included in the Windows Foundation Classes (WFC), parts of which only work on the Windows platform.

Swing Features

Swing provides many new features for those planning to write large-scale applications in Java. Here is an overview of some of the more popular features.

Pluggable Look-and-Feels

One of the most exciting aspects of the Swing classes is the ability to dictate the *look-and-feel* (L&F) of each of the components, even resetting the look-and-feel at runtime. Look-and-feels have become an important issue in GUI development over the past five years. Most users are familiar with the Motif style of user interface, which was common in Windows 3.1 and is still in wide use on Unix platforms. Microsoft has since deviated from that standard with a much more optimized look-and-feel in their Windows 95/98 and NT 4.0 operating systems. In addition, the Macintosh computer system has its own branded look-and-feel, which most Apple users feel comfortable with.

Swing is capable of emulating several look-and-feels, and currently includes support for Windows 98 and Unix Motif.[*] This comes in handy when a user would like to work in the L&F environment which he or she is most comfortable with. In addition, Swing can allow the user to switch look-and-feels at runtime without having to close the current application. This way, a user can experiment to see which L&F is best for them with instantaneous feedback. And, if you're feeling really ambitious as a developer (perhaps a game developer), you can create your own look-and-feel for each one of the Swing components!

Swing comes with a default look-and-feel called "Metal," which was developed while the Swing classes were in the beta-release phase. This look-and-feel combines some of the best graphical elements in today's L&Fs and even adds a few surprises of its own. Figure 1-3 shows an example of several look-and-feels that you can use with Swing, including the new Metal look-and-feel. All Swing L&Fs are built from a set of base classes called the Basic L&F. However, though we may refer to the Basic L&F from time to time, you can't use it on its own.

Lightweight Components

Most Swing components are *lightweight*. In the purest sense, this means that components are not dependent on native peers to render themselves. Instead, they use simplified graphics primitives to paint themselves on the screen and can even allow portions to be transparent.

The ability to create lightweight components first emerged in JDK 1.1, although the majority of AWT components did not take advantage of it. Prior to that, Java programmers had no choice but to subclass `java.awt.Canvas` or `java.awt.Panel` if they wished to create their own components. With both classes, Java allocated an opaque peer object from the underlying operating system

---

[*] An early access version of the Macintosh look-and-feel has been released. For more information see *http://developer.java.sun.com/developer/earlyAccess/jfc/*.

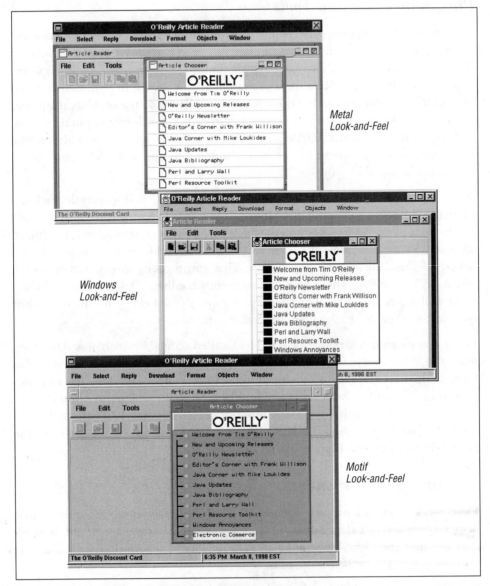

Figure 1-3. Various look-and-feels in the Java Swing environment

to represent the component, forcing each component to behave as if it were its own window, taking on a rectangular, solid shape. Hence, these components earned the name "heavyweight," because they frequently held extra baggage at the native level that Java did not use.

Heavyweight components were unwieldy for two reasons:

- Equivalent components on different platforms don't necessarily act alike. A list component on one platform, for example, may work differently than a list component on another. Trying to coordinate and manage the differences between components was a formidable task.

- The look-and-feel of each component was tied to the host operating system and could not be changed.

With lightweight components, each component renders itself using the drawing primitives of the Graphics object (e.g., drawLine(), fillRect(), etc.). Lightweight components always render themselves onto the surface of the heavyweight top-level component they are contained in. With the arrival of JDK 1.1, programmers can directly extend the java.awt.Component or java.awt.Container classes when creating lightweight components. Unlike java.awt.Canvas or java.awt.Panel, these classes do not depend on a native peer and allow the developer to render quickly to the graphics context of the container. This results in faster, less memory-intensive components than were previously available in Java.

Almost all of the Swing components are lightweight; only a few top-level containers are not. This design allows programmers to draw (and redraw) the look-and-feel of their application at runtime, instead of tying it to the L&F of the host operating system. In addition, the design of the Swing components supports easy modification of component behavior. For example, you can indicate to almost any Swing component whether you wish it to accept or decline focus, and how it should handle keyboard input.

Additional Features

Several other features distinguish Swing from the older AWT components:

- A wide variety of new components, such as tables, trees, sliders, progress bars, internal frames, and text components.

- Swing components contain support for replacing their insets with an arbitrary number of concentric borders.

- Swing components can have *tooltips* placed over them. A tooltip is a textual popup that momentarily appears when the mouse cursor rests inside the component's painting region. Tooltips can be used to give more information about the component in question.

- You can arbitrarily bind keyboard events to components, defining how they will react to various keystrokes under given conditions.

- There is additional debugging support for the rendering of your own lightweight Swing components.

We will discuss each of these features in greater detail as we move through the next three chapters.

How Can I Use Swing?

Not everyone will use Swing for the same reasons. In fact, the Swing libraries have many levels of use, each with their own level of prerequisite knowledge. Here are some potential uses:

- Use the Swing components as they are to build your own enterprise applications.

- Create your own Swing components—or extend those that already exist.

- Override or create a new look-and-feel for one or more of the Swing components.

The first approach is what the vast majority of Swing programmers will use. Here, using Swing components is just like using the AWT components. A familiar set of components, containers, and layout managers are all available in the Swing packages to help you get your application up and running quickly. If you're adept at AWT programming, you will probably need only a cursory introduction to each component to get started. Only in the event of some of the larger and newer component families, such as tables and text, will we need to get into broader issues. If you are planning to use each component as a Java Bean for visual programming, you will also fall into this category.

Creating your own component, or extending an already existing one, requires a deeper understanding of Swing. This includes a firm understanding of Swing architecture, events, and lower-level classes. Also, if you decide to subclass a Swing component, the responsibilities of that component must be adopted and handled accordingly—otherwise, your new component may perform erratically.

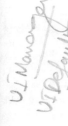

Finally, you may wish to change the look-and-feel of one or more Swing components. This is arguably the most complex of the three routes that you can take—it requires a thorough knowledge of the design, architectural fundamentals, and graphical primitives of each lightweight component. In addition, you will need to understand how Swing's `UIManager` and `UIDefaults` classes work together to "set" each component's look-and-feel.

This book strives to help you with each of these issues. Because we anticipate that the vast majority of readers will fall under the first category, we spend a great deal of time reviewing each component's properties and methods, as well as providing source code for various scenarios that use these components. We also document the protected methods and fields. Programmers can use these to extend the Swing components into their own master creations.

Programming your own look-and-feel can get pretty complex; in fact, the source code for an entire look-and-feel would far exceed the size of even this book. However, we don't want to leave you in the dark. If you are an experienced Swing programmer already, and you're looking for a concise introduction on how to get started, see Chapter 26, *Look & Feel*. This chapter provides some excellent examples of how to code your own look-and-feel for both simple and complex Swing components.com.sun.java.accessibility

Swing Packages and Classes

Swing Packages

Here is a short description of each package in the Swing libraries.

javax.accessibility[*]

Contains classes and interfaces that can be used to allow *assistive technologies* to interact with Swing components. Assistive technologies cover a broad range of items, from audible text readers to screen magnification. Although the accessibility classes are technically not part of Swing, they are used extensively throughout the Swing components. We discuss the accessibility package in greater detail in Chapter 25, *Programming with Accessibility*.

javax.swing

Contains the core Swing components, including most of the model interfaces and support classes.

javax.swing.border

Contains the definitions for the abstract border class as well as eight predefined borders. Borders are not components; instead, they are special graphical elements that Swing treats as properties and places around components in place of their insets. If you wish to create your own border, you can subclass one of the existing borders in this package, or you can code a new one from scratch.

javax.swing.colorchooser

Contains support for the JColorChooser component, discussed in Chapter 12, *Chooser Dialogs*.

---

[*] At one point, Sun intended to package Swing and Accessibility under the java.awt hierarchy. In this system, com.sun.java.accessibility would be java.awt.accessibility. The beta 2 and beta 3 releases of JDK 1.2 reflect the java.awt packaging. Sun reverted to com.sun.java for beta 4, and is using the javax.swing hierarchy for the actual release of JDK 1.2. Sun provides a free tool for automatically adjusting the package names in any code you've written for earlier releases. For more information, see *http://java.sun.com/products/jfc/PackageRenamer/*.

javax.swing.event

Defines several new listeners and events that Swing components use to communicate asynchronous information between classes. To create your own events, you can subclass various events in this package or write your own event class.

javax.swing.filechooser

Contains support for the JFileChooser component, discussed in Chapter 12.

javax.swing.pending

Contains an assortment of components that aren't ready for prime time, but may be in the future. Play here at your own risk. The contents of the pending package aren't discussed in this book.

javax.swing.plaf

Defines the unique elements that make up the pluggable look-and-feel for each Swing component. Its various subpackages are devoted to rendering the individual look-and-feels for each component on a platform-by-platform basis. (Concrete implementations of the Windows and Motif L&Fs are in subpackages of com.sun.java.swing.plaf.)

javax.swing.table

Provides models and views for the table component. The table component allows you to arrange various information in a grid-based format with an appearance similar to a spreadsheet. Using the lower-level classes, you can manipulate how tables are viewed and selected, as well as how they display their information in each cell.

javax.swing.text

Provides scores of text-based classes and interfaces supporting a common design known as *document/view*. The text classes are among the more advanced Swing classes to learn, so we will devote several chapters (19–24) to both the design fundamentals and the implementation of several text applications.

javax.swing.text.html

Used specifically for reading and formatting HTML text through an ancillary editor kit.

javax.swing.text.html.parser

Contains support for parsing HTML.

javax.swing.text.rtf

Used specifically for reading and formatting the Rich Text Format (RTF) text through an ancillary editor kit.

javax.swing.tree

Defines models and views for a hierarchal tree component, such as you might see representing a file structure or a series of properties.

javax.swing.undo

Contains the necessary functionality for implementing undoable functions.

By far the most widely-used package is `javax.swing`. In fact, almost all the Swing components, as well as several utility classes, are located inside this package. The only exceptions are borders and support classes for the trees, tables, and text-based components. Because the latter components are much more extensible and often have many more classes to work with, these classes have been broken off into separate packages. '

Class Hierarchy

Figure 1-4 shows a detailed overview of the Swing class hierarchy as it appears in the 1.2 JDK. At first glance, the class hierarchy looks very similar to AWT. Each Swing component with an AWT equivalent shares the same name, except that the Swing class is preceded by a capital "J". In most cases, if a Swing component supersedes an AWT component, it can be used as a drop-in replacement.

Upon closer inspection, however, you will discover that there are welcome differences between the Swing and AWT components. The first item that you might notice is that the menu components, including `JMenuBar`, are now descendants of the same base component as the others: `JComponent`. This is a change from the older AWT menu classes. Both the AWT 1.0 and 1.1 menu classes inherited their own high-level component, `MenuComponent`, which severely limited their capabilities. In addition, this design prevented menubars from being positioned with layout managers inside containers; instead, Java simply attached menubars to the top of frames.

Also, note that Swing has redesigned the button hierarchy. It now includes a `JToggleButton` class, which is used in dual-state components. For example, if you click on a toggle button while in the "released" position, the button switches to the "pressed" state and remains in that state. When it is clicked again, the button returns to the released state. Note that the `JToggleButton` outlines behavior seen in radio buttons and checkboxes. Hence, these classes inherit from `JToggle-Button` in the new Swing design. Also, note the addition of the `JRadioButton` and `JRadioButtonMenuItem` classes in Swing. Until now, Java forced developers to use the AWT checkbox-equivalent to mimic radio buttons.

You might have noticed an increase in the number of "frames" and "panes" in Swing. For example, consider *internal frames*. Swing can now support placing frames inside other frames—this is commonly referred to as an MDI (multiple

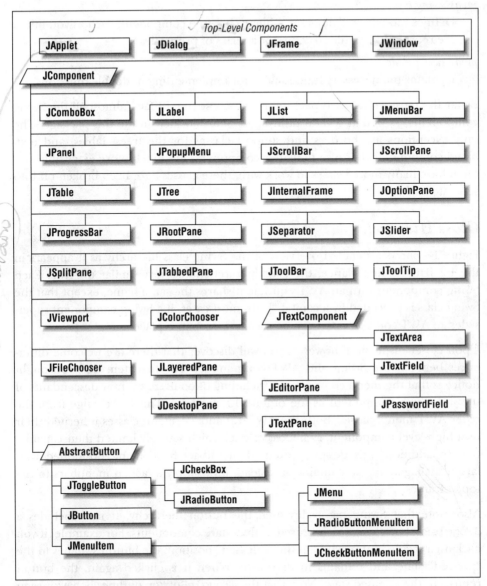

Figure 1-4. The Swing component hierarchy

document interface) in the Microsoft Windows world. You can assign these internal frames arbitrary vertical layers; these layers determine which internal frame will appear on top. In fact, even the simplest frame, JFrame, embraces the concept of layers by including support for layered *panes* on which you can position different elements of your application. These topics are discussed in more detail in Chapter 9, *Internal Frames,* and Chapter 11, *Specialty Panes and Layout Managers.*

There are many other design enhancements in Swing; too many, in fact, to discuss here. However, before we go on, we should discuss one of the fundamental designs behind every Swing component: the *model-view-controller architecture.*

The Model-View-Controller Architecture

Swing uses the *model-view-controller architecture* (MVC) as the fundamental design behind each of its components. Essentially, MVC breaks GUI components into three elements. Each of these elements plays a crucial role in how the component behaves.

Model

The model encompasses the state data for each component. There are different models for different types of components. For example, the model of a scrollbar component might contain information about the current position of its adjustable "thumb," its minimum and maximum values, and the thumb's width (relative to the range of values). A menu, on the other hand, may simply contain a list of the menu items the user can select from. Note that this information remains the same no matter how the component is painted on the screen; model data always exists independent of the component's visual representation.

View

The view refers to how you see the component on the screen. For a good example of how views can differ, look at an application window on two different GUI platforms. Almost all window frames will have a titlebar spanning the top of the window. However, the titlebar may have a close box on the left side (like the older MacOS platform), or it may have the close box on the right side (as in the Windows 95 platform). These are examples of different types of views for the same window object.

Controller

The controller is the portion of the user interface that dictates how the component interacts with events. Events come in many forms—a mouse click, gaining or losing focus, a keyboard event that triggers a specific menu command, or even a directive to repaint part of the screen. The controller decides how each component will react to the event—if it reacts at all.

Figure 1-5 shows how the model, view, and controller work together to create a scrollbar component. The scrollbar uses the information in the model to determine how far into the scrollbar to render the thumb and how wide the thumb should be. Note that the model specifies this information relative to the minimum and the maximum. It does not give the position or width of the thumb in screen pixels—the view calculates that. The view determines exactly where and how to draw the scrollbar, given the proportions offered by the model. The view knows whether it is a horizontal or vertical scrollbar, and it knows exactly how to shadow the end buttons and the thumb. Finally, the controller is responsible for handling mouse events on the component. The controller knows, for example, that dragging the thumb is a legitimate action for a scroll bar, and pushing on the end buttons is acceptable as well. The result is a fully functional MVC scrollbar.

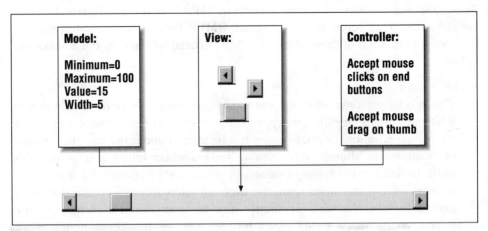

Figure 1-5. The three elements of a model-view-controller architecture

MVC Interaction

With MVC, each of the three elements—the model, the view, and the controller—requires the services of another element to keep itself continually updated. Let's continue discussing the scrollbar component.

We already know that the view cannot render the scrollbar correctly without obtaining information from the model first. In this case, the scrollbar will not know where to draw its "thumb" unless it can obtain its current position and width relative to the minimum and maximum. Likewise, the view determines if the component is the recipient of user events, such as mouse clicks. (For example, the view knows the exact width of the thumb; it can tell whether a click occurred over the thumb or just outside of it.) The view passes these events on to the controller, which decides how to handle them best. Based on the controller's decisions, the values in the model may need to be altered. If the user drags the scrollbar thumb, the controller will react by incrementing the thumb's position in the model. At that point, the whole cycle can repeat. The three elements, therefore, communicate their data as shown in Figure 1-6.

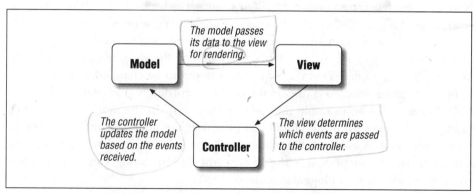

Figure 1-6. Communication through the model-view-controller architecture

MVC in Swing

Swing actually makes use of a simplified variant of the MVC design called the *model-delegate*. This design combines the view and the controller object into a single element that draws the component to the screen and handles GUI events known as the *UI delegate*. Bundling graphics capabilities and event handling is somewhat easy in Java, since much of the event handling is taken care of in AWT. As you might expect, the communication between the model and the UI delegate then becomes a two-way street, as shown in Figure 1-7.

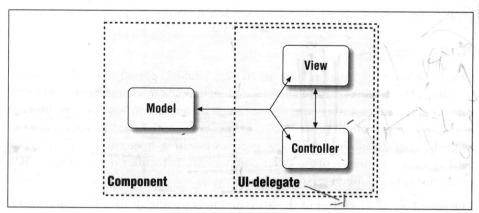

Figure 1-7. With Swing, the view and the controller are combined into a UI-delegate object

So let's review: each Swing component contains a model and a UI delegate. The model is responsible for maintaining information about the component's state. The UI delegate is responsible for maintaining information about how to draw the component on the screen. In addition, the UI delegate (in conjunction with AWT) reacts to various events that propagate through the component.

Note that the separation of the model and the UI delegate in the MVC design is extremely advantageous. One unique aspect of the MVC architecture is the ability to tie multiple views to a single model. For example, if you want to display the same data in a pie chart and in a table, you can base the views of two components on a single data model. That way, if the data needs to be changed, you can do so in only one place—the views update themselves accordingly (Chapter 16, *Advanced Table Examples,* has an example that does exactly this). In the same manner, separating the delegate from the model gives the user the added benefit of choosing what a component will look like without affecting any of its data. By using this approach, in conjunction with the lightweight design, Swing can provide each component with its own pluggable look-and-feel.

By now, you should have a solid understanding of how MVC works. However, we won't yet spoil the fun of using MVC. Chapter 2, *Jump Starting a Swing Application,* and Chapter 3, *Swing Component Basics,* go into further detail on how you can use MVC to your advantage in even the simplest of applications.

Working with Swing

Our introduction to Swing wouldn't be complete unless we briefly mentioned some caveats of the new libraries. There are two areas to briefly mention: multi-threading issues and lightweight/heavyweight issues. Being aware of these issues will help you make informed decisions while working with Swing. Chapter 28, *Swing Under the Hood,* gives you in-depth guidance in these difficult areas.

Multithreading

Shortly before the initial release of Swing, JavaSoft posted an article recommending that developers not use independent threads to change model states in components.[*] Instead, they suggest that once a component has been painted to the screen (or is about to be painted), updates to its model state should only occur from the *event-dispatching queue.* The event-dispatching queue is a system thread used to communicate events to other components. It handles the posting of GUI events, including those to repaint components.

The issue here is an artifact of the MVC architecture and deals with performance and potential race-conditions. As we mentioned above, a Swing component draws itself based on the state values in its model. However, if the state values change while the component is in the process of repainting, the component can repaint incorrectly—this is unacceptable. To compound matters, placing a lock on the

---

[*] Hans Muller and Kathy Walrath. "Threads and Swing" on *The Swing Connection,* at *http://java.sun.com/ products/jfc/tsc/swingdoc-archive/threads.html.*

entire model, as well as on some of the critical component data, or even cloning the data in question, could seriously hamper performance for each refresh. The only feasible solution, therefore, is to place state changes in serial with refreshes. This ensures that modifications in component state do not occur at the same time that Swing is repainting any components, and no race conditions will occur.

The Z-Order Caveat: Lightweight and Heavyweight Components

One of the most frequent issues to come out of the lightweight/heavyweight component debate is the idea of depth, or *z-order*—that is, a well-defined method for how elements are stacked on the screen. Because of z-order, it is not advisable to mix lightweight and heavyweight components in Swing.

To see why, remember that heavyweight components depend on peer objects used at the operating system level. However, with Swing only the top-level components are heavyweight: `JApplet`, `JFrame`, `JDialog`, and `JWindow`. Also, recall that heavyweight components are always "opaque"—they have a rectangular shape and are non-transparent. This is because the host operating system typically allocates the entire painting region to the component, clearing it first.

The remaining components are lightweight. So here is the crux of the dilemma: when a lightweight component is placed inside of a heavyweight container, it shares (and actually borrows) the graphics context of the heavyweight component. The lightweight component must always draw itself on the same plane as the heavyweight component that contains it, therefore it must share the same z-order as the component. In addition, lightweight components are bound to the clipping region of the top-level window or dialog that contains them. In effect, lightweight components are all "drawings" on the canvas of a heavyweight component. The drawings cannot go beyond the boundaries of the canvas, and can always be covered by another canvas. Heavyweight components, however, are free from this restriction. Therefore, they always appear on top of the lightweight components—whether that is the intent or not.

Heavyweight components have other ramifications in Swing as well. Heavyweight components do not work well in scroll panes, where they can extend beyond the clipping boundaries; they don't work in front of lightweight menus and menubars (unless certain precautions are taken) or inside internal frames. Some Swing classes, however, offer an interesting approach to this problem. These classes allow you to specify whether the component will draw itself using a lightweight or a heavyweight window. Hence, with a bit of judicious programming, you can keep your components correctly rendered—no matter where they are located.

The Swing Set Demo

If you're in a hurry to see all the components that Swing has to offer, be sure to check out the Swing Set demonstration provided with the standalone Swing distribution. The demonstration is extremely easy to set up. Assuming you're using JDK 1.1, after downloading and extracting the Swing classes on your computer, you will need to the following:

1. Edit your CLASSPATH environment variable to include the file *swingall.jar*, which resides in the base directory of the distribution. Also, set the SWING_HOME environment variable to point to the base directory.

2. Change directory to the *examples/SwingSet* directory in the Swing distribution.

3. Execute the *runnit* script or *runnit.bat* file, depending on your platform.[*]

If you are using JDK 1.2, just find the directory *demo/SwingSet* (unfortunately, it has moved around in different pre-releases) and type java SwingSet. You should immediately see a progress bar indicating that the Swing Set demo is loading. When it finishes, a window appears, similar to the one in Figure 1-8.

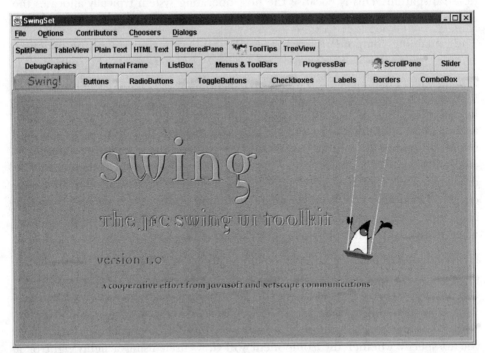

Figure 1-8. The Swing Set demo

---

[*] If this doesn't work, you can probably enter the classes directory and type in java SwingSet.

This demo contains a series of tabs that demonstrate almost all of the components in the Swing libraries. Be sure to check out the internal frames demo and the new Metal look-and-feel. In addition, some of the Swing creators have added "Easter eggs" of their own throughout the Swing Set demo. See if you can find some!

Reading this Book

We're well aware that most readers don't read the Preface. You have our permission to skip it, provided that you look at the Conventions section. That section is particularly important because in this book, we're experimenting with a few new techniques for explaining the Swing classes. As we said earlier, everything in Swing is a Java Bean. This means that much of an object's behavior is controlled by a set of properties, which are manipulated by accessor methods. For example, the property color would be accessed by the methods getColor() (to find out the color) and setColor() (to change the color). If a property has a boolean value, the get method is often replaced by an is method; for example, the visible property would have methods isVisible() and setVisible().

We found the idea of properties very powerful in helping us understand Swing. Therefore, rather than listing all of a class's accessor methods, we decided to present a table for each class, listing the class's properties and showing the property's data type, which accessor methods are present, whether the property is "bound" (i.e., changing the property generates a PropertyChangeEvent), and the property's default value. This approach certainly saves paper (you didn't really want a 2000 page book, did you?) and should make it easier to understand what a component does and how it is structured. Furthermore, if you're not already in the habit of thinking in terms of the JavaBeans architecture, you should get in the habit. It's a very useful and powerful tool for understanding component design.

The conventions we use in the property tables—plus some other conventions that we use in class diagrams—are explained in the Preface. So we'll let you ignore the rest of the Preface, as long as you familiarize yourself with the conventions we're using.

The next chapter will help you get a jumpstart on Swing by presenting some simple applications that ease the Java AWT developer into the latest additions. In Chapter 3, we continue our discussion by presenting some of the fundamental classes of Swing and discussing how you can use the features inherent in each of these classes to shorten your overall development time. Don't stop now—the best is yet to come!

2

Jump Starting a Swing Application

Now that you have an overview of Swing, let's look at a few quick Swing components you can put into your applications right now. This chapter will show you how to add images to buttons, and then go on to the more complicated, but more interesting, internal frames. We won't belabor the theory and background. You'll find everything we talk about now (and tons more we don't discuss here) presented in later chapters in much greater detail. We just want to show you some of the fun stuff right away.

Upgrading Your Programs

One of the benefits of object-oriented languages is that you can upgrade pieces of a program without rewriting the rest of it. While practice is never as simple as theory, with Swing it's close. You can use most of the Swing components as drop-in replacements for AWT components with ease. The components sport many fancy new features worth exploiting, but they still maintain the functionality of the AWT components you're familiar with. As a general rule, you can stick a "J" in front of your favorite AWT component and put the new class to work as a Swing component. Constructors for components such as JButton, JTextField, and JList can be used with the same arguments and generate the same events as Button, Text-Field, and List. Some Swing containers, like JFrame, take a bit of extra work, but not much.

One of the first steps a programmer takes when building a modern user interface for commercial or internal use is to add a graphical button. Nice monitors and cheap hardware have made icons almost a necessity. The AWT package in Java does not directly support image buttons, but they are fairly easy to create by extending the Canvas or Component class. However, none of the extensions you write will be compatible with any extensions written by other programmers. The

JButton class from the Swing package provides (finally) a standard way to add image buttons.

A Simple AWT Application

Undoubtedly, you have some programs lying around that use regular AWT buttons that you'd love to replace with image buttons, but don't have the time or, honestly, the necessity to produce your own image button class. Let's look at a simple application that demonstrates an upgrade path you can use on your own programs.

First, let's look at the code for this very simple application:

```
// ToolbarFrame1.java
// A simple frame containing a "toolbar" made up of several java.awt.Button
// objects. We'll be converting the Buttons to JButtons in the
// ToolbarFrame2.java file.
//
import java.awt.*;
import java.awt.event.*;

public class ToolbarFrame1 extends Frame implements ActionListener {

  Button cutButton, copyButton, pasteButton;
  public ToolbarFrame1() {
    super("Toolbar Example (AWT)");
    setSize(450, 250);
    addWindowListener(new BasicWindowMonitor());

    Panel toolbar = new Panel();
    toolbar.setLayout(new FlowLayout(FlowLayout.LEFT));

    cutButton = new Button("Cut");
    cutButton.addActionListener(this);
    toolbar.add(cutButton);

    copyButton = new Button("Copy");
    copyButton.addActionListener(this);
    toolbar.add(copyButton);

    pasteButton = new Button("Paste");
    pasteButton.addActionListener(this);
    toolbar.add(pasteButton);

    // the new "preferred" BorderLayout add call
    add(toolbar, BorderLayout.NORTH);
  }
```

```
public void actionPerformed(ActionEvent ae) {
  System.out.println(ae.getActionCommand());
}

public static void main(String args[]) {
  ToolbarFrame1 tf1 = new ToolbarFrame1();
  tf1.setVisible(true);
}
}
```

To close the window on cue, we use a simple extension to the WindowAdapter class. This is a fairly useful utility; you'll see it often throughout the book.

```
import java.awt.event.*;
import java.awt.Window;

public class BasicWindowMonitor extends WindowAdapter {

  public void windowClosing(WindowEvent e) {
    Window w = e.getWindow();
    w.setVisible(false);
    w.dispose();
    System.exit(0);
  }
}
```

Our application presents the very simple interface you see in Figure 2-1.

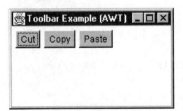

Figure 2-1. A simple application using three java.awt.Button objects

These buttons don't really do anything except report being pressed. A standard 1.1-style handler for action events reports button presses to standard output. It's not exciting, but it will let us demonstrate that Swing buttons work the same way as the AWT buttons.

Including Your First Swing Component

The first step in adding a Swing component to your application is getting the Swing package ready for use. If you're preparing an application to run with JDK 1.1, you'll need to put the *swingall.jar* file on the CLASSPATH so that the Swing components are available during compilation and at runtime. If you're using JDK

1.2 or later, the Swing components are included with the distribution, so you don't need to mess with the CLASSPATH; the Swing classes should already be available.

In your source code, you'll first need to include that new Swing package in your import statements by adding an import statement:

```
import javax.swing.*;
```

Now you're ready to replace your Button objects with JButton objects. We'll also set up the application to take advantage of Swing's look-and-feel capabilities; we've put another row of buttons at the bottom of the frame that let you select one of the three standard look-and-feels:

```
// ToolbarFrame2.java
// The Swing-ified button example.
//
import java.awt.*;
import java.awt.event.*;
import javax.swing.*;

public class ToolbarFrame2 extends Frame implements ActionListener {

  // This time, let's use JButtons!
  JButton cutButton, copyButton, pasteButton;
  JButton winButton, javaButton, motifButton;

  public ToolbarFrame2() {
    super("Toolbar Example (Swing)");
    setSize(450, 250);
    addWindowListener(new BasicWindowMonitor());

    // JPanel works similarly to Panel, so we'll use it
    JPanel toolbar = new JPanel();
    toolbar.setLayout(new FlowLayout(FlowLayout.LEFT));

    cutButton = new JButton("Cut");
    cutButton.addActionListener(this);
    toolbar.add(cutButton);

    copyButton = new JButton("Copy");
    copyButton.addActionListener(this);
    toolbar.add(copyButton);

    pasteButton = new JButton("Paste");
    pasteButton.addActionListener(this);
    toolbar.add(pasteButton);

    add(toolbar, BorderLayout.NORTH);  // the new BorderLayout add
```

```
    // Add the look-and-feel controls
    JPanel lnfPanel = new JPanel();
    LnFListener lnfListener = new LnFListener(this);
    javaButton = new JButton("Metal");
    javaButton.addActionListener(lnfListener);
    lnfPanel.add(javaButton);
    motifButton = new JButton("Motif");
    motifButton.addActionListener(lnfListener);
    lnfPanel.add(motifButton);
    winButton = new JButton("Windows");
    winButton.addActionListener(lnfListener);
    lnfPanel.add(winButton);
    add(lnfPanel, BorderLayout.SOUTH);
  }

  public void actionPerformed(ActionEvent ae) {
    System.out.println(ae.getActionCommand());
  }

  public static void main(String args[]) {
    ToolbarFrame2 tf2 = new ToolbarFrame2();
    tf2.setVisible(true);
  }
}
```

As you can see, the application is more or less the same. All we did was change Button to JButton, and add three more JButtons for look-and-feel selection. We update the application's look-and-feel in the LnFListener class, which gets its event from the simple Swing buttons at the bottom of the application. Apart from figuring out which button was pressed, we must also force the look-and-feel to change. That's pretty simple. The first step is setting the new look-and-feel using the UIManager.setLookAndFeel() method. (That's the method that needs the correct name for the look-and-feel we want.) Once the look-and-feel is set, we want to make the change visible immediately, so we update the look-and-feel for all of the components using the SwingUtilities.updateComponentTreeUI() method.

```
// LnFListener.java
// A listener that can change the look-and-feel of a frame based on
// the actionCommand of an ActionEvent object. Supported look-and-feels are:
//   * Metal
//   * Windows
//   * Motif
//
import java.awt.*;
import java.awt.event.*;
import javax.swing.*;
```

```java
public class LnFListener implements ActionListener {
  Frame frame;

  public LnFListener(Frame f) {
    frame = f;
  }

  public void actionPerformed(ActionEvent e) {
    String lnfName = null;
    if (e.getActionCommand().equals("Metal")) {
      lnfName = "javax.swing.plaf.metal.MetalLookAndFeel";
    } else if (e.getActionCommand().equals("Motif")) {
      lnfName = "com.sun.java.swing.plaf.motif.MotifLookAndFeel";
    } else {
      lnfName = "com.sun.java.swing.plaf.windows.WindowsLookAndFeel";
    }

    try {
      UIManager.setLookAndFeel(lnfName);
      SwingUtilities.updateComponentTreeUI(frame);
    }
    catch (UnsupportedLookAndFeelException ex1) {
      System.err.println("Unsupported LookAndFeel: " + lnfName);
    }
    catch (ClassNotFoundException ex2) {
      System.err.println("LookAndFeel class not found: " + lnfName);
    }
    catch (InstantiationException ex3) {
      System.err.println("Could not load LookAndFeel: " + lnfName);
    }
    catch (IllegalAccessException ex4) {
      System.err.println("Cannot use LookAndFeel: " + lnfName);
    }
  }
}
```

With the JButton objects in place we get the application shown in Figure 2-2.

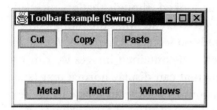

Figure 2-2. The same application with JButtons for Cut, Copy, and Paste (in the Metal L&F)

When we run the new version of the application, we still get ActionEvent objects from pressing the buttons, and the events still get delivered to the actionPerformed() method. Okay, big deal. Now we have buttons that work just like before and don't look particularly great. So what? Well, for one thing, we can now take advantage of the new UI management capabilities of Swing components. The *swingall.jar* file Swing uses defines new look-and-feels that we can use with any of the Swing components. If you punch the "Metal," "Motif," or "Windows" button on this application, it switches from the current look-and-feel to the appropriate version. Figure 2-3 shows the effect.

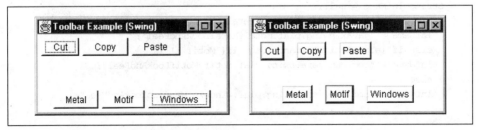

Figure 2-3. JButtons using the Windows (left) and Motif (right) look-and-feel modes

Now we've got a bunch of JButtons. We're still using the old AWT Panel and Frame objects as containers for our applications. You can change them easily, too. Changing Panel to JPanel is as simple as updating the buttons: just do a global replace, and you're done. Updating Frame is a little more complex. Once you've replaced Frame with JFrame, you must also look at the calls to add() that put things in the JFrame. A JFrame has something in it called a "content pane"; when we add something to a JFrame, we usually want to add it to this content pane:

```
getContentPane().add(something);    // formerly just add(something)
```

With these changes, the JFrame and JPanel will also change their appearance when you change the application's look-and-feel. It may not be noticeable. But you'll also get the other new features that Swing gives you. We'll stick with the old Frame and Panel for now, but we'll use JFrame and JPanel later in this chapter and throughout the book.

This is all very nice, but it's still not what we came for. We weren't interested in making minor changes in the way our buttons looked, though that's a nice side effect. So let's get to those images! First, we need to create what the Swing components refer to as an Icon. You can get the details on icons in Chapter 4, *Labels and Icons*, but for now, just think of them as nicely self-contained images we can use inside just about any of the Swing components that can display normal text (such as labels, buttons, and menu items). We'll start out by adding an image to the text we're currently displaying in each button. We can use all of the graphics formats Java supports (GIF, JPEG, and others) with icons, including transparent and animated GIF-89a images. Here's the code to add images to each of our buttons:

```
cutButton = new JButton("Cut", new ImageIcon("cut.gif"));
cutButton.addActionListener(this);
toolbar.add(cutButton);
```

```
copyButton = new JButton("Copy", new ImageIcon("copy.gif"));
copyButton.addActionListener(this);
toolbar.add(copyButton);

pasteButton = new JButton("Paste", new ImageIcon("paste.gif"));
pasteButton.addActionListener(this);
toolbar.add(pasteButton);
```

That creates buttons with little icons to the left of the text. Any look-and-feel can display the images. Figure 2-4 shows the result.

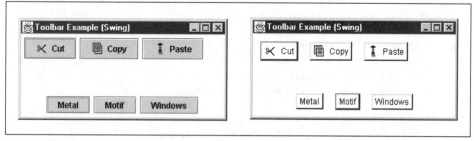

Figure 2-4. Icon and text buttons in Metal (left) and Motif (right) look-and-feel modes

Adding the icons hasn't changed anything. In particular, our action event handlers are exactly the same as they were with normal AWT buttons. But you probably see a problem developing. Our handler uses the buttons' text labels to decide which button was pressed. That's not a problem, since our buttons still display some text. What happens if we throw that text out? How can we tell which button was pressed? Well, first, let's look at the code to create an image-only button.

```
copyButton = new JButton(new ImageIcon("copy.gif"));
copyButton.addActionListener(this);
toolbar.add(copyButton);
```

If we do this for every button, the application will look like Figure 2-5.

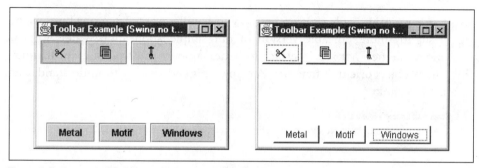

Figure 2-5. Icon-only JButtons in Metal (left) and WJavaindows (right) look-and-feel modes

Now let's look back at the event handler we use:

```
public void actionPerformed(ActionEvent e) {
    System.out.println(e.getActionCommand());
}
```

Doesn't do much. Normally, you would need to distinguish between the various buttons or other components that report to this handler. Since we implement the `ActionListener` interface directly in the application class, we can use the simple route of checking the source of the event against the buttons we know we have. For example, we could differentiate the cut, copy, and paste buttons like this:

```
public void actionPerformed(ActionEvent ae) {
    if (ae.getSource() == cutButton) {
    System.out.println("Got Cut event");
    }
    else if (ae.getSource() == copyButton) {
        System.out.println("Got Copy event");
    }
    else if (ae.getSource() == pasteButton) {
        System.out.println("Got Paste event");
    }
}
```

However, we don't always have the luxury of implementing the event handler directly in our application, and we might not want to pass around a huge list of button references to make it possible to write such code in other classes. Instead, you can use the `actionCommand` property of the `Button` class to distinguish your buttons from one another. The `JButton` class also implements this property, so we can just call `setActionCommand()` for each of the buttons and pass in a unique string that we can check in the `actionPerformed()` method—regardless of which class that method sits in. Using the `actionCommand` property to distinguish a component works for components whose appearance might be changing for any of a variety of reasons. (For example, you might be writing an international application where the text on the button changes depending on the user's native language.)

Now, this is not the only or even best way to handle events from our buttons, but it's a slightly more portable version of our simple application. Later, we'll be looking at the new `Action` interface to better support this type of event handling in a more object-oriented manner. For now, this code is easy to understand, even if it is a bit clunky.

```
// ToolbarFrame4.java
// The Swing-ified button example. The buttons in this toolbar all carry images
// but no text.
//
import java.awt.*;
import java.awt.event.*;
```

```java
import javax.swing.*;

public class ToolbarFrame4 extends Frame {

  // This time, let's use JButtons!
  JButton cutButton, copyButton, pasteButton;
  JButton winButton, javaButton, motifButton;

  public ToolbarFrame4() {
    super("Toolbar Example (Swing no text)");
    setSize(450, 250);
    addWindowListener(new BasicWindowMonitor());

    // JPanel works much like Panel does, so we'll use it
    JPanel toolbar = new JPanel();
    toolbar.setLayout(new FlowLayout(FlowLayout.LEFT));

    CCPHandler handler = new CCPHandler();

    cutButton = new JButton(new ImageIcon("cut.gif"));
    cutButton.setActionCommand(CCPHandler.CUT);
    cutButton.addActionListener(handler);
    toolbar.add(cutButton);

    copyButton = new JButton(new ImageIcon("copy.gif"));
    copyButton.setActionCommand(CCPHandler.COPY);
    copyButton.addActionListener(handler);
    toolbar.add(copyButton);

    pasteButton = new JButton(new ImageIcon("paste.gif"));
    pasteButton.setActionCommand(CCPHandler.PASTE);
    pasteButton.addActionListener(handler);
    toolbar.add(pasteButton);

    add(toolbar, BorderLayout.NORTH);

    // Add the look-and-feel controls
    JPanel lnfPanel = new JPanel();
    LnFListener lnfListener = new LnFListener(this);
    javaButton = new JButton("Metal");
    javaButton.addActionListener(lnfListener);
    lnfPanel.add(javaButton);
    motifButton = new JButton("Motif");
    motifButton.addActionListener(lnfListener);
    lnfPanel.add(motifButton);
    winButton = new JButton("Windows");
    winButton.addActionListener(lnfListener);
    lnfPanel.add(winButton);
    add(lnfPanel, BorderLayout.SOUTH);
  }
```

```
public static void main(String args[]) {
  ToolbarFrame4 tf4 = new ToolbarFrame4();
  tf4.setVisible(true);
}
}
```

Here's the new event handler for this simple application. Notice that we set up some constants for the different actions we plan to take. We can now use these constants in the setActionCommand() call of any application whenever we're setting up cut, copy, or paste buttons—regardless of what we display on the screen for the buttons. We can now easily tell which action to take in the actionPerformed() method, however, you may still need to pass around a reference to object that contains the buttons, since you will most likely need to take a real action when the user presses a button. We'll look at such a program a bit later in the chapter.

```
// CCPHandler.java
// A Cut, Copy, and Paste event handler. Nothing too fancy, just define some
// constants that can be used to set the actionCommands on buttons.
//
import java.awt.event.*;

public class CCPHandler implements ActionListener {

  public final static String CUT   = "cut";
  public final static String COPY  = "copy";
  public final static String PASTE = "paste";

  public void actionPerformed(ActionEvent e) {
    String command = e.getActionCommand();
    if (command == CUT) { // we can do this since we're comparing statics
      System.out.println("Got Cut event");
    }
    else if (command == COPY) {
      System.out.println("Got Copy event");
    }
    else if (command == PASTE) {
      System.out.println("Got Paste event");
    }
  }
}
```

Beyond Buttons

Buttons are very useful, but even with great images forming the buttons, they still lack a certain glamour—every application has buttons. For the next example, let's take a look at something a bit more exciting. (Well, exciting might be a bit of an exaggeration, but it definitely has more impact than buttons.) The Swing package contains a new class called JInternalFrame, which allows you to create free-standing frames with menus, titlebars, and everything else a Frame needs right inside your application.

What Is an Internal Frame?

Before we start coding, here's a brief rundown of the features of an internal frame:

- Same functions as a normal Frame object, but confined to the visible area of the container it is placed in
- Can be iconified (icon stays inside main application frame)
- Can be maximized (frame consumes entire main application frame area)
- Can be closed using the standard controls for popup windows
- Can be placed in a "layer," which dictates how the frame displays itself relative to other internal frames (a frame in layer 1 can never hide a frame in layer 2)

Figure 2-6 shows a simple internal frame using the Metal L&F.

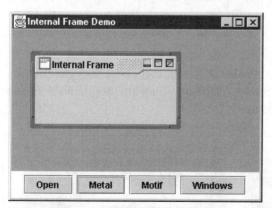

Figure 2-6. The SimpleInternalFrame application using the Metal look-and-feel

For this first example, we'll add an empty internal frame to an application. Once that's working, we'll expand the simple frame to create a couple of different types of internal frames and create the framework for a simple application.

One of the prerequisites for using internal frames is that you need a window capable of managing them. The swing package provides the JDesktopPane class for this purpose. You'll see the details of the JDesktopPane in Chapter 9, *Internal Frames*, but for now, here's how to get one started:

```
// Set up the layered pane
JDesktopPane desktop = new JDesktopPane();
add(desktop, BorderLayout.CENTER);
```

With the desktop in place, you can create a new internal frame and show it. The
JInternalFrame constructor we'll use takes five arguments that tailor the look
and functionality of the frame:

```
public JInternalFrame(String title,
                         boolean resizable,
                         boolean closable,
                         boolean maximizable,
                         boolean iconifiable);
```

We'll turn on every feature for the example. To make the internal frame visible,
then:

```
internalFrame = new JInternalFrame("Internal Frame",
                                    true, true, true, true);
internalFrame.setBounds(50, 50, 200, 100);
desktop.add(internalFrame, new Integer(1));
```

The desktop.add() call does the real work here. You supply the internal frame
and the "layer" your frame belongs in. Layers are Integer objects. The values
determine the order of your layers and what shows on top of what. For example,
frames in layer 2 will always show on top of frames in layer 1, even if the frame in
layer 1 has the keyboard focus. But you do need to remember to give your frame
both a size and a location. The internal frames have default preferred and
minimum sizes of 0 × 0.

Figure 2-7 shows how the JInternalFrame class also takes advantage of the new
pluggable look-and-feel feature of Swing. You can switch the appearance of the
frames, just like you did with the buttons.

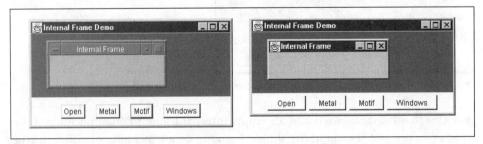

Figure 2-7. The SimpleInternalFrame in Motif (left) and Windows (right) look-and-feel modes

You can even iconify these frames. They turn into an "iconified box" appropriate
for the current look-and-feel. Figure 2-8 shows an iconified frame in the Metal
look-and-feel.

Here's the complete application with an open button and an internal frame.
When you click the button, it pops up the internal frame. You can use the button

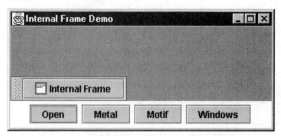

Figure 2-8. An iconified internal frame in the Metal look-and-feel

in the upper right corner of the frame to close it (providing you're using either the Metal or the Windows look-and-feel). You can use the other buttons in the main frame to adjust the look-and-feel of the internal frame:

```
// SimpleInternalFrame.java
// A quick demonstration of setting up an Internal Frame in an application.
//
import java.awt.*;
import java.awt.event.*;
import javax.swing.*;

public class SimpleInternalFrame extends Frame implements ActionListener {

    JButton openButton, winButton, javaButton, motifButton;
    JLayeredPane desktop;
    JInternalFrame internalFrame;

    public SimpleInternalFrame() {
        super("Internal Frame Demo");
        setSize(500,400);
        openButton = new JButton("Open");
        winButton = new JButton("Windows");
        javaButton = new JButton("Metal");
        motifButton = new JButton("Motif");
        Panel p = new Panel();
        p.add(openButton);
        p.add(javaButton);
        p.add(motifButton);
        p.add(winButton);
        add(p, BorderLayout.SOUTH);
        addWindowListener(new BasicWindowMonitor());
        openButton.addActionListener(this);
        LnFListener lnf = new LnFListener(this);
        winButton.addActionListener(lnf);
        javaButton.addActionListener(lnf);
        motifButton.addActionListener(lnf);
```

```
    // Set up the layered pane
    desktop = new JDesktopPane();
    desktop.setOpaque(true);
    add(desktop, BorderLayout.CENTER);
  }

  public void actionPerformed(ActionEvent e) {
    if ((internalFrame == null) || (internalFrame.isClosed())) {
      internalFrame = new JInternalFrame("Internal Frame",
                                     true, true, true, true);
      internalFrame.setBounds(50, 50, 200, 100);
      desktop.add(internalFrame, new Integer(1));
    }
  }

  public static void main(String args[]) {
    SimpleInternalFrame sif = new SimpleInternalFrame();
    sif.setVisible(true);
  }
}
```

The internal frame examples use the same look-and-feel listener and basic window monitor as the JButton example starting on page 25. You'll notice some nasty flickering when you move the internal frame around. That's because we put it inside a Frame, not a JFrame. In our next example, the problem disappears.

A Bigger Application

Now that you've seen how to create internal frames and played around with them a bit, let's tackle a slightly larger problem. We want to build an application that can pop up internal frames that you can honestly use. This starter application is a web-site manager that shows us a list of HTML pages at a site and, for any of those pages, allows us to pop up the page in a separate frame and edit it. We'll keep the main list of HTML pages in one "site" frame that contains a simple list box.

Once you have a site built up with a couple of pages, you can click on any entry in the list, and if the file exists, we'll create a new "page" frame and load the file into a JTextArea object for you to edit. You can modify the text and then save the file using the File menu in the page frame.

As a bonus, we'll put those cut, copy, and paste icons to use as well. You can manipulate text in any of the open page frames. The icons work as Action objects by looking at the selected text and insertion point of the active frame. (We'll look at the Action class below.) If the active frame is a site frame, nothing happens.

You could certainly add a lot of features to this application and make it a real working program, but we don't want to get mired down in details just yet. (If you want to get really fancy, you could look at some of the editor kits discussed in Chapter 24, *EditorKits and TextActions,* and build yourself a real HTML editor.) Figure 2-9 shows the finished application with a couple of frames open.

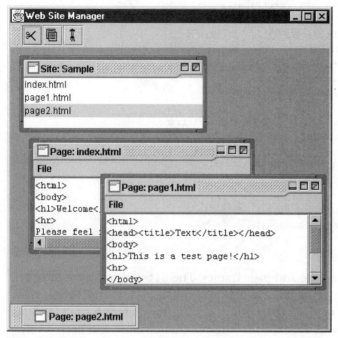

Figure 2-9. The SiteManager application running (set to use the Metal look-and-feel)

We'll break the code for this application into three separate classes to make it more manageable for discussing. The first class handles the real application frame. The constructor handles all of the interface setup work. It sets up the toolbar, as well as the cut, copy, and paste buttons. It also uses the Metal look-and-feel from the beginning, instead of shifting it on the fly. (You could certainly attach the LnFListener from above, if you wanted to.) Here's the source code:

```
// SiteManager.java
//
import java.awt.*;
import java.io.*;
import java.util.*;
import java.awt.event.*;
import javax.swing.*;

public class SiteManager extends JFrame {

  JLayeredPane desktop;
  Vector popups = new Vector();
```

```
public SiteManager() {
  super("Web Site Manager");
  setSize(450, 250);
  addWindowListener(new BasicWindowMonitor());
  Container contentPane = getContentPane();

  JToolBar jtb = new JToolBar();
  jtb.add(new CutAction(this));
  jtb.add(new CopyAction(this));
  jtb.add(new PasteAction(this));
  contentPane.add(jtb, BorderLayout.NORTH);

  // Add our LayeredPane object for the Internal frames
  desktop = new JDesktopPane();
  contentPane.add(desktop, BorderLayout.CENTER);
  addSiteFrame("Sample");
}

public static void main(String args[]) {
  SiteManager mgr = new SiteManager();
  mgr.setVisible(true);
}
```

Now for the creation of the site and page frames. The SiteFrame class and Page-Frame class, discussed later in this chapter, extend the JInternalFrame class. These classes handle all of the hard work in getting the frames to look and act correctly. Here we just need to make the internal frame visible and keep a reference to the frame. By keeping the popups vector around, we could eventually add "Save All," "Close Site," and other features. For now we just use it to help find the current frame.

```
// Methods to create our internal frames
  public void addSiteFrame(String name) {
    SiteFrame sf = new SiteFrame(name, this);
    popups.addElement(sf);
    desktop.add(sf, new Integer(2));  // Keep sites on top for now
  }

  public void addPageFrame(String name) {
    PageFrame pf = new PageFrame(name, this);
    desktop.add(pf, new Integer(1));
    pf.setIconifiable(true);
    popups.addElement(pf);
  }

  public JInternalFrame getCurrentFrame() {
    for (int i = 0; i < popups.size(); i++) {
      JInternalFrame currentFrame = (JInternalFrame)popups.elementAt(i);
      if (currentFrame.isSelected()) {
```

```
        return currentFrame;
      }
    }
    return null;
  }
}
```

The getCurrentFrame() method runs through a list of all the frames currently open in the site manager and returns the active frame. (Yes, this is a bit inefficient, but we're ignoring that for right now.)

Notice that we're using a JToolBar object in our example. This is a great shortcut if you just want a few buttons along the top (or side or bottom) of your application. A JToolBar can contain almost any kind of component, though it's most often used for buttons. We don't actually use buttons; instead, we use Action objects, which are automatically converted into buttons when placed in a toolbar. The Action interface encapsulates an icon and an actionPerformed() method so that you don't have to do that lengthy if/else-if testing. When you add an Action to the toolbar, the toolbar displays the Action's icon, and when you click on the icon, the Action's actionPerformed() method is called automatically. Here's the code for the CopyAction class:

```java
// CopyAction.java
// A simple Action that copies text from a PageFrame object.
//
import java.awt.event.ActionEvent;
import javax.swing.*;

public class CopyAction extends AbstractAction {
  SiteManager manager;

  public CopyAction(SiteManager sm) {
    super("", new ImageIcon("copy.gif"));
    manager = sm;
  }

  public void actionPerformed(ActionEvent ae) {
    JInternalFrame currentFrame = manager.getCurrentFrame();
    if (currentFrame == null) { return; }
    // can't cut or paste sites
    if (currentFrame instanceof SiteFrame) { return; }
    ((PageFrame)currentFrame).copyText();
  }
}
```

The cut and paste action classes work in a similar fashion. (We won't show them here.) Eventually, you'll see that editor kits (Chapter 24) include a lot of prebuilt Actions, so you may not even need to write your own.

Next we need a way to create the site frames. We can set up a separate class that extends the JInternalFrame class and contains the functionality appropriate to the site manager. Namely, we must be able to list available pages in the site and open any of those pages for editing.

We can create a frame that has a listbox as its primary component. This won't be a fancy manager, but it will do what we want. The nice thing about internal frames, from the frame's point of view, is that they look just like regular frames. You can use the constructor to add all of the graphical interface elements and put in event listeners. The only difference with internal frames is that they need to be added to an appropriate desktop pane, but again, that's not a difference we can see here in the code for the individual frames. You can upgrade existing popup Frame classes to these new JInternalFrame classes with very little effort:

```java
// SiteFrame.java
// A simple extension of the JInternalFrame class that contains a list
// object. Elements of the list represent HTML pages for a web site.
//
import java.awt.*;
import javax.swing.*;
import javax.swing.event.*;

public class SiteFrame extends JInternalFrame
    implements ListSelectionListener {

  JList nameList;
  SiteManager parent;
  // Hardcode the pages of our "site" to keep things simple
  String[] pages = {"index.html", "page1.html", "page2.html"};

  public SiteFrame(String name, SiteManager sm) {
    super("Site: " + name, true, true, true);
    parent = sm;
    setBounds(50,50,250,100);

    nameList = new JList(pages);
    nameList.setSelectionMode(ListSelectionModel.SINGLE_SELECTION);
    nameList.addListSelectionListener(this);

    Container contentPane = getContentPane();
    contentPane.add(nameList, BorderLayout.CENTER);
  }
```

In the valueChanged() method for the site frames, we handle the basic functions of the page list. Single-clicking on an entry in the list creates a new PageFrame object for that file. If the file doesn't exist, you get a blank text area to create the page from scratch. Note that very little error checking is going on here. But you probably have already discovered that robust error checking just gets in the way of having fun, and that's all we're really trying to accomplish with this application.

```
public void valueChanged(ListSelectionEvent lse) {
  // We know this is the list, so pop up the page
  if (!lse.getValueIsAdjusting()) {
    parent.addPageFrame((String)nameList.getSelectedValue());
  }
}
}
```

Now you have the site frame going. The new page frame needs to be able open the file (if it exists) and display the file for editing. The cut, copy, and paste buttons from our earlier example allow you to move text around in a file and between open files in the application.

Like the site frame, we'll create a subclass of JInternalFrame for our page frame. We can use the constructor for the interface work again, and then allow the text area to manage all of the text display and editing work:

```
// PageFrame.java
// A simple extension of the JInternalFrame class that contains a list
// object. Elements of the list represent HTML pages for a web site.
//
import java.awt.*;
import java.io.*;
import java.awt.event.*;
import javax.swing.*;

public class PageFrame extends JInternalFrame implements ActionListener {

  SiteManager parent;
  String filename;
  JTextArea ta;

  public PageFrame(String name, SiteManager sm) {
    super("Page: " + name, true, true, true, true);
    parent = sm;
    setBounds(50,50,300,150);

    // Use the JFrame's content pane to store our desktop
    Container contentPane = getContentPane();

    // Create a text area to display the contents of our file and put it in a
    // scrollable pane so we can get at all of it
    ta = new JTextArea();
    JScrollPane jsp = new JScrollPane(ta);
    contentPane.add(jsp, BorderLayout.CENTER);
```

```
    // Add a "File->Save" option to the menubar for this frame
    JMenuBar jmb = new JMenuBar();
    JMenu fileMenu = new JMenu("File");
    JMenuItem saveItem = new JMenuItem("Save");
    saveItem.addActionListener(this);
    fileMenu.add(saveItem);
    jmb.add(fileMenu);
    setJMenuBar(jmb);

    // Now get the content, based on the filename passed in
    filename = name;
    loadContent();
  }

  public void actionPerformed(ActionEvent ae) {
    // Can only be the save menu in this simple example
    saveContent();
  }
}
```

Here we need to add some load and save routines to the `PageFrame` class for the text areas. You'll learn more about the `read()` and `write()` methods in Chapter 19, *Text 101*, but for now we'll just use them, since they provide such a convenient way to read and write text files:

```
public void loadContent() {
  try {
    FileReader fr = new FileReader(filename);
    ta.read(fr, null);
    fr.close();
  }
  catch (Exception e) { System.err.println("Could not load page: "+filename); }
}

public void saveContent() {
  try {
    FileWriter fw = new FileWriter(filename);
    ta.write(fw);
    fw.close();
  }
  catch(Exception e) { System.err.println("Could not save page: "+filename); }
}
```

To make the cut and paste operations simpler, we'll put in some public access methods to manipulate the text. All three of these routines are built to function regardless of the clipboard implementation you use. We'll be using the system clipboard (via some convenience methods found in `JTextComponent`) for this example, but you could just as easily use your own clipboard, or eventually, drag-and-drop text. You can get more information on the system clipboard in *Java AWT*, by John Zukowski (O'Reilly).

```
public void cutText() { ta.cut(); }
public void copyText() { ta.copy(); }
public void pasteText() { ta.paste(); }
```

Now you can start the program and bring up the individual HTML files by selecting them from the list. Each file will have its own internal frame that you can move around, resize, iconify, maximize, and close. You can cut, copy, and paste text between files. You can save edits using menus attached to each popup frame. You can even detach the toolbar and let it "float." All this for about 250 lines of code!

Well, now that we've had a bit of fun, it's time to move on to the details. The next chapter plunges into the world of Swing with the JComponent class. Good luck, and have fun!

3

Swing Component Basics

The previous chapter showed you how easy it was to create some impressive-looking programs with Swing components. Now it's time to dig in a little deeper. We begin this chapter by presenting an overview of Action, a key class in Swing, and briefly discussing ChangeEvent and PropertyChangeEvent, two central event classes in Swing. Finally, we spend the remainder of the chapter introducing the JComponent class, the heart and soul of all Swing components.

Understanding Actions

Actions are a popular addition to Swing. An action allows a programmer to bundle a commonly used procedure and its bound properties (including an image to represent it) into a single class. This construct comes in handy if an application needs to call upon a particular function from multiple sources. For example, let's say that a Swing programmer creates an action that saves data to disk. The application could then invoke this action from both the Save menu item of the File menu, and the Save button on a toolbar. Both components reference the same action object, which performs the task of saving the data. If the save function is disabled for some reason, this property can be set in the action as well. The menu and toolbar objects are automatically notified that they can no longer save any data, and can relay that information to the user.

Actions and Containers

Swing containers, such as JMenu, JPopupMenu, and JToolBar, can each accept action objects with their add() methods. When an action is added, these containers automatically create a GUI component, which the add() method then returns to you for customization. For example, a JMenu or a JPopupMenu creates and returns a JMenuItem from an Action, while a JToolBar creates and returns a JButton. The action is then paired with the newly-created GUI component in two ways: the GUI component registers as a PropertyChangeListener for any property changes that might occur in the action object, while the action object registers as an ActionListener on the GUI component. Figure 3-1 shows the interactions between a menu item or toolbar and an Action.

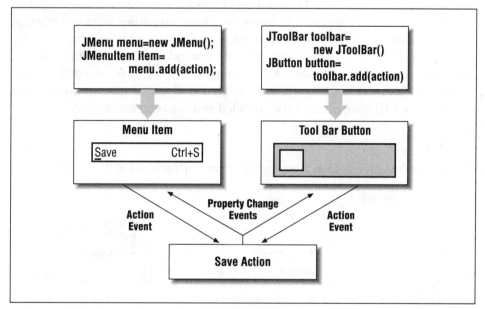

Figure 3-1. An action in conjunction with a Swing menu item and toolbar

Essentially, this means that if the menu item or button is selected by the user, the functionality inside of the action is invoked. On the other hand, if the action is disabled, it sends a PropertyChangeEvent to both the menu item and the toolbar, causing them to disable and turn gray.

The Action Interface

An action is defined by the interface it implements, which in this case is javax.swing.Action. Action extends the ActionListener interface from AWT; this forces concrete classes that implement Action to provide an action-Performed() method. The programmer uses the actionPerformed() method to implement whatever behavior is desired. For example, if you are creating a Save action, you want to put the code to save the data inside of your actionPer-formed() method.

When the action is added to an accepting container, such as JMenu, JPopupMenu, or JToolBar, the container automatically registers the action as an ActionListener of the GUI component it creates. Consequently, if the GUI component is selected by the user, it simply invokes the actionPerformed() method of the action to do its job.

The Action interface defines five constants, which serve as keys for storing standardized Action properties. The method of storage varies from implementer to implementer, but a Hashtable is common. These properties store information such as the name of the action, its description, and a representative icon. Also, the Action interface defines a boolean property that indicates whether the action is enabled or disabled. Recall that the GUI component created for the action registers itself as a PropertyChangeListener. Hence, if any of these properties are modified, the GUI component will be notified and can react accordingly.

Property

The Action interface defines the property shown in Table 3-1.

Table 3-1. Action Property

Property	Data Type	get	is	set	bound	Default Value
enabled	boolean		•	•		

See also java.awt.ActionListener.

The enabled property defines whether anyone can invoke the action. When this property changes, the action should fire a PropertyChangeEvent describing the change.

Note that the keyed properties are not shown. These are really properties because changing one should fire a PropertyChangeEvent. However, because they do not use standard accessors, they do not fit the true JavaBeans property model, so we have omitted them from Table 3-1.

Methods

public abstract Object getValue(String key)
public abstract void putValue(String key, Object value)
    Store various keyed properties for the action. A string-based key is used to index the values. Several string constants representing the keys are shown in Table 3-2. When putValue() is called with any property, and the value passed in is different than what was there previously, the implementing object must fire a PropertyChangeEvent to all registered listeners describing the change.

Table 3-2. String-Based Key Constants for the Action Interface

Constant	Meaning
DEFAULT	Default setting
NAME	Name of the action
SHORT_DESCRIPTION	Short text description of what the action does
LONG_DESCRIPTION	Long text description of what the action does
SMALL_ICON	Represents a small icon typically used in a toolbar

public abstract void actionPerformed(ActionEvent e)

This method is required by the `ActionListener` interface (it does not actually exist in the `Action` interface). Any concrete class that implements the `Action` interface must provide an `actionPerformed()` method that performs whatever task the action is supposed to accomplish.

Events

Objects implementing the `Action` interface must fire a `PropertyChangeEvent` when any keyed property is changed, or when the action is enabled or disabled. Containers that accept actions typically listen for these `PropertyChangeEvent` notifications so they can update their own properties or appearances.

public abstract void addPropertyChangeListener(PropertyChangeListener listener)
public abstract void removePropertyChangeListener(PropertyChangeListener listener)

Add or remove the specified `PropertyChangeListener` from the event listener list.

The AbstractAction Class

The `AbstractAction` class is an abstract implementation the `Action` interface. `AbstractAction` provides the default functionality for almost all of the methods defined in the `Action` interface. You can extend this class to create your own specific actions. If you do so, the only method for which you must provide an implementation is the `actionPerformed()` method. This method is where you provide the functionality for the action. Here is a simple example:

```
class MyAction extends AbstractAction {

    public MyAction(String text, Icon icon) {
        super(text,icon);
    }
    public void actionPerformed(ActionEvent e) {
        System.out.println("Action ["+e.getActionCommand()+"]!");
    }
}
```

Here, we simply print out the action command that was sent with the `Action-Event`. You can add more features based on the contents of the `ActionEvent`.

Properties

The `AbstractAction` class stores its keyed properties in a `Hashtable` object. Beyond that, the `AbstractAction` object contains a single property, as shown in Table 3-3. The `enabled` property defines whether the application can invoke the action. When this property changes, `AbstractAction` fires a `PropertyChangeEvent`. The set accessor for this property, `setEnabled()` is synchronized.

Table 3-3. AbstractAction Properties

Property	Data Type	get	is	set	bound	Default Value
enabled *	boolean		•	•	•	true

Events

The `AbstractAction` class fires a `PropertyChangeEvent` when any property in the hashtable is changed or when the action is enabled or disabled.

public synchronized void addPropertyChangeListener(PropertyChangeListener listener)
public synchronized void removePropertyChangeListener(PropertyChangeListener listener)
> Add or remove the specified `PropertyChangeListener` from the event listener list.

protected void firePropertyChange(String propertyName, Object oldValue, Object newValue)
> Notifies all registered listeners that a property change has occurred in the action. It specifies the name of the property, as well as the old and new values.

Protected Fields

The following are protected fields in the `AbstractAction` class:

protected boolean enabled
> Defines whether the action is enabled or disabled.

protected javax.swing.event.PropertyChangeSupport changeSupport
> Manages the change listeners for the `AbstractAction`. Event-related methods in this class typically call upon their `PropertyChangeSupport` equivalents here. Notice that Swing is using its own `PropertyChangeSupport` class in JDK 1.2/Swing 1.1. In Swing 1.0, it used the `PropertyChangeSupport` class from `java.beans`.

Constructors

public AbstractAction()
public AbstractAction(String name)
public AbstractAction(String name, Icon icon)

The constructors for the `AbstractAction` object can be used to set the name and icon hashtable properties of the action under the `NAME` or `SMALL_ICON` keys, respectively.

Methods

public Object getValue(String key)
public void putValue(String key, Object value)

Store or retrieve various elements in a private `Hashtable`. A string-based key is used to index the `Hashtable` values. See the `Action` interface earlier in the chapter for an enumeration of common string-based keys.

Using an Action

This example creates an `Action` for both a menu item and a toolbar, displaying both components and allowing the user to click on either one. When the components are clicked, the `actionPerformed()` method of the action is called. Don't worry if you don't understand all the methods behind the toolbar or the menu; these classes will be discussed later. For now, it is important to see that selecting either one performs the action.

```
// ActionExample.java
//
import java.awt.*;
import java.awt.event.*;
import javax.swing.*;
import javax.swing.border.*;

public class ActionExample extends JPanel {

    public JMenuBar menuBar;
    public JToolBar toolBar;

    public ActionExample() {
        super(true);

        // Create a menu bar and give it a bevel border
        menuBar = new JMenuBar();
        menuBar.setBorder(new BevelBorder(BevelBorder.RAISED));

        // Create a menu and add it to the menu bar
        JMenu menu = new JMenu("Menu");
```

```
        menuBar.add(menu);

        // Create a toolbar and give it an etched border
        toolBar = new JToolBar();
        toolBar.setBorder(new EtchedBorder());

        // Instantiate a sample action with the NAME property of
        // "Download" and the appropriate SMALL_ICON property
        SampleAction exampleAction = new SampleAction("Download",
                                    new ImageIcon("action.gif"));

        // Finally, add the sample action to the menu and the toolbar.
        menu.add(exampleAction);
        toolBar.add(exampleAction);
    }


    class SampleAction extends AbstractAction {

        // This is our sample action. It must have an actionPerformed() method,
        // which is called when the action should be invoked.
        public SampleAction(String text, Icon icon) {
            super(text,icon);
        }

        public void actionPerformed(ActionEvent e) {
            System.out.println("Action [" + e.getActionCommand() + "] performed!");
        }
    }

    public static void main(String s[]) {
        ActionExample example = new ActionExample();

        JFrame frame = new JFrame("Action Example");
        frame.addWindowListener(new BasicWindowMonitor());
        frame.setJMenuBar(example.menuBar);
        frame.getContentPane().add(example.toolBar, BorderLayout.NORTH);
        frame.setSize(200,200);
        frame.setVisible(true);
    }
}
```

The preceding example creates a toolbar with a single button and a menu with a single menu item. Both are generated from the SampleAction class, and are shown in Figure 3-2. Note that we used the BasicWindowMonitor that we developed in Chapter 2, *Jump Starting a Swing Application*, inside our main() function to close the window properly.

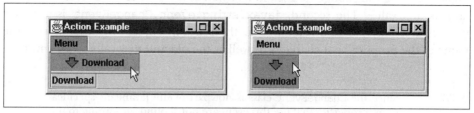

Figure 3-2. An action in a menu and in a toolbar

Selecting the menu item or clicking on the toolbar button a few times both yield the same results to the console:

```
Action [Download] performed!
Action [Download] performed!
Action [Download] performed!
```

Now for something interesting. You can add the following line to the constructor to disable the action:

```
exampleAction.setEnabled(false);
```

With this line, the `PropertyChangeEvent` propagates to listeners in the menu item and in the toolbar button, causing both components to turn gray and become disabled. Figure 3-3 shows what happens when an action is disabled.

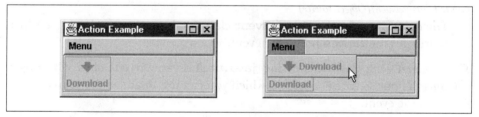

Figure 3-3. A disabled action in a menu and in a toolbar

Of course, you can enable the menu item and toolbar button again at any time with the following line of code:

```
exampleAction.setEnabled(true);
```

Upon execution, the property change again propagates, re-enabling both components simultaneously.

Sending Change Events in Swing

Swing actually uses two different change event classes. The first is the standard `java.beans.PropertyChangeEvent` class. This class passes a reference to the object, sending the change notification, as well as the property name, its old value, and its new value. The second, `javax.swing.event.ChangeEvent`, is a lighter version that only passes a reference to the sending object—in other words, the name of the property that changed, as well as the old and new values, are omitted.

NOTE   Since the `ChangeEvent` class is not part of the JavaBeans specifications, properties that use this event are not "bound" according to the JavaBeans standard. In order to prevent confusion, properties that use a `ChangeEvent` to notify listeners of property changes have not been marked as bound in our property tables.

Because the `ChangeEvent` only includes a reference to the event originator, which never changes, you can always define a single, static `ChangeEvent` and reuse it over and over when firing events from your component.

The ChangeEvent Class

The `ChangeEvent` is a stripped-down version of the `java.beans.PropertyChangeEvent` class. This class has no methods or properties, only a constructor:

Constructor

public ChangeEvent(Object source)
     The constructor for the `ChangeEvent` class. It takes only a single object, which represents the entity sending the event.

The `ChangeEvent` class extends the `java.util.EventObject` class. This object contains the `getSource()` method, which you can use to access the source object that fired the event.

The ChangeListener Interface

Objects that intend to receive change events must implement the `com.sun.java.swing.event.ChangeListener` interface. They can then register to receive `ChangeEvent` objects from a publisher class. The `ChangeListener` interface only consists of one method:

Method

public abstract void stateChanged(ChangeEvent e)
     Implemented in a listener object to receive `ChangeEvent` notifications.

The JComponent Class

JComponent is an abstract class that almost all Swing components extend; it provides much of the underlying functionality common throughout the Swing component library. Just as the java.awt.Component class serves as the guiding framework for most of the AWT components, the javax.swing.JComponent class serves an identical role for the Swing components. We should note that the JComponent class extends java.awt.Container (which in turn extends java.awt.Component), so it is accurate to say that Swing components carry with them a great deal of AWT functionality as well.

Because JComponent extends Container, many Swing components can serve as containers for other AWT and Swing components. These components may be added using the traditional add() method of Container. In addition, they can be positioned with any Java layout manager while inside the container. The terminology remains the same as well: components that are added to a container are said to be its *children*; the container is the *parent* of those components. Following the analogy, any component that is higher in the tree is said to be its *ancestor*, while any component that is lower is said to be its *descendant.*

Recall that Swing components are considered "lightweight." In other words, they do not rely on corresponding peer objects within the operating system to render themselves. As we mentioned in Chapter 1, *Introducing Swing*, lightweight components draw themselves using the standard features of the abstract Graphics object, which not only decreases the amount of memory each component uses, but allows components to have transparent portions and take on nonrectangular shapes. And, of course, lightweight components are free from a dedicated look-and-feel.

It's not out of the question to say that a potential benefit of using lightweight components is a decrease in testing time. This is because the functionality necessary to implement lightweight components in the Java virtual machine is significantly less than that of heavyweight components. Heavyweight components must be individually mapped to their own native peers. On the other hand, one need only implement a single lightweight peer on each OS for all the Swing components to work correctly. Hence, there is a far greater chance that lightweight components will execute as expected on any operating system and not require rounds of testing for each platform.

NOTE   Because all Swing components extend Container, you should be careful that you don't add() to Swing components that aren't *truly* containers. The results can range from amusing to destructive.

In JDK 1.2, JComponent reuses some of the functionality of the `java.awt.Graphics2D` class. This consists primarily of responsibilities for component painting and debugging.

Inherited Properties

Swing components carry with them several properties that can be accessed through JComponent, but otherwise originate with AWT. Before we go any further, we should review those properties of `java.awt.Container` and `java.awt.Component` that can be used to configure all Swing components. This discussion is relatively brief; if you need a more thorough explanation of these AWT classes, see our sister book *Java AWT* by John Zukowski (O'Reilly). Table 3-4 lists the properties that JComponent inherits from its AWT superclasses.

Table 3-4. Properties Inherited from the AWT Component and Container Classes

Property	Data Type	get	is	set	bound	Default Value
background	Color	•		•		
colorModel	ColorModel	•				
component (indexed)	Component	•				
componentCount	int	•				
components	Component[]	•				
cursor	Cursor	•		•		Cursor.DEFAULT_CURSOR
enabled	boolean		•	•		true
font	Font	•		•		
foreground	Color	•		•		
insets	Insets	•				Insets(0,0,0,0)
layout	LayoutManager	•		•		BorderLayout()
locale	Locale	•		•		
location	Point	•		•		
locationOnScreen	Point	•		•		
name	String	•		•		""
parent	Container	•		•		null
size	Dimension	•		•		
showing	boolean		•			true
valid	boolean		•			
visible	boolean		•	•		true

Let's briefly discuss these properties. The `background` and `foreground` properties indicate which colors the component will use to paint itself. We should mention that with Swing the background property will be disabled if the component is transparent (not opaque). The read-only colorModel property returns the current model used to translate colors to pixel values; the user generally does not need to access this property. The font property lets you get or set the font used for displaying text in the component.

The indexed component property maintains a list of all the components inside the container. You can tell how many there are through the use of the integer componentCount property. If you want to access all of them through a Component array, retrieve the components property. The insets property tells the current insets of the container, while the layout property indicates which layout manager is managing the components of the container. Technically, this means that you can use any component as a container. Don't be misled; if a component doesn't seem like a reasonable conainer, it probably can't be used as one. (Don't, for example, try to add a JButton to a JScrollBar.) A number of components use these properties for internal, specialized layout managers and components.

The locale property specifies the internationalization locale for the application. The location property indicates the x,y coordinates of the component's upper-left corner in the container's coordinate space. If you want to see the location of the component's upper-left corner in screen coordinates, use the read-only locationOnScreen property.

The name property gives this component a string-based name that components can display if they choose. The parent property references the container that is acting as this component's parent, or null if there is none. The size property tells the component's current height and width in pixels.

The showing property indicates whether the component is currently showing on the screen, while the visible property tells if the component is marked to be drawn on the screen. There's an odd, nonintuitive relationship between visible and showing. A component that is visible isn't necessarily showing. "Visible" means that a component is capable of being displayed; "showing" means that the component is actually displayed (though it may be obscured by something else). Most containers (JPanel, JFrame, etc.) are invisible by default; most other components (JButton, etc.) are visible by default. So if you add a JButton to an invisible JFrame, for example, the button will be visible but not showing. It's ready to be displayed, but happens to be in a container that isn't currently displayed.

Finally, if the valid property is false, the component needs to be resized or moved by the component's layout manager. If it is true, the component is ready to be displayed.

Other Methods

Here are some other methods you will frequently call when working with Swing components:

public Component add(Component comp)
public Component add(Component comp, int index)
public void add(Component comp, Object constraints)
public void add(Component comp, Object constraints, int index)

> Add a component to the container, given the optional constraints and the current index.

public void remove(int index)
public void remove(Component comp)
public void removeAll()

> Remove the appropriate component from the container. The final method empties the entire container.

public void pack()

> This method of `java.awt.Window` resizes the window to encompass the preferred size of all the contained components, as placed by the current layout manager. It's a good idea to call `pack()` after you've added components to a top level container with a layout manager, such as `JFrame`, `JApplet`, `JDialog`, and `JWindow`.

public void validate()
public void invalidate()

> The `invalidate()` method is typically called on a `Container` to indicate that its children need to be laid out, or on a `Component` to indicate that it needs to be re-rendered. This method is often called automatically. However, certain changes to a `Component` (such as changing the size of a button by changing its label or font) do not cause it to be invalidated. In such cases, `invalidate()` must be called on the `Component` to mark it as invalid, and `validate()` must be called on its `Container`. The `validate()` method is typically called to cause a `Container` to be validated, laid out, and repainted. Calling this method is especially important when you add or remove `Components` in a `Container` that is already displayed.
>
> Swing improves the `validate()`/`invalidate()` situation a bit by calling `invalidate()` in response to many property changes, saving you from having to make the call. Unfortunately, there are still situations (such as changing a `JButton`'s font) that still do not trigger an automatic `invalidate()` call, so you'll still have to explicitly call `invalidate()` in some situations.

The key things to take away from these methods are:

- You may need to call invalidate() if you make changes to the appearance of a displayed component.

- You must call validate() on Containers that have been invalidated (typically by the addition or invalidation of a child).

As a result of deprecation and the movement toward JavaBeans accessors, AWT has some methods with multiple names. For example, show() and setVisible(true) are essentially the same. It is always better to use the JavaBeans-style name—setVisible()—when working with Swing; the newer name will be less confusing for people familiar with the JavaBeans conventions.

JComponent Properties

Now to the heart of the matter. JComponent has many properties of its own, and overrides (or otherwise modifies) the behavior of many of its inherited properties. This is where the new and interesting stuff happens. Table 3-5 shows a summary of JComponent's properties.

Table 3-5. JComponent Properties

Property	Data Type	get	is	set	bound	Default Value
UIClassID	String	•				"ComponentUI"
accessibleContext	Accessible-Context	•				null
alignmentX*	float	•		•		
alignmentY*	float	•		•		
autoscrolls	boolean	•		•		false
border	Border	•		•	•	null
bounds*	Rectangle	•		•		
debugGraphicsOptions	int	•		•		DebugGraphics.NONE_OPTION
doubleBuffered	boolean		•	•		false
focusCycleRoot	boolean		•			false
focusTraversable	boolean		•			true
graphics*	Graphics	•				
height[a]	int	•				bounds.height
insets*	Insets	•		•		
location*	Point	•		•		Point(bounds.x, bounds.y)
managingFocus	boolean		•			false

See also java.awt.Container and java.awt.Component (Table 3-4).

Table 3-5. JComponent Properties (continued)

Property	Data Type	get	is	set	bound	Default Value
maximumSize*	Dimension	•		•		
minimumSize*	Dimension	•		•		
nextFocusable-Component	Component	•		•	•	
opaque[a]	boolean		•	•	•	false
optimizedDrawing-Enabled	boolean		•			true
paintingTile	boolean		•			
preferredSize*	Dimension	•		•		
registeredKeyStrokes	KeyStroke[]	•				
requestFocusEnabled	boolean		•	•		true
rootPane	JRootPane	•				
size*	Dimension	•		•		Dimension (bounds.height, bounds.width)
toolTipText	String	•		•	•	null
topLevelAncestor	Container	•				
validateRoot	boolean		•			false
visible*	boolean		•	•		true
visibleRect	Rectangle	•				
width[a]	int	•				bounds.width
x[a]	int	•				bounds.x
y[a]	int	•				bounds.y

See also java.awt.Container and java.awt.Component (Table 3-4).

[a] In JDK 1.2, these properties move to java.awt.Component.

UI Delegates and UIClassIDs

As we mentioned in Chapter 1, all Swing components use a modified MVC architecture. Each Swing component is responsible for maintaining two unique objects: a model and a UI delegate. The object representing the model handles the state information specific to the component, while the UI delegate determines how the component paints itself based on the model's state information.

Note that there is no property for a model in JComponent. You typically access the model property at the level of a JComponent subclass. This is because each Swing component defines its own data model, unique from all other components. The UI delegate property, on the other hand, can be handled at the JComponent level, because the methods that handle the rendering of lightweight components are always the same. These methods (e.g., `installUI()`, `uninstallUI()`, `paint()`) can be traced back to the abstract class `javax.swing.plaf.ComponentUI`, which serves as the superclass for all UI delegates.

`JComponent` contains a reference to the current UI delegate for the object. `JComponent` allows a subclass to alter the component's UI delegate with the protected `setUI()` method; this method effectively resets the look-and-feel of the component. The UI therefore acts like a write-only property, but we hesitate to call it a property because its accessor isn't public. Invoking `setUI()` by itself, however, does not change the display. A call to `updateUI()` is also required, which forces the component to redraw itself. If you are looking to change the entire look-and-feel of the application, it is better to change it universally with the `setLookAndFeel()` method of `UIManager`, than to change it one component at a time. See Chapter 2 for a simple example of how to work with various look-and-feels.

Each Swing component maintains a read-only string constant, `UIClassID`, that identifies the type of UI delegate that it uses. Most Swing components override the accessor `getUIClassID()` and return a string constant, typically the letters "UI" appended to the name of the component (without the "J"). This string is then used by Swing's UI manager to match the component with a UI delegate for the current look-and-feel. For example, a `JButton` object has a `UIClassID` string of `ButtonUI`. If the current look-and-feel is "Metal," the `UIManager` can figure out that the `MetalButtonUI` is the correct UI-delegate class to use. See Chapter 26, *Look & Feel*, for more information about the `UIManager` and using look-and-feels.

Invalidating and Repainting

Sometimes entire components need to be drawn to the screen. At other times, only parts of components can (or should) be drawn. For example, if an internal frame is dragged across the container, the entire internal frame is redrawn along the way until it reaches its destination. However, only the parts of the container uncovered by the internal frame need to be repainted. We typically do not repaint the entire component, as this would be an unnecessary waste of processing time. (See Figure 3-4.)

Swing uses a *repaint manager* to repaint lightweight components. The repaint manager maintains a queue of rectangular areas that need to be repainted; it calls these areas "dirty regions." Sometimes the rectangles are the size of entire components; other times they are smaller. The repaint manager processes repaint requests as they are added to the queue, updating dirty regions as quickly as possible while preserving the visual order of the components. Recall that in AWT, the `Component` class contains an overloaded `repaint()` method that allows you to repaint only a subrectangle of the component. The same is true with `JComponent`. If only part of a component needs to be repainted, the repaint manager

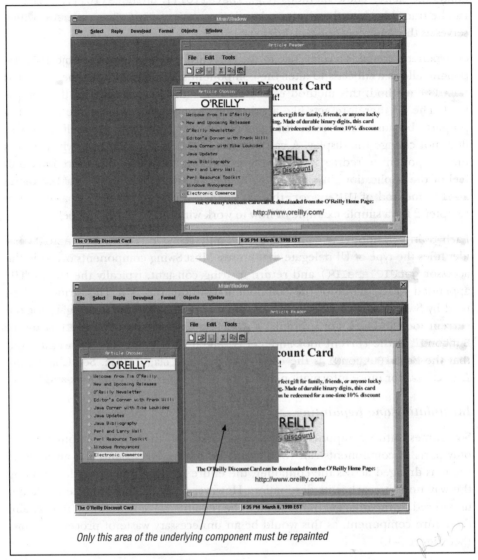

Only this area of the underlying component must be repainted

Figure 3-4. Performing repaints for components in Java

invokes an overloaded version of the repaint() method that takes a Rectangle parameter.

JComponent contains two repaint() methods that each add specified rectangles directly to the dirty region. Like AWT, you want call upon these methods instead of invoking the paint() method directly, which bypasses the RepaintManager. The RepaintManager class is discussed in more detail in Chapter 28, *Swing Under the Hood*.

The paint() Method and Opaqueness

Because JComponent is the direct subclass of the AWT Container class, it is the official recipient of repaint requests through its paint() method. As you might guess, JComponent must delegate this request by passing it on to the paint() method of the UI-delegate object. The responsibility, however, does not end there. JComponent is actually responsible for painting three items: the component itself, any borders associated with the component, and any children that it contains.

The order is intentional. Swing assumes that the components drawn last are always on top; hence, child components always paint over their parents. JComponent contains three protected methods that it uses to complete this functionality:

- paintComponent()
- paintBorder()
- paintChildren()

Because of the complexity involved in painting and repainting Swing components, you should always try to override these three methods while creating your own components. Again, do not try to override paint() unless you call super-paint() while you're at it.

The boolean property opaque dictates the transparency of each Swing object.[*] If this property is set to false, the component's background color is transparent. This means that any areas left untouched by the component's rendering allow graphics in the background to show through. If the property is set to true, the rectangular painting region is completely filled with the component's background color before it is rendered. Incidentally, transparency was not possible before lightweight components. Native peer objects in Java 1.0 always drew their component on a solid rectangle; anything that was behind the component was erased. Figure 3-5 shows the difference between an opaque and a transparent (non-opaque) label without a dark background color. The label on the left is transparent, so its background color is ignored; the label's text appears on top of the container's relatively light background.

JComponent can optimize its repainting time if none of its children overlap; this is because the repaint manager does not have to compute the hidden and visible areas for each child component before rendering them. Some containers, such as JSplitPane, are designed so that overlap between child components is impossible, so this optimization works nicely. Other containers, such as JLayeredPane, have support for child components that can overlap. JComponent contains a property that Swing frequently calls upon to see if it can optimize component

---

[*] In JDK1.2, the isOpaque() method is defined in java.awt.Component.

Figure 3-5. Transparency and opaqueness

drawing: `optimizedDrawingEnabled`. In `JComponent`, the property is set to `true` by default. If overlap occurs in a subclass of `JComponent`, the subclass should override the `isOptimizedDrawingEnabled()` accessor and return `false`. This prevents the repaint manager from using the optimized drawing process when rendering the container's children.

`JComponent` contains a boolean read-only property `paintingTile` that indicates whether the component is currently in the process of painting a *tile*—that is, a child component that does not overlap any other children. The `isPaintingTile()` method will return `true` until all tiles have been painted.

The `visibleRect` property is a `Rectangle` that indicates the intersection of the component's visible rectangles with the visible rectangles of all of its ancestors. Why the *intersection*? Remember that you can have a contained object that is clipped by its parent. For example, you can move an internal frame so that a portion of it falls outside the parent window's clipping region. Therefore, the visible portion (the portion that is actually drawn to the screen) will consist only of the intersection of the parent's visible portion and the child's visible portion. You typically will not need to access this property.

The `validateRoot` property is `false` by default. If it is set to `true`, it designates this component as the root component in a validation tree. Recall that each time a component in a container is invalidated, its container is invalidated as well, along with all of its children. This causes an invalidation to move all the way up the component hierarchy, stopping only when it reaches a component for which `isValidateRoot()` returns `true`. Currently, the only components that set this property to `true` are `JRootPane` (which is used by all the Swing top-level components), `JScrollPane`, and `JTextField`.

The `topLevelAncestor` property contains a reference to the top-level window that contains this component, usually a `JWindow` or `JApplet`. The `rootPane` property contains the low-level `JRootPane` for this component; `JRootPane` is covered in more detail in Chapter 8, *Swing Containers*.

Finally, `JComponent` contains a property called `autoscrolls`, which indicates whether a component is capable of supporting autoscrolling. This property is false by default. If the property is true, an Autoscroller object has been set over this component. The Autoscroller object monitors mouse events on the target component. If the mouse is dragged outside the component, the auto-scroller will force the target component to scroll itself. Autoscrolling is typically used in containers such as JViewport.

Position, Size, and Alignment

You can set and retrieve a Swing component's current position and size on the screen through the bounds property, or more precisely, through the location and size properties of JComponent. The location property is defined as a Point in the parent's coordinate space where the upper-left corner of the component's bounding box resides. The size property is a Dimension that specifies the current width and height of the component. The bounds property is a Rectangle object that gives the same information: it bundles both the location and the size properties. Figure 3-6 shows how Swing measures the size and location of a component.

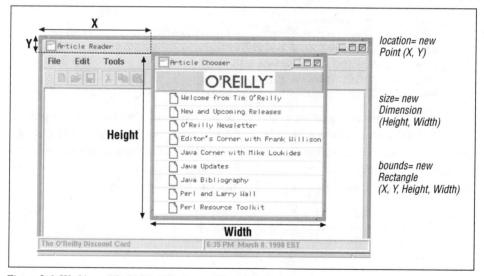

Figure 3-6. Working with the bounds, size, and location properties

Unlike the AWT Component class, the getBounds() accessor in JComponent can take a pre-instantiated Rectangle object, as shown below:

```
Rectangle myRect = new Rectangle();
myRect = component.getBounds(myRect);
```

If a Rectangle is supplied, the getBounds() method alters each of the fields in the passed-in Rectangle to reflect the component's current size and position, returning a copy of it. If the reference passed in is a `null`, the method instantiates a new `Rectangle` object, sets its values, and returns it. You can use the former approach to conserve memory if there are several calls to `getBounds()`.

The `setBounds()` method resets the component's size and position. This method also takes a `Rectangle` object. If the new settings are a change from the previous settings, the component is moved, typically resized, and invalidated. If the component has a parent, it is invalidated as well. Be warned that various layout managers may override any changes you attempt to make to the bounds property. Invalidating a component with a call to `setBounds()` may force the layout manager to recompute and reset the bounds of the component in relation to the other components—resolving it to the same size as before.

Here is a short example that shows how to retrieve the current position and size of any Swing component:

```
JFrame frame = new JFrame("Test Frame");
frame.setBounds(20,20,200,200);
frame.setVisible(true);

Rectangle r = new Rectangle();
r = frame.getBounds(r);
System.out.println("X      = " + r.x());
System.out.println("Y      = " + r.y());
System.out.println("Width  = " + r.width());
System.out.println("Height = " + r.height());
```

There is a shorthand approach for retrieving each of the bounds properties. `JComponent` contains four methods that directly access them: `getX()`, `getY()`, `getWidth()`, and `getHeight()`. You can use these accessors directly instead of instantiating a `Rectangle` object on the heap with a call to `getBounds()`. Consequently, you can replace the last six lines with the following four:

```
System.out.println("X      = " + frame.getX());
System.out.println("Y      = " + frame.getY());
System.out.println("Width  = " + frame.getWidth());
System.out.println("Height = " + frame.getHeight());
```

In addition, if it is just the size or location you are concerned with, you can use the `getSize()` and `getLocation()` accessors to set or retrieve the size or location. The size is specified as a `Dimension`, while the location is given as a `Point`. Like `getBounds()`, the `getLocation()` accessor also allows the programmer to pass in a pre-instantiated `Point` object. If one is passed in, the method alters the coordinates of the `Point` instead of instantiating a new object.

```
Point myPoint = new Point();
myPoint = component.getLocation(myPoint);
```

You can still use the `setSize()` and `setLocation()` methods of `java.awt.Component` if you prefer to code with those as well. Again, note that when resetting the size of the component, the layout manager may override the new value and reset it back to its previous value, thus ignoring your new size values.

The three well-known AWT sizing properties, `minimumSize`, `preferredSize`, and `maximumSize`, are accessible through `JComponent`. `minimumSize` indicates the smallest size that the component is allowed to be when it exists in a container. `preferredSize` contains the size at which the container's layout manager should strive to draw the component. `maximumSize` indicates the largest size the component should be when displayed in a container. If none of these properties are set by the user, they are always calculated by the component's UI delegate or directly by the layout manager of the container, in that order. An important new feature of `JComponent` is the addition of the methods `setMinimumSize()`, `setPreferredSize`, and `setMaximumSize()`, allowing you to change these properties without subclassing.

Finally, `JComponent` contains two read/write properties that help interested layout managers align the component in a container: `alignmentX` and `alignmentY`. Both of these properties contain floating-point values between 0.0 and 1.0; the numbers determine the position of the component relative to any siblings. A number closer to 0 indicates that the component should be positioned closer to the left or top side, respectively. A perfect 0.5 indicates that the component should be placed at the center, while a number nearing 1 indicates that the component should be positioned closer to the right or bottom. Currently, the only layout managers that use these properties are the `BoxLayout` and `OverlayLayout` managers; all AWT 1.1 layout managers ignore these properties and position their children by other means. We discuss these managers further in Chapter 11, *Specialty Panes and Layout Managers*.

Adding Borders

One widely requested feature of AWT is the ability to provide components with borders. Swing has defined a `border` property in `JComponent` that accepts objects that implement the `javax.swing.border.Border` interface. Figure 3-7 shows a component with a border.

Figure 3-7. Borders in Swing

Swing currently provides seven different styles of borders, including an empty border. Each one extends the `javax.swing.border.Border` interface.

In addition, you can surround a Swing component with multiple borders through the use of the CompoundBorder class. This class allows you to combine any two borders into a single border by specifying one as the outer border and the other as the inner. Because CompoundBorder accepts other compound borders, you can recursively layer as many borders as you like into a single border.

Using borders is extremely easy. For example, one of the border styles that is provided with Swing is an etched border. Here is how you might create a bevel border similar to the one in Figure 3-7:

```
JLabel label = new JLabel("A Simple Label");
label.setBorder(new EtchedBorder());
```

One important characteristic of Swing is that if a border property is set on a component, the border overrides the component's insets property. Swing allows the programmer to specify an empty border, so you can still pad the component with extra space as well as provide a border if you use a CompoundBorder. If the border property is null, the default insets are used for the component instead. Borders are covered in more detail in Chapter 13, *Borders*.

Working with Tooltips

JComponent also provides Swing components with support for *tooltips*. Tooltips are small windows of text that pop up when the user rests the mouse over the target component. They are typically used to supplement the meaning of an icon or button, but they can also provide the user with instructions or important information about the underlying component. The tooltip usually disappears after a designated amount of time (four seconds by default) or if the mouse is moved outside of the component's bounds.

Simple string-based tooltips can be automatically set or retrieved using the tool-TipText property of JComponent, as shown here:

```
JButton button = new JButton("Press Me!"); // JButton extends JComponent
button.setToolTipText("Go Ahead!");
System.out.println(button.getToolTipText());
```

Figure 3-8 shows what a tooltip looks like on the screen.

Figure 3-8. A tooltip for a component

JComponent does not manage tooltips by itself; it gets help from the ToolTipManager class. The ToolTipManager continually scans for mouse events on components that have tooltips. When the mouse passes into a component with a tooltip set, the ToolTipManager begins a timer. If the mouse has not left the component's region in three-quarters of a second, a tooltip is drawn at a preset location near the component. If the mouse has moved out of a region for longer than a half-second, the tooltip is removed from the screen.

With the default setToolTipText() and getToolTipText() methods, JComponent handles the creation of an appropriate tooltip. If you want to get more creative, however, Swing provides a separate object for tooltips: JToolTip. With it, you can completely redefine the characteristics of a tooltip by declaring your own JToolTip object and overriding the createToolTip() method of JComponent to return it to the ToolTipManager on demand.

We cover the JToolTip object and the ToolTipManager in more detail in Chapter 27, *Swing Utilities*.

Client Properties

Swing components can maintain a special table of properties called "client properties." The purpose is to provide specialized properties that can be meaningful in components only in certain instances. For example, let's assume that a specific look-and-feel uses a client property to store information about how a component should display itself when that L&F is activated. As you might guess, this client property would be meaningless when another look-and-feel is activated. Using the client properties approach allows various look-and-feels to expand their component properties without deluging the Swing source base with L&F-specific data.

The name "client properties" is somewhat confusing, because client properties are distinct from JavaBeans-style properties. Obviously, there's a big difference: unlike JavaBeans properties, you can create new client properties without subclassing; you can even create new client properties at runtime. These two methods in JComponent store and retrieve client properties:

```
myComponent.putClientProperty("aClientProperty", Boolean.TRUE);
Boolean result = (Boolean)getClientProperty("aClientProperty");
```

Note that because we are using a hashtable, the properties must be objects and not primitive data types. Hence, we are forced to use the Boolean object, instead of simplysetting true and false.

Double Buffering

The JComponent class allows all Swing components to take advantage of *double buffering*. The idea behind double buffering is that it takes longer for a component to render its individual parts on screen than it does for a rectangular area-copy to take place. If the former occurs with multiple refreshes, the human eye is likely to catch the component in the process of being drawn, and it may appear to flicker. With the latter, the screen is usually updated as fast as the monitor can refresh itself.[*]

When double buffering is activated in Swing, all component rendering performed by the repaint manager is done to an off-screen buffer. Upon completion, the contents of the off-screen buffer are quickly copied (not redrawn) on the screen at the component's position. You can activate double buffering by accessing the boolean doubleBuffered property of JComponent. Passing in true to the setDoubleBuffered() method enables double buffering; false shuts it off:

```
JButton button = new JButton("Test Button");
button.setDoubleBuffered(true);     // Turns on double buffering
```

You can use the isDoubleBuffered() method to check if double buffering is currently enabled on a Swing component.

With double buffering, transparency is maintained in non-opaque components because the graphics underneath the component are copied into the buffer first before any off-screen rendering takes place. However, there is a slight penalty for double buffering non-opaque components, because Swing is performing two area copies instead of one: one to copy the background over, and one to copy the background plus the component back.

Buffers also chew up a great deal of memory. Therefore, the repaint manager tries to avoid initializing and using more than one off-screen buffer at a time. For example, if an off-screen buffer has been set for both a container and one of its children, the buffer for the parent container is used for both components.

Serialization

Objects that extend JComponent are serializable; that is, the object's data at that point can be written out, or *serialized*, and written onto an output stream, which might send it over a network or save it in a file.[†] The serialized output can later be *deserialized* back into memory, where the object will continue to operate from its original state. Object serialization gives Java programmers a powerful and convenient way to store and retrieve object data, as opposed to saving or transmitting state data in custom-made storage files. Serialization also provides the ability to transfer quickly active components from one virtual machine to another, which

---

[*] Area copies are always faster because they are performed by the operating system or even the graphics card of the computer. At this level, they are commonly referred to as "bit-block transfers" or BitBLTs.

[†] The only exceptions to this are fields marked with the transient keyword.

can be useful in remote method invocation (RMI) and other forms of distributed computing.

You can serialize components in Swing as you normally would in Java: by passing a reference to the object into the `writeObject()` method of an `ObjectOutput-Stream` object. In the event that the serialized object contains a reference to another object, the serialization algorithm recursively calls `writeObject()` on that object as well, continuing until all objects in the class hierarchy are serialized. The resulting *object graph* is then written out to the output stream. Conversely, you can deserialize a component back in by using the `readObject()` method of an `ObjectInputStream`, which reverses the entire process.

NOTE   The baseline for serialization is JDK 1.2. If you serialized objects with JDK 1.1/Swing 1.0, they may be incompatible with JDK 1.2/Swing 1.1 objects.

Debug Graphics

Lightweight components are rendered entirely in Java, as opposed to off-loading their work to a native heavyweight peer. The abstract `Graphics` class outlines platform-independent implementations for line-drawing, image-painting, and area-copying and filling that a lightweight peer can call upon to draw itself. If you create your own component, or extend an already existing one, a `Graphics` object is often passed to the UI delegate's `paint()` method to help out with the drawing.

Sometimes the way you intend a component to be painted, however, isn't how it appears on the screen. Debugging painting problems can prove to be troublesome, especially when dealing with transparency, opaqueness, and double buffering. `JComponent`, however, can generate a special version of the `Graphics` object, called `DebugGraphics`, which it can pass to a UI delegate's `paint()` method that aids in debugging. This object can take a set of user-configurable debugging options that modify how a component is drawn to the screen.

If you wish to activate debugging for the component's graphics, you can pass one or more debugging flags into the `setDebugGraphicsOptions()` method of `JComponent`. The debugging flags are given in Table 3-6.

The debug options outlined in Table 3-6 are bits in a binary mask; you can set more than one at the same time by using the bitwise OR (|) operator, as shown here:

```
JButton myButton = new JButton("Hello");  // JButton extends JComponent
myButton.setDebugGraphicsOptions(DebugGraphics.FLASH_OPTION
                            | DebugGraphics.LOG_OPTION);
```

Table 3-6. Constants for Debug Graphics Options

DebugGraphics Constant	Description
DebugGraphics.FLASH_OPTION	Causes each graphics primitive to flash a user-configurable number of times as it is being rendered.
DebugGraphics.LOG_OPTION	Prints a text message to the screen as each graphics primitive is drawn.
DebugGraphics.BUFFERED_OPTION	Raises a window that shows the drawing that is taking place in the offscreen buffer. This is useful in the event that the double-buffered feature has been activated.
DebugGraphics.NONE_OPTION	Disables all debug graphics options.

When any of the debug graphics options are set, the getComponentGraphics() method of JComponent returns a DebugGraphics object, instead of a normal Graphics object. As we mentioned above, this is the same type of object that is passed to the UI delegate of the component. When a component draws itself, it calls upon the functionality of the DebugGraphics object to perform the task, just as it would with a typical Graphics object. The drawing primitives are then slowed or logged so that the user can help identify any problems.

Focus and Focus Cycle

The term *focus* refers to the active component on the screen. We typically think of the active component as the frame or window that is the current recipient of mouse and keyboard events. Other components, such as buttons and text fields, can have the focus as well. Visual cues, like a colored title bar or a dashed outline, often help us determine where the current focus resides.

When we click on another component with the mouse, the focus is typically shifted, and that component is now responsible for consuming mouse and keyboard events. You can also *traverse* the focus by pressing the TAB key to move forward or the TAB and the SHIFT key together to move backward. This causes the focus to cycle from one component to the next, eventually completing a loop and returning to its original position. This loop is called the *focus cycle*.

A group of components within a single container can define a focus cycle of its own. If the container has its own focus cycle, the focus repeatedly traverses through all of its children that accept the focus. The focus cycle is typically determined by the location of components in the container, although you can create your own focus manager if you require a different behavior. With the default focus manager, the component closest to the top-left corner of the container always receives the focus first. The focus then moves from left to right across the components, and from top to bottom. Figure 3-9 shows how the default focus cycle shifts focus between components in a container.

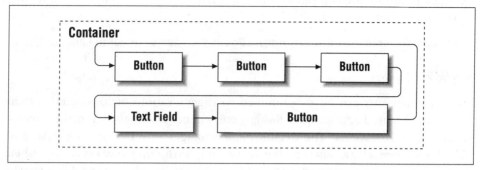

Figure 3-9. The default container focus cycle

If a container has a focus cycle of its own, it should override the JComponent method isFocusCycleRoot() and return true. If the method returns true, then the container is known as the *root container* of the focus cycle.

The root container is allowed to indicate whether or not it is *managing focus*. If it is, it should override the isManagingFocus() method and return true. When a container is managing focus, the focus manager is disabled and all key events are sent to the container for processing. By default, the isManagingFocus() method returns false, allowing the Swing focus manager to handle the task of shifting and traversing the focus.

With any JComponent, you can explicitly name the component that should receive the focus next by setting the nextFocusableComponent property. In addition, focus can be programmatically requested through the JComponent method requestFocus(), which the focus manager can call to shift the focus to this component. This is often done when the user selects the object (i.e., presses a JButton). If you don't want your component to be able to respond to request-Focus() calls, you can set the requestFocusEnabled property of JComponent to false.

There is an important distinction here: setting the requestFocusEnabled property to false does not mean that the focus cannot be *traversed* onto your component; it simply means that it cannot be programmatically requested. JComponent provides a similar property, focusTraversable, that you can enable or disable to specify whether a component receives the focus when traversed. Note the difference between the two. If you wanted to allow a JButton to gain the focus when clicked, but skipped in the focus cycle, you would set the requestFocusEnabled property to true and the focusTraversable property to false. If you wanted to prevent focus from being shifted to the JButton when clicked, you would set the requestFocusEnabled property to false. If you wanted the

JButton to ignore focus traversal and focus requests (i.e., never have the focus), you would set both properties to false.

We discuss the concept of focus and the FocusManager in detail in Chapter 28.

Keyboard Events

Swing components can be programmed to trigger various actions when certain keystrokes occur. For example, Swing components automatically handle focus-related keyboard events. The default focus manager searches only for TAB and SHIFT-TAB keystrokes, altering the focus and consuming the keystrokes when detected. If the focus manager does not know how to handle a keystroke, it checks to see whether the processComponentKeyEvent() method can consume it. This method currently does nothing. However, you can override it in a subclass if you want to react to a keystroke in your own way. If neither of these succeeds in consuming the key event, the JComponent class checks to see if a *keyboard action* has been registered for that keystroke. A keyboard action binds a Swing action and a keystroke to a specific component.

You can associate keyboard actions to a component through one of two regis-terKeyboardAction() methods:

```
void registerKeyboardAction(ActionListener anAction, String aCommand,
                    KeyStroke aKeyStroke, int aCondition)
void registerKeyboardAction(ActionListener anAction, KeyStroke aKeyStroke,
                    int aCondition)
```

In order to use these methods, you need a couple of things: a KeyStroke object that represents the keystroke combination you wish to monitor, and an Action that occurs when that keystroke has taken place. (Actions are covered earlier in the chapter.) If you want the keyboard event to insert a specific string as the event's action command, you can specify that as well. A final parameter to the registerKeyboardAction() method places restrictions on when the action is fired. Table 3-7 shows the constants for the final parameter.

Table 3-7. Constants for Keystroke Registration

Constant	Description
WHEN_FOCUSED	The Action takes place only when the target component has the focus.
WHEN_IN_FOCUSED_WINDOW	The Action takes place when the target component has the focus or resides in a container that has the focus.
WHEN_ANCESTOR_OF_ FOCUSED_WINDOW	The Action takes place when the target component has the focus, or is the ancestor of the component that currently has the focus.

The latter two constants come in handy in different situations. JCompo-nent.WHEN_IN_FOCUSED_WINDOW can be used in a situation where you want to define a keystroke that works on a specific component in a container, but func-tions even when the parent container has the focus. For example, a dialog could have a save button that captures the letter "S" in conjunction with a modifier key (ALT, CTRL, or SHIFT). It could register this keyboard action with the button to perform a save when the "S" key was pressed. The keyboard action would work even if the button didn't explicitly have the focus—as long as the parent dialog did. On the other hand, if you want to define a keyboard event that is standard-ized throughout a container and its components, register a keyboard event at the container level and use the JComponent.WHEN_ANCESTOR_OF_FOCUSED_WINDOW option. This allows keyboard events to be recognized at the container level, even if the descendant has the focus.

You can use the registeredKeyStrokes property of JComponent to get access to all the keystrokes registered for a component. The getRegisteredKey-Strokes() method returns this information as an array of KeyStroke objects. If you want to see what condition is tied to any particular keystroke, you can use the getConditionForKeyStroke() method. If you want to obtain the action associ-ated with the keystroke, use getActionForKeyStroke(). In both cases, you will have to specify the target keystroke as the search key.

Accessibility

As we mentioned in Chapter 1, one entirely new feature about Swing components is that they support accessibility options. Accessibility options are constructed for users who have trouble with traditional user interfaces, and include support for alternative input and output devices and actions. There are several parts to accessi-bility; they are covered in more detail in Chapter 25, *Programming with Accessibility*, and Chapter 26. JComponent implements the methods required by the Acces-sible interface, though it does not implement the interface itself.

The accessibleContext property holds an AccessibleContext object that is the focal point of communication between the component and auxilliary accessi-bility tools. There's a different default context for each kind of JComponent. For nore information, see Chapter 25.

Events

Table 3-8 shows the events fired by JComponent (not counting the many events it inherits from the AWT classes).

Table 3-8. JComponent Events

Event	Description
PropertyChangeEvent	A change has occurred in JComponent.
VetoablePropertyChangeEvent	A change has occurred in JComponent that can be vetoed by interested listeners.
AncestorEvent	An ancestor of a JComponent has moved or changed its visible state.

Event Methods

The following methods may move to `java.awt.Component` in the future.

protected void firePropertyChange(String propertyName, Object oldValue, Object newValue)
public void firePropertyChange(String propertyName, byte oldValue, byte newValue)
public void firePropertyChange(String propertyName, char oldValue, char newValue)
public void firePropertyChange(String propertyName, short oldValue, short newValue)
public void firePropertyChange(String propertyName, int oldValue, int newValue)
public void firePropertyChange(String propertyName, long oldValue, long newValue)
public void firePropertyChange(String propertyName, float oldValue, float newValue)
public void firePropertyChange(String propertyName, double oldValue, double newValue)
public void firePropertyChange(String propertyName, boolean oldValue, boolean newValue)
> Fire a `PropertyChangeEvent` to all registered listeners if `newValue` differs from `oldValue`. There are overloaded versions of this method for each primitive data type, as well as a protected version for the generic `Object` class.

protected void fireVetoableChange(String propertyName, Object oldValue, Object newValue)
> *throws PropertyVetoException*
> Fires a vetoable `PropertyChangeEvent` to all registered listeners if `newValue` differs from `oldValue`.

public synchronized void addPropertyChangeListener(PropertyChangeListener listener)
public synchronized void removePropertyChangeListener(PropertyChangeListener listener)
> Add and remove a `PropertyChangeListener` to the event registration list.

public synchronized void addVetoableChangeListener(VetoableChangeListener listener)
public synchronized void removeVetoableChangeListener(VetoableChangeListener listener)
> Add and remove a `VetoableChangeListener` to the event registration list. A `VetoableChangeListener` is allowed to veto any property changes that occur inside a component. If only one veto occurs, the property is not changed.

public void addAncestorListener(AncestorListener listener)
public void removeAncestorListener(AncestorListener listener)
> Add and remove an `AncestorListener` to the event registration list. All registered objects are notified if any of the components' ancestors change position or are made visible or invisible.

JComponent also inherits all the event listener registration methods from its AWT superclasses, Container and Component. From Component, it inherits the methods to add or remove a ComponentListener, FocusListener, KeyListener, MouseListener, or MouseMotionListener. From Container, it inherits the methods to add or remove a ContainerListener. We won't describe all the listener interfaces here; for more information, see *Java AWT* by John Zukowski (O'Reilly). However, you should note that Swing only supports the JDK 1.1 event model. To receive an event, you always must register as a listener with the JComponent that generates the event—events are never propagated through the containment hierarchy, as they were with JDK 1.0.

Fields and Methods

Protected Fields

protected AccessibleContext accessibleContext
Holds the AccessibleContext for the component.

protected EventListenerList listenerList
The event listener list for the component. See Chapter 27 for more information on the EventListenerList class.

protected ComponentUI ui
The UI delegate for the component.

Constructor

public JComponent()
Initializes a simple JComponent and sets the layout manager to null.

Graphics

protected Graphics getComponentGraphics(Graphics g)
Accepts a graphics context and modifies its foreground color and font to match the current defaults. If the debug graphics option has been activated, the method returns a special graphics object that the programmer can configure for debugging component drawing with the color and font modifications.

public void update(Graphics g)
Equivalent to paint(g). This is significantly different from the update() method of Component, which first cleared the component's background. In Swing, clearing the component is handled by ComponentUI, based on whether the component is opaque.

public boolean contains(int x, int y)

Returns true if the coordinates passed in are inside the bounding box of the component, false otherwise. The method always asks the UI delegate first, giving it an opportunity to define the bounding box as it sees fit. If the UI delegate does not exist for this component, or cannot define the bounding box, the standard component contains() method is invoked.

publicInsets getInsets (Insets insets)

Copies the JComponent's insets into the given Insets object, and returns a reference to this object.

public void paint(Graphics g)

The primary method that the AWT subsystem calls upon for components to draw themselves if they are not obscured. This method delegates most of its work to the protected methods paintComponent(), paintBorder(), and paintChildren(), which it calls in that order. Because this method performs its own internal calculations, it is generally not a good idea to override it in a subclass; if you want to redefine how a component draws itself, override paintComponent() instead.

public void reshape(int x, int y, int w, int h)

Resets the bounds property of the component.

protected void paintComponent(Graphics g)

Draws the component using the graphics context provided. Unless overridden, it simply turns around and calls the paint() method of the delegate. If there is no delegate, the method does nothing.

protected void paintChildren(Graphics g)

Cycles through each of the component's children, invoking the paint() method on each one.

protected void paintBorder(Graphics g)

Paints the border (or borders) outlined in by the border property of JComponent. Note that if a border is defined, JComponent ignores its own insets and uses the border instead.

public void repaint(long tm, int x, int y, int width, int height)
public void repaint(Rectangle r)

These methods place a request to repaint the specified region on the repaint manager's update queue. The initial variable tm of the first repaint() method is no longer used and can be ignored. Because the redrawing queue knows the correct order to draw various component layers, it is widely preferred that you call these methods, instead of directly invoking paint().

public void paintImmediately(int x, int y, int w, int h)
public void paintImmediately(Rectangle r)

These methods force an immediate repaint of the specified region in the component. This method is invoked by the repaint manager when it is time for the component to draw itself; the programmer should not call this method. This method may move to `java.awt.Component` in the future.

public void revalidate()

Adds the current component to the repaint manager's revalidation queue, which is located on the system event queue.

public void computeVisibleRect(Rectangle visibleRect)

Calculates a `Rectangle` that represents the intersection of the component's own visible rectangle and each of its ancestors. The result is placed in the `visibleRect` property and is used to determine how much of a component is drawn to the screen.

Focus

public void requestFocus()

Shifts the focus to this component if the `requestFocusEnabled` property is `true`.

public boolean requestDefaultFocus()

Shifts the focus to a default component, typically the first focus-traversable component in the current container. If the method is unable to find such a component, it returns `false`.

public void grabFocus()

Used by focus managers to shift the focus to this component, regardless of the state of the `requestFocusEnabled` property. Because of this, it is generally better to use `requestFocus()` instead of this method.

public boolean hasFocus()

Returns `true` if this component currently has the focus. This method is defined in `java.awt.Component` in JDK 1.2.

Keyboard Actions

public void registerKeyboardAction(ActionListener anAction, String aCommand,
    KeyStroke aKeyStroke, int aCondition)
public void registerKeyboardAction(ActionListener anAction, KeyStroke aKeyStroke,
    int aCondition)

These methods register a specific keyboard action with the component. When the keystroke `aKeyStroke` occurs under the appropriate conditions, `JCompo-nent` invokes the `actionPerformed()` method of the object implementing anAction. If the programmer desires, the action command can be set to aCommand. The conditions involved are listed in Table 3-7.

public void unregisterKeyboardAction(KeyStroke aKeyStroke)

Unregisters a keyboard action from the component.

public int getConditionForKeyStroke(KeyStroke aKeyStroke)

Returns the conditions defined for the keyboard action triggered by aKeyStroke.

public ActionListener getActionForKeyStroke(KeyStroke aKeyStroke)

Returns the Action that is registered to be triggered by aKeyStroke.

public void resetKeyboardActions()

Clears all keyboard actions for the component.

protected void processComponentKeyEvent(KeyEvent e)

This protected method is called if there are no keyboard actions matching the keystroke directed at the component. The method currently does nothing; you can override it in your own components to perform component-specific keyboard handling.

Tooltips

public String getToolTipText(MouseEvent event)

Retrieves the text used for the component's tooltip, given the appropriate mouse event. JComponent always returns the current toolTipText property. However, you can override this method in your own component if you want to return different strings based on various mouse events.

public Point getToolTipLocation(MouseEvent event)

Currently returns null. You can override it in your own component to specify the local component coordinates where its tooltip should be displayed. If the method returns null, Swing chooses a location for you.

public JToolTip createToolTip()

Returns a new instance of JToolTip by default. If you want to extend the JToolTip class with a tooltip creation of your own, you can override this method in your components, forcing it to return the new class to the tooltip manager.

Client Properties

public final Object getClientProperty(Object key)

Searches the client property list for the Object specified under the appropriate key. It returns null if no object is found.

public final void putClientProperty(Object key, Object value)

Inserts the specified client property value under the appropriate key. If the value passed in is null, the property is cleared from the list.

Event Handlers

protected void processFocusEvent(FocusEvent e)

Sets an internal flag that indicates whether the JComponent has gained or lost the focus. You can override this method in a subclass to determine how your component reacts to super.processFocusEvent().

protected void processComponentKeyEvent (KeyEvent e)

This method currently does nothing. You can override it if you want to handle KeyEvents in your component independent of those consumed by the focus handler and key listeners. If you hanle any KeyEvent notifications in this method, be sure to consume them.

protected void processKeyEvent(KeyEvent e)

Handles the key events for each component. It first checks with the focus manager to see if it can consume the key event, then checks for any interested listeners, and (if it has not been consumed) invokes the processComponent-KeyEvent() above. If the key event still has not been consumed at this point, it will check to see if there are any keyboard actions registered with the component.

protected void processMouseMotionEvent(MouseEvent e)

Tracks mouse drags in the event that the Swing component supports auto-scrolling. You can override this method in a subclass to determine how your component reacts to mouse motion events. If you do so, be sure to call super.processMouseMotionEvent().

Miscellaneous

protected void setUI(ComponentUI u)

Installs u as the UI delegate for the component, effectively changing the component's look-and-feel. This change doesn't appear onscreen until updateUI() is called.

public void updateUI()

Called by the current UIManager to notify the component that the look-and-feel for the component has changed, and the UI delegate should repaint itself.

public void addNotify()

Called by Swing to notify the component that it has gained a parent. The method fires a notification to all AncestorListeners, passing in a reference to the new parent component. The parent component (and its ancestors) inherit each of the appropriate keyboard actions and AWT event masks, as appropriate. addNotify() also fires a property change event indicating that the "ancestor" property has changed.

public void removeNotify()

Called by Swing to notify the component that it has lost a parent. The method fires a notification to all AncestorListeners, informing them that the parent component is no longer an ancestor. removeNotify() also fires a property change event indicating that the "ancestor" property has changed.

public void scrollRectToVisible(Rectangle aRect)

Calls similar methods up the component hierarchy. You can override this method at any level if you want to explicitly handle scrolling updates.

public static boolean isLightweightComponent(Component c)

A convenience method that returns a boolean indicating whether the component passed is a lightweight component. If it is, the method returns true. Otherwise, it returns false. This method may move to java.awt.Component in the future.

4

Labels and Icons

We'll begin our look at the Swing components with the `JLabel` class. In addition, we'll look at Swing's new `Icon` interface and an implementation of this interface called `ImageIcon`. With just these few new constructs, you'll begin to see how much Swing has done to improve UI development in Java.

Labels

Swing allows you to create labels that can contain text, images, or both. We'll begin this chapter with a look at the `JLabel` class.

The JLabel Class

The `JLabel` class allows you to add basic, nonfunctional labels to a user interface. Because of their inherent simplicity, there is no model class for `JLabel` components. Figure 4-1 shows a class diagram for `JLabel`. We'll get into the two relations to `Icon` a little later.

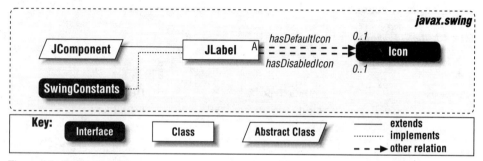

Figure 4-1. JLabel class diagram

Unlike java.awt.Label objects, JLabel objects may consist of both text and graphics (icons). For simple text labels, the interface to JLabel is very similar to that of java.awt.Label. The code to create and display a very simple text label looks like this:

```
// SimpleJLabelExample.java
//
import javax.swing*;

public class SimpleJLabelExample {
  public static void main(String[] args) {
    JLabel label = new JLabel("A Very Simple Text Label");

    JFrame frame = new JFrame();
    frame.addWindowListener(new BasicWindowMonitor());
    frame.getContentPane().add(label);
    frame.pack();
    frame.setVisible(true);
  }
}
```

Running this simple program produces the display shown in Figure 4-2.

Figure 4-2. A simple JLabel

Properties

The JLabel class contains the properties shown in Table 4-1. The icon and disabledIcon properties specify the icon to be displayed by default and when the label is disabled respectively. If no disabledIcon is specified, a grayscale version of the default icon is created automatically. The font property is shown in this table only because the setFont() method is overridden to call repaint() after calling super.setFont().

Table 4-1. JLabel Properties

Property	Data Type	get	is	set	bound	Default Value
UI	LabelUI	•		•		from L&F
UIClassID*	String					"LabelUI"
accessibleContext*	Accessible-Context	•				JLabel.Accessible-JLabel

See also properties from the JComponent class (Table 3-5).

Table 4-1. JLabel Properties (continued)

Property	Data Type	get	is	set	bound	Default Value
disabledIcon	Icon	•		•	•	null
displayedMnemonic	int	•		•	•	'\0'
font*	Font	•		•		from L&F
horizontalAlignment	int	•		•	•	LEFT
horizontalTextPosition	int	•		•		RIGHT
icon	Icon	•		•	•	null
iconTextGap	int	•		•	•	4
labelFor	Component	•		•	•	null
text	String	•		•	•	" "
verticalAlignment	int	•		•	•	CENTER
verticalTextPosition	int	•		•	•	CENTER

See also properties from the JComponent class (Table 3-5).

displayedMnemonic indicates the character to be rendered as an accelerator key (typically meaning that the first occurrence of this character in the label text is underlined). If the labelFor property has been set, the referenced component will gain focus when the mnemonic is pressed in conjunction with the ALT key.[*] One common use of this feature is to apply mnemonics to labels appearing next to text fields, allowing the fields to gain focus when the shortcut key is pressed. We'll see an example of this strategy later in this section.

NOTE   displayedMnemonic is an integer property. However, a setDisplayedMnemonic() method is defined, which takes a char. If you use the version that takes an int, be aware that specifying the value of a lowercase character will cause the character to appear underlined, but will not generate the expected action when pressed. Even if the character appears in lowercase in the labels, the mnemonic should still be set to uppercase. Typically, it makes more sense to use the char method anyway.

The horizontalAlignment and verticalAlignment properties are used to specify the alignment of the label's content (text and icon). The values for these properties are defined in SwingConstants, and must be LEFT, RIGHT, or CENTER for horizontalAlignment; for verticalAlignment it must be TOP, BOTTOM, or

---

[*] This is actually up to the look-and-feel, but the basic look-and-feel implements it this way, and none of the other Swing L&Fs change this behavior.

CENTER. horizontalTextPosition and verticalTextPosition indicate the position of the label's text relative to the its icon (if both icon and text are defined). Like the alignment properties, the valid values for the text position properties are LEFT, RIGHT, TOP, BOTTOM, and CENTER. We'll cover these properties in more detail in the sections that follow. Note that JLabel implements SwingConstants, so you can refer to the constant values listed in this paragraph as either SwingConstants.XYZ or JLabel.XYZ—whichever you prefer.

The iconTextGap property reflects the space (in pixels) between the label's icon and text (if both are defined). The text property is simply the label's textual content. Finally, the UI property holds a reference to the LabelUI object used to render the label.

displayedMnemonic and labelFor Properties

The following example shows how the displayedMnemonic and labelFor properties can be used to direct focus to a component, based on the mnemonic assigned to a label. All we do here is create three labels and three text fields, assigning one field to each label:

```
// MnemonicLabels.java
//
import javax.swing.*;
import java.awt.*;

// Shows how displayedMnemonic and labelFor properties work together
public class MnemonicLabels {
  public static void main(String[] args) {

    // Create labels and text fields
    JLabel lastName = new JLabel("Last Name", JLabel.RIGHT);
    JLabel middleName = new JLabel("Middle Name", JLabel.RIGHT);
    JLabel firstName = new JLabel("First Name", JLabel.RIGHT);

    JTextField lastField = new JTextField(10);
    JTextField middleField = new JTextField(10);
    JTextField firstField = new JTextField(10);

    // Add displayedMnemonic and labelFor property values
    lastName.setDisplayedMnemonic('L');
    middleName.setDisplayedMnemonic('M');
    firstName.setDisplayedMnemonic('F');
    lastName.setLabelFor(lastField);
    middleName.setLabelFor(middleField);
    firstName.setLabelFor(firstField);

    // Layout and Display
    JPanel p = new JPanel();
```

```
        p.setLayout(new GridLayout(3,2,5,5));
        p.add(lastName);
        p.add(lastField);
        p.add(middleName);
        p.add(middleField);
        p.add(firstName);
        p.add(firstField);

        JFrame f = new JFrame();
        f.addWindowListener(new BasicWindowMonitor());
        f.setContentPane(p);
        f.pack();
        f.setVisible(true);
    }
}
```

When executed, this example produces the display shown in Figure 4-3. The first letter in each label is underlined, based on the assigned mnemonic. Pressing ALT-L, ALT-M, or ALT-F will cause focus to shift to the corresponding text field.

Figure 4-3. JLabels with mnemonics

Alignment

Like `java.awt.Labels`, JLabels allow the specification of a horizontal alignment to indicate whether the label's contents should be left justified, right justified, or centered. These values can be set in the constructor or by a call to the setHorizontalAlignment() method. In addition, the JLabel class provides the same type of flexibility for specifying the vertical position of the label. However, since the JLabel constructors were modeled after those of java.awt.Label, vertical alignment may only be specified via the setVerticalAlignment() method.

The following example shows the effects of horizontal and vertical alignment:

```
// AlignmentExample.java
//
import javax.swing.*;
import java.awt.*;

public class AlignmentExample {
  public static void main(String[] args) {
```

```
// Create the labels and set alignment
JLabel label1 = new JLabel("BottomRight", SwingConstants.RIGHT);
JLabel label2 = new JLabel("CenterLeft", SwingConstants.LEFT);
JLabel label3 = new JLabel("TopCenter", SwingConstants.CENTER);
label1.setVerticalAlignment(SwingConstants.BOTTOM);
label2.setVerticalAlignment(SwingConstants.CENTER);
label3.setVerticalAlignment(SwingConstants.TOP);

// Add borders to the labels . . . more on Borders later in the book!
label1.setBorder(BorderFactory.createLineBorder(Color.black));
label2.setBorder(BorderFactory.createLineBorder(Color.black));
label3.setBorder(BorderFactory.createLineBorder(Color.black));

// Put it all together . . .
JFrame frame = new JFrame();
frame.addWindowListener(new BasicWindowMonitor());
Container c = frame.getContentPane();
c.setLayout(new GridLayout(3,1));
c.add(label1);
c.add(label2);
c.add(label3);
frame.setSize(200,200);
frame.setVisible(true);
  }
}
```

Figure 4-4 shows the result of running this program.

Figure 4-4. JLabel alignment

Working with Images

To this point, there have not been many striking differences between Swing JLabels and good old AWT Labels. The fundamental difference between the two is that JLabel allows the label to be composed of text, graphics, or both, while the old `Label` class only allowed simple text labels. This is a powerful enhancement, making it very simple to add graphics to your user interface. Images used in `JLabels` (as well as buttons) are of type `javax.swing.Icon`, an interface described in detail in the next section.

The following two lines of code show how simple it is to create a label containing an image:

```
ImageIcon icon = new ImageIcon("images/smile.gif");
JLabel label = new JLabel(icon);
```

For labels that contain both graphics and text, Swing provides considerable flexibility with respect to the relative location of the text and image. The text for the label may be displayed at any one of nine locations relative to the image. These locations are specified via the `setVerticalTextPosition()` and `setHorizontalTextPosition()` methods, which take values from the `SwingConstants` class discussed earlier. Note the distinction between the label's text position and its alignment; text position reflects the position of the text relative to the image, while alignment specifies the location of the label's contents (image and text) relative to the borders of the label.

Another useful feature of the `JLabel` class is the ability to enable and disable the label by "graying out" the label and text. By default, a call to `JLabel.setEnabled(false)` will switch the image to an automatically generated grayscale version of the original image and alter the text rendering in some (L&F-specific) way. However, the grayscale image is only used if no disabled icon has been set. The `setDisabledIcon()` method can be used to set an alternate image for the disabled label.

Additionally, the spacing between the image and the text can be specified by a call to `setIconTextGap()`, which takes a single parameter specifying the number of pixels between the image and the icon. This setting has no effect if both the horizontal and the vertical text positions have been set to `SwingConstants.CENTER`, since in this case the text will be placed directly over the image.

Figure 4-5 shows a group of labels with text and image, with the text at each of the nine locations relative to the image. Labels 0 and 1 are disabled, the first one using the default disabled image and the second one using an explicitly specified alternate image. Labels 2 and 3 show nondefault text gap settings. Here's the source code that produces these labels:

```
// ImageLabelExample.java
//
import javax.swing.*;
import java.awt.*;
```

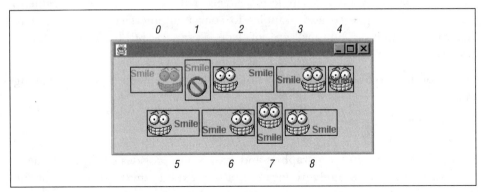

Figure 4-5. JLabel text position and properties

```
public class ImageLabelExample {
  public static void main(String[] args) {
    JLabel[] labels= new JLabel[9];

    labels[0] = makeLabel(JLabel.TOP, JLabel.LEFT);
    labels[1] = makeLabel(JLabel.TOP, JLabel.CENTER);
    labels[2] = makeLabel(JLabel.TOP, JLabel.RIGHT);
    labels[3] = makeLabel(JLabel.CENTER, JLabel.LEFT);
    labels[4] = makeLabel(JLabel.CENTER, JLabel.CENTER);
    labels[5] = makeLabel(JLabel.CENTER, JLabel.RIGHT);
    labels[6] = makeLabel(JLabel.BOTTOM, JLabel.LEFT);
    labels[7] = makeLabel(JLabel.BOTTOM, JLabel.CENTER);
    labels[8] = makeLabel(JLabel.BOTTOM, JLabel.RIGHT);

    // Disable label 0
    labels[0].setEnabled(false);

    // Disable label 1 with a disabled icon
    labels[1].setDisabledIcon(new ImageIcon("images/no.gif"));
    labels[1].setEnabled(false);

    // Change text gap on labels 2 and 3
    labels[2].setIconTextGap(15);
    labels[3].setIconTextGap(0);

    // Add the labels to a frame and display it
    JFrame frame = new JFrame();
    frame.addWindowListener(new BasicWindowMonitor());
    Container c = frame.getContentPane();
    c.setLayout(new FlowLayout(FlowLayout.CENTER, 3, 3));
    for (int i=0;i<9;i++)
      c.add(labels[i]);
    frame.setSize(350,150);
    frame.setVisible(true);
  }
```

```
    protected static JLabel makeLabel(int vert, int horiz) {
      JLabel l = new JLabel("Smile", icon, SwingConstants.CENTER);
      l.setVerticalTextPosition(vert);
      l.setHorizontalTextPosition(horiz);
      l.setBorder(BorderFactory.createLineBorder(Color.black));
      return l;
    }

    private static Icon icon = new ImageIcon("images/smile.gif");
  }
```

Don't worry if you don't understand everything we did in this example. We'll explain icons in more detail in this chapter, and will get to borders and frames later in the book. For now, just concentrate on the various properties we set on the different labels and compare the code to the display it produced in Figure 4-5.

Events

The only events explicitly fired by JLabel are PropertyChangeEvents.

Constant

JLabel defines a single constant as shown in Table 4-2. A client property set with this constant as a key is used by JComponent.AccessibleJComponent to derive a name for components that haven't explicitly set one. If the component has a LABELED_BY_PROPERTY defined, the text from the JLabel referenced by the property value will be used as the accessible name of the component.

Table 4-2. JLabel Constant

Constant	Type	Description
LABELED_BY_PROPERTY	String	Client property key used as a back-pointer by the labelFor property.

Field

protected Component labelFor
Contains the value of the labelFor property.

Constructors

JLabel()
Creates a label with no text or icon.

JLabel(Icon image)
JLabel(Icon image, int horizontalAlignment)
Create labels displaying the given icon. If specified, the horizontal alignment must be one of the following values taken from SwingConstants: LEFT, RIGHT, or CENTER.

JLabel(String text)

JLabel(String text, int horizontalAlignment)

Create labels displaying the given text. If specified, the horizontal alignment must be one of the following values taken from SwingConstants: LEFT, RIGHT, or CENTER.

JLabel(String text, Icon image, int horizontalAlignment)

Creates a label with an image, text, and specified horizontal alignment. The horizontal alignment must be one of the following values taken from Swing-Constants: LEFT, RIGHT, or CENTER.

User Interface Method

public void updateUI()

Indicates that the look-and-feel (L&F) has changed.

Other Public Method

public void setDisplayedMnemonic(char aChar)

Provides a convenient way to set the mnemonic property by passing in a char (instead of the property's actual type, int). The character is converted to uppercase and passed to the other setDisplayedMnemonic() method as an int.

Protected Methods

protected int checkHorizontalKey(int x, String s)

Used internally to validate horizontalAlignment and horizontalTextPosition values. It returns the given integer if its value is LEFT, CENTER, or RIGHT. Otherwise, it throws an IllegalArgumentException, with the given string as the exception text. You should never need to call this method directly.

protected int checkVerticalKey(int y, String s)

Used internally to validate verticalAlignment and verticalTextPosition values. It returns the given integer if its value is TOP, CENTER, or BOTTOM. Otherwise, it throws an IllegalArgumentException, with the given string as the exception text. You should never need to call this method directly.

Icons

Swing introduces the concept of an icon for use in a variety of components. The Icon interface and ImageIcon class make dealing with simple images extremely easy.

The Icon Interface

The Icon interface is very simple, specifying just three methods used to determine the size of the Icon and to display it. Implementors of this interface are free to store and display the image in any way, providing a great deal of flexibility. In other words, icons don't have to be bitmaps or GIF images, but are free to render themselves any way they choose; as we'll see later, an icon can simply draw on the component if that's more efficient. The examples at the end of this section show a couple of different ways the interface might be implemented.

Properties

The Icon interface defines the properties listed in Table 4-3. The iconHeight and iconWidth properties specify the size of the Icon in pixels.

Table 4-3. Icon Properties

Property	Data Type	get	is	set	bound	Default Value
iconHeight	int	•				
iconWidth	int	•				

Method

public abstract void paintIcon(Component c, Graphics g, int x, int y)
Paints the Icon at the specified location on the given Graphics. The Component is provided to allow its properties (such as foreground or background color) to be used when painting, or to allow the component to be used as an image observer (see "The ImageIcon Class," later in this chapter).

Implementing Your Own Icons

Here's a class that implements the Icon interface and uses ovals as simple icons:

```
// OvalIcon.java
//
import javax.swing.*;
import java.awt.*;

// A simple Icon implementation that draws ovals
public class OvalIcon implements Icon {

  public OvalIcon(int w, int h) {
    width = w;
    height = h;
  }
```

```
    public void paintIcon(Component c, Graphics g, int x, int y) {
      g.drawOval(x, y, width-1, height-1);
    }

    public int getIconWidth() { return width; }
    public int getIconHeight() { return height; }

    private int width, height;
}
```

And a simple class that creates a few labels to show how it works:

```
// TestOval.java
//
import javax.swing.*;
import java.awt.*;

public class TestOval {
  public static void main(String[] args) {
    JFrame f = new JFrame();
    f.addWindowListener(new BasicWindowMonitor());

    JLabel label1 = new JLabel(new OvalIcon(20,50));
    JLabel label2 = new JLabel(new OvalIcon(50,20));
    JLabel label3 = new JLabel
        ("Round!", new OvalIcon(60,60), SwingConstants.CENTER);
    label3.setHorizontalTextPosition(SwingConstants.CENTER);

    Container c = f.getContentPane();
    c.setLayout(new FlowLayout());
    c.add(label1);
    c.add(label2);
    c.add(label3);
    f.pack();
    f.setVisible(true);
  }
}
```

Running this test program produces the display shown in Figure 4-6.

Figure 4-6. OvalIcon labels

Dynamic Icons

Icons are under no obligation to paint themselves the same way every time they are displayed. It's perfectly reasonable (and often quite useful) to have an icon that uses some sort of state information to determine how to display itself. In the next example, we create two sliders (JSlider is explained in detail in Chapter 6, *Bounded Range Components*) that can be used to change the width and height of a dynamic icon.

```
// DynamicIconExample
//
import javax.swing.*;
import javax.swing.event.*;
import java.awt.*;

// Example of an icon that changes form.
public class DynamicIconExample {
  public static void main(String[] args) {

    // Create a couple sliders to control the icon size
    final JSlider width = new JSlider(JSlider.HORIZONTAL, 1, 150, 75);
    final JSlider height = new JSlider(JSlider.VERTICAL, 1, 150, 75);

    // A little Icon class that uses the current slider values.
    class DynamicIcon implements Icon {
      public int getIconWidth() { return width.getValue(); }
      public int getIconHeight() { return height.getValue(); }

      public void paintIcon(Component c, Graphics g, int x, int y) {
        g.fill3DRect(x, y, getIconWidth(), getIconHeight(), true);
      }
    };
    Icon icon = new DynamicIcon();
    final JLabel dynamicLabel = new JLabel(icon);

    // A listener to repaint the icon when sliders are adjusted.
    class Updater implements ChangeListener {
      public void stateChanged(ChangeEvent ev) {
        dynamicLabel.repaint();
      }
    };
    Updater updater = new Updater();

    width.addChangeListener(updater);
    height.addChangeListener(updater);

    // Lay it all out
    JFrame f = new JFrame();
    f.addWindowListener(new BasicWindowMonitor());
```

```
        Container c = f.getContentPane();
        c.setLayout(new BorderLayout());
        c.add(width, BorderLayout.NORTH);
        c.add(height, BorderLayout.WEST);
        c.add(dynamicLabel, BorderLayout.CENTER);
        f.setSize(210,210);
        f.setVisible(true);
    }
}
```

Figure 4-7 shows the dynamic icon in its initial state, and then again after we've moved the sliders around a bit.

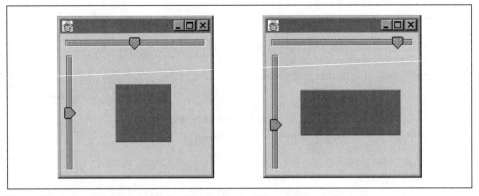

Figure 4-7. A dynamic Icon; its size is controlled by the sliders

The important thing to notice is that the Icon class does not actually store any information. In this case, we've made the Icon class an inner class, giving it direct access to the sliders. Whenever the icon is told to paint itself, it gets its width and height from the values of the sliders. You could also choose to make your Icon class an event listener and have it update itself according to changes in certain events. The options here are wide open.

No matter how your icon gets its data, you need to make sure that any time you want to change the way the icon looks, you trigger a repaint of the icon. In this example, we've done this by listening to change events from the sliders and calling repaint() on the label that's holding the icon any time one of the sliders changes.

The ImageIcon Class

Swing provides a concrete implementation of the Icon interface which is considerably more useful than our OvalIcon class. ImageIcon uses a java.awt.Image object to store and display any graphic and provides synchronous image loading (i.e., the Image is loaded completely before returning), making ImageIcons very powerful and easy to use. You can even use an `ImageIcon` to display an animated GIF.89a, making the ubiquitous "animation applet" as simple as this:

```
// AnimationApplet.java
//
import javax.swing.*;

// A simple animation applet
public class AnimationApplet extends JApplet {
  public void init() {
    ImageIcon icon = new ImageIcon("images/rolling.gif");    // animated gif
    getContentPane().add(new JLabel(icon));
  }
}
```

All we did here was load an animated GIF in the `init()` method and then add it to the applet in `start()`. For more information on `JApplet`, see Chapter 8, *Swing Containers*.

Properties

The `ImageIcon` class defines the properties listed in Table 4-4. The `description` property allows an arbitrary description of the image to be specified. One possible use of this property might be to give a blind user an audio description of the image.

Table 4-4. ImageIcon Properties

Property	Data Type	get	is	set	bound	Default Value
description	String	•		•		null
iconHeight*	int	•				-1
iconWidth*	int	•				-1
image	Image	•		•		null
imageLoadStatus	int	•				0
imageObserver	ImageObserver	•		•		null

The `iconHeight` and `iconWidth` properties default to –1 if no image is loaded by the constructor, while the `image` property simply contains the `Image` object rendered by the icon. `ImageLoadStatus` indicates the success or failure of the image load process, using the constants defined in `java.awt.MediaTracker` (ABORTED, ERRORED, or COMPLETE). The default for this property is zero, which does not map to any of these constants.

The `imageObserver` property contains the `ImageObserver` specified to receive notifications of changes to the image. If this property is `null` (as it is by default), the component containing the icon will be treated as the image observer when the image is painted.

Figure 4-8 shows a class diagram for `ImageIcon` and the classes related to it.

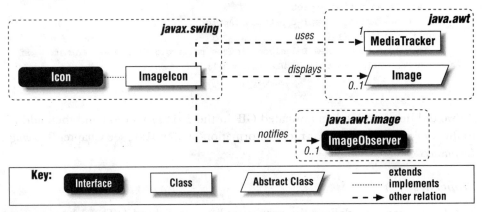

Figure 4-8. ImageIcon class diagram

Serialization

Like most Swing classes, `ImageIcon` implements `Serializable`. The keen observer may see a problem with this: the `java.awt.Image` class used by `Image-Icon` is *not* serializable. By default, this would keep `ImageIcon` objects from serializing properly. The good news is that `ImageIcon` implements the `readObject()` and `writeObject()` methods, so that the pixel representation of the image is stored and retrieved correctly.

Protected Constants

The protected constants defined in `ImageIcon` are in Table 4-5.

Table 4-5. ImageIcon Constants

Constant	Type	Description
component	Component	An empty-implementation inner class of Component used only to satisfy the MediaTracker constructor signature.
tracker	MediaTracker	The MediaTracker used by all ImageIcons when loading images.

Constructors

ImageIcon()
    Creates an uninitialized `ImageIcon`.

ImageIcon(Image image)

ImageIcon(Image image, String description)

Create `ImageIcon` objects from existing images. A textual description of the image may be provided. If no description is provided, an attempt is made to retrieve the "comment" property from the input `Image`. If this is a non-null string, it will be used as the description.

ImageIcon(String filename)

ImageIcon(String filename, String description)

Create `ImageIcon` objects from the contents of the specified GIF or JPEG file. The image is guaranteed to be completely loaded (unless an error occurs) when the constructor returns.

ImageIcon(URL location)

ImageIcon(URL location, String description)

Create `ImageIcon` objects from the contents of the specified URL. The image is guaranteed to be completely loaded (unless an error occurs) when the constructor returns.

public ImageIcon(byte imageData[])

public ImageIcon(byte imageData[], String description)

Create `ImageIcon` objects from an array of bytes containing an image in a supported format, such as GIF or JPEG. The image is guaranteed to be completely loaded (unless an error occurs) when the constructor returns.

User Interface Method

public synchronized void paintIcon(Component c, Graphics g, int x, int y)

Paints the `Image` at the specified location on the input `Graphics`. The given `Component` is passed to the `Graphic`'s `drawImage()` method as the `ImageObserver` (recall that `java.awt.Component` implements `ImageObserver`), if no image observer has been explicitly set.

Protected Method

protected void loadImage(Image image)

Called by the constructors and `setImage()`. It uses a `java.awt.MediaTracker` object to load an image synchronously. On completion, the image is guaranteed to be completely loaded, unless an error occurred, in which case the `imageLoadStatus` property will reflect the error.

5

Buttons

Buttons

Buttons are simple UI components used to generate events when the user presses them. In AWT, buttons were very basic, able to display only simple text strings. In much the same way as JLabel provided improvements over java.awt.Label, the Swing button classes improve on java.awt.Button and java.awt.Checkbox by introducing the ability to display icons, text, or both. In this section, we'll introduce both the ButtonModel interface and DefaultButtonModel class (which define the state of the button). Next, we'll look at the AbstractButton class (which defines much of the functionality for all button types). Finally, we'll look at four concrete subclasses of AbstractButton and see how they can be grouped together using a ButtonGroup.

Figure 5-1 shows the class hierarchy, with significant relationships between the button-related Swing classes. Notice that, as we discussed in the introductory chapters, each button (AbstractButton) keeps a reference to a ButtonModel, which represents its state.

The JMenuItem class shown here (and its subclasses, not shown) is not covered in this chapter. Instead, they are covered in Chapter 14, *Menus and Toolbars*.

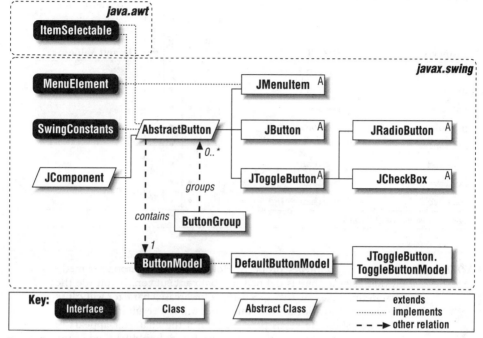

Figure 5-1. Swing Button class diagram

The ButtonModel Interface

The state of any Swing button is maintained by a `ButtonModel` object. This interface defines methods for reading and writing the model's properties and for adding and removing various types of event listeners.

Properties

The properties for the `ButtonModel` interface are listed in Table 5-1. The `actionCommand` property specifies the name of the command to be sent as part of the `ActionEvent` fired when the button is pressed. This can be used by event handlers that are listening to multiple buttons, to determine which button has been pressed. The `group` property contains a reference to the `ButtonGroup` that contains the button (if any).

`mnemonic` contains the key that can be pressed in conjunction with the L&F-specific modifier key in order to produce the same effect as clicking the button with the mouse. The modifier key is currently the ALT key for all Swing L&Fs.

Table 5-1. ButtonModel Properties

Property	Data Type	get	is	set	bound	Default Value
actionCommand	String	•		•		
armed	boolean		•	•		
enabled	boolean		•	•		
group	ButtonGroup			•		
mnemonic	int	•		•		
pressed	boolean		•	•		
rollover	boolean		•	•		
selected	boolean		•	•		

See also java.awt.ItemSelectable.

NOTE   mnemonic is an integer property. However, a setMnemonic() method that takes a char is defined in AbstractButton. If you use the version that takes an int, specifying a lowercase character will cause the character to appear underlined, but will not result in the expected action when the key is pressed. Even if the character appears in lowercase on the button, the uppercase letter should be used as the mnemonic. Typically, it makes more sense to use the char method, unless you are working with the model directly.

The other properties are boolean flags that reflect certain aspects of the button's state. These flags are defined by the constants in Table 5-4. The properties are:

armed

Indicates whether or not releasing the button causes an action to be performed. This becomes false when a button is pressed and the cursor is moved away from the button while the mouse button is still being held down.

enabled

Indicates whether or not the button is currently enabled. A button must be enabled to be pressed.

pressed

Indicates whether or not the button is currently being pressed (meaning that the button is being held down).

rollover

Indicates whether or not the mouse cursor is currently over the button. This allows an alternate image to be displayed.

selected

> Indicates whether or not the button is currently selected. Only JToggle-Button and its subclasses may be selected. This property toggles on and off each time the button is clicked.

Events

Objects implementing the ButtonModel interface fire action events, change events, and item events, as shown in Table 5-2.

Table 5-2. ButtonModel Events

Event	Description
ActionEvent	The button has been pressed.
ChangeEvent	A change has occurred in one or more properties of the button model.
ItemEvent	The button has been toggled on or off.

The ButtonModel interface contains the following standard methods for maintaining event subscribers:

public abstract void addActionListener(ActionListener l)
public abstract void removeActionListener(ActionListener l)
public abstract void addItemListener(ItemListener l)
public abstract void removeItemListener(ItemListener l)
public abstract void addChangeListener(ChangeListener l)
public abstract void removeChangeListener(ChangeListener l)

The DefaultButtonModel Class

Swing provides a default implementation of the ButtonModel interface called DefaultButtonModel. This class is used directly by the JButton class. The other button classes (JToggleButton and its descendants) use an extension of DefaultButtonModel (defined as an inner class within JToggleButton) to handle their state data.

Properties

The DefaultButtonModel class gets most of its properties from ButtonModel. The default values set by this class are shown in Table 5-3.

The only property here that does not come from the ButtonModel interface is the selectedObjects property. This property comes as part of the ItemSelectable interface implemented by this class. The accessor method always returns null.

Table 5-3. DefaultButtonModel Properties

Property	Data Type	get	is	set	bound	Default Value
actionCommand*	String	•		•		null
armed*	boolean		•	•		false
enabled*	boolean		•	•		true
group*	ButtonGroup			•		null
mnemonic*	int	•		•		0
pressed*	boolean		•	•		false
rollover*	boolean		•	•		false
selected*	boolean		•	•		false
selectedObjects	Object[]	•				null

Events

The events fired by `DefaultButtonModel` are those required by `ButtonModel` and listed in Table 5-2. An `ActionEvent` is fired when the button is pressed, an `ItemEvent` is fired when the button's state is changed, and a `ChangeEvent` is fired when a change has occurred in the button's properties.

The following methods are implemented in this class using the `EventListener-List` class:

public void addActionListener(ActionListener l)
public void removeActionListener(ActionListener l)
public void addItemListener(ItemListener l)
public void removeItemListener(ItemListener l)
public void addChangeListener(ChangeListener l)
public void removeChangeListener(ChangeListener l)

In addition, the following protected methods are added in this class:

protected void fireActionPerformed(ActionEvent e)
protected void fireItemStateChanged(ItemEvent e)
protected void fireStateChanged()

These methods use the standard `EventListenerList` to dispatch events to registered listeners. `ChangeEvents` are fired when the values of any of the following properties are set: `armed`, `enabled`, `selected`, `pressed`, `rollover`, `mnemonic`.

Constants

`DefaultButtonModel` tracks its five boolean properties using a single state mask. Though they are generally not useful outside the class, the constants used in this mask are defined as public integers, so we'll list them here. Note that none of the methods defined in `DefaultButtonModel` accept these constants as method parameters. In short, you should never need these constants at all. Even if you subclass `DefaultButtonModel` for some reason, you should still use the public methods to access these properties.

Table 5-4. DefaultButtonModel Constants

Constant	Type	Description
ARMED	int	The button is armed.
ENABLED	int	The button is enabled.
PRESSED	int	The button is pressed.
ROLLOVER	int	The button is rolled-over.
SELECTED	int	The button is selected.

Protected Fields

protected transient ChangeEvent changeEvent
> The single `ChangeEvent` fired whenever a property value changes.

protected EventListenerList listenerList
> The listener list used to track all listeners added to the model.

protected int stateMask
> The current state of properties `armed`, `enabled`, `pressed`, `rollover`, and `selected`. See the "Constants" section for more information.

protected String actionCommand
protected ButtonGroup group
protected int mnemonic
> The values of the properties of the same names.

Constructor

public DefaultButtonModel()
> Creates a new model. The model's properties are set as defined in Table 5-3.

The AbstractButton Class

`AbstractButton` is an abstract base class for all button components (`JButton`, `JToggleButton`, `JCheckBox`, and `JRadioButton`, as well as `JMenuItem` and its subclasses).

`AbstractButton` provides much of the functionality associated with the interaction between the various concrete button classes and their `ButtonModel` objects. As we mentioned earlier, buttons in Swing can be made up of an image (`Icon`), text, or both. The relative positions of the text and icon are specified just as they are with the JLabel class.

Image buttons may actually specify as many as seven different images, allowing the button to be displayed differently depending on its current state. The seven icons are described in Table 5-5, with the other properties defined by AbstractButton.

Properties

The AbstractButton class defines the properties shown in Table 5-5.

Table 5-5. AbstractButton Properties

Property	Data Type	get	is	set	bound	Default Value
UI	ButtonUI	•		•	•	from L&F
model	ButtonModel	•		•	•	null
actionCommand	String	•		•		null
borderPainted	boolean		•	•	•	true
contentAreaFilled	boolean		•	•	•	true
disabledIcon	Icon	•		•	•	null
disabledSelectedIcon	Icon	•		•	•	null
enabled*	boolean		•	•		true
focusPainted	boolean		•	•	•	true
horizontalAlignment	int	•		•	•	CENTER
horizontalTextPosition	int	•		•	•	RIGHT
icon	Icon	•		•	•	null
label	String	•		•		
mnemonic	int	•		•	•	0
margin	Insets	•		•	•	null
pressedIcon	Icon	•		•	•	null
rolloverEnabled	boolean		•	•	•	false
rolloverIcon	Icon	•		•	•	null
rolloverSelectedIcon	Icon	•		•	•	null
selected	boolean		•	•		false
selectedIcon	Icon	•		•	•	null
selectedObjects	Object[]	•				null
text	String	•		•	•	" "
verticalAlignment	int	•		•	•	CENTER
verticalTextPosition	int	•		•	•	CENTER

See also properties from the JComponent class (Table 3-5).

There are seven different icons available for a button. Each is shown when the button is in a certain state, as defined below:[*]

icon

The default icon for the button.

disabledIcon

The icon shown when the button is disabled (if not specified, a grayscale version of the default icon is generated automatically).

selectedIcon

The icon shown when the button has been selected.

disabledSelectedIcon

The icon shown when the button is selected and also disabled (if not specified, a grayscale version of the selected icon is generated; if no selected icon has been set, the disabled icon is used). If you're following closely, you'll notice that there's a potential problem here—if there is no `disabledSelectedIcon` defined and also no `selectedIcon` or `disabledIcon` defined, the `getDisabledSelectedIcon()` method will return `null`. It would really be more consistent to return a grayscale version of the default `icon` in this case.

pressedIcon

The icon shown while the button is being pressed.

rolloverIcon

The icon shown (if `rolloverEnabled == true`) when the cursor is moved over the unselected button.

rolloverSelectedIcon

The icon shown (if `rolloverEnabled == true`) when the cursor is moved over the selected button.

The `horizontalAlignment` and `verticalAlignment` properties specify where the button's content (text, icon, or both) should be drawn within the button's borders. These properties are only significant when the button's size is larger than the default size. `HorizontalTextPosition` and `verticalTextPosition` specify the location of the text relative to the icon. These are only meaningful if both an icon and text have been specified.[†]

The `margin` property specifies the distance between the button's borders and its contents (text, icon, or both). However, it's up to the border implementation to take advantage of the value of this property. The Swing L&Fs define borders that

---

[*] Actually, `disabledSelectedIcon` and `rolloverSelectedIcon` are ignored by the current Swing L&Fs.

[†] See the examples in Chapter 4, *Labels and Icons*, in the section called "The JLabel Class," for further explanation of the alignment and text position properties.

take the value of margin into affect, but if you replace a button's border with one of your own, be aware that the margin space will not be used unless you access it explicitly in your border code. Model reflects the ButtonModel containing state information about the button. The text property contains the text, if any, displayed on the button (note that this property replaces the deprecated label property). BorderPainted indicates whether or not a border (recall from Chapter 3, *Swing Component Basics*, that border is a property of JComponent) should be painted around the button. This assumes the button has a border defined. This is the default, but the border could be removed; then setting this property to true would still not cause a border to be drawn. The contentArea-Filled property indicates whether or not the rectangular content area of the button should be filled. This should be set to false if you want to define an image-only button. Note that this is the preferred mechanism, rather than calling setOpaque(false) because the value of the opaque property for buttons is set by the L&F. FocusPainted indicates whether or not something special (such as a dashed line inside the button's border) should be painted to show that the button has focus.

Finally, the rolloverEnabled property indicates whether or not moving the cursor over the button should cause the rolloverIcon or rolloverSelected-Icon to be displayed. Calling setRolloverIcon() will cause this property to be set to true.

The actionCommand, mnemonic, and selected properties are taken directly from the AbstractButton's ButtonModel object. AbstractButton adds its own implementation of setEnabled(), inherited from java.awt.Component which updates the enabled property of the ButtonModel.

UI holds the ButtonUI used to render the button.

Events

AbstractButton fires the events, required by the ButtonModel interface, and listed in Table 5-6. An ActionEvent is fired when the button is pressed, an ItemEvent is fired when the button's state is changed, and a ChangeEvent is fired when a change has occurred in the button's properties.

Table 5-6. AbstractButton Events

Event	Description
ActionEvent	The button has been pressed.
ChangeEvent	A change has occurred in one or more properties of the button's model.
ItemEvent	The button has been toggled on or off.

All of these events are generated by the button's model. `AbstractButton` registers a listener for each type of event with the model and refires any events fired by the model to any registered listeners. The following standard listener management methods are implemented in this class:

public void addActionListener(ActionListener l)
public void removeActionListener(ActionListener l)
public void addItemListener(ItemListener l)
public void removeItemListener(ItemListener l)
public void addChangeListener(ChangeListener l)
public void removeChangeListener(ChangeListener l)

Several additional protected methods are defined to assist in the event firing process:

protected ActionListener createActionListener()
protected ChangeListener createChangeListener()
protected ItemListener createItemListener()

> Used internally to create listeners to be added to the `ButtonModel`. Each listener uses the button's "fire" methods (see below) to forward events fired by the model to the button's listeners. This allows users to add listeners to the button itself, rather than having to listen to the model. Subclasses wanting to change how model events are handled could override these methods.

protected void fireActionPerformed(ActionEvent e)
protected void fireItemStateChanged(ItemEvent e)
protected void fireStateChanged()

> Use the standard `EventListenerList` to dispatch events to registered listeners. They are called any time events are fired by the button model.

Constants

The following constants shown in Table 5-7 are defined by `AbstractButton` for use in `PropertyChangeEvents`.

Table 5-7. AbstractButton Constants

Constant	Type	Description
BORDER_PAINTED_CHANGED_PROPERTY	String	indicates that the `borderPainted` property has changed
CONTENT_AREA_FILLED_CHANGED_PROPERTY	String	indicates that the `contentAreaFilled` property has changed
DISABLED_ICON_CHANGED_PROPERTY	String	indicates that the `disabledIcon` property has changed
DISABLED_SELECTED_ICON_CHANGED_PROPERTY	String	indicates that the `disabledSelectedIcon` property has changed

Table 5-7. AbstractButton Constants (continued)

Constant	Type	Description
FOCUS_PAINTED_CHANGED_PROPERTY	String	indicates that the focusPainted property has changed
HORIZONTAL_ALIGNMENT_CHANGED_PROPERTY	String	indicates that the horizontalAlignment property has changed
HORIZONTAL_TEXT_POSITION_CHANGED_PROPERTY	String	indicates that the horizontalTextPosition property has changed
ICON_CHANGED_PROPERTY	String	indicates that the icon property has changed
MARGIN_CHANGED_PROPERTY	String	indicates that the margin property has changed
MNEMONIC_CHANGED_PROPERTY	String	indicates that the mnemonic property has changed
MODEL_CHANGED_PROPERTY	String	indicates that the model property has changed
PRESSED_ICON_CHANGED_PROPERTY	String	indicates that the pressedIcon property has changed
ROLLOVER_ENABLED_CHANGED_PROPERTY	String	indicates that the rolloverEnabled property has changed
ROLLOVER_ICON_CHANGED_PROPERTY	String	indicates that the rolloverIcon property has changed
ROLLOVER_SELECTED_ICON_CHANGED_PROPERTY	String	indicates that the rollovedSelectedIcon property has changed
SELECTED_ICON_CHANGED_PROPERTY	String	indicates that the selectedIcon property has changed
TEXT_CHANGED_PROPERTY	String	indicates that the text property has changed
VERTICAL_ALIGNMENT_CHANGED_PROPERTY	String	indicates that the verticalAlignment property has changed
VERTICAL_TEXT_POSITION_CHANGED_PROPERTY	String	indicates that the verticalTextPosition property has changed

Protected Fields

protected ActionListener actionListener
protected ChangeListener changeListener
protected ItemListener itemListener

These fields hold the listeners responsible for receiving events from the model.

protected transient ChangeEvent changeEvent

The single instance of ChangeEvent used any time a ChangeEvent needs to be fired. There is no need to create new ChangeEvent objects each time one is fired, since they contain no information other than the object that fired them (this).

protected ButtonModel model

Provides direct access to the button's model.

Constructor

public AbstractButton()

The default constructor does nothing.

User Interface Methods

protected void paintBorder(Graphics g)

Paints the button's border (by calling `super.paintBorder()`) only if the `borderPainted` property is set to `true`.

public void updateUI()

Called to indicate that the look-and-feel has changed. The default implementation does nothing.

Other Public Methods

public void doClick(int pressTime)

Programmatically simulates a user pressing the button for a specified number of milliseconds. Calling this method has the same effect as pressing the button—the button will even give the visual appearance of being pressed.

public void doClick()

This version of `doClick()` calls the first version with a value of 68 milliseconds.

public void setMnemonic(char mnemonic)

Provides a convenient way to set the `mnemonic` property by passing in a `char` (as opposed to the property's actual type, `int`). The character is converted to uppercase and passed to the other `setMnemonic()` method as an `int`.

Protected Methods

protected void init(String text, Icon icon)

Initializes a button with the given text and icon. It also calls `updateUI()`, adds a focus listener to the button, and sets the `JComponent` `alignmentX` property to `LEFT_ALIGNMENT`. This method is called by the constructors of the `AbstractButton` subclasses.

protected int checkHorizontalKey(int x, String s)

> Used internally to validate `horizontalAlignment` and `horizontalText-Position` values. It returns the input integer if it is LEFT, CENTER, or RIGHT. Otherwise, it throws an `IllegalArgumentException` with the given string as the exception text. You should never need to call this method.

protected int checkVerticalKey(int y, String s)

> Used internally to validate `verticalAlignment` and `verticalTextPosition` values. It returns the input integer if it is TOP, CENTER, or BOTTOM. Otherwise, it throws an `IllegalArgumentException` with the given string as the exception text. You should never need to call this method.

The JButton Class

`JButton` is the simplest of the button types, adding very little to what is provided by the `AbstractButton` class. `JButtons` are buttons that are not toggled on and off, but instead act as "push" buttons, which perform some action when clicked. They are typically used much like `java.awt.Buttons`. Figure 5-2 shows what these buttons look like in the three Swing look-and-feels.

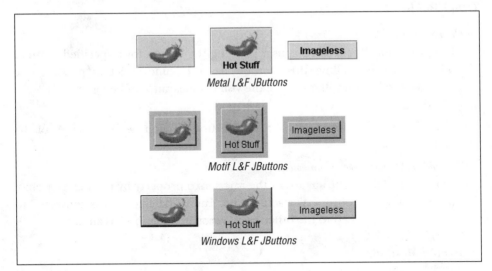

Figure 5-2. *JButtons in three look-and-feels*

Properties

The `JButton` class inherits most of its properties and default values from its super-classes. The exceptions to this are shown in Table 5-8. The `model` property is set to a new instance of `DefaultButtonModel` when a `JButton` is created.

Table 5-8. JButton Properties

Property	Data Type	get	is	set	bound	Default Value
model*	ButtonModel	•		•		DefaultButtonModel()
UIClassID*	String	•				"ButtonUI"
accessibleContext*	AccessibleContext	•				JButton.Accessible-JButton()
defaultButton	boolean		•			false
defaultCapable	boolean		•	•		true

See also properties from AbstractButton (Table 5-6).

The defaultButton property indicates whether the button will be activated by default when some event occurs within the JRootPane containing the button. Typically, the event that would trigger the button would be an ENTER key press, but this is actually up to the look-and-feel implementation.

The defaultButton property cannot be set directly. Instead, it is set by telling the JRootPane that contains the button which button should be the default. We'll cover JRootPane in Chapter 8, *Swing Containers*—at this point, it's enough to know that the new Swing containers JApplet, JDialog, JFrame, and JWindow all use a JRootPane as their primary content container. If the button is inside one of these Swing containers, this property may be set to true.

The other new property, defaultCapable, indicates whether or not the button may be set as a root pane's default button. A button may only be treated as the default button if this property is set to true.

Using the Default Button

Here's a quick example showing how the default button property can be used:

```
// DefaultButtonExample.java
//
import javax.swing.*;
import java.awt.*;

// Example using defaultButton and JRootPane.setDefaultButton()
public class DefaultButtonExample {
  public static void main(String[] args) {

    // Create some buttons
    JButton ok = new JButton("OK");
    JButton cancel = new JButton("Cancel");
    JPanel buttonPanel = new JPanel();
    buttonPanel.add(ok);
    buttonPanel.add(cancel);
```

```
      JLabel msg = new JLabel("Is this OK?", JLabel.CENTER);

      // Create a frame, get its root pane, and set the "ok" button as the
      // default. This button will be "pressed" if we hit <ENTER> while the
      // frame has focus.
      JFrame f = new JFrame();
      f.addWindowListener(new BasicWindowMonitor());
      JRootPane root = f.getRootPane();
      root.setDefaultButton(ok);

      // Layout and Display
      Container content = f.getContentPane();
      content.setLayout(new BorderLayout());
      content.add(msg, BorderLayout.CENTER);
      content.add(buttonPanel, BorderLayout.SOUTH);
      f.setSize(200,100);
      f.setVisible(true);
    }
  }
```

The first thing we do here is create two buttons and a label. We then create a
JFrame and get its "root pane." Next, we call setDefaultButton() on this pane,
passing in a reference to the "OK" button. When executed, the "OK" button will
typically be drawn with a different border around it, as shown with the Metal look-
and-feel in Figure 5-3. More important, when we press ENTER while the frame has
focus, the default button will be pressed automatically.

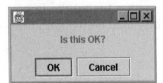

Figure 5-3. Default button

Events

JButton does not define any new events, but it's important to understand which
of the events defined by its superclasses are fired when the button is pressed. The
most important thing to know about JButton events is that JButtons fire
ActionEvents when they are clicked. This type of event is sent after the button is
released, and only if the button is still armed (meaning that the cursor is still over
the button). The following example creates event listeners for action, change, and
item events to show which events get fired when we press the button:

```
// JButtonEvents
//
import javax.swing.*;
```

```
import javax.swing.event.*;
import java.awt.*;
import java.awt.event.*;

public class JButtonEvents {
  public static void main(String[] args) {
    JButton jb = new JButton("Press Me");

    jb.addActionListener(new ActionListener() {
      public void actionPerformed(ActionEvent ev) {
        System.out.println("ActionEvent!");
      }
    });
    jb.addItemListener(new ItemListener() {
      public void itemStateChanged(ItemEvent ev) {
        System.out.println("ItemEvent!");
      }
    });
    jb.addChangeListener(new ChangeListener() {
      public void stateChanged(ChangeEvent ev) {
        System.out.println("ChangeEvent!");
      }
    });
    JFrame f = new JFrame();
    f.addWindowListener(new BasicWindowMonitor());
    f.getContentPane().add(jb);
    f.pack();
    f.setVisible(true);
  }
}
```

Running this program and pressing the button produces the following output:

```
ChangeEvent!
ChangeEvent!
```

When the button is released, the following additional output is produced:

```
ActionEvent!
ChangeEvent!
```

The initial change events are fired, indicating that the button has been "armed" and "pressed." When the button is released, the action event is fired, along with another change event to indicate that the button is no longer pressed.

Pressing the button a second time results in only a single change event, followed by the action event and change event when the button is released. This is because the button's armed property remains set to true after the button is clicked. This property only gets set to false again if you hold the mouse button down and then move the cursor away from the button. If the button is released while the pointer is no longer over the button, no `ActionEvent` will be fired.

In practice, you will typically only be interested in the `ActionEvents` fired by a `JButton`.

Constructors

public JButton()
> Creates a button with no image or text.

public JButton(Icon icon)
> Creates a button displaying the specified icon.

public JButton(String text)
> Creates a button displaying the specified text.

public JButton(String text, Icon icon)
> Creates a button displaying the specified text and icon.

User Interface Method

public void updateUI()
> Indicates that the look-and-feel has changed. It calls `setUI()`, passing in the new UI delegate.

Using Mnemonics

The following example shows how to create a set of `JButtons` that use mnemonics to allow the buttons to be selected by holding down the ALT key and pressing the mnemonic (in addition to responding to mouse clicks):

```
// Mnemonic.java
//
import javax.swing.*;
import java.awt.*;
import java.awt.event.*;

public class Mnemonic extends JFrame {

   // Create a new frame with some buttons on it.
   public Mnemonic() {
      buttonPanel.setLayout(new GridLayout(1, 4, 4, 4));

      // Create the buttons.
      addButton("Sports", new ImageIcon("images/sports.gif"));
      addButton("Music", new ImageIcon("images/music.gif"));
      addButton("Travel", new ImageIcon("images/travel.gif"));
      addButton("Art", new ImageIcon("images/art.gif"));
```

```
    // Layout.
    Container c = getContentPane();
    c.setLayout(new BorderLayout());
    c.add(new JLabel("Select an Activity"), BorderLayout.NORTH);
    c.add(buttonPanel, BorderLayout.CENTER);
    pack();
}


// Add a button to the button panel with the specified text and icon. The
// first character of the text is used as a mnemonic key.
private void addButton(String label, Icon icon) {

    // Use the first char as our key mnemonic
    final char key = label.charAt(0);
    JButton button = new JButton(label, icon);

    // this will register keystrokes with the ALT mask
    button.setMnemonic(key);

    button.setVerticalTextPosition(SwingConstants.BOTTOM);
    button.setHorizontalTextPosition(SwingConstants.CENTER);

    // add this button to the panel
    buttonPanel.add(button);
}


// button panel
private JPanel buttonPanel = new JPanel();

// A simple test program
public static void main(String[] args) {
    Mnemonic acc = new Mnemonic();
    acc.setVisible(true);
}
}
```

Figure 5-4 shows the initial display. Pressing ALT-S, ALT-M, ALT-T, or ALT-A causes the corresponding button to be "pressed." As we noted earlier, the use of the ALT key is actually up to the L&F, but currently all Swing L&Fs use ALT.

Figure 5-4. JButtons with mnemonics

Fancy Buttons

In the AbstractButton section, we learned that there are quite a few things that can be done with Swing buttons to make them more visually interesting. In this example, we'll see how we can spice up a user interface by adding rollover and selected icons to our buttons. We'll also take away the button borders, focus painting, and filled content area to give our display a nice clean look.

```java
// FancyButton.java
//
import javax.swing.*;
import java.awt.*;

public class FancyButton extends JButton {
    // Create a JButton that does not show focus, does not paint a border, and
    // displays different icons when rolled-over and pressed.
    public FancyButton(Icon icon, Icon pressed, Icon rollover) {
        super(icon);
        setFocusPainted(false);
        setRolloverEnabled(true);
        setRolloverIcon(rollover);
        setPressedIcon(pressed);
        setBorderPainted(false);
        setContentAreaFilled(false);
    }

    // A simple test program
    public static void main(String[] args) {

        FancyButton b1 = new FancyButton(
            new ImageIcon("images/redcube.gif"),
            new ImageIcon("images/redpaw.gif"),
            new ImageIcon("images/reddiamond.gif"));
        FancyButton b2 = new FancyButton(
            new ImageIcon("images/bluecube.gif"),
            new ImageIcon("images/bluepaw.gif"),
            new ImageIcon("images/bluediamond.gif"));
        JFrame f = new JFrame();
        f.addWindowListener(new BasicWindowMonitor());
        Container c = f.getContentPane();
        c.setLayout(new FlowLayout());
        c.add(b1);
        c.add(b2);
        f.pack();
        f.setVisible(true);
    }
}
```

Figure 5-5 shows a few screenshots of our new button class with the different states of the buttons. Of course, this is just one example of a "fancy" button implementation. You can create your own special button classes using some or all of the features shown in FancyButton, as well as other features, such as adding icons for other button states.

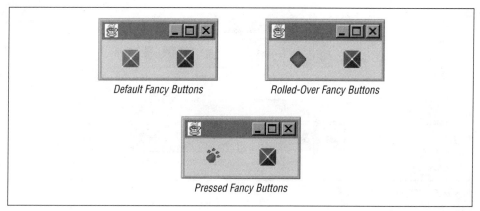

Figure 5-5. Buttons using "rollover" and "pressed" icons

The JToggleButton Class

JToggleButton is an extension of AbstractButton, used to represent buttons that can be toggled on and off (as opposed to buttons like JButton which, when pushed, "pop back up"). It should be noted that while the subclasses of JToggle-Button (JCheckBox and JRadioButton) are the types of JToggleButtons most commonly used, JToggleButton is not an abstract class. When used directly, it typically (though this is ultimately up to the L&F) has the appearance of a JButton that does not pop back up when pressed (see Figure 5-6).

Properties

The JToggleButton class inherits all of its properties and most of its default values from its superclasses. The exceptions are shown in Table 5-9. The model property is set to a new instance of ToggleButtonModel when a JToggleButton is created. ToggleButtonModel (described in the next section) is a public inner class that extends DefaultButtonModel.

Events

Like JButton, JToggleButton defines no new events. However, the events fired by JToggleButtons are slightly different than those fired by JButton. Let's look

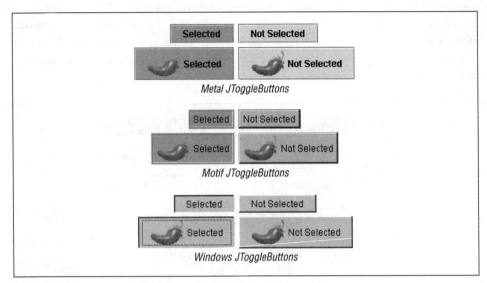

Figure 5-6. JToggleButtons

Table 5-9. JToggleButton Properties

Property	Data Type	get	is	set	bound	Default Value
model*	ButtonModel	•		•		ToggleButtonModel()
UIClassID*	String	•				"ToggleButtonUI"
accessibleContext*	AccessibleContext	•				JToggleButton.Accessible-JToggleButton()

See also properties from AbstractButton (Table 5-6).

at these events by running a simple program like the one used in the JButton event section. This time, we'll create a JToggleButton instead of a JButton:

```
// JToggleButtonEvents.java
//
import javax.swing.*;
import javax.swing.event.*;
import java.awt.*;
import java.awt.event.*;

public class JToggleButtonEvents {
  public static void main(String[] args) {
    JToggleButton jtb = new JToggleButton("Press Me");

    jtb.addActionListener(new ActionListener() {
      public void actionPerformed(ActionEvent ev) {
```

```
        System.out.println("ActionEvent!");
      }
    });
    jtb.addItemListener(new ItemListener() {
      public void itemStateChanged(ItemEvent ev) {
        System.out.println("ItemEvent!");
      }
    });
    jtb.addChangeListener(new ChangeListener() {
      public void stateChanged(ChangeEvent ev) {
        System.out.println("ChangeEvent!");
      }
    });
    JFrame f = new JFrame();
    f.addWindowListener(new BasicWindowMonitor());
    Container c = f.getContentPane();
    c.setLayout(new FlowLayout());
    c.add(jtb);
    f.pack();
    f.setVisible(true);
  }
}
```

When we run this program and press the button, we get the following output:

```
ChangeEvent!
ChangeEvent!
```

After releasing the button, we see:

```
ChangeEvent!
ItemEvent!
ChangeEvent!
ActionEvent!
```

As in our JButton example, the first two events are fired to indicate that the button has been *armed* and *pressed*. When the button is released, we get another change event, indicating that the button has now been *selected*. Additionally, toggle buttons fire an ItemEvent to indicate button selection. The final two events match those of JButton, indicating that the button is no longer being pressed and that an action (button press) has occurred.

Subsequent button presses result in one less ChangeEvent (just like we saw with JButton), because the button remains *armed* after it has been pressed.

Constructors

public JToggleButton()
    Creates a button that has no text or icon and is not selected.

public JToggleButton(Icon icon)

public JToggleButton(Icon icon, boolean selected)

> Create a button that displays the specified icon. If included, the `boolean` parameter indicates the initial selected state of the button.

public JToggleButton(String text)

public JToggleButton(String text, boolean selected)

> Create a button that displays the specified text. If included, the `boolean` parameter indicates the initial selected state of the button.

public JToggleButton(String text, Icon icon)

public JToggleButton(String test, Icon icon, boolean selected)

> Create a button that displays the specified text and icon. If included, the `boolean` parameter indicates the initial selected state of the button.

User Interface Method

public void updateUI()

> Indicates that the look-and-feel (L&F) has changed.

The JToggleButton.ToggleButtonModel Class

As we mentioned earlier, `JToggleButton` does not use the `DefaultButtonModel` class as its model. `ToggleButtonModel`, a public static inner class that extends `DefaultButtonModel`, is used instead.

Properties

`ToggleButtonModel` modifies the methods for working with the properties listed in Table 5-10. New implementations of `isSelected()` and `setSelected()` are provided that use the button's `ButtonGroup` (if defined) to keep track of which button is selected. This is done to ensure that even if multiple selected buttons are added to a group, only the first one will be considered selected (since the group keeps track of the "officially" selected button). In addition, the `setPressed()` method is redefined to call `setSelected()` when the button is released (if it is armed).

Table 5-10. JToggleButton.ToggleButtonModel Properties

Property	Data Type	get	is	set	bound	Default Value
pressed*	boolean		•	•		false
selected*	boolean		•	•		false

See also properties from DefaultButtonModel (Table 5-3).

The JCheckBox Class

The look-and-feels for the JCheckBox[*] class are shown in Figure 5-7. JCheckBox is a subclass of JToggleButton typically used to allow the user to turn a given feature on or off, or to make multiple selections from a set of choices. A JCheckBox is usually rendered by showing a small box into which a "check" is placed when selected (as shown in Figure 5-7). If you specify an icon for the checkbox, this icon replaces the default box. Therefore, if you choose to specify an icon, you should always also supply a selected icon—otherwise, there will be no way to tell if a check box has been selected or not .

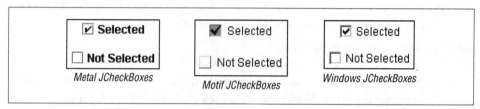

Figure 5-7. JCheckBoxes in the three look-and-feels

Properties

The JCheckBox class inherits all of its properties and most of its default values from its superclasses. The only exceptions are shown in Table 5-11. By default, no border is painted on JCheckBoxes, and their horizontalAlignment is to the left.

Table 5-11. JCheckBox Properties

Property	Data Type	get	is	set	bound	Default Value
UIClassID*	String	•				"CheckBoxUI"
accessibleContext*	AccessibleContext	•				AccessibleJCheckBox
borderPainted*	boolean		•	•		false
horizontalAlignment*	int	•		•		LEFT

See also properties from JToggleButton (Table 5-10).

Events

See the discussion of JToggleButton (JCheckBox's superclass) events.

---

* Note the difference in capitalization from AWT's Checkbox class.

Constructors

public JCheckBox()

Creates a checkbox that has no text or icon and is not selected.

public JCheckBox(Icon icon)
public JCheckBox(Icon icon, boolean selected)

Create a checkbox that displays the specified icon. If included, the selected parameter indicates the initial selected state of the button.

public JCheckBox(String text)
public JCheckBox(String text, boolean selected)

Create a checkbox that displays the specified text. If included, the selected parameter indicates the initial selected state of the button.

public JCheckBox(String text, Icon icon)
public JCheckBox(String text, Icon icon, boolean selected)

Create a checkbox that displays the specified text and icon. If included, the selected parameter indicates the initial selected state of the button.

User Interface Method

public void updateUI()

Indicates that the look-and-feel has changed.

The JRadioButton Class

JRadioButton is a subclass of JToggleButton, typically used with other JRadioButtons, allowing users to make a single selection from a set of options (Figure 5-8). Because of this intended behavior, JRadioButtons are usually used in groups, managed by a ButtonGroup (described in the next section). JRadioButtons have the same behavior with respect to images as JCheckBoxes, meaning that a selected icon should always be specified if a default icon is supplied.

Figure 5-8. JRadioButtons in the three look-and-feels

Properties

The JRadioButton class inherits all of its properties and most of its default values from its superclasses. The only exceptions are shown in Table 5-12. By default, no border is painted on JRadioButtons and their horizontalAlignment is to the left.

Table 5-12. JRadioButton Properties

Property	Data Type	get	is	set	bound	Default Value
UIClassID*	String	•				"RadioButtonUI"
accessibleContext*	AccessibleContext	•				JRadioButton.Accessi-bleJRadioButton()
borderPainted*	boolean		•	•		false
horizontalAlignment*	int	•		•		LEFT

See also properties from JToggleButton (Table 5-10).

Events

See the discussion of JToggleButton (JRadioButton's superclass) events.

Constructors

public JRadioButton()
> Creates a button that has no text or icon and is not selected.

public JRadioButton(Icon icon)
public JRadioButton(Icon icon, boolean selected)
> Create a button that displays the specified icon. If included, the boolean parameter indicates the initial selected state of the button.

public JRadioButton(String text)
public JRadioButton(String text, boolean selected)
> Create a button that displays the specified text. If included, the boolean parameter indicates the initial selected state of the button.

public JRadioButton(String text, Icon icon)
public JRadioButton(String text, Icon icon, boolean selected)
> Create a button that displays the specified text and icon. If included, the boolean parameter indicates the initial selected state of the button.

User Interface Method

public void updateUI()
> Indicates that the look-and-feel has changed.

Opaque JRadioButtons and JCheckBoxes

Typically, JRadioButtons and JCheckBoxes should be left transparent (not opaque) with their contentAreaFilled property explicitly set to false. These components usually do not fill most of their allocated space, and making them opaque or filled causes an awkward-looking rectangle to be painted behind them, as shown in Figure 5-9.

Figure 5-9. Opaque JCheckBox and JRadioButton

The ButtonGroup Class

The ButtonGroup class allows buttons to be logically grouped together, guaranteeing that no more than one button in the group will be selected at any given time. In fact, once one of the buttons has been selected, the ButtonGroup will ensure that exactly one button remains selected at all times. Note that this allows for an initial state (in which no button has been selected) that can never be reached again once a selection has been made.

As mentioned earlier, ButtonGroups are usually used to hold JRadioButtons (or JRadioButtonMenuItems, discussed in Chapter 14), but this is purely a convention and is not enforced by ButtonGroup. ButtonGroup's add() method takes objects of type AbstractButton, so any button type may be added—even a mix of types. Of course, adding a JButton to a ButtonGroup would not be very useful, since JButtons do not have selected and deselected states. In fact, JButtons added to ButtonGroups have no effect on the state of the other buttons if they are pressed.

ButtonGroup objects do not have any visual appearance; they simply provide a logical grouping of a set of buttons. Buttons in a ButtonGroup still must be added to a Container and laid out just as though no ButtonGroup were being used.

It's worth noting that some methods defined in the ButtonGroup class deal with AbstractButton objects and some deal with ButtonModel objects. The add(), remove(), and getElements() methods all use AbstractButton, while the getSelection(), isSelected(), and setSelection() methods use ButtonModel objects.

Properties

ButtonGroup defines the properties listed in Table 5-13. The `elements` property is an `Enumeration` of the `AbstractButton` objects contained by the group. The `selection` property contains the `ButtonModel` of the currently selected button.

Table 5-13. ButtonGroup Properties

Property	Data Type	get	is	set	bound	Default Value
elements	Enumeration	•				Empty
selection	ButtonModel	•				null

Voting with a Button Group

The following example demonstrates the use of a `ButtonGroup` to ensure that only a single selection is made from a list of presidential candidates. Listeners are added to the buttons to show which events are fired each time a new button is selected:

```
// SimpleButtonGroupExample.java
//
import javax.swing.*;
import java.awt.*;
import java.awt.event.*;

// A ButtonGroup voting booth.
public class SimpleButtonGroupExample {
  public static void main(String[] args) {

    // Some choices
    JRadioButton dem = new JRadioButton("B. Clinton", false);
    dem.setActionCommand("Bill");
    JRadioButton rep = new JRadioButton("R. Dole", false);
    rep.setActionCommand("Bob");
    JRadioButton ind = new JRadioButton("R. Perot", false);
    ind.setActionCommand("Ross");

    // A group, to ensure that we only vote for one.
    final ButtonGroup group = new ButtonGroup();
    group.add(dem);
    group.add(rep);
    group.add(ind);

    // A simple ActionListener, showing each selection using the ButtonModel.
    class VoteActionListener implements ActionListener {
      public void actionPerformed(ActionEvent ex) {
```

```
        String choice = group.getSelection().getActionCommand();
        System.out.println("ACTION Candidate Selected: " + choice);
    }
}


// A simple ItemListener, showing each selection and deselection.
class VoteItemListener implements ItemListener {
    public void itemStateChanged(ItemEvent ex) {
        String item =
            ((AbstractButton)ex.getItemSelectable()).getActionCommand();
        boolean selected = (ex.getStateChange() == ItemEvent.SELECTED);
        System.out.println("ITEM Candidate Selected: " + selected +
            " Selection: " + item);
    }
}


// Add listeners to each button.
ActionListener al = new VoteActionListener();
dem.addActionListener(al);
rep.addActionListener(al);
ind.addActionListener(al);

ItemListener il = new VoteItemListener();
dem.addItemListener(il);
rep.addItemListener(il);
ind.addItemListener(il);

// Throw everything together.
JFrame frame = new JFrame();
frame.addWindowListener(new BasicWindowMonitor());
Container c = frame.getContentPane();
c.setLayout(new GridLayout(4,1));
c.add(new JLabel("Please Cast Your Vote"));
c.add(dem);
c.add(rep);
c.add(ind);
frame.pack();
frame.setVisible(true);
    }
}
```

We first create three radio buttons and add them to a button group. Then, we
define an ActionListener and an ItemListener to print out some information
each time a selection is made. We add both listeners to each button. The rest of
the code is just layout.

When executed, the initial selection of a candidate produces the following output:

```
ITEM Candidate Selected: true Selection: Ross
ACTION Candidate Selected: Ross
```

Changing the selection causes two item events to be fired, showing which button was toggled off and which was toggled on:

```
ITEM Candidate Selected: false Selection: Ross
ITEM Candidate Selected: true Selection: Bill
ACTION Candidate Selected: Bill
```

Protected Field

protected Vector buttons
>The collection of buttons managed by the group.

Constructor

public ButtonGroup()
>Creates an empty group.

Methods

public void add(AbstractButton b)
>Adds a button to the group. If there is no selected button in the group, and the given button is selected, it becomes the group's selection. It's important to remember that all JToggleButtons use an extension of DefaultButton-Model, which relies on the ButtonGroup (when defined) to determine whether or not a button is selected. The following brief example shows how adding multiple selected buttons to a group actually changes the state of the buttons. Be sure to read the comments in the code:

```
// ButtonGroupSelection.java
//
import javax.swing.*;

public class ButtonGroupSelection {
  public static void main(String[] args) {

    // create two selected buttons
    JToggleButton one = new JToggleButton();
    one.setSelected(true);
    JToggleButton two = new JToggleButton();
    two.setSelected(true);

    // both are selected (prints "true true")
    System.out.println(one.isSelected() + " " + two.isSelected());

    // put them in a group
    ButtonGroup group = new ButtonGroup();
    group.add(one);
    group.add(two);
```

```
      // Only first one is selected now (prints "true false"). This is because
      // ToggleButtonModel.isSelected() first checks to see if the button is in
      // a group and, if so, asks the group if it is selected.
      System.out.println(one.isSelected() + " " + two.isSelected());
    }
  }
```

The first thing we do here is create two unrelated toggle buttons, both of which are selected. We print out their selected state to show that they both return true from isSelected(). Then, we add them both to a Button-Group and print their response to isSelected() again. This time, only the first one returns true, because the second one was toggled off by the button group when it was added, since the group already had a selected button.

public void remove(AbstractButton b)

Removes a button from the group. If the removed button was the currently selected button, the group's selection is set to null.

public void setSelected(ButtonModel m, boolean b)

Selects the given button if the boolean parameter is true. If there was a previously selected button in the group, it is unselected. Calling this method with a false argument has no effect.

public boolean isSelected(ButtonModel m)

Indicates whether or not the given button is the group's currently selected button.

6

Bounded Range Components

This chapter groups several Swing components together by the model that drives them: the *bounded-range model*. Bounded-range components in Swing include JSlider, JProgressBar, and JScrollBar. In addition, we discuss two classes that make use of progress bars: ProgressMonitor and ProgressMonitorInput-Stream. These classes display status dialogs using a JOptionPane that you can assign to a variety of tasks.

The Bounded-Range Model

Components that make use of the bounded-range model typically consist of an integer value that is constrained within two integer boundaries. The lower boundary, the *minimum*, should always be less than or equal to the model's current *value*. In addition, the model's value should always be less than the upper boundary, the *maximum*. The model's value can cover more than one unit; this size is referred to as its *extent*. With bounded range, the user is allowed to adjust the value of the model according to the rules of the component. If the value violates any of the rules, the model can adjust the values accordingly.

The interface javax.swing.BoundedRangeModel outlines the data model for such an object. The interface is very similar to the java.awt.Adjustable interface presented in AWT 1.1 and retains many of its characteristics.

Objects implementing the `BoundedRangeModel` interface must contain an adjustable integer value, an extent, and a minimum and maximum. Swing contains three bounded-range components: `JScrollBar`, `JSlider`, and `JProgressBar`. These components are shown in Figure 6-1.

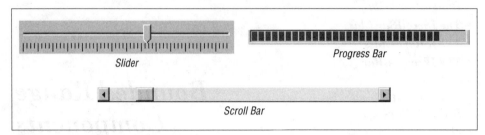

Figure 6-1. Bounded-range components in Swing

Properties

Table 6-1 shows the properties of the `BoundedRangeModel` interface.

Table 6-1. BoundedRangeModel Properties

Property	Data Type	get	is	set	bound	Default Value
minimum	int	•		•		
maximum	int	•		•		
value	int	•		•		
extent	int	•		•		
valueIsAdjusting	boolean	•		•		

The `minimum`, `maximum`, and `value` properties form the actual bounded range. The `extent` property can give the value its own subrange. Extents can be used in situations where the model's value exceeds a single unit; they can also be changed dynamically. For example, the sliding "thumbs" of many scrollbars resize themselves based on the percentage of total information displayed in the window. If you wish to emulate this behavior with Swing, you could declare a bounded-range scrollbar and set the `extent` property to grow or shrink as necessary.

Figure 6-2 illustrates a bounded range with the properties:

```
minimum = 1; maximum = 24; value = 9; extent = 3
```

Extents always define a range greater than the model's value and never less. If you do not wish the value to have a subrange, you can set the extent to 0.

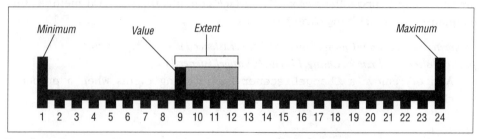

Figure 6-2. Properties of the BoundedRangeModel interface

Here are some rules to remember when working with bounded ranges:

- If the user sets a new value that is outside the bounded range, the value is set to the closest boundary (minimum or maximum).

- If the user sets a new value so that extent exceeds the maximum, the model resets the value to the amount of the maximum minus the extent—thus preserving the width of the extent.

- If the user sets the extent to a negative number, it is reset to 0.

- If the user sets the extent large enough to exceed the maximum, the model resets the extent to be the remaining width, if any, between the model's current value and its maximum.

- If the user resets the minimum or maximum so that the model's value now falls outside the bounded range, the value is adjusted to become the boundary closest to its original value.

- If a user resets a minimum so that it exceeds the maximum, the maximum and the value are reset to the new minimum. Conversely, if a new maximum is less than the current minimum, the minimum and value are adjusted to be the new maximum. In both cases, the bounded range has no width and the extent is reset to 0.

- If the user resets a minimum or maximum so that the extent goes beyond the maximum, the extent is shrunk so it does not exceed the maximum.

Finally, the valueIsAdjusting property is a boolean that indicates this change is one in a series. JSlider, for example, toggles this property to true when the user is dragging the component. This alerts any ChangeEvent listeners on the component that this event is probably one in a series, and it may choose not to react immediately.

Events

Objects implementing the BoundedRangeModel interface must fire a Change-Event when the model modifies its minimum, maximum, value, or extent property. The `BoundedRangeModel` interface contains the standard methods for maintaining a list of `ChangeEvent` subscribers.

public abstract void addChangeListener(ChangeListener 1)
public abstract void removeChangeListener(ChangeListener 1)

Add or remove a `ChangeListener` for receiving events when a property changes.

Method

public abstract void setRangeProperties(int value, int extent, int min, int max,
boolean adjusting)

Typically, one event is generated per property change. However, if you wish to make multiple changes without triggering as many events, you can call the `setRangeProperties()` method to change all five properties at once. This method generates a single `ChangeEvent` per call. For example:

```
setRangeProperties(newValue, newExtent, newMin, newMax,
        newValueIsAdjusting);        // Generates a single change event
```

The DefaultBoundedRangeModel Class

Swing provides a standard implementation of the `BoundedRangeModel` interface with the `DefaultBoundedRangeModel` class. This class provides the minimum functionality necessary to correctly implement the bounded-range model. Programmers are free to use and extend this class as they see fit.

Properties

The properties of the `DefaultBoundedRangeModel` class are identical to the properties of the interface it implements; it provides default values, but doesn't otherwise add or change properties, as shown in Table 6-2. See the `BoundedRangeModel` interface earlier in this chapter for a description of the rules this component follows when the values of its properties are changed.

Table 6-2. DefaultBoundedRangeModel Properties

Property	Data Type	get	is	set	bound	Default Value
extent*	int	•		•		0
maximum*	int	•		•		100
minimum*	int	•		•		0
value*	int	•		•		0
valueIsAdjusting*	boolean	•		•		false

Events

As specified by the bounded-range interface, the `DefaultBoundedRangeModel` fires a `ChangeEvent` when the model modifies its `minimum`, `maximum`, `value`, or `extent` properties.

public void addChangeListener(ChangeListener l)
public void removeChangeListener(ChangeListener l)
> Add or remove a change listener from the list of objects that receive a `ChangeEvent` when a property changes.

protected void fireStateChanged()
> Fires a `ChangeEvent` to all registered listeners, indicating that a property of the bounded-range model has changed.

Fields

The `DefaultBoundedRangeModel` contains two protected fields:

protected transient ChangeEvent changeEvent
> The change event used by the `DefaultBoundedRangeModel`. Because the event only contains one variable, the source (which always points back to this object), the same `ChangeEvent` object can be used each time an event is generated.

protected EventListenerList listenerList
> Contains a list of the change listeners interested in receiving notification when a bounded-range property changes.

Constructors

public DefaultBoundedRangeModel()
> The default constructor for this class. It initializes a bounded range model with a minimum of 0, a maximum of 100, and a value and extent of 0.

public DefaultBoundedRangeModel(int value, int extent, int minimum, int maximum)
> Initializes the bounded-range model with the values specified.

Miscellaneous

public void setRangeProperties(int newValue, int newExtent, int newMin, int newMax, int newValueIsAdjusting)
> Sets multiple bounded-range properties, while generating a single `ChangeEvent`.

public string toString()
> Returns the values of the bounded range model as a `String`.

Working with the Bounded-Range Model

Here is a program that helps to demonstrate some of the peculiarities of the
`DefaultBoundedRangeModel` class and the bounded-range interface. We
intentionally try to confuse the interface to show how the model reacts to
inappropriate property values.

```java
//  Bounded.java
//
import java.awt.*;
import java.awt.event.*;
import java.util.*;
import javax.swing.*;
import javax.swing.event.*;

public class Bounded {
    public Bounded() {
        try {
            DefaultBoundedRangeModel model = new DefaultBoundedRangeModel();
            ChangeListener myListener = new MyChangeListener();
            model.addChangeListener(myListener);

            System.out.println(model.toString());
            System.out.println("Now setting minimum to 50 . . .");
            model.setMinimum(50);
            System.out.println(model.toString());
            System.out.println("Now setting maximum to 40 . . .");
            model.setMaximum(40);
            System.out.println(model.toString());
            System.out.println("Now setting maximum to 50 . . .");
            model.setMaximum(50);
            System.out.println(model.toString());
            System.out.println("Now setting extent to 30 . . .");
            model.setExtent(30);
            System.out.println(model.toString());

            System.out.println("Now setting several properties . . .");
            if (!model.getValueIsAdjusting()) {
                model.setValueIsAdjusting(true);
                System.out.println(model.toString());
                model.setMinimum(0);
                model.setMaximum(100);
                model.setExtent(20);
                model.setValueIsAdjusting(false);
            }
            System.out.println(model.toString());
        } catch (Exception e) { e.printStackTrace(); }
    }
```

```
    class MyChangeListener implements ChangeListener {
        public void stateChanged(ChangeEvent e) {
            System.out.println("A ChangeEvent has been fired!");
        }
    }


    public static void main(String args[]) { new Bounded(); }
}
```

Let's go through the output step by step. The first step is to define a Default-BoundedRangeModel and attach a ChangeListener to it. After doing so, we print out the default values of the model below:

```
DefaultBoundedRangeModel[value=0, extent=0, min=0, max=100, adj=false]
```

Here we set the minimum to 50 and the maximum to a value smaller than the minimum, 40. Looks like trouble ahead...

```
Now setting minimum to 50 . . .
A ChangeEvent has been fired!
DefaultBoundedRangeModel[value=50, extent=0, min=50, max=100, adj=false]
Now setting maximum to 40 (smaller than min) . . .
A ChangeEvent has been fired!
DefaultBoundedRangeModel[value=40, extent=0, min=40, max=40, adj=false]
```

There are two things to note here. First, by resetting the minimum to 50 we let the value property fall outside the bounded range. The model compensated by raising the value to match the new minimum. Second, we threw a monkey wrench into the model by setting the maximum less than the minimum. However, the bounded-range model adjusted the minimum and the value accordingly to match the newly specified maximum.

Now let's try a different tactic:

```
Now setting maximum to 50 . . .
A ChangeEvent has been fired!
DefaultBoundedRangeModel[value=40, extent=0, min=40, max=50, adj=false]
Now setting extent to 30 (greater than max) . . .
A ChangeEvent has been fired!
DefaultBoundedRangeModel[value=40, extent=10, min=40, max=50, adj=false]
```

Here we see what happens when we try to set an extent with a subrange greater than the current maximum—the model shortens the extent so that it falls within the bounded range. The same thing occurs if we reset the value of the extent's subrange so that it violates the maximum.

Finally, we activate the valueIsAdjusting property to notify any listeners that this is one in a series of changes, and the listener need not react immediately:

```
Now setting several properties . . .
A ChangeEvent has been fired!
```

```
DefaultBoundedRangeModel[value=40, extent=10, min=40, max=50, adj=true]
A ChangeEvent has been fired!
A ChangeEvent has been fired!
A ChangeEvent has been fired!
A ChangeEvent has been fired!
DefaultBoundedRangeModel[value=40, extent=20, min=0, max=100, adj=false]
```

The JScrollBar Class

JScrollBar is the Swing implementation of a scrollbar. It is the lightweight successor to the AWT 1.1 counterpart java.awt.Scrollbar, and is intended as a direct replacement for programmers converting their applications to Swing. The JScrollBar class is shown with various look-and-feels in Figure 6-3.

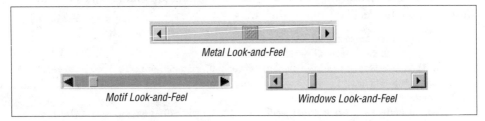

Figure 6-3. Scrollbars in the three look-and-feels

To program with a scrollbar, it is important to understand its anatomy. Scrollbars are composed of a rectangular tab, called a *slider* or *thumb*, located between two arrow buttons. The arrow buttons on either end increment or decrement the slider's position by an adjustable number of units, generally one. In addition, clicking in the area between the thumb and the end buttons (often called the *paging area*) moves the slider one *block*, or ten units by default. The user can modify the value of the scrollbar in one of three ways: by dragging the thumb in either direction, by pushing on either of the arrow buttons, or by clicking in the paging area.

As with AWT, scrollbars can have one of two orientations: horizontal or vertical. Figure 6-4 provides an illustration of a horizontal scrollbar. JScrollBar makes use of the bounded-range model to represent the scrollbar's data. The assignment of each bounded-range property is also shown in Figure 6-5. The minimum and maximum of the scrollbar fall on the interior edges of the arrow buttons. The scrollbar's value is defined as the left (or top) edge of the slider. Finally, the extent of the scrollbar defines the width of the thumb in relation to the total range. (The older Adjustable interface referred to the extent property as the "visible amount.") Note that horizontal scrollbars increment to the right and vertical scrollbars increment downward.

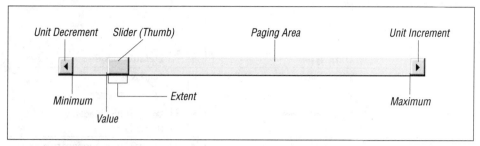

Figure 6-4. Anatomy of a horizontal scrollbar

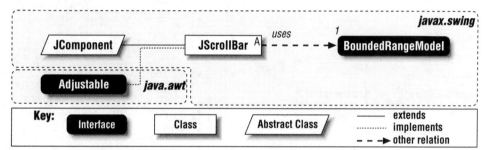

Figure 6-5. JScrollBar class diagram

Properties

Table 6-3 shows the properties of the JScrollBar component. Most of these properties come from the java.awt.Adjustable interface. The orientation property gives the direction of the scroll-bar, either JScrollBar.HORIZONTAL or JScrollBar.VERTICAL. The unitIncrement property represents the integer amount that the bounded range value changes when the user clicks on either of the arrow buttons. The blockIncrement property represents the integer amount that the scrollbar value changes by when the user clicks in either of the paging areas. The enabled property indicates whether the scrollbar can generate or respond to events. The minimum, maximum, value, and valueIsAdjusting properties match the equivalent properties in the BoundedRangeModel of the scroll bar. The visibleAmount property matches to the extent property in the model; it indicates the thickness of the thumb. The minimumSize and maximumSize properties allow the scrollbar to behave appropriately when it is resized.

Events

JScrollBar objects trigger java.awt.event.AdjustmentEvent whenever the component undergoes a change. Recall, however, that the bounded-range model generates a ChangeEvent when one of its properties changes. It becomes the

Table 6-3. JScrollBar Properties

Property	Data Type	get	is	set	bound	Default Value
UI	ScrollBarUI	•		•	•	from L&F
UIClassID*	String	•				"ScrollBarUI"
model	BoundedRangeModel	•		•	•	DefaultBoundedRange-Model()
accessible-Context*	AccessibleContext	•				JScrollBar.Accessible-JScrollBar()
blockIncrement*	int	•		•	•	10
enabled*	boolean			•		true
minimum*	int	•		•		0
minimumSize*	Dimension	•				
maximum*	int	•		•		100
maximumSize*	Dimension	•				
orientation*	int	•		•	•	JScrollBar.VERTICAL
unitIncrement*	int	•		•	•	1
value*	int	•		•		0
valueIsAdjusting	int	•		•		false
visibleAmount*	int	•		•		10

See also the properties of the JComponent class (Table 3-5).

responsibility of the JScrollBar class to convert change events to adjustment events and pass them on to registered listeners. Figure 6-6 shows the sequence of events between the component, model, and delegate when the user drags the scrollbar. JScrollBar also generates PropertyChangeEvent when any of its bound properties change.

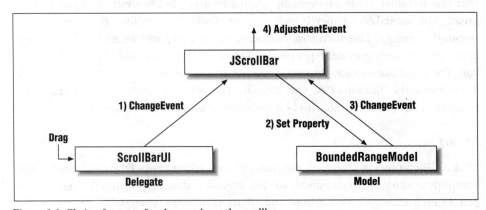

Figure 6-6. Chain of events after the user drags the scrollbar

Because JScrollBar was meant as a drop-in replacement for the AWT scrollbar, the older event system has been preserved to maintain consistency with the AWT 1.1 Adjustable interface.

The following methods are defined in the JScrollBar class:

public void addAdjustmentListener(AdjustmentListener l)
public void removeAdjustmentListener(AdjustmentListener l)
   Add or remove a specific listener for AdjustmentEvents from the scrollbar.

protected void fireAdjustmentValueChanged(AdjustmentEvent e)
   Notifies all registered listeners that a change has occurred in any of the scrollbar's bound properties.

Protected Fields

The JScrollBar class contains four protected fields:

protected BoundedRangeModel model
   The data model of the scrollbar object.

protected int orientation
protected int unitIncrement
protected int blockIncrement
   These fields store the values of the properties of the same name.

Constructors

public JScrollBar()
public JScrollBar(int orientation)
public JScrollBar(int orientation, int value, int extent, int minimum, int maximum)
   These constructors set the initial values of the scrollbar. If either of the first two constructors is invoked, the scrollbar initializes itself using the default values shown in Table 6-3. The orientation must be either JScrollBar.HORI-ZONTAL or JScrollBar.VERTICAL, or the constructor will throw a runtime IllegalArgumentException. If desired, the last four parameters in the third constructor can be used to initialize the scrollbar's bounded-range model to new values.

Miscellaneous

public int getUnitIncrement(int direction)
public int getBlockIncrement(int direction)
   Convenience methods that return the scrollbar unit and block increments for a particular direction. The direction is –1 for down and left, and 1 for up and right. These methods are typically invoked by the UI delegate to determine

how far to increment in a particular direction. Subclasses can override these methods to specify the units to increment in either direction, based on the content represented. For example, if a scrollbar was attached to a word-processing document, the variable-sized text in the document could result in different unit increments at any particular time for a vertical scrollbar.

public void updateUI()

Signals that a new look-and-feel has been set using the `setUI()` accessor. Invoking this method forces the component to reset its view using the new UI delegate.

public void setValues(int newValue, int newExtent, int newMinimum, int newMaximum)

Maps to the `setRangeValues()` method in the `BoundedRangeModel` interface.

Handling Events from a Scrollbar

The following program demonstrates how to monitor events generated by a pair of scrollbars:

```
// ScrollBarExample.java
//
import java.awt.*;
import java.awt.event.*;
import javax.swing.*;

public class ScrollBarExample extends JPanel {

    JLabel label;

    public ScrollBarExample() {
        super(true);
        label=new JLabel();
        setLayout(new BorderLayout());

        JScrollBar hbar=new JScrollBar(JScrollBar.HORIZONTAL, 30, 20, 0, 300);
        JScrollBar vbar=new JScrollBar(JScrollBar.VERTICAL, 30, 40, 0, 300);

        hbar.setUnitIncrement(2);
        hbar.setBlockIncrement(1);

        hbar.addAdjustmentListener(new MyAdjustmentListener());
        vbar.addAdjustmentListener(new MyAdjustmentListener());

        add(hbar, BorderLayout.SOUTH);
        add(vbar, BorderLayout.EAST);
        add(label, BorderLayout.CENTER);
    }
```

```
class MyAdjustmentListener implements AdjustmentListener {
    public void adjustmentValueChanged(AdjustmentEvent e) {
        label.setText("    New Value is " + e.getValue() + "        ");
        repaint();
    }
}

public static void main(String s[]) {
    JFrame frame = new JFrame("Scroll Bar Example");
    frame.addWindowListener(new BasicWindowMonitor());
    frame.setContentPane(new ScrollBarExample());
    frame.setSize(200,200);
    frame.setVisible(true);
}
}
```

The code is relatively easy to follow. The application creates a single panel and adds two scrollbars, one on the right side and one on the bottom. It then listens for any adjustments in either scrollbar and paints the scrollbar's new value in the middle of the panel. Figure 6-7 shows the result.

Figure 6-7. A simple scrollbar example

The JSlider Class

The JSlider class represents a graphical slider, a new component in Swing. Like scrollbars, sliders can have either a horizontal or a vertical orientation. With sliders, however, you can enhance their appearance with both tick marks and labels. The class hierarchy is illustrated in Figure 6-8.

The JSlider class allows you to set the spacing of two types of tick marks: major and minor. Major tick marks are longer than minor tick marks and are generally used at wider intervals. Figure 6-9 shows various sliders that can be composed in Swing.

The setPaintTicks() method sets a boolean, which is used to activate or deactivate the slider's tick marks. In some look-and-feels, the slider changes from a

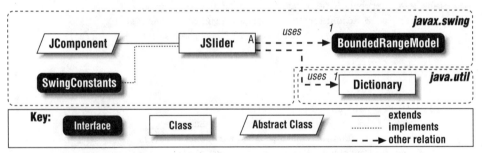

Figure 6-8. JSlider class diagram

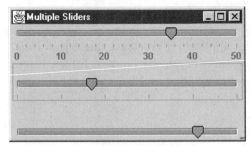

Figure 6-9. Various sliders in Swing

rectangular shape to a pointer when tick marks are activated. This is often done to give the user a more accurate representation of where the slider falls.

You can create a Dictionary of Component objects to annotate the slider. Each field in the Dictionary consists of two fields: an integer key, which tells the index to draw the various component, followed by the component itself. If you do not wish to create your own label components, you can use the createStandardLabels() method to create a series of JLabel objects for you. In addition, if you set the paintLabels property to true and give a positive value to the majorTick-Spacing property, a set of labels will be created automatically that matches the major tick marks. Figure 6-10 shows what a JSlider looks like in three different look-and-feels.

Properties

Table 6-4 shows the properties of the JSlider component. The slider object has several properties in addition to those of its data model. The orientation property determines which way the slider moves. It can be one of two values: JSlider.HORIZONTAL or JSlider.VERTICAL.

The labelTable is a Dictionary of slider values and JLabel objects. The labels in this dictionary are used to label the slider; they can be explicitly set by the user,

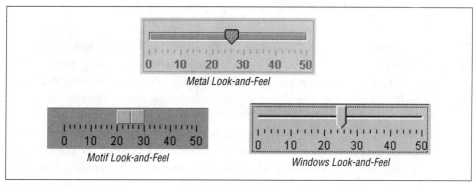

Figure 6-10. Sliders in the three look-and-feels

Table 6-4. JSlider Properties

Property	Data Type	get	is	set	bound	Default Value
UI	SliderUI	•		•	•	from L&F
UIClassID*	String	•				"SliderUI"
model	BoundedRangeModel	•		•	•	DefaultBoundedRangeModel
accessible-Context*	AccessibleContext	•				JSlider.Accessible-JSlider()
extent	int	•		•		0
inverted	boolean	•		•	•	false
labelTable	Dictionary	•		•	•	null
majorTickSpacing	int	•		•	•	10
maximum	int	•		•		100
minimum	int	•		•		0
minorTickSpacing	int	•		•	•	2
orientation	int	•		•	•	JSlider.HORIZONTAL
paintTicks	boolean	•		•	•	false
paintLabels	boolean	•		•	•	false
paintTrack	boolean	•		•	•	true
snapToTicks	boolean	•		•	•	true
value	int	•		•		50
valueIsAdjusting	boolean	•		•		false

See also properties from the JComponent class (Table 3-5).

or generated automatically by calling `createStandardLabels()`, which we'll discuss later. The `paintLabels` property is a `boolean` that determines whether to paint the textual labels associated with the slider. If `paintLabels` is set to `true`, the JLabel objects in the labelTable are painted at the appropriate locations in the slider.

The paintTicks property is a boolean; it decides if the major and minor tick marks are drawn. If it is true, *both* types of tick marks are drawn (unless their spacing is set to zero—see the last paragraph in this section). The snapToTicks property indicates whether the slider adjusts its value to reside directly above the nearest value, not the nearest tick mark as its name suggests. This may be fixed in a later release, and would be useful if you only want values that match the tick marks. The paintTrack property controls whether the "track" on the slider is painted. If the inverted property is false, then the table increments from left-to-right or from bottom-to-top; if the property is true, the table increments from right-to-left or from top-to-bottom. All tick marks and labels are shifted accordingly.

The minimum, maximum, value, and valueIsAdjusting properties match the equivalent properties in the BoundedRangeModel of the slider. The extent property is slightly different from the model; it tells how much the slider will increment up or down when L&F-specific keys are pressed (generally, PageUp and PageDown).

The majorTickSpacing and minorTickSpacing properties decide the repetition rate of the tick marks. In the event that both a major and minor tick mark occupy the same position, the major wins out. Neither property should ever be less than zero. If you wish to prevent either type of tick mark from being drawn you can give it a spacing value of zero.

Client Properties

The JSlider object contains one client property that works only with the Metal look-and-feel, JSlider.isFilled. When this client property is set to true, as shown below, the result is a slider component that fills itself only on its descending half. See Figure 6-11.

```
JSlider slider = new JSlider();
slider.putClientProperty("JSlider.isFilled", Boolean.TRUE);
```

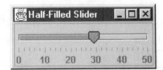

Figure 6-11. JSlider with the isFilled client property set (Metal look-and-feel)

Events

JSlider triggers a ChangeEvent whenever the user modifies any of its properties. It also generates a PropertyChangeEvent whenever any of its properties change.

public void addChangeListener(ChangeListener l)
public void removeChangeListener(ChangeListener l)
> Add and remove a specific listener from receiving property change events generated by the JSlider object.

protected void fireStateChanged()
> Fires a ChangeEvent to each of the registered listeners. The method is protected and is designed to be invoked only by objects that subclass JSlider.

protected ChangeListener createChangeListener()
> Returns an internal listener class, ModelListener, which is used to propagate change events from the bounded-range model. Subclasses of JSlider can override this method to return their own ChangeListener if they wish to handle changes from the model differently.

Protected Fields

protected transient ChangeEvent changeEvent
> Represents the change event for the JSlider object. Because the ChangeEvent does not contain information about the property that has changed, but instead only highlights that a change has occurred, only one instance of this object is needed for each event that JSlider fires.

protected ChangeListener changeListener
> Includes support for the ChangeEvent event model, including managing the ChangeListener event listeners.

protected int majorTickSpacing
protected int minorTickSpacing
protected int orientation
protected boolean snapToTicks
> These fields store the values of the properties of the same name.

protected BoundedRangeModel sliderModel
> Holds the BoundedRangeModel that serves as the data model for the slider.

Constructors

public JSlider()
public JSlider(int orientation)
public JSlider(int min, int max)

public JSlider(int min, int max, int value)

public JSlider(int orientation, int minimum, int maximum, int value)

public JSlider(BoundedRangeModel brm)

> These constructors set the initial values of the slider. The orientation must be either `JSlider.HORIZONTAL` or `JSlider.VERTICAL`. If anything else is passed in, the `JSlider` object throws a runtime `IllegalArgumentException`. The remaining parameters are used to initialize the slider's bounded-range model. If the parameters are not given, they are initialized to the default values in the table above. The final constructor accepts a bounded range model object to initialize the slider.

Labels

public Hashtable createStandardLabels(int increment)

public Hashtable createStandardLabels(int increment, int start)

> Utility functions that create a hashtable of numeric labels, starting at the value specified by `start` (or the minimum if omitted), and incrementing by the value specified by `increment`. The resulting `Hashtable` can be placed in the `labelTable` property and drawn if the `drawLabels` property is set to `true`.

protected updateLabelUIs()

> Called internally by the `updateUI()` function. It redraws the latest version of the slider labels.

Miscellaneous

public void updateUI()

> The `updateUI()` method is called to signal that a new look-and-feel has been set using the `setUI()` accessor. Invoking this method forces the slider component to reset its view using the new UI delegate.

Creating a Slider

The following program shows how to create a full-featured slider:

```
//  SliderExample.java
//
import java.awt.*;
import java.awt.event.*;
import javax.swing.*;
import javax.swing.border.*;

public class SliderExample extends JPanel {

    public SliderExample() {
```

```
        super(true);
        this.setLayout(new BorderLayout());
        JSlider slider = new JSlider(JSlider.HORIZONTAL, 0, 50, 25);

        slider.setMinorTickSpacing(2);
        slider.setMajorTickSpacing(10);
        slider.setPaintTicks(true);
        slider.setPaintLabels(true);

        // Note that the following line is really unnecessary. By setting a
        // positive integer to the major tick spacing and setting the paintLabel
        // property to true, it's done for us!
        slider.setLabelTable(slider.createStandardLabels(10));

        add(slider, BorderLayout.CENTER);
    }

    public static void main(String s[]) {
        JFrame frame = new JFrame("Slider Example");
        frame.addWindowListener(new BasicWindowMonitor());
        frame.setContentPane(new SliderExample());
        frame.pack();
        frame.setVisible(true);
    }
}
```

This code yields the slider shown in Figure 6-12.

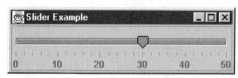

Figure 6-12. Swing slider

The JProgressBar Class

Like sliders, progress bars are also a new feature in Swing. The bars themselves are simply rectangles of an arbitrary length, a percentage of which is filled in based on the value of their model. Applications typically use progress bars to report the status of time-consuming jobs, such as software installation or large amounts of copying. Swing progress bars come in two flavors: horizontal and vertical. If the orientation is horizontal, the bar fills from left to right. If the bar is vertical, it fills from bottom to top. The class hierarchy is illustrated in Figure 6-13.

Different look-and-feels can contain different filling styles. Metal, for example, uses a solid fill, while the Windows look-and-feel uses an LED style. The latter means that the bar indicates progress by filling itself with dark, adjacent rectangles

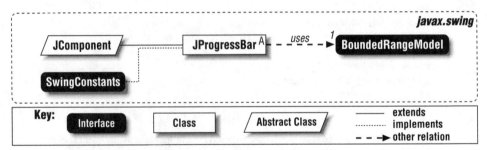

Figure 6-13. JProgressBar class diagram

instead of using a fluid line. The `JProgressBar` class also contains a `boolean` that specifies whether the progress bar draws a dark border around itself. You can override this default border by setting the border property of the `JComponent`. Figure 6-14 shows a Swing progress bar with three different look-and-feels.

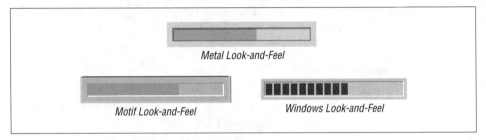

Figure 6-14. Progress bars in the three look-and-feels

Properties

The basic properties of the `JProgressBar` object are listed in Table 6-5. The `orientation` decides which way the progress bar lies; it must be either `JProgressBar.HORIZONTAL` or `JProgressBar.VERTICAL`. The `minimum`, `maximum`, and `value` properties mirror those in the bounded-range model. The `boolean` `borderPainted` indicates whether the component's border should appear around the progress bar. Borders are routinely combined with progress bars—they not only tell the user where its boundaries lie, but they also help to set off the progress bar from other components. An important note about the `JProgressBar` class: there are no methods to access the `extent` variable of its bounded-range model. This property is irrelevant in the progress bar component.

Three properties (all new in Swing 1.1/JDK 1.2) control whether a string is painted onto the progress bar. `StringPainted` is `true` if the string should appear. The `string` property is the actual string to be painted. If it is `null`, the progress bar displays the value of `percentComplete`, converted to a percentage

Table 6-5. JProgressBar Properties

Property	Data Type	get	is	set	bound	Default
UI	progressBarUI	•		•	•	from L&F
UIClassID*	String	•				"ProgressBarUI"
model	BoundedRangeModel	•		•		DefaultBoundedRangeModel()
accessible-Context*	AccessibleContext	•				JProgressBar.Accessible-JProgressBar()
borderPainted	boolean		•	•		true
maximum	int	•		•		100
minimum	int	•		•		0
orientation	int	•		•		JProgressBar.HORIZONTAL
percent-Complete	double		•	•		
string	String	•		•		null
stringPainted	boolean	•				false
value	int	•		•		0

See also properties from the JComponent class (Table 3-5).

between 0 and 100 (e.g., "35%"). Finally, `percentComplete` holds the completion value as a number between 0 and 1.

Events

`JProgressBar` triggers a `ChangeEvent` whenever the user modifies any of its properties and a `PropertyChangeEvent` when its bound property changes.

public void addChangeListener(ChangeListener l)
public void removeChangeListener(ChangeListener l)

Add or remove a specific listener for `ChangeEvent` notifications from the component.

protected void fireStateChanged()

Fires a `ChangeEvent` to each of the registered listeners. It is designed to be invoked only by objects that subclass `JProgressBar`.

protected ChangeListener createChangeListener()

Returns an internal class, `ModelListener`, which is used to propagate change events from the bounded-range model. Subclasses of `JProgressBar` can override this method to return their own `ChangeListener` if they wish to handle changes from the model differently.

Protected Fields

protected BoundedRangeModel model

Holds the `BoundedRangeModel` that serves as the data model for the progress bar.

protected transient ChangeEvent changeEvent

Represents the change event for the `JProgressBar` object. Because the `ChangeEvent` does not contain information about the property that has changed, but instead only that a change has occurred, only one instance of this object is needed for each event that `JProgressBar` fires.

protected ChangeListener changeListener

Includes support for the `ChangeEvent` event model, including managing the `ChangeListener` event listeners.

protected int orientation

Indicates the orientation of the progress bar.

protected boolean paintBorder

Indicates whether the progress bar's border should be painted.

Constructors

public JProgressBar()

Creates a horizontal progress bar with a lowered border. The `DefaultBoundedRangeModel` is used as the data model for the progress bar.

public JProgressBar(BoundedRangeModel model)
public JProgressBar(int orient, int min, int max)
public JProgressBar(int min, int max)
public JProgressBar(int orient)

These constructors create progress bars with initial values specified by their arguments. In the first of these constructors, `model` supplies the initial values and serves as the data model of the progress bar.

Miscellaneous

public void paintBorder()

Overrides the `paintBorder()` method in `JComponent` to paint the border for the progress bar, if the `borderPainted` property is currently `true`.

public void updateUI()

Signals that a new look-and-feel has been set using the `setUI()` accessor. Invoking this method forces the slider component to reset its UI delegate.

Working with Progress Bars

Like the other bounded-range components, progress bars are easy to work with. This example displays a simple progress bar that fills from left to right by updating itself every tenth of a second:

```java
// ProgressBarExample.java
//
import java.awt.*;
import java.awt.event.*;
import javax.swing.*;

public class ProgressBarExample extends JPanel {

    JProgressBar pbar;
    static final int MY_MINIMUM=0;
    static final int MY_MAXIMUM=100;

    public ProgressBarExample() {
    super(true);

        pbar = new JProgressBar();
        pbar.setMinimum(MY_MINIMUM);
        pbar.setMaximum(MY_MAXIMUM);
        add(pbar);
    }

    public void updateBar(int newValue) {
        pbar.setValue(newValue);
    }

    public static void main(String args[]) {

        final ProgressBarExample it = new ProgressBarExample();

        JFrame frame = new JFrame("Progress Bar Example");
        frame.addWindowListener(new BasicWindowMonitor());
        frame.setContentPane(it);
        frame.pack();
        frame.setVisible(true);

        for (int i = MY_MINIMUM; i <= MY_MAXIMUM; i++) {
            final int percent=i;
            try {
                SwingUtilities.invokeAndWait({
                    new Runnable() {
                        public void run() {
                            it.updateBar(percent);
                        }
                    });
```

```
        java.lang.Thread.sleep(100);

    } catch (Exception e) {;}
}
```

We used SwingUtilities.invokeAndWait() here because we are updating the user interface from within our own thread (rather than from the event handling thread). For more information on working with multiple threads in Swing, see Chapter 28, *Swing Under the Hood*.

Monitoring Progress

By themselves, progress bars are pretty boring. Swing, however, combines progress bars with the dialog capabilities of JOptionPane to create the ProgressMonitor and ProgressMonitorInputStream classes. You can use the first of these to report on the current progress of a potentially long task. You can use Progress-MonitorInputStream to automatically monitor the amount of data that has been read in with an InputStream. With both, you can define various strings to be posted in the progress monitor dialogs to offer a better explanation of the task at hand.

The ProgressMonitor Class

The ProgressMonitor class is a generic progress dialog box that can be used for practically anything. There are two string descriptions that can be set on a ProgressMonitor dialog box. The first is a static component that can never change; it appears on the top of the dialog and is set in the constructor. The second is a variable string-based property that can be reset at any time. It appears below the static string, slightly above the progress bar. Figure 6-15 shows the structure for this class.

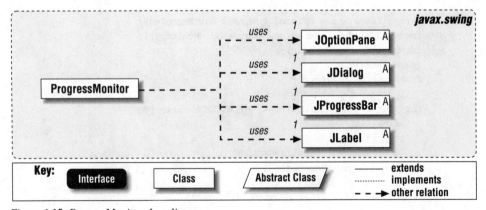

Figure 6-15. ProgressMonitor class diagram

Once instantiated, the ProgressMonitor dialog (shown in Figure 6-16) does not pop up immediately. The dialog waits a configurable amount of time before deciding whether the task at hand is long enough to warrant the dialog. If it is, the dialog is displayed. When the current value of the progress bar is greater than or equal to the maximum, as specified in the constructor, the progress monitor dialog closes. If you need to close the progress monitor early, you can call upon the close() method. The user can close this dialog as well by pressing the "OK" or the "Cancel" buttons (they do the same thing—the "OK" button is redundant); you can test the canceled property to see if this has happened.

Figure 6-16. The ProgressMonitor dialog

NOTE   When this book went to press, the ProgressMonitor class worked well on Windows, but would often crash the virtual machine on Solaris and Linux. This typically happens when the user sets the progress property to anything other than zero. This may be fixed by the time you read this.

You should be aware that the ProgressMonitor class does not fire any events indicating that it is complete. Hence, you should test the isCancelled() method each time you call setProgress() to see if the user has canceled the dialog.

Properties

Table 6-6 shows the properties for the ProgressMonitor class. The canceled property is a boolean that indicates whether the progress monitor has been canceled. This is useful if you need to determine whether the user dismissed the dialog halfway through. The minimum and maximum properties define the range of the progress bar; the progress property is analogous to the progress bar's current value. The note property is a string that can be updated as the progress monitor works; it serves to indicate what the progress monitor is currently doing.

As we mentioned previously, the progress monitor dialog does not pop up immediately. Instead, it waits millisToDecideToPopup milliseconds before estimating

Table 6-6. ProgressMonitor Properties

Property	Data Type	get	is	set	bound	Default Value
canceled	boolean		•			false
maximum	int	•		•		100
minimum	int	•		•		0
note	String	•		•		
progress	int	•		•		0
millisToDecideToPopup	int	•		•		500
millisToPopup	int	•		•		2000

how long the current progress might take. If it appears that it will take longer than millisToPopup milliseconds, it will pop up a progress monitor dialog.

Constructor

public ProgressMonitor(Component parentComponent, Object message, String note, int min, int max)

Creates a ProgressMonitor dialog box, placed above the component specified as parentComponent. The dialog contains a static message that is constant throughout the life of the dialog (see JOptionPane in Chapter 10 for a discussion of valid values) and a note that changes throughout the life of the dialog. If the note value is initially null, the note cannot be updated throughout the life of the dialog. The min and max values specify the minimum and maximum of the progress bar.

Miscellaneous

public void close()

Forces the ProgressMonitor to shut down, even if it has not completed all of its tasks.

Using a Progress Monitor

The following example shows a ProgressMonitor in action. With it, we simulate updating the dialog with a timer that fires off events every half-second. We use the invokeLater() method to place the actual update on the system event queue; this is always a prudent idea when working with multiple threads in Swing. We use invokeLater() runs a section of code that's implemented by the inner class Update. The run() method of Update simply increments the progress bar's progress property, updates the text on the progress bar, and updates the counter. The result is shown in Figure 6-16.

```
// ProgressMonitorExample
//
import java.awt.*;
import java.awt.event.*;
import javax.swing.*;

public class ProgressMonitorExample extends JPanel implements
            ActionListener {

    static ProgressMonitor pbar;
    static int counter = 0;

    public ProgressMonitorExample() {
        super(true);
        pbar = new ProgressMonitor(this, "Monitoring Progress",
                                "Initializing . . .", 0, 100);

        // Fire a timer every once in a while to update the progress
        Timer timer = new Timer(500, this);
        timer.start();
    }

    public static void main(String args[]) {
        new ProgressMonitorExample();
    }

    public void actionPerformed(ActionEvent e) {

        // Invoked by the timer every half second. Simply place
        // the progress monitor update on the event queue.
        SwingUtilities.invokeLater(new Update());
    }

    class Update implements Runnable {
        public void run() {
            if (pbar.isCanceled()) {
                pbar.close();
                System.exit(1);
            }
            pbar.setProgress(counter);
            pbar.setNote("Operation is "+counter+"% complete");
            counter += 2;
        }
    }
}
```

The ProgressMonitorInputStream

The ProgressMonitorInputStream allows the programmer to monitor the amount of data read from an input stream. It includes a ProgressMonitor object

...e of itself that the user can access to update the progress of the reading of the ...put stream as it progresses. Figure 6-17 shows the class diagram for this object.

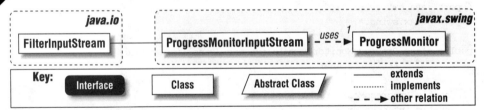

Figure 6-17. ProgressMonitorInputStream class diagram

For the most part, the `ProgressMonitorInputStream` class contains many of the methods found in `java.io.InputStream`. Like all `InputStream` objects, you can tie this class together with a `FilterInputStream` for better control over the input. Figure 6-18 shows the progress monitor dialog associated with a typical `ProgressMonitorInputStream`.

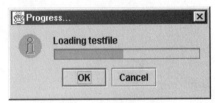

Figure 6-18. The ProgressMonitorInputStream dialog

Property

Table 6-7 shows the only property of the `ProgressMonitorInputStream`: `progressMonitor`, which contains the progress monitor defined inside this object. The read-only accessor allows you to change the progress or the note string, as well as close the dialog.

Table 6-7. ProgressMonitorInputStream Property

Property	Data Type	get	is	set	bound	Default Value
progressMonitor	ProgressMonitor	•				ProgressMonitor()

When it's created, the `ProgressMonitorInputStream` attempts to read the amount of data available and updates the progress monitor's `progress` property as bytes are read from the stream. This can lead to strange results if you wrap a `ProgressMonitorInputStream` around some other input stream for which the amount of data waiting to be read isn't well defined—for example, a `PipedIn-putStream`. It's a good idea to read small amounts of data from a

ProgressMonitorInputStream at a time. This way, the dialog has a chance to update its progress frequently. Finally, as with any blocking request, try not to perform a read() while on the event dispatching queue. That way, if the call blocks for an inordinate amount of time, you won't drag down any repainting requests and give the illusion that your application has crashed. It's best to handle read()s in a separate thread.

Constructor

public ProgressMonitorInputStream(Component parentComponent, Object message, InputStream in)

Creates a ProgressMonitorInputStream dialog box, placed above the parentComponent. The dialog contains a static message that is constant throughout the life of the dialog (see JOptionPane in Chapter 10 for a discussion of valid values). The constructor also takes a reference to the target input stream.

Methods

public int read() throws IOException

Reads in a single byte and updates the progress monitor.

public int read(byte b[]) throws IOException

Reads in an array of bytes and updates the progress monitor.

public int read(byte b[], int off, int len) throws IOException

Reads in an array of bytes and updates the progress monitor.

public long skip(long n) throws IOException

Skips a series of bytes and updates the progress monitor.

public void close() throws IOException

Closes the input stream and the progress monitor.

public synchronized void reset() throws IOException

Resets the current reading position back to the beginning and updates the progress monitor.

Using a ProgressMonitorInputStream

Here is a simple example that demonstrates using a ProgressMonitorInput-Stream class to monitor the progress of loading a file. You can specify the name of the file on the command line as follows:

```
java ProgressMonitorInputExample myfile
```

This program reads in the file a little bit at a time, dumping out the results to the screen. If the file is not found, an error dialog is displayed. If you run the program, load a text file (not a binary file). Here is the source code:

```java
// ProgressMonitorInputExample.java
//
import java.io.*;
import java.awt.*;
import javax.swing.*;

public class ProgressMonitorInputExample extends JPanel {

    public ProgressMonitorInputExample(String filename) {

        ProgressMonitorInputStream monitor;

        try {
            monitor = new ProgressMonitorInputStream(
                this, "Loading "+filename, new FileInputStream(filename));
            InputStream in = new BufferedInputStream(monitor);
            while (in.available() > 0) {
                byte[] data = new byte[38];
                in.read(data);
                System.out.write(data);
            }
        } catch (FileNotFoundException e) {
            JOptionPane.showMessageDialog(null, "Unable to find file: "
                + filename, "Error", JOptionPane.ERROR_MESSAGE);
        } catch (IOException e) {;}
    }

    public static void main(String args[]) {
        new ProgressMonitorInputExample(args[0]);
    }
}
```

7

Lists and Combo Boxes

This chapter deals with two similar components: *lists* and *combo boxes*. Both components present a catalog of choices to the user. A list allows the user to make single or multiple selections. A combo box permits only a single selection, but can be combined with a text field that allows the user to type in a selection as well. From a design standpoint, both lists and combo boxes share similar characteristics, and as you will soon see, both can be extended in ways that many Swing components cannot.

Lists

A *list* is a graphical component from which the user can select choices. Lists typically display several items at a time, allowing the user to make either a single selection or multiple selections. In the event that the inventory of the list exceeds the component's display, the list is often coupled with a scrollbar to navigate through the entire contents.

AWT limited the contents of its `List` component to strings. The Swing `JList` component lifts this restriction. List elements can now be strings, images—any Java component capable of painting itself. Swing offers a wide degree of flexibility with list components; they can be as simple or as complex as the programmer's needs dictate.

Let's get our feet wet with a simple list. The following example uses the Swing list class, `JList`, to create a single-selection list composed only of strings. Figure 7-1 shows the result.

```
// SimpleList.java
//
import java.awt.*;
import java.awt.event.*;
```

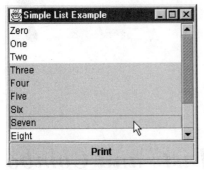

Figure 7-1. A simple Swing list

```java
import javax.swing.*;

public class SimpleList extends JPanel implements ActionListener {
    String label[] = { "Zero","One","Two","Three","Four","Five","Six",
                       "Seven","Eight","Nine","Ten","Eleven" };
    JList list;

    public SimpleList() {
        this.setLayout(new BorderLayout());
        list = new JList(label);
        JScrollPane pane = new JScrollPane(list);
        JButton button = new JButton("Print");
        button.addActionListener(this);

        add(pane, BorderLayout.CENTER);
        add(button, BorderLayout.SOUTH);
    }

    public static void main(String s[]) {
        JFrame frame = new JFrame("Simple List Example");
        frame.addWindowListener(new BasicWindowMonitor());
        frame.setContentPane(new SimpleList());
        frame.setSize(250, 180);
        frame.setVisible(true);
    }

    public void actionPerformed(ActionEvent e) {
        int selected[] = list.getSelectedIndices();
        System.out.println("Selected Elements:  ");

        for (int i=0; i < selected.length; i++) {
            String element =
                (String)list.getModel().getElementAt(selected[i]);
            System.out.println("  " + element);
        }
    }
}
```

Take a close look at the source. The first thing you might notice is that we were forced to embed the Swing list inside the viewport of a scroll pane object. Unlike AWT, the Swing JList class does not support scrolling through its data. Instead, it hands off the responsibility to the JScrollPane class. This is a significant design change from its predecessor, java.awt.List, which automatically manages a scrollbar for you. However, making a list the view of a scroll pane object fits better into the overall philosophy of Swing. This allows developers to reuse a customized scrollbar (or scroll pane) with their own lists, instead of simply accepting a default provided with the list component. It also enables autoscrolling support, so you can drag the mouse above or below the list, and its contents will scroll automatically.

Try selecting multiple numbers (you can do this by holding down the "Shift" button while clicking). Note that you are only allowed to select one *range*, or continuous set of numbers, at a time. If you select a number beyond the current selection range, the range is extended to cover everything in between. The first number selected (i.e., the one you didn't have to hold "Shift" down for) becomes the initial endpoint for the range. This endpoint is called the *anchor*. The most recent selection (which is outlined) forms the second endpoint. This element is called the *lead*. Together, the anchor and the lead form a range of selections in the list, as shown in Figure 7-2.

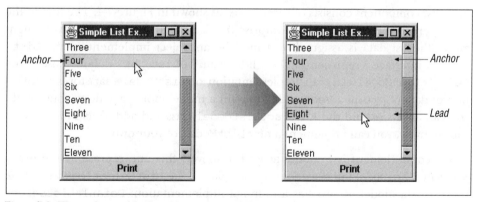

Figure 7-2. The anchor and lead positions in a single list selection

Finally, the example contains an actionPerformed() method that is called when the user presses the button. This method reports all the items that are currently selected in the list:

```
Selected Elements:
   Four
   Five
   Six
   Seven
   Eight
```

Anatomy of a Swing List

Now that we've seen the basics, let's take a closer look at JList. Figure 7-3 shows a high-level class diagram for Swing's list classes. In particular, note the three interfaces on the far right side.

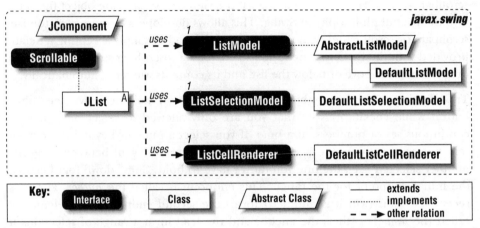

Figure 7-3. Swing List class diagram

Each list component consists of three parts, as shown in Figure 7-4. The first of the three parts is the elements that comprise the list, called the *list data*. As you might guess, the list data is assigned to a model—an object implementing the List-Model interface represents the list data. JList by default uses the DefaultListModel class, an implementation of ListModel that stores a collection of data objects in a Vector. If you want a model more specific to your needs, you can always extend the AbstractListModel class and add to its functionality. Alternatively, you can implement a new ListModel of your own.

The second element is a model as well; however, this one represents the user's *selections*. The model interface for selection data is the ListSelectionModel. Like the list data model, it also has a minimal implementation: DefaultListSelectionModel. With the default JList, for example, you can select several ranges simultaneously. However, you can also program the DefaultListSelectionModel to allow only one element to be selected at a given time.

The final piece is called a *cell renderer*. A cell renderer defines how each cell displays its data in the list, including when the cell is selected. Why an entire class for rendering list elements? As we mentioned previously, list data is no longer constrained to strings. Icons and animations can be displayed in place of or next to descriptive text. A cell renderer is common in many Swing components as a way to render complex data. In fact, if you write one carefully, it can be reused in several locations.

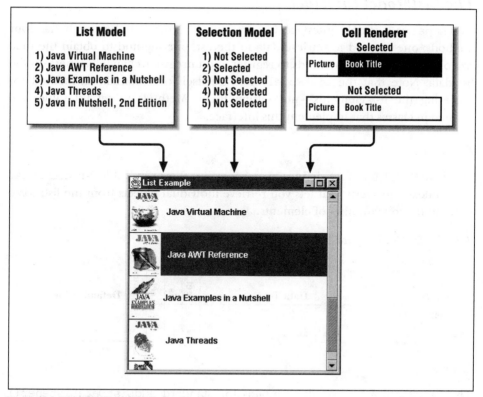

Figure 7-4. The three parts of a Swing list

Where To Go from Here?

The following sections outline the various models and support classes that make up a Swing list. If you simply want to get to know the Swing JList class as is, you can skip ahead to the section on JList, where we create a graphical list of selected O'Reilly Java books. On the other hand, if you want to learn more about the data and selection models of the JList, then read on!

Representing List Data

Swing uses one interface and two classes to maintain a model of the list elements. When programming with lists, you will often find that you can reuse these classes without modification. Occasionally, you may find it necessary to extend or even rewrite these classes to obtain functionality that is lacking. In either case, it's important to examine all three in detail. Let's start with the easiest: ListModel.

The ListModel Interface

ListModel is a simple interface for accessing the data of the list. It has four methods: one method to retrieve data in the list, one method to obtain the total size of the list, and two methods to register and unregister change listeners on the list data. Note that the ListModel interface itself only contains a method for retrieving the list elements—not setting them. Methods to set list values are defined in classes that implement this interface.

Properties

The ListModel interface defines two properties, shown in Table 7-1. elementAt is an indexed property that lets you retrieve individual objects from the list; size tells you the total number of elements.

Table 7-1. ListModel Properties

Property	Data Type	get	is	set	bound	Default Value
elementAt (indexed)	Object	•				
size	int	•				

Events

The ListModel interface also contains the standard addListDataListener() and removeListDataListener() event subscription methods. These methods accept listeners that wish to be notified when the contents of the list have changed. A ListDataEvent should be generated when elements in the list are added, removed, or modified.

public abstract void addListDataListener(ListDataListener l)
public abstract void removeListDataListener(ListDataListener l)
    Add or remove a specific listener for ListDataEvent notifications.

The AbstractListModel Class

The AbstractListModel class supplements the ListModel interface by providing implementations of the required addListDataListener() and removeListDataListener() event registration classes. It also provides three methods for firing ListDataEvent objects. These methods are triggered when an addition, subtraction, or modification to the list data has taken place. Note that a ListDataEvent is not the same as a PropertyChangeEvent, which is more general in nature. (ListDataEvent is covered later in this chapter.)

Protected Fields

protected EventListenerList listenerList
  Contains the event listeners for the data model.

Methods

protected void fireContentsChanged(Object source, int index1, int index2)
  Called by subclasses to trigger a `ListDataEvent`. The event indicates that a modification has occurred in the list elements between `index1` and `index2`. `index2` can be less than `index1`. The `source` variable provides a reference to the object that signaled the change.

protected void fireIntervalAdded(Object source, int index1, int index2)
  Called by subclasses to trigger a `ListDataEvent`. The event indicates that the list elements between `index1` and `index2` (inclusive) have been added to the list. Assuming that `index2` is the greater index, the element previously at `index1` in the list is now element (`index2+1`). All subsequent elements are shifted as well. `index2` can be less than `index1`. The `source` variable provides a reference to the object that signaled the change.

protected void fireIntervalRemoved(Object source, int index1, int index2)
  Called by subclasses to trigger a `ListDataEvent`. The event indicates to a listener that the list elements from `index1` to `index2` have been removed from the list. Assuming that `index2` is the larger index, the element previously at (`index2+1`) now becomes `index1` and all elements greater are shifted down accordingly. `index2` can be less than `index1`. The `source` variable provides a reference to the object that signaled the change.

Although the `AbstractListModel` class completes the event framework defined by the list model interface, it does not implement the remaining two methods of the `ListModel` interface: `getSize()` and `getElementAt()`. Instead, it defines these as abstract (making the entire class abstract) and leaving data storage and retrieval to a subclass, such as `DefaultListModel`.

The DefaultListModel Class

Swing provides a default implementation of the `AbstractListModel` class called `DefaultListModel`. This class is based on the `java.util.Vector` class, a resizable array of objects that most Java programmers are comfortable using. A majority of the methods of the `DefaultListModel` class are identical to those of `Vector`, with the added (and required) feature that those methods fire a `ListDataEvent` each time the contents or size of the vector changes.

We should briefly review some `Vector` concepts here. A `Vector` holds an array of objects that can grow or shrink in capacity as necessary. The *size* of the vector is the amount of elements that it currently contains, while the *capacity* of the vector is the maximum number of elements the vector can hold before it must allocate more space for itself. The capacity is typically larger than the size; however, a `Vector` can trim its capacity to match its size on command.

NOTE   Sun plans to modify this class in future releases of Swing to adhere to the Java Collections framework more closely. See the Java home page (*http://java.sun.com/*) for more information about Java Collections.

Properties

The `DefaultListModel` class has three properties, shown in Table 7-2. The `size` property indicates how many elements are currently stored in the vector. You can use the `setSize()` method to reset the size of the vector. If the new size is larger than the previous size, the additional elements are populated with `null` references and the method fires a `ListDataEvent` describing the range that was added. If the new size is smaller, the vector is truncated, and the method fires a `ListDataEvent` describing the range that was removed.

Table 7-2. DefaultListModel Properties

Property	Data Type	get	is	set	bound	Default Value
elementAt (indexed)	Object	•		•		
empty	boolean		•			true
size	int	•		•		0

The `empty` property is a `boolean` that indicates whether the vector has no elements. `elementAt` is an indexed property that you can use to access the vector elements. If you set a new element using the `setElementAt()` method, the method fires a `ListDataEvent` describing the element that was changed.

Constructor

public DefaultListModel()
     Creates an empty vector to be used as the list model.

Methods

public void copyInto(Object anArray[])
     Copies all of the objects in the vector into the array `anArray`.

public void trimToSize()

Collapses the capacity of the vector to match its current size, removing any empty storage.

public void ensureCapacity(int minCapacity)

Tells the vector to make sure that its capacity is at least `minCapacity`.

public int capacity()

Returns the current capacity of the vector. The capacity is the number of objects the vector can hold without reallocating for more space.

public int size()

Returns the number of elements currently contained in the vector. It is equivalent to `getSize()`.

public Enumeration elements()

Returns an `Enumeration` of each of the elements in the vector.

public boolean contains(Object elem)

Returns a boolean indicating whether the object referenced by the variable `elem` is currently contained in the vector.

public int indexOf(Object elem)

Returns the index of the object referenced by the variable `elem`, or −1 if the object is not contained in the vector.

public int indexOf(Object elem, int index)

Returns the index of the first object referenced by the variable `elem`, beginning its search at the element specified by `index` and moving forward through the vector. The method returns −1 if the object is not contained in the vector.

public int lastIndexOf(Object elem)

Returns the index of the last object referenced by the variable `elem`, searching backward from the last element in the vecto to the front of the list. The method returns −1 if the object is not contained in the vector.

public int lastIndexOf(Object elem, int index)

Returns the index of the last object referenced by the variable `elem`, searching backward from the element referenced by `index` to the front of the list. The method returns −1 if the object is not contained in the vector.

public Object elementAt(int index)

Returns a reference to the object at the specified index. It is equivalent to `getElementAt(index)`.

public Object firstElement()

Returns a reference to the first object in the vector.

public Object lastElement()

Returns a reference to the last object in the vector.

public void removeElementAt(int index)

Removes the element at the specified index. It then fires off a `ListData-Event` to all registered listeners, describing the element that was removed.

public void insertElementAt(Object obj, int index)

Inserts the object `obj` into the vector at the given index, incrementing the index of the element previously at that index and any elements above it. (That is, it adds `obj` before the element at `index`.) The total size of the vector is increased by one. The method then fires off a `ListDataEvent` to all registered listeners, describing the element that was inserted.

public void addElement(Object obj)

Adds the object `obj` to the end of the vector and fires off a `ListDataEvent` to all registered listeners, describing the element that was appended.

public boolean removeElement(Object obj)

Attempts to remove the first occurrence of the object `obj` from the vector, returning `true` if successful and `false` if no such object exists in the vector. If the method is successful, all subsequent element indices are decremented, and the size of the vector is reduced by one. The method then fires off a `ListDataEvent` to all registered listeners, describing the element that was removed.

public void removeAllElements()

Removes all the elements from the vector. It then fires off a `ListDataEvent`, indicating that the entire range was removed.

public String toString()

Provides a comma-separated list of each element currently in the vector.

public Object[] toArray()

Returns the contents of the vector as an array of type `Object`. It is functionally equivalent to the `copyInto()` method, except that the results are explicitly returned.

public Object get(int index)

Equivalent to `getElementAt(index)`.

public Object set(int index, Object element)

Equivalent to `setElementAt(element, index)`.

public void add(int index, Object element)

Equivalent to `insertElementAt(element, index)`.

public Object remove(int index)

Equivalent to `removeElementAt(element, index)`.

public void clear()

Equivalent to `removeAllElements()`.

public void removeRange(int fromIndex, int toIndex)
> Removes all elements between the first and second index (including the boundary elements) from the list. The method fires a `ListDataEvent` describing the interval that was removed.

A JList with Changing Contents

Here's a simple program that dynamically adds and removes elements from a JList. To do so, we work with the `DefaultListModel` that keeps track of the list's contents.

```java
//  ListModelExample.java
//
import java.awt.*;
import java.awt.event.*;
import javax.swing.*;

public class ListModelExample extends JPanel implements ActionListener {

    JList list;
    DefaultListModel model;
    int counter = 16;

    public ListModelExample() {
        super(true);
        setLayout(new BorderLayout());
        model = new DefaultListModel();
        list = new JList(model);
        JScrollPane pane = new JScrollPane(list);
        JButton addButton = new JButton("Add Element");
        JButton removeButton = new JButton("Remove Element");
        for (int i = 0; i < 15; i++)
            model.addElement("Element " + i);

        addButton.addActionListener(this);
        removeButton.addActionListener(this);

        add(pane, BorderLayout.NORTH);
        add(addButton, BorderLayout.WEST);
        add(removeButton, BorderLayout.EAST);
    }

    public static void main(String s[]) {
        JFrame frame = new JFrame("List Model Example");
        frame.addWindowListener(new BasicWindowMonitor());
        frame.setContentPane(new ListModelExample());
        frame.setSize(250, 220);
        frame.setVisible(true);
    }
```

```
    public void actionPerformed(ActionEvent e) {
        if (e.getActionCommand() == "Add Element") {
            model.addElement("Element " + counter);
            counter++;
        } else {
            if (model.getSize() > 0)
                model.removeElementAt(0);
        }
    }
}.
```

The result is shown in Figure 7-5.

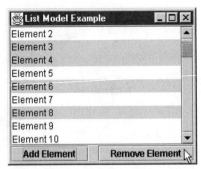

Figure 7-5. Dynamically adding and removing elements from a list

This example demonstrates a few important concepts. First, we instantiated our own `DefaultListModel` instead of using the default provided with the `JList`. if we hadn't done this, we wouldn't have been able to add anything to the list. Working with your own instantiation is generally easier when you need to make runtime changes to any model—again, assigning new models is a wonderful benefit of the MVC architecture in Swing.

We've provided two ways for changing the list's contents: the "Add Element" button and the "Remove Element" button at the bottom. Pressing "Add Element" calls our `actionPerformed()` method and appends an element to the end of the list. Pressing "Remove Element" calls the same method and deletes an element from the front of the list. After either button is pressed, the `JList` is notified of the change in the model and updates itself automatically. If you watch carefully, you can see the scrollbar thumb grow or shrink as the list size changes.

Try selecting some elements, then press the "Remove Element" button a couple of times. Here's a gotcha: the selections don't decrement with the elements. This introduces an important difference in responsibilities between the data model and the selection model: the selection model simply remembers the indices of the elements that are selected; it doesn't care what those elements contain, or even if they have shifted over time!

ListDataEvent

ListDataEvent is an extension of `java.util.EventObject` that holds information about a change in the list data model. The event describes the nature of the change, as well as the bounding indices of the elements involved. However, it does not send data about the resulting elements. Listeners must query the source of the event to determine the new contents of the affected elements.

There are three types of changes that can occur to the list data: elements can be altered, inserted, or removed from the list. Note that the indices passed in form a closed interval (i.e., both indices are included in the affected range). If a ListDataEvent is received claiming that list elements have been altered, the bounding indices typically describe the smallest range of data elements that have changed. If elements have been removed, the indices describe the range of elements that have been deleted. If elements have been added, the indices describe the new elements that have been inserted into the list.

Properties

The ListDataEvent contains four properties, each with its own read-only accessor, as shown in Table 7-3. Each of these properties must be set in the List-DataEvent constructor. The source property indicates the object that is firing the event. The type property represents the type of change that has occurred; it must be one of the constants listed in Table 7-4. The index0 and index1 properties outline the range of affected elements. index0 does not need to be less than index1 for the ListDataEvent to be valid.

Table 7-3. ListDataEvent Properties

Property	Data Type	get	is	set	bound	Default Value
index0	int	•				
index1	int	•				
source*	Object	•				
type	int	•				

Constants

The static integer event types of the ListDataEvent are listed in Table 7-4.

Table 7-4. Constants for ListDataEvent

Constant	Data Type	Description
CONTENTS_CHANGED	int	The elements between the two indices (inclusive) have been altered.
INTERVAL_ADDED	int	The elements now between the two indices (inclusive) have just been inserted into the list.
INTERVAL_REMOVED	int	The elements previously between the two indices (inclusive) have now been removed from the list.

Constructor

public ListDataEvent(Object source, int type, int index0, int index1)

   The constructor for the event. It takes a reference to the object that fires the event, as well as the event type and bounding indices.

The ListDataListener Interface

The ListDataListener interface, which is the conduit for receiving the ListDataEvent objects, contains three methods. Each method receives a different ListDataEvent type that can be generated. This interface must be implemented by any listener object that wishes to be notified of changes to the list model.

Methods

public abstract void intervalAdded(ListDataEvent e)

   Called when the interval of elements specified in the ListDataEvent has already been added to the list. The specified interval includes both endpoints. Listeners will typically want to query the source of the event for the contents of the new interval.

public abstract void intervalRemoved(ListDataEvent e)

   Called when the interval of elements specified in the ListDataEvent has already been deleted. The specified interval includes both endpoints.

public abstract void contentsChanged(ListDataEvent e)

   Called when the interval of elements specified in the ListDataEvent has been altered. The specified interval includes both endpoints, although not all elements are guaranteed to have changed. Listeners will typically want to query the source of the event for the contents of those objects.

Handling Selections

The JList class in Swing depends on a second model, this one to monitor the elements that have been selected by the user. As with the list data model, the programmer is given a wide latitude of control when dealing with selections. Swing uses a simple interface for models that handle list selections—ListSelection-Model—and also provides a default implementation—DefaultListSelection-Model.

The ListSelectionModel Interface

The ListSelectionModel interface outlines the methods necessary for managing list selections. Selections are represented by a series of ranges, where each range is defined by its endpoints. For example, if the elements "One," "Two," "Three," "Six," "Seven," and "Nine" were selected in the opening example of the chapter, the list selection model would contain three entries that specified the ranges {1,3} and {6,7} and {9,9}. All selection range endpoints are zero-based. If only one element is present in a range, such as with "Nine," both endpoints are identical.

Properties

Table 7-5 shows the properties of the ListSelectionModel interface. The first four properties of the list selection model can be used to retrieve various indices in the list that are currently selected. The anchorSelectionIndex and leadSelectionIndex properties represent the anchor and lead indices of the most recent range of selections. The maxSelectionIndex and minSelectionIndex properties return the largest and smallest selected index in the entire list, respectively.

Table 7-5. ListSelectionModel Properties

Property	Data Type	get	is	set	bound	Default Value
anchorSelectionIndex	int	•		•		
leadSelectionIndex	int	•		•		
maxSelectionIndex	int	•				
minSelectionIndex	int	•				
selectionEmpty	boolean		•			
selectionMode	int	•		•		
valueIsAdjusting	boolean	•		•		

The selectionMode property defines the type of selections that the user may make in the list. This property can take one of three constants, representing a single selection, a single range of selections, or multiple ranges of selections. The default is the single range of selections. (The selectionMode constants are outlined in greater detail in Table 7-6.) The selectionEmpty property is a boolean indicating whether there are any selections. If there are no selections anywhere in the list, the property is set to false.

Setting the valueIsAdjusting property to true indicates that the object is sending a series of selection change events. For example, when the user is dragging the mouse across the list, the object can set this property to true, which indicates that the selection change events are part of a series. When the series has been completed, the property should be set to false. The receiver may wish to delay action until all events have been received.

NOTE   As of Swing 1.0.2, selection events generated by clicking and hold-
            ing down "Shift" or "Ctrl" set the valueIsAdjusting property to
            true, without sending a closing event with the property equal to
            false. Until this inconsistency is worked out, it is better to recog-
            nize this property only on lists that support a single selection.

Constants

The constants shown in Table 7-6 are used in conjunction with the selection-Mode property of the ListSelectionModel interface.

Table 7-6. Constants for the ListSelectionModel Interface

Constant	Data Type	Description
MULTIPLE_INTERVAL_SELECTION	int	Indicates that the user can make selections of several ranges at the same time
SINGLE_INTERVAL_SELECTION	int	Indicates that the user can select only one range of items at a time
SINGLE_SELECTION	int	Indicates that the user can select only one item at a time

Methods

public abstract void addSelectionInterval(int index1, int index2)

Adds a group of list elements, ranging from index1 to index2 (including both endpoints), to the selection list. If the current selection mode supports only single selections, the method selects only the element at index2. This method must trigger a ListSelectionEvent describing the resulting change.

public abstract void removeSelectionInterval(int index1, int index2)

Removes the group of list elements from index1 to index2 (including both endpoints) from the selection list, whether the elements are selected or not.

This method must trigger a `ListSelectionEvent` describing any changes it makes.

public abstract void clearSelection()

Clears all selections from the data model. This method must trigger a `List-SelectionEvent`, indicating that the entire selection has been cleared.

public abstract void insertIndexInterval(int index, int length, boolean before)

Synchronizes the selection list after an addition occurs in the list data. If `before` is `true`, this method inserts `length` elements into the selection list starting before `index`. If `before` is `false`, the method inserts `length` elements after `index`. All added elements are unselected. This method must trigger a `ListSelectionEvent`, indicating that insertions have been made to the selection list.

public abstract void removeIndexInterval(int index1, int index2)

Synchronizes the selection list after a deletion occurs in the list data. This method removes the indices between `index1` and `index2` from the selection model. This method must trigger a `ListSelectionEvent`, indicating that the selections following the deletion have shifted in position.

public abstract boolean isSelectedIndex(int index)

Returns `true` if the specified index is currently selected.

public abstract void setSelectionInterval(int index1, int index2)

Clears all selections and resets the selection to cover the range between `index1` and `index2`. If the selection mode allows only a single selection, the element referenced by `index2` is selected. This method must trigger a `List-SelectionEvent` describing the change, if there is one.

Events

The `ListSelectionModel` interface declares the `addListSelectionListener()` and `removeListSelectionListener()` event subscription methods for notifying other objects of selection changes. These selection changes come in the form of `ListSelectionEvent` objects.

public void addListSelectionListener(ListSelectionListener l)
public void removeListSelectionListener(ListSelectionListener l)

Add or remove a listener interested in receiving list selection events. The listener objects are notified each time a change to the list selection occurs.

The DefaultListSelectionModel Class

Swing provides a default implementation of the list selection interface called `DefaultListSelectionModel`. This class implements accessors for each of the properties listed above, and maintains an `EventListenerList` of change listeners.

The `DefaultListSelectionModel` is capable of chaining `ListSelectionEvent` objects in a series in order to notify listeners that a change has occurred in the selection list. This is common, for example, when the user is dragging the mouse across the list. In this case, a series of selection change events can be fired off with a `valueIsAdjusting` property set to `true`, which indicates that this event is only one of many. The listener may wish to delay any activity until all the events are received. When the chain of selections has completed, the `valueIsAdjusting` property is set to `false`, which tells the listener that the series has completed.

Properties

Table 7-7 lists the properties of the `DefaultListSelectionModel`. Almost all the properties are implementations of the properties defined by the `ListSelection-Model` interface. The only new property, `leadAnchorNotificationEnabled`, designates whether the class fires change events over the `leadSelectionIndex` and `anchorSelectionIndex` each time it fires a series of notification events. (Recall that the anchor selection is at the beginning of the selection range, while the lead selection is the most recent addition to the selection range.) If the property is `false`, only the elements that have been selected or deselected since the last change are included in the series.

Table 7-7. DefaultListSelectionModel Properties

Property	Data Type	get	is	set	bound	Default Value
anchorSelectionIndex	int	•		•		-1
leadAnchorNotificationEnabled	boolean		•	•		true
leadSelectionIndex	int	•		•		-1
maxSelectionIndex	int	•				-1
minSelectionIndex	int	•				Integer.MAX_VALUE
selectionEmpty	boolean		•			true
selectionMode	int	•		•		SINGLE_INTERVAL_ SELECTION
valueIsAdjusting	boolean	•		•		false

Events

The `DefaultListSelectionModel` uses the `ListSelectionEvent` to signal that the list selection has changed. The event notifies interested listeners that a modification to the selection data has taken place; it also tells which elements were affected. The `DefaultListSelectionModel` class contains three unique methods that can fire off a `ListSelectionEvent`.

protected void fireValueChanged(boolean isAdjusting)

Sends a `ListSelectionEvent` that serves as the beginning or ending marker for a series of changes, which are also `ListSelectionEvent` objects. Passing in a value of `true` signifies that this is part of a series of `ListSelection-Event` objects being sent, while passing in `false` signifies that there is only one event or that the series has completed.

protected void fireValueChanged(int firstIndex, int lastIndex)

Notifies all registered listeners that the list selection has changed between the indices `firstIndex` and `lastIndex`, including the two endpoints.

protected void fireValueChanged(int firstIndex, int lastIndex, boolean isAdjusting)

Notifies all registered listeners that the list selection has changed between `firstIndex` and `lastIndex`, including the two endpoints. You can use the boolean `isAdjusting` to signify whether or not this is one of a series of events. Passing in a value of `true` signifies that this is part of a series of `List-SelectionEvent` objects being sent, while passing in `false` signifies that there is only one event or that the series has completed.

public void addListSelectionListener(listSelectionListener 1)
public void removeListSelectionListener(listSelectionListener 1)

Add or remove a listener from the list of objects interested in receiving `ListSelectionEvents`.

Protected Field

protected EventListenerList listenerList

The list of event listeners that have subscribed to this model for receiving `ListSelectionEvent` notifications.

Constructor

public DefaultListSelectionModel()

The default constructor. It initializes a list selection model that can be used by a `JList` or `JComboBox` component.

Method

public Object clone() throws CloneNotSupportedException

Returns a clone of the current selection list. You should be aware that the event listener list is not cloned.

Working with the ListSelectionModel

The following example is a modified version of our earlier list example. This one, however, has its own `ListSelectionListener` that reports each of the list selection events as they occur:

```java
// SimpleList2.java
//
import java.awt.*;
import java.awt.event.*;
import javax.swing.*;
import javax.swing.event.*;

public class SimpleList2 extends JPanel implements ListSelectionListener,
            ActionListener {

    String label[] = { "Zero","One","Two","Three","Four","Five","Six",
                       "Seven","Eight","Nine","Ten","Eleven" };
    JList list;

    public SimpleList2() {
        setLayout(new BorderLayout());

        list = new JList(label);
        JButton button = new JButton("Print");
        JScrollPane pane = new JScrollPane(list);

        DefaultListSelectionModel m = new DefaultListSelectionModel();
        m.setSelectionMode(ListSelectionModel.SINGLE_SELECTION);
        m.setLeadAnchorNotificationEnabled(false);
        list.setSelectionModel(m);

        list.addListSelectionListener(this);
        button.addActionListener(this);

        add(pane, BorderLayout.NORTH);
        add(button, BorderLayout.SOUTH);
    }

    public static void main(String s[]) {
        JFrame frame = new JFrame("List Example");
        frame.addWindowListener(new BasicWindowMonitor());
        frame.setContentPane(new SimpleList2());
        frame.pack();
        frame.setVisible(true);
    }
```

```
public void valueChanged(ListSelectionEvent e)
{
    System.out.println(e.toString());
}

public void actionPerformed(ActionEvent e) {

    int selected[] = list.getSelectedIndices();
    System.out.println("Selected Elements:   ");

    for (int i=0; i < selected.length; i++) {
        String element = (String)list.getModel().
                                   getElementAt(selected[i]);
        System.out.println("   " + element);
    }
}
}
```

Try running this code and selecting a couple of items in the list. If you drag the mouse from item 0 to item 5, you get the following output:

```
javax.swing.event.ListSelectionEvent[source=javax.swing.JList[,0,0,86x204]
firstIndex= 0 lastIndex= 1 isAdjusting= true ]

javax.swing.event.ListSelectionEvent[source=javax.swing.JList[,0,0,86x204]
firstIndex= 1 lastIndex= 2 isAdjusting= true ]

javax.swing.event.ListSelectionEvent[source=javax.swing.JList[,0,0,86x204]
firstIndex= 2 lastIndex= 3 isAdjusting= true ]

javax.swing.event.ListSelectionEvent[source=javax.swing.JList[,0,0,86x204]
firstIndex= 3 lastIndex= 4 isAdjusting= true ]

javax.swing.event.ListSelectionEvent[source=javax.swing.JList[,0,0,86x204]
firstIndex= 4 lastIndex= 5 isAdjusting= true ]

javax.swing.event.ListSelectionEvent[source=javax.swing.JList[,0,0,86x204]
firstIndex= 5 lastIndex= 5 isAdjusting= false ]
```

Each entry describes a change in selection. The first five entries recognize that a change of selection has occurred between one element and the next as the mouse was dragged. In this case, the former was deselected, and the latter was selected. However, note that the isAdjusting property was set to true, indicating that this is potentially one in a series of changes. When the mouse button is released, the list knows that the drag has stopped, and fires a ListSelectionEvent with the isAdjusting property set to false, repeating the last changed index.

ListSelectionEvent

Much like the `ListDataEvent`, the `ListSelectionEvent` specifies a change by highlighting those elements in the selection list that have altered. Note that a `ListSelectionEvent` does not indicate the new selection state of the list element, only that some change has occurred. You should not assume that the new state is the opposite of the previous state; always check with the event source to see what the current selection state really is.

Properties

There are four properties in the `ListSelectionEvent`, each with its own read-only accessor, as shown in Table 7-8.

Table 7-8. ListSelectionEvent Properties

Property	Data Type	get	is	set	bound	Default Value
firstIndex	int	•				
lastIndex	int	•				
source*	Object	•				
valueIsAdjusting	boolean	•				

Constructor

public ListSelectionEvent(Object source, int firstIndex, int lastIndex, boolean isAdjusting)
   Takes a reference to the object that fires the event, as well as the bounding indices and a boolean indicating whether the event is one in a series. Note that `firstIndex` should always be less than or equal to `lastIndex`.

Methods

public String toString()
   Provides a comma-separated string output of the properties above.

ListSelectionListener

The `ListSelectionListener` interface, which is the conduit for receiving the `ListSelectionEvent` objects, consists of only one method: `valueChanged()`. This method must be implemented by any listener object that wishes to be notified of changes to the list selection model.

public abstract void valueChanged(ListSelectionEvent e)
   Notifies the listener that one or more selection elements have changed.

Listening for ListSelectionEvents

Here is a brief example that demonstrates using the `ListSelectionListener` and the `ListSelectionEvent`. The example creates a series of radio buttons that listen for selection events and accurately mirror the current selections in the list. Some results from running this program are shown in Figure 7-6.

```
//  SelectionMonitor.java
//
import java.awt.*;
import java.awt.event.*;
import javax.swing.*;
import javax.swing.event.*;

public class SelectionMonitor extends JPanel implements
    ListSelectionListener {

    String label[] = { "Zero","One","Two","Three","Four","Five","Six",
                        "Seven","Eight","Nine","Ten","Eleven","Twelve" };
    JRadioButton buttons[];
    JList list;

    public SelectionMonitor() {
        setLayout(new BorderLayout());

        list = new JList(label);
        JScrollPane pane = new JScrollPane(list);
        buttons = new JRadioButton[label.length];

        // Format the list and the buttons in a vertical box
        Box rightBox = new Box(BoxLayout.Y_AXIS);
        Box leftBox = new Box(BoxLayout.Y_AXIS);

        // Monitor all list selections
        list.addListSelectionListener(this);

        for(int i=0; i < label.length; i++) {
            buttons[i] = new JRadioButton("Selection " + i);
            rightBox.add(buttons[i]);
        }
        leftBox.add(pane);
        add(rightBox, BorderLayout.EAST);
        add(leftBox, BorderLayout.WEST);
    }

    public static void main(String s[]) {
        JFrame frame = new JFrame("Selection Monitor");
        frame.addWindowListener(new BasicWindowMonitor());
        frame.setContentPane(new SelectionMonitor());
```

```
            frame.pack();
            frame.setVisible(true);
        }

    public void valueChanged(ListSelectionEvent e) {

        //  If either of these are true, the event can be ignored.
        if ((e.getValueIsAdjusting() == false) || (e.getFirstIndex() == -1))
            return;

        //  Change the radio button to match the current selection state
        //  for each list item that reported a change.
        for (int i = e.getFirstIndex(); i <= e.getLastIndex(); i++) {
            buttons[i].setSelected(((JList)e.getSource()).isSelectedIndex(i));
        }
    }
}
```

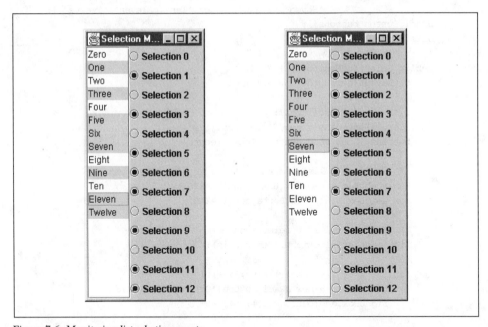

Figure 7-6. Monitoring list selection events

Remember that a `ListSelectionEvent` does not inform you of the new selection state of an element that has changed. You might be tempted to conclude that if you receive a `ListSelectionEvent`, the selection state for the target element would simply be the opposite of what it was before. This is not true. The selection state *cannot* be determined from the `ListSelectionEvent`; it must be determined by querying the event source.

Displaying Cell Elements

Swing gives the programmer the option to specify how each element in the list (called a *cell*) should be displayed on the screen. The list itself maintains a reference to a *cell renderer*. Cell renderers are common in Swing components, including lists and combo boxes. Essentially, a cell renderer is a component whose paint() method is called each time the component needs to draw or redraw an element. To create a cell renderer, you need only register a class that extends the List-CellRenderer interface. This registration can be done with the setCell-Renderer() method of JList or JComboBox:

```
JList list = new JList();
list.setCellRenderer(new myCellRenderer());
```

The ListCellRenderer Interface

The ListCellRenderer interface must be implemented by cell renderers for lists and combo boxes. It has only one method.

public abstract Component getListCellRendererComponent(JList list, Object value, int index, boolean isSelected, boolean cellHasFocus)
This method must return a Component that can be used to draw the cell given the five variables passed in. The JList variable is a callback reference to the list itself. The object represented by value is the object in the list data that this cell corresponds to. The index of the cell in the list is given by the variable index. isSelected tells the renderer if the cell has been selected, and cellHasFocus tells the renderer if the cell currently has the input focus.

NOTE   Occasionally, Swing can call this method with an index of –1, which indicates that it requires the default selection. This is common with combo boxes that need to update their text fields with the current selection. To figure out the default selection, you could try using the getSelectedIndex() method of the passed-in list.

It may be necessary to set the preferred size of the component returned by the cell renderer before returning it, so that the requesting list knows how large to paint the component. This can be done by calling the setPreferredSize() method on the component.

Implementing a Cell Renderer

Here is an inner class of the JList example (later in the book) that implements a cell renderer. We've included some fields of the enclosing class to make the

renderer code easier to understand. This renderer renders each cell in a list of
O'Reilly books by placing its title side-by-side with a small icon of its cover.

```java
// These fields are populated with book titles and images
private String titles[];
private ImageIcon bookImage[] = new ImageIcon[];

// Inner class BookCellRenderer
class BookCellRenderer extends JLabel implements ListCellRenderer
{
    Color highlightColor = new Color(0, 0, 128);

    BookCellRenderer() {
        setOpaque(true);
    }
    public Component getListCellRendererComponent(
        JList list,
        Object value,
        int index,
        boolean isSelected,
        boolean cellHasFocus)
    {
        // If this is the selection value request from a combo box
        // then find out the current selected index from the list.
        if (index == -1) {
            int selected = list.getSelectedIndex();
            if (selected == -1)
                return this;
            else
                index = selected;
        }
        setText(" " + titles[index]);
        setIcon(bookImage[index]);
        if(isSelected) {
            setBackground(highlightColor);
            setForeground(Color.white);
        } else {
            setBackground(Color.white);
            setForeground(Color.black);
        }
        return this;
    }
}
```

Assuming that our initial data was populated correctly, our custom cell renderer
will display images similar to those in Figure 7-7. Before we put the O'Reilly books
example together, however, we need to discuss the central list class in Swing:
JList. We'll do that after a brief detour for DefaultListCellRenderer.

Figure 7-7. The ListCellRenderer results

The DefaultListCellRenderer Class

Swing contains a default list cell renderer class that is used by JList whenever the programmer does not explicitly set a cell renderer. This class, DefaultListCell-Renderer, implements the ListCellRenderer interface defined above. The class, as you might expect, contains only one method:

public Component getListCellRendererComponent(JList list, Object value, int index,
boolean isSelected, boolean cellHasFocus)

This method returns a Component that is used to draw a default list cell. If isSelected is true, then the cell is drawn with the selectedBackground and selectedForeground properties defined in the list variable. If the cell is not selected, it uses the standard background and foreground colors of the list component are used. If the cell has focus, a border is placed around the component that is UI-specific (typically a 1-pixel LineBorder). The cell renderer can handle both text and icons. If the value is text, the default font of the list is used.

The JList Class

The JList class is the generic Swing implementation of a list component. The class works reasonably well as a drop-in replacement for the AWT List class. If the selection mode is set appropriately, you can make multiple selections by clicking with the mouse while holding down the "Shift" or "Ctrl" modifier keys. Unlike AWT, the JList class does not provide scrolling capabilities; it must be set as the viewport of a JScrollPane in order to support scrolling. Figure 7-8 shows the JList component with three separate look-and-feels.

Properties

The JList class essentially combines the features of the data model, the selection model, and the cell renderer into a single Swing component. The properties of the JList class are shown in Table 7-9.

The model property contains an object that implements the ListModel interface; this object holds the element data of the list. If you don't supply a model (or the

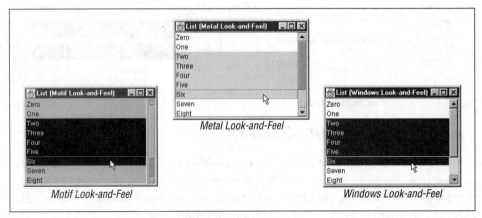

Figure 7-8. The JList component in the three look-and-feels

Table 7-9. JList Properties

Property	Data Type	get	is	set	bound	Default
model	ListModel	•		•	•	
selectionModel	ListSelec-tionModel	•		•	•	DefaultListSelection-Model()
UI	ListUI	•		•	•	from L&F
UIClassID*	String	•				"ListUI"
accessibleContext*	Accessible-Context	•				JList.AccessibleJList()
anchorSelectionIndex	int	•				
cellRenderer	ListCell-Renderer	•		•	•	from L&F
firstVisibleIndex	int	•				
fixedCellHeight	int	•		•	•	-1
fixedCellWidth	int	•		•	•	-1
lastVisibleIndex	int	•				
leadSelectionIndex	int	•				
maxSelectionIndex	int	•				
minSelectionIndex	int	•				
opaque*	boolean		•	•		true
preferredScroll-ableViewportSize*	Dimension	•				
prototypeCellValue	Object	•		•	•	null

See also properties from JComponent (Table 3-5).

Table 7-9. JList Properties (continued)

Property	Data Type	get	is	set	bound	Default
scrollableTracksView-portHeight*	boolean	•				
scrollableTracksView-portWidth*	boolean	•				
selectedIndex	int	•		•		-1
selectedIndex (Indexed)	boolean		•			
selectedIndices	int[]	•		•		
selectedValue	Object	•				
selectedValues	Object[]	•				
selectionBackground	Color	•		•	•	null
selectionEmpty	boolean		•			true
selectionForeground	Color	•		•	•	null
selectionMode	int	•		•		MULTIPLE_INTERVAL_SELECTION
valueIsAdjusting	boolean	•		•		false
visibleRowCount	int	•		•	•	8

See also properties from JComponent (Table 3-5).

data from which to build a model) when you construct the JList, a useless default is created that contains zero entries (and cannot be added to). The selection-Model property contains an object that implements the ListSelectionModel interface; this object manages the current selections in the list. Both interfaces were covered earlier in the chapter.

The selectionMode mirrors the selectionMode property of the ListSelec-tionModel. This property indicates how many ranges can be selected at a time. The selectionForeground and selectionBackground properties set the foreground and background colors of the selected cells. The opaque property is always set to true to indicate that the JList is opaque.

The firstVisibleIndex property represents the topmost element that is at least partially visible in the list's "window," while the lastVisibleIndex property represents the bottommost element at least partially visible. visibleRowCount indicates the number of elements currently visible in the list. You can set this property to ensure that the list shows no more than a certain number of elements at a time.

The next series of properties mirror those in the ListSelectionModel: the anchorSelectionIndex and leadSelectionIndex give the anchor and lead positions for the most recent selection; the minSelectionIndex and maxSelec-tionIndex give the smallest and largest indices of all selected components; selectedIndex gives the first selected index in the list (or -1 if there is none), while selectedIndices holds an ordered integer array of all current selections. There is also an indexed selectedIndex property that indicates whether or not a specific index is selected. The selectedValue property lets you retrieve the first selected object, and selectedValue lets you retrieve an array that contains all the selected objects. Finally, the selectionEmpty property is a boolean that tells whether there are any elements currently selected.

The fixedCellHeight and fixedCellWidth properties allow the user to explic-itly set a fixed height in pixels for the cells in the list. The prototypeCellValue is a reference to an object that the list can use to calculate the minimum width of every cell in the list; you can use this property to define the size needed for each cell. This keeps the list from having to compute the size by checking each item in the list. For example, you might set this property to the string "mmmmm" to ensure that each cell could contain five characters. The preferredScrollable-ViewportSize indicates the Dimension necessary to support the visibleRowCount property. The valueIsAdjusting property is used to indicate that a series of ListSelectionEvent objects is being generated by the selection model, such as when a drag is occurring.

This scrollableTracksViewportWidth and scrollableTracksViewport-Height properties report whether the JList will be resized to match the size of the viewport containing it. They are true if the preferred size of the JList is smaller than the viewport (in the appropriate direction), allowing a JList to stretch. They are false if the JList is larger than the viewport. The standard JViewport adds scrollbars when these properties become false.

Constructors

public JList()
> Creates an empty JList. Nothing can be added to this list without changing the model.

public JList(ListModel model)
> Creates a JList using the specified data model.

public JList(Object[] objects)
> Creates a JList using the array of objects passed in to populate the data model.

public JList(Vector vector)
> Creates a JList using a Vector of objects passed in to populate the data model.

Miscellaneous

public void ensureIndexIsVisible(int index)

Automatically scrolls the viewport associated with the list until the element specified by index is visible.

public Rectangle getCellBounds(int index1, int index2)

Returns a Rectangle object that outlines the area covered by the range of list elements. In the event that the range is invalid, the method returns null.

public Point indexToLocation(int index)

Returns a point representing the upper-left corner of the list element in local coordinates. In the event that the element is not currently displayed on the screen, or does not exist, the method returns null.

public int locationToIndex(Point p)

Returns the index of the list element that contains the graphical point p.

Selection Model

protected void fireValueChanged(int firstIndex, int lastIndex, boolean isAdjusting)

Notifies all registered listeners added at the JList level that the list selection from firstIndex to lastIndex has changed, including the two endpoints. The isAdjusting variable can be set to true if this event is one in a series.

public void setSelectionInterval(int index0, int index1)

Resets the selection interval to the inclusive range specified by the two indices passed in.

public void setSelectedValue(Object obj, boolean shouldScroll)

Sets the list element that matches the reference obj as the only selection in the list. If the shouldScroll boolean is true, the list automatically scrolls to ensure that the element is visible.

public void addSelectionInterval(int index0, int index1)

Adds the interval specified by the two indices passed in to the current selection.

public void removeSelectionInterval(int index0, int index1)

Removes the interval specified by the two indices passed in from the current selection.

public void clearSelection()

Clears the entire selection.

protected ListSelectionModel createSelectionModel()

Returns a new instance of the selection model: DefaultListSelection-Model.

Scrolling

The following methods are used for internal configuration purposes. Along with the methods `getPreferredScrollableViewportSize()`, `getScrollable-TracksViewportHeight()`, and `getScrollableTracksViewportWidth()` (accessors for three of the properties listed in Table 7-9), these methods implement the `Scrollable` interface. `Scrollable` allows a `JScrollPane` to be more intelligent about scrolling. It is rare that the programmer would need to call these methods.

public int getScrollableBlockIncrement(Rectangle visibleRect, int orientation, int direction)
   If the orientation is vertical, this method returns the height of the visibleRect rectangle. If the orientation is horizontal, this methods returns the width. The `direction` variable is not used.

public int getScrollableUnitIncrement(Rectangle visibleRect, int orientation, int direction)
   Returns the number of pixels that it takes to expose the next element in the list. If `direction` is positive, it is assumed that the user is scrolling downward and the method returns the height of the first element visible or partially visible on the list. If the direction is negative, it is assumed that the user is scrolling upwards and the method returns the height of the last element visible or partially visible on the list.

Data Model

public void setListData(Object[] objects)
   Creates a `ListDataModel` from the array of objects passed in and resets the current data model of the `JList` to reference it.

public void setListData(Vector vector)
   Creates a `ListDataModel` from the vector of objects passed in and resets the current data model of the `JList` to reference it.

User Interface

public void updateUI()
   Signals that a new look-and-feel has been selected by the user. Invoking this method forces the component to reset its UI-delegate.

Events

The `JList` component fires a `ListSelectionEvent` when any of its selections change. These methods mirror the `ListSelectionEvent` objects that are fired directly from the selection model and are used to notify any selection listeners that have registered directly with the `JList` itself. The source of the event is always the `JList` object.

public void addListSelectionListener(ListSelectionListener)

public void removeListSelectionListener(ListSelectionListener)

Add or remove a selection listener from the event registration list.

The Java Books Example

Here is the code for the O'Reilly Java books list. It makes use of the custom cell renderer offered earlier in the chapter:

```java
// ListExample.java
//
import java.awt.*;
import java.awt.event.*;
import javax.swing.*;

public class ListExample extends JPanel implements ActionListener {

    private String titles[] = { "Designing With JavaScript",
                                "Exploring Java, 2nd Edition",
                                "Developing Java Beans",
                                "Database Programming with JDBC and Java",
                                "Java in a Nutshell, Deluxe Edition",
                                "Java Fundamental Classes Reference",
                                "Java Language Reference, 2nd Edition",
                                "Java Networking",
                                "Java Virtual Machine",
                                "Java AWT Reference",
                                "Java Examples in a Nutshell",
                                "Java Threads",
                                "Java in a Nutshell, 2nd Edition" };
    private ImageIcon bookImage[] = new ImageIcon[13];
    private JList booklist;

    public ListExample() {
        super(true);
        bookImage[0] = new ImageIcon("designjs.s.gif");
        bookImage[1] = new ImageIcon("expjava2.s.gif");
        bookImage[2] = new ImageIcon("javabeans.s.gif");
        bookImage[3] = new ImageIcon("javadata.s.gif");
        bookImage[4] = new ImageIcon("javadeluxe.s.gif");
        bookImage[5] = new ImageIcon("javafund.s.gif");
        bookImage[6] = new ImageIcon("javalang2.s.gif");
        bookImage[7] = new ImageIcon("javanetwk.s.gif");
        bookImage[8] = new ImageIcon("javavm.s.gif");
        bookImage[9] = new ImageIcon("javawt.s.gif");
        bookImage[10] = new ImageIcon("jenut.s.gif");
        bookImage[11] = new ImageIcon("jthreads.s.gif");
        bookImage[12] = new ImageIcon("javanut2.s.gif");
```

```
        this.setLayout(new BorderLayout());
        JButton button = new JButton("Print");
        button.addActionListener(this);

        booklist = new JList(titles);
        booklist.setCellRenderer(new BookCellRenderer());
        booklist.setVisibleRowCount(4);
        JScrollPane pane = new JScrollPane(booklist);

        add(pane, BorderLayout.CENTER);
        add(button, BorderLayout.SOUTH);
    }

    public static void main(String s[]) {
        JFrame frame = new JFrame("List Example");
        frame.addWindowListener(new BasicWindowMonitor());
        frame.setContentPane(new ListExample());
        frame.pack();
        frame.setVisible(true);
    }

    public void actionPerformed(ActionEvent e) {

        int selected[] = booklist.getSelectedIndices();
        System.out.println("Selected Elements:   ");

        for (int i=0; i < selected.length; i++) {
            String element = (String)booklist.getModel().
                                        getElementAt(selected[i]);
            System.out.println("   " + element);
        }
    }

    // Include cell renderer inner class earlier in the chapter.
}
```

The code to create the list is relatively short. First, the list is instantiated, populating the data model with an array of strings that is passed into the constructor. Second, we inform the JList to use the cell renderer that we created earlier when displaying each of the books in the list. Last, we add the list to a JScrollPane object to allow support for scrolling. The result appears in Figure 7-9.

Combo Boxes

A combo box component is actually a combination of a Swing list (embedded in a popup window) and a text field. Because combo boxes contain a list inside of them, many of the classes you read about previously with lists are used here as well. Unlike lists, a combo box only allows the user *one* selection at a time, which is

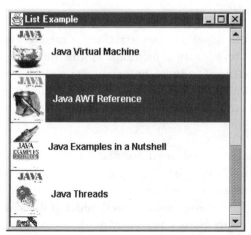

Figure 7-9. A complete JList with a custom cell renderer

usually copied into an editable component at the top, such as a text field. The user can be permitted, however, to manually enter in a selection as well. Figure 7-10 shows a high-level class diagram for Swing's combo box classes.

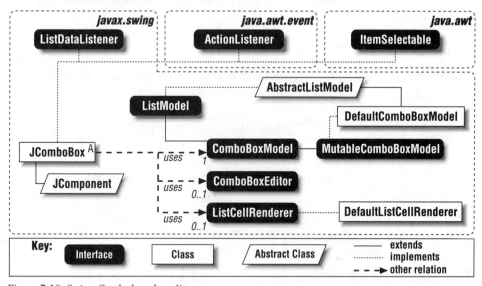

Figure 7-10. Swing Combo box class diagram

Like lists, the combo box component uses a data model to track its list data; the model is called `ComboBoxModel`.

The ComboBoxModel Interface

The ComboBoxModel interface extends the ListModel interface and is used as the primary model for combo box data. It adds two methods to the interface, setSelectedItem() and getSelectedItem(), thus eliminating the need for a separate selection model. Recall that with a JComboBox there can be only one selected item at a time. Hence, what would be the selection model in lists is collapsed into these two methods.

Because the data of the ComboBoxModel is stored in an internal list, the ComboBoxModel also reuses the ListDataEvent to report changes in the model state. However, with the addition of methods to monitor the current selection, the model is now obligated to report changes in the selection as well, which it does by firing a modification ListDataEvent with both endpoints as –1. Again, you should always query the event source to determine the resulting change in the elements.

You can create your own ComboBoxModel, or use the default that is provided with the JComboBox class. The default model is an inner class of JComboBox. If you need to create your own, it is always a good idea to extend the AbstractListModel class and go from there.

Property

Table 7-10 shows the property defined by the ComboBoxModel interface. The selectedItem property lets you set or retrieve the currently selected object.

Table 7-10. JComboBoxModel Properties

Property	Data Type	get	is	set	bound	Default Value
selectedItem	Object	•		•		

See also properties of the ListModel interface (Table 7-1).

Events

The ComboBoxModel interface reuses the ListDataEvent to indicate that the selection or the contents of the list has changed. No new event-related methods are added to the ComboBoxModel interface.

The MutableComboBoxModel Interface

In addition to the ComboBoxModel that is presented, Swing 1.1 introduces an interface called MutableComboBoxModel. This model, which extends the Combo-

BoxModel interface, adds four new methods to the mix, giving a more refined data model that can support growing or shrinking as necessary:

public abstract void addElement(Object obj)
    This method adds a specific element to the data model.

public abstract void removeElement(Object obj)
    This method removes a specific element from the data model.

public abstract void insertElementAt(Object obj, int index)
    This method inserts a specific element at the given index.

public abstract void removeElement(int index)
    This method deletes a specific element from the list.

A data model that implements the `MutableComboBoxModel` interface also implements `ComboBoxModel` and `ListModel`, which gives the model the ability to add, remove, and retrieve elements, set a selection, and support change listeners.

The DefaultComboBoxModel Class

If you're getting lost with all these interfaces, don't despair: Swing provides a `DefaultComboBoxModel` that can be used that implements each of these interfaces. In fact, it is highly encouraged that you use this class whenever possible, as some of the methods in `JComboBox` require an object that implements `MutableComboBoxModel`.

Table 7-11 shows the properties of the `DefaultComboBoxModel` class. The indexed `elementAt` property allows you to retrieve any particular element in the vector. The `selectedItem` property points to the currently selected item in the model. Note that the `setSelectedItem()` method fires a modification `ListDataEvent`, specifying both endpoints of the "change" as –1, to indicate that the selection has changed. Finally, the read-only `size` property lets you find out the number of elements in the vector.

Table 7-11. DefaultComboBoxModel Properties

Property	Data Type	get	is	set	bound	Default Value
elementAt	Object	•				null
selectedItem	Object	•		•		null
size	int	•				0

Constructors

public DefaultComboBoxModel()
public DefaultComboBoxModel(final Object items[])
public DefaultComboBoxModel(Vector v)

Create a default combo box model using a vector. In the first case, an empty vector is created. In the second, the objects in the items variable are copied into a new vector. In the third case, an existing vector is used.

Methods

public void addElement(Object obj)

Adds a specific element to the data model, firing an addition `ListDataEvent` that describes the change.

public void removeElement(Object obj)

Removes a specific element from the data model, firing a `ListDataEvent` that describes the removal.

public void removeAllElements()

Removes all elements from the data model, firing a `ListDataEvent` that describes the removal.

public void insertElementAt(Object obj, int index)

Inserts a specific element at the given index, firing an additional `ListDataE-vent` that describes the change.

public void removeElementAt(int index)

Deletes a specific element from the list, firing a `ListDataEvent` that describes the removal.

public int getIndexOf(Object obj)

Returns the index of the object referenced by the variable `obj`.

Events

The `DefaultComboBoxModel` interface reuses the `ListDataEvent` to indicate that the contents of the model or its selection have changed. See Table 7-12.

Table 7-12. DefaultComboBoxModel Events

Event	Description
ListDataEvent	Indicates that a change in the contents of the combo box model has occurred.

public void addListDataListener(ListDataListener l)

public void removeListDataListener(ListDataListener l)

> These methods can be used to add and remove a specific listener from receiving `ListDataEvent` notifications about the default combo box model.

ComboBoxEditor

The `ComboBoxEditor` is an interface that defines a component that can be used for editing in the combo box. By default, `JComboBox` uses a text field for its editor. However, you can create your own combo box editor by implementing the methods of this interface.

Creating your own combo box editor takes a bit of imagination. You might notice that the methods are heavily biased toward text editing. This is not a coincidence, since most of the editable components in Swing deal with text. However, there is nothing to prevent you from mixing various components together and using the editor to specify how they react.

Properties

The `ComboBoxEditor` interface defines the two properties shown in Table 7-13. The `editorComponent` is a component that can be used to edit the contents of a field in the combo box. The `getEditorComponent()` accessor is typically called once, when the combo box is first displayed. You would implement this method to return the component you want to use for editing.

Table 7-13. JComboBoxEditor Properties

Property	Data Type	get	is	set	bound	Default Value
editorComponent	Component	•				
item	Object	•		•		

The `item` property is the object being edited. The `setItem()` accessor lets the editor kinow which item is being edited; it is called after the user selects an item from the list or completes an edit (e.g., by pressing RETURN in a text field). The `getItem()` accessor returns the item currently being edited.

Events

The `ComboBoxEditor` interface uses an `ActionListener` to indicate that the user has finished modifying the item in the `ComboBoxEditor`. For example, the default text editor of the combo box component fires this event after the user completes typing in the text box and hits RETURN. After the editing has been completed, the combo box generally calls setItem() to ensure that the results are set correctly in the editor.

public abstract void addActionListener(ActionListener l)

public abstract void removeActionListener(ActionListener l)

> Add or remove a specific listener interested in receiving `ActionEvents` concerning the item currently being edited.

public abstract void selectAll()

> Selects everything, allowing the user to begin editing.

Implementing a Custom Editor

The following example shows a simple custom editor for a combo box:

```java
// ComboBoxEditorExample.java
//
import java.awt.*;
import java.awt.event.*;
import java.util.*;
import javax.swing.*;
import javax.swing.border.*;

public class ComboBoxEditorExample implements ComboBoxEditor
{
    Hashtable hashtable;
    ImagePanel panel;
    ImageIcon questionIcon;

    public ComboBoxEditorExample(Hashtable h, String defaultTitle) {
        hashtable = h;
        Icon defaultIcon = ((JLabel)hashtable.get(defaultTitle)).getIcon();
        panel = new ImagePanel(defaultIcon, defaultTitle);
        questionIcon = new ImageIcon("question.gif");
    }

    public void setItem(Object anObject)
    {
        if (anObject != null) {
            panel.setText(anObject.toString());
            JLabel label = (JLabel)hashtable.get(anObject.toString());
            if (label != null)
                panel.setIcon(label.getIcon());
            else
                panel.setIcon(questionIcon);
        }
    }

    public Component getEditorComponent() { return panel; }
```

```
        public Object getItem() { return panel.getText(); }
        public void selectAll() { panel.selectAll(); }

        public void addActionListener(ActionListener l) {
            panel.addActionListener(l);
        }

        public void removeActionListener(ActionListener l) {
            panel.removeActionListener(l);
        }

        //  We create our own inner class to handle setting and
        //  repainting the image and the text.
        class ImagePanel extends JPanel {

            JLabel imageIconLabel;
            JTextField textField;

            public ImagePanel(Icon icon, String text) {
                setLayout(new BorderLayout());

                imageIconLabel = new JLabel(icon);
                imageIconLabel.setBorder(new BevelBorder(BevelBorder.RAISED));

                textField = new JTextField(text);
                textField.setColumns(45);
                textField.setBorder(new BevelBorder(BevelBorder.LOWERED));

                add(imageIconLabel, BorderLayout.WEST);
                add(textField, BorderLayout.EAST);
            }

            public void setText(String s) { textField.setText(s); }
            public String getText() { return (textField.getText()); }

            public void setIcon(Icon i) {
                imageIconLabel.setIcon(i);
                repaint();
            }

            public void selectAll() { textField.selectAll(); }

            public void addActionListener(ActionListener l) {
                textField.addActionListener(l);
            }
            public void removeActionListener(ActionListener l) {
                textField.removeActionListener(l);
            }
        }
    }
```

This example is tightly coupled with the example for the JComboBox class (later in the chapter). However, the source is not hard to understand. When the combo box is initialized, Swing calls getEditorComponent() to position and paint the combo box editor at the top of the JComboBox component. This is our inner class, and essentially consists of a JPanel with both the name of a book and its cover image.

The user is allowed to interact freely with the text field. Whenever a list element is selected by the user, however, or the user completes an edit in the text field, the setItem() method is called to update the book icon. If an icon cannot be found for the text, a question mark is displayed. Whenever the editor needs to retrieve the currently edited object, it makes a call to getItem(). Note that our addActionListener() and removeActionListener() methods pass the listener on to the JTextField defined in the editor. After all, when you boil it down, the text field is the component that is used for editing, and any notifications sent should come from it.

The JComboBox Class

JComboBox is the Swing version of a combo box component. It is very similar to the AWT Choice component, and even implements the ItemSelectable interface for backward compatibility. By default, the JComboBox component provides a single text edit field adjacent to a small button with a downward arrow. When the button is pressed, a popup list of choices is displayed below the text edit field, one of which can be selected by the user. If a selection is made, the choice is copied into a text edit field and the popup disappears. If there was a previous selection, it is erased. You can also remove the popup by pressing the TAB key while the combo box has the focus. Figure 7-11 shows combo boxes for three look-and-feels.

The text field in the JComboBox component can have one of two states: *editable* or *static.* This state is given by the editable property. If the text field is editable, the user is allowed to type information into the text box, as well as make selections from the list. If the component is not editable, the user can only make selections from the list.

Unless you specify a set of objects in the constructor, the combo box comes up empty. You can use the addItem() method to add objects to the combo box list. Conversely, the removeItem() and removeItemAt() methods remove a specified object from the list. You also have the ability to insert objects at specific locations in the combo box list with the insertItemAt() method. If you wish to retrieve the current amount of objects in the list, use the getItemCount() method, and if you wish to retrieve an object at a specific index, use the getItemAt() method.

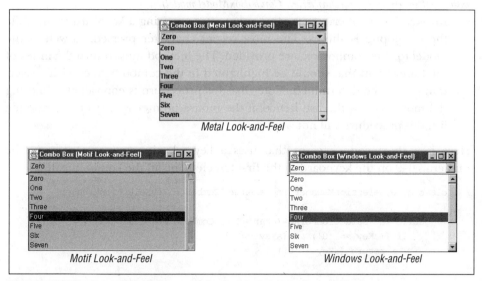

Figure 7-11. The JComboBox component in the three look-and-feels

Note that the list component inside the JComboBox is not part of the component itself, but rather is part of its UI delegate. Hence, there is no property to access the list component directly. However, you should be able to get any information you need through the component properties or the ComboBoxModel.

Like regular popup menus, you have the ability to specify whether the popup in the JComboBox component should be drawn as a lightweight or a heavyweight component. The advantage to having a lightweight component is that it takes less memory and resources to work with. However, if you are mixing lightweight and heavyweight components together, you should also consider forcing the combo box to use a heavyweight popup. This can be done by setting the lightWeight-PopupEnabled property to false. If the property is set to true, the combo box uses a lightweight popup when appropriate.

Combo boxes in Swing use the same ListCellRenderer as the JList component, discussed earlier in this chapter, to paint selected and nonselected items in its list.

The Key Selection Manager

With combo boxes, you have the ability to map keystrokes to item selections in the list. In order to do this, you can create an object that implements the internal interface JComboBox.KeySelectionManager. This interface contains only one method:

public int selectionForKey(char aKey, ComboBoxModel model)

Invoked by the `JComboBox` component after receiving a keyboard event while the list popup is shown. The most recent character pressed, as well as the model for the combo box, are provided. The method must return the index of the list element that should be highlighted in the combo box, or –1 if a selection cannot be determined. Note that this procedure is equivalent to moving the mouse across the list; hence, if the mouse pointer is anywhere inside the list, this procedure will not work.

Here is a short code excerpt that uses a key selection manager to map the numerals 0–9 on the keyboard to the first ten elements in the combo box list:

```
class myKeySelectionManager implements JComboBox.KeySelectionManager
{
    public int selectionForKey(char aKey, ComboBoxModel aModel) {
        if ((aKey >= '0') && (aKey <= '9'))
            return (aKey - '0');
        else
            return -1;
    }
}
```

You can install the key selection manager using the `setKeySelectionManager()` method of `JComboBox`:

```
myComboBox.setKeySelectionManager(new myKeySelectionManager());
```

And that's all there is to it!

Properties

Table 7-14 shows the properties that can be found in the `JComboBox` component. As we mentioned earlier, the `editable` property defines whether the text field of the combo box allows text to be manually entered. The `lightWeightPopupEnabled` property allows you to specify whether `JComboBox` should use a lightweight component to draw the list popup. The `popupvisible` property controls whether the popup associated with the combo box is visible. The `maximumRowCount` property represents the total amount of list elements that can be displayed in the popup. If the list contains more than `maximumRowCount`, it uses a scrollbar for navigation.

The following properties mimic those in `JList`: the `selectedItem` property represents the object currently selected in the combo box. If you call the `setSelectedItem()` method with an object that does not exist, the first object in the list is selected instead. The `selectedIndex` property gives the index of the selected item, or –1 if there is none. The `selectedObjects` property holds an array of size 1—the object currently selected. The `getSelectedObjects()` method is present

Table 7-14. JComboBox Properties

Property	Data Type	get	is	set	bound	Default Value
UI	ComboBoxUI	•		•	•	from L&F
UIClassID*	String	•				"ComboBoxUI"
model	ComboBoxModel	•		•	•	JComboBox.Default-ComboBoxModel()
accessibleContext	AccessibleContext	•				JComboBox.Accessible-JComboBox()
actionCommand	String	•		•		"comboBoxChanged"
editable	boolean		•	•	•	false
editor	ComboBoxEditor	•		•	•	ComboBoxEditor()
enabled*	boolean			•	•	true
focusTraversable*	boolean		•			false
itemAt (indexed)	Object	•				null
itemCount	int	•				0
keySelectionManager	JComboBox.Key-SelectionManager	•		•		JComboBox.DefaultKey-SelectionManager()
lightWeightPopup-Enabled	boolean		•	•		true
maximumRowCount	int	•		•	•	8
opaque*	boolean		•	•		true
popupVisible	boolean		•	•		
renderer	ListCellRenderer	•		•	•	
selectedIndex	int	•		•		-1
selectedItem	Object	•		•		null
selectedObjects	Object[]	•				null

See also properties from the JComponent class (Table 3-5).

to provide backward compatibility with the AWT Choice component. The read-only itemCount property tells how many elements are currently in the combo box's list.

The enabled property overrides that of the java.awt.Component class. If the property is set to false, the method prevents the user from selecting items from the list and typing text into the text field or editor. The opaque property, on the other hand, is always set to true. This indicates that the component is opaque at all times. Finally, the focusTraversable property is set to false, overriding the isFocusTraversable() method of JComponent. This tells Swing not to traverse focus onto the `JComboBox` itself, but rather to skip directly to the text field or editor inside the combo box.

The `actionCommand` property is coupled to an `ActionEvent` that is fired when the user makes a selection inside the list. The `actionCommand` typically contains a string-based representation of the item that was selected.

Events

Combo boxes fire both an `ItemEvent` and an `ActionEvent` when the selection in the list has changed. The `ItemEvent` is fired when there is a change in the current selection of the list, from any source. The `ActionEvent` is fired when the user explicitly makes a selection; it is coupled with the `actionCommand` property shown above. (Note that the `actionCommand` does not by default tell you the item that was selected.) The `ItemEvent` and its listener list maintain backward compatibility with the `ItemSelectable` interface of AWT 1.1.

public void addItemListener(ItemListener aListener)
public void removeItemListener(ItemListener aListener)
> Add or remove an `ItemListener` from the list. These methods maintain backward compatibility with the `ItemSelectable` interface of AWT 1.1.

public void addActionListener(ActionListener l)
public void removeActionListener(ActionListener l)
> Add or remove an `ActionListener` for `ActionEvents` sent when the user makes a selection.

protected void fireItemStateChanged(ItemEvent e)
> Can be called to signify that an item selection of the combo box has changed.

protected void fireActionEvent()
> Can be called to signify that the user has made a new selection.

protected void selectedItemChanged()
> Equivalent to `fireItemStateChanged()`.

Constructors

public JComboBox(ComboBoxModel aModel)
> Initializes its items from an existing `ComboBoxModel`.

public JComboBox(Object items[])
> Creates a `JComboBox` using the items specified in the array.

public JComboBox(Vector items)
> Creates a `JComboBox` using the items specified in the `Vector` passed in.

public JComboBox()

Creates an empty JComboBox using the DefaultComboBoxModel as its data model.

Methods

public void updateUI()

Called by the UIManager when the look-and-feel of the component has changed.

public void showPopup()

Raises the popup that contains the combo box list.

public void hidePopup()

Lowers the popup that contains the combo box list.

public void configureEditor(ComboBoxEditor anEditor, Object anItem)

Initializes the specified ComboBoxEditor with the object passed in.

List Methods

public void addItem(Object anObject)

Adds a specific object to the end of the list. This method must work in conjunction with a MutableComboBoxModel; otherwise, an error will be thrown.

public void insertItemAt(Object anObject, int index)

Inserts an object into the list after the index specified. This method must work in conjunction with a MutableComboBoxModel; otherwise, an error will be thrown.

public void removeItem(Object anObject)

Removes the specified object from the list after the specified index. This method must work in conjunction with a MutableComboBoxModel; otherwise, an error will be thrown.

public void removeItemAt(int anIndex)

Removes an object from the list at the specified index.

public void removeAllItems()

Removes all items from the list. This method must work in conjunction with a MutableComboBoxModel; otherwise, an error will be thrown.

Key Selection

protected JComboBox.KeySelectionManager createDefaultKeySelectionManager()

Returns a new instance of the default key selection manager. This selection manager matches keystrokes against the first character of each item in the list starting with the first item below the selected item (if there is one).

public boolean selectWithKeyChar(char keyChar)

Attempts to select a list item that corresponds to the character passed in. If the method is successful, it returns `true`. If there is no list item that corresponds to that character, the method returns `false`.

Internal Methods

Because the `JComboBox` maintains both a text field and a list, it implements several methods that are not intended to be invoked by the user.

public void processKeyEvent(KeyEvent e)

Overrides `processKeyEvent()` in `JComponent`. The method calls `hide-Popup()` if the user presses the TAB key. It should not be invoked by the programmer.

public void actionPerformed(ActionEvent e)

Monitors internal action events from the embedded list component and must be public. It should not be invoked or overridden by the programmer.

public void contentsChanged(ListDataEvent e)

Monitors model events from the list component and must be public. It should not be invoked or overridden by the programmer.

public void intervalAdded(ListDataEvent e)

This method is invoked when an interval of list items has been added to the list. It should not be called by the programmer.

public void intervalRemoved(ListDataEvent e)

This method is invoked when an interval of list items has been removed from the list. It should not be called by the programmer.

Java Books Revisited

Here is the list of O'Reilly Java books implemented as a combo box. We make use of our new combo box editor to allow the user to see which book he or she has selected.

```
//   EditableComboBox.java
//
import java.awt.*;
import java.awt.event.*;
import java.util.*;
import javax.swing.*;
```

```java
public class EditableComboBox extends JPanel implements ActionListener {

    private String title[] = { "Designing with JavaScript",
                               "Exploring Java, 2nd Edition",
                               "Developing Java Beans",
                               "Database Programming with JDBC and Java",
                               "Java in a Nutshell, Deluxe Edition",
                               "Java Fundamental Classes Reference",
                               "Java Language Reference, 2nd Edition",
                               "Java Networking",
                               "Java in a Nutshell, 2nd Edition",
                               "Java Virtual Machine",
                               "Java AWT Reference",
                               "Java Examples in a Nutshell",
                               "Java Threads" };
    Hashtable hashtable;

    public EditableComboBox() {
      super(true);

      hashtable = new Hashtable();
      hashtable.put(title[0],new JLabel(new ImageIcon("designjs.s.gif")));
      hashtable.put(title[1],new JLabel(new ImageIcon("expjava2.s.gif")));
      hashtable.put(title[2],new JLabel(new ImageIcon("javabeans.s.gif")));
      hashtable.put(title[3],new JLabel(new ImageIcon("javadata.s.gif")));
      hashtable.put(title[4],new JLabel(new ImageIcon("javadeluxe.s.gif")));
      hashtable.put(title[5],new JLabel(new ImageIcon("javafund.s.gif")));
      hashtable.put(title[6],new JLabel(new ImageIcon("javalang2.s.gif")));
      hashtable.put(title[7],new JLabel(new ImageIcon("javanetwk.s.gif")));
      hashtable.put(title[8],new JLabel(new ImageIcon("javanut2.s.gif")));
      hashtable.put(title[9],new JLabel(new ImageIcon("javavm.s.gif")));
      hashtable.put(title[10],new JLabel(new ImageIcon("javawt.s.gif")));
      hashtable.put(title[11],new JLabel(new ImageIcon("jenut.s.gif")));
      hashtable.put(title[12],new JLabel(new ImageIcon("jthreads.s.gif")));

      setLayout(new BorderLayout());

      JComboBox bookCombo = new JComboBox(title);
      bookCombo.setEditable(true);
      bookCombo.setEditor(new ComboBoxEditorExample(hashtable, title[10]));
      bookCombo.setMaximumRowCount(4);
      bookCombo.addActionListener(this);
      bookCombo.setActionCommand("Hello");
      add(bookCombo, BorderLayout.CENTER);
    }

    public static void main(String s[]) {
        JFrame frame = new JFrame("Combo Box Example");
        frame.addWindowListener(new BasicWindowMonitor());
```

```
        frame.setContentPane(new EditableComboBox());
        frame.pack();
        frame.setVisible(true);
    }

    public void actionPerformed(ActionEvent e) {
        System.out.println("You chose " + ((JComboBox)e.getSource()).
                                    getSelectedItem() + "!");
    }
}
```

The code to initialize the combo box is relatively simple. After the combo box is instantiated, we set the `editable` property to `true` and inform the combo box of our custom editor. Finally, we set the `maximumRowCount` property to four, ensuring that the user cannot see more than four books in the list at a time. If the user types in a book that cannot be found inside our list, the example displays a question mark instead of a cover. Whenever a selection is made, the results are printed on the screen. Figure 7-12 shows the result.

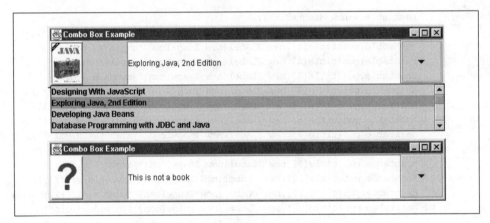

Figure 7-12. A custom JComboBox component

8

Swing Containers

In this chapter, we'll take a look at a number of components Swing provides for grouping other components together. In AWT, such components extended `java.awt.Container` and included `Panel`, `Window`, `Frame`, and `Dialog`. With Swing, you get a whole new set of options, providing greater flexibility and power.

A Simple Container

Not everything in this chapter is more complex than its AWT counterpart. As proof of this claim, we'll start the chapter with a look at the `JPanel` class, a very simple Swing container.

The JPanel Class

`JPanel` is an extension of `JComponent` (which, remember, extends `java.awt.Container`) used for grouping together other components. It gets most of its implementation from its superclasses. Typically, using `JPanel` amounts to instantiating it, setting a layout manager (this can be set in the constructor and defaults to a `FlowLayout`), and adding components to it using the `add()` methods inherited from `Container`.

Properties

`JPanel` does not define any new properties. Table 8-1 shows the default values that differ from those provided by `JComponent`.

Table 8-1. JPanel Properties

Property	Data Type	get	is	set	bound	Default Value
UIClassID	String	•				"PanelUI"
accessibleContext*	AccessibleContext	•				JPanel.AccessibleJPanel()
doubleBuffered*	true		•	•		true
layout*	LayoutManager	•		•		FlowLayout()
opaque*	boolean	•	•		•	true

See also properties from the JComponent class (Table 3-5).

The doubleBuffered and opaque properties default to true, while the layout-Manager defaults to a new FlowLayout.

Constructors

public JPanel()

Creates a new panel with a FlowLayout and double buffering.

public JPanel(boolean isDoubleBuffered)

Creates a new panel with a FlowLayout and double buffering enabled if isDoubleBuffered is true.

public JPanel(LayoutManager layout)

Creates a new panel with the specified layout manager and double buffering.

public JPanel(LayoutManager layout, boolean isDoubleBuffered)

This constructor (called by all the others) creates a new panel with the specified layout manager and double-buffering policy.

Method

public void updateUI()

Called to indicate that the L&F has changed.

Opacity

Here's a simple program showing what it means for a JPanel to be opaque. All we do is create two JPanels. Inside the first JPanel, we place another JPanel, which is opaque. In the second, we place a transparent (non-opaque) JPanel. In both cases, we set the background of the outer panel to white and the background of the inner panel to black. We'll place a JButton inside each inner panel to give it some size. Figure 8-1 shows the result.

Figure 8-1. Opaque and non-opaque JPanels

On the left, we see the black panel inside the white one. But on the right, since the inner panel is not opaque, its black background is never painted and the background of the outer panel shows through. Here's the code:

```
// OpaqueExample.java
//
import javax.swing.*;
import java.awt.*;

public class OpaqueExample {
  public static void main(String[] args) {

    // Create 2 JPanels (opaque), one containing another opaque JPanel, and
    // the other containing a nonopaque JPanel
    JPanel opaque = createNested(true);
    JPanel notOpaque = createNested(false);

    // Throw it all together in a JFrame
    JFrame f = new JFrame();
    f.addWindowListener(new BasicWindowMonitor());
    f.getContentPane().setLayout(new FlowLayout());
    f.getContentPane().add(opaque);
    f.getContentPane().add(notOpaque);
    f.pack();
    f.setVisible(true);
  }

  // Create a JPanel containing another JPanel. The inner JPanel's opacity
  // is set according to the parameter. A JButton is placed inside the inner
  // JPanel to give it some content.
  public static JPanel createNested(boolean opaque) {
    JPanel outer = new JPanel(new FlowLayout());
    JPanel inner = new JPanel(new FlowLayout());
    outer.setBackground(Color.white);
    inner.setBackground(Color.black);

    inner.setOpaque(opaque);
    inner.setBorder(BorderFactory.createLineBorder(Color.gray));
```

```
        inner.add(new JButton("Button"));
        outer.add(inner);

        return outer;
    }
}
```

The Box Class

Another very useful Swing container is the Box. A Box makes it easy to lay out a series of components end-to-end. Since it's supported by a special new layout manager (BoxLayout), we'll cover it later in Chapter 11, *Specialty Panes and Layout Managers.*

The Root Pane

Now that we've seen the simplest example of a Swing container, we'll move on to something a bit more powerful. Most of the other Swing containers (JFrame, JApplet, JWindow, JDialog, and even JInternalFrame) contain an instance of another class, JRootPane, as their only component, and implement a common interface, RootPaneContainer. In this section, we'll look at JRootPane and RootPaneContainer, as well as another class JRootPane uses, JLayeredPane.

Before jumping into the descriptions of these classes, let's take a look at how the classes and interfaces that make up the Swing root containers fit together. Figure 8-2 shows that JApplet, JFrame, JDialog, and JWindow do not extend JComponent like the other Swing components. Instead, they extend their AWT counterparts, serving as top-level user interface windows. This implies that these components (unlike the lightweight Swing components) have native AWT peer objects.

Notice that these Swing containers (as well as JInternalFrame) implement a common interface, RootPaneContainer. This is an interface that gives access to the JRootPane's properties. Furthermore, each of the five containers uses a JRootPane as the "true" container of child components managed by the container. This class is discussed later in this chapter.

The JRootPane Class

JRootPane is a special container that extends JComponent and is used by many of the other Swing containers. It's quite different from most containers you're probably used to using. The first thing to understand about JRootPane is that it contains a fixed set of components: a Component called the glass pane and a JLayeredPane called, logically enough, the layered pane. Furthermore, the layered pane contains two more components: a JMenuBar and a Container called

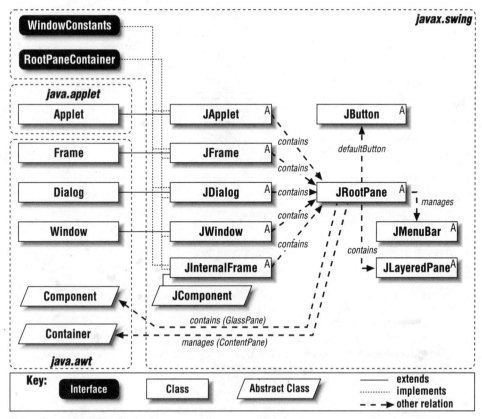

Figure 8-2. Swing "Root" containers

the content pane.* Figure 8-3 shows a schematic view of the makeup of a JRootPane.

Attempts to add additional components to a JRootPane are ignored by its custom layout manager (a protected inner class called RootLayout).† Instead, children of the root pane should be added to its content pane. In fact, for most uses of JRootPane, all you'll need to do is get the content pane and add your components to it. Here's a simple example (using a JFrame) that adds a single button to the content pane.

---

* In general, JLayeredPanes can contain any components they wish. This is why Figure 8-2 does not show JLayeredPane as containing the menubar and content pane. In the case of the JRootPane, a JLayeredPane is used to hold these two specific components.

† It is possible to change the layout manager to one of your own choosing, but it would be responsible for handling all details of laying out the JRootPane. Using any of the other AWT or Swing layouts will not work properly.

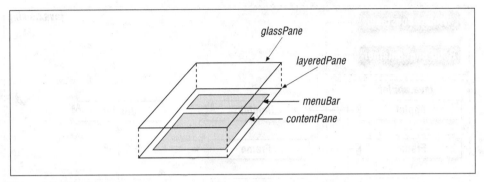

Figure 8-3. JRootPane

```
// RootExample.java
//
import javax.swing.*;
import java.awt.*;

public class RootExample {
  public static void main(String[] args) {
    JFrame f = new JFrame();
    f.addWindowListener(new BasicWindowMonitor());
    JRootPane root = f.getRootPane();          // XXX
    Container content = root.getContentPane(); // XXX
    content.add(new JButton("Hello"));          // XXX
    f.pack();
    f.setVisible(true);
  }
}
```

This may seem like a lot of complexity just to add something to a frame. Thankfully, as we'll see in the next section, each of the containers that use JRootPane implement the RootPaneContainer interface, which provides direct access to each of the root's subcomponents. This allows the three lines marked with "XXX" to be replaced with:

```
f.getContentPane().add(new JButton("Hello"));
```

In the next example, we'll see how to add a menu to a root pane, producing a display like the one in Figure 8-4.

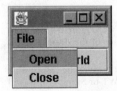

Figure 8-4. JRootPane with a JMenuBar

```
// RootExample2.java
//
import javax.swing.*;
import java.awt.*;

public class RootExample2 {
  public static void main(String[] args) {
    JFrame f = new JFrame();
    f.addWindowListener(new BasicWindowMonitor());
    JRootPane root = f.getRootPane();

    // Create a menu bar
    JMenuBar bar = new JMenuBar();
    JMenu menu = new JMenu("File");
    bar.add(menu);
    menu.add("Open");
    menu.add("Close");
    root.setJMenuBar(bar);

    // Add a button to the content pane
    root.getContentPane().add(new JButton("Hello World"));

    // Display the UI
    f.pack();
    f.setVisible(true);
  }
}
```

In this case, the getRootPane() and setJMenuBar() calls could have been replaced with a single f.setJMenuBar(bar) call. Note that the menubar property on the Swing containers is called JMenuBar.

The previous two root pane examples were intended to give you an understanding of how the JRootPane really works. Typically, however, your code will not be working with JRootPane directly. We'll get a better understanding of why when we get to the discussion of RootPaneContainer. For now, here's a version of the last example that shows how you'd really write that code:

```
// RootExample3.java
//
import javax.swing.*;
import java.awt.*;

public class RootExample3 {
  public static void main(String[] args) {
    JFrame f = new JFrame();
    f.addWindowListener(new BasicWindowMonitor());
    JMenuBar bar = new JMenuBar();
    JMenu menu = new JMenu("File");
```

```
    bar.add(menu);
    menu.add("Open");
    menu.add("Close");

    // Shortcuts provided by JFrame (and other RootPaneContainers)...
    f.setJMenuBar(bar);
    f.getContentPane().add(new JButton("Hello World"));

    f.pack();
    f.setVisible(true);
  }
}
```

Understanding the Glass Pane

JRootPane may seem a bit confusing at first glance. The important thing to remember is that in most cases, all you'll need to worry about is adding your component to the content pane and possibly setting a menubar. In this section, we'll explain the other component contained by JRootPane: the "glass pane."

The glass pane is a component that is laid out to fill the entire pane. By default, it is an instance of JPanel, but it can be replaced with any Component. JRootPane's implementation of the addImpl() method ensures that the glass pane is the first component in the container, meaning that it will be painted last. In other words, the glass pane allows you to place components "above" any other components in the pane. Because of this, it generally makes sense for the glass pane to be non-opaque; otherwise it will cover everything in the layered pane. It's important to remember that when the layout of the JRootPane is performed, the placement of the contents of the glass pane will have no effect on the placement of the contents of the layered pane (and its content pane). Both sets of components are placed within the same component space, overlapping each other as necessary. It's also important to realize that the components in the various panes are all equal when it comes to receiving input: mouse events are sent to any component in the JRootPane, whatever part of the pane it happens to be in.

This last note brings us a common use of the glass pane—blocking mouse events from the other components. As a rule, mouse events are sent to the "top" component if components are positioned on top of each other. If the top component has registered mouse listeners, the events will not be sent to the covered components. In the next chapter, we'll see how JInternalFrame takes advantage of this technique.

For now, we'll look at an example in which we use the glass pane to display a single button above the rest of the root pane's content. The panel will listen for all mouse events (and do nothing with them). Once the "start" button in the glass pane is pressed, the glass pane will be removed, allowing the underlying components to be used again. This example is not intended to be particularly useful. It's here for the purpose of demonstrating how the glass pane works.

```java
// GlassExample.java
//
import javax.swing.*;
import java.awt.*;
import java.awt.event.*;

// Show how a glass pane can be used to block mouse events
public class GlassExample {
  public static void main(String[] args) {

      // Create a frame and its content pane's contents
      JFrame f = new JFrame();
      f.addWindowListener(new BasicWindowMonitor());
      final JPanel p1 = new JPanel();
      p1.add(new JLabel("Foo, Bar & Baz", JLabel.CENTER));
      p1.add(new JButton("Foo"));
      p1.add(new JButton("Bar"));
      f.getContentPane().add(p1);

      // Place a button in the center of the glass pane and make it visible
      final JPanel glass = (JPanel)f.getGlassPane();

      glass.setVisible(true);
      glass.setLayout(new GridBagLayout());
      JButton glassButton = new JButton("Start");
      glass.add(glassButton);

      // Register for all the mouse events in the glass pane (and do nothing).
      // This registration keeps the components in the content pane from being
      // clickable. We could have created our own panel that called
      // enableEvents(AWTEvent.MOUSE_EVENT_MASK |
      // AWTEvent.MOUSE_MOTION_EVENT_MASK) to get the same effect.
      glass.addMouseListener(new MouseAdapter() {});
      glass.addMouseMotionListener(new MouseMotionAdapter() {});

      // Add a listener to the glass pane's button that will make the glass
      // pane invisible when the button is clicked.
      glassButton.addActionListener(new ActionListener() {
        public void actionPerformed(ActionEvent ev) {
          glass.setVisible(false);
          p1.repaint();
        }
      });
```

```
      // Display the example . . .
      f.setSize(150, 80);
      f.setVisible(true);
   }
 }
```

Note that the lines:

```
   glass.addMouseListener(new MouseAdapter() {});
   glass.addMouseMotionListener(new MouseMotionAdapter() {});
```

block mouse events from reaching the hidden components (remember, the glass pane fills the entire frame), because the events are sent to the first component (starting at the top) with registered listeners. Any time a mouse event method is called, it will do nothing, since we just extended the empty-implementation adapter classes.

Once the start button is clicked, the glass pane is no longer visible, so the previously hidden components will now receive the events.

Figure 8-5 shows how the glass pane is drawn above the content pane when this example is run. If you were to call setOpaque(true) on the glass pane, only the start button would be visible.

Figure 8-5. Glass pane

Avoiding Unnecessary Layers

The following code fragment shows a common mistake that's easy to make:

```
   JPanel panel = new JPanel();
   panel.add(someStuff);
   JFrame f = new JFrame();
   f.getContentPane().add(panel);
```

There's nothing fundamentally wrong with this code. It will work just fine. However, there's an extra layer added here that's just not necessary. Recall from the beginning of this section that the content pane is initialized to an instance of JPanel. There's nothing special about that panel, and you should feel free to use it. A better implementation of the code fragment we just looked at would be:

```
   JFrame f = new JFrame();
   Container panel = f.getContentPane(); // cast to JPanel if you want to
   panel.add(someStuff);
```

It's also important to keep in mind that the content pane can be any arbitrary container—it doesn't have to be a JPanel. If you want to fill the content pane with a scrollable region, or perhaps with a tabbed pane, you can replace the content pane with a JScrollPane or JTabbedPane. For example:

```
JScrollPane scroll = new JScrollPane(new JTextPane());
JFrame f = new JFrame();
f.setContentPane(scroll); // not f.getContentPane().add(scroll);
```

A reasonable rule of thumb is that if you are only going to add a single component to the content pane, and you want it to fill the entire pane, don't add to the content pane—replace it.

Properties

Table 8-2 shows the properties and default values defined by JRootPane. The background property is set to the default "control" color defined in the UIManager.

Table 8-2. JRootPane Properties

Property	Data Type	get	is	set	bound	Default Value
accessibleContext*	AccessibleContext	•				JRootPane.Accessible-JRootPane()
background*	Color	•		•		UIManager.getColor ("control")
contentPane	Container	•		•		JPanel()
defaultButton	JButton	•		•	•	null
doubleBuffered	boolean	•		•		true
glassPane	Component	•		•		JPanel()
JMenuBar[a]	JMenuBar	•		•		null
layeredPane	JLayeredPane	•		•		JLayeredPane()
layout*	LayoutManager	•		•		RootLayout()
validateRoot*	boolean		•			true

See also properties from the JComponent class (Table 3-5).

[a] This property replaces the deprecated menuBar property.

The contentPane is initially set to a JPanel with a BorderLayout, while glassPane is set to a non-opaque, invisible JPanel with a default (FlowLayout) layout manager. A new instance of JLayeredPane is the default value for layeredPane, and by default the JMenuBar property is set to null. The contentPane is contained by the layered pane's `FRAME_CONTENT_LAYER` (see the section on `JLayeredPane` for further explanation).

Note that the `set()` methods for the `JMenuBar` and `contentPane` properties take care of placing these components within the `JLayeredPane`, so you don't typically have to worry about the layered pane at all.

The inherited `doubleBuffered` property is `true` by default and `layout` defaults to a new instance of the protected inner class `RootLayout`.

The `defaultButton` property was introduced back in Chapter 5, *Buttons*. This property allows a `JButton` to be specified as the default for the container. The default button is the button that will be "pressed" if the user presses "enter" (or some other UI-defined key) while the pane has focus (unless some other focused component, like a `JTextField`, handles the key). This is a very convenient feature when presenting a user with information to be viewed and acknowledged, because it keeps the user from having to use the mouse.

Revalidate

The last property listed in Table 8-2 is the `validateRoot` property. `JRootPane` overrides `isValidateRoot()` to return `true`. This causes the container to be validated (meaning that its contents will be redisplayed) as a result of any call to `revalidate()` on one of its children or their descendants. This simplifies the process of dealing with components that change dynamically.

Previously, if the font size (for example) of a component changed, you needed to call `invalidate()` on the component and then `validate()` on its container to ensure that the component would be resized appropriately. Using `revalidate()`, only one call is necessary. Furthermore, the way `revalidate()` is implemented allows multiple `revalidate()` calls to be handled at once, much like multiple `repaint()` calls are handled at the same time by the AWT.

Here's a simple example that shows how `revalidate()` can be used:

```
// RevalidateExample.java
//
import javax.swing.*;
import java.awt.*;
import java.awt.event.*;

public class RevalidateExample {
  public static void main(String[] args) {
    JFrame f = new JFrame();
    f.addWindowListener(new BasicWindowMonitor());
```

```
    // Create a single button
    Font font = new Font("Dialog", Font.PLAIN, 10);
    final JButton b = new JButton("Add");
    b.setFont(font);

    Container c = f.getContentPane();
    c.setLayout(new FlowLayout());
    c.add(b);

    // Increase the size of the button's font each time it's clicked
    b.addActionListener(new ActionListener() {
      int size = 10;

      public void actionPerformed(ActionEvent ev) {
        b.setFont(new Font("Dialog", Font.PLAIN, ++size));
        b.revalidate();    // invalidates the button & validates its root pane
      }
    });
    f.setSize(150, 120);
    f.setVisible(true);
  }
}
```

In this example, we create a single button and add it to the content pane of a
JFrame (which uses a JRootPane). Each time the button is clicked, we increase
the size of the button's font. As a result, the button needs to be resized to accommodate the larger label. To make this happen, we simply call revalidate() on
the button. Note that the button could have been nested inside any number of
other containers below the root pane and this would still work properly. As long as
there is an ancestor of the revalidated component that returns true to isVali-
dateRoot(), the container will be validated.

Protected Fields

The following fields are available to subclasses of JRootPane:

protected JMenuBar menuBar
protected Container contentPane
protected JLayeredPane layeredPane
protected Component glassPane
protected JButton defaultButton

   These fields just hold the components described in the Properties section.

protected JRootPane.DefaultAction defaultPressAction
protected JRootPane.DefaultAction defaultReleaseAction

   These fields contain the Actions used to implement the behavior associated
   with defaultButton. DefaultAction is a package-level inner class.

Constructors

public JRootPane()

Creates a new pane with the default property values specified in Table 8-2. It uses the four protected *create* methods listed below, so subclasses may choose to override certain aspects of the creation process.

Public Methods

public void addNotify()

This method (initially defined in `java.awt.Component`) is called when the root pane first appears. It sets up a special event queue management strategy, calls `super.addNotify()`, and enables key events. You should not need to call this method directly.

public void removeNotify()

This method (initially defined in `java.awt.Component`) is called when the root pane is disposed. It stops the special event queue management strategy and calls `super.addNotify()`. You should not need to call this method directly.

Protected Methods

protected void addImpl(Component comp, Object constraints, int index)

Overrides the default implementation from `Component` to ensure that the glass pane will always be the first component in the container.

protected Container createContentPane()
protected Component createGlassPane()
protected JLayeredPane createLayeredPane()
protected LayoutManager createRootLayout()

Called by the constructor to build the pane's subcomponents and set the default layout manager. The default implementations set the default properties as described in the "Properties" section.

Inner Classes

protected class RootLayout implements LayoutManager2, Serializable

The default layout manager for `JRootPane`. It places the glass pane so that it covers the entire pane (remember, the glass pane usually should not be opaque). It also lays out the menubar and content pane, even though they are technically part of the layered pane, by placing the menubar (if one has been set) at the top of the pane, with the content pane just below it, filling the remainder of the pane.

The RootPaneContainer Interface

As we've already mentioned, the top-level Swing containers all use the JRootPane class as their single child component. In order to make it easier to work with these containers, Swing provides a common interface that each of them implement. This interface, RootPaneContainer, defines methods for accessing the common properties available in JRootPane, as well as for the root pane itself. This is what allows the shortcuts we described in the previous section.

The classes that implement this interface typically delegate the methods to their contained JRootPane. For example, getContentPane() would be implemented like this:

```
public Container getContentPane() {
    return getRootPane().getContentPane();
}
```

Properties

This interface is made up entirely of accessors for the JRootPane and its properties, shown in Table 8-3. Notice that the root pane's JMenuBar is not available in this interface. This is because certain containers (JWindow, specifically) don't typically contain menus. This is not to say that you couldn't use one if you really wanted to (accessing it from the JRootPane), but access to the menubar is not directly supported by the interface.

Table 8-3. RootPaneContainer Properties

Property	Data Type	get	is	set	bound	Default Value
contentPane	Container	•		•		
glassPane	Component	•		•		
layeredPane	JLayeredPane	•		•		
rootPane	JRootPane	•				

The JLayeredPane Class

Though it didn't make much use of it directly, JRootPane introduced a class called JLayeredPane. JLayeredPane is a container that manages its components via layers so that components in the upper layers are painted on top of components in the lower layers. This gives you something that was difficult to get with AWT: complete control over which components are painted on top and which are hidden.

The easiest way to understand how this works is to look at a very simple example.

```java
// SimpleLayers.java
//
import javax.swing.*;
import java.awt.Color;

public class SimpleLayers {
  public static void main(String[] args) {

    // Create a frame & gets its layered pane
    JFrame f = new JFrame();
    f.addWindowListener(new BasicWindowMonitor());
    JLayeredPane lp = f.getLayeredPane();

    // Create 3 buttons
    JButton top = new JButton();
    top.setBackground(Color.white);
    top.setBounds(20, 20, 50, 50);
    JButton middle = new JButton();
    middle.setBackground(Color.gray);
    middle.setBounds(40, 40, 50, 50);
    JButton bottom = new JButton();
    bottom.setBackground(Color.black);
    bottom.setBounds(60, 60, 50, 50);

    // Place the buttons in different layers
    lp.add(middle, new Integer(2));
    lp.add(top, new Integer(3));
    lp.add(bottom, new Integer(1));

    // Show the frame
    f.setSize(150, 150);
    f.setVisible(true);
  }
}
```

In this example, we add three colored buttons to a JLayeredPane. The top button is placed in layer 3, the middle in layer 2, and the bottom in layer 1. Recall that the Component.add() method takes an Object as a second parameter, so we must create Integer objects to identify the layers, rather than just passing in ints. When we run this example, we see (in Figure 8-6) that the white button (the one with the highest layer—3) is drawn above the gray button (in layer 2), which is drawn above the black button (layer 1). The order in which the buttons were added has no significance.

The actual values used for the layers are not important, only their relative ordering. We could just as easily have used 10, 20, and 30 as the layer values.

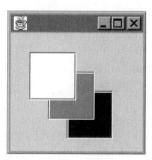

Figure 8-6. JLayeredFrame example

Properties

JLayeredPane defines default values for properties listed in Table 8-4. The Layout property is set to null by default. This works fine when the pane's layers are containers themselves, each managing the layout of a particular layer, or when only a single component is added to each layer. If multiple components are added to a single layer, however, they will be laid out with no layout manager. This is why the RootLayout class described in the JRootPane section explicitly lays out the components it adds to a single layer of its layered pane.

Table 8-4. JLayeredPane Properties

Property	Data Type	get	is	set	bound	Default Value
accessibleContext*	AccessibleContext	●				AccessibleJLay-eredPane()
layout*	LayoutManager	●		●		null
optimizedDrawingEnabled*	boolean	●				true

See also properties from the JComponent class (Table 3-5).

OptimizedDrawingEnabled is a property defined in JComponent that allows a component's children to be drawn more efficiently if they can be guaranteed not to overlap. In JComponent, this property is always true. In JLayeredPane, it is true only if the components in the pane do not overlap.

Constants

JLayeredPane defines several constants. The first six shown in Table 8-5 (and in Figure 8-7) are Integer objects, used to define specific layers available to users of the class.

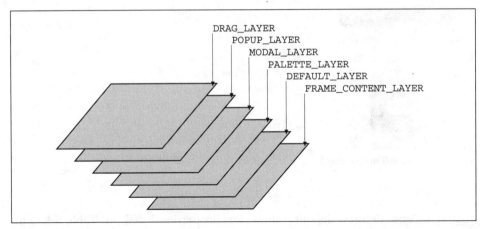

Figure 8-7. Predefined layers

Remember, any number can be used as a layer number; these are just provided as useful defaults. However, it's generally not a good idea to mix your own values with these constants, since there's no guarantee they won't change (this would be very unlikely, but it's definitely poor coding practice to assume the exact values of symbolic constants). Instead, you should choose to either use these constants or define your own layer values.

Table 8-5. JLayeredPane Constants

Constant	Type	Description
DEFAULT_LAYER	Integer	Used for most components (0)
DRAG_LAYER	Integer	Used when dragging objects on the screen to ensure that they appear on top of everything else as they are being dragged (400)
FRAME_CONTENT_LAYER	Integer	Used only for the content pane and menu bar (-30000)
MODAL_LAYER	Integer	Used to display modal popup windows above other components (200)
PALETTE_LAYER	Integer	Used to display floating toolbars or palettes (100)
POPUP_LAYER	Integer	Used to ensure that popups (including tool-tips) are displayed above the components that generate them (300)
LAYER_PROPERTY	String	The name of the layer client property

The last constant in this table, LAYER_PROPERTY, is used as a client property name on JComponents added to the pane. A property with this name will be set on any JComponent added to the pane. The property value will be an Integer representing the component's layer.

Constructor

public JLayeredPane()

This constructor creates a new pane with a `null` layout manager.

Adding Components to Layers

The `add()` methods described below (implemented in `java.awt.Container`) are not actually reimplemented in this class, but it's important to understand how they can be used with `JLayeredPane`. In order to gain this understanding, we'll first explain the use of the term *position* with respect to this class.

A component's position in a layer determines the order in which it will be drawn. This is no different from a component's position in a simple container. Components with the lowest position numbers are drawn last (on top). Components with a position of –1 are added with the next highest position number, so they will drawn first (on bottom). This is best understood by looking at a quick example. Assume we have three components in a layer at positions 0, 1, and 2. We have:

A B C

Now, if we add D to position 1, we have:

A D B C

Adding E to position –1 yields:

A D B C E

Adding F to position 5 gives us:

A D B C E F

If we paint these components, they will be painted in the following order:

F E C B D A

That is, F will be drawn first (on bottom) and A will be drawn last.

When working with multiple layers, nothing changes. The only difference is that all components in a given layer are painted before any components in the next layer, regardless of their positions within a layer. Note that the ordering of layers places the components in the *highest* numbered layer on top, while the ordering of positions places the component with the *lowest* numbered position on top. So, if we have:

Layer 1: A B (A is at position 0, B is at position 1)

Layer 2: C D

Layer 3: E F

The components will be painted in this order:

B A D C F E

The component (E) with the highest layer (3) and lowest position (0) is painted last (on top), as shown in Figure 8-8.

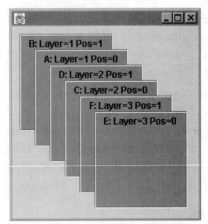

Figure 8-8. Paint order of layered components

Here's how the various versions of Component.add() work with JLayeredPane. Again, these add() methods are *not* reimplemented in JLayeredPane; they're covered here only for the purpose of explaining how they work in this context. Each version of add() is explained in terms of how it will call addImpl(), a protected method that *is* implemented in this class and is also described below.

public Component add(Component comp)
    Results in a call to addImpl(comp, null, -1).

public Component add(Component comp, int index)
    Results in a call to addImpl(comp, null, index).

public void add(Component comp, Object constraints)
    Results in a call to addImpl(comp, constraints, -1). The input object should be an Integer specifying which layer to add the component to.

public void add(Component comp, Object constraints, int index)
    Results in a call to addImpl(comp, constraints, index). The input object should be an Integer specifying the layer to add the component to.

public Component add(String name, Component comp)
    Should not be used with JLayeredPane. If it is, it results in a call to addImpl(comp, name, -1). Since name is not an Integer, it is ignored.

protected void addImpl(Component comp, Object constraints, int index)

> This implementation of `addImpl` checks to see if the given constraint object is an `Integer`, and if so, uses it as the component's layer. If the constraint object is `null` (or anything other than an `Integer`), the component's layer is set by calling `getLayer()` (described later in this chapter).

Layer Management Methods

`JLayeredPane` makes it easy to manipulate layers and the components within them by providing the following methods:

public int getComponentCountInLayer(int layer)

> Returns the number of components currently in the specified layer.

public Component[] getComponentsInLayer(int layer)

> Returns an array containing the `Components` currently in the specified layer.

public int getIndexOf(Component c)

> Returns the absolute index of the given component. This ignores the pane's layers completely. The component with the highest index is the first component painted, meaning it will appear under all other components (which are painted in decreasing order). Since this method ignores the abstractions the layered pane provides, you will not typically use it in application code.

public int getLayer(Component c)

> Returns the layer in which the given component has been placed. If the given component is a `JComponent`, the layer is determined by getting its `LAYER_PROPERTY` client property. If it is not a `JComponent`, it is looked up in an internal hash table used for mapping non-`JComponents` to layers. In either case, if the layer cannot be determined as described, the `DEFAULT_LAYER` is returned.

public int getPosition(Component c)

> Returns a component's position within its layer.

public int highestLayer()

> Returns the highest numbered layer in which a child is contained. If there are no children, zero is returned.

public int lowestLayer()

> Returns the lowest numbered layer in which a child is contained. If there are no children, zero is returned.

public void moveToBack(Component c)

> Moves the specified component to the "back" of its layer.

public void moveToFront(Component c)

> Moves the specified component to the "front" of its layer (position 0).

public void remove(int index)

    Removes the specified component (the index is an absolute index, not layer-based) from the pane.

public void setLayer(Component c, int layer)
public void setLayer(Component c, int layer, int position)

    Set the layer and position (which defaults to −1 in the first case) for the given component and repaint the component. Note that these methods do not add the component to the pane; add() must still be called. Alternatively, a single call to add(c, new Integer(layer)) or add(c, new Integer(layer), positon) could be made. If the given component is a JComponent, its layer is stored by setting the LAYER_PROPERTY client property on the component itself. If not, the component's layer is stored in an internal hash table that maps from non-JComponents to layers.

public void setPosition(Component c, int position)

    Sets a component's position within its layer (determined by calling getLayer(c)).

Other Public Method

public void paint(Graphics g)

    Overridden to explicitly paint the background rectangle if the pane is opaque. It also calls super.paint().

Static Methods

public static int getLayer(JComponent c)

    Uses the LAYER_PROPERTY to get the layer for a given Swing component. Normally, the getLayer() instance method should be used.

public static JLayeredPane getLayeredPaneAbove(Component c)

    Searches the component hierarchy from the given component upward, returning the first JLayeredPane it finds. This allows you to find the layered pane in which a component has been placed. If none is found, it returns null.

public static void putLayer(JComponent c, int layer)

    Sets a component's layer by assigning a value to its LAYER_PROPERTY client property. It does not cause a repaint like the setLayer() instance method does. Normally, setLayer() should be used.

Protected Methods

In addition to the addImpl() method already described, JLayeredPane defines the following protected methods:

protected Hashtable getComponentToLayer()
> Provides access to an internal table, mapping (non JComponent) child components to layers.

protected Integer getObjectForLayer(int layer)
> Returns an Integer object for the given layer number.

protected int insertIndexForLayer(int layer, int position)
> Determines the absolute index for a component to be added to the specified layer at the specified position.

Basic RootPaneContainers

For the rest of this chapter, we'll look at some basic containers (JFrame, JWindow, and JApplet) that implement RootPaneContainer and use JRootPane. First, we'll take a quick look at a simple interface called WindowConstants.

The WindowConstants Interface

WindowConstants is a simple interface containing only constants. It is implemented by JFrame, JDialog, and JInternalFrame.

Constants

The constants defined in WindowConstants specify possible behaviors in response to a window being closed. These values are shown in Table 8-6.

Table 8-6. WindowConstants Constants

Constant	Type	Description
DISPOSE_ON_CLOSE	int	Dispose window when closed.
DO_NOTHING_ON_CLOSE	int	Do nothing when closed.
HIDE_ON_CLOSE	int	Hide window when closed.

In the next section, we'll look at a strategy for exiting the application in response to a frame being closed.

The JFrame Class

The most common Swing container for Java applications is the JFrame. Like java.awt.Frame, JFrame provides a top-level window with a title, border, and other platform-specific adornments (e.g., minimize, maximize, and close buttons). Because it uses a JRootPane as its only child, working with a JFrame is slightly different than working with an AWT Frame. An empty JFrame is shown in Figure 8-9.

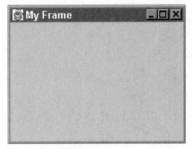

Figure 8-9. JFrame

The primary difference is that calls to `add()` must be replaced with calls to `getContentPane().add()`. In fact, the `addImpl()` method is implemented so that a call made directly to `add()` throws an `Error`. For more information, please refer to the previous sections of this chapter.

Properties

`JFrame` defines the properties shown in Table 8-7. The `accessibleContext` property is as expected. `ContentPane`, `glassPane`, `layeredPane`, and `JMenuBar` are really properties of `JRootPane`, described earlier in the chapter. `JFrame` provides direct access to these panes, as required by the `RootPaneContainer` interface.

Table 8-7. JFrame Properties

Property	Data Type	get	is	set	bound	Default Value
accessibleContext*	AccessibleContext	•				JFrame.Accessible-JFrame()
background*	Color	•		•		UIManager.getColor ("control")
contentPane*	Container	•		•		from rootPane
defaultCloseOperation	int	•		•		HIDE_ON_CLOSE
glassPane*	Component	•		•		from rootPane
layeredPane*	JLayeredPane	•		•		from rootPane
layout*	LayoutManager	•		•		BorderLayout()
JMenuBar*	JMenuBar	•		•		from rootPane
rootPane*	JRootPane	•				JRootPane()
title*	String	•	•			" "

See also the java.awt.Frame class.

The `defaultCloseOperation` is set to `HIDE_ON_CLOSE`, a value taken from `WindowConstants`. This indicates that closing a `JFrame` window results in a call to `setVisible(false)`.

The `layout` property is listed here because `JFrame` overrides `setLayout()` to throw an `Error` if an attempt is made to change the layout manager, rather than set the layout manager of the frame's content pane.

The `rootPane` property is set to a new instance of `JRootPane` when the frame is created and cannot be changed (via public methods).

The accessors for the `title` property are inherited from `Frame`. This property can be set in the `JFrame` constructor.

Protected Fields

The following fields are available to subclasses of `JFrame`:

protected AccessibleContext accessibleContext
Contains the `AccessibleJFrame` for this frame.

protected JRootPane rootPane
Contains the frame's root pane.

protected boolean rootPaneCheckingEnabled
Indicates whether the frame will throw an `Error` if an attempt is made to add components directly to the frame (rather than to its content pane) or to set the layout manager. By default, this is set to `true` once the frame has been built. Subclasses could change this property if necessary, but this is not recommended.

Constructors

public JFrame()
Creates a new unnamed, invisible frame.

public JFrame(String title)
Creates an invisible frame with the specified title.

User Interface Methods

public void update(Graphics g)
Overrides `Container.update()`, to do nothing but call `paint()`. This is consistent with the implementation of `update()` provided by `JComponent`.

Protected Methods

protected void addImpl(Component comp, Object constraints, int index)

This method (called by add()) is overridden to throw an Error when an attempt is made to add a component directly to the JFrame. The only component allowed to be added is the JRootPane, which fills the entire frame (using BorderLayout.CENTER).

protected JRootPane createRootPane()

Called by the constructor to create the frame's JRootPane.

protected void frameInit()

Called by the constructor to enable key and window events, set the root pane, and set the background color. The last thing this method does is set the root-PaneCheckingEnabled field to true.

protected boolean isRootPaneCheckingEnabled()

Indicates whether the frame will throw an Error if an attempt is made to add a component directly to the frame.

protected void processKeyEvent(KeyEvent e)

Forwards the event to JComponent's processKeyBindingsForAllComponents static method.

protected void processWindowEvent(WindowEvent e)

Allows the superclass implementation to process the event. It then handles window closing events based on the current default close operation for the frame. For HIDE_ON_CLOSE, the frame is made invisible, for DISPOSE_ON_CLOSE, the frame is made invisible and disposed, and for DO_NOTHING_ON_CLOSE, nothing is done.

protected void setRootPane(JRootPane root)

Used internally to set the root pane. It temporarily allows components (the root pane) to be added to the frame (keeping addImpl() from throwing an error).

protected void setRootPaneCheckingEnabled(boolean enabled)

Sets the rootPaneCheckingEnabled field.

Exiting Frames

In many applications, closing the main application frame should cause the program to exit (shutting down the virtual machine). The default implementation, however, is only to hide the frame when it is closed, leaving the VM running with no visible frame. We'll briefly look at two simple ways to get the program to exit when the frame is closed.

The simplest thing to do is to add a `WindowListener` to the frame, calling `System.exit()` in the `windowClosing()` method. Here's a simple example:

```java
// FrameClose1.java
//
import javax.swing.JFrame;
import java.awt.event.*;

public class FrameClose1 {
  public static void main(String[] args) {
    JFrame mainFrame = new JFrame();

    // Exit app when frame is closed.
    mainFrame.addWindowListener(new WindowAdapter() {
      public void windowClosing(WindowEvent ev) {
        System.exit(0);
      }
    });

    mainFrame.setSize(320, 240);
    mainFrame.setVisible(true);
  }
}
```

If you get tired of writing this same block of code in every frame that needs to close properly, you might want to use an extension of `JFrame` that supports this feature. Here's one possible implementation of such a class:

```java
// ExitFrame.java
//
import javax.swing.JFrame;
import java.awt.event.WindowEvent;

// A very simple extension of JFrame that adds another option for the
// defaultCloseOperation called EXIT_ON_CLOSE.  This is the default
// for this class, but it can be changed just as it is changed with JFrame.
public class ExitFrame extends JFrame {

  // Exit the VM when the frame is closed
  public static final int EXIT_ON_CLOSE = 100;

  protected int closeOp;

  public ExitFrame() {
    super();
    setDefaultCloseOperation(EXIT_ON_CLOSE);
  }

  public ExitFrame(String title) {
    super(title);
```

```
      setDefaultCloseOperation(EXIT_ON_CLOSE);
   }

   // Overrides JFrame implementation to store the operation locally
   public void setDefaultCloseOperation(int operation) {
      super.setDefaultCloseOperation(operation);
      closeOp = operation;
   }

   // Override JFrame implementation to exit if the close operation is set
   // to EXIT_ON_CLOSE
   protected void processWindowEvent(WindowEvent e) {
      if (e.getID() == WindowEvent.WINDOW_CLOSING) {
         if (closeOp == EXIT_ON_CLOSE)
            System.exit(0);
      }
      super.processWindowEvent(e);
   }
}
```

You can use this class just like you'd use a JFrame. If you don't want the program to exit when the user closes the frame, just change the default close action to one of the values defined in WindowConstants.

A more common strategy is to display a dialog box asking something like *are you sure?* when the user tries to close the frame. JOptionPane (which we'll get to in detail in Chapter 10, *Swing Dialogs*) makes this very easy to do. All you need to do is reimplement your processWindowEvent() method like this:

```
   public static final int MAYBE_EXIT_ON_CLOSE = 101;
   protected void processWindowEvent(WindowEvent e) {
      if (e.getID() == WindowEvent.WINDOW_CLOSING) {
         if (closeOp == MAYBE_EXIT_ON_CLOSE) {
            int exit = JOptionPane.showConfirmDialog(this, "Are you sure?");
            if (exit == JOptionPane.YES_OPTION) {
               System.exit(0);
            }
         }
      }
      super.processWindowEvent(e);
   }
```

The JWindow Class

JWindow is an extension of java.awt.Window that uses a JRootPane as its single component. Other than this core distinction, JWindow does not change anything defined by the Window class.

In AWT, one common reason for using the `Window` class was to create a popup menu. Since Swing explicitly provides a `JPopupMenu` class (see Chapter 14, *Menus and Toolbars*), there is no need to extend `JWindow` for this purpose. The only time you'll use `JWindow` is if you've got something that needs to be displayed in its own window without the adornments added by `JFrame`. Remember, this means that the window can only be moved or closed programmatically (or via the user's platform-specific window manager controls, if available).

One possible use for `JWindow` would be to display a splash screen when an application is starting up. Many programs display such a screen, possibly containing copyright information, resource loading status, etc. Here's such a program:

```java
// Splash.java
//
import javax.swing.*;
import java.awt.*;

public class Splash {
  public static void main(String[] args) {

    // Throw a nice little title page up on the screen first
    showSplash(10000);

    System.exit(0); // replace with application code!
  }

  // A simple little method to show a title screen in the
  // center of the screen for a given amount of time.
   public static void showSplash(int duration) {
     JWindow splash = new JWindow();
     JPanel content = (JPanel)splash.getContentPane();

    // set the window's bounds, centering the window
    int width = 240;
    int height = 120;
    Dimension screen = Toolkit.getDefaultToolkit().getScreenSize();
    int x = (screen.width-width)/2;
    int y = (screen.height-height)/2;
    splash.setBounds(x,y,width,height);

    // build the splash screen
    JLabel label = new JLabel(new ImageIcon("splash.gif"));
    JLabel copyrt = new JLabel
      ("Copyright 1998, PussinToast Inc.", JLabel.CENTER);
    copyrt.setFont(new Font("Sans-Serif", Font.BOLD, 12));
    content.add(label, BorderLayout.CENTER);
    content.add(copyrt, BorderLayout.SOUTH);
    content.setBorder(BorderFactory.createLineBorder(Color.red, 10));
```

```
    // display it
    splash.setVisible(true);

    // Wait a little while, maybe while loading resources
    try { Thread.sleep(duration); } catch (Exception e) {}

    splash.setVisible(false);
  }
}
```

All this program does is create a JWindow containing a pair of labels and display it in the center of the screen. In a real application, the title screen might be displayed while various system resources are being loaded (consider using a ProgressMonitor in this case). When run, this example displays a simple window in the center of the screen, as shown in Figure 8-10.

Figure 8-10. JWindow used as a splash screen

Properties

JWindow defines the properties shown in Table 8-8. The contentPane, glass-Pane, and layeredPane are really properties of JRootPane, as described earlier in the chapter. Direct access is provided for convenience. Unlike JFrame (and JApplet, below), JWindow does not provide direct access to the root pane's menubar. This is just an indication of JWindow's intended usage. If you have some compelling reason to display a menubar on a JWindow, you can always access it via the root pane or just add it as a component.

Table 8-8. JWindow Properties

Property	Data Type	get	is	set	bound	Default Value
accessibleContext*	AccessibleContext	•				JWindow.Accessible-JWindow()
contentPane*	Container	•		•		from rootPane
glassPane*	Component	•		•		from rootPane
layeredPane*	JLayeredPane	•		•		from rootPane

See also the java.awt.Window class.

Table 8-8. JWindow Properties (continued)

Property	Data Type	get	is	set	bound	Default Value
layout*	LayoutManager	•		•		BorderLayout()
rootPane*	JRootPane	•				JRootPane()

See also the java.awt.Window class.

The `layout` property is listed here because `JWindow` overrides `setLayout()` to throw an `Error` if an attempt is made to change the layout manager, rather than set the layout manager of the window's content pane.

The `rootPane` property is set to a new instance of `JRootPane` when the frame is created and cannot be changed using public methods.

Protected Fields

The following fields are available to subclasses of `JWindow`:

protected AccessibleContext accessibleContext
Contains the `AccessibleJWindow` for this window.

protected JRootPane rootPane
Contains the window's root pane.

protected boolean rootPaneCheckingEnabled
Indicates whether the window will throw an `Error` if an attempt is made to add components directly to the window (rather than to its content pane) or to set the layout manager. By default, this is set to `true` once the window has been built. Subclasses could change this property if necessary, though it is not recommended.

Constructors

public JWindow()
Creates a new, invisible window associated with no particular owner. This makes use of `SwingUtilities.getSharedOwnerFrame()`.

public JWindow(JFrame frame)
Creates a new, invisible window associated with the given frame.

Protected Methods

protected void addImpl(Component comp, Object constraints, int index)
This method (called by `add()`) is overridden to throw an `Error` when an attempt is made to add a component directly to the `JWindow`. The only

component allowed to be added is the JRootPane, which fills the entire window (using BorderLayout.CENTER).

protected JRootPane createRootPane()
Called by the constructor to create the window's JRootPane.

protected boolean isRootPaneCheckingEnabled()
Indicates whether the window will throw an Error if an attempt is made to add a component directly to the window.

protected void setRootPane(JRootPane root)
Used internally to set the root pane.

protected void setRootPaneCheckingEnabled(boolean enabled)
Sets the rootPaneCheckingEnabled field.

protected void windowInit()
Called by the constructor set the root pane and set the rootPaneChecking-Enabled field to true.

The JApplet Class

JApplet is a simple extension of java.applet.Applet, for use when creating Swing programs designed to be used in a web browser (or *appletviewer*). As a direct subclass of Applet, JApplet is used in much the same way, with the init(), start(), and stop() methods still playing critical roles. The primary thing JApplet provides over Applet is the use of a JRootPane as its single display component. The properties and methods described below should look a lot like those described in the previous sections on JFrame and JWindow. Figure 8-11 shows a JApplet running in *appletviewer*.

Figure 8-11. A JApplet running in the JDK appletviewer

Hiding the Warning Message

At the time of this writing, the current popular browsers do not allow applets to access the system event queue. As a result, a warning message is printed to the Java console, indicating that the applet attempted to access the system event queue and failed. If you find this warning sufficiently annoying, Swing provides a workaround that allows you to suppress it. Just implement a constructor for your applet with the following code:

```
getRootPane().putClientProperty("defeatSystemEventQueueCheck", Boolean.TRUE);
```

In AWT, applets rarely (if ever) had constructors. With Swing, a constructor (which must have no arguments) is a good place to set client properties like this one.

Threading Issues

Since JApplets are typically used within an existing Java application (the web browser), you need to be careful about Swing threading issues. A good rule of thumb is that any adding or manipulation of components should be done in the init() method. If you choose to interact with Swing components in the start() method, you should be sure to execute the code in the event dispatch thread using the SwingUtilities.invokeLater() or SwingUtilities.invokeAnd-Wait() methods. Here's a simple applet that uses this technique; we also use a constructor to suppress the warning message:

```
// SimpleApplet.java
//
import javax.swing.*;
import java.awt.*;

public class SimpleApplet extends JApplet {
  public SimpleApplet() {

    // supress warning message
    getRootPane().putClientProperty("defeatSystemEventQueueCheck",
    Boolean.TRUE);
  }

  public void start() {
    SwingUtilities.invokeLater(new Runnable() {
      public void run() { // run in the event thread . . .
        JPanel p = new JPanel();
        p.setLayout(new GridLayout(2, 2, 2, 2));
        p.add(new JLabel("Username"));
        p.add(new JTextField());
        p.add(new JLabel("Password"));
        p.add(new JPasswordField());
        Container content = getContentPane();
        content.setLayout(new GridBagLayout()); // used to center the panel
```

```
        content.add(p);
        validate();
      }
    });
  }
}
```

Of course, in this example, we could just move this code to init() and safely do away with the use of invokeLater(). For more information on threading issues in Swing, please see Chapter 1, *Introducing Swing* (for an introduction), and Chapter 28, *Swing Under the Hood.*

Properties

JApplet defines the properties and default values shown in Table 8-9. The contentPane, glassPane, layeredPane, and JMenuBar properties are really properties of JRootPane, as described earlier in the chapter. Direct access is provided to them for convenience.

Table 8-9. JApplet Properties

Property	Data Type	get	is	set	bound	Default Value
accessibleContext*	AccessibleContext	•				JApplet.Accessible-JApplet()
contentPane*	Container	•		•		from rootPane
glassPane*	Component	•		•		from rootPane
layeredPane*	JLayeredPane	•		•		from rootPane
layout*	LayoutManager	•		•		BorderLayout()
JMenuBar*	JMenuBar	•		•		from rootPane
rootPane*	JRootPane	•				JRootPane()

See also the java.applet.Applet class.

The layout property is listed here because JApplet overrides setLayout() to throw an Error if an attempt is made to change the layout manager, rather than set the layout manager of the applet's content pane.

The rootPane property is set when the applet is created. It cannot be changed via public methods.

Protected Fields

The following fields are available to subclasses of JApplet.

protected AccessibleContext accessibleContext

Contains the `AccessibleJApplet` for this window.

protected JRootPane rootPane

Contains the applet's root pane.

protected boolean rootPaneCheckingEnabled

Indicates whether the applet will throw an `Error` if an attempt is made to add components directly to the applet (rather than to its content pane) to set the layout manager. By default, this is set to `true` once the applet has been built. Subclasses could change this property if necessary.

Constructor

public JApplet()

Creates a new applet and ensures that the timerQueue is running. This is how browsers (and *appletviewer*) create new applets. If you supply a constructor with an applet, perhaps to disable event queue checking, remember that browsers expect an applet constructor to have no arguments. The constructor sets the applet's foreground color to black and its background color to white.

User Interface Methods

public void update(Graphics g)

Overrides `Container.update()` to do nothing but call `paint()`. This is consistent with the implementation of `update()` provided by `JComponent` (and the implementation used by `JFrame`).

Protected Methods

protected void addImpl(Component comp, Object constraints, int index)

This method (called by `add()`) is overridden to throw an `Error` when an attempt is made to add a component directly to the `JApplet`. The only component allowed to be added is the `JRootPane`, which fills the entire applet (using `BorderLayout.CENTER`).

protected JRootPane createRootPane()

Called by the constructor to create the applet's `JRootPane`.

protected boolean isRootPaneCheckingEnabled()

Indicates whether the applet will throw an `Error` if an attempt is made to add a component directly to the applet.

protected void processKeyEvent(KeyEvent e)

Forwards the event to `JComponent`'s `processKeyBindingsForAllComponents()` static method.

protected void setRootPane(JRootPane root)

Used internally to set the root pane. It temporarily allows components (the root pane) to be added to the applet, ensuring that `addImpl()` will not throw an `Error`.

protected void setRootPaneCheckingEnabled(boolean enabled)

Sets the `rootPaneCheckingEnabled` field.

9

Internal Frames

Managing a Desktop

Certain GUI applications need to simulate a desktop environment by allowing multiple "frames" to be displayed within a single root window. These frames look like the normal frames you'd see on a real desktop, but are not actually known to the window manager, because they are not really windows in the normal sense of the term. For some types of applications (word processors, IDEs, etc.), this can be a very powerful approach to UI design.

In this chapter, we'll look at a collection of classes Swing provides to allow you to create this type of application in Java. At the end of the chapter, we'll provide a large sample program that shows how to implement a variety of useful features.

Overview

Before looking at each of the classes involved in the Swing desktop/internal frame model, we'll take a moment for an overview of how they all work together. Figure 9-1 shows the relationships between the classes we'll be covering in this chapter.

A JInternalFrame is a container that looks much like a JFrame. The key difference is that internal frames can only exist within some other Java container. JInternalFrame implements the following three interfaces: Accessible, WindowConstants, RootPaneContainer.

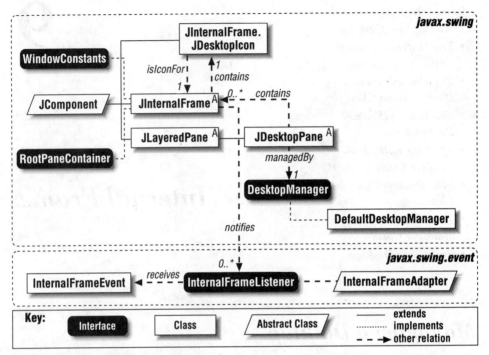

Figure 9-1. Internal Frame and Desktop class diagram

Each internal frame keeps a reference to an instance of the static inner class called JDesktopIcon. Like real frames, JInternalFrames can be iconified. JDesktop-Icon is the class responsible for taking the place of the frame when it gets iconified.

Though it is not required, JInternalFrames are typically used inside of a JDesk-topPane. JDesktopPane is an extension of JLayeredPane that adds direct support for managing a collection of JInternalFrames in layers. JDesktopPane uses an object called a DesktopManager to control how different behavior, like iconification or maximization, is carried out. A default implementation of this interface, DefaultDesktopManager, is provided. We'll see how all of this functionality is broken out as we cover the various classes and interfaces involved.

One more thing to notice about Figure 9-1 is that JInternalFrame supports a new type of listener called InternalFrameListener. This interface contains methods that match those defined by the AWT WindowListener class, but have slightly different names and take InternalFrameEvents, rather than Window-Events, as input.

The JInternalFrame Class

JInternalFrame is a powerful addition to Java, providing the ability to create lightweight frames that exist inside other components. An internal frame is managed entirely within some other Java container, just like any other component, allowing the program complete control over iconification, maximization, resizing, etc. Despite looking like "real" windows, the underlying windowing system knows nothing of the existence of internal frames.[*] Figure 9-2 shows what an internal frame looks like in the different look-and-feels.[†]

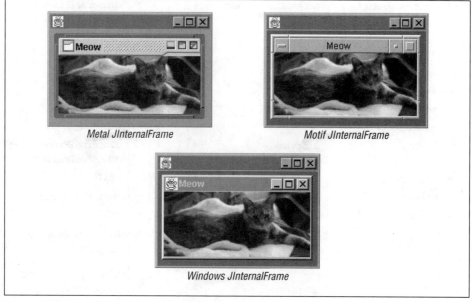

Figure 9-2. JInternalFrames in the three look-and-feels

There's quite a lot to discuss about JInternalFrames, but most of their power comes when they are used inside a JDesktopPane. In this section, we will give a quick overview of the properties, constructors, and methods available in JInternalFrame, but we'll leave the more detailed discussion of using internal frames to the sections that follow.

---

[*] Note that JInternalFrame extends JComponent, not JFrame or Frame, so this statement should seem logical.

[†] The appearance of an internal frame in the Metal look-and-feel has changed very slightly since these screen shots were taken.

Properties

JInternalFrame defines the properties and default values shown in Table 9-1.

Table 9-1. JInternalFrame Properties

Property	Data Type	get	is	set	bound	Default Value
UI	InternalFrameUI	•		•	•	from L&F
UIClassID*	String	•				"InternalFrameUI"
accessibleContext*	AccessibleContext	•				JInternalFrame.AccessibleJInternalFrame()
background*	Color	•		•		from contentPane()
closable	boolean		•	•		false
closed[a]	boolean		•	•	•	false
contentPane*	Container	•		•	•	from rootPane
defaultCloseOperation	int	•		•		HIDE_ON_CLOSE
desktopIcon	JInternal-Frame.JDesktopIcon	•		•		JInternalFrame.JDesktopIcon()
desktopPane	JDesktopPane	•				null
foreground*	Color	•		•		from contentPane()
frameIcon	Icon	•		•	•	null
glassPane*	Component	•		•	•	from rootPane()
icon[a]	boolean		•	•	•	false
iconifiable	boolean		•	•		false
JMenuBar*[b]	JMenuBar	•		•	•	from rootPane()
layer	int	•				0
layeredPane*	JLayeredPane	•		•	•	from rootPane()
maximizable	boolean		•	•		false
maximum[a]	boolean		•	•	•	false
resizable	boolean		•	•		false
rootPane*	JRootPane	•			•	JRootPane()
selected[a]	boolean		•	•	•	false
title	String	•		•	•	""
warningString	String	•				null

See also properties from the JComponent class (Table 3-5).

[a] These properties are the only constrained properties in Swing. The set() methods for each of them fire PropertyChangeEvents to any registered VetoablePropertyChangeListeners. Consequently, calls to these set() methods must be wrapped in a try-catch block, checking for PropertyVetoException. See the example at the end of the chapter for more information.
[b] This property replaces the deprecated menuBar parperty.

The `background` and `foreground` properties are delegated to the frame's content pane.

Three pairs of properties indicate whether or not something can be done to a frame and whether or not that thing is currently done to the frame. They are: `closable`/`closed`, `iconifiable`/`icon`, and `maximizable`/`maximum`. Note that `closed`, `icon`, and `maximum` are constrained properties.

The `contentPane`, `glassPane`, `layeredPane`, and `JMenuBar` properties come from the `RootPaneContainer` interface and are taken directly from the frame's `JRootPane`. The `rootPane` property is set to a new `JRootPane` when the frame is constructed.

The value of the `defaultCloseOperation` property defaults to `WindowConstants.HIDE_ON_CLOSE`. This implies that when the frame is closed, its `setClosed()` method will be called. The frame could be reopened at a later time.

The `desktopIcon` reflects how the frame will be displayed when iconified. A `JDesktopIcon` (which leaves the rendering to the L&F) is created for the frame when it is instantiated. The `desktopPane` property provides a convenient way to access the `JDesktopPane` containing the frame, if there is one.

`frameIcon` is the icon painted inside the frame's titlebar (usually on the far left). By default, there is no icon. However, the basic look-and-feel checks to see if a `frameIcon` has been set and, if not, paints the "java cup" icon. This explains why an icon appears in the Windows L&F frame shown in Figure 9-2, but not in the others (which provide their own `paint()` implementations, rather than using the one provided by the basic L&F).*

The `layer` property indicates the frame's current layer, if it has been placed in a `JLayeredPane`. The `resizable` property indicates whether the frame can be resized by dragging its edges or corners, and `selected` indicates whether the frame has been selected (this typically determines the color of the titlebar). `selected` is a constrained property. `title` contains the string for the titlebar.

The `UI` property holds the current L&F implementation for the frame, and `UIClassID` reflects the class ID for internal frames.

Finally, the `warningString` property, which is always `null`, is used to specify the string that should appear in contexts where the frame might be insecure. This is the technique used by `java.awt.Window` to display a string like "Warning: Applet Window" when a Java window is displayed from an applet. Since `JInternalFrames` are always fully enclosed by some other top-level container, this property is always `null`.

---

* The `BasicLookAndFeel` is an abstract base class from which all the Swing L&Fs extend. For more information, see Chapter 26, *Look & Feel*.

Events

JInternalFrame fires an InternalFrameEvent (discussed later in this chapter) whenever the frame's state changes.

The following standard methods are provided for working with events.

public synchronized void addInternalFrameListener(InternalFrameListener l)
public synchronized void removeInternalFrameListener(InternalFrameListener l)
protected void fireInternalFrameEvent(int id)
> Fire an event to registered internal frame listeners. The input id must be one of the valid constants defined in InternalFrameEvent.

Like all the other Swing classes, JInternalFrame fires PropertyChangeEvents when the value of any bound property is changed. JInternalFrame is unique in that it is the only Swing class that uses vetoable changes for some properties (closed, icon, maximum, and selected).

Constants

Table 9-2 shows the constants defined in this class. They are all strings and contain the names of the bound properties.

Table 9-2. JInternalFrame Constants

Constant	Property
CONTENT_PANE_PROPERTY	Indicates that the content pane has changed
FRAME_ICON_PROPERTY	indidcaes that the frame's icon has changed
GLASS_PANE_PROPERTY	Indicates that the glass pane has changed
IS_CLOSED_PROPERTY	Indicates that the frame has been opened or closed
IS_ICON_PROPERTY	Indicates that the frame as been iconified or deiconified
IS_MAXIMUM_PROPERTY	Indicates that the frame has been maximized or minimized
IS_SELECTED_PROPERTY	Indicates that the frame has been selected or deselected
LAYERED_PANE_PROPERTY	Indicates that the layered pane has changed
MENU_BAR_PROPERTY	Indicates that the menubar has changed
ROOT_PANE_PROPERTY	Indicates that the root pane has changed
TITLE_PROPERTY	Indicates that the frame's title has changed

Protected Fields

protected boolean closable
protected JInternalFrame.JDesktopIcon desktopIcon
protected Icon frameIcon
protected boolean iconable

protected boolean isClosed
protected boolean isIcon
protected boolean isMaximum
protected boolean isSelected
protected boolean maximizable
protected boolean resizable
protected JRootPane rootPane
protected String title

These fields hold the values of many of the properties listed in Table 9-1. Subclasses should access them through the accessor methods, rather than using these fields directly.

protected boolean rootPaneCheckingEnabled

Indicates whether the frame throws an `Error` if an attempt is made to add components directly to the frame (rather than to its content pane). By default, this is set to `true` once the frame has been built. Subclasses could change this property if necessary.

Constructors

`JInternalFrame` provides constructors that allow several of its boolean properties to be set at creation time. By default, `resizable`, `closable`, `maximizable`, and `iconifiable` are all set to `false`.

public JInternalFrame()
public JInternalFrame(String title)

Create a new frame with all four properties set to false.

public JInternalFrame(String title, boolean resizable)
public JInternalFrame(String title, boolean resizable, boolean closable)
public JInternalFrame(String title, boolean resizable, boolean closable, boolean maximizable)
public JInternalFrame(String title, boolean resizable, boolean closable, boolean maximizable, boolean iconifiable)

Allow one to four of the frame's boolean properties to be set at creation time.

JLayeredPane Methods

These methods are applicable only if the frame is contained by a `JLayeredPane` (otherwise, they do nothing).

public void moveToBack()
public void toBack()

Call the containing layered pane's `moveToBack()` method, causing the frame to be the first (bottom) component painted in its layer.

public void moveToFront()

public void toFront()

> Call the containing layered pane's `moveToFront()` method, causing the frame to be the last (top) component painted in its layer.

Miscellaneous Public Methods

public void dispose()

> Makes the frame invisible, unselected, and closed.

public void pack()

> Works like `Frame`'s `pack()` method, causing the frame to be resized according to the preferred size of its components.

public void reshape(int x, int y, int width, int height)

> Calls its superclass implementation and then forces a repaint of the frame, so that decorations such as the title bar will be painted.

public void show()

> Makes the frame visible and selects it, bringing it to the front of its layer.

public void updateUI()

> Called to indicate that the L&F for the frame has changed.

Protected Methods

protected void addImpl(Component comp, Object constraints, int index)

> Called by the various `add()` methods. If `rootPaneCheckingEnabled` is set to `true`, this method throws an `Error`, indicating that components should be added to the frame's content pane, not to the frame itself.

protected JRootPane createRootPane()

> Used by the constructor to create a new `JRootPane`.

protected boolean isRootPaneCheckingEnabled()

> Indicates the current value of `rootPaneCheckingEnabled`.

protected void setRootPane(JRootPane root)

> Called by the constructor to set the frame's root pane.

Use of Glass Pane

`JInternalFrame` is the only Swing class that makes use of the glass pane (see Chapter 8 for a general discussion of the glass pane). To be precise, `JInternal-Frame` itself doesn't do anything special with the glass pane, but the default UI implementation (`BasicInternalFrameUI`) does. This class toggles the visibility of an internal frame's glass pane each time the state of the frame's selected property changes. When the frame is selected, the glass pane is made invisible, allowing components inside the frame to be accessed with the mouse. But when the frame is not selected, the glass pane is made visible. This means that the first time you click anywhere within a non-selected internal frame, the mouse click will not get through to the component within the frame that you clicked on, but will instead be intercepted by the glass pane, causing the frame to be selected (and causing the glass pane to be removed).

The Metal L&F JInternalFrame.isPalette Client Property

If you plan to use the Metal L&F in your application, you can take advantage of a special custom property supported by `MetalInternalFrameUI`. This client property allows you to define an internal frame as a palette. This effectively amounts to removing the thick border from the frame. This is a technique commonly used in word processing or graphics editing programs to provide small windows that contain a set of convenient edit buttons. If you couple the use of this client property with the use of the desktop's PALETTE_LAYER (discussed later), you'll have a nice borderless frame that will float above your other internal frames. Here's an idea of how you'd use this property:

```
JInternalFrame palette = new JInternalFrame(); // use any constructor you
want
palette.putClientProperty("JInternalFrame.isPalette", Boolean.TRUE);
palette.setBounds(0, 0, 50, 150);
JDesktopPane desk = new JDesktopPane();
desk.add(palette, JDesktopPane.PALETTE_LAYER);
```

Other L&Fs will quietly ignore this property.

The JInternalFrame.JDesktopIcon Class

`JDesktopIcon` is a static inner class of `JInternalFrame`, used to provide an iconified view of a frame. `JInternalFrame` instantiates a `JDesktopIcon` when the frame is created. The class extends `JComponent` and, like other Swing components, leaves all details of its visual appearance to its UI delegate.

Note that this class has no relation at all to the Swing `Icon` interface.

NOTE   You should not work with the `JDesktopIcon` class directly—the java-doc for this inner class indicates that it will go away in a future Swing release. We are including this brief description of the class for completeness until the change is made.

Properties

JDesktopIcon defines the properties shown in Table 9-3. The desktopPane property simply provides convenient, direct access to the JDesktopPane containing the icon, if applicable. This property comes directly from the icon's internal frame. The internalFrame property reflects the icon's tight coupling with the JInternalFrame class. The icon's frame is set when the icon is constructed and typically should not be changed. As usual, the UI property provides access to the object's UI implementation, and UIClassID is set to the expected value.

Table 9-3. JDesktopIcon Properties

Property	Data Type	get	is	set	bound	Default Value
UI	DesktopIconUI	•		•		from L&F
UIClassID*	String	•				"DesktopIconUI"
accessibleContext*	AccessibleContext	•				JDesktopIcon.Acces- sibleJDesktopIcon()
desktopPane	JDesktopPane	•				from internal frame
internalFrame	JInternalFrame	•		•		from constructor

See also properties from the JComponent class (Table 3-5).

Constructors

public JDesktopIcon(JInternalFrame f)
    Creates an icon for the specified internal frame.

Methods

There is only one method other than the accessors for the icon's properties.

public void updateUI()
    Indicates that the icon's L&F should be updated.

The InternalFrameEvent Class

As we described earlier in the chapter, JInternalFrames fire Internal-FrameEvents when the state of the frame changes. This is a standard AWTEvent subclass, providing a number of constants to define the type of change that was made to the frame.

Constants

Table 9-4 shows constants defined as possible values for the event ID.

Table 9-4. InternalFrameEvent Constants

Constant	Type	Description
INTERNAL_FRAME_ACTIVATED	int	The frame has been activated, typically causing the title bar to change to a special color and the frame to gain focus
INTERNAL_FRAME_CLOSED	int	The frame has been closed (sent any time the frame is closed)
INTERNAL_FRAME_CLOSING	int	The frame is about to be closed (sent when the user clicks the closebox on the frame)
INTERNAL_FRAME_DEACTIVATED	int	The frame has been deactivated, typically causing the title bar to change to a default color and the frame to lose focus
INTERNAL_FRAME_DEICONIFIED	int	The frame has been restored from an icon
INTERNAL_FRAME_ICONIFIED	int	The frame has been iconified
INTERNAL_FRAME_OPENED	int	The frame has been opened
INTERNAL_FRAME_FIRST	int	The first integer value used to represent the above event IDs
INTERNAL_FRAME_LAST	int	The last integer value used to represent the above event IDs

Constructor

public InternalFrameEvent(JInternalFrame source, int id)

Creates a new event. The `id` should be taken from the list of constants provided above.

Method

public String paramString()

This method, used by `toString()`, returns a parameter string describing the event.

The InternalFrameListener Interface

`JInternalFrame` fires `InternalFrameEvents` to registered `InternalFrameListeners`. This interface defines the following set of methods (which have a one-to-one correspondence to the methods in the `java.awt.event.WindowListener` interface).

Methods

All of these methods except `internalFrameClosing()` are called by the `JInternalFrame` when its properties are changed.

public abstract void internalFrameActivated(InternalFrameEvent e)
> The frame has been activated, typically meaning that it will gain focus and be brought to the front.

public abstract void internalFrameClosed(InternalFrameEvent e)
> The frame has been closed.

public abstract void internalFrameClosing(InternalFrameEvent e)
> The frame is closing. This is called by the L&F when the close button is clicked.

public abstract void internalFrameDeactivated(InternalFrameEvent e)
> The frame has been deactivated.

public abstract void internalFrameDeiconified(InternalFrameEvent e)
> The frame has been restored from an icon.

public abstract void internalFrameIconified(InternalFrameEvent e)
> The frame has been reduced to an icon.

public abstract void internalFrameOpened(InternalFrameEvent e)
> A previously closed frame has been opened.

The InternalFrameAdapter Class

This class follows the standard AWT 1.1 listener/adapter pattern by providing empty implementations of the seven methods defined in the `InternalFrameListener` interface. If you are only interested in certain types of events, you can create a subclass of this adapter that implements only the methods you care about.

Methods

The following methods have empty implementations in this class:

public void internalFrameActivated(InternalFrameEvent e)
public void internalFrameClosed(InternalFrameEvent e)
public void internalFrameClosing(InternalFrameEvent e)
public void internalFrameDeactivated(InternalFrameEvent e)
public void internalFrameDeiconified(InternalFrameEvent e)
public void internalFrameIconified(InternalFrameEvent e)
public void internalFrameOpened(InternalFrameEvent e)

The JDesktopPane Class

JDesktopPane is an extension of JLayeredPane, which uses a DesktopManager to control the placement and movement of frames. Figure 9-3 shows what JDesktopPane looks like in the different look-and-feels. Like its superclass, JLayeredPane has a null layout manager. Components added to it must be placed at absolute locations with absolute sizes, because it is intended to be used to house JInternalFrames, which rely on the user to determine their placement.

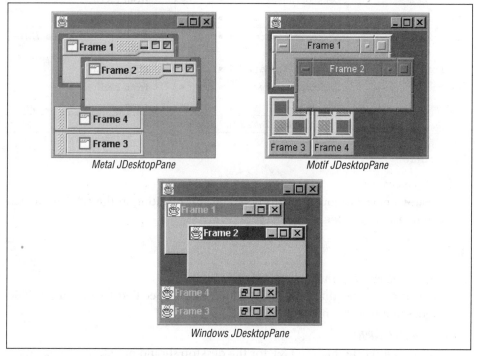

Figure 9-3. JDesktopPanes in the three look-and-feels

Another reason for using JDesktopPane is to allow popup dialog boxes to be displayed using JInternalFrames. This is discussed in detail in the next chapter.

Properties

Table 9-5 shows the properties defined by JDesktopPane. The allFrames property provides access to all JInternalFrames contained by the desktop. The desktopManager property holds the DesktopManager object supplied by the pane's L&F. We'll cover the responsibilities of the DesktopManager in the next section. The opaque property defaults to true for JDesktopPanes and isOpaque() is overridden so that it always returns true. UI contains the Desk-topPaneUI implementation, and UIClassID contains the class ID for JDesktopPane.

Table 9-5. JDesktopPane Properties

Property	Data Type	get	is	set	bound	Default Value
UI	DesktopPaneUI	•		•		from L&F
UIClassID*	String	•				"DesktopPaneUI"
accessibleContext*	AccessibleContext	•				JDesktopPane.Accessible-JDesktopPane()
allFrames	JInternalFrame[]	•				empty array
desktopManager	DesktopManager	•		•		from L&F
opaque*	boolean		•	•		true

See also properties from the JLayeredPane class (Table 8-4).

Constructor

public JDesktopPane()

Creates a new desktop and calls updateUI(), resulting in the L&F implementation installing a DesktopManager.

Methods

public JInternalFrame[] getAllFramesInLayer(int layer)

Returns all frames that have been added to the specified layer. This includes frames that have been iconified.

public void updateUI()

Called to indicate that the L&F for the desktop should be set.

The DesktopManager Interface

This interface is responsible for much of the management of internal frames contained by JDesktopPanes. It allows a look-and-feel to define exactly how it wants to manage things such as frame activation, movement, and iconification. Most of the methods in InternalFrameUI implementations should delegate to a DesktopManager object. As described earlier, DesktopManagers are contained by JDesktopPane objects and are intended to be set by the L&F.

Methods

The majority of the methods in this interface act on a given JInternalFrame. However, those methods that could be applied to other types of components do not restrict the parameter unnecessarily (they accept any JComponent), despite the fact that they will typically only be used with JInternalFrames. The exception to this in the current Swing release is a single use of setBoundsForFrame(), (called from BasicDesktopIconUI), which passes in a JDesktopIcon rather than a JInternalFrame. If you implement your own DesktopManager or other L&F classes, you may find a need for this flexibility.

public abstract void activateFrame(JInternalFrame f)

Called to indicate that the specified frame should become active.

public abstract void beginDraggingFrame(JComponent f)

Called to indicate that the specified frame is now being dragged. The given component will normally be a JInternalFrame.

public abstract void beginResizingFrame(JComponent f, int direction)

Called to indicate that the specified frame is going to be resized. The direction comes from SwingConstants and must be NORTH, SOUTH, EAST, WEST, NORTH_EAST, NORTH_WEST, SOUTH_EAST, or SOUTH_WEST. The given component will normally be a JInternalFrame. When resizing is complete, endResizingFrame() will be called.

public abstract void closeFrame(JInternalFrame f)

Called to indicate that the specified frame should be closed.

public abstract void deactivateFrame(JInternalFrame f)

Called to indicate that the specified frame is no longer active.

public abstract void deiconifyFrame(JInternalFrame f)

Called to indicate that the specified frame should no longer be iconified.

public abstract void dragFrame(JComponent f, int newX, int newY)

Called to indicate that the specified frame should be moved from its current location to the newly specified coordinates. The given component will normally be a JInternalFrame.

public abstract void endDraggingFrame(JComponent f)

Called to indicate that the specified frame is no longer being dragged. The given component will normally be a JInternalFrame.

public abstract void endResizingFrame(JComponent f)

Called to indicate that the specified frame is no longer being resized. The given component will normally be a JInternalFrame.

public abstract void iconifyFrame(JInternalFrame f)

Called to indicate that the specified frame should be iconified.

public abstract void maximizeFrame(JInternalFrame f)

Called to indicate that the specified frame should be maximized.

public abstract void minimizeFrame(JInternalFrame f)

Called to indicate that the specified frame should be minimized. Note that this is not the same as iconifying the frame. Typically, calling this method will cause the frame to return to its size and position from before it was maximized.

public abstract void openFrame(JInternalFrame f)

Called to add a frame and display it at a reasonable location. This is not normally called, because frames are normally added directly to their parent.

public abstract void resizeFrame(JComponent f, int newX, int newY, int newWidth,
    int newHeight)

Called to indicate that the specified frame has been resized. Note that resizing is still in progress (many calls to this method may be made while the frame is being resized) after this method completes. The given component will normally be a `JInternalFrame`.

public abstract void setBoundsForFrame(JComponent f, int newX, int newY, int newWidth,
    int newHeight)

Called to set a new size and location for a frame. The given component will normally be a `JInternalFrame`.

The DefaultDesktopManager Class

`DefaultDesktopManager` is a default implementation of the `DesktopManager` interface. It serves as the base class for the Windows and Motif L&Fs, while the Metal L&F uses it without modification. In this section, we'll give a brief explanation of how each of the methods in the interface is implemented by this class.

Methods

public void activateFrame(JInternalFrame f)

Calls `setSelected(false)` on all other `JInternalFrames` contained by the specified frame's parent that are in the same layer as the given frame. It then moves the given frame to the front of its layer, selecting it.

public void closeFrame(JInternalFrame f)

Removes the given frame from its parent. It also removes the frame's icon (if displayed). It sets the frame's previous bounds to `null`.

public void deiconifyFrame(JInternalFrame f)

Removes the given frame's icon from its parent and adds the frame. It then tries to select the given frame.

public void dragFrame(JComponent f, int newX, int newY)

Calls `setBoundsForFrame()` with the given location and current dimensions.

public void iconifyFrame(JInternalFrame f)

Removes the given frame from its parent and adds the frame's desktop icon. Before adding the icon, it checks to see if it has ever been iconified. If not, it calls `getBoundsForIconOf()` to set the icon's bounds. This is only done once for a given frame, ensuring that each time a frame is iconified, it returns to the same location on the desktop.

public void maximizeFrame(JInternalFrame f)

Maximizes the given frame so that it fills its parent. It also saves the frame's previous bounds for use in `minimizeFrame()`. Once the frame has been maximized, it is also selected.

This method can be called on an iconified frame, causing it to be deiconified and maximized.

public void minimizeFrame(JInternalFrame f)

Sets the frame's bounds to its previous bounds. If there are no previous bounds (previous bounds are set by calling `maximizeFrame()`), the frame is not resized.

public void openFrame(JInternalFrame f)

Gets the desktop icon for the given frame. If the icon's parent is non-`null`, the icon is removed from the parent, and the frame is added. If its parent is `null`, this method does nothing.

public void resizeFrame(JComponent f, int newX, int newY, int newWidth, int newHeight)

Calls `setBoundsForFrame()` with the given location and dimensions.

public void setBoundsForFrame(JComponent f, int newX, int newY, int newWidth, int newHeight)

Moves and resizes the given frame (using `setBounds()`) and validates the frame if the size was actually changed.

public void beginDraggingFrame(JComponent f)
public void beginResizingFrame(JComponent f, int direction)
public void deactivateFrame(JInternalFrame f)
public void endDraggingFrame(JComponent f)
public void endResizingFrame(JComponent f)

These methods have empty implementations in this class.

Protected Methods

This default implementation provides several convenience methods, which it uses in the methods described above. The methods relate to desktop icon management and the management of a frame's previous size (when maximized). If you subclass `DefaultDesktopManager`, these methods will probably be of use to you.

The frame's previous bounds and an indication of whether or not it has ever been iconified are stored in client properties on the frame itself.[*] The property names used are previousBounds (which holds a Rectangle) and wasIconOnce (which holds a Boolean).

protected Rectangle getBoundsForIconOf(JInternalFrame f)

Gets the bounds for the given frame's icon. The width and height are taken directly from the size of the icon. The icon's location will be the lower-left corner of the desktop. If an icon has already been placed in this corner, the icon is placed directly to the right, continuing until an unclaimed position along the bottom of the frame is found. If there is no space along the bottom, a new row of icons is started directly above the first row. Once a frame has been iconified, its icon's location is set and the icon will always return to the same spot (unless the icon is moved by the user).

protected Rectangle getPreviousBounds(JInternalFrame f)

Returns the frame's previous bounds (set when the frame is maximized). These bounds are retrieved from the frame's previousBounds client property.

protected void removeIconFor(JInternalFrame f)

Removes the given frame's icon from its parent and repaints the region under the icon.

protected void setPreviousBounds(JInternalFrame f, Rectangle r)

Saves the previous bounds of a frame. This is done by saving the frame's previous bounds in the frame itself, using the client property, previous-Bounds. This is generally called by maximizeFrame() with the data being used in a subsequent minimizeFrame() call.

protected void setWasIcon(JInternalFrame f, Boolean value)

Called by iconifyFrame() to indicate whether or not the frame has, at some time, been iconified. This is done by saving the boolean value in the frame itself, using the client property wasIconOnce. This is used to determine whether or not the icon's bounds have been defined.

protected boolean wasIcon(JInternalFrame f)

Determines whether or not a frame has ever been iconified (if it has, bounds will already be defined for the icon). This is done by returning the was-IconOnce client property on the frame.

---

* See Chapter 3, *Swing Component Basics*, for an explanation of JComponent's client property feature.

Building a Desktop

In this section, we'll pull together some of the things we've discussed in the previous pages to create an application using JDesktopPane, JInternalFrame, and a custom DesktopManager. The example shows:

- The effect of adding frames to different layers of the desktop.

- How to display a background image ("wallpaper") on the desktop.

- How to keep frames from being moved outside of the desktop.

- How to deiconify, move, and resize internal frames by frame "tiling."

- How to take advantage of JInternalFrame's constrained properties by requiring that there be at least one non-iconified frame on the desktop.

Figure 9-4 shows what the application looks like when it's running.

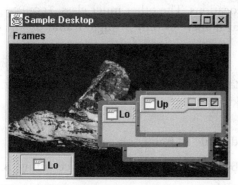

Figure 9-4. SampleDesktop layered frames and background image

Here we see the desktop with three frames, plus a fourth that has been iconified. The frames titled "Lo" are in a lower layer than the "Up" frame. No matter which frame is active or how the frames are arranged, the "Up" frame will always appear on top of the others. Frames in the same layer can be brought to the front of that layer by clicking on the frame. This display also shows the use of a background image (what good is a desktop if you can't put your favorite image on the background, right?). This image is added to a very low layer (the lowest possible integer, actually) to ensure that it is always painted behind anything else in the desktop. Figure 9-5 shows the same display after the frames have been "tiled."

Now, let's take a look at some of the code used to create this example. There are three primary classes:

SampleDesktop

This is the main class, which we chose to create as a JFrame that uses a JDesktopPane as its content pane. SampleDesktop has two inner classes.

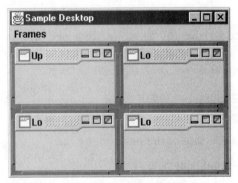

Figure 9-5. SampleDesktop with tiled frames

AddFrameAction is an **Action** used to add frames to the desktop. Recall from Chapter 3 that actions are a nice way to encapsulate functionality that you might want to invoke from multiple locations. The other inner class, **IconPolice**, is responsible for ensuring that if there is only a single frame on the desktop, it cannot be iconified.

SampleDesktopMgr

An extension of **DefaultDesktopManager** that keeps frames from being moved outside the bounds of the desktop.

TileAction

A generic action class that can be used to tile all frames on a given desktop.

Let's take a look at these classes piece by piece. The complete source listing is provided at the end of the chapter.

Setting Things Up

The first thing to look at is the **SampleDesktop** constructor:

```
public SampleDesktop(String title) {
    super(title);
    addWindowListener(new BasicWindowMonitor());

    // Create a desktop and set it as the content pane. Don't set the layered
    // pane, since it needs to hold the menubar too.
    desk = new JDesktopPane();
    setContentPane(desk);

    // Install our custom desktop manager
    desk.setDesktopManager(new SampleDesktopMgr());
    createMenuBar();
    loadBackgroundImage();
}
```

We set the frame's content pane to our new JDesktopPane. Since we won't be adding anything else to the body of the frame, this is a good idea. We could also have called getContentPane().add(desk), but as we discussed in Chapter 8, this just introduces an unnecessary extra level (the content pane would then be a JPanel holding only our JDesktopPane). The more important thing to avoid is calling setLayeredPane(desk). Remember, the layered pane is responsible for rendering the menubar too. If you did this, the menubar would still be drawn at the top of the frame, but your desktop would be filling the same space, allowing frames to be placed over the menu.

The createMenuBar() method called here just adds a few options to the frame's menubar. It uses instances of AddFrameAction for adding new frames (at "Up" and "Lo" levels), and it uses an instance of TileAction to support frame tiling. See the complete code listing at the end of this section for more details on this method.

The loadBackgroundImage() method looks like this:

```
protected void loadBackgroundImage() {
   ImageIcon icon = new ImageIcon("images/matterhorn.gif");
   JLabel l = new JLabel(icon);
   l.setBounds(0, 0, icon.getIconWidth(), icon.getIconHeight());

   desk.add(l, new Integer(Integer.MIN_VALUE));
}
```

This method just creates a large JLabel containing an image and adds this label to the lowest possible layer of the desktop. This ensures that nothing will ever be painted behind the background. In this example, we don't make any effort to resize or tile the background image, but it certainly could be done.

Adding Frames to the Desktop

The AddFrameAction class is an Action we've added to the menubar. When fired, AddFrameAction instantiates a JInternalFrame and adds it to the specified layer of the desktop. Here's the code for the actionPerformed() method of this class:

```
public void actionPerformed(ActionEvent ev) {
   JInternalFrame f = new JInternalFrame(name, true, true, true, true);
   f.addVetoableChangeListener(iconPolice);
   f.setBounds(0, 0, 120, 60);
   desk.add(f, layer);
}
```

The important thing to notice here is that we set the bounds, not just the size, of the new frame. If you don't specify a location (we've specified [0,0], the upper-left corner) for the frame, it won't appear on the desktop when you add it. Remember, there's no layout manager controlling the location of the components in a JDesktopPane.

Veto Power

In the previous code block, we added a VetoableChangeListener to each new frame we created. This listener is an instance of another inner class called Icon-Police. The purpose of this class is to ensure that the last frame on the desktop cannot be iconified. This may not be the most useful thing in the world to do, but it shows how to use JInternalFrame's constrained properties. Here's the code for this class.

```
class IconPolice implements VetoableChangeListener {
  public void vetoableChange(PropertyChangeEvent ev)
    throws PropertyVetoException {
    String name = ev.getPropertyName();
    if (name.equals(JInternalFrame.IS_ICON_PROPERTY)
    && (ev.getNewValue() == Boolean.TRUE)) {
      JInternalFrame[] frames = desk.getAllFrames();
      int count = frames.length;
      int nonicons = 0; // how many are not icons?
      for (int i=0; i<count; i++) {
        if (frames[i].isIcon() == false) {
          nonicons++;
        }
      }
      if (nonicons <= 1) {
        throw new PropertyVetoException("Invalid Iconification!", ev);
      }
    }
  }
}
```

If you haven't used constrained properties before, this code may look a little strange. The idea behind constrained properties is that before a property is changed, all registered listeners are given the opportunity to "veto" the change. This is done by throwing a PropertyVetoException from the veto-ableChange() method as we've done here.

Bounding the Frames

The next class to look at is our custom desktop manager called SampleDesk-topMgr. This class is an extension of DefaultDesktopManager which overrides the default implementation of setBoundsForComponent(). This is the method called any time the frame is moved or resized. The new implementation simply checks the new location of the frame to see if the requested change of bounds will result in part of the frame moving outside of the desktop. If so, it adjusts the coordinates so that the frame will only be moved to the edge of the desktop. The code for this method is included at the end of the chapter.

In order to correctly handle invalid bounds changes, we need to know if the frame is being moved or if it is being resized. This will affect how we adjust the frame's size and location in the setBoundsForComponent(). In this example, we do this by storing a client property* called RESIZING in each frame. In beginResizing-Frame(), we set this property to true. When endResizingFrame() is called, we switch it to false. Here's how we do this:

```
protected static final String RESIZING = "RESIZING";

public void beginResizingFrame(JComponent f, int dir) {
  f.putClientProperty(RESIZING, Boolean.TRUE);
}

public void endResizingFrame(JComponent f) {
  f.putClientProperty(RESIZING, Boolean.FALSE);
}
```

This class is included only as a useful example of the type of thing you might want to do with a desktop manager. If you don't mind frames being moved off the desktop, you can always just use DefaultDesktopManager (the default).

Moving Things Around

The last class in this example is called TileAction. Its job is to resize all of the frames and lay them out in a grid on a desktop. There are a few interesting things that take place in the actionPerformed() method of this class. First, we get all of the frames on the desktop and determine where each frame should be placed and how big it should be based on the size of the desktop and the total number of frames. For the details of how this is calculated, see the full code listing at the end of the chapter.

Next, we iterate over all of the frames on the desktop, deiconifying any iconified frames and then setting the size and location of each frame. Here's the block of code that does this work:

```
for (int i=0; i<rows; i++) {
  for (int j=0; j<cols && ((i*cols)+j<count); j++) {
    JInternalFrame f = allframes[(i*cols)+j];
    if ((f.isClosed() == false) && (f.isIcon() == true)) {
      try {
        f.setIcon(false);
```

---

* For an explanation of client properties, see Chapter 3.

```
        }
            catch (PropertyVetoException ex) {}
        }
        desk.getDesktopManager().resizeFrame(f, x, y, w, h);
        x += w;
    }
    y += h;        // start the next row
    x = 0;
}
```

We call setIcon() on the frame, rather than calling deiconifyFrame() on the
DesktopManager. We do this because deiconifyFrame() does not actually
change the state of the icon property in the frame, which can result in unexpected behavior down the road. Figure 9-6 shows the sequence of calls (only
certain significant calls are identified) made when we call setIcon(false).

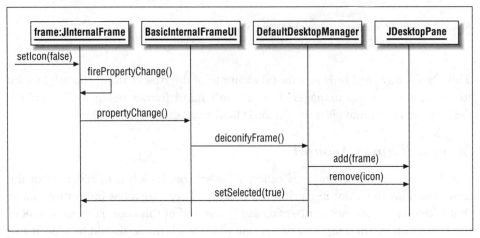

Figure 9-6. setIcon() sequence diagram

Note that the UI delegate is registered as a listener for property change events.
When it hears that a frame is being deiconified, it calls deiconifyFrame() on the
desktop manager. This object then adds the frame to its container (the desktop
pane in this case), removes the icon, and selects the newly added frame.

Once we've got the frame deiconified, we relocate and resize it by calling the
resizeFrame() method on the desktop manager:

```
        desk.getDesktopManager().resizeFrame(f, x, y, w, h);
```

We call this method (instead of just calling setBounds() on the frame) because it
validates the frame after setting its bounds.

Source Code

Here's the complete source code (three files) for this example:

```
// SampleDesktop.java
//
import javax.swing.*;
import java.awt.event.*;
import java.awt.*;
import java.util.*;
import java.beans.*;

// An example that shows how to do a few interesting things using
// JInternalFrames, JDesktopPane, and DesktopManager.
public class SampleDesktop extends JFrame {

  private JDesktopPane desk;
  private IconPolice iconPolice = new IconPolice();

  public SampleDesktop(String title) {
    super(title);
    addWindowListener(new BasicWindowMonitor());

    // Create a desktop and set it as the content pane. Don't set the layered
    // pane, since it needs to hold the menubar too.
    desk = new JDesktopPane();
    setContentPane(desk);

    // Install our custom desktop manager
    desk.setDesktopManager(new SampleDesktopMgr());

    createMenuBar();
    loadBackgroundImage();
  }

  // Create a menubar to show off a few things.
  protected void createMenuBar() {
    JMenuBar mb = new JMenuBar();
    JMenu menu = new JMenu("Frames");

    menu.add(new AddFrameAction(true)); // add "upper" frame
    menu.add(new AddFrameAction(false)); // add "lower" frame
    menu.add(new TileAction(desk)); // add tiling capability

    setJMenuBar(mb);
    mb.add(menu);
  }

  // Here we load a background image for our desktop.
  protected void loadBackgroundImage() {
```

```java
    ImageIcon icon = new ImageIcon("images/matterhorn.gif");
    JLabel l = new JLabel(icon);
    l.setBounds(0,0,icon.getIconWidth(),icon.getIconHeight());

    // Place the image in the lowest possible layer so nothing
    // can ever be painted under it.
    desk.add(l, new Integer(Integer.MIN_VALUE));
  }

// This class will add a new JInternalFrame when requested.
class AddFrameAction extends AbstractAction {
  public AddFrameAction(boolean upper) {
    super(upper ? "Add Upper Frame" : "Add Lower Frame");
    if (upper) {
      this.layer = new Integer(2);
      this.name = "Up";
    }
    else {
      this.layer = new Integer(1);
      this.name = "Lo";
    }
  }

  public void actionPerformed(ActionEvent ev) {
    JInternalFrame f = new JInternalFrame(name,true,true,true,true);
    f.addVetoableChangeListener(iconPolice);

    f.setBounds(0, 0, 120, 60);
    desk.add(f, layer);
  }

  private Integer layer;
  private String name;
}

// A simple vetoable change listener that insists that there is always at
// least one noniconified frame (just as an example of the vetoable
// properties).
class IconPolice implements VetoableChangeListener {
  public void vetoableChange(PropertyChangeEvent ev)
    throws PropertyVetoException {

    String name = ev.getPropertyName();
    if (name.equals(JInternalFrame.IS_ICON_PROPERTY)
    && (ev.getNewValue() == Boolean.TRUE)) {
      JInternalFrame[] frames = desk.getAllFrames();
      int count = frames.length;
      int nonicons = 0; // how many are not icons?
      for (int i=0; i<count; i++) {
```

```
              if (frames[i].isIcon() == false) {
                nonicons++;
              }
          }
          if (nonicons <= 1) {
            throw new PropertyVetoException("Invalid Iconification!", ev);
          }
        }
      }
    }

    // A simple test program.
    public static void main(String[] args) {
      SampleDesktop td = new SampleDesktop("Sample Desktop");

      td.setSize(300, 220);
      td.setVisible(true);
    }
}


// SampleDesktopMgr.java
//
import javax.swing.*;
import java.awt.event.*;
import java.awt.*;
import java.util.*;
import java.beans.*;

// A DesktopManager that keeps its frames inside the desktop.
public class SampleDesktopMgr extends DefaultDesktopManager {

  // We'll tag internal frames that are being resized using a client
  // property with the name RESIZING.  Used in setBoundsForFrame().
  protected static final String RESIZING = "RESIZING";

  public void beginResizingFrame(JComponent f, int dir) {
    f.putClientProperty(RESIZING, Boolean.TRUE);
  }

  public void endResizingFrame(JComponent f) {
    f.putClientProperty(RESIZING, Boolean.FALSE);
  }

  // This is called any time a frame is moved or resized.  This
  // implementation keeps the frame from leaving the desktop.
  public void setBoundsForFrame(JComponent f, int x, int y, int w, int h) {
    if (f instanceof JInternalFrame == false) {
      super.setBoundsForFrame(f, x, y, w, h); // only deal w/internal frames
    }
```

```
else {
  JInternalFrame frame = (JInternalFrame)f;

  // Figure out if we are being resized (otherwise it's just a move)
  boolean resizing = false;
  Object r = frame.getClientProperty(RESIZING);
  if (r != null && r instanceof Boolean) {
    resizing = ((Boolean)r).booleanValue();
  }

  JDesktopPane desk = frame.getDesktopPane();
  Dimension d = desk.getSize();

  // Nothing all that fancy below, just figuring out how to adjust
  // to keep the frame on the desktop.
  if (x < 0) {              // too far left?
    if (resizing)
      w += x;               // don't get wider!
    x=0;                    // flush against the left side
  }
  else {
    if (x+w>d.width) {      // too far right?
     if (resizing)
       w = d.width-x;       // don't get wider!
     else
       x = d.width-w;       // flush against the right side
    }
  }
  if (y < 0) {              // too high?
    if (resizing)
      h += y;               // don't get taller!
    y=0;                    // flush against the top
  }
  else {
    if (y+h > d.height) {   // too low?
      if (resizing)
        h = d.height - y;   // don't get taller!
      else
        y = d.height-h;     // flush against the bottom
    }
  }

  // Set 'em the way we like 'em
  super.setBoundsForFrame(f, x, y, w, h);
  }
 }
}
```

```java
// TileAction.java
//
import javax.swing.*;
import java.awt.event.*;
import java.awt.*;
import java.beans.*;

// An action that tiles all internal frames when requested.
public class TileAction extends AbstractAction {
  private JDesktopPane desk; // the desktop to work with

  public TileAction(JDesktopPane desk) {
    super("Tile Frames");
    this.desk = desk;
  }

  public void actionPerformed(ActionEvent ev) {

    // How many frames do we have?
    JInternalFrame[] allframes = desk.getAllFrames();
    int count = allframes.length;
    if (count == 0) return;

    // Determine the necessary grid size
    int sqrt = (int)Math.sqrt(count);
    int rows = sqrt;
    int cols = sqrt;
    if (rows*cols < count) {
      cols++;
      if (rows*cols < count) {
        rows++;
      }
    }

    // Define some initial values for size & location
    Dimension size = desk.getSize();

    int w = size.width/cols;
    int h = size.height/rows;
    int x = 0;
    int y = 0;

    // Iterate over the frames, deiconifying any iconified frames and then
    // relocating & resizing each
    for (int i=0; i<rows; i++) {
      for (int j=0; j<cols && ((i*cols)+j<count); j++) {
        JInternalFrame f = allframes[(i*cols)+j];
```

```
      if ((f.isClosed() == false) && (f.isIcon() == true)) {
        try {
          f.setIcon(false);
        }
        catch (PropertyVetoException ex) {}
      }

      desk.getDesktopManager().resizeFrame(f, x, y, w, h);
      x += w;
    }
  y += h; // start the next row
  x = 0;
  }
 }
}
```

10

Swing Dialogs

In most GUI applications, certain information needs to be displayed for a brief period of time, often just long enough for the user to read it and click "OK" or perhaps enter some information, such as a username and password. In AWT, such interactions were typically carried out using the Dialog class.

As you'd probably expect if you've already read Chapter 8, *Swing Containers*, Swing extends Dialog with a class called JDialog that implements the RootPaneContainer interface. This in itself is not a particularly exciting enhancement, though it does give you the ability to add a menu to a dialog box if you have some reason to do so.

The much more interesting new Swing feature is the JOptionPane class. This class makes creating simple dialog boxes extremely easy—in many cases requiring just one line of code. We'll look at both of these new classes in this chapter.

The JDialog Class

JDialog is the Swing replacement for its superclass, java.awt.Dialog. It provides the same key changes described in Chapter 8,[*] in the discussion of JWindow, JFrame, and JApplet—it uses a JRootPane as its container, and it provides default window-closing behavior. Since JDialog extends java.awt. Dialog, it has a heavyweight peer and is managed by the native windowing system. Figure 10-1 shows how JDialog fits into the class hierarchy.

---

[*] Certain parts of this chapter assume that you have read at least part of Chapter 8.

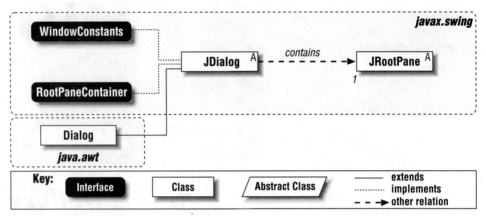

Figure 10-1. The JDialog class hierarchy

Properties

JDialog defines the properties and default values listed in Table 10-1. The contentPane, glassPane, JMenuBar, and layeredPane properties are taken from rootPane, which is set to a new JRootPane by the constructor.

Table 10-1. JDialog Properties

Property	Data Type	get	is	set	bound	Default Value
accessibleContext*	AccessibleContext	•				JDialog.Accessible-JDialog()
contentPane*	Container	•		•		from rootPane
defaultCloseOperation	int	•		•		HIDE_ON_CLOSE
glassPane*	Component	•		•		from rootPane
JMenuBar*	JMenuBar	•		•		null
layeredPane*	JLayeredPane	•		•		from rootPane
layout*	LayoutManager	•		•		BorderLayout
modal*	boolean		•	•		false
parent*	Container	•				SwingUtilities.get-SharedOwnerFrame()
rootPane*	JRootPane	•				JRootPane
title*	String	•		•		" "

See also the java.awt.Dialog class.

The defaultCloseOperation specifies how the dialog should react if its window is closed. The valid values come from the WindowConstants class, and the default operation is to hide the dialog.

The `layout` property is listed here because `JDialog` overrides `setLayout()` to throw an `Error` if an attempt is made to change the layout manager, rather than set the layout manager of the dialog's content pane.

The `parent` and `title` properties are inherited from `Component` and `Dialog`, respectively. Both are listed here because they can be set in the `JDialog` constructors.

The `modal` property is listed in this table because the `JDialog` constructors allow this property (inherited from `Dialog`) to be set. If a dialog is modal, no other window can be active while the dialog is displayed.

NOTE   Due to AWT 1.1 constraints, modal `JDialogs` are not allowed to contain heavyweight popup components. All popup components (`JComboBox`, `JPopupMenu`, or `JMenuBar`) will be forced to be lightweight. This restriction implies that heavyweight components should not be used in `JDialogs`, since any popups (lightweight) would be hidden by the heavyweight components.

Constructors

The following constructors are provided. Note that it is valid not to set a parent (by using the zero argument constructor, or by passing in `null` as the first argument to any of the others). The primary role of the parent `Frame` is to dispose of any windows (including dialogs) that it owns when the frame itself is disposed.

public JDialog()
> Creates a new dialog without a specified parent frame. An invisible owner frame is obtained from `SwingUtilities.getSharedOwnerFrame()`.

public JDialog(Frame parent)
> Creates a nonmodal dialog with the specified parent.

public JDialog(Frame parent, boolean modal)
> Creates a dialog with the specified parent and modal setting.

public JDialog(Frame parent, String title)
> Creates a nonmodal dialog with the given parent and title.

public JDialog(Frame parent, String title, boolean modal)
> Creates a dialog with the given parent, title, and modal setting.

Protected Fields

protected AccessibleContext accessibleContext
> Holds the dialog's accessible context.

protected JRootPane rootPane

Holds the dialog's root pane.

protected boolean rootPaneCheckingEnabled

Indicates whether the dialog will throw an `Error` if an attempt is made to add components directly to the dialog (rather than to its content pane) or to set the layout manager. By default, this is set to `true` once the dialog has been built. Subclasses could change this property if necessary.

Public Methods

public void setLocationRelativeTo(Component c)

Sets the dialog's location based on the location of the given component. The dialog will be centered within (if the component is larger than the dialog) or over (if the dialog is larger) the input component. If the specified component is not currently displayed, this method centers the dialog on the screen. Note that this method has no effect on the dialog's parent, even if the input component is a different `Frame`.

public void update(Graphics g)

This implementation of `update()` just calls `paint()`.

Protected Methods

protected void addImpl(Component comp, Object constraints, int index)

This method (called by `add()`) is overridden to throw an `Error` when an attempt is made to add a component directly to the `JDialog`. The only component allowed to be added is the `JRootPane`, which fills the entire frame (using `BorderLayout.CENTER`).

protected JRootPane createRootPane()

Called by the constructor to create a new `JRootPane` for the dialog.

protected void dialogInit()

Called by the constructor to enable events and set the root pane.

protected boolean isRootPaneCheckingEnabled()

Indicates whether the dialog will throw an `Error` if an attempt is made to add a component directly to the dialog.

protected void processWindowEvent(WindowEvent e)

This method allows the superclass implementation to process the event. It then handles window-closing events based on the current default close operation for the frame. For `HIDE_ON_CLOSE`, the frame is made invisible; for `DISPOSE_ON_CLOSE`, the frame is made invisible and disposed; and for `DO_NOTHING_ON_CLOSE`, nothing is done.

The JOptionPane Class

JOptionPane is a utility class used to create complex JDialog and JInternal-Frame (for use as lightweight dialogs) objects. Figure 10-2 shows where JOptionPane fits into the class hierarchy; Figure 10-3 shows JOptionPane in the three look-and-feels. It provides a range of convenient ways to create common popup dialog boxes, significantly reducing the amount of code you are required to write.

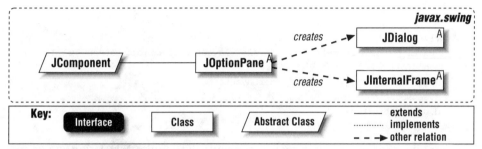

Figure 10-2. The JOptionPane class hierarchy

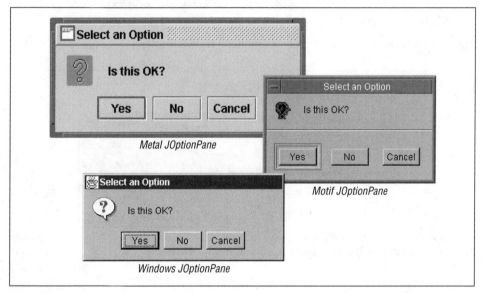

Figure 10-3. JOptionPanes (showing internal confirm dialogs) in the three look-and-feels

For example, to create a very simple dialog window with the text "Click OK after you read this" and an "OK" button without JOptionPane, you'd have to write something like the code that follows.

```
public void showSimpleDialog(JFrame f) {
  final JDialog d = new JDialog(f, "Click OK", true);
  d.setSize(200, 150);
  JLabel l = new JLabel("Click OK after you read this", JLabel.CENTER);
  d.getContentPane().setLayout(new BorderLayout());
  d.getContentPane().add(l, BorderLayout.CENTER);
  JButton b = new JButton("OK");
  b.addActionListener(new ActionListener() {
    public void actionPerformed(ActionEvent ev) {
      d.setVisible(false);
      d.dispose();
    }
  });
  JPanel p = new JPanel();        // flow layout will center button
  p.add(b);
  d.getContentPane().add(p, BorderLayout.SOUTH);
  d.setLocationRelativeTo(f);
  d.setVisible(true);
}
```

That's quite a lot of work for such a conceptually simple task. Using JOption-Pane, the above method can be replaced with:

```
JOptionPane.showMessageDialog(f, "Click OK after you read this",
  "Click OK", JOptionPane.INFORMATION_MESSAGE);
```

Figure 10-4 shows the dialogs created by these two examples.

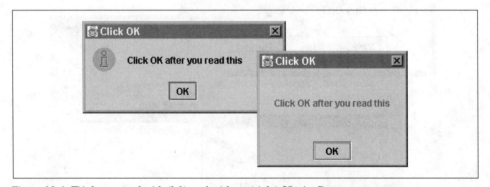

Figure 10-4. JDialogs created with (left) and without (right) JOptionPane

Properties

JOptionPane defines the properties listed in Table 10-2. The maxCharacters-PerLine property specifies the maximum number of characters the L&F should display on a single line. By default there is no limit. To change this value, you must subclass JOptionPane.[*]

Table 10-2. JOptionPane Properties

Property	Data Type	get	is	set	bound	Default Value
UI	JOptionPaneUI	•		•		from L&F
UIClassID*	String	•				"OptionPaneUI"
accessibleContext*	Accessible-Context	•				JOptionPane.Accessi-bleJOptionPane()
icon	Icon	•		•	•	null
initialSelectionValue	Object	•		•	•	null
initialValue	Object	•		•	•	null
inputValue	Object	•		•	•	null
maxCharactersPerLineCount	int	•				Integer.MAX_VALUE
message	Object	•		•	•	"JOptionPaneMessage"
messageType	int	•		•	•	PLAIN_MESSAGE
options	Object[]	•		•	•	null
optionType	int	•		•	•	DEFAULT_OPTION
selectionValues	Object[]	•		•	•	null
value	Object	•		•	•	null
wantsInput	boolean	•		•	•	false

See also properties from the JComponent class (Table 3-5).

The UI and UIClassID properties are defined as usual. Value specifies the value selected by the user. This will be set by the L&F when the user closes the dialog. WantsInput indicates whether or not the pane is expecting input (beyond just clicking a JButton) from the user.

The other properties (as well as more detail on value and wantsInput) will be discussed in detail throughout the chapter.

JOptionPane Structure

The dialogs created by JOptionPane are made up of four basic elements, some of which may be null. These elements are shown in Figure 10-5.

---

* If you subclass JOptionPane for this purpose, you'll need to construct instances of your subclass, rather than using the static methods (which will just construct JOptionPane objects, ignoring your subclass).

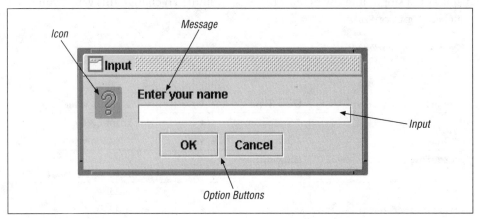

Figure 10-5. JOptionPane structure

The elements are:

An icon

> The icon usually provides some visual indication of the type of message being displayed. The icons used for the three Swing L&Fs are shown in Figure 10-7.

A message area

> The message area usually contains a simple textual message. However, it can actually be any arbitrary Object. We'll discuss how different types of objects are displayed later.

A data input area

> This area allows the user to enter a value or make a selection in response to the message. Typically, this will be a JTextField, JComboBox, or JList, but this is entirely up to the look-and-feel.

A set of options buttons

> For example, "OK" and "CANCEL."

Using JOptionPane

There are basically two ways to use JOptionPane. The simplest, demonstrated by the example at the beginning of this section, is to invoke one of the many static methods of the class. These methods all result in a JDialog or JInternalFrame being displayed immediately for the user. The methods return when the user clicks one of the buttons in the dialog.

The other way to use JOptionPane is to instantiate one using one of the many constructors and then call createDialog() or createInternalFrame(). These methods give you access to the JDialog or JInternalFrame and allow you to control when and where they are displayed. In most cases, the static methods will do everything you need.

It's worth noting here that JOptionPane extends JComponent. When you instantiate one, you've actually got a perfectly usable component, laid out with the structure we described earlier. If you wanted to, you could display the component directly, but it typically only makes sense to use it in a dialog or internal frame.

NOTE   All of the methods in JOptionPane that result in the creation of a JDialog create modal dialogs, where the methods that display JInternalFrames do not enforce modality. When the internal frame dialog is displayed, the other windows in your application are still able to receive focus.

Events

JOptionPane fires a PropertyChangeEvent any time one of the bound properties listed in Table 10-6 changes value. This is the mechanism used to communicate changes from the JOptionPane to the JOptionPaneUI, as well to the anonymous inner class listeners JOptionPane creates to close the dialog when the value or inputValue property is set by the L&F.

Constants

Tables 10-3 through 10-6 list the many constants defined in this class. They fall into four general categories:

Message Types
Used to specify what type of message is being displayed.

Option Types
Used to specify what options the user should be given.

Options
Used to specify which option the user selected.

Properties
Contains the string names of the pane's bound properties.

Table 10-3. JOptionPane Constants for Specifying the Desired Message Type

Constant	Type	Description
ERROR_MESSAGE	int	Used for error messages
INFORMATION_MESSAGE	int	Used for informational messages
PLAIN_MESSAGE	int	Used for arbitrary messages

Table 10-3. JOptionPane Constants for Specifying the Desired Message Type (continued)

Constant	Type	Description
QUESTION_MESSAGE	int	Used for question dialogs
WARNING_MESSAGE	int	Used for warning messages

Table 10-4. JOptionPane Constants for Specifying the User's Options

Constant	Type	Description[a]
DEFAULT_OPTION	int	"OK" button
OK_CANCEL_OPTION	int	"OK" and "Cancel" buttons
YES_NO_CANCEL_OPTION	int	"Yes." "No," and "Cancel" buttons
YES_NO_OPTION	int	"Yes" and "No" buttons

[a] The actual button labels are determined by the L&F. Currently, Swing L&Fs use the strings shown here. In future releases, these strings will be internationalized.

Table 10-5. JOptionPane Selected Option (and Other "Value") Constants

Constant	Type	Description
CANCEL_OPTION	int	"Cancel" button pressed
CLOSED_OPTION	int	No button pressed, e.g., when the window is closed
NO_OPTION	int	"No" button pressed
OK_OPTION	int	"OK" button pressed
YES_OPTION	int	"Yes" button pressed
UNINITIALIZED_VALUE	Object	Value indicating that no value has been set for the pane

Table 10-6. JOptionPane Bound Property Name Constants

Constant	Type	Description
ICON_PROPERTY	String	Displayed icon
INITIAL_SELECTION_VALUE_PROPERTY	String	Initially selected value
INITIAL_VALUE_PROPERTY	String	Initially focused button
INPUT_VALUE_PROPERTY	String	Value entered by the user
MESSAGE_PROPERTY	String	Message displayed to the user
MESSAGE_TYPE_PROPERTY	String	Type of message displayed
OPTION_TYPE_PROPERTY	String	Type of options provided
OPTIONS_PROPERTY	String	list of nondefault options provided
SELECTION_VALUES_PROPERTY	String	Selection values available to user
VALUE_PROPERTY	String	Option selected by user
WANTS_INPUT_PROPERTY	String	Whether or not pane requires input

Protected Fields

The following fields are available to subclasses of JOptionPane. They all correspond to properties in Table 10-2. It's generally a good idea to use the accessors for these properties, rather than accessing the fields directly.

protected transient Icon icon
protected transient Object initialSelectionValue
protected transient Object initialValue
protected transient Object inputValue
protected transient Object message
protected int messageType
protected transient Object options[]
protected int optionType
protected transient Object selectionValues[]
protected transient Object value
protected boolean wantsInput

Four Dialog Types

JOptionPane provides static methods for creating four types of dialogs.[*] Each of these types can automatically be enclosed in either a JDialog or a JInternal-Frame. The four types are:

Input Dialog
  Provides some way (typically a JTextField, JComboBox, or JList) for the user to enter data. Always includes two buttons: "OK" and "Cancel."

Confirm Dialog
  Asks a user to confirm some information. Includes buttons such as "Yes" and "No" or "OK" and "Cancel."

Message Dialog
  Displays information to the user. Includes a single "OK" button.

Option Dialog
  Displays arbitrary data to the user. May contain any set of buttons for the user to choose from.

The first three types are somewhat restrictive, making it easy to create the most common types of dialogs. Option Dialog is more flexible, giving you complete control. Also, remember that you can instantiate JOptionPane objects directly. These objects will be Option Dialogs, again allowing you complete control.

---

[*] Note that these dialog types are not different Java classes. They simply represent common types of dialog boxes used in GUI applications.

Constructors

public JOptionPane()

public JOptionPane(Object message)

public JOptionPane(Object message, int messageType)

public JOptionPane(Object message, int messageType, int optionType)

public JOptionPane(Object message, int messageType, int optionType, Icon icon)

public JOptionPane(Object message, int messageType, int optionType, Icon icon,
    Object[] options)

public JOptionPane(Object message, int messageType, int optionType, Icon icon,
    Object[] options, Object initialValue)

These constructors allow JOptionPanes to be created and held over time
(unlike the static methods listed next, which create panes that are used only
once). We'll discuss the parameters in detail shortly.

Static Dialog Display Methods

Here's a complete list of the static "show" methods used to create and display
JDialog and JInternalFrame objects that contain JOptionPanes. All of the
information listed here is summarized in Table 10-7.

public static String showInputDialog(Object message)

public static String showInputDialog(Component parentComponent, Object message)

public static String showInputDialog(Component parentComponent, Object message,
    String title, int messageType)

public static Object showInputDialog(Component parentComponent,
    Object message, String title, int messageType, Icon icon, Object[] selectionValues,
    Object initialSelectionValue)

public static String showInternalInputDialog(Component parentComponent, Object message)

public static String showInternalInputDialog(Component parentComponent, Object message,
    String title, int messageType)

public static Object showInternalInputDialog(Component parentComponent,
    Object message, String title, int messageType, Icon icon, Object[] selectionValues,
    Object initialSelectionValue)

public static void showMessageDialog(Component parentComponent, Object message)

public static void showMessageDialog(Component parentComponent, Object message,
    String title, int messageType)

public static void showMessageDialog(Component parentComponent, Object message,
    String title, int messageType, Icon icon)

public static void showInternalMessageDialog(Component parentComponent,
    Object message)

public static void showInternalMessageDialog(Component parentComponent,
    Object message, String title, int messageType)

public static void showInternalMessageDialog(Component parentComponent,
    Object message, String title, int messageType, Icon icon)

public static int showConfirmDialog(Component parentComponent, Object message)
public static int showConfirmDialog(Component parentComponent, Object message,
    String title, int optionType)
public static int showConfirmDialog(Component parentComponent, Object message,
    String title, int optionType, int messageType)
public static int showConfirmDialog(Component parentComponent, Object message,
    String title, int optionType, int messageType, Icon icon)
public static int showInternalConfirmDialog(Component parentComponent, Object message)
public static int showInternalConfirmDialog(Component parentComponent, Object message,
    String title, int optionType)
public static int showInternalConfirmDialog(Component parentComponent, Object message,
    String title, int optionType, int messageType)
public static int showInternalConfirmDialog(Component parentComponent, Object message,
    String title, int optionType, int messageType, Icon icon)

public static int showOptionDialog(Component parentComponent, Object message,
    String title, int optionType, int messageType, Icon icon, Object[] options,
    Object initialValue)
public static int showInternalOptionDialog(Component parentComponent, Object message,
    String title, int optionType, int messageType, Icon icon, Object[] options,
    Object initialValue)

Dialog Creation Method Parameters

Table 10-7 summarizes the parameter types, names, and default values for
JOptionPane's various constructors and static dialog creation methods. The
parameters are listed (top to bottom) in the order they occur in the constructors
and methods. Parameters that do not apply to a given column are left blank. The
vertical brackets indicate the required grouping of parameters (for example, when
creating a Message Dialog, you can specify the first two parameters, the first four
parameters, or all five). In the rest of this section, we'll explain how each of these
parameters affects the dialog's display. After that, we'll show some examples of
dialogs and internal frames created using specific JOptionPane methods and
constructors.

Component parentComponent
    For JDialogs, this is the dialog's parent. The dialog will be centered on this
    component when it is displayed. For JInternalFrames, this parameter is used
    to find a container for the frame. If parentComponent is a JDesktopPane,
    the internal frame is added to its MODAL_LAYER. Otherwise, an attempt is
    made to see if parentComponent is contained (possibly recursively) by a

Table 10-7. JOptionPane Constructor/Dialog Creation Method Parameters, Defaults, and Return Types

Parameter Type	Parameter Name	JOptionPane constructors	InputDialog[a]	ConfirmDialog	MessageDialog	OptionDialog
Component	parentComponent		*Required*	*Required*	*Required*	*Required*
Object	message	"JOptionPane Message"	*Required*	*Required*	*Required*	*Required*
String	title		"Input"	"Select an Option"	"Message"	*Required*
int	optionType	PLAIN_MESSAGE[b]		YES_NO_CANCEL_OPTION		*Required*
int	messageType	DEFAULT_OPTION[b]	QUESTION_MESSAGE	QUESTION_MESSAGE	INFORMATION_MESSAGE	*Required*
Icon	icon	null	null	null	null	*Required*
Object[]	selectionValues		null			
Object	initialSelectionValue		null			
Object[]	options	null				*Required*
Object	initialValue	null				*Required*
Return Type			String/Object	int	void	int

[a] There's one static method that doesn't quite fit this table: showInputDialog(Object message). This version does not require a parentComponent (it calls the static getRootFrame() method to get one). It's not clear why this one exception was made for *Input Dialogs* only, but it's there.

[b] The order of the optionType and messageType parameters for the constructors is reversed—messageType must come first.

JDesktopPane. If so, the frame is added to the containing desktop's MODAL_ LAYER. If neither of these apply, the parentComponent's parent (if it has no parent, a RuntimeException will be thrown) is used as the container, and the frame is added with BorderLayout.CENTER constraints.

This last option, while supported, will rarely give you what you're looking for. Since the dialog is added with BorderLayout constraints, your parentComponent's parent should be using a BorderLayout, or you may have various problems (e.g., GridBagLayout throws an exception if you add a component with constraints, other than a GridBagConstraints object). Even if you've got a container with a BorderLayout, remember that the entire center of the container will be filled with the dialog, causing it to be resized as necessary, possibly to an unusable size. All of this leads to a simple rule: to make your life easier, only create internal dialogs within JDesktopPanes. See the example at the end of the chapter to see how to do this when you're not already using a JDesktopPane in your GUI.

Object message

This is the message to be displayed in the dialog. Typically, this will be a simple String object. However, the methods allow this to be any arbitrary object. It's up to the look-and-feel to determine how to handle other objects. Typically (for the Swing L&Fs), if the message is a Component, it is displayed as-is. If it is an Icon, it is wrapped in a JLabel and displayed. If message is an Object[], the elements of the array are recursively expanded (applying these same rules) and added to form a vertical column. Any other types passed in are added as strings by calling the object's toString() method.

Note that the flexibility of this parameter allows you to use any arbitrary component (including containers with many other components inside) as the "message" for the dialog. Figure 10-6 shows an internal dialog that was created by passing in a custom calendar component as the message parameter.

Figure 10-6. Custom component in a JOptionPane internal dialog

String title

This parameter contains the string that will appear on the dialog's titlebar. Note that this parameter does not apply to the JOptionPane constructors, since JOptionPane itself does not have a titlebar.

int messageType

This parameter indicates the type of dialog to create. The possible values are WARNING_MESSAGE, QUESTION_MESSAGE, INFO_MESSAGE, ERROR_MESSAGE, and PLAIN_MESSAGE. It's up to the L&F to determine how to interpret these options. In the Swing L&Fs, the value of the parameter determines the icon displayed in the dialog. Figure 10-7 shows the various icons for the different look-and-feels. There is no icon associated with PLAIN_MESSAGE. The icon can be changed by passing in a non-null value for the icon parameter (see below).

int optionType

This parameter determines what options the user will be given for exiting the dialog. This parameter only applies to Confirm Dialogs, Option Dialogs, and JOptionPane constructors. As a rule, Input Dialogs will have an "OK" button and a "Cancel" button. Message Dialogs only have an "OK" button. For the other types of dialogs, this parameter may be one of these values: DEFAULT_OPTION, YES_NO_OPTION, YES_NO_CANCEL_OPTION, or OK_CANCEL_OPTION. Again, it's up to the L&F to determine how to interpret these, but you can confidently assume that YES_NO_OPTION will provide a "Yes" and a "No" button, and so on. The DEFAULT_OPTION value provides a single "OK" button. If you want a different set of buttons, you need to use an Option Dialog, which allows you to specify any arbitrary set of buttons via the options parameter (below).

Icon icon

This parameter specifies the Icon to display in the dialog, allowing you to further customize the display. If it is set to null, the icon is determined based on the message type. To have no icon displayed, pass PLAIN_MESSAGE as the messageType. Figure 10-7 shows the default icons used by the different L&Fs.

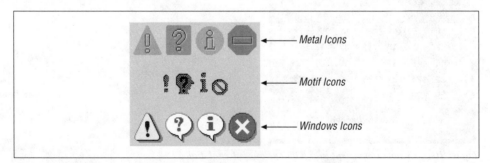

Figure 10-7. JOptionPane icons (Warning, Question, Info, and Error)

Object[] selectionValues

This parameter is used only in Input dialogs. It allows you to specify a set of selections for the user to choose from. As you might expect, it's up to the L&F to determine how to supply these options to the user. The Swing L&Fs place the selections in a JComboBox unless there are 20 or more, in which case a scrolling JList (with 10 visible rows and a selection mode of MULTIPLE_INTERVAL_SELECTION) is used. In either case, the array of objects is passed directly to the list or combo box for interpretation. See the documentation on these components for details on how different object types are interpreted. If the *selectionValues* parameter is null, a JTextField is used for data entry.

Object initialSelectionValue

This parameter also applies only to Input Dialogs. It allows you to specify which of the options supplied in the selectionValues parameter should be initially selected.

Object[] options

This parameter applies to JOptionPane constructors and Option Dialogs only. It allows you to specify the set of option buttons the user will see. Using null here indicates that the optionType should be used to determine the set of buttons displayed. Useful parameter types for this parameter are String and Icon. These will used to construct JButton objects. Components passed in via this parameter are added as-is. This is generally not useful, since no event listeners will be added to them by the Swing L&Fs. In a future release, I hope the input of JButtons (at least) will be supported by having the L&F add an action listener (like the one it adds to the JButtons it creates) to any input buttons. Any other input objects are used to create JButtons with a label generated by calling toString() on the object.

Object initialValue

This parameter (also available for constructors and Option Dialogs only) allows you to specify a default option from the list supplied by the options parameter. Note that this *only* works if the options parameter is non-null. This value determines which button has initial focus. In addition, if the initial value is a JButton, it will be set as the default button on the root pane that contains it (if there is one). For example, specifying {"Retry", "Abort"} as the options and "Abort" as the initialValue will cause the "Abort" button to have initial focus and be defined as the default button.

Simple Examples

The following are a few examples that show some of things you can do with JOptionPane static methods and constructors.

Here's an input dialog with more than 20 selection values. This results in the creation of a JList (Figure 10-8):

```
JOptionPane.showInputDialog(f, "Please choose a name", "Example 1",
    JOptionPane.QUESTION_MESSAGE, null, new Object[] {
    "Audrey", "Brenda", "Connie", "Dave", "David", "Haji", "Holly", "Jake",
    "Jill", "Josh", "Kathy", "Lauren", "Marilyn", "Nicole", "Peggy", "Rex",
    "Rick", "Robin", "Shannon", "Stephanie", "Steve", "Tahlaad"}, "Audrey");
```

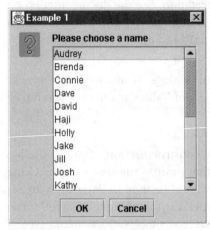

Figure 10-8. Input dialog (JList)

Here's another input dialog. This time, we don't provide any selection values, so we get a JTextField. The default value we supply is entered in the field when it comes up (Figure 10-9):

```
JOptionPane.showInputDialog(f, "Please enter your name", "Example 2",
    JOptionPane.QUESTION_MESSAGE, null, null, "Shannon");
```

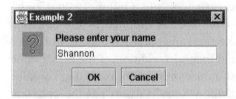

Figure 10-9. Input dialog (JTextField)

Next, we'll try a message dialog with a custom icon (Figure 10-10):

```
JOptionPane.showMessageDialog(f, "Have a nice day.", "Example 3",
    JOptionPane.INFORMATION_MESSAGE, new ImageIcon("images/smile.gif"));
```

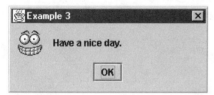

Figure 10-10. Message dialog with a custom Icon

Here's a very simple confirm dialog (Figure 10-11):

```
JOptionPane.showConfirmDialog(f, "Are you sure?", "Example 4",
    JOptionPane.YES_NO_CANCEL_OPTION);
```

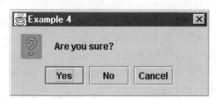

Figure 10-11. Confirm dialog

Next, we'll get a little fancy and create an internal frame dialog with custom option buttons (Figure 10-12):

```
JOptionPane.showInternalOptionDialog(desk, "Please select a color",
    "Example 5", JOptionPane.DEFAULT_OPTION, JOptionPane.QUESTION_MESSAGE,
    null, new Object[] {"Red", "Green", "Blue"}, "Blue");
```

Figure 10-12. Internal frame dialog with custom buttons

Finally, let's use a JOptionPane constructor and place the new pane inside a regular Swing container. This is a strange thing to do, but it's perfectly valid (Figure 10-13):

```
JFrame f = new JFrame();
Container c = f.getContentPane();
c.setLayout(new BorderLayout());
JOptionPane op = new JOptionPane("Stop!", JOptionPane.WARNING_MESSAGE);
JPanel p = new JPanel(new FlowLayout());
p.add(op);
```

```
c.add(p);
c.add(new JLabel("Example 6", JLabel.CENTER), BorderLayout.NORTH);
```

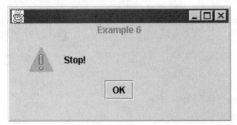

Figure 10-13. A JOptionPane inside a Swing container

Getting the Results

Now that we've seen how to create all sorts of useful dialog boxes, it's time to take a look at how to retrieve information about the user's interaction with the dialog while it was open. Table 10-7 showed the return types of the various methods. Here's a quick summary of what the returned values mean.

Input Dialogs

The versions that do not take an array of selection values return a String. This is the data entered by the user. The methods that do take an array of selection values return an Object reflecting the selected option.[*] In any case, if the user presses the "Cancel" button, null is returned.

Confirm Dialogs

These methods return an int reflecting the button pressed by the user. The possible values are YES_OPTION, NO_OPTION, CANCEL_OPTION, and OK_OPTION. CLOSED_OPTION is returned if the user closes the window without selecting anything.

Message Dialogs

These methods have void return types.

Option Dialogs

If no options are specified, this method returns one of the constant values YES_OPTION, NO_OPTION, CANCEL_OPTION, and OK_OPTION. If options are explicitly defined, the return value gives the index into the array of options that matches the button selected by the user. CLOSED_OPTION is returned if the user closes the window without selecting anything.

Getting a value from a JOptionPane you've instantiated directly is also very simple. The value is obtained by calling the pane's getValue() method. This

---

[*] Unfortunately, if you supply 20 or more selections, the Swing L&Fs create a JList that allows multiple selections. Only the first user selection is returned by the static methods.

method returns an `Integer` value using the same rules as those described above for Option Dialogs with two small variations. Instead of returning an `Integer` containing `CLOSED_OPTION`, `getValue()` returns `null` if the dialog is closed. Also, if you call `getValue()` before the user has made a selection (or before displaying the dialog at all, for that matter), it will return `UNINITIALIZED_VALUE`. To get the value of user input (from a `JTextField`, `JComboBox`, or `JList`), call `getInputValue()`. This will return the entered `String` or the selected `Object` (which may also be a `String`).

The following example contains code to retrieve results from `JOptionPanes`.

A Comparison: Constructors vs. Static Methods

We've talked quite a bit about the two fundamental ways to create dialogs using `JOptionPane`: instantiate a `JOptionPane` and ask it to put itself into a `JDialog` or `JInternalFrame`, which you then display; or create and display the dialog in a single step by invoking one of the many static "show" methods.

The basic trade-off is this: using the static methods is a bit easier, but using a constructor allows you to hold on to and reuse the `JOptionPane` instance, a useful feature if the pane is fairly complex, and you expect to be displaying it frequently (if you use the static methods, the option pane gets re-created each time you call). The significance of this difference depends largely on the complexity of the pane.

The following example shows the differences between using `JOptionPane`'s static methods and its constructors. It allows both internal and noninternal dialogs to be created, showing how each is done.

```java
// OptPaneComparison.java
//
import javax.swing.*;
import java.awt.event.*;
import java.awt.*;
import java.beans.*;

public class OptPaneComparison extends JFrame {

  public static void main(String[] args) {
    JFrame f = new OptPaneComparison("Enter your name");
    f.setVisible(true);
  }

  public OptPaneComparison(final String message) {
    addWindowListener(new BasicWindowMonitor());

    final int msgType = JOptionPane.QUESTION_MESSAGE;
    final int optType = JOptionPane.OK_CANCEL_OPTION;
    final String title = message;
```

```
    setSize(350, 200);

    // Create a desktop for internal frames
    final JDesktopPane desk = new JDesktopPane();
    setContentPane(desk);

    // Add a simple menubar
    JMenuBar mb = new JMenuBar();
    setJMenuBar(mb);

    JMenu menu = new JMenu("Dialog");
    JMenu imenu = new JMenu("Internal");
    mb.add(menu);
    mb.add(imenu);
    final JMenuItem construct = new JMenuItem("Constructor");
    final JMenuItem stat = new JMenuItem("Static Method");
    final JMenuItem iconstruct = new JMenuItem("Constructor");
    final JMenuItem istat = new JMenuItem("Static Method");
    menu.add(construct);
    menu.add(stat);
    imenu.add(iconstruct);
    imenu.add(istat);

    // Create our JOptionPane.  We're asking for input, so we call setWantsInput.
    // Note that we cannot specify this via constructor parameters.
    optPane = new JOptionPane(message, msgType, optType);
    optPane.setWantsInput(true);

    // Add a listener for each menu item that will display the appropriate
    // dialog/internal frame
    construct.addActionListener(new ActionListener() {
      public void actionPerformed(ActionEvent ev) {

        // Create and display the dialog
        JDialog d = optPane.createDialog(desk, title);
        d.setVisible(true);

        respond(getOptionPaneValue());
      }
    });

    stat.addActionListener(new ActionListener() {
      public void actionPerformed(ActionEvent ev) {
        String s = JOptionPane.showInputDialog
          (desk, message, title, msgType);
        respond(s);
      }
    });
```

```
iconstruct.addActionListener(new ActionListener() {
  public void actionPerformed(ActionEvent ev) {

    // Create and display the dialog
    JInternalFrame f = optPane.createInternalFrame(desk, title);
    f.setVisible(true);

    // Listen for the frame to close before getting the value from it.
    f.addPropertyChangeListener(new PropertyChangeListener() {
      public void propertyChange(PropertyChangeEvent ev) {
        if ((ev.getPropertyName().equals
        (JInternalFrame.IS_CLOSED_PROPERTY))
        && (ev.getNewValue() == Boolean.TRUE)) {
          respond(getOptionPaneValue());
        }
      }
    });
  }
});

istat.addActionListener(new ActionListener() {
  public void actionPerformed(ActionEvent ev) {
    String s = JOptionPane.showInternalInputDialog
      (desk, message, title, msgType);
    respond(s);
  }
});
}


// This method gets the selected value from the option pane and resets the
// value to null so we can use it again.
protected String getOptionPaneValue() {

  // Get the result . . .
  Object o = optPane.getInputValue();
  String s = "<Unknown>";
  if (o != null)
    s = (String)o;

  Object val = optPane.getValue(); // which button?

  // Check for cancel button or closed option
  if (val != null) {
    if (val instanceof Integer) {
      int intVal = ((Integer)val).intValue();
      if((intVal == JOptionPane.CANCEL_OPTION) ||
        (intVal == JOptionPane.CLOSED_OPTION))
        s = "<Cancel>";
    }
  }
```

```
      // A little trick to clean the text field. It is only updated if the initial
      // value gets changed. To do this, we'll set it to a dummy value ("X")
      // and then clear it.
      optPane.setInitialValue("X");
      optPane.setInitialValue("");

      return s;
    }

  protected void respond(String s) {
    if (s == null)
      System.out.println("Never mind.");
    else
      System.out.println("You entered: " + s);
  }


  protected JOptionPane optPane;
}
```

The user interface for this example (Figure 10-14) is simple. We provide two menus, one to create standard dialogs, and one to create internal frame dialogs. Each menu allows us to create a dialog using the JOptionPane we're holding (created via a constructor) or create a new dialog with a static method call.

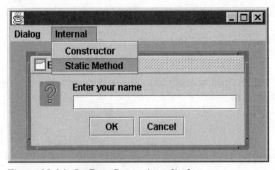

Figure 10-14. OptPaneComparison display

There are a few details here worth pointing out. First, notice that we called setWantsInput(true) on our JOptionPane object. This is how we create a pane that looks like those created by the showInputDialog() methods. Without this call, there would not be a text field in our dialog.

The next point of interest is the way we handle the JInternalFrame we get from the JOptionPane. Since this is just an ordinary internal frame, we don't have any simple way to block, waiting for input. Instead, we add a property change listener to the frame, which will wait for the frame to be closed. Alternatively we could have added a property change listener to the `JOptionPane` and listened for the `INPUT_VALUE_PROPERTY`.

One last thing to point out is the little trick at the end of our `getOption-PaneValue()` method. We want to clear the value from the text field so that it won't show up there the next time we use the same option pane. Since we have no way of getting to the text field directly, and no way of explicitly clearing the value, we resort to making two changes to the initial value of the field. The reason we have to make two calls is that the text field only gets cleared when the `initialValue` property *changes*. If we just set it to an empty string every time, that wouldn't be considered a change, so the field wouldn't be updated.

In this example, we held on to the `JOptionPane` object. You might be tempted to hold on to the `JDialog` you get from the pane instead. This is not generally a good idea. The `JOptionPane` "disposes" the dialog when it closes, meaning that, among other things, its peer is destroyed. It's much easier to reuse the `JOptionPane`. Similar difficulties arise if you try to reuse the `JInternalFrame` created by the `JOptionPane`. Again, reusing the `JOptionPane` is the preferred strategy.

Non-Static Methods

Most of the methods defined in `JOptionPane` are static (or accessors for the pane's properties). Here are the only other nonstatic methods in the class:

public JDialog createDialog(Component parentComponent, String title)
> Creates a new `JDialog` containing this `JOptionPane`. The dialog's parent will be the specified component, and the input string will be used as the window's title. The dialog will be centered on the input parent component. This method is used by all of the static "show dialog" methods, and it is also the method to use when you construct a `JOptionPane` directly and want to use it in a dialog.

public JInternalFrame createInternalFrame(Component parentComponent, String title)
> Creates a new `JInternalFrame` containing this `JOptionPane`. The frame's parent will be the specified component, and the input string will be used as the frame's title. The parent component will be used to search (up the parent chain) for an enclosing `JDesktopPane`. See the detailed discussion of the `parentComponent` parameter that appears earlier in this chapter. This method is used by all of the static "show internal frame" methods; it is the method to use when you construct a `JOptionPane` directly and want to use it in an internal frame.

public void selectInitialValue()

Selects the initial value, causing the default button to receive focus. If you are going to use a JOptionPane to display a dialog multiple times, you should call this method before making the dialog visible.

public void updateUI()

Indicates that the L&F has changed.

Miscellaneous Static Methods

In addition to all of the static methods defined for showing dialogs (which we'll get to next), several other static methods are also defined:

public static Frame getFrameForComponent(Component parentComponent)

Searches up the parent hierarchy of the given Component until it finds a Frame, which it returns. If it encounters a null parent (or if the input component is null), it returns the result of a call to getRootFrame().

public static JDesktopPane getDesktopPaneForComponent(Component parentComponent)

Searches up the parent hierarchy of the given Component until it finds a JDesktopPane, which it returns. If it encounters a null parent (or if the input component is null), it returns null.

public static void setRootFrame(Frame newRootFrame)

Sets a default Frame to be used when an attempt is made to create a dialog, and a parent Frame cannot be found.

public static Frame getRootFrame()

Returns the value set by setRootFrame(). The value is initially null.

Using Internal Frame Dialogs with JDesktopPane

In order to get the best results when using internal frame dialogs created by JOptionPane, the dialogs need to be placed in a JDesktopPane. However, this may not seem convenient if your application does not use a JDesktopPane. In this section, we'll show how you can easily adapt your application to use a JDesktopPane so that you can use internal frame dialogs.

Recall that JDesktopPane has a null layout manager, leaving the management of the location of its contents up to the DesktopManager and the user. This makes JDesktopPane a poor choice when you just need a container in which to build your main application. As a result, if you want to have an internal frame dialog displayed in a "normal" container, you need a solution that gives you the features of both JDesktopPane and a more layout-friendly container.

This is actually a pretty straightforward goal to achieve. You need to create a JDesktopPane and add your application container to it, so that it fills an entire layer of the desktop. When there are no internal frames displayed, this will look the same as if you were displaying the application container alone. The benefit is that when you need to add an internal frame dialog, you've got a desktop to add it to.

Here's a simple example that shows how this works. It also shows how you can make sure your container will fill the desktop, even if the desktop changes size (since there's no layout manager, this won't happen automatically).

```java
// DialogDesktop.java
//
import javax.swing.*;
import java.awt.event.*;
import java.awt.*;

// A frame that can easily support internal frame dialogs.
public class DialogDesktop extends JFrame {

  public DialogDesktop(String title) {
    super(title);
    addWindowListener(new BasicWindowMonitor());

    final JDesktopPane desk = new JDesktopPane();
    setContentPane(desk);

    // Create our "real" application container; use any layout manager we want.
    final JPanel p = new JPanel(new GridBagLayout());

    // Listen for desktop resize events so we can resize p. This will ensure that
    // our container always fills the entire desktop.
    desk.addComponentListener(new ComponentAdapter() {
      public void componentResized(ComponentEvent ev) {
        Dimension deskSize = desk.getSize();
        p.setBounds(0, 0, deskSize.width, deskSize.height);
        p.validate();
      }
    });

    // Add our application panel to the desktop. Any layer below the MODAL_LAYER
    // (where the dialogs will appear) is fine. We'll just use the default in
    // this example.
    desk.add(p);

    // Fill out our app with a few buttons that create dialogs
    JButton input = new JButton("Input");
    JButton confirm = new JButton("Confirm");
    JButton message = new JButton("Message");
```

```
    p.add(input);
    p.add(confirm);
    p.add(message);

    input.addActionListener(new ActionListener() {
      public void actionPerformed(ActionEvent ev) {
        JOptionPane.showInternalInputDialog(desk, "Enter Name");
      }
    });

    confirm.addActionListener(new ActionListener() {
      public void actionPerformed(ActionEvent ev) {
        JOptionPane.showInternalConfirmDialog(desk, "Is this OK?");
      }
    });

    message.addActionListener(new ActionListener() {
      public void actionPerformed(ActionEvent ev) {
        JOptionPane.showInternalMessageDialog(desk, "The End");
      }
    });
  }

  // A simple test program
  public static void main(String[] args) {
    DialogDesktop td = new DialogDesktop("Desktop");
    td.setSize(350, 250);
    td.setVisible(true);
  }
}
```

Most of this class is just a sample program proving that the strategy works. The key ideas come early on in the code. The first important thing is the creation of a JDesktopPane, which we set as the frame's content pane. We then add the "real" application container to the desktop. The last important detail is the little ComponentListener we add to the desktop pane to ensure that our main application container gets resized when the size of the desktop changes.

11

Specialty Panes and Layout Managers

With all the new Swing components, you might expect to see a few new layout managers to help place them, and you wouldn't be disappointed. The Swing package includes several new layout managers. However, most of these managers are meant for use with specific containers—JScrollPane has its own ScrollPaneLayout manager, for example. The Swing package also includes several new convenience containers that handle varied things such as scrolling and tabs. We'll be taking a close look at these containers and their associated layout managers in this chapter. Figure 11-1 shows the class hierarchy of Swing's specialty panes and layout managers.

The JSplitPane Class

The JSplitPane component allows you to place two (and only two) components side by side in a single pane. You can separate the pane horizontally or vertically, and the user can adjust this separator graphically at runtime. You have probably seen such a split pane approach in things like a file chooser or a news reader. The top or left side holds the list of directories or news subject lines, while the bottom side (or right side) contains the files or body of the currently selected directory or article. To get started, Figure 11-2 shows a simple split pane example that shows two text areas and horizontal split. You can adjust the width of the split by grabbing the divider and sliding it left or right.

Even with the code required to make the text areas behave (more on that in Chapter 19, *Text 101*), this example is still fairly simple. If you are looking to get up and running with a quick split pane, this is the way to go:

```
// SimpleSplitPane.java
// A quick test of the JSplitPane class.
//
```

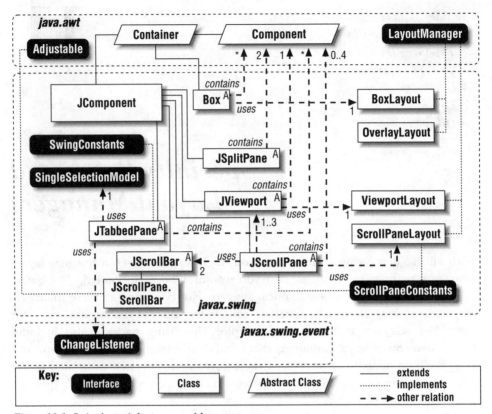

Figure 11-1. Swing's specialty panes and layout managers

```
import java.awt.*;
import java.awt.event.*;
import javax.swing.*;

public class SimpleSplitPane extends JFrame {

    static String sometext = "This is a simple text string that is long enough " +
        "to wrap over a few lines in the simple demo we're about to build.  We'll " +
        "put two text areas side by side in a split pane.";

    public SimpleSplitPane() {
        super("Simple SplitPane Frame");
        setSize(450, 200);
        addWindowListener(new BasicWindowMonitor());

        JTextArea jt1 = new JTextArea(sometext);
        JTextArea jt2 = new JTextArea(sometext);
```

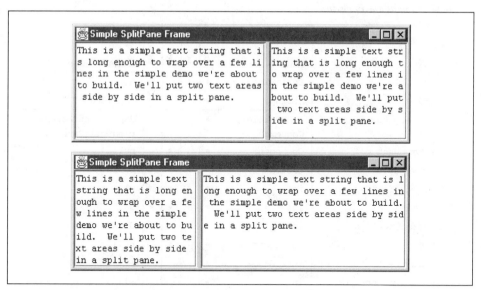

Figure 11-2. Simple JSplitPane with two text areas

```
    // Make sure our text boxes do line wrapping and have reasonable
    // minimum sizes.
    jt1.setLineWrap(true);
    jt2.setLineWrap(true);
    jt1.setMinimumSize(new Dimension(150, 150));
    jt2.setMinimumSize(new Dimension(150, 150));
    jt1.setPreferredSize(new Dimension(250, 200));
    JSplitPane sp = new JSplitPane(JSplitPane.HORIZONTAL_SPLIT, jt1, jt2);
    getContentPane().add(sp, BorderLayout.CENTER);
  }

  public static void main(String args[]) {
    SimpleSplitPane ssb = new SimpleSplitPane();
    ssb.setVisible(true);
  }
}
```

Properties

Table 11-1 shows the properties contained in the JSplitPane class. The properties of JSplitPane center primarily around the divider. You can get and set its size, location, and orientation, and its minimum and maximum bounds. Of particular interest is the oneTouchExpandable property. If this value is set to true, the UI should provide a component that can quickly collapse or expand the divider. For your programming convenience, you'll find four component properties available. Note that the component properties bottomComponent and rightComponent refer to the same object, as do the topComponent and leftComponent. This

Table 11-1. JSplitPane Properties

Property	Data Type	get	is	set	bound	Default Value
UI	SplitPaneUI	•			•	from L&F
UIClassID*	String	•				"SplitPaneUI"
accessibleContext*	Accessible-Context	•				JSplitPane.Accessi-bleJSplitPane()
bottomComponent	Component	•		•		null
continuousLayout	boolean		•	•	•	false
dividerLocation[a]	int	•		•		-1
dividerSize	int	•		•	•	5
lastDividerLocation	int	•		•		0
leftComponent	Component	•		•		null
maximumDividerLocation[a]	int	•				-1
minimumDividerLocation[a]	int	•				-1
oneTouchExpandable	boolean		•	•	•	false
orientation	int	•		•	•	HORIZONTAL_SPLIT
rightComponent	Component	•		•		null
topComponent	Component	•		•		null

See also properties from the JComponent class (Table 3-5).

[a] These properties return -1 only if no UI is defined for this component. Normally, the UI is queried for its current value.

way, you can refer to your components in a fashion that's consistent with the orientation of your split pane. If the continuousLayout property is true, both sides of the pane will be updated as often as possible while the user moves the divider. Otherwise, the components will only be resized and redrawn once the divider location is set. Continuous layout can be a performance problem, and is often just awkward. The lastDividerLocation property saves the previous location of the divider, and could be used to undo a change in the divider's position.

Constants

Several constants are defined for use with the JSplitPane class. Some of these constants name the various properties in a split pane, others provide constraints for where to place a component or where to place the split.

Table 11-2. JSplitPane Constants

Constant	Type	Description
BOTTOM	String	Add a component to the bottom of a vertically split pane
CONTINUOUS_LAYOUT_PROPERTY	String	Used in property change events to specify that the continuousLayout property has been changed
DIVIDER	String	Add a component as the divider for the pane
DIVIDER_SIZE_PROPERTY	String	Used in property change events to specify that the dividerSize property has changed
HORIZONTAL_SPLIT	int	One of the valid values for the orientation property of a JSplitPane object. This type of split creates a vertical divider, resulting in a set of left/right components
LAST_DIVIDER_LOCATION_PROPERTY	String	Used in property change events to specify that the lastDividerLocation property has changed
LEFT	String	Add a component to the left of a horizontally split pane
ONE_TOUCH_EXPANDABLE_PROPERTY	String	Used in property change events to specify that the oneTouchExpandable property has changed
ORIENTATION_PROPERTY	String	Used in property change events to specify that the orientation property has changed
RIGHT	String	Add a component to the right of a horizontally split pane
TOP	String	Add a component to the top of a vertically split pane
VERTICAL_SPLIT	int	One of the valid values for the orientation property of a JSplitPane object. This type of split creates a horizontal divider, resulting in a set of top/bottom components

Fields

protected boolean continuousLayout
protected int dividerSize
protected Component leftComponent
protected boolean oneTouchExpandable
protected int orientation
protected Component rightComponent

These fields hold the values of the properties of the same names. Note that leftComponent and rightComponent are equivalent to topComponent and bottomComponent, respectively.

Constructors

public JSplitPane()

> This constructor is a "demo" constructor. It sets up a horizontal split with a left button and right button (both JButton components) already defined and added.

public JSplitPane(int orientation)
public JSplitPane(int orientation, boolean continuousLayout)

> These constructors allow you to pick your initial split (horizontal or vertical) using the constants HORIZONTAL_SPLIT and VERTICAL_SPLIT. No components are added to either pane. If you give a true value as the continuousLayout argument to the second constructor, both panes with be repainted continuously as the user moves the divider. (This property is false by default—you just see a line showing the proposed divider location while you move the divider.)

public JSplitPane(int orientation, Component leftOrTop, Component bottomOrRight)
public JSplitPane(int orientation, boolean continuousLayout, Component leftOrTop,
> *Component bottomOrRight)*

> These constructors allow you to pick your orientation and the initial components for each pane. Depending on the orientation you pick, the first component will be placed in the left or top pane, with the second component filling the other pane. If you give a true value as the continuousLayout argument to the second constructor, both panes will be repainted continuously as the user moves the divider.

Control Methods

protected void addImpl(Component comp, Object constraint, int index)

> Adds the specified component to the appropriate location (one of left or top, right or bottom, or divider). If the location is already occupied, the current component is removed and comp is added in its place.

public void remove(Component comp)
public void remove(int index)
public void removeAll()

> Remove components from the split pane. Typically, you will use the first of these methods to remove one component at a time.

public void resetToPreferredSizes()

> Resets the sizes of the components to their preferred sizes. The preferred size of a component is determined by the UI manager for the split pane. The preferred size of a split pane is the sum of the preferred sizes of its children (including the divider).

public void setDividerLocation(double position)

> This convenience method does the pixel calculating for you so that you can specify a position for the divider. The position you give will be the fraction of the whole pane given to the left of the pane (for a horizontal split) or the top of the pane (for a vertical split). For example, with a horizontal split, a value of 0.75 assigns $\frac{3}{4}$ of the pane to the component on the left. The position must be a value between 0 and 1. If it isn't, you get an `IllegalArgument-Exception`.

UI Methods

protected void paintChildren(Graphics g)

> Calls finished `PaintingChildren()` on the UI after the children have been painted.

public void updateUI()

> Updates the component using the current UI dictated by the `UIManager`.

Minimum and Preferred Sizes

When setting up your split panes, watch out for the minimum and preferred sizes of the two components. If you look back at the code for Figure 11-2, you can see we forcibly set the minimum sizes of the two text areas. The boundaries observed by the divider in a split pane are dictated by the minimum sizes of the two components. Some components, such as `JTextArea`, define their minimum size as the size they are initially shown with. That often works fine, but in the case of the split pane, it means that you cannot adjust the division between the two text areas (as both are already at their minimum sizes). The same is true for containers such as panels or the `JScrollPane` we discuss in the next section.

You also need to set the preferred size of the first component if you want the split pane to come up correctly the first time. In the previous example, if you remove the line that sets the preferred size of `jt1`, then `jt1` comes up as big as the entire window, and `jt2` has no width at all. As soon as you try to click on the divider, it jumps to the middle, giving `jt2` its appropriate minimum size. By setting the preferred size of `jt1`, you avoid this problem.

The JScrollPane Class

The `JScrollPane` class offers a more flexible version of the `ScrollPane` class found in the AWT package. Beyond the automatic scrollbars, you can put in horizontal and vertical headers as well as active components in the corners of your pane. (Figure 11-6, later in the chapter, shows the exact areas available in a `JScrollPane`, which is managed by the `ScrollPaneLayout` class.)

Many of the Swing components you have seen make use of the `JScrollPane` to handle their scrolling. The `JList` component, for example, does not handle scrolling on its own. Instead, it concentrates on presenting the list and making selection easy, assuming you'll put it inside a `JScrollPane` if you need scrolling.

Figure 11-3 shows a simple `JScrollPane` in action with a `JList` object.

Figure 11-3. JScrollPane with a list too long to be shown

This particular example does not take advantage of the row or column headers. The scroll pane adds the scrollbars automatically, but only "as needed." If we were to resize the window to make it much larger, the scrollbars would disappear. Here's the code that builds this pane:

```java
// ScrollList.java
// A simple JScrollPane.
//
import javax.swing.*;
import java.awt.*;

public class ScrollList extends JFrame {

  JScrollPane scrollpane;

  public ScrollList() {
    super("JScrollPane Demonstration");
    setSize(300, 200);
    addWindowListener(new BasicWindowMonitor());

    String categories[] = { "Household", "Office", "Extended Family",
                    "Company (US)", "Company (World)", "Team",
```

```
                              "Will", "Birthday Card List", "High School",
                              "Country", "Continent", "Planet" };
        JList list = new JList(categories);
        scrollpane = new JScrollPane(list);

        getContentPane().add(scrollpane, BorderLayout.CENTER);
    }

    public static void main(String args[]) {
        ScrollList sl = new ScrollList();
        sl.setVisible(true);
    }
}
```

A similar technique can be used with many of the Swing components, including
JPanel, JTree, JTable, and JTextArea. Chapter 15, *Tables*, discusses the JTable
class and its use of JScrollPane.

While you will certainly use JScrollPane with many of the Swing components,
you can also build your own components and drop them into a scrollable area.
You will often bundle up a piece of your user interface into one panel, and make
that panel scrollable.

Here's a short example that takes the items from our previous list and turns them
into a basic census form. As you can see in Figure 11-4, the form itself is a panel
with a size of 600x400 pixels. We display it inside a JScrollPane and make the
application 300x200.

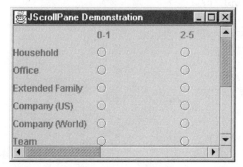

Figure 11-4. A JScrollPane with a component larger than the application window

The only change from our first program is that we now have to build the census
panel from scratch. We build a JPanel containing various labels and radio
buttons, and slap it into a JScrollPane. The only logic involved is figuring out
whether we're adding a label or a button, and getting the buttons into appropriate ButtonGroups (one group per row).

```java
// ScrollDemo.java
// A simple JScrollPane demonstration.
//
import javax.swing.*;
import java.awt.*;
import java.awt.event.*;

public class ScrollDemo extends JFrame {

  JScrollPane scrollpane;

  public ScrollDemo() {
    super("JScrollPane Demonstration");
    setSize(300, 200);
    addWindowListener(new BasicWindowMonitor());
    init();
    setVisible(true);
  }

  public void init() {
    JRadioButton form[][] = new JRadioButton[12][5];
    String counts[] = { "", "0-1", "2-5", "6-10", "11-100", "101+" };
    String categories[] = { "Household", "Office", "Extended Family",
                            "Company (US)", "Company (World)", "Team",
                            "Will", "Birthday Card List", "High School",
                            "Country", "Continent", "Planet" };
    JPanel p = new JPanel();
    p.setSize(600, 400);
    p.setLayout(new GridLayout(13, 6, 10, 0));
    for (int row = 0; row < 13; row++) {
      ButtonGroup bg = new ButtonGroup();
      for (int col = 0; col < 6; col++) {
        if (row == 0) {
          p.add(new JLabel(counts[col]));
        }
        else {
          if (col == 0) {
            p.add(new JLabel(categories[row - 1]));
          }
          else {
            form[row - 1][col - 1] = new JRadioButton();
            bg.add(form[row -1][col - 1]);
            p.add(form[row -1][col - 1]);
          }
        }
      }
    }
    scrollpane = new JScrollPane(p);
    getContentPane().add(scrollpane, BorderLayout.CENTER);
  }
```

```
    public static void main(String args[]) {
      new ScrollDemo();
    }
  }
```

Properties

Table 11-3 shows how the JScrollPane properties grant you access to the five main components (not the corners) and the scrollbar policies. The valid values for horizontalScrollBarPolicy and verticalScrollBarPolicy are defined in the ScrollPaneConstants interface (see Table 11-5). The validateRoot property is always true to ensure that revalidation calls to any of the pane's descendants cause the scroll pane and all of its descendants to be validated and that revalidation doesn't go any further than the JScrollPane, whoch would be redundant.

Table 11-3. JScrollPane Properties

Property	Data Type	get	is	set	bound	Default Value
UI	ScrollPane-UI	•		•		from L&F
UIClassID*	String					"ScrollPaneUI"
accessibleContext*	Accessible-Context	•				JScrollPane.Accessible-JScrollPane()
columnHeader	JViewport	•			•	null
columnHeaderView	Component			•		
horizontalScrollBar	JScrollBar	•			•	null
horizontalScrollBarPolicy	int	•		•	•	HORIZONTAL_SCROLLBAR_AS_NEEDED
opaque	boolean		•			false
rowHeader	JViewport	•			•	null
rowHeaderView	Component			•		
validateRoot	boolean		•			true
verticalScrollbar	JScrollBar	•			•	null
verticalScrollBarPolicy	int	•		•	•	VERTICAL_SCROLLBAR_AS_NEEDED
viewport	JViewport	•			•	null
viewportBorder	Border	•		•	•	null
viewportBorderBounds	Rectangle	•				
viewportView	Component			•		

See also properties from the JComponent class (Table 3-5).

Given that you already have a viewport set up for the row and column headers, or the main viewport itself, you can use the `columnHeaderView`, `rowHeaderView`, and `viewportView` properties to modify the contents of these viewports. Note that the `set` accessors for these properties don't create new viewport objects; they simply set the view to display the given component.

Fields

protected JViewport columnHeader
protected JScrollBar horizontalScrollBar
protected int horizontalScrollBarPolicy
protected JViewport rowHeader
protected JScrollBar verticalScrollBar
protected int verticalScrollBarPolicy
protected JViewport viewport

These fields store the values of the properties with the same names.

protected Component lowerLeft
protected Component lowerRight
protected Component upperLeft
protected Component upperRight

These fields hold the components displayed in the scroll plane's corners.

Constructors

public JScrollPane()
public JScrollPane(Component view)
public JScrollPane(Component view, int verticalScrollBarPolicy,
    int horizontalScrollBarPolicy)
public JScrollPane(int verticalScrollBarPolicy, int horizontalScrollBarPolicy)

Create new scroll panes. You can start off by specifying the `view` (i.e., the component to scroll), the scrollbar policies, or both. Just make sure you get the scrollbar policies in the right order! Of course, any of these pieces can be specified or changed after the scroll pane has been created. See the `setView-portView()` method later in this chapter.

Pane Component Methods

public JScrollBar createHorizontalScrollBar()
public JScrollBar createVerticalScrollBar()

Used by the UI for the scroll pane to create the scrollbars you see. You can override these methods if you want to use a specific subclass of the `JScrollBar` class.

public JViewport createViewport()

> Creates the JViewport object that contains the main view you see. You can override this to use your own subclass of JViewport.

public Component getCorner(String whichCorner)
public void setCorner(String whichCorner, Component corner)

> Get or set the component in the corner of a scroll pane. The whichCorner argument can be any one of the corner strings from the ScrollPaneConstants class (see Table 11-4). You can add any component you like to the corners.

UI Methods

public void updateUI()

> Updates the component using the current UI dictated by the UIManager.

Headers and Corners

Neither of the first examples took advantage of the additional features provided by JScrollPane over the AWT ScrollPane class. You can add headers to your scrolling panes and even put active components in the corners. Figure 11-5 shows an expanded example of our census program with headers and an "info" button in the upper-left corner.

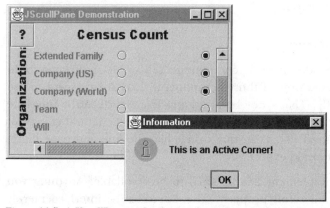

Figure 11-5. A JScrollPane with a button that opens a popup in the upper-left corner

The code to add to the constructor for our demo is straightforward:

```
// Add in some JViewports for the column and row headers
JViewport jv1 = new JViewport();
jv1.setView(new JLabel(new ImageIcon("columnlabel.gif")));
scrollpane.setColumnHeader(jv1);
JViewport jv2 = new JViewport();
```

```
jv2.setView(new JLabel(new ImageIcon("rowlabel.gif")));
scrollpane.setRowHeader(jv2);

// And throw in an information button
JButton jb1 = new JButton(new ImageIcon("question.gif"));
jb1.addActionListener(new ActionListener() {
  public void actionPerformed(ActionEvent ae) {
    JOptionPane.showMessageDialog(null,
          "This is an Active Corner!", "Information",
          JOptionPane.INFORMATION_MESSAGE);
  }
} );
scrollpane.setCorner(ScrollPaneConstants.UPPER_LEFT_CORNER, jb1);
```

We use a JLabel inside a JViewport for each header. The use of the viewport in the headers allows the JScrollPane to synchronize header scrolling with the main viewport. We'll look at the JViewport class in more detail later in this chapter.

When you set up corner components, remember that if your scrollbars are on an as-needed basis, your corners could disappear. In our example, if we moved the information button to the upper-right corner and then made the window tall enough to contain the entire census form, the vertical scrollbar would disappear, and so would the information button. You can alleviate this problem by setting the appropriate scrollbar policy to "always." That way your corners stick around even when the scrollbars are not active.

The Scrollable Interface

You may have noticed that several Swing components rely on JScrollPane to do the scrolling work for them. Most of those components, like JList, seem to use the scrollpane intelligently. That's not by accident. The Scrollable interface defines five methods that a component can implement to get a natural effect out of the scrollpane. By "natural" we mean that things like the line and page increments behave the way you would expect.

A component need not implement Scrollable to be scrollable. Anything you add to a JScrollPane will scroll properly. The Scrollable interface merely provides some intelligence to make scrolling more convenient.

Increment Methods

public int getScrollableBlockIncrement(Rectangle visibleRect, int orientation,
  int direction)
public int getScrollableUnitIncrement(Rectangle visibleRect, int orientation,
  int direction)

These methods should be used to return the appropriate increment amount required to display the next logical row or column of the component, depending on the value of `orientation`. The possibilities for `orientation` are either `SwingConstants.HORIZONTAL` or `SwingConstants.VERTICAL`. The unit increment specifies how to display the next logical row or column; the bolck increment specifies how to "page" horizontally or vertically. The current position of the component is determined by `visibleRect`. The `direction` argument will have a positive (> 0) value for moving down or right and a negative value (< 0) for moving up or left.

Viewport Dimension Methods

The other methods of the interface dictate the relation between the visible area of the scrollable component and the viewport it will be displayed in.

public Dimension getPreferredScrollableViewportSize()

This method should return the preferred size of the viewport containing the component. This value may or may not be the same as the value returned by `getPreferredSize()` for the component. If you think of `JList` again, the preferred size of the component itself is a dimension big enough to display all of the items in the list. The preferred size for the viewport, however, would only be big enough to display some particular number of rows in the list.

public boolean getScrollableTracksViewportHeight()
public boolean getScrollableTracksViewportWidth()

These methods can be used to effectively disable horizontal or vertical scrolling in a scrollpane. If you return `true` for either of these methods, you force the component's height (or width) to match that of its containing viewport. An example might be a text area component that supports word wrapping. Since the text will wrap regardless of the width of the component, you could have `getScrollableTracksViewportWidth()` return `true`. As the scrollpane is resized, the vertical scrollbar will still move up and down through the text, but the horizontal scrollbar will not be used. Returning `false`, then, indicates that the component's height (or width) is determined irrespective of the viewport's dimensions. A scrollpane might then display a scrollbar to allow the user to view the entire component.

The JScrollPane.ScrollBar Class

protected class JScrollPane.ScrollBar extends JScrollBar inplements UIResource

By default, the scrollbars used in a `JScrollPane` are instances of this class. These scrollbars are a bit smarter than regular scrollbars. They check with the view to see if if implements the `Scrollable` interface. If it does (and you did not explicitly set the unit and block increments), then these scrollbars ask the view to provide what it thinks are the appropriate values.

ScrollPaneLayout

The `JScrollPane` class is actually just a panel with a hard-working layout manager and some convenient access methods for the manager. While you probably will not use this class on its own, the `ScrollPaneLayout` class is the manager that provides layout control for the nine areas of a `JScrollPane` object:

- Viewport
- Row header
- Column header
- Vertical scrollbar
- Horizontal scrollbar
- Four corners (upper left, upper right, lower left, and lower right)

These nine components are laid out as shown in Figure 11-6.

The column headers and scrollbars behave similar to the four compass positions (North, South, East, and West) of a `BorderLayout` managed panel. The vertical components are as wide as they need to be and as tall as the viewport. The horizontal components are as tall as they need to be and as wide as the viewport. The difference from the `BorderLayout`-managed panels is that the `ScrollPaneLayout` panels have four corners. Each corner can be a regular component (or be blank). The corners appear based on the visibility of the headers and scrollbars. For example, if the both of the scrollbars are visible, the lower-right corner component would be available.

protected void addSingletonComponent(Component oldComp, Component newComp)
public void addLayoutComponent(String location, Component comp)
public void removeLayoutComponent(Component comp)

These methods come from the `LayoutManager` interface. The `JScrollPane` class uses these to add and remove each of the nine components. (The `addSingletonComponent()` method provides a convenient way to replace components regardless of location.) The `location` string determines which component is being added. The valid values for this parameter are defined in the `ScrollPaneConstants` interface (see Table 11-4).

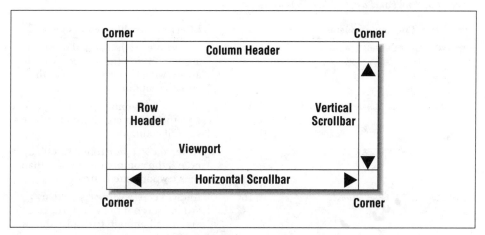

Figure 11-6. The layout areas managed by ScrollPaneLayout

Table 11-4. ScrollPaneLayout Constant Values

Location String from ScrollPaneConstants	Component Location
VIEWPORT	Main viewing area, typically a JViewport component
COLUMN_HEADER	The column header (a row), typically a JViewport component
ROW_HEADER	The row header (a column), typically a JViewport component
HORIZONTAL_SCROLLBAR	The horizontal scrollbar for the viewport, must be a JScrollBar component
VERTICAL_SCROLLBAR	The vertical scrollbar for the viewport, must be a JScrollBar component
LOWER_LEFT_CORNER	The southwest corner, typically empty
LOWER_RIGHT_CORNER	The southeast corner, typically empty
UPPER_LEFT_CORNER	The northwest corner, typically empty
UPPER_RIGHT_CORNER	The northeast corner, typically empty

public int getHorizontalScrollbarPolicy()
public void setHorizontalScrollbarPolicy(int policy)
public int getVerticalScrollbarPolicy()
public void setVerticalScrollbarPolicy(int policy)

The ScrollPaneLayout class also contains several methods for manipulating the scrollbars associated with the viewport. Both the horizontal and vertical scrollbars have policies that determine when (and if) they show up. You can set and retrieve the scrollbar policies using these methods with constants defined in the ScrollPaneConstants interface listed in Table 11-5.

Table 11-5. ScrollPaneLayout Policy Constants

ScrollPaneConstants constant	Type	Effect on Scrollbar component
HORIZONTAL_SCROLLBAR_ALWAYS	int	Always keeps a horizontal scrollbar around, even if the viewport extent area is wide enough to display the entire component.
HORIZONTAL_SCROLLBAR_AS_NEEDED	int	Shows a horizontal scrollbar whenever the extent area is smaller than the full component.
HORIZONTAL_SCROLLBAR_NEVER	int	Never shows a horizontal scrollbar, even if the component is wider than the viewport extent area.
VERTICAL_SCROLLBAR_ALWAYS	int	Always keeps a vertical scrollbar around, even if the viewport extent area is tall enough to display the entire component.
VERTICAL_SCROLLBAR_AS_NEEDED	int	Shows a vertical scrollbar whenever the extent area is smaller than the full component.
VERTICAL_SCROLLBAR_NEVER	int	Never shows a vertical scrollbar, even if the component is taller than the viewport extent area.
HORIZONTAL_SCROLLBAR_POLICY	int	The name of the horizontal scrollbar policy property for use with property change events.
VERTICAL_SCROLLBAR_POLICY	int	The name of the vertical scrollbar policy property for use with property change events.

Properties

This layout manager treats the various components as properties, with the usual property access methods. However, since ScrollPaneLayout really is just a layout manager, you don't set the components, you add them to the JScrollPane. Table 11-6 shows the components managed by a ScrollPlaneLayout.

Table 11-6. ScrollPaneLayout Properties

Property	Data Type	get	is	set	bound	Default Value
columnHeader	JViewport	•				null
corner	Component	•				null
horizontalScrollBar	JScrollBar	•				null
rowHeader	JViewport	•				null
verticalScrollbar	JScrollBar	•				null
viewport	JViewport	•				null

The columnHeader, rowHeader, and viewport components are all of type JViewport. We'll be looking at that class in the next section, but basically it provides easy access to placing a viewable rectangle over a component. If the entire component fits in the rectangle, you can see all of the component. If not, the parts outside the rectangle get cropped. The corner property is indexed using constant values from Table 11-4.

As with other layout managers, you rarely add or remove components directly through the manager; that task is handled by the container. As you saw above, the JScrollPane class contains the methods necessary to add or replace any of these nine components. It also contains methods to retrieve these components, but the retrieval methods are provided through the layout manager, too, for convenience.

Fields

protected JViewport viewport
> The value for the viewport property.

protected JScrollBar hsb
protected JScrollBar vsb
> The values for the horizontal and vertical scrollbars, respectively.

protected JViewport colHead
protected JViewport rowHead
> The values for the column and row header viewport properties, respectively.

protected java.awt.Component lowerLeft
protected java.awt.Component lowerRight
protected java.awt.Component upperLeft
protected java.awt.Component upperRight
> The values for the indexed corner property.

protected int hsbPolicy
protected int vsbPolicy
> The values for the horizontal and vertical scrollbar policies, respectively.

public Rectangle getViewportBorderBounds(JScrollPane sp)
> Returns the bounding rectangle for sp's viewport border.

public void syncWithScrollPane(JScrollPane sp)
> This method canbe used with your own customized scrollpane layout manager to synchronize the components associated with the scrollpane sp and this manager. That way, any components already added to sp are appropriately recognized by your layout manager.

Inner Classes

public static class ScrollPaneLayout.UIResource extends ScrollPaneLayout implements
UIResource

The inner class can be used to create a UIResource instance of the Scroll-
PaneLayout manager to distinguish it from a layout manager set specifically
by the developer. See Chapter 26, *Look & Feel*, for more details.

JViewport

You use the JViewport class to create a view of a potentially large component in a
potentially small place. We say potentially because the view can encompass the
entire component or just a piece of it. In the JScrollPane class, a view port is
used to show a piece of the main component, and the scrollbars provide the user
with control over which piece they see. JViewport accomplishes this using the
normal clipping techniques, but it guarantees that an appropriately sized view of
the component is displayed. The JScrollPane class also uses JViewport objects
for the row and column headers.

Most of the time, you'll leave JViewport alone and use one of the bigger panes,
like JScrollPane, to display your components. However, nothing prevents you
from using JViewport objects and you could certainly subclass this to create some
interesting tools, such as an image magnifier pane. In such a pane, you'd still have
to write the magnifying code—JViewport would just make it easy to see pieces of
a magnified image.

Properties

The JViewport class has the properties shown in Table 11-7. The useful properties of JViewport deal with the view component. The view property lets you get
or set the component this viewport is viewing. The viewSize and viewPosition
control the size and position of the area that's displayed. viewSize is normally
equal to the size of the viewport, unless the component is smaller than the viewport. In that case, viewSize equals the component's size, and all of it is displayed.
viewPosition is relative to the top-left corner of the component being displayed.
If the backingStoreEnabled property is true, this JViewport object double-
buffers the display of its contents. The isOptimizedDrawingEnabled() call
always returns false to force the viewport's paint() method to be called, rather
than allowing repaint calls to notify the viewport's children individually.

Events

The JViewport class fires a ChangeEvent whenever the view size, view position,
or extent size changes.

Table 11-7. JViewport Properties

Property	Data Type	get	is	set	bound	Default Value
accessibleContext	Accessible-Context	•				JViewport.Accessible-JViewport()
extentSize	Dimension	•		•		size of the component
insets[a]	Insets	•				Insets(0, 0, 0, 0)
view	Component	•		•		null
viewPosition	Point	•		•		Point(0, 0)
viewRect	Rectangle	•				Rect(getViewPosition(), getExtentSize())
viewSize	Dimension	•		•		Dimension(0, 0)
backingStoreEnabled	boolean		•	•		false
optimizedDrawingEnabled*	boolean		•			false

See also properties of the JComponent class (Table 3-5).

[a] These get methods override JComponent and are final. See also ViewportLayout later in the chapter.

public void addChangeListener(ChangeListener l)
public void removeChangeListener(ChangeListener l)

Add or remove a change listener for the viewport's ChangeEvents.

protected void fireStateChanged()

Subclasses can use this convenience method to report a change of their own.

Fields

protected boolean backingStore

The value for the backingStoreEnabled property.

protected transient Image backingStoreImage

The image used for the backing store (if enabled).

protected boolean isViewSizeSet

Set to true when the size of the viewport has been set.

protected Point lastPaintPosition

Stores the last painted position so that as much of the backing store as possible (but not more) can be reused.

protected boolean scrollUnderway

Rather than force components (such as JList) to manage the backing store directly, this property is managed inside the JViewport class to keep the use of the backing store efficient. This flag is only set to true when positioning a view using the setLocation() method.

Constructors

public JViewport()

Creates an empty JViewport object. You can put something in the viewport using the setView() method.

Helper Methods

protected void addImpl(Component view, Object constraint, int index)
protected boolean computeBlit(int dx, int dy, Point blitFrom, Point blitTo,
Dimension blitSize, Rectangle blitPaint)
protected LayoutManager createLayoutMunager()
protected JViewport.ViewListener createViewListener()

These methods do most of the dirty work of making the viewport function. Any one of them can be overridden in a subclass to get different behavior. It's common to override the createLayoutManager() method, which allows you to create a viewport object with a layout manager other than Viewport-Layout (discussed later in this chapter).

public final Insets getInsets(Insets insets)

Returns an Insets object just like the getInsets() call for the regular insets property listed in Table 11-7. However, this version reinitializes the insets object passed to the method (all values go to 0) and returns that object.

public Dimension toViewCoordinates(Dimension size)
public Point toViewCoordinates(Point p)

Translate the incoming Dimension or Point objects into corresponding objects relative to the current view. If your viewport supported logical coordinates, these methods would need to be overridden.

public void scrollRectToVisible(Rectangle rect)

Tries to make the area represented by rect visible in the viewport.

public void setBounds(int x, int y, int width, int height)

Overrides the resize method in JComponent to make sure the backing store for this image is correct if the width or height changes from the current dimensions.

Miscellaneous Methods

public void paint(Graphics g)

Overrides the usual paint() call to make sure it uses the backing store (if enabled) efficiently.

public void remove(Component comp)

Allows you to remove the view component if you need to.

public void repaint(long delay, int x, int y, int width, int height)

Overrides the usual `repaint()` call to make sure that only one `repaint()` is performed. It does this by translating the repaint rectangle to the parent's coordinate system and telling the parent to `repaint()`. Presumably, if the rectangle doesn't need to be repainted, nothing happens, although the parent could have its own overridden `repaint()` method.

The ViewportLayout Class

As with the `ScrollPaneLayout` class, this class is for use with a `JViewport` object, and not meant for general use.

Layout Methods

public void addLayoutComponent(String s, Component comp)
public void removeLayoutComponent(Component comp)

These methods are empty and serve only to meet the requirements of the `LayoutManager` interface. The addition or removal of a view component must be done on the `JViewport` object.

public void layoutContainer(Container parent)

Forces a refresh of the container. This might be needed if the view position or size changes.

public Dimension minimumLayoutSize(Container parent)
public Dimension preferredLayoutSize(Container parent)

These methods determine the preferred and minimum sizes for the viewport. The viewport can grow if you resize the container, but it will not shrink below the minimum size. While the viewport is being resized, it will bottom-justify the view until the entire view is visible.

The JTabbedPane Class

The tabbed pane is now a fixture in applications for option displays, system configuration displays and other multiscreen UIs. In the AWT, you have access to the `CardLayout` layout manager, which can be used to simulate the multiscreen behavior, but it contains nothing to graphically activate screen switching—you must write that yourself. Figure 11-7 shows that with the `JTabbedPane`, you can create your own tabbed pane, with tab activation components, very quickly.

Here's the code that generated this simple application. We use the tabbed pane as our real container and create new tabs using the `addTab()` method. Note that each tab can contain exactly one component. As with a `CardLayout`-managed

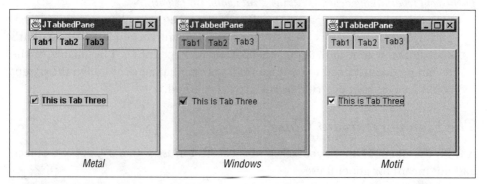

Figure 11-7. A simple tabbed pane with three tabs in Metal, Windows, and Motif look-and-feels

container, you quite often add a container as the one component on the tab. That way, you can then add as many other components to the container as necessary.

```
// SimpleTab.java
// A quick test of the JTabbedPane component.
//
import java.awt.*;
import java.util.*;
import java.awt.event.*;
import javax.swing.*;

public class SimpleTab extends JFrame {

  JTabbedPane jtp;

  public SimpleTab() {
    super("JTabbedPane");
    setSize(200, 200);
    Container contents = getContentPane();
    jtp = new JTabbedPane();
    jtp.addTab("Tab1", new JLabel("This is Tab One"));
    jtp.addTab("Tab2", new JButton("This is Tab Two"));
    jtp.addTab("Tab3", new JCheckBox("This is Tab Three"));
    contents.add(jtp);

    addWindowListener(new BasicWindowMonitor());
    setVisible(true);
  }

  public static void main(String args[]) {
    new SimpleTab();
  }
}
```

Properties

The JTabbedPane class has the properties list in Table 11-8. For a tabbed pane, the properties are much simpler than for the scroll pane. You have access to the selection model; (see Chapter 14, *Menus and Toolbars*, for a discussion of Single-SelectionModel and DefaultSingleSelectionModel). The currently selected tab—available by component (selectedComponent) or index (selectedIndex) and the total number of tabs for this panel. The tabRunCount property tells you how many rows (or runs) the pane is using currently to display all of the tabCount tabs. You can also control the location of the tabs using the tabPlacement property. That property can be any of the TOP, BOTTOM, LEFT, or RIGHT constants defined in SwingConstants.

Table 11-8. . JTabbedPane Properties

Property	Data Type	get	is	set	Bound	Default Value
UI	TabbedPaneUI	•		•		null
UIClassID*	String					"TabbedPaneUI"
model	SingleSelection-Model	•		•	•	DefaultSingleSelection-Model()
accessibleContext*	AccessibleCon-text	•				JTabbedPane.Accessible-JTabbedPane()
selectedComponent	Component	•		•		null
selectedIndex	int	•		•		-1
tabCount	int	•				0
tabPlacement	int	•		•	•	SwingConstants.TOP
tabRunCount	int	•				0

See also properties from the JComponent class (Table 3-5).

Events

In addition to the property change events generated for the model and tabPlacement properties, JTabbedPane also generates change events whenever the tab selection changes. On its own, a JTabbedPane listens to the change events coming from the tabs to keep the user interface in sync with the selected tab. Of course, you can add your own listener to the pane. The SingleSelectionModel uses the ChangeEvent class to report a new tab selection.

public void addChangeListener(ChangeListener l)
public void removeChangeListener(ChangeListener l)

Add or remove a listener for change events from this tabbed pane.

protected ChangeListener createChangeListener()

Creates a listener that can route change events from the selection model for the pane to the `fireStateChanged()` method. The protected inner class `JTabbedPane.ModelListener` is used to accomplish the redirection.

protected void fireStateChanged()

The `fireStateChanged()` method is used to report changes in the selected tab with the tabbed pane (and not the selection model) listed as the source of the event.

Fields

protected SingleSelectionModel model

The values for the `tabPlacement` and `model` properties

protected ChangeListener changeListener

The change listener (created with `createChangeListener()`) attached to the pane to help redirect events from the selection model.

protected transient ChangeEvent changeEvent

Since change events only carry the source of the event, which is always the tabbed pane itself, the `JTabbedPane` class keeps a single reference to an appropriate `ChangeEvent` for use with the `fireStateChanged()` method discussed earlier.

protected int tabPlacement

Stores the value for the `tabPlacement` property.

Constructors

public JTabbedPane()

Creates an empty tabbed pane to which you can add new tabs with one of the tab methods listed below. The tabs are placed along the top of the pane.

public JTabbedPane(int tabPlacement)

Creates an empty tabbed pane that you can add new tabs to with one of the tab methods listed below. The tabs are placed according to `tabPlacement`, which can be one of TOP, BOTTOM, LEFT, or RIGHT.

Tab Methods

Once you have a tabbed pane set up, you can add, remove, and modify tabs at any time.

public void addTab(String title, Component comp)

public void addTab(String title, Icon tabIcon, Component comp)

public void addTab(String title, Icon tabIcon, Component comp, String tip)

These methods allow you to add (append, really) a tab to the pane. You must specify the tab's component and title. If the component is `null`, the tab will still appear, but it will not behave appropriately. When you select a tab with a `null` component, the previously selected tab's component remains visible. The title may be null. Optionally, you can also specify an icon and a tooltip for the tab. As with the title, `null` values for these arguments do not cause any problems. Each of these methods builds up an appropriate call to `insertTab()`.

public void insertTab(String title, Icon tabIcon, Component comp, String tip, int index)

This method does all of the work for getting tabs into place on the pane. You specify the tab's title, icon, tooltip (all of which can be `null`), component, and the index to insert the component. If you supply an index larger than the tab count, an `ArrayIndexOutOfBoundsException` will be thrown.

public Component add(Component component)

public Component add(String title, Component component)

public Component add(Component component, int index)

public void add(Component component, Object constraints)

public void add(Component component, Object constraints, int index)

These methods are alternatives for adding tabs to a tabbed pane, in you don't want to use `addTab()` or `insertTab()`. They are more with the standard `add()` method for containers. If you supply an index, the tab will be inserted at that index. If you supply constraints, they should be either `String` or `Icon` objects for use in the tab. (If the `constraints` object isn't a `String` or an `Icon`, it is ignored.) If you do not supply a title or constraint to label the tab, the tabbed pane uses `component.getName()`.

public void remove(Component component)

Removes the tab with a match to `component`. If a match cannot be found, nothing happens.

public void removeAll()

Removes all tabs from the tabbed pane.

public void removeTabAt(int index)

This method allows you to remove a given tab. As with `insertTab()`, an inappropriate `index` value will cause an `ArrayIndexOutOfBoundsException`.

The next series of methods for tabs resemble indexed property accessor methods, but they don't quite follow the usual JavaBeans property naming conventions. All of the methods throw an `ArrayIndexOutOfBoundsException` if the index is not valid.

public Color getBackgroundAt(int index)
public void setBackgroundAt(int index, Color c)

Deal with the background color property of the tab at `index`.

public Component getComponentAt(int index)
public void setComponentAt(int index, Component comp)

Allow you to work with the component displayed on the tab at `index`.

public Rectangle getBoundsAt(int index)

Returns the bounds of the tab (not the component) at `index`. Returns `null` if the tab is not visible.

public Icon getDisabledIconAt(int index)
public void setDisabledIconAt(int index, Icon icon)

These methods allow you to set and access the icon used when the tab is disabled, but still visible. The default disabled look for a tab with an icon is a grayed-out icon.

public Color getForegroundAt(int index)
public void setForegroundAt(int index, Color c)

Deal with the foreground color property of the tab at `index`.

public Icon getIconAt(int index)
public void setIconAt(int index, Icon tabIcon)

These methods allow you to set and access the icon for an enabled tab. You can also use the icon to look up a tab using the `indexOf()` method described later in the chapter.

public String getTitleAt(int index)
public void setTitleAt(int index, String title)

Give you access to a tab's title, which can be `null`.

public boolean isEnabledAt(int index)
public void setEnabledAt(int index, boolean enabled)

These methods allow you enable and disable (and check the enabled status of) tabs in the pane without removing them. This can be very useful in configuration panes where not all tabs may be applicable based on the state of other tabs.

public int indexOfComponent(Component comp)
public int indexOfTab(String title)
public int indexOfTab(Icon icon)

These methods allow you to look up a tab at runtime. If you use the second or third methods, the first tab with a matching `title` or `icon` will be returned.

Miscellaneous Methods

Tabbed panes also support the notion of tooltips and do most of the work for you. However, you do need to set the tooltip text when you add the tab, no `setToolTipText()` method exists.

public String getToolTipText(MouseEvent event)
> This method overrides the `getToolTipText()` call from `JComponent` to return the tooltip appropriate for the tab your mouse cursor is on.

Figure 11-8 shows our previous tabbed pane with tooltips active.

Figure 11-8. A tabbed pane with tooltips active

And here are the modifications to the code needed to make this work. We just add a null icon and the tooltip text (the last arguments) to the `addTab()` methods:

```
jtp = new JTabbedPane();
jtp.addTab("Tab1", null, new JLabel("This is Tab One"), "Tab #1");
jtp.addTab("Tab2", null, new JButton("This is Tab Two"), "Tab #2");
jtp.addTab("Tab3", null, new JCheckBox("This is Tab Three"), "Tab #3");
contents.add(jtp);
```

UI Methods

public void UpdateUI()
> Updates the component using the current UI dictated by the `UIManager`.

Layout Managers

Beyond these specialty panes with their dedicated layout managers, the Swing package also includes some general layout managers you can use with your own code. You can use the new `BoxLayout` to make things like toolbars and `OverlayLayout` to make things like layered labels.

The Box and BoxLayout Classes

The BoxLayout class is a manager that gives you one row or column to put every-thing in. It's great for toolbars and button ribbons. It also comes with its very own convenience container called Box. The Box class is a lightweight container that requires a BoxLayout manager. While you can certainly use the BoxLayout class to control your own panel, frame, or other container, the Box class provides several shortcuts for dealing with components in a boxed layout. You'll often find using a Box is easier than creating a panel or frame that you control with a BoxLayout manager.

The Box Class

Let's start with a look at the convenience container that puts the BoxLayout manager to use. The Box class is a lightweight container object whose primary purpose is to let you add components to a horizontal or vertical box without having to think about getting the constraints right. You use the normal Container.add() method to place components in the box. Components are placed left to right (or top to bottom) in the order you add them.

Properties

Table 11-9 shows the properties of the Box class. You are not allowed to change a box's layout manager, so the setLayout accessor always throws an AWTError.

Table 11-9. Box Properties.

Property	Data Type	get	is	set	Bound	Default Value
accessibleContext	AccessibleContext	•				box.AccessibleBox
layout	layoutManager			•		BoxLayout

See also properties from the JComponent class (Table 3-5).

Constructors

public Box(int alignment)

> Creates a container with a BoxLayout manager using the specified align-ment. The possible values for the alignment are BoxLayout.X_AXIS (a horizontal box) and BoxLayout.Y_AXIS (a vertical box). You can refer to Figure 11-11 for an example of vertical and horizontal boxes. Usually, you'll use the createVerticalBox() or createHorizontalBox() methods to make new boxes.

Creation Methods

Two convenience routines exist for creating boxes. You can create your own using the constructor, but these are sometimes easier.

public static Box createHorizontalBox()
public static Box createVerticalBox()
    These methods create new Box components with the appropriate alignment.

Spacing and Resizing Methods

The Box class provides several static helper components for spacing and resizing controls. You can add these components just as you would add any other component to the box.

public static Component createGlue()
public static Component createHorizontalGlue()
public static Component createVerticalGlue()
    These methods create "glue" components that you can place between two fixed-size components. Glue might be a misnomer; it doesn't cause the components to stay in one place. Rather, glue acts like a gooey filler—it lets a component shift when the parent container is resized and takes up the slack. The idea is that glue is malleable and stretchable compared to a strut or rigid area. Rather than forcing the components to change their sizes to consume new space, you can put glue components anywhere you want blank space. It's important to remember, however, that glue components really are components. When resizing a box, all of the components—the glue and the buttons in our examples—will have their sizes adjusted, up to their minimum or maximum limits.

    The horizontal and vertical glue components stretch along the appropriate axis, while the generic glue component can stretch in both directions, if necessary. Figure 11-9 shows how a resize affects buttons in a Box. Without glue, the buttons grow as the contour is resized. With glue, the buttons still change, but they don't change as much; the glue takes up much of the extra space.

Here's the code to add glue to both sides of the buttons:

```
// HBoxWithGlue.java
// A quick test of the box layout manager using the Box utility class.
//
import java.awt.*;
import java.awt.event.*;
import javax.swing.*;

public class HBoxWithGlue extends JFrame {
```

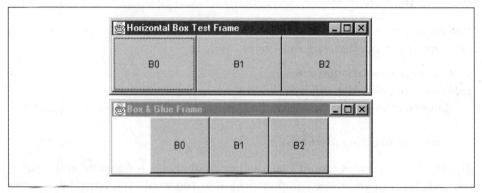

Figure 11-9. A Box container after being resized without (top) and with glue components (bottom)

```
public HBoxWithGlue() {
    super("Box & Glue Frame");
    setSize(350, 100);
    Box box = Box.createHorizontalBox();
    setContentPane(box);
    box.add(Box.createHorizontalGlue());
    for (int i = 0; i < 3; i++) {
        Button b = new Button("B" + i);
        box.add(b);
    }
    box.add(Box.createHorizontalGlue());
    addWindowListener(new BasicWindowMonitor());
    setVisible(true);
}

public static void main(String args[]) {
    HBoxWithGlue bt = new HBoxWithGlue();
}
}
```

public static Component createRigidArea(Dimension d)
public static Component createHorizontalStrut(int width)
public static Component createVerticalStrut(int width)

These methods create rigid spaces. You can use these methods to force gaps between components. This is useful if you are trying to create groups of components in a toolbar. The rigid area creates an invisible component that has a fixed width and height. The horizontal strut has a fixed width and a variable height. The vertical strut has a fixed height and a variable width. Figure 11-10 has some examples of strut components before and after a resize.

Here's the code for the strut example:

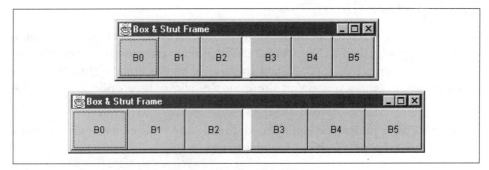

Figure 11-10. Strut components being resized inside a Box container

```java
// HBoxWithStrut.java
// A quick test of the box layout manager using the Box utility class.
//
import java.awt.*;
import java.awt.event.*;
import javax.swing.*;

public class HBoxWithStrut extends JFrame {

  public HBoxWithStrut() {
    super("Box & Strut Frame");
    setSize(350, 80);
    Box box = Box.createHorizontalBox();
    setContentPane(box);
    for (int i = 0; i < 3; i++) {
      Button b = new Button("B" + i);
      box.add(b);
    }

    // Add a spacer between the first three buttons and the last three
    box.add(Box.createHorizontalStrut(10));
    for (int i = 3; i < 6; i++) {
      Button b = new Button("B" + i);
      box.add(b);
    }
    addWindowListener(new BasicWindowMonitor());
    setVisible(true);
  }

  public static void main(String args[]) {
    HBoxWithStrut bt = new HBoxWithStrut();
  }
}
```

The Box.Filler Class

The struts and glue components used in the various create methods above use a public inner class called `Filler`. The `Filler` inner class extends `Component` and provides mechanisms to specify fixed or variable widths and heights. It has no visual presence, but as you saw in the examples above, it can play a role in the layout process for a container.

While this class is public and can be used directly, the static convenience methods found in the `Box` class are probably easier to use.

Properties

Table 11-10 shows the properties found in the `Filler` class. The size properties all store their values in protected fields inherited from `Component`. Glue components are created by putting zeros in the minimum and preferred sizes, and `Short.MAX_VALUE` in the maximum sizes. Strut (and rigid area) components are created by putting exactly the same value in each of the three size categories.

Table 11-10. Box.Filler Properties

Property	Data Type	get	is	set	bound	Default Value
accessibleContext	AccessibleContext	•				Box.Filler.AccessibleBox-Filler()
maximumSize*	Dimension	•				Set by constructor
minimumSize*	Dimension	•				Set by constructor
preferredSize*	Dimension	•				Set by constructor

See also the java.awt.Component class.

Constructors

public Filler(Dimension min, Dimension pref, Dimension max)
   Creates a new `Filler` object with the given minimum, preferred and maximum sizes.

Shape Methods

The `Filler` class has only one other method beyond those required to support accessibility.

public void changeShape(Dimension min, Dimension pref, Dimension max)
   Sets the `Filler` object's minimum, preferred, and maximum sizes.

The BoxLayout Class

If you do want just the manager for your own container, this is the class you need. The BoxLayout class implements the LayoutManager2 interface from the java.awt package. This class and its predecessor, LayoutManager, are discussed in detail in John Zukowski's *Java AWT Reference*, which provides an excellent background on layout managers in general.

Constants

The BoxLayout class contains the following two constants listed in Table 11-11.

Table 11-11. JSplitPaneConstants

Constant	Type	Description
X_AXIS	int	Used with the constructor to create a manager that will lay out components along a horizontal axis. This constant can also be used with the constructor for the Box class.
Y_AXIS	int	Used with the constructor to create a manager that will lay out components along a vertical axis. This constant can also be used with the constructor for the Box class.

Constructors

public BoxLayout(Container target, int axis)

The only constructor for this layout manager; it takes as input the container to manage and how the components should be laid out: left to right (X_AXIS) or top to bottom (Y_AXIS). Figure 11-11 shows an example of a horizontal panel (A) and a vertical panel (B). To prove this BoxLayout is just a layout manager, we'll use regular AWT panels and buttons.

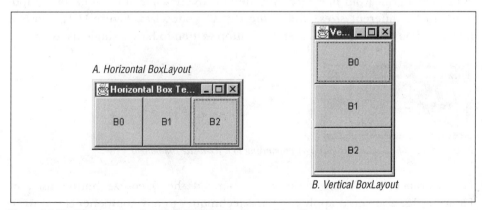

Figure 11-11. Horizontal and vertical BoxLayout-managed panels

Here's a look at the code to generate these boxes:

```
// HBox.java
// A quick test of the box layout manager using the Box utility class.
//
import java.awt.*;
import java.awt.event.*;
import javax.swing.*;

public class HBox extends JFrame {

  public HBox() {
    super("Horizontal Box Test Frame");
    setSize(200, 100);
    Panel box = new Panel();

    // Use BoxLayout.Y_AXIS below if you want a vertical box
    box.setLayout(new BoxLayout(box, BoxLayout.X_AXIS));
    setContentPane(box);
    for (int i = 0; i < 3; i++) {
      Button b = new Button("B" + i);
      box.add(b);
    }
    addWindowListener(new BasicWindowMonitor());
    setVisible(true);
  }

  public static void main(String args[]) {
    HBox bt = new HBox();
  }
}
```

Well, maybe that's not really exciting, since you can do the same thing with a well-constructed grid-layout manager. But the BoxLayout class does allow for components to be different sizes, unlike the GridLayout class. Figure 11-12 shows a horizontal box with a simple extended button written to have a single fixed size.

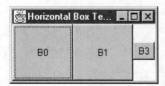

Figure 11-12. The BoxLayout manager responding to a fixed-size component

For reference, here's the code that generated the fixed-size button used in Figure 11-12. You could apply the same techniques to any components you write or extend.

```
// FixedButton.java
// A simple extension to the button class that gives the button a fixed size.
// Basically the "maximum" and "minimum" just return the same size.
//
import java.awt.*;

public class FixedButton extends Button {

  public FixedButton(String name) { super(name); }

  public Dimension getMinimumSize() { return getPreferredSize(); }

  public Dimension getMaximumSize() { return getPreferredSize(); }
}
```

Methods

public void addLayoutComponent(String name, Component comp)
public void addLayoutComponent(Component comp, Object constraints)
public void removeLayoutComponent(Component comp)

These methods do nothing in this class. The container handles adding and removing components. These are primarily set up for peerless components in later releases.

public void invalidateLayout(Container target)

Tells the layout manager that one or more of the child components has modified its layout constraints, and it should ignore any layout decisions it might be caching.

This method throws an AWTError if the container given as the target does not match the container specified in the constructor.

public Dimension preferredLayoutSize(Container target)
public Dimension maximumLayoutSize(Container target)
public Dimension minimumLayoutSize(Container target)

Return dimension objects for the preferred, maximum, and minimum sizes of the container respectively. The manager calculates the sizes based on the preferred, maximum and minimum sizes of its children.

These methods throw an AWTError if the container given as the target does not match the container specified in the constructor.

public float getLayoutAlignmentX(Container target)
public float getLayoutAlignmentY(Container target)

These methods return floating-point numbers that can be used to align components along the appropriate axis. If you have a horizontal box, getLayoutAlignmentX() returns the default alignment of 0.5 and getLayoutAlignmentY() returns the alignment needed for components that have a fixed or maximum size. On the other hand, for a vertical box, getLay-outAlignmentX() returns the needed alignment for fixed- or maximum-size components and getLayoutAlignmentY() returns the default.

Alignments range from extreme left or top (0.0) to extreme right or bottom (1.0). These alignments are similer to the alignments used in the sizeRe-quirements class discussed with the ScrollPaneLayout class

These methods throw an AWTError if the container given as the target does not match the container specified in the constructor.

public void layoutContainer(Container target)

Lays out the container according to the rules of the layout manager and the current constraints attached to the child components. You typically do not call this method directly, but rather rely on the doLayout() method from the Container class.

This method throws an AWTError if the container given as the target does not match the container specified in the constructor.

OverlayLayout

One other layout manager in the Swing package is the OverlayLayout class. This layout manager is more of a facilitating manager for some of the Swing compo-nents, such as JMenuItem and AbstractButton. The purpose of this layout manager is to place components on top of each other based on some alignment points. This allows things like buttons and menu items to manage icons and text in the same visual area. For example, if two components share exactly the same hori-zontal and vertical alignments, one will be placed directly on top of the other. However, if one component has a horizontal alignment of 0.0, while the other component has a horizontal alignment of 1.0, the two will appear side by side.

Constructor

publicOverlayLayout(container target)

Create a layout manager for managing the components in a given container.

LayoutManager2 Methods

public void addLayoutComponent(Component comp, Object constraints)
public void addLayoutComponent(String name, Component comp)

These standard layout manager methods are not used by the OverlayLayout manager.

public float getLayoutAlignmentX(Container target)

Returns the alignment along the x axis for the container.

public float getLayoutAlignmentY(Container target)

Returns the alignment along the y axis for the container.

public void invalidateLayout(Container target)

Indicates that a child has changed its layout-related information, which causes any cached calculations to be flushed.

public void layoutContainer(Container target)

After checking the insets for the container, children are laid out according to their alignments.

public Dimension maximumLayoutSize(Container target)
public Dimension minimumLayoutSize(Container target)
public Dimension preferredLayoutSize(Container target)

These layout manager methods return the various sizes of the container, calculated by looking at the children associated with this manager. These sizes are determined using the `javax.swing.SizeRequirements` convenience class.

public void removeLayoutComponent(Component comp)

Not used by the `OverlayLayout` manager.

The SizeRequirements Class

Laying out all of these components for the different layout manager involves a lot of calculations that can be quite similar. The layout manager needs to end up with a list of (x,y) coordinates for each component as well as a list of widths and heights. The `SizeRequirements` class provides several convenience methods for doing exactly these kinds of calculations.

The type of calculations fall into two basic categories, aligned and tiled. You have seen both of these in the simplest layout manager available in Java, the `FlowLayout` manager. If you place two buttons and a list on a panel managed by `FlowLayout`, you get the components laid out left to right, each vertically centered relative to the others. The left to right x coordinates and widths for each component are an example of tiled requirements. The y coordinates and heights are an example of aligned requirements. You can perform both types of calculations with the static methods of this class. One thing to remember when using `SizeRequirements`, however, is that it calculates only one axis at a time—you can't make one call to get both the (x, y) and (width, height) lists. It's not really a big hassle though, just make one call for the x and width values, and another for the y and height values.

Fields

public float alignment

This field represents the actual alignment used for the component. A "center" alignment would be 0.5. A "left" alignment (when calculating widths) would be 0.0.

public int maximum

This field represents the maximum size allowed for this component. If you are calculating widths, this should be the same as `getMaximumSize().width` for the component. For heights, this should be the same as `getMaximum-Size().height`.

public int minimum

This field represents the minimum size required for this component. If you are calculating widths, this should be the same as `getMinimumSize().width` for the component. For heights, this should be the same as `getMinimum-Size().height`.

public int preferred

This field represents the preferred size for this component. If you are calculating widths, this should be the same as `getPreferredSize().width` for the component. For heights, this should be the same as `getPreferred-Size().height`.

Constructors

public SizeRequirements()

This constructor creates a `SizeRequirements` object with centered alignment and all sizes set to 0.

public SizeRequirements(int min, int pref, int max, float a)

This constructor creates a `SizeRequirements` object with the given alignment a, minimum size min, preferred size pref, and maximum size max.

Methods

public static int[] adjustSizes(int delta, SizeRequirements[] children)

Returns an array of new preferred sizes for children based on `delta`. `delta` should be a change in the allocated space. The sizes of the children will be shortened or lengthened to accommodate the new allocation.

public static void calculateAlignedPositions(int allocated, SizeRequirements total,
    SizeRequirements[] children, int[] offsets, int[] spans)
public static void calculateTiledPositions(int allocated, SizeRequirements total,
    SizeRequirements[] children, int[] offsets, int[] spans)

These methods calculate the offsets (x or y coordinates) and spans (widths or heights) for components that are to be laid out in an aligned or tiled manner, respectively. For example, if you were laying out a single row of buttons, you could use this method to calculate the x coordinate for the upper-left corner and the width of the button. The allocated parameter dictates how much space is allocated, while total determines the overall SizeRequirements for the children. (This value can be null, or can be easily retrieved by calling getAlignedSizeRequirements() or getTiledSizeRequirements(), respectively.)

public static SizeRequirements getAlignedSizeRequirements(SizeRequirements[] children)

This method calculates the space required for a group of children (themselves described by a SizeRequirements object in the array) that should be aligned according to their individual alignments. The resulting SizeRequirements object will have an alignment of 0.5. If children has zero elements, a default SizeRequirements object will be returned.

public static SizeRequirements getTiledSizeRequirements(SizeRequirements[] children)

This method calculates the space required for a group of children (themselves described by a SizeRequirements object in the array) that should be placed end to end, or tiled. The resulting SizeRequirements object will have an alignment of 0.5. If children has zero elements, a default SizeRequirements object will be returned.

public String toString()

This method overrides the definition in Object to provide a string containing the minimum, preferred, and maximum sizes as well as the alignment for this object.

An OverlayLayout Example

Rather than contrive an example using the OverlayLayout manager, Figure 11-13 shows a simple program that lets you play with three buttons inside a panel, with an OverlayLayout manager running. You can type in the X- and Y-alignment values between 0.0 and 1.0 into text fields along the bottom. The text fields are organized as X and Y fields for each of the three buttons ("B1," "Button 2," and "Another Button," respectively). Then click the "Update" button. The buttons in the panel above will rearrange themselves according to the values you entered. The gridlines show the bounds of the panel and its center. Try changing several of the values; this will give you an idea of how this layout manager might be useful.

Admittedly, you probably won't be lining up buttons using this layout manager, but imagine controlling a multiline, multi-icon label. This layout manager could prove useful in such situations.

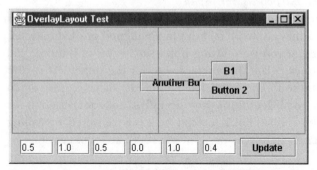

Figure 11-13. A demonstration of the OverlayLayout manager on three components

Here's the code that produced this example. As with many of the examples, this one is more fun if you compile and run the program itself:

```
// OverlayTest.java
// A test of the OverlayLayout manger . . .
//
import java.awt.*;
import java.awt.event.*;
import javax.swing.*;

public class OverlayTest extends JFrame {

    public OverlayTest(float[] alignments) {
        super("OverlayLayout Test");
        setSize(400, 200);
        addWindowListener(new BasicWindowMonitor());

        Container c = getContentPane();

        final JPanel p1 = new GridPanel();
        final OverlayLayout overlay = new OverlayLayout(p1);
        p1.setLayout(overlay);

        final JButton jb1 = new JButton("B1");
        final JButton jb2 = new JButton("Button 2");
        final JButton jb3 = new JButton("Another Button");

        SimpleReporter reporter = new SimpleReporter();
        jb1.addActionListener(reporter);
        jb2.addActionListener(reporter);
        jb3.addActionListener(reporter);
```

```
          p1.add(jb1);
          p1.add(jb2);
          p1.add(jb3);

          JPanel p2 = new JPanel();
          p2.setLayout(new GridLayout(1, 7));
          final JTextField x1 = new JTextField("0", 4);    // Button1 x alignment
          final JTextField y1 = new JTextField("0", 4);    // Button1 y alignment
          final JTextField x2 = new JTextField("0", 4);
          final JTextField y2 = new JTextField("0", 4);
          final JTextField x3 = new JTextField("0", 4);
          final JTextField y3 = new JTextField("0", 4);

          p2.add(x1);
          p2.add(y1);
          p2.add(x2);
          p2.add(y2);
          p2.add(x3);
          p2.add(y3);

          JButton updateButton = new JButton("Update");
          // Note that we expect real values in the text fields
          updateButton.addActionListener(new ActionListener() {
            public void actionPerformed(ActionEvent ae) {
                jb1.setAlignmentX(Float.valueOf(x1.getText().trim()).floatValue());
                jb1.setAlignmentY(Float.valueOf(y1.getText().trim()).floatValue());
                jb2.setAlignmentX(Float.valueOf(x2.getText().trim()).floatValue());
                jb2.setAlignmentY(Float.valueOf(y2.getText().trim()).floatValue());
                jb3.setAlignmentX(Float.valueOf(x3.getText().trim()).floatValue());
                jb3.setAlignmentY(Float.valueOf(y3.getText().trim()).floatValue());

                overlay.invalidateLayout(p1);
                p1.doLayout();
            }
          } );

        p2.add(updateButton);

        c.add(p1, BorderLayout.CENTER);
        c.add(p2, BorderLayout.SOUTH);
    }

    public static void main(String args[]) {
      float alignments[] = { 0.0f, 0.0f, 0.0f, 0.0f };
      if (args.length == 4) {
        for (int i = 0; i < 4; i++) {
          alignments[i] = Float.valueOf(args[i]).floatValue();
        }
      }
```

```java
    OverlayTest ot = new OverlayTest(alignments);
    ot.setSize(500, 300);
    ot.setVisible(true);
  }


  public class SimpleReporter implements ActionListener {
    public void actionPerformed(ActionEvent ae) {
      System.out.println(ae.getActionCommand());
    }
  }


  public class GridPanel extends JPanel {
    public void paint(Graphics g) {
      super.paint(g);
      int w = getSize().width;
      int h = getSize().height;

      System.out.println("w: " + w + " h: " + h);
      g.setColor(Color.red);
      g.drawRect(0, 0, w-1, h-1);
      g.drawLine(w/2, 0, w/2, h);
      g.drawLine(0, h/2, w, h/2);
    }
  }
}
```

When the user clicks the "Update" button, we receive an ActionEvent. The
listener for this event does all the real work. We then query all the text fields,
convert their contents into numbers, and set the alignment values. To make the
new alignments take effect, we invalidate the layout and tell our panel to re-do its
layout.

Other Panes

While these panes provide a number of professional containers to use in your
applications, they are not the only utility classes in the Swing package. Chapter 12,
Chooser Dialogs, discusses some of the other panes available, including a file
chooser and a color chooser.

12

Chooser Dialogs

Just about any application you write these days needs to have a mechanism for opening and saving files. In the AWT, you can use the `FileDialog` class, but that is a heavyweight dialog that lacks the flexibility of the Swing components we've seen so far. The `JFileChooser` is Swing's answer to the `FileDialog`. The Swing package also contains a helper dialog for choosing colors (a common task in the configuration area of applications). We'll look at both of these dialogs in this chapter.

NOTE   Some of the classes discussed in this chapter were still being updated as of JDK 1.2 beta4. You should check the online documentation that ships with the JDK for any late-breaking updates or additions.

To get things started, Figure 12-1 shows the class hierarchy of the pieces we'll be looking at in this chapter.

The JFileChooser Class

Since it plays such an integral role in just about every commercial application, let's look at the file chooser first. The `JFileChooser` class bundles a directory pane and typical selection buttons into a handy interface. Figure 12-2 shows the dialog window you get when you select the Save option of a simple application. As you might expect, other look-and-feels can also be applied to this chooser. Figure 12-3 shows the Windows and Motif L&Fs.

Here's the code that generated the application. The application itself only reports which file was chosen to open or save. Our application has a "Pick Directory" button that restricts the chooser to directories. The event handlers for each button

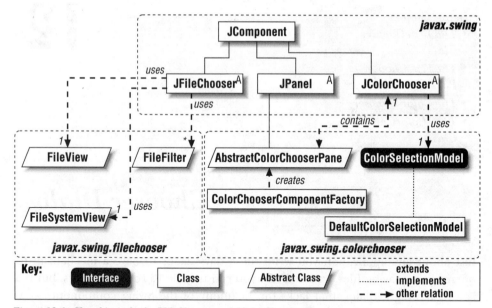

Figure 12-1. *Class hierarchy for JFileChooser and JColorChooser*

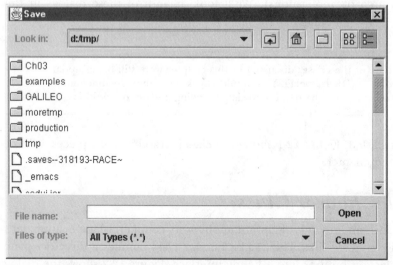

Figure 12-2. *The JFileChooser save dialog (Metal look-and-feel)*

do most of the interesting work. In each case, we create a new `JFileChooser` object, make any changes to the default properties that we need for the particular action, and then show the dialog. As you will see from the constants discussed later, the `int` returned from the `showDialog()` method indicates whether the user accepted a file selection or canceled the dialog. If we have a successful selection, we put the name of the file into a display label.

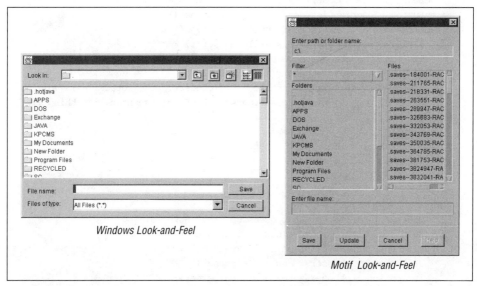

Figure 12-3. The Windows and Motif look-and-feel for JFileChooser

For this quick test, we create each file chooser dialog as we need it. You do not have to do this. You can save a reference to these dialogs and reuse them, just as you would other popups.

```
// SimpleFileChooser.java
// A simple file chooser to see what it takes to make one of these work.
//
import java.awt.*;
import java.awt.event.*;
import java.io.*;
import javax.swing.*;

public class SimpleFileChooser extends JFrame {
  JFrame parent;
  public SimpleFileChooser() {
    super("Table Test Frame");
    setSize(350, 200);
    addWindowListener(new BasicWindowMonitor());
    parent = this;

    Container c = getContentPane();
    c.setLayout(new FlowLayout());

    JButton openButton = new JButton("Open");
    JButton saveButton = new JButton("Save");
    JButton dirButton = new JButton("Pick Dir");
    final JLabel statusbar =
              new JLabel("Output of your selection will go here");
```

```java
// Create a file chooser that opens up as an "Open" dialog
openButton.addActionListener(new ActionListener() {
  public void actionPerformed(ActionEvent ae) {
    JFileChooser chooser = new JFileChooser();
    int option = chooser.showOpenDialog(parent);
    if (option == JFileChooser.APPROVE_OPTION) {
      statusbar.setText("You chose " + ((chooser.getSelectedFile()!=null)?
                        ((chooser.getSelectedFile().getName():"nothing"));
    }
    else {
      statusbar.setText("You canceled.");
    }
  }
});

// Create a file chooser that opens up as a "Save" dialog
saveButton.addActionListener(new ActionListener() {
  public void actionPerformed(ActionEvent ae) {
    JFileChooser chooser = new JFileChooser();
    int option = chooser.showSaveDialog(parent);
    if (option == JFileChooser.APPROVE_OPTION) {
      statusbar.setText("You saved " + ((chooser.getSelectedFile()!=null)?
                        chooser.getSelectedFile().getName():"nothing"));
    }
    else {
      statusbar.setText("You canceled.");
    }
  }
});

// Create a file chooser that allows you to pick a directory
// rather than a file
dirButton.addActionListener(new ActionListener() {
  public void actionPerformed(ActionEvent ae) {
    JFileChooser chooser = new JFileChooser();
    chooser.setFileSelectionMode(JFileChooser.DIRECTORIES_ONLY);
    int option = chooser.showOpenDialog(parent);
    if (option == JFileChooser.APPROVE_OPTION) {
      statusbar.setText("You opened " + ((chooser.getSelectedFile()!=null)?
                        chooser.getSelectedFile().getName():"nothing"));
    }
    else {
      statusbar.setText("You canceled.");
    }
  }
});

c.add(openButton);
c.add(saveButton);
```

```
      c.add(dirButton);
      c.add(statusbar);
   }

   public static void main(String args[]) {
      SimpleFileChooser sfc = new SimpleFileChooser();
      sfc.setVisible(true);
   }
}
```

Properties

The JFileChooser class uses properties for configuring most of the dialog's functionality. The properties shown in Table 12-1 are available.

Table 12-1. FileChooser Properties

Property	Data Type	get	is	set	bound	Default Value
UI	SplitPaneUI	•		•	•	from L&F
UIClassID*	String	•				"FileChooserUI"
acceptAllFileFilter	FileFilter	•				from L&F
accessibleContext	Accessible-Context	•				FileChooser.accessibleJFileChooser()
accessory	JComponent	•		•	•	null
approveButtonMnemonic		•		•	•	
approveButtonText	String	•		•	•	null
approveButtonToolTipText	String	•		•	•	null
choosableFileFilters[a]	FileFilter[]	•			•	{getAcceptAllFileFilter()}
currentDirectory	File	•		•	•	User's home directory
dialogTitle	String	•		•		null
dialogType	int	•		•	•	OPEN_DIALOG
directorySelectionEnabled[b]	boolean		•			false
fileFilter	FileFilter	•		•	•	AcceptAllFileFilter()
fileHidingEnabled	boolean		•	•	•	true
fileSelectionEnabled[b]	boolean		•			true
fileSelectionMode	int	•		•	•	FILES_ONLY
fileSystemView	FileSystem-View	•		•	•	FileSystem-View.getFileSystemView()
fileView	FileView	•		•	•	null

See also properties from the JComponent class (Table 3-5).

Table 12-1. FileChooser Properties (continued)

Property	Data Type	get	is	set	bound	Default Value
multiSelectionEnabled	boolean		•	•	•	false
selectedFile	File	•		•	•	null
selectedFiles[c]	File[]	•		•	•	File[0]

See also properties from the JComponent class (Table 3-5).

[a] File filters are set using separate add, remove, and reset methods discussed later.
[b] These properties are based on the fileSelectionMode property.
[c] These properties should be bound, but currently this functionality is pending.

The acceptAllFileFilter property provides access to the most common filter which, not surprisingly, accepts all files. You can set a more restrictive filter through the fileFilter property, or get a list of all the filters this dialog knows about with the choosableFileFilters property. The filters can also be affected by the fileHidingEnabled property, which if true, does not display hidden files (such as files starting with "." on Unix systems). You can determine whether or not the dialog looks for files, directories, or both during selection, using the directorySelectionEnabled and fileSelectionEnabled convenience properties. The fileSelectionMode property is the real determining factor. You can use this property to select files, directories, or both with some of the constants presented later. Regardless of whether or not directories are selectable, double-clicking a directory opens that directory and makes it the new currentDirectory for the chooser. The number of files that can be selected (one or many) is determined by the multiSelectionEnabled property, which was not implemented at the time of this writing. The selectedFile property contains the lead selection, while the selectedFiles property holds several files, if multiple selections are allowed.

The remaining properties dictate the visual appearance of the dialog. You can create save, open, and custom dialogs with the dialogType property and some of the constants discussed later. The icons and descriptions used for files and folders are managed with the fileView and fileSystemView properties. (The data types supporting these properties are discussed in more detail in the next section.) You can customize the text in the dialog by setting the dialogTitle property for the popup's title, and the approveButtonText and approveButtonToolTipText properties for the "Ok" button equivalent in your dialog.

The accessory property provides developers with an interesting hook into the dialog. You can create a custom component and attach it to the dialog. A typical example of such an accessory is an image viewer that shows you a thumbnail of any image file you have selected in the file selection window. Figure 12-4 shows a similar component that allows you to play *.au* files.

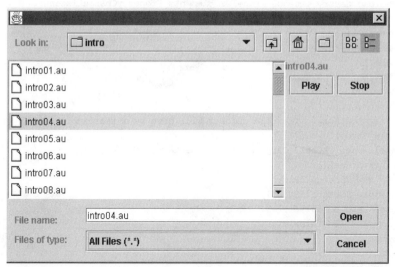

Figure 12-4. A file chooser with an audio accessory that can play a selected .au file

Here's the code for the accessory. To react to the user selecting a new file, your accessory needs to implement the PropertyChangeListener interface. (We attach it as a listener in the main application below this code.) Notice how we check the property change being reported in the propertyChange() method, so that we only react to new file selections. If it is a file selection event, we grab the new filename from the PropertyChangeEvent object. The propertyChange() method is the heart of the program. You should use this method to update your accessory as the user moves around the file system. We also use the setCurrent-Clip() method to keep the accessory's GUI in sync with the selected file. This keeps the play and stop buttons inactive for non-audio files, so that users don't try to play a text file.

```java
// AudioAccessory.java
// A simple accessory for JFileChooser that lets you play .au clips.
//
import javax.swing.*;
import java.awt.*;
import java.net.*;
import java.beans.*;
import java.io.*;
import java.applet.*;
import java.awt.event.*;

// Caveat programmer: you should replace this with a JMF equivalent when that's
// ready for all of your delivery platforms.
import sun.applet.*;
```

```java
public class AudioAccessory extends JPanel implements PropertyChangeListener {

  AudioClip currentClip;
  String currentName="";
  JLabel fileLabel;
  JButton playButton, stopButton;

  public AudioAccessory() {
    // Set up the accessory.  The file chooser will give us a reasonable size.
    setLayout(new BorderLayout());
    add(fileLabel = new JLabel("Clip Name"), BorderLayout.NORTH);
    JPanel p = new JPanel();
    playButton = new JButton("Play");
    stopButton = new JButton("Stop");
    playButton.setEnabled(false);
    stopButton.setEnabled(false);
    p.add(playButton);
    p.add(stopButton);
    add(p, BorderLayout.CENTER);

    playButton.addActionListener(new ActionListener() {
      public void actionPerformed(ActionEvent e) {
        if (currentClip != null) {
          currentClip.stop();
          currentClip.play();
        }
      }
    });
    stopButton.addActionListener(new ActionListener() {
      public void actionPerformed(ActionEvent e) {
        if (currentClip != null) {
          currentClip.stop();
        }
      }
    });
  }

  public void propertyChange(PropertyChangeEvent e) {
    if (e.getPropertyName()
        .equals(JFileChooser.SELECTED_FILE_CHANGED_PROPERTY)) {

      // Ok, the user selected a file in the chooser
      File f = (File)e.getNewValue();

      // Make reasonably sure it's an audio file
      if (f.getName().toLowerCase().endsWith(".au")) {
        setCurrentClip(f);
      }
      else {
```

```
            setCurrentClip(null);
        }
    }
}

public void setCurrentClip(File f) {
    // Make sure we have a real file, otherwise, disable the buttons
    if ((f == null) || (f.getName() == null)) {
        fileLabel.setText("no audio selected");
        playButton.setEnabled(false);
        stopButton.setEnabled(false);
        return;
    }

    // Ok, seems the audio file is real, so load it and enable the buttons
    String name = f.getName();
    if (name.equals(currentName)) {
        return;
    }
    if (currentClip != null) { currentClip.stop(); }
    currentName = name;
    try {
        URL u = new URL("file:///" + f.getAbsolutePath())
        currentClip = new AppletAudioClip(u);
    }
    catch (Exception e) {
        e.printStackTrace();
        currentClip = null;
        fileLabel.setText("Error loading clip.");
    }
    fileLabel.setText(name);
    playButton.setEnabled(true);
    stopButton.setEnabled(true);
    }
}
```

And here's the application code that inserts the accessory into the chooser. The only real change we make is to the open button's `actionPerformed()` method. Before we make the chooser visible, we use `setAccessory()` to get our audio accessory in place. Then we attach the accessory as a property change listener to the chooser, so that the accessory is appropriately notified as the user selects new files.

```
// AccessoryFileChooser.java, just a simple file chooser example
// to see what it takes to make one of these work.
//
import java.awt.*;
import java.awt.event.*;
import java.io.*;
```

```
import com.sun.java.swing.*;

public class AccessoryFileChooser extends JFrame {
  JFrame parent;
  public AccessoryFileChooser() {
    super("Accessory Test Frame");
    setSize(350, 200);
    addWindowListener(new BasicWindowMonitor());
    parent = this;
    Container c = getContentPane();
    c.setLayout(new FlowLayout());

    JButton accButton = new JButton("Accessory");
    final JLabel statusbar =
                new JLabel("Output of your selection will go here");

    accButton.addActionListener(new ActionListener() {
      public void actionPerformed(ActionEvent ae) {
        JFileChooser chooser = new JFileChooser();
        AudioAccessory aa = new AudioAccessory();
        chooser.setAccessory(aa);
        chooser.addPropertyChangeListener(aa);
        int option = chooser.showOpenDialog(parent);
        if (option == JFileChooser.APPROVE_OPTION) {
          statusbar.setText("You chose " + ((chooser.getSelectedFile()!=null)?
                        chooser.getSelectedFile().getName():"nothing"));
        }
        else {
          statusbar.setText("You canceled.");
        }
      }
    });
    c.add(accButton);
    c.add(statusbar);
  }

  public static void main(String args[]) {
    AccessoryFileChooser afc = new AccessoryFileChooser();
    afc.setVisible(true);
  }
}
```

Events

In addition to the property change events generated like most other Swing components, the JFileChooser also generates action events when the user presses the
approve or cancel buttons. The event is fired after the dialog is hidden.

public void addActionListener(ActionListener l)

public void removeActionListener(ActionListener l)

> If you want to listen directly to the approve or cancel button events, you can add an `ActionListener` to the dialog. The accessory example listened to such events to stop playing any active audio clip.

public void approveSelection()

public void cancelSelection()

> You can programmatically fire an approval or a cancellation using these methods, simulating pressing the "Ok" or "Cancel" buttons. This can be useful if your accessory provides its own way of saying yes or no to the current selection. Both methods use the `fireActionPerformed()` method below to send out the events. The `APPROVE_SELECTION` and `CANCEL_SELECTION` constants listed later are used for the appropriate command string.

protected void fireActionPerformed(String command)

> This protected method fires off a newly generated `ActionEvent` with the given command as the `actionCommand` of the event.

Constants

The `JFileChooser` class has several constants. These constants can be broken into two categories:

- The constants used for property change events, shown in Table 12-2

- The constants used as various property values, shown in Table 12-3

Table 12-2. FileChooser Property Names (for Property Change Events)

Constant	Type	Description
ACCESSORY_CHANGED_PROPERTY	String	The name of the `accessory` property
APPROVE_BUTTON_MNEMONIC_ CHANGED_PROPERTY	String	The name of the `approveButtonMne-monic` property
APPROVE_BUTTON_TEXT_CHANGED_ PROPERTY	String	The name of the `approveButtonText` property
APPROVE_BUTTON_TOOL_TIP_ TEXT_CHANGED_PROPERTY	String	The name of the `approveButtonTool-TipText` property
CHOOSABLE_FILE_FILTER_ CHANGED_PROPERTY	String	The name of the `choosableFile-Filters` property
DIALOG_TYPE_CHANGED_PROPERTY	String	The name of the `dialogType` property
DIRECTORY_CHANGED_PROPERTY	String	The name of the `currentDirectory` property
FILE_FILTER_CHANGED_PROPERTY	String	The name of the `fileFilter` property
FILE_HIDING_CHANGED_PROPERTY	String	The name of the `fileHidingEnabled` property

Table 12-2. FileChooser Property Names (for Property Change Events) (continued)

Constant	Type	Description
FILE_SELECTION_MODE_CHANGED_ PROPERTY	String	The name of the fileSelectionMode property
FILE_SYSTEM_VIEW_CHANGED_ PROPERTY	String	The name of the fileSystemView property
FILE_VIEW_CHANGED_PROPERTY	String	The name of the fileView property
MULTI_SELECTION_ENABLED_ CHANGED_PROPERTY	String	The name of the multiSelection-Enabled property
SELECTED_FILE_CHANGED_ PROPERTY	String	The name of the selectedFile property

The constants in Table 12-3 provide values for many of the properties in the JFileChooser class.

Table 12-3. FileChooser Dialog Constants

Constant	Type	Description
APPROVE_OPTION	int	The return value from the showDialog() methods, indicating the user selected the "approve" option
APPROVE_SELECTION	String	The string to be used for the action-Command property of the ActionEvent generated when the user approves the current selection
CANCEL_OPTION	int	The return value from the showDialog() methods, indicating the user selected the "cancel" option
CANCEL_SELECTION	String	The string to be used for the action-Command property of the ActionEvent generated when the user cancels the current selection
CUSTOM_DIALOG	String	A valid option for the dialogType property, indicating this dialog supports a user-defined operation
DIRECTORIES_ONLY	int	A valid option for the fileSelection-Mode property, indicating that only directories can be selected
ERROR_OPTION	int	The return value from the showDialog() methods, indicating an error occurred
FILES_AND_DIRECTORIES	int	A valid option for the fileSelection-Mode property, indicating that both files and directories can be selected
FILES_ONLY	int	A valid option for the fileSelection-Mode property, indicating that only files can be selected

Table 12-3. FileChooser Dialog Constants (continued)

Constant	Type	Description
OPEN_DIALOG	int	A valid option for the dialogType property, indicating this dialog is selecting files to be opened
SAVE_DIALOG	int	A valid option for the dialogType property, indicating this dialog is selecting a file to be saved

Constructors

public JFileChooser()

Creates a file chooser starting at the user's home directory. File choosers do not make a distinction between open and save at creation time. That aspect of a chooser is dictated by the dialogType property, which can be set at any time.

public JFileChooser(File directory)
public JFileChooser(String path)

These constructors create new choosers starting at the specified directory.

FileFilter Methods

The choosableFileFilters property does not have a proper "set" method, but you can modify the set of available filters using these methods.

public void addChoosableFileFilter(FileFilter filter)
public void removeChoosableFileFilter(FileFilter filter)

Add or remove filters. The FileFilter class is discussed in detail below.

public void resetChoosableFileFilters()

Resets the list of choosable file filters to contain only the original "accept all" filter.

File Methods

The file methods check files to find the appropriate names, descriptions and icons to display in the chooser according to the active FileView and FileFilter objects.

public boolean accept(File f)

Returns true if the file f should be displayed.

public void ensureFileIsVisible(File f)

Ensures the file f is visible in the chooser, which may mean changing the scroll location of the file list.

public String getDescription(File f)

Returns a description of the file f. A common description is simply the file's name.

public Icon getIcon(File f)

Returns an icon to display in the chooser for the file f. The icon could change depending on the type of file.

public String getName(File f)

Returns the name of the file f. The chooser relies on the active `FileView` object to decide a file's name. The `FileView` object could alter the file's name for display, for example, to create an ISO 9660 compliant name.

public String getTypeDescription(File f)

Returns a brief description of the type of file f. The details view of a directory might use this information.

public boolean isTraversable(File f)

Returns `true` if the file is a folder and can be opened.

Dialog Methods

public int showDialog(Component parent, String approveButtonText)

Makes the dialog visible. If `parent` is not an instance of `Frame`, then the containing `Frame` object for `parent` is located and used. This method returns 0 if the user accepts a file, -1 if the user cancels or otherwise closes the dialog. Use this version of `showDialog()` to create a custom dialog that has text you specify for the "Ok" button (as opposed to one of the other show methods below).

public int showOpenDialog(Component parent)
public int showSaveDialog(Component parent)

You can use these methods to display chooser dialogs that have "Open" or "Save" on the approve button. The dialogs will be shown relative to the `parent` component.

Miscellaneous Methods

public void changeToParentDirectory()

Programmatically moves the current directory up one level. At the root level, this method has no effect.

protected void init()

Initializes the properties of the dialog and picks the default file view for your system.

public void rescanCurrentDirectory()

Reloads the current directory if its contents have changed.

public void updateUI()
> Updates the chooser dialog with the look-and-feel dictated by the UI manager.

The File Chooser Package

Under `javax.swing`, you'll find a package of helper classes for the `JFileChooser`. The `javax.swing.filechooser` package contains several classes for displaying and filtering files. (More classes are planned for this package, but they are currently located in the file chooser demo area in the *examples/* directory of the Swing download package.)

The FileFilter Class

The `FileFilter` class can be used to create filters for `JFileChooser` dialogs. The class contains only two abstract methods, but default implementations based on filename extensions should become a standard part of the Swing package with the next release. It's important to note that extensions are not the only way to judge a file's fitness for a particular filter. The Mac filesystem, for example, can understand the creator of a file regardless of the file's name. On Unix systems, you might write a filter to display only files that are readable by the current user.

Constructors

public FileFilter()

The `FileFilter` class receives this default constructor at compile time, it is not defined in the class itself.

Filter Methods

public abstract boolean accept(File f)
> Returns `true` if the file `f` matches this filter.

public abstract String getDescription()
> Returns a short description to appear in the filters pull-down on the chooser. An example would be "Java Source Code" for any *.java* files.

Figure 12-5 shows a file chooser with custom filters for multimedia file types.

Here's the code for the application. Before we make this chooser visible, we create and insert the three new filters for our media types. Other than that, it's much the same code as our previous applications. In a future release of Swing, you should have access to a similar extension-based file filter class. However, we use this example anyway, as it illustrates the inner workings of a filter that should seem familiar to most programmers.

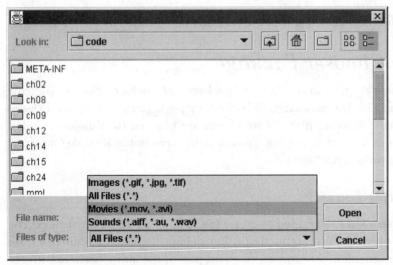

Figure 12-5. A custom set of filters for use with JFileChooser

```
// MyFilterChooser.java
// Just a simple example to see what it takes to make one of these filters work.
//
import java.awt.*;
import java.awt.event.*;
import java.io.*;
import javax.swing.*;

public class MyFilterChooser extends JFrame {
  JFrame parent;
  public MyFilterChooser() {
    super("Filter Test Frame");
    setSize(350, 200);
    addWindowListener(new BasicWindowMonitor());
    parent = this;

    Container c = getContentPane();
    c.setLayout(new FlowLayout());

    JButton openButton = new JButton("Open");
    final JLabel statusbar =
              new JLabel("Output of your selection will go here");

    openButton.addActionListener(new ActionListener() {
      public void actionPerformed(ActionEvent ae) {
        String[] pics = new String[] {"gif", "jpg", "tif"};
        String[] movies = new String[] {"mov", "avi"};
        String[] audios = new String[] {"au", "aiff", "wav"};
        JFileChooser chooser = new JFileChooser();
```

```
        chooser.setMultiSelectionEnabled(false);
        chooser.addChoosableFileFilter(new SimpleFileFilter(pics,
                                "Images (*.gif, *.jpg, *.tif)"));
        chooser.addChoosableFileFilter(new SimpleFileFilter(movies,
                                "Movies (*.mov, *.avi)"));
        chooser.addChoosableFileFilter(new SimpleFileFilter(audios,
                                "Sounds (*.aiff, *.au, *.wav)"));
        int option = chooser.showOpenDialog(parent);
        if (option == JFileChooser.APPROVE_OPTION) {
          if (chooser.getSelectedFile()!=null)
            statusbar.setText("You chose " +
                        chooser.getSelectedFile().getName());
        }
        else {
          statusbar.setText("You canceled.");
        }
      }
    });

    c.add(openButton);
    c.add(statusbar);
    setVisible(true);
  }

  public static void main(String args[]) {
    MyFilterChooser bt = new MyFilterChooser();
  }
}
```

And here is the implementation of the filter class. You pass in an extension (or list of extensions) and a description of the extension to the constructor. If you don't supply a description, the constructor builds a simple one for you based on the extensions you passed in. The only real work this class does happens in the accept() method, where we look to see if the file presented matches one of the supplied extensions.

```
// SimpleFileFilter.java
// A straightforward extension-based example of a file filter. This should be
// replaced by a "first class" Swing class in a later release of Swing.
//
import javax.swing.filechooser.*;
import java.io.File;

public class SimpleFileFilter extends FileFilter {

  String[] extensions;
  String description;
```

```
  public SimpleFileFilter(String ext) {
    this (new String[] {ext}, null);
  }

  public SimpleFileFilter(String[] exts, String descr) {
    // clone and lowercase the extensions
    extensions = new String[exts.length];
    for (int i = exts.length - 1; i >= 0; i--) {
      extensions[i] = exts[i].toLowerCase();
    }
    // make sure we have a valid (if simplistic) description
    description = (descr == null ? exts[0] + " files" : descr);
  }

  public boolean accept(File f) {
    // we always allow directories, regardless of their extension
    if (f.isDirectory()) { return true; }

    // ok, it's a regular file so check the extension
    String name = f.getName().toLowerCase();
    for (int i = extensions.length - 1; i >= 0; i--) {
      if (name.endsWith(extensions[i])) {
        return true;
      }
    }
    return false;
  }

  public String getDescription() { return description; }
}
```

The FileView Class

Another abstract helper class in the `filechooser` package is the `FileView` class. This class is implemented by the various look-and-feels to supply icons and descriptions for the basic file and folder entries in the filesystem. While each look-and-feel has a default implementation of this class, you can write your own and attach it to a file chooser to supply custom icons and descriptions for interesting types of files.

Constructor

public FileView()
     The `FileView` class has only this default constructor.

Methods

All of the methods for the `FileView` class are abstract and take one `File` as an argument. You fill in these methods to present a clean, consistent view of all files throughout the file chooser. Most views end up making decisions based on file information, such as the file's name or extension, before returning its result.

public abstract String getName(File f)

> Returns the name of the file f. While it's quite easy to return f.getName(), you might want to return an all-uppercase version, or a cross-platform CD-ROM–compliant (ISO 9660) name, etc.

public abstract String getDescription(File f)

> Returns a description of the file. The description could be something of a short abstract of the file's contents. Your file chooser might not necessarily display this information.

public abstract String getTypeDescription(File f)

> Returns a description of the type of the file, such as "Directory" or "Bitmap Image."

public abstract Icon getIcon(File f)

> Returns an icon appropriate for the file f. This could be a folder icon, a file icon, or some specific icon based on other file information, such as its extension.

public abstract boolean isTraversable(File f)

> Answers questions about whether or not a directory can be opened. For example, Unix and Windows NT can prevent users from accessing directories for which they don't have permission. You could check permissions and return false if the user is not allowed to open a given folder. Rather than get an error when trying to open the folder, the user doesn't get the chance to try.

Figure 12-6 is an example of a custom FileView that (slowly!) displays tiny representations of any *.gif* or *.jpg* files in the directory, instead of the generic icons. Since it loads the real image and scales it, rather than storing some separate folder of real icons, you don't want to try this on your collection of 5,000 JPEG clip art images. It's great on small directories, though. Notice, too, the "hard drive" icon on Win32 systems (for *C:* and similar directories) has been replaced by a generic folder icon, since we don't distinguish between root-level and regular directories.

Following is the code for this particular file view. Look at the getIcon() method. That's where we decide which icon to return for a particular file. In this implementation, we list all directories as traversable and return a rather generic type description for our files. Notice that in the getName() method we check for an empty string. On Windows platforms, this empty string corresponds to one of the drive letters. The "name" of the file is empty, but the path contains the appropriate information, so we return that. If you're curious about the Metal-IconFactory that we use to get the file and folder icons, check out Chapter 26, *Look & Feel.*

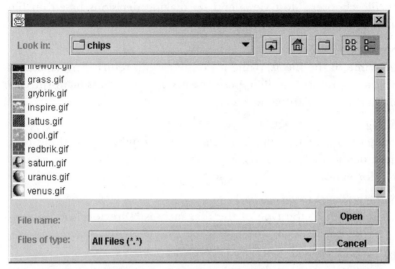

Figure 12-6. A custom file view for a file chooser that displays icons of image files

You might notice that we store a Component object (rather than JComponent) as our image observer. The reason for this is twofold. First, that's one class the createImage() method is defined in. Second, one obvious choice for the observer is the frame containing the application, which will frequently be a JFrame, and JFrame does not descend from JComponent.

```java
// ThumbNailFileView.java
// A simple implementation of the FileView class that provides a 16x16 image of
// each GIF or JPG file for its icon. This could be SLOW for large images, as we
// simply load the real image and then scale it.
//
import java.io.File;
import java.awt.*;
import javax.swing.*;
import javax.swing.filechooser.*;
import javax.swing.plaf.metal.MetalIconFactory;

public class ThumbNailFileView extends FileView {

  private Icon fileIcon = MetalIconFactory.getTreeLeafIcon();
  private Icon folderIcon = MetalIconFactory.getTreeFolderIcon();
  private Component observer;

  public ThumbNailFileView(Component c) {
    // we need a component around to create our icon's image
    observer = c;
  }
```

```
public String getDescription(File f) {
  // we won't store individual descriptions, so just return the
  // type description
  return getTypeDescription(f);
}

public Icon getIcon(File f) {
  // is it a folder?
  if (f.isDirectory()) { return folderIcon; }

  // ok, it's a file, so return a custom icon if it's an image file
  String name = f.getName().toLowerCase();
  if (name.endsWith(".jpg") || name.endsWith(".gif")) {
    return new Icon16(f.getAbsolutePath());
  }

  // and return the generic file icon if it's not
  return fileIcon;
}

public String getName(File f) {
  String name = f.getName();
  return name.equals("") ? f.getPath() : name;
}

public String getTypeDescription(File f) {
  String name = f.getName().toLowerCase();
  if (f.isDirectory()) { return "Folder"; }
  if (name.endsWith(".jpg")) { return "JPG Image"; }
  if (name.endsWith(".gif")) { return "GIF Image"; }
  return "Generic File";
}

public Boolean isTraversable(File f) {
  // we'll mark all directories as traversable
  return f.isDirectory() ? Boolean.TRUE : Boolean.FALSE;
}

public class Icon16 extends ImageIcon {
  public Icon16(String f) {
    super(f);
    Image i = observer.createImage(16, 16);
    i.getGraphics().drawImage(getImage(), 0, 0, 16, 16, observer);
    setImage(i);
  }

  public int getIconHeight() { return 16; }
  public int getIconWidth() { return 16; }
```

```
    public void paintIcon(Component c, Graphics g, int x, int y) {
      g.drawImage(getImage(), x, y, c);
    }
  }
}
```

Here's the application that uses this file view implementation. The only real change from the previous applications is in the properties we set for the chooser.

```
// MyViewChooser.java
// A simple example to see what it takes to make one of these FileViews work.
//
import java.awt.*;
import java.awt.event.*;
import java.io.*;
import javax.swing.*;

public class MyViewChooser extends JFrame {
  JFrame parent;
  public MyViewChooser() {
    super("File View Test Frame");
    setSize(350, 200);
    addWindowListener(new BasicWindowMonitor());
    parent = this;

    Container c = getContentPane();
    c.setLayout(new FlowLayout());

    JButton openButton = new JButton("Open");
    final JLabel statusbar =
              new JLabel("Output of your selection will go here");

    openButton.addActionListener(new ActionListener() {
      public void actionPerformed(ActionEvent ae) {
        JFileChooser chooser = new JFileChooser();

        // ok, set up our own file view for the chooser
        chooser.setFileView(new ThumbNailFileView(MyViewChooser.this));

        int option = chooser.showOpenDialog(parent);
        if (option == JFileChooser.APPROVE_OPTION) {
          statusbar.setText("You chose " +
                          chooser.getSelectedFile().getName());
        }
        else {
          statusbar.setText("You cancelled.");
        }
      }
    });
```

```
    c.add(openButton);
    c.add(statusbar);
  }

  public static void main(String args[]) {
    MyViewChooser vc = new MyViewChooser();
    vc.setVisible(true);
  }
}
```

The FileSystemView Class

Another detail missing from the normal `FileChooser` dialog is a system independent way of asking for a look at the entire filesystem. On Windows machines, for example, there are several "root" directories—one for each floppy drive, hard drive, CD drive, etc. On Unix systems, there is only one root directory, named "/". Mac systems have a notion of a volume which is different still. The `FileSystem-View` class is meant to be a source for system-independent views that map nicely to the real filesystem underneath your application. Currently, only Unix and Win32 systems have real implementations, but others are planned for release shortly. Systems that do not have a full implementation rely on a generic filesystem view, similar to what is available through the standard `java.io.File` class.

Constructor

public FileSystemView()

Like the `FileView` class, this class contains only the default constructor.

Class Method

public static FileSystemView getFileSystemView()

This method checks the file separator character to decide which filesystem view to return. A / returns a Unix view, \ returns a Win32 view, and everything else gets the generic view.

File and Folder Methods

public File createFileObject(File dir, String filename)

Returns a new `File` object, based on `dir` and `filename`. This method checks `dir` and if it's `null`, returns a `File` object based solely on `filename`.

public File createFileObject(String path)

Returns a new `File` object created with `path`.

public abstract File createNewFolder(File containingDir) throws IOException

Creates a new folder with some default name appropriate to the filesystem.

public File[] getFiles(File dir, boolean useFileHiding)

Returns a list of all of the files in `dir`. If `useFileHiding` is `true`, each file in `dir` will be checked before being added to the list.

public File getParentDirectory(File dir)

Returns the parent directory of `dir` as a file object. If `dir` is `null`, `null` will be returned.

public abstract File[] getRoots()

Returns a list of "root" directories. On Unix systems, this is the / directory. On Windows machines, this is a list of the active drive letters. Presumably, this would also be used to get things such as a list of volumes on a Mac system, but that functionality is not present in any of the current implementations.

public abstract boolean isHiddenFile(File f)

Returns `true` if the file `f` is a hidden file. What makes a file a hidden file differs from system to system.

public abstract boolean isRoot(File f)

Returns `true` if the file `f` maps to a root directory.

The Color Chooser

As the name indicates, the `JColorChooser` component is designed to allow users to pick a color. If your application supports customized environments (like the foreground, background, and highlight colors for text) this control might come in handy. You can pick colors from a palette and then look at that color in a preview panel that shows you how your color looks with black and white. The dialog also has an RGB mode that allows you to pick the exact amounts of red, blue, and green using sliders. The standard color chooser window looks like Figure 12-7.[*]

The `JColorChooser` class provides a static method for getting this popup going quickly. Here's the code that produced the screen shots in Figure 12-7:

```
// ColorPicker.java
// A quick test of the JColorChooser dialog.
//
import java.awt.*;
import java.awt.event.*;
import javax.swing.*;

public class ColorPicker extends JFrame {

  public ColorPicker() {
```

---

[*] JColorChooser has had a complicated history. It disappeared briefly into a `preview` package, and then returned for JDK 1.2 beta4 in a completely different form. We discuss the JDK 1.2 beta4 chooser.

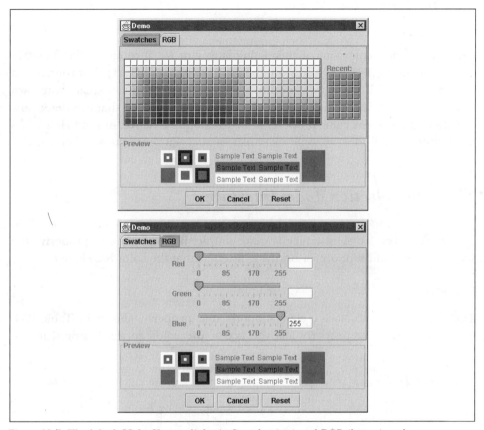

Figure 12-7. The default JColorChooser dialog in Swatches (top) and RGB (bottom) modes

```
    super("JColorChooser Test Frame");
    setSize(200, 100);
    final JButton go = new JButton("Show JColorChooser");
    go.addActionListener(new ActionListener() {
      public void actionPerformed(ActionEvent e) {
        Color c;
        c = JColorChooser.showDialog(
                ((Component)e.getSource()).getParent(),
                "Demo", Color.blue);
        go.setBackground(c);
      }
    });
    getContentPane().add(go);
    addWindowListener(new BasicWindowMonitor());
  }

  public static void main(String args[]) {
    ColorPicker cp = new ColorPicker();
```

```
      cp.setVisible(true);
  }
}
```

One way to get a color out of this dialog is to wait for it to close (the showDi-alog() method will block) and store the result of showDialog(). But you are not limited to a modal dialog that produces a single color. You can create your own color choosers to which you attach a ChangeListener object that can detect any change in the current color property while the popup is active, or even after it has been closed. We'll look at some examples of such custom choosers later in this chapter.

The ColorSelectionModel Interface

The JColorChooser uses a model to represent the currently selected color. The ColorSelectionModel interface is quite simple, having only one property (the selected color) and support for notifying listeners that the color has changed.

Property

The ColorSelectionModel class supports one property, shown in Table 12-4. The selectedColor property lets you access the color currently stored in the model.

Table 12-4. ColorSelectionModel Property

Property	Data Type	get	is	set	bound	Description
selectedColor	Color	•		•		

Events

To indicate the selected color has changed, implementations of ColorSelec-tionModel should fire a ChangeEvent whenever the selectedColor property changes.

Following the standard naming conventions, the following methods are required for managing ChangeEvent listeners:

public void addChangeListener(ChangeListener l)
public void removeChangeListener(ChangeListener l)

> As you might expect, these methods allow you to add and remove listener objects interested in receiving event notifications.

The DefaultColorSelectionModel Class

The `DefaultColorSelectionModel` class provides a straightforward implementation of the `ColorSelectionModel` interface. This is the selection model used by default in the `JColorChooser` class.

Property

Table 12-5 shows the default value `DefaultColorSelectionModel` provides for the property inherited from `ColorSelectionModel`.

Table 12-5. DefaultColorSelectionModel Property

Property	Data Type	get	is	set	bound	Default Value
selectedColor	Color	•		•		Color.white

Events

Since `DefaultColorChooserModel` implements the `ColorChooserModel`, it fires a `ChangeEvent` whenever the `selectedColor` property changes.

In addition to the usual `addChangeListener()` and `removeChangeListener()` methods required by `ColorChooserModel`, the following method is provided to aid in dispatching change events:

public void addChangeListener(ChangeListener l)
public void removeChangeListener(ChangeListener l)
> Add or remove a change listener interested in changes to the state of this model.

protected fireStateChanged()
> You can use this method to fire a `ChangeEvent` whenever the color in the model is updated.

Fields

protected transient ChangeEvent changeEvent
> Since we only report change events when the selected color changes, we only need one event. That event is stored in this field.

protected EventListenerList listenerList
> This field stores the list of listeners interested in receiving notification when the selected color changes.

Constructors

public DefaultColorSelectionModel()
public DefaultColorSelectionModel(Color color)

These constructors create new `DefaultColorSelectionModel` objects. If you call the first constructor with no color, `Color.white` is used.

The JColorChooser Class

Properties

In addition to the typical UI properties of Swing components, the color chooser has the following properties listed in Table 12-6. The `chooserPanels` property contains an array of all the chooser panels currently associated with this color chooser. You can get and set the entire array at once or, more commonly, you can add and remove chooser panels using some of the methods described later. The `color` property contains the currently selected color in the chooser. The `previewPanel` property contains the `JComponent` subclass that previews your color choice. (You can see an example of the default preview panel in Figure 12-7.) The `selectionModel` property dictates which selection model the chooser uses.

Table 12-6. JColorChooser Properties

Property	Data Type	get	is	set	bound	Default Value
UI	ColorChooserUI	•		•	•	from L&F
UIClassID*	String	•				"ColorChooserUI"
selectionModel	ColorSelectionModel	•		•	•	DefaultColorSelec-tionModel
accessibleContext	AccessibleContext	•				JColorChooser.Acces-sibleJColorChooser()
chooserPanels	AbstractColorChooser-Panel[]	•		•	•	null
color	Color	•		•		Color.white
previewPanel	JComponent	•		•	•	null

See also properties from the JComponent class (Table 3-5).

Events (Inherited from JComponent)

On its own, `JColorChooser` only supports `PropertyChangeEvents`, like all other Swing components. Using the static `createDialog()` method described below, you can attach your own `ChangeListener` to the color selection model for your chooser and react to changes in color anywhere in your program. You can even create a standalone chooser and add it to the container of your choice.

Constants

The JColorChooser class defines several constants for the property names shown in Table 12-7.

Table 12-7. JColorChooser Property Names for Use in Property Change Events

Constant	Type	Description
CHOOSER_PANELS_PROPERTY	String	The name of the chooserPanels property
PREVIEW_PANEL_PROPERTY	String	The name of the previewPanel property
SELECTION_MODEL_PROPERTY	String	The name of the selectionModel property

Constructors

public JColorChooser()
public JColorChooser(Color initialColor)
public JColorChooser(ColorSelectionModel model)
> These constructors create new JColorChooser panes. The first two versions use a DefaultColorSelectionModel. In the first two versions, where you do not specify an initial color, Color.white will be used. In the last version, the color is extracted from the model.

Dialog Methods

public static JDialog createDialog(Component c, String title, boolean modal,
> *JColorChooser chooserPane, ActionListener okListener, ActionListener cancelListener)*
> Creates a (possibly modal) dialog window, with chooserPane as its main component. With this convenience method, you can add your own action listeners for the "Ok" and "Cancel" buttons.

public static Color showDialog(Component c, String title, Color initialColor)
> Creates a modal dialog that waits for the user to press either the "Ok" or the "Cancel" button. If the user chose "Ok," the current color in the chooser is returned, otherwise, null is returned. No errors or exceptions are raised if the user cancels.

Chooser Panel Methods

public void addChooserPanel(AbstractColorChooserPanel panel)
> Adds a new tab to the color chooser and places panel on that tab. An example using a custom chooser panel appears later in this chapter.

public AbstractColorChooserPanel removeChooserPanel(AbstractColorChooserPanel panel)

> Removes a panel from the chooser. If `panel` is found on one of the tabs, it is removed and returned. If the panel is not found, `null` is returned.

UI Methods

public void setColor(int c)
public void setColor(int r, int g, int b)

> You can use these methods as alternate ways of setting the color. They both affect the `color` property of `JColorChooser`. The first method expects a single ARGB color (where the alpha channel is effectively ignored). The second method takes red, green, and blue values ranging from 0 to 255.

public void updateUI()

> Updates the chooser's UI to the current one, according to the `UIManager`.

The AbstractColorChooserPanel Class

If you don't find the two chooser panels sufficient for your needs, you can write your own chooser panel and add it to the chooser along with the others. If you decide to do that, the `AbstractColorChooserPanel` is your starting point. This class has several properties you can fill in and a few abstract methods you must supply. Both of the panels you saw in Figure 12-7 were based on this class. Later, we'll take a look at writing our own custom chooser panel using this class.

Properties

The `AbstractColorChooserPanel` supports the properties shown in Table 12-8. The `smallDisplayIcon` and `displayName` properties should return values used in the tabs of the JColorChooser's tabbed pane. They can be `null`, but you should have at least one return a valid object, so that your tab contains some form of identification. The `colorSelectionModel` property accesses the `colorSelectionModel` of the enclosing chooser.

Protected Helper Method

protected Color getColorFromModel()

> This protected method retrieves the current color from the `ColorSelectionModel` attached to this chooser panel.

Chooser Panel Methods

protected abstract void buildChooser()

> Called to build your chooser panel when the color chooser is ready for it. It should only be called once.

Table 12-8. AbstractColorChooserPanel Properties

Property	Data Type	get	is	set	bound	Default Value
colorSelection- Model	ColorSelection- Model	•				DefaultColorSelection- Model()
displayName[a]	String	•				
largeDisplayIcon	Icon	•				
smallDisplayIcon[a]	Icon	•				

See also properties from the JPanel class (Table 8-1).

[a] The get call is abstract and must be supplied by the programmer, so no default value is available.

public void installChooserPanel(JColorChooser enclosingChooser)

This method is called when you add your chooser panel to the color chooser's tabbed pane. It registers this panel as a listener for change events coming from the chooser's ColorSelectionModel. You don't normally need to override this method, but if you do, be sure to call the corresponding method from the superclass.

public void uninstallChooserPanel(JColorChooser enclosingChooser)

Called when the panel is removed from the chooser's tabbed pane. As you might expect, the panel is unregistered from the selection model. And, as with installChooserPanel(), call the corresponding method from the superclass if you plan to override this. (You aren't required to call the superclass, but if you don't, you need to be sure that your install() and uninstall() methods cooperate.)

public void paint(Graphics g)

Watches to see if any color changes have been caught. If so, a call to update-Chooser() is made before repainting.

public abstract void updateChooser()

This method should update your chooser panel to reflect the current color in the ColorSelectionModel for the chooser. It will be called automatically when the panel is added to the chooser, so you do not have to figure out the current color in the constructor or buildChooser() method.

The ColorChooserComponentFactory Class

The ColorChooserComponentFactory class provides a few small methods for creating components common to a color chooser panel. The default chooser panels you see in JColorChooser come from this class, but you are certainly not restricted to using these components.

Methods

public static AbstractColorChooserPanel getAdvancedChooserPanel()

    Returns an instance of the package private `DefaultRGBChooserPanel` class. This is the "RGB" panel in Figure 12-7.

public static AbstractColorChooserPanel getSimpleChooserPanel()

    Returns an instance of the package private `DefaultSwatchChooserPanel` class. This is the "Swatches" panel in Figure 12-7.

public static JComponent getPreviewPanel()

    Returns an instance of the package private `DefaultPreviewPanel` class. This is the preview panel used in both screenshots in Figure 12-7.

Developing a Custom Chooser Panel

If you look very long at the `JColorChooser` component, you'll realize that it is really just a tabbed pane with a color previewer below it. You can have as many chooser panels in it as you like. Let's take a brief look at a panel that can be added to a color chooser. We'll create a simple panel for selecting a shade of gray with one slider, rather than pushing each slider for red, green, and blue to the same exact value. Figure 12-8 shows the resulting panel; following is the source code.

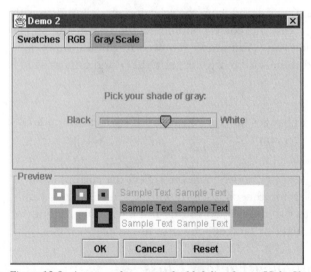

Figure 12-8. A custom chooser panel added directly to a JColorChooser object

```
// GrayScalePanel.java
// A simple implementation of the AbstractColorChooserPanel class. This class
// provides a slider for picking out a shade of gray.
//
import java.awt.*;
```

```
import javax.swing.*;
import javax.swing.event.*;
import javax.swing.colorchooser.*;

public class GrayScalePanel extends AbstractColorChooserPanel
                            implements ChangeListener {

  JSlider scale;

  // Set up our list of grays.  We'll assume we have all 256 possible shades, and
  // we'll do it when the class is loaded.
  static Color[] grays = new Color[256];
  static {
    for (int i=0; i<256; i++) { grays[i] = new Color(i, i, i); }
  }

  public GrayScalePanel() {
    setLayout(new GridLayout(0, 1));

    // create the slider and attach us as a listener
    scale = new JSlider(JSlider.HORIZONTAL, 0, 255, 128);
    scale.addChangeListener(this);

    // Set up our display for the chooser
    add(new JLabel("Pick your shade of gray:", JLabel.CENTER));
    JPanel jp = new JPanel();
    jp.add(new JLabel("Black"));
    jp.add(scale);
    jp.add(new JLabel("White"));
    add(jp);
  }

  // We did this work in the constructor so we can skip it here.
  protected void buildChooser() { }

  // Make sure the slider is in sync with the other chooser panels. We rely on
  // the red channel, but we could do a fancier averaging if we really wanted to.
  public void updateChooser() {
    scale.setValue(getColorSelectionModel().getSelectedColor().getRed());
  }

  // Pick a name for our tab in the chooser
  public String getDisplayName() { return "Gray Scale"; }

  // No need for an icon.
  public Icon getSmallDisplayIcon() { return null; }
  public Icon getLargeDisplayIcon() { return null; }
  // And lastly, update the selection model as our slider changes.
  public void stateChanged(ChangeEvent ce) {
```

```
      getColorSelectionModel().setSelectedColor(grays[scale.getValue()]);
  }
}
```

Here's the application that produced the new chooser. The only real change is that we manually build the list of chooser panels for our chooser in the ColorPicker2 constructor:

```
// ColorPicker2.java
// A quick test of the JColorChooser dialog.
//
import java.awt.*;
import java.awt.event.*;
import javax.swing.*;
import javax.swing.colorChooser.*;

public class ColorPicker2 extends JFrame {

  JFrame parent;
  Color c;

  public ColorPicker2() {
    super("JColorChooser Test Frame");
    setSize(200, 100);
    parent = this;
    final JButton go = new JButton("Show JColorChoser");
    go.addActionListener(new ActionListener() {
      final JColorChooser chooser = new JColorChooser();
      boolean first = true;
      public void actionPerformed(ActionEvent e) {
        if (first) {
          first = false;
          GrayScalePanel gsp = new GrayScalePanel();

          // Bug workaround--you should eventually be able to replace the
          // remainder of this if statement with one line:
          // chooser.addChooserPanel(gsp);
          // Can also cause odd side effects that should go away with bug fixes
          AbstractColorChooserPanel[] oldPanels =
                                chooser.getChooserPanels();
          AbstractColorChooserPanel[] newPanels =
            new AbstractColorChooserPanel[oldPanels.length + 1];
          int i;
          for (i = 0; i < oldPanels.length; i++) {
            newPanels[i] = oldPanels[i];
          }
          newPanels[i] = gsp;
          chooser.setChooserPanels(newPanels);
        }
        JDialog dialog = JColorChooser.createDialog(parent, "Demo 2", true,
```

```
                              chooser, new ActionListener() {
                                  public void actionPerformed(ActionEvent e) {
                                    c = chooser.getColor();
                                  }}, null);
        dialog.setVisible(true);
        go.setBackground(c);
      }
    });
    getContentPane().add(go);
    addWindowListener(new BasicWindowMonitor());
  }

  public static void main(String args[]) {
    ColorPicker2 cp2 = new ColorPicker2();
    cp2.setVisible(true);
  }
}
```

Custom Preview Panel

In addition to creating custom color chooser panels, you can also create your own preview panel to replace the default. At the time of this writing, however, this ability was not fully supported. Refer to the most recent API for details on this process.

Developing a Custom Dialog

While you might rely entirely on the standard color chooser dialog, it is possible to create a color chooser component and use that inside your own dialogs or applications. Let's take a look at a fancy font chooser that lets you pick the face, style, and color. Figure 12-9 shows an example of such a dialog.

It looks like a lot is going on in the code that built this dialog window, but it's not really that bad. The first part of the code is devoted to the tedious business of setting up the graphical interface pieces. Notice that we create a regular JColorChooser object and never call either the showDialog() or createDialog() methods. You can also see the piece of code required to catch color updates in that section. We attach a ChangeListener to the ColorSelectionModel for the chooser. The event handler for that listener simply calls updatePreviewColor() to keep our custom previewer in sync with the color shown in the chooser.

You'll notice that we're storing our font information in a SimpleAttributeSet object. This object gets used with the JTextPane class, and you can find out more about it in Chapter 21, *Styled Documents and JTextPane*. For right now, just know that it has some convenient methods for storing text attributes, such as the font name, bold/italic, and size.

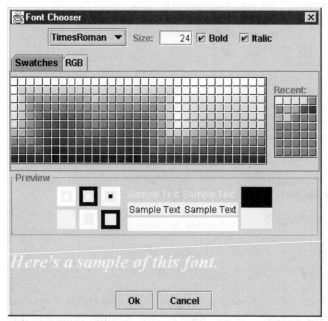

Figure 12-9. A custom dialog window, with a JColorChooser as one piece of it

Here's that startup code:

```
// FontChooser.java
// A font chooser that allows users to pick a font by name, size, style, and
// color.  The color selection will be provided by a JColorChooser pane.  This
// dialog builds an AttributeSet suitable for use with JTextPane.
//
import javax.swing.*;
import javax.swing.event.*;
import javax.swing.colorchooser.*;
import javax.swing.text.*;
import java.awt.*;
import java.awt.event.*;

public class FontChooser extends JDialog implements ActionListener {

    JColorChooser colorChooser;
    JComboBox fontName;
    JCheckBox fontBold, fontItalic;
    JTextField fontSize;
    JLabel previewLabel;
    SimpleAttributeSet attributes;
    Font newFont;
    Color newColor;
```

```java
public FontChooser(Frame parent) {
  super(parent, "Font Chooser", true);
  setSize(400, 400);
  attributes = new SimpleAttributeSet();

  // make sure that any way they cancel the window does the right thing
  addWindowListener(new WindowAdapter() {
    public void windowClosing(WindowEvent e) {
      closeAndCancel();
    }
  });

  // Start the long process of setting up our interface
  Container c = getContentPane();

  JPanel fontPanel = new JPanel();
  fontName = new JComboBox(new String[] {"TimesRoman",
                                         "Helvetica", "Courier"});
  fontName.setSelectedIndex(1);
  fontName.addActionListener(this);
  fontSize = new JTextField("12", 4);
  fontSize.setHorizontalAlignment(SwingConstants.RIGHT);
  fontSize.addActionListener(this);
  fontBold = new JCheckBox("Bold");
  fontBold.setSelected(true);
  fontBold.addActionListener(this);
  fontItalic = new JCheckBox("Italic");
  fontItalic.addActionListener(this);

  fontPanel.add(fontName);
  fontPanel.add(new JLabel(" Size: "));
  fontPanel.add(fontSize);
  fontPanel.add(fontBold);
  fontPanel.add(fontItalic);

  c.add(fontPanel, BorderLayout.NORTH);

  // Set up the color chooser panel and attach a change listener so that color
  // updates get reflected in our preview label.
  colorChooser = new JColorChooser(Color.black);
  colorChooser.getSelectionModel()
              .addChangeListener(new ChangeListener() {
    public void stateChanged(ChangeEvent e) {
      updatePreviewColor();
    }
  });
  c.add(colorChooser, BorderLayout.CENTER);

  JPanel previewPanel = new JPanel(new BorderLayout());
```

```
    previewLabel = new JLabel("Here's a sample of this font.");
    previewLabel.setForeground(colorChooser.getColor());
    previewPanel.add(previewLabel, BorderLayout.CENTER);

    // Add in the Ok and Cancel buttons for our dialog box
    JButton okButton = new JButton("Ok");
    okButton.addActionListener(new ActionListener() {
      public void actionPerformed(ActionEvent ae) {
        closeAndSave();
      }
    });
    JButton cancelButton = new JButton("Cancel");
    cancelButton.addActionListener(new ActionListener() {
      public void actionPerformed(ActionEvent ae) {
        closeAndCancel();
      }
    });

    JPanel controlPanel = new JPanel();
    controlPanel.add(okButton);
    controlPanel.add(cancelButton);
    previewPanel.add(controlPanel, BorderLayout.SOUTH);

    // Give the preview label room to grow.
    previewPanel.setMinimumSize(new Dimension(100, 100));
    previewPanel.setPreferredSize(new Dimension(100, 100));

    c.add(previewPanel, BorderLayout.SOUTH);
  }
```

Let's take a look now at the next section of code. The `actionPerformed()` method monitors our font choices from the buttons and text field at the top of our dialog. As font attributes change, we keep the `AttributeSet` object updated, and also update our display label. (The listener for the color part of our dialog was attached directly to the color chooser in the code above.) The `updatePreview-Font()` and `updatePreviewColor()` methods allow us to change the font and color of the preview label separately. That's a bit more efficient, especially when the user is picking a color with an RGB slider.

```
    // Ok, something in the font changed, so figure that out and make a
    // new font for the preview label
    public void actionPerformed(ActionEvent ae) {
      // Check the name of the font
      if (!StyleConstants.getFontFamily(attributes)
                        .equals(fontName.getSelectedItem())) {
        StyleConstants.setFontFamily(attributes,
                                  (String)fontName.getSelectedItem());
      }
```

```
      // Check the font size (no error checking yet)
      if (StyleConstants.getFontSize(attributes) !=
                                      Integer.parseInt(fontSize.getText())) {
        StyleConstants.setFontSize(attributes,
                                    Integer.parseInt(fontSize.getText()));
      }
      // Check to see if the font should be bold
      if (StyleConstants.isBold(attributes) != fontBold.isSelected()) {
        StyleConstants.setBold(attributes, fontBold.isSelected());
      }
      // Check to see if the font should be italic
      if (StyleConstants.isItalic(attributes) != fontItalic.isSelected()) {
        StyleConstants.setItalic(attributes, fontItalic.isSelected());
      }
      // and update our preview label
      updatePreviewFont();
    }


    // Get the appropriate font from our attributes object and update
    // the preview label
    protected void updatePreviewFont() {
      String name = StyleConstants.getFontFamily(attributes);
      boolean bold = StyleConstants.isBold(attributes);
      boolean ital = StyleConstants.isItalic(attributes);
      int size = StyleConstants.getFontSize(attributes);

      //Bold and italic don't work properly in beta 4.
      Font f = new Font(name, (bold ? Font.BOLD : 0) +
                              (ital ? Font.ITALIC : 0), size);
      previewLabel.setFont(f);
    }


    // Get the appropriate color from our chooser and update previewLabel
    protected void updatePreviewColor() {
      previewLabel.setForeground(colorChooser.getColor());
      // manually force the label to repaint
      previewLabel.repaint();
    }
```

The last segment of code helps us with the shutdown stage for our dialog. The getNewFont() and getNewColor() methods allow you to retrieve the selected font and color once the dialog has been closed. You can also get the complete attribute set using getAttributes(). The closeAndSave() method stores the font and color information from our preview label into newFont and newColor, while closeAndCancel() puts null into both fields. After showing this dialog, the application using it should check the value of newFont or newColor to determine whether or not the user accepted a font choice.

```
  public Font getNewFont() { return newFont; }
  public Color getNewColor() { return newColor; }
  public AttributeSet getAttributes() { return attributes; }

  public void closeAndSave() {
    // save font & color information
    newFont = previewLabel.getFont();
    newColor = previewLabel.getForeground();

    // and then close the window
    setVisible(false);
  }

  public void closeAndCancel() {
    // erase any font information and then close the window
    newFont = null;
    newColor = null;
    setVisible(false);
  }
}
```

And here's the application that puts this dialog to use. It's similar to our first color picker. A single button in the application causes the font chooser dialog to be displayed, and whatever font the user picks through the dialog becomes the font for the button. As with that first program, the main work is done here in the actionPerformed() method of the button's event handler. Notice how the application does indeed check the new font choice to see if it is null or not.

```
// FontPicker.java
// A quick test of the JColorChooser dialog.
//
import java.awt.*;
import java.awt.event.*;
import javax.swing.*;
import javax.swing.colorchooser.*;

public class FontPicker extends JFrame {

  JFrame parent;
  Color c;

  public FontPicker() {
    super("JColorChooser Test Frame");
    setSize(200,100);
    final JButton go = new JButton("Show FontChooser");
    go.addActionListener(new ActionListener() {
      final FontChooser chooser = new FontChooser(FontPicker.this);
      boolean first = true;
      public void actionPerformed(ActionEvent e) {
```

```
      chooser.setVisible(true);
      // If we got a real font choice, then update our go button
      if (chooser.getNewFont() != null) {
        go.setFont(chooser.getNewFont());
        go.setForeground(chooser.getNewColor());
      }
    }
  });
  getContentPane().add(go);
  addWindowListener(new BasicWindowMonitor());
}

public static void main(String args[]) {
  FontPicker fp = new FontPicker();
  fp.setVisible(true);
}
}
```

As Swing matures, many other choosers will be added to this set. Choosers for currency and dates are in the pending package, and may eventually graduate to the real release. In the meantime, the current set of choosers provide high-quality, controllable components for your application.

13

Borders

Borders were one of the most commonly requested extensions to the Java AWT. Swing provides seven unique styles of borders and allows you to "compound" borders to form more intricate combinations. This chapter introduces you to the Swing borders, and shows you how to work with and configure them. At the end of the chapter, we also show you how to create a border of your own.

Introducing Borders

Figure 13-1 shows the standard borders that Swing provides. There are eight border styles: *Bevel, Soft Bevel, Empty, Etched, Line, Matte, Titled,* and *Compound.* The MatteBorder gives you two borders in one: the border area can be filled with a solid color or an icon. (The figure only shows the icon version; we'll leave it up to you to imagine the solid line.)

You can place a border around any Swing component that extends JComponent. The JComponent class contains a border property that is inherited by all Swing components. (Top-level components that don't inherit from JComponent, like JFrame and JDialog, can't have borders.) By default, the border property is null (no border), but you can access and modify it using the getBorder() and setBorder() methods. Once you've set a component's border, the component always paints itself using that border, and the insets of the border replace the component's default insets.

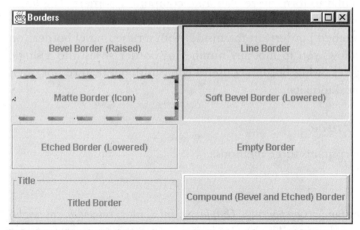

Figure 13-1. Borders in Swing

Here's how to set a component's border:

```
JLabel label = new JLabel("A Border");
mylabel.setBorder(new BevelBorder(BevelBorder.LOWERED));
```

Borders are grouped into a separate package within the Swing hierarchy: `javax.swing.border`. Figure 13-2 shows the classes within this package. All Swing borders directly or indirectly extend the `AbstractBorder` class, which in turn implements the more fundamental `Border` interface. The `Border` interface outlines a minimal set of methods that Swing requires for an object to qualify as a border.

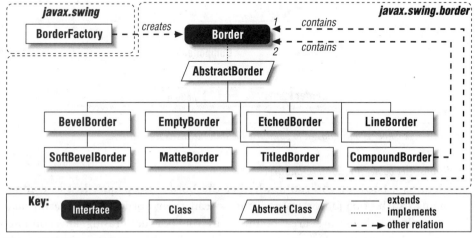

Figure 13-2. Border class diagram

Borders can be combined to form more elaborate compound borders. The lower right corner of Figure 13-1 shows an example of a compound border. Here, we have "combined" an etched border (on the inside) with a raised bevel border (on the outside). Swing allows you to mix any number of border styles into a single border object. This gives Swing borders a useful compositional feature not often found in other graphical toolkits.

The Border Interface

The Border interface contains three methods.

Methods

public abstract void paintBorder(Component c, Graphics g, int x, int y, int width, int height)
Performs the actual drawing. The border is drawn onto the graphics context g with the location and dimensions provided. If the border is not opaque, paintBorder() should calculate exactly what area it can paint by acquiring the border's insets (see getBorderInsets()).

public abstract Insets getBorderInsets(Component c)
Returns an Insets object that reports the minimum amount of space the border needs to paint itself around the given component. Borders must never paint outside this insets region (shown shaded in Figure 13-3). When the border property is set, it replaces the native insets of the component with those of the border.

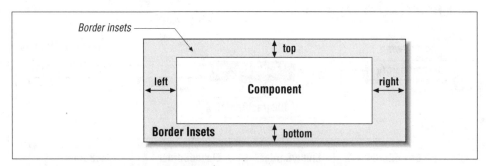

Figure 13-3. A border is only allowed to paint itself within the insets it declares

public abstract boolean isBorderOpaque()
Returns a boolean indicating whether the border is opaque. Just as components can be opaque or transparent, so can their borders. Opaque borders typically fill the entire area bounded by the border, erasing any contents drawn there previously. Non-opaque borders fill only the region given by their insets, and leave the interior blank. In the areas left untouched, the background graphics of the bordered component are preserved. Note that if a

border returns true for its isBorderOpaque() method, Swing will expect it to paint every pixel given to it.

Painting Borders Correctly

The golden rule of creating borders is: *Never paint in the component's region.* Here's a border that violates this rule:

```
public class WrongBorder extends AbstractBorder {
    public WrongBorder() {}
    public void paintBorder(Component c, Graphics g, int x, int y,
                            int width, int height) {
        g.setColor(Color.black);
        g.fillRect(x, y, width, height);        // Bad
    }
    public boolean isBorderOpaque() { return true;}
    public Insets getBorderInsets(Component c) {
        return new Insets(20, 20, 20, 20);
    }
}
```

Look carefully at the paintBorder() method. The last four parameters passed in to the method can be used to calculate the total screen area of the component—*including* the border insets. We decided to paint our border by creating a single filled rectangle that fills the entire component space. While drawing the border, however, we painted over the underlying component, and violated the golden rule.

A safer approach would be to acquire the insets of the border region and draw rectangles only in that space, as shown below:

```
public void paintBorder(Component c, Graphics g, int x, int y,
                        int width, int height) {
    Insets insets = getBorderInsets(c);
    g.setColor(Color.black);

    //  Draw rectangles around the component, but do not draw
    //  in the component area itself.
    g.fillRect(x, y, width, insets.top);
    g.fillRect(x, y, insets.left, height);
    g.fillRect(x+width-insets.right, y, insets.right, height);
    g.fillRect(x, y+height-insets.bottom, width, insets.bottom);
}
```

The AbstractBorder Class

AbstractBorder is the superclass that all Swing borders extend. Although not required, borders of your own design can also extend AbstractBorder.

AbstractBorder provides default implementations of the three methods of the Border interface. If you subclass AbstractBorder to create your own border, you should override at least the paintBorder() and getBorderInsets() methods. The only additional functionality that AbstractBorder provides is a method that calculates the area of the component being bordered. Borders can use this function to ensure that their drawing does not paint over the respective component.

AbstractBorder has one property, shown in Table 13-1. The borderOpaque property returns false by default. If you create a border that is opaque, you should override the isBorderOpaque() method and return true.

Table 13-1. AbstractBorder Properties

Property	Data Type	get	is	set	bound	Default Value
borderOpaque*	boolean		•			false

Constructor

public AbstractBorder()
  The only constructor; it takes no arguments.

Methods

public void paintBorder(Component c, Graphics g, int x, int y, int width, int height)
  This empty method is required by the Border interface; it should be overridden by a subclass to perform the actual rendering of the border.

public Insets getBorderInsets(Component c)
  Returns an Insets object with 0 for each inset. Subclasses should override both of these methods to report the true area required by their border. The second version of this method modifies and returns the Insets object, i.

public Rectangle getInteriorRectangle(Component c, int x, int y, int width, int height)
  This non-static method calls the static version below, using a reference to the current border.

public static Rectangle getInteriorRectangle(Border b, int x, int y, int width, int height)
  This static method calculates the area representing the component being bordered. It returns the result as a Rectangle object. This method is useful for pinpointing the area of the inner component in which borders shouldn't draw.

Now that we're done with the preliminaries, let's look at the borders that Swing provides.

Swing Borders

The following sections discuss Swing's border classes in detail.

The BevelBorder and SoftBevelBorder Classes

A *bevel* is another name for a slanted edge. The `BevelBorder` class can be used to simulate a raised or lowered edge with a slant surrounding the component, similar to the appearance of a button. The default bevel edge is two pixels wide on all sides. Figure 13-4 shows two bevel borders, the first raised and the second lowered.

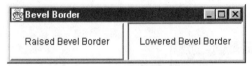

Figure 13-4. Raised and lowered bevel borders

Notice how the border creates the illusion of three dimensions. Like many components, the bevel border simulates a light source above and to the left of the object. The border is then drawn with four colors: an outer and inner *highlight* color, and an outer and inner *shadow* color. The highlight colors represent the two surfaces of the bevel facing toward the light, while the shadow colors represent the surfaces facing away from the light. Figure 13-5 shows how a bevel border uses the highlight and shadow colors.

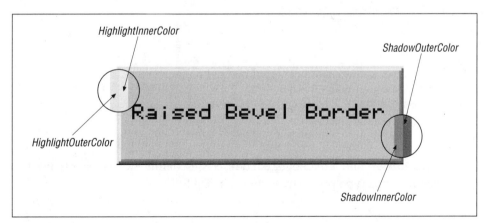

Figure 13-5. The four colors of a bevel border

When the bevel is raised, the top and left sides of the border are highlighted and the bottom and right sides of the border are shadowed. This presents the appearance of the surface protruding above the background. When the bevel is lowered, the highlighted and shadowed surfaces are reversed, and the border appears to sink into the background. A bevel border is two pixels wide on all sides. The *inner* color represents the inner pixels for the border, while the *outer* color represents the outer pixels.

The beveled border in Swing has a baby brother: `SoftBevelBorder`. `SoftBevel-Border` can also be used to simulate a subtle raised or lowered edge around a component. In fact, the only difference from the regular `BevelBorder` is that the soft beveled edge is slightly thinner on two of its four sides and provides for small rounded corners. Figure 13-6 shows a pair of soft bevel borders; if your eyes are really good, you may be able to tell the difference between these and the "plain" bevel borders.

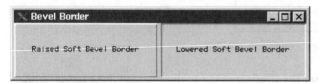

Figure 13-6. Soft bevel borders in Swing

Table 13-2 shows the properties of `BevelBorder` and `SoftBevelBorder`[*]. The `bevelTypes` property shows whether the border appears raised or lowered. The `borderOpaque` property is `true` by default for a bevel border, and `false` for a soft bevel border.

Table 13-2. BevelBorder and SoftBevelBorder Properties

Property	Data Type	get	is	set	bound	Default Value
bevelType	int	•				BevelBorder.RAISED
borderOpaque*	boolean		•			see below

Constants

The `BevelBorder` and `SoftBevelBorder` classes define two constants used to initialize the `bevelType` property, as shown in Table 13-3.

---

[*] In Swing 1.0, there were two additional properties, `highlight` and `shadow`. These properties and their accessors have disappeared in Swing 1.1.

Table 13-3. BevelBorder and SoftBevelBorder Constants

Constant	Data Type	Definition
RAISED	int	Raised bevel border
LOWERED	int	Lowered bevel border

Protected Fields

protected int bevelType

Stores the value of the bevelTypes property, which determines whether the border is raised or lowered.

protected Color highlightOuterColor
protected Color highlightInnerColor
protected Color shadowOuterColor
protected Color shadowInnerColor

These fields hold the colors used to draw the border. If the colors are not specified in the constructor, they are derived from the component that uses the border, as shown in Table 13-4. In this table, background refers to the component's background color.

Table 13-4. Default Colors for Bevel Borders

Property	Color
highlightOuterColor	background.brighter().brighter()
highlightInnerColor	background.brighter()
shadowOuterColor	background.darker().darker()
shadowInnerColor	background.darker()

Constructors

public BevelBorder(int type)
public BevelBorder(int type, Color highlight, Color shadow)
public BevelBorder(int type, Color highlightOuter, Color highlightInner, Color shadowOuter, Color shadowInner)

These constructors can be used to set the initial property values of the Bevel-Border. The constructor is the only location where the colors of the bevel border can be set; there are no "set" accessors for each of the color variables.

public SoftBevelBorder(int bevelType)
public SoftBevelBorder(int bevelType, Color highlight, Color shadow)
public SoftBevelBorder(int bevelType, Color highlightOuter, Color highlightInner, Color shadowOuter, Color shadowInner)

These constructors can be used to set the initial property values of the Soft-BevelBorder. The definitions are identical to BevelBorder constructors.

In the constructors with two Color arguments, the given colors set the high-lightInner and shadowOuter properties. highlightOuter is set to highlight.darker() and shadowInner is set to shadow.Brighter().

Methods

public Insets getBorderInsets(Component c)
public Insets getBorderInsets(Component c, Insets i)

> Returns an Insets object specifying an inset of 2 pixels on each side for BevelBorder and 3 pixels on each side for SoftBevelBorder. The second version of this method modifies and returns the given Insets object, i.

public Color getHighlightInnerColor(Component c)
public Color getHighlightOuterColor(Component c)
public Color getShadowInnerColor(Component c)
public Color getShadowOuterColor(Component c)

> Retrieve various colors used to draw the border; the colors are used as shown in Figure 13-5.

public void paintBorder(Component c, Graphics g, int x, int y, int width, int height)

> Forces the border to paint itself with the graphics context of the component.

Miscellaneous

The following protected methods are defined in BevelBorder:

protected void paintRaisedBevel(Component c, Graphics g, int x, int y, int width, int height)
protected void paintLoweredBevel(Component c, Graphics g, int x, int y, int width,
> *int height)*

> These methods are used by BevelBorder.paintBorder() to paint the two different bevel types.

Changing Borders on the Fly

Here is a short program that creates four labels. Each label draws a bevel border around itself when the mouse pointer enters the component's region, and erases it when the mouse leaves the region. Modifying this program to use soft bevel borders is trivial.

```
//  BevelExample.java
//
import java.awt.*;
import java.awt.event.*;
import javax.swing.*;
import javax.swing.border.*;

public class BevelExample extends JPanel implements MouseListener {
```

```
    BevelBorder bevel;
    EmptyBorder empty;
    JLabel label[] = new JLabel[4];

    public BevelExample() {
        super(true);
        setLayout(new GridLayout(1, 4));

        bevel = new BevelBorder(BevelBorder.RAISED);
        empty = new EmptyBorder(5, 5, 5, 5);

        label[0] = new JLabel("Home");
        label[1] = new JLabel("Back");
        label[2] = new JLabel("Forward");
        label[3] = new JLabel("Stop");

        for (int i = 0; i < label.length; i++) {
            label[i].setHorizontalAlignment(JLabel.CENTER);
            label[i].addMouseListener(this);
            label[i].setBorder(empty);
            add(label[i]);
        }
    }

    public static void main(String s[]) {
        JFrame frame = new JFrame("Bevel Border");
        frame.addWindowListener(new BasicWindowMonitor());
        frame.setSize(400, 100);
        frame.setContentPane(new BevelExample());
        frame.setVisible(true);
    }

    public void mouseEntered(MouseEvent e) {
        ((JLabel)e.getComponent()).setBorder(bevel);
        repaint();
    }

    public void mouseExited(MouseEvent e) {
        ((JLabel)e.getComponent()).setBorder(empty);
        repaint();
    }

    public void mouseClicked(MouseEvent e) {
        String text = ((JLabel)e.getComponent()).getText();
        System.out.println("You clicked " + text + "!");
    }

    public void mousePressed(MouseEvent e) {}
    public void mouseReleased(MouseEvent e) {}
}
```

Figure 13-7 shows the results of our example.

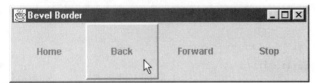

Figure 13-7. Working with bevel borders

The Empty Border Class

The EmptyBorder class is used to place empty space around a component. The size of the space on each side is defined by the border's insets, which are set in the constructor. The EmptyBorder class has only one property inherited from AbstractBorder. Figure 13-8 shows an empty border with 20 pixels on all sides surrounding a JLabel. (Note that we use two other borders to denote the boundaries of the EmptyBorder.)

Figure 13-8. An empty border with two etched borders surrounding it

Property

Table 13-5 shows the only property of the EmptyBorder class.

Table 13-5. EmptyBorder Property

Property	Data Type	get	is	set	Bound	Default Value
borderOpaque*	boolean		•			false

Protected Fields

protected int bottom
protected int left
protected int right
protected int top
    These fields hold the border's inset on each side.

Constructors

public EmptyBorder(int top, int left, int bottom, int right)
public EmptyBorder(Insets insets)
> Create an empty border with the given insets.

public void paintBorder(Component c, Graphics g, int x, int y, int width, int height)
> Since this is an empty border, this method does nothing.

Method

public Insets getBorderInsets(Component c)
public Insets getBorderInsets(Component c, Insets i)
> Return an `Insets` object with the insets specified in the constructor. The second version of this method modifies and returns the `Insets` object, `i`.

The EtchedBorder Class

An etched border is a single etching that surrounds the target component. The etching consists of adjacent lines of two colors, a highlight and a shadow, and can be raised or lowered. Like bevel borders, etched borders render themselves by simulating a light source above and to the left. The highlight is the color of the etching that faces the light source, while the shadow is the color of the etching that faces away from the light source. An etched border is shown in Figure 13-9.

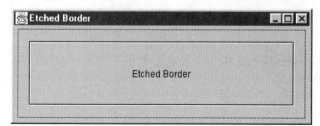

Figure 13-9. A lowered etched border in Swing

An etched border is very similar to a bevel border. By carefully manipulating the colors, you can create an `EtchedBorder` from a `BevelBorder`.

Properties

The properties for the `EtchedBorder` class are shown in Table 13-6[*]. The `borderOpaque` property always returns `true`, indicating that this border paints

---

[*] In Swing 1.0, there were two additional properties, `highlight` and `shadow`. These properties and their accessors have disappeared in Swing 1.1.

over all of its allocated pixels. The `etchType` tells whether the etch appears as raised or lowered. Finally, the `highlightColor` and `shadowColor` properties indicate the two colors used to simulate the etching. If no values are given, brighter and darker variations of the background color of the component are used for the `highlightColor` and `shadowColor`, respectively.

Table 13-6. EtchedBorder Properties

Property	Data Type	get	is	set	bound	Default Value
borderOpaque*	boolean		•			true
etchType	int			•		EtchedBorder.LOWERED

Constants

`EtchedBorder` contains two constants used to initialize the `etchType` property, as shown in Table 13-7.

Table 13-7. EtchedBorder Constants

Constant	Data Type	Definition
RAISED	int	A raised border
LOWERED	int	A lowered border

Protected Fields

protected int etchType

Stores the value of the `etchType` property, which determines whether the border is raised or lowered.

protected Color highlight

protected Color shadow

These fields hold the colors used to paint the highlighted and shadowed parts of the border. If the colors are not specified in the constructor, `highlight` is set to `background.brighter()`, and shadow is set to `background.darker()`, where `background` is the background color of the component using the border.

Constructors

public EtchedBorder()

Creates a simple lowered etched border. The colors of the border's highlight and shadow default to the `brighter()` and `darker()` shades of the background color of the bordered component.

public EtchedBorder(Color highlight, Color shadow)
> Creates a lowered etched border using the specified highlight and shadow colors for the etching. There are no "set" accessors for the color fields; they can only be set by this constructor.

public EtchedBorder(int etchType)
> Creates a simple etched border of the etch type passed in. The colors of the border's highlight and shadow default to the `brighter()` and `darker()` shades of the background color of the bordered component.

public EtchedBorder(int etchType, Color highlight, Color shadow)
> Creates an etched border of the type passed in using the specified highlight and shadow colors for the etching. Note that there are no "set" accessors for the color fields; they can only be set by this constructor.

Miscellaneous

public Insets getBorderInsets(Component c)
public Insets getBorderInsets(Comonent c, Insets i)
> Returns an `Insets` object specifying an inset of 2 on each side. The second version of this method modifies and returns the given `Insets` object, `i`.

public Color getHighlightColor(Component c)
public Color getShadowColor(Component c)
> Retreive the colors used to draw the shadowed and highlighted parts of the border.

public void paintBorder(Component c, Graphics g, int x, int y, int width, int height)
> Forces the border to paint itself with the graphics context of the component.

The LineBorder Class

The `LineBorder` class creates a border consisting of a line of arbitrary thickness around the component. Unlike the beveled or etched borders, the line is a single color and is not shaded. If you wish to create a slightly more elegant border, there is code inside the `LineBorder` class to round its corners. There is currently no way to create a `LineBorder` with rounded corners unless you extend `LineBorder` and do it yourself. Figure 13-10 shows two different line borders, each with a different thicknesses.

Figure 13-10. Line borders in Swing

The properties for the `LineBorder` object are shown in Table 13-8. The border-Opaque property always returns `true`, indicating that this border paints over all of its allocated pixels. The `lineColor` property tells the current color of the line border. Note that the `roundedCorners` property is read-only and cannot be set, except in a subclass.

Table 13-8. LineBorder properties

Property	Data Type	get	is	set	bound	Default Value
lineColor	Color	•				from constructor
borderOpaque*	boolean		•			true
roundedCorners	boolean	•				false
thickness	int	•				1

Protected Fields

protected int thickness
protected Color lineColor
> These fields hold the values of the respective `LineBorder` properties.

protected boolean roundedCorners
> Determines whether borders are rounded.

Constructors

public LineBorder(Color color)
public LineBorder(Color color, int thickness)
> Create a lined border with a specific color and an optional thickness. The thickness defaults to 1.

Methods

public Insets getBorderInsets(Component c)
public Insets getBorderInsets(Component c, Insets i)
> Returns an `Insets` object; the inset on each side is equal to the thickness of the line, as specified in the constructor. The second version of this method modifies and returns the given `Insets` object, i.

public void paintBorder(Component c, Graphics g, int x, int y, int width, int height)
> Forces the border to paint itself with the graphics context of the component.

Miscellaneous

The LineBorder class contains two shortcut methods for programmers in a hurry. These methods save on memory by returning the same object each time they are called.

public static Border createBlackLineBorder()
> Returns the equivalent of LineBorder(Color.black, 1).

public static Border createGrayLineBorder()
> Returns the equivalent of LineBorder(Color.gray, 1).

The MatteBorder Class

In art and photography, a *mat* is often used to offset a picture from its frame.[*] In Swing, matte[†] borders perform the same function, separating a component from everything else. A matte border in Swing can be either a solid color or a repeated image icon. The color or icon fills the entire space reserved by the border's insets.

With a MatteBorder, you have the choice of instantiating the object with either a Color or an Icon. If you choose a color, the color will flood-fill the entire space reserved for the border. If you use an icon, the icon will replicate or "wallpaper" itself throughout the entire area of the MatteBorder. Figure 13-11 shows both kinds of MatteBorder.

Figure 13-11. Various matte borders in Swing

Property

MatteBorder extends the EmptyBorder class. The resulting property in the MatteBorder class is shown in Table 13-9. This borderOpaque property can be either true or false, depending on how the border is used. If the MatteBorder

---

[*] Perhaps you've heard of *matte paintings* in motion picture special effects. Historically, these were skilled oil paintings done on glass, the center of which remained clear. Before computers or complex optical printers, the paintings were physically placed on location between the camera and the action, fooling the viewer into believing the scene contained items that were not really there.

[†] This is Sun's misspelling, not ours. While mat only refers to the frame around a picture, another definition describes a dull or rough finish, spelled either mat or matte.

is drawn exclusively with a solid color, then the border is opaque and the property has the value of true. If the border is used with an image, the image may contain transparency and the property has the value false.

Table 13-9. MatteBorder Property

Property	Data Type	get	is	set	bound	Default Value
borderOpaque*	boolean		•			

| NOTE | Be careful if you use an image icon with a MatteBorder and do not explicitly set the insets. The resulting border insets will be the width and height of the icon used, which (depending on how much space the layout manager gives) could paint over part of your component. |

Fields

protected Color color
protected Icon icon

These fields hold the color or icon used to draw the border.

Constructors

public MatteBorder(Icon tileIcon)

Creates a matte border by calculating the insets from the icon passed in. The border's top and bottom height will match the height of the icon, while the border's left and right width will match the width of the icon.

public MatteBorder(int top, int left, int bottom, int right, Color color)

Creates a matte border with the specified insets using the solid color specified by Color.

public MatteBorder(int top, int left, int bottom, int right, Icon tileIcon)

Creates a matte border with the specified insets. Instead of using a flood-filled color, however, the specified icon is "wallpapered" throughout the border's space.

Method

public Insets getBorderInsets(Component c)
public Insets getBorderInsets(Component c, Insets i)

Returns an Insets object. The insets depend on how the border is constructed. If the insets are specified explicitly in the constructor, those insets are returned. If the border uses an icon and insets aren't specified explicitly, the width of the icon is used as the inset on the left and right sides, and the height of the icon is used on the top and bottom. The second version of this method modifies and returns the given Insets object, i.

public void paintBorder(Component c, Graphics g, int x, int y, int width, int height)
Forces the border to paint itself with the graphics context of the component.

Both Kinds of Matte Border

Here is a program that displays the two types of matte borders. The result is shown in Figure 13-11.

```java
//  MatteExample.java
//
import java.awt.*;
import javax.swing.*;
import javax.swing.border.*;

public class MatteExample extends JPanel {

    public MatteExample() {
        super(true);
        this.setLayout(new GridLayout(1, 2, 5, 5));

        JLabel label1 = new JLabel("Matte Border");
        JLabel label2 = new JLabel("Matte Border (Icon)");

        label1.setHorizontalAlignment(JLabel.CENTER);
        label2.setHorizontalAlignment(JLabel.CENTER);

        Icon icon = new ImageIcon("plant.gif");
        MatteBorder matte = new MatteBorder(35, 35, 35, 35, Color.blue);
        MatteBorder matteicon = new MatteBorder(35, 35, 35, 35, icon);
        label1.setBorder(matte);
        label2.setBorder(matteicon);

        add(label1);
        add(label2);
    }

    public static void main(String s[]) {
        JFrame frame = new JFrame("Matte Borders");
        frame.addWindowListener(new BasicWindowMonitor());
        frame.setSize(500, 200);
        frame.setContentPane(new MatteExample());
        frame.setVisible(true);
    }
}
```

The TitledBorder Class

The `TitledBorder` class takes an arbitrary border and adds a descriptive string to it. This title string can be placed in one of six different positions around the component, and can be set to appear above, below, or on top of the border. In addition, you can specify the font and color of the title string. Figure 13-12 enumerates all of the title positions and justifications available.

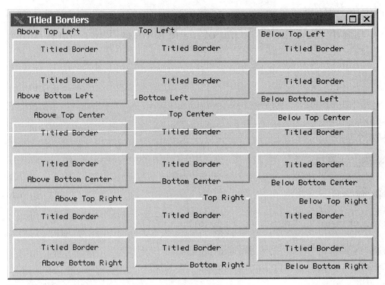

Figure 13-12. Title positions and justifications

You can use any style of border in conjunction with a `TitledBorder` by setting its border property. For example, the borders in Figure 13-12 are used in conjunction with a `BevelBorder`. The default border style, however, is an `EtchedBorder`.

Properties

The properties for the `TitledBorder` class are given in Table 13-10. The `border` property contains the border that is being titled. It can be any border that implements the `Border` interface. The read-only `borderOpaque` property always returns `false`; this border does not color all of its pixels. The `title` property holds the string that is displayed with this border. `titleColor` is the string's color, `title-Font` represents its font, size, and style. `titleJustification` and `titlePosition` tell where the title will appear in relation to the component and the border. See Table 13-12 and Table 13-13 for their values.

Table 13-10. TitledBorder Properties

Property	Data Type	get	is	set	bound	Default Value
border	Border	•		•		from L&F
borderOpaque*	boolean		•			false
title	String	•		•		" "
titleColor	Color	•		•		from L&F
titleFont	Font	•		•		from L&F
titleJustification	int	•		•		LEFT
titlePosition	int	•		•		TOP

Constants

The constants in Table 13-11 are protected members of the `TitledBorder` class and can only be used by subclasses.

Table 13-11. TitledBorder Constants

Constant	Data Type	Definition
EDGE_SPACING	int	The space that the title string is offset from the edge of the border component
TEXT_SPACING	int	The space that the title string is offset from the border
TEXT_INSET_H	int	The horizontal inset from the edge of the border with text that is left or right justified

Protected Fields

protected String title
protected Border border
protected int titlePosition
protected Font titleFont
protected int titleJustification
protected Color titleColor

These fields hold the values of the respective `TitledBorder` properties.

Constructors

public TitledBorder(String title)
public TitledBorder(Border border)
public TitledBorder(Border border, String title)
public TitledBorder(Border border, String title, int titleJustification, int titlePosition)

public TitledBorder(Border border, String title, int titleJustification, int titlePosition,
    Font titleFont)
public TitledBorder(Border border, String title, int titleJustification, int titlePosition,
    Font titleFont, Color titleColor)

> Create a `TitledBorder` instance with the specified properties. Any border that implements the `Border` interface can be used for the `border` property. The justification and position are enumerated in Table 13-12 and Table 13-13.

Table 13-12. Justification Constants

Constant	Data Type	Definition
DEFAULT_JUSTIFICATION	int	Use the default justification, which is LEFT
LEFT	int	Place the title string on the left side of the border
CENTER	int	Place the title string in the center of the border
RIGHT	int	Place the title string on the right side of the border

Table 13-13. Position Constants

Constant	Data Type	Definition
DEFAULT_POSITION	int	Place the text in the default position, TOP
ABOVE_TOP	int	Place the text above the top line of the border
TOP	int	Place the text on the top line of the border
BELOW_TOP	int	Place the text below the top line of the border
ABOVE_BOTTOM	int	Place the text above the bottom line of the border
BOTTOM	int	Place the text on the bottom line of the border
BELOW_BOTTOM	int	Place the text below the bottom line of the border

Miscellaneous

public Insets getBorderInsets(Component c)
public Insets getBorderInsets(Component c, Insets i)

> Returns an `Insets` object; the insets depend on the font and position of the border's title. The second version of this method modifies and returns the given `Insets` object, `i`.

public void paintBorder(Component c, Graphics g, int x, int y, int width, int height)

> Forces the border to paint itself with the graphics context of the component.

public Dimension getMinimumSize(Component c)

> Returns the minimum size of this border, including the border and the text.

protected getFont(Component c)

Retrieves the current font of the border title or the target component. The method defaults to a 12-point `Dialog` font if neither the `titleFont` or the component's font are set.

Using a Titled Border

Here is a short program that creates the image displayed in Figure 13-13:

```
//  TitledExample.java
//
import java.awt.*;
import javax.swing.*;
import javax.swing.border.*;

public class TitledExample extends JPanel {

    public TitledExample() {
        super(true);

        this.setLayout(new GridLayout(1, 1, 5, 5));

        JLabel label = new JLabel("Titled Border");
        label.setHorizontalAlignment(JLabel.CENTER);

        TitledBorder titled = new TitledBorder("Title");
        label.setBorder(titled);

        add(label);
    }

    public static void main(String s[]) {
        JFrame frame = new JFrame("Borders");
        frame.addWindowListener(new BasicWindowMonitor());
        frame.setSize(200, 100);
        frame.setContentPane(new TitledExample());
        frame.setVisible(true);
    }
}
```

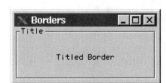

Figure 13-13. A simple title border

The CompoundBorder Class

You can combine two borders to create more eye-catching displays with the
CompoundBorder class. The insets of both borders are added together to form the
insets of the resulting compound border object. The component renders the
outside border first, followed by the inside border. You can compound borders
recursively so that any number of borders can be embedded inside of a
CompoundBorder object:

```
CompoundBorder comp = new CompoundBorder(
              new CompoundBorder(new EtchedBorder(),
                         new EmptyBorder(10, 10, 10, 10)),
              new MatteBorder(20, 20, 20, 20, Color.red)
              );
```

The preceding code yields the border in Figure 13-14.

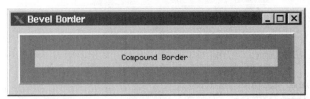

Figure 13-14. A compound border

Properties

Table 13-14 lists the properties of the CompoundBorder class. The insideBorder
and outsideBorder properties hold the borders that are combined. If both of the
borders in the compound border are opaque, the borderOpaque property is set to
true. Otherwise, the property is false.

Table 13-14. CompoundBorder Properties

Property	Data Type	get	is	set	bound	Default Value
borderOpaque*	boolean		•			
insideBorder	Border	•				null
outsideBorder	Border	•				null

Constructors

public CompoundBorder()

Initializes a default compound border with no outside and inside borders. Because there are no "set" accessors for either border property, you probably won't ever need to invoke this constructor.

public CompoundBorder(Border outsideBorder, Border insideBorder)

Creates a compound border object with the specified inside and outside borders.

Miscellaneous

public Insets getBorderInsets(Component c)
public Insets getBorderInsets(Component c, Insets i)

Returns an `Insets` object; the inset on each side is the sum of the insets of the borders being combined in this compound border. The second version of this method modifies and returns the given `Insets` object, `i`.

public void paintBorder(Component c, Graphics g, int x, int y, int width, int height)

Forces the border to paint itself with the graphics context of the component.

The BorderFactory Class

The `BorderFactory` class (which is in the `javax.swing` package) allows the user to call various static methods to create borders. Instead of declaring new instances for each border, the factory class attempts to reuse previously defined (cached) borders, thus saving memory. It's a good idea to get in the habit of using this factory if you create a lot of borders in your application. Currently, only a few borders are actually cached. But in future releases, additional border caching may be added to this class.

Methods

public static Border createBevelBorder(int type)

Creates a `BevelBorder` of the specified type (either raised or lowered). This method returns a cached border, rather than creating a new one.

public static Border createBevelBorder(int type, Color highlight, Color shadow)

Creates a `BevelBorder` of the specified type (either raised or lowered), with the appropriate highlight and shadow colors.

public static Border createBevelBorder(int type, Color highlightOuter, Color highlightInner, Color shadowOuter, Color shadowInner)

Creates a `BevelBorder` of the specified type (either raised or lowered), with the appropriate highlight and shadow colors.

public static Border createEmptyBorder()
    Creates an EmptyBorder. This method returns a cached border rather than
    creating a new one.

public static Border createEmptyBorder(int top, int left, int bottom, int right)
    Creates an EmptyBorder with the specified size.

public static Border createEtchedBorder()
    Creates a default EtchedBorder. This method returns a cached border rather
    than creating a new one.

public static Border createEtchedBorder(Color highlight, Color shadow)
    Creates an EtchedBorder with the appropriate highlight and shadow colors.

public static Border createLineBorder(Color color)
    Creates a LineBorder with the specified color.

public static Border createLineBorder(Color color, int thickness)
    Creates a LineBorder with the specified color and thickness.

public static Border createLoweredBevelBorder()
    Creates a lowered BevelBorder. This method returns a cached border rather
    than creating a new one.

public static Border createRaisedBevelBorder()
    Creates a raised BevelBorder. This method returns a cached border rather
    than creating a new one.

public static CompoundBorder createCompoundBorder()
    Creates an empty CompoundBorder.

public static CompoundBorder createCompoundBorder(Border outsideBorder,
    Border insideBorder)
    Creates a CompoundBorder by combining the two borders passed in.

public static MatteBorder createMatteBorder(int top, int left, int bottom, int right,
    Color color)
    Creates a MatteBorder with the specified size and color.

public static MatteBorder createMatteBorder(int top, int left, int bottom, int right,
    Icon titleIcon)
    Creates a MatteBorder with the specified size, flood-filling it with instances of
    the specified icon titleIcon.

public static TitledBorder createTitledBorder(Border border)
    Creates a TitledBorder from the Border.

public static TitledBorder createTitledBorder(Border border, String title)
    Creates a TitledBorder from the Border. The border's title will be the
    title string passed in, positioned at the upper left of the border.

public static TitledBorder createTitledBorder(Border border, String title, int titleJustification,
  int titlePosition)

Creates a `TitledBorder` from the `Border` passed in. The border's title, justification, and position are also passed in.

public static TitledBorder createTitledBorder(Border border, String title, int titleJustification,
  int titlePosition, Font titleFont)

Creates a `TitledBorder` from the `Border` passed in. The border's title, justification, and position, as well as the font, are all passed in.

public static TitledBorder createTitledBorder(Border border, String title, int titleJustification,
  int titlePosition, Font titleFont, Color titleColor)

Creates a `TitledBorder` from the `Border` passed in. The border's title will be the `title` string passed in. The justification, position, font, and color of the border are also dictated by the variables passed in.

public static TitledBorder createTitledBorder(String title)

Creates a `TitledBorder` with the given title.

Creating Your Own Border

Creating your own border is simple when you extend the `AbstractBorder` class. You need to define three things: whether the border is opaque, what its insets are, and how to draw the border. To accomplish this, you must implement `paint-Border()`, both `isBorderOpaque()` methods, and `getBorderInsets()`. The hard part of coming up with your own border is doing something creative with the `Graphics` primitives in the `paintBorder()` method. A reminder: make sure that you do not paint inside the insets region that you define for yourself. Otherwise, you could be painting over the component you intend to border.

Let's take a look at a simple border:

```
// CurvedBorder.java
//
import java.awt.*;
import javax.swing.border.*;

public class CurvedBorder extends AbstractBorder
{
    private Color wallColor = Color.gray;
    private int sinkLevel = 10;

    public CurvedBorder() { }
    public CurvedBorder(int sinkLevel) { this.sinkLevel = sinkLevel; }
    public CurvedBorder(Color wall) { this.wallColor = wall; }
    public CurvedBorder(int sinkLevel, Color wall)     {
        this.sinkLevel = sinkLevel;
```

```
        this.wallColor = wall;
    }

    public void paintBorder(Component c, Graphics g, int x, int y,
                            int w, int h)
    {
        g.setColor(getWallColor());

        //  Paint a tall wall around the component
        for (int i = 0; i < sinkLevel; i++) {
            g.drawRoundRect(x+i, y+i, w-i-1, h-i-1, sinkLevel-i, sinkLevel);
            g.drawRoundRect(x+i, y+i, w-i-1, h-i-1, sinkLevel, sinkLevel-i);
            g.drawRoundRect(x+i, y, w-i-1, h-1, sinkLevel-i, sinkLevel);
            g.drawRoundRect(x, y+i, w-1, h-i-1, sinkLevel, sinkLevel-i);
        }
    }

    public Insets getBorderInsets(Component c) {
        return new Insets(sinkLevel, sinkLevel, sinkLevel, sinkLevel);
    }
    public Insets getBorderInsets(Component c, Insets i) {
        i.left = i.right = i.bottom = i.top = sinkLevel;
        return i;
    }
    public boolean isBorderOpaque() { return true; }
    public int getSinkLevel() { return sinkLevel; }
    public Color getWallColor() { return wallColor; }
}
```

This border draws round rectangles in succession around the component. The rectangles are offset from each other so that it appears that the component is depressed into the surface. The sinkLevel property defines how "deep" the depression should appear. Note that we define the border insets to match the sinkLevel property. We draw four round rectangles on each pass, instead of just one—this ensures that each pixel is filled between rectangles, which won't be the case if we use just one. (If you want to see what I mean, try commenting out some of the drawRoundRect() calls.) Finally, the wallColor property specifies the border's color.

Here is an excerpt from the source that you can use to surround a slider with this border; Figure 13-15 shows the result.

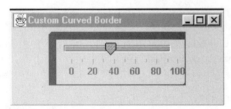

Figure 13-15. A custom curved border

```
JSlider mySlider = new JSlider();
mySlider.setMajorTickSpacing(20);
mySlider.setMinorTickSpacing(10);
mySlider.setPaintTicks(true);
mySlider.setPaintLabels(true);

CurvedBorder border = new CurvedBorder(10, Color.darkGray);
mySlider.setBorder(border);
```

14

Menus and Toolbars

This chapter discusses Swing menus and toolbars. Menus are by far the larger and more extensible of the two, so they encompass most of the chapter. Swing offers the programmer a fully reimplemented menu system from AWT 1.1. This re-engineering allows you to use the Swing menus in a variety of eye-catching ways, and provides much more freedom to lay out menu components.

Toolbars are a new addition to Swing. Toolbars allow the programmer to group buttons, combo boxes, and other components together in repositionable panels; these tools can assist the user in performing many common tasks. You can add any component to a Swing toolbar, even non-Swing components. In addition, Swing allows the toolbar to be dragged from the frame and positioned inside a child window for convenience.

Introducing Swing Menus

If you've worked with menus before, you know that one of the most frustrating issues with AWT is that almost all of its menu components extend the abstract `java.awt.MenuComponent` class. This is an awkward design, as the remaining AWT components extend the more versatile `java.awt.Component` class. Consequently, menu components are divorced from regular components in AWT, since subclasses of `MenuComponent` can perform only a fraction of the others' functionality. In addition, AWT programmers are locked into placing a single menubar at the top of each `Frame` and cannot position menu components in containers using layout managers.

With Swing, this hierarchy has been redesigned. Menu components are now subclasses of `JComponent`. Consequently, they now have all the benefits of a true

Swing component, and you can treat them as such with respect to layout managers and containers.

Here are some other notable additions to the Swing menu system:

- Icons can augment or replace menu items

- A radio-button menu item

- Keyboard accelerators can be assigned to menu items that appear next to the menu item text

- Most standard Swing components can be used as menu items

Most of the Swing menu classes have been designed as drop-in replacements for their AWT equivalents. Swing provides the familiar menu separators, checkbox menu items, popup menus, and submenus for use in your applications. In addition, Swing menus maintain support for the older AWT-style "underline" (mnemonic) shortcuts, and you can still attach menu bars to the top of Swing frames with a single function that adjusts the frame insets accordingly. If you're well versed with AWT menus, you'll find that transitioning to the Swing menu system is a piece of cake. Figure 14-1 defines the various elements that make up the menu system in Swing.

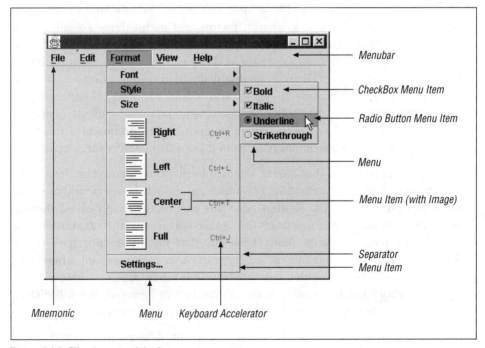

Figure 14-1. The elements of the Swing menu system

Menu Hierarchy

The class hierarchy for Swing menus is shown in Figure 14-2.

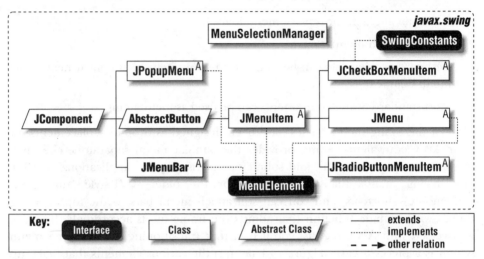

Figure 14-2. The Swing menu classes

The first question that you might be asking yourself is, "What's AbstractButton doing in there?" Well, believe it or not, menus and menu items actually retain characteristics of Swing buttons. For example, menu items can be highlighted—in this case, when the mouse passes over them. They can be clicked to indicate that the user has made a choice. They can be disabled and grayed like buttons, and can be assigned action commands to assist with event handling. Some, such as JCheckBoxMenuItem and JRadioButtonMenuItem, can even be toggled between two selection states. In short, Swing menu components reuse much of the functionality of Swing buttons, so it makes sense to inherit from AbstractButton.

It may also seem awkward that JMenu would inherit from JMenuItem, instead of vice-versa. This is because each JMenu contains an implicit menu item that serves as the title of the menu. You'll often hear this part of the menu called the *title button*. When the user presses or drags the mouse cursor over the title button, the corresponding menu appears. Note, however, that menus do not have to be anchored to a menubar. You can embed them in other menus as well, where they act as submenus. This means that the title button must be able to mimic a menu item, which would not be possible if the hierarchy was reversed. We will discuss this behavior in more detail when we cover the JMenu class later in this chapter.

Finally, note that almost all of the menu classes implement the MenuElement interface. The MenuElement interface outlines standardized methods that dictate how each Swing menu component will behave when it encounters various user input, such as keyboard or mouse events. Swing menu classes typically process these mouse and keyboard events and pass notifications to the component delegates, which handle any necessary redrawing of the component. These methods work in tandem with the `MenuSelectionManager` class. While it is rare that you will need to implement the `MenuElement` interface, it helps to know how it works. We show how to implement this interface later in the chapter.

Getting Your Feet Wet

Okay, it's time to get your feet wet. Here is a flashy program that introduces much of the basic Swing menu functionality:

```
//   IntroExample.java
//
import java.awt.*;
import java.awt.event.*;

import javax.swing.*;

public class IntroExample extends JMenuBar implements ActionListener {

    String[] fileItems = new String[] { "New", "Open", "Save", "Exit" };
    String[] editItems = new String[] { "Undo", "Cut", "Copy", "Paste" };
    char[] fileShortcuts = { 'N','O','S','X' };
    char[] editShortcuts = { 'Z','X','C','V' };

    public IntroExample() {

        JMenu fileMenu = new JMenu("File");
        JMenu editMenu = new JMenu("Edit");
        JMenu otherMenu = new JMenu("Other");
        JMenu subMenu = new JMenu("SubMenu");
        JMenu subMenu2 = new JMenu("SubMenu2");

        // Assemble the File menus with mnemonics
        for (int i=0; i < fileItems.length; i++) {
            JMenuItem item = new JMenuItem(fileItems[i], fileShortcuts[i]);
            item.addActionListener(this);
            fileMenu.add(item);
        }

        // Assemble the File menus with keyboard accelerators
        for (int i=0; i < editItems.length; i++) {
            JMenuItem item = new JMenuItem(editItems[i]);
            item.setAccelerator(KeyStroke.getKeyStroke(editShortcuts[i],
                            java.awt.Event.CTRL_MASK, false));
            item.addActionListener(this);
            editMenu.add(item);
        }
```

```
        //  Insert a separator in the Edit Menu in Position 1 after "Undo"
        editMenu.insertSeparator(1);

        //  Assemble the submenus of the Other Menu
        JMenuItem item;
        subMenu2.add(item = new JMenuItem("Extra 2"));
        item.addActionListener(this);
        subMenu.add(item = new JMenuItem("Extra 1"));
        item.addActionListener(this);
        subMenu.add(subMenu2);

        //  Assemble the Other Menu itself
        otherMenu.add(subMenu);
        otherMenu.add(item = new JCheckBoxMenuItem("Check Me"));
        item.addActionListener(this);
        otherMenu.addSeparator();
        ButtonGroup buttonGroup = new ButtonGroup();
        otherMenu.add(item = new JRadioButtonMenuItem("Radio 1"));
        item.addActionListener(this);
        buttonGroup.add(item);
        otherMenu.add(item = new JRadioButtonMenuItem("Radio 2"));
        item.addActionListener(this);
        buttonGroup.add(item);
        otherMenu.addSeparator();
        otherMenu.add(item = new JMenuItem("Potted Plant",
                                    new ImageIcon("image.gif")));
        item.addActionListener(this);

        //  Finally, add all the menus to the menubar
        add(fileMenu);
        add(editMenu);
        add(otherMenu);
    }

    public void actionPerformed(ActionEvent event) {
        System.out.println("Menu item [" + event.getActionCommand() +
                            "] was pressed.");
    }

    public static void main(String s[]) {
        JFrame frame = new JFrame("Simple Menu Example");
        frame.addWindowListener(new BasicWindowMonitor());
        frame.setJMenuBar(new IntroExample());
        frame.pack();
        frame.setVisible(true);
    }
}
```

This example creates a menubar with three simple menus, attaching mnemonics to the menu items of the "File" menu, and keyboard accelerators to the menu items of the "Edit" menus. Figure 14-3 shows a mosaic of the different menus that the program produces.

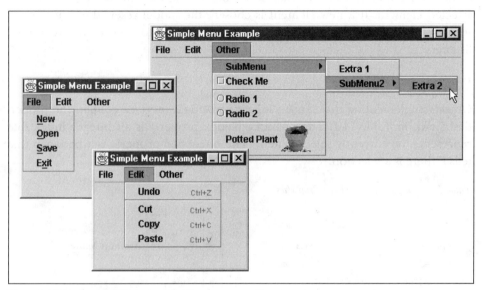

Figure 14-3. A sample of Swing menu effects

In the third menu, we've enhanced the last item with a GIF image of a potted plant. In addition, the first menu item in the "Other" menu is actually a submenu that pops out to a second submenu, underscoring the recursive nature of menus. If you select any of the menus, you are rewarded with a simple text output that tells you what you clicked:

```
Menu item [New] was pressed.
Menu item [Radio 1] was pressed.
```

Don't worry if you do not understand all the classes and methods at this point. We will examine each menu component in detail shortly.

Menu Bar Selection Models

In all GUI environments, menu components only allow one selection to be made at a time. Swing is no exception. Swing provides a data model that menubars and menus can use to emulate this behavior: the SingleSelectionModel.

The SingleSelectionModel Interface

Objects implementing the SingleSelectionModel interface do exactly what the name suggests: they maintain an array of possible selections, and allow one element in the array to be chosen at a time. The model holds the index of the selected element. If a new element is chosen, the model resets the index representing the chosen element and fires a ChangeEvent to each of the registered listeners.

Properties

Objects implementing the SingleSelectionModel interface contain the properties shown in Table 14-1. The selectedIndex property is an integer index that represents the currently selected item. The selected property is a boolean that tells if there is a selection.

Table 14-1. SingleSelectionModel Properties

Property	Data Type	get	is	set	bound	Default Value
selected	boolean		•			
selectedIndex	int	•		•		

Events

Objects implementing the SingleSelectionModel interface must fire a ChangeEvent (not a PropertyChangeEvent) when the object modifies its selectedIndex property, i.e., when the selection has changed. The interface contains the standard addChangeListener() and removeChangeListener() methods for maintaining a list of ChangeEvent listeners.

void addChangeListener(ChangeListener listener)
void removeChangeListener(ChangeListener listener)
   Add or remove the specified ChangeListener from the list of listeners receiving this model's change events.

Methods

The SingleSelectionModel interface contains one other method:

public void clearSelection()
   Clears the selection value, forcing the selected property to return false.

The DefaultSingleSelectionModel Class

Swing's default implementation of the SingleSelectionModel interface is the DefaultSingleSelectionModel class. DefaultSingleSelectionModel allows only one selection element to be chosen at a time, which it represents with a non-negative integer. The value –1 indicates that there is no selection.

Properties

The DefaultSingleSelectionModel contains the same properties as the SingleSelectionModel interface, as shown in Table 14-2. The selectedIndex property is an integer index that represents the currently selected item. The default value of –1 indicates that there is no selection. The selected property is a boolean that returns true if the selectedIndex is anything other than –1, false otherwise.

Table 14-2. DefaultSingleSelectionModel Properties

Property	Data Type	get	is	set	bound	Default Value
selected	boolean		•			false
selectedIndex	int	•		•		–1

Events

The DefaultSingleSelectionModel object fires a ChangeEvent when the selectedIndex property is modified, i.e., when the selection has changed. The object incorporates addChangeListener() and removeChangeListener() methods for maintaining a list of ChangeEvent listeners.

public void addChangeListener(ChangeListener listener)
public void removeChangeListener(ChangeListener listener)
> Adds or removes the specified ChangeListener from the list of listeners recieving this model's change events.

protected void fireStateChanged()
> Fires a ChangeEvent to all of this model's registered change event listeners.

Protected Fields

The DefaultSingleSelectionModel contains two protected fields:

protected transient ChangeEvent changeEvent
> Represents the ChangeEvent that is sent to all listeners.

protected EventListenerList listenerList

Manages the change listeners for the menu selection model.

Method

public void clearSelection()

Resets the `selectedIndex` property to -1, forcing the `selected` property to return `false`.

The JMenuBar Class

Swing's `JMenuBar` class supersedes the older AWT `MenuBar` class. This class creates a horizontal menubar component with zero or more menus attached to it. `JMenuBar` uses the `DefaultSingleSelectionModel` as its data model; this is because the user can raise, or *activate*, only one of its menus at a given time. Once the mouse pointer leaves that menu, the class removes the menu from the screen (or *cancels* it, in Swing lingo), and all menus again become eligible to be raised. Figure 14-4 shows the class hierarchy for the `JMenuBar` component.

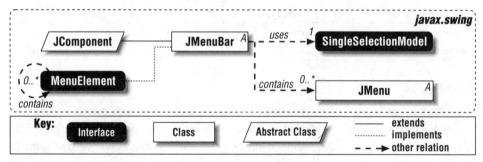

Figure 14-4. A sample of Swing menu effects

You can add `JMenu` objects from the menubar with the `add()` method of the `JMenuBar` class. `JMenuBar` then assigns an integer index based on the order in which the menus were added. The menubar displays the menus from left to right on the bar according to their assigned index. There is one exception: the help menu. You are allowed to mark one menu as the help menu; the location of the help menu is up to the look-and-feel.

NOTE   As of JDK 1.2 beta 4, the help menu feature was not implemented.

Menubar Placement

You can attach menubars to Swing frames or applets in one of two ways. First, you can use the setJMenuBar() method of JFrame, JDialog, JApplet, or JInternalFrame:

```
JFrame frame = new JFrame("Menu");
JMenuBar menuBar = new JMenuBar();

//  Attach the menu bar to the frame
frame.setJMenuBar(menuBar);
```

The setJMenuBar() method is analogous to the setMenuBar() method of java.awt.Frame. Like its predecessor, setJMenuBar() anchors the menubar to the top of a frame, adjusting the frame's internal Insets accordingly. Both JDialog and JApplet now contain a setJMenuBar() method—this means that you can finally add menubars to both applets and dialogs (not possible in AWT). Either way, be sure not to confuse the setJMenuBar() method with the older setMenuBar() method of AWT when working with Swing menus, or the compiler will complain bitterly.

The second way to add a menubar is more inspiring. Recall that the JMenuBar class extends JComponent. This means it can be positioned by a Swing layout manager like other Swing components. For example, we could replace the call to setJMenuBar() with the following code:

```
menuBar.setBorder(new BevelBorder(BevelBorder.RAISED));
frame.getContentPane().add(menuBar, BorderLayout.SOUTH);
```

This places the menubar at the bottom of the frame, as shown in Figure 14-5. (Note that we set a beveled border around the menubar to help outline its location.) Don't like the menubar at the bottom? Place it in the middle! Add two or three menubars in different locations if you like. The important thing to remember is that Swing does not require a single menubar to be anchored to the top of a frame. Because they extend JComponent, multiple menubars can now be positioned anywhere inside a container.

NOTE   You have to add at least one named menu to a menubar for it to gain any "thickness." Otherwise, it appears as a thin line— similar to a separator.

Properties

The properties of the JMenuBar class are shown in Table 14-3. menu is an indexed property that references each JMenu attached to the menubar. The read-only

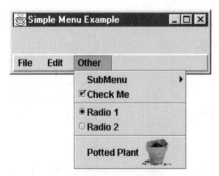

Figure 14-5. JMenuBar positioned as a Swing component

menuCount property maintains a count of those attached menus. Remember that the single selection model allows only one menu to be activated at a time. If any menu is currently activated, the selected property will return true; otherwise, the property will return false. The componentAtIndex property accesses the menu associated with the given index. It is similar to the indexed menu property, except the contents are cast to a Component. If there is no component associated with that index, the getComponentAtIndex() accessor returns null. The component property returns a reference to this (i.e., the menu bar itself); subElements returns an array consisting of the menus on the menu bar.

Table 14-3. JMenuBar Properties

Property	Data Type	get	is	set	bound	Default
UI	MenuBarUI	•		•	•	from L&F
UIClassID*	String	•				"MenuBarUI"
selectionModel	SingleSelection-Model	•		•		DefaultSingleSelection-Model()
accessibleContext*	AccessibleContext	•				JMenuBar.Accessible-JMenuBar()
borderPainted	boolean		•	•		true
component	Component	•				this
componentAtIndex (indexed)	Component	•				true
helpMenu	JMenu	•		•		null
layout*	LayoutManager	•		•		BoxLayout(X_AXIS)
margin	Insets	•		•		null
managingFocus	boolean		•			true

See also properties from the JComponent class (Table 3-5).

Table 14-3. JMenuBar Properties (continued)

Property	Data Type	get	is	set	bound	Default
menu (indexed)	JMenu	•				null
menuCount	int	•				0
selected	boolean			•		false
subElements	MenuElement[]	•				

See also properties from the JComponent class (Table 3-5).

The `margin` property controls the amount of space between the menubar's border and its menus, while the `borderPainted` property is a boolean that indicates whether the menubar should paint its border. As we demonstrated above, you can set a Swing border around any subclass of `JComponent`, including `JMenuBar`.[*] For more information about Swing borders, see Chapter 13, *Borders*.

You can assign one `JMenu` the role of the menubar's help menu. The `helpMenu` property represents this `JMenu`.

NOTE   As of JDK1.2 beta4, any attempt to set the `helpMenu` property results in an error exception.

Constructor

public JMenuBar()

Creates and initializes an empty `JMenuBar` object.

Menus

public JMenu add(JMenu menu)

You can use this method to attach a `JMenu` to the menubar set. Because of the `BoxLayout` of `JMenuBar`, menus are displayed on the menubar from left to right in the order that you `add()` them. The method returns a reference to the `JMenu` that was passed in, allowing you to string together calls. For example: `menubar.add(menu).add(menuitem)`.

---

[*] Note that in `JComponent`, there is no boolean `borderPainted` property. A border simply paints itself if the `border` property is set to a non-null value. This `borderPainted` property exists because the default menubar uses a border while rendering itself.

Miscellaneous

public int getComponentIndex(Component c)

Returns the index associated with the component reference passed in. If there is no match to the component, the method returns a –1. You can typically assume that the component passed in is a JMenu.

protected void paintBorder(Graphics g)

Paints the border if the borderPainted property is set to true.

public void setSelected(Component c)

Forces the menubar (and its associated model) to select a particular menu, which will fire a ChangeEvent in the menubar's single selection model. This method, for example, is called when a mnemonic key for a particular menu has been pressed. Note that this is different than the boolean selected property listed in Table 14-3.

public void updateUI()

Forces the UIManager to refresh the look-and-feel of the component, based on the current UI-delegate.

Menu Element Interface

public void menuSelectionChanged(boolean isIncluded)
public MenuElement[] getSubElements()
public Component getComponent()
public void processMouseEvent(MouseEvent event, MenuElement path[],
    MenuSelectionManager manager)
public void processKeyEvent(KeyEvent event, MenuElement path[],
    MenuSelectionManager manager)

These methods implement the MenuElement interface, which is covered later in this chapter.

The JMenuItem Class

Before discussing menus, we should introduce the JMenuItem class first. Figure 14-6 shows the class diagram for the JMenuItem component.

A JMenuItem serves as a wrapper for strings and images to be used as elements in a menu. We mentioned earlier that the JMenuItem class is essentially just a specialized button. In fact, the JMenuItem class extends the AbstractButton class. Its logic, however, is somewhat different from the standard button. When the mouse passes over a menu item, Swing considers the menu item to be *selected*. If the user releases the mouse over the menu item, it is considered chosen and should perform its action.

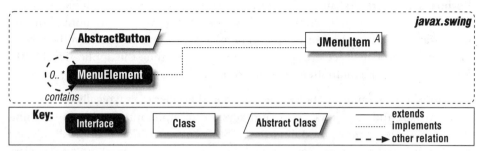

Figure 14-6. JMenuItem class diagram

There is an unfortunate conflict in terminology here. Swing considers a menu item "selected" when the mouse moves over it, as updated by the `MenuSelectionManager` and classes that implement the `MenuElement` interface. On the other hand, Swing considers a button "selected" when it remains in one of two persistent states, such as a checkbox button remaining in the checked state until clicked again. So when a menu item is *selected*, its button model is really *armed*. Conversely, when a menu item is deselected, its button model is disarmed. Finally, when the user releases the mouse button over the menu item, the button is considered *clicked* and the `AbstractButton`'s `doClick()` method is invoked.

Menu Item Shortcuts

Menu items can take both keyboard accelerators or mnemonics. Mnemonics are an artifact of buttons; they appear as a single underline below the character that represents the shortcut. Keyboard accelerators, on the other hand, are inherited from `JComponent`. With menu items, they have the unique side effect of being printed directly to the right of the menu item. (This is actually up to the installed L&F.) Figure 14-7 shows both mnemonics and keyboard accelerators.

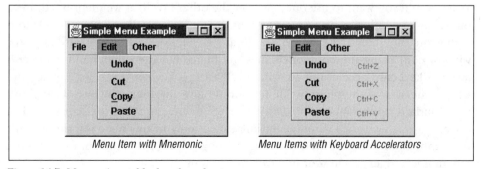

Figure 14-7. Mnemonics and keyboard accelerators

Keyboard accelerators and mnemonics perform the same function: users can abbreviate common GUI actions with keystrokes. However, a mnemonic can only be activated when the button (or menu item) it represents is visible on the screen. Menu item keyboard accelerators can be invoked any time the application has the focus—whether the menu item is visible or not.

Let's look at programming both cases. Keyboard accelerators typically use a variety of keystrokes: function keys, command keys, or an alphanumeric key in combination with a one or more modifiers (e.g., "Shift," "Control," or "Alt"). All of these key combinations can be represented by the `javax.swing.KeyStroke` class. Hence, you can assign a keyboard accelerator to a menu item by setting its `accelerator` property with a `KeyStroke` object, as follows:

```
JMenuItem m = new JMenuItem("Copy");
m.setAccelerator(KeyStroke.
                getKeyStroke('C', java.awt.Event.SHIFT_MASK, false));
```

This sets the accelerator to "Shift-C," which is the letter "C" typed in combination with the "Shift" key. The accelerator appears at the right side of the menu item (though again, the position is up to the L&F). The `KeyStroke` class is covered in more detail in Chapter 27, *Swing Utilities*.

The second way to set a shortcut is to set the `mnemonic` property of the `Abstract-Button` superclass:

```
JMenuItem mi = new JMenuItem("Copy");
mi.setMnemonic('C');
```

The `mnemonic` property underlines the character you pass into the `setMnemonic()` method. Note that mnemonic characters cannot take modifiers; they are simple letters. Be sure to use a letter that exists in the menu item's label. Otherwise, nothing will be underlined and the user will not know how to activate the keyboard shortcut.

When would you want to use one way over the other? Well, as we mentioned previously, you can only use a mnemonic when the menu item that it corresponds to is visible on the screen. Keyboard accelerators will work whenever any ancestor window containing the component has the focus. On the other hand, you can't assign a keyboard accelerator to a menu. Placing a keyboard accelerator description to the side of the menu's title text would give the menubar a confusing and non-standard appearance. (In fact, if you try to use `setAccelerator()` with a `JMenu` object, Swing will throw a runtime exception.) In this case, you should only use a mnemonic. Alternatively, there is nothing to prevent you from using both a mnemonic and an accelerator in a true menu item.

Images

In Swing, menu items can now contain (or consist entirely of) icons. This gives the user the option of adding or a visual aid to the menu item if the icon can convey the intended meaning more clearly. You can pass an `Icon` object to the constructor of the `JMenuItem` class as follows:

```
JMenu menu = new JMenu("Justify");

// The first two menu items contain text and an image. The third
// uses only the image.
menu.add(new JMenuItem("Center", new ImageIcon("center.gif")));
menu.add(new JMenuItem("Right", new ImageIcon("right.gif")));
menu.add(new JMenuItem(new ImageIcon("left.gif")));
```

By default, the text is placed to the left of the image. This is shown on the left in Figure 14-8. As you can see, this often misaligns the images to the right of the text, especially if there is a menu item consisting only of an image. If the menu item images are all the same width, you can improve the appearance of your menus by resetting the text's position using the `setHorizontalTextAlignment()` method:

```
JMenu menu = new JMenu("Justify");

// The first two menu items contain text and an image. The third
// uses only the image. The text is now set to the right.
JMenuItem item1= new JMenuItem("Center", new ImageIcon("center.gif")));
item1.setHorizontalTextAlignment(SwingConstants.RIGHT);
JMenuItem item2= new JMenuItem("Right", new ImageIcon("right.gif")));
item2.setHorizontalTextAlignment(SwingConstants.RIGHT);

// Now add the menu items to the menu
menu.add(item1);
menu.add(item2);
menu.add(new JMenuItem(new ImageIcon("left.gif")));
```

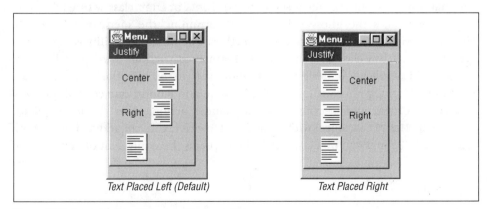

Figure 14-8. Image and text placement in menu items

This positions the text on the other side of the images, as shown on the right of Figure 14-8. You can trace the setHorizontalTextAlignment() method up the class hierarchy to the AbstractButton class. As we mentioned before, the JMenu-Item class uses a button object to represent its text and image. AbstractButton contains the corresponding setVerticalTextAlignment() method as well, so if the accompanying image is taller than the menu item text, you can use this method to set the text's vertical position as well. See the AbstractButton class (Chapter 5, *Buttons*) and the OverlayLayout class (Chapter 11, *Specialty Panes and Layout Managers*) for more information about alignment with menu items and buttons. The image is placed to the left of the text if you construct a menu item from an Action object (more on this later in the chapter).

Java supports alpha channeling of images, so if you require some parts of an image to be transparent, you can specify a "transparent" color in the GIF file (many paint programs will allow you to do this), or you can create a specialized color filter that seeks out specific pixel colors and changes their opacity before passing the resulting Image onto the menus. The former is much easier.

Event Handling

There are a couple of ways that you can process events from menu items. Because menu items inherit ActionEvent functionality from AbstractButton, the traditional approach is to assign an action command to each menu item (this is often done automatically with named components) and attach all of the menu items to the same ActionListener. Then, in the actionPerformed() method of the listener, use the event's getActionCommand() method to obtain the action command of the menu item generating the event. This reveals to the listener the menu item that has been clicked, allowing it to react accordingly. This is the approach used in the IntroExample.java earlier and PopupMenuExample.java discussed later.

Alternatively, you can register a separate ActionListener class with each menu item, which takes the guesswork out of determining the menu item selected. However, Swing allows you to go a step further. The other possibility is to create a specialized Action class in lieu of each JMenuItem. Actions are generally more efficient for application design—they allow you to bundle the code for each program action together with the action's name and icon in one centralized location. Both JMenu and JPopupMenu can handle actions. You cannot explicitly initialize a JMenuItem object with an action. However, you can add actions to both JMenu and JPopupMenu objects, which then creates the equivalent JMenuItem for you.

Properties

The properties for the JMenuItem class are shown in Table 14-4. Most of the properties shown are superclass properties reconfigured to ensure that the menu item's "button" acts more like a traditional menu item. The borderPainted property is always set to false; the menu item will never take a border. The focusPainted property is also set to false to ensure that a focus rectangle is never drawn around the menu item. horizontalTextPosition and horizontalAlignment are both initialized to JButton.LEFT. This places the text to the left of the image icon, and places the text and image icon on the left side of the menu item. (See our earlier example for reconfiguring this.) Finally, if only an icon is used for the menu item, the requestFocusEnabled property is always set to return false, indicating that the menu item cannot request focus.

Table 14-4. JMenuItem Properties

Property	Data Type	get	is	set	bound	Default Value
UI	MenuItemUI			•		from L&F
UIClassID*	String	•				"MenuItemUI"
model*	ButtonModel	•		•		DefaultButtonModel()
accelerator	KeyStroke	•		•		null
accessibleContext*	Accessible Context	•				JMenuItem.Accessible-JMenuItem()
armed*	boolean		•	•		false
borderPainted*	boolean		•	•		false
component*	Component	•				
enabled*	boolean		•	•		true
focusPainted*	boolean		•	•		false
horizontalTextPosi-tion*	int	•		•		JButton.LEFT
horizontalAlignment*	int	•		•		JButton.LEFT
requestFocusEnabled*	boolean			•		(Discussed later)
subElements*	MenuElement[]	•				

See also properties from the AbstractButton class (Table 5-6).

The accelerator property sets the keyboard accelerator for the menu item; the accelerator is typically drawn to the right of the menu item string. The armed property simply maps a boolean down to the armed state of the component model: ButtonModel. You can use this to programmatically select the menu item if needed. The enabled property is a boolean that indicates whether the user can select the menu item. If the menu item is disabled, JMenuItem automatically grays the text and associated image. The `subElements` property provides an array of submenus contained in this menu item.

Constructors

JMenuItem()
JMenuItem(Icon icon)
JMenuItem(String string)
JMenuItem(String string, Icon icon)
JMenuItem(String string, int mnemonic)

> Create a menu item with the appropriate icon or string. You also have the option to specify a mnemonic if you initialize with a string.

Events

`JMenuItems` send many different kinds of events. Perhaps the most important are `Action` `Events`, which are fired when an item is selected. Likewise, `Change` `Events` are fired when various button properties change. Methods for adding and removing listeners for these events are inherited from `AbstractButton`.

`JMenuItem` also uses special events for reporting mouse motions and key presses on top of the menu item. These are the `MenuDragMouseEvent` and `MenuKeyEvent`. Here are the methods for registering listeners for these events:

addMenuDragMouseListener (MenuDragMouseListener 1)
removeMenuDragMouseListener (MenuDragMouseListener 1)

> These methods add or remove a specific `MenuDragMouseListener` interested in being notified when there is a `MenuDragMouseEvent`.

addMenuKeyListener (MenuKeyListener 1)
removeMenuKeyListener (MenuKeyListener 1)

> These methods add or remove a specific `MenuKeyListener` interested in being notified when there is a `MenuKeyEvent`.

The following methods provide support for firing these events:

public void processMenuDragMouseEvent (MenuDragMouseEvent e)

> Fires a specific `MenuDragMouseEvent` notification based on the type of `MouseEvent` that was observed. If the `MouseEvent` listed was `MOUSE_ENTERED`, for example, the menu invokes the `fireMenuDragMouseEntered()` method.

public void processMenuKeyEvent (MenuKeyEvent e)

> Fires a specific `MenuKeyEvent` notification based on the type of `MenuKeyEvent` that was observed. If the `MenuKeyEvent` listed was `KEY_` `RELEASED`, for example, the menu invokes the `fireMenuKeyReleased()` method.

protected void fireMenuDragMouseEntered (MenuDragMouseEvent e)

Invokes the `menuDragMouseEntered()` method of all registered `MenuDrag-MouseListener` classes, passing in the appropriate `MenuDragMouseEvent` to describe the change.

protected void fireMenuDragMouseExited (MenuDragMouseEvent e)

Invokes the `menuDragMouseExited()` method of all registered `MenuDrag-MouseListener` classes, passing in the appropriate `MenuDragMouseEvent` to describe the change.

protected void fireMenuDragMouseDragged (MenuDragMouseEvent e)

Invokes the `menuDragMouseDragged()` method of all registered `MenuDrag-MouseListener` classes, passing in the appropriate `MenuDragMouseEvent` to describe the change.

protected void fireMenuDragMouseReleased (MenuDragMouseEvent e)

Invokes the `menuDragMouseReleased()` method of all registered `MenuDrag-MouseListener` classes, passing in the appropriate `MenuDragMouseEvent` to describe the change.

protected void fireMenuKeyPressed (MenuKeyEvent e)

Invokes the `menuKeyPressed()` method of all registered `MenuKeyPressed` classes, passing in the appropriate `MenuKeyEvent` to describe the change.

protected void fireMenuKeyReleased (MenuKeyEvent e)

Invokes the `menuKeyReleased()` method of all registered `MenuKeyReleased` classes, passing in the appropriate `MenuKeyEvent` to describe the change.

protected void fireMenuKeyPressed (MenuKeyEvent e)

Invokes the `menuKeyTyped()` method of all registered `MenuKeyTyped` classes, passing in the appropriate `MenuKeyEvent` to describe the change.

Methods

public void updateUI()

Forces the current UI manager to reset the current delegate for the component, thus updating the component's look-and-feel.

protected void init(String text, Icon icon)

Initializes the menu item with the specified text and icon. If you wish to omit either one, you can pass in `null`.

Menu Element Interface

public void menuSelectionChanged(boolean isIncluded)
public MenuElement[] getSubElements()
public Component getComponent()

public void processMouseEvent(MouseEvent event, MenuElement path[],
    MenuSelectionManager manager)
public void processKeyEvent(KeyEvent event, MenuElement path[],
    MenuSelectionManager manager)
    Implement the MenuElement interface, which is covered later in this chapter.

The MenuDragMouseEvent Class

Swing generates a series of events while the mouse is dragging across an open menu. This event, MenuDragMouseEvent, describes the drag in relation to a particular menu item. You can listen for these events by adding an object that implements MenuDragMouseListener to the addMenuDragMouseListener() method of JMenuItem. The object implementing MenuDragMouseListener will have four separate methods that can be invoked in response to a mouse drag inside a menu; each one indicates exactly what happened with the drag. Table 14-5 shows the properties of the MenuDragMouseEvent.

Table 14-5. MenuDragMouseEvent Properties

Property	Data Type	get	is	set	bound	Default Value
source	Object	•				
id*	int	•		•		
when*	long	•				
modifiers*	Object	•		•		
x*	int	•				
y*	int	•		•		
clickCount*	int	•				
popupTrigger*	boolean		•			
path	MenuElement[]	•				
manager	MenuSelectionManager	•				

See also java.awt.event.MouseEvent.

There are no defaults for the event; all properties are set in the constructor. The source property indicates the object that sent the event. The id property describes the type of event that was fired. The when property gives the event a timestamp. The modifiers property allows you to test various masks to see which mouse button is being pressed, as well as the "Alt," "Ctrl," "Shift," and "Meta" keys. The x and y properties give the current location of the mouse pointer relative to the component in question. The clickCount property describes how many times a mouse button has been clicked prior to this drag. The popupTrigger property describes whether this mouse event can be considered a popup menu event. The path property gives an ordered array of `MenuElement` objects, describing the path to this specific menu. Finally, the `manager` property contains a reference to the current `MenuSelectionManager` for this menu system.

Constructor

public MenuDragMouseEvent(Component source, int id, long when, int modifiers, int x, int
y, int clickCount, boolean popupTrigger, MenuElement[] path, MenuSelectionManager
manager)
   Initializes each of the properties described in Table 14-5 with the values specified.

The MenuDragMouseListener Interface

The `MenuDragMouseListener` interface, which is the conduit for receiving the `MenuDragMouseEvent` objects, contains four methods. One method is called when the mouse is dragged inside the menu item, the second when the mouse is released inside the menu item. Finally, the last two are called when the mouse is dragged into a menu item, or dragged out of a menu item.

Methods

public abstract void menuDragMouseDragged(PopupMenuEvent e)
   Called when the mouse has been dragged inside of a menu item.

public abstract void menuDragMouseReleased(PopupMenuEvent e)
   Called when the mouse has been released inside of a menu item.

public abstract void menuDragMouseEntered(PopupMenuEvent e)
   Called when the mouse is being dragged, and has entered a menu item.

public abstract void menuDragMouseExited(PopupMenuEvent e)
   Called when the mouse is being dragged, and has exited a menu item.

The MenuKeyEvent Class

Swing also generates an event when a specific menu item receives a key event. Note that the key event does not have to be directed at the specific menu (i.e., an accelerator or mnemonic). Instead, the menu item will respond to any key events that are generated while the menu popup containing it is showing on the screen. You can listen for these events by adding an object that implements `MenuKeyListener` to the `addMenuKeyListener()` method of `JMenuItem`. The object implementing `MenuKeyListener` will have three separate methods that can be invoked in response to a menu key event.

Table 14-6 shows the properties of MenuKeyEvent. There are no defaults for the event; all properties are set in the constructor. The source property indicates the object that sent the event. The id property describes the type of event that was fired. The when property gives the event a timestamp. The modifiers property allows you to test various masks to see which mouse button is being pressed, as well as the ALT, CTRL, SHIFT, and META keys. The keyCode and keyChar properties describe the key that was actually pressed. The path property gives an ordered array of MenuElement objects, describing the path to this specific menu. Finally, the manager property contains a reference to the current MenuSelection-Manager.

Table 14-6. MenuKeyEvent Properties

Property	Data Type	get	is	set	bound	Default Value
source	Object	•				
id*	int	•		•		
when*	long	•				
modifiers*	Object	•		•		
keyCode*	int	•				
keyChar*	char	•		•		
path	MenuElement[]	•				
manager	MenuSelectionManager	•				

See also java.awt.event.keyEvent.

Constructor

public MenuDragMouseEvent(Component source, int id, long when, int keyCode, char keyChar, MenuElement[] path, MenuSelectionManager manager)
    Takes each of the properties described from Table 14-6.

The MenuKeyListener Interface

The MenuKeyListener interface, which is the conduit for receiving the MenuKeyEvent objects, contains three methods. One method is called when a key has been typed (i.e., pressed and released), while the second is called after a key has been pressed. This third is called after a key has been released. Note that if a key is pressed and held down for a few seconds, Swing emulates the traditional key bahavior: it considers the key both "typed" and "pressed" again.

Methods

public abstract void menuKeyTyped(MenuKeyEvent e)
    Called when a key intended for this menu element has been both pressed and released.

public abstract void menuKeyPressed(MenuKeyEvent e)
    Called when a key intended for this menu element has been pressed.

public abstract void menuKeyReleased(MenuKeyEvent e)
    Called when a key intended for this menu element has been released.

Menu items cannot exist by themselves; they must be embedded in menus. Like AWT, Swing implements two closely related styles of menus: the traditional anchored menu and the popup menu. Swing uses the JMenu and JPopupMenu classes to implement these menus.

The JPopupMenu Class

Popup menus were first introduced in AWT 1.1. These menus are not attached to a menubar; instead, they are free-floating menus that associate themselves with an underlying component. This component is called the *invoker*. Popup menus are brought into existence by a platform-dependent popup trigger event that occurs while the mouse is over the invoking component. In AWT and Swing, this trigger is typically a mouse event. Once raised, the user can interact with the menu normally. Figure 14-9 is an example of a popup menu in Swing.

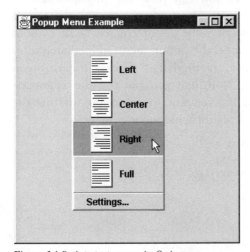

Figure 14-9. A popup menu in Swing

You can add or insert JMenuItem, Component, or Action objects to the popup menu by calling the add() and insert() methods. The JPopupMenu class assigns an integer index to each menu item and orders them based on the layout manager of the popup menu. In addition, you can add separators to the menu by using the `addSeparator()` method; these separators also count as an index. Figure 14-10 shows the class diagram for the `JPopupMenu` component.

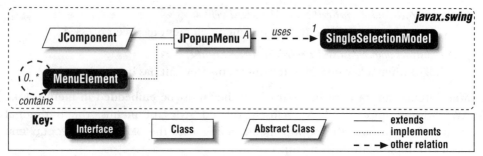

Figure 14-10. JPopupMenu class diagram

Displaying the Popup Menu

Popup menus are usually raised by invoking the `show()` method in conjunction with the platform-dependent popup trigger. The `show()` method sets the `location` and `invoker` properties of the popup before setting the `visible` property to true. Popups are automatically canceled by any of a variety of events, including clicking a menu item; resizing an invoking component; or moving, minimizing, maximizing, or closing the parent window. (For the most part, you will never need to worry about canceling popup menus.) You can raise the popup menu by querying all `MouseEvent` objects passed to the host component for the popup trigger. A word to the wise: if the `MouseEvent` is the popup trigger, be sure not to pass it to the superclass, or Swing could cancel the popup menu immediately after raising it! Here's a `processMouseEvent()` method that raises a popup menu upon recieving the appropriate trigger. Note that you can use the `isPopup-Trigger()` method of `java.awt.event.MouseEvent` to determine whether the mouse event is the appropriate trigger in a platform-independent way:

```
public void processMouseEvent(MouseEvent e) {
    if (e.isPopupTrigger()) {
        popup.show(this, e.getX(), e.getY());
    }
    else {
        super.processMouseEvent(e);
    }
}
```

When the mouse moves outside the component, Swing will no longer send popup trigger events to that component, and its popup menu cannot be raised. This gives you the opportunity to define different popup menus for different underlying components.

Properties

The properties of the `JPopupMenu` class are shown in Table 14-7. Popup menus have many properties. The `visible` property tells whether the popup menu is currently showing on the screen; you can use the `setVisible()` method to show or hide the popup, but if it is a free-floating popup it is much easier to use the `show()` method. The `location` property provides the coordinates on the screen where the popup menu is or has been raised. The read-only `margin` property gives the amount of space between the popup window border and an imaginary rectangle surrounding the individual menu items.

Table 14-7. JPopupMenu Properties

Property	Data Type	get	is	set	bound	Default Value
UI	PopupMenuUI	•		•	•	BasicPopupMenuUI()
UIClassID*	String	•				"PopupMenuUI"
selectionModel	SingleSelec-tionModel	•		•		DefaultSingleSelection-Model()
accessibleContext*	AccessibleContext	•				JPopupMenu.accessible-JPopupMenu()
borderPainted	boolean		•	•		true
component	Component	•				
componentAtIndex (indexed)	Component	•				
invoker	Component	•		•		
label	String	•		•	•	""
layout*	LayoutManager	•		•		GridBagLayout()
lightWeightPopupEn-abled	boolean		•	•		getDefaultLightWeightPop-upEnabled()
location*	Point			•		
margin	Insets	•				
popupSize	Dimension			•		
subElements	MenuElement[]	•				
visible*	boolean		•	•		false

See also properties from the JMenuItem class (Table 14-4).

The `invoker` property is a reference to the component that is responsible for hosting the popup menu. The `borderPainted` property indicates whether the popup menu should paint its border. The `label` property gives each popup menu a specific label; the individual look-and-feel is free to use or ignore this property as it sees fit. Note that `label` is a `String` and not a `JLabel`. `componentAtIndex` is an indexed property that returns the component at the specified index. If there is no component at the index passed to `getComponentAtIndex()`, the method returns −1.

The `lightWeightPopupEnabled` property allows the programmer to enable or disable the potential use of lightweight components to represent the popup menu. If the property is set to `true`, Swing will use a lightweight component when the popup is inside the top-level component's drawing space, and a heavyweight when the popup extends beyond its space. When the property is set to `false`, an AWT `Panel` is used if the menu is entirely inside the top-level component, while a new heavyweight top-level `Window` is used if it extends outside those boundaries. You are also allowed to set the default value of this property for all other popup menus using the static `setDefaultLightWeightPopupEnabled()` method.

Events

`JPopupMenu` objects fire a `PopupMenuEvent` under three conditions: when the menu has received instructions to become visible or invisible, or when the popup menu has been canceled without a menu item selection. The class contains the standard `addPopupMenuListener()` and `removePopupMenuListener()` methods for maintaining a list of `PopupMenuEvent` subscribers.

public void addPopupMenuListener(PopupMenuListener l)
public void removePopupMenuListener(PopupMenuListener l)
　　Add or remove a `PopupMenuListener` from the object's event queue.

protected void firePopupMenuWillBecomeVisible()
　　Fires a `PopupMenuListener` event stating that the popup menu is about to become visible.

protected void firePopupMenuWillBecomeInvisible()
　　Fires a `PopupMenuListener` event stating that the popup menu is about to become invisible.

protected void firePopupMenuCanceled()
　　Fires a `PopupMenuListener` event stating that the popup menu has been cancelled without a menu item selection. This can occur if the host component is resized, or the component's window is minimized, maximized, closed, or moved.

Note that when the popup menu is canceled, it also becomes invisible, so two events are actually triggered.

Constructor

public JPopupMenu()
public JPopupMenu(String title)

Create an empty popup menu. The second constructor accepts a `String` as the title of the popup menu.

Menu Items

public JMenuItem add(JMenuItem menuItem)
public Component add(Component c)
public JMenuItem add(Action a)

Add various elements to the popup menus. Objects of both `JMenuItem` and `JComponent` can be added, but the latter functions best if it implements the `MenuElement` interface. If you specify an `Action`, its text and image properties are used to derive an appropriate `JMenuItem`, and its text is placed to the right of the image icon. The resulting `JMenuItem` is then returned, which you can use to alter its formatting.

public JMenuItem insert(Action a, int index)
public Component insert(Component component, int index)

Insert a specific menu item at a particular index. You can pass in a `JComponent` or an `Action` to these methods. If you use a `JComponent`, it's best if it implements the `MenuElement` interface. If you specify an `Action`, its text and image properties are used to derive an appropriate `JMenuItem`, and its text is placed to the right of the image icon. The resulting `JMenuItem` is then returned, which you can use to alter its formatting. All menu item indices that were previously at or after the specified position are incremented.

public void addSeparator()

Adds a separator to the popup menu. Typically, a separator consists of a single horizontal line drawn across the popup menu. Note that, like menu items, the separator counts as an index in the menu. The separator used is an instance of an inner class, not the regular `JSeparator`; it is always horizontal.

Display

public void pack()

Forces the menu items inside the popup menu to be compressed to the smallest size possible without violating any requested minimum sizes.

public void show(Component invoker, int x, int y)

Paints the popup menu at the requested coordinates. The method takes a reference to the invoking component. It is functionally equivalent to the following calls: `setInvoker()`, `setLocation()`, and `setVisible()`.

public void setPopupSize(int width, int height)

Resets the size of the popup menu, accepting a pair of coordinate integers instead of a Dimension. A default size is computed after the pack() method is invoked on the popup menu. This computed size will remain in effect unless reset by this method or the standard accessor for the popupSize property.

Miscellaneous

protected PropertyChangeListener createActionChangeListener(JMenuItem mi)

This protected method is an internal utility method that creates an individual property change listener for a specific menu item.

public int getComponentIndex(Component c)

Returns the index associated with the component reference c. If there is no match to the component passed in, the method returns –1.

public static boolean getDefaultLightWeightEnabled

Returns the default value for the lightWeightPopupEnabled property.

public void menuSelectionChanged(boolean b)

This is an internal change listener used to monitor menu events; it typically should not be called by the programmer.

protected void paintBorder(Graphics g)

Paints the border only if the borderPainted property is set to true.

public static void setDefaultLightWeightPopupEnabled(boolean aFlag)

Sets the default value of the lightWeightPopupEnabled property, which controls whether a lightweight or heavyweight component is used for the popup.

public void setSelected(Component c)

Forces the popup menu's model to select a particular menu item. This forces a property change event in the popup menu's single selection model.

public void updateUI()

Forces the default user interface manager to update itself, thus resetting the delegate to display a new PopupMenuUI.

Menu Element Interface

public void menuSelectionChanged(boolean isIncluded)
public MenuElement[] getSubElements()
public Component getComponent()
public void processMouseEvent(MouseEvent event, MenuElement path[],
    MenuSelectionManager manager)

public void processKeyEvent(KeyEvent event, MenuElement path[],
*   MenuSelectionManager manager)*
Implement the `MenuElement` interface, which is covered later in this chapter.

Using Popup Menus

Here is a program that demonstrates the use of the `JPopupMenu` class. The example is similar to Figure 14-9, except that the popup communicates events from the popup menu and from each of its menu items.

```java
//  PopupMenuExample.java
//
import java.awt.*;
import java.awt.event.*;

import javax.swing.*;
import javax.swing.border.*;
import javax.swing.event.*;

public class PopupMenuExample extends JPanel
    implements ActionListener, PopupMenuListener, MouseListener {

    public JPopupMenu popup;

    public PopupMenuExample() {
        popup = new JPopupMenu();

        JMenuItem item;
        popup.add(item = new JMenuItem("Left", new ImageIcon("left.gif")));
        item.setHorizontalTextPosition(JMenuItem.RIGHT);
        item.addActionListener(this);
        popup.add(item = new JMenuItem("Center",
                                        new ImageIcon("center.gif")));
        item.setHorizontalTextPosition(JMenuItem.RIGHT);
        item.addActionListener(this);
        popup.add(item = new JMenuItem("Right", new
                                        ImageIcon("right.gif")));
        item.setHorizontalTextPosition(JMenuItem.RIGHT);
        item.addActionListener(this);
        popup.add(item = new JMenuItem("Full", new ImageIcon("full.gif")));
        item.setHorizontalTextPosition(JMenuItem.RIGHT);
        item.addActionListener(this);
        popup.addSeparator();
        popup.add(item = new JMenuItem("Settings . . ."));
        item.addActionListener(this);

        popup.setLabel("Justification");
        popup.setBorder(new BevelBorder(BevelBorder.RAISED));
```

```java
        popup.addPopupMenuListener(this);

        addMouseListener(this);
    }

    public void mousePressed(MouseEvent e) { checkPopup(e); }
    public void mouseClicked(MouseEvent e) { checkPopup(e); }
    public void mouseEntered(MouseEvent e) {}
    public void mouseExited(MouseEvent e) {}
    public void mouseReleased(MouseEvent e) { checkPopup(e); }

    private void checkPopup(MouseEvent e) {
        if (e.isPopupTrigger()) {
            popup.show(this, e.getX(), e.getY());
        }
    }

    public void popupMenuWillBecomeVisible(PopupMenuEvent e) {
        System.out.println("Popup menu will be visible!");
    }
    public void popupMenuWillBecomeInvisible(PopupMenuEvent e) {
        System.out.println("Popup menu will be invisible!");
    }
    public void popupMenuCanceled(PopupMenuEvent e) {
        System.out.println("Popup menu is hidden!");
    }

    public void actionPerformed(ActionEvent event) {
        System.out.println("Popup menu item [" + event.getActionCommand() +
                           "] was pressed.");
    }

    public static void main(String s[]) {
        JFrame frame = new JFrame("Popup Menu Example");
        frame.addWindowListener(new BasicWindowMonitor());
        frame.setContentPane(new PopupMenuExample());
        frame.setSize(300, 300);
        frame.setVisible(true);
    }
}
```

The intersting parts of this program are the methods that implement MouseListener. These call a private method CheckPopup(), that verifies that we've received an event that should raise the popup menu. If we had a valid trigger event, we show the popup at the mouse location. You could implement this somewhat more efficiently by overriding processMouseEvent(). If you do, make sure to call super.processMouseEvent() if (and only if) you don't receive a valid trigger.

The PopupMenuEvent Class

This is a simple event that tells listeners that the target popup menu is about to become visible or invisible, or that it has been canceled. Note that it doesn't tell which one has occurred. The object implementing `PopupMenuListener` will actually have three separate methods that can be called by a menu; each one indicates exactly what happened with the target popup menu object.

Constructor

public PopupMenuEvent(Object source)
   The constructor takes a reference to the object that fired the event.

The PopupMenuListener Class

The `PopupMenuListener` interface, which is the conduit for receiving the `PopupMenuEvent` objects, contains three methods. One method is called when the popup is canceled, the other two react to various events that could force the popup to show or hide itself. This interface must be implemented by any listener object that wishes to be notified of changes to the popup menu.

Methods

public abstract void popupMenuCanceled(PopupMenuEvent e)
   Called when the target popup menu has been canceled or removed from the screen.

public abstract void popupMenuWillBecomeInvisible(PopupMenuEvent e)
   Called when the popup menu has received instructions to remove itself from the screen for either internal or external events.

public abstract void popupMenuWillBecomeVisible(PopupMenuEvent e)
   Called when the popup menu has received instructions to show itself on the screen.

The JMenu Class

The `JMenu` class represents the anchored menus that are attached to a `JMenuBar` or another `JMenu`. Menus that are directly attached to a menubar are called *top-level* menus. Submenus, on the other hand, are not attached to a menubar but instead to an already existing menu item that serves as its title. This menu item title is typically marked by a right arrow, indicating that its menu will appear alongside the menu item if the user selects it. See Figure 14-11.

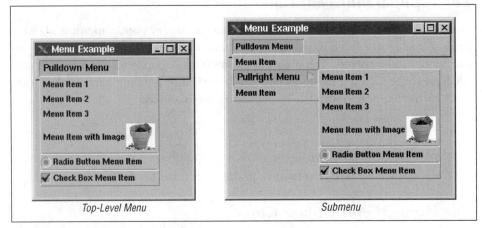

Figure 14-11. Top-level menus and submenus

JMenu is a curious class. It contains a MenuUI delegate, but it uses a ButtonModel for its data model. To see why this is the case, it helps to visualize a menu as two components: a menu item and a popup menu. The menu item serves as the title. When it is pressed, it signals the popup menu to show itself either below or directly to the right of the menu item. JMenu actually extends the JMenuItem class, which makes it possible to implement the title portion of the menu. This, in effect, makes it a specialized button. Remember that you can use the mnemonic property of the JMenuItem superclass to define the shortcut for the menu's title, and consequently the menu. In addition, you can use the enabled property of JMenuItem to disable the menu if desired.

As with popup menus, you can add or insert JMenuItem, Component, or Action objects to the popup portion of the menu by calling the add() and insert() methods. You can also add a simple string to the menu; JMenu will create the corresponding JMenuItem object internally for you. The JMenu class then assigns an integer index to each menu item and orders them based on the layout manager used for the menu. You can also add separators to the menu by using the addSeparator() method.

NOTE   You cannot use keyboard accelerators with JMenu objects (top-level or submenu), because Swing assumes that you intend to set an accelerator on the menu's title button. It is better to use the setMnemonic() method to assign a shortcut to the menu instead.

You can programmatically cause the popup portion to appear on the screen by setting the popupMenuVisible property to true. Be aware that the popup will not appear if the menu's title button is not showing.

Figure 14-12 shows the class diagram for the JMenu component.

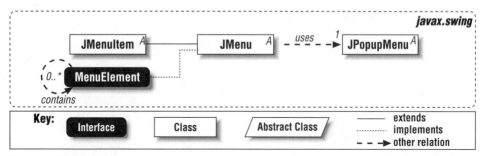

Figure 14-12. JMenu class diagram

Properties

The JMenu properties are listed in Table 14-8. JMenu uses a JPopupMenu to represent its list of menu items. If you wish to access that underlying menu, you can do so using the popupMenu property. The popupMenuVisible property is a read-only boolean that signals whether the menu's popup portion is currently visible. If it is, this property is set to true. JMenu also contains a selected property, which indicates if the user has selected the title button of the menu. Both properties should mirror each other.

Table 14-8. JMenu Properties

Property	Data Type	get	is	set	Bound	Default Value
model*	ButtonModel	•		•		DefaultButtonModel()
UI	MenuUI			•	•	from L&F
UIClassID	String	•				"MenuUI"
accessibleContext*	AccessibleContext	•				JMenu.accessible-JMenu()
component	Component	•				
delay	int	•		•		0
item (indexed)	JMenuItem	•				null
itemCount	int	•				0
layout*	LayoutManager	•		•		OverlayLayout()

See also properties from the JMenuItem class (Table 14-4).

Table 14-8. JMenu Properties (continued)

Property	Data Type	get	is	set	Bound	Default Value
menuComponent (indexed)	Component	•				null
menuComponentCount	int	•				0
menuComponents	Component[]	•				
popupMenu	JPopupMenu	•				
popupMenuVisible	boolean		•	•		false
selected	boolean		•	•		false
subElements	MenuElement[]	•				
tearOff	boolean		•			false
topLevelMenu	boolean		•			

See also properties from the JMenuItem class (Table 14-4).

The topLevelMenu property has the value true if this JMenu is directly attached to a menubar and is not a submenu. item is an indexed property that allows access to each of the JMenuItem objects in the menu, while itemCount maintains a count of all of the JMenuItem objects present. The delay property specifies the amount of time, in milliseconds, that the underlying menu waits to appear or disappear after receiving the corresponding event. The delay must be set to a positive integer or setDelay() will throw an IllegalArgumentException.

The menuComponent property is a more generalized version of the item property; it returns the component at the given index as a Component, rather than as a JMenuItem. In addition, the menuComponentCount property retains a count of the menu items, separators, and other components currently in the menu. The menuComponents property lets you access each of the items in the menu, returned as an array of Component objects.

NOTE   The tearOff property is not yet implemented and is reserved for future use in Swing.

Constructor

public JMenu()
public JMenu(String s)
public JMenu(String s, boolean b)

Initialize a default JMenu. You have the option of specifying the string that the JMenu will display, as well as a boolean for the tearOff property.

Menu Items

public JMenuItem add(JMenuItem menuItem)
public Component add(Component c)
public void add(String s)
public JMenuItem add(Action a)

Add various elements to the menus. Objects of both JMenuItem and JCompo-nent can be added, but the latter functions best if it implements the MenuElement interface. If you specify a String as the parameter, a menu item with the appropriate label is created. If you specify an Action, its text and icon properties are used to derive an appropriate JMenuItem, and its text is placed to the right of the icon. The resulting JMenuItem is returned, which you can use to alter its formatting.

public void addSeparator()

Adds a separator to the menu. Typically, a separator consists of a single hori-zontal line drawn across the menu.

public void doClick()

Overrides the doClick() method of AbstractButton, the popup portion of the menu.

public void insert(String s, int index)
public JMenuItem insert(JMenuItem mi, int index)
public JMenuItem insert(Action a, int index)

Insert a specific menu item at a particular index. The index must be positive, or the method will throw an IllegalArgumentException. You can pass in a JMenuItem, a String, or an Action to these methods. If you specify a String as the parameter, a menu item with the appropriate label is created. If you specify an Action, its text and icon properties are used to derive an appro-priate JMenuItem, and its text is placed to the right of the icon. The resulting JMenuItem is then returned, which you can use to alter its formatting. All menu items that were previously at or after the specified position are shifted by one.

public void insertSeparator(int index)

Inserts a horizontal separator at the position specified by the integer index. The index must be positive, or the method will throw an IllegalArgument-Exception. All menu items that were previously at or after the specified position are shifted by one.

public void remove(JMenuItem item)
public void remove(int index)

Removes the menu item that matches the JMenuItem passed in or that currently occupies the specified integer index. If there are no matches (or the position does not exist) no changes are made to the menu. If the function is successful, all menu items indices following the removed menu item are reduced by one.

public void removeAll()

Removes all of the items from the menu.

Miscellaneous

public void updateUI()

Forces the default user interface manager to update itself, thus resetting the delegate to display a new MenuUI.

public void setMenuLocation(int x, int y)

Sets the location of the popup menu, in horizontal and vertical coordinates, on the screen.

public boolean isMenuComponent(Component c)

Determines whether the component c is present anywhere in the menu. This method searches all submenus as well.

public String paramString()

Returns a String specifying the current state of the menu properties.

public void menuSelectionChanged(boolean b)

This internal change listener monitors menu events; it typically should not be called by the programmer.

protected PropertyChangeListener createActionChangeListener(JMenuItem mi)

This protected method is an internal utility method that creates an individual property change listener for a specific menu item. The programmer typically will not need to call this method.

protected JMenu.WinListener createWinListener(JPopupMenu menu)

This protected method is an internal utility method that creates an individual window listener for a specific popup menu. The programmer typically will not need to call this method.

Events

JMenu objects fire a MenuEvent when the user has selected or deselected the menu's title button. The JMenu object contains the standard addChangeListener() and removeChangeListener() methods for maintaining a list of MenuEvent subscribers.

public void addMenuListener(MenuListener listener)
public void removeMenuListener(MenuListener listener)

Add or remove a MenuListener from the list of listeners recieving this menu's events.

protected void fireMenuCanceled()

Invokes the `menuCanceled()` method of all registered `MenuListener` classes, passing in the appropriate `MenuEvent`.

protected void fireMenuSelected()

Fires a `MenuListener` event stating that the user has selected the menu's title button.

protected void fireMenuDeselected()

This protected method is used to fire a `MenuListener` event stating that the user has deselected the menu's title button.

Menu Element Interface

public void menuSelectionChanged(boolean isIncluded)
public MenuElement[] getSubElements()
public Component getComponent()
public void processKeyEvent(KeyEvent event, MenuElement path[],
   MenuSelectionManager manager)

Implement the `MenuElement` interface, which is covered later in this chapter.

Working with Menus

Here is a program that demonstrates the use of the `JMenu` class. In this program, we make use of Swing's `Action` class to process the menu events. We will continue to use actions as we discuss toolbars below.

```java
// MenuExample.java
//

import java.awt.*;
import java.awt.event.*;
import javax.swing.*;
import javax.swing.border.*;

public class MenuExample extends JPanel {

    public JTextPane pane;
    public JMenuBar menuBar;

    public MenuExample() {
        super(true);

        menuBar = new JMenuBar();

        JMenu formatMenu = new JMenu("Justify");
        formatMenu.setMnemonic('J');
```

```
        MenuAction leftJustifyAction = new MenuAction("Left",
                                    new ImageIcon("left.gif"));
        MenuAction rightJustifyAction = new MenuAction("Right",
                                    new ImageIcon("right.gif"));
        MenuAction centerJustifyAction = new MenuAction("Center",
                                    new ImageIcon("center.gif"));
        MenuAction fullJustifyAction = new MenuAction("Full",
                                    new ImageIcon("full.gif"));

        JMenuItem item;
        item = formatMenu.add(leftJustifyAction);
        item.setMnemonic('L');
        item = formatMenu.add(rightJustifyAction);
        item.setMnemonic('R');
        item = formatMenu.add(centerJustifyAction);
        item.setMnemonic('C');
        item = formatMenu.add(fullJustifyAction);
        item.setMnemonic('F');

        menuBar.add(formatMenu);
        menuBar.setBorder(new BevelBorder(BevelBorder.RAISED));

    }

    class MenuAction extends AbstractAction {

        public MenuAction(String text, Icon icon) {
            super(text,icon);
        }

        public void actionPerformed(ActionEvent e) {
            try { pane.getStyledDocument().insertString(0 ,
                "Action ["+e.getActionCommand()+"] performed!\n", null);
            } catch (Exception ex) {;}
        }
    }

    public static void main(String s[]) {

        MenuExample example = new MenuExample();
        example.pane = new JTextPane();
        example.pane.setPreferredSize(new Dimension(250, 250));
        example.pane.setBorder(new BevelBorder(BevelBorder.LOWERED));

        JFrame frame = new JFrame("Menu Example");
        frame.addWindowListener(new BasicWindowMonitor());
        frame.getContentPane().add(example.menuBar, BorderLayout.NORTH);
        frame.getContentPane().add(example.pane, BorderLayout.CENTER);
        frame.pack();
```

```
        frame.setVisible(true);
    }
}
```

Our `Actions` are all instances of the inner class `MenuActions`. As we add each `Action` to the menu, it creates an appropriate `JMenuItem` (with the image left-justified) and returns it to us. This allows us to manipulate the resulting menu item in any way we want; in this case, we add a mnemonic for each item.

The resulting program produces a menubar with a single menu as shown in Figure 14-13. The menu contains four menu items and is similar in appearance to the popup example above. When the user clicks any menu item, Swing generates an `ActionEvent` to be processed by the `actionPerformed()` method of our `MenuAction` class. Much like the previous examples, this results in the name of the menu item being printed. For variety, we have added a simple `JTextPane` to display the results of our menu choice, instead of using the system output. See Chapter 19, *Text 101*, and Chapter 21, *Styled Documents and JTextPane*, for more information on `JTextPane`.

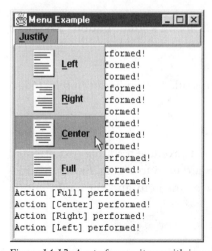

Figure 14-13. A set of menu items with icons and mnemonics.

The MenuEvent Class

This is a simple event that tells listeners that the target menu has been raised, selected, or canceled. Note that it doesn't tell which one has occurred. The listener will have three separate methods that can be called to deliver the menu event; each one tells exactly what happened.

Constructor

public MenuEvent(Object source)
    The constructor takes a reference to the object that fires the event.

The MenuListener Interface

The MenuListener interface, which is the conduit for receiving the MenuEvent objects, contains three methods. One method is called when the menu is canceled, the other two occur when the title button of the menu is selected or deselected. This interface must be implemented by any listener object that needs to be notified of changes to the menu object.

Methods

public abstract void menuCanceled(MenuEvent e)
    This method is called when the menu has been canceled or removed from the screen.

public abstract void menuDeselected(MenuEvent e)
    This method is called when the target menu's title button has been deselected.

public abstract void menuSelected(MenuEvent e)
    This method is called when the target menu's title button has been selected.

Selectable Menu Items

So far, we've covered traditional menu items that produce a simple text-oriented label. But that's not the only type of item users are used to seeing. Swing provides for two selectable menu items: the check box menu item and the radio button menu item.

The JCheckBoxMenuItem Class

Check box menu items are represented by the JCheckBoxMenuItem class. As you might have guessed, this object behaves similarly to the JCheckBox object. By clicking on a check box menu item, you can toggle a UI-defined checkmark that generally appears to the left of the menu item's label. There is no mutual exclusion between adjoining JCheckBoxMenuItem objects—the user can check any item without affecting the state of the others. Figure 14-14 shows the class diagram for the JCheckBoxMenuItem component.

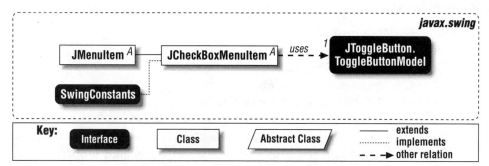

Figure 14-14. JCheckBoxMenuItem class diagram

Properties

Table 14-9 shows the properties of the JCheckBoxMenuItem class. JCheckBox-MenuItem inherits the JMenuItem model (ButtonModel) and its accessors. The JCheckBoxMenuItem class also contains two additional component properties. The state property has the value true if the menu item is currently in the checked state and false if it is not. The setState() accessor is synchronized. The selectedObjects property contains an Object array of size one, consisting of the text of the menu item if it is currently in the checked state. If it is not, getSelectedObjects() returns null. The synchronized getSelectedObjects() method exists for compatibility with the java.awt.ItemSelectable interface.

Table 14-9. JCheckBoxMenuItem Properties

Property	Data Type	get	is	set	bound	Default Value
UI	CheckBoxMenuItemUI	•		•	•	from L&F
UIClassID*	String	•				"CheckBoxMenuItem"
accessibleContext*	AccessibleContext	•				JCheckBoxMenu-Item.AccessibleJCheck-BoxMenuItem()
state	boolean	•		•		false
selectedObjects*	Object[]	•				

See also properties from the JMenuItem class (Table 14-4).

Constructors

public JCheckBoxMenuItem()
public JCheckBoxMenuItem(Icon icon)
public JCheckBoxMenuItem(String text)
public JCheckBoxMenuItem(String text, Icon icon)
public JCheckBoxMenuItem(String text, boolean checked)
public JCheckBoxMenuItem(String text, Icon icon, boolean checked)

These constructors initialize the JCheckBoxMenuItem with a specified icon or string. The additional boolean value initializes the state property, specifying whether the menu item is initially checked.

Miscellaneous

protected void init(String text, Icon icon)

This protected method is used by the JCheckBoxMenuItem constructors to initialize the text and icon of the object. If you extend JCheckBoxMenuItem, you should invoke this method from your constructors to initialize the menu item's display text and icon, or pass in null for either if it is not needed.

public void updateUI()

Forces the current UI manager to reset and repaint the delegate for the component, thus updating the component's look-and-feel.

public void requestFocus()

This method does nothing. It overrides requestFocus() in the superclass to take no action if the focus is offered.

Using Checkbox Menu Items

Here's a program using the JCheckBoxMenuItem class. It is similar to the JMenu example, except that each menu item now has a checkmark next to it. We've done nothing to make the items mutually exclusive; that comes next.

```
//   CheckBoxMenuItemExample.java
//

import java.awt.*;
import java.awt.event.*;
import javax.swing.*;
import javax.swing.border.*;

public class CheckBoxMenuItemExample extends JPanel implements
    ActionListener {

    public JTextPane pane;
    public JMenuBar menuBar;
```

```
public JToolBar toolBar;

public CheckBoxMenuItemExample() {
    super(true);

    menuBar = new JMenuBar();

    JMenu justifyMenu = new JMenu("Justify");
    justifyMenu.setMnemonic('J');

    JCheckBoxMenuItem leftJustify = new
        JCheckBoxMenuItem("Left", new ImageIcon("left.gif"));
    leftJustify.setHorizontalTextPosition(JMenuItem.RIGHT);
    leftJustify.setMnemonic('L');
    leftJustify.addActionListener(this);
    JCheckBoxMenuItem rightJustify = new
        JCheckBoxMenuItem("Right", new ImageIcon("right.gif"));
    rightJustify.setHorizontalTextPosition(JMenuItem.RIGHT);
    rightJustify.setMnemonic('R');
    rightJustify.addActionListener(this);
    JCheckBoxMenuItem centerJustify = new
        JCheckBoxMenuItem("Center", new ImageIcon("center.gif"));
    centerJustify.setHorizontalTextPosition(JMenuItem.RIGHT);
    centerJustify.setMnemonic('C');
    centerJustify.addActionListener(this);
    JCheckBoxMenuItem fullJustify = new
        JCheckBoxMenuItem("Full", new ImageIcon("full.gif"));
    fullJustify.setHorizontalTextPosition(JMenuItem.RIGHT);
    fullJustify.setMnemonic('F');
    fullJustify.addActionListener(this);

    justifyMenu.add(leftJustify);
    justifyMenu.add(rightJustify);
    justifyMenu.add(centerJustify);
    justifyMenu.add(fullJustify);

    menuBar.add(justifyMenu);
    menuBar.setBorder(new BevelBorder(BevelBorder.RAISED));

}

public void actionPerformed(ActionEvent e) {
    try { pane.getStyledDocument().insertString(0 ,
        "Action ["+e.getActionCommand()+"] performed!\n", null);
    } catch (Exception ex) {;}
}

public static void main(String s[]) {
    CheckBoxMenuItemExample example = new CheckBoxMenuItemExample();
```

```
        example.pane = new JTextPane();
        example.pane.setPreferredSize(new Dimension(250, 250));
        example.pane.setBorder(new BevelBorder(BevelBorder.LOWERED));

        JFrame frame = new JFrame("Menu Example");
        frame.addWindowListener(new BasicWindowMonitor());
        frame.getContentPane().add(example.menuBar, BorderLayout.NORTH);
        frame.getContentPane().add(example.pane, BorderLayout.CENTER);
        frame.pack();
        frame.setVisible(true);
    }
}
```

Figure 14-15 shows the result of this code.

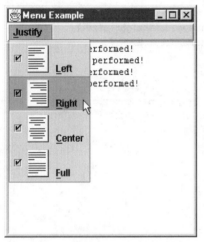

Figure 14-15. A series of checkbox menu items

The JRadioButtonMenuItem Class

Swing implements radio button menu items with the JRadioButtonMenuItem class. The radio button menu item is a new type of menu item in Swing. As you might expect, it shares the characteristics of the JRadioButton class. By clicking on a radio button menu item, you can toggle a UI-defined circle that appears to the left of the menu item's text or image.

Although you might expect otherwise, radio button menu items don't enforce mutual exclusion by themselves. Instead, you need to use a ButtonGroup class to limit the user to a single selection. Figure 14-16 shows the class diagram for the JRadioButtonMenuItem component.

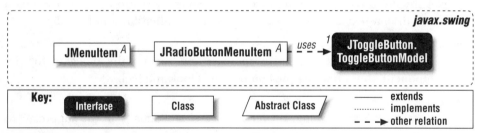

Figure 14-16. RadioButton class diagram

Properties

Table 14-10 shows the properties of the JRadioButtonMenuItem class. Unlike JCheckBoxMenuItem, there is no state property that indicates the current selection state of the menu item. Instead, you typically use this class in conjunction with a ButtonGroup, which contains a getSelected() method for extracting the correct object.

Table 14-10. JRadioButtonMenuItem Properties

Property	Data Type	get	is	set	bound	Default
UI	RadioButtonMenu- ItemUI	•		•	•	from L&F
UIClassID*	String	•				"RadioButtonMenuItem"
accessibleContext*	Accessible Context	•				JRadioButtonMenu- Item.AccessibleJRadio- ButtonMenuItem()

See also properties from the JMenuItem class (Table 14-4).

Constructors

public JRadioButtonMenuItem()
public JRadioButtonMenuItem(Icon icon)
public JRadioButtonMenuItem(String text)
public JRadioButtonMenuItem(String text, Icon icon)
> Initialize the JRadioButtonMenuItem with an optional icon or string.

Miscellaneous

protected void init(String text, Icon icon)
> This protected method is used by the JCheckBoxMenuItem constructors to initialize the text and icon of the object. If you extend JCheckBoxMenuItem,

you should invoke this method from your constructors to initialize the menu item's display text and icon, or pass in `null` for either if it is not needed.

public void updateUI()

Forces the current UI manager to reset and repaint the delegate for the component, thus updating the component's look-and-feel.

public void requestFocus()

This method does nothing. It overrides `requestFocus()` in the superclass to take no action if the focus is offered.

Enforcing Mutual Exclusion

The following program shows how to implement the mutually exclusive nature of radio button menu items:

```
// RadioButtonMenuItemExample.java
//

import java.awt.*;
import java.awt.event.*;
import javax.swing.*;
import javax.swing.border.*;

public class RadioButtonMenuItemExample extends JPanel implements ActionListener
{

    public JTextPane pane;
    public JMenuBar menuBar;
    public JToolBar toolBar;

    public RadioButtonMenuItemExample() {
        super(true);

        menuBar = new JMenuBar();

        JMenu justifyMenu = new JMenu("Justify");
        justifyMenu.setMnemonic('J');

        JRadioButtonMenuItem leftJustify = new
                JRadioButtonMenuItem("Left", new ImageIcon("left.gif"));
        leftJustify.setHorizontalTextPosition(JMenuItem.RIGHT);
        leftJustify.setMnemonic('L');
        leftJustify.addActionListener(this);
        JRadioButtonMenuItem rightJustify = new
                JRadioButtonMenuItem("Right", new ImageIcon("right.gif"));
        rightJustify.setHorizontalTextPosition(JMenuItem.RIGHT);
        rightJustify.setMnemonic('R');
        rightJustify.addActionListener(this);
```

```
        JRadioButtonMenuItem centerJustify = new
                JRadioButtonMenuItem("Center", new ImageIcon("center.gif"));
        centerJustify.setHorizontalTextPosition(JMenuItem.RIGHT);
        centerJustify.setMnemonic('C');
        centerJustify.addActionListener(this);
        JRadioButtonMenuItem fullJustify = new
                JRadioButtonMenuItem("Full", new ImageIcon("full.gif"));
        fullJustify.setHorizontalTextPosition(JMenuItem.RIGHT);
        fullJustify.setMnemonic('F');
        fullJustify.addActionListener(this);

        ButtonGroup group = new ButtonGroup();
        group.add(leftJustify);
        group.add(rightJustify);
        group.add(centerJustify);
        group.add(fullJustify);

        justifyMenu.add(leftJustify);
        justifyMenu.add(rightJustify);
        justifyMenu.add(centerJustify);
        justifyMenu.add(fullJustify);

        menuBar.add(justifyMenu);
        menuBar.setBorder(new BevelBorder(BevelBorder.RAISED));

    }


    public void actionPerformed(ActionEvent e) {
        try { pane.getStyledDocument().insertString(0 ,
            "Action ["+e.getActionCommand()+"] performed!\n", null);
        } catch (Exception ex) {;}
    }

    public static void main(String s[]) {

        RadioButtonMenuItemExample example = new
                                    RadioButtonMenuItemExample();
        example.pane = new JTextPane();
        example.pane.setPreferredSize(new Dimension(250, 250));
        example.pane.setBorder(new BevelBorder(BevelBorder.LOWERED));

        JFrame frame = new JFrame("Menu Example");
        frame.addWindowListener(new BasicWindowMonitor());
        frame.getContentPane().add(example.menuBar, BorderLayout.NORTH);
        frame.getContentPane().add(example.pane, BorderLayout.CENTER);
        frame.pack();
        frame.setVisible(true);
    }
}
```

Figure 14-17 shows the result. We use a `ButtonGroup` object, `group`, to make our `JRadioButtonMenuItems` mutually exclusive. Selecting any of the menu items deselects the others. Since text justification is mutually exclusive, this example shows how you would implement a true justification menu. All you need is a more sophisitcated `actionPerformed()` method to do the actual work.

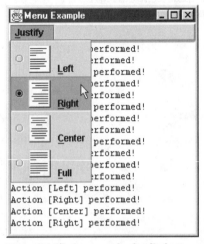

Figure 14-17. An example of radio button menu items

The JSeparator Class

You may have noticed that both `JMenu` and `JPopupMenu` contain `addSeparator()` methods to add separators to menus. In doing so, each class instantiates a `JSeparator` object and positions it in the menu. However, `JSeparator` exists as a component unto itself outside of menus, and because it extends `JComponent`, it can be positioned inside a container like any other Swing component. `JSeparator` is a simple component that consists only of a horizontal line drawn across its entire width. It has no model, only a delegate.

Properties

Table 14-11 shows the properties of `JSeparator`.

Table 14-11. JSeparator Properties

Property	Data Type	get	is	set	bound	Default
UI	SeparatorUI	•		•	•	*from L&F*
UIClassID*	String	•				"SeparatorUI"

See also properties from the JComponent class (Table 3-5).

Table 14-11. JSeparator Properties (continued)

Property	Data Type	get	is	set	bound	Default
accessibleContext*	AccessibleContext	•				JSeparator.accessible-JSeparator()
orientation	int	•		•		SwingConstants.HORI-ZONTAL

See also properties from the JComponent class (Table 3-5).

Constructor

JSeparator()
JSeparator(int orientation)

Creates a separator. By default, this separator is horizontal; if you specify an orientation, it should be either SwingConstants.HORIZONTAL or Swing-Constants.VERTICAL.

Miscellaneous

public void updateUI()

Forces the current UI manager to reset and repaint the delegate for the component, thus updating the component's look-and-feel.

Using a Separator Outside of a Menu

We've already seen how a separator can be used in menus to provide more grouping between menu items. However, separators are components in themselves, and can be used for a variety of tasks. Here is a program that adds a separator between a series of buttons:

```
import java.awt.*;
import java.awt.event.*;
import javax.swing.*;
import javax.swing.border.*;

public class SeparatorExample extends JPanel {

    public SeparatorExample() {
        super(true);

        setLayout(new BoxLayout(this, BoxLayout.Y_AXIS));
        Box box1 = new Box(BoxLayout.X_AXIS);
        Box box2 = new Box(BoxLayout.X_AXIS);
        Box box3 = new Box(BoxLayout.X_AXIS);

        box1.add(new JButton("Press Me"));
```

```
        box1.add(new JButton("No Me!"));
        box1.add(new JButton("Ignore Them!"));
        box2.add(new JSeparator());
        box3.add(new JButton("I'm the Button!"));
        box3.add(new JButton("It's me!"));
        box3.add(new JButton("Go Away!"));

        add(box1);
        add(box2);
        add(box3);
    }

    public static void main(String s[]) {
        WindowListener l = new WindowAdapter() {
            public void windowClosing(WindowEvent e) {System.exit(0);}
        };

        SeparatorExample example = new SeparatorExample();

        JFrame frame = new JFrame("Separator Example");
        frame.addWindowListener(l);
        frame.setContentPane(example);
        frame.pack();
        frame.setVisible(true);
    }
}
```

This code yields the application shown in Figure 14-18.

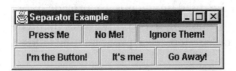

Figure 14-18. A standalone separator between two groups of buttons

The MenuElement Interface

As we saw in the previous examples, one nice feature of Swing menus is that we are no longer constrained to using text for menu items. However, the possibilities don't have to stop with icons either. In fact, with a little work you can create or extend any Java component to serve as a menu item. There is one catch: your new menu item must implement the MenuElement interface. Swing declares five methods in the MenuElement interface; these methods are called by Swing's internal MenuSelectionManager when various actions take place.

Why is this necessary? Let's look at the traditional menu item, such as the "Paste" menu item in the "Edit" menu. When the user raises the "Edit" menu, and the mouse passes over the "Paste" menu item, the menu item typically changes its colors. This tells us that if the user clicks the mouse button, he or she will have chosen the "Paste" option. When the mouse leaves the menu item, it returns to its normal color. However, what if we wanted to make the text bold instead of highlighting it? What if we wanted to substitute another icon image in the menu item when the mouse passes over it? By calling the methods of this interface, menus can allow menu items to define their own unique behavior.

Let's look at the methods of this interface:

public void processMouseEvent(MouseEvent event,MenuElement path[],
  MenuSelectionManager manager)
  Handles events triggered by the mouse. In addition to the `MouseEvent`, the current path of selected menu elements is provided, as well as a reference to the current menu selection manager. You can take whatever action you feel is necessary in this method.

public void processKeyEvent(KeyEvent event, MenuElement path[], MenuSelectionManager
  manager)
  Handles events triggered by keystrokes. In addition to the `KeyEvent`, the current path of selected menu elements is provided, as well as a reference to the current menu selection manager. You can take whatever action you feel is necessary in this method.

public void menuSelectionChanged(boolean isIncluded)
  Called when the menu element is added or removed from the current target menu.

public MenuElement[] getSubElements()
  Returns an array of subelements for the target `MenuElement`. This is needed in the event that a particular menu element has a submenu.

public Component getComponent()
  Returns a reference to the component responsible for painting the menu item.

Making arbitrary components into menu elements

It is relatively easy to convert any Swing component into a menu element and drop it in a menu. Here is a program that places a `JSlider` inside of a popup menu and use it as a hidden control for an underlying component.

```
//  MenuElementExample.java
//

import java.awt.*;
import java.awt.event.*;
```

```java
import javax.swing.*;
import javax.swing.border.*;
import javax.swing.event.*;

public class MenuElementExample extends JPanel implements ActionListener,
    PopupMenuListener, MouseListener {

    public JPopupMenu popup;
    SliderMenuItem slider;
    int theValue = 0;

    public MenuElementExample() {

        popup = new JPopupMenu();
        slider = new SliderMenuItem();

        popup.add(slider);
        popup.add(new JSeparator());

        JMenuItem ticks = new JCheckBoxMenuItem("Slider Tick Marks");
        JMenuItem labels = new JCheckBoxMenuItem("Slider Labels");
        ticks.addActionListener(this);
        labels.addActionListener(this);

        popup.add(ticks);
        popup.add(labels);
        popup.addPopupMenuListener(this);

        addMouseListener(this);
    }

    public void mousePressed(MouseEvent e) { popupCheck(e); }
    public void mouseClicked(MouseEvent e) { popupCheck(e); }
    public void mouseReleased(MouseEvent e) { popupCheck(e); }
    public void mouseEntered(MouseEvent e) {}
    public void mouseExited(MouseEvent e) {}

    private void popupCheck(MouseEvent e) {
        if (e.isPopupTrigger()) {
            popup.show(this, e.getX(), e.getY());
        }
    }

    public void popupMenuWillBecomeVisible(PopupMenuEvent e) { }

    public void popupMenuWillBecomeInvisible(PopupMenuEvent e) {
        theValue = slider.getValue();
        System.out.println("The value is now " + theValue);
    }
```

```
    public void popupMenuCanceled(PopupMenuEvent e) {
        System.out.println("Popup menu is hidden!");
    }


    public void actionPerformed(ActionEvent event) {
        if (event.getActionCommand() == "Slider Tick Marks")
            slider.setPaintTicks(!slider.getPaintTicks());
        if (event.getActionCommand() == "Slider Labels")
            slider.setPaintLabels(!slider.getPaintLabels());
    }


    public static void main(String s[]) {
        JFrame frame = new JFrame("Menu Element Example");
        frame.addWindowListener(new BasicWindowMonitor());
        frame.setContentPane(new MenuElementExample());
        frame.setSize(300, 300);
        frame.setVisible(true);
    }


    class SliderMenuItem extends JSlider implements MenuElement {

        public SliderMenuItem() {
            setBorder(new CompoundBorder(new TitledBorder("Control"),
                            new EmptyBorder(10, 10, 10, 10)));

            setMajorTickSpacing(20);
            setMinorTickSpacing(10);
        }

        public void processMouseEvent(MouseEvent e, MenuElement path[],
                            MenuSelectionManager manager) {}

        public void processKeyEvent(KeyEvent e, MenuElement path[],
                            MenuSelectionManager manager) {}

        public void menuSelectionChanged(boolean isIncluded) {}

        public MenuElement[] getSubElements() {return new MenuElement[0];}

        public Component getComponent() {return this;}
    }
}
```

As with our previous popup example, PopupMenuExample, we implement MouseListener and check incoming mouse events to see whether or not to show the popup. The inner class SliderMenuItem implements the MenuElement interface, and is the focus of our attention. In this case, it's fairly easy. Our menu slider will never have subelements, and doesn't have a concept of a selection, and doesn't need to do anything special with mouse or key events.

The output of our example is shown in Figure 14-19. We provide a `JSlider` object, a separator, and two `JCheckBoxMenuItem` objects, which control the state of the slider. The slider is also surrounded by a titled border. When the user adjusts the slider and closes the popup, we print the current value of the slider out to the standard output. With a little bit of imagination, you can do just about anything with a popup menu!

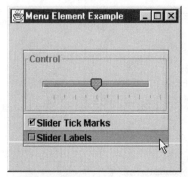

Figure 14-19. A JSlider masquerading as a popup menu element

Toolbars

Swing gives the ability to add a toolbar to a `JFrame` or `JApplet` in addition to a menubar. While toolbars are traditionally located below menubars, they are extensions of the `JComponent` class and, like `JMenuBar`, can be positioned by a Swing layout manager in any desired location.

Toolbars have the unique ability to tear themselves from their current location and embed their components in a moveable stand-alone window. This gives the user the freedom to drag the toolbar anywhere on the screen. In addition, toolbars can "dock" in locations where the layout manager can support them.

The JToolBar Class

Like the menubar, the `JToolBar` class is a container for various components to be added. You can add any component to the toolbar, including buttons, combo boxes, and even additional menus. The toolbar is easier to work with, however, when it uses Swing `Action` objects.

When a component is added to the toolbar, it is assigned an integer index that determines its display order from left to right. While there is no restriction on the type of component that can be added, the toolbar will generally look best if it uses components that are the same vertical height. Note that toolbars have a default border installed by the L&F. If you don't like the default, you can override the border with one of your own using the `setBorder()` method. Alternatively, you can deactivate the drawing of the border by setting the `borderPainted` property to `false`.

`JToolBar` has its own separator that inserts a blank space on the toolbar; you can use the `addSeparator()` method to access this separator. Separators are useful if you want to add space between groups of related toolbar components. The separator for toolbars is actually an inner class. Be sure not to confuse this separator with the `JSeparator` class.

Figure 14-20 shows the class diagram for the `JToolBar` component.

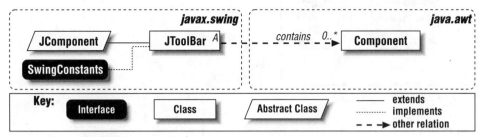

Figure 14-20. JToolBar class diagram

Floating Toolbars

Although toolbars can be easily positioned in Swing containers, they do not have to stay there. Instead, you can "float" the toolbar by holding the mouse button down while the cursor is over an empty section of the toolbar (that is, not over any of its components) and dragging. This will place the toolbar in a moveable child window; you can position it anywhere in the viewing area. Toolbars can then reattach themselves to specific locations, or *hotspots*, within the frame. Letting go of the toolbar while dragging it over a hotspot anchors the toolbar back into the container. Figure 14-21 is an example of a floating toolbar.

It is best to place a toolbar in a container that supports the `BorderLayout`. If you intend to make the toolbar floatable, place it along either the north, south, east, or west side of the container, and leave the remaining sides open. This allows the toolbar to define anchor spots when it is being dragged and ensures that the resulting layout will not be ambiguous.

If you want to disable floating, you can reset the `floatable` property to `false`:

```
JToolBar toolBar = new JToolBar();
toolBar.setFloatable(false);
```

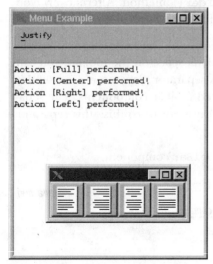

Figure 14-21. A floating toolbar

Properties

The properties of the JToolBar class are shown in Table 14-12. The border-Painted property defines whether the toolbar should paint its border. The JToolBar constructor resets the layout manager of the component to a BoxLayout along the x axis (this becomes a y-axis BoxLayout if the orientation is VERTICAL), which it uses to place any child components. The margin property defines the insets that will appear between the toolbar's edges and its components. The floatable property defines whether the toolbar can be separated from the container and "floated" in a standalone window. You can use the indexed componentAtIndex property to access any of the components on the toolbar. Finally, orientation determines whether the toolbar is horizontal or vertical. Its value must be either HORIZONTAL or VERTICAL (constants defined in SwingConstants). Attempting to set orientation to some other value throws an IllegalArgumentException.

Table 14-12. JToolBar Properties

Property	Data Type	get	is	set	bound	Default
UI	ToolBarUI	•		•	•	*from L&F*
UIClassID*	String	•				"ToolBarUI"
accessibleContext	AccessibleContext	•				JToolBar.Accessible-JToolBar()

See also properties from the JComponent class (Table 3-5).

Table 14-12. JToolBar Properties (continued)

Property	Data Type	get	is	set	bound	Default
borderPainted	boolean		•	•		true
componentAtIndex (indexed)	Component	•				
floatable	boolean		•	•		true
layout*	LayoutManager	•		•		BoxLayout(X_AXIS)
margin	Insets	•		•	•	Insets(0,0,0,0)
orientation	int	•		•		SwingConstants.HORIZONTAL

See also properties from the JComponent class (Table 3-5).

Events

JToolbar generates a `PropertyChangeEvent` when any of its bound properties are changed.

Constructors

public JToolBar()
public JToolBar(int orientation)

Creates a `JToolBar`. The orientation is horizontal by default; if you specify the orientation, it must be `SwingConstants.HORIZONTAL` or `SwingConstants.VERTICAL`.

Adding Actions

public JButton add(Action a)

Adds an `Action` to the toolbar. The method creates a simple `JButton` with the text of the action placed below its image. It then returns the `JButton`, allowing you to reset any of the button's attributes. (As you'd expect, the method for adding a component to a toolbar is inherited from `Container`.)

Miscellaneous

public void updateUI()

Forces the current `UIManager` to repaint the UI delegate for the component, updating the component's look-and-feel.

public int getComponentIndex(Component c)

Returns the integer index of the component c.

public void addSeparator()

public void addSeparator(Dimension size)

> Adds a separator to the toolbar. Be sure not to confuse the toolbar separator with `JSeparator`, which is a separate Swing component. The toolbar separator created by this method is simply a blank area of space used to provide spacing between groups of toolbar components. The size is normally up to the toolbar, though you can specify the separator's size explicitly if you wish.

protected void paintBorder(Graphics g)

> Overrides the `paintBorder()` method in `JComponent` in order to observe the `borderPainted` property.

protected PropertyChangeListener createActionChangeListener(JButton b)

> An internal utility method that creates an individual property change listener for a specific menu item. The programmer typically will not need to call this method.

protected void addImpl(Component comp, Object constraints, int index)

> Adds the given component to the toolbar, with the specified constraints, and at the position specified by `index`.

Creating a Toolbar

The following example adds a toolbar to the `JMenu` example above, creating a set of buttons from the `Action` objects we added to the menu. Just for fun, we added tool tips to the buttons on the toolbar. We also allow the user to choose from a specified font combo box, showing that you can use other kinds of components in a toolbar. Note that we add the combo box and a `JLabel` for the combo box as separate components, and that the combo box uses its own `actionPerformed()` method:

```
//  ToolBarExample.java
//
import java.awt.*;
import java.awt.event.*;
import javax.swing.*;
import javax.swing.border.*;
import javax.swing.event.*;

public class ToolBarExample extends JPanel implements ActionListener {

    public JTextPane pane;
    public JMenuBar menuBar;
    public JToolBar toolBar;
    String fonts[] =
            {"Serif","SansSerif","Monospaced","Dialog","DialogInput"};
```

```java
public ToolBarExample() {
    super(true);

    menuBar = new JMenuBar();

    JMenu formatMenu = new JMenu("Justify");
    formatMenu.setMnemonic('J');

    MenuAction leftJustifyAction = new MenuAction("Left",
                                   new ImageIcon("left.gif"));
    MenuAction rightJustifyAction = new MenuAction("Right",
                                   new ImageIcon("right.gif"));
    MenuAction centerJustifyAction = new MenuAction("Center",
                                   new ImageIcon("center.gif"));
    MenuAction fullJustifyAction = new MenuAction("Full",
                                   new ImageIcon("full.gif"));

    JMenuItem item;
    item = formatMenu.add(leftJustifyAction);
    item.setIcon((Icon)leftJustifyAction.getValue(Action.SMALL_ICON));
    item.setHorizontalTextPosition(JMenuItem.RIGHT);
    item.setMnemonic('L');
    item = formatMenu.add(rightJustifyAction);
    item.setIcon((Icon)rightJustifyAction.getValue(Action.SMALL_ICON));
    item.setHorizontalTextPosition(JMenuItem.RIGHT);
    item.setMnemonic('R');
    item = formatMenu.add(centerJustifyAction);
    item.setIcon((Icon)centerJustifyAction.getValue(Action.SMALL_ICON));
    item.setHorizontalTextPosition(JMenuItem.RIGHT);
    item.setMnemonic('C');
    item = formatMenu.add(fullJustifyAction);
    item.setIcon((Icon)fullJustifyAction.getValue(Action.SMALL_ICON));
    item.setHorizontalTextPosition(JMenuItem.RIGHT);
    item.setMnemonic('F');

    menuBar.add(formatMenu);
    menuBar.setBorder(new BevelBorder(BevelBorder.RAISED));

    toolBar = new JToolBar();

    JButton button;
    button = toolBar.add(leftJustifyAction);
    button.setActionCommand((String)leftJustifyAction.getValue(Action.NAME));
    button.setToolTipText((String)leftJustifyAction.getValue(Action.NAME));
    button = toolBar.add(rightJustifyAction);
    button.setActionCommand((String)rightJustifyAction.getValue(Action.NAME));
    button.setToolTipText((String)rightJustifyAction.getValue(Action.NAME));
    button = toolBar.add(centerJustifyAction);
    button.setActionCommand((String)centerJustifyAction.getValue(Action.NAME));
    button.setToolTipText((String)centerJustifyAction.getValue(Action.NAME));
```

```
    button = toolBar.add(fullJustifyAction);
    button.setActionCommand((String)fullJustifyAction.getValue(Action.NAME));
    button.setToolTipText((String)fullJustifyAction.getValue(Action.NAME));

    toolBar.addSeparator();
    JLabel label = new JLabel("Font");
    toolBar.add(label);

    toolBar.addSeparator();
    JComboBox combo = new JComboBox(fonts);
    combo.addActionListener(this);
    toolBar.add(combo);

    //  Disable one of the Actions
    fullJustifyAction.setEnabled(false);
}

public void actionPerformed(ActionEvent e) {
    try { pane.getStyledDocument().insertString(0,
          "Font ["+((JComboBox)e.getSource()).getSelectedItem()+
                "] chosen!\n", null);
    } catch (Exception ex) {;}
}

public static void main(String s[]) {

    ToolBarExample example = new ToolBarExample();
    example.pane = new JTextPane();
    example.pane.setPreferredSize(new Dimension(250, 250));
    example.pane.setBorder(new BevelBorder(BevelBorder.LOWERED));
    example.toolBar.setMaximumSize(example.toolBar.getSize());

    JFrame frame = new JFrame("Menu Example");
    frame.addWindowListener(new BasicWindowMonitor());
    frame.setJMenuBar(example.menuBar);
    frame.getContentPane().add(example.toolBar, BorderLayout.NORTH);
    frame.getContentPane().add(example.pane, BorderLayout.CENTER);
    frame.pack();
    frame.setVisible(true);
}

class MenuAction extends AbstractAction {

    public MenuAction(String text, Icon icon) {
        super(text, icon);
    }

    public void actionPerformed(ActionEvent e) {
        try { pane.getStyledDocument().insertString(0,
```

```
                "Action ["+e.getActionCommand()+"] performed!\n", null);
            } catch (Exception ex) {;}
        }
    }
}
```

This demonstrates one of the nice things about using Action objects. Not only can you populate a toolbar with buttons generated from Action icons, but you can also disable the Action directly with one method call. For example, ToolBar-Example.java includes the line:

```
fullJustifyAction.setEnabled(false);
```

Once the action is disabled, all the triggering components are notified of the property change. In our program, both the menu item and the toolbar button for left justification are grayed, as shown in Figure 14-22.

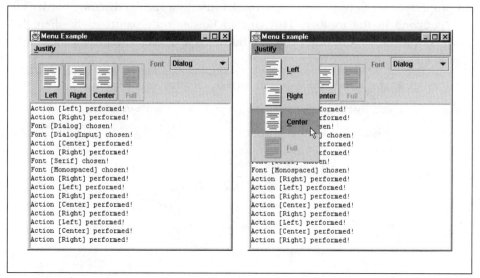

Figure 14-22. Disabling actions automatically grays the toolbar and menu representations

As we mentioned, this program added a combobox to the toolbar as well. The layout of the combo box was not quite what was expected—Swing placed it towards the top of the toolbar, instead of in the middle. This is primarily an artifact of the layout used with the toolbar, the BoxLayout. You can override this layout manually (GridBagLayout() works effectively), but it is best to set the floatable property to false when you do so. Otherwise, the layout manager resets itself when the toolbar is repositioned.

You can define the alignment of the components in the toolbar by setting the alignmentY (or alignmentX) property on each component you add. For example, adding the following lines to the previous example causes everything to line up nicely:

```
label.setAlignmentY(0);
combo.setAlignmentY(0);
```

Finally, a JToolBar is a regular Swing component, so you can use more than one in an application. Again, if you do so, and you wish to make the toolbars floatable, it is best to place each toolbar in a concentric BorderLayout container, leaving the other three sides unpopulated. This will ensure that the toolbars maintain their respective positions if they are both dragged to a new side.

The MetalToolBarUI isRollover property

The MetalLookAndFeel checks for a special client property called "JToolBar.isRollover" when it installs the MetalToolBarUI. If the value of this property is set to Boolean.TRUE, the UI installs a special dynamic border on any JButtons in the toolbar. This custom border only paints itself when the cursor is over the button; otherwise, the border is invisible. This gives a nice highlighting effect to the toolbar.

If you are using the Metal L&F, you can turn this feature on by calling:

```
MyToolbar.setClientProperty("JToolbar.isRollover", Boolean.TRUE);
```

The other Swing L&Fs ignore this property.

In this chapter:

- *Table Columns*
- *Table Data*
- *The JTable Class*
- *Editing and Rendering*
- *Selecting Table Entries*

15

Tables

Tables represent one of the most common formats for viewing data. Database records are easy to sort and choose from a table. Statistics on disk usage can be displayed for several computers or several time periods all at once. Stock market quotes can be tracked. And where would sales presentations be without tables? Well, the `JTable` class in the Swing package now gives you access to a single component that can handle all of the preceding examples and more.

Without getting fancy, you can think of tables as an obvious expression of two-dimensional data. In fact, the `JTable` class has a constructor that takes an `Object[][]` argument and displays the contents of that two-dimensional array as a table with rows and columns. For example, Figure 15-1 shows how a table of string objects falls out very quickly.

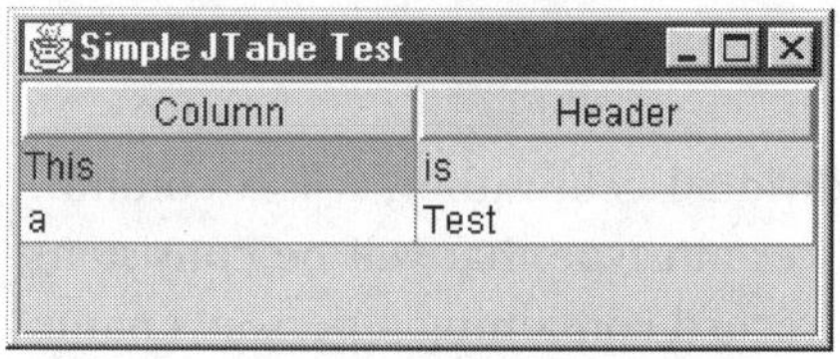

Figure 15-1. Two-dimensional array of strings for data

This program was generated with very little code. All we did was set up a `JTable` object with an `String[][]` argument for the table data, and a `String[]` argument for the table's headers. Rather than adding the table itself directly to our window, we enclose it in a scroll pane:

```
// SimpleTable.java
// A test of the JTable class using default table models and a convenience
// constructor.
//
```

```java
import java.awt.*;
import com.sun.java.swing.*;

public class SimpleTable extends JFrame {

  public SimpleTable() {
    super("Simple JTable Test");
    setSize(300, 200);
    addWindowListener(new BasicWindowMonitor());

    JTable jt = new JTable(new String[][] {
                          {"This", "is"}, {"a", "Test"}},
                      new String[] {"Column", "Header"});
    JScrollPane jsp = new JScrollPane(jt);
    getContentPane().add(jsp, BorderLayout.CENTER);
  }

  public static void main(String args[]) {
    SimpleTable st = new SimpleTable();
    st.setVisible(true);
  }
}
```

As you can see, we rely entirely on the data models built for us and simply pass in our data (a `String[][]` object) and our column headers (a `String[]` object). `JTable` takes care of the rest of it. With the default models, you can select multiple rows, edit individual cells, and listen for selection events. But of course, you are not restricted to the default models, and you can produce some pretty interesting effects if you decide to roll your own. To get there, you need to know about the basics of a `JTable`, beginning with columns.

Table Columns

With Swing tables, the basic unit is not an individual cell; rather, it is a column. Most columns in real-world tables represent a certain type that will be consistent for all of the records displayed. For example, a record containing a person's name will have a `String` type and might be the first column of the table. For every other record (row), the first cell is always a `String`. The columns do not need to all have the same type. The same record could hold not only a person's name, but whether or not they owned a computer. That column would hold `boolean` values, not `String` values.

The ability to store different types of data also affects how the table draws the data. The table column that maps to the "owns a computer" field could use a `JCheckBox` object for the cells of this column, while using regular `JLabel` objects for the cells of other columns. But again, each column will have one data type and one class responsible for drawing it.

Now, as the JTable class evolves, you may find alternate ways to think about tables without relying so heavily on columns. You'll want to keep an eye on the API in future releases of the JFC package. Figure 15-2 shows how the classes of the JTable package fit together.

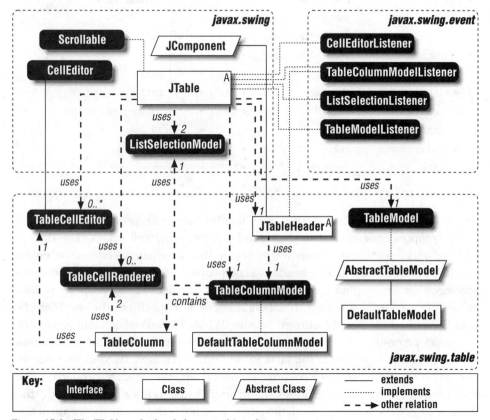

Figure 15-2. The JTable and related classes and interfaces

The TableColumn Class

The starting point for building your columns is this class. The TableColumn class supplies access to all the basic components of an individual column. But, this class should not be confused with the TableColumnModel interface. That model, discussed in the next section, dictates the form of a collection of table columns, which then makes up a full table.

Properties

The `TableColumn` class has the properties listed in Table 15-1.

Table 15-1. TableColumn Properties

Property	Data Type	get	is	set	bound	Default Value
cellEditor	TableCellEditor	•		•		null
cellRenderer	TableCellRenderer	•		•	•	null
headerRenderer	TableCellRenderer	•		•	•	null
headerValue	Object	•		•	•	null
identifier	Object	•		•		null
maxWidth	int	•		•		Integer.MAX_VALUE
minWidth	int	•		•		15
modelIndex	int	•		•		0
resizable	boolean	•		•		true
width	int	•		•	•	75

The `cellEditor`, `cellRenderer`, and `headerRenderer` properties determine which components are used to draw (and possibly edit) cell values. The default value of `null` for these properties indicates that a default renderer or editor should be built and used. The `headerValue` property is accessible to the header-Renderer for drawing an appropriate header. The `identifier` property is used to identify a column uniquely. If `identifier` is not specified, the `getIdentifier()` method returns the current `headerValue`. The `minWidth` and `maxWidth` properties determine the minimum and maximum width in pixels for the column. By setting these properties to the same value, you can create a fixed-width column. The current width of the column is stored in the `width` property. The `modelIndex` determines the index value used when rendering or editing the column to get the appropriate data values. It is normally set in the constructor, and does not need to be modified after that. Relocating the column on-screen has no effect on the model index. The `resizable` property only affects the user's ability to manually resize columns—you can programmatically resize a column at any time.

Constants

Four of the properties are associated with constants that describe them, for use with property change events. These constants are listed in Table 15-2.

Table 15-2. TableColumn Constants

Constant	Type	Description
CELL_RENDERER_PROPERTY	String	The property name of the cellRenderer property
COLUMN_WIDTH_PROPERTY	String	The property name of the columnWidth property
HEADER_RENDERER_PROPERTY	String	The property name of the headerRenderer property
HEADER_VALUE_PROPERTY	String	The property name of the headerValue property

Events

The only events generated by the TableColumn class are property change events generated when any of the column's bound properties (cellRenderer, header-Renderer, headerValue, and width) are changed.

public void addPropertyChangeListener(PropertyChangeListener l)
public void removePropertyChangeListener (PropertyChangeListener l)

> Add or remove a property change listener interested in receiving events from this column.

Fields

protected TableCellEditor cellEditor
protected TableCellRenderer cellRenderer
protected TableCellRenderer headerRenderer
protected Object headerValue
protected Object identifier
protected boolean isResizable
protected int maxWidth
protected int minWidth
protected int modelIndex
protected int resizedPostingDisableCount
protected int width

> The fields in the TableColumn class store their respective properties from Table 15-1. (The isResizable field corresponds to the resizable property.)

Constructors

The following constructors exist for building TableColumn objects:

public TableColumn()

> Creates an empty column with the default property values.

public TableColumn(int modelIndex)

> Creates an empty column with the specified `modelIndex`.

public TableColumn(int modelIndex, int width)

> Creates an empty column with the specified `modelIndex` and `width` in pixels. The `minWidth` and `maxWidth` properties keep their default values.

public TableColumn(int modelIndex, int width, TableCellRenderer cellRenderer,
TableCellEditor cellEditor)

> This constructor creates an empty column with the specified `modelIndex`, `width` in pixels, `cellRenderer`, and `cellEditor`. Either (or both) of the renderer or editor arguments can be `null`, in which case the appropriate default will be used.

Miscellaneous Methods

While the get/set methods for the properties constitute a majority of the `Table-Column` class, the following methods provide some additional functionality:

protected TableCellRenderer createDefaultHeaderRenderer()

> Creates a `TableCellRenderer` object using an anonymous inner class to create a `JLabel` with a distinct border and background that reflects the fact that this is a header cell, and not a regular part of the table data.

public void disableResizedPosting()
public void enableResizedPosting()

> Increment and decrement a counter to determine whether or not column resize events are reported during or after a resize. A counter is used so that if two calls to disable the resize posting are received (presumably from two separate sources), two complementary enable calls must be received before resize posting is re-enabled. These methods are not commonly used.

public void sizeWidthToFit()

> Forces the width of the column to match that of its header, even if it means modifying the `minWidth` or `maxWidth` properties.

The TableColumnModel Interface

A single column is not a very interesting table—an interesting list, maybe, but not a table. To handle real tables (even ones with only one column) we need a model for storing several columns as a collection. The `TableColumnModel` interface provides that functionality in the Swing package. As you may have noticed from Figure 15-2, the `JTable` class uses a column model in addition to a table model. While the table model provides the specific values for the cells in a column, the column model provides information such as the column margins and whether or not column selections are allowed.

The purpose of the `TableColumnModel` interface falls into two areas: managing column selections and column spacing. For managing selections, you have access to the usual selection properties, such as the number of selected columns and the selection model in place. For dealing with column spacing, you can control the column margins and view the total column width.

Properties

`TableColumnModel` has the properties listed in Table 15-3. The `columnCount` property returns the number of columns supported by this model. While this might seem like redundant information, given that table model (discussed later in this chapter) knows how many columns it supports, the next chapter examines some column models that do not use all of the columns available in the table model. The `columnMargin` property dictates how much space should be left between columns. That spacing is included when calculating the value of the `totalColumnWidth`. You can turn column selection on or off with the `columnSelectionAllowed` property. If column selections are allowed, you can then use the `selectionModel`, `selectedColumns`, and `selectedColumnCount` properties to work with the selections. As with other selections, you can use the `selectionModel` to programmatically affect the selected columns if needed.

The `column` and `columns` properties let you access the table's columns themselves. The index used as an argument to `getColumn()` refers to the column's index in the column model, which doesn't necessarily match the index of the column in the table model, or the order in which columns appear on the screen.

Table 15-3. TableColumnModel Properties

Property	Data Type	get	is	set	bound	Default Value
column (indexed)	TableColumn	•				
columns	Enumeration	•				
columnCount	int	•				
columnMargin	int	•		•		
columnSelectionAllowed	boolean	•		•		
selectedColumnCount	int	•				
selectedColumns	int[]	•				
selectionModel	ListSelectionModel	•		•		
totalColumnWidth	int	•				

Events

Any class implementing the TableColumnModel interface will have to support the ColumnModelEvent, which is generated when a column's view size, position, or extent size changes. The interface defines the standard addColumnModelListener() and removeColumnModelListener() methods, but the implementing class will be responsible for writing the code to fire the events when columns are added, removed, or moved.

public void addColumnModelListener(TableColumnModelListener l)
public void remove ColumnModelListener(TableColumnModelListener l)

    Add or remove a listener interested in changes to this column model.

Column Methods

The TableColumnModel interface defines several methods for working with the columns in the model.

public void addColumn(TableColumn column)

    Appends column to the current column model.

public int getColumnIndex(Object identifier)
public int getColumnIndexAtX(int xPixel)

    Return the column model (screen) index of a column, either with a header matching identifier, or at the specified xPixel location on the screen.

public void moveColumn(int index, int newIndex)

    Moves the column at index to newIndex. Other columns should be shifted around as needed to accommodate the moved column. This visually relocates the column on the screen only. The table model does not change.

public void removeColumn(TableColumn column)

    Deletes column from the column model. Columns following the removed column will be shifted one index to fill the gap.

The DefaultTableColumnModel Class

The DefaultTableColumnModel class implements the TableColumnModel interface and serves as the column model if you do not specify a model in the JTable constructor. It also works as a good starting point for creating your own column models. You inherit everything you need; just override the methods you want to change.

Properties

The DefaultTableColumnModel class inherits all of its properties from the TableColumnModel interface and supplies the default values shown in Table 15-4.

Table 15-4. DefaultTableColumnModel Properties

Property	Data Type	get	is	set	bound	Default Value
column (indexed)*	TableColumn	•				
columns*	Enumeration	•				
columnCount*	int	•				0
columnMargin	int	•		•		1
columnSelectionAllowed*	boolean	•		•		false
selectedColumnCount*	int	•				0
selectedColumns*	int[]	•				null
selectionModel*	ListSelec- tionModel	•		•		DefaultListSelection- Model()
totalColumnWidth*	int	•				0

Events

The `DefaultTableColumnModel` supports the `ColumnModelEvent` events that are dictated by the `TableColumnModel` interface, but it includes several convenience methods beyond simply attaching listeners:

protected void fireColumnAdded(TableColumnModelEvent e)
protected void fireColumnMarginChanged()
protected void fireColumnMoved(TableColumnModelEvent e)
protected void fireColumnRemoved(TableColumnModelEvent e)
protected void fireColumnSelectionChanged(ListSelectionEvent e)

These helper methods are used to fire events when columns are added, resized, relocated, removed, or selected. They also give you access to firing column-based events to create your own column model by extending this class.

public void addColumnModelListener(TableColumnModelListener x)
public void removeColumnModelListener(TableColumnModelListener x)

Add or remove a listener for `TableColumnModelEvents` fired by this model.

protected void propertyChange(PropertyChangeEvent e)
protected void valueChanged(ListSelectionEvent e)

The `DefaultTableColumnModel` listens to some of these events to keep the visual state of the table in sync. The `COLUMN_WIDTH_PROPERTY` change events (from one of the added `TableColumn` objects) cause the width cache for the table to be recalculated. The `valueChanged()` method listens for new column selections and fires off a column selection changed event.

Fields

protected ChangeEvent changeEvent
Since only one change event is ever needed for the column model, one is kept around as a field.

protected EventListenerList listenerList
Holds the list of listeners for table column events.

protected Vector tableColumns
Holds the actual columns currently in the model.

protected int columnMargin
protected boolean columnSelectionAllowed
protected ListSelectionModel selectionModel
protected int totalColumnWidth
These remaining fields hold the values for their respective properties listed in Table 15-4.

Constructors

public DefaultTableColumnModel()
This sets up a new `DefaultTableColumnModel` with the default values for properties listed in Table 15-4.

Methods

protected ListSelectionModel createSelectionModel ()
Create a list selection model to manage selections in this table column model.

public void addColumn(TableColumn Column)
public int getColumnIndex(Object identifier)
public int getColumnIndexAtx(int xPixell)
public void moveColumn(int index, int newindex)
public void removeColumn(TableColumn column)
These methods provide straightforward implementation of the abstract methods required by the `TableColumnModel` interface.

protected void recalcWidthCache()
Runs through an enumeration of the columns, adding up their widths as it goes. This method is called whenever columns are added, removed, or resized. This width is used to determine the values on a horizontal scrollbar, if one exists.

The TableColumnModelEvent Class

Many of the events fired by the DefaultTableColumnModel class use this event class to encode which columns were affected. Notice that these events describe something happening to a contiguous group of columns, unlike the selection events. There is no direct support for things like removing a discontiguous selection of columns. You must generate a different event for each contiguous range of columns that needs to be removed.

Fields

protected int fromIndex
protected int toIndex

These fields hold the index values representing the first and last columns affected by the event, respectively.

Constructors

public TableColumnModelEvent(TableColumnModel source, int from, int to)

As the only constructor for these events, you must supply the from and to column indices of the affected columns. If only one column is affected, from and to will have the same value.

Event Methods

public int getFromIndex()
public int getToIndex()

Use these methods to find the affected columns.

The TableColumnModelListener Interface

If you want to listen to any of the column model events you must implement the TableColumnModelListener interface and register as a listener for these events. Not surprisingly, the event-firing methods from the DefaultTableColumnModel class reflect the types of events this interface defines:

public void columnAdded(TableColumnModelEvent e)
public void columnMarginChanged(ChangeEvent e)
public void columnMoved(TableColumnModelEvent e)
public void columnRemoved(TableColumnModelEvent e)
public void columnSelectionChanged(ListSelectionEvent e)

Use these methods to react to changes in the column model. While you cannot add a ListSelectionListener directly to the column model if you only care about column selections, you can retrieve the selection model (using getSelectionModel()) and attach a listener to that object.

Implementing A Column Model

Here's a custom column model that keeps all of its columns in alphabetical order as they get added:

```
// SortingColumnModel.java
// A simple extension of the DefaultTableColumnModel class that sorts
// incoming columns.
//
import javax.swing.table.*;

public class SortingColumnModel extends DefaultTableColumnModel {

  public void addColumn(TableColumn tc) {
    super.addColumn(tc);
    int newIndex = sortedIndexOf(tc);
    if (newIndex != tc.getModelIndex()) {
      moveColumn(tc.getModelIndex(), newIndex);
    }
  }

  protected int sortedIndexOf(TableColumn tc) {
    // just do a linear search for now
    int stop = getColumnCount();
    String name = tc.getHeaderValue().toString();

    for (int i = 0; i < stop; i++) {
      if (name.compareTo(getColumn(i).getHeaderValue().toString()) <= 0) {
        return i;
      }
    }
    return stop;
  }
}
```

Implementing the model is simple. We just override addColumn() to add the column to the superclass and then move it into the appropriate position. You can use this column model with any data model. The next section goes into much more detail on the table model used to store the real data, so for this simple example, we'll use the DefaultTableModel class to hold the data. Once we have our table model and our column model, we can build a JTable with them. Then, any columns we add are listed in alphabetical order (by the header), regardless of the order in which they were added. The result looks like Figure 15-3.

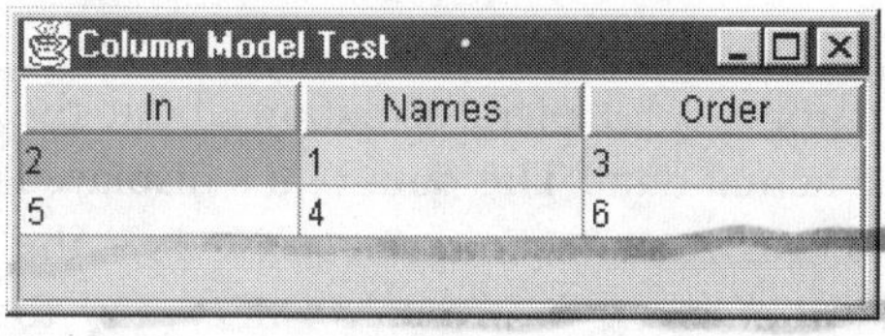

Figure 15-3. A sorting column model; the columns were added as "In," "Names," "Order"

Here's the code that puts the table and column models together:

```java
// ColumnExample.java
// A test of the JTable class using default table models and a convenience
// constructor.

import java.awt.*;
import javax.swing.*;
import javax.swing.table.*;

public class ColumnExample extends JFrame {
  public ColumnExample() {
    super("Abstract Model JTable Test");
    setSize(300, 200);
    addWindowListener(new BasicWindowMonitor());

    DefaultTableModel dtm = new DefaultTableModel(
                          new String[][] {
                            {"1", "2", "3"},
                            {"4", "5", "6"} },
                          new String[] {"Names", "In", "Order"});
    SortingColumnModel scm = new SortingColumnModel();
    JTable jt = new JTable(dtm, scm);
    jt.createDefaultColumnsFromModel();

    JScrollPane jsp = new JScrollPane(jt);
    getContentPane().add(jsp, BorderLayout.CENTER);
  }

  public static void main(String args[]) {
    ColumnExample ce = new ColumnExample();
    ce.setVisible(true);
  }
}
```

There's no trick here. All we do is create our sorting column model and use it when we create the JTable. You can find some other examples of custom column models in the next chapter.

Table Data

We've seen the `TableColumnModel` which stores a lot of information about the structure of a table, but doesn't contain the actual data. The data that's displayed in a `JTable` is stored in a `TableModel`. The `TableModel` interface describes the minimum requirements for a model that supplies the information necessary to display and edit a table's cells, and to show column headers. The `AbstractTableModel` fills out most of the `TableModel` interface, but leaves the methods for retrieving the actual data undefined. The `DefaultTableModel` extends `AbstractTableModel` and provides an implementation for storing data as a vector of vectors. We'll be looking at both the abstract and default table models in more detail later in this chapter.

The TableModel Interface

All of the table models start with this interface. A table model must be able to give out information on the number of rows and columns in the table and have access to the values of the cells of the table. The `TableModel` interface also has methods that can be used to encode information about the columns of the table (such as a localized name or class type), apart from the column model.

Properties

The `TableModel` interface supports the properties shown in Table 15-5. The `columnCount` is the number of columns in the data model. This does not have to match the number of columns reported by the column model. Likewise, `rowCount` is the number of rows in the data model. `columnName` and `columnClass` are indexed properties that let you retrieve the name of the column and the class of objects in the column. The name used in the table model is distinct from anything used in the `TableColumn` class. For both properties, remember that the index refers to the table model, regardless of where the column appears on the screen.

Table 15-5. TableModel Properties

Property	Data Type	get	is	set	bound	Default Value
columnCount	int	•				
rowCount	int	•				

Events

As you may have come to expect from other models in the Swing package, the `TableModel` has its own event type, `TableModelEvent`, generated whenever the table changes. A full discussion of the `TableModelEvent` class and the `TableModelListener` appears later in this chapter.

public void addTableModelListener(TableModelListener l)
public void removeTableModelListener(TableModelListener l)

    Add and remove listeners interested in receiving table model events.

Cell Methods

These methods let you obtain and change the values of individual cells.

public Object getValueAt(int rowIndex, int columnIndex)

    Returns the value of the cell at (`rowIndex`, `columnIndex`). Base types (`int`, `float`, etc.) are wrapped in an appropriate `Object`.

public boolean isCellEditable(int rowIndex, int columnIndex)

    Returns `true` if the cell at (`rowIndex`, `columnIndex`) can be edited.

public void setValueAt(Object aValue, int rowIndex, int columnIndex)

    Sets the value of the cell at (`rowIndex`, `columnIndex`) to `aValue`. As with the `getValueAt()` method, you may need to wrap primitive data types in an `Object` (like `Integer`) before using them to set the value of a cell.

The AbstractTableModel Class

This class implements many of the methods of the `TableModel` interface, leaving the really important ones to you. If you want to build your own table model, this is the place to start. (In fact, the documentation shipped with the Swing package even recommends starting here, rather than with the `DefaultTableModel` presented below.) The three unimplemented methods from `TableModel` are:

- `public abstract int getColumnCount()`
- `public abstract int getRowCount()`
- `public abstract Object getValueAt(int row, int col)`

With these methods, you can build your own table model better suited to the kinds of data you want to display. You can extend this model to support databases and even dynamic data.

As a starting point, let's look at recreating that first table with our own data model. For fun, we'll throw in support for the column headers as well. (This is not one of

the requirements of a minimal table model, but it makes the table look more
professional.) Here's the source code:

```java
// AbstractExample.java
// A test of the JTable class using default table models and a convenience
// constructor.
//
import java.awt.*;
import javax.swing.*;
import javax.swing.table.*;

public class AbstractExample extends JFrame {

  public AbstractExample() {
    super("Abstract Model JTable Test");
    setSize(300, 200);
    addWindowListener(new BasicWindowMonitor());

    TableModel tm = new AbstractTableModel() {
      String[][] data = { {"This", "is"}, {"a", "Test"} };
      String[] headers = {"Column", "Header"};

      public int getRowCount() { return data.length; }
      public int getColumnCount() { return headers.length; }
      public Object getValueAt(int r, int c) { return data[r][c]; }
      public String getColumnName(int c) { return headers[c]; }
    };

    JTable jt = new JTable(tm);

    JScrollPane jsp = new JScrollPane(jt);
    getContentPane().add(jsp, BorderLayout.CENTER);
  }

  public static void main(String args[]) {
    AbstractExample ae = new AbstractExample();
    ae.setVisible(true);
  }
}
```

Instead of supplying the data and headers in the JTable constructor, we built
them into our own table model, and then created the JTable with our own
model. Apart from changing the title of our application's frame, the resulting
table in Figure 15-4 is exactly the same as the first example.

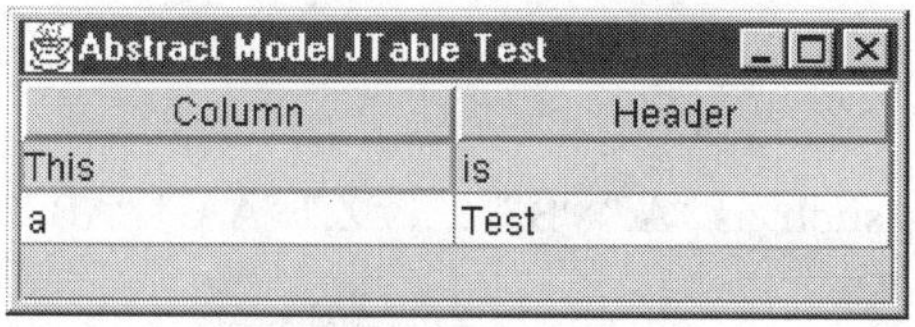

Figure 15-4. A JTable built with a custom TableModel class

Fields

protected EventListenerList listenerList

> The `AbstractTableModel` class adds a listener list for table model event listeners. You can access the list with the add and remove methods.

Events

public void addTableModelListener(TableModelListener l)
public void removeTableModelListener(TableModelListener l)

> Add and remove listeners for table model events coming from this model. The listeners are used in the various event firing methods presented below.

public void fireTableDataChanged()
public void fireTableStructureChanged()
public void fireTableRowsInserted(int first, int last)
public void fireTableRowsUpdated(int first, int last)
public void fireTableRowsDeleted(int first, int last)
public void fireTableCellUpdated(int row, int col)

> These methods all call `fireTableChanged()` after constructing an appropriate `TableModelEvent` object. `fireTableDataChanged()` indicates that all of the cells in the table might have changed, but the columns of the table are still intact. On the other hand, the `fireTableStructureChanged()` method indicates that the actual columns present in the model may have changed (in name, type or even number) as well.

public void fireTableChanged(TableModelEvent e)

> Reports event e to any registered listeners.

TableModel Methods

The other methods from the `TableModel` interface are shown below with their default implementations:

public int findColumn(String columnName)

> Provides an easy mechanism for looking up columns by their associated names. This is a linear search, so large tables may need to override this.

public Class getColumnClass(int index)

> Returns `Object.class`.

public String getColumnName(int index)

> Returns spreadsheet-style letter names such as "A," "B," …, "Z," "AA," "AB," etc.

public boolean isCellEditable(int row, int col)

> Returns `false`. You'll have to override this if you want to create an editable table.

public void setValueAt(Object value, int row, int col)

> Implemented with an empty body to support the read-only tables. You'll have to override this if you want to create an editable table.

The TableModelEvent Class

Several methods of the `AbstractTableModel` class help you fire events to report changes in your data model. All of the methods build an appropriate `TableModelEvent` object and send it out to any registered listeners through the `fireTableChanged()` method. The `TableModelEvent` class encompasses the properties listed in Table 15-6.

Table 15-6. TableModelEvent Properties

Property	Data Type	get	is	set	bound	Default Value
column	int	•				
firstRow	int	•				
lastRow	int	•				
type	int	•				

The `column` property shows the column affected by this event, which could be a specific column or `ALL_COLUMNS`. Likewise, `firstRow` and `lastRow` identify the first and last row in a range of rows affected by this event; they may be a specific column on `HEADER_ROW`; `lastRow` will be greater than or equal to the `firstRow`. Finally, `type` indicates which type of event occurred; its value will be one of the constants `INSERT`, `UPDATE`, or `DELETE`.

Constants

The properties and constructors can make use of several constants, defined in the `TableModelEvent` class and shown in Table 15-7.

Table 15-7. TableModelEvent Constants

Constant	Data Type	Description
ALL_COLUMNS	int	Indicates that the event is not localized on one column.
DELETE	int	One of the values that can be returned by the getType() call; indicates that rows have been deleted from the model.
HEADER_ROW	int	This constant can be used in place of a normal first row value to indicate that the metadata (such as column names) of the table has changed.
INSERT	int	One of the values that can be returned by the getType() call; indicates that rows have been inserted into the model.
UPDATE	int	One of the values that can be returned by the getType() call; indicates that data in some of the rows has changed. The number of rows and columns has not changed.

Fields

protected int column
protected int firstRow
protected int lastRow
protected int type

All of the fields for TableModelEvent store the values of their respective properties.

Constructors

You can build a TableModelEvent using any one of the following constructors:

public TableModelEvent(TableModel source)

Use this constructor when everything has changed. For example, in a database query display table, a new query will likely have new (or at least different) columns. This constructor would build an object appropriate for reporting such an event.

public TableModelEvent(TableModel source, int row)

If the data in one row has changed, use this constructor. This is an update event that affects all columns in row.

public TableModelEvent(TableModel source, int firstRow, int lastRow)

If the data in a range of rows (firstRow ... lastRow inclusive) has changed, use this constructor. This is an update event that affects all columns in the range.

public TableModelEvent(TableModel source, int firstRow, int lastRow, int column)

If a cell or range of cells in one column has changed, use this constructor. (For a single cell, the firstRow and lastRow values are the same.) This is an update event. The ALL_COLUMNS value can be used in column to indicate that all columns need to be updated.

public TableModelEvent(TableModel source, int firstRow, int lastRow, int column, int type)
Use this method to specify an insert or delete event (rather than an update event). You can specify the range of rows, the column (or ALL_COLUMNS), and the event type (INSERT, DELETE, or UPDATE).

The TableModelListener Interface

As you saw in the previous examples, the JTable class listens to model events to keep the view of the table consistent with the model. If you want to monitor changes in a table yourself, implement this interface. Only one method exists for event notification, and you register the listener with the model itself, not with the JTable.

public void tableChanged(TableModelEvent e)
Called for any table model events your model generates. You can use getType() to distinguish between events of different types.

The DefaultTableModel Class

While you will most likely create your own table models by extending the AbstractTableModel class as we did earlier in this chapter, the Swing package includes a DefaultTableModel class that contains a Vector of Vector objects to house the data. This class itself extends AbstractTableModel and provides a few methods for manipulating the data. The default model presumes that every cell is editable.

Properties

The DefaultTableModel class provides default values to the properties inherited from the TableModel interface. These values are shown in Table 15-8.

Table 15-8. DefaultTableModel Properties

Property	Data Type	get	is	set	bound	Default Value
columnCount*	int	•				0
rowCount*	int	•				0

Events

The `DefaultTableModel` class does not support any new event types, but since it does contain real data, it provides the following helper methods to generate events:

public void newDataAvailable(TableModelEvent e)
public void newRowsAdded(TableModelEvent e)
public void rowsRemoved(TableModelEvent e)

> These methods all fire the appropriate table model events. If e is `null`, the model assumes all of the associated data has changed, and creates an appropriate event.

Fields

protected Vector dataVector

> Holds a vector of data representing the table. Most entries in this vector will be other vectors or arrays.

protected Vector columnIdentifiers

> Holds the names of the columns in the model.

Constructors

public DefaultTableModel()

> Builds a `DefaultTableModel` with zero rows and zero columns

public DefaultTableModel(int numRows, int numColumns)

> Builds a `DefaultTableModel` with the specified number of rows and columns

public DefaultTableModel(Vector columnNames, int numRows)
public DefaultTableModel(Object[] columnNames, int numRows)

> Build a `DefaultTableModel` with the specified number of rows. The number of columns matches the number of elements in the `columnNames` vector (or array), which also supplies the names for the columns in the column header.

public DefaultTableModel(Vector data, Vector columnNames)
public DefaultTableModel(Object[] [] data, Object[] columnNames)

> Build a `DefaultTableModel` with the number of rows determined by the data object and the number of columns determined by the `columnNames` object. The data vector `columns` will be padded or truncated to match the number of columns dictated by the `columnNames` vector.
>
> The `Object` arrays get converted to vectors (or vectors of vectors in the case of `Object[] []`) using the `convertToVector()` methods discussed below.

Data Methods

With the DefaultTableModel class, you can get and set the data directly. These methods work in addition to the usual getValueAt() and setValueAt() methods for individual cells.

public Vector getDataVector()

Returns the row vector, which itself contains vectors representing the collection of cells (one for each column) for each row.

public void setDataVector(Object[][] newData, Object[] columnIDs)
public void setDataVector(Vector newData, Vector columnIDs)

Set the new data (as a vector of vectors) for the model. The columnIDs field can be null, or it can contain the names of columns that will be returned by getColumnName(). (Although you can create column IDs that are not of String type, the getColumnName() method will convert them to strings using the toString() method.) The first column ID is mapped to the first column in newData, the second column ID to the second column, and so on.

protected static Vector convertToVector(Object[] array)
protected static Vector convertToVector(Object[] [] array)

Return a Vector consisting of the objects in the given array. The second method returns a Vector of Vectors, each holding one column of the array.

Row and Column Methods

All of these methods for modifying the rows or columns in the table generate the appropriate table change event for you.

public void addColumn(Object columnID)
public void addColumn(Object columnID, Object[] columnData)
public void addColumn(Object columnID, Vector columnData)

Add a new column to the model. The first version inserts null values into the rows currently in the table. Both the second and third versions insert values into the current rows up to their size or the number of rows, and null values after that if more rows exist. (If, for example, you had 20 rows but supplied a vector of 18 objects, the last two rows would receive null values.) The columnID field must not be null.

public void addRow(Object[] rowData)
public void addRow(Vector rowData)

These methods append new rows to the table. Like the padding that occurs with adding columns, the row's data is truncated or extended as necessary to match the current number of columns in the table.

public String getColumnName(int index)

Returns the name of the column indicated by index. If the column names array (from the constructor or a setData() call) is null or does not contain a name for the specified column, the spreadsheet default inherited from the AbstractTableModel class is used. If the column names array contains a non-String object, the toString() method for that object will be used and returned.

public Object getValueAt(int row, int column)

Returns the object at the specified location in the table model.

public void insertRow(int row, Object[] rowData)
public void insertRow(int row, Vector rowData)

Inserts a new row at row in the table. As with the addRow() methods, the size of the rowData vector is adjusted to match the number of columns in the table.

public boolean isCellEditable(int row, int column)

Returns true because all cells in a DefaultTableModel are editable.

public void moveRow(int startIndex, int endIndex, int toIndex)

Moves a range of rows (from startIndex to endIndex inclusive) to a new location (toIndex). The other rows are shifted accordingly.

public void removeRow(int index)

Deletes the row at index from the table.

public void setColumnIdentifiers(Object[] columnIDs)
public void setColumnIdentifiers(Vector columnIDs)

Set the identifiers for the columns in the table to columnIDs. The number of identifiers passed in dictates the number of columns in the table.

public void setNumRows(int newSize)

Changes the number of rows in the current table. If newSize is less than the current table size, the extra rows are truncated. If newSize is larger than the current table size, extra rows (new Vector(getColumnCount()) objects) are added to pad the table to newSize rows.

public void setValueAt(Object balue, int row, int column)

Sets the table cell and the given row and column to value. This method overrides the implementiation in AbstractTableModel. (The implementation in AbstractTableModel does nothing.)

Dynamic Table Data

Since we've already seen some simple examples of table models at work in a JTable object, let's look at some more interesting ones.

You can take advantage of the convenience methods that generate TableMod-elEvent objects to create a table model that responds to dynamic data. A classic example of dynamic table data is stock market quotes. Of course, you have to pay for the quote feed, but if you've done that, you could use a JTable to show off your portfolio.

Just to try out dynamic data, we'll simulate a stock market where Swing components are the traded commodities. The heart of this simulator is MYOSM, which sets up a thread to play with the values of the components so that we have changing data to look at. The example contains two different constructors. One constructor for MYOSM simply starts the updater thread. This is the version our final application will use, since the JTable we build will be showing off the stock quotes; the other constructor creates its own JFrame that monitors and displays the changes. If you run MYOSM as an application, that's the version you'll see.

Here's the code that will serve as our stock market. (The Stock class is available online, but isn't particularly interesting, so we didn't list it.)

```java
// MYOSM.java
// Make Your Own Stock Market: A simple stock market simulator that contains a
// few stocks and their current prices (and deltas).  It randomly adjusts the
// prices on stocks to give a dynamic feel to the data.
//
import javax.swing.*;
import java.awt.*;
import java.util.*;

public class MYOSM extends JFrame implements Runnable {

  Stock[] market = {
    new Stock("JTree", 14.57),
    new Stock("JTable", 17.44),
    new Stock("JList", 16.44),
    new Stock("JButton", 7.21),
    new Stock("JComponent", 27.40)
  };
  boolean monitor;
  Random rg = new Random();
  Thread runner;

  public MYOSM() {
    // not meant to be shown as a real frame
    super("Thread only version . . .");
    runner = new Thread(this);
    runner.start();
  }
```

```java
// This version creates a real frame so that you can see how the typical stocks
// get updated.  It's not meant to be used with other programs, but rather as a
// debugging tool to make sure the market runs ok.
public MYOSM(boolean monitorOn) {
  super("Stock Market Monitor");
  setSize(400, 100);
  addWindowListener(new BasicWindowMonitor());
  monitor = monitorOn;

  getContentPane().add(new JLabel("Trading is active.  " +
      "Close this window to close the market."),
      BorderLayout.CENTER);
  runner = new Thread(this);
  runner.start();
}


// Here's the heart of our stock market. In an infinite loop, just pick a
// random stock and update its price.  To make the program interesting, we'll
// update a price every second.
public void run() {
  while(true) {
    int whichStock = Math.abs(rg.nextInt()) % market.length;
    double delta = rg.nextDouble() - 0.4;
    market[whichStock].update(delta);
    if (monitor) {
      market[whichStock].print();
    }
    try {
      Thread.sleep(1000);
    }
    catch(InterruptedException ie) {
    }
  }
}


public Stock getQuote(int index) {
  return market[index];
}


// This method returns the list of all the symbols in the market table
public String[] getSymbols() {
  String[] symbols = new String[market.length];
  for (int i = 0; i < market.length; i++) {
    symbols[i] = market[i].symbol;
  }
  return symbols;
}
```

```
  public static void main(String args[]) {
    MYOSM myMarket = new MYOSM(args.length > 0);
    myMarket.setVisible(true);
  }
}
```

With this stock market class producing dynamic data, we need a model that can listen for that data. We'll use a polling method to extract new data at intervals. If your data source generated events, you could also create a table model that listened for the events and updated your table immediately after receiving a change event. (If updating your table is costly, the polling route might make more sense.)

Here's the table model that works in conjunction with the dynamic data source. Notice that we implement Runnable so that we can start a thread to control the polling frequency. Apart from that, the data model handles the same tasks as the previous data models. We return the appropriate column names and values for individual cells.

```
// MarketDataModel.java
//
import javax.swing.table.*;
import javax.swing.*;

public class MarketDataModel extends AbstractTableModel
implements Runnable {

  Thread runner;
  MYOSM market;
  int delay;

  public MarketDataModel(int initialDelay) {
    market = new MYOSM();
    delay = initialDelay * 1000;
    Thread runner = new Thread(this);
    runner.start();
  }

  Stock[] stocks = new Stock[0];
  int[] stockIndices = new int[0];
  String[] headers = {"Symbol", "Price", "Change", "Last updated"};

  public int getRowCount() { return stocks.length; }
  public int getColumnCount() { return headers.length; }

  public String getColumnName(int c) { return headers[c]; }

  public Object getValueAt(int r, int c) {
    switch(c) {
```

```
    case 0:
      return stocks[r].symbol;
    case 1:
      return new Double(stocks[r].price);
    case 2:
      return new Double(stocks[r].delta);
    case 3:
      return stocks[r].lastUpdate;
    }
    throw new IllegalArgumentException("Bad cell (" + r + ", " + c +")");
  }

  public void setDelay(int seconds) { delay = seconds * 1000; }
  public void setStocks(int[] indices) {
    stockIndices = indices;
    updateStocks();
    fireTableDataChanged();
  }

  public void updateStocks() {
    stocks = new Stock[stockIndices.length];
    for (int i = 0; i < stocks.length; i++) {
      stocks[i] = market.getQuote(stockIndices[i]);
    }
  }

  public void run() {
    while(true) {
      // blind update . . . we could check for real deltas if necessary
      updateStocks();

      // Now, we know there are no new columns, so don't fire a data change, only
      // fire a row update . . . this keeps the table from flashing
      fireTableRowsUpdated(0, stocks.length - 1);
      try { Thread.sleep(delay); }
      catch(InterruptedException ie) {}
    }
  }
}
```

Most of the code is fairly simple. getValueAt() merely looks up the appropriate value from the table's data, taking into account the column requested so it can return an appropriate type of object. The one trick is that our model doesn't necessarily track all the stocks simulated by MYOSM. The model provides a setStocks() method that lets you select the stocks that interest you, and populates the model's data accordingly. setStocks() fires a TableModelEvent indicating that the table's data has changed; in particular, rows (but not columns) may have been added or deleted. The model's run() method fires a similar event with each update, indicating that the data in the rows has been updated. With this model in place, we can create a table using the same simple code, but this time, we update the table every five seconds. Figure 15-5 shows the results.

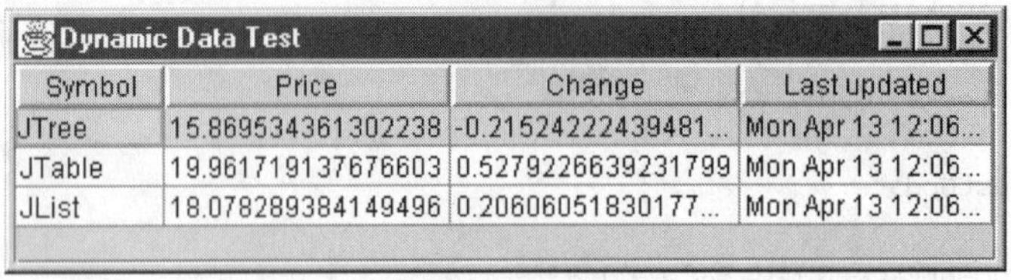

Symbol	Price	Change	Last updated
JTree	15.869534361302238	-0.21524222439481...	Mon Apr 13 12:06...
JTable	19.961719137676603	0.5279226639231799	Mon Apr 13 12:06...
JList	18.078289384149496	0.20606051830177...	Mon Apr 13 12:06...

Figure 15-5. A table model that generates dynamic (and precise!) data

Just to be complete, here's the code for this application that displays our market simulator. Notice that only the model passed to the JTable constructor really changed from the previous table application.

```
// MarketTable.java
// A test of the JTable class using default table models and a convenience
// constructor.
//
import java.awt.*;
import javax.swing.*;

public class MarketTable extends JFrame {

  public MarketTable() {
    super("Dynamic Data Test");
    setSize(300, 200);
    addWindowListener(new BasicWindowMonitor());

    // set up our table model with a 5 second polling delay
    MarketDataModel mdm = new MarketDataModel(5);

    // Pick which stocks we want to watch . . .
    mdm.setStocks(new int[] { 0, 1, 2 });

    // And pop up the table
    JTable jt = new JTable(mdm);
    JScrollPane jsp = new JScrollPane(jt);
    getContentPane().add(jsp, BorderLayout.CENTER);
  }

  public static void main(String args[]) {
    MarketTable mt = new MarketTable();
    mt.setVisible(true);
  }
}
```

Database Data

Another popular source of information for table displays is database records. You can create a table model that connects to a database and produces rows and columns based on the results of queries you send. Figure 15-6 shows a simple application that passes any query you type to the database. The table displays the results from your query. The column headings (and even the number of columns) are taken directly from the database and depend entirely on the query and the database contents.

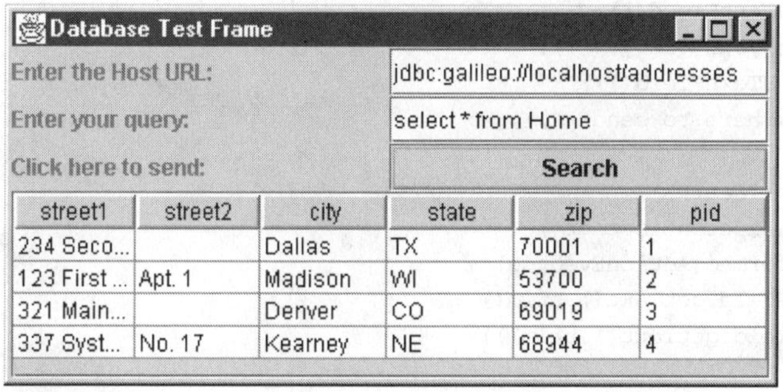

street1	street2	city	state	zip	pid
234 Seco...		Dallas	TX	70001	1
123 First...	Apt. 1	Madison	WI	53700	2
321 Main...		Denver	CO	69019	3
337 Syst...	No. 17	Kearney	NE	68944	4

Enter the Host URL: `jdbc:galileo://localhost/addresses`
Enter your query: `select * from Home`
Click here to send: **Search**

Figure 15-6. A database query result table example

In this example, each new search causes a `fireTableChanged()`, since the query may have new columns. If we could count on the columns remaining the same, we could use the `fireTableRowsUpdated()` method, like we did with the dynamic data example.

Here is the code to build this application. Most of the work is setting up the labels and textfields that serve as our graphical interface, but take a look at the anonymous event handler for the "Search" button. This is where we pass the database URL and query to our model. We'll use the URL and query as the starting point for discussing the model code below.

```
// DatabaseTest.java
// Let's try to make one of these work . . .
//
import java.awt.*;
import java.awt.event.*;
import javax.swing.*;
import javax.swing.table.*;

public class DatabaseTest extends JFrame {

  JTextField hostField;
  JTextField queryField;
  QueryTableModel qtm;
```

```
public DatabaseTest() {
  super("Database Test Frame");
  addWindowListener(new BasicWindowMonitor());
  setSize(350, 200);

  qtm = new QueryTableModel();
  JTable table = new JTable(qtm);
  JScrollPane scrollpane = new JScrollPane(table);
  JPanel p1 = new JPanel();
  p1.setLayout(new GridLayout(3, 2));
  p1.add(new JLabel("Enter the Host URL: "));
  p1.add(hostField = new JTextField());
  p1.add(new JLabel("Enter your query: "));
  p1.add(queryField = new JTextField());
  p1.add(new JLabel("Click here to send: "));

  JButton jb = new JButton("Search");
  jb.addActionListener(new ActionListener() {
    public void actionPerformed(ActionEvent e) {
      qtm.setHostURL(hostField.getText().trim());
      qtm.setQuery(queryField.getText().trim());
    }
  } );
  p1.add(jb);
  getContentPane().add(p1, BorderLayout.NORTH);
  getContentPane().add(scrollpane, BorderLayout.CENTER);
}

public static void main(String args[]) {
  DatabaseTest tt = new DatabaseTest();
  tt.setVisible(true);
}
}
```

And here's the code for the query model. Rather than hold a vector of vectors, we'll store a vector of String[] objects to facilitate retrieving the values. This query table contains all of the code required to connect to a database server using a JDBC driver. The server and driver we are using were both written by Brian Cole of Galileo Systems, LLC, and are available on the website along with the rest of the code in this chapter.

We have code similar to all of our previous examples for the basic methods from the AbstractTableModel class, which we extend. But we have to add support for a changing host and query. If the host stays the same from the last query that was run, we can continue to use the same connection. If not, we'll close the old connection and build a new one. When we set the query, however, we have to send it to the database server, and then update the table once we get the response. Notice that this example fires a full table changed event at the end of the setQuery() call. With our open-ended query form, chances are we'll get back some very different results from query to query, so we don't bother trying to send only modification events. If you're unfamiliar with SQL or the JDBC code throughout this class, check out *Database Programming with JDBC and Java,* by George Reese (O'Reilly & Associates).

```java
// QueryTableModel.java
// A basic implementation of the TableModel interface that fills out a Vector of
// String[] structure from a query's result set.
//
import java.sql.*;
import java.io.*;
import java.util.Vector;
import javax.swing.*;
import javax.swing.table.*;

public class QueryTableModel extends AbstractTableModel {
  Vector cache;  // will hold String[] objects . . .
  int colCount;
  String[] headers;
  Connection db;
  Statement statement;
  String currentURL;

  public QueryTableModel() {
    cache = new Vector();
    new gsl.sql.driv.Driver();
  }

  public String getColumnName(int i) { return headers[i]; }
  public int getColumnCount() { return colCount; }
  public int getRowCount() { return cache.size();}

  public Object getValueAt(int row, int col) {
    return ((String[])cache.elementAt(row))[col];
  }

  public void setHostURL(String url) {
    if (url.equals(currentURL)) {
      // same database, we can leave the current connection open
      return;
    }
    // Oops . . . new connection required
    closeDB();
    initDB(url);
    currentURL = url;
  }
```

```java
// All the real work happens here; in a real application,
// we'd probably perform the query in a separate thread.
public void setQuery(String q) {
  cache = new Vector();
  try {
    // Execute the query and store the result set and its metadata
    ResultSet rs = statement.executeQuery(q);
    ResultSetMetaData meta = rs.getMetaData();
    colCount = meta.getColumnCount();

    // Now we must rebuild the headers array with the new column names
    headers = new String[colCount];
    for (int h=1; h <= colCount; h++) {
      headers[h-1] = meta.getColumnName(h);
    }

    // and file the cache with the records from our query.  This would not be
    // practical if we were expecting a few million records in response to our
    // query, but we aren't, so we can do this.
    while (rs.next()) {
      String[] record = new String[colCount];
      for (int i=0; i < colCount; i++) {
        record[i] = rs.getString(i + 1);
      }
      cache.addElement(record);
    }
    fireTableChanged(null); // notify everyone that we have a new table.
  }
  catch(Exception e) {
    cache = new Vector(); // blank it out and keep going.
    e.printStackTrace();
  }
}

public void initDB(String url) {
  try {
    db = DriverManager.getConnection(url);
    statement = db.createStatement();
  }
  catch(Exception e) {
    System.out.println("Could not initialize the database.");
    e.printStackTrace();
  }
}

public void closeDB() {
  try {
    if (statement != null) { statement.close(); }
    if (db != null) {        db.close(); }
  }
```

```
  catch(Exception e) {
    System.out.println("Could not close the current connection.");
    e.printStackTrace();
  }
 }
}
```

This model does not support database updates using any of the entries you see in the table. You could certainly support that feature if you needed to. The Swing package has a more complete result-set model call the JDBCAdapter in the table examples directory if you want another example of database and JTable communication.

The JTable Class

Well, we made it this far without officially discussing the JTable class itself. Dynamic data and database queries are all handled entirely by the table model underneath the display. So what can you do with a JTable object? The JTable class gives you control over the appearance and behavior of the table. You can control the spacing of columns, their resizability, their colors, and so on. The JTable object will be the source of row selections, and through delegation, you can add and remove rows and columns directly with the JTable object.

Properties

The appearance of a JTable is manipulated almost entirely through its properties. To make things a bit more manageable, we'll break the properties up into three smaller tables: one for row, column and cell properties; one for selection properties; and one for the visual properties. Table 15-9 covers the row, column, and cell properties.

Table 15-9. JTable Row, Column, and Cell Properties

Property	Data Type	get	is	set	bound	Default Value
columnModel	TableColumn-Model	•		•		DefaultTableColumn-Model()
model	TableModel	•		•		DefaultTableModel()
autoCreateColumnsFrom-Model	boolean	•		•		false
autoResizeMode	int	•		•		AUTO_RESIZE_ALL_COLUMNS
columnCount*	int	•				0
rowCount*	int	•				0
rowHeight	int	•		•		16

The autoCreateColumnsFromModel property determines whether or not the column model is loaded automatically with data from the table model. This value gets set to true in the initializeLocalVars() method which is called by the constructor. (You can always replace an existing column model with the setColumnModel() method.) The autoResizeMode property determines how the table reacts to being resized. Using the constants presented in Table 15-12, you can adjust all of the columns, only the last column, or shut resizing off altogether. You must turn off autoresizing if you want to use the horizontal scrollbar in your scroll pane. The columnCount and rowCount properties allow you to ask the JTable object how many rows and columns it has. These values come from the models in place. The columnModel property holds the current column model and can be replaced at runtime, if necessary. The rowHeight property dictates how tall rows are, in pixels. This property must be a number greater than or equal to one. Other values cause the setRowHeight() method to throw an IllegalArgumentException. The value of rowHeight includes the vertical intercell spacing.

Table 15-10 lists the selection-related properties of the JTable class. The selectionModel property holds the ListSelectionModel object that handles row selections, and the selectionMode property applies to that model. (You can control the column selections with the selectionModel property of the TableColumnModel for your table.) The cellSelectionEnabled, columnSelectionAllowed, and rowSelectionAllowed properties determine whether or not you can select cells, columns, or rows. If cells are selectable, only cells can be selected, regardless of the row and column properties. With cell selection turned on and row and column selection turned off, you can still select a range of cells. With an active selection on your table, the selectedColumn, selectedColumnCount, selectedColumns, selectedRow, selectedRowCount, and selectedRows give you access to the various parts of that selection. The selectedRow and selectedColumn properties store the anchor selection (i.e., the first selection) from their respective selection models.

Table 15-10. JTable Selection Properties

Property	Data Type	get	is	set	bound	Default Value
cellSelectionEnabled	boolean	•		•		false
columnSelection-Allowed	boolean	•		•		false
rowSelectionAllowed	boolean	•		•		true
selectedColumn	int	•				-1
selectedColumnCount	int	•				0
selectedColumns	int[]	•				int[0]
selectedRow	int	•				-1

Table 15-10. JTable Selection Properties (continued)

Property	Data Type	get	is	set	bound	Default Value
selectedRowCount	int	•				0
selectedRows	int[]	•				int[0]
selectionMode	int			•		MULTIPLE_INTERVAL_SELECTION
selectionModel	ListSelectionModel	•		•		DefaultListSelectionModel

Table 15-11 covers the remaining properties of the JTable class. The cellEditor property determines the cell editor currently in use. When you start editing, the JTable class looks up your column and asks it for an editor. If the column has one, that editor is used, otherwise a default editor for the column's class type is used. If no cell is currently being edited, this property will be null. The gridColor, selectionBackground, and selectionForeground properties determine the color used for the grid lines and selection text. The intercellSpacing property determines the horizontal and vertical spacing around each cell in the table. The preferredScrollableViewportSize property determines the preferred size of the scrollpane for the table. The scrollableTracksViewportHeight and scrollableTracksViewportWidth properties are always false, to indicate that making the viewport around the table should not resize the table to fit the viewport (assuming you have placed the table in a scrollpane). You can control which lines show up on the your table with showGrid, showHorizontalLines, and showVerticalLines. Use setShowGrid() as a convenient way to turn both horizontal and vertical lines on or off at the same time. The tableHeader property is used to store a JTableHeader object for your table. That header can be used in a scrollpane as the column header for your table. No row header is provided, but you can see an example of that in the next chapter. The rowMargin property determines the amount of empty space between rows. This is really just a more convenient way of getting at the height information in the internalSpacing property.

Table 15-11. JTable Visual and Editing Properties

Property	Data Type	get	is	set	bound	Default Value
UI*	TableUI	•		•	•	from L&F
UIClassID*	String	•				"TableUI"
accesibleContext*	AccessibleContext	•				JTable.AccessibleJTable

See also properties from the JComponent class (Table 3-5).

Table 15-11. JTable Visual and Editing Properties (continued)

Property	Data Type	get	is	set	bound	Default Value
cellEditor	TableCell-Editor	•		•		null
gridColor	Color	•		•		
intercellSpacing	Dimension	•		•		Dimension(1, 1)
preferredScrollable-ViewportSize*	Dimension	•		•		Dimension(450, 400)
rowMargin	int	•		•		1
scrollableTracksView-portHeight*	boolean	•				false
scrollableTracksView-portWidth*	boolean	•				false
selectionBackground	Color	•		•	•	
selectionForeground	Color	•		•	•	
showGrid	boolean			•		true
showHorizontalLines	boolean	•		•		true
showVerticalLines	boolean	•		•		true
tableHeader	JTableHeader	•		•		JTableHeader(column-Model)

See also properties from the JComponent class (Table 3-5).

Events

All table-specific events you would expect to see from the JTable class are routed through its data model and column model. You must get a reference to these models and attach listeners to the models directly, using code like this:

```
TableModel myModel = new MyTableModel();  // some valid TableModel class
JTable table = new JTable(myModel);
// Listen for added/removed/updated rows
myModel.addTableModelListener(new MyTableModelListener());
TableColumnModel columnModel = table.getColumnModel();
// Listen for added/removed/moved columns
columnModel.addTableColumnModelListener(new MyColumnModelListener());
// Listen for row selections
ListSelectionListener simpleListener = new ListSelectionListener();
myTable.getSelectionModel().addListSelectionListener(simpleListener);
// Listen for column selections
columnModel.getSelectionModel.addListSelectionListener(simpleListener);
```

You can see a more detailed example using the selection listeners later in this chapter. Examples using model listeners are in Chapter 16, *Advanced Table Examples*.

Constants

Table 15-12 shows the constants defined in `JTable`. These constants specify how columns behave when you resize the entire table or adjust a single column; they are used for the `autoResizeMode` property.

Table 15-12. JTable Constants

Constant	Data Type	Description
AUTO_RESIZE_ALL_COLUMNS	int	When a table is resized, all columns should be resized proportionately.
AUTO_RESIZE_LAST_COLUMN	int	When a table is resized, resize the last column only.
AUTO_RESIZE_NEXT_COLUMN	int	When a column is resized, resize the next column too. For example, if you make column N bigger, column N+1 will shrink.
AUTO_RESIZE_OFF	int	When a table is resized, do not resize the columns at all.
AUTO_RESIZE_SUBSEQUENT_ COLUMNS	int	When a column is resized, resize all subsequent columns proportionally to preserve the overall width of the table.

Fields

protected boolean autoCreateColumnsFromModel

protected int autoResizeMode

protected transient TableCellEditor cellEditor

protected boolean cellSelectionEnabled

protected TableColumnModel columnModel

protected TableModel dataModel

protected transient int editingColumn

protected transient int editingRow

protected transient Component editorComp

protected Color gridColor

protected Dimension preferredViewportSize

protected int rowHeight

protected int rowMargin

protected boolean rowSelectionAllowed

protected Color selectionBackground

protected Color selectionForeground

protected ListSelectionModel selectionModel

protected boolean showHorizontalLines

protected boolean showVerticalLines

protected JTableHeader tableHeader

These fields store the values for their respective properties. The `editorComp` field corresponds to the `editorComponent` property.

protected transient Hashtable defaultRenderersByColumnClass

protected transient Hashtable defaultEditorsByColumnClass

These two fields hold the renderers and editors for various `Class` types of columns. The fields are accessed through methods such as `getCellEditor()` and `setDefaultCellRenderer()`, discussed later in this chapter.

Constructors

public JTable()

Creates a new `JTable` object using a `DefaultTableModel`, a `DefaultTable-ColumnModel`, and a `DefaultListSelectionModel` for its models.

public JTable(TableModel dm)

public JTable(TableModel dm, TableColumnModel cm)

public JTable(TableModel dm, TableColumnModel cm, ListSelectionModel sm)

These constructors allow you to specify the exact table model, table column model, and (row) list selection model you want to use. If you only want to specify the column or list selection model, you can pass `null` as an argument for the other models and the appropriate default model will be created and used.

public JTable(int numRows, int numColumns)

This constructor builds a default table model with the specified number of rows and columns. Default table column and list selection models are also used.

public JTable(Vector data, Vector columnNames)

public JTable(Object data[][], Object columnNames[])

Populate tables by filling the custom table model with `data` and naming the columns with `columnNames`. In the case of the first constructor, it is assumed that the data vector will be a vector containing other vectors, one for each row of data. The data argument can contain any type of object. The table will do its best to appropriately render the objects in the array, using labels generated by calling `toString()` on the objects if necessary. While the `columnNames` argument can also contain an array of any type of object, a `String[]` is the most common. The default table header renderer uses column names (or the `toString()` result of nonstring objects) to label columns.

The table models used by these constructors are not instances of `DefaultTableModel`. If you retrieve the table model, you will only be able to interact with through the `TableModel` interface.

Protected Initialization and Helper Methods

protected TableColumnModel createDefaultColumnModel()

Returns a new `DefaultColumnModel` object. It is used by constructors that were not given a specific column model to use.

protected TableModel createDefaultDataModel()

Returns a new `DefaultTableModel` object. It is used by constructors that were not given a specific table model to use.

protected void createDefaultEditors()

Creates editors for the following column classes: `Object`, `Number` and `Boolean`. `Boolean` columns use a centered `JCheckBox` component. `Number` columns use a right-justified `JTextField`. `Object` columns (i.e., everything else) use a left-justified `JTextField`.

protected void createDefaultRenderers()

Sets up renderers for the following column classes: `Object`, `Number`, `Boolean`, and `Icon`. `Icon` columns use a centered `JLabel` object. `Boolean` columns use a centered `JCheckBox` component. `Number` columns use a right-justified `JTextField`. `Object` columns (i.e., everything else) use a left-justified `JText-Field`. The inner class used to render `Boolean` values does not support row selection. If you want the cell containing the check box to change color when its row is selected, you'll need to install your own boolean renderer.

protected ListSelectionModel createDefaultSelectionModel()

Returns a new `DefaultListSelectionModel` object. It also sets the `leadAnchorNotificationEnabled` property of the selection model (for the rows) to `false` to improve rendering performance.

protected JTableHeader createDefaultTableHeader()

Returns a new `JTableHeader` object, based on the current column model.

protected void initializeLocalVars()

Initializes the default properties listed in Table 15-9, installs the default editors and renderers using `createDefaultEditors()` and `createDefaultRenderers()`, and sets the table header using `createDefaultTableHeader()`.

protected void resizeAndRepaint()

Resizes the table and header views (by calling `revalidate()`) and then calls `repaint()`. It is called by many of the event support methods.

Editor and Renderer Methods

public TableCellEditor getDefaultEditor(Class columnClass)

Returns the `TableCellEditor` object associated with the `columnClass` class type. This method is called when the table is told to start editing a cell.

public TableCellEditor getCellEditor(int row, int col)

Return an appropriate editor for the cell at `col`. If the table column at `col` has an associated editor, use that, otherwise use the default editor for the data type of the column. You could potentially extend the `JTable` and override this method to return unique editors for every cell (which might be useful in a spreadsheet where not all cells in a column have the same type).

public Component prepareEditor(TableCellEditor editor, int row, int column)

Gets the appropriate `editor` ready for use with the currently selected cell. "Getting ready" includes making sure the editor starts with values that reflect the current values of the cell. The `Component` returned is the component provided by the `TableCellEditor.getTableCellEditor()` method.

public void removeEditor()

Usually called whenever the table is editing a cell and the user changes the selection. It finds the current editor, cancels the editing session, and then removes the editor component from the table.

public TableCellRenderer getCellRenderer(int row, int column)

Returns the renderer appropriate for the cell at `row`, `col`. As with the editor for the cell, if the table column at `col` has a renderer, that renderer is used. Otherwise, the default renderer for the data type in the column will be returned.

public Compinent prepareRenderer(TableCellRenderer renderer, int row, int column)

Figures out all of the necessary parameters to call the `getTableCellRendererComponent()` method (discussed later in the chapter) from the specified renderer. This includes deciding whether the cell is selected and whether it has focus. Once these values are known, the method returns an appropriate rendering component.

public void setDefaultRenderer(Class columnClass, TableCellRenderer renderer)

Adds a new renderer for a particular type of data, given by the `columnClass`.

Selection Methods

public void addColumnSelectionInterval(int index0, int index1)
public void addRowSelectionInterval(int index0, int index1)

Programmatically add an interval of rows or columns to the current selection. The appropriate `selectionAllowed` property must be set to `true` for this to work.

public void clearSelection()

Clears any selection that might exist on the table. Nothing happens if no selection exists.

public boolean isCellSelected(int row, int column)
public boolean isColumnSelected(int column)
public boolean isRowSelected(int row)

These methods return `true` if the specified `row`, `column`, or cell is currently part of any selection interval.

public void removeColumnSelectionInterval(int index0, int index1)
public void removeRowSelectionInterval(int index0, int index1)

Remove row or column intervals from the current selection.

public void selectAll()

Selects the entire table.

public void setColumnSelectionInterval(int index0, int index1)
public void setRowSelectionInterval(int index0, int index1)

Set the selection on the table to the given column or row interval.

Row and Column Methods

public void addColumn(TableColumn aColumn)
public void removeColumn(TableColumn aColumn)

These methods add and remove columns from the table. The `addColumn()` method appends the specified column to the end of the table.

public int columnAtPoint(Point point)
public int rowAtPoint(Point point)

Locate the column or row that matches an (x, y) coordinate given in `point`. While you can certainly use these methods for your own purposes, the `JTable` class uses them to determine the cell under the mouse when tooltips are active.

public int convertColumnIndexToModel(int viewColumnIndex)
public int convertColumnIndexToView(int modelColumnIndex)

Translate between the model index of a column and its view index. Recall that users can manually rearrange the columns displayed on the screen, so the view and model indices for a given column can be two distinct numbers. (The model indices should never change from what they are in your original `TableModel`.) To maintain a robust program, you should use these methods, rather than relying on your knowledge of the column model in place.

public void createDefaultColumnsFromModel()

Creates columns for the table based on the table model in place. It calls the `getColumnCount()` method from `TableModel` to find out how many columns exist. These columns are then added to the current column model.

public TableColumn getColumn(Object identifier)

> Given an identifier object (such as a `String` containing the column's name), this method returns the column whose identifier matches. If `identifier` is `null` or no column matches, an `IllegalArgumentException` will be thrown.

public Class getColumnClass(int column)

> Gets the `Class` type for `column` from the table model in place.

public String getColumnName(int column)

> Returns the name for the `column` by delegating the question to the table model.

public void moveColumn(int column, int targetColumn)

> Moves the column at the index given by `column` to the new index `target-Column` by delegating the request to the column model. Other columns are shifted as needed to make room for (and close the gap left by) the relocated column.

public void sizeColumnsToFit(boolean lastColumnOnly)

> Tries to resize the columns in the table to fit the allotted space. If `lastColumnOnly` is `true`, the last column is stretched (or shrunk) to fit the table's space, until any limits on the maximum or minimum width are reached. If that happens, the next to the last column is resized to its available limit, and then the next column is used and so on. If `lastColumnOnly` is `false`, the change in column widths is spread across all columns. You can force a particular column to bear the brunt of resizing by fixing the widths of all the columns to its right and calling `sizeColumnsToFit(true)`. This method is deprecated in JDK 1.2/Swing 1.1

public void sizeColumnsToFit(int resizingColumn)

> Resizes the columns in a table to fit the bounds allocated to the table based on the `autoResizeMode` property, while still working within the minimum and maximum sizes set on any given column. The various resize modes are associated with the constants you can see in Table 15-12.

Cell Methods

public boolean editCellAt(int row, int column)
public boolean editCellAt(int row, int column, EventObject e)
public boolean isCellEditable(int row, int column)

> Given that `isCellEditable()` returns `true` for a given `row` and `column`, `editCellAt()` prepares an editor and puts it on the table so that the user can edit the value. The second version of `editCellAt()` passes the event `e` to the cell editor, which may decide not to allow editing. The first version simply calls the second version with a `null` event.

public Rectangle getCellRect(int row, int column, boolean includeSpacing)

Returns a bounding rectangle for the cell given by row and column. If includeSpacing is true, the rectangle includes all of the padding around the cell (dictated by the intercellSpacing property). If it's false, half of the intercell spacing is included.

public Object getValueAt(int row, int column)
public void setValueAt(Object aValue, int row, int column)

These methods delegate to the table model to get and set the value for a particular cell. Note that the table model must support setValueAt() to make a cell truly editable.

Event Listener Support Methods

The following methods help the table's visual appearance remain consistent with the state of the data, column, and list selection models that support it. While you can call these manually, the table normally registers itself as a listener for all three categories of events (table model, table column model, and list selection), so these methods are called automatically.

public void tableChanged(TableModelEvent e)
public void columnAdded(TableColumnModelEvent e)
public void columnRemoved(TableColumnModelEvent e)
public void columnMoved(TableColumnModelEvent e)
public void columnMarginChanged(ChangeEvent e)

These methods keep the visual representation of the table intact when changes occur. For each method, the table stops any active editing and calls resizeAndRepaint().

public void columnSelectionChanged(ListSelectionEvent e)
public void valueChanged(ListSelectionEvent e)

These methods clean up the table after a selection has changed. Both methods calculate the bounding region of affected cells and repaint that area.

public void editingStopped(ChangeEvent e)
public void editingCanceled(ChangeEvent e)

Update the table by removing any active editor currently on the screen. The editingStopped() method reports the new value to the data model by retrieving the editor's current value and passing that through the setValueAt() method. The editingCanceled() method simply removes the editor without reporting any value changes.

Miscellaneous Methods

public String getToolTipText(MouseEvent event)

Returns the tooltip for the current cell's renderer, found by using the (x,y) location of the mouse in event. If the renderer doesn't supply a tooltip, the table's own tooltip(if defined) will be returned.

public void updateUI()

Overrides the JComponent updateUI() call to replace the table's UI with the version from the interface manager. As with other components, you can use this to refresh the table after the look-and-feel has changed.

public int getScrollableUnitIncrement(Rectangle visibleRect, int orientation, int direction)

This method from the Scrollable interface returns a value sufficient to view the entire row or column, depending on the value of orientation.

public int getScrollableBlockIncrement(Rectangle visibleRect, int orientation, int direction)

This method from the Scrollable interface returns a value (height or width of the viewport, depending on the orientation value) sufficient to view the entire next screen (based on the size of visibleRect).

The JTableHeader Class

The JTableHeader class is an extension of JComponent and serves as the header component for tables. The JTableHeader class not only dictates the basic color and font used for the header, but also the resizability and relocatability of the columns in the table. If you have an appropriate renderer for the header, you can also enable tooltips for the header. An example of custom renderers appears in "Editing and Rendering" later in this chapter.

Properties

The JTableHeader class has the properties listed in Table 15-13.

Table 15-13. JTableHeader Properties

Property	Data Type	get	is	set	bound	Default Value
UI	TableHeaderUI	•		•	•	from L&F
UIClassID*	String	•				"TableHeaderUI"
columnModel	TableColumn-Model	•		•		DefaultColumnModel()
accessibleContext*	Accessible-Context	•				JTableHeader.Accessible-JTableHeader()

See also properties from the JComponent class (Table 3-5).

Table 15-13. JTableHeader Properties (continued)

Property	Data Type	get	is	set	bound	Default Value
draggedColumn	TableColumn	•		•		null
draggedDistance	int	•		•		0
opaque*	boolean		•	•		true
reorderingAllowed	boolean	•		•		true
resizingAllowed	boolean	•		•		true
resizingColumn	TableColumn	•		•		null
table	JTable	•		•		null
updateTableInRealTime	boolean	•		•		true

See also properties from the JComponent class (Table 3-5).

The `columnModel` property is the `TableColumnModel` in place for the header. This is normally set through the constructor during the `JTable initializeLocalVars()` call. The `draggedColumn` and `resizingColumn` properties return the `TableColumn` object that the user has moved or resized. You can control whether the user is allowed to move or resize columns using the `reorderingAllowed` and `resizingAllowed` properties. The `updateTableInRealTime` property dictates whether or not the column being moved or resized is visually updated during the move or after. If this property is `false`, only the column headers move until the action is complete, and then the table is updated. The `table` property represents the companion table for the header.

Fields

protected TableColumnModel columnModel
protected transient TableColumn draggedColumn
protected transient int draggedDistance
protected boolean reorderingAllowed
protected boolean resizingAllowed
protected transient TableColumn resizingColumn
protected JTable table
protected boolean updateTableInRealTime

All of the fields of the `JTableHeader` class store the values for their respective properties.

Constructors

public JTableHeader()
public JTableHeader(TableColumnModel cm)

> Build new table headers. If cm is null or you use the first constructor, a DefaultTableColumnModel is built and used. While you can create a JTableHeader with only a table column model, as of the 1.1 release of Swing it must be paired with a JTable using the setTable() call before it can be made visible.

Column Methods

public int columnAtPoint(Point point)

> Returns the index for the column containing (or nearest to) point.

public void columnAdded(TableColumnModelEvent e)
public void columnMarginChanged(ChangeEvent e)
public void columnMoved(TableColumnModelEvent e)
public void columnRemoved(TableColumnModelEvent e)
public void columnSelectionChanged(ListSelectionEvent e)

> Implements the TableColumnModelListener interface and keeps the header in sync with the table, as columns are modified.

Miscellaneous Methods

protected TableColumnModel createDefaultColumnModel()

> Creates a DefaultColumnModel object for use with the no-argument constructor.

public Rectangle getHeaderRect(int columnIndex)

> Returns the bounding rectangle of the header for the column at columnIndex.

protected void initializeLocalVars()

> Initializes the properties in Table 15-13.

public void resizeAndRepaint()

> Forces redisplay of the table and header by calling revalidate() and repaint().

Tooltip and UI Methods

public String getToolTipText(MouseEvent event)

> Returns a tooltip string for a header cell. If the cell renderer is a JComponent, this method checks to see if the renderer has its own tooltip. If not, the tooltip

for the header is used. (That means if your header renderer doesn't supply tooltips, all of the header cells get the same tooltip.)

public void updateUI()

Overrides the JComponent updateUI() call to replace the header's UI with the version from the interface manager. As with other components, you can use this to refresh the header after the look-and-feel has changed.

Editing and Rendering

You can build your own editors and renderers for the cells in your table. By default, you get renderers and editors for Boolean types (JCheckBox for display and editing), ImageIcon types, Number types (right-justified JTextField for an editor), and Object types (JTextField for editing). However, you can specify a particular editor or renderer for a class type or a particular column, or even a particular cell.

The TableCellRenderer Interface

This interface provides access to a rendering component without defining what the component will do. This works because a renderer functions by rubber-stamping a component's image in a given location. The only method this interface defines initializes and returns just such a component:

public abstract Component getTableCellRendererComponent(JTable table, Object value, boolean isSelected, boolean hasFocus, int row, int column)

Takes a value, which could also be retrieved by getting the cell at row, column of table, and returns a component capable of drawing the value in a table cell (or anywhere, really). The resulting drawing can be affected by the selection state of the object and whether or not it currently has the keyboard focus.

The DefaultTableCellRenderer Class

The javax.swing.table package includes a default renderer that produces a JLabel to display text for each cell in the table. The JTable class uses this renderer to display Numbers, Icons, and Objects. JTable creates a new default renderer and then aligns it correctly and attaches an appropriate icon, depending on the type of data. Object objects are shown as regular labels, Number objects are shown right-aligned, and Icons are shown using centered labels. Boolean values do not use DefaultTableCellRenderer; instead, they use a private renderer class that extends JCheckBox.

Properties

The DefaultTableCellRenderer modifies three properties of the JLabel class as shown in Table 15-14. The color values are used as the "unselected" foreground and background colors for text. You might recall that the selected foreground and background colors are governed by the JTable class. If you set either of these properties to null, the foreground and background colors from JTable will be used.

Table 15-14. DefaultTableCellRenderer Properties

Property	Data Type	get	is	set	bound	Default Value
background	Color	•		•		null
foreground	Color	•		•		null
opaque	boolean		•	•		true

See also properties from the JComponent class (Table 3-5).

Protected Constants

protected static Border noFocusBorder
> By default, this is an empty border with a few pixels of padding around it. It is used when rendering any cells whose hasFocus value is false in the getTableCellRendererComponent() method.

Constructors

public DefaultTableCellRenderer()
> Creates the default cell renderer.

Inner Classes

public static class DefaultTableCellRender.UIResource extends DefaultTableCellRenderer
> *implements UIResource*
> This inner class can be used to create a UIResource instance of the DefaultTableCellRenderer to distinguish it from a renderer set specifically by the developer. See Chapter 26, *Look & Feel*, for more details.

Renderer Methods

public Component getTableCellRendererComponent(JTable table, Object value,
> *boolean isSelected, boolean hasFocus, int row, int column)*
> Returns a reference to this component (which is a subclass of JLabel) after setting the foreground and background colors according to isSelected,

placing a border based on `hasFocus`, and calling `setValue(value)` to register the appropriate text to display.

protected void setValue(Object value)

Uses `value.toString()` as the text to display in the label.

public void updateUI()

Overrides the `JComponent.updateUI()` method to replace the label's UI with the version from the interface manager.

Figure 15-7 shows a table containing audio tracks in a mixer format, using the default renderer. We have some track information, such as the track name, its start and stop times, and two volumes (left and right channels, both using integer values from 0 to 100) to control.

Track	Start	Stop	Left Volume	Right Volume
Bass	0:00:000	1:00:000	56	56
Strings	0:00:000	0:52:010	72	52
Brass	0:08:000	1:00:000	99	0
Wind	0:08:000	1:00:000	0	99

Figure 15-7. A standard table with cells drawn by the DefaultTableCellRenderer

We'd really like to show our volume entries as scrollbars. The scrollbars give us a better indication of the volumes relative to each other. Figure 15-8 shows the application after we have attached a custom renderer for the volumes.

Track	Start	Stop	Left Volume	Right Volume
Bass	0:00:000	1:00:000		
Strings	0:00:000	0:52:010		
Brass	0:08:000	1:00:000		
Wind	0:08:000	1:00:000		

Figure 15-8. A standard table with the Volume cells drawn by VolumeRenderer

The code for this example involves two new pieces and a table model for our audio columns. First, we must create a new renderer by implementing the `Table-CellRenderer` interface ourselves. Then, in the application code, we have to attach our new renderer to our volume columns. The model code looks similar to the models we have built before. The only real difference is that we now have two columns using a custom `Volume` class. Following is the `Volume` class that encodes an integer. The interesting thing about this class is the `setVolume()` method, which can parse a `String`, a `Number`, or another `Volume` object.

```
// Volume.java
// A simple data structure for track volumes on a mixer.
//
public class Volume {
  private int volume;

  public Volume(int v) { setVolume(v); }
  public Volume() { this(50); }

  public void setVolume(int v) { volume = (v < 0 ? 0 : v > 100 ? 100 : v); }
  public void setVolume(Object v) {
    if (v instanceof String) {
      setVolume(Integer.parseInt((String)v));
    }
    else if (v instanceof Number) {
      setVolume(((Number)v).intValue());
    }
    else if (v instanceof Volume) {
      setVolume(((Volume)v).getVolume());
    }
  }

  public int getVolume() { return volume; }

  public String toString() { return "" + volume; }
}
```

And here's the model code. We store a simple `Object[][]` structure for our data, a separate array for the column headers, and one for the column class types. We'll make every cell editable by always returning `true` in the `isCellEditable()` method. The `setValue()` method checks to see if we're setting one of the volumes, and if so, we don't simply stick the new object into the array. Rather, we set the volume value for the current object that's in the data array. Then, if someone builds an editor that returns a `String` or a `Number` rather than a `Volume` object, we still keep our `Volume` object intact.

```
// MixerModel.java
// An audio mixer table data model. This model contains the following columns:
//   + Track name (String)
//   + Track start time (String ?)
//   + Track stop time (String?)
//   + Left channel volume (Bounded range, 0 . . 100)
//   + Right channel volume (Bounded range, 0 . . 100)
//
import javax.swing.table.*;

public class MixerModel extends AbstractTableModel {
```

```
String headers[] = {"Track", "Start", "Stop",
                    "Left Volume", "Right Volume"};
Class columnClasses[] = {String.class, String.class, String.class,
                         Volume.class, Volume.class};
Object  data[][] = {
  {"Bass", "0:00:000", "1:00:000", new Volume(56), new Volume(56)},
  {"Strings", "0:00:000", "0:52:010", new Volume(72), new Volume(52)},
  {"Brass", "0:08:000", "1:00:000", new Volume(99), new Volume(0)},
  {"Wind", "0:08:000", "1:00:000", new Volume(0), new Volume(99)},
};

public int getRowCount() { return data.length; }
public int getColumnCount() { return data[0].length; }
public Class getColumnClass(int c) { return columnClasses[c]; }
public String getColumnName(int c) { return headers[c]; }
public boolean isCellEditable(int r, int c) { return true; }
public Object getValueAt(int r, int c) { return data[r][c]; }

// Ok, do something extra here so that if we get a String object back (from a
// text field editor) we can still store that as a valid Volume object.  If
// it's just a string, then stick it directly into our data array.
public void setValueAt(Object value, int r, int c) {
  if (c >= 3) { ((Volume)data[r][c]).setVolume(value);}
  else {data[r][c] = value;}
}

// A quick debugging utility to dump out the contents of our data structure
// (regardless of what shows on the screen)
public void dump() {
  for (int i = 0; i < data.length; i++) {
    System.out.print("|");
    for (int j = 0; j < data[0].length; j++) {
      System.out.print(data[i][j] + "|");
    }
    System.out.println();
  }
}
}
```

Here's the application that brings up the window and table. Notice how we attach a specific renderer to the Volume class type without specifying which columns contain that data type, using the setDefaultRenderer() method. The table uses the results of the TableModel's getColumnClass() call to decide class of a given column, and then uses getDefaultRenderer() to get an appropriate renderer for that class.

```
// MixerTest.java
// A test of the JTable class using default table models and a convenience
// constructor.
//
import java.awt.*;
import javax.swing.*;

public class MixerTest extends JFrame {

  public MixerTest() {
    super("Customer Editor Test");
    setSize(600,160);
    addWindowListener(new BasicWindowMonitor());

    MixerModel test = new MixerModel();
    test.dump();
    JTable jt = new JTable(test);
    jt.setDefaultRenderer(Volume.class, new VolumeRenderer());
    JScrollPane jsp = new JScrollPane(jt);
    jsp.setColumnHeaderView(jt.getTableHeader());
    getContentPane().add(jsp, BorderLayout.CENTER);
  }

  public static void main(String args[]) {
    MixerTest mt = new MixerTest();
    mt.setVisible(true);
  }
}
```

So now we need to build our renderer. As you saw with the `DefaultTableCell-Renderer` class, to create a new renderer we often just extend the component that will do the rendering. Then we can use the `getTableCellRendererCompo-nent()` method to initialize the component, and return a reference to that same component. That is exactly what we do with this rather simple `VolumeRenderer` class. We extend the `JScrollBar` class, and in the `getTableCellRendererCom-ponent()` method, we set the position of the scrollbar's slider and then return the scrollbar. This doesn't allow us to edit the volume values, but at least we get a better visual representation.

```
// VolumeRenderer.java
// A slider renderer for volume values in a table.
//
import java.awt.Component;
import javax.swing.*;
import javax.swing.table.*;

public class VolumeRenderer extends JScrollBar implements TableCellRenderer {
```

```
public VolumeRenderer() {
  super(JScrollBar.HORIZONTAL);
}


public Component getTableCellRendererComponent(JTable table, Object value,
                                               boolean isSelected,
                                               boolean hasFocus,
                                               int row, int column) {
    if (value == null) {
      return this;
    }
    if (value instanceof Volume) {
      setValue(((Volume)value).getVolume());
    }
    else {
      setValue(0);
    }
    return this;
  }
}
```

The TableCellEditor Interface

Of course, the next obvious question is how to make the scrollbars usable for editing the volume values. To do that, we can write our own VolumeEditor class that implements the TableCellEditor interface.

public Component getTableCellEditorComponent(JTable table, Object value, boolean isSelected, int row, int column)

Returns a component capable of editing a value. This method should initialize the editor (to reflect the value and isSelected arguments) and may also affect the table. You could dull the color of the rest of the row or table while editing one cell, for example.

While this is the only method present in the TableCellEditor interface, this interface extends CellEditor (discussed in Chapter 27, *Swing Utilities*), so you need to supply the same methods.

The following code implements a TableCellEditor for Volume objects from scratch. The fireEditingCanceled() method shows how to cancel an editing session, and fireEditingStopped() shows how to end a session and update the table. In both cases, it's a matter of firing a ChangeEvent identifying the editor to the appropriate listeners. When editing is cancelled, you also have to restore the cell's original value.

```java
// VolumeEditor.java
// A slider Editor for volume values in a table.
//
import java.awt.Component;
import java.util.*;
import javax.swing.*;
import javax.swing.table.*;
import javax.swing.event.*;

public class VolumeEditor extends JScrollBar implements TableCellEditor {

  protected transient Vector listeners;
  protected transient int originalValue;

  public VolumeEditor() {
    super(JScrollBar.HORIZONTAL);
    listeners = new Vector();
  }

  public Component getTableCellEditorComponent(JTable table,Object value,
                                               boolean isSelected,
                                               int row,int column) {
    if (value == null) {
      return this;
    }
    if (value instanceof Volume) {
      setValue(((Volume)value).getVolume());
    }
    else {
      setValue(0);
    }
    table.setRowSelectionInterval(row, row);
    table.setColumnSelectionInterval(column, column);
    originalValue = getValue();
    return this;
  }

  // CellEditor methods
  public void cancelCellEditing() {fireEditingCanceled();}

  public Object getCellEditorValue() {return new Integer(getValue());}

  public boolean isCellEditable(EventObject eo) {return true;}

  public boolean shouldSelectCell(EventObject eo) {
    return true;
  }
```

```
public boolean stopCellEditing() {
  fireEditingStopped();
  return true;
}

public void addCellEditorListener(CellEditorListener cel) {
  listeners.addElement(cel);
}

public void removeCellEditorListener(CellEditorListener cel) {
  listeners.removeElement(cel);
}

protected void fireEditingCanceled() {
  setValue(originalValue);
  ChangeEvent ce = new ChangeEvent(this);
  for (int i = listeners.size(); i >= 0; i--) {
    ((CellEditorListener)listeners.elementAt(i)).editingCanceled(ce);
  }
}

protected void fireEditingStopped() {
  ChangeEvent ce = new ChangeEvent(this);
  for (int i = listeners.size() - 1; i >= 0; i--) {
    ((CellEditorListener)listeners.elementAt(i)).editingStopped(ce);
  }
}
}
```

You can make this the active editor for volume objects using the setDefaultEditor() method:

```
JTable table = new JTable(new MixerModel());
table.setDefaultEditor(Volume.class, new VolumeEditor());
```

Once it's active, you can use the scrollbars to edit the volumes. Because we always return true when asked isCellEditable(), the scrollbars are always active. If you want, you can make them a muted color until the user double-clicks on one, and then make that scrollbar active. When the user stops editing by selecting another entry, the active scrollbar should return to its muted color. The Default-CellEditor does a lot of the work for you for free.

Selecting Table Entries

All this, and all we can do is render and edit data in a table. "What about selecting data?" you ask. Yes, we can do that, too. And, as you might expect, the ListSe-lectionModel (discussed in Chapter 7, *Lists and Combo Boxes*) drives us through these selections. Unlike most of the other components, however, the two-dimensional JTable has two selection models, one for the rows and one for the columns.

Figure 15-9 shows an application that allows you to turn on and off the various selections allowed on a table (cell, row, and column). As you select different rows and columns, two status labels show you the indices of the selected items.

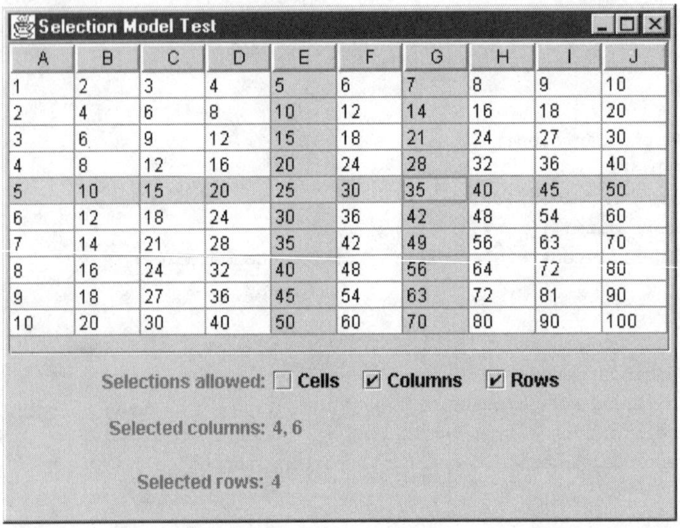

Figure 15-9. A table that lets you select rows, columns, or cells

Let's look at the code for this example. Most of the work is getting the interface you see running. Once that's done, we attach our two reporting labels as listeners to the row selection and column selection models. The interesting part of the code is the ListSelectionListener, written as an inner class. This class tracks any ListSelectionModel, and every time it changes, updates a label with the currently selected indices. (Those indices are retrieved using the getSelected-Indices() method we wrote ourselves.) Since we rely on only the list selection model, we can use the same event handler for both the row and the column selections.

```java
// SelectionExample.java
// A test of the JTable class using default table models and a convenience
// constructor.
//
import java.awt.*;
import java.awt.event.*;
import javax.swing.*;
import javax.swing.event.*;
import javax.swing.table.*;
```

```java
public class SelectionExample extends JFrame {

  public SelectionExample() {
    super("Selection Model Test");
    setSize(450, 350);
    addWindowListener(new BasicWindowMonitor());

    TableModel tm = new AbstractTableModel() {
      // We'll create a simple multiplication table to serve as a noneditable
      // table with several rows and columns
      public int getRowCount() { return 10; }
      public int getColumnCount() { return 10; }
      public Object getValueAt(int r, int c) { return "" + (r+1)*(c+1); }
    };

    final JTable jt = new JTable(tm);

    JScrollPane jsp = new JScrollPane(jt);
    getContentPane().add(jsp, BorderLayout.CENTER);

    // Now set up our selection controls
    JPanel controlPanel, buttonPanel, columnPanel, rowPanel;

    buttonPanel = new JPanel();
    JCheckBox cellBox, columnBox, rowBox;
    cellBox = new JCheckBox("Cells", jt.getCellSelectionEnabled());
    cellBox.addActionListener(new ActionListener() {
      public void actionPerformed(ActionEvent ae) {
        jt.setCellSelectionEnabled(!jt.getCellSelectionEnabled());
      }
    } );

    columnBox = new JCheckBox("Columns", jt.getColumnSelectionAllowed());
    columnBox.addActionListener(new ActionListener() {
      public void actionPerformed(ActionEvent ae) {
        jt.setColumnSelectionAllowed(!jt.getColumnSelectionAllowed());
      }
    } );

    rowBox = new JCheckBox("Rows", jt.getRowSelectionAllowed());
    rowBox.addActionListener(new ActionListener() {
      public void actionPerformed(ActionEvent ae) {
        jt.setRowSelectionAllowed(!jt.getRowSelectionAllowed());
      }
    } );

    buttonPanel.add(new JLabel("Selections allowed:"));
    buttonPanel.add(cellBox);
    buttonPanel.add(columnBox);
    buttonPanel.add(rowBox);
```

```
    columnPanel = new JPanel();
    ListSelectionModel csm = jt.getColumnModel().getSelectionModel();
    JLabel columnCounter = new JLabel("(Selected Column Indices Go Here)");
    csm.addListSelectionListener(new SelectionDebugger(columnCounter,
                                                       csm));
    columnPanel.add(new JLabel("Selected columns:"));
    columnPanel.add(columnCounter);

    rowPanel = new JPanel();
    ListSelectionModel rsm = jt.getSelectionModel();
    JLabel rowCounter = new JLabel("(Selected Row Indices Go Here)");
    rsm.addListSelectionListener(new SelectionDebugger(rowCounter, rsm));
    rowPanel.add(new JLabel("Selected rows:"));
    rowPanel.add(rowCounter);

    controlPanel = new JPanel(new GridLayout(0, 1));
    controlPanel.add(buttonPanel);
    controlPanel.add(columnPanel);
    controlPanel.add(rowPanel);

    getContentPane().add(controlPanel, BorderLayout.SOUTH);
  }

  public static void main(String args[]) {
    SelectionExample se = new SelectionExample();
    se.setVisible(true);
  }

  public class SelectionDebugger implements ListSelectionListener {
    JLabel debugger;
    ListSelectionModel model;

    public SelectionDebugger(JLabel target, ListSelectionModel lsm) {
      debugger = target;
      model = lsm;
    }
    public void valueChanged(ListSelectionEvent lse) {
      if (!lse.getValueIsAdjusting()) {
        // skip all the intermediate events . . .
        StringBuffer buf = new StringBuffer();
        int[] selection = getSelectedIndices(model.getMinSelectionIndex(),
                                             model.getMaxSelectionIndex());
        if (selection.length == 0) {
          buf.append("none");
        }
        else {
          for (int i = 0; i < selection.length -1; i++) {
            buf.append(selection[i]);
            buf.append(", ");
          }
```

```
            buf.append(selection[selection.length - 1]);
        }
        debugger.setText(buf.toString());
    }
}


// This method returns an array of selected indices. It's guaranteed to
// return a nonnull value.
protected int[] getSelectedIndices(int start, int stop) {
    if ((start == -1) || (stop == -1)) {
        // no selection, so return an empty array
        return new int[0];
    }

    int guesses[] = new int[stop - start + 1];
    int index = 0;
    // manually walk through these . . .
    for (int i = start; i <= stop; i++) {
        if (model.isSelectedIndex(i)) {
            guesses[index++] = i;
        }
    }

    // ok, pare down the guess array to the real thing
    int realthing[] = new int[index];
    System.arraycopy(guesses, 0, realthing, 0, index);
    return realthing;
    }
  }
}
```

Now, it is definitely worth pointing out that for this specific application we could have retrieved the array of selected row indices from the JTable object and the array of selected column indices from the table's column model. Those classes have methods similar to our getSelectedIndices() method. However, that would have required two separate handlers. But quite honestly, outside this example, two separate handlers might be easier to write and maintain.

There are many other things you can do with JTable and its various supporting models. While we don't have time or space to present all of them, we will take a look at a few more interesting examples of JTable features in Chapter 16, *Advanced Table Examples.*

16

Advanced Table Examples

In this chapter, we're going to take a different approach. Tables are extremely flexible, useful gadgets. Here, we're going to show you how to put tables to work in more advanced situations. Most of these require working on the TableModel itself or the TableColumnModel. But once you know what you're doing, subclassing these models is fairly easy and gives you a lot of flexibility.

We're going to look at three particular examples:

- A scrollable table with row headers. Remember that a JTable understands column headers, but doesn't have any concept of a row header. Also, remember that a JScrollPane understands both column and row headers. In this example, we'll show you how to add row headers to a JTable and make them work properly within a JScrollPane.

- A table that has an extremely large numbers of rows. Scrolling stops working well when you have more than a few hundred rows to work with. We'll build a table with 10,000 rows, let you page up and down to select a range of 100 rows within the table, and then scroll back and forth within that more limited range.

- A TableChart component that builds pie charts based on the TableModel class used by JTable. In this example, the JTable is almost superfluous, although it provides a convenient way to edit the data in the pie chart. The real point is that the TableModel is a powerful abstraction that can be put to use even when there's no table around.

A Table with Row Headers

As we promised, this is a table with headers for both rows and columns. The JTable handles the column headers itself; we need to add machinery for the rows.

Figure 16-1 shows what the resulting table looks like. It shows column labels, plus two data columns from a larger table. Scrolling works the way you would expect. When you scroll vertically, the row headers scroll with the data. You can scroll horizontally to see other data columns, but the row headers always remain on the screen.

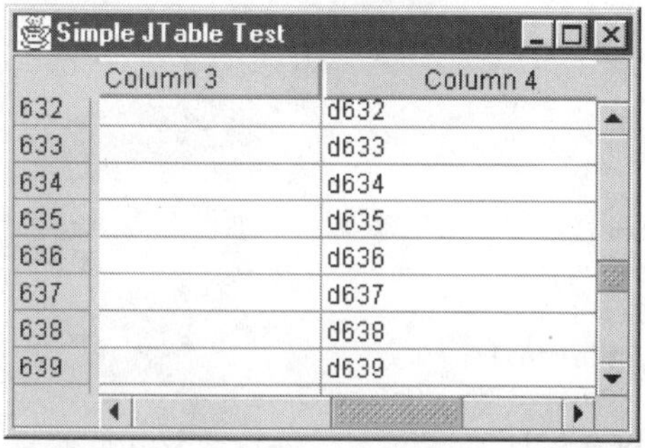

Figure 16-1. A table with row and column headers

The trick is that we really have two closely coordinated tables: one for the row headers (a table with only one column) and one for the data columns. There is a single `TableModel`, but separate `TableColumnModels` for the two parts of the larger table. In the figure, the gray column on the left is the row header; it's really column 0 of the data model.

To understand what's going on, it helps to remember how a Swing table models data. The `TableModel` itself keeps track of all the data for the table, i.e., the values that are used to fill in the cells. There's no reason why we can't have two tables that share the same table model—that's one of the advantages of the model-view-controller architecture. Likewise, there's no reason why we can't have data in the table model that isn't displayed; the table model can keep track of a logical table that is much larger than the table we actually put on the screen. This will be particularly important in the next example, but it's also important here. The table that implements the row headers uses the first column of the data model and ignores everything else; the table that displays the data ignores the first column.

The `TableColumnModel` keeps track of the columns and is called whenever we add, delete, or move a column. One way to implement tables that use or ignore parts of our data is to build table column models that do what we want: only add a particular column (or group of columns) to the table. That's the approach we've chosen. Once we have our models, it is relatively simple to create two `JTables` that use the same `TableModel`, but different `TableColumnModels`. Each table displays only the columns that its column model allows. When we put the tables next to each other, one will serve as the row header, and the other will display the body. Following is the code for our not-so-simple table.

```java
// SimpleTable2.java
//
import java.awt.*;
import java.awt.event.*;
import javax.swing.*;
import javax.swing.table.*;

public class SimpleTable2 extends JFrame {

  public SimpleTable2() {
    super("Simple JTable Test");
    setSize(300, 200);
    addWindowListener(new BasicWindowMonitor());

    TableModel tm = new AbstractTableModel() {
      String data[] = {"", "a", "b", "c", "d", "e"};
      String headers[] = {"", "Column 1", "Column 2", "Column 3",
                          "Column 4", "Column 5"};
      public int getColumnCount() { return data.length; }
      public int getRowCount() { return 1000; }
      public String getColumnName(int col) { return headers[col]; }

      // Synthesize some entries using the data values & the row #
      public Object getValueAt(int row, int col) {
        return data[col] + row;
      }
    };

    // Create a column model for the main table. This model ignores the first
    // column added, and sets a minimum width of 150 pixels for all others.
    TableColumnModel cm = new DefaultTableColumnModel() {
      boolean first = true;
      public void addColumn(TableColumn tc) {
        // Drop the first column . . . that'll be the row header
        if (first) { first = false; return; }
        tc.setMinWidth(150);
        super.addColumn(tc);
      }
    };

    // Create a column model that will serve as our row header table. This
    // model picks a maximum width and only stores the first column.
    TableColumnModel rowHeaderModel = new DefaultTableColumnModel() {
      boolean first = true;
      public void addColumn(TableColumn tc) {
        if (first) {
          tc.setMaxWidth(35);
          super.addColumn(tc);
          first = false;
        }
```

```
        // Drop the rest of the columns . . . this is the header column only
      }
    };

    JTable jt = new JTable(tm, cm);

    // Set up the header column and get it hooked up to everything
    JTable headerColumn = new JTable(tm, rowHeaderModel);
    jt.createDefaultColumnsFromModel();
    headerColumn.createDefaultColumnsFromModel();

    // Make sure that selections between the main table and the header stay
    // in sync (by sharing the same model)
    jt.setSelectionModel(headerColumn.getSelectionModel());

    // Make the header column look pretty
    headerColumn.setMaximumSize(new Dimension(40, 10000));
    headerColumn.setBackground(Color.lightGray);
    // If you want to make the header selection invisible, uncomment this
    // next line:
    // headerColumn.setSelectionBackground(Color.lightGray);
    headerColumn.setColumnSelectionAllowed(false);
    headerColumn.setCellSelectionEnabled(false);

    // Put it in a viewport that we can control a bit
    JViewport jv = new JViewport();
    jv.setView(headerColumn);
    jv.setPreferredSize(headerColumn.getMaximumSize());

    // Without shutting off autoResizeMode, our tables won't scroll
    // correctly (horizontally, anyway)
    jt.setAutoResizeMode(JTable.AUTO_RESIZE_OFF);
    headerColumn.setAutoResizeMode(JTable.AUTO_RESIZE_OFF);

    // We have to manually attach the row headers, but after that, the scroll
    // pane keeps them in sync
    JScrollPane jsp = new JscrollPane(jt);
    jsp.setRowHeader(jv);

    getContentPane().add(jsp, BorderLayout.CENTER);
  }

  public static void main(String args[]) {
    SimpleTable2 st = new SimpleTable2();
    st.setVisible(true);
  }
}
```

The various models we use—our subclasses of `AbstractTableModel` and `DefaultTableColumnModel`—are anonymous inner classes. The new table model doesn't do anything really interesting; it just keeps track of the raw data. There's an array of column headers; the data itself is computed in the `getValueAt()` method. Of course, in a real example, you'd have some way of looking up real data.

Our `TableColumnModels` are where the magic happens. The `addColumn()` method, which they override, is called whenever a column is added to a table. The first of our two models, `cm`, keeps track of the body of the table. The first time it is called, it returns without doing anything—effectively ignoring the first column in the table, which is the column of row headers. (It does set the local variable `first` to `false`, indicating that it's already processed the headers.) For subsequent columns, `addColumn()` behaves the way you would expect: it sets a minimum column width, then calls the method in the superclass to insert the column in the table.

The other table column model, `rowHeaderModel`, overrides `addColumn()` to do the opposite: it inserts the first column (the row header) into the table, and ignores all the other columns. These classes make the assumption that column 0 (the row headers) is added to the table first, and never added again. As long as the table isn't editable, that assumption will be valid. If the table were editable, we would have to add some logic to make sure we always know what column we're working on.

The rest of the code is almost self-explanatory. We create two `JTable` objects, `jt` (for the body) and `headerColumn` (for the row headers). We start by telling our tables to build their columns, since we specified our own column models. Our tables use the same `TableModel`, and the appropriate `TableColumnModel`. To make sure that row selection for the two tables is always in sync, we give them both the same `SelectionModel`. We give `headerColumn` a different color and disable column and cell selection. The only thing left is to arrange the display. We create a separate `JViewport` to display the row headers and put the header column in it. We set the viewport's width to match the header column's size. Then we disable autoresize mode for both tables (`jt` and `headerColumn`); this is necessary to make the scrollbars work appropriately. (Things get confusing if a table inside a scroll pane tries to resize itself.) Finally, we create a `JScrollPane` from `jt`. To get the row headers into the scroll pane, we add the viewport, which already contains `headerColumn` to the `JScrollPane` by calling `setRowHeader()`. Then we just slap the `JScrollPane`, which now contains both tables, into our `JFrame`'s content pane, and we're done.

Large Tables with Paging

Working conveniently with very large tables can be a pain. Scrolling up and down is fine as long as the table is only a few hundred lines long, but when it gets larger, a tiny movement in the scrollbar can change your position by a few thousand rows. One way to solve this is by combining paging with scrolling. We'll create a table with 10,000 rows (large enough to make scrolling through the entire table a real hassle) and add buttons to page up and down 100 rows at a time. Within any group of 100 rows, you can use the scrollbar as usual to move around. Figure 16-2 shows the result.

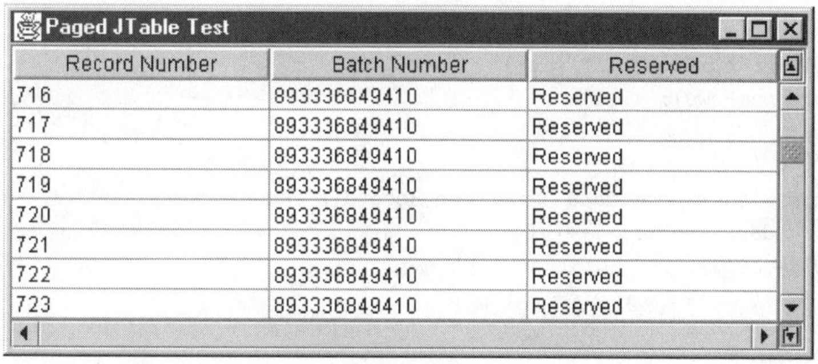

Figure 16-2. A paging (and scrolling) table

In this example, we're using a simple trick. There are really two tables to worry about: a logical table that contains all 10,000 rows, which might represent records that were read from a database, and the physical table that's instantiated as a JTable object and displayed on the screen. To do this trick, we implement a new table model, PagingModel, which is a subclass of AbstractTableModel. This table model keeps track of the data for the entire logical table: all 10,000 rows. However, when a JTable asks it for data to display, it pretends it only knows about the 100 rows that should be on the screen at this time. It's actually quite simple. (And we don't even need to worry about any column models; the default column model is adequate.)

Here's the PagingModel code used to track the 10,000 records:

```
// PagingModel.java
// A larger table model that performs "paging" of its data.  This model
// reports a small number of rows (like 100 or so) as a "page" of data.  You
// can switch pages to view all of the rows as needed using the pageDown()
// and pageUp() methods.  Presumably, access to the other pages of data is
// dictated by other GUI elements such as up/down buttons, or maybe a text
// field that allows you to enter the page number you want to display.
//
import javax.swing.table.*;
```

```java
import javax.swing.*;
import java.awt.event.*;
import java.awt.*;

public class PagingModel extends AbstractTableModel {

  protected int pageSize;
  protected int pageOffset;
  protected Record[] data;

  public PagingModel() {
    this(10000, 100);
  }

  public PagingModel(int numRows, int size) {
    data = new Record[numRows];
    pageSize = size;

    // fill our table with random data (from the Record() constructor)
    for (int i=0; i < data.length; i++) {
      data[i] = new Record();
    }
  }

  // Return values appropriate for the visible table part
  public int getRowCount() { return pageSize; }
  public int getColumnCount() { return Record.getColumnCount(); }

  // Only works on the visible part of the table
  public Object getValueAt(int row, int col) {
    int realRow = row + (pageOffset * pageSize);
    return data[realRow].getValueAt(col);
  }

  public String getColumnName(int col) {
    return Record.getColumnName(col);
  }

  // use this method to figure out which page you are on
  public int getPageOffset() { return pageOffset; }

  public int getPageCount() {
    return (int)Math.ceil((double)data.length / pageSize);
  }

  // use this method if you want to know how big the real table is . . . we
  // could also write "getRealValueAt()" if we needed.
  public int getRealRowCount() {
    return data.length;
```

```
}

public int getPageSize() { return pageSize; }
public void setPageSize(int s) {
  if (s == pageSize) { return; }
  int oldPageSize = pageSize;
  pageSize = s;
  if (pageSize < oldPageSize) {
    fireTableRowsDeleted(pageSize, oldPageSize - 1);
  }
  else {
    fireTableRowsInserted(oldPageSize, pageSize - 1);
  }
}

// update the page offset and fire a data changed (all rows)
public void pageDown() {
  if (pageOffset < getPageCount() - 1) {
    pageOffset++;
    fireTableDataChanged();
  }
}

// update the page offset and fire a data changed (all rows)
public void pageUp() {
  if (pageOffset > 0) {
    pageOffset--;
    fireTableDataChanged();
  }
}

// we'll provide our own version of a scroll pane that includes
// the page up and page down buttons by default.
public static JScrollPane createPagingScrollPaneForTable(JTable jt) {
  JScrollPane jsp = new JScrollPane(jt);

  // Don't choke if this is called on a regular table . . .
  if (! (jt.getModel() instanceof PagingModel)) {
    return jsp;
  }

  // Okay, go ahead and build the real scroll pane
  final PagingModel model = (PagingModel)jt.getModel();
  final JButton upButton = new JButton(new ArrowIcon(ArrowIcon.UP));
  upButton.setEnabled(false);  // starts off at 0, so can't go up
  final JButton downButton = new JButton(new ArrowIcon(ArrowIcon.DOWN));

  upButton.addActionListener(new ActionListener() {
    public void actionPerformed(ActionEvent ae) {
```

```
      model.pageUp();

      // If we hit the top of the data, disable the up button
      if (model.getPageOffset() == 0) {
        upButton.setEnabled(false);
      }
      downButton.setEnabled(true);
    }
  } );

  downButton.addActionListener(new ActionListener() {
    public void actionPerformed(ActionEvent ae) {
      model.pageDown();

      // If we hit the bottom of the data, disable the down button
      if (model.getPageOffset() == (model.getPageCount() - 1)) {
        downButton.setEnabled(false);
      }
      upButton.setEnabled(true);
    }
  } );

  // Turn on the scrollbars; otherwise we won't get our corners
  jsp.setVerticalScrollBarPolicy
      (ScrollPaneConstants.VERTICAL_SCROLLBAR_ALWAYS);
  jsp.setHorizontalScrollBarPolicy
      (ScrollPaneConstants.HORIZONTAL_SCROLLBAR_ALWAYS);

  // add in the corners (page up/down)
  jsp.setCorner(ScrollPaneConstants.UPPER_RIGHT_CORNER, upButton);
  jsp.setCorner(ScrollPaneConstants.LOWER_RIGHT_CORNER, downButton);

  return jsp;
  }
}
```

The PagingModel constructor fills an array with all our data. (The Record object does something simple to generate meaningless data; in real life, it would probably use JDBC to read data from a database.) Most of the methods in the PagingModel are fairly self-explanatory. The interesting ones have something to do with the table's rows. getRowCount() isn't computationally complex, but is typical of what we'll see: instead of returning the number of rows of data, it returns pageSize, which is the number of rows we want to display. getValueAt() is only slightly more complex: it translates the desired row from the physical table into the actual row within the much larger logical table, and returns the appropriate data. (We don't need to do anything to the column, but we would if we were making a table that paged in two directions.) We've added some convenience methods, `getPageOffset()`, `getPageCount()`, and `getRealRowCount()`, to provide information about the table's actual size, and the portion we're looking at.

The `pageDown()` and `pageUp()` methods are a bit more interesting. These get called when the user clicks on either of the paging buttons that we'll display with the table. When the user pages, these methods increment or decrement the model's `pageOffset` variable, which records the current offset into the table. This effectively means that the data in the physical table (the table we display) has changed, although nothing has changed in the logical table at all. Because the physical table has changed, we call `fireTableDataChanged()`, which fires a `TableModelEvent` that tells the `JTable` to reload all the data. When it's created, the `JTable` will register itself as a listener for table model events.

Our table doesn't let you change the page increment, but that would be a useful feature. Therefore, we provide a `setPageSize()` method that you could use to alter the page size. This method is interesting because, again, changing the page size does nothing to the logical table, but it effectively adds or deletes rows from the physical `JTable` on the screen. Therefore, this method figures out whether we're adding or deleting rows; which rows are added or deleted, and then calls `fireTableRowsInserted()` or `fireTableRowsDeleted()` accordingly.

The last important task that our table model has to perform is to build a `JScroll-Pane` that knows how to work properly with our table. This is implemented in the `createPagingScrollPaneForTable()` method. This method starts by getting a `JScrollPane` and then modifying it to work appropriately. The modifications are really quite simple. We create a pair of buttons to control the paging (the icons for the buttons are implemented by the rather simple `ArrowIcon` class, which we haven't shown); we wire the buttons to the `pageUp()` and `pageDown()` methods of our table model; and we include some logic to disable buttons when we reach the top or bottom of the table. Finally, we turn on the scroll pane's scrollbars, and add the buttons in the upper- and lower-right corners. Remember that if the scrollbars aren't enabled, there won't be any place to put the buttons.

Our table is currently static: it displays data, but doesn't have any means for updating the data. How would you implement table updates? We'll leave this as a thought experiment. There's some simple bookkeeping that you'd have to do, but the most interesting part would be implementing `setValueAt()` in the `Paging-Model` class. Like `getValueAt()`, it would have to translate between logical rows in the data and physical rows in the `JTable`. It would have to call `fireTable-DataChanged()` to generate a table model event and cause the `JTable` to update the display. But, you would also need a way to set the value of the cells that are not visible. For real applications, you might consider writing your own `getRealVal-ueAt()` and `setRealValueAt()` that do not map incoming row values.

Here's the very simple `Record` class; it just provides column names and generates meaningless data, one record (row) at a time:

```
// Record.java
// A simple data structure for use with the PagingModel demo.
//
public class Record {
    static String headers[] = { "Record Number", "Batch Number", "Reserved" };
    static int counter;
    String[] data;

    public Record() {
        data = new String[] { "" + (counter++), "" + System.currentTimeMillis(),
                "Reserved" };
    }

    public String getValueAt(int i) { return data[i]; }

    public static String getColumnName(int i) { return headers[i]; }
    public static int getColumnCount() { return headers.length; }
}
```

And here's the application that brings up the `JTable` using our paging model:

```
// PagingTester.java
//
import java.awt.*;
import java.awt.event.*;
import javax.swing.*;
import javax.swing.table.*;

public class PagingTester extends JFrame {

    public PagingTester() {
        super("Paged JTable Test");
        setSize(300, 200);
        addWindowListener(new BasicWindowMonitor());

        PagingModel pm = new PagingModel();
        JTable jt = new JTable(pm);

        // Use our own custom scrollpane.
        JScrollPane jsp = PagingModel.createPagingScrollPaneForTable(jt);
        getContentPane().add(jsp, BorderLayout.CENTER);
    }

    public static void main(String args[]) {
        PagingTester pt = new PagingTester();
        pt.setVisible(true);
    }
}
```

We just create an instance of our `PagingModel` to hold the data and construct a `JTable` with that model. Then we get a paging scroll pane from the `JTable`, and add that scroll pane to the content pane of a `JFrame`.

Charting Data with a TableModel

Our last example shows that the table machinery isn't just for building tables; you can use it to build other kinds of components, like the pie chart in Figure 16-3. If you think about it, there's no essential difference between a pie chart, a bar chart, and many other kinds of data displays; they are all different ways of rendering data that's logically kept in a table. When that's the case, it is easy to use a `TableModel` to manage the data, and build your own component for the display.

With AWT, building a new component was easy: you simply created a subclass of `Component`. With Swing, it's a little more complex because of the distinction between the component itself and the user interface implementation. But it's not terribly hard, particularly if you don't want to brave the waters of pluggable look-and-feel. In this case, there's no good reason to make pie charts that look different on different platforms, so we'll opt for simplicity. We'll call our new component a `TableChart`; it extends `JComponent`. Its big responsibility is keeping the data for the component updated; to this end, it listens for `TableModelEvents` from the `TableModel` to determine when changes have been made.

To do the actual drawing, `TableChart` relies on a "delegate." Our delegate will be a `PieChartPainter`, which is responsible for rendering the data on the screen. To keep things flexible, `PieChartPainter` is a subclass of `ChartPainter`, which gives us the option of building other kinds of chart painters—bar chart painters, etc.—in the future. `ChartPainter` extends `ComponentUI`, which is the base class for user interface delegates. Here's where the model-view-controller architecture comes into play. The table model contains the actual data; `TableChart` is a controller that tells a delegate what and when to paint; and `PieChartPainter` is the "view" that actually paints a particular kind of representation on the screen.

Just to prove that the same `TableModel` can be used with any kind of display, we also display an old fashioned `JTable` using the same data—which turns out to be convenient, because we can use the `JTable`'s built-in editing capabilities to modify the data. If you change any field (including the name), the pie chart will immediately change to reflect the new data.

The `TableChart` class is particularly interesting because it shows the "other side" of table model event processing. In the `PagingModel` of the previous example, we had to generate events as the data changed. Here, you see how those events might be handled. The `TableChart` has to register itself as a `TableModelListener` and respond to events so that it can redraw itself when you edit the table. The Table-Chart also implements one (perhaps unsightly) short cut: it presents the data by summing and averaging along the columns. It would have been more work (but not much more work) to present the data in any particular column, letting the user choose the column to be displayed.

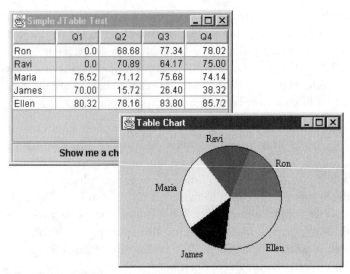

Figure 16-3. A Chart component using a TableModel

Here's the application that produces both the pie chart and the table. It includes the TableModel as an anonymous inner class. This inner class is very simple, much simpler than the models we used earlier in this chapter; it just provides an array for storing the data, methods to get and set the data, and methods to provide other information about the table. Notice that we provided an isCellEdit-able() method that always returns true (the default method always returns false). Because we're allowing the user to edit the table, we must also override setValueAt(); our implementation updates the data array and calls fireTable-RowsUpdated() to notify any listeners that data has changed and they need to redraw. The rest of ChartTester just sets up the display; we display the pie chart as a popup, to make things somewhat more interesting.

```
// ChartTester.java
//
import java.awt.*;
import java.awt.event.*;
import javax.swing.*;
import javax.swing.table.*;

public class ChartTester extends JFrame {
```

```
    public ChartTester() {
      super("Simple JTable Test");
      setSize(300, 200);
      addWindowListener(new BasicWindowMonitor());


      TableModel tm = new AbstractTableModel() {
        String data[][] = {
          {"Ron", "0.00", "68.68", "77.34", "78.02"},
          {"Ravi", "0.00", "70.89", "64.17", "75.00"},
          {"Maria", "76.52", "71.12", "75.68", "74.14"},
          {"James", "70.00", "15.72", "26.40", "38.32"},
          {"Ellen", "80.32", "78.16", "83.80", "85.72"}
        };
        String headers[] = { "", "Q1", "Q2", "Q3", "Q4" };
        public int getColumnCount() { return headers.length; }
        public int getRowCount() { return data.length; }
        public String getColumnName(int col) { return headers[col]; }
        public Class getColumnClass(int col) {
          return (col == 0) ? String.class : Number.class;
        }

        public boolean isCellEditable(int row, int col) { return true; }
        public Object getValueAt(int row, int col) { return data[row][col]; }
        public void setValueAt(Object value, int row, int col) {
          data[row][col] = (String)value;
          fireTableRowsUpdated(row,row);
        }
      };

      JTable jt = new JTable(tm);
      JScrollPane jsp = new JScrollPane(jt);
      getContentPane().add(jsp, BorderLayout.CENTER);

      final TableChartPopup tcp = new TableChartPopup(tm);
      JButton button = new JButton("Show me a chart of this table");
      button.addActionListener(new ActionListener() {
        public void actionPerformed(ActionEvent ae) {
          tcp.setVisible(true);
        }
      } );
      getContentPane().add(button, BorderLayout.SOUTH);
    }

    public static void main(String args[]) {
      ChartTester ct = new ChartTester();
      ct.setVisible(true);
    }
  }
```

The TableChart object is actually made of three pieces. The TableChart class extends JComponent, which provides all the machinery for getting a new component on the screen. It implements TableModelListener because it has to register and respond to TableModelEvents.

```java
// TableChart.java
// A chart-generating class that uses the TableModel interface to get
// its data.
//
import java.awt.*;
import java.awt.event.*;
import javax.swing.*;
import javax.swing.event.*;
import javax.swing.table.*;

public class TableChart extends JComponent implements TableModelListener {

  protected TableModel model;
  protected ChartPainter cp;
  protected double[] percentages;   // pie slices
  protected String[] labels;        // labels for slices
  protected String[] tips;          // tooltips for slices

  protected java.text.NumberFormat formatter =
              java.text.NumberFormat.getPercentInstance();

  public TableChart(TableModel tm) {
    setUI(cp = new PieChartPainter());
    setModel(tm);
  }

  public void setTextFont(Font f) { cp.setTextFont(f); }
  public Font getTextFont() { return cp.getTextFont(); }

  public void setTextColor(Color c) { cp.setTextColor(c); }
  public Color getTextColor() { return cp.getTextColor(); }

  public void setColor(Color[] clist) { cp.setColor(clist); }
  public Color[] getColor() { return cp.getColor(); }

  public void setColor(int index, Color c) { cp.setColor(index, c); }
  public Color getColor(int index) { return cp.getColor(index); }

  public String getToolTipText(MouseEvent me) {
    if (tips != null) {
      int whichTip = cp.indexOfEntryAt(me);
      if (whichTip != -1) {
        return tips[whichTip];
      }
    }
```

```
  }
  return null;
}

public void tableChanged(TableModelEvent tme) {
  // only rebuild the arrays if the structure changed.
  updateLocalValues(tme.getType() != TableModelEvent.UPDATE);
}

public void setModel(TableModel tm) {
  // get listener code correct.
  if (tm != model) {
    if (model != null) {
  model.removeTableModelListener(this);
    }
    model = tm;
    model.addTableModelListener(this);
    updateLocalValues(true);
  }
}

public TableModel getModel() { return model; }

// Run through the model and count every cell (except the very first column
// which we assume is the slice label column
protected void calculatePercentages() {
  double runningTotal = 0.0;
  for (int i = model.getRowCount() - 1; i >= 0; i--) {
    percentages[i] = 0.0;
    for (int j = model.getColumnCount() - 1; j >=0; j--) {

      // First try the cell as a Number object
      try {
        percentages[i] += ((Number)model.getValueAt(i, j)).doubleValue();
      }
      catch(ClassCastException cce) {  // oops, it wasn't numeric...
        // Ok, so try it as a string
        try {
          percentages[i]+=Double.valueOf(model.getValueAt(i,j).toString())
                            .doubleValue();
        }
        catch (Exception e) { // give up.
        }
      }
    }
    runningTotal += percentages[i];
  }
```

```
    // make each entry a percentage of the total
    for (int i = model.getRowCount() - 1; i >= 0; i--) {
      percentages[i] /= runningTotal;
    }
  }


  // This method just takes the percentages and formats them for use as
  // tooltips
  protected void createLabelsAndTips() {
    for (int i = model.getRowCount() - 1; i >= 0; i--) {
      labels[i] = (String)model.getValueAt(i, 0);
      tips[i] = formatter.format(percentages[i]);
    }
  }


  // Call this method to update the chart.  We try to be a bit efficient here
  // in that we only allocate new storage arrays if the new table has a
  // different number of rows
  protected void updateLocalValues(boolean freshStart) {
    if (freshStart) {
      int count = model.getRowCount();
      if ((tips == null) || (count != tips.length)) {
        percentages = new double[count];
        labels = new String[count];
        tips = new String[count];
      }
    }
    calculatePercentages();
    createLabelsAndTips();

    // Now that everything's up-to-date, reset the chart painter with the new
    // values
    cp.setValues(percentages);
    cp.setLabels(labels);

    // and finally, repaint the chart.
    repaint();
  }
}
```

The constructor for TableChart sets the user interface for this class to be the PieChartPainter that we'll discuss later in this chapter. It also saves the Table-Model for the component by calling our setModel() method; providing a separate setModel() (rather than saving the model in the constructor) lets us change the model at a later time–a nice feature for a real component, though we don't take advantage of it. We also override getToolTipText() that is called with a MouseEvent as an argument. This method calls the ChartPainter's index-OfEntryAt() method to figure out which of the model's entries corresponds to the current mouse position, looks up the appropriate tooltip, and returns it.

tableChanged() is the method we implement to listen for TableModelEvents. It just delegates the call to another method, updateLocalValues(), with an argument of true if the table's structure has changed (e.g., rows added or deleted), and false if only the values have changed. The rest of TableChart takes care of updating the data when the change occurs. The focal point of this work is updateLocalValues(); calculatePercentages() and createLabelsAnd-Tips() are helper methods that keep the work modular. If up-dateLocal-Values() is called with its argument set to true, it finds out the new number of rows for the table and creates new arrays to hold the component's view of the data. It calculates percentages, retrieves labels, makes up tool tips, and calls the Chart-Painter (the user interface object) to give it the new information. It ends by calling repaint() to redraw the screen with updated data.

ChartPainter is the actual user interface class. It is abstract; we subclass it to implement specific kinds of charts. It extends the ComponentUI class, which makes it sound rather complex. But in fact, it isn't. We've made one tremendously simplifying assumption: the chart will look the same for any look-and-feel. (The component in which the chart is embedded will change its appearance, but that's another issue—and one we don't have to worry about.) All our ComponentUI has to do is implement paint(), which we leave abstract, forcing the subclass to implement it. Our other abstract method, indexOfEntryAt(), is required by TableChart.

```
// ChartPainter.java
// A simple chart-drawing UI base class. This class tracks the basic fonts
// and colors for various types of charts including pie and bar. The paint()
// method is abstract and must be implemented by subclasses for each type.
//
import java.awt.*;
import java.awt.event.*;
import javax.swing.*;
import javax.swing.plaf.*;

public abstract class ChartPainter extends ComponentUI {

  protected Font textFont = new Font("Serif", Font.PLAIN, 12);
  protected Color textColor = Color.black;
  protected Color colors[] = new Color[] {
    Color.red, Color.blue, Color.yellow, Color.black, Color.green,
    Color.white, Color.gray, Color.cyan, Color.magenta, Color.darkGray
  };
  protected double values[] = new double[0];
  protected String labels[] = new String[0];

  public void setTextFont(Font f) { textFont = f; }
  public Font getTextFont() { return textFont; }
```

```
    public void setColor(Color[] clist) { colors = clist; }
    public Color[] getColor() { return colors; }

    public void setColor(int index, Color c) { colors[index] = c; }
    public Color getColor(int index) { return colors[index]; }

    public void setTextColor(Color c) { textColor = c; }
    public Color getTextColor() { return textColor; }

    public void setLabels(String[] l) { labels = l; }
    public void setValues(double[] v) { values = v; }

    public abstract int indexOfEntryAt(MouseEvent me);
    public abstract void paint(Graphics g, JComponent c);
  }
```

There's not much mystery here. Except for the two abstract methods, these methods just maintain various simple properties of ChartPainter: the colors used for painting, the font, and the labels and values for the chart.

The real work takes place in the PieChartPainter class, which provides the implementation of the indexOfEntryAt() and paint() methods. The indexOfEntryAt() method allows our TableChart class to figure out which tooltip to show. The paint() method allows us to draw a pie chart of our data.

```
// PieChartPainter.java
// A pie chart implementation of the ChartPainter class.
//
import java.awt.*;
import java.awt.event.*;
import javax.swing.*;
import javax.swing.plaf.*;

public class PieChartPainter extends ChartPainter {

  protected static PieChartPainter chartUI = new PieChartPainter();
  protected int originX, originY;
  protected int radius;

  private static double piby2 = Math.PI / 2.0;
  private static double twopi = Math.PI * 2.0;
  private static double d2r   = Math.PI / 180.0; // degrees to radians.

  public int indexOfEntryAt(MouseEvent me) {
    int x = me.getX() - originX;
    int y = originY - me.getY();  // upside down coordinate system.

    // is (x,y) in the circle?
    if (Math.sqrt(x*x + y*y) > radius) { return -1; }
```

```
      double percent = Math.atan2(Math.abs(y), Math.abs(x));
      if (x >= 0) {
        if (y <= 0) { // (IV)
          percent = (piby2 - percent) + 3 * piby2; // (IV)
        }
      }
      else {
        if (y >= 0) { // (II)
          percent = Math.PI - percent;
        }
        else { // (III)
          percent = Math.PI + percent;
        }
      }
      percent /= twopi;
      double t = 0.0;
      if (values != null) {
        for (int i = 0; i < values.length; i++) {
          if (t + values[i] > percent) {
            return i;
          }
          t += values[i];
        }
      }
      return -1;
    }

    public void paint(Graphics g, JComponent c) {
      Dimension size = c.getSize();
      originX = size.width / 2;
      originY = size.height / 2;
      int diameter = (originX < originY ? size.width - 40
                                        : size.height - 40);
      radius = (diameter / 2) + 1;
      int cornerX = (originX - (diameter / 2));
      int cornerY = (originY - (diameter / 2));

      int startAngle = 0;
      int arcAngle = 0;
      for (int i = 0; i < values.length; i++) {
        arcAngle = (int)(i < values.length - 1 ?
                         Math.round(values[i] * 360) :
                         360 - startAngle);
        g.setColor(colors[i % colors.length]);
        g.fillArc(cornerX, cornerY, diameter, diameter,
                  startAngle, arcAngle);
        drawLabel(g, labels[i], startAngle + (arcAngle / 2));
        startAngle += arcAngle;
      }
```

```
      g.setColor(Color.black);
      g.drawOval(cornerX, cornerY, diameter, diameter);  // cap the circle
  }

  public void drawLabel(Graphics g, String text, double angle) {
    g.setFont(textFont);
    g.setColor(textColor);
    double radians = angle * d2r;
    int x = (int) ((radius + 5) * Math.cos(radians));
    int y = (int) ((radius + 5) * Math.sin(radians));
    if (x < 0) {
      x -= SwingUtilities.computeStringWidth(g.getFontMetrics(), text);
    }
    if (y < 0) {
      y -= g.getFontMetrics().getHeight();
    }
    g.drawString(text, x + originX, originY - y);
  }

  public static ComponentUI createUI(JComponent c) {
    return chartUI;
  }
}
```

There's nothing really complex here; it's just a lot of trigonometry and a little bit of simple AWT drawing. `paint()` is called with a graphics context and a JCompo-nent as arguments; the JComponent allows you to figure out the size of the area we have to work with.

And here's the code for the popup containing the chart:

```
// TableChartPopup.java
//
import java.awt.*;
import java.awt.event.*;
import javax.swing.*;
import javax.swing.table.*;

public class TableChartPopup extends JFrame {

  public TableChartPopup(TableModel tm) {
    super("Table Chart");
    setSize(300,200);
    TableChart tc = new TableChart(tm);
    getContentPane().add(tc, BorderLayout.CENTER);

    // Turn on the tooltips, we can use any string to get going.
    tc.setToolTipText("Demo Chart");
  }
}
```

As you can see, the `TableChart` component can be used on its own without a `JTable`. We just need a model to base it on. You could expand this example to chart only selected rows or columns, but we'll leave that as an exercise for the reader.

17

Trees

One crucial component that found its way into the Swing set is the tree. Tree components help you visualize hierarchical information and make traversal and manipulation of that information much more manageable. A tree consists of *nodes,* which can contain either a user-defined object along with references to other nodes, or a user-defined object only. (The nodes that have no references to other nodes are commonly called *leaves.*) In modern windowing environments, the directory list is an excellent example of a tree. The top of the component is the root directory or drive, and under that is a list of subdirectories. If the subdirectories contain further subdirectories, you can look at those as well. The actual files found in any directory in this component are the leaves of the tree.

Any data that contains parent-child relationships between chunks of information can be displayed as a tree. Another common example is an organizational chart. In such a chart, every management position is a node, with child nodes representing the employees under the manager. The organizational chart's leaves are the employees who are not in management positions, and its root is the president or CEO. Of course, real organization don't always adhere to a strict tree structure. In a tree, each node has exactly one parent node, with the exception of the root node, which cannot have a parent (so trees are not cyclic). This means two managers cannot manage the same employee.

In short, whenever you have a clearly defined hierarchy, you can express that hierarchy as a tree. Swing implements trees with the `JTree` class and its related models. With trees, as with tables, it's particularly important to understand the models. The `JTree` itself merely coordinates the tree's display.

A Simple Tree

Before we look at the models supporting the JTree class, let's look at a very simple example of a tree built with the default implementations in the Swing package (as shown in Figure 17-1).* The javax.swing.DefaultMutableTreeNode class serves as our node class. You don't have to worry about specifically making a node a leaf. If the node has no references to other nodes by the time you display it, it's a leaf.

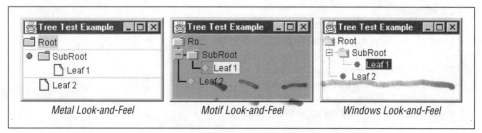

Figure 17-1. A simple JTree in the Metal, Motif, and Windows look-and-feels

This example works by building up a series of unconnected nodes (using the DefaultMutableTreeNode class) and then connecting them. As long as we stick to the default classes provided with the tree package, we can build a regular model out of our nodes quite quickly. In this example, we build the model based on an empty root node, and then populate the tree by attaching the other nodes to the root or to each other. You can also build the tree first, and then create the model from the root node. Both methods have the same result. With a valid tree model in place, we can make a real JTree object and display it.

```
// TestTree.java
// A Simple test to see how we can build a tree and populate it.
//
import java.awt.*;
import java.awt.event.*;
import javax.swing.*;
import javax.swing.tree.*;

public class TestTree extends JFrame {

  JTree tree;
  DefaultTreeModel treeModel;

  public TestTree() {
    super("Tree Test Example");
    setSize(400, 300);
    addWindowListener(new BasicWindowMonitor());
  }
```

---

* The appearance of an internal frame in the Metal look-and-feel has changed slightly since these screen shots were taken.

```
public void init() {
    // Build up a bunch of TreeNodes. We use DefaultMutableTreeNode because the
    // DefaultTreeModel can use that to build a complete tree.
    DefaultMutableTreeNode root = new DefaultMutableTreeNode("Root");
    DefaultMutableTreeNode subroot = new DefaultMutableTreeNode("SubRoot");
    DefaultMutableTreeNode leaf1 = new DefaultMutableTreeNode("Leaf 1");
    DefaultMutableTreeNode leaf2 = new DefaultMutableTreeNode("Leaf 2");

    // Build our tree model starting at the root node, and then make a JTree out
    // of that.
    treeModel = new DefaultTreeModel(root);
    tree = new JTree(treeModel);

    // Build the tree up from the nodes we created
    treeModel.insertNodeInto(subroot, root, 0);
    treeModel.insertNodeInto(leaf1, subroot, 0);
    treeModel.insertNodeInto(leaf2, root, 1);

    // And display it
    getContentPane().add(tree, BorderLayout.CENTER);
}

public static void main(String args[]) {
    TestTree tt = new TestTree();
    tt.init();
    tt.setVisible(true);
}
}
```

As you can see here, all of the action happens in the `init()` method. We create several nodes using the `DefaultMutableTreeNode` class. The `DefaultTree-Model` class provides us with a basis for working with the tree, and we add our nodes into that model. All of the trees we will look at in this chapter contain the same basic steps—gathering nodes, creating a tree, and populating the tree—though again, not necessarily in that order. We will also look at the other types of things you can do with trees, including how to catch selection events and how to change the presentation of the nodes and leaves.

And just to prove that it's not hard to listen to selections from a tree, Figure 17-2 shows an expanded example that displays the most recently selected item in a JLabel at the bottom of the application.

To make this work, we add a listener directly to the `JTree` object. The listener looks and behaves much like a `ListSelectionListener`, but is slightly modified to handle the specifics of tree selections. (For example, selection intervals may have to cross over an expanded node, and all the nodes under the expanded entry must also be selected.) Even though we allow multiple entries to be selected, we

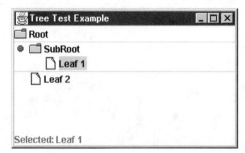

Figure 17-2. The TestTree program with a TreeSelectionListener label active

only show the lead entry of the selection, to keep output simple. Here's the chunk of code we need to add to the `init()` method in the `TestTree` class:

```
// Create and add our message label for the selection output
final JLabel messageLabel = new JLabel("Nothing selected.");
add(messageLabel, BorderLayout.SOUTH);

// Add in our selection listener and have it report to
// our messageLabel
tree.addTreeSelectionListener(new TreeSelectionListener() {
  public void valueChanged(TreeSelectionEvent tse) {
    TreePath tp = tse.getNewLeadSelectionPath();
    messageLabel.setText("Selected: " + tp.getLastPathComponent());
  }
} );
```

Of course, you should be sure to import `javax.swing.event.*` to get access to the `TreeSelectionListener` and `TreeSelectionEvent` classes.

Tree Terminology

Let's look at a simple tree made up of the letters A–Z, shown in Figure 17-3.

Here are a few definitions for terms used to work with trees. We'll be using them throughout this chapter.

Node
> Any entry in the tree. A, J, and T are all nodes.

Root
> The top-level entry of the tree. A root cannot have a parent, and a tree can have only one root. The root in this example is A.

Child
> Any of the nodes attached below a given node. M is a child of G.

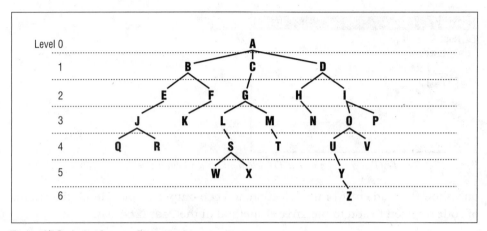

Figure 17-3. A simple tree

Parent

The node attached above a given node. Any typical node has only one parent, but the root of the tree is the only node with no parent. G is the parent of M and C is the parent of G.

Sibling

Any child of a node's parent. A node is also its own sibling. B's siblings are B, C, and D.

Descendant

Any child, or child of a child, or child of a child of a child, etc. A node is also its own descendant. L, S, W, and X are the descendants of L.

Ancestor

Any parent, or parent's parent, or parent's parent's parent, etc. A node is also its own ancestor. A, D, I, and P are the ancestors of P.

Level

The distance (measured in number of ancestors) from a node to the root node. The biggest level is also called the height or depth of a tree. A's level is 0, while T's level is 4.

Path

A list of nodes leading from one node to another. Typically, a path is from the root to another node.

Row

In a graphical representation of a tree, the mapping of a path to a corresponding row number on the screen. A would always be row 0, while other nodes might map to different rows, depending on which nodes are expanded and which are collapsed. If you think of taking a snapshot of a JTree and converting it to a `JList`, the row of the entry in the tree would correspond to the index of the entry in the list.

Collapsed

In a visual representation of a tree, a node is "collapsed" if you cannot see any of its children. In our example, none of the nodes are collapsed.

Expanded

In a visual representation of a tree, a node is "expanded" if you can see its children. In our example, all of the nodes are expanded. (While you can expand or collapse a leaf, it has no effect, as leaves have no children by definition).

As a quick overview, Figure 17-4 details how the various tree classes work together to produce a tree on screen. We'll be looking at each of these classes in depth below. `JTrees` use `TreeCellRenderers` to graphically display a tree represented by a `TreeModel`. `TreeModels` encode a tree using `TreeNodes` that contain an `Object` (your data for that node) and possibly references to other `TreeNodes`. Once displayed, the nodes of the tree can be selected according to the rules of a `TreeSelectionModel`. If supported, you can edit any one of the nodes in the tree using a `TreeCellEditor`.

Tree Models

Looking at Figure 17-4 you can get an overview of where all the tree pieces come from. As with many of the Swing components you've seen already, the models supporting the data for trees play a crucial role in making the component run. Two interfaces are particularly important: `TreeModel`, which describes how to work with tree data, and `TreeSelectionModel`, which describes how to select nodes. We'll be looking at the model for the tree data first, and later the model supporting tree selections.

The TreeModel Interface

To get started, you need a tree model. The `TreeModel` interface is the starting point for your model. You don't have to start from scratch, there is a default implementation you can subclass or just look at for ideas. (We'll look at this class, `DefaultTreeModel`, later in the chapter.)

Property

The `TreeModel` has one `root` property, listed in Table 17-1. This read-only property designates the root of a tree: by definition, the node that has no parent. All other nodes in your tree will be descendants of this node.

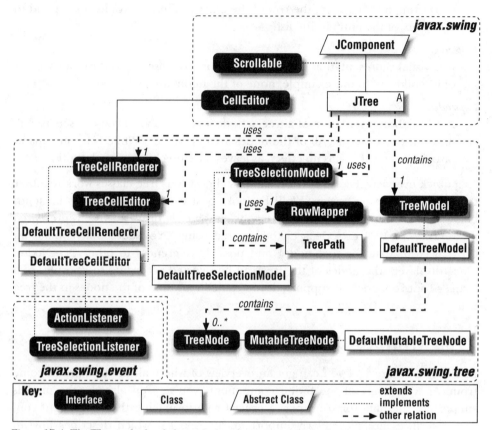

Figure 17-4. The JTree and related classes (using the various default classes available)

Table 17-1. TreeModel Property

Property	Data Type	get	is	set	bound	Default Value
root	Object	•				

Events

The tree model uses the `TreeModelEvent` class defined in the `javax.swing.event` package. A `TreeModelEvent` indicates that the tree has been changed; one or more nodes have been added, modified, or deleted. You will find a more detailed discussion of the tree events in the section "Tree Events," later in this chapter.

public void addTreeModelListener(TreeModelListener l)

public void removeTreeModelListener(TreeModelListener l)

Add and remove listeners interested in receiving tree model events.

Miscellaneous Methods

Several miscellaneous methods are defined in this model for querying the tree and its structure. Although the actual data structures are defined by the classes that implement the model, the model works as if every node maintains an array of its children, and that children can be identified by an index into the array.

public Object getChild(Object parent, int index)

Given a parent object, returns the child node at the given index. In many cases, if you specify an invalid index or try to get a child from a leaf, you should receive an ArrayIndexOutOfBoundsException. Of course, this is user-definable. It would also be possible to create a model that simply returned a null or default child.

public int getChildCount(Object parent)

Given a parent node, returns the number of children this node has. Leaves return a value of zero.

public int getIndexOfChild(Object parent, Object child)

Given a parent node and an object, returns the index of the child in the parent's children array. If the child object is not a child of this parent, it returns -1.

public boolean isLeaf(Object node)

This method checks to see if the given node is a leaf. By definition, a leaf has no children. This method does not distinguish between a "real" leaf (a node that should never have a child) and nodes that simply do not have a child at the time you query them. If you need to distinguish these types of nodes, look at the allowsChildren property of the TreeNode class.

public void valueForPathChanged(TreePath path, Object newValue)

Notifies the tree of a change to the user-defined object contained in the node pointed to by path.

The DefaultTreeModel Class

The DefaultTreeModel class puts together a basic tree model using TreeNode objects. We'll look at TreeNode in the next section. This DefaultTreeModel is the basis for the first example we built above. It implements the TreeModel interface also adds a few new methods. If you're in a mood to go creating your own tree, this is a great place to start. Each node's data is really just an Object reference, pointing to just about anything you could want to represent. (Base types, of course, must be wrapped up in objects.) You can usually get away with building on a `DefaultTreeModel`, unless you need to impose a specific structure, such as limiting the number of children a node can have. Normally, the children of a node are just kept in a vector, so no limits exist.

One other note about tree models: if you plan on allowing multiple threads to access your model, you need to find a synchronization point. A conservative approach to thread safety dictates that you lock on the root node of the tree. Less conservative approaches require a bit of searching to make sure that you are not locking on a descendant of an already locked node. (If you did, it's possible the other thread would delete one of your ancestors, and thus delete you.)

Properties

The `DefaultTreeModel` contains the properties listed in Table 17-2. The `DefaultTreeModel` class provides a `root` property (inherited from `TreeModel`) and a `boolean` property `asksAllowsChildren` to determine whether or not the tree model asks a node if it can accept children before inserting them. This property allows you to write nodes that can reject the addition of a child at runtime.

Table 17-2. DefaultTreeModel Properties

Property	Data Type	get	is	set	bound	Default Value
asksAllowsChildren[a]	boolean			•		false
root*	Object	•		•		null

[a] The read method for the `asksAllowsChildren` property is `asksAllowsChildren()`.

Events

The `DefaultTreeModel` fires a `TreeModelEvent` whenever the tree has been changed. It implements the standard methods for registering listeners, plus a number of helper methods for firing different versions of the `TreeModelEvent`.

public void addTreeModelListener(TreeModelListener l)
public void removeTreeModelListener(TreeModelListener l)
  Add or remove listeners interested in receiving tree model events.

protected void fireTreeNodesChanged(Object source, Object path[], int childIndices[], Object children[])
protected void fireTreeNodesInserted(Object source, Object path[], int childIndices[], Object children[])
protected void fireTreeNodesRemoved(Object source, Object path[], int childIndices[], Object children[])

protected void fireTreeStructureChanged(Object source, Object path[], int childIndices[], Object children[])

These protected methods send a `TreeModelEvent` to the appropriate method of all registered `TreeModelListeners`. The main difference between `fire-TreeNodesChanged()` and `fireTreeStructureChanged()` is that the latter represents a significant change to the overall structure of the tree, while the former typically is used for minor changes, such as notifying listeners that the user data stored in a particular set of nodes has changed, or the visual representation of those nodes has changed. These methods should be called from one of the public node change methods below. All of these methods assume an ascending order for the child indices.

public void nodeChanged(TreeNode node)

Use this method any time you update a node to notify the model that the representation of this node may have changed. This is used most often to indicate that the user data in a node was edited.

public void nodesChanged(TreeNode node, int childIndices[])

Similar to `nodeChanged()`, but you use this method any time you update the *children* of a node and need to notify the model that the representation of those children may have changed.

public void nodesWereInserted(TreeNode node, int childIndices[])

Indicates that you have added children to a node. The indices of the children you added must be sorted in ascending order.

public void nodesWereRemoved(TreeNode node, int childIndices[])

Indicates that you have removed children from a node. The indices of the children you added must be sorted in ascending order.

public void nodeStructureChanged(TreeNode node)

If you have completely rearranged the children (and possibly grandchildren and great grandchildren, etc.) of the node, call this method. It in turn calls the `fireTreeStructureChanged()` method.

public void valueForPathChanged(TreePath path, Object newValue)

Use this method to set the value of the user-defined object stored in this node. This method calls `nodesChanged()` for you. If you have subclassed `Default-TreeModel` to create your own tree model and that model uses specific user-defined objects in its nodes, you will want to override this method to make sure that the appropriate type of object gets put into the node. For example, if your tree nodes store base types, you will need to manually extract the base value out of the wrapper object passed to this method.

Fields

protected boolean asksAllowsChildren

Holds the value for the `asksAllowsChildren` property.

protected EventListenerList listenerList

Holds the list of listeners attached to the model.

protected TreeNode root

Holds the value for the `root` property (the root of the tree).

Constructors

public DefaultTreeModel(TreeNode root)

public DefaultTreeModel(TreeNode root, boolean asksAllowsChildren)

Creates a new tree model implemented with `TreeNode` objects for the nodes. These constructors set the given node up as the root of the tree. If you specify `true` for the `asksAllowsChildren` argument of the second constructor, the model will check the node to see if it allows children before deciding whether or not the node is a leaf.

Miscellaneous Methods

The `DefaultTreeModel` contains several methods to help you query and update the contents of your tree. These methods should help you add and remove nodes, as well as update the tree whenever you make other changes (such as changing user data).

public TreeNode[] getPathToRoot(TreeNode node)

protected TreeNode[] getPathToRoot(TreeNode node, int depth)

Return an array of `TreeNode` objects from the root down to the specified node. (The protected version uses `depth` as a marker to aid in its recursive discovery of the path. Normally, you would just use the public method.)

public void insertNodeInto(MutableTreeNode child, MutableTreeNode parent, int index)

Attaches the node `child` to the node `parent` at the given `index`. If the index is larger than the child count (meaning more than just "the next possible index") an `ArrayIndexOutOfBoundsException` is thrown.

public void reload()

public void reload(TreeNode node)

These methods refresh a tree, presumably after it has been modified in some fashion. The first method reloads the tree from the root down, while the second call starts with the specified node.

public void removeNodeFromParent(MutableTreeNode node)

Removes a node from its parent. The node is not destroyed, but is placed in an array for use with `nodesWereRemoved()`, which generates the appropriate model event for you.

Working with Tree Models

The `TestTree` example earlier in the chapter shows the `DefaultTreeModel` in action. However, if you want to build a tree out of something other than `TreeNode` objects, you need to build your own tree model directly from the `TreeModel` interface. (Of course, you can also extend the `DefaultTreeModel` and build a more tailored model that includes some knowledge about the tree nodes you intend to build, using the `TreeNode` and `MutableTreeNode` interfaces discussed later.)

As an example, we will build an algebraic expression tree model from scratch and then build an operator node for use in the tree. We want to represent expressions like 1 + 2 * 3 as a tree. The operators (+ and *) will be the "folders" and we'll use integers as the leaves, or "files." For example, a + must have two children; each child can be either another operator, or an `Integer`. Once completed, an example expression might look like Figure 17-5.

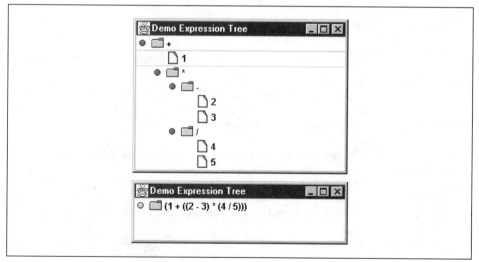

Figure 17-5. Expression Tree in expanded (top) and collapsed (bottom) views

We'll be sprucing up this example a bit as we go on, but first, let's define our node types. We can use the `java.lang.Integer` class for our leaves, but we'll need our own class for the operators. We can build an `OpNode` class to handle the four basic operations, add (+), subtract (−), multiply (*), and divide (/).

The OpNode class is responsible for storing operators and their child expressions. Because we're modeling algebraic expressions, an OpNode only needs to hold two children, which it stores in an array. The constructor for OpNode takes a string as an argument and parses that string. Notice that we do not implement the TreeNode interface. Since we're building our own tree model, we do not need that interface. Our tree model will have methods to access OpNodes directly. Most of the work in OpNode revolves around parsing the strings you pass in for operators or children. We also have to make the toString() method a bit dynamic, so that it checks to see if the node is currently expanded or collapsed before returning a value.

```java
// OpNode.java
// A node structure containing an operator in our calculation tree. This node
// will hold two children.
//
import javax.swing.tree.*;

public class OpNode {
  public static final String MULTIPLY = "*";
  public static final String DIVIDE   = "/";
  public static final String ADD      = "+";
  public static final String SUBTRACT = "-";

  String operator;
  Object[] children = new Object[2];
  boolean expanded = false;

  public OpNode() { this(ADD); }
  public OpNode(String op) { operator = op; }

  public void setExpanded(boolean b) { expanded = b; }

  // Add in a child (which can be either another OpNode or an Integer. If the
  // index isn't 0 or 1, throw an exception
  public void setChild(int index, Object child) {
    if (index == 0) { children[0] = buildChild(child); }
    else if (index == 1) { children[1] = buildChild(child); }
    else {
      throw new IllegalArgumentException("child index " + index
                                    + " must be 0 or 1");
    }
  }

  // return the child for the given index, may return null
  public Object getChild(int index) {
    if (index == 0) { return children[0]; }
    else if (index == 1) { return children[1]; }
    throw new IllegalArgumentException("child index must be 0 or 1");
  }
```

```java
// return the index of the given child
public int getIndexOfChild(Object child) {
  if (child.equals(children[0])) { return 0;  }
  else if (child.equals(children[1])) { return 1; }
  return -1;
}

public int getChildCount() {
  int count = 0;
  if (children[0] != null) { count++; }
  if (children[1] != null) { count++; }
  return count;
}

// Get and set the current operator. We'll need to support the set method when
// we start to make the tree editable
public String getOperator() { return operator; }
public void setOperator(Object op) {
  if (op instanceof String) { operator = (String)op; }
  else {
    throw new IllegalArgumentException("operators must be strings");
  }
}

// Here's the workhorse for OpNode. This method parses an Object and returns
// either a valid OpNode or an Integer. If the object can't be parsed, an error
// is printed and an Integer(0) is returned. (This keeps the tree from crashing
// out . . . )
protected Object buildChild(Object o) {
  if ((o instanceof Integer) || (o instanceof OpNode)) {
    return o;
  }
  String op = null;
  if (o instanceof String) {
    op = ((String)o).trim();
    if (op.equals(ADD)) { return new OpNode(ADD); }
    else if (op.equals(SUBTRACT)) { return new OpNode(SUBTRACT); }
    else if (op.equals(MULTIPLY)) { return new OpNode(MULTIPLY); }
    else if (op.equals(DIVIDE)) { return new OpNode(DIVIDE); }
    else {
      try { return Integer.valueOf(op); }
      catch (NumberFormatException nfe) { return new Integer(0); }
    }
  }
  System.err.println("Fell through new child: " + op);
  return new Integer(0);
}
```

```
// Return a string representing this node. If the tree is collapsed, build up
// the expression below this node and return that as the string.
public String toString() {
  if (expanded) { return operator; }
  else {
    StringBuffer buf = new StringBuffer(40);
    buildCollapsedString(buf, this);
    return buf.toString();
  }
}

// put together an expression of (leftside op rightside), but do it recursively
// so we get the entire subtree
protected void buildCollapsedString(StringBuffer buf, Object node) {
  if (node == null) { return; }
  if (node instanceof OpNode) {
    buf.append("(");
    buildCollapsedString(buf, ((OpNode)node).getChild(0));
    buf.append(" ");
    buf.append(((OpNode)node).getOperator());
    buf.append(" ");
    buildCollapsedString(buf, ((OpNode)node).getChild(1));
    buf.append(")");
  }
  else { buf.append(node); }
}
```

Now that we have all the node types we need, we must build a model that knows how to use them. We must implement the TreeModel interface; most of this ExpressionTreeModel is devoted to that task. We tailor the TreeModel methods to deal with OpNode and Integer objects. Several of the methods simply call the equivalent method in OpNode; an OpNode knows how to insert, find, and count its children. Beyond the basic TreeModel methods, we only have two support methods: insertNode() to add new nodes to the tree and fireTreeNodes-Changed() to hand out tree model events.

Here is the ExpressionTreeModel class:

```
// ExpressionTreeModel.java
// An implementation of the TreeModel interface for use with our calculation
// trees.
//
import javax.swing.tree.*;
import javax.swing.event.*;
import java.util.Vector;

public class ExpressionTreeModel implements TreeModel {
```

```
  Vector listeners;
  OpNode root;

  public ExpressionTreeModel(OpNode r) {
    if (r == null) {
      throw new IllegalArgumentException("root is null");
    }
    root = r;
  }

  public void insertNode(OpNode parent, Object node, int index) {
    parent.setChild(index, node);
  }

  // Methods from TreeModel
  public Object getChild(Object node, int index) {
    if (node instanceof OpNode) { return ((OpNode)node).getChild(index); }
    return null;
  }

  public int getIndexOfChild(Object parent, Object child) {
    if (parent instanceof OpNode) {
      return ((OpNode)parent).getIndexOfChild(child);
    }
    else { return -1; }
  }

  public Object getRoot() { return root; }

  public int getChildCount(Object parent) {
    if (parent instanceof OpNode) { return ((OpNode)parent).getChildCount(); }
    else { return 0; }
  }

  public boolean isLeaf(Object node) { return (!(node instanceof OpNode)); }

  // A new value has been entered into our tree, so make sure we record it
  // correctly, and then fire off a node Change event to any TreeModelListeners.
  public void valueForPathChanged(TreePath path, Object newValue) {
    Object[] p = path.getPath();
    Object[] pp = p;
    Object node;
    int index;
    if (p.length == 1) { //editing root . . .
      root.setOperator(newValue);
      node = root;
      index = -1;
    }
    else {
```

```
      node = p[p.length - 1];
      OpNode parent = (OpNode)p[p.length - 2];
      index = parent.getIndexOfChild(node);
      if (node instanceof OpNode) {((OpNode)node).setOperator(newValue);}
      else {
         // Play a few path games since Integer is a noneditable object. We'll say
         // that the changed node is our parent, not us.
         parent.setChild(index, newValue);
         node = parent.getChild(index);
         // Create a new path down to our parent, but don't include us
         pp = new Object[p.length - 1];
         for (int i = 0; i < pp.length; i++) {pp[i]=p[i];}
      }
   }
   int[] ci = new int[] { index };        // child indices in parent
   Object [] cc = new Object[] { node };  // child objects in parent
   fireTreeNodesChanged(this, pp, ci, cc);
}


public void addTreeModelListener(TreeModelListener tml) {
   if (listeners == null) { listeners = new Vector(); }
   listeners.addElement(tml);
}


public void removeTreeModelListener(TreeModelListener tml) {
   if (listeners != null) { listeners.removeElement(tml); }
}


// Update our tree because expanding and collapsing changes the way we
// represent OpNodes.
public void refresh(TreeExpansionEvent tee) {
   int[] ci = new int[] { -1 };
   fireTreeNodesChanged(tee.getSource(), tee.getPath().getPath(), ci, null);
}


// And last but not least, fire off an event to anyone who cares to hear about
// model changes.
protected void fireTreeNodesChanged(Object source, Object[] path,
                                    int[] ci, Object[] cc)
{ // Short, but not very thread safe!!
   if (listeners != null) {
      TreeModelEvent tme = new TreeModelEvent(source, path, ci, cc);
      for (int i = 0; i < listeners.size(); i++) {
         ((TreeModelListener)listeners.elementAt(i)).treeNodesChanged(tme);
      }
   }
}
}
```

Tree Nodes and Paths

You probably noticed that the DefaultTreeModel class depends on TreeNode and TreePath objects. In a tree, a TreeNode represents an individual piece of data stored at a particular point in a tree, and a path represents a collection of these pieces that are directly related to each other (in an ancestor/descendant relationship). Let's look at the classes that make up the typical nodes and paths.

The TreeNode Interface

A TreeNode is the basic unit of a tree. This interface defines the minimum properties and access routines a typical tree model expects to see in its nodes.

Properties

The TreeNode interface contains the properties listed in Table 17-3. The TreeNode properties are straightforward and deal with the structure of the node. The parent property holds a valid value for every node in a tree, except the root. The childAt property lets you access a particular child in the tree. The childCount property contains the number of children associated with this node, if it allows children. If the node does not allow children, it is probably a leaf, but it is possible to have a mutable tree node that has no children, does not allow children, and yet is not a leaf. (An empty directory with no write permissions in a filesystem would be an example of such a node.)

Table 17-3. TreeNode Properties

Property	Data Type	get	is	set	bound	Default Value
allowsChildren	boolean	•				
childAt (indexed)	TreeNode	•				
childCount	int	•				
leaf	boolean		•			
parent	TreeNode	•				

Notice that the children are not properties of a TreeNode. This is not to say that a TreeNode does not have children, but rather the accessor methods do not fit the "property" definition.

Child Access Methods

public int getIndex(TreeNode node)
public Enumeration children()

> Allow you to access the children associated with a particular node. You can pick the child by node getIndex(); you can also use the childAt property accessor, getChildAt(), to pick a child by index number. If you want all of the nodes under a parent, the children() method returns an enumeration of those nodes.

The MutableTreeNode Interface

This interface extends the TreeNode interface to include basic manipulation methods for the children and the user data. If you set about defining your own nodes, this is a good place to start.

Properties

The MutableTreeNode class contains the properties listed in Table 17-4. MutableTreeNode adds write access to the parent property from the TreeNode interface and gives you access to user data. You should note, however, that setParent() expects a MutableTreeNode, while getParent() simply returns a TreeNode. The userObject property contains the data that makes a TreeNode interesting. You can use this property to store any arbitrary object. All other properties are inherited without change.

Table 17-4. MutableTreeNode Properties

Property	Data Type	get	is	set	bound	Default Value
parent*	MutableTreeNode	•		•		
userObject	Object			•		

See also properties of the TreeNode interface (Table 17-3).

Mutation Methods

The mutation methods of MutableTreeNode allow you to access and modify the node's children as well as its parent:

public void insert(MutableTreeNode child, int index)

> Inserts a child into the children array maintained by the node. The position of the new child is given by index. If you want to append a child, the index should be the node's getChildCount() + 1.

public void remove(int index)
public void remove(MutableTreeNode node)

> Remove a child from the node; the child may be specified by its index or by the child node itself.

public void removeFromParent()

> Removes the node from its parent. This assumes that the parent is also a mutable node and allows the removal of children.

The DefaultMutableTreeNode Class

Properties

DefaultMutableTreeNode inherits all of its properties from the Mutable-TreeNode and TreeNode interfaces. It supplies the default values shown in Table 17-5.

Table 17-5. DefaultMutableTreeNode Properties

Property	Data Type	get	is	set	bound	Default Value
allowsChildren*	boolean	•		•		false
childAt* (indexed)	TreeNode	•				
childCount*	int	•				0
leaf*	boolean		•			
parent*	MutableTreeNode[a]	•		•		null
userObject*	Object	•		•		null

[a] The read() method for the parent property returns a TreeNode object.

Constant

The DefaultMutableTreeNode class contains one constant, shown in Table 17-6.

Table 17-6. DefaultMutableTreeNode Constant

Constant	Type	Description
EMPTY_ENUMERATION	Enumeration	The enumeration methods listed below return this constant if the enumeration you ask for is empty.

Fields

protected MutableTreeNode parent
protected transient Object userObject
protected boolean allowsChildren

> Store the values for their respective properties.

protected Vector children

> Stores the children attached to this node. While not a direct property, you can use the `getChildAt()` methods to get a particular child, or the `children()` method to get an enumeration of all children.

Constructors

public DefaultMutableTreeNode()
public DefaultMutableTreeNode(Object userObject)
public DefaultMutableTreeNode(Object userObject, boolean allowsChildren)

> These constructors build new tree nodes that carry an optional `userObject`. You can also specify whether or not this child should be allowed to contain children. If you set `allowsChildren` to `false`, an `IllegalStateException` is thrown any time you try to insert or add a child to this node. By default, the user object is `null`, and children are allowed.

Structure Methods

The structure methods listed here provide you with easy ways of modifying and querying the structure of a tree. You can check the relation of a given node to any other node, and even retrieve specific relatives (children, parent, siblings) of a node. Many of these methods could be considered accessors for various properties; we thought it would be easier to discuss and contrast their behavior if we listed them as methods. In our discussion, we'll refer frequently to the tree made out of letters from Figure 17-3. Figure 17-6 shows a `JTree` built with the same structure using `DefaultMutableTreeNode` nodes and the `DefaultTreeModel`.

public void add(MutableTreeNode child)

> Removes the node `child` from its current position (if any) and appends it to the end of the child array for this node. It throws `IllegalStateException` if this node does not allow children and it throws `IllegalArgumentException` if `child` is `null`.

public TreeNode getChildAfter(TreeNode child)

> Use this method to retrieve the next child for this node after the specified child. If `child` is the last node in the child array, it returns `null`. If `child` does not exist at this node, an `IllegalArgumentException` is thrown. (For node A, the child after B is C, and the child after C is D.)

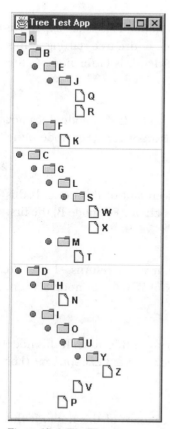

Figure 17-6. The JTree representation of the tree in Figure 17-3

public TreeNode getChildAt(int index)

Returns the child at the given index. If the index is invalid, you'll receive an `ArrayIndexOutOfBoundsException`. (For node G, the child at index 1 is M.)

public TreeNode getChildBefore(TreeNode child)

Use this method to retrieve the previous child for this node after the specified child. If `child` is the first node in the child array, it returns `null`. If `child` does not exist at this node, an `IllegalArgumentException` will be thrown. (For node A, the child before node B is null, the child before node C is B.)

public int getChildCount()

Returns a count of all the children found at this node. If this node currently has no children or does not allow children, a value of zero is returned. (For node E the child count is 1, for node J the child count is 2.)

public int getDepth()

> Returns the depth of the tree starting from this node. This is an expensive operation because you basically have to traverse the entire tree starting at this node to get the correct answer. (For node A the depth is 6, for node G the depth is 3.)

public TreeNode getFirstChild()

> Retrieves the first child in the child array of this node. If this node does not have any children, it will throw a NoSuchElementException. (For node I, the first child is O.)

public DefaultMutableTreeNode getFirstLeaf()

> Use this method to get the first leaf that is a descendant of this node. If this node has no children, it is itself a leaf, so it returns this. (For node B, the first leaf is Q, for node W, the first leaf is W.)

public int getIndex(TreeNode child)

> Returns the index of child in the node's child array. It returns –1 if child does not exist at this node. (For node S, the index of W is 0. For node S again, the index of T is –1.)

public TreeNode getLastChild()

> This method retrieves the last child in the child array of this node. If this node does not have any children, it will throw a NoSuchElementException. (For node I, the last child is P.)

public DefaultMutableTreeNode getLastLeaf()

> Use this method to get the last leaf that is a descendant of this node. If this node has no children, it is itself a leaf, so it returns this. (For node B, the last leaf is K. For node D, the last leaf is P.)

public int getLeafCount()

> Returns the number of leaves that are descendants of this node. If this node has no children, it is itself a leaf, so it returns 1. If a node has children, however, it is not a leaf, so it will not count itself. (For both nodes C and G, the leaf count is 3.)

public int getLevel()

> Returns the current level of this node with relation to the root of the tree (i.e., its distance from the root). If this node is the root, its level is zero. (For node A, the level is 0. For node M, the level is 3.)

public DefaultMutableTreeNode getNextLeaf()

> Returns the next node in its parent's tree that is a leaf. If this is the last node in its parent's tree, it returns null. It does not matter whether this node is a leaf or not. (For node H, the next leaf is Z.)

public DefaultMutableTreeNode getNextNode()

Returns the next node in the tree, where "next" is defined in terms of a preorder traversal of the tree. If this node is the last in a preorder traversal, it returns `null`. See the `preorderEnumeration()` method later for a more detailed discussion of preorder traversals. (For node E, the next node is J. For node T, the next node is D.)

public DefaultMutableTreeNode getNextSibling()

Returns the next child in this parent's child array. If this node is the last (or only) child, it returns `null`. (For Node Q, the next sibling is R. For Node D, the next sibling is null.)

public TreeNode[] getPath()

Returns the path from the root to this node as an array of `TreeNode` objects. (The path for node R is A B E J R.)

protected TreeNode[] getPathToRoot(TreeNode node, int depth)

This protected helper method recursively walks up a tree from `node` to the root. The `getPath()` method calls this method with `this` and 0 as arguments, creating an array of tree nodes with root at index 0 and this `node` as the last element of the array. Normally, you would just use the public `getPath()` call. (For node R, with an initial depth of 0, this method would return an array containing nodes A B E J R.)

public DefaultMutableTreeNode getPreviousLeaf()

Returns the previous node in its parent's tree that is a leaf. If this is the first node in its parent's tree, it returns `null`. It does not matter whether this node is a leaf or not. (For node H, the previous leaf is null. For node T, the previous leaf is X.)

public DefaultMutableTreeNode getPreviousNode()

Returns the previous node in the tree, where "previous" is defined in terms of a preorder traversal of the tree. If this node is the first in a preorder traversal, it returns `null`. See the `preorderEnumeration()` method later in the chapter for a more detailed discussion of preorder traversals. (For node E, the previous node is B. For node C, the previous node is K.)

public DefaultMutableTreeNode getPreviousSibling()

Returns the previous child in this parent's child array. If this node is the first (or only) child, it returns null. (For node Q, the previous sibling is null. For node D, the previous sibling is C.)

public TreeNode getRoot()

You can use this method to retrieve the root of the tree this node belongs to. Any given tree will have exactly one root, where a root is defined as the node

with a null parent. (For any node in the example tree, including A, the root
is A.)

public TreeNode getSharedAncestor(DefaultMutableTreeNode node2)

This method finds the closest shared ancestor for this node and the given
node2. If node2 is a descendant of this node, this node is the common
ancestor (and vice versa). The "worst" case for two nodes in the same tree
would be to have the root as the only shared ancestor. If node2 is not in this
node's tree, it returns null. (For nodes J and K, the shared ancestor is B. For
nodes J and V, the shared ancestor is A.)

public int getSiblingCount()

Returns the number of siblings for this node. Since a node is its own sibling,
this method returns the child count for this node's parent. (For node Q, the
sibling count is 2. For node K, the sibling count is 1.)

public Object[] getUserObjectPath()

Returns all user objects along the path from the root to this node. May
contain nulls if some nodes along the path have no user object. Recall that a
user object is any arbitrary piece of data you wish to store with a node. In a filesystem tree that stores file and folder names as user objects, for example, this
method would return an array of String objects where each string represents a
directory in the path and the last string represents the selected file.

public void insert(MutableTreeNode node, int index)

Inserts a new node as a child to this node at the given index. If index is larger
than getChildCount() + 1, it generates an ArrayIndexOutOfBoundsException. If node is null or is an ancestor of this node, it generates an
IllegalArgumentException. If this node doesn't accept children (allows-
Children is false), it generates an IllegalStateException.

public boolean isLeaf()

Returns true if this node has no children. It does not check the allowsChildren property. (Node B returns false. Node R returns true.)

public boolean isNodeAncestor(TreeNode node2)

Returns true if node2 is an ancestor of this node. (E, B, and A are all ancestors of node E.)

public boolean isNodeChild(TreeNode node2)

Returns true if node2 is in this node's child array. (For node G, L returns
true, while S returns false.)

public boolean isNodeDescendant(DefaultMutableTreeNode node2)

Returns true if node2 is a descendant of this node. (For node G, both L and S
return true, but C and H return false.)

public boolean isNodeRelated(DefaultMutableTreeNode node2)

> Returns `true` if `node2` is in the same tree as this node. (Any two nodes listed in our example are part of the same tree, so they would all return true.)

public boolean isNodeSibling(TreeNode node2)

> Returns `true` if `node2` is a sibling of this node. (For node Q, R is a sibling, but S is not.)

public boolean isRoot()

> Returns `true` if this node is the root of its tree. "Rootness" is determined by having a `null` parent. (A is the root of the tree.)

public void remove(int index)
public void remove(MutableTreeNode node)

> Remove a child from this node. In the first version, if an invalid index number is given, you receive an `ArrayIndexOutOfBoundsException`. In the second version, if the node given does not exist as a child, you receive `IllegalArgumentException`. The child is given a `null` parent after removal.

public void removeAllChildren()

> Removes all of the children attached to this node. It does nothing if no children exist.

public void removeFromParent()

> Removes this node from its parent. This works like a call to `getParent()`. `remove(this)`, by creating a new tree rooted at this node.

Enumeration Methods

If you want to look at all of the nodes in a tree, you should use one of the following enumeration methods to get that list of nodes. The enumeration does not build a copy of the tree, but it does keep track of where you are in the tree, and when you call the `nextElement()` method, you get the correct next element according to the traversal you picked. The code to traverse (or search) a tree looks something like this:

```
Enumeration e = root.breadthFirstEnumeration();
while (e.hasMoreElements()) {
    DefaultMutableTreeNode node = (DefaultMutableTreeNode)e.nextElement();
    System.out.print(node.getUserObject() + " ");
    // or do something else more interesting with the node . . .
}
System.out.println();
```

public Enumeration breadthFirstEnumeration()

> A breadth-first traversal starts looking at the root node, then goes to its children, in ascending index order. After each child has been looked at, the

traversal moves on to the children of the root's first child and so on. The tree in Figure 17-3 produces the following breadth-first output:

A B C D E F G H I J K L M N O P Q R S T U V W X Y Z

A breadth-first traversal might be good if you were searching a very large tree for some item, and you expected to find the item near the top of the tree.

public Enumeration depthFirstEnumeration()
public Enumeration postorderEnumeration()

Depth-first (sometimes called *postorder*) traversals start with the root, go to its first child, go to that node's first child, and so on. The first node it actually "looks" at is the first leaf it hits. Then it backs up one level and goes to other children of that first leaf's parent. In our example, the depth-first traversal produces this output:

Q R J E K F B W X S L T M G C N H Z Y U V O P I D A

A depth-first traversal would be useful if you expected to find the leaves of a tree interesting and want to start working with them quickly. For example, in a filesystem a depth-first enumeration would get you to a file object right away.

public Enumeration preorderEnumeration()

Preorder traversals start at the root, look at it, then move on to the first child, look at it, then move on to its first child, look at it, and so on. The preorder output of the example looks like this:

A B E J Q R F K C G L S W X M T D H N I O U Y Z V P

A preorder traversal is useful for dumping out a tree that represents some parsed data. In the filesystem example, such a traversal would be useful if you needed information about each directory you visited, before you looked at any of its children, but you didn't want to look at all of the top-level directories first (like you would with a breadth-first search).

public Enumeration children()
public Enumeration pathFromAncestorEnumeration(TreeNode ancestor)

These last two enumerations do not give you the entire tree, but rather, an interesting piece of it. The `children()` call is inherited from `TreeNode` and gives an enumeration of the immediate children of this node. The `pathFrom-AncestorEnumeration()` gives you a list of all the nodes from the root down to this node. (The children of A are B, C, and D. The path from ancestor for node N is A, D, H, N.)

Miscellaneous Methods

public Object clone()

> The `clone()` method is overridden to make it public. This provides a dupli-
> cate of the node with a minimum of effort. The cloned node has no parent,
> no children, and shares the same reference to the `userObject`, if one exists.

public String toString()

> Returns the `toString()` call on the node's user object. If the node has no
> user object, it returns `null`

public Enumeration getExpandedDescendants(TreePath parent)

> Returns an enumeration of all currently expanded nodes that are descen-
> dants of `parent`. If `parent` is `null` or is not expanded itself, `null` is returned.

protected Enumeration getDescendantToggledPaths(TreePath parent)

> Returns an enumeration of descendant nodes (from `parent`) that have been
> expanded. This differs from `getExpandedDescendants()` in that the node
> does not currently have to be expanded. The only requirement is that the
> node was expanded at some point.

The TreePath Class

If you look at a collection of these node objects from one node to one of its
descendants, you have a path. The `TreePath` class is straightforward, but it does
have some convenience methods for comparing and dealing with paths. A `Tree-`
`Path` is a read-only object. If you want to change the structure of the path, you
need to interact with the model, not the path. (These paths serve as a "view" of a
tree branch, but are not part of an existing tree.)

Properties

The `TreePath` class has five simple properties. The values of these properties,
shown in Table 17-7, are set by the constructor, and after that are read-only.

Table 17-7. TreePath Properties

Property	Data Type	get	is	set	bound	Default Value
lastPathComponent	Object	•				
parentPath	TreePath	•				
path	Object[]	•				
pathComponent (indexed)	Object	•				
pathCount	int	•				

The path property is the array of tree nodes from the root to another node. Since the path is an Object array and not a TreeNode array, you can still use a Tree-Path to describe a path in a tree with custom nodes, such as our expression tree. The parentPath is a TreePath leading up to (and including) the parent of this node. pathCount is the number of nodes in the path property. lastPathComponent lets you access the last node on the path, and the indexed property, pathComponent, lets you retrieve any node.

Fields

protected transient Object[] path
   This field holds the value for the path property.

Constructors

public TreePath(Object singlePath)
public TreePath(Object[] path)
   These constructors build a TreePath object out of one or several Objects. If you want a path represented by just one node, you can use the first version of the constructor. Typically, paths will consist of several nodes from the root down to some interesting node, so you will use the second version. A Tree-Path should reflect all the nodes from the root down, but there is no check involved if you tried to create a "partial" path from an ancestor node that was not necessarily the root. However, other classes dealing with TreePath objects expect the first entry in the path to be the root of the tree.

protected TreePath(TreePath parent, Object lastElement)
protected TreePath(Object[] path, int length)
   These protected constructors build a normal TreePath object and fill out the parentPath property for this object.

protected TreePath()
   This constructor is meant for subclasses that do not want to use the regular constructors, which (among other things) force building up the parentPath property. The *javadoc* for this method warns that if you subclass TreePath and use this constructor, you should also override the getPath(), getPath-Count(), getPathComponent(), and equals() methods.

Miscellaneous Methods

public boolean equals(Object otherPath)
   Returns true if otherPath is the same as this path. Paths are considered equal if each node along this path equals the corresponding node in otherPath.

public boolean isDescendant(TreePath path)

> Returns true if subPath is a descendant of this path. The given path is considered a descendant of this path if path contains all of the nodes found in this path. This differs from equals() in that path could be longer than this path and still be a descendant. If this path is null, it returns false.

public TreePath pathByAddingChild(Object child)

> This method returns a new TreePath object created by appending child to this path. The child argument cannot be null.

public String toString()

> Returns a string representation of the path. It includes a comma-separated list of the individual toString() calls on all of the objects in the path.

The JTree Class

Now that you've seen all of the tree and node models and some of the default implementations, let's look at the visual representation we can give them. The JTree class can build up trees out of several different objects, including a Tree-Model. JTree extends directly from JComponent and just represents the visual side of any valid tree structure.

Here's the source code that built the expression tree example in Figure 17-5. In this example, the init() method does all of the real work by creating a series of OpNode nodes and several Integer objects and connecting them in a valid expression. That tree model is passed to the JTree constructor, which in turn creates the component that we add to the content pane. Like many other components, JTree does not scroll automatically, so you would need to place it in a JScrollPane if you expected the tree to be large. (JTree implements Scrollable, which allows a JScrollPane to be intelligent about scrolling.)

```
// ExprTree1.java
// An expression tree for holding algebraic expressions, built up using
// ExpressionTreeModel for use with a JTree object.
//
import java.awt.*;
import java.awt.event.*;
import java.util.*;
import javax.swing.*;
import javax.swing.tree.*;
import javax.swing.event.*;

public class ExprTree1 extends JFrame implements TreeExpansionListener {

    JTree tree;
    ExpressionTreeModel treeModel;
    OpNode[] operators = new OpNode[4];
```

```java
Integer[] operands = new Integer[5];

public ExprTree1() {
  super("Demo Expression Tree");
  setSize(400, 300);
  addWindowListener(new BasicWindowMonitor());
}

public void init() {
  // create the nodes and the leaves
  operators[0] = new OpNode("+");
  operators[1] = new OpNode("*");
  operators[2] = new OpNode("-");
  operators[3] = new OpNode("/");
  operands[0] = new Integer(1);
  operands[1] = new Integer(2);
  operands[2] = new Integer(3);
  operands[3] = new Integer(4);
  operands[4] = new Integer(5);

  // start our tree with a root of "+"
  treeModel = new ExpressionTreeModel(operators[0]);

  // build the tree from the root down
  treeModel.insertNode(operators[0], operands[0], 0);
  treeModel.insertNode(operators[0], operators[1], 1);
  treeModel.insertNode(operators[1], operators[2], 0);
  treeModel.insertNode(operators[1], operators[3], 1);
  treeModel.insertNode(operators[2], operands[1], 0);
  treeModel.insertNode(operators[2], operands[2], 1);
  treeModel.insertNode(operators[3], operands[3], 0);
  treeModel.insertNode(operators[3], operands[4], 1);

  tree = new JTree(treeModel);
  tree.setShowsRootHandles(true);
  tree.collapseRow(0);

  // Listen to our own expand/collapse events to keep the labels in sync
  tree.addTreeExpansionListener(this);
  getContentPane().add(tree, BorderLayout.CENTER);
}

// Make sure that we get the correct label after we have expanded the node
public void treeExpanded(TreeExpansionEvent tee) {
  OpNode node = (OpNode)tee.getPath().getLastPathComponent();
  node.setExpanded(true);
  treeModel.refresh(tee);
}
```

```
// Likewise, make sure that we get the correct label after we have collapsed
// the node
public void treeCollapsed(TreeExpansionEvent tee) {
  OpNode node = (OpNode)tee.getPath().getLastPathComponent();
  node.setExpanded(false);
  treeModel.refresh(tee);
}

public static void main(String args[]) {
  ExprTree1 et = new ExprTree1();
  et.init();
  et.setVisible(true);
}
}
```

In this example, we listen and react to tree expansion events, and therefore implement `TreeExpansionListener`. An expansion event occurs any time you open or close a folder. We listen to these events because our nodes change their labels depending on whether they are collapsed or expanded. When an expansion event arrives, `treeExpanded()` and `treeCollapsed()` call our model's `refresh()` method, which updates the tree. (This method is unique to our `Expression-TreeModel`.) Normally, you do not need to worry about nodes suddenly changing their appearance. We'll look more closely at expansion events in the "Tree Events" section.

Properties

The `JTree` class contains properties (shown in Table 17-8) for manually displaying and editing tree cells if you need this control. The `editable` property specifies whether cells can be edited (i.e., modified by users). The `cellEditor`, `cellRenderer`, and `invokesStopCellEditing` properties affect the components used to display and manipulate trees. Setting `invokesStopCellEditing` to true forces changes to a cell to be saved if editing is interrupted. The `JTree` class also provides properties that allow you to control how the tree appears regardless of the display and editing mechanisms used. Many aspects of the tree's appearance are based on the concept of a "row," which is a single item currently displayed in the tree. You can control the row height and root display style with the `rowHeight`, `fixedRowHeight`, `rootVisible`, and `showsRootHandles` properties. `fixedRowHeight` specifies that all rows must have the same height; if it is `false`, row heights may vary. `rootVisible` is true if the tree's root is displayed; if it is `false`, the root is omitted. Its initial value depends on which constructor you call. If `scrollsOnExpand` is true, expanding any node automatically scrolls the tree so that as many of the node's children as possible are visible. Finally, `shows-RootHandles` determines whether or not the one-touch expand/collapse control (or "handle") appears for the root node.

Table 17-8. JTree Properties

Property	Data Type	get	is	set	bound	Default Value
UI*	TreeUI	•		•	•	from L&F
UIClassID*	String	•				"TreeUI"
model	TreeModel	•		•	•	null
selectionModel	TreeSelection-Model	•		•	•	DefaultTreeSelec-tionModel()
accessibleContext*	AccessibleCon-text	•				JTree.Accessible-JTree()
cellEditor	TreeCellEditor	•		•	•	null
cellRenderer	TreeCellRenderer	•		•	•	null
editable	boolean		•	•	•	false
fixedRowHeight	boolean		•			true
invokesStopCellEditing	boolean	•		•	•	false
largeModel	boolean		•	•	•	false
opaque*	boolean		•	•	•	true
rootVisible	boolean		•	•	•	true
rowHeight[a]	int	•		•	•	16
scrollsOnExpand	boolean	•		•	•	true
showsRootHandles	boolean	•		•	•	false
visibleRowCount	int	•		•	•	20

See also properties of the JComponent class (Table 3-5).

[a] A value of –1 indicates variable row heights.

Another interesting property of trees is largeModel. Some UI managers pay attention to this property, and if it is set to true, alter their behavior, presumably to increase the efficiency of certain things, such as updates and model events. What size tree merits using this property depends largely on your application, but if you're wondering if your tree could benefit from a large model, try turning the property on and play with your tree to see if you notice a performance gain.

Many methods of the JTree class should properly be considered accessors for properties we haven't listed in Table 17-8. This omission is intentional (though not undebated). We felt it would be clearer if these methods were discussed with similar methods that don't fit the "property" patterns.

Events

The JTree class adds support for expansion and selection events as shown in Table 17-9. We'll be looking at these events in greater detail (with examples) in "Tree Events" later in this chapter.

Table 17-9. JTree Events

Event	Description
TreeExpansionEvent	A tree node has been expanded or collapsed.
TreeSelectionEvent	A row (path) has been selected or, if more than one row can be selected, a row has been added or removed from the current selection.

These events are supported by the following methods:

public void addTreeExpansionListener(TreeExpansionListener l)
public void removeTreeExpansionListener(TreeExpansionListener l)

   Add or remove listeners interested in receiving tree expansion events.

public void addTreeWillExpandListener (TreeWillExpandListener tel)
public void removeTreeWillExpandListener (TreeWillExpandListener tel)

   Ad or remove listeners interested in receiving "tree will expand" events. Note that no TreeWillExpandEvent class exists. The methods of the TreeWillExpandListener interface (discussed later in this chapter) use TreeExpansionEvent objects.

public void addTreeSelectionListener(TreeSelectionListener l)
public void removeTreeSelectionListener(TreeSelectionListener l)

   Add or remove listeners interested in receiving tree selection events.

public void fireTreeCollapsed(TreePath collapsedPath)
public void fireTreeExpanded(TreePath expandedPath)

   These methods notify any registered TreeExpansionListener objects that a path has collapsed or expanded. The collapsedPath and expandedPath arguments are used to construct a new TreeExpansionEvent with this JTree as the source.

public void fireTreeWillExpand(TreePath path) throws ExpandVetoException
public void fireTreeWillCollapse(TreePath path) throws ExpandVetoException

   These methods notify registered listeners that a tree node is about to expand or collapse. The path argument will be used to construct a new TreeExpansionEvent object sent to the listeners. The ExpandVetoException class is discussed later in the "Tree Events" section of this chapter.

protected void fireValueChanged(TreeSelectionEvent selectionEvent)

Notifies registered `TreeSelectionListener` objects that a selection event has occurred. Whenever a listener registers with this `JTree`, an event redirector is set up to grab the selection events coming from the tree selection model and pass them on to the listener with this `JTree` as the source. You do not need to worry about the selection model in place to attach a listener. You attach the listener to the `JTree` itself, and the redirector does all of the work.

`JTree` also generates property change events whenever any of its bound properties are modified.

Constants

The constants provided with the `JTree` class are used for reporting the names of bound properties in property change events and are listed in Table 17-10.

Table 17-10. JTree Constants for Use with Property Change Events

Constant	Type	Description
CELL_EDITOR_PROPERTY	String	The name of the cellEditor property
CELL_RENDERER_PROPERTY	String	The name of the cellRenderer property
EDITABLE_PROPERTY	String	The name of the editable property
INVOKES_STOP_CELL_EDITING_ PROPERTY	String	The name of the invokesStopCellEditing property
LARGE_MODEL_PROPERTY	String	The name of the largeModel property
ROOT_VISIBLE_PROPERTY	String	The name of the rootVisible property
ROW_HEIGHT_PROPERTY	String	The name of the rowHeight property
SELECTION_MODEL_PROPERTY	String	The name of the selectionModel property
SCROLLS_ON_EXPAND_PROPERTY	String	The name of the scrollsOnExpand property
SHOWS_ROOT_HANDLES_PROPERTY	String	The name of the showsRootHandles property
TREE_MODEL_PROPERTY	String	The name of the model property
VISIBLE_ROW_COUNT_PROPERTY	String	The name of the visibleRowCount property

Fields

protected transient TreeCellEditor cellEditor
protected transient TreeCellRenderer cellRenderer
protected boolean editable
protected boolean invokesStopCellEditing
protected boolean largeModel
protected boolean rootVisible
protected int rowHeight
protected boolean scrollsOnExpand

protected transient TreeSelectionModel selectionModel

protected boolean showsRootHandles

protected transient TreeModel treeModel

protected int visibleRowCount

These fields store the values for their respective properties. The `treeModel` field corresponds to the `model` property.

protected transient JTree.TreeSelectionRedirector selectionRedirector

Holds a selection redirector object, which listens for tree selection events coming from the selection model. The `TreeSelectionRedirector` inner class inserts this tree as the source of the event, and then redistributes the modified event to any registered listeners.

Constructors

public JTree()

Creates a tree using a `DefaultTreeModel` object as its base. You probably want to use one of the other constructors to get an interesting tree. The default tree is populated with some meaningless sample content.

public JTree(TreeNode root)

public JTree(TreeNode root, boolean asksAllowsChildren)

These constructors build new trees using the node `root` as the root of the tree. They also use the `DefaultTreeModel` as their model.

public JTree(TreeModel model)

Builds a tree using the model provided. The `model` argument contains the root of the tree.

public JTree(Object value[])

public JTree(Vector value)

public JTree(Hashtable value)

These convenience constructors build a `DefaultTreeModel` object and use the inner class `JTree.DynamicUtilTreeNode` to populate the tree using the `value` argument as children. If any element in `value` is itself an `Object[]`, a `Vector`, or a `Hashtable`, a node will be built for that element and its contents become children of the node. This recursive process continues until all elements and their contents have been explored.

The last constructor is great for simple data structures that you want to display as a tree. Figure 17-7 shows the tree that results when you display a hash table.

Even though this tree is larger than the tree of Figure 17-1, it takes less code to set it up, as follows.

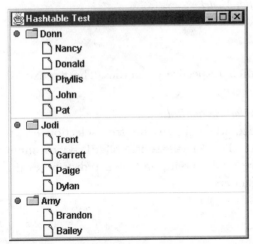

Figure 17-7. A JTree built using a Hashtable and the DefaultTreeModel

```java
// ObjectTree.java
// A Simple test to see how we can build a tree and populate it.
//
import java.awt.*;
import java.awt.event.*;
import javax.swing.*;
import javax.swing.tree.*;
import java.util.*;

public class ObjectTree extends JFrame {

  JTree tree;
  String[][] sampleData = {
    {"Amy"}, {"Brandon", "Bailey"},
    {"Jodi"}, {"Trent", "Garrett", "Paige", "Dylan"},
    {"Donn"}, {"Nancy", "Donald", "Phyllis", "John", "Pat"}
  };

  public ObjectTree() {
    super("Hashtable Test");
    setSize(400, 300);
    addWindowListener(new BasicWindowMonitor());
  }

  public void init() {
    Hashtable h = new Hashtable();
    // build up the hashtable using every other entry in the String[][] as a key
    // followed by a "value" which is a String[]
    for (int i = 0; i < sampleData.length; i+=2) {
      h.put(sampleData[i][0], sampleData[i + 1]);
```

```
      }
      tree = new JTree(h);
      getContentPane().add(tree, BorderLayout.CENTER);
    }

  public static void main(String args[]) {
    ObjectTree tt = new ObjectTree();
    tt.init();
    tt.setVisible(true);
  }
}
```

Tree Model Methods

The JTree class provides two static methods that can build a tree model for use with JTree components.

protected static TreeModel getDefaultTreeModel()

Creates and populates a "demo" tree. This is useful for visual builders, where you start with an essentially empty tree and add, delete, or configure components graphically.

protected static TreeModel createTreeModel(Object value)

Generates a tree on the fly by creating a DefaultTreeModel object and populating it with the objects present in value. The value object is quite often an Object array, a Vector, or a Hashtable. The constructors with value arguments use this method.

Selection Methods

One of the primary functions the JTree class provides is programmer access to the selection status of the tree. Most of these functions work with a selection model discussed in "Tree Selections." We'll say more about this later, but selections may be based either on rows or paths. A row is a displayed element in a tree; you refer to a row by its index. A path is a list of nodes from the root to the selected node.

addSelectionInterval(int row1, int row2)

Adds the paths between row1 and row2 to the current selection. It uses getPathBetweenRows() to collect the list of paths to add.

public void addSelectionPath(TreePath path)
public void addSelectionPaths(TreePath paths[])
public void addSelectionRow(int row)
public void addSelectionRows(int rows[])

You can use one of these methods to add to the current selection on the tree. If you supply an array of paths or integers, each of the paths or rows indicated will be selected. If any path or row is not currently visible, it will be made visible.

public void clearSelection()

Clears the current selection completely.

public Object getLastSelectedPathComponent()

Returns the path component representing the last path entry in the current selection. If the selection is empty, this returns `null`.

public TreePath getLeadSelectionPath()
public int getLeadSelectionRow()

Return the lead path or row for a selection. A "lead" path is the last path that was added to the selection.

public int getMaxSelectionRow()

Returns the last row in the current selection. If only one row is selected, that row index is returned.

public int getMinSelectionRow()

Returns the first row in the current selection. If only one row is selected, that row index is returned.

public int getSelectionCount()

Returns the number of paths that are currently selected.

public TreePath getSelectionPath()
public TreePath[] getSelectionPaths()
public int[] getSelectionRows()

Retrieve the current selected paths (or rows). The `getSelectionPath()` convenience method returns the first path in the selection. The equivalent method for rows is `getMinSelectionRow()`.

public boolean isPathSelected(TreePath path)
public boolean isRowSelected(int row)

These methods return `true` if the given path or row is in the current selection.

public boolean isSelectionEmpty()

Returns `true` if the selection is currently empty (i.e., nothing is selected).

public void removeSelectionInterval(int row1, int row2)

Removes the paths between `row1` and `row2` from the current selection. It uses `getPathBetweenRows()` to collect the list of paths to deselect.

public void removeSelectionPath(TreePath path)
public void removeSelectionPaths(TreePath paths[])

public void removeSelectionRow(int row)

public void removeSelectionRows(int rows[])

Remove pieces of the current selection dictated by the rows or paths provided as arguments. If a path or row specified in one of these methods is not in the current selection, it is ignored and any remaining rows or paths are deselected.

public void setSelectionInterval(int row1, int row2)

Sets the current selection to represent the paths between `row1` and `row2`. It uses `getPathBetweenRows()` to collect the list of paths to select.

public void setSelectionPath(TreePath path)

public void setSelectionPaths(TreePath paths[])

public void setSelectionRow(int row)

public void setSelectionRows(int rows[])

Set the current selection on the tree. If you supply an array of paths or integers, each of the paths or rows indicated will be selected. If any path or row is not currently visible, it will be made visible.

Expansion Methods

For any entry in your tree, you can check to see if it is currently expanded or collapsed. A node is considered expanded if all of the nodes in its path are also expanded. (This applies to leaves as well.) You can also programmatically control the collapsing and expanding of parts of your tree. All of the methods below accept either a `TreePath` or a row (`int`) argument.

public void collapsePath(TreePath path)

public void collapseRow(int row)

These methods collapse the path or row given if needed. (In the case of the path argument, the last component of the path is collapsed.) Once collapsed, it tries to make the path visible as well.

public void expandPath(TreePath path)

public void expandRow(int row)

These methods expand the given path or row if needed. Once expanded, it tries to make the path visible as well.

public boolean isCollapsed(int row)

public boolean isCollapsed(TreePath path)

These methods return `true` if any node in the given path or row is not currently expanded. If every node is expanded, these methods return false.

public boolean isExpanded(int row)

public boolean isExpanded(TreePath path)

> Return true if the given path or row is currently fully expanded. If any nodes in the path are not expanded, these methods return false.

public boolean hasBeenExpanded(TreePath path)

> Returns true if the path has ever been expanded.

protected void setExpandedState(TreePath path, boolean state)

> As long as no TreeWillExpandListener vetoes the move, this helper method sets the state of the path to state, and marks all parents of path as expanded, regardless of the state for path. The JTree class keeps track of the fact that a node has been expanded in a private hashtable called expanded-State.

protected void removeDescendantToggledPaths(Enumeration toRemove)

> Removes references to the descendants of nodes in the toRemove list from the expandedState cache.

protected void clearToggledPaths()

> This method clears the expandedState cache of all entries.

Path and Row Methods

public TreePath getClosestPathForLocation(int x, int y)

public int getClosestRowForLocation(int x, int y)

> These methods return the path or row closest to a given location (x,y) in the component, relative to its upper-left corner. These methods only return null if nothing is visible. If you need to be sure that the point (x,y) is actually inside the bounds for the path or row returned, you need to check that yourself. The getPathForLocation() and getRowForLocation() methods do a basic check for you and return null if the point falls outside the closest row, if that's all you need.

protected TreePath[] getPathBetweenRows(int row1, int row2)

> You can use this method to retrieve the various different paths between row1 and row2 (including row2). If no tree exists, this method returns null. This protected method is used by the different selection interval methods.

public Rectangle getPathBounds(TreePath path)

> Returns the Rectangle object that encompasses the specified path, if that path is not currently visible. The scrollPathToVisible() method calls this to show a particular path on the screen. If the path is already visible, this method returns null.

public TreePath getPathForLocation(int x, int y)

This method is a more restricted version of `getClosestPathForLocation()`. If `x` or `y` ends up outside the bounds of the path returned by the closest path call, this method returns `null`.

public TreePath getPathForRow(int row)

Returns the path associated with the specified row. If `row` is an invalid value (less than zero or greater than the number of rows in the current tree), or the row is not currently visible, this method returns `null`.

public Rectangle getRowBounds(int row)

This method functions like `getPathBounds()` for the given row.

public int getRowCount()

Returns the number of rows that are currently visible. See the `isVisible()` method below.

public int getRowForLocation(int x, int y)

This method is a more restricted version of `getClosestRowForLocation()`. If `x` or `y` ends up outside the bounds of the row returned by the closest row call, this method will return `-1`.

public int getRowForPath(TreePath path)

Returns the row number for the last component in `path`. If any part of `path` is not visible, or `path` is null, this method returns `-1`.

public boolean isVisible(TreePath path)

Returns `true` if the path given is currently visible. A "visible" path is any path you can see in the tree without expanding another node. If you have the tree in a scroll pane, a path could be off the screen, but still be considered visible.

public void makeVisible(TreePath path)

Makes `path` visible, if it is not already visible.

public void scrollPathToVisible(TreePath path)
public void scrollRowToVisible(int row)

If the tree is in a scroll pane, scroll the given path or row to make it appear in the pane. A path is expanded up to its last component, if need be, to make it visible. (By definition, rows are always visible.) The tree must be in a scrollable environment (like a `JScrollPane` or `JViewport`) for this to work.

Editing Methods

public void cancelEditing()

Cancels editing of a tree cell. If no cell is being edited, this method has no effect.

public TreeNode getEditingPath()

Returns the path to the element in the tree that is currently being edited. If the tree is not being edited, this method returns `null`.

public boolean isEditing()

Returns `true` if the current selection is being edited.

public boolean isPathEditable(TreePath path)

Returns the value of the `editable` property for a given path. If it returns `true`, the path can be edited. It gets called by the UI manager before starting to edit a node so that a subclass of `JTree` can override this method and say yes or no based on some appropriate criteria. (For example, you could allow editing of leaves, but not allow editing of folders.)

public void startEditingAtPath(TreePath path)

Tries to start editing the last element in `path`. This might fail if the cell editor will not edit that element.

public boolean stopEditing()

Stops the tree from being edited. If the tree is not being edited, then this method has no effect. It returns `true` if the tree was being edited, and the cell editor stopped successfully. It returns `false` otherwise—for example, if the tree was not being edited or the editor could not be stopped.

Miscellaneous Methods

public String convertValueToText(Object value, boolean selected, boolean expanded, boolean leaf, int row, boolean hasFocus)

Converts `value` to a string for the cell's renderer by calling `value.toString()`. You could subclass `JTree` and override this to prepare a more meaningful string.

public String getToolTipText(MouseEvent event)

Returns the tooltip text from a cell's renderer. For this to work properly, however, this `JTree` must be registered manually with the `ToolTipManager`, and your cell renderer must have some tooltip text:

```
ToolTipManager.sharedInstance().registerComponent(tree);
((JComponent)tree.getCellRenderer()).setToolTipText("This is a tip.");
```

The default renderer displays the same tip for every cell in your tree. To get more interesting tips, you'll need to create your own renderer. An example of such a renderer is discussed later in the "Custom Renderers" section.

public void treeDidChange()

Updates the tree when nodes have expanded or collapsed, or when nodes have been inserted.

protected TreeModelListener createTreeModelListener()

This method returns a new `TreeModelHandler` object (see the section on "Inner Classes" below) for use with this tree. The `TreeModelHandler` manages the private `expandedState` hashtable.

JTree Inner Classes

protected class JTree.AccessibleJTree

This class represents the accessible implementation for `JTree`.

public static class JTree.DynamicUtilTreeNode

Various constructors of the `JTree` class use this inner class to build tree nodes out of arrays, vectors and hashtables.

protected static class JTree.EmptySelectionModel

As its name implies, this inner class provides an implementation of the `Tree-SelectionModel` interface (by extending `DefaultTreeSelectionModel`) that does not allow any selections.

protected class JTree.TreeModelHandler

This class manages the `expandedState` cache by listening to expansion and modification events coming from the model.

protected class JTree.TreeSelectionRedirector

This class contains methods for redirecting the source of events. Typically this is done when the tree model generates an event, but the `JTree` object associated with that model needs to be listed as the source of the event.

UI Methods

The methods in this group (with the exception of `UpdateUI()`) implement the scrollable interface, which allow a `JScrollPane` or `JViewport` to be "intelligent" when scrolling a `JTree`.

public Dimension getPreferredScrollableViewportSize()

Returns the preferred size of a scrollable viewport for this tree based on the visible row count (for height) and the current preferred width.

public int getScrollableBlockIncrement(Rectangle visibleRect, int orientation, int direction)

Returns the appropriate block increment (the amount needed to expose one "page" or "screen") for the viewport's scrollbars based on this tree and the parameters provided. The `visibleRect` argument is the viewable area of the viewport. Its size determines how much to scroll. You can use either `SwingConstants.VERTICAL` or `SwingConstants.HORIZONTAL` for orientation, and `direction` takes −1 for up or left, and 1 for down or right.

public boolean getScrollableTracksViewportHeight()

public boolean getScrollableTracksViewportWidth()

> Both of these methods return `false` to indicate that changing the size of the viewport containing the tree does not affect the calculated width or height of the tree. They can be overridden for specialized behavior. For example, if you placed your tree in a `JScrollPane` and the width of that pane were suddenly changed so that a given node might not be visible without scrolling, you could turn on tooltips for the long node and supply a string that contained the entire path for that node. The tooltip popup would show the whole path without scrolling, regardless of the viewport size.

public int getScrollableUnitIncrement(Rectangle visibleRect, int orientation, int direction)

> Returns the amount needed to expose the next row. If the direction is HORIZONTAL, it returns 4.

public void updateUI()

> Overrides the `JComponent` `updateUI()` call to replace the tree's UI with the version from the interface manager. As with other components, you can use this to refresh the tree after the look-and-feel has changed.

Tree Selections

After you have the tree built and looking the way you want it to, you need to start working with selections so it does something useful. The `JTree` class introduced many of the selection manipulation methods already, but let's take a closer look at the model for selecting paths in a tree and the `DefaultSelectionModel` provided in the `javax.swing.tree` package. If you're comfortable with selection models, you probably won't find anything surprising here and may want to skip to "Editing and Rendering."

Selections are based on rows or paths. It's important to realize the distinction between a "row" and a "path" for trees. A path contains the list of nodes from the root of the tree to another node. Paths exist regardless of whether or not you plan to display the tree.

Rows, however, are completely dependent on the graphical display of a tree. The easiest way to think about a row is to think of the tree as a `JList` object. Each item in the list is a row on the tree. That row corresponds to some particular path. As you expand and collapse folders, the number of rows associated with the tree changes. It's the `RowMapper` object's job to relate a row number to the correct path.

Depending on your application, you may find rows or paths more efficient to deal with. If your program deals mostly with the user object data, paths will most likely be the thing to use. If you're working with the graphical interface (automatically expanding folders and things like that) the rows may be more useful.

The RowMapper Interface

Tree selections make extensive use of the RowMapper interface. It is a simple interface with one method:

public int[] getRowsForPaths(TreePath paths[])

> The UI for your tree should implement this to return a list of row indices matching the paths supplied. If any of the paths are null or not visible, a –1 should be placed in the return int array. While this may seem like an obvious task, you must account for the expanded or collapsed state of the nodes in the tree; remember that there's no such thing as a collapsed row. This is one reason the JTree class cannot simply use a ListSelectionModel.

The TreeSelectionModel Interface

Now for the heart of selections. The TreeSelectionModel determines what a tree selection can look like.

Properties

The TreeSelectionModel contains the properties listed in Table 17-11. The selection model properties deal primarily with the current selection on the tree. The notion of a "lead" selection stems from the fact that a selection can happen as a process, not only as a single event. The lead selection is the most recently added cell in the selection. It might be the only path selected, but it might also be the most recent selection out of several in a range or discontiguous group of selections. If the selection contains more than one path, the getSelectionPath() method returns the first selection in the path, which may or may not be the same thing as getLeadSelectionPath(). It's also good to remember that selecting a "folder" node in a tree does not imply selecting all of the nodes underneath it, if it has children.

Having said that, the rest of the properties are fairly self-explanatory. minSelectionRow and maxSelectionRow let you get the smallest and largest selected row numbers. rowMapper holds a utility that manages the mapping between rows and row numbers. selectionPaths and selectionRows let you access the rows or paths that are currently selected. selectionCount tells you the number of rows that are selected.

Table 17-11. TreeSelectionModel Properties

Property	Data Type	get	is	set	bound	Default Value
leadSelectionPath	TreePath	•				
leadSelectionRow	int	•				
maxSelectionRow	int	•				
minSelectionRow	int	•				
rowMapper	RowMapper	•		•		
selectionCount	int	•				
selectionMode	int	•		•		
selectionPath	TreePath	•		•		
selectionPaths	TreePath[]	•		•		
selectionRows	int[]	•				
selectionEmpty	boolean		•			

Constants

The value of the selectionMode property must be one of the constants listed in Table 17-12 and defined in the TreeSelectionModel interface.

Table 17-12. TreeSelectionModel Constants

Constant	Type	Description
SINGLE_TREE_SELECTION	int	Allows only one path in the tree to be selected at any one time. Choosing a new path deselects the previous choice.
CONTIGUOUS_TREE_SELECTION	int	Allows several paths to be selected; they must be in a continuous block. The block ranges from the minSelectionRow to the maxSelectionRow.
DISCONTIGUOUS_TREE_SELECTION	int	Allows several paths to be selected; they can be any set of nodes, contiguous or otherwise.

Events

The TreeSelectionModel requires classes that implement the model to implement methods for registering listeners for property change events and tree selection events. TreeSelectionEvent is discussed in greater detail in "Tree Events," later in this chapter.

public void addPropertyChangeListener(PropertyChangeListener l)
public void removePropertyChangeListener(PropertyChangeListener l)
    Add and remove listeners interested in receiving property change events.

public void addTreeSelectionListener(TreeSelectionListener l)
public void removeTreeSelectionListener(TreeSelectionListener l)

Add and remove listeners interested in receiving tree selection events. These methods differ from the `JTree` methods for adding or removing listeners, in that the event source sent to these listeners is the selection model, whereas the event source sent to the `JTree` selection listeners is the tree itself.

Selection Methods

Many of these will look familiar if you read through the section on the `JTree` class. Trees pass along many of the selection calls to the selection model that supports it, so that you can deal primarily with the tree itself.

public void addSelectionPath(TreePath path)
public void addSelectionPaths(TreePath paths[])

These methods augment the current selection with the supplied path or paths.

public void clearSelection()

Clears the current selection, leaving the selection empty. If nothing is selected before calling `clearSelection()`, this method should have no effect.

public boolean isPathSelected(TreePath path)
public boolean isRowSelected(int row)

Return `true` if the path or row specified is in the current selection.

public void removeSelectionPath(TreePath path)
public void removeSelectionPaths(TreePath paths[]))

Remove the listed path or paths from the current selection. Any selected paths not specified remain selected.

public void resetRowSelection()

Updates the set of currently selected rows. This would be done if the row mapper changes, for example.

The DefaultTreeSelectionModel Class

Swing provides a default implementation of the tree selection model that supports all three modes of selection. You can see this model in use in an example near the beginning of this chapter.

Properties

The `DefaultTreeSelectionModel` inherits all of its properties from the `TreeSelectionModel` interface and supplies the default values listed in Table 17-13.

Table 17-13. DefaultTreeSelectionModel Properties

Property	Data Type	get	is	set	bound	Default Value
leadSelectionPath*	TreePath	•				null
leadSelectionRow*	int	•				-1
maxSelectionRow*	int	•				-1
minSelectionRow*	int	•				-1
rowMapper*	RowMapper	•		•		null
selectionCount*	int	•				0
selectionMode*	int	•		•	•	DISCONTIGUOUS_TREE_SELECTION
selectionPath*	TreePath	•		•		null
selectionPaths*	TreePath[]	•		•		null
selectionRows*	int[]	•				null
selectionEmpty*	boolean		•			true

Events

The DefaultTreeSelectionModel supports the same property change and tree selection events as the TreeSelectionModel interface.

public void addPropertyChangeListener(PropertyChangeListener l)
public void removePropertyChangeListener(PropertyChangeListener l)
    Add or remove listeners interested in receiving property change events.

public void addTreeSelectionListener(TreeSelectionListener l)
public void removeTreeSelectionListener(TreeSelectionListener l)
    Add or remove listeners interested in receiving tree selection events. These events come from the DefaultTreeSelectionModel, rather than the JTree itself.

Constant

The DefaultTreeSelectionModel contains one constant, shown in Table 17-14.

Table 17-14. DefaultTreeSelectionModel Constant

Constant	Type	Description
SELECTION_MODE_PROPERTY	String	The name of the selection mode property used in property change events

Fields

protected SwingPropertyChangeSupport changeSupport
protected EventListenerList listenerList

> Support the event listeners for property change and selection events, respectively.

protected TreePath[] selection

> Stores the current selection for the tree. You can access it through the `getSelectionPaths()` or `getSelectionRows()` methods.

protected transient RowMapper rowMapper

> Stores the value for the `rowMapper` property.

protected int leadIndex
protected TreePath leadPath
protected int leadRow

> Store the lead path information associated with the `leadSelectionPath` and `leadSelectionRow` properties. The `leadIndex` is the index of the `leadPath`. The `leadRow` is the row number of the `leadPath`.

protected DefaultListSelectionModel listSelectionModel

> Stores the list selection model that this `DefaultListSelectionModel` class is based on.

protected int selectionMode

> Stores the value for the `selectionMode` property.

Constructors

public DefaultTreeSelectionModel()

> Creates an instance of the default selection model with all of the properties initialized to the default values listed in Table 17-13.

Additional Methods

The following protected methods support some of the types of selections available and support the events for the `TreeSelectionModel`. These might be useful if you subclass `DefaultTreeSelectionModel`.

protected boolean arePathsContiguous(TreePath paths[])

> Returns `true` if the entries in `paths` are contiguous. The paths do not need to be sorted in any order to be contiguous.

protected boolean canPathsBeAdded(TreePath paths[])

> Returns `true` if the entries in `paths` can be added to the current selection. For example, entries might not be "addable" if they are not part of a contiguous block, and the selection mode is set for contiguous.

protected boolean canPathsBeRemoved(TreePath paths[])

Returns true if the entries in paths can be removed without disrupting the selection with respect to the current selection mode.

protected void fireValueChanged(TreeSelectionEvent event)

Notifies all of the registered TreeSelectionListener objects associated with this selection that the selection has changed.

protected void insureRowContinuity()

Ensures that a selection is made up of continuous rows. To do this, it starts with the minimum selected row (*min*), and works its way up to the maximum selected row (*max*). If any intermediate row, say *r*, is not selected, the selection is reset to contain the rows from *min* to *r* − 1.

protected void insureUniqueness()

Ensures that all entries listed in the selection are unique. Any duplicate entries are removed. A null selection is unique.

protected void notifyPathChange(Vector paths, TreePath oldLeadSelection)

Indicates that a change in the selection has occurred. It builds a new TreeSelectionEvent and then calls fireValueChanged(). The paths argument is a vector of PathPlaceHolder objects. The PathPlaceHolder class is a non-public class that holds one TreePath object and a boolean variable to indicate whether or not the tree path is new.

protected void updateLeadIndex()

Updates the leadIndex property to match the current lead path in the selection. If the selection is null, the leadIndex property is reset to –1.

Tree Events

Trees generate three new types of events that are worth mentioning. Apart from the obvious selection and expansion events from the graphical side, you can also catch structural changes with model events.

The TreeModelEvent Class

The TreeModelEvent class encapsulates model changes in the form of the path that has changed, as well as information on the children of that path.

Fields

protected int[] childIndices
protected Object[] children

Hold the children and their indices in the parent node associated with this event.

protected TreePath path

> Holds the path to the parent of the children associated with this event.

Constructors

public TreeModelEvent(Object source, Object path[], int childIndices[], Object children[])
public TreeModelEvent(Object source, TreePath path, int childIndices[], Object children[])

> These constructors allow you to build an event that encompasses the children of a modified node. This type of event is useful if the references to the node's children have changed, or if the number of children has changed.

public TreeModelEvent(Object source, Object path[])
public TreeModelEvent(Object source TreePath path)

> If the modified node is the only interesting node for this event (if its value changed, but nothing happened to its children, for example) then you can use these constructors.

Methods

public int[] getChildIndices()
public Object[] getChildren()

> If the event contains information about the affected children of a node, you can retrieve those indices and the children themselves with these methods.

public Object[] getPath()
public TreePath getTreePath()

> These methods supply access to the main node of the event. Whether you look at that node through a TreePath object or through an Object array depends on your program; both methods lead to the same node.

The TreeModelListener Interface

The TreeModelListener requires that listeners implement the following methods:

public void treeNodesChanged(TreeModelEvent e)
public void treeNodesInserted(TreeModelEvent e)
public void treeNodesRemoved(TreeModelEvent e)

> Indicate that nodes have changed, have been inserted, or have been removed, respectively.

public void treeStructureChanged(TreeModelEvent e)

> Indicates that the tree structure has changed significantly (such as several subtrees being deleted) and may require more analysis than can be performed on the nodes and children retrievable through the event object e.

We can use this class of events to monitor the state of the tree. For example, with our expression tree, we could write a simple expression evaluator class that displays the current calculated value of the expression. Any time we change the tree, we'll want to update the calculated value. For this simple example, we react the same to the various subtypes of events, since we have to recalculate the entire tree to get the correct response. In a large model tree, we might decide to cache the results of a subtree in the OpNode class, and then we would only have to evaluate portions of the tree to update the total calculated value.

We'll bundle this expression evaluator into a JLabel object so we can monitor it. Figure 17-8 shows the results.

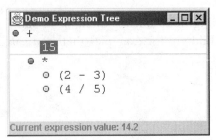

Figure 17-8. A tree event listener label that updates the current value of our expression

The code for the EvaluatorLabel is listed below. The evaluate() method does the recursive work of calculating the answer to the expression. The various Tree-ModelListener methods ensure that any time the tree changes, we re-evaluate the expression.

```
// EvaluatorLabel.java
// An extension of the JLabel class that evaluates the value of an expression
// tree. This class is specifically designed to work with OpNodes and Integer
// objects, but it returns a double value so that odd expressions will show an
// interesting value instead of 0 . . .
//
import javax.swing.*;
import javax.swing.event.*;
import javax.swing.tree.*;

public class EvaluatorLabel extends JLabel implements TreeModelListener {

  public EvaluatorLabel() { super("No tree specified"); }

  public void showEvaluation(Object node) {
    double value = evaluate(node);
    setText("Current expression value: " + value);
    repaint();
  }
```

```
protected double evaluate(Object n) {
  if (n instanceof Integer) {
    return ((Integer)n).doubleValue();
  }
  // must be an OpNode . . .
  OpNode node = (OpNode) n;
  double leftSide = evaluate(node.getChild(0));
  double rightSide = evaluate(node.getChild(1));
  String op = node.getOperator();

  // Ok, do the correct calculation of leftside OP rightside
  if (op.equals( OpNode.ADD )) return leftSide + rightSide;
  if (op.equals( OpNode.SUBTRACT )) return leftSide - rightSide;
  if (op.equals( OpNode.MULTIPLY )) return leftSide * rightSide;
  if (op.equals( OpNode.DIVIDE )) return leftSide / rightSide;

  // Shouldn't get here, but just in case
  return Double.NaN;
}

// Implement the TreeModelListener methods. Regardless of the change, we just
// need to recalculate and redisplay the tree's value from the root down.
public void treeNodesChanged(TreeModelEvent tme) {
  Object source = tme.getSource();
  if (source instanceof JTree) {
    showEvaluation(((JTree)source).getModel().getRoot());
  }
  else if (tme.getSource() instanceof TreeModel) {
    showEvaluation(((TreeModel)source).getRoot());
  }
}

public void treeNodesInserted(TreeModelEvent tme) {
  treeNodesChanged(tme);
}
public void treeNodesRemoved(TreeModelEvent tme) {
  treeNodesChanged(tme);
}
public void treeStructureChanged(TreeModelEvent tme) {
  treeNodesChanged(tme);
}
}
```

The modifications to the **ExprTree** class `init()` method are fairly minimal. To make sure that the label follows changes to the tree, we have to add it as a listener to the model events:

```
// Add the Evaluator stuff . . .
EvaluatorLabel el = new EvaluatorLabel();
getContentPane().add(el, BorderLayout.SOUTH);
```

```
el.showEvaluation(operators[0]);
treeModel.addTreeModelListener(el);
```

The TreeSelectionEvent Class

Selection events occur whenever a user (or program for that matter) changes the selection on a tree. For example, if you went through a directory tree and manually selected 12 discontiguous files, that would generate 12 selection events, each building on the last. If you were to pick 12 contiguous files by selecting the first file and using a modifier to pick the last, that would generate only two selection events. (Both of these examples assume that nothing was originally selected.) As with list selections, *unselecting* something also counts as a selection event. In many cases where more than one file can be selected, you don't want to listen for selection events directly, but rather, you should provide an "OK" button or some other means for the user to indicate the current selection is the final, desired selection.

Fields

protected boolean[] areNew

> For all the paths in this event, this array stores a corresponding true value if the path is new to the selection.

protected TreePath newLeadSelectionPath
protected TreePath oldLeadSelectionPath

> Store the lead path and previous lead path associated with the event.

protected TreePath[] paths

> Stores all of the paths associated with this event.

Constructors

public TreeSelectionEvent(Object source, TreePath path, boolean isNew,
> *TreePath oldLeadSelectionPath, TreePath newLeadSelectionPath)*
> Builds a TreeSelectionEvent centered on one path. The isNew argument determines whether the selection is an addition to (true) or a removal from (false) the current selection.

public TreeSelectionEvent(Object source, TreePath paths[], boolean areNew[], TreePath
> *oldLeadSelectionPath, TreePath newLeadSelectionPath)*
> This version of the constructor allows you to build a selection event that starts off with multiple selections in place. This would be useful in a filesystem tree for selecting things that matched a filter, like all the *.java* files.

Methods

public Object cloneWithSource(Object newSource)

This clever method allows you to clone an event and modify the source component that ostensibly generated the event. This is great for a component that delegates some or all of its visual presence to a tree. You can use this method in an event adapter to pass on the event to some other listener, with the new component listed as the source.

public TreePath getNewLeadSelectionPath()
public TreePath getOldLeadSelctionPath()

These methods give you access to the old and new lead selection path objects respectively. The old lead selection path may be empty (null).

public TreePath getPath()
public TreePaths[] getPaths()

These methods allow you to retrieve the currently selected path or paths. If the selection has multiple paths and you call getPath(), you'll receive the first path in the array that would be returned by getPaths().

public boolean isAddedPath()

Determines whether a particular selection event reflects an addition to an ongoing selection, such as a range or discontiguous selection. Only the first entry in the selection event is checked, even if multiple selections are part of the event.

public boolean isAddedPath(TreePath path)

This version of isAddedPath() checks the specified path to see if it was added to the current selection.

The TreeSelectionListener Interface

The TreeSelectionListener interface carries only one method:

public void valueChanged(TreeSelectionEvent e)

Called whenever the selection on a tree changes. The DefaultTreeModel puts this method to use even for selections caused programmatically.

The TreeExpansionEvent Class

Normally, expanding and collapsing elements of a tree is handled for you by the tree UI. However, if you want to listen and react to these events, you can do so. The TreeExpansionEvent class covers both expanding and collapsing a tree node.

Fields

protected TreePath path
> Stores the path associated with this event.

Constructors

public TreeExpansionEvent(Object source, TreePath path)
> The source for this constructor is most often the tree itself, but it's certainly possible to imagine a GUI trigger being considered the source for a collapse or expand call.

Methods

public TreePath getPath()
> This sole method of the `TreeExpansionEvent` returns the path that was collapsed or expanded. You can query the path to see whether or not it is currently expanded, but the listener interface allows you to easily distinguish which event occurred.

The TreeExpansionListener Interface

To catch these events yourself, you can implement the `TreeExpansionListener` interface, which provides the following two methods to easily separate tasks for collapsing and expanding paths:

public void treeExpanded(TreeExpansionEvent e)
public void treeCollapsed(TreeExpansionEvent e)
> Called when a path is collapsed or expanded.

Pending Expansion Events

The JDK1.2 beta4 release introduced two new classes that help you listen and react to expansion events before they occur. The `TreeWillExpandListener` interface allows you to register interest in pending expansion events. Implementations of that interface throw an `ExpandVetoException` if they decide that the expansion or collapse should not be allowed.

The TreeWillExpandListener Interface

This interface gives you access to the expansion events (both expanding and collapsing) before the event takes place in the tree itself. The only reason you would want to hear about such an event rather than listening for the real expansion event is if you want to do something with the tree before it changes.

The interface provides the following two methods: one for expand events, the other for collapse events.

public void treeWillExpand(TreeExpansionEvent event) throws ExpandVetoException
public void treeWillCollapse(TreeExpansionEvent event) throws ExpandVetoException
  Implement these methods to react to pending expansion events.

The ExpandVetoException Class

The most common reason for listening to pending expansion events is that you may want to stop one of those events from occurring. If the user did not have permission to expand a folder in a filesystem, for example, you could have a listener checking each expand event. If you find such a case where an expansion or collapse should not occur, your listener can throw an `ExpandVetoException`. Each of the listener methods mentioned above can throw this exception. The `JTree setExpandedState()` method catches these exceptions, and if one is thrown, the `fireTreeExpanded()` or `fireTreeCollapsed()` methods are never called.

Constructors

public ExpandVetoException(TreeExpansionEvent event)
public ExpandVetoException(TreeExpansionEvent event, String message)
  Similar to other exception classes, these constructors build new exceptions with the proposed expansion `event`, and an optional `message`.

Fields

protected TreeExpansionEvent event
  While the `ExpandVetoException` class does not provide any public read access to the event used in constructing the exception, that event is stored in this protected field for use by subclasses.

Implementing the Expansion Listener Interface

If you look back at our expression tree, you'll notice that the nodes are never told that they have been expanded or collapsed. That has the side effect of leaving the entire expression represented below a given operator as the displayed string. Without listening to any of these events, a completely expanded expression tree might look like Figure 17-9. We would like an expanded branch to show only the operator associated with that branch, as in Figure 17-10.

We can accomplish that by implementing the `TreeExpansionListener` interface and adding the following bits of code to the `ExprTree` class.

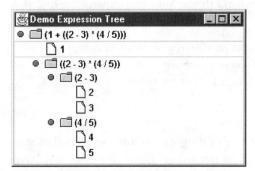

Figure 17-9. Expression tree with static labels for the operator nodes

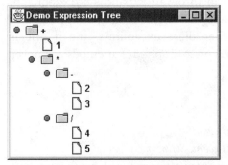

Figure 17-10. Expression tree with "dynamic" operator labels updated by expansion events

```
public void treeExpanded(TreeExpansionEvent tee) {
  OpNode node = (OpNode)te.getPath().getLastPathComponent();
  node.setExpanded(true);
  treeModel.refresh(tee);
}

public void treeCollapsed(TreeExpansionEvent tee) {
  OpNode node = (OpNode)te.getPath().getLastPathComponent();
  node.setExpanded(false);
  treeModel.refresh(tee);
}
```

Of course, we also need to register the listener for these events in our `init()` method:

```
tree.addTreeExpansionListener(this);
```

Rendering and Editing

As with the table cells covered in previous chapters, you can create your own tree cell renderers and editors. The default renderers and editors usually do the trick, but you're probably reading this because they don't do the trick for you, so forge onward! If you went through building your own renderers and editors for tables, you'll find this material quite familiar. The tree uses renderers and editors in much the same way that tables do.

Rendering Nodes

Why would I want to render a node? Good question. One reason is that you want to modify the look-and-feel of a tree without writing a whole UI package for trees. If you had some special way of presenting the "selected" look, for example, you could write your own tree renderer, and still use the default look-and-feel stuff for all of your other components. You might want to render something other than a string with an icon for the nodes of your tree. Or, as we mentioned above, you might want tooltips that vary based on the particular node you rest your cursor on. As always, "because I can" is also a good reason.

But I only want to change the icons!

Before we tackle creating our own renderers, we should point out that the Metal look-and-feel lets you modify the set of icons used by a tree for the leaves and folders. To change the icons, you use the UIManager class and the look-and-feel icons for trees. You can also use the client property JTree.lineStyle to affect the type of lines drawn from folders to leaves. Chapter 26, *Look & Feel*, has much more detail on look-and-feels, but this short example should get you started for the tree-specific properties.

You call the putClientProperty() method on your instance of the tree to set its line style. Your choices for styles are:

Horizontal
> Thin horizontal lines drawn above each top-level entry in the tree (the default)

Angled
> The Windows-style right-angle lines from a folder to each of its leaves

None
> No lines at all

You call the UIManager.put() method to modify the icons used by all trees. The icons you can replace are:

Tree.openIcon
> Used for opened folders

Tree.closedIcon
> Used for closed folders

`Tree.leafIcon`
>   Used for leaves

`Tree.expandedIcon`
>   Used for the one-touch expander when its node is expanded

`Tree.collapsedIcon`
>   Used for the one-touch expander when its node is collapsed

Thus, if `t` is a `JTree`, and `icon` is some kind of `Icon`, the code:

```
t.putClientProperty ("JTree.lineStyle", "Angled");
UIManager.put ("Tree.openIcon", icon);
```

sets the tree's line style to `Angled`, and sets the icon for opened folders to `icon`.

Figure 17-11 shows a tree with custom icons and angled lines connecting the nodes. (This is also a sample of a `JTree` used for some hierarchical data other than a filesystem. Here we have a VRML world builder with the containers representing composite scenes and the leaves representing atomic objects in the world.)

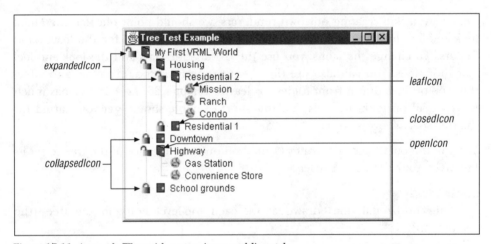

Figure 17-11. A sample JTree with custom icons and line style

And here's the code that installed these customizations. The customizations happen in two places. The various icons used throughout the tree are installed in our constructor and apply to any tree instance we create. The `lineStyle` property is something we associated with the particular instance of `JTree` in our `init()` method. Again, this property only has an effect when you are using the Metal look-and-feel.

```
// TestTree3.java
// A Simple test to see how we can build a tree and customize its icons.
//
```

```java
import java.awt.*;
import java.util.*;
import java.awt.event.*;
import javax.swing.*;
import javax.swing.plaf.*;
import javax.swing.tree.*;

public class TestTree3 extends JFrame {

  JTree tree;
  DefaultTreeModel treeModel;

  public TestTree3() {
    super("Tree Test Example");
    setSize(200, 150);
    addWindowListener(new BasicWindowMonitor());

    // Add in our own customized tree icons
    UIManager.put("Tree.leafIcon", new ImageIcon("world.gif"));
    UIManager.put("Tree.openIcon", new ImageIcon("door.open.gif"));
    UIManager.put("Tree.closedIcon", new ImageIcon("door.closed.gif"));
    UIManager.put("Tree.expandedIcon", new ImageIcon("unlocked.gif"));
    UIManager.put("Tree.collapsedIcon", new ImageIcon("locked.gif"));
  }

  public void init() {
    // Build the hierarchy of containers & objects
    String[] schoolyard = {"School", "Playground", "Parking Lot", "Field"};
    String[] mainstreet = {"Grocery", "Shoe Shop", "Five & Dime",
                           "Post Office"};
    String[] highway = {"Gas Station", "Convenience Store"};
    String[] housing = {"Victorian_blue", "Faux Colonial",
                        "Victorian_white"};
    String[] housing2 = {"Mission", "Ranch", "Condo"};
    Hashtable homeHash = new Hashtable();
    homeHash.put("Residential 1", housing);
    homeHash.put("Residential 2", housing2);

    Hashtable cityHash = new Hashtable();
    cityHash.put("School grounds", schoolyard);
    cityHash.put("Downtown", mainstreet);
    cityHash.put("Highway", highway);
    cityHash.put("Housing", homeHash);

    Hashtable worldHash = new Hashtable();
    worldHash.put("My First VRML World", cityHash);
```

```
    // Build our tree out of our big hashtable
    tree = new JTree(worldHash);

    // Pick an angled line style
    tree.putClientProperty("JTree.lineStyle", "Angled");
    getContentPane().add(tree, BorderLayout.CENTER);
  }

  public static void main(String args[]) {
    TestTree3 tt = new TestTree3();
    tt.init();
    tt.setVisible(true);
  }
}
```

The DefaultTreeCellRenderer Class

The JDK1.2 beta4 release introduced another alternative to the look-and-feel setup
for trees. In addition to setting up icons and line styles as we do in the previous
example, you can use the DefaultTreeCellRenderer class and its properties to
customize tree display. DefaultTreeCellRenderer is an extension of the JLabel
class that implements the TreeCellRenderer interface (discussed later), and is
devoted to making your tree appear on screen the way you want it to look.

Properties

Table 17-15 shows the properties associated with this new class:

Table 17-15. DefaultTreeCellRenderer Properties

Property	Data Type	get	is	set	bound	Default Value
background*[a]	Color	•		•		From L&F
backgroundNonSelectionColor	Color	•		•		From L&F
backgroundSelectionColor	Color	•		•		From L&F
borderSelectionColor	Color	•		•		From L&F
closedIcon	Icon	•		•		From L&F
defaultClosedIcon	Icon	•				From L&F
defaultLeafIcon	Icon	•				From L&F
defaultOpenIcon	Icon	•				From L&F
font*[a]	Font	•		•		From L&F
leafIcon	Icon	•		•		From L&F
openIcon	Icon	•		•		From L&F
preferredSize*[b]	Dimension	•		•		From L&F

Table 17-15. DefaultTreeCellRenderer Properties (continued)

Property	Data Type	get	is	set	bound	Default Value
textNonSelectionColor	Color	•		•		From L&F
textSelectionColor	Color	•		•		From L&F

[a] This property has an overridden set() method that does not allow UIResource objects (such as ColorUIResource and FontUIResource) as its argument.
[b] This property overrides the get() method to increase the width of the preferred size by 3 pixels.

The various properties let you configure the icons to use for leaves, open folders and closed folders. You can also control the colors used for the text and selected cells.

Constructors

The `DefaultTreeCellRenderer` class has only one constructor:

public DefaultTreeCellRenderer()
    This constructor simply returns a new instance of the class.

Fields

protected Color backgroundNonSelectionColor
protected Color backgroundSelectionColor
protected Color borderSelectionColor
protected transient Icon closedIcon
protected transient Icon leafIcon
protected transient Icon openIcon
protected Color textNonSelectionColor
protected Color textSelectionColor
    These fields store the values for their respective properties.

protected boolean selected
    This field tracks whether or not the cell is currently selected.

Rendering Methods

Beyond simple property accessors and mutators, you will find two other methods in this class that help display the cell the way you would expect.

public void paint(Graphics g)
    This overridden method paints the background for a cell based on its selected status.

public Component getTreeCellRendererComponent(JTree tree, Object value, boolean sel,
boolean expanded, boolean leaf, int row, boolean hasFocus)

This method comes from the `TreeCellRenderer` interface. It returns the actual `Component` that will be used to display the cell. The various parameters to the method configure the cell renderer and are discussed in more detail later.

Custom Renderers

Now let's look at writing our own renderer. Our expression tree uses the default folder and leaf icons, which are more appropriate to files and filesystems. We can write a more formal renderer that uses a nice big monospaced font and does away with the little folder icons on the operators. Figure 17-12 shows the results.

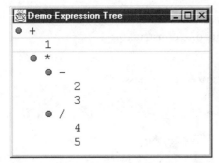

Figure 17-12. Expression tree with a custom renderer

The TreeCellRenderer Interface

With this interface and your favorite `Component` subclass, you can render a tree cell any way you like, regardless of the look-and-feel in place. While you can return any component as a renderer, because of the problems with mixing heavyweight and lightweight components, you'll probably want to return a subclass of `JComponent`. If you want multiple components to do your rendering (or your editing, for that matter), extending `Container` is a good place to start.

This interface defines one method:

public Component getTreeCellRendererComponent(JTree tree, Object value, boolean selected,
boolean expanded, boolean leaf, int row, boolean hasFocus)

This method takes as arguments all of the information relevant to rendering a tree node. You are free to ignore any argument that doesn't interest you, or you can go directly to the tree node, `value`. You can then create and return a component that will draw your node correctly.

A simple way to build your first renderer is to extend the `JLabel` class. You'll probably want to keep some other state information around, as well. Here's the code that built the expression renderer above. In the constructor, we create a center-aligned label with a medium-sized monospaced font. When the program renders a cell or displays a cell's tooltip (by calling `getTreeCellRendererComponent()`) we set the current color for the foreground and background according to the selected status of our object. We could also query our object for other bits of information if needed.

To get the (slightly) more interesting tooltips working, we override the `getTool-TipText()` method to return a different string, depending on whether the mouse is over is a node or a leaf. We use the `opaque` property to determine whether we see the blue background.

```java
// ExpressionTreeCellRenderer.java
// A renderer for our expression cells.
//
import java.awt.*;
import javax.swing.*;
import javax.swing.tree.*;

public class ExpressionTreeCellRenderer extends JLabel
implements TreeCellRenderer {

  Color backColor;
  boolean isLeaf;

  public ExpressionTreeCellRenderer() {

    // Pick a nice, big, fixed width font for our labels
    setFont(new Font("Monospaced", Font.PLAIN, 16));
    setHorizontalAlignment(SwingConstants.CENTER);
  }

  public Component getTreeCellRendererComponent(JTree tree, Object value,
                                    boolean selected,
                                    boolean expanded, boolean leaf,
                                    int row, boolean hasFocus) {
    if (selected) {
      setOpaque(true);
      setForeground(Color.white);
    }
    else {
      setOpaque(false);
      setForeground(Color.black);
    }
    setText(value.toString());
    isLeaf = leaf;
```

```
    return this;
  }

  // Override the default to send back different strings for folders and leaves
  public String getToolTipText() {
    if (isLeaf) { return "Leaf"; }
    return "Node";
  }

  // Override the default to give us a bit of horizontal padding
  public Dimension getPreferredSize() {
    Dimension dim = super.getPreferredSize();
    if(dim != null) { dim = new Dimension(dim.width + 4, dim.height); }
    return dim;
  }
}
```

And here's the line in `ExprTree.java` that tells our tree to use our renderer instead of the default one:

```
    tree.setCellRenderer(new ExpressionTreeCellRenderer());
```

If you want the tooltips to be active, you have to register the tree with the `Tool-TipManger` (discussed earlier in this chapter).

Editing Nodes

One of the other things you may want to do with a tree node is edit it. Each look-and-feel shipped with Swing implement's basic text field editors for tree nodes, but it is possible to use other components to edit nodes. In fact, since editors are just subclasses of `Component`, you can even build your own editor.

For example, we can create an expression editor like you see in Figure 17-13 that picks one of two possible components. If you want to edit an operator, you'll get a `JComboBox` with the four various supported operators in the list. If you want to edit an integer, you'll get a `JTextField`.

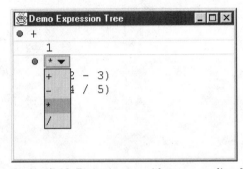

Figure 17-13. Expression tree with a custom editor for the operator nodes

The TreeCellEditor Interface

Like the `TreeCellRenderer` interface, the `TreeCellEditor` interface has one method:

public Component getTreeCellRendererComponent(JTree tree, Object value, boolean selected,
boolean expanded, boolean leaf, int row)
Allows you to configure the editor just before it pops up on the screen. In our example, we use this method to select the current operator in the combo box or to set the current text value for the text field.

In addition to this method, you also need to keep track of things like whether or not you can even edit this tree node. Most of that information will come from the `CellEditor` interface (which `TreeCellEditor` extends).

The DefaultTreeCellEditor Class

The JDK1.2 beta4 release gives us another useful addition to the tree package: the `DefaultTreeCellEditor` class. This class can be used to supply an editor for your tree cells that lets icons associated with the cells remain. (That was a problem in previous releases.) You can use a default text field to edit cells, or you can wrap your own custom editor in this class to make use of the start-up and rendering features. The `DefaultTreeCellEditor` class will start editing a cell after a triple-click of the mouse, or after a "click-pause-click wait for 1200 milliseconds" sequence.

Properties

The `DefaultTreeCellEditor` properties are shown below in Table 17-16:

Table 17-16. DefaultTreeCellEditor Properties

Property	Data Type	get	is	set	bound	Default Value
borderSelectionColor	Color	•		•		from L&F
cellEditorValue*	Object	•				
font*	Font	•		•		from L&F
tree[a]	JTree			•		from constructor

[a] This property has a protected set() method.

The `font` and `borderSelectionColor` properties determine the visible qualities of the editor. The `cellEditorValue` property comes from the `CellEditor` interface discussed in detail in Chapter 27, *Swing Utilities.* (It just contains the current value stored in the editor.) The `tree` property is the `JTree` whose cell is being edited.

Events

As dictated by the `CellEditor` interface, the `DefaultTreeCellEditor` class generates `ChangeEvent` objects for cell editor events. The usual add and remove methods are present:

public void addCellEditorListener()
public void removeCellEditorListener()
> These methods register and unregister listeners interested in finding out that the editor has a new value for the cell. One such listener would be the tree currently under edit.

Fields

protected Color borderSelectionColor
> Stores the value for the `borderSelectionColor` property.

protected boolean canEdit
> Stores the value used by the `isCellEditable()` method. It gets its value during the `getTreeCellEditorComponent()` call based on the values passed in.

protected transient Component editingComponent
protected Container editingContainer
> These fields store the component that will perform the editing and its container, respectively.

protected transient Icon editingIcon
> Stores the `Icon` to use when editing a cell. This is not a means to allow a different icon to show up during editing. In the current implementation, it merely serves to reflect the correct icon already associated with the cell in the tree and make that icon available for the rest of the class. (In other words, if you start editing a cell with an open folder icon, the text field will have an open folder icon to its left when it pops up.)

protected Font font
> Stores the value for the `font` property. A `null` value indicates the font from the renderer should be used.

protected transient TreePath lastPath
> Stores the last path that was selected in the tree.

protected transient int lastRow

Set during the `getTreeCellEditorComponent()` call, it contains the row of the cell that should be edited.

protected transient int offset

Contains the x position (offset for the current cell) for placing the editing component or for calculating what constitutes the "interesting" part of the cell. In this context, interesting means "without the tree's icon."

protected TreeCellEditor realEditor

The editor that handles the editing. The various `CellEditor` methods implemented for this class delegate to this object.

protected DefaultTreeCellRenderer renderer

Contains a reference to a renderer used for determining the font and offsets to use for the editor component. It can only be set through the constructor for this class.

protected transient Timer timer

The `timer` determines when an editing session should start. Chapter 27, *Swing Utilities*, has more on the `Timer` class.

protected transient JTree tree

Stores the value for the `tree` property. It can also be set by passing in a new tree object through the `getTreeCellEditorComponent()` method.

Constructors

Two constructors exist that allow you to build your own version of the "default" editor.

public DefaultTreeCellEditor(JTree tree, DefaultTreeCellRenderer renderer)

This constructor just calls the next constructor with the supplied `tree` and `renderer` arguments, and passes `null` for the editor.

public DefaultTreeCellEditor(JTree tree, DefaultTreeCellRenderer renderer,
TreeCellEditor editor)

This constructor builds a default editor with the given tree and renderer used. If you supply `null` for the editor, a `DefaultCellEditor` with a text field will be created for you. (You can see more on the `DefaultCellEditor` class in Chapter 27.)

Event Methods

Apart from the events generated by a cell editor, the `DefaultTreeCellEditor` class implements the `ActionListener` and `TreeSelectionListener` interfaces.

public void actionPerformed(ActionEvent e)

Listens for events coming from the timer. If the timer fires and the editor has valid (non-null) tree and lastPath fields, an editing session starts.

public void valueChanged(TreeSelectionEvent e)

Tracks the selection events happening on the tree and updates the lastPath field as things change.

CellEditor and TreeCellEditor Methods

The DefaultTreeCellEditor class implements the TreeCellEditor interface (and by extension, the CellEditor interface). The methods from those interfaces are present in the class. The methods for CellEditor are usually delegated to the realEditor component.

public Component getTreeCellEditorComponent(JTree tree, Object value, boolean isSelected, boolean expanded, boolean leaf, int row)

This is the sole method from the TreeCellEditor interface, discussed previously in this section.

public void cancelCellEditing()
public Object getCellEditorValue()
public boolean isCellEditable(EventObject event)
public boolean shouldSelectCell(EventObject event)
public boolean stopCellEditing()

These methods (along with the add and remove methods for cell editor listeners above) come from the CellEditor interface. You can find more details on this interface in Chapter 27, Swing Utilities.

Helper Methods

This class uses several protected helper classes to do everything from determining when to start editing to laying out the editor appropriately.

protected boolean canEditImmediately(EventObject event)

Returns true if event is null or a mouse click inside the cell with a click count greater than two.

protected Container createContainer()

Creates a container of type DefaultTreeCellEditor.EditorContainer. This container is used to manage the editing component and icon objects.

protected TreeCellEditor createTreeCellEditor()

The constructor uses this method if null is passed for the TreeCellEditor parameter. This method returns a new DefaultCellEditor built with a DefaultTreeCellEditor.DefaultTextField component.

protected void determineOffset(JTree tree, Object value, boolean isSelected, boolean expanded, boolean leaf, int row)

Determines the value of the offset field based on the location and desired gap for the icon. If the icon is null, 0 will be used for the offset field.

protected boolean inHitRegion(int x, int y)

Returns true if the (x, y) coordinate is located inside the cells bounds, but not inside the region delimited by the offset field. This ensures that the mouse click was not on the folder or leaf icon, which often has a different meaning.

protected void prepareForEditing()

Adds the editing component to the editing container.

protected boolean shouldStartEditingTimer(EventObject event)

Returns true if event is a MouseEvent inside the hit region.

protected void startEditingTimer()

Starts (and creates, if necessary) a timer set to go off in 1200 milliseconds. The "click-pause-click" method of beginning an edit session relies on this method.

Inner Classes

The DefaultTreeCellEditor class contains two inner classes to help out with the editor component.

public class DefaultTreeCellEditor.DefaultTextField extends JTextField

This extension of the JTextField class uses the border and font specified by the DefaultTreeCellEditor class. It also overrides the getPreferred-Size() method to use information from the renderer, if one was supplied.

public class DefaultTreeCellEditor.EditorContainer extends Container

This container paints in the editingIcon object and locates the editing-Component to the left of the icon and forces it to fill the remaining space occupied by the container. Any editor you pass in to the constructor will be placed inside this container.

For our expression tree, we really need two different editors. One editor (pictured in Figure 17-13) should be a combo box with the four supported operators in it. The other editor must be a text field to type in any arbitrary integer. By default, we would get text fields for both of our node types. While that would be sufficient to do our work, it's not as convenient, and more important, not very robust. With a generic text field, we don't have any control over what the user enters. The user could pick an unsupported operator, or maybe type in a name instead of a number for one of the integers. If we build our own editors, we can guard against that.

For the tree itself, we need one class that we can designate as our editor. That class will, in turn, delegate its editing capabilities to one of the two editors mentioned above. This class does not have to be a component itself, since the actual editor the tree uses comes from the getTreeCellEditorComponent() call, which returns the actual component to do the editing. In our case, it returns an Editor-TextField or an EditorComboBox, depending on whether we're editing a node or a leaf. However, ExpressionTreeCellEditor does have to implement the TreeCellEditor interface; as you can see from the code below, after the real editors are set up, it delegates every other method to the current editor.

```java
// ExpressionTreeCellEditor.java
// A customized editor for our expression tree. This editor only kicks in if the
// node you try to edit is an OpNode, otherwise the default text field is used
// for integers.
//
import javax.swing.*;
import javax.swing.event.*;
import java.awt.*;
import java.awt.event.*;
import java.util.*;
import javax.swing.tree.*;

public class ExpressionTreeCellEditor implements TreeCellEditor {

    EditorComboBox nodeEditor;
    EditorTextField leafEditor;
    CellEditor currentEditor;

    static String[] operators = { "+", "-", "*", "/" };

      public ExpressionTreeCellEditor() {

          EditorTextField tf = new EditorTextField();
          tf.setFont(new Font("Monospaced", Font.PLAIN, 14));
          EditorComboBox cb = new EditorComboBox(operators);
          cb.setFont(new Font("Monospaced", Font.PLAIN, 14));

          nodeEditor = cb;
          leafEditor = tf;
      }

      public Component getTreeCellEditorComponent(JTree tree, Object value,
                                          boolean isSelected,
                                          boolean expanded,
                                          boolean leaf, int row) {
          if (leaf) {
            currentEditor = leafEditor;
            leafEditor.setText(value.toString());
          }
```

```
        else {
          currentEditor = nodeEditor;
          nodeEditor.setSelectedItem(((OpNode)value).getOperator());
        }
        return (Component)currentEditor;
    }

    public Object getCellEditorValue() {
      return currentEditor.getCellEditorValue();
    }

    public boolean isCellEditable(EventObject event) {
      return currentEditor.isCellEditable(event);
    }

    public boolean shouldSelectCell(EventObject event) {
      return currentEditor.shouldSelectCell(event);
    }

    public boolean stopCellEditing() {
      return currentEditor.stopCellEditing();
    }

    public void cancelCellEditing() {
      currentEditor.cancelCellEditing();
    }

    public void addCellEditorListener(CellEditorListener l) {
      nodeEditor.addCellEditorListener(l);
      leafEditor.addCellEditorListener(l);
    }

    public void removeCellEditorListener(CellEditorListener l) {
      nodeEditor.removeCellEditorListener(l);
      leafEditor.removeCellEditorListener(l);
    }
}
```

Next, we need to set up our first custom editor. For the OpNode class, we want a combo box that gives us the four supported operators as choices. The EditorComboBox class is really a bit more flexible than that. It accepts an array of objects as an argument to its constructor and returns a JComboBox editor containing that list as its choices.

This class also implements the CellRenderer interface, so that it can perform the duties required of an editor. As you saw above, the ExpressionTreeCellEditor delegates most of its responsibilities here. In setting up the constructor, we attach an action listener that stops the editing process when the user chooses one of the

items in the list. The JTree object using this editor registers as a CellEditorListener when you begin editing a node. It then waits for the ChangeEvent that we
distribute in the fireEditingStopped() method before removing your editor
component from the screen. Using the isCellEditable() method, we'll start
editing if the user clicks on our node with the right mouse button.

```java
// EditorComboBox.java
// A CellEditor JComboBox subclass for use with Trees (and possibly tables). This
// particular editor also checks to verify that the value entered is an integer.
//
import javax.swing.*;
import javax.swing.event.*;
import java.awt.event.*;
import java.awt.*;
import java.util.*;

public class EditorComboBox extends JComboBox implements CellEditor {

  String value;
  Vector listeners = new Vector();
  private static final int minWidth = 36;

  // mimic all of the constructors people expect with ComboBoxes
  public EditorComboBox(Object[] list) {
    super(list);
    setEditable(false);
    value = list[0].toString();

    // listen to our own action events, so we know when to stop editing
    addActionListener(new ActionListener() {
      public void actionPerformed(ActionEvent ae) {
        if (stopCellEditing()) {
          fireEditingStopped();
        }
      }
    });
  }

  // Implement the CellEditor methods
  public void cancelCellEditing() { }

  // only stop editing if the user entered a valid value
  public boolean stopCellEditing() {
    try {
      value = (String)getSelectedItem();
      if (value == null) { value = (String)getItemAt(0); }
      return true;
    }
```

```
      catch (Exception e) {
        // something went wrong
        return false;
      }
  }

  public Object getCellEditorValue() {
    return value;
  }

  // start editing when the right mouse button is clicked
  public boolean isCellEditable(EventObject eo) {
    if ((eo == null) ||
        ((eo instanceof MouseEvent) && (((MouseEvent)eo).isMetaDown())))) {
      return true;
    }
    return false;
  }

  public boolean shouldSelectCell(EventObject eo) { return true; }

  // Add in support for listeners
  public void addCellEditorListener(CellEditorListener cel) {
    listeners.addElement(cel);
  }

  public void removeCellEditorListener(CellEditorListener cel) {
    listeners.removeElement(cel);
  }

  protected void fireEditingStopped() {
    if (listeners.size() > 0) {
      ChangeEvent ce = new ChangeEvent(this);
      for (int i = listeners.size() - 1; i >= 0; i--) {
        ((CellEditorListener)listeners.elementAt(i)).editingStopped(ce);
      }
    }
  }

  // override setBounds() to make sure that JTree gives our editor enough space
  public void setBounds(Rectangle r) {
    r.width = Math.max(minWidth, r.width);
    super.setBounds(r);
  }

  public void setBounds(int x, int y, int w, int h) {
    w = Math.max(minWidth, w);
    super.setBounds(x, y, w, h);
  }
}
```

The next step is to build our editor delegate for the `Integer` nodes. We'll use the same approach, but this time, we want to make sure the value the user enters is valid. We do this in the `stopCellEditing()` method. If the value in the text field does not convert to an `Integer`, we return `false` and do *not* fire the Change-Event. See Chapter 20, *Document Model and Events*, for a proactive approach to restricting the text field input. This leaves the text field on the screen. Until the user types a valid integer into the text field, hitting RETURN has no effect, and the editor remains visible.

```java
// EditorTextField.java
// A CellEditor.JTextField subclass for use with Trees (and possibly tables).
// This particular editor also checks that the value entered is an integer.
//
import javax.swing.*;
import javax.swing.event.*;
import java.awt.event.*;
import java.awt.*;
import java.util.*;

public class EditorTextField extends JTextField implements CellEditor {

  Integer value = new Integer(1);
  Vector listeners = new Vector();
  private static final int minWidth = 64;

  // mimic all of the constructors people expect with text fields
  public EditorTextField() { this("", 5); }
  public EditorTextField(String s) { this(s, 5); }
  public EditorTextField(int w) { this("", w); }
  public EditorTextField(String s, int w) {
    super(s, w);
    // listen to our own action events, so we know when to stop editing
    addActionListener(new ActionListener() {
      public void actionPerformed(ActionEvent ae) {
        if (stopCellEditing()) { fireEditingStopped(); }
      }
    });
  }

  // Implement the CellEditor methods
  public void cancelCellEditing() { setText(""); }

  // only stop editing if the user entered a valid value
  public boolean stopCellEditing() {
    try {
      value = Integer.valueOf(getText());
      return true;
    }
```

```
    catch (Exception e) {
      // something went wrong (most likely we don't have a valid integer)
      return false;
    }
  }

  public Object getCellEditorValue() { return value; }

  // start editing when the right mouse button is clicked
  public boolean isCellEditable(EventObject eo) {
    if ((eo == null) ||
        ((eo instanceof MouseEvent) &&
          (((MouseEvent)eo).isMetaDown())))) {
      return true;
    }
    return false;
  }

  public boolean shouldSelectCell(EventObject eo) { return true; }

  // Add in support for listeners
  public void addCellEditorListener(CellEditorListener cel) {
    listeners.addElement(cel);
  }

  public void removeCellEditorListener(CellEditorListener cel) {
    listeners.removeElement(cel);
  }

  protected void fireEditingStopped() {
    if (listeners.size() > 0) {
      ChangeEvent ce = new ChangeEvent(this);
      for (int i = listeners.size() - 1; i >= 0; i--) {
        ((CellEditorListener)listeners.elementAt(i)).editingStopped(ce);
      }
    }
  }

  // override setBounds() to make sure that JTree gives us enough space
  public void setBounds(Rectangle r) {
    r.width = Math.max(minWidth, r.width);
    super.setBounds(r);
  }

  public void setBounds(int x, int y, int w, int h) {
    w = Math.max(minWidth, w);
    super.setBounds(x, y, w, h);
  }
}
```

And of course, as the last step, we must register this new delegating editor with our JTree object in the init() method of the ExprTree class:

```
tree.setCellEditor(new ExpressionTreeCellEditor());
tree.setEditable(true);
```

Look-and-Feel Helper Classes

The JDK1.2 beta4 release added three other classes to the tree package devoted to helping the look-and-feel code do its job. These classes are:

AbstractLayoutCache
> This class serves as the abstract base class for calculating layout information for a look and feel. This includes dealing with icons and row height information. The details of these calculations are left to subclasses.

FixedHeightLayoutCache (extends AbstractLayoutCache)
> This class assumes a fixed height for all tree cells and does not accept heights less than or equal to 0.

VariableHeightLayoutCache (extends AbstractLayoutCache)
> This class allows variable heights for cells, checking with the cell renderer if a specified height is given as less than or equal to 0.

The documentation for these classes notes that they will become "more open" with future releases of the JDK. The JTree class itself is not concerned with these classes—there are no methods for setting or modifying the layout cache. The look-and-feel classes, however, do use these, and developers building their own look-and-feels will want to watch for new information coming from releases after beta4.

What Next?

With all of this control over the look of a tree and its contents, you can create some impressive interfaces for a wide variety of data. You can create your own network management software that lets you browse domains and subdomains and computers and users. Any hierarchy of information you can think of can now be shown graphically.

It is worth pointing out, however, that you are not restricted to graphical applications with these models. You can use the DefaultTreeModel to store regular, hierarchical data, even if you have no intention of displaying the data on a screen. The model is flexible and provides a good starting point if you don't have any tree data structures of your own lying around.

18

Undo

In many applications (word processors, spreadsheets, board games, etc.) the user is given the opportunity to undo changes made to the state of the application. In a word processor you can (thankfully!) undo deletions. In a chess game, you're often allowed to take back undesirable moves (typically after realizing your queen has just been banished from the board). Without support, providing these undo capabilities can be a lot of work for the programmer, especially if you want to provide a powerful undo system that keeps a history of undoable operations and allows them to be undone and redone indefinitely.

Thankfully, Swing provides a collection of classes and interfaces that support this advanced undo functionality. Within the Swing packages, only the classes in the `javax.swing.text` package currently use these facilities, but you are free to use undo in any component you create or extend. You can even use it for undoing things that may not be directly associated with a UI component (like a chess move). It's important to realize that the undo facility is not tied, in any way, to the Swing components themselves. One could easily argue that the package might be more logically called `java.util.undo`. None of the classes or interfaces in the `javax.swing.undo` package uses any other Swing object.

In this chapter, we'll look at everything Swing provides to support undo, but we won't get into the details of how the text components use this facility. That discussion will be left to the text chapters that follow.

The Swing Undo Facility

The `javax.swing.undo` package contains two interfaces and seven classes (two of which are just exception classes). These, along with a listener interface and event class from the `javax.swing.event` package make up the undo facility shown in Figure 18-1.

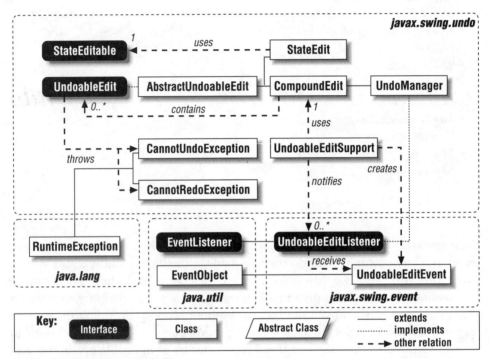

Figure 18-1. The Swing undo facility

Before describing each interface and class in detail, here is a brief overview of each one and how they work together:

`UndoableEdit`

   This is the base interface for just about everything else in the undo package. It serves as an abstraction for anything in an application that can be undone.

`AbstractUndoableEdit`

   This default implementation of `UndoableEdit` provides a starting point for building new `UndoableEdit` classes. It provides a simple set of rules for determining whether undo and redo requests are allowable (based on whether or not the edit has already been undone, redone, or killed). Despite its name, it is not an abstract class. This is really just a technicality since the default implementation is not at all useful as it is, so you'd never want to instantiate one.

CompoundEdit

This extension of `AbstractUndoableEdit` allows multiple edits to be grouped together into a single edit. Those familiar with *Design Patterns,* by Gamma et al., will recognize this construct as a basic implementation of the Composite pattern.

UndoableEditEvent

This event class can be used to notify listeners that an undoable edit has been made.

UndoableEditListener

The listener interface to which `UndoableEditEvents` are sent. It contains a single method called `undoableEditHappened()`.

UndoManager

An extension of `CompoundEdit`, it can be used to manage a list of edits, which may be undone and redone in sequence. `UndoManager` implements `UndoableEditListener`, so it can be added to many components that generate `UndoableEditEvents`, allowing it to manage edits from multiple sources in a single undo list.

StateEdit

An extension of `AbstractUndoableEdit`, it can be used for edits that are undone or redone by changing a set of property values representing the state of the application (or some aspect of it) before and after the edit.

StateEditable

This interface must be implemented by objects wishing to use `StateEdit`. The `StateEdit` constructor accepts a `StateEditable` and calls its two methods, `storeState()` and `restoreState()`, to manage the editable's state.

UndoableEditSupport

This class provides support facilities for classes that need to support undo. It simplifies the processes of managing listeners, firing events, and grouping together multiple edits.

CannotUndoException *and* CannotRedoException

These exception classes extend `RuntimeException` and are thrown when an undo or redo attempt is made while the edit is not in the correct state (e.g., calling `redo()` on an edit that has not yet been undone).

Now that we've got a basic understanding of what we've got to work with, let's look at the details of each of these interfaces and classes.

The UndoableEdit Interface

The `UndoableEdit` interface defines a set of operations that may be performed on any object that needs to provide undo and redo functionality. Typically, classes that implement this interface are fairly small, instances of which represent single, undoable changes ("edits") made to the state of the application or some component of the application.

UndoableEdits can be thought of as being in one of three states, as shown in the state chart in Figure 18-2. Since UndoableEdit is just an interface, it can't really enforce this state model. However, this is the intended state model and the AbstractUndoableEdit class described in the next section does enforce it. Alternate implementations of this interface should not deviate from this model.

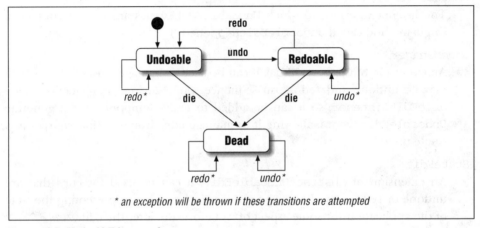

Figure 18-2. UndoableEdit state chart

When initially created, the edit represents some change that has just been done and is now *undoable*.[*] Once the edit is undone, it becomes *redoable*. Having been undone, it may be redone, causing it to become *undoable* again. This sequence can be repeated indefinitely. If, for whatever reason, an edit can no longer be used, it can be "killed," taking it to the *dead* state. Once killed, the edit can no longer be undone or redone. Dead is dead.

NOTE   The die() method provides a mechanism for edits to explicitly release any resources they may be holding, rather than waiting until the edits are garbage-collected.

---

[*] Throughout this chapter, we'll use *italics* when we refer to the "state" of an edit. These states do not usually map directly to any field or method provided by the undo classes, they just provide an easy way to talk about the state of an edit.

Properties

Table 18-1 shows the properties defined by `UndoableEdit`.

Table 18-1. UndoableEdit Properties

Property	Data Type	get	is	set	bound	Default Value
presentationName	String	•				
redoPresentationName	String	•				
significant	boolean		•			
undoPresentationName	String	•				

`UndoableEdit`s are typically displayed to a user, allowing the user to decide to undo or redo some action performed. In support of this, `UndoableEdit` provides three properties that name an edit: `presentationName`, `undoPresentation-Name`, and `redoPresentationName`. These properties might have values such as "delete," "undo delete," and "redo delete," respectively. The last two names are typically just variations on the first.

The `significant` property may be used to distinguish edits of different levels of importance. An insignificant edit, for example, might not be displayed to the user, instead being performed as a side effect of some other edit.

To understand the idea of an insignificant edit, think of a computer chess game. The process of making a move might consist of clicking on a piece, causing the square the piece is sitting on to change color, then clicking on the destination square, completing the move. You might implement the game's undo capability by having an edit responsible for changing the color of the square of the selected piece and another edit representing the move itself. The first edit is not the type of edit you'd want to display to the user. Instead, you'd track this as an insignificant edit.

Edit Merging Methods

`UndoableEdit` provides two methods for merging the changes described by two edits into a single edit. Implementations of these methods are under no obligation to support this merging feature. Such implementations simply return `false`, indicating that no merging of the edits was done.

The `addEdit()` and `replaceEdit()` methods are similar. `addEdit()` asks the edit it is invoked upon to absorb an input edit, and `replaceEdit()` asks the edit if it would like to replace the input edit. The idea is that `addEdit()` is called on an existing edit, passing in a new one, while `replaceEdit()` is called on a new edit, passing in an existing one.

Absorbing edits can be useful in a variety of scenarios. One use of this feature might be to group together a series of "delete-character" edits created as a user holds down the delete or backspace key. By merging these into a single edit, the user would be able to undo the series of deletions with a single undo operation, rather than having to undo each individual character.

For another example, consider our chess game again. If a user clicked on three different pieces before deciding which one to move, each subsequent piece selection edit would probably want to replace the previous one so that the temporary selections don't become part of the undoable history.

public abstract boolean addEdit(UndoableEdit anEdit)
> This method asks the edit to absorb `anEdit`. If the edit is able to do so, it returns `true`. If not, it returns `false`. If `anEdit` is absorbed, it is no longer undoable or redoable by itself (i.e., `canUndo()` and `canRedo()` should return `false`, and `undo()` and `redo()` should throw exceptions). If `anEdit` is no longer needed, `die()` should be called on it.

public abstract boolean replaceEdit(UndoableEdit anEdit)
> This method asks this edit to replace `anEdit`. If the edit is able to do so, it returns `true`. If not, is returns `false`. If `anEdit` is replaced, it is should no longer be undoable or redoable by itself (i.e., `canUndo()` and `canRedo()` should return `false` and `undo()` and `redo()` should throw exceptions). If `anEdit` is no longer needed, `die()` should be called on it.

For more information on these methods, see the discussion of `CompoundEdit`.

Other Methods

public abstract boolean canRedo()
> This method should return `true` if the edit currently can be redone, implying that a subsequent `redo()` call should not throw a `CannotRedoException`.

public abstract boolean canUndo()
> This method should return `true` if the edit currently can be undone, implying that a subsequent `undo()` call should not throw a `CannotUndoException`.

public abstract void die()
> This method is called to indicate that the edit can no longer be undone or redone. Any state being held by the edit can be released and subsequent calls to `undo()` or `redo()` should throw exceptions.

public abstract void redo() throws CannotRedoException
> This method is called to redo an edit that has previously been undone. If the edit cannot be redone (perhaps because it has not been undone yet), a `CannotRedoException` should be thrown.

public abstract void undo() throws CannotUndoException

> Called to undo an edit. If the edit cannot be undone (perhaps because it has already been undone), a CannotUndoException should be thrown.

The AbstractUndoableEdit Class

This implementation of UndoableEdit provides useful default behavior for the methods defined in the interface. It enforces the state model described in the previous section using two internal boolean properties, *alive* and *done*. A new AbstractUndoableEdit is both *alive* and *done*. A call to die() makes it no longer *alive*. A call to undo() makes it no longer *done*, while redo() makes it *done* again. In order for an edit to be undone, it must be both *alive* and *done*. To be redone, it must be *alive* but not *done*.

Subclasses of AbstractUndoableEdit should take advantage of this fundamental state support by calling super.undo() and super.redo() in the first line of their undo() and redo() methods, respectively. This frees the subclass from having to worry about enforcing the edit's state model.

Properties

Table 18-2 shows the default values AbstractUndoableEdit specifies for the properties defined in UndoableEdit.

Table 18-2. AbstractUndoableEdit Properties

Property	Data Type	get	is	set	bound	Default Value
presentationName*	String	•				" "
redoPresentationName*	String	•				"Redo"
significant*	boolean		•			true
undoPresentationName*	String	•				"Undo"

The presentationName property is empty by default. RedoPresentationName and undoPresentationName are formed by appending presentationName to RedoName and UndoName (protected constants, see below) respectively. By default, all AbstractUndoableEdits are significant.

There is no way to change the values of these properties once the object is created. Concrete edit classes need to provide some way (possibly just returning a constant value from the property accessor) to define the presentation name.

Constants

`AbstractUndoableEdit` defines two protected constants used by default when forming the `redoPresentationName` and `undoPresentationName` properties. These are shown in Table 18-3.

NOTE   As of JDK 1.2 beta4, these are hardcoded English strings. In future releases, look for a more internationally friendly implementation.

Table 18-3. AbstractUndoableEdit Constants

Constant	Type	Description
UndoName	String	String ("Undo") prepended to the presentation name to form the undo presentation name.
RedoName	String	String ("Redo") prepended to the presentation name to form the undo presentation name.

Constructors

public AbstractUndoableEdit()

Creates a new edit. The edit is initially *alive* and *done*.

UndoableEdit Methods

The following methods provide a simple default implementation of the `UndoableEdit` interface.

public boolean addEdit(UndoableEdit anEdit)

Always returns `false`. Merging of edits is not directly supported by this class.

public boolean canRedo()

Returns `true` if the edit is *alive* (`die()` has not been called) and not *done* (it has been undone).

public boolean canUndo()

Returns `true` if the edit is *alive* (`die()` has not been called) and *done* (it has not already been undone, or it has been undone and redone).

public void die()

Sets a flag indicating that the edit is no longer *alive*.

public void redo() throws CannotRedoException

Calls `canRedo()` and throws an exception if it returns `false`. Otherwise, it sets a flag to indicate that the edit is *done*.

public boolean replaceEdit(UndoableEdit anEdit)

>   Always returns `false`. Merging of edits is not directly supported by this class.

public void undo() throws CannotUndoException

>   Calls `canUndo()` and throws an exception if it returns `false`. Otherwise, it sets a flag to indicate that the edit is no longer *done*.

Other Methods

public String toString()

>   Returns a textual representation of the edit, including whether or not the edit is *done* and whether or not it is *alive*.

Creating a Toggle Edit

In this example, we'll create a simple extension of `AbstractUndoableEdit` called `UndoableToggleEdit`.* This edit provides the ability to undo pressing a JToggleButton (or one of its subclasses, JRadioButton or JCheckBox). A program using this new edit creates a new `UndoableToggleEdit` each time the toggle button is pressed. If `undo()` is called on the edit, it changes the state of the button back to its previous state. A `redo()` call sets the button back to the state it was when it was passed into the `UndoableToggleEdit` constructor. Here's the source code for this new edit class:

```
// UndoableToggleEdit.java
//
import javax.swing.*;
import javax.swing.undo.*;


// An UndoableEdit used to undo the pressing of a JToggleButton
public class UndoableToggleEdit extends AbstractUndoableEdit {

  // Create a new edit for a JToggleButton which has just been toggled.
  public UndoableToggleEdit(JToggleButton button) {
    this.button = button;
    selected = button.isSelected();
  }

  // Return a reasonable name for this edit.
  public String getPresentationName() {
    return "Toggle " + button.getText() + " " +
    (selected ? "on" : "off");
  }
```

---

* We'll use this class throughout the examples in this chapter, so it's probably a good idea to make sure you understand its purpose.

```
  // Redo by setting the button state as it was initially.
  public void redo() throws CannotRedoException {
    super.redo();
    button.setSelected(selected);
  }

  // Undo by setting the button state to the opposite value.
  public void undo() throws CannotUndoException {
    super.undo();
    button.setSelected(!selected);
  }

  private JToggleButton button;
  private boolean selected;
}
```

We inherit most of our behavior from AbstractUndoableEdit. The most important thing to learn from this class is that the edit keeps track of enough information to undo or redo an operation. In our case, this is done by holding a reference to the toggle button the edit applies to, as well as by keeping a boolean to hold the value of the toggle. For more complex undo capabilities, your edit classes will probably need more information than this.

Another important thing to notice is that both undo() and redo() call their super implementations to ensure that the edit is in the appropriate state.

Next, let's look at a small application that shows how we might use this new edit class. In this (admittedly worthless) application, we create three toggle buttons which we place in the center of a frame. Below these toggle buttons, we add two JButtons—one for undo and one for redo. Each time one of the toggle buttons is pressed (see the main actionPerformed() method), we create a new Undoable-ToggleEdit (discarding any previous edit). At this time, we also update the labels on our undo and redo buttons using the names defined by the new edit.

If the undo button is pressed, we call undo() on the edit, which changes the state of the last toggle button we pressed. Pressing the redo button switches it back again by calling redo() on the edit.

When we initially create the edit, as well as each time we perform an undo or redo (note the finally blocks in the two anonymous listener classes), we enable or disable the undo and redo buttons based on the edit's response to canUndo() and canRedo().

For now, we're only able to undo the most recent edit. Later in the chapter, we'll present a similar example that supports multiple undo operations. Here's the source code for this sample application:

```java
// UndoableToggleApp.java
//
import javax.swing.*;
import javax.swing.event.*;
import javax.swing.undo.*;
import java.awt.*;
import java.awt.event.*;

// A sample app showing the use of UndoableToggleEdit
public class UndoableToggleApp extends JFrame implements ActionListener {

  // Create the main frame and everything in it.
  public UndoableToggleApp() {

    // Create some toggle buttons (and subclasses)
    JToggleButton tog = new JToggleButton("ToggleButton");
    JCheckBox cb = new JCheckBox("CheckBox");
    JRadioButton radio = new JRadioButton("RadioButton");

    // Add this object as a listener to each toggle button
    tog.addActionListener(this);
    cb.addActionListener(this);
    radio.addActionListener(this);

    // Lay out the buttons
    Box buttonBox = new Box(BoxLayout.Y_AXIS);
    buttonBox.add(tog);
    buttonBox.add(cb);
    buttonBox.add(radio);

    // Create undo and redo buttons (initially disabled)
    undoButton = new JButton("Undo");
    redoButton = new JButton("Redo");
    undoButton.setEnabled(false);
    redoButton.setEnabled(false);

    // Add a listener to the undo button. It attempts to call undo() on the
    // current edit, then enables/disables the undo/redo buttons as appropriate.
    undoButton.addActionListener(new ActionListener() {
      public void actionPerformed(ActionEvent ev) {
        try {
          edit.undo();
        } catch (CannotUndoException ex) { ex.printStackTrace(); }
        finally {
          undoButton.setEnabled(edit.canUndo());
          redoButton.setEnabled(edit.canRedo());
        }
      }
    });
```

```
    // Add a redo listener: just like the undo listener, but for redo this time.
    redoButton.addActionListener(new ActionListener() {
      public void actionPerformed(ActionEvent ev) {
        try {
          edit.redo();
        } catch (CannotRedoException ex) { ex.printStackTrace(); }
        finally {
          undoButton.setEnabled(edit.canUndo());
          redoButton.setEnabled(edit.canRedo());
        }
      }
    });

    // Lay out the undo/redo buttons
    Box undoRedoBox = new Box(BoxLayout.X_AXIS);
    undoRedoBox.add(Box.createGlue());
    undoRedoBox.add(undoButton);
    undoRedoBox.add(Box.createHorizontalStrut(2));
    undoRedoBox.add(redoButton);
    undoRedoBox.add(Box.createGlue());

    // Lay out the main frame
    Container content = getContentPane();
    content.setLayout(new BorderLayout());
    content.add(buttonBox, BorderLayout.CENTER);
    content.add(undoRedoBox, BorderLayout.SOUTH);
    setSize(400, 150);
  }

  // When any toggle button is clicked, we create a new UndoableToggleEdit (which
  // replaces any previous edit). We then get the edit's undo/redo names and set
  // the undo/redo button labels. Finally, we enable/disable these buttons by
  // asking the edit what we are allowed to do.
  public void actionPerformed(ActionEvent ev) {
    JToggleButton tb = (JToggleButton)ev.getSource();
    edit = new UndoableToggleEdit(tb);
    undoButton.setText(edit.getUndoPresentationName());
    redoButton.setText(edit.getRedoPresentationName());
    undoButton.getParent().validate();
    undoButton.setEnabled(edit.canUndo());
    redoButton.setEnabled(edit.canRedo());
  }

  private UndoableEdit edit;
  private JButton undoButton;
  private JButton redoButton;
```

```
  // Main program just creates the frame and displays it.
  public static void main(String[] args) {
    JFrame f = new UndoableToggleApp();
    f.addWindowListener(new BasicWindowMonitor());
    f.setVisible(true);
  }
}
```

Figure 18-3 shows what this application looks like after we've played with it for a while. We just got through toggling on the radio button and then pressing the undo button.

Figure 18-3. Sample ToggleButtonApp display

The CompoundEdit Class

CompoundEdit is a subclass of AbstractUndoableEdit which supports the aggregation of multiple edits into a single composite edit. After a CompoundEdit is created, UndoableEdits can be added to it by calling addEdit(). Once all edits have been added, a new method, end(), must be called on the CompoundEdit to indicate that the creation of the edit is complete (after this point, addEdit() will just returns false). Only after end() has been called can the edit be undone. CompoundEdit implements undo() and redo() by calling the appropriate method on each of the edits added to it, allowing all of them to be executed at once.

Figure 18-4 shows a state chart very similar to the one we saw for UndoableEdit. The key difference is that a CompoundEdit is initially *inProgress* and does not allow either undo() or redo(). The end() method must be called after adding the edits to the CompoundEdit to enable undo.

Properties

CompoundEdit defines the properties and default values shown in Table 18-4. inProgress is the only property new to this class. It indicates whether or not edits may be added to the CompoundEdit. Initially true, this property is set to false when end() is called. It never changes back to true after that.

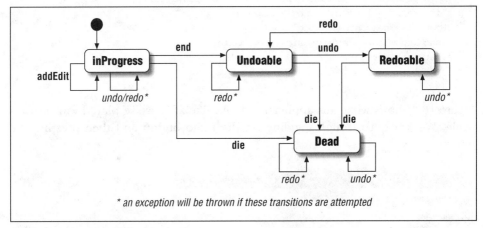

Figure 18-4. CompoundEdit state chart

Table 18-4. CompoundEdit Properties

Property	Data Type	get	is	set	bound	Default Value
inProgress	boolean		•			true
presentationName*	String	•				""
redoPresentationName*	String	•				"Redo"
significant*	boolean		•			false
undoPresentationName*	String	•				"Undo"

See also properties from the AbstractUndoableEdit class (Table 18-2).

The values of presentationName, redoPresentationName, and undoPresenta-tionName are initially the same as the values defined in Abstract-UndoableEdit. However, once edits are added, these values are set to the values of the corresponding properties of the last edit added.

The significant property is initially false. Once edits are added, this value is determined by checking the significance of the child edits. If any of them are set to true, the CompoundEdit is considered to be significant.

Protected Fields

protected Vector edits

This is where the CompoundEdit stores its edits. New edits are added to the end of the vector.

Constructors

public CompoundEdit()

> This constructor creates a new edit with no children that is initially *inProgress*. The undo() and redo() methods will throw exceptions until end() is called.

UndoableEdit Methods

The following methods override the implementations of the UndoableEdit methods defined in AbstractUndoableEdit.

public boolean addEdit(UndoableEdit anEdit)

> This method returns false if the edit is not currently *inProgress*. Otherwise, the first time the method is called, the input edit is added as the first element of a list of child edits. Subsequent calls are given the opportunity to merge with the last edit in the list. This is done by calling addEdit(anEdit) on the last edit in the list. If this returns false (indicating that the last edit did not absorb the new edit), anEdit.replaceEdit(lastEdit) is called to see if the new edit can replace the last edit. If this returns true (indicating that the new edit can replace the last edit), the last edit is removed from the list and the new edit is added in its place. If not, the last edit is left in the list and the new edit is added to the end of the list.

> Figure 18-5 shows a sequence diagram for this method. In this example, the last edit does not absorb the new edit, but the new edit does replace the previous last edit. We show the last two operations in italics to indicate that these are not actual method calls on the compound edit.

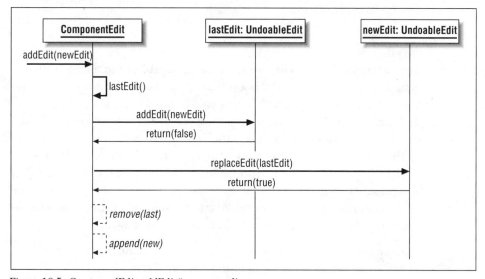

Figure 18-5. CompoundEdit.addEdit() sequence diagram

public boolean canRedo()

Returns `true` if the edit is *inProgress* and `super.canRedo()` returns `true`.

public boolean canUndo()

Returns `true` if the edit is *inProgress* and `super.canUndo()` returns `true`.

public void die()

Calls `die()` on each of its child edits in reverse order. It then calls `super.die()`.

public void redo() throws CannotRedoException

Calls `super.redo()` to make sure redo is allowed. It then calls `redo()` on each of its children in the order they were added.

public void undo() throws CannotUndoException

Calls `super.undo()` to make sure undo is allowed. It then calls `undo()` on each of its children in the reverse of the order they were added.

Other Methods

public void end()

Indicates that no more edits will be added. After this method is called, the edit is no longer *inProgress*.

protected UndoableEdit lastEdit()

Returns the last edit added, or `null` is no edits have been added yet.

public String toString()

Returns a textual representation of the edit, including the value of `super.toString()`, plus the status of `inProgress` and the number of edits the `CompoundEdit` contains.

Using Compound Edits

The following example is a modification of the `UndoableToggleApp` from the previous section. This version uses `CompoundEdit` to allow multiple button toggles to be undone at once. Each time one of the toggle buttons is pressed, a new `UndoableToggleEdit` is created and added to a `CompoundEdit`. Once you've toggled as many buttons as you want, you can press the end button, which causes `end()` to be called on the `CompoundEdit` and enables the undo button. Pressing this button causes `undo()` to be called on the `CompoundEdit`, which in turn calls `undo()` on each of the `UndoableToggleEdits` that were added to it. Pressing one of the toggle buttons again causes the `CompoundEdit` to be replaced with a new one, to which new edits will be added until the end button is pressed again.

Here's the source code for this example. Much of it is unchanged from the `UndoableToggleApp` example, so we've highlighted the significant changes.

```java
// UndoableToggleApp2.java
//
import javax.swing.*;
import javax.swing.event.*;
import javax.swing.undo.*;
import java.awt.*;
import java.awt.event.*;

// A sample app showing the use of UndoableToggleEdit and CompoundEdit
public class UndoableToggleApp2 extends JFrame implements ActionListener {

  // Create the main frame and everything in it.
  public UndoableToggleApp2() {

    // Create some toggle buttons (and subclasses)
    JToggleButton tog = new JToggleButton("ToggleButton");
    JCheckBox cb = new JCheckBox("CompoundEdit ExampleCheckBox");
    JRadioButton radio = new JRadioButton("RadioButton");

    // Add this object as a listener to each toggle button
    tog.addActionListener(this);
    cb.addActionListener(this);
    radio.addActionListener(this);

    // Lay out the buttons
    Box buttonBox = new Box(BoxLayout.Y_AXIS);
    buttonBox.add(tog);
    buttonBox.add(cb);
    buttonBox.add(radio);

    // Create undo and redo buttons (initially disabled)
    undoButton = new JButton("Undo");
    redoButton = new JButton("Redo");
    endButton = new JButton("End");
    undoButton.setEnabled(false);
    redoButton.setEnabled(false);
    endButton.setEnabled(false);

    // Add a listener to the undo button. It attempts to call undo() on the
    // current edit, then enables/disables the undo/redo buttons as appropriate.
    undoButton.addActionListener(new ActionListener() {
      public void actionPerformed(ActionEvent ev) {
        try {
          edit.undo();
        } catch (CannotUndoException ex) { ex.printStackTrace(); }
        finally {
          undoButton.setEnabled(edit.canUndo());
          redoButton.setEnabled(edit.canRedo());
        }
```

```
      }
    });

    // Add a redo listener: just like the undo listener, but for redo this time.
    redoButton.addActionListener(new ActionListener() {
      public void actionPerformed(ActionEvent ev) {
        try {
          edit.redo();
        } catch (CannotRedoException ex) { ex.printStackTrace(); }
        finally {
          undoButton.setEnabled(edit.canUndo());
          redoButton.setEnabled(edit.canRedo());
        }
      }
    });

    // Add an end listener. This listener will call end() on the CompoundEdit and
    // update the undo/redo buttons.
    endButton.addActionListener(new ActionListener() {
      public void actionPerformed(ActionEvent ev) {
        edit.end();
        endButton.setEnabled(false);
        undoButton.setEnabled(edit.canUndo());
        redoButton.setEnabled(edit.canRedo());
      }
    });

    // Lay out the undo/redo/end buttons
    Box undoRedoEndBox = new Box(BoxLayout.X_AXIS);
    undoRedoEndBox.add(Box.createGlue());
    undoRedoEndBox.add(undoButton);
    undoRedoEndBox.add(Box.createHorizontalStrut(2));
    undoRedoEndBox.add(redoButton);
    undoRedoEndBox.add(Box.createHorizontalStrut(2));
    undoRedoEndBox.add(endButton);
    undoRedoEndBox.add(Box.createGlue());

    // Lay out the main frame
    Container content = getContentPane();
    content.setLayout(new BorderLayout());
    content.add(buttonBox, BorderLayout.CENTER);
    content.add(undoRedoEndBox, BorderLayout.SOUTH);
    setSize(400, 150);
  }

  // When any toggle button is clicked, we check to see if there is an inProgress
  // CompoundEdit. If there is not, we create a new one (replacing the old
  // CompoundEdit if there was one). We then create a new UndoableToggleEdit and
  // add it to the CompoundEdit. Next, the end button is enabled and we enable/
```

```
// disable the Undo/Redo buttons by asking the edit what we are allowed to do.
public void actionPerformed(ActionEvent ev) {
  if (edit == null || edit.isInProgress() == false)
    edit = new CompoundEdit();

  JToggleButton tb = (JToggleButton)ev.getSource();
  UndoableEdit togEdit = new UndoableToggleEdit(tb);
  edit.addEdit(togEdit);
  endButton.setEnabled(true);
  undoButton.setEnabled(edit.canUndo());
  redoButton.setEnabled(edit.canRedo());
}

private CompoundEdit edit;
private JButton undoButton;
private JButton redoButton;
private JButton endButton;

// Main program just creates the frame and displays it.
public static void main(String[] args) {
  JFrame f = new UndoableToggleApp2();
  f.addWindowListener(new BasicWindowMonitor());
  f.setVisible(true);
}
}
```

The UndoableEditEvent Class

UndoableEditEvent is an event class (it extends java.util.EventObject)
defined in the javax.swing.event package. It is used by components that
support undo to notify interested listeners (implementing UndoableEditListener) that an UndoableEdit has been performed.

A little later in the chapter, we'll see an example that uses the Undoable-
EditEvent class and the UndoableEditListener interface.

Property

UndoableEditEvent defines the property shown in Table 18-5. The edit property contains the UndoableEdit that was generated, causing this event to be fired.

Table 18-5. UndoableEditEvent Property

Property	Data Type	get	is	set	bound	Default Value
edit	UndoableEdit	•				

See also the java.util.EventObject class.

Constructors

public UndoableEditEvent(Object source, UndoableEdit edit)
    Creates a new event with the specified event source and `UndoableEdit`.

The UndoableEditListener Interface

Classes that generate `UndoableEditEvents` fire these events to `Undoable-EditListeners`. This is a simple interface (like `UndoableEditEvent`, it can be found in the `javax.swing.event` package), defining the single method described below.

Methods

public abstract void undoableEditHappened(UndoableEditEvent e)
    Called when an undoable operation is performed on an object which supports undo. The event e can be used to obtain the new `UndoableEdit`.

The UndoManager Class

`UndoManager` is an extension of `CompoundEdit` that can be used to track a history of edits, allowing them to be undone or redone one at time. Additionally, it implements `UndoableEditListener` by calling `addEdit()` each time an `Undoable-EditEvent` is fired. This allows a single `UndoManager` to be added as a listener to many components that support undo, providing a single place where all edits can be tracked. This can then be used to populate an undo menu for the entire application.

It may seem a bit strange that `UndoManager` extends `CompoundEdit`. We'll explain why this was done shortly, but first it's important to understand the important ways in which `UndoManager` acts differently than `CompoundEdit`. For starters, when you add an edit to an `UndoManager`, it is placed in a list of edits available for undo. When you call `undo()`, only the first (significant) edit is undone. This is different from the behavior of `CompoundEdit`, in which a call to `undo()` results in a call to `undo()` on all of the added edits.

Another major difference between `UndoManager` and its superclass is the semantics of the `inProgress` property. In `CompoundEdit`, we were only allowed to add new edits when we were *inProgress*, and only after calling `end()` could `undo()` or `redo()` be called. In contrast, `UndoManager` allows `undo()` and `redo()` to be called while it is *inProgress*. Furthermore, when `end()` is called, it stops supporting sequential undo/redo behavior and starts acting like a `CompoundEdit` (`undo()` and `redo()` call their superclass implementations when the `UndoManager` is not *inProgress*).

For the strong-hearted,[*] Figure 18-6 shows a state chart for the `UndoManager` class.[†] For several reasons, this chart is considerably more complicated than the ones in the previous sections. First, as mentioned earlier, `UndoManager` has the curious behavior that once `end()` is called, it begins to act (for the most part) like a `CompoundEdit`. This is why we have the transition from the *inProgress* state to a new super-state (*notInProgress*, for lack of a better name), the contents of which look just like the `CompoundEdit` state chart (see Figure 18-4).

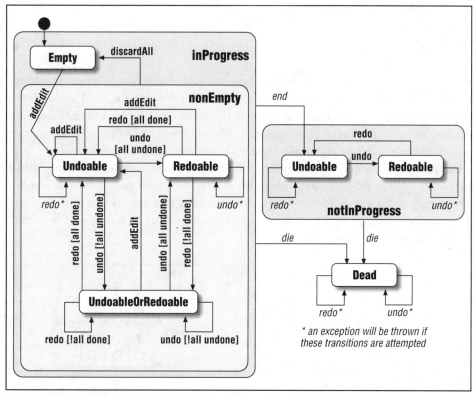

Figure 18-6. UndoManager state chart

This state chart is also complicated because, within the *inProgress* state, whether we are *undoable, redoable,* or both (*undoableOrRedoable*) depends on whether or not all of the edits have been undone or redone. For example, if there are two edits in the `UndoManager` and we've undone one, we are *undoableOrRedoable*. We can undo the remaining edit, or redo the one we've undone. If we choose to undo the

---

* All others might want to skip ahead to the description of Figure 18-7.

† This chart assumes all edits are `significant`. For details on why this is important, see the descriptions of the `editToBeUndone()` and `editToBeRedone()` methods later in this section.

remaining edit, we go from *undoableOrRedoable* to *redoable* since there are no more edits to undo. However, if there had still been more undoable edits, we'd have stayed in the *undoableOrRedoable* state. Or, if we'd chosen to redo the undone edit, there would be no more redoable edits, so we'd go from *undoableOrRedoable* to *undoable*.

One more thing that adds to the complexity is that any time we add a new edit, we are no longer able to redo past undos, because the new edit takes the place of the last undone edit and all pending redoable edits are dropped. Therefore, any time we add an edit, we go to the *undoable* state.

A Codeless Example

Figure 18-7 attempts to simplify the explanation of UndoManager state transitions by showing how the UndoManager handles additions, undos, and redos for a sample scenario. This example shows that the most typical use of UndoManager is straightforward, despite all its complexity. We add three edits to the UndoManager and then undo each of them. We then redo the first edit. At this point, we could redo the second edit or undo the first edit again. In the example, we instead add a new edit. Adding an edit causes any edits that appear later in the list (those edits which originated latest) to be lost. In this example, that causes our initial second and third edits to be dropped from the manager before the new edit is added. Finally, we undo this new edit.

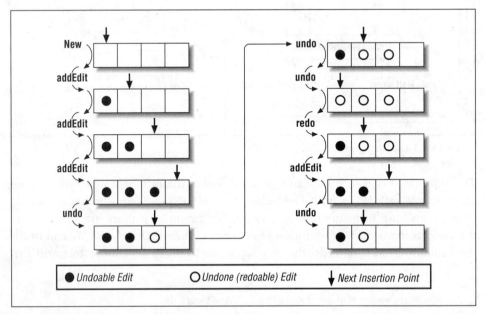

Figure 18-7. UndoManager example

Transformer?

Probably the most nonintuitive things to understand about the design of UndoManager is its extension from CompoundEdit and the fact that after its end() method is called, an UndoManager is essentially transformed into a Compound-Edit. The idea here is to use an UndoManager in a temporary capacity during a specific editing task and then later be able to treat all of the edits given to the UndoManager as a single CompoundEdit.

As an example, consider a spreadsheet application. The process of editing the formula for a single cell can be managed by an UndoManager, allowing small changes to be undone and redone. Once the formula has been committed, the UndoManager's end() method can be called and the manager will begin to act like a CompoundEdit. This edit can then be handed off to a primary undo manager, allowing the entire formula change to be undone as a single edit.

Properties

UndoManager defines the properties and default values shown in Table 18-6.

Table 18-6. UndoManager Properties

Property	Data Type	get	is	set	bound	Default Value
limit	int	•		•		100
redoPresentationName*	String	•				"Redo"
undoOrRedoPresentationName	String	•				"Undo"
undoPresentationName*	String	•				"Undo"

See also properties from the CompoundEdit class (Table 18-4).

The limit property represents the maximum number of edits the UndoManager will hold. Setting this value so that limit is less than the current number of edits in the manager causes the list of edits to be reduced to fit inside the new limit. The strategy for decreasing the list size is described in trimForLimit(), below.

If the manager is *inProgress*, the redoPresentationName and undoPresentationName properties are set to the values returned by the next edit to be redone or undone, respectively. If redo or undo is not possible, AbstractUndoEdit.Redo or AbstractUndoableEdit.Undo is returned. If the manager is not *inProgress*, these values revert to the values defined by CompoundEdit.

A new property, undoOrRedoPresentationName is defined in this class. This property is only intended for use when limit is set to 1. It returns the value of undoPresentationName if the single edit has not been undone, or the value of redoPresentationName if it has.

Constructor

public UndoManager()
> Creates a new manager containing no edits, with a limit of 100.

UndoableEditListener Method

This method is defined in the UndoableEditListener interface implemented by UndoManager:

public void undoableEditHappened(UndoableEditEvent e)
> Calls addEdit(), passing in the UndoableEdit stored in the input event.

UndoableEdit Methods

UndoManager overrides the following UndoableEdit methods:

public synchronized boolean addEdit(UndoableEdit anEdit)
> If the manager is *inProgress*, this method adds anEdit at the current insertion point. Any undone edits are removed from the manager and die() is called on each of these in reverse order (the last edit added is killed first). If the manager is not *inProgress*, this method returns false.

NOTE   In versions of Swing prior to JDK 1.2, there are several problems with this method. The most notable is that it always returns true. Furthermore, any redoable edits are removed the first time addEdit() is called after an end() call. Starting with the JDK 1.2 release, end() will be implemented in this class to remove any redoable edits and addEdit() will be fixed to return false once end() has been called. If you are using an earlier release, be aware that this method always returns true and that undone edits will still be part of the edit after end() is called.

---

public synchronized boolean canRedo()
> If the UndoManager is *inProgress*, this method uses editToBeRedone() (described later) to find the next significant redoable edit. If an edit is found, and it returns true when canRedo() is called on it, this method returns true. If the manager is not *inProgress*, super.canRedo() is called, making the manager act like a CompoundEdit.

public synchronized boolean canUndo()

If the UndoManager is *inProgress*, this method uses editToBeUndone() to find the next significant undoable edit. If an edit is found and it returns true when canUndo() is called on it, this method returns true. If the manager is not *inProgress*, super.canUndo() is called, making the manager act like a CompoundEdit.

public synchronized void redo() throws CannotRedoException

If the UndoManager is *inProgress*, this method uses editToBeRedone() to find the next significant redoable edit (the most recently undone edit). If an edit is found, redoTo() is called to redo all edits up to the next significant one. If no edit is found, an exception is thrown. If the manager is not *inProgress*, super.redo() is called, making the manager act like a CompoundEdit.

public synchronized void undo() throws CannotUndoException

If the UndoManager is *inProgress*, this method uses editToBeUndone() to find the next significant undoable edit. If an edit is found, undoTo() is called to undo all edits up to the next significant one. If no edit is found, an exception is thrown. If the manager is not *inProgress*, super.undo() is called, making the manager act like a CompoundEdit.

Calling undo() and then calling redo() does not necessarily put you right back where you started. Any insignificant edits undone by the undo() call will not be redone by a subsequent redo() call.

New Public Methods

The following are new methods introduced in the UndoManager class:

public synchronized void discardAllEdits()

Removes all edits from the UndoManager, calling die() on them in the order they were added.

public synchronized boolean canUndoOrRedo()

This method is intended to be used when the manager is limited to holding a single edit (limit == 1). If the edit has been undone, it returns the result of a call to canRedo(), otherwise it returns the result of a call to canUndo().

public synchronized void undoOrRedo() throws CannotRedoException, CannotUndoException

This method is intended to be used when the manager is limited to holding a single edit (limit == 1). If the edit has been undone, it calls redo(), otherwise, it calls undo().

Protected Methods

These methods are used internally by the UndoManager to manage its list of edits. They provide support for ignoring insignificant edits and removing edits that are no longer accessible.

protected UndoableEdit editToBeRedone()

Returns the next edit to be redone. This is simply the last significant edit that was undone. Any insignificant edits are skipped. If there are no significant redoable edits available, this method returns null.

protected UndoableEdit editToBeUndone()

Returns the next edit to be undone. This is the last significant edit that was either redone or added. Any insignificant edits are skipped. If there are no significant undoable edits available, this method returns null.

protected void trimEdits(int from, int to)

Removes the specified range of edits from the manager (if *from* is greater than *to*, it does nothing). The die() method is called on each removed edit in reverse order (*to* down to *from*). If the insertion point was within the trimmed range, it is reset to the value of *from*.

protected void trimForLimit()

Reduces the number of edits to fit within the set limit for this manager. If the number of edits is not greater than limit, it does nothing. Otherwise, it removes edits from either end of the list (or both), trying to end up with equal numbers of undoable and redoable edits (or as close as possible). For example, if there are 10 edits, half of which had been undone, and limit is reduced to six, the first two undone edits (those that were undone first) and the first two edits added (those that would be undone last) are removed. This leaves six edits (the new limit), three of which have been undone.

protected void redoTo(UndoableEdit edit) throws CannotRedoException

Starts with the last undone edit and calls redo() on each edit in the list, stopping after it has called redo() on the input edit. An ArrayIndex-OutOfBoundsException will be thrown if the input edit is not found before reaching the end of the edit list.

protected void undoTo(UndoableEdit edit) throws CannotUndoException

Starts with the last redone or added edit and calls undo() on each edit in the list, stopping after it has called undo() on the input edit. An ArrayIndex-OutOfBoundsException will be thrown if the input edit is not found before reaching the beginning of the edit list.

Other Methods

public String toString()

    Returns a string representation of the `UndoManager`, formed by calling `super.toString()` and appending the value of the `limit` property and the current insertion point.

Using an Undo Manager

In the previous examples, we created `UndoableEdits` in our main program each time we were notified of an action that we wanted to allow the user to undo. A more desirable strategy is to make the component that generated the action responsible for creating the `UndoableEdit` and firing an `UndoableEditEvent`, passing us the edit. Using an `UndoManager`, we can then easily provide the user with the ability to undo and redo as many changes as necessary.

For this example to work, we need to provide a component that generates `UndoableEdits` and allows `UndoableEditListeners` to be added and removed. In keeping with the examples provided so far in this chapter, we'll do this by creating an extension of `JToggleButton` that fires an `UndoableEditEvent` each time its state is toggled. This event will contain an `UndoableToggleEdit` (the class introduced near the beginning of the chapter) which can be used to undo the toggle. To keep the example as simple as possible, we'll allow only a single listener to be added to the button. In a real application, you'd likely want to maintain a list of interested listeners instead.[*] Here's the code for this event-generating button class:

```
// UndoableJToggleButton.java
//
import java.awt.event.*;
import javax.swing.*;
import javax.swing.event.*;
import javax.swing.undo.*;

// Sample undoable toggle button class. Supports only a single listener to
// simplify the code.
public class UndoableJToggleButton extends JToggleButton {
  // For this example, we'll just provide one constructor . . .
  public UndoableJToggleButton(String txt) {
    super(txt);
  }
}
```

---

[*] Later in the chapter, we'll introduce `UndoableEditSupport`, a class that simplifies this process.

```
// Set the UndoableEditListener
public void addUndoableEditListener(UndoableEditListener l) {
  listener = l; // should ideally throw an exception if listener != null
}

// Remove the UndoableEditListener
public void removeUndoableEditListener(UndoableEditListener l) {
  listener = null;
}

// We override this method to call the super implementation first (to fire the
// action event) and then fire a new UndoableEditEvent to our listener.
protected void fireActionPerformed(ActionEvent ev) {

  // Fire the ActionEvent as usual
  super.fireActionPerformed(ev);

  if (listener != null) {
    listener.undoableEditHappened(new UndoableEditEvent(this,
      new UndoableToggleEdit(this)));
  }
}

private UndoableEditListener listener;
}
```

As you can see, all we've done here is override `fireActionPerformed()`, so that each time an `ActionEvent` is fired (indicating that the button was toggled), we also create and fire a new `UndoableEditEvent`. Of course, the strategy for generating edits will vary considerably based on the type of class you're making undoable.

Now let's look at a program that uses an `UndoManager` to allow undo of multiple toggle button edits. In this example, we'll create three `UndoableJToggleButtons` and provide undo and redo buttons that allow the user to undo and redo up to 100 (the default limit) button toggles.

In this example, we don't take advantage of the fact that `UndoManager` implements `UndoableEditListener` by adding the manager as a listener to our undoable buttons. We want to do more than track the edit when it is generated; we also want to update the user interface so that the user knows the undo and redo options available. To support this, we instead add our main application object as an `UndoableEditListener`, calling `addEdit()` on the `UndoManager` each time an event is fired and then updating our undo and redo buttons appropriately.

NOTE   Lack of listener support has been identified by the Swing team as an
            important hole in the current UndoManager. Look for more sup-
            port in this area in a future release. At the end of the chapter, we
            show how you can extend the current UndoManager to give it better
            listener support.

Here's the source code, again similar in structure to the previous examples:

```java
// UndoableToggleApp3.java
//
import javax.swing.*;
import javax.swing.event.*;
import javax.swing.undo.*;
import java.awt.*;
import java.awt.event.*;

// A sample app showing the use of UndoManager.
public class UndoableToggleApp3 extends JFrame implements UndoableEditListener {

  // Create the main frame and everything in it.
  public UndoableToggleApp3() {

    // Create some toggle buttons
    UndoableJToggleButton tog1 = new UndoableJToggleButton("One");
    UndoableJToggleButton tog2 = new UndoableJToggleButton("Two");
    UndoableJToggleButton tog3 = new UndoableJToggleButton("Three");

    // Add this object as a listener to each toggle button
    tog1.addUndoableEditListener(this);
    tog2.addUndoableEditListener(this);
    tog3.addUndoableEditListener(this);

    // Lay out the buttons
    Box buttonBox = new Box(BoxLayout.Y_AXIS);
    buttonBox.add(tog1);
    buttonBox.add(tog2);
    buttonBox.add(tog3);

    // Create undo and redo buttons (initially disabled)
    undoButton = new JButton("Undo");
    redoButton = new JButton("Redo");
    undoButton.setEnabled(false);
    redoButton.setEnabled(false);

    // Add a listener to the undo button. It attempts to call undo() on the
    // UndoManager, then enables/disables the undo/redo buttons as appropriate.
    undoButton.addActionListener(new ActionListener() {
```

```
  public void actionPerformed(ActionEvent ev) {
    try {
      manager.undo();
    } catch (CannotUndoException ex) { ex.printStackTrace(); }
    finally {
      updateButtons();
    }
  }
});

// Add a redo listener: just like the undo listener.
redoButton.addActionListener(new ActionListener() {
  public void actionPerformed(ActionEvent ev) {
    try {
      manager.redo();
    } catch (CannotRedoException ex) { ex.printStackTrace(); }
    finally {
      updateButtons();
    }
  }
});

// Lay out the undo/redo buttons
Box undoRedoBox = new Box(BoxLayout.X_AXIS);
undoRedoBox.add(Box.createGlue());
undoRedoBox.add(undoButton);
undoRedoBox.add(Box.createHorizontalStrut(2));
undoRedoBox.add(redoButton);
undoRedoBox.add(Box.createGlue());

// Lay out the main frame
getContentPane().setLayout(new BorderLayout());
getContentPane().add(buttonBox, BorderLayout.CENTER);
getContentPane().add(undoRedoBox, BorderLayout.SOUTH);
setSize(400, 150);
}


// When an UndoableEditEvent is generated (each time one of the buttons is
// pressed), we add it to the UndoManager and then get the manager's undo/redo
// names and set the undo/redo button labels. Finally, we enable/disable these
// buttons by asking the manager what we are allowed to do.
public void undoableEditHappened(UndoableEditEvent ev) {
  manager.addEdit(ev.getEdit());
  updateButtons();
}


// Method to set the text and state of the undo/redo buttons.
protected void updateButtons() {
  undoButton.setText(manager.getUndoPresentationName());
```

```
      redoButton.setText(manager.getRedoPresentationName());
      undoButton.getParent().validate();
      undoButton.setEnabled(manager.canUndo());
      redoButton.setEnabled(manager.canRedo());
    }

    private UndoManager manager = new UndoManager();
    private JButton undoButton;
    private JButton redoButton;

    // Main program just creates the frame and displays it.
    public static void main(String[] args) {
      JFrame f = new UndoableToggleApp3();
      f.addWindowListener(new BasicWindowMonitor());
      f.setVisible(true);
    }
}
```

Figure 18-8 shows the application running. Before taking this screen shot, we toggled each of the buttons in order and then undid the third toggle. Notice that we can now re-toggle button three or undo the previous toggle (button two).

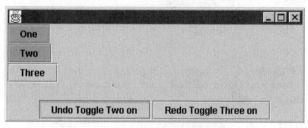

Figure 18-8. Undoing and redoing toggle buttons

Understanding the UndoManager in-depth

There are a lot of subtle details about UndoManager that may be hard to understand without seeing them in action. In this section, we'll try to provide a concrete example of how all these little things work. To do so, let's create a very simple UndoableEdit implementation, not actually associated with any component. It will serve to help us see what the UndoManager is doing in certain situations. All it does is output various bits of useful information when its methods are called. Here's the code for this class:

```
// SampleUndoableEdit.java
//
import javax.swing.undo.*;
import java.util.*;

public class SampleUndoableEdit extends AbstractUndoableEdit {
```

```java
// Create a new edit with an identifying number. The boolean arguments define
// the edit's behavior.
public SampleUndoableEdit(int number, boolean allowAdds,
                          boolean isSignificant,
                          boolean isReplacer) {
  this.number = number;
  this.allowAdds = allowAdds;
  if (allowAdds)
    addedEdits = new Vector();
  this.isSignificant = isSignificant;
  this.isReplacer = isReplacer;
}


// "Undo" the edit by printing a message to the screen.
public void undo() throws CannotUndoException {
  super.undo();
  System.out.print("Undo " + number);
  dumpState();
}


// "Redo" the edit by printing a message to the screen.
public void redo() throws CannotRedoException {
  super.redo();
  System.out.print("Redo " + number);
  dumpState();
}


// If allowAdds is true, we store the input edit. If not, just return false.
public boolean addEdit(UndoableEdit anEdit) {
  if (allowAdds) {
    addedEdits.addElement(anEdit);
    return true;
  }
  else
    return false;
}


// If isReplacer is true, we store the edit we are replacing.
public boolean replaceEdit(UndoableEdit anEdit) {
  if (isReplacer) {
    replaced = anEdit;
    return true;
  }
  else
    return false;
}


// Significance is based on constructor parameter.
public boolean isSignificant() {
  return isSignificant;
}
```

```
  // Just return our identifier.
  public String toString() {
    return "<" + number + ">";
  }


  // Debug output.
  public void dumpState() {
    if (allowAdds && addedEdits.size() > 0) {
      Enumeration e = addedEdits.elements();
      System.out.print(" (absorbed: ");
      while (e.hasMoreElements()) {
        System.out.print(e.nextElement());
      }
      System.out.print(")");
    }
    if (isReplacer && replaced != null) {
      System.out.print(" (replaced: " + replaced + ")");
    }
    System.out.println();
  }

  private boolean isSignificant;
  private boolean isReplacer;
  private int number;
  private boolean allowAdds;
  private Vector addedEdits;
  private UndoableEdit replaced;
}
```

In our main program, we'll add instances of this new edit class to an UndoManager to show how different features work. We won't step through this program line-by-line. The comments in the code and in the output should serve as an explanation of the different UndoManager features (and quirks) being shown:.

```
// UndoManagerDetails.java
//
import javax.swing.undo.*;

// An example that shows lots of little UndoManager details.
public class UndoManagerDetails {
  public static void main(String[] args) {
    UndoManager mgr = new UndoManager();

    // Show how insignificant edits are skipped over
    //
    //                                # adds? sig? replace?
    mgr.addEdit(new SampleUndoableEdit(1, false, true, false));
    mgr.addEdit(new SampleUndoableEdit(2, false, true, false));
    mgr.addEdit(new SampleUndoableEdit(3, false, false, false));
    mgr.addEdit(new SampleUndoableEdit(4, false, false, false));
```

```
      System.out.println("-------------------------");
      System.out.println("Insignificant edit example");
      System.out.println("-------------------------");
      mgr.undo();
      mgr.redo();
      System.out.println(mgr.canRedo()); // no more sig. edits

      // Show how edits which call add/replace are used
      //
      //                                    #  adds? sig? replace?
      mgr.addEdit(new SampleUndoableEdit(5, true,  true, false));
      mgr.addEdit(new SampleUndoableEdit(6, false, true, false));
      System.out.println("--------------------------------");
      System.out.println("Absorbed (by addEdit) edit example");
      System.out.println("--------------------------------");
      mgr.undo();
      mgr.discardAllEdits();

      //                                    #  adds? sig? replace?
      mgr.addEdit(new SampleUndoableEdit(1, false, true, false));
      mgr.addEdit(new SampleUndoableEdit(2, false, true, true));
      System.out.println("------------------------------------");
      System.out.println("Absorbed (by replaceEdit) edit example");
      System.out.println("------------------------------------");
      mgr.undo();
      System.out.println(mgr.canUndo());

      // Show how changing limit works
      mgr.discardAllEdits();

      //                                    #  adds? sig? replace?
      mgr.addEdit(new SampleUndoableEdit(1, false, true, false));
      mgr.addEdit(new SampleUndoableEdit(2, false, true, false));
      mgr.addEdit(new SampleUndoableEdit(3, false, true, false));
      mgr.addEdit(new SampleUndoableEdit(4, false, true, false));
      mgr.addEdit(new SampleUndoableEdit(5, false, true, false));
      mgr.addEdit(new SampleUndoableEdit(6, false, true, false));
      System.out.println("----------------------");
      System.out.println("Changing limit example");
      System.out.println("----------------------");
      mgr.undo();
      mgr.undo();
      mgr.undo(); // now 3 undoable, 3 redoable
      mgr.setLimit(4); // now 2 undoable, 2 redoable!
      while (mgr.canUndo())
        mgr.undo();
      while (mgr.canRedo())
        mgr.redo();
```

```
    // undoOrRedo example
    mgr.discardAllEdits();
    mgr.setLimit(1);

    //                              # adds? sig? replace?
    mgr.addEdit(new SampleUndoableEdit(1, false, true, false));
    System.out.println("------------------");
    System.out.println("undoOrRedo example");
    System.out.println("------------------");
    System.out.println(mgr.getUndoOrRedoPresentationName());
    mgr.undoOrRedo();
    System.out.println(mgr.getUndoOrRedoPresentationName());
    mgr.undoOrRedo();

    // Show how UndoManager becomes a CompositeEdit
    mgr.discardAllEdits();
    mgr.setLimit(100);

    //                              # adds? sig? replace?
    mgr.addEdit(new SampleUndoableEdit(1, false, true, false));
    mgr.addEdit(new SampleUndoableEdit(2, false, true, false));
    mgr.addEdit(new SampleUndoableEdit(3, false, true, false));
    System.out.println("----------------------------");
    System.out.println("Transform to composite example");
    System.out.println("----------------------------");
    mgr.end();
    mgr.undo();
    mgr.redo();

    // Show that adds are no longer allowed. Note that addEdit() returns true in
    // pre-JDK 1.2 Swing releases. This is fixed in JDK 1.2.
    System.out.println(mgr.addEdit(
     new SampleUndoableEdit(4, false, true, false)));
    mgr.undo(); // note that edit 4 is not there
  }
}
```

Here's the output generated by this program. We've added some comments to the output in *italic*.

```
    ------------------------
    Insignificant edit example
    ------------------------
    Undo 4 // 3 undos from a single mgr.undo() call . . .
    Undo 3
    Undo 2
    Redo 2 // but mgr.redo() only redoes the significant one!
    false  // . . . and there are no more redos
```

```
-----------------------------------
Absorbed (by addEdit) edit example
-----------------------------------
Undo 5 (absorbed: <6>) // edit 6 was absorbed by edit 5 and undone
-------------------------------------
Absorbed (by replaceEdit) edit example
-------------------------------------
Undo 2 (replaced: <1>) // edit 1 was replaced by edit 2 and undone
false // no more edits to undo
----------------------
Changing limit example
----------------------
Undo 6 // we do three undos . . .
Undo 5
Undo 4 // . . . and then set the limit to 4 which trims from both ends
Undo 3 // only 2 undos left . . .
Undo 2
Redo 2 // and then 4 redos are available . . .
Redo 3
Redo 4
Redo 5
------------------
undoOrRedo example
------------------
Undo    // undoOrRedoPresentationName is "Undo" here...
Undo 1 // ...then we do an undoOrRedo()...
Redo    // ...and it's now "Redo"
Redo 1
-----------------------------
Transform to composite example
-----------------------------
Undo 3 // because we called end(), undo() undoes all the edits . . .
Undo 2
Undo 1
Redo 1 // . . . and redo() redoes them all . . .
Redo 2
Redo 3
true    // addEdit() claims the edit was added. . . (returns false in JDK 1.2)
Undo 3 // but edit 4 never got added because end() had been called . . .
Undo 2
Undo 1
```

All of the details shown in this example can be a little overwhelming, but don't let this keep you from using UndoManager. For most applications, the basic features of UndoManager (shown in the first example in this section) will give you everything you need to provide powerful undo capabilities to your users.

Extending UndoManager

At the end of this chapter, we'll show how you might extend `UndoManager` to add additional functionality. We'll create an undo manager that gives us access to the edits it contains and notifies us any time an edit is added.

The StateEditable Interface

So far in this chapter, we've seen that the responsibility for undoing or redoing an edit lies in the `UndoableEdit` object itself. The Swing undo package also provides another mechanism for handling undo and redo, which is based on the idea of letting an "outside object" define its state before and after a series of changes are made to it. Once these *pre* and *post* states of the object have been defined, a `StateEdit` can be used to toggle back and forth between these states, undoing and redoing the changes. The "outside object" is responsible for defining the object's significant state, and must implement the `StateEditable` interface, which defines the methods listed below.

Methods

`StateEditable` defines two simple methods:

public void storeState(Hashtable state)
> This method is called to ask the object to store its current state by inserting attributes and values as key/value pairs into the given `Hashtable`.

public void restoreState(Hashtable state)
> This method is called to tell the object to restore its state, based on the key/value pairs found in the given `Hashtable`.

The StateEdit Class

`StateEdit` is an extension of `AbstractUndoableEdit` that is used to toggle between two arbitrary states. These states are defined by a `StateEditable` associated with the `StateEdit`. When the edit is created, it gets the current (*pre*) state from the `StateEditable`. Later, when `end()` is called on the edit (presumably after some changes have been made to the state of the `StateEditable`), it again gets the current (*post*) state from the `StateEditable`. After this point, `undo()` and `redo()` calls result in the state of the `StateEditable` being toggled back and forth between the *pre* and *post* states. Figure 18-9 shows a typical sequence of method calls between an application object (some object in the system that is managing edits), a `StateEdit`, its `StateEditable`, and the two `Hashtables` used to store the state of the `StateEditable`.

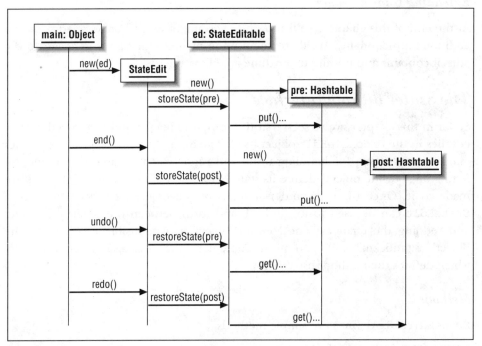

Figure 18-9. StateEdit sequence diagram

State Optimization

It's important to understand that StateEdit optimizes its representation of the states returned by the StateEditable. This is done by removing all duplicate key/value pairs from the *pre* and *post* Hashtables, keeping only those values that have changed. This is important to understand because it means the StateEditable cannot assume that all keys and values stored by its storeState() method will be in the table that gets passed into restoreState().

Figure 18-10 shows an example of how this works. The top two tables show the complete state as returned by the StateEditable. The bottom two tables show the tables as they appear after StateEdit.end() has compressed them to remove duplicate data. This is how the tables would look when passed to State-Editable.restoreState().

Property

Table 18-7 shows the default property values defined by StateEdit. The presentationName property defaults to null if not specified in the StateEdit constructor. All other properties are defined by the superclass.

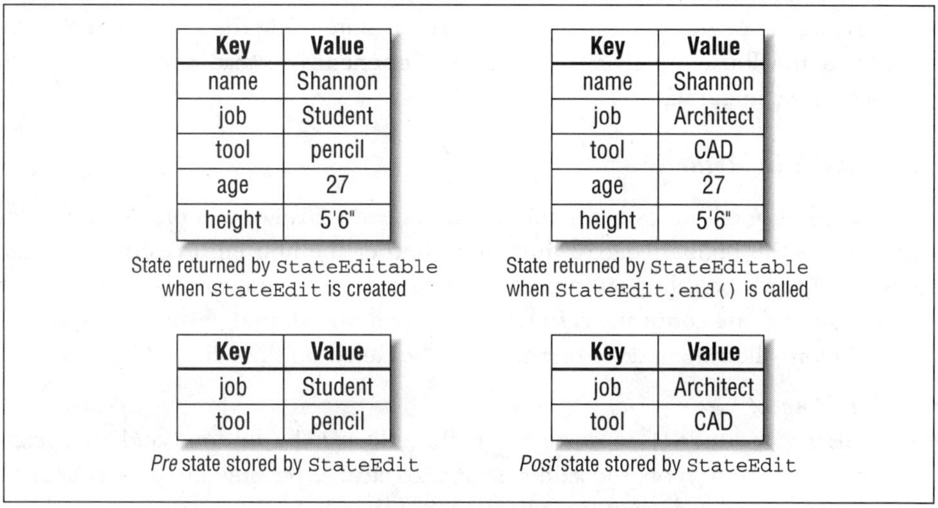

Key	Value
name	Shannon
job	Student
tool	pencil
age	27
height	5'6"

State returned by `StateEditable`
when `StateEdit` is created

Key	Value
name	Shannon
job	Architect
tool	CAD
age	27
height	5'6"

State returned by `StateEditable`
when `StateEdit.end()` is called

Key	Value
job	Student
tool	pencil

Pre state stored by `StateEdit`

Key	Value
job	Architect
tool	CAD

Post state stored by `StateEdit`

Figure 18-10. Example of state compression done by StateEdit

Table 18-7. StateEdit Property

Property	Data Type	get	is	set	bound	Default Value
presentationName*	String	•				null

See also properties from the AbstractUndoableEdit class (Table 18-2).

Protected Fields

The following fields are available to subclasses of `StateEdit`:

protected StateEditable object
> The `StateEditable` associated with this edit.

protected Hashtable preState
protected Hashtable postState
> The `Hashtable`s used to store the state information.

protected String undoRedoName
> The presentation name used for this edit.

Constructors

public StateEdit(StateEditable anObject)
> Creates a new edit that saves and restores its state using the given `StateEditable`. It calls `init()` to set up the initial state.

public StateEdit(StateEditable anObject, String name)

Creates a new edit that saves and restores its state using the given `StateEdit-able`. It will use the given name as its `presentationName`. It calls `init()` to set up the initial state.

UndoableEdit Methods

The following methods override the `AbstractUndoableEdit` implementations of methods in the `UndoableEdit` interface. Neither method enforces the fact that they should only be called after `end()`. This is not consistent with the intent of the class and can cause confusing results.[*] In practice, you should ensure that `end()` is called before allowing `undo()` or `redo()` to be called on the edit.

public void undo()[†]

Calls `super.undo()` to ensure that the edit can be undone and then calls `restoreState()` on the edit's `StateEditable`, passing in the `Hashtable` that was populated when the edit was constructed.

public void redo()[‡]

Calls `super.redo()` to ensure that the edit can be redone and then calls `restoreState()` on the edit's `StateEditable`, passing in the `Hashtable` that was populated when `end()` was called on the edit.

New Public Methods

The following new method is defined in this class.

public void end()

Called to indicate that the state of the `StateEditable` has changed. The `storeState()` method is called on the `StateEditable` to determine its *post* state. This method then uses `removeRedundantState()` to compress the *pre* and *post* state `Hashtable`s. Note that the `StateEdit` is not fully ready to handle `undo()` and `redo()` requests until this method has been called.

---

[*] Calling `undo()` will basically work. The problem is that a subsequent call to `canRedo()` would then return true. However, if you then called `redo()`, the `Hashtable` passed to `restoreState()` would be null since it is not created until `end()` is called. Future Swing releases will probably throw exceptions in these abnormal cases.

[†] `CannotUndoException` is not listed in the throws clause of this method as it was in the superclass version. This is valid only because this exception extends `RuntimeException`. Since `super.undo()` is called, this method *will* throw a `CannotUndoException` if the edit has already been undone.

[‡] `CannotRedoException` is not listed in the throws clause of this method as it was in the superclass version. This is valid only because this exception extends `RuntimeException`. Since `super.redo()` is called, this method *will* throw a `CannotRedoException` if the edit has already been undone.

Protected Methods

protected void init (StateEditable anObject, String name)

Called by the constructors to set the initial state of the edit. It stores the input `StateEditable` and edit name (used for the `presentationName` property) and creates a new `Hashtable`, which it passes to the input `StateEditable`'s `storeState()` method. This new `Hashtable` now holds the edit's *pre* state.

protected void removeRedundantState()

This method is called by `end()` to remove any duplicate key/value pairs from the *pre* and *post* `Hashtables`. Only entries that have the same key and value are removed from the tables. Comparisons are done using the `equals()` method. See Figure 18-10 for an illustration of how this method is used.

StateEdit Example

Here's one last version of our toggle button application. In this example, we'll use a `StateEdit` to store the state of all three toggle buttons. The user can determine when we start and stop the creation of the edit (buttons will be provided for these functions). The main application frame serves as the `StateEditable`, and its `storeState()` method stores the `selected` property of each of its buttons in the input `Hashtable`. The highlighted code shows the differences between this example and `UndoableToggleApp2`:

```
// UndoableToggleApp4.java
//
import javax.swing.*;
import javax.swing.event.*;
import javax.swing.undo.*;
import java.awt.*;
import java.awt.event.*;
import java.util.Hashtable;

// A sample app showing the use of StateEdit(able).
public class UndoableToggleApp4 extends JFrame
   implements StateEditable, ActionListener {

  // Create the main frame and everything in it.
  public UndoableToggleApp4() {

    // Create some toggle buttons (and subclasses)
    tog = new JToggleButton("ToggleButton");
    cb = new JCheckBox("CheckBox");
    radio = new JRadioButton("RadioButton");

    // Add this frame as a listener to the buttons
    tog.addActionListener(this);
    cb.addActionListener(this);
    radio.addActionListener(this);
```

```
// Lay out the buttons
Box buttonBox = new Box(BoxLayout.Y_AXIS);
buttonBox.add(tog);
buttonBox.add(cb);
buttonBox.add(radio);

// Create undo, redo, start, and end buttons
startButton = new JButton("Start");
endButton = new JButton("End");
undoButton = new JButton("Undo");
redoButton = new JButton("Redo");
startButton.setEnabled(true);
endButton.setEnabled(false);
undoButton.setEnabled(false);
redoButton.setEnabled(false);

// Add a listener to the start button. It creates a new StateEdit, passing in
// this frame as the StateEditable.
startButton.addActionListener(new ActionListener() {
  public void actionPerformed(ActionEvent ev) {
    edit = new StateEdit(StateEditable.this);
    startButton.setEnabled(false);
    endButton.setEnabled(true);
    //undoButton.setEnabled(edit.canUndo());
    //
    // NOTE: We really don't want to be able to undo until end() is pressed,
    // but StateEdit does not enforce this for us!
    undoButton.setEnabled(false);
    redoButton.setEnabled(edit.canRedo());
  }
});

// Add a listener to the end button. It will call end() on the StateEdit.
endButton.addActionListener(new ActionListener() {
  public void actionPerformed(ActionEvent ev) {
    edit.end();
    startButton.setEnabled(true);
    endButton.setEnabled(false);
    undoButton.setEnabled(edit.canUndo());
    redoButton.setEnabled(edit.canRedo());
  }
});

// Add a listener to the undo button. It attempts to call undo() on the
// current edit, then enables/disables the undo/redo buttons as appropriate.
undoButton.addActionListener(new ActionListener() {
  public void actionPerformed(ActionEvent ev) {
    try {
      edit.undo();
```

```
        } catch (CannotUndoException ex) { ex.printStackTrace(); }
        finally {
          undoButton.setEnabled(edit.canUndo());
          redoButton.setEnabled(edit.canRedo());
        }
      }
    });

    // Add a redo listener: just like the undo listener.
    redoButton.addActionListener(new ActionListener() {
      public void actionPerformed(ActionEvent ev) {
        try {
          edit.redo();
        } catch (CannotRedoException ex) { ex.printStackTrace(); }
        finally {
          undoButton.setEnabled(edit.canUndo());
          redoButton.setEnabled(edit.canRedo());
        }
      }
    });

    // Lay out the state/end and undo/redo buttons
    Box undoRedoBox = new Box(BoxLayout.X_AXIS);
    undoRedoBox.add(Box.createGlue());
    undoRedoBox.add(startButton);
    undoRedoBox.add(Box.createHorizontalStrut(2));
    undoRedoBox.add(endButton);
    undoRedoBox.add(Box.createHorizontalStrut(2));
    undoRedoBox.add(undoButton);
    undoRedoBox.add(Box.createHorizontalStrut(2));
    undoRedoBox.add(redoButton);
    undoRedoBox.add(Box.createGlue());

    // Lay out the main frame
    Container content = getContentPane();
    content.setLayout(new BorderLayout());
    content.add(buttonBox, BorderLayout.CENTER);
    content.add(undoRedoBox, BorderLayout.SOUTH);
    setSize(400, 150);
  }

  // When any toggle button is clicked, we turn off the undo and redo buttons,
  // reflecting the fact that we can only undo/redo the last set of state changes
  // as long as no additional changes have been made.
  public void actionPerformed(ActionEvent ev) {
    undoButton.setEnabled(false);
    redoButton.setEnabled(false);
  }
```

```
// Save the state of the app by storing the current state of the three buttons.
// We'll use the buttons themselves as keys and their selected state as values.
public void storeState(Hashtable ht) {
  ht.put(tog, new Boolean(tog.isSelected()));
  ht.put(cb, new Boolean(cb.isSelected()));
  ht.put(radio, new Boolean(radio.isSelected()));
}

// Restore state based on the values we saved when storeState() was called.
// Note that StateEdit discards any state info that did not change from between
// the start state and the end state, so we can't assume that the state for all
// 3 buttons is in the Hashtable.
public void restoreState(Hashtable ht) {
  Boolean b1 = (Boolean)ht.get(tog);
  if (b1 != null)
    tog.setSelected(b1.booleanValue());
  Boolean b2 = (Boolean)ht.get(cb);
  if (b2 != null)
    cb.setSelected(b2.booleanValue());
  Boolean b3 = (Boolean)ht.get(radio);
  if (b3 != null)
    radio.setSelected(b3.booleanValue());
}

private JToggleButton tog;
private JCheckBox cb;
private JRadioButton radio;

private JButton undoButton;
private JButton redoButton;
private JButton startButton;
private JButton endButton;

private StateEdit edit;

// Main program just creates the frame and displays it.
public static void main(String[] args) {
  JFrame f = new UndoableToggleApp4();
  f.addWindowListener(new BasicWindowMonitor());
  f.setVisible(true);
}
}
```

Note that we could have used whatever keys and values we needed to store the current state in the storeState() method. In this example, an easy strategy was to use the button itself as the key and a Boolean to hold the value. There are no restrictions on the keys and values you choose, as long as they are Objects and the storeState() and restoreState() methods are implemented to use the same keys.

The UndoableEditSupport Class

UndoableEditSupport is a simple utility class for classes that need to support undo.[*] It provides methods for adding and removing UndoableEditListeners, as well as a postEdit() method used to send an UndoableEditEvent to the added listeners. Additionally, it allows multiple edits to be added to it and then fired as a single CompoundEdit.

Property

UndoableEditSupport is a direct subclass of Object and defines the updateLevel property shown in Table 18-8. updateLevel reflects the current level of nesting of beginUpdate() calls. See the discussion of "Nested Edit Support" for more information on this property.

Table 18-8. UndoableEditSupport Property

Property	Data Type	get	is	set	bound	Default Value
updateLevel	int	•				0

Protected Fields

The following fields are available to subclasses of UndoableEditSupport.

protected CompoundEdit compoundEdit
> This is the edit used to group together multiple edits that are added between beginUpdate() and endUpdate() calls. See the discussion of "Nested Edit Support" later in this section.

protected Vector listeners
> This is where the list of listeners is stored.

protected Object realSource
> Holds the event source used for all events fired by this object. If the source is set when the UndoableEditSupport is created, that object will be sent as the source of all events. Otherwise, the UndoableEditSupport itself will become the source.

protected int updateLevel
> This is where the updateLevel property is stored.

---

[*] Presently, none of the Swing classes that support undo actually use this class. Instead, they manage their edits and listeners themselves.

Constructors

public UndoableEditSupport()

> Creates a new support object, which will use itself as the source object for any events it fires.

public UndoableEditSupport(Object r)

> Creates a new support object, which will use the given object as the source for any events it fires.

UndoableEditEvent/Listener Support Methods

The following methods allow an undo-capable object to use an UndoableEdit-Support object to manage event listeners.

public synchronized void addUndoableEditListener(UndoableEditListener l)

> Adds the given listener to a list of listeners to be notified of new UndoableEdits.

public synchronized void removeUndoableEditListener(UndoableEditListener l)

> Removes the specified listener.

public synchronized void postEdit(UndoableEdit e)

> If updateLevel is 0, this method uses _postEdit() to send an Undoable-EditEvent to all added listeners. If updateLevel is not 0, this method adds the input edit to a CompoundEdit to be fired later. See the beginUpdate() and endUpdate() methods for more details on the use of the CompoundEdit.

protected void _postEdit(UndoableEdit e)

> This protected method is used by postEdit() and endUpdate(). It creates a new UndoableEditEvent containing the input edit and sends it to all registered listeners by calling undoableEditHappened() on each.

Nested Edit Support

The following methods allow the UndoableEditSupport class to consolidate multiple edits into a single CompoundEdit, to be fired after a series of edits have been added. To use these methods, the object using the support object first calls beginUpdate(). Each subsequent postEdit() call will cause the input edit to be added to a single CompoundEdit. When endUpdate() is called, an Undoable-EditEvent containing the CompoundEdit is fired.

If multiple beginUpdate() calls are made, the support object keeps track of the level of nesting using the updateLevel property. Only when the number of endUpdate() calls matches the number of beginUpdate() calls is the Compound-Edit finally fired. Regardless of how many times beginUpdate() is called, only a single CompoundEdit is created.

public synchronized void beginUpdate()

Indicates that subsequent `postEdit()` calls should result in the input edit being added to a `CompoundEdit`. This method increments `updateLevel` and, if the `updateLevel` is 0, creates a new `Compound-Edit`.

public synchronized void endUpdate()

Decrements `updateLevel`. If `updateLevel` is now 0, it calls `end()` on the `CompoundEdit` and then calls `_postEdit()` to deliver the edit to the support object's listeners.

protected CompoundEdit createCompoundEdit()

Returns a new `CompoundEdit`. A subclass could override this method to return a different `CompoundEdit` implementation if desired.

Figure 18-11 shows how to use `beginUpdate()` and `endUpdate()`. We add a total of four edits to the support object. Notice that the first `endUpdate()` call does nothing but decrement the current level. The next `endUpdate()`, which brings the level to zero, causes the composite edit containing the four added edits to be fired.

Other Methods

public String toString()

Returns a `String` representation of the support object including the current `updateLevel`, and `String` representations of the listener vector and `CompoundEdit`.

Using Undoable Edit Support

Earlier in this chapter, we created a simple undoable toggle button class. To keep that example simple, we allowed only a single listener to be added to the button. In this example (just a new implementation of the same class), we'll show how easily we can use `UndoableEditSupport` to allow multiple listeners to be added and notified. Differences from our earlier implementation are highlighted.

```
import java.awt.event.*;
import javax.swing.*;
import javax.swing.event.*;
import javax.swing.undo.*;


// Sample undoable toggle button class using UndoableEditSupport.
public class UndoableJToggleButton2 extends JToggleButton {

  // For this example, we'll just provide one constructor.
  public UndoableJToggleButton2(String txt) {
    super(txt);
    support = new UndoableEditSupport(this);
  }
```

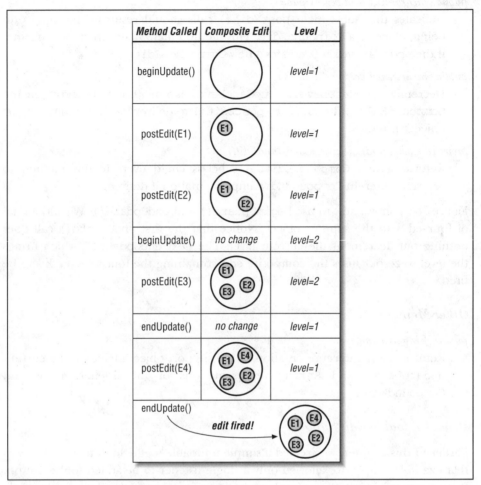

Method Called	Composite Edit	Level
beginUpdate()		level=1
postEdit(E1)		level=1
postEdit(E2)		level=1
beginUpdate()	no change	level=2
postEdit(E3)		level=2
endUpdate()	no change	level=1
postEdit(E4)		level=1
endUpdate()	edit fired!	

Figure 18-11. Using beginUpdate() and endUpdate()

```
// Add an UndoableEditListener using our support object.
public void addUndoableEditListener(UndoableEditListener l) {
  support.addUndoableEditListener(l);
}


// Remove an UndoableEditListener using our support object.
public void removeUndoableEditListener(UndoableEditListener l) {
  support.addUndoableEditListener(l);
}


// Override this method to call the super implementation first (to fire the
// action event) and then fire a new UndoableEditEvent to our listeners using
// our support object.
protected void fireActionPerformed(ActionEvent ev) {
```

```
    // Fire the ActionEvent as usual
    super.fireActionPerformed(ev);

    support.postEdit(new UndoableToggleEdit(this));
  }

  private UndoableEditSupport support;
}
```

The CannotRedoException Class

This class is an extension of RuntimeException thrown when an attempt is made to redo an UndoableEdit that cannot be redone (typically because it has not yet been undone, or because it has been "killed").

There are no properties, constructors (other than the implicit default), or methods defined in this class.

The CannotUndoException Class

This class is an extension of RuntimeException thrown when an attempt is made to undo an UndoableEdit that cannot be undone (typically because it has already been undone, or because it has been "killed").

There are no properties, constructors (other than the implicit default), or methods defined in this class.

Extending UndoManager

Now that we've looked at all of the classes and interfaces in the undo framework, we'll look at a few ideas for extending the functionality it provides.

In this example, we'll extend UndoManager to add a few extra features. The first thing we'll add is the ability to get a list of the edits stored in the manager. This is a simple task of returning the contents of the edits vector inherited from CompoundEdit. We also provide access to an array of significant undoable edits and an array of significant redoable edits. These might be useful in a game like chess in which we want to provide a list of past moves.

The next major feature we'll add in this extended UndoManager is support for listeners. At the time of this writing, the current UndoManager did not have any way of notifying you when it received edits. As we saw in an earlier example, this means that you have to listen to each edit-generating component if you want to update the user interface to reflect new undoable or redoable edits as they occur. In our manager, we simply add the ability to add and remove undoable edit listeners to the undo manager itself. Each time an edit is added, the undo manager fires an `UndoableEditEvent` to any registered listeners. This way, we can just add the undo manager as a listener to each edit-generating component and then add a single listener to the undo manager to update the UI.

The methods of our new undo manager can be divided into two groups, each supporting one of the two features we're adding. We'll split the source code listing along these lines so we can talk about each set of methods independently. Here's the first half.

```java
// ExtendedUndoManager.java
//
import javax.swing.event.*;
import javax.swing.undo.*;
import java.util.Enumeration;
import java.util.Vector;

// An extension of UndoManager that provides two additional features:
// (1) The ability to add & remove listeners and (2) the ability to gain more
// extensive access to the edits being managed.
public class ExtendedUndoManager extends UndoManager
  implements UndoableEditListener {

  // Return the complete list of edits in an array.
  public synchronized UndoableEdit[] getEdits() {
    UndoableEdit[] array = new UndoableEdit[edits.size()];
    edits.copyInto(array);
    return array;
  }

  // Return all currently significant undoable edits. The first edit will be the
  // next one to be undone.
  public synchronized UndoableEdit[] getUndoableEdits() {
    int size = edits.size();
    Vector v = new Vector(size);
    for (int i=size-1;i>=0;i--) {
      UndoableEdit u = (UndoableEdit)edits.elementAt(i);
      if (u.canUndo() && u.isSignificant())
        v.addElement(u);
    }
    UndoableEdit[] array = new UndoableEdit[v.size()];
    v.copyInto(array);
    return array;
  }

  // Return all currently significant redoable edits. The first edit will be the
  // next one to be redone.
  public synchronized UndoableEdit[] getRedoableEdits() {
    int size = edits.size();
    Vector v = new Vector(size);
```

```
   for (int i=0; i<size; i++) {
     UndoableEdit u = (UndoableEdit)edits.elementAt(i);
     if (u.canRedo() && u.isSignificant())
       v.addElement(u);
   }
   UndoableEdit[] array = new UndoableEdit[v.size()];
   v.copyInto(array);
   return array;
 }
```

The first method here is simple. All we do is copy the edits from the edits vector into an array and return it. The other two methods are nearly identical. They are a little more complicated than they ideally should be because we don't have access to the current insertion point into the edits vector (which would split the list right between the undoable and redoable edits). Instead, we just iterate over the elements, building up a list of undoable or redoable significant edits.

Here are the methods we added to support listeners.

```
// UndoableEditListener Method Support (ExtendedUndoManager.java, part 2)
//

// Add an edit and notify our listeners.
public synchronized boolean addEdit(UndoableEdit anEdit) {
  boolean b = super.addEdit(anEdit);
  if (b)
    support.postEdit(anEdit); // if the edit was added, notify listeners
  return b;
}

// When an edit is sent to us, call addEdit() to notify any of our listeners.
public synchronized void undoableEditHappened(UndoableEditEvent ev) {
  UndoableEdit ue = ev.getEdit();
  source = ev.getSource();
  addEdit(ue);
}

// Add a listener to be notified each time an edit is added to this manager.
// This makes it easy to update undo/redo menus as edits are added.
public synchronized void addUndoableEditListener(UndoableEditListener l) {
  support.addUndoableEditListener(l);
}

// Remove a listener from this manager.
public synchronized void removeUndoableEditListener(UndoableEditListener l) {
  support.removeUndoableEditListener(l);
}
```

```
private ExtendedUndoableEditSupport support =
  new ExtendedUndoableEditSupport();

private Object source; // the source of the last edit

// A simple extension of UndoableEditSupport that lets us specify the event
// source each time we post an edit.
class ExtendedUndoableEditSupport extends UndoableEditSupport {

  // Post an edit to added listeners.
  public synchronized void postEdit(UndoableEdit ue) {
    realSource = source; // from our enclosing manager object
    super.postEdit(ue);
  }
}
}
```

The first method here is a customized implementation of addEdit(). For the most part, we leave this method to the superclass. The only thing we've added is a call to UndoableEditSupport.postEdit(). Any time an edit is added to the undo manager, we'll notify its listeners. The idea is that a single listener, probably responsible for updating an *Undo* menu, will be added to the undo manager.

The next method is the undoableEditHappened() method from the Undoable-EditListener interface. This is the method called each time any edit-generating component in the application fires an UndoableEdit. In this method, we first store the source of the event (we'll see how we use this shortly) and then call addEdit().

The next two methods simply use UndoableEditSupport to manage interested listeners.

Finally, we define a small inner class called ExtendedUndoableEditSupport. This is an extension of UndoableEditSupport that we will use to set the correct event source each time the ExtendedUndoManager fires an UndoableEditEvent. Rather than declaring the undo manager as the source of the event, we use the real source of the event that was passed to the undo manager's undoableEdit-Happened() method. Note that realSource, which is a protected field in UndoableEditSupport, becomes the source object in the fired UndoableEdit-Event.

19

Text 101

Swing provides an extensive collection of classes for working with text in user interfaces. In fact, there's so much provided for working with text, Swing's creators placed most of it into its own package: `javax.swing.text`. This package's dozens of interfaces and classes (plus the five concrete component classes in `javax.swing`) provide a rich (and complex!) set of text-based models and components. Over the course of the next six chapters, we'll cover each of these classes and interfaces in detail. Figure 19-1 shows a very high-level view of the structure of the Swing text components. The arrows in the figure can be read as "knows about," or "uses."

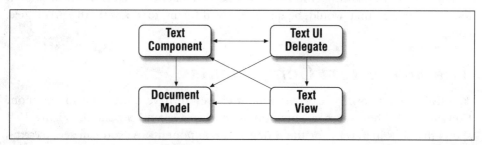

Figure 19-1. High-level view of the Swing text framework

The text content for any component is stored in a model object called a Document. Chapter 20, *Document Model and Events,* and Chapter 21, *Styled Documents and JTextPane,* cover the complex Swing document model in considerable detail. This model allows you to represent highly structured text supporting multiple fonts and colors, and even embedded Icons and Components.

Swing text components allow you to customize certain aspects of the look-and-feel without much work. This includes the creation of custom carets (cursor) and custom highlighting, as well as the definition of custom key bindings, allowing you to associate `Actions` with special key combinations. These features are covered in Chapter 22, *Carets, Highlighters, and Keymaps*.

As usual, each text component delegates its painting tasks to a UI delegate. Unlike the other Swing UI delegates, the `TextUI` relies heavily on a large number of additional classes that extend a common base class called `View`. These classes are responsible for the details of layout, including issues such as alignment and text wrapping. We'll cover all of these classes in detail in Chapter 23, *Text Views*.

Finally, all of this is tied together by something called an `EditorKit`. `EditorKits` allow you to define how your documents will be input and output via streams, what view objects should be used in which situations, and what special actions your editor will support. `EditorKits` (and `TextActions`) are covered in Chapter 24, *EditorKits and TextActions*.

This may all seem a bit overwhelming. The good news is that despite all the complexity and power Swing's text components provide, it's still pretty simple to do most things. That is the focus of this chapter. Here, we'll look at `JTextComponent`, the base class for all of the text components, and its five subclasses: `JTextField`, `JPasswordField`, `JTextArea`, `JEditorPane`, and `JTextPane`. We won't cover the complex text model and view classes until later, but we'll occasionally reference things you may want to investigate further in the upcoming chapters. In the case of `JTextPane`, we won't cover the properties and methods of this class in this chapter, because they rely pretty heavily on the document model. Instead, we'll just provide a brief overview and an example that shows how to do a few basic things that would be particularly difficult to do with the AWT text components.

The Swing Text Components

The five concrete Swing text component classes all have quite a bit in common. Consequently, they share a common base class, `JTextComponent`. Figure 19-2 shows the class hierarchy for the Swing text components. As you can see, `JTextComponent` is the only one of these classes defined in the `text` package; the rest can be found in `javax.swing`[*] with the rest of the Swing component classes.

---

[*] All of the other text-related classes (discussed in the subsequent chapters) are part of the `javax.swing.text` package.

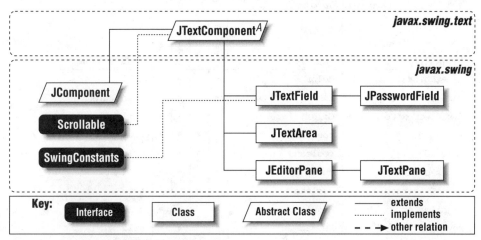

Figure 19-2. The Swing text components

The JTextComponent Class

JTextComponent is an abstract class that serves as the base class for all text-based Swing components. It defines a large number of properties and methods that apply to its subclasses. In this introductory chapter, we'll pass quickly over many of these properties, as they require an understanding of the underlying model and view aspects of the text framework.

Properties

JTextComponent defines the properties and default values shown in Table 19-1. document is a reference to the Document model for the component. This is where the component's data is stored. We'll get into a lot of detail on the Document interface and its implementations in the next chapter. The UI property for all text components is a TextUI.

Table 19-1. JTextComponent Properties

Property	Data Type	get	is	set	bound	Default Value
document	Document	•		•	•	null
UI	TextUI	•		•	•	from L&F
accessibleContext*	AccessibleContext	•				AccessibleJTextCompo-nent
actions	Action[]	•				From the UI's EditorKit
caret	Caret	•		•	•	null

See also properties from the JComponent class (Table 3-5).

Table 19-1. JTextComponent Properties (continued)

Property	Data Type	get	is	set	bound	Default Value
caretColor	Color	●		●	●	null
caretPosition	int	●		●		From caret
disabledTextColor	Color	●		●	●	null
editable	boolean		●	●	●	true
enabled*	boolean		●	●		true
focusAccelerator	char	●		●	●	'0'
focusTraversable*	boolean		●			true
highlighter	Highlighter	●		●	●	null
keymap	Keymap	●		●	●	null
layout*	LayoutManager	●		●		null
margin	Insets	●		●	●	TextUI.getDefault-Margin()
opaque*	boolean	●		●		false
preferredScrollable-ViewportSize*	Dimension	●				Preferred size of component
scrollableTracks-ViewportHeight*	boolean	●				see below
scrollableTracks-ViewportWidth*	boolean	●				see below
selectedText	String	●				From document
selectedTextColor	Color	●		●	●	null
selectionColor	Color	●		●	●	null
selectionEnd	int	●		●		From caret
selectionStart	int	●		●		From caret
text	String	●		●		From document

See also properties from the JComponent class (Table 3-5).

accessibleContext refers to an instance of the inner class AccessibleJText-Component which implements the AccessibleText interface, described in Chapter 25, *Programming with Accessibility*. The actions property specifies the Actions (see Chapter 3, *Swing Component Basics*, for an introduction to Swing's new Action interface) available for the component. These actions might include things such as *cut*, *paste*, or *change-font*. The supported actions are defined by the component's EditorKit, which we'll cover in detail in Chapter 24.

caret represents the location at which data will be inserted into the document. We'll discuss the Caret interface in Chapter 22. caretColor, disabledText-Color, selectionColor, and selectedTextColor simply specify the color used to render the caret, disabled text, selection background, and selected text, respectively.* CaretPosition provides quick access to the Caret's current position.

The editable property indicates whether or not the document can be edited. If this property is set to false, characters typed into the component will not be inserted—the component will be used only for displaying text. We list the enabled property here only because JTextComponent overrides setEnabled() to explicitly call repaint().

Next, the focusAccelerator property specifies the key that can be used to give focus to the text component. focusTraversable is true by default, because the implementation of isFocusTraversable() is overridden to return true if the component is editable and enabled.

The highlighter property is a reference to the object responsible for making highlights in the text. Like Caret, the Highlighter interface will be introduced in Chapter 22. Yet another new interface we'll get to later in that chapter is Keymap, which is used to define the keymap property. This is an important property that allows you to specify, for example, what keys will cause text to be cut (e.g., CTRL-X) or paste (e.g, CTRL-V).

The inherited layout property defaults to null, because the layout of text components is handled by the view hierarchy (see Chapter 23). The margin property specifies the distance between the component's text and its border (using Insets, an AWT class).

JTextComponent redefines the setOpaque() and isOpaque() methods, and the opaque property defaults to false (though the DefaultTextUI class sets it to true, which is the normal case).

NOTE   These opaque accessors are probably left over from an earlier release and may be removed in a future release. As they are currently implemented, opaque is not a bound property in JTextComponent, even though it *is* bound in JComponent.

The preferredScrollableViewportSize property (from the Scrollable interface) just delegates to getPreferredSize(). The values of the other two properties from the Scrollable interface, scrollableTracksViewportHeight and scrollableTracksViewportWidth, are determined based on the size of the JViewport containing the component. If the viewport is larger than the preferred

---

* The regular text color is stored in the inherited foreground property.

size of the text component, these properties will be true. If not, they'll be false. If the component's parent is not a JViewport, these properties are always false.

The selectedText and text properties are managed by the component's Document, while selectionStart and selectionEnd are delegated to the Caret.

Events

JTextComponent fires a CaretEvent any time the state of the component's Caret changes. Any time the cursor position changes, an event is fired. The only exception is that while a selection is being made (the mouse is being dragged), events are not fired as the cursor moves, only when the mouse is released and the selection has been created.

The following standard methods are provided for working with caret events.

public void addCaretListener(CaretListener listener)
protected void fireCaretUpdate(CaretEvent e)
public void removeCaretListener(CaretListener listener)

The CaretEvent class and CaretListener interface are described in detail in Chapter 22.

In addition to firing CaretEvents, JTextComponents fire property change events when the values of the following properties are changed: caret, caretColor, disabledTextColor, document, editable, focusAccelerator, highlighter, keymap, margin, selectedTextColor, and selectionColor.

Constants

Table 19-2 defines the JTextComponent constants. FOCUS_ACCELERATOR_KEY is the only property name that is explicitly defined as a static string. There is apparently nothing special about it, and its existence as a constant does not appear to be meaningful.

Table 19-2. JTextComponent Constants

Constant	Type	Description
DEFAULT_KEYMAP	String	The name of the default keymap used by all text components. This string can be used as a parameter to the static getKeymap() method.
FOCUS_ACCELERATOR_KEY	String	The bound property name for the focus accelerator.

Constructors

public JTextComponent()

Creates a new editable component and updates the UI (causing many of the null properties listed in Table 19-1 to be set).

Clipboard Methods

These methods allow you to move data to and from the system clipboard:

public void copy()

Copies the currently selected range in the component's model to the system clipboard. No change is made to the document itself.

public void cut()

Copies the currently selected range in the component's model to the system clipboard. The selected range is removed from the document.

public void paste()

Copies the contents of the system clipboard into the document. If there is an active selection, it is replaced by the pasted contents. If there is no selection, the contents are inserted in front of the current insert position.

Selection Methods

These methods are concerned with selecting (highlighting) text.

public void moveCaretPosition(int pos)

Forms a selection by moving the caret to the specified position. The selection begins at the location defined when setCaretPosition() was previously called.

public void replaceSelection(String content)

Replaces the currently selected area with the input string. If there is no current selection, the input text is inserted at the current insert position.

public void select(int selectionStart, int selectionEnd)

Selects an area of the document bounded by the input offsets. This method is implemented by calling setCaretPosition() and moveCaretPositon(). According to the documentation for JTextComponent, these methods should be used directly, rather than using select(), which is provided only for backward compatibility.

public void selectAll()

Selects all of the text in the component.

View Methods

These methods provide mappings between model and view coordinate systems (e.g., pixel (53,71) is part of character 42 in the document) and information for scrolling the text component:

public int getScrollableBlockIncrement(Rectangle visibleRect, int orientation, int direction)
> Returns the "block" scroll increment (in pixels) desired by the component. The default implementation returns the size of the visible area, meaning that the entire visible area will be scrolled off the screen. Subclasses are intended to compute a scroll increment that exposes some logical portion of the display, such as a row or column of data. The input `Rectangle` defines the size of the current view area. The orientation must be either `SwingConstants.VERTICAL` or `SwingConstants.HORIZONTAL`. The direction indicates which direction to scroll. Negative values indicate a scroll up or left, positive values indicate down or right. For more information on scrolling, see the explanation of the `Scrollable` interface in Chapter 11, *Specialty Panes and Layout Managers*.

public int getScrollableUnitIncrement(Rectangle visibleRect, int orientation, int direction)
> Returns the "unit" scroll increment (in pixels) desired by the component. The default implementation returns 10% of the visible area. Subclasses are intended to compute a scroll increment that exposes some logical portion of the display, such as a row or column of data. The input `Rectangle` defines the size of the current view area. The orientation must be either `SwingConstants.VERTICAL` or `SwingConstants.HORIZONTAL`. The direction indicates which direction to scroll. Negative values indicate a scroll up or left, positive values indicate down or right. For more information on scrolling, see the explanation of the `Scrollable` interface in Chapter 11.

public Rectangle modelToView(int pos) throws BadLocationException
> Converts the input position to an area in the view coordinate system. The input position is an offset into the content of the text component.

public int viewToModel(Point pt)
> Returns the offset of the character found at the input view location.

Working with Keymaps

The Swing text components allow you to map certain keystrokes to specified actions. This feature can be used to add shortcut editing features (e.g., CTRL-C to copy text) to text components. We'll discuss the `Keymap` interface in more detail in Chapter 22. The following methods are defined in the `JTextComponent` base class.

public static Keymap addKeymap(String nm, Keymap parent)

Creates a new Keymap with the specified parent. If the input map name (nm) is not null, the new Keymap is added to an internal table that can be accessed using the map name.

public static Keymap getKeymap(String nm)

Returns the Keymap associated with the given name.

public static Keymap loadKeymap(Keymap map, JTextComponent.KeyBinding[] bindings,
Action[] actions)

Allows you to populate a given Keymap using the KeyBinding inner class (described later in the chapter). Each input KeyBinding contains an action name and a KeyStroke (see Chapter 27, *Swing Utilities*). Each action name is looked up in the array of Actions. If there is a match, a mapping is added from the KeyStroke to the Action.

public static Keymap removeKeymap(String nm)

Removes (and returns) the Keymap specified by the input map name.

protected void processComponentKeyEvent(KeyEvent e)

This method is called each time a key is pressed. If the input event is a KEY_TYPED event, it tries to map the key to an action. If there is no action for the given keystroke, the default action (typically a simple character insertion) is performed. The handling of KEY_PRESSED and KEY_RELEASED events is similar, but if the keystroke cannot be mapped to an action, no default action is performed.

This method is called by JComponent.processKeyEvent() only if neither the FocusManager nor registered KeyListeners consumed the event.

Other Methods

public String getText(int offs, int len) throws BadLocationException

Returns a portion of the text starting at the input offset (the distance, in characters, from the beginning of the document), containing the requested number of characters.

public void read(Reader in, Object desc) throws IOException

Initializes the component from a stream. The default implementation reads this stream as plain text, but subclasses may handle more complex formats, such as HTML. The second parameter, an Object, may contain any type of information useful to the processing of the data.

public void updateUI()

This method is called to indicate that the look-and-feel (L&F) has changed.

public void write(Writer out) throws IOException
> Writes the contents of the document to the given stream. The default implementation stores the document as plain text, but subclasses may produce alternate data formats, such as HTML.

The JTextComponent.KeyBinding Class

This very simple static inner class is used to map a `KeyStroke` to an action name. We saw this class used in the `JTextComponent.loadKeymap()` method.

Fields

The two data members of the class are defined as public fields:

public KeyStroke key
> The `KeyStroke` (see Chapter 27) to be mapped to an action.

public String actionName
> The name of the action corresponding to `key`.

Constructors

public KeyBinding(KeyStroke key, String actionName)
> Creates a new binding.

The JTextField Class

`JTextField` provides similar functionality to the `java.awt.TextField` class. It allows the user to enter a single line of text, firing an `ActionEvent` when the enter key is pressed. Key improvements over the AWT text field include simple text alignment (left, right, or center) and a better design for text filtering. Figure 19-3 shows what Swing text fields look like.

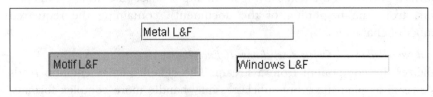

Figure 19-3. JTextFields in the three look-and-feels

The following program dumps the contents of a right-justified field to standard output each time the enter key is pressed:

```
// JTextFieldExample.java
//
```

```
import javax.swing.*;
import java.awt.event.*;

public class JTextFieldExample {

  public static void main(String[] args) {

    final JTextField field = new JTextField(20);
    field.setHorizontalAlignment(SwingConstants.RIGHT);

    field.addActionListener(new ActionListener() {
      public void actionPerformed(ActionEvent ev) {
        System.out.println("Entered: " + field.getText());
      }
    });

    JFrame frame = new JFrame();
    frame.addWindowListener(new BasicWindowMonitor());
    frame.getContentPane().add(field);
    frame.pack();
    frame.setVisible(true);
  }
}
```

Properties

Table 19-3 shows the properties defined by `JTextField`. The `document` property defaults to a new instance of `PlainDocument`, and the `UIClassID` is `TextFieldUI`.

Table 19-3. JTextField Properties

Property	Data Type	get	is	set	bound	Default Value
document*	Document	●		●	●	PlainDocument
UIClassID*	String	●				"TextFieldUI"
accessibleContext*	AccessibleContext	●				AccessibleJTextField
actionCommand	String			●		null
actions*	Action[]	●				adds NotifyAction
columns	int	●		●		0
font*	Font	●		●	●	From superclass
horizontalAlignment	int	●		●	●	LEFT
horizontalVisibility	BoundedRangeModel	●				DefaultBoundedRange-Model

See also properties from the JTextComponent class (Table 19-1).

Table 19-3. JTextField Properties (continued)

Property	Data Type	get	is	set	bound	Default Value
minimumSize*	Dimension	•		•	•	Preferred size
preferredSize*	Dimension	•		•	•	Width based on columns and font
scrollOffset	int	•		•		From horizontal visibility
validateRoot*	boolean			•		true

See also properties from the JTextComponent class (Table 19-1).

The `accessibleContext` property is as expected. Note that `AccessibleJText-Field` extends `JTextComponent.AccessibleJTextComponent`. `actionCommand` specifies the value that will be used in `ActionEvents` generated by the text field. If this value is not explicitly set, the current contents of the field are used as the action command.

The `actions` property appears here because `JTextField` adds a `notifyAction`, used to indicate that the contents of the field have been "accepted" by the user (typically by pressing Enter).

The `columns` property specifies the number of columns in the field. Note that for variable-width fonts, the width of a single column is defined by the width of the lowercase character m, using the field's specified font. This property (`font`) is included here because `setFont()` is overridden to clear the internal column width field and revalidate the component (so the new font will take effect).

`horizontalAlignment` indicates where the text will appear within the field. Valid values are `LEFT`, `CENTER`, and `RIGHT` (defined in `SwingConstants`). `horizontal-Visiblity` is a `BoundedRangeModel` (see Chapter 6, *Bounded Range Components*) that defines the portion of the text that will be displayed if the text is too long to fit in the field. Its `minimum` is zero and it's `maximum` is equal to the size of the text field or the total length of the text, whichever is bigger (in pixels). Its `extent` is the width of the text field (in pixels), and its `value` is the offset from the beginning of the text that is currently showing at the left edge of the field.

The `minimumSize` and `preferredSize` properties for `JTextField` are determined by calling `super.getPreferredSize()` and then adjusting the width based on the value of `columns`. `shiftOffset` just provides direct access to horizontalVisibility's `value` property.

The `validateRoot` property is returned as `true` by `JTextField`. This means that calls to `revalidate()` on the text field will be handled by validating the field.

Events

JTextField objects fire ActionEvents any time the enter key is pressed, indicating that the user is finished with the field.

The JTextField class contains the following standard methods for working with ActionEvents:

public synchronized void addActionListener(ActionListener l)
public synchronized void removeActionListener(ActionListener l)
protected void fireActionPerformed()

Additionally, the following method is provided:

public void postActionEvent()
   This public method just calls the protected fireActionPerformed().

In addition to firing ActionEvents, a JTextField will fire a PropertyChange-Event whenever the horizontalAlignment property is updated.

Constants

JTextField defines the constant shown in Table 19-4.

Table 19-4. JTextField Constants

Constant	Type	Description
notifyAction	String	The name of the action used to send notification that the field's contents have been accepted.

This action name is used by TextFieldUI implementations to map a keystroke (typically Enter) to the Action provided by JTextField, which notifies listeners that something has been entered into the field.

Constructors

public JTextField()
   Creates a new text field with zero columns.

public JTextField(String text)
   Creates a new text field displaying the given text.

public JTextField(int columns)
   Creates a new text field with the requested number of columns.

public JTextField(String text, int columns)
   Creates a new text field with the specified number of columns, displaying the given text.

public JTextField(Document doc, String text, int columns)

> Creates a new text field that uses the specified document model (Document is covered in detail in the next chapter), displays the specified string of text, and contains the requested number of columns.

Public Methods

Almost all of the public methods are property accessors or event management methods that have already been covered. The only exception is listed below:

public void scrollRectToVisible(Rectangle r)

> Adjusts the field's visibility based on the x value (in pixels) of the input rectangle (the other values in the rectangle are ignored). It ensures that the specified x coordinate, relative to the left edge of the field, will be visible. To scroll text to the right, r.x must be greater than the width of the field. To scroll text to the left, r.x must be negative.

Protected Methods

protected Document createDefaultModel()

> Creates the default document model to be used, if one is not specified as a constructor argument. This implementation returns a new PlainDocument.

protected int getColumnWidth()

> Returns the width (in pixels) of a single column. The default implementation returns the width of the character "m" using the FontMetrics of the current font.

protected String paramString()

> Returns the string of parameters used to create a string representation of the text field. This method is used by Component.toString().

A Simple Form

One of the most common and simplest user-interface constructs is the basic form. Typically, forms are made up of labels and fields, with the label text describing the text to be entered in the field. Here's a primitive TextForm class that shows the use of tooltips and basic accessibility support. Note that we call setLabelFor() on each label to associate it with a field. This gives an accessibleName to the text field.

```
// TextForm.java
//
import javax.swing.*;
import java.awt.event.*;
import java.awt.*;
```

```java
// A simple label/field form panel
public class TextForm extends JPanel {

  // Create a form with the given labels, tooltips, and sizes
  public TextForm(String[] labels, String[] tips, int[] widths) {
    tf = new JTextField[labels.length];

    // Define layout
    setLayout(new GridBagLayout());
    GridBagConstraints gbc = new GridBagConstraints();
    gbc.anchor = GridBagConstraints.WEST;
    gbc.insets = new Insets(2, 2, 2, 2);

    // Add labels and fields as specified
    for (int i=0; i<labels.length; i++) {
      JLabel l = new JLabel(labels[i]);

      // Create an accessibility-friendly field
      tf[i] = new JTextField(widths[i]);
      tf[i].setToolTipText(tips[i]); // sets accessible desc too!
      l.setLabelFor(tf[i]);          // sets accessibleName for tf[i]!

      // lay out label & field
      gbc.gridy = i;
      gbc.gridx = 0;
      add(l, gbc);
      gbc.gridx = 1;
      add(tf[i], gbc);
    }
  }

  // Get the contents of one of the TFs.
  public String getEnteredText(int index) {
    return tf[index].getText();
  }

  private JTextField[] tf;

  // A simple example program
  public static void main(String[] args) {
    String[] labels =
      { "First Name", "Middle Initial", "Last Name", "Age" };

    String[] descs = { "First Name","Middle Initial",
      "Last Name", "Age" };

    int[] widths = { 15, 1, 15, 3 };

    final TextForm form = new TextForm(labels, descs, widths);
```

```
    // A button that dumps the field contents
    JButton dump = new JButton("Dump");
    dump.addActionListener(new ActionListener() {
      public void actionPerformed(ActionEvent ev) {
        System.out.println(form.getEnteredText(0));
        System.out.println(form.getEnteredText(1));
        System.out.println(form.getEnteredText(2));
        System.out.println(form.getEnteredText(3));
      }
    });

    // layout
    JFrame f = new JFrame();
    f.addWindowListener(new BasicWindowMonitor());
    Container c = f.getContentPane();
    c.setLayout(new BorderLayout());
    c.add(form, BorderLayout.CENTER);
    c.add(dump, BorderLayout.SOUTH);
    f.pack();
    f.setVisible(true);
  }
}
```

We've included a simple `main()` method here to show how this form class might
be used. Clearly, much could be done to make this simple class more flexible and
powerful. That aside, Figure 19-4 shows what we get.

Figure 19-4. A simple text form

Understanding JTextField Sizing

Depending on how you construct your `JTextField`, you may be a bit surprised by
its size when you display it on the screen. The rules for determining the preferred
width of a `JTextField` are a bit complicated. They are:

- If the number of columns has been set (either in the constructor or by a call
  to `setColumns()`), multiply the number of columns by the width of the letter
  "m," using the field's current font. Note that specifying default text when constructing the field does *not* set the number of columns.

- If the number of columns has not been specified, but the `preferredSize` for the field has been explicitly set, use the preferred size.

- If neither the number of columns nor the `preferredSize` has been specified, allow the size to be determined by the `TextUI` (the UI delegate) associated with the component. This behavior is inherited from `JComponent`, which delegates `getPreferredSize()` to the UI if no size has been explicitly set. The default behavior (from `DefaultTextUI`) is to return a size that will allow the entire content of the field (based on the field's font) to be displayed.

The size returned by UI is not cached anywhere; each time a call is made to `getPreferredSize()`, a new value is calculated based on the current contents of the field. This means that your field can change size whenever its container is validated. The following program shows several different text fields and different ways of managing their widths:

```
// TFExample.java
//
import javax.swing.*;
import java.awt.*;
import java.awt.event.*;

public class TFExample {
  public static void main(String[] args) {
    JFrame f = new JFrame();
    f.addWindowListener(new BasicWindowMonitor());

    // Create several fields using different constructors
    JTextField t1 = new JTextField();
    JTextField t2 = new JTextField(11);
    JTextField t3 = new JTextField("mmmmmmmmmmmm");
    JTextField t4 = new JTextField("Hello World");
    JTextField t5 = new JTextField("Hello World", 11);
    JTextField t6 = new JTextField("Hello World");
    JTextField t7 = new JTextField(2);
    JTextField t8 = new JTextField();

    // Validate the container when we hit 'enter' in t4.
    final JTextField ref = t4;
    ref.addActionListener(new ActionListener() {
      public void actionPerformed(ActionEvent ev) {
        ref.getParent().validate();
        ref.setScrollOffset(0);
      }
    });

    // Make sure t6 won't grow on us (like t4 will)
    t6.setPreferredSize(t6.getPreferredSize());
```

```
    // Use a fixed-width font on t7-2 characters wide . . . not!
    t7.setFont(new Font("Monospaced", Font.PLAIN, 12));

    // A little trick to make t8 _really_ 2 characters wide
    t8.setText("  "); // 2 characters . . .
    t8.setFont(new Font("Monospaced", Font.PLAIN, 12));
    t8.setPreferredSize(t8.getPreferredSize());
    t8.setText(""); // empty the field

    // Shift all the fields with content back to the left
    t3.setScrollOffset(0);
    t4.setScrollOffset(0);
    t5.setScrollOffset(0);
    t6.setScrollOffset(0);

    // Display all the fields . . .
    Container content = f.getContentPane();
    content.setLayout(new GridBagLayout());
    GridBagConstraints gbc = new GridBagConstraints();
    gbc.gridy = 0;
    content.add(t1, gbc); gbc.gridy++;
    content.add(t2, gbc); gbc.gridy++;
    content.add(t3, gbc); gbc.gridy++;
    content.add(t4, gbc); gbc.gridy++;
    content.add(t5, gbc); gbc.gridy++;
    content.add(t6, gbc); gbc.gridy++;
    content.add(t7, gbc); gbc.gridy++;
    content.add(t8, gbc);

    f.setSize(150, 200);
    f.setVisible(true);
  }
}
```

Each of the eight fields in this example shows something of interest:

t1

Using the zero-argument constructor makes for very small fields. You'll need to set the columns or add text and validate the container at some point if you use this constructor.

t2

An 11 column field with no data.

t3

An 11-column field with 11 "m"s. Note that this field is actually a little larger than *t2*. This demonstrates an important fact: specifying the number of columns does not make the usable part of the field quite big enough to fit the specified number of characters. More on this in *t7* & *t8*.

t4

The text here is also 11 characters, but we didn't specify the number of columns. The field is much smaller using a variable-width font. We've added a listener to this field to validate the frame any time we hit enter. This will show that the size of the field actually grows to fit its content.

t5

The specified number of columns is more significant than the specified text. This field is the same width as *t2*.

t6

This field is just like *t4*, but we explicitly set its size so it won't grow. See Figure 19-5.

t7

An attempt at a 2-character fixed-width field. Unfortunately, the borders of the field take up some of the space, so we can't really fit two characters in it.

t8

A 2-character fixed-width field that works. This is a little bit a of a hack, but we use the field's preferred size to set the field width to fit 2 full characters. We could achieve the same effect by adding the field's insets to the preferred size.

Figure 19-5 shows the result. The first frame shows the initial output, while the second frame shows the display after adding ". Goodbye." to the end of *t4* and *t6*, and adding the text "12" to *t7* and *t8*. Notice that *t4* has grown to fit the entire content of the field while t6 has not. Also note that, despite being defined with a width of 2 columns, *t7* is not large enough to display two characters.

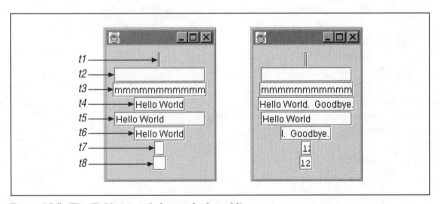

Figure 19-5. JTextField sizing, before and after adding text

Keep in mind that this entire discussion of text field sizing assumes you are using a layout manager that respects the component's preferred size. Figure 19-6 shows the output from the program `GridTFs`, which uses a `GridLayout` to manage the display of its text fields; a `GridLayout` ignores the preferred size of the components it manages, so the text fields won't change size as text is added.

Figure 19-6. Default JTextFields in a GridLayout

```
// GridTFs.java
//
import java.awt.*;
import javax.swing.*;
import javax.swing.text.*;

public class GridTFs {
  public static void main(String[] args) {
    JLabel l1 = new JLabel("Last Name");
    JLabel l2 = new JLabel("Middle Name");
    JLabel l3 = new JLabel("First Name");
    JTextField tf1 = new JTextField();
    JTextField tf2 = new JTextField();
    JTextField tf3 = new JTextField();

    JPanel p = new JPanel();
    p.setLayout(new GridLayout(3, 2, 2, 2)); // ignores preferred size

    p.add(l1);
    p.add(tf1);
    p.add(l2);
    p.add(tf2);
    p.add(l3);
    p.add(tf3);

    JFrame f = new JFrame();
    f.addWindowListener(new BasicWindowMonitor());
    f.setContentPane(p);
    f.pack();
    f.setVisible(true);
  }
}
```

Restricting Input

One of the most common extensions of a text field is a field that defines some type of restriction on the text that may be entered into it (uppercase only, numbers only, no more than 10 characters, etc.). In Swing, the proper way to provide such functionality is to create a new document model that only allows the desired input to enter the component. Since this solution focuses on the document model, we'll defer this discussion to the next chapter, when we look at `PlainDocument`.

The JPasswordField Class

The AWT `TextField` class provides methods to set an echo character to be used to replace the characters typed by the user. This feature is generally used when entering passwords, to avoid echoing the password to the screen. In Swing, this functionality has been moved to a subclass of `JTextField` called `JPassword-Field`. The class provides the ability to set an echo character ("*" by default) for the field. In all other respects, `JPasswordField` behaves just like an ordinary `JTextField`, though some steps have been taken to enhance a password field's security.

Properties

Table 19-5 shows the properties defined by `JPasswordField`. `JPasswordField` has its own unique `UIClassID` value. It is up to the L&F to hide the input characters, so a different UI delegate class is typically used. The `accessibleContext` property is as expected. `AccessibleJPasswordField` extends the `JText-Field.AccessibleJTextField` class. The `echoChar` property specifies the character to be displayed in the field each time a key is pressed. This character is used to hide the actual input characters.

Table 19-5. JPasswordField Properties

Property	Data Type	get	is	set	bound	Default Value
UIClassID*	String	•				`"PasswordFieldUI"`
accessibleContext*	AccessibleContext	•				`AccessibleJPassword-Field`
echoChar	char	•		•		`'*'`
text*	string	•		•		
password	char[]	•				

See also properties from the JTextField class (Table 19-3).

In the interest of security, the `getText()` accessor methods have been deprecated in the `JPassword` field. To get the entered password, it is recommended that the new `getPassword()` method be used instead. For additional security, the characters in the returned array should be set to 0 once the password has been read.

Constructors

public JPasswordField()

Creates a new password field with zero columns.

public JPasswordField(String text)

Creates a new text field displaying the input text (using the echo character).

public JPasswordField(int columns)

Creates a new text field with the requested number of columns.

public JPasswordField(String text, int columns)

Creates a new text field with the specified number of columns, displaying the input text (using the echo character).

public JPasswordField(Document doc, String text, int columns)

This constructor (called by all the others) creates a new text field that uses the specified document model, displays the specified string of text (using the echo character), and contains the requested number of columns. The echo character is set to "*" by this constructor.

Data Protection Methods

public void cut()
public void copy()

These methods are overridden to disable cut and copy behavior in password fields. They simply call `getToolkit().beep()`. If these methods were not overridden, it would be possible for hidden passwords to be copied from password fields and pasted into nonhidden fields.

public string getText(int offs, int len) throws BadLocationException

Defined in this class only for the purpose of being marked as deprecated. The `getPassword()` method should be used instead.

Miscellaneous Methods

public boolean echoCharIsSet()

Indicates whether or not an echo character has been set. Note that a default echo character (*) is defined, so this method always returns `true` unless the echo character is explicitly set to "\u0000."

The JTextArea Class

The `JTextArea` class is modeled after AWT's `TextArea`, providing much of the same functionality. Generally, it is used to allow the user to enter a textual message, or to display textual information to the user. Figure 19-7 shows a `JTextArea`.

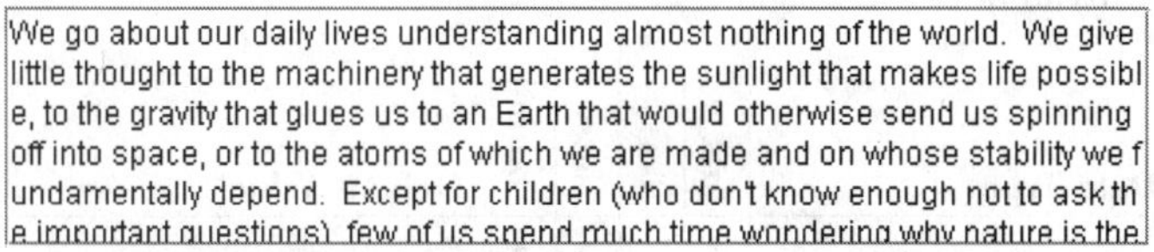

> We go about our daily lives understanding almost nothing of the world. We give
> little thought to the machinery that generates the sunlight that makes life possibl
> e, to the gravity that glues us to an Earth that would otherwise send us spinning
> off into space, or to the atoms of which we are made and on whose stability we f
> undamentally depend. Except for children (who don't know enough not to ask th
> e important questions) few of us spend much time wondering why nature is the

Figure 19-7. JTextArea

One significant change from the AWT `TextArea` is that `JTextArea` does not directly support scrolling. However, adding the ability to scroll the contents of a `JTextArea` is very simple; just add the `JTextArea` to the viewport of a `JScroll-Pane` (`JScrollPanes` are described in more detail in Chapter 11). `JTextArea` implements `Scrollable`, so a scroll pane can be intelligent about scrolling it.

Properties

`JTextArea` defines properties shown in Table 19-6. The `document` property defaults to a new `PlainDocument`. `AccessibleJTextArea` extends the `JText-Component.AccessibleJTextComponent` class.

Table 19-6. JTextArea Properties

Property	Data Type	get	is	set	bound	Default Value
document*	Document	•		•	•	`PlainDocument`
UIClassID*	String	•				`"TextAreaUI"`
accessibleContext*	AccessibleContext	•				`AccessibleJTextArea`
columns	int	•		•		0
font*	Font	•		•	•	From superclass
lineCount	int	•				From document
lineWrap	boolean	•		•	•	false
managingFocus*	boolean		•			true
minimumSize*	Dimension	•		•	•	Preferred size (if columns or rows !=0) or super.minimumSize
preferredScrolla-bleViewportSize*	Dimension	•				See comments below
preferredSize*	Dimension	•		•	•	See comments below
rows	int	•		•		0
scrollableTracks-ViewportWidth*	boolean	•				see comments below

See also properties from the javax.swing.text.JTextComponent class (Table 19-1).

Table 19-6. JTextArea Properties (continued)

Property	Data Type	get	is	set	bound	Default Value
tabSize	int	•		•	•	8
wrapStyleWord	boolean	•		•	•	false

See also properties from javax.swing.text.JTextComponent class.

The `columns` attribute specifies the number of columns to be displayed by the component. For variable-width fonts, the width of each column is based on the width of the lowercase character m. The `font` property is listed here because `getFont()` has been overridden to revalidate the component, allowing it to resize based on the size of the new font. `lineCount` provides access to the number of lines contained by the text area's document. What constitutes a "line" is document-dependent, but typically a line is a sequence of characters that end with a \n. This is not the same as `rows`, which is simply the number of rows of text displayed by the component.

The `lineWrap` property indicates whether or not text should wrap around to the next line when the end of a line is reached. This should be set to `true` when using a nonscrollable `JTextArea` (otherwise, text which runs off the edge of the component cannot be seen) and set to `false` when horizontal scrolling is enabled. Remember that scrolling is enabled by placing the text area in a `JScrollPane`. The `wrapStyleWord` property allows you to specify how the text should be broken up if `lineWrap` is `true`. By default, `wrapStyleWord` is set to `false`, so lines are broken on character boundaries. If set to `true`, lines are only broken on word boundaries. Figure 19-8 shows a `JTextArea` with `wrapStyleWord` set to `true`.

> We go about our daily lives understanding almost nothing of the world. We give little thought to the machinery that generates the sunlight that makes life possible, to the gravity that glues us to an Earth that would otherwise send us spinning off into space, or to the atoms of which we are made and on whose stability we fundamentally depend. Except for children (who don't know enough not to ask the important questions) few of us spend much time wondering why

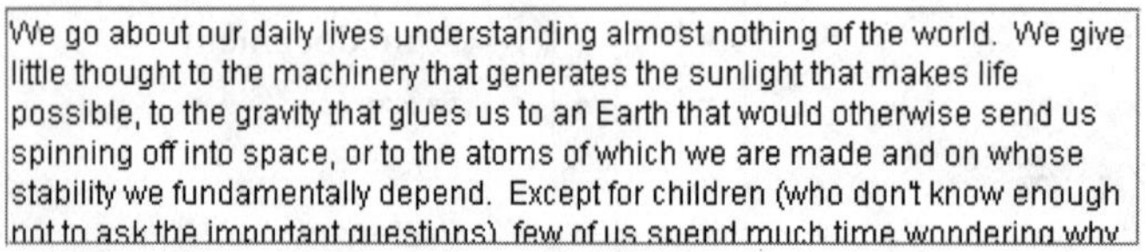

Figure 19-8. JTextArea with wrapStyleWord set to true

The `managingFocus` property is always `true`. This indicates that pressing the TAB key does not cause focus to be moved to the next component (it just inserts a tab). If you want to be able to use the TAB key to exit the text area, you'll need to subclass `JTextArea` and override `isManagingFocus()` to return `false`.

The `minimumSize` property is returned as the `preferredSize` if either `rows` or `columns` is nonzero. Otherwise, it is as defined in the superclass. `preferred-ScrollableViewportSize` reflects the preferred size of the component if used in a JScrollPane. It is returned as the column width times the number of columns and the row height times the number of rows. If either of these values is zero, the value returned by the superclass method is used. The preferredSize property uses the superclass implementation, but adjusts the width and height if the columns and rows properties are set. The scrollableTracksViewportWidth property will be true if lineWrap is true. If not, its value is determined by the superclass.

The tabSize property specifies the number of characters that a tab character should expand to.

Events

JTextArea does not fire any new event types. It fires PropertyChangeEvents when its lineWrap, tabSize, or wrapStyleWord properties change.

NOTE   The names of the properties fired by this class do not follow the standard property naming convention. The names used are "Line-Wrap," "TabSize," and "WrapStyleWord."

Constructors

public JTextArea()
> Creates a default text area.

public JTextArea(Document doc)
> Creates a text area using the input document.

public JTextArea(int rows, int columns)
> Creates a text area with the specified number of rows and columns.

public JTextArea(String text)
> Creates a text area displaying the specified text.

public JTextArea(String text, int rows, int columns)
> Creates a text area with the specified number of rows and columns displaying the given text.

public JTextArea(Document doc, String text, int rows, int columns)
> Uses the given Document, populated with the given text to create a text area of the specified size. All of the other constructors use this one.

Text Manipulation Methods

The following convenience methods make it easy to modify the contents of the text area's document model.

public void append(String str)

Appends the given text to the end of the document.

public void insert(String str, int pos)

Inserts the specified text at the given position (offset from the beginning of the document). To insert text at the beginning of the document, use a value of 0 for the second argument.

public void replaceRange(String str, int start, int end)

Uses the input text to replace a section of the document, beginning with the character at the `start` position and ending with the character at the `end` position.

Line Transformation Methods

These methods can be used to find the character offset of a given line (see the distinction between `line` and `row` in the Properties section earlier in the chapter) and vice-versa. Note that the first line of the document is line 0.

public int getLineEndOffset(int line) throws BadLocationException

Returns the character offset (from the beginning of the document) which marks the end of the specified line. This is actually the offset of the *first character* of the *next* line.

public int getLineOfOffset(int offset) throws BadLocationException

Returns the line number that contains the given character offset (from the beginning of the document).

public int getLineStartOffset(int line) throws BadLocationException

Returns the character offset (from the beginning of the document) that marks the beginning of the specified line.

The following example shows how these three methods work:

```
// OffsetTest.java
//
import javax.swing.*;
import javax.swing.text.*;

public class OffsetTest {
  public static void main(String[] args) {

    // Create a JTextField with three lines of text
    JTextArea ta = new JTextArea();
    ta.setLineWrap(true);
    ta.append("The first line.\n");
    ta.append("Line Two!\n");
    ta.append("This is the 3rd line of the document.");
```

```
      // Print some results . . .
      try {
        System.out.println(ta.getLineEndOffset(0) + " (end of line 0)");
        System.out.println(ta.getLineStartOffset(1) + " (start of line 1)");
        System.out.println(ta.getLineOfOffset(20) +
                        " (line containing position 20)");

        int theEnd = ta.getLineEndOffset(2);
        System.out.println(theEnd + " (end of last line)");
        System.out.println(ta.getText(ta.getLineEndOffset(2), 2));
      }
      catch (BadLocationException ex) { System.out.println("BAD!"); }

      // Layout . . .
      JFrame f = new JFrame();
      f.addWindowListener(new BasicWindowMonitor());
      f.setContentPane(ta);
      f.setSize(150, 150);
      f.setVisible(true);
    }
}
```

When run, this little program produces the following output, along with the frame shown in Figure 19-9. Note that the '\n' counts as a character in the document.

Figure 19-9. OffsetTest frame

```
16 (end of line 0)
16 (start of line 1)
1 (line containing position 20)
64 (end of last line)
BAD!
```

The last line of output shows that getLineEndOffset() returns an index of the character *after* the last character in the specified line. When called on the last line, this offset is not a valid document offset.

Protected Methods

protected Document createDefaultModel()

Creates a default model object to be used if one is not provided as a constructor argument. The default object created by `JTextArea` is a `PlainDocument`.

protected int getColumnWidth()

Returns the width (in pixels) of a single column. The default implementation returns the width of the character m in the current font. It's important to realize that unless you are using a fixed-width font (e.g., Courier), this method is only useful for determining a maximum column width.

protected int getRowHeight()

Returns the height (in pixels) of each row. This is defined by the height of the current font.

protected String paramString()

Returns the parameter string used to represent this text area as a string. This is the result of `super.paramString()` with the number of rows and columns in the component appended to the string.

Understanding JTextArea Sizing

The following code produces a result you might not expect:

```
// UnstableTA.java
//
import javax.swing.*;
import java.awt.*;

public class UnstableTA {
  public static void main(String[] args) {
    JTextArea area = new JTextArea(3, 10);

    JFrame f = new JFrame();
    f.addWindowListener(new BasicWindowMonitor());
    f.getContentPane().setLayout(new FlowLayout());
    f.getContentPane().add(area);
    f.setSize(200, 110);
    f.setVisible(true);
  }
}
```

At first glance, this looks fine.[*] However, things start getting a little strange if you enter text into the area. Figure 19-10 shows the display when it's first displayed and then after adding some data to the text area.

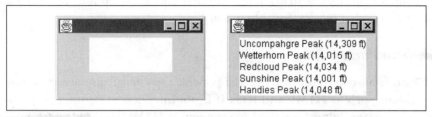

Figure 19-10. Unstable JTextArea—size changes after adding data

The text area expanded both horizontally and vertically to accommodate the text we entered. Chances are this is not the behavior you'd like. Fortunately, there are several strategies we can use to get more usable results. They include:

- Place the `JTextArea` in a `JScrollPane`.
- Explicitly specify the `preferredSize` of the `JTextArea`.
- Use a layout manager that doesn't use the `preferredSize` of its components.

The first strategy is useful when you want to fix the size of the displayed area without restricting the total amount of text the user can enter. A simple change to our previous example accomplishes this goal. Just replace the old `add()` call with:

```
f.getContentPane().add(new JScrollPane(area));
```

The second strategy gives you complete control over the size of the text area. If you just want the size to reflect the dimensions you supplied in the constructor, you can use the `preferredScrollableViewportSize`, which uses the rows and columns you specified, and add in the text area's insets. Adding the following lines to our example is one way to make this change:

```
Dimension d = area.getPreferredScrollableViewportSize();
Insets in = area.getInsets();
d.width = d.width + in.left + in.right;
d.height = d.height + in.top + in.bottom;
area.setPreferredSize(d);
```

The last strategy allows the text area to fill the available space. Note that using this strategy does not tie the size of the text area to the specified number of rows and columns. The `JTextArea` grows to fill the space available in the current layout. To see an example of this strategy, change the `setLayout()` and `add()` calls from the original example to this:

```
f.getContentPane().setLayout(new BorderLayout());
f.getContentPane().add(area, BorderLayout.CENTER);
```

---

* Prior to the Swing 1.0.2 release, this example would have produced a tiny 1x1 character text area.

Another common strategy is to combine the first and third options to create a scrollable text area that fills all available space.

The JEditorPane Class

JEditorPane is an extension of JTextComponent capable of displaying various types of content, such as HTML and RTF. It is not intended to be used as a full-featured web browser, but can be used to view simple HTML and is ideal for integrating online help into Java applications.

JEditorPanes work closely with EditorKit objects which are plugged into the editor pane to customize it for a particular content type. Without an EditorKit telling it how to work, a JEditorPane can't function. In this chapter, we are going to ignore this complexity and just look at how we might use a JEditorPane as a very simple web browser. We'll get into the details of JEditorPane and EditorKit in Chapter 24.

Figure 19-11. JEditorPane showing an HTML page

Figure 19-11 shows the JEditorPane in action, displaying a portion of the old style javadoc for the JEditorPane class. Here's the code:

```
// HTMLExample.java
//
import javax.swing.*;
import javax.swing.event.*;
```

```
import java.io.*;

public class HTMLExample {
  public static void main(String[] args) {
    JEditorPane pane = null;
    try {
      pane = new JEditorPane(args[0]);
    }
    catch (IOException ex) {
      ex.printStackTrace(System.err);
      System.exit(1);
    }
    pane.setEditable(false);

    // Add a hyperlink listener
    final JEditorPane finalPane = pane;
    pane.addHyperlinkListener(new HyperlinkListener() {
      public void hyperlinkUpdate(HyperlinkEvent ev) {
        try {
          if (ev.getEventType() == HyperlinkEvent.EventType.ACTIVATED)
            finalPane.setPage(ev.getURL());
        } catch (IOException ex) { ex.printStackTrace(System.err); }
      }
    });

    JFrame frame = new JFrame();
    frame.addWindowListener(new BasicWindowMonitor());
    frame.setContentPane(new JScrollPane(pane));
    frame.setSize(350,400);
    frame.setVisible(true);
  }
}
```

We've created a very minimal HTML browser.[*] In a real application, you'd want to do things like change the cursor while new pages are being loaded and handle exceptions more elegantly. The anonymous inner class in this example shows a quick way to enable hyperlinks when viewing text in a JEditorPane. We'll look at the classes and methods used here in the next few pages.

Properties

Table 19-7 shows the properties defined by JEditorPane. The accessibleContext property depends on the type of EditorKit in use. If an HTMLEditorKit is installed, a special AccessibleJEditorPaneHTML object will be used. Otherwise,

---

* This simple browser will not handle all HTML pages. The Swing html package is still being enhanced to provide better HTML support. However, significant progress has been made since earlier releases.

its superclass, `AccessibleJEditorPane` is used. `AccessibleJEditorPane` extends the `JTextComponent.AccessibleJTextComponent` class.

Table 19-7. JEditorPane Properties

Property	Data Type	get	is	set	bound	Default Value
UIClassID*	String	•				"EditorPaneUI"
accessibleContext*	AccessibleContext	•				AccessibleJEditor-Pane or Accessible-JEditorPaneHTML
contentType	String	•		•		From editorKit
editorKit	EditorKit	•		•	•	null
managingFocus*	boolean		•			true
page	URL	•		•		null
scrollableTracks-ViewportWidth*	boolean	•				true

See also properties from the JTextComponent class (Table 19-1).

The `contentType` property reflects the type of content displayed by the editor. This value is taken from the installed `EditorKit` and typically has values such as "text/plain," "text/html," and "text/rtf." The `editorKit` supplies everything needed to work with a particular content type. `EditorKit` and its default implementations are described in detail in Chapter 24.

`ManagingFocus` is set to `true` for `JEditorPane`, reflecting the fact that using the TAB key will not cause focus to move to the next component. The `page` property specifies the URL of the current page being displayed. The `scrollableTracks-ViewportWidth` property is set to `true` in this class.

Events

`JEditorPanes` fire a new type of event called a `HyperlinkEvent`. Typically, this is fired when the user clicks on a hyperlink in the currently displayed document; the program normally responds by loading a new page. To support this new event type, a new event class and listener interface are available in the `javax.swing.event` package. These are described briefly at the end of this section.

As you'd expect, the following methods are provided for working with these events.

public synchronized void addHyperlinkListener(HyperlinkListener listener)
public synchronized void removeHyperlinkListener(HyperlinkListener listener)
public void fireHyperlinkUpdate(HyperlinkEvent e)

`JEditorPane` objects also fire `PropertyChangeEvents` when the `editorKit` property is changed.

Constructors

The following constructors are provided. Note that the last two may throw an `IOException` if they are unable to load the specified URL.

public JEditorPane()
    Creates an empty pane.

public JEditorPane(String url) throws IOException
public JEditorPane(URL initialPage) throws IOException
    Create a pane displaying the specified URL. `contentType` and `editorKit` are set based on the content type of the `URLConnection` created from the given URL. Because these constructors attempt to open a URL, they may throw an `IOException` if the URL cannot be found.

EditorKit Methods

The following methods are available for managing `EditorKits`. You won't need to use any of these methods if you're not defining your own `EditorKits` for working with various content types.

public EditorKit getEditorKitForContentType(String type)
    Returns an `EditorKit` for the given content type. An attempt is made to create the appropriate `EditorKit` if one has not already been set (via a call to `setEditorKitForContentType()`). If the appropriate `EditorKit` cannot be created, a `DefaultEditorKit` is returned.

public void setEditorKitForContentType(String type, EditorKit k)
    Explicitly sets the `EditorKit` to be used for a given content type.

public static EditorKit createEditorKitForContentType(String type)
    Attempts to create a new `EditorKit` instance for the given content type. In order for this method to return a non-`null` object, the content type must have been associated with an editor kit class name by a call to `register-EditorKitForContentType()`.

public static void registerEditorKitForContentType(String type, String classname)
    Called to associate a content type to an editor kit class name. It is called three times in the `JEditorPane` initializer block. These calls define the mappings shown in Table 19-8.

Table 19-8. Default Content-Type Mappings

Content Type	Class
application/rtf	javax.swing.text.rtf.RTFEditorKit
text/plain	javax.swing.JEditorPane.PlainEditorKit[a]
text/html	javax.swing.text.html.HTMLEditorKit
text/rtf	javax.swing.text.rtf.RTFEditorKit

[a] A package private subclass of DefaultEditorKit.

protected EditorKit createDefaultEditorKit()

> Called to create a default editor kit. It returns a new instance of a package private subclass of DefaultEditorKit called PlainEditorKit. This method is not used typically, as it is only called by getEditorKit() if no editor kit has been set for the pane.

Miscellaneous Methods

public void setPage(String url) throws IOException

> A convenience method used to set the current page, given a URL string. An IOException will be thrown if the given URL cannot be loaded.

protected void scrollToReference(String reference)

> Used by setPage() to scroll the display to the specified reference within the current document. This provides support for URLs containing references like JComponent updateUI. Note that this method only works with HTML documents.

The HyperlinkListener Interface

This interface (found in javax.swing.event) defines a single method, used to respond to hyperlink activations.

public abstract void hyperlinkUpdate(HyperlinkEvent e)

> Called to indicate that a hyperlink request has been made. Typical implementations of this method obtain the new URL from the event and call setPage() on the associated JEditorPane. See the JEditorPane example earlier in the chapter to see how this method can be used.

The HyperlinkEvent Class

This event class (found in javax.swing.event) describes a hyperlink request.

Properties

HyperlinkEvent defines the properties shown in Table 19-9. The description property allows a description of the link (typically the URL text string) to be defined. This is useful when a URL can't be formed from the text, meaning that the URL will be null. The eventType property defines the type of event that has occurred. The possible values are described below. The URL property reflects the URL the event refers to.

Table 19-9. HyperlinkEvent Properties

Property	Data Type	get	is	set	bound	Default Value
description	string	•				null
eventType	HyperlinkEvent.EventType	•				From constructor
URL	URL	•				From constructor

See also the java.util.EventObject class (not covered in this book).

Constructors

public HyperlinkEvent(Object source, HyperlinkEvent.EventType type, URL u)
public HyperlinkEvent(Object source, HyperlinkEvent.EventType type, URL u, string desc)

Creates a new event with the specified arguments. The value of the type parameter is taken from the constant values defined in the HyperlinkEvent.EventType class: ENTERED, EXITED, and ACTIVATED. The only value currently used is ACTIVATED. The desc parameter is optional.

Inner Classes

public static final class EventType

This simple inner class just holds a single String value and defines three constants of type HyperlinkEvent.EventType. These constants are ENTERED, EXITED, and ACTIVATED. Currently, only ACTIVATED is fired by the HTMLEditorKit. It is used to indicate that a hyperlink has been activated (clicked) by the user. The other values could be used to change the cursor type when the cursor is moved over (or away from) a hyperlink.

The JTextPane Class

JTextPane is a complex extension of JEditorPane that provides functionality typical of a basic word processor, including features such as multicolored text, multiple fonts and text styles, image embedding, and more. There's a great deal to discuss with respect to JTextPane and the many classes it interacts with.

In this chapter, we'll just touch the surface, showing how you can do a few simple things using a JTextPane that you couldn't easily do with the AWT or JTextArea. Since most of the properties and methods defined in JTextPane use classes and interfaces that we've not yet defined, we'll omit all of the details of JTextPane properties and methods from this section. For a more complete discussion of JTextPane, refer to Chapter 21.

Using the JTextPane

In this example, we'll show how to use a JTextPane as a more powerful text window for displaying diagnostic information. In AWT, or with a Swing JTextArea, you are limited to a single font, style, and foreground color. Using a JTextPane, we can easily add text using a variety of formats. This is done using AttributeSets to define the features of the displayed text. For the purpose of this example, it's enough to understand that an AttributeSet (we'll actually use SimpleAttributeSet, a mutable extension of AttributeSet) defines a group of attributes and that the values of these attributes can be set by calling various static methods on the StyleConstants class.

Here's a simple utility for displaying diagnostic messages to a user. Three types of messages (informational, warning, and error) are displayed using different colors and text styles.

```
// Diagnostic.java
//
import javax.swing.*;
import javax.swing.text.*;
import java.awt.*;

public class Diagnostic {
  // Create new new Diagnostic display using a black JTextPane
  public Diagnostic() {
    pane = new JTextPane();
    pane.setBackground(Color.black);
    pane.setEditable(false);
  }

  // Show an informational message (green, plain text)
  public void showInfo(String msg) {
    SimpleAttributeSet attrs = new SimpleAttributeSet();
    StyleConstants.setForeground(attrs, Color.green);
    showMsg(msg, attrs);
  }
```

```java
// Show a warning message (yellow, italic text)
public void showWarning(String msg) {
  SimpleAttributeSet attrs = new SimpleAttributeSet();
  StyleConstants.setForeground(attrs, Color.yellow);
  StyleConstants.setItalic(attrs, true);
  showMsg(msg, attrs);
}

// Show an error message (red, bold/italic text)
public void showError(String msg) {
  SimpleAttributeSet attrs = new SimpleAttributeSet();
  StyleConstants.setForeground(attrs, Color.red);
  StyleConstants.setItalic(attrs, true);
  StyleConstants.setBold(attrs, true);
  showMsg(msg, attrs);
}

// Return the visual component to be displayed
public Component getComponent() { return pane; }

// Show a text message using the specified AttributeSet
protected void showMsg(String msg, AttributeSet attrs) {
  Document doc = pane.getDocument();
  msg += "\n";
  try {
    doc.insertString(doc.getLength(), msg, attrs);
  } catch (BadLocationException ex) { ex.printStackTrace(); }
}

private JTextPane pane;

// A sample test program
public static void main(String[] args) {
  Diagnostic diag = new Diagnostic();
  JFrame f = new JFrame();
  f.addWindowListener(new BasicWindowMonitor());
  f.getContentPane().add(diag.getComponent());
  f.setSize(300,200);
  f.setVisible(true);

  // Display a few messages...
  diag.showInfo("System normal");
  diag.showWarning("Disk space low");
  diag.showError("Out of memory");
  diag.showError("Program performed an illegal operation");
  diag.showInfo("System normal");
}
}
```

Over the course of the next two chapters, we'll explain all of the strange-looking methods used in this example. You might want to refer back to this example as you read those chapters. Figure 19-12 shows the display generated by this class. Unfortunately, we can't show you the colors.

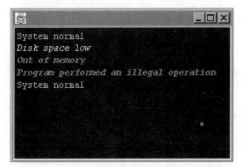

Figure 19-12. JTextPane diagnostic example

More to Come

In this chapter, we've shown how easy it is to do simple things with the Swing text framework. However, if you want to do more than we've demonstrated in this chapter, Swing has a lot to offer. Over the next five chapters, we'll examine every class and interface in the Swing text package, building many interesting and powerful sample programs as we go.

The order of the next five chapters is fairly important. You should read the next two chapters in sequence to gain an understanding of the interfaces and classes used to describe the document model. The chapter discussing *Text Views*, Chapter 23, is fairly advanced and will be optional for many readers. Most of the material covered in the last chapter will make sense even if you skip the *Views* chapter.

20

Document Model
and Events

In the previous chapter, we introduced the Swing text components, ignoring many of the details in order to simplify the introduction. In this chapter,[*] we'll give a detailed explanation of the many classes and interfaces that make up the basic text model. Additionally, we'll look at the classes and interfaces involved in delivering events to provide notification of document model changes.

The Document Model

Before getting into the details of the classes and interfaces that make up the Swing text model, we'll give a brief overview of the top-level interfaces that serve as the model's key abstractions. These interfaces, and the relationships between them, are shown in Figure 20-1.

The first—and arguably most important—interface to look at is called Document. The model representation of any text component (even a simple text field) in Swing is defined by this interface. A Document is little more than an arbitrary collection of text (though Swing's implementations of the interface provide much more).

Document objects are partitioned by Elements that describe the structural pieces of a Document, such as paragraphs or sections of specially formatted text (e.g., *italics*). Elements are made up of child Elements, forming a tree with a "root" Element as the base and arbitrary levels of child Elements below it. Each Document defines one or more Elements as its root Elements, from which the entire

---

[*] Certain sections of this chapter refer to Swing's undo facility, and assume that you already understand the basics of it. If you've not yet read Chapter 18, *Undo*, we recommend that you read at least the introductory section of it before continuing here.

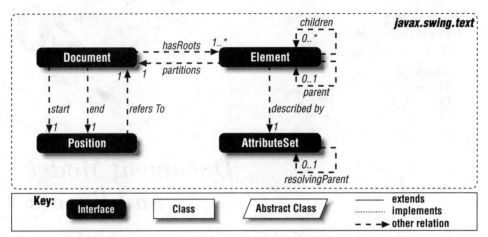

Figure 20-1. High-level Document class diagram

structure of the Document can be determined. Typically, only a single root Element is defined. However, more complex document types might contain multiple root elements, to support multiple ways of structuring the same document content. The key thing to understand is that the Document contains the data; the Elements just give it structure.

Each Element has an associated AttributeSet, which defines things such as the font or text style to be applied to the Element. The attributes themselves may be any arbitrary Object (the *value*), indexed by another Object (the *key*).

Arbitrary positions in the document may be represented using Position objects. Position provides the ability to track a given location in the document as its absolute offsets change. For example, if you created a position that pointed to the beginning of a given sentence, that position would always refer to the beginning of the sentence, no matter what other changes were made to the document.

The Document, Element, Position, and AttributeSet interfaces are all described in detail later in this section.

The Document Interface

We've described the Document interface a bit already. Now let's take a look at its properties, constructors, and methods.

Properties

Table 20-1 shows the properties defined by the Document interface. The properties defined by the Document interface are fairly straightforward. A property called defaultRootElement is provided to access the Element at the root of the default

Table 20-1. Document Properties

Property	Data Type	get	is	set	bound	Default Value
defaultRootElement	Element	•				
endPosition	Position	•				
length	int	•				
rootElements	Element[]	•				
startPosition	Position	•				

Element structure hierarchy. In addition, the rootElements property specifies an array of all root elements (including the default) available in the Document. Most Document types only define a single root.

Two Positions, startPosition and endPosition, are provided. These properties always reference the beginning and end of the document, regardless of changes made to it throughout its lifetime. Finally, the length property specifies the total number of characters[*] in the Document.

Events

Implementations of the Document interface fire DocumentEvents and Undoable-EditEvents to indicate changes that have been made to the Document's contents. UndoableEditEvent and UndoableEditListener were covered in Chapter 18. The corresponding DocumentEvent classes will be discussed at the end of this chapter.

Document defines the following standard methods for managing event listeners.

public abstract void addDocumentListener(DocumentListener listener)
public abstract void removeDocumentListener(DocumentListener listener)
public abstract void addUndoableEditListener(UndoableEditListener listener)
public abstract void removeUndoableEditListener(UndoableEditListener listener)

Constants

Document defines the two constants, shown in Table 20-2, which may be used as keys when calling getProperty() or putProperty().

---

[*] We'll see in the next chapter that Documents are not limited to holding text. In most cases, length refers to the number of characters in the Document, but embedded images and components may also be included in this count, each being stored as a single character. Newline characters count as well, so a document containing "Hello\nWorld" would have a length of 11.

Table 20-2. Document Constants

Constant	Type	Description
StreamDescriptionProperty	String	The property name used to describe any information known about the stream from which the Document was initialized (if it was initialized from a stream)
TitleProperty	String	The property name used to store the Document's name, if it has one

Text Manipulation Methods

These methods manipulate the contents of the document. They can all throw a BadLocationException. This is an exception (defined later in the chapter) used throughout the text package to indicate that an attempt has been made to reference a document offset that does not exist. For example, attempting to insert text at offset 200 of a 100-character document would result in a BadLocation-Exception.

public abstract String getText(int offset, int length) throws BadLocationException
  Retrieves the text at the specified location in the Document. The returned string will be of the requested length, beginning at the specified offset.

public abstract void getText(int offset, int length, Segment txt) throws BadLocationException
  Retrieves the text at the specified location in the Document. The returned text will be of the requested length, beginning at the specified offset, and is returned in the input Segment (defined later in the chapter) object.

public abstract void insertString(int offset, String str, AttributeSet a) throws
  BadLocationException
  Inserts the specified string at the given offset in the Document. The new String should be described by the given AttributeSet, and the Document should update its Element structures as necessary to reflect this.

public abstract void remove(int offs, int len) throws BadLocationException
  Removes the specified section of text from the Document. The Document should update its Element structures to reflect the change.

Other Methods

public abstract Position createPosition(int offs) throws BadLocationException
  Creates a Position object used to track the contents of the Document at the specified offset. The section "The Position Interface," later in this chapter, contains an example showing how this might be used.

public abstract Object getProperty(Object key)
public abstract void putProperty(Object key, Object value)

> Retrieves and inserts (respectively) arbitrary properties associated with the document. These properties can be used to store things such as the document title, author, etc.

public abstract void render(Runnable r)

> Executes the given `Runnable`, guaranteeing that the contents of the model will not be changed while the `Runnable` is running. The input `Runnable` may not modify the model. This method allows the `Document` to be painted without concerns about its contents changing during the painting process. It is called by the `TextUI`'s `paint()` method.

The Element Interface

`Element` is an interface used to describe an arbitrary portion of a document. However, it's important to realize that `Element`s do not actually *contain* a portion of the document, they just define a way of structuring it. Because of this, a `Document` may be described by multiple sets of `Element`s, each defining a different logical structure.

Each `Element` is described by an `AttributeSet`, which defines things such as the font style or color used in the `Element`. Note that this means that all `Document` content described by a given `Element` will have the same set of attributes. `Element`s may contain other `Element`s, allowing a document to be described by an arbitrary tree structure. Figure 20-2 shows a purely hypothetical example of the structure of a series of `Element`s. In this diagram, there is a single "document" element made up of two "paragraph" elements, each of which is, in turn, made up of a pair of "sentence" elements. Finally, one of the sentences is further split into two more elements, one for a plain text area and the other for a section of bold text. Remember, this is only an example of how elements fit together; the element types here do not map directly to anything provided by Swing.

Another way to understand the concept of an `Element` is to look at mark-up languages such as HTML or XML. Documents defined by such mark-up languages can be easily represented using the Swing `Document`/`Element` model. Each "element" from the mark-up language simply maps to an `Element` in the document model. Consider the following short HTML document.

```
<HTML>
<H1>
The Document Model
</H1>
<H2>
The Document Interface
```

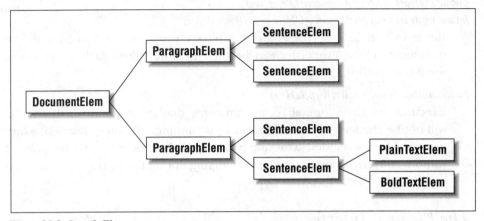

Figure 20-2. Sample Element structure

```
</H2>
<H2>
The Element Interface
</H2>
<P>
Element is an interface used to describe an arbitrary portion of a document.
<BR>
Each Element is described by an AttributeSet.
</P>
</HTML>
```

A possible element representation of this document is shown in Figure 20-3. Attributes that define the appearance of different elements types (such as H1, H2, P) are stored in the branch elements, while each line of text within an element is stored in a leaf element.

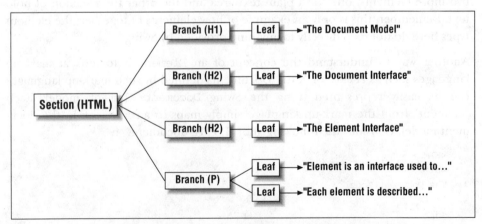

Figure 20-3. Sample Element structure for a simple HTML document

Properties

The Element interface defines the properties[*] shown in Table 20-3. The attributes property defines a set of attributes, which apply to the text represented by the Element. The AttributeSet interface is described in more detail in the next section. For now, it's enough to understand that any arbitrary information relevant to the Element can be stored by the attributes property.

Table 20-3. Element Properties

Property	Data Type	get	is	set	bound	Default Value
attributes	AttributeSet	•				
document	Document	•				
element (indexed)	Element	•				
elementCount	int	•				
endOffset	int	•				
leaf	boolean		•			
name	String	•				
parentElement	Element	•				
startOffset	int	•				

The document property provides access to the Document this Element describes while parentElement defines the Element that contains this Element (if this is not a root Element). The element property is an indexed property containing the Element's child elements, while elementCount specifies the number of children (possibly zero) the Element contains. The child elements are always kept in order, so you are assured that element[0] will reference offsets in the document that appear before those referenced by element[1].

The startOffset and endOffset properties specify the offsets from the beginning of the document that the Element covers. These values change as data is added to or before the Element. The leaf property indicates whether or not this is a leaf Element (one that has no children), and the name specifies an arbitrary name for the Element.

---

[*] elementIndex could technically be considered an indexed property. However, the argument passed to getElementIndex() is actually an offset into the Document, not a simple array index.

Miscellaneous Method

public abstract int getElementIndex(int offset)

Returns the index of the child element closest to the given offset (character offset from the beginning of the Document). This index can be used as input to the getElement() method to retrieve the appropriate child.

The ElementIterator Class

This class, first introduced in the JDK1.2 beta4 release, provides a strategy for iterating over some or all of the elements that make up a document. It's used by the AbstractWriter class (see Chapter 24, *EditorKits and TextActions*), but could be used for other purposes as well.

ElementIterator orders the elements depth-first, meaning that the root element (or whatever element you specify as a starting point) will be the first element returned. The root's first child is then returned, followed by the first child of that child, and so on until a leaf is reached. Once a leaf is reached, the next leaf is returned, and so on, until the last leaf of a child is reached, at which point the next sibling of that child is returned (and continues with its descendants).

Common use of this class would look like this:

```
ElementIterator it = new ElementIterator(myDocument);
Element e = it.first();
do {
  // do something with "e"
  e = it.next();
} while (e != null);
```

Constructors

public ElementIterator(Document document)

Creates an iterator that will begin at document's default root element.

public ElementIterator(Element root)

Creates an iterator that will begin at root.

Methods

ElementIterator defines the following public methods.

public synchronized Object clone()

Returns a copy of the iterator. The clone is set at the same point in the iteration as the original iterator. You must call current(), first(), or next() before calling clone(), or a NullPointerException will be thrown.

public Element current()
> Returns the current element in the iteration.

public int depth()
> Returns the current depth of the internal stack used by the iterator. This indicates the number of non-leaf elements at or above the level of the current element.

public Element first()
> Resets the iterator to the first element and returns it.

public Element next()
> Returns the current element and moves the iterator to the next element.

public Element previous()
> Returns the previous element. It does not change the state of the iterator (i.e., calling `next();previous();next();previous()` would actually move you forward two elements).

The AttributeSet Interface

`AttributeSet` is an interface used to collect an arbitrary set of key/value pairs. An attribute value is any arbitrary `Object`, accessible by an attribute key (another `Object`). Typically, as we'll see in much more detail in the next chapter, attributes are used to define things such as the font or color of the text described by the `Elements` this `AttributeSet` is applied to.

The interface provides methods for accessing the attributes, but not for setting them. In the next section, we'll introduce the `MutableAttributeSet` interface, which provides methods for settings attributes.

An `AttributeSet` may have a resolving parent which is another `AttributeSet`. The relationship between an `AttributeSet` and its resolving parent is much like the relationship between a Java class and its superclass: attributes not found in a given `AttributeSet` will be searched for in the set's resolving parent, just as method implementations not found in a class are searched for in its superclass. This can go on indefinitely until the attribute is found or a set with no parent is reached.

Properties

Table 20-4 shows the properties defined by the `AttributeSet` interface. The `attributeCount` property simply specifies the number of attributes contained by the set. `attributeNames` is an `Enumeration` containing the attribute keys (not necessarily names, since keys are of type `Object`). Note that this property does not contain the attributes defined in the set's parent. `resolveParent` represents the parent set used to resolve attribute keys not found in the current set. This property will be `null` if there is no parent set.

Table 20-4. AttributeSet Properties

Property	Data Type	get	is	set	bound	Default Value
attributeCount	int	•				
attributeNames	Enumeration	•				
resolveParent	AttributeSet	•				

Methods

public abstract boolean containsAttribute(Object name, Object value)

Returns `true` if the set (or its resolving parent) contains the given attribute and its value matches that of the second given object. Equality is tested using the `equals()` method.

public abstract boolean containsAttributes(AttributeSet attributes)

Returns `true` if the set (or its resolving parent) contains values for all of the attributes in the `AttributeSet` and all of these values are equal. Equality is tested using the `equals()` method on each attribute.

public abstract AttributeSet copyAttributes()

Creates and returns a copy of the `AttributeSet`.

public abstract Object getAttribute(Object key)

Searches for an attribute whose key matches the given object. If the attribute is not found locally, the set's resolving parent is searched (if it exists). This process repeats until the attribute is found. If the value cannot be found, `null` is returned.

public abstract Enumeration getAttributeNames()

Returns an `Enumeration` of objects representing the keys of the attributes in the set. Only the attributes defined locally in the set are returned.

public abstract boolean isDefined(Object attrName)

Returns `true` if the given attribute key is defined in the set. The resolving parent is not checked.

public abstract boolean isEqual(AttributeSet attr)

Returns `true` if the set's attributes and values exactly match those of the given set. Equality is tested using the `equals()` method on each attribute.

Inner Interfaces

`AttributeSet` contains four inner-interfaces. Each of these is entirely empty, serving only to identify attribute keys as belonging to a particular category. There is no requirement for attribute keys to implement these interfaces, but we'll see in the next chapter that Swing provides several pre-defined attribute keys that do.

public interface CharacterAttribute
public interface ColorAttribute
public interface FontAttribute
public interface ParagraphAttribute

The MutableAttributeSet Interface

MutableAttributeSet is an extension of the AttributeSet interface that adds methods for modifying (as opposed to just accessing) the attributes in a set.

Properties

MutableAttributeSet does not define any properties. It inherits those defined in its super-interface AttributeSet. It does add a setResolveParent() method for the resolveParent attribute, since this was a read-only attribute in the AttributeSet interface. (See Table 20-5.)

Table 20-5. MutableAttributeSet Properties

Property	Data Type	get	is	set	bound	Default Value
resolveParent*	AttributeSet	•		•		

See also properties from the AttributeSet interface (Table 20-4).

Methods

public abstract void addAttribute(Object name, Object value)
   Adds an attribute with the specified key and value.

public abstract void addAttributes(AttributeSet attributes)
   Adds all of the attributes in the given set.

public abstract void removeAttribute(Object name)
   Removes the attribute with the specified key.

public abstract void removeAttributes(AttributeSet attributes)
   Removes all attributes that match those in the given set in both key and value. Equality is defined by the equals() method.

public abstract void removeAttributes(Enumeration names)
   Removes all attributes that have keys that match those found in the Enumeration.

The SimpleAttributeSet Class

Swing provides a simple implementation of the MutableAttributeSet interface, which maintains attributes using a Hashtable. The class structure is shown in Figure 20-4.

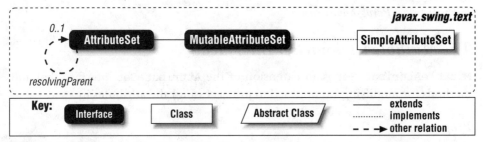

Figure 20-4. The SimpleAttributeSet class hierarchy

Properties

Table 20-6 shows the default property values defined by SimpleAttributeSet. A newly created SimpleAttributeSet contains an empty Hashtable. The resolveParent (when set) is stored in the table just like any other attribute, using the attribute key StyleConstants.ResolveParent. This means that the attributeCount property will include this attribute and that attributeNames will include this object. The empty property is false if the set has any attributes, even if the only attribute in the set is the resolveParent.

Table 20-6. SimpleAttributeSet Properties

Property	Data Type	get	is	set	bound	Default Value
attributeCount*	int	•				0
attributeNames*	Enumeration	•				empty
empty*	boolean	•				true
resolveParent*	AttributeSet	•		•		null

Constant

SimpleAttributeSet defines the constant shown in Table 20-7.

Table 20-7. SimpleAttributeSet Constant

Constant	Type	Description
EMPTY	AttributeSet	An empty SimpleAttributeSet

Constructors

public SimpleAttributeSet()

Creates a new set containing no attributes.

public SimpleAttributeSet(AttributeSet source)

Creates a set containing the attributes and values from the given set. It does not use the set as a resolving parent; it just copies the set's contents.

Add/Remove Methods

public void addAttribute(Object name, Object value)

Adds the specified value for the specified name. If the key already exists, its value is changed to the new value. Note that the use of a `Hashtable` as the attribute storage mechanism prohibits an attribute from having a value of `null` (`Hashtable.put()` would throw a `NullPointerException`).

public void addAttributes(AttributeSet attributes)

Iterates over the given set of attributes, adding each one to the set using `addAttribute()`.

public void removeAttribute(Object name)

Removes the specified attribute from the set. If the given key is not found, this method does nothing. It does not attempt to find the attribute in the resolving parent.

public void removeAttributes(AttributeSet attributes)

Removes each element found in the given set from the current set. Only attributes whose key *and* value match will be removed. Equality is defined by the `equals()` method. This method does not attempt to remove attributes from the resolving parent.

public void removeAttributes(Enumeration names)

Removes each of the attributes in the given `Enumeration` from the set. The `Enumeration` should contain attribute keys to be removed. Equality is defined by the `equals()` method. This method does not attempt to remove attributes from the resolving parent.

Query Methods

public boolean containsAttribute(Object name, Object value)

Checks whether the specified attribute exists in the set and has a value matching the input. Equality is defined by the `equals()` method. This method searches the resolving parent if the attribute is not found locally.

public boolean containsAttributes(AttributeSet attributes)

> Checks whether every attribute in the given set is found in the current set. This method only returns `true` if every attribute is found with a matching value. It searches the resolving parent for attributes not found locally. Equality is defined by the `equals()` method.

public Object getAttribute(Object name)

> Returns the value for the named attribute. If the attribute is not found, the resolving parent (if one has been set) is searched. If the attribute is not found up the parent chain, `null` is returned.

public boolean isDefined(Object attrName)

> Indicates whether or not a value has been set for the given attribute key. It does not search the resolving parent.

public boolean isEqual(AttributeSet attr)

> Returns `true` only if the given set has the same contents (attribute names and values, including resolving parent) as the current set. The precise definition of this method is that it returns `true` if the input set has the same number of attributes as this set and `containsAttributes(attr)` returns `true`.

public boolean equals(Object obj)

> Returns `true` if the given object is an `AttributeSet` and `isEqual(obj)` returns `true`.

Miscellaneous Methods

public String toString()

> Returns a string containing the names and values (shown as `name=value`) of the local attributes. The resolving parent is shown as `"resolver=**AttributeSet**"` if it has been set.

public AttributeSet copyAttributes()
public Object clone()

> Creates a new `SimpleAttributeSet` by cloning the existing `Hashtable`.

public int hashCode()

> Returns the internal `Hashtable`'s hash code, allowing attribute sets to be properly stored in hashtables.

Using a Resolving Parent

The following example shows how a resolving parent can be used to store information applicable to multiple attribute sets. The attributes in this example are not actually applied to a document. The goal is only to show how to use a `SimpleAttributeSet` with a resolving parent.

```java
// ResParentExample.java
//
import javax.swing.text.*;
import java.awt.Color;

// An example showing how to use attribute sets and resolving parents.
public class ResParentExample {
  public static void main(String[] args) {

    // Create a set with 2 attributes
    SimpleAttributeSet elway = new SimpleAttributeSet();
    elway.addAttribute("name", "John Elway");
    elway.addAttribute("number", new Integer(7));

    // Create a "super" set :-)
    SimpleAttributeSet broncos = new SimpleAttributeSet();
    broncos.addAttribute("teamname", "Denver Broncos");
    Color[] colors = {Color.blue, Color.orange};
    broncos.addAttribute("colors", colors);
    broncos.addAttribute("superBowlChamps", Boolean.TRUE);

    // Set the new set as the resolveParent of the first
    elway.setResolveParent(broncos);

    // Show some attributes from the sets
    System.out.println("Name: " + elway.getAttribute("name"));
    System.out.println("Number: " + elway.getAttribute("number"));
    System.out.println("Team: " + elway.getAttribute("teamname"));

    // Note that we can get an attribute from a parent set, but if we ask if it's
    // defined, we get "no".
    colors = (Color[])elway.getAttribute("colors");
    System.out.println("Colors: " + colors[0] + " & " + colors[1]);
    System.out.println("Colors Defined?: " + elway.isDefined("colors"));

    // containsAttribute matches attribute AND value
    System.out.println("----------");
    System.out.println("Contains number 8: "
      + elway.containsAttribute("number", new Integer(8)));
    System.out.println("Contains number 7: "
      + elway.containsAttribute("number", new Integer(7)));

    // copy an attribute set
    System.out.println("----------");
    AttributeSet copyElway = elway.copyAttributes();
    System.out.println("Copy works: " + elway.containsAttributes(copyElway));

    // use the same resolveParent for a second set
    SimpleAttributeSet davis = new SimpleAttributeSet();
```

```
    davis.setResolveParent(broncos);
    System.out.println("----------");
    System.out.println("Davis' Team: "
      + davis.getAttribute("teamname"));
    System.out.println("Davis won Super Bowl?: "
      + davis.getAttribute("superBowlChamps"));

    // show toString output
    System.out.println("----------");
    System.out.println(elway);
    System.out.println(broncos);
  }
}
```

Here's the output; comments are in italics.

```
Name: John Elway
Number: 7
Team: Denver Broncos        // This came from the resolving parent
Colors: java.awt.Color[r=0,g=0,b=255] & java.awt.Color[r=255,g=200,b=0]
Colors Defined?: false      // We get colors from res. parent, but it's not defined
----------
Contains number 8: false   // containsAttribute() must match key AND value
Contains number 7: true
----------
Copy works: true
----------
Davis' Team: Denver Broncos
Davis won Super Bowl?: true
----------
name=John Elway resolver=**AttributeSet** number=7
teamname=Denver Broncos colors=[Ljava.awt.Color;@1cc851 superBowlChamps=true
```

The Position Interface

Position is an interface used to represent a location in a Document. Positions are intended to be more stable than simple Document offsets. For example, if you set a Position at the beginning of a sentence and then insert text before the sentence, the Position will still be located at the beginning of the sentence, even though its offset will have changed.

Property

Table 20-8 shows the property defined by the Position interface. The offset property indicates the Position's current offset from the start of the Document. The only method in this interface is the accessor for this property, getOffset().

Table 20-8. Position Property

Property	Data Type	get	is	set	bound	Default Value
offset	int	•				

An Example

The following simple example shows how a `Position` can be used. In the example, we create a `Document` with some initial text ("One Three Four") and set a `Position` at the beginning of the word "Three". We then insert some text in front of this word and show that the position still points to the beginning of the word "Three", even though its absolute offset has changed.

```java
// PositionExample.java
//
import javax.swing.text.*;

public class PositionExample {
  public static void main(String[] args) {
    try {

        // Create a document with some initial text
        PlainDocument doc = new PlainDocument();
        doc.insertString(0, "One Three Four", null);

        // Create a Position starting at "Three"
        Position pos = doc.createPosition(4);
        int offset = pos.getOffset();
        System.out.println("Offset Before: " + offset);
        System.out.println(doc.getText(0, doc.getLength()));
        for (int i=0;i<offset;i++)
          System.out.print(" ");
        System.out.println("* <- Position before\n");

        // Add some text before the Position
        doc.insertString(4, "Two ", null);

        // Offset has shifted due to the insertion
        offset = pos.getOffset();
        System.out.println("Offset After: " + offset);
        System.out.println(doc.getText(0, doc.getLength()));
        for (int i=0;i<offset;i++)
          System.out.print(" ");
        System.out.println("* <- Position after");
    } catch (BadLocationException ex) {}
  }
}
```

Here's the output from this program. We show the position by printing a number of blank spaces equal to the position's offset.

```
Offset Before: 4
One Three Four
    * <- Position before

Offset After: 8
One Two Three Four
        * <- Position after
```

The Position.Bias Class

This is a very simple static inner class used to define a type-safe enumeration. The values of the enumeration indicate a position's bias toward the character before or after an actual Position value.

Constants

The class defines two constants, the only allowable instances (since the constructor is private) of this class.

Table 20-9. Position.Bias constants

Constant	Type	Description
Forward	Position.Bias	A bias toward the previous character in the model.
Backward	Position.Bias	A bias toward the next character in the model.

Methods

public String toString()
    Returns either "Forward" or "Backward".

The Segment Class

We saw the Segment class back in the Document interface's getText() method. It's a very basic class used to allow fast access to a segment of text. To do so, it breaks some fundamental rules of object-oriented programming by exposing it's data as public fields. Therefore, when using it, it's important not to modify the contents of Segment's fields directly.

Fields

public char array[]
    The array of characters used to store the data. It should not be modified.

public int count
> The number of characters considered to be part of the Segment. It may be less than the number of characters stored in array.

public int offset
> The offset into the array that represents the beginning of the text of interest.

Constructors

public Segment()
> Creates a Segment with no data.

public Segment(char array[], int offset, int count)
> Creates a Segment that references an existing array. The offset and count define the subset of the array of interest.

Methods

public String toString()
> Returns the Segment as a String of length count.

The AbstractDocument Class

Much of the implementation of the Document interface is provided by the AbstractDocument class. The most significant thing provided by this default implementation is a basic locking mechanism.[*] In addition, several important inner classes and interfaces (described in the pages that follow) are defined within AbstractDocument.

Two of these inner classes make up the fundamental structure of an Abstract-Document, as shown in Figure 20-5. An AbstractDocument stores its content in an instance of a class that implements the Content interface (all Swing Document types currently use a class called StringContent, but another implementation called GapContent is also available). In addition, the attributes that define the Elements of the Document are managed by an instance of a class that implements the AttributeContext interface. The purpose of this interface is to allow frequently occurring attributes to be managed efficiently.

Properties

AbstractDocument defines the properties shown in Table 20-10. Most of these properties are defined in the Document interface. AbstractDocument defers the

---

[*] Unlike most of the methods in Swing, certain methods in the classes that make up the document model are thread-safe. AbstractDocument is specifically designed so that it may be used in a multi-threaded environment.

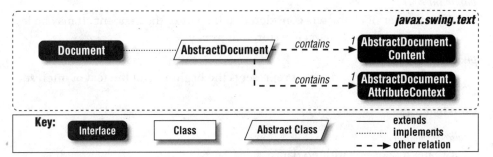

Figure 20-5. High-level AbstractDocument class diagram

creation of the a bi-directional[*] defaultRootElement to its subclasses (getDe-faultRootElement is abstract in this class). This single root element becomes the single root element held in the rootElements property. The startPosition and endPosition are set to new instances of inner classes AbstractDocument.TmpPosition and AbstractDocument.EndPosition, respectively. The length is initially zero by default.

Table 20-10. AbstractDocument Properties

Property	Data Type	get	is	set	bound	Default Value
defaultRootElement*	Element	•				abstract
documentProperties	Dictionary	•		•		null
endPosition*	Position	•				AbstractDocument.EndPosition()
length*	int	•				0
rootElements*	Element[]	•				{ defaultRootElement }
startPosition*	Position	•				AbstractDocument.TmpPosition()

The only new property added in this class is called documentProperties. This property (a java.util.Dictionary) allows direct access to the storage mechanism used in support of the getProperty() and putProperty() methods defined in Document.

Events

Table 20-11 shows that AbstractDocument fires DocumentEvents and Undoable-EditEvents when changes are made to the document.

---

* Preliminary support for bi-directional text has been added as of JKD1.2 beta4. We will not cover these features in detail, as they are still under development, but we'll identify classes and methods that include this support as we come across them.

Table 20-11. Document Events

Event	Description
DocumentEvent	Indicates that a change has been made to the document.
UndoableEditEvent	Indicates that an undoable change has been made to the document.

The following standard methods are implemented in this class:

public void addDocumentListener(DocumentListener listener)

public void removeDocumentListener(DocumentListener listener)

public void addUndoableEditListener(UndoableEditListener listener)

public void removeUndoableEditListener(UndoableEditListener listener)

protected void fireChangedUpdate(DocumentEvent e)

protected void fireInsertUpdate(DocumentEvent e)

protected void fireRemoveUpdate(DocumentEvent e)

protected void fireUndoableEditUpdate(UndoableEditEvent e)

Constants

AbstractDocument defines the constants shown in Table 20-12.

Table 20-12. AbstractDocument Constants

Constant	Type	Description
BAD_LOCATION	String	Error message indicating a bad location
ContentElementName	String	Name of elements used to represent content (the default name for BranchElements)—"content"
ElementNameAttribute	String	Name of attribute used to specify element names
ParagraphElementName	String	Name of elements used to represent paragraphs (the default name for BranchElements)—"paragraph"
SectionElementName	String	Name of elements used to represent sections (the default name for SectionElements)—"section"

BAD_LOCATION is a protected constant. The others are public and are intended to be used as Element names, except for ElementNameAttribute, which should be used as the key for an attribute that contains an Element's name.

Field

protected EventListenerList listenerList

Contains the list of listeners that have been added to the document. See the discussion of EventListenerList in Chapter 27, *Swing Utilities*, for more information.

Constructors

protected AbstractDocument(AbstractDocument.Content data)

Creates a document containing the specified content. The `Content` inner class is discussed later.

protected AbstractDocument(AbstractDocument.Content data,
AbstractDocument.AttributeContext context)

Creates a document containing the specified content, using the given attribute context. The `Content` and `AttributeContext` inner classes are discussed later in this chapter.

Locking

`AbstractDocument` implements a basic locking mechanism which ensures that at any given time, there is either a single writer of the document, or zero or more readers. That is, if no one is writing to the document, anyone is allowed to begin reading it or writing to it. Once someone begins writing, no one is able to read until the writer has finished.

Certain methods that technically "read" the document (such as `getText()`) do not actually obtain a read lock to do so. The only method that obtains a read lock is the `render()` method, meaning that you are not guaranteed document stability during other access methods.

This locking scheme is supported by the methods described next. It's important to understand how this works if you decide to implement your own document type. If you decide to use the existing document types, it's not too important to understand all the details.

protected final synchronized Thread getCurrentWriter()

Returns the thread currently holding the write lock (if there is one). If the document is not currently being updated, `null` is returned.

protected final synchronized void readLock()

Blocks until it is able to obtain a read lock. If another thread holds the write lock, this method waits until it is notified that the lock has been released before trying to obtain the lock again.

protected final synchronized void readUnlock()

Called to indicate that the current thread is no longer reading the document. If this was the only reader, writing may begin (threads waiting for the lock are notified).

protected final synchronized void writeLock()

Blocks until it is able to obtain the write lock. If the write lock is held by another thread, or there are any readers, this method will wait until it is notified that the state of the locks has changed before making an attempt to obtain the lock. Once the lock has been obtained, this method returns, and no other read or write locks can be obtained until the lock is released.

protected final synchronized void writeUnlock()
Releases the write lock, allowing waiting readers or writers to obtain locks.

public void render(Runnable r)
Called to render the Document visually. It obtains a read lock, ensuring that no changes will be made to the Document during the rendering process. It then calls the input Runnable's run()[*] method. This method *must not* attempt to modify the Document, since deadlock will occur if it tries to obtain a write lock. When the run() method completes (either naturally or by throwing an exception), the read lock is released. Note that there is nothing in this method directly related to rendering the Document. It could technically be used to execute any arbitrary code while holding a read lock.

Reading and Writing

These methods read and write the underlying Document content. The methods that modify the content must obtain a write lock before proceeding.

public String getText(int offset, int length) throws BadLocationException
public void getText(int offset, int length, Segment txt) throws BadLocationException
Returns the text starting at the specified offset, continuing for the specified length. The second version returns the requested text in the input Segment object. These methods do *not* obtain a read lock while accessing the Document's content.

public void insertString(int offs, String str, AttributeSet a) throws BadLocationException
Inserts the specified string, with the given attributes, at the input offset in the Document. This method blocks until it is able to obtain the Document's write lock. After making the requested insertion, it calls insertUpdate(), fireInsertUpdate() and, if this is an undoable edit, fireUndoableEditUpdate().

public void remove(int offs, int len) throws BadLocationException
Removes text from the Document, starting at the specified offset and continuing for the given number of characters. Like insertString(), this method blocks until it is able to obtain a write lock. After removing the specified text, it calls removeUpdate(), fireRemoveUpdate() and, if this is an undoable edit, fireUndoableEditUpdate().

---

[*] This method is called directly. The Runnable is not passed to a new Thread object.

Other Public Methods

public synchronized Position createPosition(int offs) throws BadLocationException
Returns a new `Position` object, capable of tracking change as the `Document` is modified.

public void dump(PrintStream out)
Dumps diagnostic information to the specified stream. This is done by calling `dump()` on the default root element, if it is an instance of `AbstractElement`.

public Object getProperty(Object key)
Returns the value of the requested property. Properties may have any arbitrary key and any arbitrary value. This method uses the `Dictionary` managed by the `documentProperties` property.

public void putProperty(Object key, Object value)
Sets an arbitrary property value for the document. Properties may have any arbitrary key and any arbitrary value. This method uses the `Dictionary` managed by the `documentProperties` property.

Other Protected Methods

protected Element createBranchElement(Element parent, AttributeSet a)
Returns a new `BranchElement` (described later) with the given parent and attribute set.

protected Element createLeafElement(Element parent, AttributeSet a, int p0, int p1)
Returns a new `LeafElement` (described later) with the given parent and attribute set, covering the specified range.

protected final AbstractDocument.AttributeContext getAttributeContext()
Returns the `AttributeContext` (described later) used for managing the document's attributes.

protected final AbstractDocument.Content getContent()
Returns the `Content` (described later) object used to manage the actual contents of the document.

protected void insertUpdate(AbstractDocument.DefaultDocumentEvent chng,
AttributeSet attr)
Called to indicate that text has been inserted into the document. The default implementation does nothing.

protected void removeUpdate(AbstractDocument.DefaultDocumentEvent chng)
Called to indicate that text has been removed from the document. The default implementation does nothing.

Document Locking Example

This example shows that multiple Document renderers can read a Document simultaneously, but that this rendering process will block an attempted write operation. The code creates two DocRenderer objects, which it asks to render a simple document.[*] In this example, we "render" the document by just printing its contents to the screen. These rendering requests are made in separate threads, started at roughly the same time. The rendering method contains a three-second sleep() call to simulate a lengthy rendering process. After starting these two rendering threads, the main program sleeps for one second and then attempts to add text to the document. The output shows that this write attempt blocks until the two rendering threads have completed. Here's the source code for this example:

```java
// LockingExample.java
//
import javax.swing.*;
import javax.swing.text.*;

// Sample program showing how AbstractDocument locking works.
public class LockingExample {
  public static void main(String[] args) {

    // Create a document with some initial text
    Document doc = new PlainDocument();
    try {
      doc.insertString(0, "Three blind mice", null);
    } catch (BadLocationException ex) {ex.printStackTrace();}

    // Create two "renderers" which will simulate painting the document
    DocRenderer r1 = new DocRenderer("One", doc);
    DocRenderer r2 = new DocRenderer("Two", doc);

    // Start the renderers in new threads. We'll print out timing data to show
    // how things work.
    long startTime = System.currentTimeMillis();
    r1.renderInThread(startTime);
    r2.renderInThread(startTime);

    // Wait one second before writing
    try {
      Thread.sleep(1000);
    } catch (InterruptedException ex) {}
```

---

[*] We use a very simple subclass of AbstractDocument called PlainDocument in this example. This class will be defined later in this chapter. For now, there's nothing special you need to know about this class.

```
    // Attempt to add some content to the document
    System.out.println("Start writing: "
      + (System.currentTimeMillis()-startTime));

    try {
      doc.insertString(doc.getLength(), ", see how they run.", null);
    } catch (BadLocationException ex) {ex.printStackTrace();}

    System.out.println("Done writing: "
      + (System.currentTimeMillis()-startTime));

    // Render the modified document
    r1.renderInThread(startTime);
  }
}


// A simple class that implements Runnable and provides a method to run itself
// in a new Thread.
class DocRenderer implements Runnable {

  // Create a new renderer for the given document. A name is provided to
  // distinguish the output of different renderers.
  public DocRenderer(String rname, Document doc) {
    this.rname = rname;
    this.doc = doc;
  }


  // This method is called by AbstractDocument.render(). It "renders" the
  // document by sleeping for 3 sec, then dumping the doc contents to stdout.
  public void run() {
    try {
      System.out.println(rname + " start renderer.run(): "
        + (System.currentTimeMillis()-startTime));

      // Simulate a slow rendering process.
      Thread.sleep(3000);
    } catch (InterruptedException ex) {}

    // "render" by writing the text to stdout
    try {
      System.out.println(rname + ":" + doc.getText(0, doc.getLength()));
    } catch (BadLocationException ex) {ex.printStackTrace();}
  }

  // Calls render() on the document in a new Thread.
  public void renderInThread(final long startTime) {
    this.startTime = startTime;
```

```
      // An anonymous inner class for a new Thread
      new Thread() {
        public void run() {
          System.out.println(rname + " start rendering: "
            + (System.currentTimeMillis() - startTime));

          doc.render(DocRenderer.this);

          System.out.println(rname + " done rendering: "
            + (System.currentTimeMillis()-startTime));
        }
      }.start();          // start the new thread
    }

    private Document doc;
    private String rname;
    private long startTime;
}
```

Here's the output created by this program. The writing process, which contains no `sleep()` calls, was not able to complete until the rendering processes finished.

```
One start rendering: 0
One start renderer.run(): 0
Two start rendering: 0
Two start renderer.run(): 0
Start writing: 990     // writer is blocked until readers are done
One:Three blind mice
One done rendering: 3030
Two:Three blind mice
Two done rendering: 3030
Done writing: 3030     // only after readers release their locks can writer get in
One start rendering: 3080
One start renderer.run(): 3140
One:Three blind mice, see how they run.
One done rendering: 6100
```

The first four lines show that both readers start rendering at the same time. The next line shows the writer attempting to start after about one second. The next four lines shows the two readers finishing their rendering at about the same time, three seconds after they began. Only after these reads completed was the write able to get in. This is why we see the `"Done writing"` output after the reader output even though the write processing takes very little time (there is no `sleep()` call for the writer). The last four lines show the output of a single read after the document has been modified.

The AbstractDocument.AbstractElement Class

`AbstractElement` is a public abstract inner class used to represent `Element`s of an `AbstractDocument`. It defines some default behavior useful for any `Element` implementation. In addition to implementing the `Element` interface, `Abstract-Element` also implements `MutableAttributeSet`, which is an extension of the `AttributeSet` interface that allows the set to be modified. This multiple inter-face inheritance allows an `AbstractElement` to act both as an `Element` and as the `AttributeSet` that defines the `Element`'s properties.

`AbstractDocument` also provides two concrete subclasses of `AbstractElement` called `BranchElement` and `LeafElement` (defined next). Figure 20-6 shows the inheritance hierarchy for these classes.

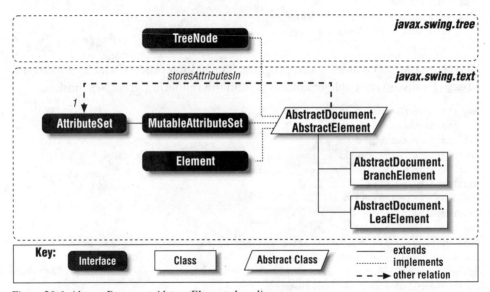

Figure 20-6. AbstractDocument.AbstractElement class diagram

Note that `AbstractElement` also implements the `TreeNode` interface from the `javax.swing.tree` package. This makes it easy to represent the document struc-ture visually using a `JTree`.

Properties

Table 20-13 shows the properties defined by `AbstractDocument.Abstract-Element`. See the "Property" sections of the `Element` and `MutableAttributeSet` interfaces for descriptions of most of these properties. Most of the properties either are abstract (`allowsChildren`, `element`, `elementCount`, `endOffset`, `leaf`, and `startOffset`) or are obtained from the `AttributeSet` passed to the

AbstractElement constructor. The resolveParent property is taken from the AttributeSet, but if this is null, the resolveParent will be the Element's parent's AttributeSet.

Table 20-13. AbstractDocument.AbstractElement Properties

Property	Data Type	get	is	set	bound	Default Value
allowsChildren*	boolean	•				abstract
attributeCount*	int	•				from attribute set
attributeNames*	Enumeration	•				from attribute set
attributes*	AttributeSet	•				this
childAt (indexed)*	TreeNode	•				same as element
childCount*	int	•				same as elementCount
document*	Document	•				AbstractDocument.this
element (indexed)*	Element	•				abstract
elementCount*	int	•				abstract
endOffset*	int	•				abstract
leaf*	boolean		•			abstract
name*	String	•				from attribute set
parent*	TreeNode	•				same as parentElement
parentElement*	Element	•				from constructor
resolveParent*	MutableAttributeSet	•		•		from attribute set
startOffset*	int	•				abstract

Several of these properties may appear to be duplicates. This is because AbstractElement implements the TreeNode interface. The allowsChildren, childAt, childCount, and parent properties come from this interface.

Constructors

public AbstractElement(Element parent, AttributeSet a)

Creates a new Element with the specified parent and attributes. The AttributeSet is stored and used in the methods defined in the AttributeSet and MutableAttributeSet interfaces.

AttributeSet Methods

The following methods are defined in the AttributeSet interface.

public boolean isDefined(String attrName)
public boolean isEqual(AttributeSet attr)
public boolean containsAttribute(String name, Object value)
public boolean containsAttributes(AttributeSet attrs)
> Delegate to the `Element`'s `AttributeSet`.

public AttributeSet copyAttributes()
> Returns the element's `AttributeSet`. It does not actually copy anything.

public Object getAttribute(String attrName)
> Delegates this call to its `AttributeSet`. If `null` is returned, it tries to retrieve the attribute value from its `resolveParent`.

MutableAttributeSet Methods

These methods are defined in the `MutableAttributeSet` interface:

public void addAttribute(String name, Object value)
public void addAttributes(AttributeSet attr)
public void removeAttribute(Object name)
public void removeAttributes(Enumeration names)
public void removeAttributes(AttributeSet attrs)
> The first thing each of these methods does is ensure that the current thread is actively holding the write lock on the document containing this `Element`. If not, a `StateInvariantError` (a non-public class in the text package) is thrown. Because of this check, you cannot call these methods directly on the `Elements` in a `Document`. They may only be called while a write lock is held. If the write lock is currently held, these methods use the `Document`'s current `AttributeContext` to modify the attribute set to reflect the desired change.

TreeNode Methods

In addition to the accessors for the `TreeNode` properties, the following methods from the `TreeNode` interface are defined:

public abstract Enumeration children()
> Must be implemented to return an `Enumeration` of the `Element`'s children.

public int getIndex(TreeNode node)
> Returns the index of the given node. If the given node is not a child of this element, −1 will be returned.

Other Methods

public void dump(PrintStream out, int indentAmount)
> Dumps the `Element` hierarchy to the given stream for debugging purposes.

public abstract int getElementIndex(int offset)
>   Returns the `Element` that corresponds to the specified character offset in the
>   `Document`.

protected void finalize() throws Throwable
>   This method, called when the `Element` is being garbage collected, notifies the
>   `AttributeContext` that it may reclaim the `Element`'s attributes.

The AbstractDocument.LeafElement Class

This is a public inner class used to refer to a block of text in the document. `Leaf-`
`Elements` do not contain child elements. This class is a concrete subclass of
`AbstractDocument.AbstractElement`.

Properties

`AbstractDocument.LeafElement` defines the property values in Table 20-14. See
the "Property" section of the `Element` interface for descriptions of these elements.
The `startOffset` and `endOffset` values are maintained by `Position` objects
created in the constructor. The other default values listed here reflect the fact that
`LeafElements` have no children.

Table 20-14. AbstractDocument.LeafElement Properties

Property	Data Type	get	is	set	bound	Default Value
allowsChildren*	boolean	•				false
element (indexed)*	Element	•				null
elementCount*	int	•				0
endOffset*	int	•				
leaf*	boolean		•			true
name*	String	•				From attribute set, or ContentElementName if null
startOffset*	int	•				

See also properties from the AbstractDocument.AbstractElement class (Table 20-13).

Constructor

public LeafElement(Element parent, AttributeSet a, int offs0, int offs1)
>   Creates a new `Element` with the specified parent and attributes. The element
>   covers the specified range of the `Document`. The offsets of this element are
>   managed by two `Position` objects created in this constructor based on the
>   offset values.

Methods

public Enumeration children()

This method (from `TreeNode`) returns `null`, since leaf elements have no children.

public int getElementIndex(int pos)

Since leaves have no children, this method always returns `-1`.

public String toString()

Returns a `String` representation of the `Element`. The value is formed by concatenating `Leaf Element`, the `Element`'s name, and its start and end positions.

The AbstractDocument.BranchElement Class

This is a public inner class used to represent composite `Elements`, which contain other `Elements`. It is a concrete subclass of `AbstractDocument.Abstract-Element`.

Properties

`AbstractDocument.BranchElement` defines the property values shown in Table 20-15. See the "Property" section of the `Element` interface for descriptions of these properties. The `startOffset` and `endOffset` values are maintained by `Position` objects created in the constructor. `StartOffset` always maps to the first character of `element[0]`, while `endOffset` maps to the last character of the last child element. The `leaf` property is always `false`, and `allowsChildren` is always `true`.

Table 20-15. AbstractDocument.BranchElement Properties

Property	Data Type	get	is	set	bound	Default Value
allowsChildren*	boolean	•				true
element (indexed)*	Element	•				null
elementCount*	int	•				0
endOffset*	int	•				element[elementCount-1].endOffset
leaf*	boolean		•			false
name*	String	•				From attribute set, or ParagraphEle-mentName if null
startOffset*	int	•				element[0].startOffset

See also properties from the AbstractDocument.AbstractElement class (Table 20-13).

Constructor

public BranchElement(Element parent, AttributeSet a)

Creates a new element with the specified parent and attributes. The element initially has no children.

Methods

public Enumeration children()

This method (from the `TreeNode` interface) returns an `Enumeration` of the element's children.

public int getElementIndex(int offset)

Maps an absolute character offset to the child `Element` containing the given offset. It performs a binary search of the `Element`'s children, looking for a child that contains the given document offset. It returns the index of the closest `Element` it can find. If this branch does not contain the given offset, the index of either the first or last child is returned, depending on which side of this `Element` the given offset is located. If this element has no children, this method returns 0 (the same value returned if the input offset is found in the element's first child).

public Element positionToElement(int pos)

Uses `getElementIndex()` to return the `Element` object at the given Document offset. If `getElementIndex()` returns the index of an `Element` that does not actually contain the given offset (which is possible, since it just returns the *closest* `Element`), `null` is returned.

public void replace(int offset, int length, Element[] elems)

Removes the requested number (`length`) of child `Elements`, starting at the specified offset, and replaces them with the input array of `Elements`. Note that the `offset` and `length` parameters specify the first child to remove and the number of children to remove. That is, they refer to the `Element`'s children, not `Document` characters.

Note that this method performs as a delete operation if `elems` is empty, or to an insert operation if the `length` is zero. Also note that removed `Elements` may contain other `Elements`, which will also be removed.

public String toString()

Returns a `String` representation of the `Element`, formed by concatenating `Branch Element`, the `Element`'s name, and the `Element`'s start and end offsets.

The AbstractDocument.Content Interface

This interface is used to represent a sequence of data that may be edited. This is where an AbstractDocument actually stores its content. Many of the methods in AbstractDocument simply delegate the call to the document's Content object.

Methods

public abstract Position createPosition(int offset) throws BadLocationException
Creates a Position that will track changes at the specified offset.

public abstract void getChars(int where, int len, Segment txt) throws BadLocationException
Returns the specified range of text. The result is passed back in the input Segment object.

public abstract String getString(int where, int len) throws BadLocationException
Returns a String containing the specified range of text.

public abstract UndoableEdit insertString(int where, String str)
throws BadLocationException
Inserts the specified string at the requested offset in the content. If the Content implementation supports undo, an UndoableEdit object will be returned; otherwise this method returns null.

public abstract int length()
Returns the current length of the content.

public abstract UndoableEdit remove(int where, int nitems) throws BadLocationException
Removes the specified number of items (characters, icons, or components) from the document content. If the Content implementation supports undo, an UndoableEdit object will be returned, otherwise this method returns null.

The StringContent Class

This is a basic implementation of the AbstractDocument.Content interface. At present, this is the implementation used by all of the Swing text components, though there may be a change to the newer GapContent class in a later release. The content is stored in a character array, and changes are made by modifying the array's contents and copying the array when necessary to support growth. String-Content supports undoable edits, so the insertString() and remove() methods always return non-null UndoableEdit objects.

Constructors

public StringContent()
> Creates an array sized to hold a default (10) number of characters, initially containing a single newline character.

public StringContent(int initialLength)
> Creates an array of the specified size, initially containing a single newline character.

Public Methods

public Position createPosition(int offset) throws BadLocationException
> Creates a `Position` that will track changes at the specified offset. This is done by keeping a `Vector` of "marks," which are updated each time content is inserted or removed. The returned `Position` is of type `StringContent.StickyPosition` (a non-public inner class).

public void getChars(int where, int len, Segment txt) throws BadLocationException
> Returns the specified range of text. The entire data array is returned in the `Segment` with the specified offset and length set.

public String getString(int where, int len) throws BadLocationException
> Creates and returns a new `String` containing the specified range of text.

public UndoableEdit insertString(int where, String str) throws BadLocationException
> Inserts the specified string at the requested offset in the content. If necessary, the array size is increased (by doubling, or by adding the size of the new string, whichever is larger) to accommodate the new text. All of the `Positions` previously created by `createPosition()` calls are updated to reflect the newly added text. An `UndoableEdit` (a non-public inner class called `InsertUndo`) is returned, which allows this insert to be undone.

public int length()
> Returns the current length of the content. This is the number of characters in the array, not the total allocated size of the array.

public UndoableEdit remove(int where, int nitems) throws BadLocationException
> Removes the specified number of characters from the content by copying the appropriate segments of the array. All of the `Positions` previously created by `createPosition()` calls are updated to reflect the removed text. An `UndoableEdit` (a non-public inner class called `RemoveUndo`) is returned, which allows this removal to be undone.

Protected Methods

The following methods are used by the non-public undoable edit inner classes to provide undo support.

protected Vector getPositionsInRange(Vector v, int offset, int length)
> Obtains a vector of position references spanning the specified range. The return value can be passed to `updateUndoPositions()` to update the positions.

protected void updateUndoPositions(Vector positions)
> Updates the position references returned by `getPositionsInRange()`.

The GapContent Class

This implementation of the `AbstractDocument.Content` interface made its Swing debut in Swing 1.0.2. As of JDK 1.2 beta4, it was not actually used within the Swing text package, possibly because it did not yet support undoable edits. Look for this feature to be added in a future release, but for now you can use it in your own applications if you don't need undo support.

The idea behind `GapContent` is to take advantage of the fact that text is typically inserted sequentially. In other words, if the user inserts a character at position 10 in the document, chances are good that the next insertion will be at position 11. With `StringContent`, each insertion results in an array copy to make room for the new text. In contrast, `GapContent` keeps a "gap" in its character array, located at the current insertion point. When the insertion point changes, the gap is moved to the new input location by shifting the contents of the array to the end. The easiest way to understand this is by example.

Figure 20-7 shows how `GapContent` would manage a 35-character array (you can specify the initial size when you create the content object). Each line represents the state of the array at some point of the insertion process. We show the "gap" by shading that portion of the array.

Initially, the entire array is the gap (actually, `GapContent` starts with a single \n in the array, but we'll ignore that detail). As text is inserted (lines 1 and 2), the right edge of the gap is shifted, staying just beyond that last inserted character.

Line 3 is the most important. This line shows what happens when we go back and insert text into the middle of the document. At this point, everything to the right of the insertion point is copied to the end of the array via a single array copy.

We're now (line 4) able to insert additional data into the middle of the document without having to pay for additional array copies. Contrast this approach with the approach used by `StringContent` in which the insertion of the letter w would

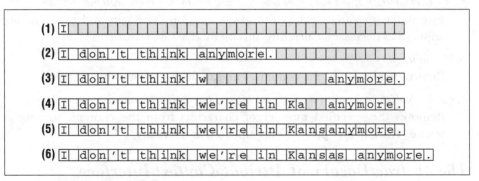

Figure 20-7. GapContent example

have shifted "anymore." down one space, the insertion of e would have shifted it down again, and so on.

Once we've filled the gap (line 5), the array must be enlarged (line 6) to hold the entire document.

Constructors

public GapContent()
> Creates a content object with an initial array size of 10.

public GapContent(int initialLength)
> Creates a content object with the specified size.

AbstractDocument.Content Methods

The following methods implement the `AbstractDocument.Content` interface.

public Position createPosition(int offset) throws BadLocationException
> Creates a `Position` at the specific document offset. This implementation manages a sorted array of positions to make it easy to find the marks that need to be updated when the gap is shifted.

public void getChars(int where, int len, Segment chars) throws BadLocationException
> Populates the given `Segment` with the requested text (`len` characters, starting at `where`). If the requested text falls entirely on one side of the gap, the whole internal array is returned. If not, a new array is constructed, containing the specified range with the gap removed.

public String getString(int where, int len) throws BadLocationException
> Uses `getChars()` to return the requested portion of the content.

public UndoableEdit insertString(int where, String str) throws BadLocationException

Inserts the specified text at the given location. The gap and positions are adjusted as necessary. Currently, this method always returns null.

public int length()

Returns the length of the content. The gap does not count in this value.

public UndoableEdit remove(int where, int nitems) throws BadLocationException

Removes the specified number of characters from the content, starting at where. The gap and positions are updated as necessary.

The AbstractDocument.AttributeContext Interface

This inner-interface of AbstractDocument defines a set of methods for managing attributes in one or more documents. The idea is that replicating AttributeSets throughout a Document could be very expensive. Implementations of this interface (see the StyleContext class in Chapter 21, *Styled Documents and JTextPane*) are intended to provide intelligent management of attribute sets, eliminating costly duplication.

The methods in AbstractDocument.AbstractElement which modify an Element's attribute set use the document's AttributeContext to make the modifications.

Property

The AbstractDocument.AttributeContext interface defines the property shown in Table 20-16. The emptySet property consists of an attribute set containing no attributes.

Table 20-16. AbstractDocument.AttributeContext Property

Property	Data Type	get	is	set	bound	Default Value
emptySet	AttributeSet	•				

Attribute Management

The following methods are defined for managing attribute sets:

public abstract AttributeSet addAttribute(AttributeSet old, Object name, Object value)

Returns a set that contains the attributes of the given set, plus the newly specified attribute.

public abstract AttributeSet addAttributes(AttributeSet old, AttributeSet attr)
> Returns a set that contains the result of adding the second set of attributes to the first.

public abstract void reclaim(AttributeSet a)
> Called to indicate that a set is no longer being used. It may be removed from the context if no one else is using it.

public abstract AttributeSet removeAttribute(AttributeSet old, Object name)
> Returns a set that contains the result of removing the attribute with the specified key from the given set. Equality is defined by the `equals()` method.

public abstract AttributeSet removeAttributes(AttributeSet old, Enumeration names)
> Returns a set that contains the result of removing all of the given attribute keys from the given set.

public abstract AttributeSet removeAttributes(AttributeSet old, AttributeSet attrs)
> Returns a set that contains the result of removing all attributes in the second set from the first set. Only attributes where the keys and values match should be removed.

The BadLocationException Class

This exception is thrown by many of the text classes to indicate that an attempt has been made to access an invalid offset into the document.

Constructor

public BadLocationException(String s, int offs)
> Creates a new exception as a result of an attempt to access the specified offset.

Methods

public int offsetRequested()
> Returns the offending offset that caused the exception to be thrown.

Model Summary So Far

In this chapter, we've defined all of the abstractions that make up the Swing document model. Before going on, let's briefly review the interfaces and classes we've covered so far.

Document
> This is the root of the text model. Each Swing text component references a `Document` model that stores its text. We also looked at `AbstractDocument`, an abstract class that implements `Document` and defines some default behavior, including document locking.

Element

Documents are partitioned by Elements. An Element contains a pair of offsets into a document, referencing a collection of text with a common set of attributes. AbstractDocument defines three inner classes that implement this interface: AbstractElement, LeafElement, and BranchElement.

AttributeSet

Each Element of a Document is defined, in part, by an arbitrary set of attributes called an AttributeSet. Attribute values in an AttributeSet are arbitrary Objects, accessible by unique keys (also Objects).

MutableAttributeSet

An extension of AttributeSet that allows attributes to be added and removed. We also looked at SimpleAttributeSet, a default implementation of MutableAttributeSet that uses a Hashtable to implement the interface.

Position

A Position is simply an unchanging point within a document. It is more stable than an offset, since it moves with its attached text.

Segment

A Segment is a simple container for an array of characters used to allow fast access to some segment of text.

AbstractDocument.Content

This is where an AbstractDocument's content is actually stored. The StringContent class showed a default implementation of this interface, currently used by all text components. GapContent provides an alternate, more efficient implementation.

AbstractDocument.AttributeContext

An interface that allows AttributeSets to be managed across multiple documents for efficiency purposes.

Next, we'll finally take a look at a concrete Document implementation called PlainDocument.

The PlainDocument Class

PlainDocument is an extension of AbstractDocument used for simple documents that do not need to manage complex formatting styles. The JTextField, JPasswordField, and JTextArea classes use PlainDocument as their default model. It's worth noting that PlainDocument provides more power than these components typically need. As an extension of AbstractDocument, it supports the use of AttributeSets, allowing the document to contain different fonts, colors, font styles, etc. These attributes are ignored when rendering the simple text components that use this document type.

The Elements that make up a PlainDocument correspond to distinct lines of text that end in new line characters (\n). Each line of text maps to a single LeafElement. All of these LeafElements are then contained by a single BranchElement (the document's root element).

Property

PlainDocument defines a default property value as shown in Table 20-17. The defaultRootElement created by PlainDocument is an AbstractDocument.BranchElement object containing a single empty AbstractDocument.LeafElement child.

Table 20-17. PlainDocument Property

Property	Data Type	get	is	set	bound	Default Value
defaultRootElement*	Element	•				AbstractDocument.BranchElement()

See also properties from the AbstractDocument class (Table 20-10).

Constants

PlainDocument defines the constants shown in Table 20-18.

Table 20-18. PlainDocument Constants

Constant	Type	Description
lineLimit-Attribute	String	The name of the property used to specify the maximum length of a line, if there is one
tabSizeAttribute	String	The name of the property used to specify the size for tabs

Constructors

public PlainDocument()
> Calls the protected constructor below, passing in a new instance of StringContent.

protected PlainDocument(AbstractDocument.Content c)
> Creates a new document using the specified Content. It adds a document property reflecting a default tab size of 8 and creates a default root element by calling createDefaultRoot().

Protected Methods

The only new methods defined in this class are the following protected methods.

protected AbstractDocument.AbstractElement createDefaultRoot()

Creates the `Document`'s default root element. The returned element is an `AbstractDocument.BranchElement`, containing a single empty `Abstract-Document.LeafElement`.

protected void insertUpdate(DefaultDocumentEvent chng, AttributeSet attr)

Indicates that content has been inserted into the `Document`. It refreshes the `Element` structure, adding and removing `LeafElements` as necessary to reflect the specified insert. If any `Elements` are added or removed by this method, indicating that lines have been added or removed, an `ElementEdit` (discussed at the end of the chapter) is created and added to the given event.

protected void removeUpdate(DefaultDocumentEvent chng)

Called to indicate that content has been removed from the `Document`. If the removal spans lines, the lines outside the removal range are joined together into a single `Element`. If this happens, the added and removed lines are used to create an `ElementEdit` (discussed at the end of the chapter), which is added to the given event.

Looking at PlainDocument's Element Structures

This example shows the `Element` structure used by `PlainDocument` using the `AbstractDocument.dump()` method. We start by printing the structure of an empty `PlainDocument`. We then add three lines of text and print again. Finally, we remove part of the first line, the entire second line, and part of the third line, showing how elements are removed and merged by the `Document`. Here's the source for this simple example:

```
// PlainDocExample.java
//
import javax.swing.text.*;

public class PlainDocExample {
  public static void main(String[] args) {
    try {

      // Dump an empty document
      PlainDocument doc = new PlainDocument();
      AbstractDocument.AbstractElement root = (AbstractDocument.AbstractElement)
        doc.getDefaultRootElement();

      root.dump(System.out,0);
      System.out.println("==========");

      // Add 3 lines of text, dump again
      doc.insertString(0, "Line One\n", null);
      doc.insertString(doc.getLength(), "Line Two\n", null);
```

```
          doc.insertString(doc.getLength(), "Line Three", null);
          root.dump(System.out,0);
          System.out.println("==========");

          // Remove "One/Line Two/Line", dump again
          doc.remove(5, 18);
          root.dump(System.out,0);
      } catch (BadLocationException ex) {}
  }
}
```

Here's the output produced by running this program:

```
<paragraph>
  <content>
    [0,1][
]
==========
<paragraph>
  <content>
    [0,9][Line One
]
  <content>
    [9,18][Line Two
]
  <content>
    [18,29][Line Three
]
==========
<paragraph>
  <content>
    [0,11][Line Three
]
```

The first block of output shows the default structure of the PlainDocument. At this point, we just have a single branch element (refer to Table 20-12 to see where the strings "paragraph" and "content" come from), containing a single leaf element. The numbers inside the square brackets show the startOffset and endOffset of the leaf element.

The second block of output shows the structure described at the beginning of this section. We still have a single branch element (the paragraph), but it now contains a leaf element for each line of text.

The last block shows that removing 18 characters from the middle of the document (including two newline characters) caused the second element to be removed completely, and the first and third elements to be merged into a single new element containing the remaining text.

Filtering JTextFields

A common question encountered when working with `JTextFields` is "How can I restrict the characters entered into the field?" In the AWT, this was typically done by adding a `KeyListener` to the field and consuming the keypress event if the input text was invalid.

A much more robust way to fulfill this requirement is to use a document type that enforces the restriction for you. This ensures that any insertion into the `Document` (including keyboard entry, pasting from the clipboard, or programmatic insertions) will be checked. Using the `KeyListener` strategy only catches keyboard entry. All you need is an extension of `PlainDocument` that overrides the `insertString()` method, to verify that the requested insertion is valid. Here's a class that limits the number of characters in the field:

```java
// FixedLengthPlainDocument.java
//
import java.awt.Toolkit;
import javax.swing.*;
import javax.swing.text.*;

// An extension of PlainDocument that restricts the length of the content it
// contains.
public class FixedLengthPlainDocument extends PlainDocument {

  // Create a new document with the given max length
  public FixedLengthPlainDocument(int maxLength) {
    this.maxLength = maxLength;
  }

  // If this insertion would exceed the maximum document length, we "beep" and do
  // nothing else. Otherwise, super.insertString() is called.
  public void insertString(int offset, String str, AttributeSet a)
  throws BadLocationException {
    if (getLength() + str.length() > maxLength) {
      Toolkit.getDefaultToolkit().beep();
    }
    else {
      super.insertString(offset, str, a);
    }
  }

  private int maxLength;
}
```

To use this class, simply pass in an instance of it to the `JTextField` constructor. Or, if you plan on using this document type for many text fields, you might want to create a new subclass of `JTextField`. Here's an example:

```
// FixedLengthTextField.java
//
import javax.swing.*;

// A fixed-length JTextField
public class FixedLengthTextField extends JTextField {

  public FixedLengthTextField(int length) {
    this(null, length);
  }

  public FixedLengthTextField(String text, int length) {
    super(new FixedLengthPlainDocument(length), text, length);
  }
}
```

In this class, we just define two constructors that result in our new document type being passed up to the superclass. We do this because we want to allow the document length to be specified in the constructor. If you were using a similar technique to restrict the type of input, but not the length, it would be a bit cleaner to override the `createDefaultModel()` method to return your custom document type, rather than passing the new document into the superclass constructor.

Recall from the previous chapter that we sometimes have to perform a little magic to get text fields sized correctly. Here's a "main" program that uses our new text field extension, along with the trick from the previous chapter, to create a fixed-length text field that's just the right size:

```
// FixedLengthTFMain.java
//
import java.awt.*;
import javax.swing.*;
import javax.swing.text.*;

public class FixedLengthTFMain {

  public static void main(String[] args) {

    // create the field and make it just the right size using the little hack
    // from the previous chapter
    FixedLengthTextField tf = new FixedLengthTextField(10);
    tf.setColumns(0);
    tf.setText("1234567890");
    tf.setFont(new Font("Monospaced", Font.PLAIN, 12));
    tf.setPreferredSize(tf.getPreferredSize());
    tf.setText("");

    // show the field
    JFrame f = new JFrame();
```

```
      f.addWindowListener(new BasicWindowMonitor());
      Container c = f.getContentPane();
      c.setLayout(new FlowLayout());
      c.add(tf);
      f.pack();
      f.setVisible(true);
  }
}
```

Keep this strategy of overriding `PlainDocument.insertString()` in mind whenever you want to apply any type of filter to the input text. Other document types you might want to consider creating include `NumericDocument`, `MoneyDocument`, `UpperCaseDocument`, etc. All of these could be done easily by extending `Plain-Document` and re-implementing `insertString()`.

Document Events

When changes are made to a `Document`, observers of the `Document` are notified using the event types `DocumentEvent` and `UndoableEditEvent`, defined in the `javax.swing.event` package. `UndoableEditEvent` and its associated listener interface were discussed in Chapter 18.

In this section, we'll look at `DocumentEvent` and several related classes, which make up a surprisingly complex[*] and powerful event model. We'll also look at the `DocumentListener` interface used to receive notification of `Document` changes.

The DocumentEvent Interface

A `DocumentEvent` is fired to indicate that some change has been made to a `Document`. It contains information about the area within the `Document` that was modified, along with information about the details of the change.

Unlike most events, `DocumentEvent` is an interface rather than a class. This is done so that an undo-capable class (such as `AbstractDocument`) can create an event implementation that extends a class from the `undo` package and implements this interface. We'll see all the details of how this works over the next few pages. If you're curious, you can peek ahead to Figure 20-10 for a complete diagram of `DocumentEvent` and related classes.

A default implementation of this interface is provided by `Abstract-Document.DefaultDocumentEvent`.

---

[*] Luckily, the complexity is limited to the details of how `AbstractDocument` creates events. If you just want to listen for and interpret `DocumentEvents`, things are pretty straightforward.

Properties

Table 20-19 shows the properties defined by the DocumentEvent interface. The document property specifies the Document object whose change caused this event to be fired. Length and offset define the exact area in which the change took place (the affected characters), relative to the beginning of the document. The type property indicates what type of change this event refers to. This will be one of the following constants from the Document.EventType inner class (described next): INSERT, REMOVE, CHANGE.

Table 20-19. DocumentEvent Properties

Property	Data Type	get	is	set	bound	Default Value
document	Document	•				
length	int	•				
offset	int	•				
type	DocumentEvent.EventType	•				

Change Details

public abstract DocumentEvent.ElementChange getChange(Element elem)

Returns an object describing the Elements added or removed from the specified Element. If no new Elements were added to the specified Element, and no Elements were removed from it, this method returns null. The ElementChange interface is described below.

The DocumentEvent.EventType Class

This inner class is simply a type-safe enumeration used to define different types of DocumentEvents. It has no public constructors, so the only instances of the class are the three constants listed in Table 20-20.

Table 20-20. DocumentEvent.EventType Constants

Constant	Type	Description
INSERT	DocumentEvent.EventType	Content has been inserted
REMOVE	DocumentEvent.EventType	Content has been removed
CHANGE	DocumentEvent.EventType	Attributes have changed

Method

public String toString()

Returns the type as a string: "INSERT", "REMOVE", or "CHANGE".

The DocumentEvent.ElementChange Interface

This inner-interface of DocumentEvent defines a set of Element changes made to a single parent Element. The changes may include both additions to and deletions from the parent. An ElementChange is generated only when entire Elements are added to or removed from a parent element. Merely adding content to an Element does not result in an ElementChange.

A single ElementChange contains a set of children that have been added to an Element and another set of children that have been removed from it. If neither set is empty, the ElementChange refers to a change in which one set of elements replaced another.

Properties

Table 20-21 shows the properties defined by the DocumentEvent.ElementChange interface. The childrenAdded and childrenRemoved properties indicate the set of child Elements that were added to or removed from the Element stored by the element property. The array contents are ordered based on the order the Elements appear (or used to appear) within their parent Element. The index property indicates where, within the parent Element (element), the children were added or removed. This value is the index of a child element, not a document character offset. If childrenAdded is empty, the index indicates the location of the first element removed. If childrenRemoved is empty or if neither array is empty, index indicates the location of the first added element.

Table 20-21. DocumentEvent.ElementChange Properties

Property	Data Type	get	is	set	bound	Default Value
childrenAdded	Element[]	•				
childrenRemoved	Element[]	•				
element	Element	•				
index	int	•				

Figure 20-8 shows two instance diagrams of a sample Element (*BranchQ*) before and after a change is made to it. The second diagram shows the ElementChange and the Elements it would refer to if leaf elements *B* and *C* were removed from *BranchQ* and replaced by *X*, *Y*, and *Z*.

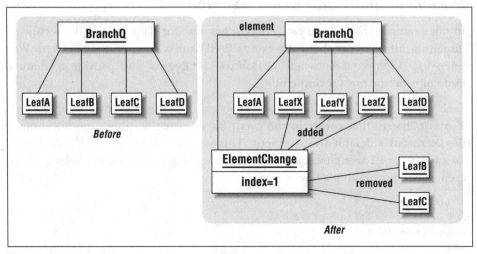

Figure 20-8. ElementChange example

The DocumentListener Interface

This is the interface implemented by an observer of a Document wishing to receive notification of changes to the Document via DocumentEvents. Its three methods correspond to the three types of events, as defined in DocumentEvent.Event-Type.

Methods

public abstract void changedUpdate(DocumentEvent e)
> Indicates that an attribute or set of attributes in the Document has changed. The range given in the event reflects the offset and length of the affected text.

public abstract void insertUpdate(DocumentEvent e)
> Indicates that text has been inserted into the Document. The range given in the event reflects the offset and length of the new text.

public abstract void removeUpdate(DocumentEvent e)
> Indicates that text has been removed from the Document. The range given by the event reflects the offset and length of the removed text, relative to the state of the Document before the text was removed. For example, if the word "blind" was removed from "three blind mice", the offset in the Document-Event would be 6 and the length would be 5.

Document and Undo Event Example

In this example, we'll create two JTextAreas, one for data entry and a second for displaying information about the events fired as text is entered or deleted. We'll listen for DocumentEvents and UndoableEditEvents and provide a menu to undo or redo the most recent edit.

Each time we print information about a DocumentEvent, we'll ask the ElementChange that comes in the event for information about modifications to the Document's default root element. This strategy works since PlainDocument uses a very flat Element tree, in which the root element holds a single level of children, each representing a line of text.

```java
// Listen.java
//
import javax.swing.*;
import javax.swing.text.*;
import javax.swing.undo.*;
import javax.swing.event.*;
import java.awt.*;
import java.awt.event.*;

// Example showing Undo & Document Events from Document
public class Listen extends JFrame
  implements DocumentListener, UndoableEditListener {

  // Set up a little GUI
  public Listen() {

    // TextArea for entering text & generating events
    editor = new JTextArea();
    editor.getDocument().addDocumentListener(this);
    editor.getDocument().addUndoableEditListener(this);

    // TextArea for showing each event as it is fired
    log = new JTextArea();
    log.setEditable(false);

    // Lay out the frame
    JScrollPane scroll1 = new JScrollPane(editor);
    JScrollPane scroll2 = new JScrollPane(log);
    getContentPane().setLayout(new GridLayout(2,1));
    getContentPane().add(scroll1);
    getContentPane().add(scroll2);

    // Add a menu with undo/redo options (just for the most recent edit to keep
    // things simple)
    JMenuBar bar = new JMenuBar();
    JMenu menu = new JMenu("Edit");
```

```
    undoItem = new JMenuItem("Undo");
    redoItem = new JMenuItem("Redo");
    bar.add(menu);
    menu.add(undoItem);
    menu.add(redoItem);
    updateMenu();

    // Call edit.undo() and update menu when undo is selected
    undoItem.addActionListener(new ActionListener() {
      public void actionPerformed(ActionEvent ev) {
        edit.undo();
        updateMenu();
      }
    });

    // Call edit.redo() and update menu when redo is selected
    redoItem.addActionListener(new ActionListener() {
      public void actionPerformed(ActionEvent ev) {
        edit.redo();
        updateMenu();
      }
    });
    setJMenuBar(bar);
    setSize(410, 400);
  }

  // Dump a DocumentEvent to the logging text area
  protected void showDocEvent(DocumentEvent ev) {
    StringBuffer buf = new StringBuffer(100);
    buf.append(ev.getType());
    buf.append(" offset:");
    buf.append(ev.getOffset());
    buf.append(" length:");
    buf.append(ev.getLength());

    // Show any ElementChanges that were provided
    Element root = editor.getDocument().getDefaultRootElement();
    DocumentEvent.ElementChange chg = ev.getChange(root);
    if (chg == null) {
      buf.append(" <NO ELEMENT CHANGES>");
    }
    else {
      buf.append(" Changes (Index/Add/Rem):");
      buf.append(chg.getIndex());
      buf.append("/");
      buf.append(chg.getChildrenAdded().length);
      buf.append("/");
      buf.append(chg.getChildrenRemoved().length);
    }
```

```java
    buf.append("\n");
    log.append(buf.toString());
  }

  // Implement the DocumentListener interface using our showDocEvent() method
  public void changedUpdate(DocumentEvent ev) {
    showDocEvent(ev);
  }

  public void insertUpdate(DocumentEvent ev) {
    showDocEvent(ev);
  }

  public void removeUpdate(DocumentEvent ev) {
    showDocEvent(ev);
  }

  // Show the UndoableEdits as they are fired. Also, update the menu.
  public void undoableEditHappened(UndoableEditEvent ev) {
    StringBuffer buf = new StringBuffer(100);
    edit = ev.getEdit();
    buf.append("UndoableEdit:");
    buf.append(edit.getPresentationName());
    buf.append("\n");
    log.append(buf.toString());
    updateMenu();
  }

  // Set menu choices based on state of the current edit.
  protected void updateMenu() {
    if (edit != null) {
      undoItem.setEnabled(edit.canUndo());
      redoItem.setEnabled(edit.canRedo());
      undoItem.setText(edit.getUndoPresentationName());
      redoItem.setText(edit.getRedoPresentationName());
    }
    else {
      undoItem.setEnabled(false);
      redoItem.setEnabled(false);
      undoItem.setText("Undo");
      redoItem.setText("Redo");
    }
  }

  private UndoableEdit edit;
  private JTextArea editor;
  private JTextArea log;
  private JMenuItem undoItem;
  private JMenuItem redoItem;
```

```
  // Test this class
  public static void main(String[] args) {
    JFrame f = new Listen();
    f.addWindowListener(new BasicWindowMonitor());
    f.setVisible(true);
  }
}
```

Let's walk through the code a little bit.

In the constructor, we just create the two text areas. Nothing fancy here. Next, we define a simple menu with undo and redo options. We then add listeners to these two menu items. Notice how easy it is to undo or redo a change. All we do is call the undo() or redo() method on the current UndoableEdit (which was set in the undoableEditHappened() method, described later). We then make a local call to updateMenu() so that we have the correct option enabled.

After the constructor is a method called showDocEvent(). This is just a diagnostic method that dumps an event into the second text area.

The next three methods implement the DocumentListener interface by calling showDocEvent() each time an event is received.

The next method, UndoableEditHappened(), implements the Undoable-EditListener interface. Here, we cache the UndoableEdit (so our undo and redo menu items can use it) and dump some information about the event to the log.

Finally, we define a method called updateMenu() which is used to enable or disable the undo and redo menu items according to the state of the current undoable edit.

The first thing you'll notice if you run this program is that a *lot* of events get generated. Each time a character is added or removed, we receive both a DocumentEvent and an UndoableEditEvent.

Another point of interest are the changes made when you press ENTER. Since the PlainDocument used by the JTextArea stores each line of text in a separate Element, you might expect the log window to show that a single Element was added to hold the newline. What actually happens is that the first Element is removed and replaced with two new Elements. Furthermore, when you type the first new character of the next line, the two Elements are *again* removed and replaced by two new ones. Figure 20-9 shows the display after several characters have been entered, including a newline.

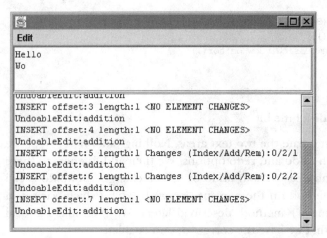

Figure 20-9. Logging DocumentEvents and UndoableEditEvents from a JTextArea

Advanced AbstractDocument
Event Model

The classes and interfaces we've covered so far (DocumentEvent, EventType, EventChange, and DocumentEventListener) are all you need to understand if you just want to receive and interpret DocumentEvents via a DocumentListener. In the next few pages, we'll cover two additional classes used by AbstractDocument and its subclasses (and subclasses you might create yourself). If you're interested in the details of how AbstractDocument actually manages undoable changes, read on. If not, you can safely skip ahead to the next chapter.

Figure 20-10 is a class diagram showing the classes and interfaces that make up the document event model. It includes the related classes and interfaces from the undo package. As we've already discussed, a DocumentEvent is characterized by its EventType and is made up of ElementChange objects. Each ElementChange describes changes made to some Element. These changes are made up of a set of Elements added to the changed Element and a set of Elements removed from it.

The rest of this diagram shows how AbstractDocument.DefaultDocumentEvent and AbstractDocument.ElementEdit implement the DocumentEvent and AbstractDocument.ElementChange interfaces, while extending classes from the undo package to provide events for both DocumentListeners and UndoableEditListeners. We'll get into the details of these classes in the next two sections.

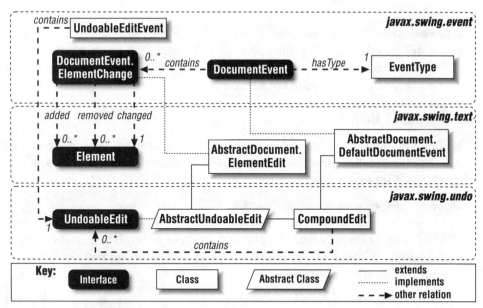

Figure 20-10. DocumentEvent class diagram

The AbstractDocument.ElementEdit Class

This static inner class is an extension of AbstractUndoableEdit that also implements the DocumentEvent.ElementChange interface described earlier. It is used by PlainDocument and DefaultStyledDocument to allow changes made to the Element hierarchy to be tracked and undone using a single object.

Properties

The AbstractDocument.ElementEdit class defines the property values shown in Table 20-22. These properties are defined in the DocumentEvent.Element-Change interface. Their values are specified in the constructor. None of the properties defined in AbstractUndoableEdit is explicitly modified in this class.

Table 20-22. AbstractDocument.ElementEdit Properties

Property	Data Type	get	is	set	bound	Default Value
childrenAdded*	Element[]	•				From constructor
childrenRemoved*	Element[]	•				From constructor
element*	Element	•				From constructor
index*	int	•				From constructor

See also properties from the AbstractUndoableEdit class (Table 18-2).

Constructor

public ElementEdit(Element e, int index, Element[] removed, Element[] added)

Creates an edit reflecting the specified changes to the given `Element`. The `index` parameter refers to the child element at which the change begins, and the `Element` arrays indicate the `Element`s removed and added to e.

UndoableEdit Methods

The following methods from the `UndoableEdit` interface are overridden in this class. They first call their superclass methods to ensure that the edit is in the correct state for the requested action.

public void redo() throws CannotRedoException

Redoes the change by replacing the removed children with the added children using `BranchElement.replace()`. If there were no removed children, the added children are re-inserted. If there were no added children, the removed children are re-removed.

public void undo() throws CannotUndoException

Undoes the change by replacing the added children with the removed children using `BranchElement.replace()`. If there were no added children, the removed children are inserted. If there were no removed children, the added children are removed.

The AbstractDocument.DefaultDocumentEvent Class

`AbstractDocument.DefaultDocumentEvent` is an implementation of the `DocumentEvent` interface, which extends `CompoundEdit` (see Chapter 18) to allow multiple undoable changes to be reflected in a single event.

There are two particularly interesting results of having this class both extend `CompoundEdit` and implement `DocumentEvent`. First, `ElementEdit`s can be added to it (via `CompoundEdit`'s `addEdit()` method). These edits can then serve as both `UndoableEdit`s (since `ElementEdit` extends `AbstractUndoableEdit`) and `ElementChange`s (since `ElementEdit` implements `ElementChange`). Second, a single `DefaultDocumentEvent` can be fired as a `DocumentEvent` and used as the `UnodableEdit` argument of the `UndoableEditEvent` constructor. The code within the `Document` implementation would look something like this:[*]

```
DefaultDocumentEvent event = new DefaultDocumentEvent
    (0, 10, DocumentEvent.EventType.INSERT);
UndoableEdit edit = new MyEdit(); // some edit implementation
```

---

[*] This is only showing the multiple uses of a `DefaultDocumentEvent`. In a real implementation, you'd have to add `ElementEdit`s to the event to reflect the changes that were made.

```
event.addEdit(edit);
event.end();
fireInsertUpdate(event);
UndoableEditEvent undo = new UndoableEditEvent(this, event);
fireUndoableEditUpdate(undo);
```

Here, we create an event indicating that an insertion of 10 characters has taken place. We then create some UndoableEdit object capable of undoing our change and add it to the event (which we can do because DefaultDocumentEvent extends CompoundEdit). We fire the event to our DocumentListeners and then use the event (again, since it's also an edit) to create an UndoableEditEvent, which we fire to our UndoableEditListeners. Both PlainDocument and DefaultStyledDocument use a strategy similar to this.

Properties

AbstractDocument.DefaultDocumentEvent defines the properties and default values shown in Table 20-23. For descriptions of these properties, see the earlier discussion of DocumentEvent (above) and UndoableEdit (Chapter 18). The document property comes from the enclosing instance, while the length, offset and type properties are all set in the constructor. The presentationName is set to addition, deletion, or style change depending on the value of the type property. RedoPresentationName and undoPresentationName are created by prepending Redo or Undo, respectively, to the presentationName.

Table 20-23. AbstractDocument.DefaultDocumentEvent Properties

Property	Data Type	get	is	set	bound	Default Value
document*	Document	•				from enclosing instance
length*	int	•				from constructor
offset*	int	•				from constructor
presentationName*	String	•				based on type
redoPresentationName*	String	•				"Redo" + presentationName
significant*	boolean		•			true
type*	Document-Event.EventType	•				from constructor
undoPresentationName*	String	•				"Undo" + presentationName

See also properties from the CompoundEdit class (Table 18-4).

Constructor

public DefaultDocumentEvent(int offs, int len, DocumentEvent.EventType type)
> Creates an event reflecting a change to the indicated portion of the document. Note that instances of this class must be associated with an enclosing `AbstractDocument` instance.

UndoableEdit Methods

The following methods override the `UndoableEdit` methods defined in `CompoundEdit`:

public boolean addEdit(UndoableEdit anEdit)
> Uses `super.addEdit()` to add the new edit. Before making this call, it checks to see if there are now more than ten edits stored in this object. If so, it creates a `Hashtable` to provide quicker access to all edits which implement `DocumentEvent.ElementChange`. This is done to speed up the `getChange()` method (see below).

public void redo() throws CannotRedoException
> Obtains a write lock on the document, then calls `super.redo()` and refires this event (using the appropriate "fire" method on `AbstractDocument`) to indicate another `Document` change. It does not fire a new `Undoable-EditEvent`. Before exiting, the write lock is released.

public void undo() throws CannotUndoException
> Obtains a write lock on the document, then calls `super.undo()` and refires this event (using one of the "fire" methods of `AbstractDocument`) to indicate another `Document` change.[*] It does not fire a new `UndoableEditEvent`. Before exiting, the write lock is released.

DocumentEvent Method

The following method (in addition to the accessors for the `DocumentEvent` properties) comes from the `DocumentEvent` interface:

public DocumentEvent.ElementChange getChange(Element elem)
> Returns the `ElementChange` associated with the input `Element`. If there have been no `Elements` added or removed from the specified `Element`, this will return `null`. Note that this method is optimized by using a `Hashtable` (see the discussion of `addEdit()`, above) to map `Elements` to `ElementChanges` when the number of edits exceeds ten.

---

[*] One potentially confusing point here is that when refiring the event, the EventType is not changed. So when you insert text, you get an event of type INSERT. If you then undo this insertion, you again get an event of type INSERT, even though text is now being removed from the Document, not added.

Other Method

public String toString()

Returns a string representation of the event which consists of a list of its `UndoableEdits`.

21

Styled Documents and JTextPane

In the previous chapter, we introduced the classes and interfaces used to represent textual models in Swing. In this chapter, we'll see how the Swing text model is extended to provide a simple mechanism for working with text "styles," greatly simplifying the process of creating a powerful text editor. Once we've defined these extensions to the text model, we'll look at the JTextPane class and see how it takes advantage of this model. At the end of the chapter, we'll look at a detailed example of a simple editor that shows the power of styles.

Style

If you've ever worked with a reasonably powerful word processor, you're probably already familiar with the concept of a style. A style is basically just a collection of attributes that describes how something should look. For example, as I sit here writing this book, the text I'm entering into my word processor looks a certain way because of the paragraph style (*Body*) and character style (*Default*) I have selected. To produce the heading just before this paragraph, I could have typed "Style," selected the text, changed the font to Bodoni BT, changed the font size to 18, and toggled on the italics button. Thankfully (believe me!), I didn't have to do all that. All I had to do was click somewhere within the text and use a menu to select the *HeadA* style, which encapsulates all of the properties described above (not to mention more interesting things, like the fact that the next paragraph should be a *Body* paragraph).

Providing this type of functionality in your own programs would be a lot of work if you had to do it all yourself. Fortunately, you don't. The Swing text package builds on the document model described in the last chapter to provide a powerful range of support for working with text styles. The new classes and interfaces involved in providing style capabilities (along with some of the ones from the last chapter that are directly related) are shown in Figure 21-1.

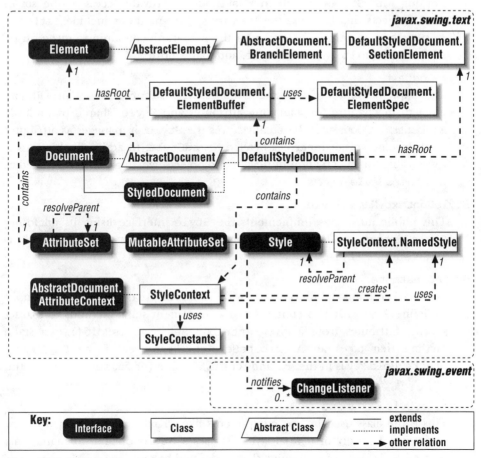

Figure 21-1. Style class diagram

Over the next few pages, we'll give a brief overview of the new classes and interfaces shown in this diagram, as well as an explanation of the relationships between them.

Style

This interface, an extension of MutableAttributeSet, adds two things not provided by its super-interface. The first is a name—every Style may (optionally) be given a name. The second is the ability to add and remove ChangeListeners. These listeners should be notified when changes are made to the definition of a Style.

StyledDocument

This interface, an extension of Document, adds a variety of methods for working with Styles and defines methods to provide access to the set of Style objects that describe the Document. New methods include setLogicalStyle(), to define the Style for the paragraph containing a given offset, addStyle(), to create a new Style, and many more.

StyleContext

This implementation of AbstractDocument.AttributeContext provides an efficient mechanism for managing attributes and Styles shared by multiple Elements or Documents. It actually stores the Styles it manages as attributes in an instance of an inner class called NamedStyle. In addition, this class is responsible for the creation of new Style objects, which are always created as new NamedStyle objects.

StyleContext.NamedStyle

This public inner class implements the Style interface using its enclosing StyleContext for efficient management of attributes. Its resolving parent is always another Style.

StyleConstants

This class contains definitions for a wide variety of pre-defined attributes used to define Styles. It also contains many convenient static methods to extract specific attributes from a given AttributeSet, e.g., isBold() is a static method that takes an AttributeSet, checks to see if the StyleConstants.Bold key is in the set, and returns its value (or false if it's not in the set).

DefaultStyledDocument

This is the class used by text components like JTextPane that want to show text using a variety of textual styles. It uses a StyleContext to manage its Styles. It also uses several inner classes, defined below.

DefaultStyledDocument.ElementBuffer

This public inner class is used to manage changes to the Element structure of a DefaultStyledDocument.

DefaultStyledDocument.ElementSpec

This public inner class is used to provide a specification of an Element to be created. ElementSpecs are created by DefaultStyledDocument (e.g., in insertUpdate()) and passed to an ElementBuffer, which uses them to determine how the Element structure needs to be updated.[*]

---

[*] Note that a containment relation should be shown from DefaultStyledDocument.ElementSpec to AttributeSet (one of the things that makes up an ElementSpec is a set of attributes), but was omitted to keep the diagram as readable as possible.

`DefaultStyledDocument.SectionElement`
This protected inner class is an extension of `AbstractDocument.BranchElement`, used to provide an additional level of nesting in the `DefaultStyledDocument` Element structure. An instance of this class serves as the document's root `Element`.

In the next part of this chapter, we'll take a closer look at each of these new classes and interfaces. Once they've all been covered, we'll look at a detailed example that shows how to use `Style`s to create a `Style`-based text editor.

The Style Interface

The `Style` interface is a simple extension of `MutableAttributeSet`, which allows a set of attributes to be given a name. This just defines a common identifier for the `Style`, allowing it to be easily referenced (e.g., by `StyledDocument`'s `getStyle()` method, which takes a single `String` and returns the matching `Style`). This name is also typically used to populate a menu in the user interface, allowing the user to select a named `Style` for some portion of text.

In addition, `Style` adds support for registering change listeners to be notified whenever the attributes that define a `Style` are modified.

Property

Table 21-1 shows the property defined by the `Style` interface. The only property added by `Style` is the name property. It is valid for a `Style` to be unnamed, in which case the accessor should simply return `null`.

Table 21-1. Style Property

Property	Data Type	get	is	set	bound	Default Value
name	String	•				

See also properties from the MutableAttributeSet interface (Table 20-9).

Events

When a change is made to the attributes that make up a `Style`, listeners registered for change events will be notified. The style interface specifies the following standard methods for registering change listeners:

public void addChangeListener(ChangeListener l)
public void removeChangeListener(ChangeListener l)

The StyleConstants Class

Many of the attributes used to describe text are very common. If each program had to choose a key (i.e., a name or symbolic constant) to represent each of these attributes, there would be little hope for consistency. In defining a key for the "bold" attribute, one developer might use the String "bold", another might use the String "BoldText", and yet another might use an Integer object that maps to some globally defined constant.

For many common attributes, this confusion can be avoided by using the Style-Constants class. This class defines a large number of type-safe constant values, intended to be used as attribute keys. This allows us to refer to the "bold" attribute as simply StyleConstants.Bold.

In addition to defining constants, StyleConstants also defines static methods that allow you to set the value for certain attributes. Using these methods allows you to replace a call like this:

```
myMutableAttrSet.addAttribute(StyleConstants.Bold, new Boolean(true));
```

with a call like this:

```
StyleConstants.setBold(myMutableAttrSet, true);
```

StyleConstants Inner Classes

StyleConstants groups its constants using the four inner classes described next. Note the different (empty) interfaces from AttributeSet implemented by each class. These allow you to determine the type of an attribute using the instanceof operator. For example:

```
if (someAttr instanceof AttributeSet.ParagraphAttribute)
    doSomething();
```

Here are the definitions of the different inner classes.

public static class CharacterConstants implements AttributeSet.CharacterAttribute
Defines constants for attributes typically applied to character content, including those defined in FontConstants and ColorConstants.

public static class ColorConstants
implements AttributeSet.ColorAttribute, AttributeSet.CharacterAttribute
Defines constants for foreground and background color.

public static class FontConstants
implements AttributeSet.FontAttribute, AttributeSet.CharacterAttribute
Defines constants related to font definition.

public static class ParagraphConstants implements AttributeSet.ParagraphAttribute
>   Defines constants used to describe an entire paragraph, such as alignment and spacing.

You don't need to worry about these inner classes, because all of the constants defined in them are also defined in the outer class, `StyleConstants`. This means that, for example, all of the following are valid (and equivalent):

```
StyleConstants.FontSize
StyleConstants.CharacterConstants.Size
StyleConstants.FontConstants.Size
```

Consistently using the first of these formats will make your code simpler to understand.

Attribute Constants

Table 21-2 shows all of the attribute constants defined by `StyleConstants`. Regardless of their actual type, which is always one of the `StyleConstants` inner classes, all of these constants are defined as type `Object`. The *Value Type* column indicates the type of *value* that should be associated with each attribute key, and the *Default* column shows the value that will be returned by the static accessor methods (described later) if the attribute is not found in a set.[*]

Table 21-2. StyleConstants Attribute Name Constants[a]

Constant	Category	Value Type	Default	Description
Alignment	Paragraph	Integer	ALIGN_LEFT	Alignment for a paragraph (see Table 21-4 for valid values)
Background	Char, Color	Color	Color.black	Background color
BidiLevel	Character	Integer	0	Bidirectional level according to the Unicode bidi algorithm
Bold	Char, Font	Boolean	false	Bold text
Component-Attribute[b]	Character	Component	null	Allows an Element to represent a Component, instead of text
FirstLineIndent	Paragraph	Float	0	Number of points to indent first line

---

[*] This is fairly important. When you create a new `JTextPane`, for example, it is these default values that define what the text will look like if you don't specify attributes for the text. This is because a default `Style` is in use that contains no attributes, so these defaults will be returned when the `Style` is examined using the static `StyleConstants` methods.

Table 21-2. StyleConstants Attribute Name Constants[a] (continued)

Constant	Category	Value Type	Default	Description
FontFamily	Char, Font	String	"Mono-spaced"	Name of the font family
FontSize	Char, Font	Integer	12	Size of the font
Foreground	Char, Color	Color	Color.black	Foreground color
IconAttribute	Character	Icon	null	Used to allow an Element to represent a Icon, instead of text
Italic	Char, Font	Boolean	false	Italic text
LeftIndent	Paragraph	Float	0	Number of points to indent from the left margin
LineSpacing	Paragraph	Float	0	Number of points between lines
Orientation[c]	Paragraph	undefined	undefined	Orientation of the paragraph
RightIndent	Paragraph	Float	0	Number of points to indent from the right margin
SpaceAbove	Paragraph	Float	0	Number of points above each line
SpaceBelow	Paragraph	Float	0	Number of points below each line
TabSet	Paragraph	TabSet[d]	null	Set of TabStops
Underline	Character	Boolean	false	Underlined text

[a] The attribute names FontFamily and FontSize are shortened to Family and Size within the Font-Constants inner class. All other attribute names are the same within their respective inner classes.
[b] The ComponentAttribute and IconAttribute constants can be used to indicate that an element should be displayed as a component or icon rather than as text. For more information, see the example later in the chapter. There is no additional significance to the "Attribute" suffix of these constants.
[c] As of JDK 1.2 beta 4, no static convenience methods are defined for this constant.
[d] The TabSet and TabStop classes are described after this section.

Other Attribute Constants

Table 21-3 shows constants used to store special information in an Attri-buteSet. The first constant shown here, ComposedTextAttribute, is intended to be used to hold an AttributedString (a new JDK 1.2 class defined in the java.text package). This constant is currently unused. The last two constants in the table are used as attribute keys to define the set's name (used for named Styles) and the set's resolving parent.

Table 21-3. StyleConstants Special Attribute Key Constants

Name	Data Type	Value Type	Description
ComposedTextAttribute	Object	java.text.At- tributedString	An attributed string describing the set's attributes (JDK 1.2 only)
NameAttribute	Object	String	The name of the attribute set
ResolveAttribute	Object	AttributeSet	Attribute set's resolving parent

Alignment Value Constants

StyleConstants also defines four attribute values for the Alignment attribute, shown in Table 21-4.

Table 21-4. StyleConstants.Alignment Attribute Value Constants

Name	Data Type	Description
ALIGN_CENTER	int	Align text to the center with equal whitespace on the left and right.
ALIGN_JUSTIFIED	int	Align text such that all whitespace is spread out, leaving text aligned on both the left and right margins. The last line should have left alignment.
ALIGN_LEFT	int	Align text to the left with whitespace on the right.
ALIGN_RIGHT	int	Align text to the right with whitespace on the left.

Element Name Constants

AbstractDocument defines a constant called ElementNameAttribute, used as a key to store the name of an Element in its AttributeSet (see Table 21-5). StyleConstants defines two possible values for this attribute, used when the Element does not contain textual data. This attribute is not limited to these two values; these are just constants for special case Element names.

Table 21-5. AbstractDocument.ElementNameAttribute Value Constants

Name	Data Type	Description
ComponentElementName	String	Used when the Element contains a Component instead of text.
IconElementName	String	Used when the Element contains an Icon instead of text.

Lookup and Update Methods

StyleConstants defines static methods to access and set each of the attributes for which it defines constant keys. Each accessor method takes an AttributeSet, while the update methods require a `MutableAttributeSet` as input. These methods handle the conversions between Java primitive types and the wrapper classes `Float`, `Integer`, and `Boolean` (remember, all attribute values are of type `Object`, so primitive attribute values must be wrapped in objects), so that all interfaces are able to use the primitive types.

public static int getAlignment(AttributeSet a)
public static Color getBackground(AttributeSet a)
public static int getBidiLevel(AttribuetSet a)
public static boolean isBold(AttributeSet a)
public static Component getComponent(AttributeSet a)
public static float getFirstLineIndent(AttributeSet a)
public static String getFontFamily(AttributeSet a)
public static int getFontSize(AttributeSet a)
public static Color getForeground(AttributeSet a)
public static Icon getIcon(AttributeSet a)
public static boolean isItalic(AttributeSet a)
public static float getLeftIndent(AttributeSet a)
public static float getLineSpacing(AttributeSet a)
public static float getRightIndent(AttributeSet a)
public static float getSpaceAbove(AttributeSet a)
public static float getSpaceBelow(AttributeSet a)
public static TabSet getTabSet(AttributeSet a)
public static boolean isUnderline(AttributeSet a)

These methods return the value found in the given set, if there is one. If the key is not found, the default values shown in Table 21-2 are returned.

public static void setAlignment(MutableAttributeSet a, int align)
public static void setBackground(MutableAttributeSet a, Color bg)
public static void setBidiLevel(MutableAttributeSet a, int 0)
public static void setBold(MutableAttributeSet a, boolean b)
public static void setFirstLineIndent(MutableAttributeSet a, float i)
public static void setFontFamily(MutableAttributeSet a, String fam)
public static void setFontSize(MutableAttributeSet a, int s)
public static void setForeground(MutableAttributeSet a, Color fg)
public static void setItalic(MutableAttributeSet a, boolean b)
public static void setLeftIndent(MutableAttributeSet a, float i)
public static void setLineSpacing(MutableAttributeSet a, float i)
public static void setRightIndent(MutableAttributeSet a, float i)
public static void setSpaceAbove(MutableAttributeSet a, float i)
public static void setSpaceBelow(MutableAttributeSet a, float i)

public static void setTabSet(MutableAttributeSet a, TabSet tabs)
public static void setUnderline(MutableAttributeSet a, boolean b)

These methods add the appropriate attribute to the given set, replacing the existing value if there is one.

The next two methods actually set two properties. In addition to setting `ComponentAttribute` or `IconAttribute`, they also set the `AbstractDocument.ElementNameAttribute`. The values used for this property were shown back in Table 21-5.

public static void setComponent(MutableAttributeSet a, Component c)
public static void setIcon(MutableAttributeSet a, Icon c)

The TabStop Class

In the last section, we came across `TabSet` and `TabStop`. Now, we'll take quick detour from our discussion of style to examine them. `TabStop`, as you might guess, is used to describe a tab position. This information is used by the text view classes to correctly handle the display of tabs encountered in the document model.

Properties

The `TabStop` class defines the properties listed in Table 21-6. The `alignment` property specifies how the text following a tab should be positioned relative to the tab position. The legal values for this property are shown in Table 21-7. The `leader` property describes what should be displayed leading up to the tab. Legal values for this property are shown in Table 21-8. Currently, none of the Swing text views use the `leader` property. The `position` property indicates where the tab should appear (in pixels).

Table 21-6. TabStop Properties

Property	Data Type	get	is	set	bound	Default Value
alignment	int	•				ALIGN_LEFT
leader	int	•				LEAD_NONE
position	float	•				from constructor

Alignment Constants

Table 21-7 shows the constants used to enumerate the possible ways that text following a tab can be aligned.

Table 21-7. TabStop Alignment Constants

Name	Data Type	Description
ALIGN_BAR	int	Text after the tab should start at the tab position (currently the same as ALIGN_LEFT)
ALIGN_CENTER	int	Text after the tab should be centered over the tab's position
ALIGN_DECIMAL	int	Text after the tab should be aligned so that the next decimal, tab, or newline is located at the tab position
ALIGN_LEFT	int	Text after the tab should start at the tab position
ALIGN_RIGHT	int	Text after the tab should end at the tab position

Here's an example that shows the effect of each of these alignment values:

```java
// TabStopExample.java
//
import javax.swing.text.*;
import javax.swing.*;

// Show how the different TabStop alignment values work.
public class TabStopExample {
  public static void main(String[] args) {
    // Create TabStops with the different alignments

    TabStop bar = new TabStop(100, TabStop.ALIGN_BAR, TabStop.LEAD_NONE);
    TabStop center = new TabStop(100, TabStop.ALIGN_CENTER, TabStop.LEAD_NONE);
    TabStop decimal= new TabStop(100, TabStop.ALIGN_DECIMAL, TabStop.LEAD_NONE);
    TabStop left = new TabStop(100, TabStop.ALIGN_LEFT, TabStop.LEAD_NONE);
    TabStop right = new TabStop(100, TabStop.ALIGN_RIGHT, TabStop.LEAD_NONE);

    // Create a JTextPane to show tabs in
    JTextPane tp = new JTextPane();
    StyledDocument doc = tp.getStyledDocument();
    SimpleAttributeSet a = new SimpleAttributeSet();

    TabSet tabs;
    int offset;

    // Insert text with each TabStop value
    try {
      offset = doc.getLength();
      doc.insertString(doc.getLength(), "\tBar\n", null);
      tabs = new TabSet(new TabStop[] {bar});
      StyleConstants.setTabSet(a, tabs);
      doc.setParagraphAttributes(offset, 1, a, false);

      offset = doc.getLength();
      doc.insertString(offset, "\tCentered\n", null);
```

```
      tabs = new TabSet(new TabStop[] {center});
      StyleConstants.setTabSet(a, tabs);
      doc.setParagraphAttributes(offset, 1, a, false);

      offset = doc.getLength();
      doc.insertString(doc.getLength(), "\t1234.99\n", null);
      tabs = new TabSet(new TabStop[] {decimal});
      StyleConstants.setTabSet(a, tabs);
      doc.setParagraphAttributes(offset, 1, a, false);

      offset = doc.getLength();
      doc.insertString(doc.getLength(), "\tLeft\n", null);
      tabs = new TabSet(new TabStop[] {left});
      StyleConstants.setTabSet(a, tabs);
      doc.setParagraphAttributes(offset, 1, a, false);

      offset = doc.getLength();
      doc.insertString(doc.getLength(), "\tRight\n", null);
      tabs = new TabSet(new TabStop[] {right});
      StyleConstants.setTabSet(a, tabs);
      doc.setParagraphAttributes(offset, 1, a, false);
    }
    catch (BadLocationException ex) {}

    // Display it
    JFrame f = new JFrame();
    f.addWindowListener(new BasicWindowMonitor());
    f.setSize(200, 110);
    f.setContentPane(tp);
    f.setVisible(true);
  }
}
```

In this example, we simply created five TabStop objects, one with each of the different alignment values. For each TabStop, we added a line of text, starting with a tab ("\t") and set its TabSet (described next) to a set containing the single TabStop. Figure 21-2 shows how these values are displayed.

Leader Constants

Table 21-8 shows constants that enumerate the possible ways the space before a tab should be filled. These constants are legal values for the leader property. Currently, changing this property's value has no effect.

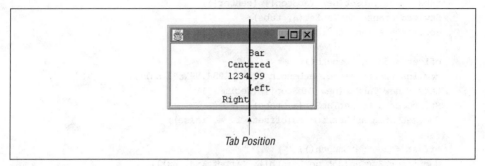

Figure 21-2. TabStop alignment

Table 21-8. TabStop Leading Constants

Constant	Description
LEAD_DOTS	Precede tab with a series of dots
LEAD_EQUALS	Precede tab with a series of equal signs
LEAD_HYPHENS	Precede tab with a series of hyphens
LEAD_NONE	Precede tab with blank space
LEAD_THICKLINE	Precede tab with a thick line
LEAD_UNDERLINE	Precede tab with a thin line

Constructors

public TabStop(float pos)

Creates a TabStop at the specified position, with alignment and leader set to ALIGN_LEFT and LEAD_NONE.

public TabStop(float pos, int align, int leader)

Creates a TabStop at the specified position, with the given alignment and leader values.

Object Methods

The following methods, defined in Object, are implemented in this class:

public boolean equals(Object other)

Returns true if the given object is a TabStop with the same alignment, leader, and position.

public int hashCode()

This method just calls super.hashCode(). Note that this breaks the contract normally defined by this method, which states that objects that are equal (according to equals()) should return the same hashCode. This should be fixed in a future release.

public String toString()
　　Returns a string that describes the values of the object's three properties.

The TabSet Class

It is often useful to define a series of TabStops that should be applied to a given block of text. TabSet allows you to do this, and defines a few convenient methods for looking up the TabStops contained in the set. TabSets are immutable—once the TabStops are defined (in the constructor), they cannot be added or removed.

Properties

The TabSet class defines the properties shown in Table 21-9. The indexed tab property is used to access a given TabStop, while the tabCount property holds the current number of TabStops defined in the set.

Table 21-9. TabSet Properties

Property	Data Type	get	is	set	bound	Default Value
tab (indexed)	TabStop	•				from constructor
tabCount	int	•				from constructor

Constructor

public TabSet(TabStop tabs[])
　　Creates a set containing the given array of TabStops.

Methods

public TabStop getTabAfter(float location)
　　Returns the first TabStop positioned after the given location.

public int getTabIndex(TabStop tab)
　　Returns the index of the given TabStop.

public int getTabIndexAfter(float location)
　　Returns the index of the first TabStop positioned after the input location.

public String toString()
　　Returns a string representation of the TabStops in the set.

The StyleContext Class

Now back to style. StyleContext is a utility class that provides a variety of features used when working with AttributeSets and Styles.

StyleContext implements the AbstractDocument.AttributeContext interface, providing mechanisms for sharing attributes that can greatly reduce the
overhead involved in storing a large number of attributes, possibly spanning
multiple documents. For large documents, a utility like StyleContext can quickly
become critical.

Consider a worst-case scenario in which we have a document containing 1000
characters that alternate between bold and italics (e.g., **abc***de***fg***hij*). Without the
use of a StyleContext, we'd have 1000 AttributeSet objects, each containing
an attribute/value pair. Using a StyleContext would reduce this number to two.
This is clearly not a particularly realistic example, but it serves to illustrate the
point that intelligent management of attributes is a good idea.

In addition to providing an efficient implementation of the AbstractDocu-
ment.AttributeContext interface, StyleContext adds methods used to track a
set of Styles and serves as a factory for new Style objects, using an inner class
called NamedStyle.

A third category of methods defined by StyleContext is methods used to retrieve
Font objects from AttributeSets and manage the Fonts efficiently. The reason
Fonts are given this special treatment is that they are typically stored using four
different attributes (FontSize, FontFamily, Bold, and Italic). This class can be
used to create and manage the actual Font objects generated from these
attributes.

Properties

Table 21-10 shows the properties defined by the StyleContext class. The
emptySet property is initialized as a StyleContext.SmallAttribute (a package
private inner class implementation of AttributeSet) object that contains no
attributes. StyleNames provides access to the names of all Styles created by this
StyleContext. Initially, a single Style named "default" is created. This Style
does not contain any attributes.

Table 21-10. StyleContext Properties

Property	Data Type	get	is	set	bound	Default Value
emptySet*	AttributeSet	•				StyleContext.SmallAttri- buteSet()
styleNames	Enumeration (String)	•				{ "default" }

Events

Whenever a new `Style` is created or an existing `Style` is removed,[*] a `Change-Event` is fired. The following two methods are provided for managing `ChangeListeners`.

public void addChangeListener(ChangeListener l)
public void removeChangeListener(ChangeListener l)

Constants

The `StyleContext` class defines the constant shown in Table 21-11.

Table 21-11. StyleContext Constants

Name	Data Type	Description
DEFAULT_STYLE	String	The name of the default (initially empty) style (`default`)

Constructor

public StyleContext()

Creates a `StyleContext` containing only a default style. The default `Style` has no attributes.

AttributeContext Methods

These methods (along with the accessor for the `emptySet` property) implement the `AbstractDocument.AttributeContext` interface. They can be used to add and remove attributes from `AttributeSets`, allowing equivalent sets to be shared within a document, or across documents sharing the same `StyleContext`.

public synchronized AttributeSet addAttribute(AttributeSet old, Object name, Object value)

Adds an attribute to the given set and returns a new attribute set. For small attribute sets, this implementation always returns a different object than the original one. Once the size of the set reaches a threshold (more than 9 attributes, by default), this method returns the original set (if it is mutable) with the specified attribute added. If the original set is immutable, a new mutable set (a `SimpleAttributeSet`) is returned.

---

[*] Note that to be notified of changes to the attributes within a `Style`, you must add a listener to the `Style` itself, not the `StyleContext`.

public synchronized AttributeSet addAttributes(AttributeSet old, AttributeSet attr)
> Adds the second set of attributes to the first and returns a new set. The same rules about returning new sets or reusing the original set apply, as for the previous method.

public synchronized AttributeSet removeAttribute(AttributeSet old, Object name)
> Removes the specified attribute and returns a new set.

public synchronized AttributeSet removeAttributes(AttributeSet old, AttributeSet attrs)
> Removes the second set of attributes from the first.

public synchronized AttributeSet removeAttributes(AttributeSet old, Enumeration names)
> Removes the specified attributes from the given set. `names` should contain the keys for the attributes to be removed.

public synchronized void reclaim(AttributeSet a)
> Tells the context that an attribute set is no longer being used, allowing it to be removed from the context.

The following example shows how `StyleContext` can be used to share `AttributeSets`. Whenever the attributes in two small sets are equal, the same set is returned. Once the sets get too large, it is more efficient to use different sets, since matching all attributes in a large set would become too time consuming.

```
// StyleContextExample.java
//
import javax.swing.text.*;
import java.awt.*;

public class StyleContextExample {
  public static void main(String[] args) {
    StyleContext con = new StyleContext();

    // Create two different attribute sets . . . .
    SimpleAttributeSet one = new SimpleAttributeSet();
    SimpleAttributeSet two = new SimpleAttributeSet();
    System.out.println("Refs are initially to the same object? "
    + (one == two)); // prints false

    // Add the same things to each set . . .
    AttributeSet oneA=con.addAttribute(one, StyleConstants.Bold, Boolean.TRUE);
    AttributeSet twoA=con.addAttribute(two, StyleConstants.Bold, Boolean.TRUE);
    System.out.println("Refs are same after setting the "
    + "same value? " + (oneA == twoA)); // prints true

    // Add a 2nd attribute to both sets
    AttributeSet oneB =
      con.addAttribute(oneA, StyleConstants.Foreground, Color.blue);
```

```
    System.out.println("Refs are same after adding a 2nd attribute "
    + "to one set? " + (oneB == twoA)); // prints false (of course)

    AttributeSet twoB = con.addAttribute(twoA,
      StyleConstants.Foreground, Color.blue);
    System.out.println("Refs are same after adding "
    + "2nd attribute to 2nd set? " + (oneB == twoB)); // prints true

    // remove the second attribute so it matches the old set . . .
    AttributeSet oneC = con.removeAttribute(oneB, StyleConstants.Foreground);
    System.out.println("Old set matches new set after removal? "
    + (oneC == oneA)); // prints true

    // show that a threshold for reusing sets is reached . . .
    AttributeSet tooBig1 = new SimpleAttributeSet();
    AttributeSet tooBig2 = new SimpleAttributeSet();
    for (int i=0; i<10; i++) {
      tooBig1 = con.addAttribute(tooBig1, Integer.toString(i), new Integer(i));
      tooBig2 = con.addAttribute(tooBig2, Integer.toString(i), new Integer(i));
      System.out.print(tooBig1 == tooBig2);
      System.out.print(" ");
    }
    System.out.println();
    System.exit(0);
  }
}
```

When executed, this program produces the following output:

```
Refs are initially to the same object? false
Refs are same after setting the same value? true
Refs are same after adding a 2nd attribute to one set? false
Refs are same after adding 2nd attribute to 2nd set? true
Old set matches new set after removal? true
true true true true true true true true true false
```

Initially, we created two new sets and checked to see if they referred to the same object. Since both were created using new(), this of course returns false. Next, we add the same attribute (bold=true) to each set and compare the sets returned from the two addAttribute() calls. The StyleContext has returned the same instance in both cases, so a comparison of oneA and twoA returns true.

We then add a second attribute (foreground=blue) to the first set. The returned value (oneB) is, as you'd expect, not the same as twoA. However, adding the second attribute to the second set as well results in another shared set. We then remove this attribute from the first set and confirm that the returned set is the same set we had before adding the second attribute.

Finally, we show that this set reuse is only done on small sets. In this last portion of the example, we add some toy attributes to two sets and show that the sets returned by addAttribute() match until we exceed the threshold, when we get separate set objects, even though they still contain the same key/value pairs.

A Look Inside

Before looking at the methods related to managing Style objects, we'll take a quick detour to look at how the StyleContext manages Styles internally. Figure 21-3 shows an object structure for a StyleContext containing two Styles, each of which has a single "real" attribute, along with its name and resolving parent, stored as attributes of the Style (if they are non-null). There are two things to note about this structure. First, the StyleContext actually uses a Style object to manage Styles. The attribute keys in this special Style are the names of the *real* Styles. In our example, there are two Styles named *style1* and *style2* (the resolving parent of *style2* is a third Style object that is not shown). The values for these keys are Style objects. Second, the NamedStyle inner class (described in a few pages) actually uses a SimpleAttributeSet to store attribute values.

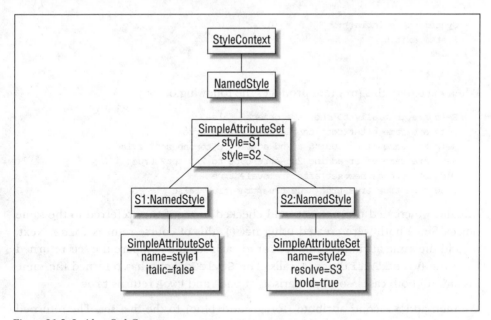

Figure 21-3. Inside a StyleContext

Style Management Methods

The following methods are used to create new Styles and manage them using a StyleContext:

public Style addStyle(String nm, Style parent)

Creates a new, empty Style with the specified name and resolving parent. If no name is specified, the new Style will not be managed by the StyleContext, so the caller is responsible for keeping track of it. The second argument should be null if there is no parent for this Style (a common case). It is helpful to understand that this method returns a new StyleContext.NamedStyle (which implements Style). This inner class uses the attribute management methods defined in the last section to keep track of the attributes that define the Style. This means that attributes directly added to the Style object will automatically be incorporated into the StyleContext, without requiring an explicit call to StyleContent.addAttribute().

public Style getStyle(String nm)

Returns a Style for the given name. If no Style has been added with the specified name, it returns null.

public void removeStyle(String nm)

Removes the named Style from the context.

Font Management Methods

These methods are used to manage Font objects. An Element's Font is not typically stored as a single attribute, so it's nice to have an easy way to obtain the Font and ensure that duplicate Font objects aren't created unnecessarily.

public Font getFont(AttributeSet attr)

Checks for four attributes (Bold, Italic, FontFamily, and FontSize) in the given set, based on the constants defined in the StyleConstants class. From the values of these attributes, it returns a Font using the getFont() method.

public Font getFont(String family, int style, int size)

Searches an internal table for a Font matching the given font family, style, and size. If the Font is found, it is returned. If not, a new Font object is created, added to the table, and returned.

The second parameter should be a logical "or" of the constants Font.PLAIN, Font.BOLD, and Font.ITALIC that defines the desired attributes.

public FontMetrics getFontMetrics(Font f)

Returns the FontMetrics object for the given Font using the default Toolkit. This method simply calls getFontMetrics() on the default Toolkit.

Color Accessor Methods

public Color getForeground(AttributeSet attr)
public Color getBackground(AttributeSet attr)

Call `StyleConstants.getForeground(attr)` and `StyleConstants.get-Background(attr)`. They could be overridden to take other attributes (brighter, darker, etc.) into account.

Serialization Methods

The following static methods define a mechanism for reading and writing an `AttributeSet` to a stream. They are written so that the constant attribute keys defined in `StyleConstants` will be recognized when the stream is read, allowing references to the existing static objects to be used, instead of creating new ones.

If these methods were not used, whenever a serialized `AttributeSet` was read in, new instances of the constants including `StyleConstants.Bold`, `StyleConstants.Foreground`, etc. were created. Each set would have its own "bold" attribute, rather than the shared `StyleConstants.Bold` instance. These methods prevent this from happening by giving special treatment to registered attribute keys.

public static void registerStaticAttributeKey(Object key)

Registers an attribute key as a well-known key. When an attribute with the given key is written to a stream, a special syntax is used so that it can be recognized when it is read back in. All attribute keys defined in `StyleConstants` are registered using this method. If you define additional attribute keys that you want to exist as nonreplicated static objects, you should register them using this method. Such keys must *not* be `Serializable`, as this is how `writeAttributeSet()` determines how to save the keys in a special format.

public static void writeAttributeSet(ObjectOutputStream out, AttributeSet a)
    throws IOException

Writes the contents of the given set to the specified stream. Any non-`Serializable` keys are looked up in the set of keys registered by calls to the `registerStaticAttributeKey()` method. All attribute *values* must be `Serializable`.

public static void readAttributeSet(ObjectInputStream in, MutableAttributeSet a)
    throws ClassNotFoundException, IOException

Reads a set of attributes from the given stream, adding them to the input set. When an attribute key is read that matches a key registered by a call to `registerStaticAttributeKey()`, the registered static key is used directly.

public void readAttributes(ObjectInputStream in, MutableAttributeSet a)
throws ClassNotFoundException, IOException
> Calls the static `readAttributeSet()` method.

public void writeAttributes(ObjectOutputStream out, AttributeSet a) throws IOException
> Calls the static `writeAttributeSet()` method.

Other Methods

public static final StyleContext getDefaultStyleContext()
> Returns a default context that is initially set up with a single (empty) default style. All documents that do not create their own context use the default context. Note that new `AbstractDocuments` use this context by default, but new `DefaultStyledDocuments` only use the default context if it is passed in as a constructor argument (otherwise, a new `StyleContext` is created by the constructor).

public String toString()
> Returns a `String` showing each of the `AttributeSets` cached in the `Style-Context`. Remember that only "small" sets (fewer than 10 attributes, by default) are cached, so the output from this method may not contain all attributes in a given set. Also, remember that `StyleContext` uses the same internal set for its own purposes (tracking the names of added styles), so you will see a line in the output containing the names of the `Styles` (but only the first 9!) added to the context.

protected int getCompressionThreshold()
> Returns the maximum number of attributes that will be stored in an internal (`StyleContext.SmallAttributeSet`) immutable set. Sets larger than this will be stored in `SimpleAttributeSet` objects to provide faster lookups. This default implementation returns 9.

The StyledContext.NamedStyle Class

This public (non-static) inner class is an implementation of the `Style` interface used by `StyleContext`. You should not need to use this class explicitly, but since it is a public class, we'll cover it briefly here. Every time you call `StyleContext.addStyle()`, a new `NamedStyle` is created for you. Since `NamedStyle` is a non-static inner class, the new object can take advantage of the `StyleContext`'s efficient attribute management whenever you change the definition of the `Style`.

`StyleContext` uses an instance of the `AttributeSet` implementation returned by `StyleContext.getEmptySet()` to store the `Style`'s attributes.

Properties

Table 21-12 shows default values defined for the properties inherited by Named-Style. A new `NamedStyle` contains no attributes and has no `name` or `resolveParent`, unless they are specified in the constructor. A new `setName()` method is added that was not available in the `Style` interface. Both the `name` and `resolveParent` properties are stored as attributes of the `Style`, using the `Name-Attribute` and `ResolveAttribute` constants defined in `StyleConstants` as keys.

Table 21-12. StyleContext.NamedStyle Properties

Property	Data Type	get	is	set	bound	Default Value
attributeCount*	int	•				0
attributeNames*	Enumeration	•				empty
name*	String	•		•		null
resolveParent*	AttributeSet	•		•		null

Events

Whenever an attribute is added to or removed from the `Style`, a `ChangeEvent` is fired to any registered listeners. The following standard methods manage the listeners.

public void addChangeListener(ChangeListener l)
public void removeChangeListener(ChangeListener l)
protected void fireStateChanged()

Fields

The following protected fields are defined:

protected transientChangeEvent changeEvent
    This is the single `ChangeEvent` fired each time an attribute is added to or removed from the style.

protected EventListenerList listenerList
    This is the `EventListenerList` used to hold the registered `ChangeListeners`.

Constructors

Since this is a non-static inner class, you can only create a new `NamedStyle` in the context of an enclosing instance. You usually won't need to do this. Instances of this class should be obtained by calling addStyle() on an instance of the Style-Context class.

public NamedStyle(String name, Style parent)

Gets an AttributeSet by calling getEmptySet() and stores the given name and parent as attributes of the Style.

public NamedStyle(Style parent)

Gets an AttributeSet by calling getEmptySet() and stores the given parent as an attribute of the Style.

public NamedStyle()

Gets an AttributeSet by calling getEmptySet(). Nothing is added to the set.

AttributeSet Methods

These methods from the AttributeSet interface are implemented by this class:

public boolean containsAttribute(Object name, Object value)
public boolean containsAttributes(AttributeSet attributes)
public Object getAttribute(Object attrName)
public boolean isDefined(Object attrName)
public boolean isEqual(AttributeSet attr)

All of these methods, as well as the property accessor methods, just delegate to the AttributeSet contained by the NamedStyle.

public AttributeSet copyAttributes()

Creates a new NamedStyle and sets its AttributeSet to the result of a call to copyAttributes() on the contained set.

MutableAttributeSet Methods

The following methods from the MutableAttributeSet interface are implemented by this class:

public void addAttribute(Object name, Object value)
public void addAttributes(AttributeSet attributes)
public void removeAttribute(Object name)
public void removeAttributes(Enumeration names)

These four methods use the corresponding methods on the NamedStyle's enclosing StyleContext instance to efficiently update the definition of the Style. When the StyleContext method returns, fireStateChanged() is called to notify listeners that the definition of the Style has changed.

public void removeAttributes(AttributeSet attributes)
> This method checks to see if the given set is the same object the `NamedStyle` the method is being called on. If so, it resets its internal set by calling `getEmptySet()`. Otherwise, it works like the other methods listed above, delegating to the enclosing `StyleContext`. In either case, `fireStateChanged()` is called at the end.

Other Method

public String toString()
> This method returns "`NamedStyle:`," followed by the name of the `Style` and then the contents of the `Style`'s `AttributeSet`.

The StyledDocument Interface

`StyledDocument` is an extension of the `Document` interface used for documents that contain more than just basic text using a single font, color, etc. It defines a number of methods to manipulate the attributes associated with different portions of the document, and to manage the collection of `Styles` available to the document. Among other things, this interface introduces the concepts of character attributes, paragraph attributes, and logical styles.

Character attributes are associated with leaf elements. They define things like the current font and text color.

Paragraph attributes are associated with nonleaf elements. They may contain the same types of attributes specified by character attributes. In addition, they may contain attributes that make sense only at a higher level, such as paragraph indentation or spacing.

Finally, logical styles are instances of objects implementing the `Style` interface. They also apply at the paragraph level, but can be overridden by paragraph or character attributes. We'll see more about how all of this fits together over the next few pages.

Properties

`StyledDocument` inherits its properties from the document interface.[*]

---

[*] `logicalStyle`, `characterElement`, and `paragraphElement` appear (by strict interpretation of the JavaBeans specification) to be indexed properties of `StyledDocument`. The index, however, is a character index into the document, not a simple array index. We'll omit these "properties" here and discuss the methods related to them in the descriptions that follow.

Specific Attribute Accessors

public abstract Color getBackground(AttributeSet attr)
public abstract Font getFont(AttributeSet attr)
public abstract Color getForeground(AttributeSet attr)

These methods provide a convenient mechanism for looking up the values of certain common attributes in a given `AttributeSet`. If the specified attribute (based on the constants defined in `StyleConstants`) is contained in the given set, its value should be returned.

Style Management

The following methods are used to manage a set of `Styles` used by the `StyledDocument`. It is reasonable (`DefaultStyledDocument` does it if you tell it to) for an implementation of this class to manage `Styles` across multiple `StyledDocuments`, providing greater optimization.

public abstract Style addStyle(String nm, Style parent)

Requests that a new, empty `Style` be added to the document's style hierarchy. The `Style` is assigned the given name, which may be `null` if the style is not named (in which case the `Style` can be used, but cannot be used in the `getStyle()` and `removeStyle()` methods). The `parent` parameter indicates the existing `Style` that will be used to resolve attributes not found in the new `Style`. A newly created `Style` object is returned.

This method's name and signature can be a bit misleading. Just remember that this method *creates* a new `Style` and that the given `Style` is the parent for the new `Style`, not the `Style` to be added.

public abstract Style getLogicalStyle(int p)

Returns the `Style` for the paragraph that contains the given document offset (from the start of the document). The definition of "paragraph" is up to the class implementing this interface.

public abstract Style getStyle(String nm)

Returns a named `Style` that has previously been added to this document.

public abstract void removeStyle(String nm)

Removes the named `Style` from this document. If multiple `StyledDocuments` are sharing the same set of `Styles` (meaning, in the default Swing implementation, that they share the same `StyleContext`), the `Style` may be removed from all documents. This is technically up to the implementation, but this is the behavior implemented by the existing Swing classes.

public abstract void setLogicalStyle(int pos, Style s)

Sets the `Style` for the paragraph that contains the given document offset (from the start of the document).

Element Query Methods

These methods are used to retrieve Elements based on a document offset:

public abstract Element getCharacterElement(int pos)
> Returns the Element that contains the character at the given position. The returned Element should be a leaf of the Element hierarchy.

public abstract Element getParagraphElement(int pos)
> Returns the Element representing the paragraph that contains the given position in the document.

AttributeSet Modification Methods

The Document interface allows attributes to be set for newly inserted text, but provides no mechanism for changing attributes once the text has been added. The following methods allow you to set attributes explicitly for a given portion of the document, overriding those specified by the Style that covers the given area.

public abstract void setCharacterAttributes(int offset, int length, AttributeSet s,
> *boolean replace)*
> This method applies the given attributes to the specified portion of the document. The boolean argument specifies whether or not the current attributes should be removed before applying the given attributes. If false, the attributes in the new set are just added to the existing set.

public abstract void setParagraphAttributes(int offset, int length, AttributeSet s,
> *boolean replace)*
> This method applies the given attributes to the paragraphs contained (or partially contained) by the specified range. The boolean argument specifies whether or not the current paragraph attributes should be removed before applying the given attributes. If false, the attributes in the new set are just added to the existing set.

The DefaultStyledDocument Class

DefaultStyledDocument is the implementation of StyledDocument that JTextPane uses by default. It defines a default Element structure, as shown in Figure 21-4. This structure consists of a default root Element, which is an instance of a protected inner class called SectionElement. The section contains Elements representing paragraphs (instances of AbstractElement.BranchElement) that contain character Elements (instances of AbstractElement.LeafElement). A character Element contains a collection of text with a common set of attributes.

Figure 21-4 should give you an idea of how the Elements in a DefaultStyled-Document are structured (by default). The next thing to understand is how

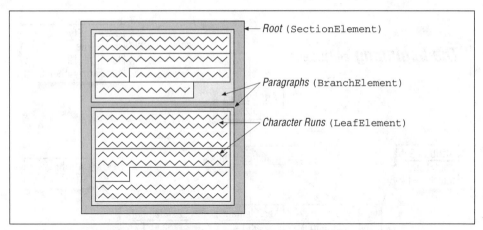

Figure 21-4. DefaultStyledDocument element structure

attributes and Styles are attached to the Elements to define how things will look. Figure 21-5 shows how this works for a small sample paragraph (represented by a BranchElement). The attributes of the paragraph Element are described by an AttributeSet that has a Style as its resolving parent. This structure lets you assign a Style to a paragraph and then use the AttributeSet to override anything you want to change for this paragraph, without directly changing the Style, which might be used by other paragraphs. In our example, we decided to override the font size, changing it from 12 (as it's defined in the Style) to 10.

Each paragraph Element contains leafElements—three of them in this example. Each leaf represents a run of text with a common set of attributes. These attributes are stored in an AttributeSet that serves to further modify the attributes and Style defined in the paragraph. In Figure 21-5, the first Element has attributes that change the font size (overriding the value defined as a paragraph attribute, which was already overriding the Style) and make the text bold (a new attribute). The second leaf defines no new attributes, so it will be defined by its enclosing paragraph. The last leaf changes the italic property from the value defined in the Style.

Keep in mind that the structure shown here reflects only the default Element structure used by this class. You are free to change this to an alternate representation if you like.

In this example, we show only one AttributeSet with a resolving parent. However, any set may have a resolving parent, in which case the parent would also be searched. Keep in mind that an Element's attributes are defined in the following order of significance. The first set in this list in which an attribute is found defines its value, hiding any values found later in the list:

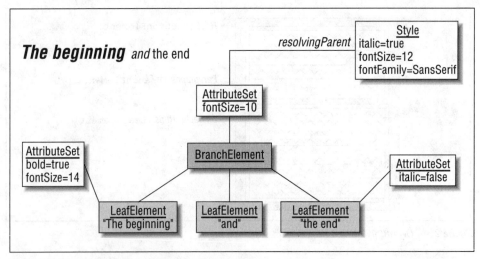

Figure 21-5. DefaultStyledDocument Style and AttributeSet example

1. Attributes defined in the `AttributeSet` directly associated with the `Element` (if there is one)

2. Attributes defined by the `AttributeSet` that is the resolving parent of the `AttributeSet` directly associated with the `Element` (if there is one)

3. Attributes defined by the resolving parent's resolving parent, and so on, until there is no parent

4. Attributes defined by the `Element`'s parent (if there is one)—the parent's attributes are defined by this same order (repeating until there is no parent)

Note that in #3, we're referring to the resolving parent of an `AttributeSet`, while in #4, we're referring to the `Element`'s parent, i.e., the `Element` that contains the `Element` in question. Don't be confused by the multiple uses of the word "parent."

One last point about `DefaultStyledDocument` is that it allows you to specify the `StyleContext` (an extension of `AbstractDocument.AttributeContext`) it should use to manage `Styles`. This enables you to share `Styles` across multiple Documents by using the same `StyleContext` in each one.

Properties

`DefaultStyledDocument` defines the property values shown in Table 21-13. The `defaultRootElement` for a `DefaultStyledDocument` is an instance of an inner class called `DefaultStyledDocument.SectionElement`, which extends `AbstractDocument.BranchElement`. This section element initially contains a single `AbstractDocument.BranchElement` which, in turn, contains a single

AbstractDocument.LeafElement. This just means that the document initially contains a single section which contains a single paragraph which contains some (empty) content.

Table 21-13. DefaultStyledDocument Properties

Property	Data Type	get	is	set	bound	Default Value
defaultRootElement*	Element	•				DefaultStyledDocu-ment.SectionElement()
rootElements*	Element[]	•				{ defaultRootElement, bidiRootElement }
styleNames	Enumeration (string)	•				{ "default" }

See also properties from the AbstractDocument class (Table 20-8).

The rootElements property defaults to an array containing the default-RootElement and the bidiRootElement defined by AbstractDocument. The styleNames property provides access to the set of named styles available to the document.

Constant

DefaultStyledDocument defines the constant shown in Table 21-14.

Table 21-14. DefaultStyledDocument Constants

Name	Data Type	Description
BUFFER_SIZE_DEFAULT	int	The default size of the StringContent object's buffer, which is created if no Content object is specified. (4096)

Constructors

public DefaultStyledDocument()

Calls the last constructor, passing it a new StringContent set to the default size, and a new StyleContext.

public DefaultStyledDocument(StyleContext styles)

Calls the last constructor, passing it a new StringContent set to the default size, and the given StyleContext.

public DefaultStyledDocument(AbstractDocument.Content c, StyleContext styles)

Creates a new document using the specified Content and StyleContext. It creates a new ElementBuffer (an inner class used for managing changes to the Element hierarchy), passing it the default root Element, and it sets the style for the initial paragraph to the default style obtained from the given `StyleContext`.

Specific Attribute Accessors

The following methods provide convenient access to a few common attributes:

public Color getBackground(AttributeSet attr)

Calls `StyleConstants.getBackground(attr)`, to search for a foreground color in the given `AttributeSet`. If the `StyleConstants.Background` attribute is defined in the given set, its value is returned.

public Color getForeground(AttributeSet attr)

Calls `StyleConstants.getForeground(attr)`, to search for a foreground color in the given `AttributeSet`. If the `StyleConstants.Foreground` attribute is defined in the given set, its value is returned.

public Font getFont(AttributeSet attr)

Uses the document's `StyleContext` to search for font attributes in the given set and return the appropriate `Font` object. Note that font is not generally stored explicitly as an attribute, but is instead made up of four attributes: `FontFamily`, `FontSize`, `Bold`, and `Italic`. For more information on this, see the earlier discussion of `StyleContext.getFont()` in "Font Management Methods."

Style Management Methods

public Style addStyle(String nm, Style parent)

Uses the document's `StyleContext` to create a new `Style` and add it to the style table.

public Style getLogicalStyle(int p)

Finds the paragraph `Element` (using `getParagraphElement()`, described later) containing the given position and returns its `Style`. Recall that the paragraph's `Style` is defined as the resolving parent of the `Element`'s `AttributeSet`.

public Style getStyle(String nm)

Returns the `Style` whose name matches the given `String`. This method is just a pass-through to the document's `StyleContext`.

public void removeStyle(String nm)

Removes a named `Style` from the `Document`. This is done by passing the request on to the document's `StyleContext`. If the `StyleContext` is being shared by multiple documents, the removed `Style` will no longer be available to any of them. Also, it's important to realize that this method only removes the Style from the set of known Styles being managed by the StyleContext. It does not directly affect the Style itself, or any paragraphs in the document that are currently using the removed Style.

public void setLogicalStyle(int pos, Style s)
Sets the logical style to be used for the paragraph containing the specified position. This is done by setting the resolving parent of the paragraph Element[*] to the given Style. Note that any attributes explicitly set on the paragraph Element will override the paragraph's Style, since attributes are always resolved locally before querying the parent.

Element Query Methods

public Element getCharacterElement(int pos)
Drills down the Element hierarchy until it reaches a leaf Element containing the specified position. If the position is negative, the first leaf Element is returned. If it is greater than the length of the document, the last leaf Element is returned.

public Element getParagraphElement(int pos)
Returns the paragraph containing the specified position. Remember that the root Element is a "section," and its children are considered paragraphs. The same rules discussed in the last method apply for handling out-of-range positions.

Attribute Modification Methods

public void setCharacterAttributes(int offset, int length, AttributeSet s, boolean replace)
Sets the character attributes for a specified range of the document. It first obtains a write lock on the document. It then uses the ElementBuffer inner class (described later) to create new Elements as necessary in cases where only a portion of an Element's content has been modified. After the updates have been made, fireChangedUpdate() and fireUndoableEditUpdate() are called to notify listeners of the changes.

The replace parameter indicates whether the given attributes should replace any existing character attributes or merge with them.

public void setParagraphAttributes(int offset, int length, AttributeSet s, boolean replace)
Sets attributes for any paragraph Elements that *intersect* the given range of text. Text outside the given range, but included in the paragraphs that

---

[*] It may seem strange to say that this method sets an Element's resolving parent (rather than an AttributeSet's resolving parent). Recall from the previous chapter that AbstractDocument.AbstractElement implements MutableAttributeSet, so setting the Element's resolveParent property is really equivalent to setting the resolveParent of the Element's AttributeSet.

intersect the range, will also be affected. Before making any changes, a write lock is obtained. Unlike setCharacterAttributes(), this method does not create new Elements. After the updates have been made, fireChangedUpdate() and fireUndoableEditUpdate() are called to notify listeners of the changes. The replace parameter indicates whether the given attributes should replace any existing paragraph attributes or merge with them.

Element Structure Methods

The following methods can be used by subclasses to make bulk changes to a document. The idea is to be able to load the document data (from a file, for example) without locking the document, and then pass in the ElementSpecs in a single call.

protected void create(ElementSpec[] data)
> Loads a collection of new Elements. Any existing data is removed from the document before the new elements are created. The document's ElementBuffer is used to create the new Elements according to the ElementSpecs (described later).

protected void insert(int offset, DefaultStyledDocument.ElementSpec data[]) throws BadLocationException
> Inserts a collection of new Elements at the specified location. The document's ElementBuffer is used to create the new Elements according to the ElementSpecs (described later).

Other Protected Methods

The following protected methods are defined in this class. These methods are called by methods in AbstractDocument and are overridden here to support the Element structure maintained by DefaultStyledDocuments.

protected AbstractDocument.AbstractElement createDefaultRoot()
> Creates a top-level AbstractDocument.SectionElement, which contains a single BranchElement containing a single LeafElement. The SectionElement is returned as the root of the document's Element hierarchy.

protected void insertUpdate(DefaultDocumentEvent chng, AttributeSet attr)
> Called by AbstractDocument.insertString() to allow the document's Element structure to be updated as a result of new text being inserted. This is done by iterating over the new text, building up a series of ElementSpecs, and passing them on to the insert() method of the document's ElementBuffer. Any changes made to the document structure are added to the given document event and will be sent to registered listeners.

Figure 21-6 shows how the implementation of this method differs from the PlainDocument implementation, which does not support the use of attributes. It shows the `Element` structure of a `PlainDocument` and a `DefaultStyledDocument` before and after inserting new text, as shown in the following code block. Notice how `PlainDocument` just expands its single content `Element`, while `DefaultStyledDocument` breaks up the old `Element` and adds a new `Element` with the new set of attributes.

```
PlainDocument plainDoc = new PlainDocument();
DefaultStyledDocument styledDoc = new DefaultStyledDocument();

SimpleAttributeSet set1 = new SimpleAttributeSet();
StyleConstants.setBold(set1, false);
StyleConstants.setItalic(set1, true);

plainDoc.insertString(0, "Swing is cool", set1); // IGNORED!
styledDoc.insertString(0, "Swing is cool", set1);

// BEFORE (see Figure 21-6)

SimpleAttributeSet set2 = new SimpleAttributeSet();
StyleConstants.setBold(set2, true);

plainDoc.insertString(9, "really ", set2); // IGNORED!
styledDoc.insertString(9, "really ", set2);

// AFTER (see Figure 21-6)
```

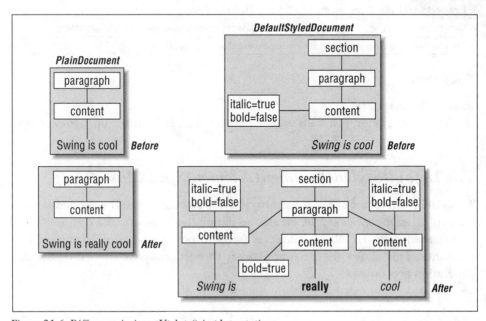

Figure 21-6. Differences in insertUpdate() implementations

protected void removeUpdate(DefaultDocumentEvent chng)

> Updates the document structure as a result of text removal by forwarding the request to the document's `ElementBuffer`, which manages affected leaves. Any changes made to the document structure are added to the given document event and sent to registered listeners.

The DefaultStyledDocument.SectionElement Class

This non-static, protected inner class is used as the default root element for `DefaultStyledDocuments`. It is an extension of `AbstractDocument.Branch-Element` that does nothing more than define a unique response to `getName()`. As we explained earlier, this class serves as a container for the document's paragraphs, which are represented by `BranchElement` objects.

Properties

Table 21-15 shows the default property value defined by `DefaultStyledDocument.SectionElement`. The `name` property for a `SectionElement` is set to `"section"`, the value of `AbstractDocument.SectionElementName`.

Table 21-15. DefaultStyledDocument.SectionElement Properties

Property	Data Type	get	is	set	bound	Default Value
name*	String	•				AbstractDocument.SectionElementName

See also properties from the AbstractDocument.BranchElement class (Table 20-14).

Constructor

public SectionElement()

> This constructor just calls `super(null, null)`, setting up a new empty `Element`.

The DefaultStyledDocument.ElementSpec Class

This public static inner class is used to describe an `Element` to be created later. A series of `ElementSpecs` can be created to define the structure of a document and then passed in to an `ElementBuffer` (see the next section) to be turned into `Elements`. This allows the parsing process to be decoupled from the `Element` generation process.

Properties

`DefaultStyledDocument.ElementSpec` defines the properties shown in Table 21-16. The `array` property contains the text to be contained by the `Element`. This is only meaningful if the `ElementSpec` is being used to generate a new document (as opposed to changing the `Element` structure of an existing one). `Attributes` defines the `Element`'s `AttributeSet`. The `length` and `offset` properties indicate the range of the document's text this `Element` maps to.

Table 21-16. DefaultStyledDocument.ElementSpec Properties

Property	Data Type	get	is	set	bound	Default Value
array	char[]	•				null
attributes	AttributeSet	•				From constructor
direction	short	•		•		OriginateDirection
length	int	•				0
offset	int	•				0
type	short	•		•		From constructor

The `direction` property is used to indicate how the `Element` should be joined with existing `Elements`. The default value is `OriginateDirection`, which indicates that the `Element` should not join with anything. Other values for this property are listed in Table 21-17.

Lastly, the `type` property is used to specify the kind of `Element` to be created. The possible values for this property are shown in Table 21-18.

Direction Constants

Table 21-17 shows the valid values for the `direction` property.

Table 21-17. DefaultStyledDocument.ElementSpec Direction Constants

Name	Data Type	Description
JoinPreviousDirection	short	The `Element` should be joined with the previous one
JoinNextDirection	short	The `Element` should be joined with the next one
OriginateDirection	short	A new `Element` should be created

Type Constants

Table 21-18 shows the valid values for the type property.

Table 21-18. DefaultStyledDocument.ElementSpec Type Constants

Name	Data Type	Description
contentType	short	ElementSpec represents the content of an Element
endTagType	short	ElementSpec represents the end of an Element
startTagType	short	ElementSpec represents the start of an Element

Constructors

Each of these constructors sets the direction property to OriginateDirection.

public ElementSpec(AttributeSet a, short type)

Creates a new ElementSpec with no content, length, or offset. This is most useful for start and end tags.

public ElementSpec(AttributeSet a, short type, int len)

Creates a new ElementSpec that specifies the length, but not the offset, of an Element. Such ElementSpecs can be processed sequentially from a known starting point.

public ElementSpec(AttributeSet a, short type, char[] txt, int offs, int len)

This constructor is used when creating new document content, typically as a result of reading a document description from some mark-up language, such as HTML.

Methods

This is the only method other than the accessors for the properties listed in Table 21-16.

public String toString()

Returns a String describing the type, direction, and length of this ElementSpec.

The DefaultStyledDocument.ElementBuffer Class

The non-static ElementBuffer inner class manages the Element structure of its enclosing DefaultStyledDocument. An instance of this class is created by the DefaultStyledDocument constructors, and all methods in DefaultStyledDocument that can modify the Element structure delegate to this buffer. Basically, this class encapsulates all activity related to the maintenance of the document's element structure.

Property

Table 21-19 shows the property defined by `DefaultStyledDocument.Element-Buffer`. The `rootElement` is given to the `ElementBuffer` in the constructor. This represents the root of the enclosing document's default `Element` structure.

Table 21-19. DefaultStyledDocument.ElementBuffer Property

Property	Data Type	get	is	set	bound	Default Value
rootElement	Element	•				From constructor

Constructor

public ElementBuffer(Element root)

Creates a new buffer, using the given `Element` as the root of the `Element` structure.

Public Methods

The first three methods below are called by `DefaultStyledDocument` to request changes to the document's `Element` hierarchy. Each of these takes a `Default-DocumentEvent` as a parameter. This event can be modified by the methods to reflect changes made to the hierarchy (recall from the last chapter that this event class extends `CompoundEdit`, so edits made to the element structure will be added to it). Eventually, the event will be fired by the `DefaultStyledDocument` method that made the call.

The last public method listed here is used internally (by the package-private `join()` method).

public void change(int offset, int length, DefaultDocumentEvent de)

Indicates that attributes are being changed for the specified portion of the document. `Element`s will be split and created as necessary to allow the specified range to be represented by a unique `Element`. Most of the work is done by `changeUpdate()`, described below. Before calling it, this method sets local variables that `changeUpdate()` will use.

The given event is updated to reflect the changes made by this call.

public void insert(int offset, int length, ElementSpec[] data, DefaultDocumentEvent de)

Inserts new `Element`s in the document at the specified position. The given offset and length indicate the range of the affected text. Most of the work is done by `insertUpdate()`, described later. Before calling it, this method sets local variables that `insertUpdate()` will use.

The given event is updated to reflect the changes made by this call.

public final void remove(int offset, int length, DefaultDocumentEvent de)

Removes `Elements` from the document. Elements that lie within the given range of text will be removed. Most of the work is done by `removeUpdate()`, described later. Before calling it, this method sets local variables that `remove-Update()` will use.

The given event is updated to reflect the changes made by this call.

public Element clone(Element parent, Element clonee)

Creates a copy of a given `Element` (including any nested structure). The newly created `Element` will have the specified parent.

Protected Methods

The following protected methods are used by the public methods described previously. In all three cases, much of the detailed work is encapsulated in methods with package-level visibility.

protected void changeUpdate()

Called by `update()` to split `Elements` based on changes made to some portion of the document.

protected void insertUpdate(ElementSpec[] data)

Called by `insert()` to add `Elements` to the document, based on the given specifications. It drills down the `Element` hierarchy until it reaches a leaf `Element`, at which point it inserts the new `Elements`. This method can result in calls to `createBranchElement()` and `createLeafElement()` on the enclosing document, causing new `Elements` to be created and added to the document.

protected void removeUpdate()

Called by `remove()`, and does the work of removing `Elements` from the document.

The JTextPane Class

Now that we've covered the complete text model for styled text, we can finally fully understand Swing's most powerful text component, `JTextPane`. This class was first introduced in Chapter 19, *Text 101*, but we didn't get into the details because so much depended on having at least a basic understanding of the underlying model. Now that this model has been explained, you'll see that the interface to `JText-Pane` is really fairly simple. Many of the methods are provided as convenient shortcuts to methods we've already discussed from the `StyledDocument` interface.

Recall that `JTextPane` is a subclass of `JEditorPane`. As such, it must have an `EditorKit` that describes much of its functionality. We'll cover `JTextPane`'s editor kit, `DefaultStyledEditorKit`, in detail in Chapter 24, *EditorKits and TextActions*.

Properties

`JTextPane` defines the properties shown in Table 21-20. Both the `document` and `styledDocument` properties refer to the pane's `StyledDocument` model. The `styledDocument` property provides type-specific access to the inherited document property. Attempting to call `setDocument()` with a `Document` that does not implement `StyledDocument` will result in an `IllegalArgumentException`.

Table 21-20. JTextPane Properties

Property	Data Type	get	is	set	bound	Default Value
document*	Document	•		•		DefaultStyledDocument
UIClassID*	String	•				"TextPaneUI"
styledDocument	StyledDocument	•		•		DefaultStyledDocument
characterAttributes	AttributeSet	•				
editorKit*	EditorKit	•		•		StyledEditorKit
inputAttributes	MutableAttributeSet	•				
logicalStyle	Style	•		•		
paragraphAttributes	AttributeSet	•				
scrollableTracks-ViewportWidth*	boolean	•				true

See also properties from the JEditorPane class (Table 19-7).

The `characterAttributes`, `logicalStyle`, and `paragraphAttributes` properties are described in the "Attribute and Style Methods" section below. We handle them this way because the `get()` and `set()` methods are more complicated than basic property accessors and mutators. The default values for these properties come from the document.

The `inputAttributes` property defines the `AttributeSet` to be used for newly inserted text. This property is managed by the `editorKit`. Newly inserted text will have the same attributes as the text before the cursor position.

The `editorKit` property reflects the `StyledEditorKit` used by this class (`EditorKits` will be covered in detail in Chapter 24, *EditorKits and TextActions*). Attempting to set `editorKit` to a kit that is not a `StyledEditorKit` (or a subclass) results in an `IllegalArgumentException`.

The scrollableTracksViewportWidth property (from the Scrollable interface) is returned as true by this class, meaning that the pane should be confined to the width of the viewport it is placed in (when used with a JScrollPane, for example). This allows text to be properly wrapped when the end of a line is reached.

Constructors

public JTextPane()

Creates an empty text pane. It creates a new StyledEditorKit and gets its document model from this kit.

public JTextPane(StyledDocument doc)

Creates a text pane displaying the given document.

StyledDocument Delegation Methods

The following methods do nothing more than delegate to the pane's model. For a detailed explanation of Style manipulation, see the description of Default-StyledDocument presented earlier in this chapter.

public Style addStyle(String nm, Style parent)
public Style getStyle(String nm)
public void removeStyle(String nm)

Attribute and Style Methods

These methods manipulate the attributes associated with either the current selection or the current cursor position. Pay close attention to which methods take the current selection into account, and which do not.

Recall from the discussion of the StyledDocument interface that character attributes are applied to leaf elements, and paragraph attributes are applied to a leaf's containing element. Styles are also applied at the paragraph level, typically serving as reusable sets of well-known attributes.

public AttributeSet getCharacterAttributes()

Returns the character attributes that apply to the text at the current cursor location. Only the current cursor position is used; any selected text is irrelevant. If the current cursor position is just after the last character in the document, this method returns an empty set, because the leaf Element containing the text up to the end of the document does not contain the position after the end of the text; there's actually an extra, empty Element there.

public Style getLogicalStyle()

Delegates to the pane's document, passing in the current cursor location. Only the current cursor position is used, any selected text is irrelevant.

public AttributeSet getParagraphAttributes()

Returns the paragraph attributes that apply to the text at the current cursor location. Only the current cursor position is used; any selected text is irrelevant.

public void setCharacterAttributes(AttributeSet attr, boolean replace)

Applies the given attributes to the selected portion of the document. If there is no selection, the attributes will be applied to any new text inserted (by updating inputAttributes) into the document. The replace argument specifies whether or not the current attributes should be removed before applying the given attributes.

public void setLogicalStyle(Style s)

Delegates to the pane's document, passing in the given Style and the current cursor location. The change is only applied to the paragraph at the current cursor location (unlike the other two set methods); any selected text is irrelevant.

public void setParagraphAttributes(AttributeSet attr, boolean replace)

Applies the given attributes to any paragraphs that intersect the selected portion of the document. If there is no selection, the attributes are applied to the paragraph at the current cursor position. The replace argument specifies whether or not the current attributes should be removed before applying the given attributes.

Adding Non-Text Content

In addition to displaying text, JTextPane can be used to display Icons and arbitrary Components. This flexibility makes it possible to display documents with embedded images, or interactive documents such as HTML forms.

public void insertComponent(Component c)

Inserts a Component into the document, replacing anything currently selected. If there is no selection, the component is inserted at the current cursor position. Inserting a Component results in a single blank space being inserted into the document. This space is represented by a single Element with attributes set to indicate that the space represents the given Component.

public void insertIcon(Icon c)

Inserts an Icon into the document, replacing anything currently selected. If there is no selection, the icon is inserted at the current cursor position. Inserting an Icon results in a single blank space being inserted into the document. This space is represented by a single Element, with attributes set to indicate that the space represents the given Icon.

Here's a short example showing how these methods work. In it, we create a JTextPane and two buttons: one inserts an Icon, and the second inserts a JButton. Figure 21-7 shows a display after playing with the editor a little bit.

```
// IconAndComp.java
//
import javax.swing.*;
import javax.swing.text.*;
import java.awt.*;
import java.awt.event.*;

// Shows that Icons and Components can be added to a JTextPane
public class IconAndComp {
  public static void main(String[] args) {
    final JTextPane pane = new JTextPane();

    // Add an icon button
    final ImageIcon icon = new ImageIcon("images/bluepaw.gif");
    JButton iconButton = new JButton(icon);
    iconButton.addActionListener(new ActionListener() {
      public void actionPerformed(ActionEvent event) {
        pane.insertIcon(icon);
      }
    });

    // Add a "Button" button
    JButton buttonButton = new JButton("Insert Button");
    buttonButton.addActionListener(new ActionListener() {
      public void actionPerformed(ActionEvent event) {
        pane.insertComponent(new Button("Click Me"));
      }
    });

    // Lay out . . .
    JPanel buttons = new JPanel();
    buttons.add(iconButton);
    buttons.add(buttonButton);

    JFrame frame = new JFrame();
    frame.addWindowListener(new BasicWindowMonitor());
    frame.setSize(300,200);
    Container c = frame.getContentPane();
    c.setLayout(new BorderLayout());
    c.add(pane, BorderLayout.CENTER);
    c.add(buttons, BorderLayout.SOUTH);
    frame.setVisible(true);
  }
}
```

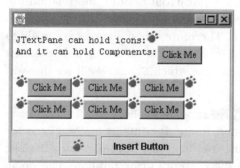

Figure 21-7. JTextPane containing JButtons and ImageIcons

Other Public Method

public void replaceSelection(String content)
> Inserts, removes, or replaces text. If there is any currently selected text, it is removed. Then, any new text is inserted in its place. If no text is passed in, this is essentially a remove operation. If no text is selected, the given text will be inserted at the current cursor position. Any new text will have the attributes currently defined for new given text (`inputAttributes`).

Protected Methods

The following protected methods are defined in `JTextPane`:

protected final StyledEditorKit getStyledEditorKit()
> Casts the result of `getEditorKit()` to a `StyledEditorKit`.

protected EditorKit createDefaultEditorKit()
> Returns a new `StyledEditorKit`. This is the method called by `JEditor-Pane.getEditorKit()`, if it is called before a kit has been set for the pane.

A Stylized Editor

We've now covered all the classes and interfaces related to the concept of document styles. The remainder of this chapter explores an in-depth example that shows how to create `Styles` and apply them to paragraphs in a document. This mini–word processor will have the following features:

- User can define `Styles`, using a simple dialog box that allows attributes such as font size, line spacing, bold, and italics to be specified.

- User can set the `Style` for the paragraph at the current cursor position.

- User can modify a `Style` and see the changes reflected in all paragraphs using the modified `Style`.

This last item requires a bit of work. This is not trivial because the relationship between an `Element` and its `Style` is one-directional. That is, a `Style` has no knowledge of the `Element`s that refer to it. Therefore, when changes are made to a `Style`, the only way we can get the `Element`s to be redrawn with the new attributes is to keep track of which `Element`s use which `Style`. We'll see one way to implement later.

The example consists of three classes: `StyleFrame`, `StyleBox`, and `StylishDocument`. `StyleFrame` is the main application frame. It contains a `JTextPane` for editing text and a `JMenuBar` that allows the user to create `Style`s, modify `Style`s, and set the `Style` for the paragraph at the current cursor position. The document used by the text pane is an instance of `StylishDocument`, an extension of `DefaultStyledDocument` that keeps track of which `Element`s use which `Style`s. Finally, `StyleBox` is a simple container containing various `JTextField`s, `JComboBox`es, and `JCheckBox`es that allow the user to define several attributes of a paragraph `Style`.

We'll look at this class first to get an idea of what the program will be able to do. Figure 21-8 shows two sample `StyleBox`es. The first one shows the "default" `Style` that we get from the document when it's created.[*] The second dialog shows a specification for a "title" `Style` that uses a large, bold font and places extra space above and below the text.

The code for this class is shown below. There's a lot of code related to the creation of all of the data entry components. Feel free to ignore these details and concentrate on the `fillStyle()` and `loadFromStyle()` methods. These show how we set attributes on a `Style` object and how we retrieve attributes from an already populated `Style` (used when the user wants to modify a `Style`).

```
// StyleBox.java
//
import javax.swing.*;
import javax.swing.text.*;
import java.awt.*;

// A class that allows several paragraph style attributes to be entered and
// provides methods to add the attributes to a Style object or set the contents
// based on an existing Style.
public class StyleBox extends Container {

  // Create the box and add the fields
  public StyleBox() {
    setLayout(new GridBagLayout());
    gbc.insets = new Insets(1, 1, 1, 1);
```

---

[*] The default values for `FontSize` and `FontFamily` are defined in Table 21-2.

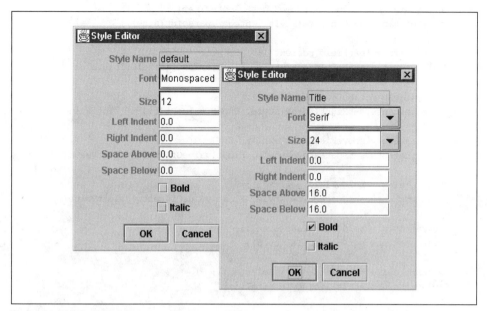

Figure 21-8. Sample StyleBoxes

```
    nameField = addField("Style Name", "");
    fontCombo = addCombo("Font", fonts, true);
    sizeCombo = addCombo("Size", sizes, true);
    leftField = addField("Left Indent", "0.0");
    rightField = addField("Right Indent", "0.0");
    aboveField = addField("Space Above", "0.0");
    belowField = addField("Space Below", "0.0");
    boldCheck = addCheck("Bold");
    italicCheck = addCheck("Italic");
  }

  // Return the name of the Style
  public String getStyleName() {
    String name = nameField.getText();
    if (name.length() > 0)
      return name;
    else
      return null;
  }

  // Fill the given Style object with the attributes entered in the fields. No
  // format checking is done in this version!
  public void fillStyle(Style style) {
    String font = (String)fontCombo.getSelectedItem();
    StyleConstants.setFontFamily(style, font);
```

```java
    String size = (String)sizeCombo.getSelectedItem();
    StyleConstants.setFontSize(style, Integer.parseInt(size));

    String left = leftField.getText();
    StyleConstants.setLeftIndent(style, Float.valueOf(left).floatValue());

    String right = rightField.getText();
    StyleConstants.setRightIndent(style, Float.valueOf(right).floatValue());

    String above = aboveField.getText();
    StyleConstants.setSpaceAbove(style, Float.valueOf(above).floatValue());

    String below = belowField.getText();
    StyleConstants.setSpaceBelow(style, Float.valueOf(below).floatValue());

    boolean bold = boldCheck.isSelected();
    StyleConstants.setBold(style, bold);

    boolean italic = italicCheck.isSelected();
    StyleConstants.setItalic(style, italic);
  }

  // Load the form from an existing Style.
  public void loadFromStyle(Style style) {
    nameField.setText(style.getName());
    nameField.setEditable(false); // don't change the name

    String fam = StyleConstants.getFontFamily(style);
    fontCombo.setSelectedItem(fam);

    int size = StyleConstants.getFontSize(style);
    sizeCombo.setSelectedItem(Integer.toString(size));

    float left = StyleConstants.getLeftIndent(style);
    leftField.setText(Float.toString(left));

    float right = StyleConstants.getRightIndent(style);
    rightField.setText(Float.toString(right));

    float above = StyleConstants.getSpaceAbove(style);
    aboveField.setText(Float.toString(above));

    float below = StyleConstants.getSpaceBelow(style);
    belowField.setText(Float.toString(below));

    boolean bold = StyleConstants.isBold(style);
    boldCheck.setSelected(bold);

    boolean italic = StyleConstants.isItalic(style);
```

```
    italicCheck.setSelected(italic);
  }


  // Reset all fields
  public void clear() {
    nameField.setText("");
    nameField.setEditable(true);
    fontCombo.setSelectedIndex(0);
    sizeCombo.setSelectedIndex(0);
    leftField.setText("0.0");
    rightField.setText("0.0");
    aboveField.setText("0.0");
    belowField.setText("0.0");
    boldCheck.setSelected(false);
    italicCheck.setSelected(false);
  }


  // Add a JLabel/JTextField pair
  protected JTextField addField(String text, String value) {
    gbc.gridx = 0;
    gbc.anchor = GridBagConstraints.EAST;
    gbc.gridy++;
    JLabel l = new JLabel(text);
    add(l, gbc);
    JTextField tf = new JTextField(value, 10);
    gbc.gridx = 1;
    gbc.anchor = GridBagConstraints.WEST;
    add(tf, gbc);
    return tf;
  }

  // Add a JLabel/JComboBox pair
  protected JComboBox addCombo(String text,String[] choices,boolean editable) {
    gbc.gridx = 0;
    gbc.anchor = GridBagConstraints.EAST;
    gbc.gridy++;
    JLabel l = new JLabel(text);
    add(l, gbc);
    JComboBox cb = new JComboBox();
    cb.setEditable(editable);
    cb.setSelectedItem(choices[0]);
    cb.setBorder(BorderFactory.createLineBorder(Color.black));
    for (int i=0; i<choices.length; i++)
      cb.addItem(choices[i]);
    gbc.gridx = 1;
    gbc.anchor = GridBagConstraints.WEST;
    add(cb, gbc);
    return cb;
  }
```

```java
// Add a JCheckBox
protected JCheckBox addCheck(String text) {
  gbc.gridx = 0;
  gbc.gridwidth = 2;
  gbc.anchor = GridBagConstraints.CENTER;
  gbc.gridy++;
  JCheckBox cb = new JCheckBox(text);
  add(cb, gbc);
  return cb;
}

private GridBagConstraints gbc = new GridBagConstraints();

private JTextField nameField;
private JComboBox fontCombo;
private JComboBox sizeCombo;
private JTextField leftField;
private JTextField rightField;
private JTextField aboveField;
private JTextField belowField;
private JCheckBox boldCheck;
private JCheckBox italicCheck;

private static final String[] fonts = {"Serif", "SansSerif", "Monospaced"};
private static final String[] sizes = {"8", "10", "12", "18", "24", "36"};
}
```

The next class used in this example is called `StylishDocument`. This is an extension of `DefaultStyledDocument` that adds a mechanism for tracking which paragraph `Elements` are used by each `Style` (using a `Hashtable` that maps a `Style` to the set of `Elements` that use it). This is done by listening for `Document-Events` fired by the document, paying attention to attribute changes (which indicate that the `Style` has changed for a paragraph) as well as the creation or removal of paragraph `Elements` (in which case, new paragraphs need to be added and removed paragraphs need to be dropped).

This new document class defines one important new public method, used by `StyleFrame` whenever an existing `Style` is modified. This method, `styleUpdated()`, checks the internal table to see which (if any) paragraphs in the document are using the modified `Style`. For each one, it generates a new `DefaultDocumentEvent` and fires it. This is done to notify the document's `View` (much more on `View` and its subclasses in Chapter 23, *Text Views*) that the attributes of the `Element` have changed. This causes the display to be updated to reflect the new `Style`. Without this code, changes to the `Style` objects would not be reflected visually, because the `View` only re-examines the `Element`'s attributes when it's explicitly told to do so.

Here's the source code for `StylishDocument`:

```java
// StylishDocument.java
//
import javax.swing.text.*;
import javax.swing.event.*;
import java.util.*;

// An extension of DefaultStyledDocument to keep track of which Elements use each
// Style, allowing changes in Styles to be reflected in Elements that use them.
public class StylishDocument extends DefaultStyledDocument
  implements DocumentListener {

  // Create a new document
  public StylishDocument(Content c, StyleContext styles) {
    super(c, styles);
    init();
  }

  // Create a new document
  public StylishDocument(StyleContext styles) {
    super(styles);
    init();
  }

  // Create a new document
  public StylishDocument() {
    super();
    init();
  }

  // We listen to ourself. Also, we add the first paragraph to our style
  // hashtable since we won't get notified that it was added.
  protected void init() {
    addDocumentListener(this);
    addToStyleHash(getParagraphElement(0));
  }

  // This method indicates that the definition of the given style has changed. It
  // goes through each of the Elements that use the style and fires an event
  // indicating that the attributes for the Element have changed. This causes the
  // View to re-check the attributes and redraw.
  public void styleUpdated(Style style) {
    // Find the set of Elements that use this style . . .

    Hashtable ht = (Hashtable)styleHash.get(style);

    if (ht != null) {
      // somebody's using it if we get here.
```

```java
    // Create a Vector of Elements that shouldn't be in this table because they
    // no longer use this Style (we don't remove them when they change Styles,
    // so they will still be here)
    Vector cleanUp = new Vector();

    // Update each Element . . .
    Enumeration e = ht.keys();
    while (e.hasMoreElements()) {
      Element el = (Element)e.nextElement();
      int start = el.getStartOffset();
      int end = el.getEndOffset();
      Style check = getLogicalStyle(start);

       // Fire an event only if this Element is still using this Style.
       if (check == style) {
         DefaultDocumentEvent ev = new DefaultDocumentEvent
           (start, end-start, DocumentEvent.EventType.CHANGE);
         fireChangedUpdate(ev);
       }
       else {
         // If not, remove this Element, since it no longer uses this Style
         cleanUp.addElement(el);
       }
    }

    // Clean up . . .
    e = cleanUp.elements();
    while (e.hasMoreElements()) {
      Element bad = (Element)e.nextElement();
      ht.remove(bad);
    }
  }
}


// Document Listener Methods

// Call updateStyleHash() whenever text is inserted
public void insertUpdate(DocumentEvent ev) { updateStyleHash(ev); }

// Call updateStyleHash() whenever text is removed
public void removeUpdate(DocumentEvent ev) { updateStyleHash(ev); }

// Whenever attributes change, add the paragraph that was changed to our hash.
public void changedUpdate(DocumentEvent ev) {
  int offset = ev.getOffset();
  Element para = getParagraphElement(offset);
  addToStyleHash(para);
}
```

```
// Internal Methods

// Called to see if there are any added or removed Elements. If there are any,
// we need to update our hash.
protected void updateStyleHash(DocumentEvent ev) {
  DocumentEvent.ElementChange chg =
    ev.getChange(getDefaultRootElement());

  if (chg != null) {

    // Something was added or removed (or both) . . .
    Element[] removed = chg.getChildrenRemoved();
    for (int i=0; i<removed.length; i++) {
      removeFromStyleHash(removed[i]);
    }

    Element[] added = chg.getChildrenAdded();
    for (int i=0;i<added.length;i++) {
      addToStyleHash(added[i]);
    }
  }
}

// Called to add an Element to our hash.
protected void addToStyleHash(Element para) {
  AttributeSet attrs = para.getAttributes();
  if (attrs != null) {
    Style style = (Style)attrs.getResolveParent();
    if (style != null) {

      // We've got the Style, now see if we've got a set of Elements that
      // use this Style
      Hashtable ht = (Hashtable)styleHash.get(style);
      if (ht == null) {
        // First user of this Style . . .add a new set
        ht = new Hashtable();
        styleHash.put(style, ht);
      }
      // If this paragraph isn't already in the set, we add it. We really want
      // a Set, not a Hashtable, but to be JDK 1.1 friendly here, we'll use a
      // Hashtable with a throw-away value. We only care about the keys.
      if (ht.containsKey(para) == false) {
        ht.put(para, new Object());
      }
    }
  }
}

// Called to remove an Element from our hash
protected void removeFromStyleHash(Element para) {
  AttributeSet attrs = para.getAttributes();
```

```
    if (attrs != null) {
      Style style = (Style)attrs.getResolveParent();
      if (style != null) {
        Hashtable ht = (Hashtable)styleHash.get(style);
        if (ht != null) {
          ht.remove(para);
        }
      }
    }
  }


  // This Hashtable maps from Style -> Hashtable<Element, null>. That is, each
  // key is a Style. The values are Hashtables, the keys of which are the
  // Elements that use the Style. The values of the inner Hashtables are useless
  // (we should use a "Set" data structure, but in JDK 1.1 there is none).
  private Hashtable styleHash = new Hashtable();
}
```

One last class ties this whole example together. StyleFrame is a JFrame subclass that provides a JTextPane for editing text and a JMenuBar for working with Styles and exiting the application. The *Style* menu (see Figure 21-9) contains one menu item (*Create Style*) and two submenus (*Set Style* and *Modify Style*). The submenus each contain a list of the Styles that have been created (plus *default*, the Style we get for free from StyleContext).

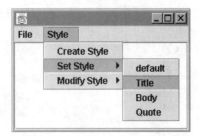

Figure 21-9. StyleFrame example menus

The different menu selections function as follows:

Create Style

When this item is selected, a dialog box is displayed showing an empty StyleBox the user can use to define a new Style. When the box is closed, a new Style is created by calling addStyle() on the document. This Style is then passed back in to the StyleBox, to be filled in with the entered data. Finally, the new Style is added to the *Modify Style* and *Set Style* menus.

Modify Style

When a Style is selected from this submenu, the StyleBox is again displayed, but this time it has been populated with the existing definition of the selected Style. Once changes have been made and the box is closed, the existing `Style` is filled by the `StyleBox`, and `styleUpdated()` is called on the `StylishDocument`, allowing it to update all paragraphs that use the modified `Style`.

Set Style

When a `Style` is selected from this menu, the `setLogicalStyle()` method is called on the frame's `JTextPane`. This method results in a call to `setLogicalStyle()` on the document, passing in the current cursor position.[*]

Here's the code for this class:

```
// StyleFrame.java
//
import javax.swing.*;
import javax.swing.text.*;
import javax.swing.event.*;
import java.awt.*;
import java.awt.event.*;
import java.util.*;

// A main frame containing a JTextPane and a menu.
public class StyleFrame extends JFrame {

  // Just creates and displays the main frame.
  public static void main(String[] args) {
    JFrame frame = new StyleFrame();
    frame.addWindowListener(new BasicWindowMonitor());
    frame.setVisible(true);
  }

  // Create a JTextPane and a JMenuBar and add them to the frame.
  public StyleFrame() {
    doc = new StylishDocument();

    textPane = new JTextPane(doc);
    setContentPane(new JScrollPane(textPane));

    JMenuBar menuBar = createMenuBar();
    setJMenuBar(menuBar);

    setSize(400, 300);
  }

  // Create a menubar with file/exit and style menus.
  protected JMenuBar createMenuBar() {
```

---

[*] With a little more work, you could handle setting the `Style` for multiple highlighted paragraphs as well.

```java
JMenuBar bar = new JMenuBar();

// Add a file/exit menu
JMenu fileMenu = new JMenu("File");
JMenuItem exitItem = new JMenuItem("Exit");
exitItem.addActionListener(new ActionListener() {
  public void actionPerformed(ActionEvent ev) { System.exit(0); }
});
fileMenu.add(exitItem);
bar.add(fileMenu);

// Add a style menu—the "Create Style" option will call our showStyleDialog()
// method (as will "Modify Style" menu items)
styleMenu = new JMenu("Style");
JMenuItem createItem = new JMenuItem("Create Style");
createItem.addActionListener(new ActionListener() {
  public void actionPerformed(ActionEvent ev) { showStyleDialog(); }
});

setStyleMenu = new JMenu("Set Style");
modifyStyleMenu = new JMenu("Modify Style");
styleMenu.add(createItem);
styleMenu.add(setStyleMenu);
styleMenu.add(modifyStyleMenu);
bar.add(styleMenu);

// Add the default style to our menus
addStyleToMenus(doc.getStyle(StyleContext.DEFAULT_STYLE));
return bar;
}

// Bring up a style-entry dialog and process the results.
protected void showStyleDialog() {
  String[] options = {"OK", "Cancel"};

  int opt = JOptionPane.showOptionDialog(this, styleBox,
    "Style Editor", JOptionPane.DEFAULT_OPTION,
    JOptionPane.PLAIN_MESSAGE, null, options, options[0]);

  if (opt == 0) { // "OK" pressed

    String name = styleBox.getStyleName();
    // Only do anything if the user named the style
    if (name != null) {
      // See if the style already exists, in which case this
      // is a change, not a creation
      Style oldStyle = doc.getStyle(name);
      if (oldStyle != null) {
```

```
                    // Redefine the Style and tell our document to
                    // repaint all Elements using this Style
                    styleBox.fillStyle(oldStyle);
                    doc.styleUpdated(oldStyle);
                }
                else {
                    // A new style has been specified. We'll add it to the document . . .
                    Style newStyle = doc.addStyle(name, null);

                    // Now fill the style with the values entered in the dialog
                    styleBox.fillStyle(newStyle);

                    // Add this Style so we can use it
                    addStyleToMenus(newStyle);
                }
            }
        }
        styleBox.clear();
    }

    // Called to add a new Style to our menus.
    protected void addStyleToMenus(final Style newStyle) {
        String styleName = newStyle.getName();

        // Add a menu item to the "Set Style" menu
        JMenuItem newItem = new JMenuItem(styleName);
        setStyleMenu.add(newItem);

        newItem.addActionListener(new ActionListener() {
            public void actionPerformed(ActionEvent ev) {
                textPane.setLogicalStyle(newStyle);
            }
        });

        // Add a menu item to the "Modify Style" menu
        newItem = new JMenuItem(styleName);
        modifyStyleMenu.add(newItem);

        newItem.addActionListener(new ActionListener() {
            public void actionPerformed(ActionEvent ev) {
                styleBox.loadFromStyle(newStyle);
                showStyleDialog();
            }
        });
    }

    private StyleBox styleBox = new StyleBox();
    private JTextPane textPane;
    private StylishDocument doc;
```

```
    private JMenu styleMenu;
    private JMenu setStyleMenu;
    private JMenu modifyStyleMenu;
    private Hashtable styleHash = new Hashtable();
}
```

Well, folks, that's it! With these three classes (just over 500 lines of code), we've created the beginnings of a potentially powerful Style-based text editor. Figure 21-10 shows several different Styles, similar to the ones used in this book.

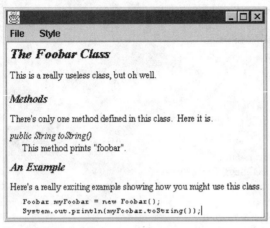

Figure 21-10. StyleFrame example

In this chapter:
- *JTextComponent UI Properties*
- *The DefaultCaret Class*
- *The DefaultHighlighter Class*
- *The DefaultHighlighter.DefaultHighlightPainter Class*
- *The Keymap Interface*

22

Carets, Highlighters, and Keymaps

Like some of the other Swing components (JTree, for example), the text components allow you to do a certain amount of customization without actually implementing your own look-and-feel. Certain aspects of these components' behavior and appearance can be modified directly using set() methods on JTextComponent. In addition, with the more powerful text components (JEditorPane, and anything that extends it, including JTextPane) you are able to control the View objects created to render each Element of the Document model.

In this chapter, we'll concentrate on the classes and interfaces related to modifying text components without dealing with View objects. This will include an explanation of carets, highlighters, and keymaps. Chapter 23, *Text Views*, will examine the various View classes.

JTextComponent UI Properties

JTextComponent has three UI-related properties that you can access and modify directly. These properties are defined by the following interfaces:

Caret

> Defines how the cursor is displayed. This includes the size and shape of the cursor, the blink rate (if any), etc.

Highlighter

> Defines how selected text is highlighted. Typically this is done by painting a solid rectangle "behind" the text, but this is up to the implementation of this interface. Highlighter also defines two inner-interfaces that we'll look at.

Keymap

> Defines the Actions performed when certain keys are pressed. For example, pressing CTRL-C may copy some text and CTRL-V may paste the cut or copied

text at the current cursor location. This is considered a look-and-feel feature because different native look-and-feels have different default keymaps.

As you might expect, Swing provides default implementations of these interfaces. Figure 22-1 shows these classes and interfaces, and the relationships between them. Note that each `Caret` and `Highlighter` is associated with a single `JText-Component` (set by their `install()` methods), while `Keymap` has no direct relation to any `JTextComponent`, and therefore can be used by multiple components.

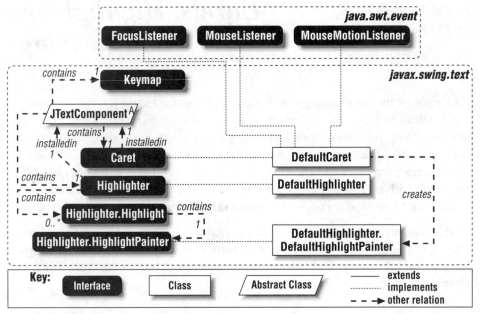

Figure 22-1. JTextComponent UI properties

In the next few pages, we'll take a closer look at these interfaces, as well as the default implementations for `Caret` and `Highlighter`. The default implementation of `Keymap` is an inner class of `JTextComponent`, which we can't subclass directly. When we get to this section, we'll see why we typically won't need to.

The Caret Interface

The `Caret` interface is used to represent the location where new data will be inserted (a caret is often referred to as a "cursor"). This interface provides a number of useful features for dealing with text insertion and selection.

Properties

The `Caret` interface defines the properties shown in Table 22-1. The `blinkRate` property specifies the number of milliseconds between `Caret` blinks. A value of zero indicates that the `Caret` doesn't blink at all.

Table 22-1. Caret Properties

Property	Data Type	get	is	set	bound	Default Value
blinkRate	int	•		•		
dot	int	•		•		
magicCaretPosition	Point	•		•		
mark	int	•				
selectionVisible	boolean		•	•		
visible	boolean		•	•		

The `dot` property reflects the current `Caret` position, while `mark` reflects a previous `Caret` position where a mark was set (used for creating selections).

`MagicCaretPosition` contains the `Point` used when moving between lines with uneven end positions, to ensure that the up and down arrow keys produce the desired effect. For example, consider the following text:

```
Line 1 is long
Line 2
Line 3 is long
```

If the caret was initially positioned before the o in "long" in line three, you'd expect the up arrow key to move the cursor to the end of line two. A second up arrow press should move the caret just before the o in "long" of the first line. That is where the "magic" comes in. The first time the up arrow is pressed, `magic-CaretPosition` is set to the old caret location, so that this position's x-coordinate can be used if the up arrow is pressed again. You will probably never need to do anything with this property, since all this happens for free in the `DefaultEditorKit`.

The `selectionVisible` property indicates whether the current selection should be shown, while `visible` indicates whether or not the `Caret` itself is visible. These properties allow the caret to decide, for example, what the display should look like when the component loses focus.

Events

Anytime the Caret's position changes, a ChangeEvent should be fired to any interested ChangeListeners. Caret defines the following standard methods for managing event listeners:

public abstract void addChangeListener(ChangeListener l)
public abstract void removeChangeListener(ChangeListener l)

Methods

In addition to the accessors for the properties listed earlier, the Caret interface defines the following four methods:

public abstract void deinstall(JTextComponent c)
    Indicates that the Caret is no longer responsible for the given component. The Caret should no longer be used once this method has been called.

public abstract void install(JTextComponent c)
    Indicates that the Caret is responsible for the given component. In addition to giving the Caret access to the component, it also provides access to the Document model (which the Caret can listen to so it can update the cursor location when text is added or removed).

public abstract void moveDot(int dot)
    Called when a selection is being made. It should move the Caret to the specified position and update the JTextComponent's Highlighter to reflect the current selection range.

public abstract void paint(Graphics g)
    Renders the Caret on the given Graphics.

The DefaultCaret Class

The DefaultCaret class provides a basic implementation of the Caret interface which renders itself as a thin vertical line. This class implements the FocusListener, MouseListener, and MouseMotionListener interfaces and reacts to these events when they are fired by the JTextComponent with which the caret is associated.

Subclassing DefaultCaret, as we'll see below, is a great way to create your own Caret without having to worry about a lot of the complicated details.

Properties

DefaultCaret does not add any properties to the Caret interface. Table 22-2 shows the default values it supplies.

Table 22-2. DefaultCaret Properties

Property	Data Type	get	is	set	bound	Default Value
blinkRate*	int	•		•		0
dot*	int	•		•		0
magicCaretPosition*	Point	•		•		null
mark*	int	•				0
selectionVisible*	boolean		•	•		false
visible*	boolean		•	•		false

Events

A `ChangeEvent` is fired to registered listeners whenever the caret's position changes. The usual implementations of the following methods are provided:

public void addChangeListener(ChangeListener l)
public void removeChangeListener(ChangeListener l)
protected void fireStateChanged()

Fields

The following protected fields are available to subclasses of `DefaultCaret`, though neither should normally be needed:

protected EventListenerList listenerList
> The list of listeners added to this component.

protected transientChangeEvent changeEvent
> The `ChangeEvent` used whenever the caret position changes. Since the source is always `this`, there is no reason to create a new event each time.

Constructors

public DefaultCaret()
> Creates a nonblinking `DefaultCaret`.

Caret Methods

`DefaultCaret` provides the following implementations of the methods defined by the `Caret` interface:

public void deinstall(JTextComponent c)
> Causes the caret to remove itself as a listener from the component and its model. If the blink rate has been set, the `Timer` responsible for the blinking is

stopped (see Chapter 27, *Swing Utilities*). The Caret should no longer be used once this method has been called.

public void install(JTextComponent c)

Adds an instance of an inner class as a DocumentListener to the component's model and as a PropertyListener of the component (so it will be notified if the Document is changed). In addition, the caret itself is added as a FocusListener, MouseListener, and MouseMotionListener of the component.

public void moveDot(int dot)

Moves the Caret to the specified position, using the component's Highlighter to highlight the area over which the cursor has been dragged.

public void paint(Graphics g)

Uses the TextUI (from the JTextComponent) to convert the current caret position to view coordinates. It then renders the caret on the Graphics by drawing a thin vertical line at the current dot position.

FocusListener Methods

These methods are implemented from the FocusListener interface:

public void focusGained(FocusEvent e)

Called when the caret's component gains focus. If the component is editable, the cursor becomes visible.

public void focusLost(FocusEvent e)

Called when the caret's component loses focus. This causes the cursor to become invisible.

Mouse Methods

These methods are implemented from the MouseListener and MouseMotion-Listener interfaces. They define the behavior of DefaultCaret in response to mouse interactions.

public void mouseClicked(MouseEvent e)

Causes a word to be selected if this is a double-click event. If this is a triple-click, a line is selected. This is done using the SelectWordAction and SelectLineAction inner classes of DefaultEditorKit (see Chapter 24, *EditorKits and TextActions*).

public void mouseDragged(MouseEvent e)

Calls moveCaret() (described later).

public void mousePressed(MouseEvent e)

Calls positionCaret() (described later) and requests focus for the caret's component if it is enabled.

public void mouseEntered(MouseEvent e)

public void mouseExited(MouseEvent e)

public void mouseMoved(MouseEvent e)

public void mouseReleased(MouseEvent e)

These methods do nothing in this implementation.

Protected Methods

In addition to implementing all of the methods defined in the `Caret` interface, `DefaultCaret` adds several useful methods of its own.

protected void adjustVisibility(Rectangle nloc)

Defines a policy for scrolling to follow the cursor. This implementation just calls the `scrollRectToVisible()` method (using `SwingUtilities.in-vokeLater()`) on the caret's component. Whenever the caret's position changes, this method is called to ensure that the caret is visible.

protected void damage(Rectangle r)

This is an important method in the `DefaultCaret` implementation. It is called whenever the `Caret` is moved and is responsible for calling `repaint()` on the area previously covered by the cursor. If `paint()` is reimplemented, this method should also be overridden to ensure that the area the cursor was in is completely repainted.

protected final JTextComponent getComponent()

Provides access to the component in which the `Caret` is being used. The `DefaultCaret`'s `install()` method (which is called when the `Caret` is added to the component) stores the component for future use, making it available here.

protected Highlighter.HighlightPainter getSelectionPainter()

Returns an object responsible for painting highlighted areas. This implementation returns a `DefaultHighlightPainter`, which is an inner class within `DefaultHighlighter`. `Highlighter` and its related classes are covered in the next section. This method is called when a new selection is made, allowing the painter to be passed in to the `Highlighter`'s `addHighlight()` method.

protected void moveCaret(MouseEvent e)

Called by `mouseDragged()` and results in a call to `moveDot()`, after converting the coordinates from the given event.

protected void positionCaret(MouseEvent e)

Called by `mousePressed()` and results in a call to `setDot()`, after converting the coordinates from the given event. It also clears the `magicCaretPosition` property.

An XOR Caret

Let's take a crack at creating our own `Caret` implementation. We'll create our class as an extension of `DefaultCaret`, so we'll only have to worry about implementing a few methods. The class we're going to create is called `XORCaret` and can be used like the common cursor seen in many applications. For those not familiar with the concept of *xor*, the idea is that if the cursor and the foreground text are the same color, we want to paint the foreground text using a different color when the cursor is over it so that the cursor doesn't cover up the text. In this example, we'll paint text that's under the cursor in the background color, so that the cursor effectively swaps the foreground and background colors.

We care about XOR because we're going to define a caret that will change size depending on the size of the letter it's positioned over, and we don't want the caret to cover the character. Figure 22-2 contains a few screenshots showing this feature.

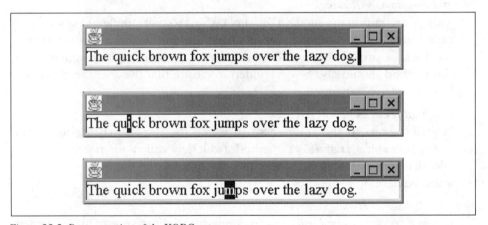

Figure 22-2. Demonstration of the XORCaret

Notice how the size of the cursor varies based on the size of the character it's covering. Changing the caret width is done using the `FontMetrics` for the text component's current `Font`.

Here's the source code for the `XORCaret` class.[*] It overrides just two of the `DefaultCaret` methods, but it uses several other methods to show how the `Caret`, `JTextComponent`, and `TextUI` work together.

---

[*] It would be a lot easier, and more effective, to implement this caret using the XOR mode implemented by the `Graphics` class. In fact, that's what we did first. However a bug was introduced in JDK1.2 beta 4 that broke our old code. When this bug has been fixed, you should be able to use our original carat (`OriginalXORCaret`), which we've included with the source code for this book. `OriginalXORCarat` has the important advantage that it can be used with text components that support multiple fonts, i.e., `JTextPane`.

```java
// XORCaret.java
//
import javax.swing.text.*;
import javax.swing.plaf.*;
import javax.swing.*;
import java.awt.*;

// An implementation of Caret that renders a variable-width XOR cursor.
public class XORCaret extends DefaultCaret {
  // Create the cursor and make it blink
  public XORCaret() {
    setBlinkRate(500); // blinking cursor
  }

  // Render the cursor
  public void paint(Graphics g) {
    if (isVisible()) {
      // Determine where to draw the cursor
      JTextComponent c = getComponent();
      TextUI ui = c.getUI();
      Rectangle r = null;
      int dot = getDot();
      try {
        r = ui.modelToView(c, dot);
      }
      catch (BadLocationException ex) { return; }

      g.setColor(c.getCaretColor());

      // Draw the rectangle, using the currentWidth() method for the width
      lastPaintedWidth = currentWidth();
      g.fillRect(r.x, r.y, lastPaintedWidth, r.height);

      // Draw the character with the background color so it shows up!
      g.setColor(c.getBackground());
      try {
        if (dot < c.getDocument().getLength()) {
          String s = getComponent().getText(dot, 1);

          // Keep \t and \n from looking funny. . .
          if (Character.isISOControl(s.charAt(0)) == false)
            g.drawString(s, r.x, r.y+currentAscent);
        }
      }
      catch (BadLocationException ex) { }
    }
  }
```

```
// This method should match the area painted by paint()
public void damage(Rectangle r) {
  if (r != null) {
    // Repaint the area where the cursor was. We don't use the current
    // width here, instead we use the width of the last caret we painted.
    getComponent().repaint(r.x, r.y, lastPaintedWidth, r.height);
  }
}


// This method determines the width of the current character based on the
// component's Font. Note that this only works porperly with single-font
// components.
protected int currentWidth() {

  Font f = getComponent().getFont();

  if (f != currentFont) {
    currentFontMetrics = Toolkit.getDefaultToolkit().getFontMetrics(f);
    currentAscent = currentFontMetrics.getAscent();
  }

  // Determine the character at the current caret position
  String current = null;
  try {
    current = getComponent().getText(getDot(), 1);
  } catch (BadLocationException ex) { /* ignore */ }

  char currentChar;
  if (current != null && current.length() > 0)
    currentChar = current.charAt(0);
  else
    currentChar = ' ';

  // Return the character's size, or the size of a space when we're adding
  // new text
  if (Character.isWhitespace(currentChar))
    return currentFontMetrics.charWidth(' ');
  else
    return currentFontMetrics.charWidth(current.charAt(0));
}

protected int lastPaintedWidth = 8;
protected Font currentFont = null;
protected int currentAscent = 0;
protected FontMetrics currentFontMetrics = null;
}
```

We did two things here to create our own cursor. First, we implemented our own
version of the paint() method. Here, we used the TextUI look-and-feel object to

map the current cursor position from model (the offset from the start of the document) to view (the pixel location on the screen) coordinates. This gives us most of what we need, but the width of the rectangle we get back from the model-ToView() call is always set to one. In order to draw our cursor so that it matches the width of the current character, we use a protected method we called current-Width(), described later. In order to give the xor effect, we switch the paint color to the component's bacground color and draw the character being covered by the cursor.

The second important method to override is damage(). Any time you reimplement paint(), you also need to reimplement damage(). This method is called when the cursor moves and is responsible for triggering a repaint of the area the cursor was previously covering. To make this work, we use the width of the last cursor we drew, which was cached in the lastPaintedWidth field.

The final method in our class is called currentWidth(). This method is not defined by any superclass or interface; it's simply a method we've defined in this class to return the width of the cursor based on the character (or lack of character) at the current location. We first get the current font from the text component. Then, we use the JTextComponent method getText() together with the Caret method getDoc() to determine the character at the current location so we can find its width.

To use this new caret, simply create a text component and call setCaret(new XORCaret()).

The CaretListener Interface

If you want to keep track of the position of a Caret in a JTextComponent, you don't actually need to interact directly with the component's Caret. Instead, you can simply add a CaretListener to the component.

Method

The CaretListener interface contains one method.

public abstract void caretUpdate(CaretEvent e)
    Called any time the caret's position changes.

The CaretEvent Class

As you'd expect, there's a CaretEvent class to go along with the CaretListener we just introduced. This is actually an abstract class. The only concrete subclass is a package private inner class within JTextComponent.

Properties

`CaretEvent` defines the properties shown in Table 22-3. `dot` indicates the current caret location, while `mark` shows the end of the selection, if there is one (otherwise it will be the same as `dot`).

Table 22-3. CaretEvent Properties

Property	Data Type	get	is	set	bound	Default Value
dot	int	•				abstract
mark	int	•				abstract

Constructor

public CaretEvent(Object source)

> Creates a new event. Subclasses must manage the `dot` and `mark` properties themselves. Since caret positions change very frequently, it's wise to ensure that only a single `CaretEvent` object is created and reused each time the caret position changes.

The Highlighter Interface

The `Highlighter` interface is responsible for marking up background areas of a text component to "highlight" selected portions of the text. A `Highlighter` is capable of describing multiple highlighted areas, each of which is referred to by an instance of an inner interface called `Highlight`. One more inner interface, `HighlightPainter`, is responsible for actually painting a highlighted area. Refer to Figure 22-1 to see how the various classes and interfaces are related.

Property

Table 22-4 shows the property defined by the `Highlighter` interface. The single property, `highlights`, contains an array of individual areas to be highlighted. This property is of yet another new type; the `Highlighter.Highlight` interface is described below. Also notice that this is an array type. While we are used to seeing one text selection highlighted at a time, the interface does not enforce this restriction.

Table 22-4. Highlighter Property

Property	Data Type	get	is	set	bound	Default Value
highlights	Highlighter.Highlight[]	•				

Methods

public abstract Object addHighlight(int p0, int p1, Highlighter.HighlightPainter p) throws BadLocationException

Adds a new highlight covering the specified range (from offset p0 to offset p1), using the specified `HighlightPainter` to perform the rendering. It may return any arbitrary object, which can be used to refer to the highlight in other methods (`changeHighlight()` and `removeHighlight()`). Implementations of this interface should define the specific type of object that this method returns.

public abstract void changeHighlight(Object tag, int p0, int p1) throws BadLocationException

Takes an existing highlight (`tag`) and changes it to refer to a different portion of the document. The tag should be an object returned from `addHighlight()` or `getHighlights()`.

public abstract void deinstall(JTextComponent c)

Called when the UI is removed from a text component. Any references stored in the `install()` method should be dropped here.

public abstract void install(JTextComponent c)

Called when a UI is installed on a text component. This provides access to the component and its `Document` model.

public abstract void paint(Graphics g)

Renders the highlights.

public abstract void removeAllHighlights()

Removes all of the `Highlighter`'s highlights.

public abstract void removeHighlight(Object tag)

Removes a single highlight. The given `tag` should be an object returned from either `getHightlights()` or `addHighlight()`.

The Highlighter.Highlight Interface

The `Hightlighter` interface contains an inner interface called `Highlight`, used to represent a single range of text to be highlighted.

Properties

Table 22-5 shows the properties defined by the `Highlighter.Highlight` interface. The `startOffset` and `endOffset` properties reflect the range of a given highlighted area in a document model. The other property, `painter`, is an object responsible for rendering the `Highlight`. The type of this property is another inner interface, defined below. The only methods in this interface are the accessors for the three properties.

Table 22-5. Highlighter.Highlight Properties

Property	Data Type	get	is	set	bound	Default Value
endOffset	int	•				
painter	Highlighter.HighlightPainter	•				
startOffset	int	•				

The Highlighter.HighlightPainter Interface

This last inner interface of Highlighter is used to render a Highlight. It consists of a single paint() method.

Method

public abstract void paint(Graphics g, int p0, int p1, Shape bounds, JTextComponent c)
Renders a highlighted area of text. The p0 and p1 parameters specify the model offsets defining the range to be highlighted, while the bounds parameter defines the bounds of the component the painter must paint within.

The DefaultHighlighter Class

The DefaultHighlighter class provides a useful implementation of the Highlighter interface.

Property

DefaultHighlighter does not add any new properties. Table 22-6 shows its inherited property.

Table 22-6. DefaultHighlighter Property

Property	Data Type	get	is	set	bound	Default Value
highlights*	Highlighter.Highlight[]	•				empty array

Constructor

public DefaultHighlighter()
Creates a new highlighter.

Methods

The following methods implement the `Highlighter` interface:

public Object addHighlight(int p0, int p1, Highlighter.HighlightPainter p) throws BadLocationException

Uses the `createPosition()` method on the component's `Document` to track the beginning and end points of the given range. It returns an instance of a nonpublic inner class called `HighlightInfo` (this class is an implementation of `Highlighter.Highlight`).

public void changeHighlight(Object tag, int p0, int p1) throws BadLocationException

Cleans up the area previously highlighted by the given highlight, and resets it. The tag should be an object returned from either `addHighlight()` or `getHighlights()`.

public void deinstall(JTextComponent c)

Called when the UI is removed from a text component. It drops the reference to the component supplied by `install()`.

public void install(JTextComponent c)

Called when a UI is installed on a text component. It stores the given component for use in other methods.

public void paint(Graphics g)

Calls `paint()` on the `HighlightPainter` defined for each `Highlight`.

public void removeAllHighlights()

Removes all of the `Highlighter`'s highlights and cleans up any areas they covered.

public void removeHighlight(Object tag)

Removes the given highlight and cleans up any area covered. The tag should be an object returned from either `getHightlights()` or `addHighlight()`.

The DefaultHighlighter.DefaultHighlightPainter Class

This inner class is the default used by the `DefaultCaret.getSelection-Painter()` method. It paints highlights as a solid background rectangle of a specified color.

Property

This inner class defines the property shown in Table 22-7. The `color` property defines the color used to draw highlights. It can only be set in the constructor.

Table 22-7. DefaultHighlighter.DefaultHighlightPainter Property

Property	Data Type	get	is	set	bound	Default Value
color	Color	•				From constructor

Constructor

public DefaultHighlightPainter(Color c)

Creates a new painter that will use the specified color.

Method

public abstract void paint(Graphics g, int offs0, int offs1, Shape bounds, JTextComponent c)

Determines the pixel locations of the given endpoints and draws a rectangle to highlight the specified region. If the two offsets are on different lines, three rectangles are drawn: one from the start point to the end of that line, another that highlights any full lines that follow, and a third from the start of the next line up to the last offset.

A Custom Highlighter

Here's a sample implementation of the `HighlightPainter` interface that paints highlights as thick underlines, instead of as the usual solid rectangle. To use this painter, we need to create a new `Caret` implementation that overrides the `getSelectionPainter()` method. An inner class called `LHCaret` is provided for this purpose. To use our new painter, we just need to make the following call on any text component:

```
textComponent.setCaret(new LineHighlightPainter.LHCaret());
```

Here's the code for the highlight painter and caret inner class:

```
// LineHighlightPainter.java
//
import java.awt.*;
import javax.swing.*;
import javax.swing.text.*;
import javax.swing.plaf.TextUI;

// A sample HighlightPainter implementation that underlines highlighted text with
// a thick line.
public class LineHighlightPainter implements Highlighter.HighlightPainter {

  // Create a new painter using the given color
  public LineHighlightPainter(Color c) { color = c; }
```

```
   public Color getColor() { return color; }

// Paint a bunch of little rectangles
public void paint(Graphics g, int p0, int p1,
  Shape bounds, JTextComponent c) {
  try {
    // Convert positions to pixel coordinates
    TextUI ui = c.getUI();

    Rectangle r1 = ui.modelToView(c, p0);
    Rectangle r2 = ui.modelToView(c, p1);
    Rectangle b = bounds.getBounds();

    int x1 = r1.x;
    int x2 = r2.x;
    int y1 = r1.y;
    int y2 = r2.y;
    int y1base = y1+r1.height-4; // start underline here
    int y2base = y2+r2.height-4; // start underline here

    // Start painting
    g.setColor(getColor());

    // Special case if points are on the same line
    if (y1 == y2) {
      g.fillRect(x1, y1base, x2 - x1, 3);
    }
    else {
      // Fill from point 1 to the end of the line
      g.fillRect(x1, y1base, b.x+b.width-x1, 3);

      // Fill all the full lines in between (assumes that
      // all lines are the same height . . . not a good assumption
      // if using a JEditorPane/JTextPane)
      int line = y1base + 1 + r1.height;
      while (line < y2) {
        g.fillRect(b.x, line-1, b.width, 3);
        line += r1.height;
      }

      // Last line . . . from the beginning to point 2
      g.fillRect(b.x, y2base, x2 - b.x, 3);
    }
  }
  catch (BadLocationException ex) {} // Can't paint
}

private Color color;
```

```
  // A Caret that uses LineHighlightPainter
  public static class LHCaret extends DefaultCaret {
    protected Highlighter.HighlightPainter getSelectionPainter() {
      return new LineHighlightPainter(getComponent().getSelectionColor());
    }
  }
}
```

All we've done here is override the paint() method to paint thin (3 pixel) rectangles under each line of text in the highlighted region. For this example, we've assumed that each line of text has the same height. This is fine for JTextField and JTextArea, but if you want to customize the highlighting of more complex text components, you need to take the different fonts into account. Figure 22-3 shows the LineHighlightPainter in action.

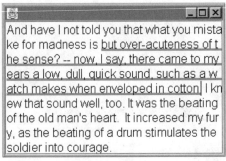

Figure 22-3. LineHighlightPainter

If you choose to implement your own Highlighter class as well, you can call setHighlighter() on any JTextComponent to cause your new class to be used.

The Keymap Interface

One last interface you can work with without implementing your own look-and-feel is called Keymap. A Keymap contains mappings from KeyStrokes[*] to Actions and provides a variety of methods for accessing and updating these mappings. Normally, a look-and-feel will define a set of meaningful keystrokes. For example, Windows users expect CTRL-C to copy text and CTRL-V to paste, while CTRL-INSERT and SHIFT-INSERT should perform the same tasks for Motif users. These different key sequences will work as expected in Swing text components because of the Keymap installed by the look-and-feel. If you want to change or add to this behavior, this interface lets you.

---

[*] KeyStroke is discussed in more detail in Chapter 27. Basically, it's just a representation of a key being typed, containing both the key code and any key modifiers (CTRL, ALT, etc.).

Properties

The `Keymap` interface defines the properties shown in Table 22-8. The `boundAction` and `boundKeyStrokes` properties contain the `Actions` and `KeyStrokes` (both of these types are defined in the `javax.swing` package) known to the `Keymap`. The `defaultAction` property represents the action to be used when there is no action defined for a key. This is typically set to an instance of the `DefaultKeyTypedAction` inner class from the `DefaultEditorKit`. However, if you want to catch all keystrokes (perhaps to implement an editor like *vi* that only echos key presses when it's in insert mode), you could define your own default action.

Table 22-8. Keymap Properties

Property	Data Type	get	is	set	bound	Default Value
boundActions	Action[]	•				
boundKeyStrokes	KeyStroke[]	•				
defaultAction	Action	•		•		
name	String	•				
resolveParent	Keymap	•		•		

The `name` is any arbitrary name given to the map. Finally, the `resolveParent` is another `Keymap` used to resolve any keys that are not defined locally in the map. This may be `null`, meaning that keys not found in the `Keymap` do not map to any `Action`.

Methods

Several methods defined in the `Keymap` interface allow `KeyStroke` to `Action` mappings to be added, removed, and queried.

public abstract void addActionForKeyStroke(KeyStroke key, Action a)
    Adds an `Action` to be performed for the given `KeyStroke`.

public abstract Action getAction(KeyStroke key)
    Determines what action to take in response to a given key sequence. If the action is not found in the `Keymap`, the `resolveParent` (if defined) should be searched.

public abstract KeyStroke[] getKeyStrokesForAction(Action a)
    Returns all `KeyStrokes` associated with the specified `Action`.

public abstract boolean isLocallyDefined(KeyStroke key)

Indicates whether or not the specified `KeyStroke` is defined in the `Keymap` (the `resolveParent` should *not* be checked).

public abstract void removeBindings()

Removes all `KeyStroke` to `Action` bindings from the `Keymap`.

public abstract void removeKeyStrokeBinding(KeyStroke keys)

Removes the binding for the specified `KeyStroke`.

Keymap Implementation

Unlike `Caret` and `Highlighter`, the `Keymap` interface does not have a public default implementation. The `JTextComponent` class defines `DefaultKeymap` as a package-level inner class. This implementation uses a hashtable to map from `KeyStokes` to `Actions`. Each `KeyStroke` maps to no more than one `Action`, and no mapping is kept in the other direction (from `Action` to `KeyStroke`). As a result, `getKeyStrokesForAction()` always returns `null`.

NOTE   The fact that `getKeyStrokesForAction()` is never called by any
              Swing class keeps the fact that it always return `null` from being an
              immediate problem, but be aware that this method will not work as
              expected if you call it yourself. Presumably, this will be implemented
              in a future release.

There are a few ways to change the `Keymap` used by your text components. One option is to call `getKeymap()` on the component, and then add any new actions directly to that map. Doing this may change the mappings for all `JTextComponents` in the application, if the look-and-feel is reusing a single `Keymap` for every component (which is what the Swing look-and-feels do). This is not a big problem if the actions you add will work with all types of text components, but it is probably not the best approach.

A much better approach is to define a new `Keymap` that uses the default `Keymap` (installed by the look-and-feel) as its parent. The new `Keymap` will contain only the mappings you define and will pass any other keys up to the default map. As the example below shows, this is done by calling `JTextComponent.addKeymap()`. This method takes the name of your new map and the parent map to be used and returns a new `Keymap` for you to add mappings to. Since this is a static method, once you've made this call and added to the new map, you can use the new map for any other `JTextComponents` by calling:

```
myComponent.setKeymap(JTextComponent.getKeymap("MyKeymapName")).
```

Adding Keyboard Actions

Here's a quick example showing how easy it is to add keyboard functionality to Swing text components. In this example, we'll enable CTRL-B and CTRL-U to act as triggers for *bold* and *underline* actions. As we'll see in the next chapter, the StyledEditorKit defines Actions, which do all the work for us. All we have to do is create a Keymap containing the mappings we want, and we'll be able to make text bold or underlined with a simple key press. Here's the code to do this:

```java
// KeymapExample.java
//
import javax.swing.*;
import javax.swing.text.*;
import java.awt.event.*;

// A simple example showing how to add Actions for KeyStrokes
public class KeymapExample {
  public static void main(String[] args) {

    // Start with a simple JTextPane. Get its Keymap to use as our parent. Create
    // a new map called "FontStyleMap" and add it to the JTextComponent static
    // table. Finally, we set the map for out JTextPane to our new map.
    JTextPane tp = new JTextPane();
    Keymap parent = tp.getKeymap();
    Keymap map = JTextComponent.addKeymap("FontStyleMap", parent);

    // Add CTRL-B -> Bold
    KeyStroke boldStroke = KeyStroke.getKeyStroke(KeyEvent.VK_B,
      InputEvent.CTRL_MASK, false);
    map.addActionForKeyStroke(boldStroke, new StyledEditorKit.BoldAction());

    // Add CTRL-U -> Underline
    KeyStroke underStroke = KeyStroke.getKeyStroke(KeyEvent.VK_U,
      InputEvent.CTRL_MASK, false);
    map.addActionForKeyStroke(underStroke,
      new StyledEditorKit.UnderlineAction());

    // Set the map for our text pane to our new map
    tp.setKeymap(map);

    // Show the TextPane
    JFrame f = new JFrame();
    f.addWindowListener(new BasicWindowMonitor());
    f.setContentPane(tp);
    f.setSize(300, 200);
    f.setVisible(true);
  }
}
```

Don't worry about understanding everything about the actions we added here. Text actions will be covered in detail in the next chapter. The important things to understand are the following basic steps:

1. Get the current map (the default set by the L&F).

2. Create a new map with the old map as its parent by calling addKeymap() on JTextComponent.

3. Get the desired KeyStrokes using the KeyStroke.getKeyStroke() method, along with a few constants defined in the java.awt.event package. The KeyEvent class defines constant values for many common keys, while InputEvent defines masks for SHIFT, CTRL, ALT, and META.

4. Add the KeyStroke/Action pair to the new Keymap.

5. Set the new map as the map for our JTextPane.

In this example, we intentionally avoided mapping CTRL-I to an ItalicAction because CTRL-I has the nasty property of being treated like a TAB by the DefaultFocusManager. As a result, the DefaultFocusManager doesn't let CTRL-I get through, so the action is never fired. If you really want to map the CTRL-I character to an action, one way to get around the problem is to create your own FocusManager. You can easily create your own manager by extending DefaultFocusManager, as the following code shows. To use this FocusManager, just call FocusManager.setCurrentManager(new CtrlIFocusManager()).

```java
// CtrlIFocusManager.java
//
import javax.swing.DefaultFocusManager;
import java.awt.event.KeyEvent;
import java.awt.event.ActionEvent;
import java.awt.Component;

// A FocusManager that doesn't treat CTRL-I like a TAB.
public class CtrlIFocusManager extends DefaultFocusManager {
  public void processKeyEvent(Component focusedComp, KeyEvent evt) {

    // If it's an "I" . . .
    if (evt.getKeyCode() == KeyEvent.VK_I) {
      // . . . and CTRL is pressed . . .
      if ((evt.getModifiers() & ActionEvent.CTRL_MASK)==ActionEvent.CTRL_MASK) {
        // . . . let it through by doing nothing . . .
        return;
      }
    }

    // Otherwise, let superclass do its thing . . .
    super.processKeyEvent(focusedComp, evt);
  }
}
```

23

Text Views

In the previous chapter, we looked at three easy ways to customize the look-and-feel of Swing text components without having to write a custom L&F. In this chapter, we'll see how the different text components are displayed by looking at the different text View classes.

This chapter probably deserves a bit of a disclaimer. The information provided here will not be of much importance to many Swing programmers. Unless you are planning to create your own types of document content that can't be displayed using the existing components and views, you probably won't need to understand the details of the classes described here. However, if you are considering creating your own text components with custom Element types, you should have at least a basic understanding of the different view classes, so you'll know which ones to create when you implement your EditorKit.

In any case, it's a good idea to read the introduction if you have any interest at all in how the text components get displayed.

Text Views

Much of the work of drawing the actual content of a text component (the text, or whatever else it displays) is done by various View classes. By installing your own EditorKit (discussed in detail in Chapter 24, *EditorKits and TextActions*), you can control which View objects are created to render the Elements that make up the display without writing your own L&F. That is why we will be covering the complete View hierarchy in this section (unlike most of the UI classes, which we have not been covering in detail).

As we already stated, most readers don't need to understand the material covered in the rest of this chapter. However, if you plan to implement your own

`EditorKit` and want to support element types not known by the existing kits, you'll need to be able to create `View` objects. Depending on your application, you may just need to know what existing class to use, or you may need to create your own `View` classes.

Figure 23-1 shows a high-level view of the relationships between Swing text components, their models, and their views. The key points of interest here are:

- Each `JTextComponent` has an associated `Document` model and `TextUI`.

- Each `TextUI` defines a root `View`, which may contain other `Views` as necessary.

- Each `TextUI` also contains a reference to an `EditorKit` (see Chapter 24 for details).

- Each `View` is responsible for rendering a single `Element` of the `Document` model.

- The `ViewFactory` interface defines how new `Views` should be created for different types of `Elements`. Views use `ViewFactory` objects to create their children.

- The `BasicTextUI` (not shown; used by all Swing L&Fs) implements `ViewFactory`. Its root view (an inner class, not shown) uses the `ViewFactory` defined by the component's `EditorKit`, if the kit defines one. If not, the UI itself is used as the factory.

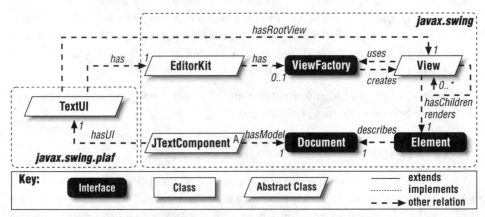

Figure 23-1. High-Level text view class diagram

The key point of this last item is that there are two ways to control what view objects get created. One way is to install an `EditorKit` that defines a `ViewFactory` responsible for creating the appropriate `View` objects (such as `StyledEditorKit`). This is the approach taken by `JEditorPane` and `JTextPane`. The other way is to use an `EditorKit` that does not define a `ViewFactory` (such as DefaultEditorKit) and have the TextUI subclass return the appropriate View objects. This is the approach used by JTextField, JPasswordField, and JTextArea.

Don't worry too much if this last paragraph about EditorKits didn't sink in. At this point, all you need to know is that EditorKits provide one way to define the Views created for different Element types.

A Few Notes

Before we go on, there are a few potentially confusing details worth noting that should make the rest of the chapter easier to understand.

Shape vs. Rectangle

Many of the methods defined in the Swing view classes take a java.awt.Shape as an argument. Shape is an interface that, in JDK 1.1, contained only a single getBounds() method. In JDK 1.2, Shape has been expanded to take advantage of the new Java 2D API. By using Shape, the Swing text package allows new view classes to be defined that take advantage of nonrectangular rendering areas. However, within the Swing view classes we'll be discussing in this chapter, all Shapes are assumed to be Rectangles.

Floats

Similarly, many of the methods in the Swing view classes use float values to specify x and y coordinates, view dimensions, etc. The current Swing classes just turn these values into the more familiar integer pixel coordinates, but future extensions could take advantage of the added flexibility using the 2D API.

Span and Allocation

The term *span* refers to a distance (typically a float) in some direction, while *allocation* refers to the area (a Shape) that a view will be rendered in. These terms are used frequently in the text view source code and documentation, so we'll use them in this chapter as well.

Overview of the View Classes

Swing provides quite a few view classes that are used by the existing text components. Figure 23-2 shows the relationships between these various classes.

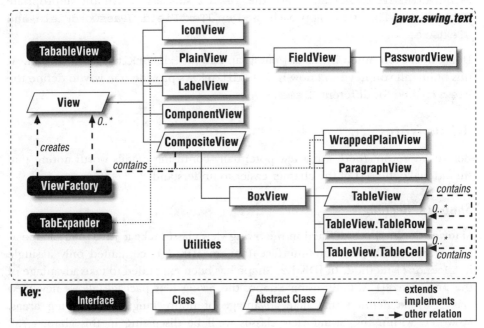

Figure 23-2. View classes

Before we get into a detailed explanation of each class, we'll give a brief overview of the interfaces and classes shown here:

View
> The abstract base class for all view objects. Defines properties common to all types of views. It implements `SwingConstants` (not shown).

TabableView
> An interface used by views whose size depends on the size of tab characters present in the displayed content.

TabExpander
> An interface implemented by views that are capable of expanding tabs.

Utilities
> A class with three static methods used for painting text that may contain tabs.

IconView
> A view class capable of painting `Icons` on a text component.

PlainView
> A view class used for displaying simple, nonwrapping text (text on one line) in a single font and color.

FieldView

An extension of `PlainView` used for text fields. Adds the ability to center the line of text if the field is expanded vertically.

PasswordView

An extension of `FieldView` that provides support for hiding input text using a special echo character.

LabelView

A view class used to render a section of styled text.

ComponentView

A view class used to render `Components` within a text component.

CompositeView

An abstract extension of `View` that allows a view to be made up of multiple child views.*

BoxView

A concrete composite view that lays out its components top-to-bottom or side-to-side. A `BoxView` might contain, for example, several `PlainViews`, one for each line of text in a `JTextArea`.

WrappedPlainView

An extension of `BoxView` used when displaying plain text that supports line-wrapping.

ParagraphView

An extension of `BoxView` used for displaying a paragraph of styled text.

TableView

An extension of `BoxView` used to display data organized in a table.

TableView.TableRow

An extension of `BoxView` used in conjunction with `TableView` to display a row of data.

TableView.TableCell

An extension of `BoxView` used in conjunction with `TableView` to display a cell of data.

Table 23-1 shows the type of Swing text component (based on the Swing L&Fs) that uses each of the available `View` classes. Note that this table includes inner classes, which you cannot use directly (and which were not shown in the above

---

* In this figure, we show `CompositeView` containing multiple child `Views`. Technically, any `View` can contain children. In practice, however, only `CompositeViews` actually have children. One exception to this is the package-level inner class of `BasicTextUI` called `RootView`. This class has a single child which is the "real" `View` of the component.

class diagram). These are included only to give the complete picture of how the different Element types are displayed. Some of these classes are also used by the HTMLFactory in the html package.

Table 23-1. View Classes Used by Swing Text Components

View Class	Visibility	Component/Element
View	public	N/A (abstract)
PlainView	public	JTextArea (no line wrap, handles all child Elements directly)
FieldView	public	JTextField
PasswordView	public	JPasswordField
LabelView	public	JTextPane (Content Elements)
LabelView.LabelFragment	package	Portion of a LabelView that is split between multiple lines
ComponentView	public	JTextPane (Component Elements)
IconView	public	JTextPane (Icon Elements)
CompositeView	public	N/A (abstract)
BoxView	public	JTextPane (Section Elements)
ParagraphView	public	JTextPane (Paragraph Elements)
ParagraphView.Row	package	Portion of a ParagraphView that fills a single row/line
WrappedPlainView	public	JTextArea (line wrap on)
WrappedPlainView.WrappedLine	package	JTextArea (children of the root Element)
TableView	public	Not used directly, but a package-private subclass is used by HTMLEditorKit
TableView.TableRow	public	Used by TableView
TableView.TableCell	public	Used by TableView
TableView.ProxyCell	package	Used by TableView
BasicTextUI.RootView	package	All JTextComponents

Figure 23-3 shows a JTextPane, highlighting some of the view objects used to display text with mixed styles, Icons, and Components. Here we have a BoxView containing three ParagraphViews. The first ParagraphView contains Label-Views for each run of text with a common attribute set (each Element).[*] The second paragraph contains a LabelView followed by a ComponentView, while the third has a LabelView and an IconView.

---

[*] We'll get into how the multiple rows of this first paragraph are handled when we get to the Paragraph-View class description. Several additional inner class view objects are actually in use here.

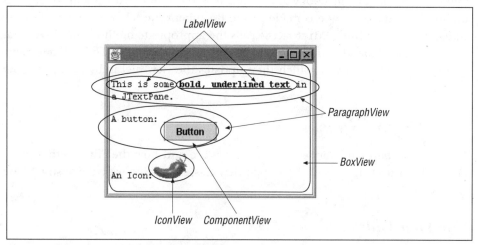

Figure 23-3. Sample view objects in a JTextPane

The "Root" View

In order to understand how all these View objects work together with the text components and the document model, it helps to know a little bit about a special view class used by BasicTextUI called RootView. This is a package private inner class, so you'll never use it directly. However, any time you use a Swing text component (unless you're using a L&F that doesn't take advantage of BasicTextUI, which is *very* unlikely) you'll be using a RootView at the top of the view object hierarchy.

RootView is not a "real" view; it only serves as a delegate to the real root view, typically a BoxView or PlainView. Most of its methods do nothing more than forward the request to the actual top-level view. The main thing this class provides is a well-known root which, by definition, has no parent. This allows all other view objects to assume that they have a parent. This is particularly important for the methods whose default implementation (in the View class) delegates to the parent view.

There are three such methods: getContainer() returns the text component the BasicTextUI has been associated with. preferenceChanged() calls revalidate() on the component, ensuring that the display will be kept up to date as views change size. This method gets called any time preferenceChanged() is called on any view since all implementations call super.preferenceChanged(). Finally, getViewFactory() is not implemented anywhere except View (which just passes it to its parent) meaning that the root view's implementation will always be used. This implementation just returns the ViewFactory of the current EditorKit. If an EditorKit does not supply a factory, the root view simply returns the BasicTextUI, which implements ViewFactory.

One last feature of the RootView is that it is the entry point for all document events. Any time a change is made to the document model, a document listener (created by the DefaultEditorKit) calls the appropriate method (we'll see what these methods look like in the next section) on the root view. This call gets delegated to the real root view which then updates the view hierarchy to support the content changes.

The View Classes

Now that we have an overview of what views are and how they fit together, we'll take a closer look at each of the public view classes, starting with the abstract base class, View.

The View Class

This abstract class represents how a single Element is displayed within a document. It defines properties and behavior common to different types of views. As we showed in Figure 23-2, all other view classes extend from View.

Properties

The View class defines the properties shown in Table 23-2. The attributes property defines the AttributeSet used by the view to render an Element. By default, the Element's attributes are used. However, view objects should access the attributes through the getAttributes() accessor, to allow view-specific attributes to be added to the Element's attributes or to allow the attributes to be converted in some way by the view subclasses.

Table 23-2. View Properties

Property	Data Type	get	is	set	bound	Default Value
alignment (indexed)	float	•				0.5
attributes	AttributeSet	•				from the Element
container	Container	•				from parent
document	Document	•				from the Element
element	Element	•				from constructor
endOffset	int	•				from the Element
maximumSpan (indexed)	float	•				if resizeWeight==0, preferredSpan, else Integer.MAX_VALUE
minimumSpan (indexed)	float	•				if resizeWeight==0, preferredSpan, else 0

Table 23-2. View Properties (continued)

Property	Data Type	get	is	set	bound	Default Value
parent	View	•		•		null
preferredSpan (indexed)	float	•				abstract
resizeWeight (indexed)	int	•				0
startOffset	int	•				from the Element
view (indexed)	View	•				null
viewCount	int	•				0
viewFactory	ViewFactory	•				from parent

The container property indicates the Container ultimately responsible for this View. In the View class itself, this is obtained from the view's parent (the View that contains this View). The element property indicates the Element this view is responsible for rendering, and the document property is taken directly from the Element for which the view was constructed. The startOffset and endOffset properties are also defined by that Element.

The viewCount property defines the number of children this View has and is always zero, unless the view is a CompositeView (or another View subclass that allows children). Consequently, the indexed view property, which gives access to specific children, returns null, unless the view is a CompositeView. viewFactory indicates the factory used to create new View objects (ViewFactory is covered later in the chapter). In View, this property is obtained from the view's parent, just like container.

The remaining properties are technically indexed properties, but their index values must be X_AXIS or Y_AXIS. In other words, each property is really two properties—one for the x axis and one for the y axis. The first such property is alignment. It describes the desired alignment for the view, where 0 indicates origin alignment, 1 indicates alignment to the full span away from the origin, and 0.5 (the default) indicates centered alignment.

The other four properties help determine the minimum, maximum, and preferred size of the component using the view. preferredSpan reflects the View's preferred size along a particular axis. resizeWeight is used to determine the minimum and maximum size of the view. A value of 0 (or less) indicates that the view should not be resized. The minimumSpan and maximumSpan of a view with a resizeWeight of zero are equal to the preferredSpan. Otherwise (if

resizeWeight > 0), the minimumSpan is considered to be 0, while the maximum-
Span is Integer.MAX_VALUE.

Constructor

public View(Element elem)
    Creates a View to represent the given Element.

Constants

View defines the constants shown in Table 23-3. The first four are used in the
getBreakWeight() method, described later. The others apply to the three properties that are indexed based on an axis.

Table 23-3. View Constants

Name	Data Type	Description
BadBreakWeight	int	The View should not be broken in fragments for formatting purposes
GoodBreakWeight	int	The View supports splitting, but that there is probably a better place to break the view
ExcellentBreakWeight	int	The View supports splitting and this is a very good place to break
ForcedBreakWeight	int	The View supports splitting and it must be broken to be displayed properly
X_AXIS	int	Used to specify the x-axis (same as SwingConstants.HORIZONTAL)
Y_AXIS	int	Used to specify the y-axis (same as SwingConstants.VERTICAL)

Miscellaneous Public Methods

public View breakView(int axis, int offset, float pos, float len)
    Requests a break in the current view along the specified axis. The offset
    indicates the document model position at which the break should begin, while
    pos and len give the view position along the specified axis that the broken
    view should occupy. The default implementation does not support breaking,
    so it returns this. Subclasses that override this method and support breaking
    should return a new view object, representing the requested subsection of this
    View.

    For text views like LabelView, breaking along the x-axis allows support for
    wrapping text to cover multiple lines. Views such as ParagraphView, which
    span multiple lines with a single view, may need to support y-axis breaking as
    well.

public View createFragment(int p0, int p1)

Creates a `View` to render some portion of the `Element` represented by the `View` the method is called on. The parameters define a character range which must be a subrange of the characters covered by this `View`'s `Element`. The range can be used to determine the size of different possible fragments of a `View`, when trying to determine where to break it. This default implementation returns `this`, since `View` does not support breaking by default.

public int getBreakWeight(int axis, float pos, float len)

Returns a "score," indicating how good a break would be in this view. The `pos` and `len` parameters indicate the potential starting point of the broken view, and the length (from `pos`) where a break is being considered. The return value may be one of the constants listed in Table 23-3, or any other integer value. The higher the number, the higher the desirability of the break. Any value less than or equal to `BadBreakWeight` indicates that the `View` should definitely not be broken. A value of `ForcedBreakWeight` or higher should always cause the `View` to be broken.

This implementation returns `BadBreakWeight`, unless the specified length is greater than the `preferredSpan` for this `View`, in which case `GoodBreakWeight` is returned (meaning that the entire `View` would be the fragment).

public Shape getChildAllocation(int index, Shape a)

Returns the allocated shape for the contained `View` at the specified index. This implementation returns `null`, since it does not directly support child `Views`.

getNextVisualPositionFrom(int pos, PositionBias b, Shape a, int direction,
PositionBias.Bias[] biasRet) throws BadLocationException

This method allows the view to specify the next location the cursor should be placed. The direction parameter should be one of `NORTH`, `SOUTH`, `EAST`, or `WEST` as defined in `SwingConstants`. For `NORTH` and `SOUTH`, this method uses `Utilities.getPostionAbove()` and `getPositionBelow()`. For `EAST` and `WEST`, it just returns the next or previous position, respectively. The `b` and `biasRet` parameters are currently unused.

public abstract Shape modelToView(int pos, Shape a, Position.Bias b)
throws BadLocationException

Returns an output rectangle (`aShape`) that gives the location of the given position pos within the model, using the view coordinates. The input rectangle a shows the area occupied by this view. If not supplied, the bias defaults to `Position.Bias.Forward`. Figure 23-4 shows how this method might work. It shows the input and output rectangles for a view for which a mapping from position 9 (the "n" in "never") was requested. The output rectangle reflects the height of the font, but typically has zero width.

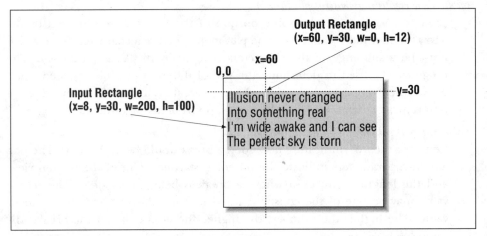

Figure 23-4. Model to view

public void preferenceChanged(View child, boolean width, boolean height)

Indicates that a child View's size has changed. The boolean parameters indicate which dimensions have been modified. The default implementation just passes the call up to the View's parent.

public void setSize(float width, float height)

Sets the size of the View, causing appropriate layout. The default implementation does nothing.

public abstract int viewToModel(float x, float y, Shape a, Position.Bias[] biasReturn)

Converts the specified view location to the closest corresponding model offset. It is up to the concrete implementations of this method to determine how to handle Shapes that encompass multiple model positions. biasReturn is an output parameter; on exit, it should be populated with a single value (Bias.Forward or Bias.Backward), indicating whether the given point was closer to the next character or the previous one.

Before looking at the subclasses of View, we'll take a quick detour to examine a few other view-related interfaces and classes.

Update Methods

These methods are variations on the methods defined in the DocumentListener interface. They are called in response to DocumentEvents being sent to the DefaultTextUI.

public void changedUpdate(DocumentEvent e, Shape a, ViewFactory f)

Indicates that attributes were changed that affect the portion of the Document this View is responsible for. This default implementation does nothing.

public void insertUpdate(DocumentEvent e, Shape a, ViewFactory f)
> Indicates that something was inserted into the portion of the Document this View is responsible for. The default implementation does nothing.

public void removeUpdate(DocumentEvent e, Shape a, ViewFactory f)
> Indicates that something was removed from the portion of the Document this View is responsible for. The default implementation does nothing.

Abstract Method

This method must be implemented by all concrete subclasses of View.

public abstract void paint(Graphics g, Shape allocation)
> Renders the View within the bounds of the given Shape on the given Graphics.

The ViewFactory Interface

ViewFactory specifies an interface for the creation of View objects used to render some portion of a Document. Classes that implement this interface must determine the type of View object to be created based on the type of Element passed in to the factory. We'll see a lot more about the ViewFactory interface, and classes that implement it, in the next chapter.

Factory Method

public abstract View create(Element elem)
> Creates a View for the specified Element. The type of View created is typically based on the name of the Element.

The TabExpander Interface

TabExpander is a simple interface implemented by certain View classes (ParagraphView, PlainView, and WrappedPlainView), to define tab expansion.

Methods

public abstract float nextTabStop(float x, int tabOffset)
> Returns the next tab stop position after the given position. Values are expressed in points. For example, a view with tab stops every 80 points, starting at zero, would return 240.0 for an input of 227.0. The second parameter is a document offset at which a tab is to be inserted. This offset may be used by implementations of this method that support different types of alignment and may need to know more than just the pixel position. For example, the view may handle tab expansion for centered text differently than for left-justified text.

The TabableView Interface

This interface is used by view classes whose size is dependent on tabs. It declares two methods used to obtain the size of some portion of the View.

Methods

public abstract float getTabbedSpan(float x, TabExpander e)

 Returns a value indicating the span for the View, starting at the specified point and using the given TabExpander to expand tabs.

public abstract float getPartialSpan(int p0, int p1)

 Returns a value indicating the span needed to cover the range defined by the given document offsets. Implementations may assume that there are no tabs in the given range.

The Utilities Class

This class defines a set of convenient static methods used by the text package. We introduce this class here because several of these methods are used by the View subclasses.

Public Static Methods

public static final int drawTabbedText(Segment s, int x, int y, Graphics g, TabExpander e, int startOffset)

 Draws the specified text Segment on the given Graphics at the desired location. Tabs will be expanded using the specified TabExpander, based on startOffset. The return value is the x-coordinate following the drawn text.

public static final int getBreakLocation(Segment s, FontMetrics metrics, int x0, int x, TabExpander e, int startOffset)

 Tries to find a suitable line-break location by looking for whitespace in the given Segment.

public static final int getNextWord(JTextComponent c, int offs)
 throws BadLocationException

 Returns the document offset of the beginning of the word that follows the given document offset.

public static final Element getParagraphElement(JTextComponent c, int offs)

 Returns the paragraph element in use at the given document offset. If the component's model is a StyledDocument, the StyledDocument.getParagraphElement() method is used. Otherwise, the document's root element is queried for the child containing the given offset.

public static final int getPositionAbove(JTextComponent c, int offs, int x)
throws BadLocationException

Returns the document position closest to the given x view coordinate in the row above the row containing the document offset offs.

public static final int getPositionBelow(JTextComponent c, int offs, int x)
throws BadLocationException

Returns the document position closest to the given x view coordinate in the row below the row containing the document offset offs.

public static final int getPreviousWord(JTextComponent c, int offs)
throws BadLocationException

Returns the document offset of the beginning of the word that comes before the given document offset.

public static final int getRowEnd(JTextComponent c, int offs) throws BadLocationException

Returns the document offset at the end of the row containing offs.

public static final int getRowStart(JTextComponent c, int offs) throws BadLocationException

Returns the document offset at the start of the row containing offs.

public static final int getTabbedTextOffset(Segment s, FontMetrics metrics, int x0, int x,
TabExpander e, int startOffset)

Returns an offset into the given Segment. The x0 parameter specifies the view location of the start of the text, while x specifies the view location to be mapped to an offset into the Segment. Tabs will be expanded using the specified TabExpander, based on the given startOffset.

public static final int getTabbedTextWidth(Segment s, FontMetrics metrics, int x,
TabExpander e, int startOffset)

Returns the width, in points, of the given Segment of text with tabs expanded. The x argument is the starting point of the text. Tabs will be expanded using the specified TabExpander, based on the given startOffset.

public static final int getWordEnd(JTextComponent c, int offs) throws BadLocationException

Returns the document offset of the character after the last character in the word containing offs.

public static final int getWordStart(JTextComponent c, int offs)
throws BadLocationException

Returns the document offset of the first character in the word containing offs.

The PlainView Class

This View class is used for simple text components rendered in a single font and color. Components that use this type of view include JTextField, JPassword-Field, and JTextArea (with line wrap turned off). The first two will actually use subclasses of PlainView, defined next, but most of the work of those subclasses is done here. Figure 23-5 shows three components using variations of the Plain-View class. Note that the JTextArea uses a single view to represent multiple lines of un-wrapped text.

Figure 23-5. Text components using PlainView (and subclasses)

Properties

The PlainView class modifies the implementation of the View properties shown in Table 23-4. See the description of View properties for details on these properties. Setting the parent causes the container (the JTextComponent) to be retrieved and cached for use in determining things such as the component's font. The preferredSpan for the X_AXIS is based on the width of the text, while the preferredSpan for the Y_AXIS is determined by multiplying the height of the containing component's font by the number of child Elements (lines) contained by element. The element property must be specified in the constructor.

Table 23-4. PlainView Properties

Property	Data Type	get	is	set	bound	Default Value
element*	Element	•				From constructor
preferredSpan (indexed)*	float	•				Described later

See also properties from the View class (Table 23-2).

Field

There is one protected field in the PlainView class:

protected FontMetrics metrics
    Contains the FontMetrics for the font currently in use.

Constructor

public PlainView(Element elem)
> Creates a View for the input Element.

Document Event Methods

The following methods override the empty implementations provided by View for the methods called when changes are made to the Element for which this View is responsible:

public void changedUpdate(DocumentEvent changes, Shape a, ViewFactory f)
public void insertUpdate(DocumentEvent changes, Shape a, ViewFactory f)
public void removeUpdate(DocumentEvent changes, Shape a, ViewFactory f)
> Call a package private method (updateDamage()), which calls repaint() on the View's JTextComponent if lines have been added or removed. If not, only the area covering the modified line is repainted.

TabExpander Method

public float nextTabStop(float x, int tabOffset)
> Returns the next tab-stop position after the given position, ignoring the second parameter. Figure 23-6 shows how this might work for a simple line of text with 8-space tabs and a fixed-width (7 pixels wide) font. An input value of 357 (the location of the end of the line of text) would result in a value of 392, the next tab stop, being returned.

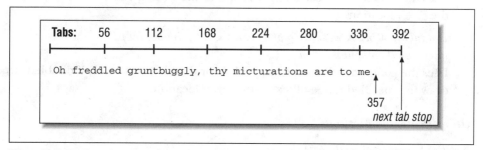

Figure 23-6. Finding the next tab stop in a PlainView

Other Public Methods

public Shape modelToView(int pos, Shape a, Position.Bias b) throws BadLocationException
> Converts the given model position to a Rectangle containing that position. The width of the rectangle is always 1, and the height is always the height of the component's font. The b parameter is currently ignored.

public void paint(Graphics g, Shape a)

Gets the font and colors from the `View`'s `JTextComponent` and then paints the lines that are currently visible, using the protected `drawLine()` method.

public void preferenceChanged(View child, boolean width, boolean height)

Indicates that the size of the view has changed. This method clears the `Plain-Document.lineLimitAttribute` from the `View`'s `Document` and calls `super.preferenceChanged()`.

public int viewToModel(float fx, float fy, Shape a, Position.Bias[] bias)

Converts the given point in the `View`'s coordinate system to an offset into the `View`'s `Document`. Currently, the output bias parameter is always populated with `Position.Bias.Forward`. In the future, this should be changed to actually calculate the correct value.

Protected Drawing Methods

These protected methods are responsible for drawing the view's text. The x and y parameters indicate the location in the view where the text is to be painted. The p0 and p1 parameters define the portion of the `Element` to be drawn.

protected void drawLine(int lineIndex, Graphics g, int x, int y)

Uses `drawSelectedText()` and `drawUnselectedText()` to render the specified line of text at the given location.

protected int drawSelectedText(Graphics g, int x, int y, int p0, int p1)
throws BadLocationException

Uses the component's selected text color to draw the specified range of text at the given location.

protected int drawUnselectedText(Graphics g, int x, int y, int p0, int p1)
throws BadLocationException

Uses the component's foreground color (or disabled text color, if disabled) to draw the specified range of text at the given location.

Other Protected Methods

protected Segment getLineBuffer()

Provides access to the buffer used to retrieve text from the `Document`.

protected int getTabSize()

Returns the size (in characters) of a tab. It checks the `Document`'s properties for the size (`PlainDocument.tabSizeAttribute`) and returns it if available. Otherwise, it returns the default value of 8.

The FieldView Class

FieldView is an extension of PlainView used for single-line editors (such as JTextField). The main thing this subclass provides is the ability to center the single line of text if the View is expanded vertically.

Properties

The FieldView class modifies the implementation of the View properties shown in Table 23-5. See the description of View properties for details on these properties. The preferredSpan for the X_AXIS is based on the width of the entire contents of the document. The preferredSpan for the Y_AXIS is defined by the superclass. resizeWeight is 1 for the X_AXIS and 0 for the Y_AXIS, indicating that the view should only be resized horizontally. As usual, the element property is set in the constructor.

Table 23-5. FieldView Properties

Property	Data Type	get	is	set	bound	Default Value
element*	Element	•				From constructor
preferredSpan (indexed)*	float	•				See below
resizeWeight (indexed)*	int	•				X_AXIS: 1, Y_AXIS: 0

See also properties from the PlainView class (Table 23-4).

Constructors

public FieldView(Element elem)
> Creates a new View for the Element.

Public Methods

The following methods override the implementations provided by PlainView. They all use the PlainView implementations, but first use the protected adjust-Allocation() method to modify the given Shape.

public void insertUpdate(DocumentEvent changes, Shape a, ViewFactory f)
> Calls super.insertUpdate() (modifying the given shape by a call to adjustAllocation()) and updates the horizontal visibility model of the JTextField rendered by this view (if there is one).

public void removeUpdate(DocumentEvent changes, Shape a, ViewFactory f)
> Calls super.removeUpdate(), modifying the given shape by a call to adjustAllocation(), and updates the horizontal visibility model of the JTextField rendered by this view (if there is one).

public void paint(Graphics g, Shape a)
public Shape modelToView(int pos, Shape a, Position.Bias b) throws BadLocationException
public int viewToModel(float fx, float fy, Shape a, Position.Bias[] bias)

> Call the appropriate super method after modifying the given Shape by calling adjustAllocation(). See Figure 23-7.

Protected Methods

protected Shape adjustAllocation(Shape a)

> Enables the single line of text to be centered vertically within the bounds of the given Shape. It returns a Rectangle that is centered vertically within the Shape and that has a height equal to the View's preferred span along y-axis. Horizontal adjustments are made according to the horizontalAlignment property of the JTextField using this view.

> Figure 23-7 shows what this method does. The larger rectangle represents the full size of the JTextField. In this case, the field's horizontal alignment is set to SwingConstants.RIGHT, indicating that the text should be right justified. This method returns the inner rectangle, indicating the exact region into which the text should be painted.

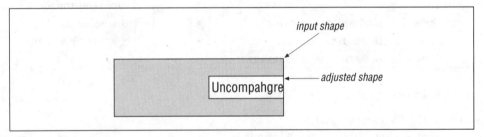

Figure 23-7. FieldView.adjustAllocation()

protected FontMetrics getFontMetrics()

> Returns the FontMetrics for the Font in use by the View's Container.

The PasswordView Class

PasswordView extends FieldView to render text using the JPasswordField's echo character. If the component using this view is not a JPasswordField, it will not render anything.

Properties

PasswordView does not modify any of the properties defined by its superclass, FieldView. The element property is set in the constructor.

Constructors

public PasswordView(Element elem)

Creates a new View for the given Element.

Protected Methods

The only methods defined in this class are two protected methods called by FieldView's paint() method and a third used by both of the others. As with FieldView, the x and y coordinates are view coordinates, while p0 and p1 are offsets in the Element being displayed.

protected int drawEchoCharacter(Graphics g, int x, int y, char c)

Draws the given character at the specified location. It returns the x-coordinate of the next character to be drawn (i.e., x plus the width of c).

protected int drawSelectedText(Graphics g, int x, int y, int p0, int p1)
throws BadLocationException

Draws the specified range of selected text using drawEchoCharacter() to draw each character in the component's selected text color. If the view's container is not a JPasswordField, nothing is drawn.

protected int drawUnselectedText(Graphics g, int x, int y, int p0, int p1)
throws BadLocationException

Draws the specified range of unselected text, using drawEchoCharacter() to draw each character in the component's foreground color. If the view's container is not a JPasswordField, nothing is drawn.

The LabelView Class

This View subclass is used to display a section of text with common attributes. A LabelView[*] is responsible for painting an Element from a StyledDocument. However, as we'll see later (Figure 23-10), if the view does not fit on a single line, it is actually replaced by multiple LabelView.LabelFragment objects, which are together responsible for painting the single Element.

LabelView supports intelligent breaking of views to allow breaks to occur on word boundaries. It implements the TabableView interface, reflecting the fact that the text it represents may contain tabs. In order for tabs to be rendered correctly, LabelViews must be embedded in views that implement TabExpander such as ParagraphView.

---

[*] Despite the somewhat misleading name, LabelView has nothing to do with rendering JLabels or even simple text fields.

Properties

The LabelView class modifies the implementation of the View properties shown in Table 23-6. See the description of View properties for details on these properties. The Y_AXIS alignment is defined as *(height-descent)/height* for the current font. In other words, LabelViews are aligned along their baselines (see Figure 23-8). X_AXIS alignment is delegated to the superclass. The X_AXIS preferredSpan is the width of the text to be displayed, computed using Utilities.getTabbedTextWidth(). The Y_AXIS preferredSpan is just the height of the font currently in use.

Table 23-6. LabelView Properties

Property	Data Type	get	is	set	bound	Default Value
alignment (indexed)*	float	•				
element*	Element	•				From constructor
preferredSpan (indexed)*	float	•				From Icon dimensions

See also properties from the View class (Table 23-2).

Figure 23-8. LabelView y-axis alignment

The element property is set in the constructor.

Constructor

public LabelView(Element elem)
    Creates a View for the given Element.

TabableView Methods

The following methods satisfy the TabableView interface implemented by this class:

public float getPartialSpan(int p0, int p1)
    Returns the width of the given document range of text, using the getTabbedTextWidth() method in the Utilities class.

public float getTabbedSpan(float x, TabExpander e)

Returns the desired span for this view, starting at the given x-coordinate, using the specified `TabExpander`.

Other Public Methods

public View breakView(int axis, int p0, float pos, float len)

Attempts to break the `View` at the whitespace character closest to the requested length from the given starting point. It returns a new `View` object (an instance of an inner class), representing a portion of this `LabelView`. The current `LabelView` is not affected. The method returns this if the given axis is not `X_AXIS`.

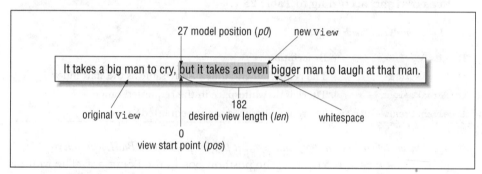

Figure 23-9. Breaking a view example

Figure 23-9 shows how this might work. In this example, the goal is to break the `View`, starting at model position 27 (the "b" in "but"), which will be at the beginning of a line (pos = 0). We want a new `View` that is about 182 points long. The `breakView()` method takes all of this into account and returns a new `View` containing a portion of the original view, broken on the first whitespace it finds prior to the requested endpoint.

public void changedUpdate(DocumentEvent e, Shape a, ViewFactory f)

Indicates that the `Document`'s attributes have changed for an area of the `Document` for which this `View` is responsible. It sets a flag so that other methods will synchronize with the `Document` before doing things such as painting the `View`.

public View createFragment(int p0, int p1)

Returns a new `View` that represents a portion of the current `View`, bound by the specified model endpoints. When a `LabelView` becomes too long to fit on a single line, it is replaced by two `LabelView.LabelFragments` (a nonpublic inner class), as shown in Figure 23-10.

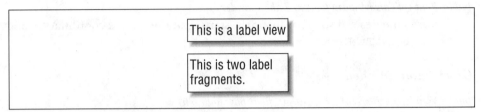

Figure 23-10. LabelView split into two LabelView.LabelFragments

public int getBreakWeight(int axis, float pos, float len)

If the given axis is Y_AXIS, this method delegates to the superclass. For X_AXIS, the result will be BadBreakWeight, GoodBreakWeight, or Excellent-BreakWeight, according to Table 23-7.

Table 23-7. LabelView Break Weights

Result	Description
BadBreakWeight	The requested end index is the same as the start index
GoodBreakWeight	There is no whitespace in the requested range
ExcellentBreakWeight	There is whitespace in the requested range

public Shape modelToView(int pos, Shape a, int p0, int p1) throws BadLocationException

Returns a Rectangle covering the position pos in the Document. The width is always 0, and the height is always the height of the font in use at this position. The p0 and p1 parameters restrict the range in which pos should be searched.

public Shape modelToView(int pos, Shape a, Position.Bias b) throws BadLocationException

This version returns modelToView(pos, a, getStartOffset(), getEndOffset()), currently ignoring b.

public void paint(Graphics g, Shape a)

Uses Utilities.drawTabbedText() to draw the text to the given Graphics, using the appropriate font and color (as specified in the Element's attributes). It uses Graphics.drawLine() to underline the text if the underline attribute has been set.

public int viewToModel(float x, float y, Shape a, int p0, int p1)

Calculates the model offset closest to the given location (only the left edge of the given Shape is taken into account). The p0 and p1 parameters are document offsets used to restrict the search range.

public int viewToModel(float x, float y, Shape a, Position.Bias[] biasReturn)

This version returns viewToModel(x, y, a, getStartOffset(), getEndOffset()). Currently, biasReturn[0] is always set to Position.Bias.Forward.

Protected Methods

protected void setPropertiesFromAttributes()

> Used to update several cached values based on the view's current attributes (which it gets from `getAttributes()`).

protected void setUnderline(boolean u)

> Used by `setPropertiesFromAttributes()` to indicate whether or not the text displayed by this view is underlined.

The ComponentView Class

This class can be used to embed AWT `Components` into the view hierarchy. As we saw in a previous chapter, a single `Element` in a `Document` can be used to represent a `Component`. A single `ComponentView` object is responsible for rendering such an `Element`.

Properties

The `ComponentView` class modifies the implementation of the `View` properties shown in Table 23-8. See the description of `View` properties for details on these properties. In `ComponentView`, the `alignment` property is taken from the `Component`'s response to `getAlignmentX()` and `getAlignmentY()` calls. Similarly, `preferredSpan` is determined based on the `preferredSize` of the `Component`. The implementation of `setParent()` actually causes the `Component` to be added (or removed if the parent is set to `null`) as a child of the view's `Container`. The `element` property must be specified in the constructor.

Table 23-8. ComponentView Properties

Property	Data Type	get	is	set	bound	Default Value
alignment (indexed)*	float	•				From Component
element*	Element	•				From constructor
parent*	View			•		null
preferredSpan (indexed)*	float	•				From preferredSize of Component

See also properties from the View class (Table 23-2).

Constructor

public ComponentView(Element elem)

> Creates a `View` for the given `Element`. It expects to get a valid `Component` from the given element's attribute set. The component is initially invisible.

Methods

ComponentView implements the three abstract methods defined in View, as well as setSize(), which had an empty implementation in View.

public Shape modelToView(int pos, Shape a, Position.Bias b) throws BadLocationException
> Returns a Rectangle with width=0 located at the given Shape's location with the shape's height. If the given position is not covered by this View, null is returned. The b parameter is currently ignored.

public void paint(Graphics g, Shape a)
> Paints the Component. This implementation just sets the bounds of the Component based on the bounds of the given Shape, and ensures that the component is visible. The actual painting of the Component will occur as a result of it being a child of some Container.

public void setSize(float width, float height)
> Converts the given arguments to integers and calls setSize() on the Component.

public int viewToModel(float x, float y, Shape a, Position.Bias[] bias)
> Returns the View's start offset, which comes from the Element it was constructed, since Elements containing Components are always only one "character" long. bias[0] is set to the appropriate value based on which half of the given Shape the x parameter falls in.

The IconView Class

This class can be used to embed Icons into the view hierarchy. Just as we saw with Components, a single Element in a Document is used to represent the Icon, and a single IconView object is responsible for rendering the Element.

Properties

The IconView class modifies the implementation of the View properties, shown in Table 23-9. See the description of View properties for details on these properties. In IconView, the alignment property is defined as 1 for the Y_AXIS (align with the bottom of the Icon). The X_AXIS alignment defaults to the value returned by View (0.5). The preferredSpan is simply the width and height of the Icon. The element property must be specified in the constructor.

Constructors

public IconView(Element elem)
> This constructor creates a View for the given Element. It expects to get a valid Icon from the given element's attribute set.

Table 23-9. IconView Properties

Property	Data Type	get	is	set	bound	Default Value
alignment (indexed)*	float	•				Y_AXIS: 1, X_AXIS: 0.5
element*	Element	•				From constructor
preferredSpan (indexed)*	float	•				From Icon dimensions

See also properties from the View class (Table 23-2).

Methods

`ComponentView` implements the three abstract methods defined in `View`, as well as `setSize()`, which had an empty implementation in `View`.

public Shape modelToView(int pos, Shape a, Position.Bias b) throws BadLocationException
> Returns a `Rectangle` with width=0, located at the given `Shape`'s location with the shape's height. If the given position is not covered by this `View`, `null` is returned. The `b` parameter is currently ignored.

public void paint(Graphics g, Shape a)
> Calls `paintIcon()` on the `View`'s icon, passing in the `View`'s `Container`, the given `Graphics`, and the x/y coordinates of the given `Shape`.

public void setSize(float width, float height)
> Since `Icons` do not support resizing, this method does nothing.

public int viewToModel(float x, float y, Shape a, Position.Bias[] bias)
> Returns the `View`'s start offset, which comes from the `Element` with which it was constructed, since `Elements` containing `Icons` are always only one "character" long. `bias[0]` is set to the appropriate value base on which half of the given `Shape` the x parameter falls in.

The CompositeView Class

This abstract class allows `Views` to be grouped and referenced as a single `View`. This is a classic use of the Composite design pattern. `CompositeViews` are used to render nonleaf nodes. The `View`'s children correspond to the `Element`'s children.

Properties

The `CompositeView` class modifies the implementation of the `View` properties shown in Table 23-10. See the description of `View` properties for details on these properties. The `setParent()` method is overridden to call `super.setParent()` and then `loadChildren()` (a protected method described later) to set up its child views. Since `CompositeView` supports child views, the `view` and `viewCount` properties are implemented to track an initially empty array of Views. The element property is set in the constructor.

Table 23-10. CompositeView Properties

Property	Data Type	get	is	set	bound	Default Value
element*	Element	•				From constructor
parent*	View			•		null
view (indexed)*	View	•				null
viewCount*	int	•				0

See also properties from the View class (Table 23-2).

Constructors

public CompositeView(Element elem)

Creates a View to represent the given Element. The View initially has zero children. Child views are not added until setParent() is called.

View Methods

The following methods override the default implementations provided by View:

public Shape getChildAllocation(int index, Shape a)

Gets the Shape's bounding Rectangle and calls childAllocation() (see list of abstract, protected methods) returning the resulting Rectangle.

public Shape modelToView(int pos, Shape a, Position.bias b) throws BadLocationException

Determines which one of the view's children contains the specified model position and passes the call on to that child.

public int viewToModel(float x, float y, Shape a, Position.bias[] bias)

Determines which one of the view's children contains the specified view location and passes the call on to that child.

New Public Methods

These methods are new to the CompositeView class. The first three are implemented by calling the fourth, replace().

public void append(View v)

Adds a new View to the end of the list of contained Views. The parent of v is set to this composite view.

public void insert(int offs, View v)

Inserts a new View at the specified child index. The parent of v is set to this composite view.

public void removeAll()

Removes all child `View`s. The parent of each is set to `null`.

public void replace(int offset, int length, View views[])

Replaces the specified range of `View`s with the given array of `View`s. The parent of any removed `View` is set to `null`. The parent of any added `View` is set to this composite view.

Protected Methods

`CompositeView` defines quite a few protected methods for working with the view's children:

protected final short getBottomInset()
protected final short getLeftInset()
protected final short getRightInset()
protected final short getTopInset()

Return the insets set by a call to `setInsets()` or `setParagraphInsets()` (both are defined later). These values reflect the amount of blank space to be displayed on a given side of the view.

protected Rectangle getInsideAllocation(Shape a)

Returns a `Rectangle` created by taking the bounds of the given `Shape` and subtracting any insets defined for this view.

protected View getViewAtPosition(int pos, Rectangle a)

Returns the child `View` containing the given model position. The given `Rectangle` gives the parent's allocation and is changed to the child's allocation on exit.

protected void loadChildren(ViewFactory f)

Initializes the `View` by loading its children. The default implementation iterates over the child `Element`s contained by the `View`'s `Element` (if there are any) and uses the given factory to create a new `View` for each `Element`.

protected final void setInsets(short top, short left, short bottom, short right)

Sets the `View`'s insets.

protected final void setParagraphInsets(AttributeSet attr)

Sets the `View`'s insets from the given `AttributeSet`. The attribute keys `SpaceAbove`, `SpaceBelow`, `LeftIndent`, and `RightIndent` (defined in `StyleConstants`) are queried.

Abstract Protected Methods

The following methods are not implemented in `CompositeView` and must be implemented by any concrete subclass.

protected abstract void childAllocation(int index, Rectangle a)

>   Modifies the given `Rectangle` a to reflect the allocation for a specified child. The `Rectangle` specifies the `View`'s allocation on input and should contain the result on exit. Figure 23-11 shows how this should work for a composite view with three children. We see that r0 is passed in, but this rectangle is modified to contain the bounds of r2 on exit.

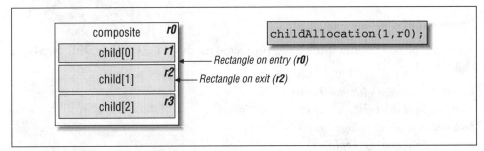

Figure 23-11. Computing the allocation for child[1]

protected abstract View getViewAtPoint(int x, int y, Rectangle alloc)

>   Returns the child `View` containing the given point. The `Rectangle` gives the parent's allocation and should be changed to the child's allocation on exit.

protected abstract boolean isAfter(int x, int y, Rectangle alloc)

>   Returns `true` if the given point is located after the given `Rectangle`. "After" is typically defined as being to the right or below.

protected abstract boolean isBefore(int x, int y, Rectangle alloc)

>   Returns `true` is the given point is located before the given `Rectangle`. "Before" is typically defined as being to the left or above.

The BoxView Class

This is a subclass of `CompositeView` that arranges its children in a box along one axis. The `StyledEditorKit` uses `BoxView` to represent its top-level section element. This provides a convenient mechanism for grouping together the paragraphs of a document; each paragraph is represented by a `ParagraphView`, which is a child of the `BoxView`.

Properties

The `BoxView` class defines two new properties and modifies the implementation of several `CompositeView` properties shown in Table 23-11. See the description of `View` properties for details on these properties. The `alignment` property for the axis being tiled will be 0.5. For the other axis, the alignment is based on the alignment and span of the children.

Table 23-11. BoxView Properties

Property	Data Type	get	is	set	bound	Default Value
alignment (indexed)*	float	•				
element*	Element	•				From constructor
height	int	•				
preferredSpan (indexed)*	float	•				
resizeWeight (indexed)*	int	•				From children
width	int	•				

See also properties from the CompositeView class (Table 23-10).

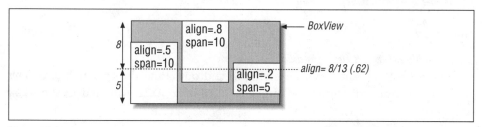

Figure 23-12. BoxView alignment

Figure 23-12 shows a BoxView with three children. Inside each child, we show its alignment and preferredSpan. The first child has a preferred span of 10 and an alignment of 0.5, indicating that it should be centered relative to the box's baseline. The second child also has a span of 10, but its alignment is 0.8, indicating that 80% of the view should be above the baseline. The last child has a span of just 5 and an alignment of 0.2, indicating that 80% of this view should be below the baseline. The figure shows the resulting BoxView which will contain these children and satisfy all of the constraints. To satisfy all of the children, the box needs to have a total span of 13 (5 below the baseline for the first child and 8 above the baseline for the second), with an alignment baseline 8/13 (0.62) from the top. This value (0.62) becomes the alignment of the box itself.

The preferredSpan properties reflect the space needed to render all of the children (13 in the example from Figure 23-12). This is the sum of the sizes for one axis and the maximum distance between the edges of its children for the other axis, as shown in Figure 23-13.

The resizeWeight is defined as the sum of the resizeWeights of the view's children. The element property is set in the constructor. width and height represent the most recently set dimensions of the view.

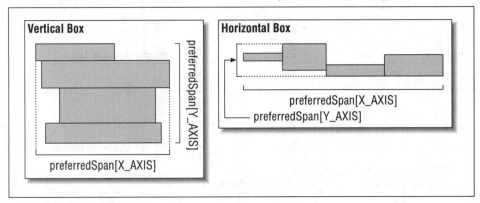

Figure 23-13. preferredSpan for vertical and horizontal BoxViews

Constructor

public BoxView(Element elem, int axis)

> Creates a View for the given element, laid out along the specified axis. The value for the axis should be either X_AXIS or Y_AXIS (defined in the View class).

Document Update Methods

The following methods update the View hierarchy in response to any changes in the Element hierarchy:

public void changedUpdate(DocumentEvent e, Shape a, ViewFactory f)

> Indicates that attributes have changed in an area of the Document for which this View is responsible. It updates the child Views to reflect the attribute changes and replaces Views as necessary. Any new children that are needed are created using the given ViewFactory.

public void insertUpdate(DocumentEvent e, Shape a, ViewFactory f)

> Indicates that content has been added to a portion of the Document for which this View is responsible. It updates its children as necessary, creating new Views (using the given factory) if appropriate.

public void removeUpdate(DocumentEvent e, Shape a, ViewFactory f)

> Indicates that content has been removed from a portion of the Document for which this View is responsible. Child Views are updated as needed, and new Views will replace other Views as necessary. Any new children that are needed are created using the given ViewFactory.

Public Methods

public Shape modelToView(int pos, Shape a, Position.bias b) throws BadLocationException
  Maps the given model position to view coordinates. It makes sure its children are allocated properly and then calls super.modelToView().

public void paint(Graphics g, Shape allocation)
  This method iterates over its children, painting them onto the given Graphics within the bounds of the specified Shape. Children are painted using the protected paintChild() method.

public void preferenceChanged(View child, boolean width, boolean height)
  Indicates that a child's span has changed. It notes which directions have changed (essentially clearing cached layout data) and passes the call up to its superclass.

public void replace(int offset, int length, View elems[])
  Calls super.replace() and clears any cached layout information. This means that any time a child is added or removed, the layout data for the parent must be recomputed.

public void setSize(float width, float height)
  Sets the overall size of the View and calls layout() to arrange the child Views, if the size specified is different than the old size.

public int viewToModel(float x, float y, Shape a, Position.bias[] bias)
  Converts the given point to an offset in the Document model. It makes sure its children are allocated properly and then calls super.viewToModel().

CompositeView Protected Methods

The following methods are defined in the CompositeView superclass and implemented here. The first two methods modify their given Rectangles. This is done (rather than just returning a new Rectangle) to avoid creating extra objects every time one of these common methods is called.

protected void childAllocation(int index, Rectangle alloc)
  Converts the given Rectangle (representing the entire View's allocation) to a Rectangle containing the specified child View.

protected View getViewAtPoint(int x, int y, Rectangle alloc)
  Returns the child View at the specified point. The given Rectangle is the View's allocation on given and is changed to the child's allocation on exit.

protected boolean isAfter(int x, int y, Rectangle innerAlloc)
  Returns true if the given point is to the right of the given Rectangle (if this is an X_AXIS BoxView), or if it is below the Rectangle (for Y_AXIS BoxViews).

protected boolean isBefore(int x, int y, Rectangle innerAlloc)
> Returns true if the given point is to the left of the given Rectangle (if this is an X_AXIS BoxView), or if it is above the Rectangle (for Y_AXIS BoxViews).

Other Protected Methods

These methods are new to the BoxView class:

protected boolean isAllocationValid()
> Returns true if nothing has been done to the View to invalidate the data cached by the view about the allocation of its children. Operations such as adding or removing children can invalidate the cache.

protected void layout(int width, int height)
> Sets the positions and sizes of the View's children, based on the given view size. Most of the work is done by layoutMajorAxis() and layoutMinor-Axis().

protected void layoutMajorAxis(int targetSpan, int axis, int[] offsets, int[] spans)
> Performs the major-axis layout. offsets and spans are output parameters that will be populated with the offsets and spans of the child components.

protected void layoutMinorAxis(int targetSpan, int axis, int[] offsets, int[] spans)
> Performs the minor-axis layout. offsets and spans are output parameters that will be populated with the offsets and spans of the child components.

protected void paintChild(Graphics g, Rectangle alloc, int index)
> Finds the child View at the specified index and calls its paint() method.

The ParagraphView Class

ParagraphView is an extension of BoxView that implements TabExpander and supports line-wrapping paragraphs with multiple fonts, colors, etc. A Paragraph-View is a vertical box containing child Views (instances of a package-private inner class called Row) to represent each row of text in the paragraph. A Row contains one or more views, each of which maps to one of the paragraph's child Elements, or a portion of a child Element, if the child cannot be displayed in a single row.

Figure 23-14 shows how the View hierarchy below a ParagraphView is affected by the size of the container in which the paragraph is to be displayed. The top box shows a simple Element structure in which a single paragraph Element contains two children. The next box shows the View hierarchy that could represent the model if the entire paragraph fit on a single line. A single Row is created, which contains LabelViews that map to each leaf Element. The last box shows what would happen if the container shrunk so that the paragraph would no longer fit on a single line. The ParagraphView creates an additional Row, and the first

`LabelView` is split (producing instances of an inner class of `LabelView` called `LabelFragment`).

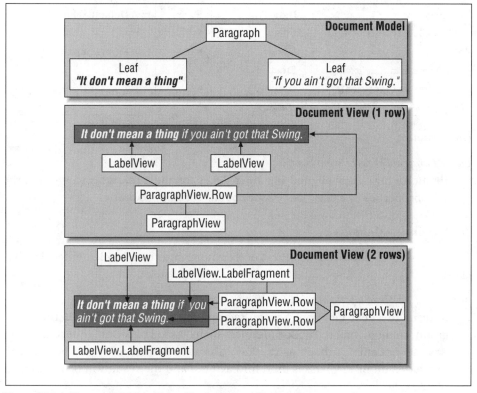

Figure 23-14. Two possible View hierarchies for a given Element structure

Instances of this class are used by the `StyledEditorKit` to represent elements whose name matches `AbstractDocument.ParagraphElementName`.

Properties

The `ParagraphView` class modifies the implementation of the `BoxView` properties shown in Table 23-12. See the description of `View` properties for details on these properties. The `alignment` property for the `X_AXIS` is handled by the superclass, while the `Y_AXIS` alignment will be based on the center of the first child (the center of the top row of text). The `preferredSpan` for the `X_AXIS` is based on the width specified when the view was laid out. For the `Y_AXIS`, this property is handled by the superclass. The `resizeWeight` is 1 for `X_AXIS` and 0 for `Y_AXIS`. The `element` property is set in the constructor.

Table 23-12. ParagraphView Properties

Property	Data Type	get	is	set	bound	Default Value
alignment (indexed)*	float	•				
element*	Element	•				From constructor
preferredSpan (indexed)*	float	•				
resizeWeight (indexed)*	int	•				X_AXIS: 1, Y_AXIS: 0

See also properties from the BoxView class (Table 23-11).

Constructor

public ParagraphView(Element elem)

Creates a new View aligned on the Y_AXIS for the Element and sets several view properties by calling setPropertiesFromAttributes().

TabExpander Methods

The following method satisfies the TabExpander interface implemented by this class:

public float nextTabStop(float x, int tabOffset)

Returns the next tab stop. Several factors determine this value. If the paragraph element has a TabSet defined in its AttributeSet (queried using StyleConstants.TabSet as the key), the tabs defined in it will be used. If not, a default of 72 pixels is used for each tab and the result will be a multiple of 72.

If a TabSet is defined, but there is no tab after the given position, this implementation returns the given position plus 5.0.

If a tab is found, the result depends on the alignment of the tab. For TabStop.ALIGN_LEFT and TabStop.ALIGN_BAR, the result is just the tab position plus the left inset. For other alignments, the result is calculated using findOffsetOfCharactersInString() and getPartialSize().

Document Change Methods

The following methods are reimplemented in this class to handle changes to the Element hierarchy displayed by this view:

public void changedUpdate(DocumentEvent changes, Shape a, ViewFactory f)
public void insertUpdate(DocumentEvent changes, Shape a, ViewFactory f)
public void removeUpdate(DocumentEvent changes, Shape a, ViewFactory f)

These methods are called when changes are made to the portion of the Document for which this View is responsible. They update the state of the view, creating new children (using the given factory) as needed, and removing children that are no longer needed.

New Public Methods

The following public methods are new to the `ParagraphView` class:

public View breakView(int axis, float len, Shape a)
> The `ParagraphView` class does not currently support breaking. This method always returns `this` until the feature is implemented.

public int getBreakWeight(int axis, float len)
> The `ParagraphView` class does not currently support breaking. This method always returns `BadBreakWeight` until the feature is implemented.

NOTE   As of JDK 1.2 beta4, the signatures of these methods do not match the signatures defined in `View`. As a result, these methods are never called. Presumably, this will be changed in a future release.

BoxView (and Superclasses) Methods

These methods override methods implemented in `BoxView` or its superclasses:

protected View getViewAtPosition(int pos, Rectangle a)
> Returns the child `View` at the specified model position. The given `rectangle` contains the `View`'s allocation on given and is constrained to the child's `View` on exit. It is implemented to iterate over the view's children until it finds one that contains the given document offset.

protected void layout(int width, int height)
> Lays out the children by calling `super.layout()`. Before doing so, it checks to see if the width has changed, in which case the rows are rebuilt.

protected void loadChildren(ViewFactory f)
> Creates a new `View` object for each child of the paragraph element using the given factory.

public void paint(Graphics g, Shape a)
> Sets the "tab base" to the left edge of the given `Shape` plus the view's left inset and then calls `super.paint()` to paint the view's children.

New Protected Methods

These new protected methods are used internally by `ParagraphView`:

protected void adjustRow(ParagraphView.Row r, int desiredSpan, int x)

> Attempts to adjust the given `Row` (a package-private inner class that extends `BoxView` and is used to represent a row of text that may contain multiple children) so that it will fit nicely in the specified span. The row's children are searched, looking for the best break point. If a valid break point is found, the row is broken accordingly. If not, the method does nothing.

protected int findOffsetToCharactersInString(char string[], int start)

> Returns the offset of the next character (after `start`) in the document that matches any character in the given array. This is used by `nextTabStop()` to search for tabs.

protected float getPartialSize(int startOffset, int endOffset)

> Returns the size used by the child views between the given document offsets.

protected TabSet getTabSet()

> Uses `StyleContants.getTabSet()` to retrieve the tabs defined for the view's element.

protected void setFirstLineIndent(float fi)
protected void setLineSpacing(float ls)
protected void setJustification(int j)

> Cache a local copy of the values of these attributes.

protected void setPropertiesFromAttributes()

> Caches several properties based on the attributes defined by `getAttributes()`. The properties set include paragraph insets, justification, line spacing, and first line indent.

The WrappedPlainView Class

This extension of `BoxView` is a simplified version of `ParagraphView`, or an enhanced version of `PlainView`, depending on how you look at it. It is used for displaying text in a single font and color (like `PlainView`), that needs to support line-wrapping (like `ParagraphView`). Like both `PlainView` and `ParagraphView`, it implements the `TabExpander` interface. The class is used to display text for `JTextArea`s that have line-wrap turned on.

`WrappedPlainView` uses a package private inner class (called `WrappedLine`) to represent each (potentially wrapped) line of text. Note that this differs from the strategy used by `ParagraphView`, in which line-wrap caused new `View` objects to be created for each row of text. With `WrappedPlainView`, there is always a one-to-one mapping from the `Document`'s `Element`s to the `WrappedLine` view objects that display them, regardless of the number of rows needed to display a single `Element`. Figure 23-15 shows these different strategies. (Although we show the

`WrappedPlainView` breaking lines on character boundaries; it can also break on word boundaries.)

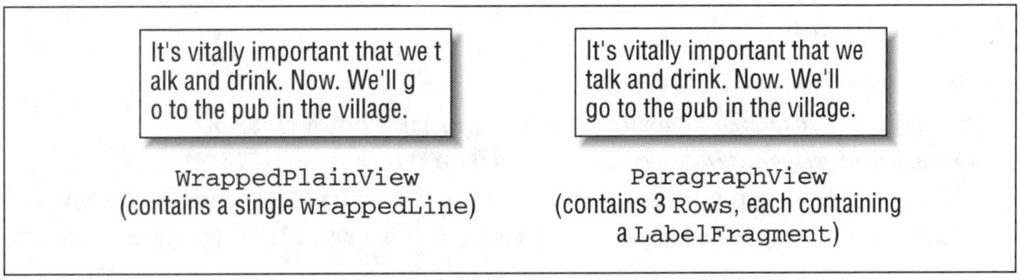

Figure 23-15. WrappedPlainView vs. ParagraphView

Properties

The `WrappedPlainView` class modifies the implementation of the `BoxView` properties shown in Table 23-13. See the description of `View` properties for details on these properties. The `getPreferredSpan()` method updates its internal cache (information about the container, font, and tab size) and then calls `super.getPreferredSpan()`. The `element` property is set in the constructor.

Table 23-13. WrappedPlainView Properties

Property	Data Type	get	is	set	bound	Default Value
element*	Element	•				From constructor
preferredSpan (indexed)*	float	•				

See also properties from the BoxView class (Table 23-11).

Constructors

public WrappedPlainView(Element elem)

 Creates a new view aligned along the `Y_AXIS` for the given `Element`. Lines will be wrapped on character boundaries.

public WrappedPlainView(Element elem, boolean wordWrap)

 Creates a new view aligned along the `Y_AXIS` for the given `Element`. Lines will be wrapped on word boundaries if `wordWrap` is `true`. Otherwise, they will be wrapped on character boundaries.

TabExpander Methods

public float nextTabStop(float x, int tabOffset)

 Returns the next tab position after the given position, ignoring the second parameter. The tab size is based on the `PlainDocument.tabSizeAttribute` property of the view's Document, multiplied by the width of the character m in the current font. If this property is not defined, a default of 8 is used.

Document Update Methods

public void changedUpdate(DocumentEvent e, Shape a, ViewFactory f)
public void insertUpdate(DocumentEvent e, Shape a, ViewFactory f)
public void removeUpdate(DocumentEvent e, Shape a, ViewFactory f)

These methods update the view hierarchy to reflect any added or removed Elements. Instances of a package private inner class called WrappedLine are created as necessary to represent any new lines of text.

BoxView Methods

These methods override the implementations provided in the BoxView class or its superclasses:

protected void loadChildren(ViewFactory f)

Creates a new view (a WrappedLine) for each child Element of the Element this view represents. The view factory is not used.

public void paint(Graphics g, Shape a)

Queries and caches font and color information from the view's component and calls super.paint() to paint its children (which, because they are instances of an inner class, can access the cached information by calling methods on the enclosing view).

public void setSize(float width, float height)

Updates the view's cache of font and tab information and calls super.setSize().

New Protected Methods

The following new protected methods are available in this class. The first four are used by the inner class responsible for displaying each line of text.

protected int calculateBreakPosition(int p0, int p1)

Returns the proper break position between the two positions. If word-wrap is turned on, it uses Utilities.getBreakLocation(). Otherwise, it uses Utilities.getTabbedTextOffset() to find the break.

protected void drawLine(int p0, int p1, Graphics g, int x, int y)

Draws a potentially wrapped line of text, using the two methods listed next to paint any selected or unselected portions of the line. p0 and p1 are document offsets, while x and y indicate the starting view position for this line.

protected int drawSelectedText(Graphics g, int x, int y, int p0, int p1)
   throws BadLocationException

protected int drawUnselectedText(Graphics g, int x, int y, int p0, int p1)
   throws BadLocationException

These two methods use `Utilities.drawTabbedText()` to paint a line of text using the appropriate text color, based on whether or not the text is selected. These methods are used by the `drawLine()` method.

protected final Segment getLineBuffer()

Provides access to the `Segment` used to retrieve text from the document.

protected int getTabSize()

Returns the size, in characters, for each tab. If the `PlainDocument.tabSize-Attribute` property has been set on the view's document, its value is used. If not, a default of 8 is returned.

The TableView Class

This abstract class extends `BoxView` and is used to render `Elements` that are structured as tables containing rows of cells. Each child of the view's top-level `Element` will be a row (an instance of `TableView.TableRow`, defined later) and each child of each row `Element` will be a cell (an instance of `TableView.TableCell`, also defined later). Figure 23-16 shows the symmetry between the model and view objects. Note that the element types shown in this diagram are not actual Swing classes. The `TableView` class does not care what type of `Element` objects it works with, as long as they follow the table/row/cell structure.

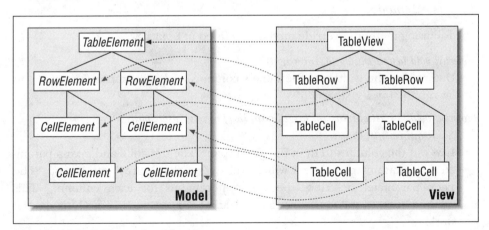

Figure 23-16. TableView and model symmetry

`TableView` allows cells to span multiple rows and columns, meaning that the rows may contain different numbers of cells. However, the `TableView` class does not actually define how an `Element` should indicate that it spans cells, requiring you to extend `TableCell` to take advantage of this feature. Figure 23-17 shows the basic structure of a `TableView` and its children.

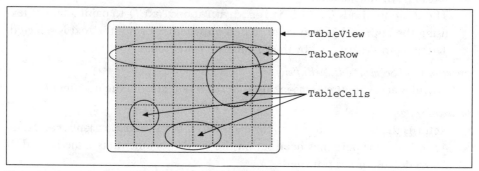

Figure 23-17. TableView structure

Properties

`TableView` does not change any of the properties defined in `BoxView`. It gets its `element` property from the constructor.

Constructor

public TableView(Element elem)
Creates a new view that contains rows aligned along the `Y_AXIS`.

BoxView Methods

The following methods override methods defined in `BoxView`:

protected void layout(int width, int height)
Determines the widths of the table's columns and calls `super.layout()` to lay out the rows.

protected void layoutColumns(int targetSpan, int[] offsets, int[] spans, SizeRequirements[] reqs)
Lays out the columns to fit in the given span. The `offsets` and `spans` parameters are output parameters which will define the appropriate layout. The `reqs` parameter describes the size requirements for each column. This method uses `SizeRequirements.calculateTiledPositions()` to do the work.

protected void loadChildren(ViewFactory f)
Creates a new `TableRow` (using `createTableRow()`) for each child of the view's `Element`. It does not use the given factory at all. Once the child rows

have been created, invisible "proxy" cells are created to fill any blank spaces left by cells that span multiple rows or columns. This is done to simplify layout.

New Protected Methods

These methods make it easy to subclass `TableView` if you want to provide your own `TableCell` or `TableRow` implementations. All children of `TableView` and `TableRow` are created using these methods:

protected TableView.TableCell createTableCell(Element elem)
> Returns a new instance of `TableCell`, to display the given `Element`.

protected TabelView.TableRow createTableRow(Element elem)
> Returns a new instance of `TableRow`, to display the given `Element`.

The TableView.TableRow Class

This inner class extends `BoxView`, and represents a horizontal row of cells.

Properties

The `TableView.TableRow` class modifies the implementation of the `BoxView` properties shown in Table 23-14. The `resizeWeight` property is set to 1 for all rows. The `element` property is defined in the constructor.

Table 23-14. TableView.TableRow Properties

Property	Data Type	get	is	set	bound	Default Value
element*	Element	•				From constructor
resizeWeight (indexed)*	int	•				1

See also properties from the BoxView class (Table 23-11).

Constructor

public TableRow(Element elem)
> Creates a new view for the given `Element`, aligned along the `X_AXIS`.

Methods

protected void layoutMajorAxis(int targetSpan, int axis, int[] offsets, int[] spans)
> Gives each child the span of the column width for the table.

protected void loadChildren(ViewFactory f)

> Iterates over the `Element`'s children, creating a new child view (using the `createTableCell()` method in the enclosing `TableView`) for each child `Element`. The given factory is not used.

The TableView.TableCell Class

This inner class extends `BoxView` and is used to represent a cell in a table. This implementation does not directly support cells that span multiple rows or columns, but subclasses can easily change this.

Properties

`TableView.TableCell` defines the properties and default values shown in Table 23-15. The `columnCount` and `rowCount` properties define the size of the cell in terms of the number of rows and columns it spans. These are always 1 in this class. The `preferredSpan` accessor is implemented to return the preferred span for the cell (according to `super.preferredSpan()`), divided by the number of rows (for `Y_AXIS`) or columns (for `X_AXIS`) covered by the cell. The `resize-Weight` is set to 1. The `element` represented by the cell is specified in the constructor.

Table 23-15. WrappedPlainView Properties

Property	Data Type	get	is	set	bound	Default Value
columnCount	int	•				1
element*	Element	•				From constructor
preferredColumnSpan	int	•				super.preferred-Span/columnCount
preferredSpan (indexed)*	float	•				Discussed later
resizeWeight (indexed)*	int	•				1
rowCount	int	•				1

See also properties from the BoxView class (Table 23-11).

Constructor

public TableCell(Element elem)

> Creates a new view to display the given `Element`, using a vertical (`Y_AXIS`) box.

New Methods

public void setGridLocation(int row, int col)
> Sets the row and column of the cell.

protected void paintCell(Graphics g, Rectangle alloc)
> This method does nothing. Subclasses can use this method to paint things such as a cell border or background.

BoxView Method

The following method overrides the implementations provided by `BoxView` and its subclasses.

public void paint(Graphics g, Shape allocation)
> Calculates the width and height of the cell, adjusting the allocation if the cell spans multiple rows or columns. It calls `paintCell()` and `super.paint()`.

24

EditorKits and TextActions

Over the last five chapters we've covered just about all of the classes and interfaces that make up the Swing text framework. In this chapter, we'll look at a class that ties everything together: EditorKit. An EditorKit is used to pull together the document model, document view, document editing actions, and document I/O strategy, serving as a central reference point for a given document type.

In addition to looking at EditorKit and its subclasses, this chapter also introduces the TextAction class (an abstract extension of AbstractAction) and the many useful concrete action classes available as inner classes of the EditorKit subclasses. These actions are used for tasks such as copying and pasting text as well as style-oriented tasks such as changing font characteristics.

Throughout the course of the chapter, we'll be building simple but powerful editors for working with increasingly complex document types.

Overview of the Editor Kits

The following sections give an overview of the components of various editor kits.

The EditorKit Class

This is the abstract base class for all editor kits. It defines a number of methods that define the model (e.g., createDefaultDocument()), the view (e.g., getViewFactory()), the capabilities (getActions()), and the I/O strategy (read() and write()) for some type of document content. Figure 24-1 shows the EditorKit class and the many classes and interfaces it interacts with.

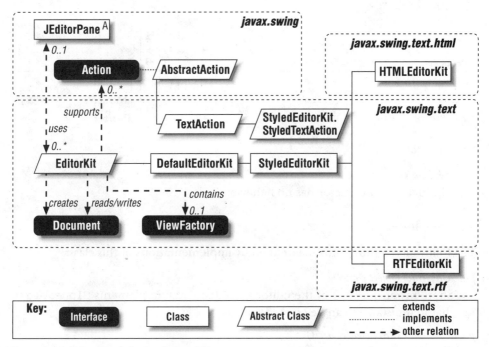

Figure 24-1. EditorKit and related classes

This figure shows several important things about the EditorKit class. First, each EditorKit instance is associated with a single JEditorPane (though in some cases, it doesn't care). The EditorKit defines how to create a default document, as well as how to read and write the document to a stream. In addition, each EditorKit may define a ViewFactory responsible for creating View objects for each Element in the document. Finally, the diagram shows that an EditorKit may define a set of Actions that it supports.

The other classes shown in the diagram are the subclasses of EditorKit and AbstractAction. We'll look at each of these classes, as well as some inner classes not shown on the diagram, throughout this chapter.

Properties

EditorKit defines the properties shown in Table 24-1. The actions property defines the set of actions that can be used on a text component, which uses a model and a view produced by this EditorKit. contentType indicates the MIME type of the data that this kit supports. The viewFactory property is the ViewFactory object used to create View objects for the Elements of the document type produced by the kit. The accessors for all three of these properties are abstract.

Table 24-1. EditorKit Properties

Property	Data Type	get	is	set	bound	Default Value
actions	Action[]	•				abstract
contentType	String	•				abstract
viewFactory	ViewFactory	•				abstract

Constructor

public EditorKit()

This default constructor has no behavior.

Abstract Methods

The following methods must be defined by implementations of this class:

public abstract Object clone()

Should return a copy of the editor kit. `EditorKit` implements `Cloneable` so that new instances can be created quickly.

public abstract Caret createCaret()

Should create a new `Caret` to be used with the `JEditorPane`.

NOTE   This method is currently not called anywhere within Swing—Carets are initially installed via the `createCaret()` method in `BasicText-UI`, and can be reset via a call to `setCaret()` on any `JTextCompo-nent`.

---

public abstract Document createDefaultDocument()

Called by the `BasicTextUI` when installing a UI for a component and by `JTextComponent` before loading a new document from a stream. It should return a new `Document` object of the appropriate type for the kit. Figure 24-2 shows how this method is called when a new `JEditorPane` is created without specifying a document.

public abstract void read(InputStream in, Document doc, int pos)
    throws IOException, BadLocationException
public abstract void read(Reader in, Document doc, int pos)
    throws IOException, BadLocationException

Should populate the given `Document`, based on data read from the stream or reader. The data read is inserted at the specified document position (use 0 if this is a new, empty document).

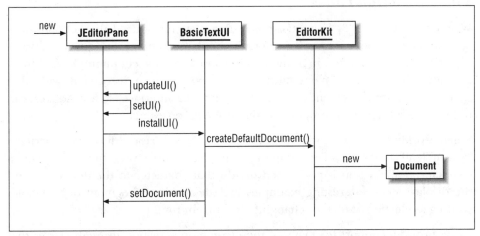

Figure 24-2. Default document creation using EditorKit

public abstract void write(OutputStream out, Document doc, int pos, int len) throws
    IOException, BadLocationException
public abstract void write(Writer out, Document doc, int pos, int len) throws IOException,
    BadLocationException
> Should write the specified portion of the document to the specified stream.
> To write the entire document, just call `write(aWriter, aDoc, 0, aDoc.getLength())`.

These `read()` and `write()` methods can support any arbitrary text format. For simple text, the data read and written will be plain text; more advanced editor kits might be able to read attribute and style information, or well-defined mark-up languages like HTML or XML.

Other Methods

These methods are not abstract, but the default implementations do nothing.

public void install(JEditorPane c)
> Called once the content type for the `JEditorPane` has been determined. It associates the kit with the editor pane. Subclasses that need to query or listen to the editor pane for any reason should take advantage of this method.

public void deinstall(JEditorPane c)
> Called when the `JEditorPane` changes its editor kit. For example, subclasses may take advantage of this method to remove listeners from the pane.

The TextAction Class

Way back in Chapter 3, *Swing Component Basics,* we introduced the `Action` interface and the `AbstractAction` default implementation. To quickly review, `Action`s are a new feature in Swing that encapsulate some common piece of functionality, along with a name and (optionally) an icon associated with that functionality. `Action` extends the `ActionListener` interface, so any `Action` can be added as a listener to components that fire `Action` events.

When working with any type of word processor or basic editor, you perform "actions" all the time. The simplest example occurs every time you type a character. Some action is performed to add that character to the document and the display. More interesting examples include making a segment of text bold, copying a selection of text, or changing the current font.

Swing provides support for many of these common activities, through classes that extend the `TextAction` abstract class. The specific actions available are defined as inner classes of the `EditorKit` subclasses. We'll cover each of these in the sections that follow. In this section, we'll briefly cover the `TextAction` class itself, so you understand what all these new actions have in common.

Constructor

public TextAction(String name)
Passes the action name up to its superclass, where it is assigned to the `Action.NAME` property. Recall from the discussion of `Action` that this property is typically the primary key used to identify actions.

Static Method

public static final Action[] augmentList(Action[] list1, Action[] list2)
Adds the actions in the second list to those in the first list. Any action names that appear in both lists will be mapped to the `Action` specified in the second list. This method can be used by an `EditorKit` that wishes to add new actions to the set of actions supported by its superclass.

Protected Methods

protected final JTextComponent getFocusedComponent()
Returns `JTextComponent.getFocusedComponent()`.

protected final JTextComponent getTextComponent(ActionEvent e)
Determines the currently active text component, allowing actions to be shared by multiple text components. If the given event has a `JTextComponent` as its target, that component is returned. If not, the result of `getFocusedComponent()` is returned.

The DefaultEditorKit Class

DefaultEditorKit is a subclass of EditorKit that provides a great deal of default behavior applicable to most document types. As we'll see below, the most interesting features available in this class are provided by the actions it supports via its numerous inner classes.

When used directly, DefaultEditorKit only supports plain text data. Its actions deal with tasks such as copying and pasting data, and its I/O methods read and write only plain text. However, the important thing about this class is that it can be extended to add more features, and the actions it defines will still be applicable. We'll see extensions of DefaultEditorKit in the sections that follow.

Properties

DefaultEditorKit defines values for the properties shown in Table 24-2. The actions provided by DefaultEditorKit are discussed below in the "Constants" section. Each action is an instance of an inner class, defined in DefaultEditorKit that is capable of performing a given action. The contentType for editors using DefaultEditorKit is text/plain, indicating that styled text is not supported. The viewFactory property is set to null, indicating that users of this class must provide ViewFactory support via the TextUI.

Table 24-2. DefaultEditorKit Properties

Property	Data Type	get	is	set	bound	Default Value
actions*	Action[]	•				Array of 47 TextAction objects
contentType*	String	•				"text/plain"
viewFactory*	ViewFactory	•				null

See also properties from EditorKit class (Table 24-1).

Constants

DefaultEditorKit defines 46[*] different action names (Strings, shown in Table 24-3) as constant values. Behind each action name is an inner class (some classes are used by multiple actions) that extends TextAction to carry out the goal of the action. Several of these action classes are public, so we will define them in more detail after this section. However, even with the nonpublic classes, you can

---

* The keen observer will notice that the properties table indicated that there were 47 actions available. One action is not defined as a constant, but is still available by the name "dump-model." This action just calls dump() on the document of the currently focused JTextComponent (assuming it's an Abstract-Document), causing the model structure to be printed to System.err.

get to an instance of the action using these constants, along with the `actions` property. The following example shows a common strategy for doing this. We'll store all of the actions in a local `Hashtable`, so that we can access any action we need by name. In this example, we then retrieve the "cut" action from the table using the `DefaultEditorKit.cutAction` constant:

```
Hashtable actionHash = new Hashtable();

Action[] actions = edKit.getActions();
for (int i=0; i<actions.length; i++) {
  String name = (String)actions[i].getValue(Action.NAME);
  actionHash.put(name, actions[i]);
}

Action cut = (Action)actionHash.get(DefaultEditorKit.cutAction);
```

Table 24-3. DefaultEditorKit Action Name Constants

Constant	Description
backwardAction	Move the caret back one position
beepAction	Create a beep (`Toolkit.beep()`)
beginAction	Move the caret to the beginning of the document
beginLineAction	Move the caret to the beginning of the current line
beginParagraphAction	Move the caret to the beginning of the current paragraph
beginWordAction	Move the caret to the beginning of the current word
copyAction	Copy the selected region and place it on the system clipboard
cutAction	Cut the selected region and place it on the system clipboard
defaultKeyTypedAction	Display the pressed key (default when there is no special keymap entry for a pressed key)
deleteNextCharAction	Delete the character following the caret position
deletePrevCharAction	Delete the character before the caret position
downAction	Move the caret down one position
endAction	Move the caret to the end of the document
endLineAction	Move the caret to the end of the current line
endParagraphAction	Move the caret to the end of the current paragraph
endWordAction	Move the caret to the end of the current word
forwardAction	Move the caret forward one position
insertBreakAction	Insert a line or paragraph break (\n) into the document; if there is a current selection, it is removed first
insertContentAction	Insert content into the document; if there is a current selection, it is removed first

Table 24-3. DefaultEditorKit Action Name Constants (continued)

Constant	Description
insertTabAction	Insert a tab character into the document; if there is a current selection, it is removed first
nextWordAction	Move the caret to the beginning of the next word
pageDownAction	Page the document down
pageUpAction	Page the document up
pasteAction	Paste the contents of the system clipboard at the caret position; if there is a current selection, it is replaced by the pasted content
previousWordAction	Move the caret to the beginning of the previous word
readOnlyAction	Set the editor to read-only mode; results in a call to setEditable(false) on the JTextComponent
selectAllAction	Highlight the entire document
selectLineAction	Select the current line
selectParagraphAction	Select the current paragraph
selectWordAction	Select the current word
selectionBackwardAction	Adjust the current selection by moving the caret back one position
selectionBeginAction	Adjust the current selection by moving the caret back to the beginning of the document
selectionBeginLineAction	Adjust the current selection by moving the caret back to the beginning of the current line
selectionBeginParagraphAction	Adjust the current selection by moving the caret back to the beginning of the current paragraph
selectionBeginWordAction	Adjust the current selection by moving the caret back to the beginning of the current word
selectionDownAction	Adjust the current selection by moving the caret down one row
selectionEndAction	Adjust the current selection by moving the caret to the end of the document
selectionEndLineAction	Adjust the current selection by moving the caret to the end of the current line
selectionEndParagraphAction	Adjust the current selection by moving the caret to the end of the current paragraph
selectionEndWordAction	Adjust the current selection by moving the caret to the end of the current word
selectionForwardAction	Adjust the current selection by moving the caret forward one position
selectionNextWordAction	Adjust the current selection by moving the caret to the beginning of the next word

Table 24-3. DefaultEditorKit Action Name Constants (continued)

Constant	Description
selectionPreviousWordAction	Adjust the current selection by moving the caret to the beginning of the previous word
selectionUpAction	Adjust the current selection by moving the caret down one row
upAction	Move the caret up one position
writableAction	Set the editor to writable mode; results in a call to setEditable(true) on the JTextComponent

Using Actions

Let's look at a simple example that shows how these actions can be used. In this program, we'll create a JTextArea and add all the available actions to a menu (the list is pretty long, so we split it into two submenus). As we discussed in the chapter on menus, we can add these Action objects directly to the menu. The default action names appear as menu selections.

Since JTextArea gets its actions from the DefaultEditorKit, you'll see each of the actions listed in Table 24-3 when you run this program. By blindly adding all of the actions, we avoid interacting with the editor kit directly in this program. At the end of this section, we'll look at a much more useful example that uses Default-EditorKit directly.

```
// TextActionExample.java
//
import javax.swing.*;
import javax.swing.text.*;

// Simple TextAction example
public class TextActionExample {
  public static void main(String[] args) {

    // Create a text area
    JTextArea ta = new JTextArea();
    ta.setLineWrap(true);

    // Add all actions to the menu (split into two menus to make it more usable)
    Action[] actions = ta.getActions();
    JMenuBar menubar = new JMenuBar();
    JMenu actionmenu = new JMenu("Actions");
    menubar.add(actionmenu);

    JMenu firstHalf = new JMenu("1st Half");
    JMenu secondHalf = new JMenu("2nd Half");
    actionmenu.add(firstHalf);
    actionmenu.add(secondHalf);
```

```
    int mid = actions.length/2;
    for (int i=0; i<mid; i++) {
      firstHalf.add(actions[i]);
    }
    for (int i=mid; i<actions.length; i++) {
      secondHalf.add(actions[i]);
    }

    // Show it . . .
    JFrame f = new JFrame();
    f.addWindowListener(new BasicWindowMonitor());
    f.getContentPane().add(ta);
    f.setJMenuBar(menubar);
    f.setSize(300, 200);
    f.setVisible(true);
  }
}
```

That's all there is to it! All we did was call getActions() on the JTextArea (which ultimately retrieved the actions from a DefaultEditorKit) and added each action to the menu. Of course, most of these actions would never be provided as menu options, and for those that would, you'd probably want to change the label (the default labels are all lowercase and the words are hyphen-separated; e.g., cut-to-clipboard). The example at the end of the section is a bit more realistic and will address these issues.

Constructor

public DefaultEditorKit()
> This default constructor defines no behavior.

Methods

The following methods provide default implementations for all of the abstract methods defined in EditorKit.

public Object clone()
> Returns a new DefaultEditorKit.

public Caret createCaret()
> Returns null. See EditorKit.createCaret().

public Document createDefaultDocument()
> Creates a new PlainDocument instance and returns it.

public void read(InputStream in, Document doc, int pos)
     throws IOException, BadLocationException
public void read(Reader in, Document doc, int pos)
     throws IOException, BadLocationException
     Read plain text from the given `Reader` (in), adding the text at the specified
     position. The version that takes an `InputStream` simply wraps the stream in
     an `InputStreamReader` and calls the other version.

public void write(OutputStream out, Document doc, int pos, int len)
     throws IOException, BadLocationException
public void write(Writer out, Document doc, int pos, int len)
     throws IOException, BadLocationException
     Write `len` plain text characters to the given `Writer` (out), starting at position
     pos. The version that takes an `OutputStream` simply wraps the stream in an
     `OutputStreamWriter` and calls the other version.

The DefaultEditorKit.DefaultKeyTypedAction Class

Over the next few pages, we'll give a brief overview of the actions defined as public
static inner classes of `DefaultEditorKit`. The first of these is the default action,
used to insert text into the active `JTextComponent`.

Constructor

public DefaultKeyTypedAction()
     Creates an action using the name `defaultKeyTypedAction`.

Method

public void actionPerformed(ActionEvent e)
     Inserts the `actionCommand` value from the given event into the active `JText-`
     `Component` using `replaceSelection()`. If the first character has a value less
     than 0x20, this does nothing.

The DefaultEditorKit.BeepAction Class

Constructor

public BeepAction()
     Creates an action using the name `beepAction`.

Method

public void actionPerformed(ActionEvent e)
     Calls `Toolkit.getDefaultToolkit().beep()`.

The DefaultEditorKit.CopyAction Class

Constructor

public CopyAction()
 Creates an action using the name copyAction.

Method

public void actionPerformed(ActionEvent e)
 Calls copy() on the active JTextComponent, if it can be determined.

The DefaultEditorKit.CutAction Class

Constructor

public CutAction()
 Creates an action using the name cutAction.

Method

public void actionPerformed(ActionEvent e)
 Calls cut() on the active JTextComponent, if it can be determined.

The DefaultEditorKit.InsertBreakAction Class

Constructor

public InsertBreakAction()
 Creates an action using the name insertBreakAction.

Method

public void actionPerformed(ActionEvent e)
 Replaces the current selection with a \n (return) character, if an active JTextComponent can be determined. If there is no selection, a \n is inserted.

The DefaultEditorKit.InsertContentAction Class

Constructor

public InsertContentAction()
 Creates an action using the name insertContentAction.

Method

public void actionPerformed(ActionEvent e)

    Inserts the `actionCommand` value from the given event into the active `JText-Component`, using `replaceSelection()`. If the action command is `null`, a beep is sounded.

The DefaultEditorKit.InsertTabAction Class

Constructor

public InsertTabAction()

    Creates an action using the name `insertTabAction`.

Method

public void actionPerformed(ActionEvent e)

    Replaces the current selection with a `\t` (tab) character, if an active `JText-Component` can be determined. If there is no selection, a tab is inserted.

The DefaultEditorKit.PasteAction Class

Constructor

public PasteAction()

    Creates an action using the name `pasteAction`.

Method

public void actionPerformed(ActionEvent e)

    Calls `paste()` on the active `JTextComponent`, if it can be determined.

A Simple Text Editor

In this first example, we'll show how to do some of things you'd expect from a basic editor. Our first editor will support the following features:

- Cut, copy, and paste via toolbar buttons, menu selection, and default key shortcuts

- Select-all capability via menu selection

- Quick keyboard navigation using the `nextWordAction`, `previousWordAc-tion`, `selectionNextWordAction`, and `selectionPreviousWordAction`

- Saving and loading documents

When we run it, our simple editor will look something like Figure 24-3.[*]

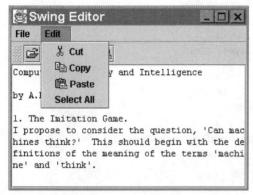

Figure 24-3. SimpleEditor

Here's the source code for SimpleEditor. It's designed to be easily extensible, allowing us to add features of the more advanced editor kits. This class serves as the base class for the other examples in this chapter.

```java
// SimpleEditor.java
//
import javax.swing.*;
import javax.swing.text.*;
import java.awt.*;
import java.io.*;
import java.awt.event.*;
import java.util.Hashtable;


// An example showing several DefaultEditorKit features. This class is designed
// to be easily extended to add additional functionality.
public class SimpleEditor extends JFrame {

  public static void main(String[] args) {
    SimpleEditor editor = new SimpleEditor();
    editor.addWindowListener(new BasicWindowMonitor());
    editor.setVisible(true);
  }

  // Create an editor
  public SimpleEditor() {
    super("Swing Editor");
    textComp = createTextComponent();
    hashDefaultActions();
```

---

[*] Text in this and following figures is from A.M. Turing, "Computing Machinery and Intelligence," *Mind*, 1950.

```
      makeActionsPretty();
      updateKeymap();

      Container content = getContentPane();
      content.add(textComp, BorderLayout.CENTER);
      content.add(createToolBar(), BorderLayout.NORTH);

      setJMenuBar(createMenuBar());

      setSize(320, 240);
      addWindowListener(new WindowAdapter() {
        public void windowClosing(WindowEvent ev) { System.exit(0); }
      });
    }

    // Create the JTextComponent subclass.
    protected JTextComponent createTextComponent() {
      JTextArea ta = new JTextArea();
      ta.setLineWrap(true);
      return ta;
    }

    // Get all of the actions defined for our text component. Hash each one by name
    // so we can look for it later.
    protected void hashDefaultActions() {
      Action[] actions = textComp.getActions();
      for (int i=0; i<actions.length; i++) {
        String name = (String)actions[i].getValue(Action.NAME);
        actionHash.put(name, actions[i]);
      }
    }

    // Get an action by name
    protected Action getHashedAction(String name) {
      return (Action)actionHash.get(name);
    }

    // Add icons and friendly names to actions we care about
    protected void makeActionsPretty() {
      Action a;
      a = getHashedAction(DefaultEditorKit.cutAction);
      a.putValue(Action.SMALL_ICON, new ImageIcon("icons/cut.gif"));
      a.putValue(Action.NAME, "Cut");

      a = getHashedAction(DefaultEditorKit.copyAction);
      a.putValue(Action.SMALL_ICON, new ImageIcon("icons/copy.gif"));
      a.putValue(Action.NAME, "Copy");

      a = getHashedAction(DefaultEditorKit.pasteAction);
```

```
    a.putValue(Action.SMALL_ICON, new ImageIcon("icons/paste.gif"));
    a.putValue(Action.NAME, "Paste");

  a = getHashedAction(DefaultEditorKit.selectAllAction);
  a.putValue(Action.NAME, "Select All");
}

// Add some key->Action mappings
protected void updateKeymap() {

  // Create a new child Keymap
  Keymap map = JTextComponent.addKeymap("NextPrevMap",
    textComp.getKeymap());

  // Define the keystrokes to be added
  KeyStroke next = KeyStroke.getKeyStroke(KeyEvent.VK_RIGHT,
    InputEvent.CTRL_MASK, false);
  KeyStroke prev = KeyStroke.getKeyStroke(KeyEvent.VK_LEFT,
    InputEvent.CTRL_MASK, false);
  KeyStroke selNext = KeyStroke.getKeyStroke(KeyEvent.VK_RIGHT,
    InputEvent.CTRL_MASK|InputEvent.SHIFT_MASK, false);
  KeyStroke selPrev = KeyStroke.getKeyStroke(KeyEvent.VK_LEFT,
    InputEvent.CTRL_MASK|InputEvent.SHIFT_MASK, false);

  // Add the new mappings used DefaultEditorKit actions
  map.addActionForKeyStroke(next, getHashedAction(
    DefaultEditorKit.nextWordAction));
  map.addActionForKeyStroke(prev, getHashedAction(
    DefaultEditorKit.previousWordAction));
  map.addActionForKeyStroke(selNext, getHashedAction(
    DefaultEditorKit.selectionNextWordAction));
  map.addActionForKeyStroke(selPrev, getHashedAction(
    DefaultEditorKit.selectionPreviousWordAction));

  // Set the Keymap for the text component
  textComp.setKeymap(map);
}

// Create a simple JToolBar with some buttons
protected JToolBar createToolBar() {
  JToolBar bar = new JToolBar();

  // Add simple actions for opening & saving
  bar.add(getOpenAction()).setText("");
  bar.add(getSaveAction()).setText("");
  bar.addSeparator();

  // Add cut/copy/paste buttons
  bar.add(getHashedAction(DefaultEditorKit.cutAction)).setText("");
```

```
    bar.add(getHashedAction(DefaultEditorKit.copyAction)).setText("");
    bar.add(getHashedAction(DefaultEditorKit.pasteAction)).setText("");
    return bar;
}

// Create a JMenuBar with file & edit menus
protected JMenuBar createMenuBar() {
  JMenuBar menubar = new JMenuBar();
  JMenu file = new JMenu("File");
  JMenu edit = new JMenu("Edit");
  menubar.add(file);
  menubar.add(edit);

  file.add(getOpenAction());
  file.add(getSaveAction());
  file.add(new ExitAction());
  edit.add(getHashedAction(DefaultEditorKit.cutAction));
  edit.add(getHashedAction(DefaultEditorKit.copyAction));
  edit.add(getHashedAction(DefaultEditorKit.pasteAction));
  edit.add(getHashedAction(DefaultEditorKit.selectAllAction));
  return menubar;
}

// Subclass can override to use a different open action
protected Action getOpenAction() { return openAction; }

// Subclass can override to use a different save action
protected Action getSaveAction() { return saveAction; }

protected JTextComponent getTextComponent() { return textComp; }

private Action openAction = new OpenAction();
private Action saveAction = new SaveAction();

private JTextComponent textComp;
private Hashtable actionHash = new Hashtable();

// ********** ACTION INNER CLASSES ********** //

// A very simple "exit" action
public class ExitAction extends AbstractAction {
  public ExitAction() { super("Exit"); }
  public void actionPerformed(ActionEvent ev) { System.exit(0); }
}

// An action that opens an existing file
class OpenAction extends AbstractAction {

  public OpenAction() {
```

```
    super("Open", new ImageIcon("icons/open.gif"));
  }

  // Query user for a filename and attempt to open and read the file into the
  // text component
  public void actionPerformed(ActionEvent ev) {
    String filename = JOptionPane.showInputDialog(
      SimpleEditor.this, "Enter Filename");
    if (filename == null)
      return;

    FileReader reader = null;
    try {
      reader = new FileReader(filename);
      textComp.read(reader, null);
    }
    catch (IOException ex) {
      JOptionPane.showMessageDialog(SimpleEditor.this,
      "File Not Found", "ERROR", JOptionPane.ERROR_MESSAGE);
    }
    finally {
      if (reader != null) {
        try {
          reader.close();
        } catch (IOException x) {}
      }
    }
  }
}

// An action that saves the document to a file
class SaveAction extends AbstractAction {
  public SaveAction() {
    super("Save", new ImageIcon("icons/save.gif"));
  }

  // Query user for a filename and attempt to open and write the text
  // component's content to the file
  public void actionPerformed(ActionEvent ev) {
    String filename = JOptionPane.showInputDialog(
      SimpleEditor.this, "Enter Filename");
    if (filename == null)
      return;

    FileWriter writer = null;
    try {
      writer = new FileWriter(filename);
      textComp.write(writer);
    }
```

```
      catch (IOException ex) {
        JOptionPane.showMessageDialog(SimpleEditor.this,
        "File Not Saved", "ERROR", JOptionPane.ERROR_MESSAGE);
      }
      finally {
        if (writer != null) {
          try {
            writer.close();
          } catch (IOException x) {}
        }
      }
    }
  }
}
```

Let's look at a few of the methods from this example. The first interesting method is called hashDefaultActions(). This method creates a Hashtable that maps action names (which we can get from the DefaultEditorKit constants) to Actions, letting us find actions we want to work with later. The next method, getHashedAction(), lets us get the actions we just hashed by providing the action name.

Next, we have a method called makeActionsPretty(). This method adds icons to the actions we're going to display, and changes the text for these actions, as well. This way, our user interface will display nice names like Cut instead of cut-to-clipboard.

Next, we've defined a method called updateKeymap(). The purpose of this method is to add some common editor functionality: the ability to skip to the next or previous word by holding down CTRL and pressing the right or left arrow key. Holding down SHIFT at the same time will highlight the word, as well. For more details on what we did with the Keymap and KeyStroke classes, refer to discussion of Keymap in Chapter 22, *Carets, Highlighters, and Keymaps*. The important thing here is to note that we used our hashed action table to map these keys to the appropriate actions. Subclasses of this editor can add mappings by overriding this method.

In createToolBar(), we get instances of two inner classes, OpenAction and SaveAction, and add them to our JToolBar. We get these actions by calling getOpenAction() and getSaveAction() to allow subclasses to provide different implementations of these actions. We then use getHashedAction() again to get the cut, copy, and paste actions. We've chosen not to display the text for the actions in the toolbar, so we call setText("") on the JButton returned by each add() call. For more details on Swing's handy new JToolBar class, see Chapter 14, *Menus and Toolbars*.

The `createMenuBar()` method is similar to `createToolBar()`. We add two additional actions here: exit and select-all. In this method, we don't strip the text from the menu items, allowing both the icon and the text to be displayed.

Finally, we define action classes for exiting the application, and for opening and saving files. These last two actions take advantage of the `DefaultEditorKit` `read()` and `write()` methods, which get called by `JTextComponent`'s `read()` and `write()` methods. For more details on another handy new Swing class we've used here, `JOptionPane`, see Chapter 10, *Swing Dialogs.*

The StyledEditorKit Class

`StyledEditorKit` extends `DefaultEditorKit` to provide additional features required for documents that allow styled text. It is the kit used by the `JTextPane` class. Like `DefaultEditorKit`, this class defines a number of new `TextActions`. In this class, all of these action classes are public. We'll look at each of them at the end of this section.

Properties

`StyledEditorKit` defines the properties and default values shown in Table 24-4. The `actions` property is the set of actions defined for `DefaultEditorKit`, augmented with actions for setting the font family, font size, font style attributes, and text alignment. The exact actions provided are shown in Table 24-5. In this table, the first column gives the name of the inner class, the next column gives the action name (`Action.NAME`), and the last column gives the parameter values that are passed to the specific action class constructor. Additional actions can be created by instantiating the desired action class, passing different values to the constructor.

Table 24-4. StyledEditorKit Properties

Property	Data Type	get	is	set	bound	Default Value
actions*	Action[]	•				DefaultEditorKit's actions plus 18 more
characterAt-tributeRun	Element	•				null
inputAttributes	MutableAttributeSet	•				
viewFactory*	ViewFactory	•				StyledViewFactory()

See also properties from the DefaultEditorKit class (Table 24-2).

The `characterAttributeRun` property is a new property that indicates the `Element` in which the caret is currently located. This is updated whenever the kit's

Table 24-5. StyledEditorKit Default Actions

Action Class	Action Name	Constructor Argument
FontFamilyAction	font-family-SansSerif	"SansSerif"
FontFamilyAction	font-family-Monospaced	"Monospaced"
FontFamilyAction	font-family-Serif	"Serif"
FontSizeAction	font-size-8	8
FontSizeAction	font-size-10	10
FontSizeAction	font-size-12	12
FontSizeAction	font-size-14	14
FontSizeAction	font-size-16	16
FontSizeAction	font-size-18	18
FontSizeAction	font-size-24	24
FontSizeAction	font-size-36	36
FontSizeAction	font-size-48	48
AlignmentAction	left-justify	StyleConstants.ALIGN_LEFT
AlignmentAction	center-justify	StyleConstants.ALIGN_CENTER
AlignmentAction	right-justify	StyleConstants.ALIGN_RIGHT
BoldAction	font-bold	N/A
ItalicAction	font-italic	N/A
UnderlineAction	font-underline	N/A

JEditorPane fires a CaretEvent. Similarly, inputAttributes provides access to the attribute set in use at the current caret position. This property is used by the JTextPane class whenever content is added to the document.

The viewFactory defined by StyledEditorKit is an inner class capable of creating View objects for different types of Elements. The View objects created by this factory depend on the name property of the Element passed to the create() method, as shown in Table 24-6.

Table 24-6. StyledEditorKit.StyledViewFactory View Creation Policy

Element Name	View Class Created
AbstractDocument.ContentElementName	LabelView
AbstractDocument.ParagraphElementName	ParagraphView
AbstractDocument.SectionElementName	BoxView
AbstractDocument.ComponentElementName	ComponentView
AbstractDocument.IconElementName	IconView
other	LabelView

Constructor

public StyledEditorKit()
> This default constructor provides no behavior.

EditorKit Methods

These methods override those defined in `DefaultEditorKit` or `EditorKit`:

public Object clone()
> Returns a new `StyledEditorKit`. that is a copy of this editor kit.

public Document createDefaultDocument()
> Returns a new instance of `DefaultStyledDocument`.

public void install(JEditorPane c)
> Called when the kit is associated with a `JEditorPane`. It adds itself (actually, an instance of a nonpublic inner class) as a `CaretListener` of the given pane.

public void deinstall(JEditorPane c)
> Indicates that the given pane is no longer using this kit. It removes the caret listener added by `install()`.

The StyledEditorKit.StyledTextAction Class

As discussed earlier, `StyledEditor` defines several public inner classes to perform actions related to styled text. This public abstract class extends `TextAction` and serves as the base class for all the other action inner classes.

Constructor

public StyledTextAction(String nm)
> Passes the action name up to the superclass.

Protected Methods

These methods are available to any subclass of `StyledTextAction`. None of them does anything really new, they just save you a few steps for certain common tasks. If you define your own styled text actions, some of these methods will come in handy.

protected final JEditorPane getEditor(ActionEvent e)
> Provides convenient access to the `JEditorPane` with which the given event is associated. If neither the event source nor the currently focused component is a `JEditorPane`, this method throws an `IllegalArgumentException`.

protected final StyledDocument getStyledDocument(JEditorPane e)

> This convenience method gets the current document from the given pane and returns it as a `StyledDocument`. If the document is not an instance of `StyledDocument` (or a subclass), this method throws an `IllegalArgument-Exception`.

protected final StyledEditorKit getStyledEditorKit(JEditorPane e)

> This convenience method gets the current editor kit from the given pane and returns it as a `StyledEditorKit`. If it is not an instance of `StyledEditorKit` (or a subclass), this method throws an `IllegalArgumentException`.

protected final void setCharacterAttributes(JEditorPane editor, AttributeSet attr,
> *boolean replace)*

> Sets the character attributes for the currently selected text, if there is a selection, or the current input attributes. The `replace` parameter indicates whether the given attributes should replace the existing ones, or just be added to them.

protected final void setParagraphAttributes(JEditorPane editor, AttributeSet attr,
> *boolean replace)*

> Calls `setParagraphAttributes()` for the currently selected range of the given editor pane.

The following seven classes are public, static extensions of the `StyledTextAction` abstract class. Instances of these classes are provided as default actions for the `StyledEditorKit`, but you can create additional instances if the exact action you want is not defined as a default. Each class contains only a constructor and an `actionPerformed(ActionEvent e)` method.

Unless otherwise noted, each of these classes uses the `setCharacterAttributes()` method, defined in `StyledTextAction`, to update the attributes for the current selection, if there is one, or the attributes for text to be inserted.

The StyledEditorKit.FontFamilyAction Class

Constructor

public FontFamilyAction(String nm, String family)

> Creates an action with the given name and font family (SansSerif, Serif, etc.).

Method

public void actionPerformed(ActionEvent e)

> By default, sets the current font family to the value defined in the constructor. However, if the target of the given event matches the current `JEditorPane`,

and the event's `actionCommand` property is not `null`, the action command is used as the new font family instead.

The StyledEditorKit.FontSizeAction Class

Constructor

public FontSizeAction(String nm, int size)
Creates an action with the given name and font size.

Method

public void actionPerformed(ActionEvent e)
By default, this method sets the current font size to the value defined in the constructor. However, if the target of the given event matches the current `JEditorPane`, and the event's `actionCommand` property is not `null`, the action command (converted from a `String` to an `int`) is used as the new font size instead.

The StyledEditorKit.ForegroundAction Class

Constructor

public ForegroundAction(String nm, Color fg)
Creates an action with the given name and color.

Method

public void actionPerformed(ActionEvent e)
By default, this method sets the current foreground color to the value defined in the constructor. However, if the target of the given event matches the current `JEditorPane`, and the event's `actionCommand` property is not `null`, the action command is used as the new color instead.

The procedure of converting the `actionCommand` string to a `Color` is handled by the `Color.decode()` method. Typically, colors are written as hexadecimal numbers in which the first 8 bits represent red, the next 8 represent green, and the last 8 represent blue. For example, `0xFF0000` is red, `0x000000` is black, and `0xFF00FF` is magenta. All `Color.decode()` does is convert such a string to the corresponding `Color`.

The StyledEditorKit.AlignmentAction Class

Constructor

public AlignmentAction(String nm, int a)
> Creates an action with the given name and alignment value. The value must be one of the alignment constants defined in SwingConstants: ALIGN_LEFT, ALIGN_CENTER, ALIGN_RIGHT, or ALIGN_JUSTIFIED.

Method

public void actionPerformed(ActionEvent e)
> By default, this method sets the current alignment to the value defined in the constructor. However, if the target of the given event matches the current JEditorPane, and the event's actionCommand property is not null, the action command (converted from a String to an int) is used as the new alignment instead.

> Note that unlike the other action classes, this one uses setParagraphAttributes(), rather than setCharacterAttributes(), since alignment is a paragraph property.

The StyledEditorKit.BoldAction Class

Constructor

public BoldAction()
> Creates an action with the name "font-bold".

Method

public void actionPerformed(ActionEvent e)
> Checks the current specified attribute set to see if the bold attribute is turned on and toggles this value for the current selection or specified attributes.

The StyledEditorKit.ItalicAction Class

Constructor

public ItalicAction()
> Creates an action with the name "font-italic".

Method

public void actionPerformed(ActionEvent e)
> Checks the current input attribute set to see if the italic attribute is turned on and toggles this value for the current selection or input attributes.

The StyledEditorKit.UnderlineAction Class

Constructor

public UnderlineAction()
> Creates an action with the name `"font-underline"`.

Method

public void actionPerformed(ActionEvent e)
> Checks the current attribute set to see if the underline attribute is turned on and toggles this value for the current selection or given attributes.

A Better Editor

Earlier in this chapter, we created a class called `SimpleEditor` that used some of the actions provided by `DefaultEditorKit`. Now we'll extend that class to create `StyledEditor`, which uses many of the new actions we've just introduced. When run, `StyledEditor` will look like Figure 24-4.

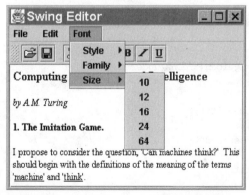

Figure 24-4. StyledEditor: A text editor that supports user-defined styles.

There's not a lot in this class that's new. We override several of the methods defined in `SimpleEditor` to add additional actions to the toolbar and menu. These include actions for changing the font's style, size, and family. We also add key mappings for CTRL-B, CTRL-I, and CTRL-U to change the font style (taking advantage of the `CtrlIFocusManager` class we wrote in Chapter 22).

Here's the code for our new and improved editor:

```java
// StyledEditor.java
//
import javax.swing.*;
import javax.swing.text.*;
import java.awt.event.*;

// An extension of SimpleEditor that adds styled-text features
public class StyledEditor extends SimpleEditor{

  public static void main(String[] args) {
    StyledEditor editor = new StyledEditor();
    editor.setVisible(true);
  }

  // Override to create a JTextPane
  protected JTextComponent createTextComponent() {
    return new JTextPane();
  }

  // Add icons & friendly names for font actions
  protected void makeActionsPretty() {
    super.makeActionsPretty();

    Action a;
    a = getHashedAction("font-bold");
    a.putValue(Action.SMALL_ICON, new ImageIcon("icons/bold.gif"));
    a.putValue(Action.NAME, "Bold");
    a = getHashedAction("font-italic");
    a.putValue(Action.SMALL_ICON, new ImageIcon("icons/italic.gif"));
    a.putValue(Action.NAME, "Italic");
    a = getHashedAction("font-underline");
    a.putValue(Action.SMALL_ICON, new ImageIcon("icons/underline.gif"));
    a.putValue(Action.NAME, "Underline");

    a = getHashedAction("font-family-SansSerif");
    a.putValue(Action.NAME, "SansSerif");
    a = getHashedAction("font-family-Monospaced");
    a.putValue(Action.NAME, "Monospaced");
    a = getHashedAction("font-family-Serif");
    a.putValue(Action.NAME, "Serif");

    a = getHashedAction("font-size-10");
    a.putValue(Action.NAME, "10");
    a = getHashedAction("font-size-12");
    a.putValue(Action.NAME, "12");
    a = getHashedAction("font-size-16");
    a.putValue(Action.NAME, "16");
    a = getHashedAction("font-size-24");
```

```
   a.putValue(Action.NAME, "24");
}


// Add key mappings for font style features. The CtrlIFocusManager used here is
// defined in Chapter 22.
protected void updateKeymap() {

   // Start with the keymap defined in SimpleEditor
   super.updateKeymap();

   FocusManager.setCurrentManager(new CtrlIFocusManager());

   // Extend the map defined by SimpleEditor
   JTextComponent comp = getTextComponent();
   Keymap map = JTextComponent.addKeymap("BoldUnderMap", comp.getKeymap());
   KeyStroke bold = KeyStroke.getKeyStroke(KeyEvent.VK_B,
      InputEvent.CTRL_MASK, false);
   KeyStroke italic = KeyStroke.getKeyStroke(KeyEvent.VK_I,
      InputEvent.CTRL_MASK, false);
   KeyStroke under = KeyStroke.getKeyStroke(KeyEvent.VK_U,
      InputEvent.CTRL_MASK, false);
   map.addActionForKeyStroke(bold, getHashedAction("font-bold"));
   map.addActionForKeyStroke(italic, getHashedAction("font-italic"));
   map.addActionForKeyStroke(under, getHashedAction("font-underline"));

   // Set the keymap for our component
   comp.setKeymap(map);
}


// Add font actions to the toolbar
protected JToolBar createToolBar() {
   JToolBar bar = super.createToolBar();
   bar.addSeparator();

   bar.add(getHashedAction("font-bold")).setText("");
   bar.add(getHashedAction("font-italic")).setText("");
   bar.add(getHashedAction("font-underline")).setText("");

   return bar;
}


// Add font actions to the menu
protected JMenuBar createMenuBar() {
   JMenuBar menubar = super.createMenuBar();
   JMenu font = new JMenu("Font");
   menubar.add(font);

   JMenu style = new JMenu("Style");
   JMenu family = new JMenu("Family");
   JMenu size = new JMenu("Size");
```

```
    font.add(style);
    font.add(family);
    font.add(size);

    style.add(getHashedAction("font-bold"));
    style.add(getHashedAction("font-underline"));
    style.add(getHashedAction("font-italic"));

    family.add(getHashedAction("font-family-SansSerif"));
    family.add(getHashedAction("font-family-Monospaced"));
    family.add(getHashedAction("font-family-Serif"));

    size.add(getHashedAction("font-size-10"));
    size.add(getHashedAction("font-size-12"));
    size.add(getHashedAction("font-size-16"));
    size.add(getHashedAction("font-size-24"));

    // Don't forget, we can define new actions too!
    size.add(new StyledEditorKit.FontSizeAction("64", 64));

    return menubar;
  }
}
```

The last thing we do in this file is create a new action using one of the StyledEditorKit inner classes, to remind you that we're not restricted to those actions
defined as defaults by the kit. We're free to create new instances when necessary.

Saving Styled Documents

One feature that's missing from our StyledEditor is the ability to read and write
styled text. Unfortunately, StyledEditorKit does not override the read() and
write() methods, so any documents saved from our StyledEditor will be saved
as plain text. To fix this problem, we'd ideally want to create a new editor kit that
saved all the Style and Element information associated with the Document.

For now, we'll provide an alternative solution by extending our editor once again
and adding the ability to serialize the Document object to a file and then read it
back in.* Note that we'll actually serialize all of the attribute and style information
that is part of the document. We can't do the same sort of thing in an editor kit
subclass because the editor kit read() methods are set up to read the contents of

---

* It's worth mentioning two drawbacks to this strategy. First, serialization is going to save the state of the
entire Document object. This is clearly less efficient than designing your own representation for saving a
document—though in these days when one common editor routinely produces multi-megabyte files for
relatively small documents, this disadvantage might not be significant. More important, serialization from
JDK 1.2/Swing 1.1 is not compatible with Swing 1.0. So you could save a document with this editor running under Swing 1.0, upgrade to JDK 1.2, and find that you couldn't read any documents you'd saved.

a file into an *existing* document. Serializing the entire document and then reading it back would not fit this model, since the process of reading a serialized object would create a new document.

Here's the source for an editor that allows styled documents to be saved and opened without losing the text attributes. All we've done is provided new implementations of the `getSaveAction()` and `getOpenAction()` methods and defined the new actions returned by these methods.

```java
// IOStyledEditor.java
//
import javax.swing.*;
import javax.swing.text.*;
import java.awt.event.*;
import java.io.*;

// An extension of StyledEditor that adds document serialization
public class IOStyledEditor extends StyledEditor {

  public static void main(String[] args) {
    IOStyledEditor te = new IOStyledEditor();
    te.setVisible(true);
  }

  // Provide a new open action
  protected Action getOpenAction() {
    if (inAction == null)
      inAction = new InAction();
    return inAction;
  }

  // Provide a new save action
  protected Action getSaveAction() {
    if (outAction == null)
      outAction = new OutAction();
    return outAction;
  }

  private Action inAction;
  private Action outAction;

  // An action that saves the document as a serialized object
  class OutAction extends AbstractAction {
    public OutAction() {
      super("Serialize Out", new ImageIcon("icons/save.gif"));
    }

    public void actionPerformed(ActionEvent ev) {
      String filename = JOptionPane.showInputDialog(
```

```
          IOStyledEditor.this, "Enter Filename");
      if (filename == null)
        return;

      FileOutputStream writer = null;
      try {
        Document doc = getTextComponent().getDocument();
        writer = new FileOutputStream(filename);
        ObjectOutputStream oos = new ObjectOutputStream(writer);
        oos.writeObject(doc); // write out the Document
      }
      catch (IOException ex) {
        JOptionPane.showMessageDialog(SimpleEditor.this,
        "File Not Saved", "ERROR", JOptionPane.ERROR_MESSAGE);
      }
      finally {
        if (writer != null) {
          try {
            writer.close();
          } catch (IOException x) {}
        }
      }
    }
  }
}


// An action that reads the document as a serialized object
class InAction extends AbstractAction {
  public InAction() {
    super("Serialize In", new ImageIcon("icons/open.gif"));
  }
  public void actionPerformed(ActionEvent ev) {
    String filename = JOptionPane.showInputDialog(
      IOStyledEditor.this, "Enter Filename");
    if (filename == null)
      return;
    FileInputStream reader = null;
    try {
      reader = new FileInputStream(filename);
      ObjectInputStream ois = new ObjectInputStream(reader);
      Object o = ois.readObject(); // read the document
      getTextComponent().setDocument((Document)o);
    }
    catch (IOException ex) {
      JOptionPane.showMessageDialog(SimpleEditor.this,
      "File Input Error", "ERROR", JOptionPane.ERROR_MESSAGE);
    }
    catch (ClassNotFoundException ex) {
      JOptionPane.showMessageDialog(SimpleEditor.this,
      "Class Not Found", "ERROR", JOptionPane.ERROR_MESSAGE);
    }
```

```
      finally {
        if (reader != null) {
          try {
            reader.close();
          } catch (IOException x) {}
        }
      }
    }
  }
}
```

As you can see from the code, all we've done is take advantage of the fact that the Swing document classes are serializable. This allows us to write the `Document` model out to a file and read it back in without losing any of the information contained in the model. If something goes wrong while reading or writing the file, we pop up an appropriate message dialog, using the `JOptionPane` class we discussed back in Chapter 10.

The HTML Package

As we saw back in Chapter 19, *Text 101*, when we introduced the `JEditorPane` class, Swing provides support for working with the web's most common markup language, HTML. Supporting HTML is no small task. In fact, there are over 10,000 lines of code in the JDK 1.2 beta 4 version of the `javax.swing.text.html` package, a number that will likely grow as the implementation is extended and improved. Unfortunately, this package has changed significantly in just about every major Swing release. As we went to print, the most recent version (JDK 1.2 beta 4) contained the following warning in the *bugs.html* file:

> `javax.swing.text.html` is being drastically revised and is not yet stable enough for serious development work. Developers working on HTML software should continue to use the beta 3 release.

Given this statement, we've chosen not to give a detailed explanation of the classes and interfaces that make up either of these versions of the HTML package. Instead, we'll give a high level overview of the most recent version so you can get a feel for how things are going to work. Keep your eye out for a word from the Swing team that the HTML package has stabilized.[*]

In providing an overview of the HTML package, we'll focus on the following key questions:

- How is HTML input parsed?

- How is HTML represented internally?

---

[*] As of JDK 1.2 Release Candidate 1, `HTMLEditorKit` looks more stable, but we're still not convinced it's fully cooked.

- How is HTML displayed?
- How is HTML output generated?

Parsing HTML

As we saw back in Chapter 19, the JEditorPane class can be used to display HTML text. As you have probably guessed by now, this is done with considerable assistance from an HTMLEditorKit class (a subclass of DefaultStyledEditorKit). When a request is made to read a file identified as containing HTML text, the read() method of HTMLEditorKit delegates to a separate parser object. Currently, HTMLEditorKit contains an abstract inner class called Parser that contains the following single method:

```
public abstract void parse(Reader r, ParserCallback cb) throws IOException
```

By defining the parser as a separate class with a very simple interface, the HTMLEditorKit makes it relatively easy to add support for newer versions of HTML. The read() method we mentioned earlier obtains a Parser by calling getParser(), allowing subclasses of HTMLEditorKit to plug in a custom editor at this point. The default implementation of this method returns an HTML 3.2 parser based on the HotJava browser source code. The source code for the parser currently lives in a separate package called javax.swing.text.html.parser. We will not get into any of the details of the classes in this package.

In the parse() method we listed earlier, you'll notice a very important parameter of type ParserCallback. This is how the parser communicates its progress. ParserCallback, another abstract inner class of HTMLEditorKit, defines a series of methods that indicate that the parser has encountered things such as start tags (e.g. <HTML>), end tags (e.g. </HTML>), or text (e.g. "Welcome to my Home Page"). These methods are expected to be called by the parser as it interprets an HTML document. It is then up to the ParserCallback implementation to decide how to turn this information into a meaningful internal representation.

The next logical question, of course, is "Where does the ParserCallback come from?" As you'd probably guess, the HTML package includes a class called HTMLDocument. This class (an extension of DefaultStyledDocument) includes a method called getReader() that returns an instance of HTMLEditorKit.ParserCallback. By default, the object returned is an instance of an HTMLDocument inner class called HTMLReader. Again, if you want to build a different structure to represent HTML, you are free to subclass HTMLDocument, override getReader(), and define your own callback implementation.

Representing HTML

This brings us to the problem of representing the structure of an HTML document using the Swing text package. This turns out to be pretty straightforward, thanks to the similarities between the basic Swing document model (see Chapter 20 for much more on this topic) and the structure of an HTML document.

As we said earlier, the task of building the element structure is handled, in part, by the `HTMLDocument.HTMLReader` object. This reader receives callbacks from the parser as it reads the document. As the HTML tags are read from the source, the parser passes instances of a class called `HTML.Tag` to the reader, identifying the type of element being interpreted. `HTML.Tag` is simply an open, typesafe enumeration used to describe all of the legal HTML 3.2 element types. It defines 68 constants (each of type `HTML.Tag`) which correspond to the element types defined by HTML.[*] By open, we mean that it is possible to create new tags if you want to add support for future or non-standard tags; this extension is done by creating an instance of a subclass of `HTML.Tag` call `HTML.UnknownTag`.

As the reader receives these tags (and the document content associated with them), it builds up a structure of `ElementSpecs` (again, see Chapter 20 for more on the concept of `ElementSpecs`). To understand how the elements are structured, and how the `HTML.Tag` objects the reader gets from the parser are used, we'll look at a simple example. Consider the following HTML source:

```
<HTML>
<TITLE>Swing HTML Demo</TITLE>
<H1>Demonstration of JDK1.2beta HTML Package</H1>
<P>We will use this small HTML file to show how the Swing HTML pacakge
models HTML text.  Here is a character attribute:
<I>This text is in italics.</I></P>
<P><A HREF=http://java.oreilly.com>The O'Reilly Java Resource Center</A></P>
</HTML>
```

The element structure created by this document is shown in Figure 24-5. In this diagram, we show each of the attributes defined for each element in the document.

There are several interesting things to note here. The first element we see maps to our `<HTML>` tag. Nothing too surprising so far—the reader simply created an element and added a single attribute to it using `StyleConstants.NameAttribute` as the key and `HTML.Tag.HTML` as the value.

Now things get a little interesting. The next tag in our document was a `<TITLE>` tag. This is real not part of the content of the document. That is, if we were to load this document into a typical browser (or `JEditorPane`, for that matter), we wouldn't see "Swing HTML Demo" anywhere on the page. However, this information is still very important, typically becoming the text in the browser's title bar. So what happens to it in Swing? It becomes a document property. Recall that the `Document` interface defines a `putProperty()` method, allowing any arbitrary information about the document to be defined. It also defines a constant called `TitleProperty`. This constant is used as a property key, allowing the title to be

---

[*] For more information, see the HTML 3.2 Reference Specification at the W3C's website: *http://www.w3.org/TR/REC-html32.*

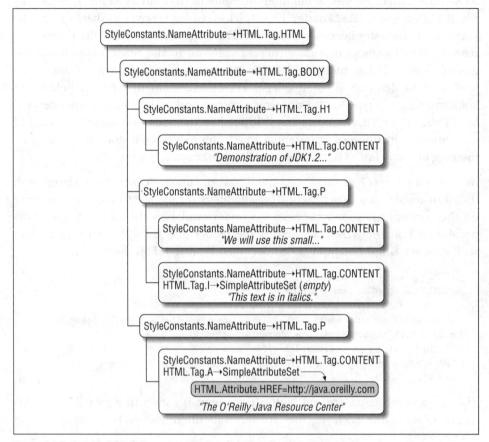

Figure 24-5. Sample HTMLDocument Element/AttributeSet structure.

stored as a document property. Therefore, retrieving the title of an HTML document is a simple matter of calling myDoc.getProperty(Document.Title-Property).

The next element shown in our hierarchy is interesting for the opposite reason. While the <TITLE> element seemed to vanish, this <BODY> element seems to have appeared out of nowhere. Well, not quite nowhere. In fact, this element is part of the default document structure created for any HTMLDocument.

Next, we see the element representation of the <H1> tag; nothing special there. What follows is a leaf element representing document content. This element contains a single attribute, again using StyleConstants.NameAttribute as a key. In this case, the value of the attribute does not map to a typical HTML tag, but instead to a special instance of HTML.Tag called HTML.Tag.CONTENT. This is the attribute value used for leaf elements containing textual content.

Below this, we see a paragraph (<P>) element. We've indicated that part of the content of this element should be in italics. Therefore, the paragraph element is broken into two content elements, the second of which contains an additional attribute. In this case, we see that the HTML.Tag.I constant is used as an attribute key. The value for this attribute is an attribute set capable of holding additional attributes associated with the tag. In this case, we don't have any such attributes, so the attribute set is empty.

In the last element, we again have an HTML.Tag (the HTML.Tag.A constant) object showing up as an attribute key. But this time, the attribute set that defines the value for the key is not empty. Instead, it contains a single entry with a key of HTML.Attribute.HREF and a value of "http://java.oreilly.com". As you might be inclined to guess, the HTML.Attribute class is very much like the HTML.Tag class–it defines a set of constants that describe the legal HTML attribute values.

That's as much detail as we're going to get into on the HTML document structure generated by the default parser and reader. If you want to create your own HTML documents in Swing, just follow this general structure and you should be in good shape.

Displaying HTML

Now that we know how the HTML document structure is represented, the next question is "How is it displayed?" If you look back at Figure 24-5, you'll notice that the element structure contains no mention of fonts, colors, or any other formatting information. This is intentional, and quite consistent with HTML itself.

In HTML, the document markup describes the type of data being displayed, but does not describe exactly how is should appear on the screen. That decision is left to the browser. For example, HTML text marked with the tag <H1> is expected to be rendered using a large "title" font. <H2> should be slightly smaller, and so on. But nowhere in the specification will you find "<H1> text shall be displayed using 18 pt. bold Helvetica."

So where does this leave us? We've got a nice, clean element structure, but we don't have the information needed to create an actual display using the Swing text components. This is where the concept of Cascading Style Sheets comes into play. A Cascading Style Sheet (CSS) provides a mechanism for mapping HTML tags to visual style data[*]. In the Swing HTML package, this mapping is managed by the StyleSheet class, an instance of which is associated with each HTMLDocument (though they are typically shared among multiple documents).

---

[*] For more informations on Cascading Style Sheets, see *http://www.w3.org/TR/REC-CSS1*.

StyleSheet defines a series of methods (several of which have not yet been implemented in JDK 1.2 beta4) to aid in this mapping process. It is then up to the various View objects to ask the StyleSheet how each element should be displayed. But how do the view objects know they're supposed to check with a style sheet? After all, we never mentioned anything about style sheets in the entire discussion of the Swing view classes in Chapter 23, *Text Views*. It turns out that every view object used by the HTMLEditorKit is some type of custom HTML view. These custom view objects are produced by the editor kit's view factory, HTMLEditorKit.HTMLFactory.

If you read Chapter 23, you might recall that the View base class defines a method called getAttributes() that returned an AttributeSet. We mentioned that view classes should always call this method, rather than obtaining the attributes directly from the Element the View is responsible for (even though the default implementation did nothing more than call getAttributes() on the view's Element). It was designed this way to handle cases like HTML in which the attributes associated with the element do not provide enough information for the view to properly display itself.

The HTML view classes convert the element's attributes to a set of view attributes via a call to getViewAttributes() on the document's StyleSheet. This method is responsible for converting the HTML.Tag attributes into a collection of view-friendly attributes. These attributes are then cached in the view, and returned any time a call is made to getAttributes(). Figure 24-6 shows the fundamental difference between the standard View-Element-AttributeSet relationship, and the structure used by the HTML views in which an additional attribute set is created by, and cached within, the view.

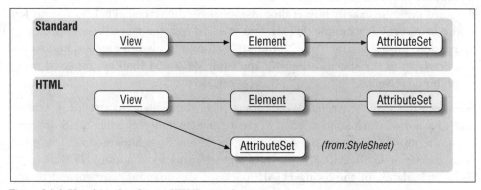

Figure 24-6. Use of AttributeSets in HTML views.

Writing HTML

Assume you've built up a nice big HTMLDocument, full of various HTML.Tag attributes. The next thing you might want to do would be to save this document as HTML text. The HTMLEditorKit will do this for you; all you need to do is call write() on the editor kit (or the JEditorPane that's using the editor kit), and your HTML output will be generated. The work of generating this output is delegated to a separate class in the HTML package called HTMLWriter.

Much, Much More

Clearly, we've only touched the surface on this topic. As we said at the outset, Swing's HTML support has been growing and changing considerably over the last few months and, as we went to print, was still doing so. We believe that the key points covered in this section will be preserved in the final design, but we obviously can't be certain.

If you're looking to do serious work using the HTML package, we recommend that you keep your eyes on *http://java.sun.com/products/jfc* for the latest and greatest Swing release, and word from the Swing team that the API has stabilized.

RTFEditorKit

One last editor kit provided by Swing is the RTFEditorKit, an extension of StyledEditorKit. This kit knows how to read and write text using RTF (Rich Text Format), a generic format that many word processors are able to work with.

Like HTMLEditorKit, RTFEditorKit has its own package (com.sun.java. swing.text.rtf) and uses many nonpublic classes defined in this package. The only public class in the package is the editor kit itself.

Property

The only modified property in RTFEditorKit is shown in Table 24-7.

Table 24-7. RTFEditorKit Property

Property	Data Type	get	is	set	bound	Default Value
contentType*	String	•				"txt/rtf"

See also properties from StyledEditorKit class (Table 24-4).

Constructor

public RTFEditorKit()

    This constructor does nothing beyond what the superclass constructors do.

Methods

public abstract Object clone()

    Returns new `RTFEditorKit`.

public abstract void read(InputStream in, Document doc, int pos)

    throws IOException, BadLocationException

    Reads RTF text from the given stream and populates the given document. The current version ignores the `pos` argument.

public abstract void write(OutputStream out, Document doc, int pos, int len)

    throws IOException, BadLocationException

    Writes RTF text to the given stream, based on the contents of the given document. The current version ignores the given `pos` and `len` arguments.

public abstract void read(Reader in, Document doc, int pos)

    throws IOException, BadLocationException

public abstract void write(Writer out, Document doc, int pos, int len)

    throws IOException, BadLocationException

    Throw an `IOException` indicating that RTF is an 8-bit format and therefore will not work with the `java.io Reader` and `Writer` classes.

Generating RTF Output

Because the version of `write()` that takes a `Writer` does nothing but throw an exception, you cannot generate RTF output by invoking the `write()` method on a `JEditorPane` (this method, defined in `JTextComponent`, takes a `Writer` and passes it through to the editor kit). Instead, you'll need to call the other `write()` method on the `RTFEditorKit` directly. If you don't already have a reference to the editor kit, the code will look something like this:

```
EditorKit edKit = myEditorPane.getEditorKit();
Document doc = myEditorPane.getDocument();
FileOutputStream out = new FileOutputStream("myfile.rtf");
edKit.write(out, doc, 0, doc.getLength());
```

Note that a similar problem does not exist for reading RTF documents using `JEditorPane` because its `setPage()` method calls the version of the editor kit's `read()` method that takes an `InputStream`.

The AbstractWriter Class

In this chapter, we've talked about a variety of strategies for saving document content. As of the JDK 1.2 beta4 release, there's a new class that can provide some assistance in creating a description of a document suitable for saving as human-readable text. It relies on the `ElementIterator` class described in Chapter 20, *Document Model and Events*. `AbstractWriter` supports indentation to clarify the document structure, as well as maximum line length to keep the generated output easy to read.

Constant

Table 24-8 shows the single, protected constant defined by `AbstractWriter`.

Table 24-8. AbstractWriter Constants

Constant	Type	Description
NEWLINE	char	the newline character (\n)

Constructors

protected AbstractWriter(Writer w, Document doc)
Creates an object that will assist in writing out the specified `Document`.

protected AbstractWriter(Writer w, Element root)
Creates an object that will assist in writing out the elements below (and including) root.

Abstract Method

abstract protected void write() throws IOException, BadLocationException
Must be implemented by subclasses to write out the document. The intention is that subclasses will call `getElementIterator()` and then iterate over the elements, using the other methods supplied by this class to produce the output.

Output Generating Methods

The following methods write text to the `Writer` supplied in the constructor.

protected void indent() throws IOException
Writes out a series of blank spaces according to the current indent level (see `setIndentSpace()`, `decrIndent()`, and `incrIndent()`, later in this chapter).

protected void text(Element elem) throws BadLocationException, IOException
Writes out the current text within the range of the given element (as returned by `getText()`, later in this chapter).

protected void write(char ch) throws IOException

Writes out the given character. If the maximum line length is reached, it will also write out a NEWLINE character and call indent().

protected void write(String str) throws IOException

Writes out the given string. If the string is too long to fit on the current line, a check is made to see if it would fit on a new line. If so, the entire string is written out on a new line. If not, the line is split between the current line and the next line.

protected void writeAttributes(AttributeSet attr) throws IOException

Writes out a textual representation of the given set of attributes. Each attribute is written as "<name>=<value>".

Other Methods

protected ElementIterator getElementIterator()

Returns the ElementIterator that subclasses should use to walk the element hierarchy.

protected Document getDocument()

Returns the Document the writer is writing.

protected String getText(Element elem) throws BadLocationException

Returns the document content associated with the given element.

protected void setLineLength(int l)

Sets the maximum line length for output. The default is 100.

protected void setIndentSpace(int space)

Sets the number of spaces for each level of indentation. The default value is 2.

protected void incrIndent()

Increments the indent level. The indent level is initially zero.

protected void decrIndent()

Decrements the indent level.

Implementing AbstractWriter

Here's a simple AbstractWriter subclass that shows how you might write out a document. In this example, we just write out the name and attributes of each element. If the element is a leaf, we write out its text.

```
// SimpleWriter.java
//
import javax.swing.text.*;
import java.io.*;
import java.awt.*;
```

```
public class SimpleWriter extends AbstractWriter {
  public SimpleWriter(Writer w, Document d) {
    super(w, d);
    setLineLength(80);
    setIndentSpace(4);
  }

  // Write the document by iterating over the elements and printing the
  // element name & attributes.  If the element is a leaf, we also print
  // its text.
  protected void write() throws IOException, BadLocationException {
    ElementIterator it = getElementIterator();

    Element e = it.first();
    while (e != null) {
      write("<" + e.getName());
      writeAttributes(e.getAttributes());
      write(">");

      if (e.isLeaf()) {
        text(e);
      }
      write(NEWLINE);
      e = it.next();
    }
  }

  // A simple test program
  public static void main(String[] args) {
    DefaultStyledDocument doc = new DefaultStyledDocument();

    try {
      // Create some simple attributed text
      SimpleAttributeSet attrs1 = new SimpleAttributeSet();
      StyleConstants.setBold(attrs1, true);
      StyleConstants.setItalic(attrs1, true);
      doc.insertString(0, "Line 2\n", attrs1);

      SimpleAttributeSet attrs2 = new SimpleAttributeSet();
      StyleConstants.setForeground(attrs2, Color.black);
      StyleConstants.setBackground(attrs2, Color.gray);
      doc.insertString(0, "Line 1\n", attrs2);

      // Write out the document
      FileWriter out = new FileWriter("test.txt");
      SimpleWriter sw = new SimpleWriter(out, doc);
      sw.write();
      out.close();
    }
```

```
        catch (BadLocationException ex) {ex.printStackTrace();}
        catch (IOException ex) {ex.printStackTrace();}
    }
}
```

The file generated by this test program looks like this:

```
<section>
<paragraph resolver=NamedStyle:default {name=default,nrefs=1}>
<content background=java.awt.Color[r=128,g=128,b=128]
 foreground=java.awt.Color[r=0,g=0,b=0]>Line 1
<paragraph resolver=NamedStyle:default {name=default,nrefs=1}>
<content italic=true bold=true>Line 2
<paragraph resolver=NamedStyle:default {name=default,nrefs=1}>
<content>
```

Building Your Own EditorKit

We've now seen everything Swing has to offer in the realm of editor kits. If you're the adventurous type, you might be thinking that it would be fun to create your own editor kit to support a particular MIME type, or perhaps to support a document type of your own creation. Depending on the type of data you want to display, this could either be a fairly easy task, or months of hard work.

NOTE   One thing to consider if you're writing an editor kit for a document type of your own creation is the use of XML. XML allows you to use a standard syntax to define element types. Furthermore, you could incorporate an existing XML parser into your editor kit's read() method, greatly simplifying the complex process of document parsing and syntax checking. For more information on XML, see the World Wide Web Consortium's XML web site found at *http://www.w3.org/XML.*

In this final section, we'll review the steps involved in creating your own editor kit. These steps include:

* Create the EditorKit class

* Define the Document type

* Define new Actions

* Create custom View classes

* Create a ViewFactory

* Create a "reader" and a "writer"

* Tell JEditorPane about your new kit

Create the EditorKit Class

The first thing to do is create your EditorKit class. Depending on the type of documents you're going to support, you can subclass the abstract EditorKit base class, or extend any of the existing kits we've covered in this chapter.

Much of the work of creating this class is covered in the steps that follow. In addition to those more complex issues, you'll want to implement the following EditorKit methods:

public abstract Object clone()

Strangely, the Swing implementations of this method just return a new instance of the editor kit subclass. It is probably a good idea to return a "true clone" here, although this method is not currently used within Swing.

public void install(JEditorPane c)

You only need to implement this method if you want to have access to the JEditorPane using your editor kit. One possibility here is to add the kit as a listener of some type.

public void deinstall(JEditorPane c)

Typically, you'll only implement this method if you implement install() to add a listener of some sort. This method should remove the listener.

public abstract String getContentType()

This method should be implemented to describe the type of content your kit will work with. The Swing-provided editor kits return text/plain, text/html, and text/rtf. This method is important if you want JEditor-Pane to be able to use your editor kit automatically when it is asked to display URLs of the appropriate type. When determining which editor kit to use, JEditorPane uses the URLConnection object from the URL passed to its setPage() method to determine the content type of the URL.

Define the Document Type

Depending on the complexity of your editor kit, you may need to define a new Document class. The HTMLEditorKit does this, defining HTMLDocument as a subclass of DefaultStyledDocument.

Whether you create your own document type or use one of the existing ones, you need to make sure createDefaultDocument() returns an instance of the type of document you want your kit to use.

Define New Actions

If you want your kit to assist in the creation of editors for your document type, you may want to define additional Action classes to perform certain activities.

Following are the three basic steps involved in this task, necessary for the creation of any document editor.

Define the new Action classes

Create any new `Action` classes you want to provide. Review the discussion of the `TextAction` and `StyledEditorKit.StyledTextAction` classes, as these may serve as useful base classes for any new `Action` classes you create.

Define Default Action Instances

Define instances of your new `Action` classes (or existing `Action` classes) that you wish to provide as default actions for the kit. This is typically done by creating a static array. For example:

```
private static final Action[] defaultActions = {
  new MyNewAction(arg1, arg2),
  new MyOtherNewAction(arg1)
};
```

Then, implement the `getActions()` method to:

```
public Action[] getActions() {
  return TextAction.augmentList(super.getActions(), this.defaultActions);
}
```

This adds your new actions to the set of actions defined by your superclass.

Define Constants for Default Actions

In order for users to be able to take advantage of your new default actions, you need to make the action names publicly available. The common pattern is to define a `String` constant for each action name. For example:

```
public static final String MY_NEW_ACTION = "my-new-action";
public static final String ANOTHER_NEW_ACTION = "another-new-action";
```

The actual values of your `String` constants should match the `Action.NAME` properties defined for each of your default actions.

Create Custom View Classes

If you want your documents to be displayed in a special way, you may need to define your own view classes. In Chapter 23, we covered the various `View` subclasses provided by Swing. It's a good idea to take a look at the available classes and see if they will do what you need, or if they can be extended to provide the look you want. Also, be sure to take advantage of the static text painting methods provided by the `javax.swing.text.Utilities` class.

Note that you are not under any obligation to keep a one-to-one mapping from `Elements` to `View` objects. It's perfectly reasonable to define a single `View` that is responsible for rendering the entire document.

Create a ViewFactory and View Classes

If you want to control the types of View objects created for the different types of Elements contained in your documents, you'll need to implement a ViewFactory. This interface contains one method, create(). A typical implementation of this interface will look something like this:

```
class MyFactory implements ViewFactory {
  public View create(Element e) {
    String name = e.getName();
    if (name != null) {
      if (name.equals(AbstractDocument.ContentElementName)) {
        return new LabelView(e);
      }
      if (name.equals(SomeOtherElementName)) {
        return new SomeOtherView(e);
      }
    }
    return new LabelView(e); // a default
  }
}
```

The key thing is to ensure that the correct type of View will be created for any Element types allowed in your documents. Note that you'll need to write this factory from scratch; there are no existing public ones, except HTMLEditorKit.HTMLFactory, to subclass.

If you do implement your own ViewFactory, remember to implement the EditorKit.getViewFactory() method to return an instance of your factory class.

Create a "Reader" and a "Writer"

Potentially the most time consuming and challenging part of creating your own editor kit is defining and implementing a strategy for reading and writing documents in the correct format. For complex document types, it makes the most sense to implement this code in separate classes outside of the editor kit.

However you choose to implement the parsing and saving operations (perhaps taking advantage of the AbstractWriterClass), you'll need to provide implementations of the read() and write() methods (unless the implementations provided by the class you're extending serve your purposes). Unless you have special requirements (as we saw with the RTF kit), you only need to implement the methods that work with the java.io Reader and Writer classes. If you're extending DefaultEditorKit, the other versions just call these.

Earlier in this chapter, we discussed the strategy of reading and writing styled documents using the built-in Java serialization mechanism. Depending on your needs, this may be a reasonable approach. Keep in mind that if you read in a serialized document, you'll have to copy all of the attributes and content over to the document passed in to the `read()` method. While this may be a pain, it may be less trouble than defining your own document format and parser.

Tell JEditorPane about Your New Kit

If you want `JEditorPane` to use your editor kit when it encounters URLs of the appropriate MIME type, you need to register your kit with the `JEditorPane` class. This is done by calling either the static method `registerEditorKitForContent-Type()` or the nonstatic `setEditorKitForContentType()`. The first method takes two strings: the content type your kit works with and the class name of your kit. You might call it like this:

```
JEditorPane.registerEditorKitForContentType("text/foo","mypackage.FooEdKit");
```

The other option takes the content type and an instance of the kit. For example:

```
JEditorPane ed = new JEditorPane();
ed.setEditorKitForContentType("text/foo", new FooEditorKit());
```

If you go with the first version (which applies to all `JEditorPane` objects), keep in mind that `JEditorPane` won't know about your kit until this call is made, so you need to be sure to make the call before you expect your kit to be used.

This step is only required if you are using a standard MIME type that the `java.net.URLConnection` class knows about. This is the class `JEditorPane` uses to determine which editor kit to use when a new URL is specified. Of course, you can still register your editor kit, even if you're not using a well-known MIME type, but you'll also need to call `setContentType()` on your `JEditorPane`, since your document type will not be recognized automatically. The other option is to skip this step altogether and just call `setEditorKit()` on the `JEditorPane`.

Phew!

At last, we've come to the close of this six-chapter novella on the Swing text framework. If you've actually read it from beginning to end, congratulations! You now know everything there is to know about the powerful new Swing text architecture.

No matter what road you took to reach this final paragraph, it's important not to let all the complexity scare you away from using the Swing text components. If you just need to do simple things, go back to Chapter 19, and revisit the examples provided there. If your requirements are more demanding, we hope the last five chapters have given you a detailed understanding of the framework.

25

Programming with Accessibility

Accessibility is a Java feature that allows you to extend your programs by interfacing an application's components with *assistive technologies* that have special permission to use them. Assistive technologies are, in the narrowest sense, specialized tools that disabled people can use to assist in interacting with your application; examples include speech-recognition and audio output. In a broader sense, however, assistive technologies can be robust application suites that can assist just about anybody with anything.

It helps to think of accessibility as a two-sided conversation. This conversation takes place between an assistive technology and the "accessibility friendly" components of applications. Assistive technologies are quite powerful: Java grants them access to all the components in the virtual machine that they can interface with, as well as the ability to interface with the windowing event queue. The latter gives an assistive technology the ability to monitor graphical events. The former means an assistive technology can directly interact with the GUI widgets of one or more applications quickly and easily—without disrupting the application beneath it.

In order for components to interface with assistive technologies, they must implement special "accessible" interfaces. (The Swing components already implement these interfaces.) There are six unique interfaces for exporting accessible functionality: one each for actions, component properties, selections, text properties, hyperlink, and bounded-range values. For each type of accessibility exported, one or more objects inside that component can be directly manipulated through that interface. For example, the `JTextField` Swing component supports text accessibility. Therefore, a speech-recognition program can insert letters in the field by obtaining the text-accessible interface and copying out the text that the user has spoken.

As there are two sides to accessibility, there are also two programming packages to deal with: the Accessibility APIs and the Accessibility Utility APIs. The first API defines the interfaces and classes that the programmer must implement on the application side in order for the components to be "accessibility friendly." The Accessibility Utility APIs, on the other hand, are a package of utilities that assistive technologies can incorporate into their own classes in order to "hook" into the Java virtual machine and interface with the application. JavaSoft bundles the former with the Swing libraries. The latter is distributed independently.

Another way of creating an assistive interface is to take advantage of the "Multi Look-and-Feel" with one or more Swing components. For example, in addition to a graphical look-and-feel, you might also redirect certain elements of the UI dele-gates to an audio output or even to a braille display. While a new look-and-feel can technically be considered an assistive technology, this approach is better explained in Chapter 26, *Look & Feel*.

NOTE   The approach described here works with the JDK1.2 version of acces-
             sibility, which was released in August 1998. This version differs from
             the JDK1.1 version. Where possible, we have tried to highlight the
             differences.

How Accessibility Works

Assistive technologies are a feature of Java. These technologies typically manifest themselves as a class archive, such as a JAR file, that resides separately on the user's local machine. As we mentioned earlier, however, Java offers assistive technologies a wide latitude of control over an application. This occurs for two reasons:

- Java loads assistive technologies into the same virtual machine as the applica-tion (or applications) with which they intend to interface.

- Assistive technologies can use or even replace the virtual machine's sole win-dowing event queue (`java.awt.EventQueue`).

Let's take a look at an accessibility-enabled Java virtual machine. When a 1.1 Java VM (1.1.5 or 1.1.6) is started, it searches the *awt.properties* configuration file for a list of specialized classes. With the 1.2 Java VM, it looks for a file called *accessi-bility.properties* in the *jre/lib* directory. If it finds them, it loads the classes into the same namespace as the application that it is about to execute. Thus, when the Java application starts, the assistive technologies start with it.

Here's a segment of the *awt.properties* file with the appropriate additions for JDK 1.1 accessibility:

```
AWT.alt=Alt
AWT.meta=Meta

# Assistive technologies
AWT.assistive_technologies=SpeechRecognition
AWT.EventQueueClass=com.sun.java.accessibility.util.EventQueueMonitor

# Key names
AWT.enter=Enter
AWT.backSpace=Backspace
```

There are two important lines under the "Assistive Technologies" heading. The line beginning `AWT.assistive_technologies=` refers to a class on the current `CLASSPATH` where Java can find an assistive technology. Each time the user starts the virtual machine, the assistive technology class is instantiated as well. The other line, `AWT.EventQueueClass=` refers to an Accessibility Utility API class that aids accessibility by replacing the Java graphical event queue. (We will talk about this class later in the chapter.) Hence, the three pieces work together to make accessibility possible. Figure 25-1 shows how an assistive technology interfaces with the Java virtual machine.

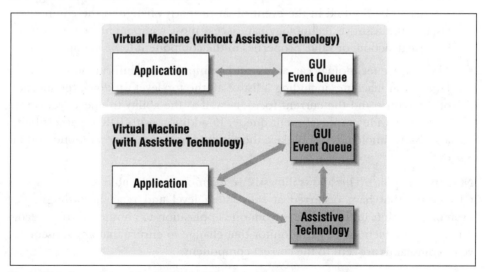

Figure 25-1. An assistive technology in the Java virtual machine

JDK 1.2 Accessibility

With the JDK 1.2 accessibility, you do not need to specify the `AWTEventQueue` property in the *accessibility.properties* file. This is now handled automatically for you.

However, you still need to specify which assistive technologies should be loaded into the Java virtual machine at startup. Hence, the *accessibility.properties* file for JDK 1.2 might look like this:

```
# Assistive technologies: only one line
assistive_technologies=SpeechRecognition
```

The Accessibility Contract

In theory, accessibility defines a "contract" between an application and an assistive technology. The contract goes like this: in exchange for providing an alternate interface that allow users greater power to interact with my application, I will allow outside control of many or all of my components. With Swing, you do this by activating accessibility properties and interfaces inside your components. If you stick to the Swing components in your application, this is a trivial task—it's already done for you. However, if you're still using AWT, it can be more difficult.

Let's take a look at the fine print:

- All accessibility friendly components return a standardized accessible object on demand. This object has standardized methods that allow assistive technologies to query each component for its name, description, role (purpose), parent, children, and its current state. In addition, the assistive technology can register to be notified in the event of an property change in the component. Finally, the assistive technology can access most component, text, selection, hypertext, action, or value properties in the component to be manipulated.

- The assistive technology can access and manipulate key information about the Java virtual machine, including a list of all the top-level windows, the location of the mouse and the current focus, as well as the ability to inject events into the system-wide graphical event queue. In addition, with JDK 1.1 accessibility, assistive technologies can replace the windowing event queue with one of their own.

Note the last point. This allows the assistive technology to be able to "sniff" various GUI events that have occurred at the system level and react accordingly. For example, if a shift in focus occurs from one application to another, a voice recognition assistive technology can monitor that change to ensure that any subsequent voice commands are sent to the correct component.

How Do I Get It?

Swing

If you are using Swing components in your application, then almost everything is taken care of for you. You only need to do two things to make your components accessibility-friendly. The first is to provide an accessible name for each of your components; the second is to provide an accessible description for each of your components. In certain cases, these properties may be set for you automatically. If not, both are trivial additions, as shown below:

```
JTextField text = new JTextField();
text.getAccessibleContext().setAccessibleName("Name");
text.getAccessibleContext().setAccessibleDescription("Enter A Name");
```

By having these two properties set in your components, any assistive technology that has been loaded into the Java virtual machine can successfully query the component to determine how it can best be used.

As we mentioned, these properties are often derived from other attributes of the Swing components. The following has the same effect as the code we just showed:

```
JTextField text = new JTextField();
JLabel label = new JLabel("Name");
label.setLabelFor(text);            // sets text's accessibleName
text.setToolTipText("Enter a name"); // sets text's accessibleDescription
```

AWT

Currently, there is no support for accessibility in AWT. However, the Java Accessibility Utility APIs intend to include a set of "translators" in the future. At the time this book went to press, the implementation was not available. Check the Accessibility home page (*http://java.sun.com/access*) for more details on this package as it is developed.

The Accessibility Package

Now, let's discuss the issues an assistive technology will encounter when hooking into an accessible friendly application.

The Path to Determining Accessibility

Almost all Swing objects support one or more forms of accessibility, which means they implement the Accessible interface. However, for an assistive technology to find out which types of accessibility an application supports, the technology needs to do some investigating. The typical course of action goes like this:

1. The assistive technology locates a desired component in the target application with the help of the Accessibility Utility APIs. Once found, it invokes the getAccessibleContext() method of the component object, which is the sole method of the Accessible interface. This method returns a customized AccessibleContext object, often an inner class of the component.

2. The assistive technology can then use the `AccessibleContext` object to retrieve the name, description, role, state, parent, and children components of the accessible component in question.

3. The assistive technology can register for any property change events in the component that it's interested in.

4. The assistive technology can call upon six standardized methods to determine whether those types of accessibility are supported. All `AccessibleContext` objects have these interface methods. If any of these methods return `null`, then the component does not support the specific accessibility type.

5. If they are not `null`, the objects returned by each of the five methods can then be used to access the functionality on the component.

Different components implement different types of accessibility. For example, a tree might export accessibility action, selection, and component properties, while a button might simply export component properties. Components do not have to support all five. Hence, assistive technologies need to determine exactly what accessible functionality each component supports by querying that component for information.

The Accessible Interface

All components that need to export functionality to outside objects must implement the `Accessible` interface. This interface consists of only one method: `getAccessibleContext()`. Assistive technologies must always call this method first to retrieve an accessible-context object from the component. This object can then be used to query the component about its accessible capabilities.

Method

public abstract AccessibleContext getAccessibleContext()
Returns the `AccessibleContext` object of the current component, or `null` if the component does not support accessibility.

NOTE   If you are creating your own component, and you do not want your component to support accessibility, you should not implement the `Accessible` interface. However, there may be circumstances where you are extending an already accessible Swing component, and you don't want the resulting component to allow accessibility. In that case, you can override the `getAccessibleContext()` method in your own component and set it to return `null`.

The AccessibleContext Class

The `AccessibleContext` class is the heart of accessibility. It bundles component information that any assistive technology can learn about. The class has three primary responsibilities. First, it allows access to the accessible properties of the host component: its name, role, description, and current state, as well as a parent object and a list of child objects, if applicable. Second, it provides the ability to register for any change events on those properties. Third, the `AccessibleContext` object is responsible for reporting the accessible functionality that the component exports. Technologies that obtain the `AccessibleContext` object of a component can then call upon these methods to determine what types of accessible functionality can be used. These methods are:

```
public AccessibleAction getAccessibleAction()
public AccessibleComponent getAccessibleComponent()
public AccessibleSelection getAccessibleSelection()
public AccessibleValue getAccessibleValue()
public AccessibleText getAccessibleText()
```

Each of these methods returns a special object that an assistive technology can use to modify properties or invoke functionality inside the component. In the event that a component does not support one or more types, the respective method returns `null`.

The `AccessibleContext` class contains several abstract methods. Hence, each component has its own subclass of `AccessibleContext` that is returned by the `getAccessibleContext()` method of the `Accessible` interface.

Properties

Table 25-1 shows the properties of the `AccessibleContext` class. The most important are `accessibleName` and `accessibleDescription`. Both properties are usually set by the programmer of the host application. The `accessibleName` property gives a name to the component; some Swing components automatically set the accessible name as the text of the component. The `accessibleDescription` gives a terse description of how the user should interact with the component.

Table 25-1. AccessibleContext Properties

Property	Data Type	get	is	set	bound	Default Value
accessibleAction	AccessibleAction	•				
accessibleChild[a] (indexed)	Accessible	•				

Table 25-1. AccessibleContext Properties (continued)

Property	Data Type	get	is	set	bound	Default Value
accessibleChildren-Count[a]	int	•				
accessibleComponent	AccessibleComponent	•				
accessibleDescription	String	•		•	•	
accessibleIndexIn-Parent[a]	int	•				
accessibleName	String	•		•	•	
accessibleParent	Accessible	•		•		
accessibleRole[a]	AccessibleRole	•				
accessibleSelection	AccessibleSelection	•				
accessibleStateSet[a]	AccessibleStateSet	•				
accessibleText	AccessibleText	•				
accessibleValue	AccessibleValue	•				
locale[a]	Locale	•				

[a] The accessors for these properties are abstract.

The read-only accessibleRole property defines the purpose of the component. Accessible roles are predefined constants, such as SCROLL_BAR or PUSHABLE_ BUTTON; they essentially tell what the component is. The accessibleStateSet property tells which states the accessible component is currently in. There are a host of states that a component can be in. Both properties are outlined in greater detail below.

The properties accessibleAction, accessibleSelection, accessibleText, accessibleValue, and accessibleComponent refer to the individual types of accessibility supported by each component. Each property contains a read-only object, used exclusively for interfacing with that accessible area of the component. The get accessors for these methods return null if there's no accessible object of the requested type for this component. Although you might think there should be, there's no accessibleHyperlink property. To get an AccessibleHyperlink, use getAccessibleText(), and check whether the result is an instance of AccessibleHypertext. Once you have an AccessibleHypertext object, call getLink() to get an AccessibleHyperlink.

The accessibleParent property places the component in its accessibility hierarchy. Note that when we say *accessibility hierarchy*, this is a component hierarchy that can differ from the regular component hierarchy. For example, a CellRenderer object inside of a Swing list component does not have the JList as its parent in the component hierarchy. However, it does have the JList as a parent in the accessibility hierarchy. That way, if an assistive technology wished to access the list itself, it would not be cut off by limitations in the component hierarchy.

The accessibleChildrenCount, accessibleChild, and accessibleIndexIn-Parent properties each give details about this component in the current accessibility hierarchy. accessibleChild is an indexed property that provides references to each of the component's accessible children, while accessible-ChildrenCount is an integer that returns the number of accessible children present. If this component is the child of a parent component in the accessibility hierarchy, the accessibleIndexInParent property indicates what index the component currently holds.

Accessible Names and Descriptions

Assistive technologies use the accessibleName property to distinguish the component from others of the same type. With named components, such as those that extend AbstractButton, the accessible name is automatically extracted from its label. For all others, you should always set the accessibleName property when including the component in your application. With Swing components, you can set the accessibility name with the following code fragment:

```
mySwingComponent.getAccessibleContext.setAccessibleName("Execute");
```

An assistive technology attempts to reference a component by keying off of its name, so it's probably a good idea to stick with standardized names. In other words, if you create a JPopupMenu object containing various chemical elements, make sure to call it something reasonable like "Elements" and not "The Elements Popup Menu of Gerald's Application." The latter would be extremely difficult for assistive technologies to identify. A good rule of thumb is to keep the names as short as possible, while maintaining their uniqueness.

You can set the accessibility description of each component with the following short segment of code:

```
myButton.getAccessibleContext().setAccessibleDescription(
    "Closes the dialog");
```

You can also set the description of a Swing component by giving it a tooltip string:

```
myButton.getAccessibleContext().setToolTipText("Closes the dialog");
```

Both approaches are equivalent. Assistive technologies can use the description property to learn more about the accessible component. The description is not as important as the name, but it frequently helps the user by providing instructions on how to work with a specific component.

Constructor

public AccessibleContext()
   This is the default constructor.

Events

Objects extending the `AccessibleContext` class must fire a `PropertyChange-Event` when one of its bound properties is modified. Assistive technologies will listen for these events and modify their states or react in some fashion if such a change occurs.

public void addPropertyChangeListener(PropertyChangeListener listener)
void removePropertyChangeListener(PropertyChangeListener listener)
   Add or remove the specified `PropertyChangeListener` from the object's list of listeners.

public void firePropertyChange(String property, Object oldValue, Object newValue)
   Fires a `PropertyChangeEvent` to all registered listeners indicating the property that has changed, and provides both the old value and the new value of the property.

Constants

`AccessibleContext` uses the string constants listed in Table 25-2 to represent various properties when communicating change events:

Table 25-2. AccessibleContext Property Constants

Constant	Description
ACCESSIBLE_CARET_PROPERTY	An `AccessibleText` component's caret property has changed
ACCESSIBLE_CHILD_PROPERTY	The `accessibleChild` property has changed
ACCESSIBLE_DESCRIPTION_PROPERTY	The `accessibleDescription` property has changed
ACCESSIBLE_NAME_PROPERTY	The `accessibleName` property has changed
ACCESSIBLE_SELECTION_PROPERTY	The `accessibleSelection` property has changed
ACCESSIBLE_STATE_PROPERTY	The `accessibleStateSet` property has changed
ACCESSIBLE_TEXT_PROPERTY	The `accessibleText` property has changed
ACCESSIBLE_VALUE_PROPERTY	The `accessibleValue` property has changed
ACCESSIBLE_VISIBLE_DATA_PROPERTY	The visual appearance of the component has changed

Other Accessible Objects

Before going further, there are several simple objects in the `Accessibility` package used by `AccessibleContext` that we should discuss in more detail.

AccessibleState

Each accessible component can have one or more states associated with it. An assistive technology can query these states at any time to determine how best to deal with the component. The accessible states can only be retrieved, however, and not set. There are two classes that the `Accessible` package uses to handle states: `AccessibleState` and `AccessibleStateSet`.

The `AccessibleState` class contains an enumeration of static objects that define states that any accessible component can have. Note that a component can be in more than one state at any time. A list of the possible states that an accessible object can be in, along with a brief description of each, is shown in Table 25-3.

Table 25-3. AccessibleState Constants

State	Meaning
ACTIVE	The window, dialog, or frame is the active one
ARMED	The object, such as a button, has been pressed but not released, and the mouse cursor is still over the button
BUSY	The object is busy processing and should not be interrupted
CHECKED	The object is checked
COLLAPSED	The object, such as a node in a tree, is collapsed
EDITABLE	The object supports any form of editing
ENABLED	The object is enabled
EXPANDABLE	The object, such as a node in a tree, can report its children
EXPANDED	The object, such as a node in a tree, is expanded
FOCUSABLE	The object can accept the focus
FOCUSED	The object has the focus
HORIZONTAL	The object's orientation is horizontal
ICONIFIED	The object is iconified
MODAL	The object is modal and must be closed before the user can switch to another window
MULTI_LINE	The object is capable of using many lines of text
MULTISELECTABLE	The object allows multiple children to be selected at the same time
OPAQUE	The object is completely filled (i.e., paints every pixel), and thus does not allow transparency

Table 25-3. AccessibleState Constants (continued)

State	Meaning
PRESSED	The object, such as a button, is being pressed but has not been released
RESIZABLE	The object is resizable
SELECTABLE	The object is capable of being selected from its parent
SELECTED	The object is selected
SHOWING	The object and each of its ancestors are visible
SINGLE_LINE	The object is only capable of using a single line of text
TRANSIENT	The object is transient. In the context of accessibility, transient objects serve only to help other components perform some underlying duty, such as rendering to the screen. These objects do not generate change events that an assistive technology would be interested in, but are necessary to allow assistive technologies to query through the component hierarchy.
VERTICAL	The object's orientation is vertical
VISIBLE	The object is visible

Some of these states are specific to various objects. For example, a JButton cannot be COLLAPSED, and a JLabel cannot be EDITABLE. An assistive technology, however, should know which objects can have which states and how to act accordingly. Note that the individual states of AccessibleState are constant static objects. In order to work with a group (or set) of them, you will need the services of the AccessibleStateSet object.

Constructor

protected AccessibleState(String key)

This protected constructor is called using any of the states listed above to instantiate an AccessibleState object. It is protected to allow each of the constants above to remain as a strongly-typed, static enumeration of states. Follow this procedure if you subclass AccessibleState with your own states.

AccessibleStateSet

Because an accessible component can have more than one accessible state at the same time, you must access each of the states through the use of an AccessibleStateSet object. This object is simply a read-only repository (or set) of accessible states, as well as various methods to search and identify particular states. You can retrieve an AccessibleStateSet for each accessible component with the getAccessibleStateSet() accessor of the AccessibleContext object.

Field

The `AccessibleStateSet` object consists of a single protected `Vector` variable that stores each of the states for the target component.

protected Vector states
> A dynamic array of `AccessibleState` constants that describe the state of the component.

Constructors

AccessibleStateSet()
> Creates an empty state set.

AccessibleStateSet(AccessibleState[])
> Creates a state set using the array of `AccessibleState` objects passed in to initialize itself.

Methods

public boolean add(AccessibleState state)
> Adds a new `AccessibleState` to the set, returning `true` if successful. If the state is already present, it is not added, and the method returns `false`.

public void addAll(AccessibleState[] states)
> Adds all the states specified in the array to the set, ignoring any that are already present.

public void clear()
> Clears all states from the state set.

public boolean contains(AccessibleState state)
> Returns a `boolean` indicating whether the given `state` is included in the set.

public boolean remove(AccessibleState state)
> Removes a specific `AccessibleState` from the set, returning `true` if successful. If the state is not present in the set, the method returns `false`.

public AccessibleState[] toArray()
> Returns an enumeration of the states in the set as an array of `AccessibleState` objects.

public String toString()
> Creates a string of the state set using the current locale.

AccessibleRole

A common way to determine the purpose or function of an accessible component is to check its *accessible role*. All accessibility roles are bundled inside an `AccessibleRole` object, which, like the `AccessibleState` object, consists only of static constants. An assistive technology can query these read-only roles from Accessi-bleContext to better determine what type of component it is dealing with. If a desired role does not exist in this object, you can always extend the Accessible-Role object into a subclass of your own and include the newly defined role there. Because they are all of type AccessibleRole, the static constants within this class can be used in conjunction with the getAccessibleRole() method of an AccessibleContext object.

Table 25-4 outlines each of the accessibility roles.

Table 25-4. AccessibleRole Constants

Constant	Meaning
ALERT	Provide an alert to the user
AWT_COMPONENT	A generic AWT component
CHECK_BOX	A dual-state button or checkbox
COLOR_CHOOSER	An object for selecting a color
COLUMN_HEADER	A header for a column of data
COMBO_BOX	A combo box component
DESKTOP_ICON	An internal frame that has been iconified
DESKTOP_PANE	A desktop pane that supports internal frames
DIALOG	A top-level dialog box
DIRECTORY_PANE	A specialty pane used to locate directories on a filesystem
FILE_CHOOSER	A specialty dialog box for choosing a file
FILLER	Any object that takes up space in a user-interface
FRAME	A top-level frame
GLASS_PANE	The glass pane of a frame or applet
INTERNAL_FRAME	An internal frame inside a desktop frame
LABEL	A string-based label
LAYERED_PANE	A layered-pane object
LIST	A list object
MENU	A standard menu that descends from a menubar
MENU_BAR	A menubar object
MENU_ITEM	A menu item inside a menu
OPTION_PANE	An object that displays a popup message
PAGE_TAB	An page tab object, typically a descendant of a page tab list
PAGE_TAB_LIST	A grouping of page tabs
PANEL	A panel object
PASSWORD_TEXT	A password text field that masks its entry text
POPUP_MENU	A popup menu
PROGRESS_BAR	A progress bar object

Table 25-4. AccessibleRole Constants (continued)

Constant	Meaning
PUSH_BUTTON	A standard button
RADIO_BUTTON	A radio button
ROOT_PANE	The root pane of a frame
ROW_HEADER	A header for a row of data
SCROLL_BAR	A scrollbar
SCROLL_PANE	A scrollpane object
SEPARATOR	A lined separator used in conjunction with a layout manager
SLIDER	A slider object
SPLIT_PANE	A pane that is split into two adjustable halves
SWING_COMPONENT	A generic Swing component
TABLE	A table object
TEXT	A generic object that displays text
TOGGLE_BUTTON	A dual-state button that does not provide a separate state
TOOL_BAR	A toolbar object
TOOL_TIP	A tooltip object
TREE	A tree object
UNKNOWN	An unknown object
VIEWPORT	A viewport used in a scroll pane
WINDOW	A top-level window without a border or title

Constructor

protected AccessibleRole(String key)

This is the only constructor for the `AccessibleRole` class. Note that the constructor is protected; there is no public constructor for this class. The constructor takes a single `String` that corresponds to the locale for each of the accessible roles. This locale determines how to translate each of the states and roles into a "human-readable" form.

The Six Types of Accessibility

Accessible components can export six types of assistive functionalities: actions, text properties, component properties, selections, hypertext, and bounded-range value properties. Most of these functions are already present in the Swing components, so if you stick closely to Swing, you probably won't need to implement these interfaces in your components. In an effort to explain how one might implement these interfaces, we have provided a simple example showing how to add `AccessibleAction` support to an AWT-based component.

The AccessibleAction Interface

The `AccessibleAction` interface outlines the methods that an accessible object or component must have to export its actions. The interface consists of only three methods. The idea is that an assistive technology can determine the correct action by obtaining the total number of actions that the component exports, then reviewing each of their descriptions to resolve the correct one. Once this has occurred, the `doAccessibleAction()` method can be called with the correct index to invoke the required method.

Properties

The properties listed in Table 25-5 must be readable through the `AccessibleAction` interface. The `accessibleActionCount` stores the number of accessible actions that the component implements. The indexed property `accessibleActionDescription` provides a string describing the action associated with the given index. The action with index 0 is the component's default action.

Table 25-5. AccessibleAction Properties

Property	Data Type	get	is	set	bound	Default Value
accessibleActionCount	int	•				
accessibleActionDescription (indexed)	Action	•				

Method

public abstract boolean doAccessibleAction(int index)

    Invokes an action based on the given index. The method returns `false` if an action with that index does not exist. It returns `true` if successful.

The AccessibleComponent Interface

The `AccessibleComponent` interface should be supported by any component that is drawn to a graphical context on the screen. Assistive technologies can use the this interface to change how the component is drawn. Almost all of the methods in this interface call equivalent methods in the `java.awt.Component` class, so you will find this accessibility type in almost every Swing component. Adding `AccessibleComponent` support to your own components is a trivial exercise.

Properties

The properties listed in Table 25-6 must be made available through the AccessibleComponent interface. These properties should be fairly self-explanatory, if you're familiar with the way JComponents work. The background and foreground properties let you manipulate the component's background and foreground colors. The cursor and font properties let you manipulate the component's cursor or font.

Table 25-6. AccessibleComponent Properties

Property	Data Type	get	is	set	bound	Default Value
background	Color	•		•		
bounds	Rectangle	•		•		
cursor	Cursor	•		•		
enabled	boolean		•	•		
focusTraversable	boolean		•			
font	Font	•		•		
foreground	Color	•		•		
location	Point	•		•		
locationOnScreen	Point	•				
showing	boolean		•			
size	Dimension	•		•		
visible	boolean		•	•		

The enabled, showing, and visible properties let you find out the component's status. A component tht is enabled will have AccessibleState.ENABLED as part of its accessibleStateSet property. Likewise, a component that is visible will have AccessibleState.VISIBLE as part of its accessibleStateSet, and a component that is showing will have AccessibleState.SHOWING as part of its accessibleStateSet. A visible component will be showing only if all of its ancestors are also visible. Remember that it's possible for a component that's showing to be hidden by another component.

The location, locationOnScreen, bounds, and size properties let you find out about the real estate occupied by the component. location gives you access to the component's position in the parent container's coordinate system; locationOnScreen gives you access to the component's position in the screen's coordinate system. The bounds property is a Rectangle that describes the component's bounding box; the size property is a Dimension that gives you the component's width and height, including any insets or borders.

The focusTraversable property tells you whether or not this object can accept focus. If its value is true, the component will also have Accessible-State.FOCUSABLE as part of its accessibleStateSet.

Methods

public abstract boolean contains(Point p)

Returns a boolean indicating whether the point passed in (in object coordinates) is within the bounding box of the component.

public abstract Accessible getAccessibleAt(Point p)

Returns a component that implements the Accessible interface under the point passed in, or null if one does not exist.

public abstract void requestFocus()

Makes a request to grab the focus. Note that the method returns void; if it does not succeed, it will not notify the caller.

Events

Objects implementing the AccessibleComponent interface must be able to register listeners for focus events generated by the component.

public abstract void addFocusListener(FocusListener l)
public abstract void removeFocusListener(FocusListener l)

Add or remove the specified FocusListener from the event listener list.

The AccessibleSelection Interface

AccessibleSelection is a simple interface that allows assistive technologies to query a component for information about its current selections. By selections, we mean choosing one or more items in a component, such as from a JList. The interface also contains methods that allow outside modification to the current set of selections.

The AccessibleSelection interface works by interfacing with two separate lists. The first is the standard *data list* of objects that have been added to the component, typically with an add() method. The second is the *selection list*; this list contains zero-based indexes into the former list. With Swing, the JList class is the most obvious candidate for implementing the AccessibleSelection interface. With that class, the interface would simply monitor both the model and the selection model of the JList to complete its functionality.

Again, this is a case where the objects in the accessibility hierarchy differ from the traditional component hierarchy. Here, the accessible children of an AccessibleSelection component should be the objects returned by the getAccessibleSelection() method; in other words, the objects added to the selectable list. As you might guess, all the objects that can be selected must implement the Accessible interface.

Properties

The properties listed in Table 25-7 must be readable through the AccessibleSelection interface. The accessibleSelectionCount property tells you how many selections the user has made. accessibleSelection, which is indexed, lets you access a particular selection given by the index. isAccessibleChildSelected, which is also indexed, lets you find out whether a particular child of the component is on the selection list; in this case, the index refers to one of the component's children, and a true value indicates that the child specified by the index is on the selection list.

Table 25-7. AccessibleSelection Properties

Property	Data Type	get	is	set	bound	Default Value
accessibleSelectionCount	int	•				
accessibleSelection (indexed)	Accessible	•				
accessibleChildSelected (indexed)	boolean		•			

Methods

public abstract void addAccessibleSelection(int index)
   Adds the child referenced by index in the data list to the selection list. If the child is already present, it is not added again. If the selection list only supports one selection at a time, the child replaces the previous selection on the list.

public abstract void removeAccessibleSelection(int index)
   Removes the child referenced by index in the data list from the current selection list. If the child is not currently selected, this method has no effect.

public abstract void clearAccessibleSelection()
   Clears the selection list.

public abstract void selectAllAccessibleSelection()
   Adds every child contained in the component to the selection list.

The AccessibleText Interface

The AccessibleText methods are used to export "editable" text to assistive technologies. By editable, we mean text that the user can normally click and change, as opposed to static text that you would see in labels or buttons. The Accessible-

Text interface provides several methods that allow you not only to change the text, but to obtain many of its attributes as well. The AccessibleText interface is generally used only with the Swing components, because much of the functionality that is required is not available in the older AWT components.

Properties

The read-only properties in Table 25-8 must be made available through the AccessibleText interface.

Table 25-8. AccessibleText Properties

Property	Data Type	get	is	set	bound	Default Value
caretPosition	int	•				
characterAttribute (indexed)	AttributeSet	•				
characterBounds (indexed)	Rectangle	•				
charCount	int	•				
selectionEnd	int	•				
selectionStart	int	•				
selectedText	String	•				

Constants

The AccessibleText interface uses the constants listed in Table 25-9. The char-Count property lets you retrieve the total number of characters in the text buffer. characterBounds lets you retrieve the Rectangle bounding the character at a given index. caretPosition gives you the index of the character directly the right of the caret.

Table 25-9. AccessibilityState Properties

State	Meaning
CHARACTER	Retrieve the current character at or near the specified index
WORD	Retrieve the current word at or near the specified index
SENTENCE	Retrieve the current sentence at or near the specified index

Methods

public abstract String getAfterIndex(int part, int index)
Returns the current character, word, or sentence after the given index, depending on which AccessibleText constant is passed in.

public abstract String getAtIndex(int part, int index)

Returns the current character, word, or sentence from the given index, depending on which `AccessibleText` constant is passed in.

public abstract String getBeforeIndex(int part, int index)

Returns the current character, word, or sentence before the given index, depending on which `AccessibleText` constant is passed in.

public abstract int getIndexAtPoint(Point p)

Takes a `Point` in local coordinates and returns an index to the text character that resides under the point. If there is no text under the given point, the method must return `-1`.

The AccessibleHypertext Interface

The `AccessibleHypertext` interface extends the `AccessibleText` interface above to allow access to hypertext, such as you'd see in an HTML browser. In order to determine whether a given component has any accessible hyperlinks in it, call the `getAccessibleText()` method of the component's `AccessibleContext` object and check to see if the object returned is an instance of the `AccessibleHypertext` interface. If it is, the resulting object is a special hypertext accessibility object that can be used to obtain not only the traditional accessible text information, but also the number of hyperlinks in the page as well as `AccessibleHyperlink` objects that represents each one.

Properties

`AccessibleHypertext` defines the properties listed in Table 25-10. The `linkcount` property tells you the number of hyperlinks in the text. The indexed property `linkIndex` gives you the index of the hyperlink at the given character offset into the text. The `link` property itself, which is also indexed, lets you access the hyperlink specified by the index. For example, to find the hyperlink associated with the character n, you could write:

```
AccessibleHyperlink h = getLink(getLinkIndex(n));
```

Table 25-10. AccessibleHypertext Properties

Property	Data Type	get	is	set	bound	Default Value
link (indexed)	AccessibleHyperlink	•				
linkCount	int	•				
linkIndex	int	•				

See also properties of the AccessibleText interface (Table 25-8).

The AccessibleHyperlink Class

The `AccessibleHyperlink` class is an abstract class that encapsulates an HTML hyperlink in a text document. Hyperlinks are only found inside the document models of a `JEditorPane`. The `AccessibleHyperlink` class implements the `AccessibleAction` interface, which normally provides support for any number of actions in accessible components. For the most part, `AccessibleHyperlink` objects only have one action associated with them, which results in loading the text pane with the HTML document or image associated with the link. `Accessi-bleHyperlink` objects are returned from the `getLink()` accessor of an `AccessibleHypertext` object.

Properties

The `AccessibleHyperlink` class defines the properties listed in Table 25-11. All of the properties are abstract. The `endIndex` and `startIndex` properties let you access the starting and ending offsets of this hyperlink in the document from which it came. The `valid` property is true if the document that this hyperlink points to is still valid (i.e., has not changed).

Table 25-11. AccessibleHyperlink Properties

Property	Data Type	get	is	set	bound	Default Value
accessibleActionAnchor (indexed)	Object	•				
accessibleActionCount	int	•				
accessibleActionDescription (indexed)	String	•				
accessibleActionObject (indexed)	String	•				
endIndex	int	•				
startIndex	int	•				
valid	boolean		•			

The remaining properties let you work with an `AccessibleAction` (or actions) associated with this hyperlink. `accessibleActionCount` lets you find out how many actions are associated with the hyperlink; this is usually one, but there can be more. If there are more, the first action is not considered the default. `acces-sibleActionDescription` lets you retrieve a `String` describing a particular action. `accessibleActionObject` lets you access an object representing the action itself. For example, given a hyperlink to the URL *http://www.oreilly.com/*, `getAccessibleActionObject` will return a Java URL pointing to *http://www.oreilly.com/*. Finally, `accessibleActionAnchor` gives you the object that is displayed on the screen to represent the link. For example, if the link is a clickable image, getAccessibleActionAnchor returns an ImageIcon; if the link is represented by text, this method returns a String containing the text.

Method

public abstract boolean doAccessibleAction(int index)
This method performs the action specified by the given integer index.

The AccessibleValue Interface

The AccessibleValue interface is responsible for handling a bounded-range value property inside a component. For example, the current value of a slider would be considered an accessible value that a component can export to an assistive technology. This is a simple interface that contains only four methods. Note that the value's data type is the generic Number; it is up to the caller to ensure that the data type passed in is correct, or the value returned is cast to the correct object.

Methods

public abstract Number getCurrentAccessibleValue()
Returns the current value as a Number. If the value has not been initialized, this method returns null.

public abstract boolean setCurrentAccessibleValue(Number n)
Attempts to set the current value to the number passed in. If the number passed in is not the correct type, or it cannot be set, the method returns false. Otherwise, the method returns true.

public abstract Number getMinimumAccessibleValue()
Returns the current minimum value as a Number. The caller is responsible for casting the returned Number to the appropriate data type.

public abstract Number getMaximumAccessibleValue()
Returns the current maximum value as a Number. The caller is responsible for casting the returned Number to the appropriate data type.

Implementing AccessibleAction

Here is a short example that implements an AccessibleContext and the AccessibleAction interface for a simple AWT button:

```
//  ActionExample2.java
//
import java.util.*;
import java.awt.*;
import java.awt.event.*;
```

```java
import javax.swing.*;
import javax.accessibility.*;

public class ActionExample2 extends Button
    implements ActionListener, Accessible {

    public ActionExample2() {
        super("Press this Button");
        addActionListener(this);
    }

    public AccessibleContext getAccessibleContext() {
        return (new ActionAccessibleContext());
    }

    public void actionPerformed(ActionEvent e) {
        system.out.println("The button was pressed!");
    }

    public void processActionEvent(ActionEvent e) {
        super.processActionEvent(e);
    }


// This class contains the accessible context for the component. Many of the
// abstract methods simply call the SwingUtilities class to get the job
// done; this is advised if you can get away with it. Otherwise, see the
// source code for SwingUtilities.
class ActionAccessibleContext extends AccessibleContext {

    public ActionAccessibleContext() {
        super();
        setAccessibleName("Button");
        setAccessibleDescription("Press the Button");
    }

    public AccessibleRole getAccessibleRole() {
        // Fill in whatever role you want here
        return (AccessibleRole.AWT_COMPONENT);
    }

    public AccessibleStateSet getAccessibleStateSet() {
        return SwingUtilities.
                getAccessibleStateSet(ActionExample.this);
    }

    public int getAccessibleIndexInParent() {
        return SwingUtilities.
                getAccessibleIndexInParent(ActionExample.this);
    }
```

```
        public int getAccessibleChildrenCount() {
            return SwingUtilities.
                        getAccessibleChildrenCount(ActionExample.this);
        }


        public Accessible getAccessibleChild(int i) {
            return SwingUtilities.getAccessibleChild(ActionExample.this, i);
        }


        public Locale getLocale() {
            //  Ask the component what its locale is
            return ActionExample.this.getLocale();
        }


        public AccessibleAction getAccessibleAction() {
            return new AccessAction();
        }
    }

// This class implements the AccessibleAction interface. Essentially, there
// is only one action that is the equivalent of pushing the button.
class AccessAction implements AccessibleAction {

    final int NUMBER_OF_ACTIONS = 1;
    final String DESCRIPTION = "Presses the button";

    public int getAccessibleActionCount() {
        return NUMBER_OF_ACTIONS;
    }

    public String getAccessibleActionDescription(int i) {
        if (i == 0)
            return (DESCRIPTION);
        else
            return null;
    }


    public boolean doAccessibleAction(int i) {
        if (i == 0) {
            // Simulate pressing a button
            ActionExample2.this.processActionEvent(new ActionEvent(this,
                ActionEvent.ACTION_PERFORMED,
                ActionExample.this.getActionCommand()));
            return true;
        } else
            return false;
    }
}
```

```
    public static void main(String s[]) {

      ActionExample2 example = new ActionExample2();

      JFrame frame = new JFrame("AccessibleAction Example");
      frame.addWindowListener(new BasicWindowMonitor());
      frame.getContentPane().add(example, BorderLayout.CENTER);
      frame.setSize(100, 100);
      frame.setVisible(true);
    }
}
```

The result is somewhat anticlimactic: the example creates a simple button on the screen, and nothing else. If you push the button, the following output is displayed:

```
    The button was pressed!
```

However, it is important to know that an assistive technology could incorporate itself into the virtual machine and find out the button's state and description, and even cause the button to be pressed. In order to understand more about how this can occur, we need to talk about the accessibility utility classes.

The Accessibility Utility Classes

So far, we've seen how the Accessibility APIs help make Swing and AWT components easier to interface with assistive technologies. However, we haven't seen what's available on the other side of the contract. In reality, there are several classes that help assistive technologies interface with the Java virtual machine on startup, communicate with accessible friendly components, and capture and interpret various system events. These classes are called the *accessibility utility* classes. These classes are not part of Swing; instead, they exist as a separate package, com.sun.java.accessibility.util, distributed by Sun Microsystems. (You can download this package from *http://java.sun.com/products/jfc/*.) The utility classes are crucial to assistive technology developers who wish to create specialized solutions that can communicate with any accessibility-friendly application.

Specifically, the accessibility utility classes can provide assistive technologies with:

- A list of the top-level windows of all Java applications currently executing under that virtual machine
- Support for locating the window that has the input focus
- Support for locating the current mouse position
- Registration for listening for when top-level windows appear and disappear
- The ability to register listeners for and insert events into the windowing event queue

For the purposes of this chapter, we will discuss only the central classes in the Accessibility Utilities API. We begin with the class that allows assistive technologies to bridge the gap into the application's component: EventQueueMonitor.

The EventQueueMonitor Class

The EventQueueMonitor class is, in effect, a gateway to the system event queue. This class provides the central functionality for any assistive technology to capture and interpret system events, monitor the mouse position, and locate components related to screen position. EventQueueMonitor is a subclass of the AWT Event-Queue class. This allows it to masquerade as the system event queue for the current Java virtual machine. Recall that the system event queue is its own thread, inserting and removing windowing events as necessary. With the EventQueueMonitor class, an application can now register listeners for and post events to the system event queue thread—a critical task for assistive technologies.

To do this in JDK 1.1, the EventQueueMonitor must replace the traditional system event queue at startup. Currently, Java allows this to occur only if the following property is set in the *awt.properties* file:

```
AWT.EventQueueClass=com.sun.java.accessibility.util.EventQueueMonitor
```

The class listed must be relative to the current value of the CLASSPATH environment variable. If successfully located, Java will instantiate this class (invoking its constructor) and use it for the windowing event queue. In JDK 1.2, the loading of the event queue monitor is not necessary.

NOTE   Some ports of the Java 1.1.x virtual machine do not allow the replacement of the windowing event queue through the awt.properties file. While the Windows and Solaris versions of the JDK follow closely to the reference specification put out by Sun Microsystems for the virtual machine, others may not. If you experience problems with accessibility on your specific port of the Java virtual machine, contact the organization that created the port and request that they support this capability.

Upon startup, the EventQueueMonitor class will also seek out any assistive technologies by looking for the following entry in the *awt.properties* file:

```
#JDK 1.1
AWT.assistive_technologies=com.xxx.SpeechRecognition,com.xxx.Brailer
```

In JDK 1.2, you make a similar addition to *accessibility.properties*:

```
#JDK 1.2
assistive_technologies=com.xxx.SpeechRecognition,com.xxx.Brailer
```

Again, the comma-separated list of classes must be relative to the CLASSPATH. When these classes are found, the EventQueueMonitor class will instantiate each of them in its own thread.

Note that the EventQueueMonitor class consists almost entirely of static methods. Because there can be only one system event queue per virtual machine, this allows assistive technologies to call upon its methods and access graphical events from any location. If you need to access the EventQueueMonitor object itself, you can always get at it through the Toolkit.getSystemEventQueue() method; however, this is rarely necessary.

Constructor

public EventQueueMonitor()

> This default constructor is used to create a new instance of an EventQueue-Monitor. The Java virtual machine invokes this at startup; it shouldn't be invoked by the user.

Initialization

In JDK 1.2, assistive technologies must not register for events before the GUI is ready. These methods allow you to find out when the GUI is ready. They don't exist in the 1.1 version of accessibility. As we show in the AssistiveExample class (later in this chapter), assistive technologies typically call isGUIInitialized(); add themselves as a GUIInitializedListener if the GUI isn't initialized; and implement the guiInitialized method (required by the GUIInitializedLis-tener interface), which is called when the GUI is ready. (Although this looks like a typical event registration pattern, no events are actually involved.)

public static void addGUIInitializedListener (GUIInitializedListener c)
public static void removeGUIInitializedListener (GUIInitializedListener c)

> These methods add or remove a listener to the list of classes which are noti-fied when the GUI subsystem of the Java VM is ready to interface with assistive technologies. You should not attempt to register for any GUI events before this has occurred.

public static boolean isGUIInitialized()

> Returns a boolean indicating whether the GUI subsystem of the Java VM is ready to interface with assistive technologies. You can check this in the constructor of your assistive technology class, and if it is false, register to be notified when it is safe to interface using the addGUIInitializedLis-tener() method.

Methods

public static void addTopLevelWindowListener(TopLevelWindowListener l)

Registers a listener method to be invoked if a top-level window is created in the current virtual machine.

public static Accessible getAccessibleAt(Point p)

Returns the object implementing the `Accessible` interface that is directly below the point passed in, or `null` if such an object does not exist. If there is a component available that does not implement the `Accessible` interface, this method will attempt to locate a translator object.

public static Point getCurrentMousePosition()

Returns the current position of the mouse in screen coordinates.

public static Window[] getTopLevelWindows()

Returns an array of each of the top-level windows in the current virtual machine.

public static Window getTopLevelWindowWithFocus()

Returns a reference to the top-level window that has the focus.

protected static void maybeLoadAssistiveTechnologies()

This protected method performs the task of loading and instantiating any assistive technologies referenced in the *awt.properties* file in the current thread. If the current virtual machine is JDK 1.2 or greater, this method returns without loading any classes; with JDK 1.2, the `Toolkit` class has inherited this responsibility.

public void postEvent(AWTEvent theEvent)

Queues an `AWTEvent` to be dispatched in the system event queue.

public static void removeTopLevelWindowListener(TopLevelWindowListener l)

Removes a listener method from the top-level window event list.

protected static void queueWindowEvent(WindowEvent e)

This protected method queues a specific `WindowEvent` to be dispatched in the system event queue.

The AWTEventMonitor Class

The `EventQueueMonitor` works with two other classes to allow assistive technologies to monitor specific events. `AWTEventMonitor` is one of those classes. This class contains a series of protected listener arrays, and allows applications to register listeners for any and all AWT events that pass through the event queue. This is done through static methods inside the class that can be called from anywhere.

Fields

protected static Component componentWithFocus
> This protected field contains a reference to the component that currently has the focus.

protected static ComponentListener componentListener
protected static ContainerListener containerListener
protected static FocusListener focusListener
protected static KeyListener keyListener
protected static MouseListener mouseListener
protected static MouseMotionListener mouseMotionListener
protected static WindowListener windowListener
protected static ActionListener actionListener
protected static AdjustmentListener adjustmentListener
protected static ItemListener itemListener
protected static TextListener textListener
protected static AWTEventListener awtListener
> These protected fields represent each of the listeners that have registered for the respective AWT event in this class. They are used in conjunction with an `AWTEventMulticaster`.

Constructor

public AWTEventMonitor()
> The default constructor. There is no need for the programmer to invoke it.

Methods

public static addActionListener(ActionListener l)
public static removeActionListener(ActionListener l)
> Add or remove a listener for AWT `ActionEvents` from the monitor.

public static addAdjustmentListener(AdjustmentListener l)
public static removeAdjustmentListener(AdjustmentListener l)
> Add or remove a listener for AWT `AdjustmentEvents` from the monitor.

public static addComponentListener(ComponentListener l)
public static removeComponentListener(ComponentListener l)
> Add or remove a listener for AWT `ComponentEvents` from the monitor.

public static addContainerListener(ContainerListener l)
public static removeContainerListener(ContainerListener l)
> Add or remove a listener for AWT `ContainerEvents` from the monitor.

public static addFocusListener(FocusListener l)
public static removeFocusListener(FocusListener l)
> Add or remove a listener for AWT `FocusEvents` from the monitor.

public static addItemListener(ItemListener l)
public static removeItemListener(ItemListener l)
> Add or remove a listener for AWT `ItemEvents` from the monitor.

public static addKeyListener(KeyListener l)
public static removeKeyListener(KeyListener l)
> Add or remove a listener for AWT `KeyEvents` from the monitor.

public static addMouseListener(MouseListener l)
public static removeMouseListener(MouseListener l)
> Add or remove a listener for AWT `MouseEvents` from the monitor.

public static addMouseMotionListener(MouseMotionListener l)
public static removeMouseMotionListener(MouseMotionListener l)
> Add or remove a listener for AWT `MouseMotionEvents` from the monitor.

public static addTextListener(TextListener l)
public static removeTextListener(TextListener l)
> Add or remove a listener for AWT `TextEvents` from the monitor.

public static addWindowListener(WindowListener l)
public static removeWindowListener(WindowListener l)
> Add or remove a listener for AWT `WindowEvents` from the monitor.

protected static getComponentWithFocus()
> Returns the component that currently has the keyboard focus.

The SwingEventMonitor Class

The `SwingEventMonitor` extends the `AWTEventMonitor` class and provides event registration for all Swing events as well. This class contains a series of protected listener arrays, and allows applications to register listeners for any and all AWT and Swing events that pass through the event queue. Note that `SwingEventMonitor` contains all the functionality of `AWTEventMonitor`; use this class to gain access to both types of windowing events.

Fields

protected static EventListenerList listenerList
> Stores all the listeners registered by other classes. The event monitor's `add` and `remove` methods are the only public means for modifying this list.

protected static SwingEventListener swingListener
> The listener that's actually installed on components.

Constructor

public SwingEventMonitor()
> The default constructor. There is no need for the programmer to invoke it.

Methods

public static addAncestorListener(AncestorListener l)
public static removeAncestorListener(AncestorListener l)
> Add or remove a listener for Swing `AncestorEvents`.

public static addCaretListener(CaretListener l)
public static removeCaretListener(CaretListener l)
> Add or remove a listener for Swing `CaretEvents`.

public static addCellEditorListener(CellEditorListener l)
public static removeCellEditorListener(CellEditorListener l)
> Add or remove a listener for Swing `CellEditorEvents`.

public static addChangeListener(ChangeListener l)
public static removeChangeListener(ChangeListener l)
> Add or remove a listener for Swing `ChangeEvents`.

public static addColumnModelListener(TableColumnModelListener l)
public static removeColumnModelListener(TableColumnModelListener l)
> Add or remove a listener for Swing `TableColumnModelEvents`.

public static addDocumentListener(DocumentListener l)
public static removeDocumentListener(DocumentListener l)
> Add or remove a listener for Swing `DocumentEvents`.

public static addListDataListener(ListDataListener l)
public static removeListDataListener(ListDataListener l)
> Add or remove a listener for Swing `ListDataEvents`.

public static addListSelectionListener(ListSelectionListener l)
public static removeListSelectionListener(ListSelectionListener l)
> Add or remove a listener for Swing `ListSelectionEvents`.

public static addMenuListener(MenuListener l)
public static removeMenuListener(MenuListener l)
> Add or remove a listener for Swing `MenuEvents`.

public static addPopupMenuListener(PopupMenuListener l)
public static removePopupMenuListener(PopupMenuListener l)
> Add or remove a listener for Swing `PopupMenuEvents`.

public static addPropertyChangeListener(PropertyChangeListener l)
public static removePropertyChangeListener(PropertyChangeListener l)
> Add or remove a listener for `PropertyChangeEvents`.

public static addTableModelListener(TableModelListener l)
public static removeTableModelListener(TableModelListener l)
    Add or remove a listener for Swing `TableModelEvents`.

public static addTreeExpansionListener(TreeExpansionListener l)
public static removeTreeExpansionListener(TreeExpansionListener l)
    Add or remove a listener for Swing `TreeExpansionEvents`.

public static addTreeModelListener(TreeModelListener l)
public static removeTreeModelListener(TreeModelListener l)
    Add or remove a listener for Swing `TreeModelEvents`.

public static addTreeSelectionListener(TreeSelectionListener l)
public static removeTreeSelectionListener(TreeSelectionListener l)
    Add or remove a listener for Swing `TreeSelectionEvents`.

public static addUndoableEditListener(UndoableEditListener l)
public static removeUndoableEditListener(UndoableEditListener l)
    Add or remove a listener for Swing `UndoableEditEvents`.

public static addVetoableChangeListener(VetoableChangeListener l)
public static removeVetoableChangeListener(VetoableChangeListener l)
    Add or remove a listener for `VetoableChangeEvents`.

The TopLevelWindowListener Interface

This is a simple listener that assistive technologies can implement and register with the `addTopLevelWindowListener()` and `removeTopLevelWindowListener()` methods of the `EventQueueMonitor` class if they want to receive notification when a top-level window is created or destroyed. The interface contains two methods:

Methods

public abstract void topLevelWindowCreated(Window w)
    Invoked when a top-level window has been created.

public abstract void topLevelWindowDestroyed(Window w)
    Invoked when a top-level window has been destroyed.

The GUIInitializedListener Interface

`GUIInitializedListener` is a simple interface that was added with the 1.2 `Accessibility` package. This interface contains a single method, `guiInitialized()`, which is called via the `EventQueueMonitor` when the GUI subsystem of the Java VM is ready to have assistive technologies interface with it (i.e., register event listeners for components).

Method

public void guiInitialized()

Invoked by the `EventQueueMonitor` when the GUI subsystem has completed initializing itself and is ready to interface with assistive technologies.

This interface is necessary because the GUI subsystem for JDK 1.2 may not be ready to deal with outside technologies by the time the assistive technology is loaded into the virtual machine. Hence, you should always check in the constructor of your assistive technology class to see if the GUI is initialized (using the static method `EventQueueMonitor.isGUIInitialized()`), and if it isn't, register a class that implements this interface with the `EventQueueMonitor`.

When the GUI is ready, it will invoke this method, and the assistive technology can complete its initialization. (See the example at the end of the chapter for the code to do this.)

Interfacing with Accessibility

The following code shows how to create a simple assistive technology that can monitor events on the system event queue and interface with accessible components. The example consists of one class, `AssistiveExample`. This class creates a small window, containing two labels and five check boxes, which are repeatedly updated when the mouse comes to rest over an accessible component for longer than half a second.

Note that while using JDK 1.2 accessibility, we had to check to see if the GUI was ready for us to start firing accessibility-related commands to it. We do this by checking the `EventQueueMonitor.isGUIInitialized()` method. This method returns a `boolean` indicating whether the GUI will accept accessibility commands. If it does, then we're fine. If it doesn't, then we must register ourselves to be notified when the GUI becomes available. This makes use of the `GUIInitialized-Listener` interface, which is explained earlier in the chapter.

Finally, note that we have a single button in our assistive example that performs to first action reported by the accessible context. You can use the TAB key to bring this button into focus while pointing with the mouse. Then, press the space bar to fire off the action.

```
// AssistiveExample.java
//

import java.awt.*;
import java.awt.event.*;
import javax.swing.*;
import javax.swing.border.*;
```

```java
import javax.accessibility.*;
import com.sun.java.accessibility.util.*;

public class AssistiveExample extends JPanel
    implements MouseMotionListener, ActionListener, GUIInitializedListener {

    Timer timer;
    static JFrame frame;

    JLabel nameLabel;
    JLabel descriptionLabel;

    JCheckBox selectionCheckBox;
    JCheckBox textCheckBox;
    JCheckBox valueCheckBox;
    JCheckBox componentCheckBox;
    JCheckBox actionCheckBox;
    JCheckBox hypertextCheckBox;
    JButton performAction;

    public AssistiveExample() {

        frame = new JFrame("Assistive Example");

        // Create and insert the appropriate labels and check boxes
        nameLabel = new JLabel();
        descriptionLabel = new JLabel();

        selectionCheckBox = new JCheckBox("Selection", false);
        textCheckBox = new JCheckBox("Text", false);
        valueCheckBox = new JCheckBox("Value", false);
        componentCheckBox = new JCheckBox("Component", false);
        actionCheckBox = new JCheckBox("Action", false);
        hypertextCheckBox = new JCheckBox("Hyperlink", false);
        performAction = new JButton("Perform Action");

        setLayout(new GridLayout(10,1));

        add(nameLabel);
        add(descriptionLabel);
        add(new JSeparator());
        add(selectionCheckBox);
        add(textCheckBox);
        add(valueCheckBox);
        add(componentCheckBox);
        add(hypertextCheckBox);
        add(actionCheckBox);
        add(performAction);
```

```
    setBorder(new TitledBorder("Accessible Component"));

    performAction.addActionListener(this);

    frame.getContentPane().add("Center", this);
    frame.pack();
    frame.show();

    //  Check to see if the GUI subsystem is initialized
    //  correctly. (This is only needed in JDK 1.2). If it
    //  isn't, then we have to wait.
    if (EventQueueMonitor.isGUIInitialized()) {
        createGUI();
    } else {
        EventQueueMonitor.addGUIInitializedListener(this);
    }

    performAction.grabFocus();
}

public void guiInitialized() {
    createGUI();
}

public void createGUI() {

    //  We want to track the mouse motions, so notify the
    //  Swing event monitor of this.
    SwingEventMonitor.addMouseMotionListener(this);

    //  Start a Timer object to measure how long the mouse stays
    //  over a particular area.
    timer = new Timer(500, this);
}

public void mouseMoved(MouseEvent e) {

    //  If the mouse moves, restart the timer.
    timer.restart();
}

public void mouseDragged(MouseEvent e) {

    //  If the mouse is dragged, restart the timer.
    timer.restart();
}

public void actionPerformed(ActionEvent e) {
```

```
    // Find the component currently under the mouse.
    Point currentPosition = EventQueueMonitor.getCurrentMousePosition();
    Accessible comp = EventQueueMonitor.getAccessibleAt(currentPosition);

    // If the user pressed the button, and the component
    // has an accessible action, then execute it.
    if (e.getActionCommand() == "Perform Action") {
        AccessibleContext context = comp.getAccessibleContext();
        AccessibleAction action = context.getAccessibleAction();

        if (action != null)
            action.doAccessibleAction(0);
        else
            System.out.println("No accessible action present!");
        return;
    }

    // Otherwise, the timer has fired. Stop it and update the window.
    timer.stop();
    updateWindow(comp);
}

private void updateWindow(Accessible component) {

    // Reset the check boxes
    actionCheckBox.setSelected(false);
    selectionCheckBox.setSelected(false);
    textCheckBox.setSelected(false);
    componentCheckBox.setSelected(false);
    valueCheckBox.setSelected(false);
    hypertextCheckBox.setSelected(false);

    // Get the accessibile context of the component in question
    AccessibleContext context = component.getAccessibleContext();

    nameLabel.setText("Name: " + context.getAccessibleName());
    descriptionLabel.setText("Desc: " +
        context.getAccessibleDescription());

    // Check the context for each of the accessibility types
    if (context.getAccessibleAction() != null)
        actionCheckBox.setSelected(true);
    if (context.getAccessibleSelection() != null)
        selectionCheckBox.setSelected(true);
    if (context.getAccessibleText() != null) {
        textCheckBox.setSelected(true);
        if (context.getAccessibleText() instanceof AccessibleHypertext)
            hypertextCheckBox.setSelected(true);
    }
```

```
        if (context.getAccessibleComponent() != null)
            componentCheckBox.setSelected(true);
        if (context.getAccessibleValue() != null)
            valueCheckBox.setSelected(true);

        repaint();
    }
}
```

Figure 25-2 below shows the result. We've connected our assistive technology to one of the menu examples from Chapter 14, *Menus and Toolbars*. Because Swing components support accessibility, we didn't need to modify the menu example. Below that, we added our assistive technology to the accessible AWT button we developed earlier, showing that we can communicate with it.

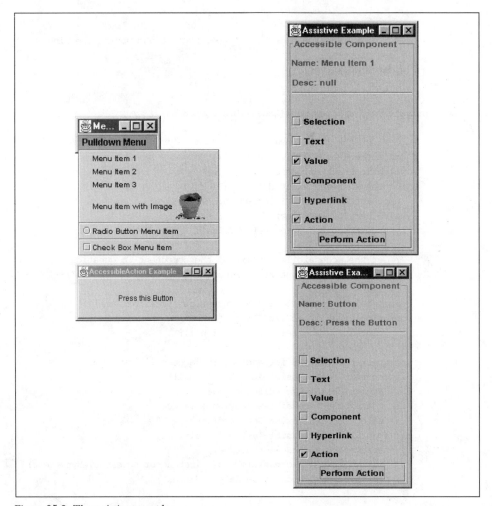

Figure 25-2. The assistive example

Note that while using JDK 1.2 accessibility, we had to check to see if the GUI was ready for us to start firing accessibility-related commands to it. We do this by checking the `EventQueueMonitor.isGUIInitialized()` method. This method returns a `boolean` indicating whether the GUI will accept accessibility commands. If it does, then we're fine. If it doesn't, then we must register ourselves to be notified when the GUI becomes available. This makes use of the `GUIInitializedListener` interface, which is explained earlier in the chapter.

Finally, note that we have a single button in our assistive example that performs to first action reported by the accessible context. You can use the TAB key to bring this button into focus while pointing with the mouse. Then, press the space bar to fire off the action.

26

Look & Feel

Way back in Chapter 1, *Introducing Swing*, we introduced the concept of Swing's pluggable look-and-feel (PLAF) architecture. In this chapter, we'll get into a variety of topics related to PLAF. The chapter includes:

- An overview of how the Swing component classes work together with the UI-delegate classes.

- A detailed explanation of the various PLAF-related classes in the `javax.swing` package, as well as some of the important classes and interfaces from `javax.swing.plaf`.

- An explanation of how PLAF fits into JFC's accessibility framework using the `MultiLookAndFeel`.

- Detailed discussions of strategies for customizing the look-and-feel of your applications using the following techniques:

  — Modification of specific component properties

  — Modification of resource defaults

  — Use of *themes* in the Metal L&F

  — Use of customized client properties in the Metal look-and-feel (L&F)

  — Replacement of specific UI delegates

  — Creation of a new L&F from scratch

This chapter contains a lot of technical detail. You can do a lot with Swing's PLAF architecture without understanding everything we cover here. If you're interested in customizing the look-and-feel of your applications, but don't mind if there are a few things that don't quite make sense, you can skim the next few sections and jump right into "Look-and-Feel Customization." If you want to understand exactly how everything works, read on.

How Does It Work?

As you probably already know, each instance of a given Swing component uses a UI delegate to render the component using the style of the currently installed L&F. To really understand how things work, it helps to peek under the hood for a moment to see what methods get called at a few key points. The first point of interest is component creation time. When a new Swing component is instantiated, it must associate itself with a UI delegate object. Figure 26-1 shows the important steps[*] in this process.

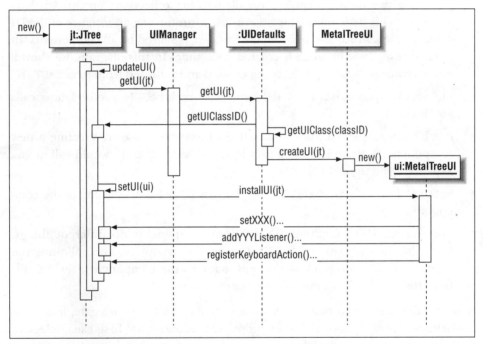

Figure 26-1. UI delegate installation

In this figure, we show what happens when a new JTree component gets created. The process is the same for any Swing component.

- First, the constructor calls updateUI(). Each Swing component class provides an updateUI() method that looks something like this:

```
public void updateUI() {
    setUI((TreeUI)UIManager.getUI(this));
}
```

---

[*] We do not show every method call. It is intended as a high-level overview of the process.

- The `updateUI()` method asks the `UIManager` class (via its static `getUI()` method) for an appropriate UI delegate object.

- The `UIManager` consults an instance of `UIDefaults` (set up when the L&F was first installed) for the appropriate UI delegate.

- The `UIDefaults` object goes back to the component to get the UI class ID. In our `JTree` example, `"TreeUI"` will be returned.

- `UIDefaults` then looks up the `Class` object for the class ID. In this case, it finds the `MetalTreeUI` class.

- The static method `createUI()` is called (using reflection) on this UI delegate class. This static method is responsible for returning an instance of the UI delegate class. In some cases, a single instance is shared by all components. In other cases, a new instance is created each time. In this diagram, we show a new instance of `MetalTreeUI` being created and returned from `createUI()`.

- At last, the `JTree` has a UI delegate. The `updateUI()` method now calls `setUI()`.

- If a UI delegate was already installed (in this example, we're creating a new component, so there is no delegate installed yet), `setUI()` would call `uninstallUI()` on the old delegate.

- `setUI()` now calls `installUI()` on the new UI delegate, passing in the component.

- The `installUI()` methods for different components do different things. Often (as shown here), `installUI()` is used to install listeners (allowing the UI delegate to keep track of changes made to the component), set defaults (e.g., fonts and colors), and add keyboard actions.

Now that the new component has been associated with its UI delegate, it can use the delegate for all L&F-related operations. The `JComponent` base class delegates the following methods to its UI:

- `paintComponent()` (called by `paint()`; calls `ui.update()`)

- `getPreferredSize()`

- `getMaximumSize()`

- `getMinimumSize()`

- `contains()`

NOTE   The three size accessors only delegate to the UI if a value has not been explicitly set on the component itself via a call to `setPreferredSize()`, `setMaximumSize()`, or `setMinimumSize()`.

Now let's take a second look under the hood and see how the delegation of the painting process actually happens. The process in Figure 26-2 is pretty straight-forward.

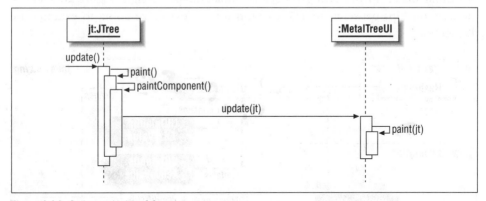

Figure 26-2. Swing painting delegation

1. When the component is asked to update itself, it simply calls `paint()`. Notice that this differs from `java.awt.Component.update()` which paints the component's background first. We'll see why this is important in a second.

2. The `JComponent.paint()` method (after doing quite a few other things we won't get into here) calls `paintComponent()`.

3. `paintComponent()` calls `update()` on the UI delegate.

4. Here (in `ComponentUI.update()`), the background is painted only if the component is opaque. Then, the `paint()` method is called on the delegate.

5. The `paint()` method, implemented by the specific UI delegate classes, gets whatever information it needs from the component (which it receives as a parameter) and renders the component.

NOTE   We've left out a lot of details about the Swing painting mechanics in this example. If you want to know more about how this works, please refer to the description of `JComponent.paint()` in Chapter 3, *Swing Component Basics*. Our goal here is just to understand where the UI delegate fits in the painting process.

You should now have a basic understanding of how the Swing component classes work together with the UI delegates. In the next section, we'll explore the key classes and interfaces that make up the PLAF architecture.

Key L&F Classes and Interfaces

In this section, we'll take an in-depth look at several of the key classes and interfaces that make up the Swing pluggable look-and-feel design. Figure 26-3 shows the relationships between the classes (and interfaces) we're going to examine in this section.

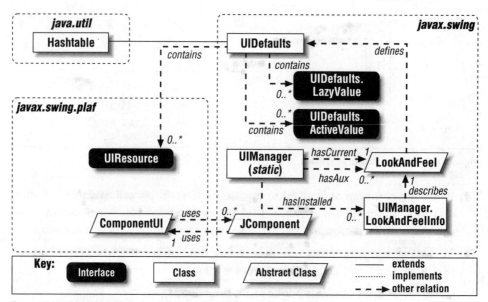

Figure 26-3. High-level look-and-feel class diagram

Before we look at the details of each of these classes, we'll quickly describe the role each one plays:

LookAndFeel

    The abstract base class from which all the different L&Fs extend. It defines a number of static convenience methods, as well as some abstract methods required by every look-and-feel.

UIDefaults

    One of the things an L&F is responsible for is defining a set of default properties. `UIDefaults` is a `Hashtable` subclass that holds these properties. The properties include `UIClassID` to `ComponentUI` subclasses mappings (e.g., `"TreeUI"` to `MetalTreeUI`) as well as lower-level defaults, such as colors and fonts.

UIDefaults.ActiveValue and UIDefaults.LazyValue

    These inner classes of `UIDefaults` enable some optimizations for resource values.

UIResource

   This is an empty interface (like `Serializable` or `Cloneable`) used to tag
   property values. It allows values defined by the L&F to be distinguished from
   values set by the user.

UIManager

   If you've ever changed the L&F of a Swing program, you're probably already
   familiar with this class. `UIManager` is responsible for tracking a global view of
   the L&Fs available in an application. It keeps track of the currently installed
   L&F and provides a mechanism to change the L&F. All of its methods are
   static, but it does provide a mechanism that allows multiple applets within a
   single virtual machine to use different L&Fs.

UIManager.LookAndFeelInfo

   This inner class is used to describe available look-and-feels without actually
   having to load the L&F classes. `UIManager` uses this class to provide a list of
   available L&Fs.

ComponentUI

   This is the base class common to all UI delegates. It defines all of the methods
   related to painting and sizing that the different delegate subclasses must
   implement.

JComponent

   You're certainly familiar with this class by now—it's the base class for all of the
   Swing components. We include it in this diagram to show that at any time,
   each `JComponent` has a reference to a single `ComponentUI`. `ComponentUI`
   objects may, however, be shared by multiple components. `JComponent` was
   covered in gory detail back in Chapter 3.

The next several sections explore the details of each of these key players. After
that, we'll be ready to look at a variety of ways that you can customize the look-and-
feel of your applications.

The LookAndFeel Class

This is the abstract base class from which all L&F implementations are derived.
Extensions of this class are responsible for defining everything that's unique to a
particular L&F. Figure 26-4 shows the inheritance hierarchy for the Swing L&F
classes.[*]

---

[*] This figure does not show the `MacLookAndFeel`, which emulates the Macintosh GUI. The Mac L&F
was released as this book went to press. The `MacLookAndFeel` isn't yet distributed with Swing, and must
be downloaded separately.

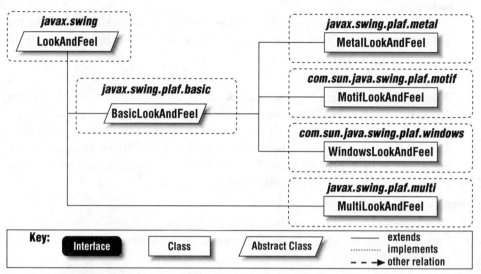

Figure 26-4. Swing LookAndFeel class diagram

Each L&F is defined in its own package.[*] This allows the numerous UI delegate classes and other support classes that make up the L&F to be conveniently grouped. The abstract `BasicLookAndFeel` class is the where the Swing L&F framework really lives. All of the abstractions for the various component UI classes are defined here. By extending the classes in the `javax.swing.plaf.basic` package, the other L&F packages (including ones you might create yourself) are relieved from having to worry about a lot of the details of the various component UI classes and can focus on rendering the components in a particular style.

Another special class in this diagram is the `MultiLookAndFeel` class, which allows you to use multiple L&Fs at the same time. This is used to provide accessibility support, perhaps by providing an L&F that speaks instead of drawing to the screen. Another possible use is for automated UI testing. We'll get into the `javax.swing.plaf.multi` package later in the chapter.

Properties

The `LookAndFeel` class defines the properties shown in Table 26-1. As you can see, none of these properties have useful values defined in this base class (those listed "abstract" have accessors that are abstract). The `defaults` property should be defined by each L&F to contain the UI delegate class defaults, default system colors and fonts, etc. We'll get into more detail on how `UIDefaults` is used later in the chapter. The `description`, `ID`, and `name` properties just describe the L&F.

---

[*] Note that the Windows and Motif look-and-feels remain in the `com.sun.java.swing.plaf` package hierarchy.

Table 26-2 shows the values of these properties for the Swing L&Fs, to give you an idea of how they are used.

Table 26-1. LookAndFeel Properties

Property	Data Type	get	is	set	bound	Default Value
defaults	UIDefaults	•				null
description	String	•				abstract
ID	String	•				abstract
name	String	•				abstract
nativeLookAndFeel	boolean		•			abstract
supportedLookAndFeel	boolean		•			abstract

Table 26-2. Look-and-Feel Properties for Swing

Look and Feel	ID	Name	Description
MetalLookAndFeel	Metal	Metal	The Java™ Look-and-Feel
MotifLookAndFeel	Motif	CDE/Motif	The CDE/Motif Look-and-Feel
WindowsLookAndFeel	Windows	Windows	The Microsoft Windows Look-and-Feel

The `nativeLookAndFeel` property indicates whether the L&F is designed to emulate the native look-and-feel of the platform on which the application is currently running. For example, if you are running on a Windows 95 machine, the `WindowsLookAndFeel` will return `true` if you invoke `isNativeLookAndFeel()`. Similarly, on a Solaris machine, the `MotifLookAndFeel` would return `true`.

Finally, the `supportedLookAndFeel` property indicates whether or not the L&F is allowed to be used on the current platform. This was put in place primarily for legal reasons—certain L&Fs[*] may not be executed on platforms other than the native platform.

Constructor

public LookAndFeel()
  This is the default constructor.

Methods

In addition to the accessors for the properties we listed earlier, the `LookAndFeel` base classes defines the following public methods:

---

* Specifically, this was added to keep the `WindowsLookAndFeel` from being used on other platforms.

public void initialize()

Performs any L&F-specific initialization needed, other than setting defaults. It is called by the UIManager just before invoking the getDefaults() method for the first time. The default implementation does nothing.

public String toString

Returns a string representation of the L&F, built from the description property and the L&F class name.

public void uninitialize()

Used to perform clean-up before the look-and-feel is replaced. This typically happens when a new look-and-feel is chosen to replace the current one.

Static Convenience Methods

The following static methods are defined in this class. They are used by L&F subclasses to simplify common tasks.

public static void installBorder(JComponent c, String defaultBorderName)

Installs a default border for the component if there is currently no border defined or if the current border is tagged as a UIResource. The border to install is retrieved from the UIManager using defaultBorderName as a key.

public static void installColors(JComponent c, String defaultBgName,
   String defaultFgName)

Installs default foreground and background colors for the component, if they are not currently defined or if the current colors are tagged as UIResources. The colors to install are retrieved from the UIManager, using defaultBgName and defaultFgName as keys.

public static void installColorsAndFont(JComponent c, String defaultBgName,
   String defaultFgName, String defaultFontName)

Calls installColors() and installs a default font using the same rules with respect to UIResources. A call to this method typically looks something like:

```
LookAndFeel.installColorsAndFont(theLabel, "Label.background",
    "Label.foreground", "Label.font");
```

public static Object makeIcon(Class baseClass, String gifFile)

Creates a UIResource from the specified filename that can be entered into a defaults table. The filename should be relative to the directory containing the L&F classes so that it can be loaded by calling baseClass.getResourceAsStream(). The returned object will be a UIDefaults.LazyValue, meaning that the GIF is only loaded if it is needed.

public static JTextComponent.KeyBinding[] makeKeyBindings(Object[] keyBindingList)

Creates an array of KeyBindings used by text components to map KeyStrokes to Actions. The object array is expected to contain alternating keystrokes and actions. The keystrokes may be actual `KeyStroke` objects or `Strings` describing a `KeyStroke`. In the latter case, an attempt will be made to convert the string to a `KeyStroke`. This string may begin with any number of modifiers taken from the following list: `shift`, `control`, `meta`, `alt`, `button1`, `button2`, `button3`. The modifiers (if any) should be followed by the name of the key (the names defined in `KeyEvent`, without the `VK_` at the beginning). For example, `x` would simply map to `new  KeyStroke(0, KeyEvent.VK_X)`, while an input key of `control-alt-DELETE` would map to:

```
new KeyStroke(InputEvent.CTRL_MASK|InputEvent.ALT_MASK, KeyEvent.VK_DELETE)
```

A L&F that wanted to define cut, copy, and paste actions, might use the method like this:

```
JTextComponent.KeyBindings[] bindings = LookAndFeel.makeKeyBindings(
  new Object[] {
    "control X", DefaultEditorKit.cutAction,
    "control C", DefaultEditorKit.copyAction,
    "control V" , DefaultEditorKit.pasteAction });
```

public static void uninstallBorder(JComponent c)
> Removes a default border from the component, if the current border is tagged as a `UIResource`.

The UIDefaults Class

One of the key things that distinguishes a look-and-feel is a set of default properties. These properties are stored in an extension of `java.util.Hashtable` called `UIDefaults`.

Any type of value that is important to a look-and-feel can be stored in this table. The most common ones are fonts, colors, borders, icons and, most importantly, UI-delegate class names. We'll get into the details of populating a `UIDefaults` object for a custom L&F in the section "Creation of a Custom L&F."

Events

`UIDefaults` fires a `PropertyChangeEvent` any time a property is added to the table.

The following event-related methods are defined:

public synchronized void addPropertyChangeListener(PropertyChangeListener listener)
public synchronized void removePropertyChangeListener(PropertyChangeListener listener)
> Define who will receive notification when changes are made to the defaults.

protected void firePropertyChange(String propertyName, Object oldValue, Object newValue)
> Fires events when properties are added, changed, or removed. The name of the property should be the default's key if a single default is being added. If a

bulk addition is made, the property name is `"UIDefaults"` and both the old and new values are `null`.

Constructors

UIDefaults()

This is the default constructor; it creates an empty hash table to hold the defaults for the look-and-feel.

UIDefaults(Object[] keyValueList)

This constructor accepts an array of objects and creates a defaults table initialized with the specified key/value pairs. The `keyValueList` array must be of even length, containing alternating keys and values. For example:

```
{ "textFont", new Font("Serif", Font.PLAIN, 12), "backgroundColor", Color.black }
```

Methods

If you are not creating your own L&F, you don't need to be concerned with the methods defined in `UIDefaults`. `UIManager` provides a set of static methods that perform the same functions on the `UIDefaults` object associated with the currently installed L&F.

public Object get(Object key)

Like its `Hashtable` equivalent, this method returns the object associated with the given key. The method is overridden to provide special handling of two special types of values: `ActiveValue` and `LazyValue`. These inner classes are described at the end of this section. Values that are not of one of these special types are returned as-is.

public Border getBorder(Object key)
public Color getColor(Object key)
public Dimension getDimension(Object key)
public Font getFont(Object key)
public Icon getIcon(Object key)
public Insets getInsets(Object key)
pulic int getInt(Object key)
public String getString(Object key)

Provide type-safe access to certain types of properties. They return the object associated with the given key, attempting to cast it to the appropriate return type. If the cast is unsuccessful, the methods return `null`.

public ComponentUI getUI(JComponent target)

Returns the UI-delegate object associated with the current look-and-feel for the target component that was passed in. It locates the correct object by invoking the `getUIClassID()` method of the input component to obtain the correct name of the delegate, cross-referencing it against the class defaults

table using the getUIClass() method (next), and invoking the UI delegate's static createUI() method to obtain an appropriate UI instance. If the
method is unsuccessful, it invokes the getUIError() method.

public Class getUIClass(String uiClassID)
public Class getUIClass(String uiClassID, ClassLoader uiClassLoader)

These methods search the defaults table for the given class ID. The value from
the table should be the class name of the appropriate UI delegate. After
retrieving the class name, the name itself is used as a key into the table in an
attempt to find the corresponding Class object. If the class is not already in
the table, it will be loaded by calling uiClassLoader.loadClass(), or by
calling Class.forName() if uiClassLoader is null. Once the class is found,
it is added to the table (with its name as the key) so that subsequent calls to
getUIClass() can get the class directly from the table. Note that the first
version of this method calls the second with a null class loader.

public Object put(Object key, Object value)

Adds the given key/value pair to the table. If the key already exists in the
table, its value is replaced. If a new key is added or an existing key is assigned a
new value, a PropertyChangeEvent is fired to all registered listeners. The
property name sent with this event is the key. If the value is null, the key is
removed from the table and a PropertyChangeEvent is fired with a new
value of null.

public void putDefaults(Object[] keyValueList)

Transfers all of the key/value pairs in the object array to the table, firing a
single PropertyChangeEvent on completion. The property name in this
event will be "UIDefaults". See the UIDefaults(Object[]) constructor for
a description of the expected format of the input array. Existing properties are
not removed by this method, unless, of course, new values are specified for
them.

protected void getUIError(String msg)

Called if the getUI() method fails to successfully retrieve a UI delegate for its
target component. By default, it just dumps a stack trace and continues. If you
want to add specific functionality to handle errors, you can override this
method in a subclass.

The UIDefaults.ActiveValue Interface

As we mentioned in the previous section, the UIDefaults.get() method handles
two types of values differently. The first of these, ActiveValue, is used for properties that need to be instantiated each time they are queried. Such properties
typically include renderers and editors.

Method

The interface defines one method:

public abstract Object createValue(UIDefaults table)
> Implementations of this method are expected to return a new instance of some class. When `UIDefaults.get()` finds an `ActiveValue`, it invokes this method and returns the resulting object, rather than returning the `ActiveValue` itself.

Creating an ActiveValue

Implementations of this interface are typically very simple. For example:

```
Object myActiveValue  = new UIDefaults.ActiveValue() {
  public Object createValue(UIDefaults table) {
    return new MyThing();
  }
};
```

The UIDefaults.LazyValue Interface

The other special type of value recognized by `UIDefaults.get()` is the `Lazy-Value`. This interface allows properties to be lazily instantiated when they are asked for, avoiding the creation of values that may not be used. This is typically used for objects which take a long time to create, such as icons, or objects that are likely to be unused.

Method

The interface defines the following method:

public abstract Object createValue(UIDefaults table)
> Implementations of this method are expected to return a new instance of some class. When `UIDefaults.get()` finds a `LazyValue`, it invokes this method and replaces the value in the table with the resulting object. See Figure 26-5.

Creating a LazyValue

The code for a `LazyValue` is just like the code we presented for `ActiveValue`. The only difference is the intent. With `ActiveValue`, `createValue()` is called every time a key is accessed. With `LazyValue`, `createValue()` is only called once because the `LazyValue` object is replaced with the real value returned by `create-eValue()`. We'll see a complete example of the use of `LazyValue` toward the end of this chapter, when we create our custom L&F.

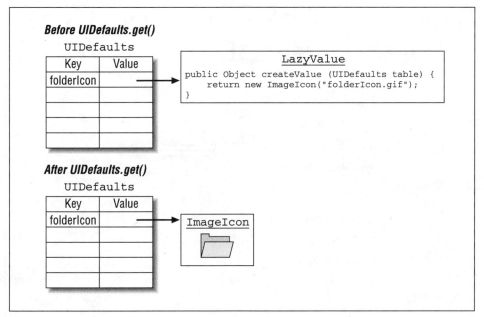

Figure 26-5. Conversion of a LazyValue

Figure 26-6 shows how LazyValues and ActiveValues are handled differently by UIDefaults. Pay special attention to the differences in handling the second get() call.

The UIResource Interface

This is an empty interface (similar in concept to java.io.Serializable or java.lang.Cloneable), used to tag L&F resource values that have been set by the L&F. The purpose of tagging these values is to allow Swing to distinguish values set by the user from values set by the L&F. This is only important if the L&F is changed during the execution of the application to avoid the following scenario:

- User creates a JFoo component
- L&F installs a default foreground property with the value Color.blue
- User calls setForeground(Color.orange) on the new JFoo object
- User (or the application logic) changes the L&F
- New L&F installs its default foreground property with the value Color.red

Without the concept of UIResources, changing the L&F would cause all of the resource values (such as the foreground color in the scenario above) to be reset when the L&F is changed, since each L&F installs its defaults as part of its initialization process. Using UIResource to tag L&F-installed resource values allows

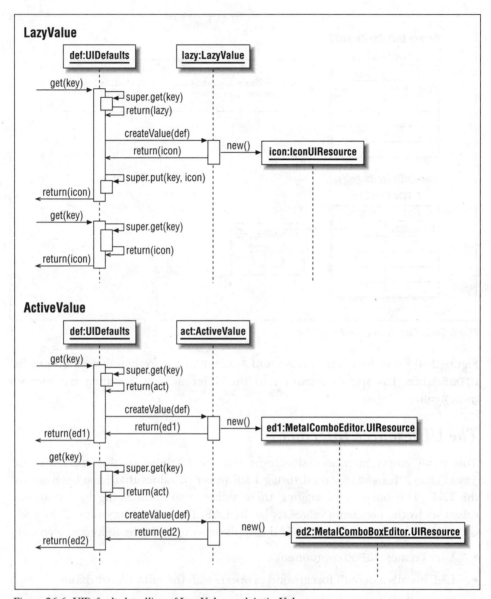

Figure 26-6. UIDefaults handling of LazyValue and ActiveValue

Swing to make an `instanceof UIResource` check before installing the default values for new resources. If this operation returns `false` (indicating that the user has changed the resource to something other than the default), the resource will not be replaced by the new L&F. In our example, the foreground color would remain orange even after changing the L&F.

Figure 26-7 shows the various implementations of this interface, used when representing different types of resource values. The resource classes that extend existing classes (`ColorUIResource`, `DimensionUIResource`, `FontUIResource`, and `InsetsUIResource`) provide nothing more than constructors that simply pass their arguments up to the superclass. In the `BorderUIResource` and `IconUIResource` classes, a delegate object, which is the "real" resource, is held. Methods called on the resource object are just forwarded to the actual border or icon.

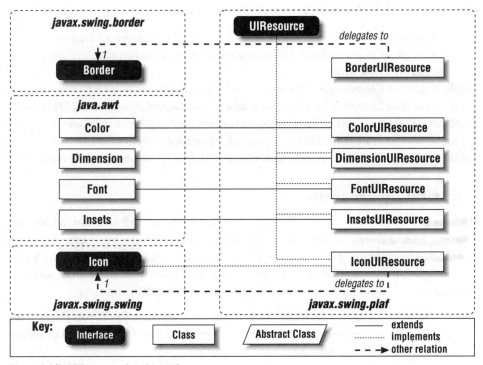

Figure 26-7. UIResource class hierarchy

Static BorderUIResource Methods

In addition to the delegation behavior described earlier, the `BorderUIResource` class defines four static methods used to access single instances of four common `Border` types tagged as `UIResources`. The methods are listed here for your convenience:

public static Border getEtchedBorderUIResource()
public static Border getLoweredBevelBorderUIResource()
public static Border getRaisedBevelBorderUIResource()
public static Border getBlackLineBorderUIResource()

This is similar to the role of the `BorderFactory` class, except that fewer borders are maintained, and they are specifically managed as `BorderUIResources`.

BorderUIResource Inner Classes

`BorderUIResource` defines static inner classes that subclass most[*] of the border classes defined in the `javax.swing.border` package. Each of these classes provides a set of constructors that map directly to the constructors provided by the real `Border` classes. See Chapter 13, *Borders*, for a list of these constructors.

public static class BevelBorderUIResource extends BevelBorder implements UIResource
public static class CompoundBorderUIResource extends CompoundBorder
    implements UIResource
public static class EmptyBorderUIResource extends EmptyBorder implements UIResource
public static class EtchedBorderUIResource extends EtchedBorderUI implements UIResource
public static class LineBorderUIResource extends LineBorder implements UIResource
public static class MatteBorderUIResource extends MatteBorder implements UIResource
public static class TitledBorderUIResource extends TitledBorder implements UIResource

The UIManager Class

`UIManager` provides a simple interface to a variety of information about the current look-and-feel, as well as to any other L&Fs that are available. All of its methods are static, so you never need to instantiate a `UIManager`; you simply call its static methods. In this section, we'll look at a variety of ways that you can control the look-and-feel of your applications using the `UIManager`.

The most common use of `UIManager` is to set the current L&F. If you don't want to use the L&F Swing selects by default, you simply call one of the `setLookAnd-Feel()` methods during initialization. For example:

```
public static void main(String[] args) {
  try {
   UIManager.setLookAndFeel(new
     com.sun.java.swing.plaf.motif.MotifLookAndFeel());
  } catch (UnsupportedLookAndFeelException e) {System.err.println("Bummer!");}
 }
```

LAFState

One issue that comes up whenever you have a static class is how to manage the fields of the class in a browser-based environment. It's important that one applet doesn't affect another by changing the value of some static field. In the case of the

---

[*] For whatever reason, there is no `SoftBevelBorderUIResource` defined.

UIManager, it's important to ensure that the L&F used in one applet doesn't affect any other applets.

UIManager gets around this by storing much of the state in a private inner class called LAFState. There is a different LAFState associated with each application context, meaning that there is no risk of an applet changing the L&F of another applet from some other source. This strategy is completely transparent to Swing developers.

UIManager L&F Concepts

The UIManager tracks a number of different look-and-feel properties. These include:

Current L&F

> The most important L&F tracked by the UIManager is the L&F currently in use. By default, this is initially set to the cross-platform L&F.

Cross-Platform L&F

> This L&F is not modeled after a pre-existing native L&F. By default, this is Swing's Metal L&F.

System L&F

> This L&F is designed to emulate the native L&F of the platform the application is currently running on. The value of this L&F is determined by calling java.lang.System.getProperty("os.name"). If the value returned by this method contains "Windows", the Windows L&F is used. If it contains "Solaris" or "SunOS", the Motif L&F is used. Otherwise, the cross-platform L&F is considered the system L&F.

Installed L&Fs

> This is the set of L&Fs currently available to the application. This set includes Metal, Motif, and Windows by default.

Auxiliary L&Fs

> This (possibly empty) set of L&Fs is used to provide accessible support from a Swing application. They exist in conjunction with the current L&F to provide some sort of nongraphical representation of the display. A typical auxiliary L&F might be called AudioLookAndFeel. There are no auxiliary L&Fs by default.

The following example shows how you can verify the L&Fs defined by your system:

```
// UIManagerDefaults.java
//
import javax.swing.*;

public class UIManagerDefaults {
  public static void main(String[] args) {
```

```
      System.out.println("Default L&F:");
      System.out.println("  " + UIManager.getLookAndFeel().getName());


      UIManager.LookAndFeelInfo[] inst = UIManager.getInstalledLookAndFeels();
      System.out.println("Installed L&Fs: ");
      for (int i=0;i<inst.length;i++) {
        System.out.println("  " + inst[i].getName());
      }


      LookAndFeel[] aux = UIManager.getAuxiliaryLookAndFeels();
      System.out.println("Auxiliary L&Fs: ");
      if (aux != null) {
        for (int i=0;i<aux.length;i++) {
          System.out.println("  " + aux[i].getName());
        }
      }
      else {System.out.println("  <NONE>");}

      System.out.println("Cross-Platform:");
      System.out.println("  " + UIManager.getCrossPlatformLookAndFeelClassName());

      System.out.println("System:");
      System.out.println("  " + UIManager.getSystemLookAndFeelClassName());

      System.exit(0);
  }
}
```

Running this program on a Windows machine produces the following output:

```
Default L&F:
  Metal Look and Feel
Installed L&Fs:
  Metal
  CDE/Motif
  Windows
Auxiliary L&Fs:
  <NONE>
Cross-Platform:
  javax.swing.plaf.metal.MetalLookAndFeel
System:
  com.sun.java.swing.plaf.windows.WindowsLookAndFeel
```

Look-and-Feel Properties File

In the previous section, we examined the default values for all of the different L&F properties we listed. These defaults are hardcoded inside the UIManager. Since this is a static class, there's no opportunity for you to change these defaults by extending UIManager. Instead, any changes to be made to these defaults must be made in the Swing properties file. During initialization, the UIManager looks for a file called *swing.properties* in the *lib* directory under the Java home directory defined by the java.home system property. Beware that the definition of java.home has changed slightly for JDK1.2, appending the directory *jre* after the installation directory. So, if you have JDK1.2 installed in */usr/local/jdk1.2*, the *swing.properties* file will be */usr/local/jdk1.2/jre/lib/swing.properties*. If you're using JDK1.1, and if your JDK is installed in */usr/local/jdk*, the UIManager looks for a file called */usr/local/jdk/lib/swing.properties*.

Table 26-3 shows the various properties that you can define in this file, along with the default values the UIManager will use if you don't define them.

Table 26-3. L&F Options in swing.properties

Property Name	UIManager Default
swing.defaultlaf	javax.swing.plaf.metal.MetalLookAndFeel
swing.auxiliarylaf	None
swing.plaf.multiplexinglaf	javax.swing.plaf.multi.MultiLookAndFeel
swing.installedlafs	Metal, Motif & Windows
swing.installedlaf.*.name	
swing.installedlaf.*.class	

The first three properties listed here must contain fully qualified class names. The values of the swing.auxiliarylaf property may contain a comma-separated list of class names. The swing.installedlafs property should contain a comma-separated list of arbitrary L&F identifiers. Each identifier listed here must also have a name and class property defined for it.

Here's a hypothetical *swing.properties* file in which we explicitly set values for all of the possible properties:

```
swing.defaultlaf=com.sun.java.swing.plaf.motif.MotifLookAndFeel
swing.auxiliarylaf=audio.AudioLookAndFeel,braille.BrailleLookAndFeel
swing.plaf.multiplexinglaf=supermulti.SuperMultiLookAndFeel
swing.installedlafs=motif,metal,audio,braille
swing.installedlaf.motif.name=CDE/Motif
swing.installedlaf.motif.class=com.sun.java.swing.plaf.motif.MotifLookAndFeel
swing.installedlaf.metal.name=Metal
swing.installedlaf.metal.class=javax.swing.plaf.metal.MetalLookAndFeel
swing.installedlaf.audio.name=Audio
swing.installedlaf.audio.class=audio.AudioLookAndFeel
swing.installedlaf.braille.name=Braille
swing.installedlaf.braille.class=braille.BrailleLookAndFeel
```

These same property values may also be defined on the command line. For example, to start your Java application using the Motif L&F, all you have to do is:

```
java -Dswing.defaultlaf=com.sun.java.swing.plaf.motif.MotifLookAndFeel MyClass
```

Events

The UIManager class fires a PropertyChangeEvent any time the active look-and-feel is changed. The property name in the event is lookAndFeel.

public static synchronized void addPropertyChangeListener(PropertyChangeListener listener)
public static synchronized void removePropertyChangeListener(PropertyChangeListener listener)
   Add or remove a PropertyChangeListener from the listener list.

UIDefaults Convenience Methods

UIManager defines a number of methods that simplify access to properties defined in the UIDefaults table of the currently installed L&F. These methods do nothing more than obtain the current UIDefaults object and call the corresponding method on it.

public static Border getBorder(Object key)
public static Color getColor(Object key)
public static Dimension getDimension(Object key)
public static Font getFont(Object key)
public static Icon getIcon(Object key)
public static Insets getInsets(Object key)
public static int getInt(Object key)
public static Object get(Object key)
public static Object put(Object key, Object value)
public static String getString(Object key)

Other Static Methods

public static void addAuxiliaryLookAndFeel(LookAndFeel laf)
   Adds an auxiliary L&F. See the section later in this chapter on the MultiLookAndFeel for more information.

public static LookAndFeel[] getAuxiliaryLookAndFeels()
   Returns an array of objects representing the currently installed auxiliary L&Fs.

public static String getCrossPlatformLookAndFeelClassName()
   Returns the name of the look-and-feel that is the default cross-platform L&F. This is hardcoded to return the Metal L&F class name.

public static UIDefaults getDefaults()
   Returns the UIDefaults object associated with the current look-and-feel, incorporating any defaults you have defined. See the "Managing Defaults" section for more information.

public static UIManager.LookAndFeelInfo[] getInstalledLookAndFeels()

Returns an array of `UIManager.LookAndFeelInfo` objects that identify the L&Fs currently installed on the system. This information is useful if you want to present the user with the names of the available look-and-feels, without actually instantiating any L&F objects.

public static LookAndFeel getLookAndFeel()

Retrieves the currently active look-and-feel.

public static UIDefaults getLookAndFeelDefaults()

Returns the `UIDefaults` table defined for the current look-and-feel, ignoring any defaults you have defined. See the "Managing Defaults" section for more information.

public static String getSystemLookAndFeelClassName()

Returns the name of the look-and-feel that is native to the current platform.

public static ComponentUI getUI(JComponent target)

Returns the appropriate UI delegate for the component passed in. The delegate is instantiated from the current look-and-feel.

public static void installLookAndFeel(String name, String className)

Creates a `UIManager.LookAndFeelInfo` entry from the two string parameters and adds it to the `installedLookAndFeels` property.

public static void installLookAndFeel(UIManager.LookAndFeelInfo info)

Adds the given `UIManager.LookAndFeelInfo` object to the `installedLookAndFeels` property.

public static boolean removeAuxiliaryLookAndFeel(LookAndFeel laf)

Removes an auxiliary L&F. Returns `true` if the L&F was found and removed.

public static void setInstalledLookAndFeels(UIManager.LookAndFeelInfo infos[])
throws SecurityException

Resets the list of currently installed look-and-feels to those specified in the array `infos`.

Changing the Look-and-Feel

The following two methods change the L&F currently in use. If you call one of these methods before creating any Swing components (at the beginning of your `main()` or `init()` method, perhaps), you don't need to do anything else.

However, if you have already created any Swing components, you'll need to notify each of them that the L&F has changed, so that they can get their new UI delegates. This is done by calling the `updateUI()` method on every component in your application. Fortunately, Swing provides a method called `SwingUtilities.updateComponentTree()` that will make all of the `updateUI()` calls for you.

All you have to do is pass in each of your top-level containers (typically `JFrames`, `JWindows`, and `JApplets`) one at a time. The `SwingUtilities` class, which is covered in detail in Chapter 27, *Swing Utilities*, will take care of updating the UI for each component contained in the component you pass in.

public static void setLookAndFeel(LookAndFeel newLookAndFeel)
    throws UnsupportedLookAndFeelException
    Resets the current look-and-feel. If the given L&F is supported, the old L&F, if there is one, will be uninitialized, and the new one will be initialized. A property change event will be fired to any registered listeners, indicating that the look-and-feel for the system has been changed. This method also calls `getDe-faults()` on the new L&F to set up the UI defaults.

public static void setLookAndFeel(String className) throws ClassNotFoundException,
    InstantiationException, IllegalAccessException, UnsupportedLookAndFeelException
    Sets the current look-and-feel, given the fully qualified name of a class that extends `LookAndFeel`. It attempts to turn the given class name into a `LookAndFeel` object and, if it is successful, passes this object to the other `setLookAndFeel()` method. Note the additional exceptions thrown by this method. These exceptions are actually thrown by the `Class.forName()` and `Class.newInstance()` methods, used to turn the given `String` into a L&F object.

Managing Defaults

The `UIManager` tracks three levels of defaults, as shown in Figure 26-8.

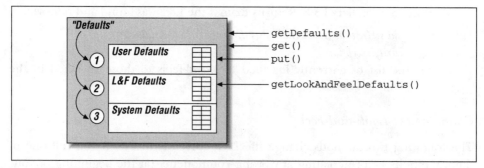

Figure 26-8. UIManager default management

As you know, each L&F defines a set of default values that are stored in a `UIDe-faults` object. But this is only the beginning of the story. You are free to modify these default values in your application. If you do, the `UIManager` will track these modifications in a separate `UIDefaults` object, which is hidden from you. When you ask for the current defaults by calling `getDefaults()`, or when you make a get() call to retrieve a specific key, you are actually accessing a sequence of UIDe-faults objects. The values you have explicitly set will have the highest priority, those set by the L&F will be considered next, and those defined as system proper-ties will be considered only if there is no user- or L&F-defined property.[*]

Any defaults that your program explicitly sets will remain defined, even if you change the L&F. If you want access to the defaults defined by the L&F, ignoring those you have overridden or added, you can call getLookAndFeelDefaults().

The UIManager.LookAndFeelInfo Class

This simple inner class is used to provide information about a look-and-feel without having to load the L&F class itself. The UIManager provides a list of the available L&Fs by providing instances these objects. The data stored in them can be used, for example, to populate a list of user-selectable L&Fs.

Properties

The properties listed in Table 26-4 make up the heart of this simple class. The name property contains a short name that describes the L&F, and the className property contains the fully qualified class name of the corresponding LookAnd-Feel implementation.

Table 26-4. UIManager.LookAndFeelInfo Properties

Property	Data Type	get	is	set	bound	Default Value
name	String	•				from constructor
className	String	•				from constructor

Constructor

public LookAndFeelInfo(String name, String className)
    Sets the object's two properties.

Method

This is the only method other than the accessors for the two properties:

public String toString()
    Returns a string built from the object's properties.

---

[*] Currently, UIManager defines only a single system default called "FocusManagerClassName". This is used by the FocusManager class do determine which FocusManager implementation to use. In the fu-ture, additional system defaults may be defined.

e *ComponentUI Class*

abstract `ComponentUI` class, found in the `com.sun.java.swing.plaf` package, is the abstract class from which all UI delegates must inherit. It defines the core set of methods called by the `JComponent` base class, which all UI delegates must implement. Very few of the Swing components invoke component-specific methods on their UI objects, so the methods defined here make up the core of the communication from the component classes to the UI classes.

In the Swing L&Fs, the individual delegate class names are typically formed by joining the L&F name, the component name (minus the `J`) and `"UI"`. For example, the Metal UI-delegate class for `JSlider` components is called `Metal-SliderUI`. This naming convention is not enforced in any way, but it's a nice simple standard that's well worth following.

Methods

Here are the methods defined in this abstract class. Note that they all take a `JCom-ponent`. As we discussed in the chapter introduction, this means that the UI delegate does not need to keep a reference to the component and that the same delegate may be used for multiple components if desired.

public boolean contains(JComponent c, int x, int y)
> Returns a `boolean` indicating whether the component specified currently encompasses the specified point x, y. The default implementation just delegates the call to the component by calling `c.inside(x, y)`.

public int getAccessibleChildrenCount(JComponent c)
> Returns the number of accessible children in this object. The reason this is delegated to the UI is that a delegate might wish to represent different parts of itself as independently accessible components which don't map directly to Swing components. However, this default implementation just uses `SwingUtilities.getAccessibleChildrenCount()`.

public Accessible getAccessibleChild(JComponent c, int i)
> Returns the accessible child at the specified index. The defaut impementation uses `SwingUtilities.getAccessbileChild ()`.

public Dimension getMaximumSize(JComponent c)
> Returns the maximum size for the given component. The default implementation returns `getPreferredSize()`.

public Dimension getMinimumSize(JComponent c)
> Should return the minimum size for the given component. The default implementation returns `getPreferredSize()`.

public Dimension getPreferredSize(JComponent c)

> Should return the preferred size for the given component. The default implementation returns `null`. If `JComponent` gets a `null` back from this method (or either of the two size methods listed previously), it defers the size query to its superclass (`Container`).

public void installUI(JComponent c)

> Called just after the UI delegate is instantiated. The default implementation does nothing. Typically, this method adds listeners to the component, so the UI can update itself when the component changes state. It is also used to set various default values, such as fonts and colors.

public void paint(Graphics g, JComponent c)

> Responsible for painting the component based on the component's current state. Since the implementation of this method is entirely component-specific, the default implementation does nothing. This method is called by the `update()` method, described later. It is not called directly by `JComponent`.

public void uninstallUI(JComponent c)

> Called as the current look-and-feel is being removed. The default implementation does nothing. Subclasses typically use this method to release any resources they may have created and, most importantly, remove any listeners they added in `installUI()`.

public void update(Graphics g, JComponent c)

> Called by `JComponent.paintComponent()`. If you're familiar with the old AWT update/paint mechanism, this method should seem familiar. The key difference is that this version of `update()` only fills the component's bounding rectangle with the background color if the component is opaque. Whatever the opaqueness, this method finishes by calling `paint()`.

Static Method

public static ComponentUI createUI(JComponent c)

> This static method, typically invoked by the `UIManager`, is used to obtain an instance of the component's UI delegate. This implementation actually throws an `Error`, since `createUI()` should not be called on the abstract `ComponentUI` class, and subclasses are expected to define a valid implementation. Concrete subclasses of `ComponentUI` should return an instance (either a new one or a shared one) of their specific class.

The MultiLookAndFeel

Before we get into creating our own L&F, we'll take a quick detour to explore the `MultiLookAndFeel`. This is the L&F that allows accessible interfaces to be incorporated into Swing applications. It can also be used to add things like audio sound effects, support for automated testing, etc.

By this point, you're probably at least aware of the concept of *accessibility* as it applies to JFC and Swing. If you read the previous chapter, you're aware of more than just the concept. The last piece of the accessibility puzzle is Swing's multiplexing L&F support.

The idea behind the `MultiLookAndFeel` is to allow multiple L&Fs to be associated with each component in a program's GUI, without the components having to do anything special to support them. By allowing multiple L&Fs, Swing makes it easy to augment a traditional L&F with auxiliary L&Fs, such as speech synthesizers or braille generators. Figure 26-9 gives a high-level view of how this might work.

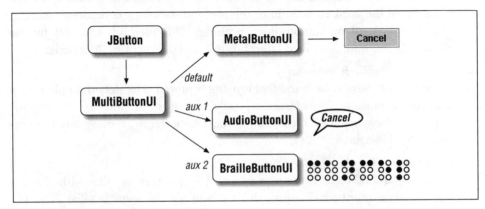

Figure 26-9. The multiplexing look-and-feel

In this diagram, we show a `JButton` in a multiplexing UI environment. The button's UI delegate is actually a `MultiButtonUI`, which is contained in the `javax.swing.plaf.multi` package. This is a special delegate that can support any number of additional `ButtonUI` objects. Here, we show the default UI delegate (`MetalButtonUI`) and two (hypothetical) auxiliary delegates, `AudioButtonUI` and `BrailleButtonUI`.

The `MultiButtonUI` (and all the other multiplexing delegates) keeps track of a vector of "real" UI objects. The first element in the vector is guaranteed to be the default, screen-based L&F. This default receives special treatment. When the `JButton` sends a query to its UI delegate, the `MultiButtonUI` forwards the query first to its default L&F, and then to each of the auxiliary L&Fs. If the method requires a return value, only the value returned from the default L&F is used; the others are ignored.

Creating an Auxilliary Look-and-Feel

Creating a fully implemented auxiliary L&F is beyond the scope of this book. However, we will throw something together to give you a feel for what it would take to build one. In many ways, it's a lot easier than building a graphical L&F.

In this example, we'll define a L&F called StdOutLookAndFeel. This simple-minded L&F prints messages to the screen to describe which component has the focus. To make the example reasonably concise, we only support JButtons and do nothing more than print messages when a button gains or loses focus.

First, let's take a look at our StdOutLookAndFeel class:

```java
// StdOutLookAndFeel.java
//
import javax.swing.*;
import javax.swing.plaf.*;

public class StdOutLookAndFeel extends LookAndFeel {

  // A few simple informational methods . . .

  public String getName() { return "Standard Output"; }
  public String getID() { return "StdOut"; }
  public String getDescription() { return "The Standard Output Look and Feel"; }
  public boolean isNativeLookAndFeel() { return false; }
  public boolean isSupportedLookAndFeel() { return true; }

  // Our only default is the UI delegate for buttons

  public UIDefaults getDefaults() {
    UIDefaults table = new UIDefaults();

    table.put("ButtonUI", "StdOutButtonUI");

    return table;
  }
}
```

As you can see, there's really not a lot to this class. Most of the space is spent in trivial one-line methods defined by the LookAndFeel base class. Of course, a real auxiliary L&F would use the getDefaults() method to define a lot more defaults in order to support all of the components. In our case, we just map "ButtonUI" (the value of the UIClassID property for JButton) to our StdOutButtonUI class. Let's take a look at that class now:

```java
// StdOutButtonUI.java
//
import java.awt.*;
```

```java
import java.awt.event.*;
import javax.accessibility.*;
import javax.swing.*;
import javax.swing.plaf.*;

public class StdOutButtonUI extends ButtonUI {

  // Use a single instance of this class for all buttons
  private static StdOutButtonUI instance;

  private AccessListener listener = new AccessListener();

  // Return the single instance. If this is the first time, we create the
  // instance in this method too.
  public static ComponentUI createUI(JComponent c) {
    if (instance == null) {
      instance = new StdOutButtonUI();
    }
    return instance;
  }

  // Add a focus listener so we know when the buttons has focus.
  public void installUI(JComponent c) {
    JButton button = (JButton)c;
    button.addFocusListener(listener);
  }

  // Remove the focus listener.
  public void uninstallUI(JComponent c) {
    JButton button = (JButton)c;
    button.removeFocusListener(listener);
  }

  // Empty paint & update methods. An empty update() is critical!
  public void paint(Graphics g, JComponent c) {
  }

  public void update(Graphics g, JComponent c) {
  }

  public Insets getDefaultMargin(AbstractButton b) {
    return null; // not called since we're auxiliary
  }

  // A focus listener. A real L&F would want to do a lot more.
  class AccessListener extends FocusAdapter {

    // We print some accessibility info when we get focus.
    public void focusGained(FocusEvent ev) {
```

```
      JButton b = (JButton)ev.getComponent();
      AccessibleContext access = b.getAccessibleContext();
      System.out.print("Focus gained by a ");
      System.out.print(access.getAccessibleRole().toDisplayString());
      System.out.print(" named ");
      System.out.println(access.getAccessibleName());
      System.out.print("Description: ");
      System.out.println(access.getAccessibleDescription());
    }

    // We print some accessibility info when we lose focus.
    public void focusLost(FocusEvent ev) {
      JButton b = (JButton)ev.getComponent();
      AccessibleContext access = b.getAccessibleContext();
      System.out.println("Focus leaving " + access.getAccessibleName());
    }
  }
}
```

The first method in this class is the static `createUI()` method, called to create an instance of our UI delegate. We chose to share an instance of `StdOutButtonUI` across all buttons, so we just return our single instance from this method. The next two methods, `installUI()` and `uninstallUI()`, are used to add and remove a `FocusListener` from the button. In a more realistic implementation, you'd likely be interested in listening for other types of events as well—this is where you'd register (and unregister) them.

Next, we define empty implementations of `paint()` and `update()`. Note the comment about the `update()` method. If we didn't override the default `update()` implementation, our auxiliary L&F, which should not affect the display in any way, would paint a solid rectangle in the location of opaque components.

We've also defined a small inner class called `AccessListener`. We've just made this class a `FocusListener` that displays a little information about the button any time it gains or loses focus. Note that we've taken advantage of Swing's support for accessibility by pulling information from the button's `AccessibleContext`.

Installing the MultiLookAndFeel

At this point, you may be wondering how exactly you get this new look-and-feel to be used. Obviously, we can't just call `UIManager.setLookAndFeel()`, because we'd lose our graphical L&F that way. Luckily, Swing provides us with three other ways to install our auxiliary L&F. The first option is to explicitly tell the UIManager about the L&F. Placing the following line in our `main()` (or `init()` for an applet) method will do the trick:

```
UIManager.addAuxiliaryLookAndFeel (new StdOutLookAndFeel () );
```

The other two options involve the swing properties we discussed earlier in the chapter. If you want to make a global addition of the L&F, add the following to your *swing.properties* file:

```
swing.auxiliarylaf=StdOutLookAndFeel
```

The last option is very convenient if you're just playing around (like we are here). All you have to do is tell the Java runtime about the L&F when you start it up, like this:

```
java -Dswing.auxiliarylaf=StdOutLookAndFeel AccessExample
```

NOTE   The `javax.swing.plaf.multi` package was not included in the *swingall.jar* file. To use auxiliary L&Fs, you just need to add *multi.jar* (part of the standard Swing distributions) to your classpath. If you're using JDK1.2, everything is included in a single *jar* file, so you won't need to do anything special.

We've now covered everything you need to do to use an auxiliary L&F. Here's a very simple program you can use to see how it works. We've added accessible descriptions to each of our buttons to describe their purpose:

```java
// AccessExample.java
//
import javax.swing.*;
import java.awt.*;

public class AccessExample {
  public static void main(String[] args) {
    JFrame f = new JFrame();
    f.addWindowListener(new BasicWindowMonitor());

    // Just create a few accessiblity friendly buttons . . .
    JButton b1 = new JButton("Start");
    JButton b2 = new JButton("Stop");
    JButton b3 = new JButton("Cancel");

    b1.getAccessibleContext().setAccessibleDescription("Start the job");
    b2.getAccessibleContext().setAccessibleDescription("Stop the job");
    b3.getAccessibleContext().setAccessibleDescription("Cancel the job");

    Container c = f.getContentPane();
    c.setLayout(new FlowLayout());
    c.add(b1);
    c.add(b2);
    c.add(b3);
```

```
      f.setSize(150, 150);
      f.setVisible(true);
   }
}
```

NOTE   Due to a change in the JDK1.2 class loading scheme, this example
          does not work properly with JDK1.2 beta4 (it works fine with
          JDK1.1). To run this example, execute the *oldjava* interpreter in-
          stead of *java*. This problem should be cleared up in the next JDK 1.2
          release.

When executed, we see the normal Metal L&F display we'd expect. In addition,
our auxiliary L&F outputs the following information as we move focus to the
various buttons:

```
Focus gained by a push button named Start
Description: Start the job
Focus leaving Start
Focus gained by a push button named Stop
Description: Stop the job
Focus leaving Stop
Focus gained by a push button named Cancel
Description: Cancel the job
Focus leaving Cancel
```

NOTE   In addition to this output, you'll notice messages sent to `stderr`
          indicating that the `createUI()` method has failed for
          `javax.swing.JPanel`. These messages are output any time an
          attempt is made to load a UI delegate for which a default has
          not been defined. In our case, since we did not define a
          `StdOutPanelUI`, the `MultiLookAndFeel` complains.

This example is certainly not very awe-inspiring. There's a lot more work involved
in creating a real auxiliary L&F. Our goal here was to give you a feel for how to get
started.

Look-and-Feel Customization

In this section, we'll look at a variety of different ways that you can change the way
components in your application appear. We'll start with the simplest approach—
making property changes on a per-component basis—and work our way through
several increasingly powerful (and complicated) strategies. In the last section, we'll
show you how to build your own L&F from the ground up.

Modification of Component Properties

This is the most obvious way to change the look of a component, and it's certainly not new to Swing. At the very top of the Java component hierarchy, `java.awt.Component` defines a number of fundamental properties, including `foreground`, `background`, and `font`. If you want to change the way a specific component looks, you can always just change the value of these properties, or any of the others defined by the specific components you are using. As we said, this is nothing new to the Swing PLAF architecture, but we don't want to lose sight of the fact that you can still make many changes in this way.

Modification of the UI Defaults

Modifying component properties lets you customize individual components. But what if you want to make more global changes? What if you want to change things that aren't exposed as component properties?

This is where `UIResources` come into play. There are more than 300 different resources defined by the Swing L&Fs that you can tweak to change the way the components are displayed. These resources include icons, borders, colors, fonts, and more. Appendix A, *Look & Feel Resources*, shows a complete list of the properties defined by the `BasicLookAndFeel`, the base class for all of the Swing-provided L&Fs. Unfortunately, not all of the Swing L&Fs adhere strictly to these resource names. In the example below, several of the resource names we've used are specific to the Metal L&F.

Making Global Changes with Defaults

In this example, we'll change the defaults for a variety of resources to give you an idea of the types of things you can affect. Specifically, we'll change the border used by buttons, the title font and icons used by internal frames, and the width used by scrollbars.

Because we're making these changes globally, any components that use these properties will be affected by what we do.

```
// ResourceModExample.java
//
import java.awt.*;
import java.awt.event.*;
import javax.swing.*;
import javax.swing.border.*;

public class ResourceModExample {
  public static void main(String[] args) {
```

```java
// A custom border for all buttons
Border border = BorderFactory.createRaisedBevelBorder();
Border tripleBorder = new CompoundBorder(new CompoundBorder(
  border, border), border);

UIManager.put("Button.border", tripleBorder);

// Custom icons for internal frames
UIManager.put("InternalFrameTitlePane.closeIcon",
  new ImageIcon("close.gif"));
UIManager.put("InternalFrameTitlePane.iconizeIcon",
  new ImageIcon("iconify.gif"));
UIManager.put("InternalFrameTitlePane.maximizeIcon",
  new ImageIcon("maximize.gif"));
UIManager.put("InternalFrameTitlePane.altMaximizeIcon",
  new ImageIcon("altMax.gif"));

// A custom internal frame title font
UIManager.put("InternalFrameTitlePane.font",
  new Font("Serif", Font.ITALIC, 12));

// Make scrollbars really wide

UIManager.put("ScrollBar.width", new Integer(30));

// Throw together some components to show what we've done.
// Nothing below here is L&F-specific.
// *********************************
JFrame f = new JFrame();
f.addWindowListener(new BasicWindowMonitor());
Container c = f.getContentPane();

JDesktopPane desk = new JDesktopPane();
c.add(desk, BorderLayout.CENTER);

JButton cut = new JButton("Cut");
JButton copy = new JButton("Copy");
JButton paste = new JButton("Paste");

JPanel p = new JPanel(new FlowLayout());
p.add(cut);
p.add(copy);
p.add(paste);
c.add(p, BorderLayout.SOUTH);

JInternalFrame inf = new JInternalFrame("MyFrame",true, true, true, true);
JLabel l = new JLabel(new ImageIcon("toast.jpg"));
JScrollPane scroll = new JScrollPane(l);
inf.setContentPane(scroll);
```

```
        inf.setBounds(10, 10, 200, 200);
        desk.add(inf);

        f.setSize(250, 350);
        f.setVisible(true);
    }
}
```

There's not really a lot to explain about the example. In the first part, we set a variety of resources, specifying our own border, icons, font, and scrollbar width. After that, we just threw together a few components to demonstrate the changes we made. We didn't have to do anything specific to our individual internal frame, scrollbar, or button objects—they used our new defaults automatically. This example produces the display shown in Figure 26-10.

Figure 26-10. UI resource customization

Use of Metal's Themes

The cross-platform Metal L&F defines a class called `MetalTheme` that allows you to customize the look of any application that uses Metal. This simple class encapsulates the colors and fonts used by the L&F. By creating your own theme, you can change the look of *every* component displayed by the `MetalLookAndFeel`.

Sound exciting? It gets better. What makes this feature especially nice is how easy it is to use. Here's an extension of the default theme (which uses three shades of blue for its primary colors) that replaces the familiar blue colors with shades of red.

```
// RedTheme.java
//
import javax.swing.plaf.*;
import javax.swing.plaf.metal.*;

public class RedTheme extends DefaultMetalTheme {
  public String getName() { return "Mars"; }

  private final ColorUIResource primary1 = new ColorUIResource(153, 102, 102);
  private final ColorUIResource primary2 = new ColorUIResource(204, 153, 153);
  private final ColorUIResource primary3 = new ColorUIResource(255, 204, 204);

  protected ColorUIResource getPrimary1() { return primary1; }
  protected ColorUIResource getPrimary2() { return primary2; }
  protected ColorUIResource getPrimary3() { return primary3; }
}
```

These last three methods are defined by `MetalTheme` to set the primary colors used by the Metal L&F. Everything Metal paints uses these colors (along with three shades of gray, plus black and white), so there's nothing more to do. To tell an application to use this new theme, we just need to add the following call to the beginning of the `main()` or `init()` method.

```
MetalLookAndFeel.setCurrentTheme(new RedTheme());
```

If you've already created any Swing components, you'll also need to call `UIManager.setLookAndFeel(new MetalLookAndFeel())` after you set the theme. Themes are only queried during the initialization phase, when all of the data from the theme is loaded into the `UIDefaults`.

MetalTheme Properties

The `RedTheme.java` example is the most basic type of theme you can create, but it doesn't show all the flexibility you get when you use Metal themes. The `MetalTheme` abstract class actually defines all the properties shown in Table 26-5 (note that some of the accessors are abstract in `MetalTheme`). The default values for all of the colors are defined by the various base colors set by the theme, along with black and white. In some cases, the defaults are defined in terms of other properties from this table.

Table 26-5. MetalTheme Properties

Property	Data Type	get	is	set	bound	Default Value
acceleratorForeground	ColorUIResource	•				primary1
acceleratorSelectedForeground	ColorUIResource	•				black

Table 26-5. MetalTheme Properties (continued)

Property	Data Type	get	is	set	bound	Default Value
control	ColorUIResource	•				secondary3
controlDarkShadow	ColorUIResource	•				secondary1
controlDisabled	ColorUIResource	•				secondary2
controlHighlight	ColorUIResource	•				white
controlInfo	ColorUIResource	•				black
controlShadow	ColorUIResource	•				secondary2
controlTextColor	ColorUIResource	•				controlInfo
controlTextFont	FontUIResource	•				Abstract
desktopColor	ColorUIResource	•				primary2
focusColor	ColorUIResource	•				primary2
highlightedTextColor	ColorUIResource	•				controlText-Color
inactiveControlTextColor	ColorUIResource	•				controlDisabled
inactiveSystemTextColor	ColorUIResource	•				secondary2
menuBackground	ColorUIResource	•				secondary3
menuDisabledForeground	ColorUIResource	•				secondary3
menuForeground	ColorUIResource	•				black
menuSelectedBackground	ColorUIResource	•				primary2
menuSelectedForeground	ColorUIResource	•				black
menuTextFont	FontUIResource	•				Abstract
name	String	•				Abstract
primaryControl	ColorUIResource	•				primary3
primaryControlDarkShadow	ColorUIResource	•				primary1
primaryControlHighlight	ColorUIResource	•				white
primaryControlInfo	ColorUIResource	•				black
primaryControlShadow	ColorUIResource	•				primary2
separatorBackground	ColorUIResource	•				white
separatorForeground	ColorUIResource	•				primary1
subTextFont	FontUIResource	•				Abstract
systemTextColor	ColorUIResource	•				primary1
systemTextFont	FontUIResource	•				Abstract
textHighlightColor	ColorUIResource	•				primary3
userTextColor	ColorUIResource	•				black
userTextFont	FontUIResource	•				Abstract
windowBackground	ColorUIResource	•				white

Table 26-5. MetalTheme Properties (continued)

Property	Data Type	get	is	set	bound	Default Value
windowTitleBackground	ColorUIResource	•				primary3
windowTitleFont	FontUIResource	•				Abstract
windowTitleForeground	ColorUIResource	•				black
windowTitleInactiveBackground	ColorUIResource	•				secondary3
windowTitleInactiveForeground	ColorUIResource	•				black

Abstract Protected Methods

As we saw in the previous table, `MetalTheme` defines six core colors (along with black and white) used to paint all Metal components. Subclasses of `MetalTheme` must implement the following six methods to define the core colors used by the theme:

protected abstract ColorUIResource getPrimary1()
protected abstract ColorUIResource getPrimary2()
protected abstract ColorUIResource getPrimary3()
protected abstract ColorUIResource getSecondary1()
protected abstract ColorUIResource getSecondary2()
protected abstract ColorUIResource getSecondary3()

Black and White

Some interesting (though arguably bizarre) effects could also be created by replacing the values of black and white. These `MetalTheme` methods return `Color.black` and `Color.white` by default:

protected ColorUIResource getBlack()
protected ColorUIResource getWhite()

Additional Customization

`MetalTheme` defines one last method that allows you to use themes to change other aspects of the L&F:

public void addCustomEntriesToTable(UIDefaults table)
> Called after the `MetalLookAndFeel` loads its default tables. The default implementation does nothing. Subclasses can take advantage of this hook to add any number of custom resource values to the defaults table. For example:

```
public void addCustomEntriesToTable(UIDefaults table) {
  table.put("Tree.openIcon", new ImageIcon("open.gif"));
```

```
        table.put("Tree.closedIcon", new ImageIcon("closed.gif"));
    }
```

DefaultMetalTheme Font Properties

DefaultMetalTheme is a concrete extension of MetalTheme. It defines the defaults for the six abstract Font properties declared in MetalTheme. Table 26-6 shows the values of these fonts.

Table 26-6. DefaultMetalTheme Fonts

Property	Font Name	Font Style	Font Size
controlTextFont	Dialog	Font.BOLD	12
menuTextFont	Dialog	Font.BOLD	12
subTextFont	Dialog	Font.PLAIN	10
systemTextFont	Dialog	Font.PLAIN	12
userTextFont	Dialog	Font.PLAIN	12
windowTitleFont	Dialog	Font.BOLD	12

Protected DefaultMetalTheme Base Colors

We saw earlier that the MetalTheme class defines abstract accessor methods for six protected color resources. Table 26-7 shows the values defined for these colors by the DefaultMetalTheme.

Table 26-7. Protected DefaultMetalTheme Colors

Name	Color
primary1	(102, 102, 153)
primary2	(153, 153, 204)
primary3	(204, 204, 255)
secondary1	(102, 102, 102)
secondary2	(153, 153, 153)
secondary3	(204, 204, 204)

The primary colors all have equal parts red and green and a higher blue component. This is how you can tell that these values represent increasingly lighter shades of blue. Similarly, the secondary colors all have the same value for red, green, and blue, indicating that they represent increasingly lighter shades of gray.

As you can see, our simple RedTheme only directly touched three of the properties defined by MetalTheme. The last few pages give you everything there is to know about making even more drastic changes to the Metal L&F using themes. All you have to decide is which of the font and color properties you want to change and override their respective accessor methods.

Remember, the team that designed the Metal L&F went to a good deal of trouble to make a clean, consistent L&F. As a rule, you're probably best off changing only the fonts and the primary and secondary colors (which define all the other colors). But if you want to, `MetalTheme` gives you the hooks to define all sorts of different color combinations.

Use of Metal's Client Properties

Another feature that's unique to the Metal L&F is the use of special client properties that allow a handful of components to be customized. To use these properties, you make a call that looks something like this:

```
myComponent.putClientProperty("JTree.lineStyle", "Angled");
```

Setting these client properties with any other look-and-feel will have no effect, unless it's a custom L&F that knows to look for these properties.

We've touched on most of these properties as they came up throughout the book, so we'll just briefly describe them here. Table 26-8 shows a breakdown of the various client properties used by Metal.

Table 26-8. Metal L&F Client Properties

Component	Property	Type	Default	Other Values
JInternalFrame	isPalette	Boolean	FALSE	TRUE
JScrollBar	isFreeStanding	Boolean	TRUE	FALSE
JSlider	isFilled	Boolean	FALSE	TRUE
JToolBar	isRollover	Boolean	FALSE	TRUE
JTree	lineStyle	String	"Horizontal"	"Angled", "None"

To create the property key, just build a string from the component type and the property name. For example, `"JToolBar.isRollover"`.

JInternalFrame.isPalette

Can be set to `Boolean.TRUE` to indicate that the border around the internal frame should not be painted.

JScrollBar.isFreeStanding

Set to `Boolean.FALSE` by the *Metal* L&F for any scrollbars used by `JScroll-Panes`. This setting just indicates that the scrollbar should be displayed flush against its borders. Normally, there is a small space around the scrollbar. Typically, you won't have reason to change this particular value.

JSlider.isFilled

Can be set to `Boolean.TRUE` to cause the slider's "track" to be filled on one side to clearly differentiate the space on either side of the "thumb."

JToolBar.isRollover

> Can be set to `Boolean.TRUE` to cause the border on each of the toolbar's buttons to be replaced with a special rollover border. This border is the same as the button's default border, except that it is only painted when the cursor is over the button, meaning that at any given time, at most one button in the toolbar will have a border. Netscape users will recognize this feature from the toolbars in *Navigator*.

JTree.lineStyle

> This property can be set to `"Angled"` or `"None"` (or the default, `"Horizontal"`) to change the way the tree structure is drawn. By default, horizontal lines are drawn to separate branches of the tree. Setting this property to `"Angled"` causes short angled lines to be drawn between the nodes. As you might guess, setting it to `"None"` turns off both features.

Replacement of Individual UI Delegates

Say you're using a L&F that you're basically happy with, but there are a few components you wish had a slightly different appearance. If the changes you want to make can't be done by simply changing resource values, one option is to implement your own custom UI delegates for the components you want to change and then tell the `UIManager` to use your new classes instead of the L&F defaults.

Modifying a Scrollbar

We'll show how this can be done with a very simple example. We've decided to toss aside the nice, clean consistent design of the Metal L&F by changing the way the "thumb" of the scrollbar is displayed. To keep the code as simple as possible, we're going to change the thumb from the Metal style with textured bumps to a simple solid black box.

We do not recommend making such random changes to existing L&Fs. In this particular example, we're breaking something the designers of the Metal L&F worked very hard to achieve—consistency. Keep in mind that this is an example that shows you *how* to do something. We'll leave it to you to have the good taste to know *when* to do it.

To do this, we need to create our own implementation of the `ScrollBarUI` class. Rather than starting from scratch, we'll extend `MetalScrollBarUI` and change only the methods we want to reimplement. In this case, we find that there's a method called `paintThumb()` that's responsible for rendering the thumb of the scrollbar. This, along with `createUI()`, are the only methods we're going to reimplement. Here's the source code for our new scrollbar UI delegate.

```java
// MyMetalScrollBarUI.java
//
import java.awt.*;
import javax.swing.*;
import javax.swing.plaf.*;
import javax.swing.plaf.metal.*;


// A simple extension of MetalScrollBarUI that draws the,thumb as a solid
// black rectangle.
public class MyMetalScrollBarUI extends MetalScrollBarUI
{
  // Create our own scrollbar UI!
  public static ComponentUI createUI( JComponent c ) {
    return new MyMetalScrollBarUI();
  }


  // This method paints the scroll thumb.  We've just taken the
  // MetalScrollBarUI code and stripped out all the
  // interesting painting code, replacing it with code that paints a
  // black box.
  protected void paintThumb(Graphics g, JComponent c, Rectangle thumbBounds)
  {
    if (!c.isEnabled()) { return; }

    g.translate( thumbBounds.x, thumbBounds.y );
    if ( scrollbar.getOrientation() == JScrollBar.VERTICAL ) {
      if ( !isFreeStanding ) {
        thumbBounds.width += 2;
      }
      g.setColor( Color.black );
      g.fillRect( 0, 0, thumbBounds.width - 2, thumbBounds.height - 1 );
      if ( !isFreeStanding ) {
        thumbBounds.width -= 2;
      }
    }
    else  { // HORIZONTAL
      if ( !isFreeStanding ) {
        thumbBounds.height += 2;
      }
      g.setColor( Color.black );
      g.fillRect( 0, 0, thumbBounds.width - 1, thumbBounds.height - 2 );
      if ( !isFreeStanding ) {
        thumbBounds.height -= 2;
      }
    }
    g.translate( -thumbBounds.x, -thumbBounds.y );
  }
}
```

Pretty simple stuff. The first thing we did was define a new `createUI()` method. Recall that this is the method `JComponent` calls when it is assigned a new UI delegate. All we do is return a new instance of our modified scrollbar delegate.

The second method in our class is basically just a stripped-down version of `Metal-ScrollBarUI`'s `paintThumb()` method. In our implementation, we've removed all the code that created a nice clean thumb, complete with shading and texture bumps, replacing it with single calls to `Graphics.fillRect()`.

Since we've extended `MetalScrollBarUI`, our new scrollbar delegate will look just like the Metal scrollbar, except for the solid black thumb.

The only thing left to do is tell the `UIManager` to use our custom scrollbar delegate instead of the L&F default. You can probably guess that this is simple. Here's what we do:

```
UIManager.put("ScrollBarUI", "MyMetalScrollBarUI");
```

NOTE   Due to a change in the JDK1.2 class loading scheme, this example does not work properly with JKD1.2 beta4 (it works fine with JDK1.1). To run this example, execute the *oldjava* interpreter instead of *java*. This problem should be cleared up in the next release of JDK1.2.

Once we make this call, any new scrollbars that get created will use our custom UI delegate, instead of the previously installed `MetalScrollBarUI`. Here's a little test program that proves that this works:

```
// MetalModExample.java
//
import javax.swing.*;
import java.awt.*;
import java.io.*;

public class MetalModExample {
  public static void main(String[] args) {
    JComponent before = makeExamplePane();

    // Replace the MetalScrollBarUI with our own!
    UIManager.put("ScrollBarUI", "MyMetalScrollBarUI");

    JComponent after = makeExamplePane();

    JFrame f = new JFrame();
    f.addWindowListener(new BasicWindowMonitor());

    Container c = f.getContentPane();
```

```
      c.setLayout(new GridLayout(2, 1, 0, 1));
      c.add(before);
      c.add(after);
      f.setSize(450, 400);
      f.setVisible(true);
    }

    // Create a scroll pane with a text area in it.
    public static JComponent makeExamplePane() {
      JTextArea text = new JTextArea();

      try {
        text.read(new FileReader("MetalModExample.java"), null);
      }
      catch (IOException ex) {}

      JScrollPane scroll = new JScrollPane(text);
      return scroll;
    }
}
```

We create two JScrollPanes, which use JScrollBars. The first one is created
with the default scrollbar delegate. Then, we tell the UIManager to use our new UI
delegate and create a second JScrollPane. Figure 26-11 shows the different
scrollbars created by this example.

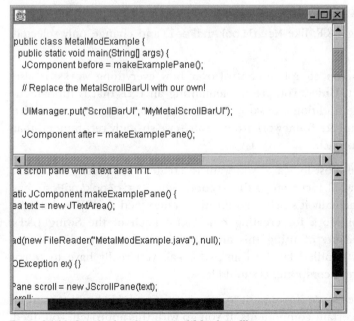

Figure 26-11. Standard and customized Metal scrollbars

In this section, we've seen how easy it is to replace a single UI delegate. If you're creating a custom application, and you want to change specific components, this is a nice, easy way to make the changes. However, if you develop a set of custom delegates that you're particularly happy with, you might want to consider rolling them into your own custom L&F, so you don't have to install each delegate in every program you write. The next section explores your options for creating a custom L&F.

Creation of a Custom L&F

Everything we've covered in this chapter up to this point has been useful background information for the ultimate application customization strategy—creating your own look-and-feel. As you might guess, this is not something you'll do in an afternoon. However, thanks to the improvements made in the L&F framework (as of the JDK 1.2 beta 4 release), it's not as difficult as you might think. You'll likely find that the most difficult part is coming up with graphical design for each component.

There are basically three different strategies for creating a new L&F:

- Start from ground zero by extending `LookAndFeel` and extending each of the UI delegates defined in `javax.swing.plaf`.

- Extend the `BasicLookAndFeel` and each of the abstract UI delegates defined in `javax.swing.plaf.basic`.

- Extend an existing L&F, like `MetalLookAndFeel`, and change only selected components.

The first option gives you complete control over how everything works. It also requires a lot of effort. Unless you are implementing an L&F that is fundamentally different from the traditional desktop L&Fs, or you have some strong desire to implement your own L&F framework from scratch, we strongly recommend that you do not use this approach.

The next option is the most logical if you want to create a completely new L&F. This is the approach we'll focus on in this section. The `BasicLookAndFeel` has been designed (well, actually it's been significantly *re*-designed as of JDK 1.2 beta 4) as an abstract framework for creating new L&Fs. Each of the Swing L&Fs extends Basic. The beauty of using this approach is that the majority of the programming logic is handled by the framework—all you really have to worry about is how the different components should look.

The third option makes sense if you want to use an existing L&F, but just want to make a few tweaks to certain components. If you go with this approach, you need to be careful not to do things that will be confusing to your users. Remember, people expect existing L&Fs to behave in certain familiar ways.

The PlainLookAndFeel

We'll discuss the process of creating a custom L&F by way of example. In this section, we'll define bits and pieces of an L&F called `PlainLookAndFeel`. The goal of this L&F is to be as simple as possible. We won't be doing anything fancy with colors, shading, or painting—this book is long enough without filling pages with fancy `paint()` implementations.

Instead, we'll focus on *how* to create an L&F. All of our painting will be done in black, white, and gray, and we'll use simple, single-width lines. It won't be pretty, but we hope it will be educational.

Creating the LookAndFeel Class

The logical first step in the implementation of a custom L&F is the creation of the `LookAndFeel` class itself. As we've said, the `BasicLookAndFeel` serves as a nice starting point. At a minimum, you'll need to implement the five abstract methods defined in the `LookAndFeel` base class (none of which is implemented in `Basic-LookAndFeel`). Here's a look at the beginning's of our custom L&F class:

```
// PlainLookAndFeel.java
//
package plain;
import java.awt.*;
import javax.swing.*;
import javax.swing.border.*;
import javax.swing.plaf.*;
import javax.swing.plaf.basic.*;

public class PlainLookAndFeel extends BasicLookAndFeel {
  public String getDescription() { return "The Plain Look and Feel"; }
  public String getID() { return "Plain"; }
  public String getName() { return "Plain"; }
  public boolean isNativeLookAndFeel() { return false; }
  public boolean isSupportedLookAndFeel() { return true; }
  // . . .
}
```

At this point, we've got an L&F that will actually compile. Let's go a little further and make it useful. The next major step is to define the defaults for the L&F. This is similar to what we did earlier when we defined a few custom resources for an application. The difference is that now we will be defining a complete set of resources for an entirely new L&F that can be used across many applications. The installation of defaults is handled by getDefaults() which has been broken down into three additional methods in BasicLookAndFeel.

NOTE   Due to a change in the JDK1.2 class loading scheme, the use of custom L&Fs does not work properly with JDK1.2 beta4 (it works fine with JDK1.1). To use the code shown in this section, execute the *old-java* interpreter instead of *java*. This problem should be cleared up in the next JDK1.2 release.

BasicLookAndFeel.getDefaults() creates a UIDefaults table and calls the following three methods (in this order):

protected void initClassDefaults(UIDefaults table)
protected void initSystemColorDefaults(UIDefaults table)
protected void initComponentDefaults(UIDefaults table)

Let's look at these three steps in detail.

Defining Class Defaults

Defining class defaults is the process of enumerating the names of the classes your L&F will use for each of the UI delegates. One nice feature of the BasicLookAnd-Feel is that it defines concrete implementations of all of the UI-delegate classes. One big benefit is that you can test your new L&F as you're creating it, without having to specify every single delegate class. Instead, just define the ones you want to test and use the basic implementations for the others. Those that you define (since they're stored in a simple Hashtable) will override any values previously defined by BasicLookAndFeel.

A typical implementation of this method looks something like this:

```
protected void initClassDefaults(UIDefaults table) {
    super.initClassDefaults(table); // install the "basic" delegates

    String plainPkg = "plain.";
    Object[] classes = {
        "ProgressBarUI", plainPkg + "PlainProgressBarUI",
            "SliderUI", plainPkg + "PlainSliderUI",
              "TreeUI", plainPkg + "PlainTreeUI",
        // . . . etc
    };
    table.putDefaults(classes);
}
```

The first line calls the BasicLookAndFeel implementation, which installs each of the basic UI delegates. Next, we create a string containing the package name for our L&F classes. This will be used in constructing the class names of each of our UI delegates. We then create an array of `UIClassID` to UI-delegate class name mappings. The items in this array should alternate between class IDs[*] and class names. Include such a mapping for each UI delegate your L&F implements.

Defining L&F Colors

The next set of defaults typically defined are the color resources used by the L&F. You have a lot of flexibility here in terms of how you handle colors. As we saw earlier in the chapter, the Metal L&F defines all colors in terms of a color "theme," allowing the colors used by the L&F to be easily customized. This feature is specific to Metal, but you can implement a similar feature in your own L&F.

Colors are typically defined according to the colors specified in the `java.awt.SystemColor` class. These are the colors used by the `BasicLookAnd-Feel`, so if you are going to default any of the painting routines to Basic, it's important to define values for the system colors. Even if you are going to handle every bit of painting in your custom L&F, it's still a good idea, though it is not required, to use the familiar color names.

`BasicLookAndFeel` adds another protected method called `loadSystem-Colors()`. For non-native L&Fs, this simply maps an array of color name/color value pairs into resource keys and `ColorUIResource` values. For example, a pair of entries in the array might be:

```
"control", "#FFFFFF"
```

This would result in a resource called `"control"` being added, with a value of the color white.

NOTE   The conversion from `#FFFFFF` to `Color.white` is done by the `java.awt.Color.decode()` method (which uses `java.lang.In-teger.decode()`). This method takes a string representation of a color and converts it to a valid `Color` object. In this case, the `#` character indicates that we are specifying a hexadecimal (base-16) number. (You can also use the familiar `0x` notation.) The first two characters (one byte) represent the red component of the color. The next two represent green, and the last two represent blue. In this example, all values are `FF` (255 decimal), which maps to the color white.

---

* The `UIClassID` property for all Swing components can be formed by dropping the `J` from the class name and adding `UI` at the end. `JButton`'s `UIClassID` is `ButtonUI`, `JTree`'s is `TreeUI`, etc.

Using `loadSystemColors()` allows you to define the color values for your L&F by creating an array of key/value pairs, like the pair we just looked at. This array is then passed to `loadSystemColors()`, along with the `UIDefaults` table. Here's a sample implementation of `initSystemColorDefaults()`:

```
protected void initSystemColorDefaults(UIDefaults table) {
    String[] colors = {
                    "desktop", "#C0C0C0",
            "activeCaption", "#FFFFFF",
        "activeCaptionText", "#000000",
      "activeCaptionBorder", "#000000"
    // more of the same . . .
    };
    loadSystemColors(table, colors, false);
}
```

Table 26-9 shows the 26 color keys defined by `SystemColor` and used by the `BasicLookAndFeel`.

Table 26-9. Standard System Color Properties

System Color Property	Description
desktop	Color of the desktop background
activeCaption	Color of the titlebar (captions) when the frame is active
activeCaptionText	Color of the titlebar text when the frame is active
activeCaptionBorder	Color of the titlebar border when the frame is active
inactiveCaption	Color of the titlebar (captions) when the frame is inactive
inactiveCaptionText	Color of the titlebar text when the frame is inactive
inactiveCaptionBorder	Color of the titlebar border when the frame is inactive
window	Color of the interior of the window
windowBorder	Color of the window border
windowText	Color of the window text
menu	Background color of menus
menuText	Color of the text in menu items
text	Background color of editable text
textText	Color of editable text
textHighlight	Background color of editable text when highlighted
textHighlightText	Color of editable text when highlighted
textInactiveText	Color of normally editable text that has been disabled.
control	Standard color for controls such as buttons or scrollbar thumbs
controlText	Color for text inside controls
controlHighlight	Highlight color for controls
controlLtHighlight	Lighter highlight color for the controls

Table 26-9. Standard System Color Properties (continued)

System Color Property	Description
controlShadow	Shadow color for controls
controlDkShadow	Darker shadow color for the controls
scrollbar	Color to use for the background area of a scrollbar (where the thumb slides)
info	Background color for informational text
infoText	Color for informational text

Defining Component Defaults

The last method called by `BasicLookAndFeel.getDefaults()` is `initCompo-nentDefaults()`. This is where you define all of the colors, icons, borders, and other resources used by each of the individual component delegates. The `BasicLookAndFeel` implementation of this method defines over 300 different resource values for 40 delegate classes. We've cataloged this long list of resources, along with the type of value expected for each, in Appendix A.

The good news is that you don't have to redefine all 300+ resource values in your custom L&F, though you certainly can if you want. Many of the resources are colors and are defined in terms of the system colors we've already defined. For example, the `Button.background` resource defaults to the value defined for `"control"` while `Button.foreground` defaults to `"controlText"`. As long as you've defined values for the system colors and you're happy with the mappings to these system colors defined by the `BasicLookAndFeel`, you can get by with little or no changes to the component-level color resources. The amount of customization done in this method is really up to you. If you like the resource choices made by the `BasicLookAndFeel`, use them. If you want your own custom defaults, you can change them.

There are a few useful steps used by the Swing L&Fs that will make the implementation of this method easier to understand. We'll discuss these in the following.

Define Fonts

Chances are there's a fixed set of fonts your L&F will use throughout its delegates. It's a good idea to define these up-front, so you're not creating duplicate font resources throughout the method. Recall from earlier in the chapter that resources defined by the L&F should implement the `UIResource` interface, so we'll create our fonts as `FontUIResource` objects. You might choose to define a few fonts like this:

```
FontUIResource sansSerifPlain10 =
   new FontUIResource("SansSerif", Font.PLAIN, 10);
FontUIResource monospacedPlain10 =
   new FontUIResource("Monospaced", Font.PLAIN, 10);
```

Define Colors

If you plan to use colors not defined by the system colors, and you're not using a flexible color strategy like Metal's themes, remember to define these colors as `ColorUIResources`. For example:

```
ColorUIResource green = new ColorUIResource(Color.green);
ColorUIResource veryLightGray = new ColorUIResource(240, 240, 240);
```

Define Insets

Several of the resource values are defined as `java.awt.Insets`. Again, it's convenient to define these values up-front. For example:

```
InsetsUIResource zeroInsets = new InsetsUIResource(0,0,0,0);
InsetsUIResource bigInsets = new InsetsUIResource(10,10,10,10);
```

Define Borders

If you're going to use the standard Swing borders for your components, recall that you can obtain singleton resource borders from the `BorderUIResource` class. For example:

```
Border etchedBorder = BorderUIResource.getEtchedBorderUIResource();
Border blackLineBorder = BorderUIResource.getBlackLineBorderUIResource();
```

This works great for defining simple borders. However, it's often useful to define dynamic borders that change based on the state of the component they are bordering. For example, when a button is pressed, it often draws its border differently than when it is in the default raised position. The Basic L&F provides a class called `BasicBorders` that includes inner classes for several common dynamic borders. We'll cover this class at the end of the chapter.

Define Icons

Several components define a variety of `Icon` resources. There are two distinct types of icons you'll want to define: static and dynamic. Static icons are usually (though not always) `ImageIcons`, loaded from small GIF files. They are used for things like tree nodes and `JOptionPane` dialogs. It's generally a good idea to define static icons using the `UIDefaults.LazyValue` class (discussed earlier in the chapter) to avoid loading the images in applications that don't use the components they are associated with. The easiest strategy is just to use `LookAndFeel.makeIcon()` method, which returns `LazyValue` objects, to load an icon from the location of your L&F classes. For example, to load an image called `warning.gif` from the `icons` directory directly under the directory containing your L&F classes, you would use the following code:

```
Object warningIcon = LookAndFeel.makeIcon(getClass(), "icons/warning.gif");
```

Table 26-10 summarizes the default icons loaded by `BasicLookAndFeel`. If you use the default resource values for these icons, be sure to supply an image for each of the icons (in the *icons* subdirectory). No default image files are defined.

Table 26-10. Image Icons Defined by BasicLookAndFeel

Resource Name	Filename
FileChooser.detailsViewIcon	DetailsView.gif
FileChooser.homeFolderIcon	HomeFolder.gif
FileChooser.listViewIcon	ListView.gif
FileChooser.newFolderIcon	NewFolder.gif
FileChooser.upFolderIcon	UpFolder.gif
FileView.computerIcon	Computer.gif
FileView.directoryIcon	Directory.gif
FileView.fileIcon	File.gif
FileView.floppyDriveIcon	FloppyDrive.gif
FileView.hardDriveIcon	HardDrive.gif
InternalFrame.icon	JavaCup.gif
OptionPane.errorIcon	Error.gif
OptionPane.informationIcon	Inform.gif
OptionPane.questionIcon	Question.gif
OptionPane.warningIcon	Warn.gif
Tree.closedIcon	TreeClosed.gif
Tree.leafIcon	TreeLeaf.gif
Tree.openIcon	TreeOpen.gif

It's more challenging to define icons that change based on the state of a component. The most obvious examples of dynamic icons are radio buttons and checkboxes. These icons paint themselves differently depending on whether or not they are selected and, typically, whether or not they are currently being pressed. We'll look at a strategy for implementing dynamic icons in a few pages.

Define Other Resources

A variety of other resources, including Dimensions and Integer values can also be defined as component resources. Remember, you can refer to Appendix A for a complete list.

Create Defaults Array

Now that you've defined all the common resources that might be shared by multiple components, it's time to put together an array of key/value pairs for the resources you want to define. This array is typically handled just like the others we've seen up to this point—entries in the array alternate between resource keys and values. Since there are potentially a very large number of resources being defined here, it's a good idea to group resources by component. Here's part of our PlainLookAndFeel defaults array definition:

```
Object[] defaults = {
  "Button.border", buttonBorder,
```

```
    "Button.margin", new InsetsUIResource(2, 2, 2, 2),
    "Button.font", sansSerifPlain10,

    "RadioButton.icon", radioButtonIcon,
    "RadioButton.pressed", table.get("controlLtHighlight"),
    "RadioButton.font", sansSerifPlain10,

    "CheckBox.icon", checkBoxIcon,
    "CheckBox.pressed", table.get("controlLtHighlight"),
    "CheckBox.font", sansSerifPlain10,

    "Slider.foreground", table.get("controlText")
};
```

Note that you aren't limited to the resources listed in Appendix A. In Table 26-10, we've added two custom resources called RadioButton.pressed and CheckBox.pressed which we'll use as background colors when the button is being pressed.

Two Little Details

We've covered almost everything you have to think about when implementing initComponentDefaults(). There are two last important steps (one at the beginning and one at the end) to remember. The first thing you will typically do is call super.initComponentDefaults(). This loads all of the defaults defined by BasicLookAndFeel. If you don't do this, you are likely to have a runtime error when the BasicLookAndFeel tries to access some undefined resource. Of course, if you define all of the resources in your L&F, you don't have to make the super call. The last thing to do in your method is to load your defaults into the input UIDefaults table. When it's complete, the initComponentDefaults() method should look something like this:

```
protected void initComponentDefaults(UIDefautls table) {
    super.initComponentDefaults(table);

    // Define any common resources, lazy/active value resources, etc . . .

    Object[] defaults = {
      // . . . define all the defaults
    };

    table.putDefaults(defaults);
}
```

Defining an Icon Factory

This is not a required step, but it can prove to be a useful one. The Swing L&Fs group the definitions of various dynamic icons into an icon factory class. This class scrves as a holder of singleton instances of the various dynamic icons used by the L&F and also contains the inner classes that actually define the icons.

Which icons, if any, you define in an icon factory is up to you. The Metal L&F uses its icon factory to draw all of its icons, except those used by JOptionPane. This allows Metal to change the color of its icons based on the current color theme, a task not easily achieved if the icons are loaded from GIF files.

For our purposes, we'll concentrate on defining dynamic icons. The PlainLook-AndFeel will use GIFs for all of the static icons.

The easiest way to understand how to implement a dynamic icon is to look at a simple example. Here's a trimmed-down version of our PlainIconFactory class, showing how we implemented the radio button icon:

```
// PlainIconFactory.java
//
package plain;

import java.awt.*;
import javax.swing.*;
import javax.swing.plaf.*;
import java.io.Serializable;

public class PlainIconFactory implements Serializable {
  private static Icon radioButtonIcon;
  private static Icon checkBoxIcon; // implemention trimmed from example

  // Provide access to the single RadioButtonIcon instance.
  public static Icon getRadioButtonIcon() {
    if (radioButtonIcon == null) {
      radioButtonIcon = new RadioButtonIcon();
    }
    return radioButtonIcon;
  }

  // An icon for rendering the default radio button icon.
  private static class RadioButtonIcon implements Icon, UIResource, Serializable
  {
    private static final int size = 15;

    public int getIconWidth() { return size; }
    public int getIconHeight() { return size; }

    public void paintIcon(Component c, Graphics g, int x, int y) {

      // Get the button & model containing the state we are supposed to show
      AbstractButton b = (AbstractButton)c;
      ButtonModel model = b.getModel();
```

```
      // If the button is being pressed (& armed), change the BG color
      // (NOTE: Could also do something different if the button is disabled)

      if (model.isPressed() && model.isArmed()) {
        g.setColor(UIManager.getColor("RadioButton.pressed"));
        g.fillOval(x, y, size-1, size-1);
      }

      // Draw an outer circle
      g.setColor(UIManager.getColor("RadioButton.foreground"));
      g.drawOval(x, y, size-1, size-1);

      // Fill a small circle inside if the button is selected
      if (model.isSelected()) {
        g.fillOval(x+4, y+4, size-8, size-8);
      }
    }
  }
}
```

We provide a static getRadioButtonIcon() method that creates the icon the first time it's called. On subsequent calls, the single instance is returned immediately. We'll do the same thing for each dynamic icon we define. Next, we have the RadioButtonIcon inner class. Recall from Chapter 4, *Labels and Icons*, that there are three methods involved in implementing the Icon interface (the other interfaces, UIResource and Serializable, have no methods). Our implementations of getIconWidth() and getIconHeight() are simple; they just return a constant size.

The interesting code is in paintIcon(). In this method, what we paint depends on the state of the button's model. In our implementation, we do two checks. First, we check to see if the button is being pressed. If so (and if the button is armed, meaning that the mouse pointer is still over the button), we paint a special background color. Then we paint a solid outer circle and perform the second check. This check is to see if the button is selected. If it is, we paint a solid circle inside the outer circle.

One thing to note here is that we chose to define a custom resource called RadioButton.pressed. Since there is no standard policy for showing that a button is pressed, we use this resource to define the background for our pressed button.

The really interesting thing about this new icon class is that for many L&Fs, defining this icon is all you need to do to for the delegate that uses it. In Plain-LookAndFeel, we don't even define a PlainRadioButtonUI class at all. Instead, we just create a RadioButtonIcon and set it as the icon using the resource "RadioButton.icon". Figure 26-12 shows some RadioButtons using the Plain-

LookAndFeel. The first button is selected, the second is selected and is being held down, and the third is unselected.

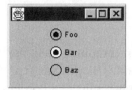

Figure 26-12. PlainIconFactory.RadioButtonIcon

Defining Custom Borders

Certain Swing components are typically rendered with some type of border around them. The javax.swing.border package defines a number of static borders that you can use. However, it's often desirable to create your own custom borders as part of your L&F. Also, certain borders (just like certain icons) should be painted differently depending on the state of the object they are being painted around.

The Swing L&Fs define custom borders in a class called *<L&FName>*Borders. Many of the inner classes defined in BasicBorders may be useful when defining your own L&F. These are the borders used by default by the BasicLookAndFeel. They include the following inner classes:

public static class ButtonBorder extends AbstractBorder implements UIResource
public static class FieldBorder extends AbstractBorder implements UIResource
public static class MarginBorder extends AbstractBorder implements UIResource
public static class MenuBarBorder extends AbstractBorder implements UIResource
public static class RadioButtonBorder extends ButtonBorder
public static class SplitPaneBorder implements Border, UIResource
public static class ToggleButtonBorder extends ButtonBorder

It's probably not too important to understand the details of most of these inner classes. The important thing to know is that these are the borders installed for certain components by the BasicLookAndFeel.

One of these inner classes, MarginBorder, does deserve special mention. This class defines a border that has no appearance, but takes up space. It's used with components that define a margin property, specifically AbstractButton, JToolBar, and JTextComponent. When defining borders for these components, it's important to create a CompoundBorder that includes an instance of BasicBorders.MarginBorder. If you don't do this, your L&F will ignore the component's margin property, a potentially confusing problem for developers

using your L&F. Here's an example from `PlainLookAndFeel` in which we use a
`MarginBorder` to define the border that we'll use for our `JButton`s:

```
Border marginBorder = new BasicBorders.MarginBorder();
Object buttonBorder = new BorderUIResource.CompoundBorderUIResource(
    new PlainBorders.ButtonBorder(), marginBorder);
```

Note that the `MarginBorder` constructor takes no arguments. It simply checks the
component's `margin` property in its `paintBorder()` method. Using a `Margin-`
`Border` with a component that has no `margin` property simply results in a border
with insets of `(0,0,0,0)`.

This example brings us back to the idea of creating a `PlainBorders` class that
defines a set of borders for our L&F. Keep in mind that you don't have to do this.
You're free to use the default borders provided by Basic, or even to use the simple
borders defined by the `swing.border` package. Here's the `PlainBorders` class in
which we define a single inner class for handling button borders:

```
// PlainBorders.java
//
package plain;

import java.awt.*;
import javax.swing.*;
import javax.swing.border.*;
import javax.swing.plaf.*;

public class PlainBorders {
  // An inner class for JButton borders.
  public static class ButtonBorder extends AbstractBorder implements UIResource
  {
    private Border raised;  // use this one by default
    private Border lowered; // use this one when pressed

    // Create the border.
    public ButtonBorder() {
      raised = BorderFactory.createRaisedBevelBorder();
      lowered = BorderFactory.createLoweredBevelBorder();
    }

    // Define the insets (in terms of one of the others).
    public Insets getBorderInsets(Component c) {
      return raised.getBorderInsets(c);
    }

    // Paint the border according to the current state.
    public void paintBorder(Component c, Graphics g, int x, int y,
        int width, int height) {
```

```
        AbstractButton b = (AbstractButton)c;
        ButtonModel model = b.getModel();

        if (model.isPressed() && model.isArmed()) {
          lowered.paintBorder(c, g, x, y, width, height);
        }
        else {
          raised.paintBorder(c, g, x, y, width, height);
        }
      }
    }
}
```

For the sake of providing a very simple example, we've implemented our Button-Border class using two other existing borders. Which of these borders is actually painted by our border is determined by the state of the button model.

The BasicGraphicsUtils Class

There's one more class from the Basic L&F worth knowing something about. BasicGraphicsUtils defines a number of static utility methods that might be useful when creating your own L&F.

Methods

public static void drawBezel(Graphics g, int x, int y, int w, int h, boolean isPressed,
    boolean isDefault, Color shadow, Color darkShadow, Color highlight)
public static void drawDashedRect(Graphics g, int x, int y, int width, int height)
public static void drawEtchedRect(Graphics g, int x, int y, int w, int h, Color control,
    Color shadow, Color darkShadow, Color highlight)
public static void drawGroove(Graphics g, int x, int y, int w, int h, Color shadow,
    Color highlight)
public static void drawLoweredBezel(Graphics g, int x, int y, int w, int h, Color shadow,
    Color darkShadow, Color highlight)
    These methods can be used to draw various different rectangles. The Basic L&F uses these for many of its borders. Figure 26-13 shows several rectangles created by these methods. The parameters shown in the four drawBezel() examples correspond to isPressed and isDefault, respectively

public static void drawString(Graphics g, String text, int underlinedChar, int x, int y)
    Draws a String at the specified location. The first occurrence of under-linedChar will be underlined. This is typically used to indicate mnemonics.

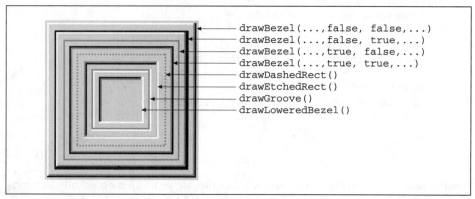

Figure 26-13. BasicGraphicsUtils

public static Insets getEtchedInsets()
public static Insets getGrooveInsets()

Return the `Insets` used by the `drawEtchedRect()` and `drawGroove()` methods.

public static Dimension getPreferredButtonSize(AbstractButton b, int textIconGap)

Returns the preferred size of a button based on its text, icon, insets, and the `textIconGap` parameter.

Create the Individual UI Delegates

The key step in developing a unique L&F is the creation of a set of UI delegate classes for the various Swing components that can't be sufficiently customized just by setting resource values or defining custom borders and icons.

Unfortunately, a description of the methods involved in each individual UI delegate is beyond the scope of this book (we're starting to fear that no one will be able to lift it as it is!). Still, we don't want to leave you in the dark after coming so far, so we'll take a detailed look at a single example. For the rest of the chapter, we'll focus on the creation of the `PlainSliderUI`, but many of the steps along the way will apply to other delegates as well.

Define a Constructor

Constructors for UI delegates don't typically do much. The main thing to concern yourself with is whether or not you want to keep a reference to the component the delegate is rendering. Generally speaking, this is not necessary because the component will always be passed as a parameter to methods on the delegate. However, if you're extending Basic, you do need to pay attention to the requirements of the Basic constructor. In the case of `BasicSliderUI`, we are required to pass a

JSlider as an argument, but since BasicSliderUI just ignores it anyway, we just pass a null. Here's the beginning of our PlainSliderUI class:

```
// PlainSliderUI.java
//
package plain;
import java.awt.*;
import javax.swing.*;
import javax.swing.plaf.*;
import javax.swing.plaf.basic.*;

public class PlainSliderUI extends BasicSliderUI {
  // ...
  public PlainSliderUI() {
    super(null); // basic ignores the parameter anyway
  }
  // ...
}
```

Define the Factory Method

The next important step is to define a createUI() factory method. This is how the delegate gets created for a given component. Typically, all you need to do here is return a new instance of your UI delegate class. In some cases, it may be better to use a single instance of the UI delegate class for all components, then createUI() will always return the same static object, rather than creating a new one each time. If you go with this approach, make sure your delegate (including its superclass) doesn't hold any instance-specific component data.

In PlainSliderUI, our createUI() method just returns a new instance of PlainSliderUI:

```
public static ComponentUI createUI(JComponent c) {
  return new PlainSliderUI();
}
```

Define installUI() and uninstallUI() (optional)

The installUI() and uninstall() methods give you an opportunity to initialize your UI delegate with information from the component it's rendering. Both methods take a single JComponent parameter, which can safely be cast to the appropriate type if needed.

If you're not extending the Basic L&F, you'll typically have quite a bit of work to do in the installUI() method. On the other hand, if you are taking advantage of the BasicLookAndFeel, you'll have little (if anything) to do here. In the case of SliderUI, the BasicSliderUI.install() method does the following things:

- Makes the slider opaque

- Adds six listeners to the slider to track its state

- Retrieves resource defaults from the UIManager

- Installs the border, background, and foreground colors (from resource values) on the component

- Adds keyboard actions to the slider, allowing it to be adjusted with keys as well as with a mouse

- Defines a Timer used when scrolling

- Calculates the bounds of each region of the slider for use in painting

We list these items to give you an idea of the types of things typically done in installUI(). In PlainSliderUI, we don't bother reimplementing this method, since the default does everything we need.

The uninstall() method should undo anything done by installUI(). In particular, any listeners should be removed. BasicSliderUI.uninstall() does the following for us:

- Removes the border

- Stops the Timer

- Uninstalls the listeners

- Sets fields to null

Again, we chose not to override uninstallUI() in PlainSliderUI.

Define Component Size

Recall that the ComponentUI base class defines the three standard sizing methods: getMinimumSize(), getMaximumSize(), and getPreferredSize(). Depending on the component, and on how much you are going to customize your L&F, you may or may not need to worry about implementing these methods. Also, some of the implementations of these methods are broken down into several additional methods.

In the case of BasicSliderUI, the preferred and minimum size methods are broken down into pairs, based on the orientation of the slider. The following four methods are used:

public Dimension getMinimumHorizontalSize()
public Dimension getMinimumVerticalSize()
public Dimension getPreferredHorizontalSize()
public Dimension getPreferredVerticalSize()

If you want to change the preferred or minimum size of the slider, these methods can be overridden. In `PlainSliderUI`, we do the following:

```
private static final Dimension PREF_HORIZ = new Dimension(250, 15);
private static final Dimension PREF_VERT = new Dimension(15, 250);
private static final Dimension MIN_HORIZ = new Dimension(25, 15);
private static final Dimension MIN_VERT = new Dimension(15, 25);

public Dimension getPreferredHorizontalSize() {
  return PREF_HORIZ;
}
public Dimension getPreferredVerticalSize() {
  return PREF_VERT;
}
public Dimension getMinimumHorizontalSize() {
  return MIN_HORIZ;
}
public Dimension getMinimumVerticalSize() {
  return MIN_VERT;
}
```

Override Component-Specific Details

So far, we've laid most of the groundwork for creating the custom UI delegate. The next thing is to look for any little details the `Basic` delegate allows you to customize. This will, of course, vary greatly from component to component. For sliders, the following two methods allow us to specify how large certain parts of the slider will be. The values returned by these methods are used in various calculations.

protected Dimension getThumbSize()
protected int getTickLength()

In `PlainSliderUI`, we provide the following implementations of these methods:

```
// Define the size of the thumb.
protected Dimension getThumbSize() {
  Dimension size = new Dimension();

  if (slider.getOrientation() == JSlider.VERTICAL) {
    size.width = 10;
    size.height = 7; // needs to be thick enough to be able to grab it
  }
  else {
    size.width = 7;  // needs to be thick enough to be able to grab it
    size.height = 10;
  }
  return size;
}
```

```
// How big are major ticks?
protected int getTickLength() {
   return 6;
}
```

There are quite a few other methods that revolve around calculating various sizes, but the defaults for these methods will serve us well enough.

Paint the Component

At last, the fun part! When all is said and done, the reason you create your own L&F is to be able to paint the components in your own special way. As you might guess, this is where the `paint()` method comes in. However, if you had to implement `paint()` from scratch, you'd have to deal with a lot of details that are the same for all L&Fs. Luckily, the Basic L&F has matured over time into a nice, clean framework with lots of hooks to allow you to customize certain aspects of the display, without worrying about every little detail.

Turning our attention to our slider delegate, we find that the `BasicSliderUI`'s `paint()` method is broken down into five other methods:

public void paintFocus(Graphics g)
public void paintLabels(Graphics g)
public void paintThumb(Graphics g)
public void paintTicks(Graphics g)
public void paintTrack(Graphics g)

> These methods let us paint the specific pieces of the slider that we want to control, without having to deal with the things we don't want to change. In `PlainSliderUI`, we've chosen to implement only `paintThumb()` and `paintTrack()`.

The `paintFocus()` method in `BasicSliderUI` paints a dashed rectangle around the slider when it has focus. This is reasonable default behavior for our L&F. The `paintLabels()` method takes care of painting the optional labels at the correct positions, and `paintTicks()` draws all the little tick marks. We have influenced how this method works by overriding the `getTickLength()` method. The `Basic-SliderUI.paintTicks()` method uses this length for major ticks and cuts it in half for minor ticks. If we didn't like this strategy, we could override `paint-Ticks()`. Better still, we could override the four methods it uses:

protected void paintMajorTickForHorizSlider(Graphics g, Rectangle tickBounds, int x)
protected void paintMajorTickForVertSlider(Graphics g, Rectangle tickBounds, int y)
protected void paintMinorTickForHorizSlider(Graphics g, Rectangle tickBounds, int x)
protected void paintMinorTickForVertSlider(Graphics g, Rectangle tickBounds, int y)

> These methods allow us to paint each tick any way we want, without having to do the calculations performed by `paintTicks()`. It's important to look for

methods like this in each UI delegate that you implement—they can be major time-savers.

Back to `PlainSliderUI`. As we said, we've chosen to implement only two of the methods `paint()` uses, making our `PlainSliderUI` as simple as possible. The first of these methods is `paintTrack()`. This is where we paint the line that the slider thumb will slide along. In fancier L&Fs, this is made up a various lines and rectangles that create a nicely shaded track. Here's our much simpler implementation:

```
// Paint the track as a single solid line.
public void paintTrack(Graphics g) {
    int x = trackRect.x;
    int y = trackRect.y;
    int h = trackRect.height;
    int w = trackRect.width;

    g.setColor(slider.getForeground());

    if (slider.getOrientation() == JSlider.HORIZONTAL) {
        g.drawLine(x, y+h-1, x+w-1, y+h-1);
    }
    else {
        g.drawLine(x+w-1, y, x+w-1, y+h-1);
    }
}
```

We've chosen to draw a single line, using the slider's foreground color, along the bottom of the available bounds defined by `trackRect`. You're probably wondering where this `trackRect` variable came from. This is a protected field defined in `BasicSliderUI` that keeps track of the area in which the slider's track should be painted. There are all sorts of protected fields like this in the Basic L&F.

The next slider painting method we've implemented is `paintThumb()`. Given our simple painting strategy, it actually looks surprisingly like `paintTrack()`.

```
// Paint the thumb as a single solid line, centered in the thumb area.
public void paintThumb(Graphics g) {
    int x = thumbRect.x;
    int y = thumbRect.y;
    int h = thumbRect.height;
    int w = thumbRect.width;

    g.setColor(slider.getForeground());
    if (slider.getOrientation() == JSlider.HORIZONTAL) {
        g.drawLine(x+(w/2), y, x+(w/2), y+h-1);
    }
```

```
      else {
        g.drawLine(x, y+(h/2), x+w-1, y+(h/2));
      }
    }
```

Here, we use another protected field called thumbRect to determine where we're supposed to paint the thumb. Recall from our getThumbSize() method, that we set the thumb width (or height for horizontal sliders) to 7. However, we only want to paint a single short line, centered relative to the total width. This is why you see (w/2) and (h/2) as part of the calculations.

Don't Forget to Use It

The last step is to make sure our PlainLookAndFeel actually uses this nice new class. All we have to do is add a line to the array we've created in the initClass-Defaults() method of PlainLookAndFeel. Since this is the only custom delegate we've created, our implementation of this method looks like this:

```
protected void initClassDefaults(UIDefaults table) {
   super.initClassDefaults(table); // install the "basic" delegates

   String plainPkg = "plain.";

   Object[] classes = {
     "SliderUI", plainPkg + "PlainSliderUI"
   };

   table.putDefaults(classes);
}
```

How's It Look?

That just about covers it for our PlainSliderUI. Let's take a look at a few "plain" sliders and see how it turned out. Figure 26-14 shows four sliders with different tick settings, labels, and orientations.

One Down...

Creating a custom look-and-feel is not a trivial task. As we've said, it's beyond the scope of this book to get into the details of every UI delegate. What we've tried to do, instead, is to give you an idea of the general procedure for implementing component-specific delegates by extending the Basic L&F. The remaining steps can be described very loosely as "repeat until done." Some of the other components will be easier to deal with than the slider, and some will be more challenging. In any case, this section has introduced the core ideas you need to implement the rest of the UI delegates.

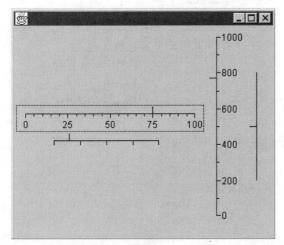

Figure 26-14. PlainSliderUI

27

Swing Utilities

There are many tasks you run into that are common and not terribly difficult. Hence, they get rewritten several times in several small variations. Ideally, you would code the task up into a method or class, and keep it around for reuse later. That's exactly what happened with the SwingUtilities class. It contains several dozen methods to handle some tasks you encounter when dealing with real applications. (There's a method to test if the mouse button pressed was the left mouse button, for example.)

And how many simple timer classes exist that fire events at useful intervals? Or more likely, how many methods out there contain while() loops wrapped around Thread.sleep(delay) calls to do the work of a clock? The Timer class in the Swing package provides a flexible timer for all your timing needs.

If you use icons, you have probably had to create a "disabled" version of the image for use in your application. Now, the GrayFilter class can help you out. There's even a tooltip manager class devoted to handling all of the common functions you might expect to have available for tooltips.

We've broken these utilities up into several categories, more for presentation than anything. You'll find the SwingUtilities, SwingConstants, Timer, and ToolTipManager classes in "General Utilities." The "Event Utilities" section covers the KeyStroke and EventListenerList classes. The "Editing Utilities" section looks at the CellEditor and CellEditorListener interfaces as well as the DefaultCellEditor and KeyStroke classes. And the "Image Utilities" section covers the GrayFilter class.

Figure 27-1 shows the classes covered in this chapter:

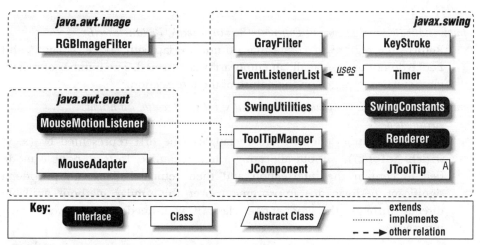

Figure 27-1. Class hierarchy for the utility classes

General Utilities

The general utilities presented here are meant for use with any part of your application. The static methods of the SwingUtilities class are called throughout the Swing source code and will probably be useful to you as well. You'll find a lot of these utilities fairly straightforward, and maybe even easy to reproduce with your own code. But try to familiarize yourself with these APIs; they're meant to keep you from reinventing wheels with each new application you write.

The SwingUtilities Class

This class serves as a collection point for several methods common in more advanced GUI development projects. You probably won't use all of the methods in any one application, but some of the methods will doubtless come in handy from time to time. While the purpose of many of these methods will be obvious from their signatures, here's a brief description of the utility calls at your disposal. If you want to see a more detailed discussion of the invokeLater() and invokeAnd-Wait() methods, check out Chapter 28, *Swing Under the Hood*.

Constructor

public SwingUtilities()

The constructor for SwingUtilities is public, but all of the public methods are static, so you will not need to create an instance.

Class Methods

public static Rectangle[] computeDifference(Rectangle rectA, Rectangle rectB)

Returns the regions in `rectA` that do not overlap with `rectB`. If `rectA` and `rectB` do not overlap at all, an empty array is returned. The number of rectangles returned depends on the nature of the intersection.

public static Rectangle computeIntersection(int x, int y, int width, int height,
Rectangle dest)

Returns the intersection of two rectangles (the first represented by (`x`, `y`, `width`, `height`)), without allocating a new rectangle. Instead, `dest` is modified to contain the intersection and then returned. This can provide a significant performance improvement over the similar methods available directly through the `Rectangle` class, if you need to do several such intersections.

public static int computeStringWidth(FontMetrics fm, String str)

Given a particular font metrics, this method returns the pixel length of the string `str`.

public static Rectangle computeUnion(int x, int y, int width, int height, Rectangle dest)

Returns the union of the rectangle represented by (`x`, `y`, `width`, `height`) and `dest`. As with `computeIntersection()`, `dest` is modified and returned; no new `Rectangle` object is allocated.

public static MouseEvent convertMouseEvent(Component source,
MouseEvent sourceEvent, Component destination)

Returns a new `MouseEvent`, based on `sourceEvent` with the (`x`, `y`) coordinates translated to `destination`'s coordinate system and the source of the event set as `destination`, provided destination is not `null`. If it is, `source` is set as the source for the new event. The actual translation of (`x`, `y`) is done with `convertPoint()`.

public static Point convertPoint(Component source, Point aPoint,
Component destination)
public static Point convertPoint(Component source, int x, int y,
Component destination)

Convert a point from the source coordinate system to the destination coordinate system. If either `source` or `destination` is `null`, the other component's root component coordinate system will be used. If both are `null`, the point is returned untranslated.

public static void convertPointFromScreen(Point p, Component c)

Converts a point on the screen, `p`, to a coordinate relative to the upper-left-hand corner of the component, `c`.

public static Component getRoot(Component c)

Returns the parent Window component, or the last applet to contain c if it is in a browser environment.

public static void convertPointToScreen(Point p, Component c)

Opposite of the previous method, this method takes a point, p, relative to the upper-left corner of the component, c, and converts it to a coordinate on the screen. Such a conversion makes light work of tiling popup windows.

public static Rectangle convertRectangle(Component source, Rectangle aRectangle, Component destination)

Translates aRectangle from the source coordinate system to the destination coordinate system, following the same rules as convertPoint().

public static Component findFocusOwner(Component c)

Returns the component at or below c that has the keyboard focus, if any. Because of security restrictions, this may not work for non-Swing components in applets.

public static Accessible getAccessibleAt(Component c, Point p)

Returns the Accessible component at point p (relative to the component c). If no such component exists, null is returned.

public static Accessible getAccessibleChild(Component c, int i)

Returns the ith accessible child of component c that implements the Accessible interface.

public static int getAccessibleChildrenCount(Component c)

Returns the number of accessible childern in component c that implements the Accessible interface.

public static int getAccessibleIndexInParent(Component c)

For a given component c, this method returns its index in its accessible parent. If the component does not have an accessible parent, –1 is returned.

public static AccessibleStateSet getAccessibleStateSet(Component c)

Returns the set of accessible states active for the component c.

public static Container getAncestorNamed(String name, Component comp)

Returns the first container named name that contains component comp. null is returned if name cannot be found.

public static Container getAncestorOfClass(Class c, Component comp)

Similar to getAncestorNamed(), this method returns the first container that is an instance of class c that contains component comp.

public static Component getDeepestComponentAt(Component parent, int x, int y)

Performs a recursive search through the component hierarchy starting at parent, and returns the last component containing the point (x, y). If parent is not a container, it is returned.

public static Rectangle getLocalBounds(Component aComponent)

Returns a rectangle containing aComponent relative to aComponent, i.e., (0, 0, width, height).

public static JRootPane getRootPane(Component c)

Finds the root pane containing c. If no JRootPane is found containing c, null is returned.

public static void invokeAndWait(Runnable obj) throws InterruptedException,
InvocationTargetException
public static void invokeLater(Runnable obj)

These methods take Runnable arguments and place them on the event queue to be executed after all pending events have been dispatched. The invoke-Later() method essentially just pushes this Runnable onto the event queue. The invokeAndWait() method pushes it onto the queue and blocks until it has been dispatched.

JComponent is an example of a Swing component that uses this technique of delayed execution. It delays revalidation of any layout components until any other events pending have been handled by calling invokeLater(). Some events rely on the location of their source to function properly (like tooltips), and moving the components before the event has been properly dispatched could cause confusion.

As mentioned earlier, Chapter 28 contains a more detailed discussion of these methods.

public static boolean isDescendingFrom(Component a, Component b)

Returns true if component a descends from b in the component hierarchy.

public static boolean isEventDispatchThread()

Returns true if the current thread is the event-dispatching thread.

public static boolean isLeftMouseButton(MouseEvent anEvent)
public static boolean isMiddleMouseButton(MouseEvent anEvent)
public static boolean isRightMouseButton(MouseEvent anEvent)

These convenience methods return true if anEvent was performed with the left, middle, or right mouse button, respectively.

public static final boolean isRectangleContainingRectangle(Rectangle a, Rectangle b)

Returns true if rectangle a completely contains rectangle b.

public static String layoutCompoundLabel(FontMetrics fm, String text, Icon icon,
int verticalAlignment, int horizontalAlignment, int verticalTextPosition,

int horizontalTextPosition, Rectangle viewR, Rectangle iconR, Rectangle textR,
int textIconGap)

Lays out a label with text and an icon, using the font metrics, alignments, and text positions supplied relative to the viewR rectangle. If text cannot be contained in the label, it is truncated and "..." is appended. The resulting string is returned; textR and iconR are updated to contain the coordinates required to accomplish the desired layout.

public static void paintComponent(Graphics g, Component c, Container p, int x, int y, int
w, int h)

public static void paintComponent(Graphics g, Component c, Container p, Rectangle r)

Paint the component c in an arbitrary graphics object g, bounded by the given rectangle, r. The container p is set as the new parent of c to stop the propagation of any validate() or repaint() calls to c. This is an easy way to rubber-stamp a component's image on a graphics area. For example, you might want to use this method in a tree or table cell renderer to draw "read-only" versions of components such as sliders. The image would look like a slider, but would just be an image, not a real component.

public static void updateComponentTreeUI(Component c)

Tells all components contained below c to update their current UI.

public static Window windowForComponent(Component aComponent)

This convenience method returns the Window object containing aComponent. If no containing window is found, null is returned.

The SwingConstants Interface

This interface defines the location constants shown in Table 0-1 that are used throughout the Swing package. Quite often, this interface is implemented by a component so that the constants appear as regular parts of the class for ease of use. (The JLabel and SwingUtilities classes are examples of such classes.)

Table 27-1. SwingConstants Constants

Constant	Type	Description
BOTTOM	int	Bottom location
CENTER	int	Center location or justification
EAST	int	East (compass) location
HORIZONTAL	int	Horizontal position or orientation
LEFT	int	Left location or justification
NORTH	int	North (compass) location
NORTH_EAST	int	Northeast (compass) location
NORTH_WEST	int	Northwest (compass) location

Table 27-1. SwingConstants Constants (continued)

Constant	Type	Description
RIGHT	int	Right location or justification
SOUTH	int	South (compass) location
SOUTH_EAST	int	Southeast (compass) location
SOUTH_WEST	int	Southwest (compass) location
TOP	int	Top location
VERTICAL	int	Vertical position or orientation
WEST	int	West (compass) location

The Timer Class

The Timer class behaves like an invisible component. It has properties and events, and thus can be used in application builders that understand JavaBeans. Its purpose is to fire an ActionEvent at a given time. The event can be set to repeat, and an optional initial delay can be set before the repeating event starts.

Properties

The Timer class properties give you access to the timer delays and nature of the event firing loops. They are listed in Table 27-2. The delay property dictates the length between repeated timer events (if repeats is true) and initialDelay determines how long to wait before starting the regular, repeating events. If your timer is not repeating, then the value of initialDelay determines when the timer fires its event. You can check to see if the timer is running with the running property. The coalesce property dictates whether or not the timer will combine pending events into one single event (to help listeners keep up). For example, if the timer fires a tick every 10 milliseconds, but the application is busy and has not handled events for 100 milliseconds, 10 action events are queued up for delivery. If coalesce is false, all 10 of these will be delivered in rapid succession. If coalesce is true (the default) only one event will be fired. The logTimers property can be turned on to generate simple debugging information to the standard output stream, each time an event is processed.

Table 27-2. Timer Propertiessv

Property	Data Type	get	is	set	bound	Default Value
delay	int	•		•		from constructor
coalesce	boolean		•	•		true
initialDelay	int	•		•		this.delay

Table 27-2. Timer Propertiesv (continued)

Property	Data Type	get	is	set	bound	Default Value
logTimers	boolean	•		•		false
repeats	boolean			•	•	true
running	boolean			•		false

Events

A `Timer` generates an `ActionEvent` whenever it "goes off." You can listen for `ActionEvent` if you want to react to a timer tick.

public void addActionListener(ActionListener l)
public void removeActionListener(ActionListener l)
Add and remove listeners interested in receiving action events from the timer.

The `Timer` class also contains its own `fireActionPerformed()` method to facilitate event reporting if you subclass `Timer`.

protected void fireActionPerformed(ActionEvent e)
Sends `ActionEvent` objects to any registered listeners.

Fields

protected EventListenerList listenerList
The list of listeners interested in receiving notification each time the timer generates an event.

Constructor

public Timer(int delay, ActionListener listener)
Creates a `Timer` object that notifies its `listener` every `delay` milliseconds. The `listener` argument can be `null`. The timer is not started right away; you must manually call the `start()` method.

Timer Control Methods

You also have a few methods to control the timer at runtime:

public void start()
Starts the timer. The first event comes after `initialDelay` milliseconds, and if it's a repeating timer, every `delay` seconds after that.

public void restart()
Restarts the timer. This method calls `stop()` and then `start()`.

public void stop()

> Stops the timer. Any timer events that have not yet been fired will be deleted.

Figure 27-2 shows a `ClockLabel` that updates itself every minute, using events from a `Timer`. The code to prouce our ticking label is remarkably short when we use a `Timer`.

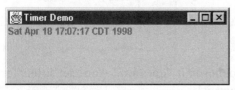

Figure 27-2. The Timer class in action with a ClockLabel

```
// ClockLabel.java
// An extension of the JLabel class that listens to events from
// a Timer object to update itself with the current date & time.
//
import java.util.*;
import java.awt.event.*;
import javax.swing.*;

public class ClockLabel extends JLabel implements ActionListener {

  public ClockLabel() {
    super("" + new Date());
    Timer t = new Timer(1000, this);
    t.start();
  }

  public void actionPerformed(ActionEvent ae) {
    setText("" + new Date());
  }
}
```

And here's the application that displays the `ClockLabel` object:

```
// ClockTest.java
// A demonstration framework for the Timer driven ClockLabel class.
//
import javax.swing.*;
import java.awt.*;

public class ClockTest extends JFrame {

  public ClockTest() {
    super("Timer Demo");
    setSize(300, 100);
    addWindowListener(new BasicWindowMonitor());
```

```
    ClockLabel clock = new ClockLabel();
    getContentPane().add(clock, BorderLayout.NORTH);
  }

  public static void main(String args[]) {
    ClockTest ct = new ClockTest();
    ct.setVisible(true);
  }
}
```

The ToolTipManager Class

This class manages the tooltips for an application. Any given virtual machine will have, at most, one ToolTipManager at any time—a new instance is created when the class is loaded. You can retrieve the current manager using the ToolTipManager.sharedInstance() method.

Properties

The ToolTipManager properties shown in Table 27-3 give you control over the delays (in milliseconds) involved in showing tooltips and determines whether or not tooltips are even active. The enabled property determines whether or not

Table 27-3. ToolTipManager Properties

Property	Data Type	get	is	set	bound	Default Value
dismissDelay	int	•		•		4000
enabled	boolean		•	•		true
initialDelay	int	•		•		750
lightWeightPopupEnabled[a]	boolean		•	•		true
reshowDelay	int	•		•		500

[a] Deprecated as of Swing 1.1/JDK1.2 beta4.

tooltips are active. The dismissDelay determines how long a tootip remains on the screen if you don't do something to dismiss it manually (such as move the mouse outside the component's borders). The initialDelay determines how long the mouse must rest inside a component before the tooltip pops up, and the reshowDelay determines how long you must wait after leaving a component before the same tooltip will show up again when you re-enter the component. If the lightWeightPopupEnabled property is true, all-Java tooltips will be used. A false value indicates native tooltips should be used.

Fields

protected boolean lightWeightPopupEnabled

Stores the value of the `lightWeightPopupEnabled` property. Deprecated in Swing 1.1/JDK1.2 beta4.

protected boolean heavyWeightPopupEnabled

This field is used to help manage heavyweight (not bound by window constraints) tooltips. It is initially set to `false`.

Mouse Event Methods

public void mouseDragged(MouseEvent event)

This method is empty. (By definition, you can't drag a tool tip.)

public void mouseEntered(MouseEvent event)

Gets the system ready to show the tooltip text (if any exists) in `initialDelay` milliseconds.

public void mouseExited(MouseEvent event)

Checks to make sure you're really exiting the component (you could be mousing out of the component but into the tooltip, for example), and if so, hides the popup and starts the reshow countdown.

public void mouseMoved(MouseEvent event)

Monitors your movements and keeps tips active as you move from one component to the next (so that they show up immediately).

public void mousePressed(MouseEvent event)

Hides the popup and stops the timer watching for the `initialDelay` to pass.

Miscellaneous Methods

If need be, you can manually register or unregister components with the manager. Normally this is done using the `JComponent.setToolTipText()` method for the component itself. If you pass in a non-`null` tip string, the component is registered. If you pass in a `null` tip string, the component is unregistered.

public void registerComponent(JComponent component)

Registers `component` with the `ToolTipManager` to make sure that its tips get shown after an appropriate mouse event occurs.

public static ToolTipManager sharedInstance()

Returns the global `ToolTipManager`. You can use this to get access to the manager and changes its delay properties. For example, you could cut the initial delay to 250 milliseconds like this:

```
ToolTipManager.sharedInstance().setInitialDelay(250);
```

public void unregisterComponent(JComponent component)

Unregisters `component` from the `ToolTipManager`. Tooltips will no longer be shown for this component.

The JToolTip Class

Of course, the whole purpose of having a tooltip manager is to manage tooltips. The tooltips themselves are simple popups containing a short, descriptive string that often shows up if you let your mouse cursor rest too long over a component. They are embodied here in the `JToolTip` class. `JToolTip` is a fairly simple class, thanks to the MVC architecture in place for Swing. All it really needs to know is what text to display, and who to display it for.

Properties

The properties that support the `JToolTip` class are shown in Table 27-4. The `component` property determines which component this tip applies to. The `tipText` property contains the text to display for the tip. Both of these properties are currently stored in package private variables.

Table 27-4. JToolTip Properties

Property	Data Type	get	is	set	bound	Default Value
UI*	TreeUI	•		•	•	From L&F
UIClassID*	String	•				"ToolTipUI"
accessibleContext	Accessible-Context	•				JToolTip.Accessible-JToolTip()
component	Component	•		•		null
tipText	String	•		•		null

Constructor

The `JToolTip` class has only one constructor:

public JToolTip()

This creates a new `JToolTip` object with no text or component association.

UI Method

public void updateUI()

As with all of the other Swing components, this method updates the look-and-feel for the tooltip based on the UIManager.

Editing and Rendering Utilities

Both the JTree and JTable classes make use of cell renderers to display cells and cell editors to modify cell values. The CellEditor interface is the basis for these editors, and the DefaultCellEditor class provides a good implementation of this interface. Unless you're doing something exotic, you should be able to base your cell editors on the DefaultCellEditor class.

The CellRendererPane Class

This utility class was built to keep renderers from propagating repaint() and validate() calls to the components using renderer components such as JTree and JList. If you played around with creating your own renderers for any of the Swing components that use them, you'll recall that you did not use this class yourself. Normally this pane is wrapped around the renderer and the paintComponent() methods below are used to do the actual drawing. Developers will not normally need to worry about this class.

Property

The CellRendererPane has only one property containing its accessible context, shown in Table 27-5.

Table 27-5. CellRendererPane Property

Property	Data Type	get	is	set	bound	Default Value
accessibleContext	AccessibleContext	•				CellRenderer-Pane.AccessibleCell-RendererPane()

Field

protected AccessibleContext accessibleContext
   This field supports the accessibleContext property.

Constructor

This class has only one constructor.

public CellRendererPane()
   This constructor creates a new renderer pane that has a null layout and is not initially visible.

Methods

protected void addImpl(Component x, Object constraints, int index)
public void invalidate()
public void paint(Graphics g)
public void update(Graphics g)

These overridden `Container` methods ensure the editor pane behaves properly and does not adversely affect the component using the editor or the editor itself. The `paint()` and `update()` methods are both empty and the documentation states that they should not be called.

public void paintComponent(Graphics g, Component c, Container p, Rectangle r)
public void paintComponent(Graphics g, Component c, Container p, int x, int y, int w,
    int h)
public void paintComponent(Graphics g, Component c, Container p, int x, int y, int w,
    int h, boolean shouldValidate)

These methods do the actual work of painting the component c on the graphics context g. These methods provide the implementation for the methods of the same signatures in the `SwingUtilities` class, discussed previously in this chapter. The `shouldValidate` parameter determines whether or not c is validated before it is painted. (The first two methods end up calling the third with a false value for shouldValidate.)

Inner Classes

protected class CellRendererPane.AccessibleCellRendererPane extends AccessibleContext
    implements Serializable, AccessibleComponent

This class defines the accessible role object for `CellRendererPane`.

The CellEditor Interface

This interface governs the basic functionality required of an editor. It has methods for retrieving a new value and determining when to start and stop editing. The basic process for editing is:

- The user clicks the required number of times on the cell (varies from editor to editor).

- The component (usually `JTree` or `JTable`) replaces the cell with its editor.

- The user types or chooses a new value.

- The user ends the editing session (e.g., hitting enter in a textfield).

- The editor fires a change event to interested listeners (usually the tree or table containing the cell), stating that editing is finished.

- The component reads the new value and replaces the editor with the cell's renderer.

Events

The CellEditor interface requires methods for adding and removing cell editor listeners, which are objects interested in finding out whether editing is finished or cancelled. The CellEditorListener class is discussed below.

public abstract void addCellEditorListener(CellEditorListener l)
public abstract void removeCellEditorListener(CellEditorListener l)

Methods

public Object getCellEditorValue()

Accesses the only property of a cell editor, which is the cell's current value. After successful editing, a table or tree will call this method to retrieve the new value for the cell.

public abstract boolean isCellEditable(EventObject anEvent)

Should return true if anEvent is a valid trigger for starting this kind of editor. For example, if you want the user to double click on a field to invoke the editor, this method would test whether anEvent is a double click mouse event. If it was only a single click, you could return false. If it was a double click, you could return true.

public abstract boolean shouldSelectCell(EventObject anEvent)

This method should return true if the cell to be edited should also be selected. While you usually want to select the cell, there are some situations in which not selecting the cell is preferable. For example, you might be implementing a table that lets the user edit cells that are part of an ongoing selection. Since you want the selection to remain in place, you would implement this method to return false. The cell can still be edited.

public abstract boolean stopCellEditing()
public abstract void cancelCellEditing()

You should use these methods to tell the editor to stop editing the cell. The stopCellEditing() method indicates that editing is over and the new value supplied should replace the old value of the cell. The cancelCellEditing() method indicates editing is over and the new value the user entered (if any) should be ignored. The stopCellEditing() method can return a false value if the editor is unable to stop editing. (This might occur if your editor validates input and currently contains an invalid entry.) As an example, you can use these to programmatically stop or cancel editing before starting to edit another cell or upon losing focus.

The CellEditorListener Interface

The `CellEditorListener` interface defines how an object can listen for events generated by a cell editor. Cell editors generate a `ChangeEvent` when editing is canceled or stopped (a better term might be "finished"). Typically, the object "hosting" the editor (for example, a `JTree` allowing the user to enter a new filename) would register as a listener. When the event occurs, the `JTree` would read the cell's new value from the editor, tear down the editor, and repaint the cell with its new value.

public void editingStopped(ChangeEvent e)

Indicates successful editing has been completed. You can get the new value of the cell from the editor component, which is contained in the `source` property of the change event.

public void editingCanceled(ChangeEvent e)

Indicates that editing has been canceled. You should ignore any partially edited value that might be present in the editor.

The DefaultCellEditor Class

Swing provides a default editor with a fair amount of flexibility. The `Default-CellEditor` class implements the `CellEditor` interface and provides constructors that let you use a text field, check box, or combo box for entering the new value.

Properties

The `DefaultCellEditor` class contains the properties listed in Table 27-6. The `cellEditorValue` property contains the value of the cell editor. This value can be used or ignored when editing stops, depending on whether editing is stopped or canceled. The `clickCountToStart` property determines how many clicks it takes to begin editing a cell. For checkboxes and combo boxes, that values is 1; for text fields, the default value of this property is 2, meaning that the user has to double click to start editing. The `component` property contains the actual component that the cell editor returns when `getTableCellEditorComponent()` or `getTree-CellEditorComponent()` is called.

Events

As dictated by the `CellEditor` interface, the `DefaultCellEditor` class implements the add and remove methods for cell editor listeners. It also provides these convenience methods for generating those events.

Table 27-6. DefaultCellEditor Properties

Property	Data Type	get	is	set	bound	Default Value
cellEditorValue*	Object	•				null
clickCountToStart	int	•		•		Determined by constructor
component	Component	•				Determined by constructor

protected void fireEditingStopped()
protected void fireEditingCanceled()

> Both of these methods notify registered listeners that editing has stopped. The cell editor is listed as the source of these events.

Constructors

You can create your own cell editor using any of the following constructors. You can pre-configure any of the components you pass in as well. For example, you might pass in a right-justified text field or a checkbox with custom icons.

public DefaultCellEditor(JTextField x)
public DefaultCellEditor(JCheckBox x)
public DefaultCellEditor(JComboBox x)

Fields

protected EventListenerList listenerList
protected transient ChangeEvent changeEvent

> These fields support the cell edit events generated by the editor. The `listenerList` field stores the list of all registered listeners interested in hearing about stop or cancel events. The `changeEvent` field holds the single change event passed to listeners when events are fired.

protected JComponent editorComponent

> This field contains the value for the `component` property.

protected DefaultCellEditor.EditorDelegate delegate

> This field contains a wrapped reference to the editor component. The `EditorDelegate` inner class delegates calls such as `isCellEditable()` to the component it contains, but also listens for events that indicate editing has stopped. For the three possible types of editors, a "stop event" from the contained component would be either an action event for text fields, or an item event for checkboxes and combo boxes.

protected int clickCountToStart

> This field stores the value for the `clickCountToStart` property.

Tree and Table Editor Methods

Most of the methods in `DefaultCellEditor` are implementations of the `CellEditor` methods. The only other methods in the `DefaultCellEditor` class that are new are the methods required to implement the `TableCellEditor` and `TreeCellEditor` interfaces.

public Component getTreeCellEditorComponent(JTree tree, Object value, boolean isSelected,
   boolean expanded, boolean leaf, int row)
   Returns a valid tree cell editor and is discussed in more detail in Chapter 17,
   Trees.

public Component getTableCellEditorComponent(JTable table, Object value, boolean
   isSelected, int row, int column)
   Returns a valid table cell editor and is discussed in more detail in Chapter 15,
   Tables.

Event Utilities

If you extend one of the Swing components to add functionality, or indeed, build your own component from scratch, you need to handle event listeners for any events you might generate. The `EventListenerList` class is designed to aid in that task. This class is similar in many ways to the `AWTEventMulticaster`; however, it supports any type of listener and assumes you'll use only the appropriate listeners for a given event type. Unlike the AWT multicaster, it does not assume all of the listeners support the same events.

The `KeyStroke` class can also help handle keyboard events. Rather than listening to every key that gets pressed and throwing out the things you don't care about, you can use the `KeyStroke` class to register specific actions with specific keys.

The EventListenerList Class

If your component generates events, it must contain methods to add and remove interested listeners. Following the JavaBeans design patterns, these are the `add`*Type*`Listener()` and `remove`*Type*`Listener()` methods. Typically you store the listeners in a vector, and then use the vector as a rollcall for who to send events to when the time comes. This is a very common task for components that generate events, and the `EventListenerList` can help lift some (but certainly not all) of the burden of coding the event firing.

The `EventListenerList` stores listeners as pairs of objects, one object to hold the listener's type and one to hold the listener itself. At any time, you can retrieve all of the current listeners as an array of `Objects` and use that array to fire off any events you need.

Here is a `SecretLabel` class that extends `JLabel` and fires `ActionEvent` messages when clicked. The label does not give any indication it has been clicked, hence its secret nature. The code for this label demonstrates how an `EventListenerList` is typically used. Figure 27-3 shows the `SecretLabel` up and running.

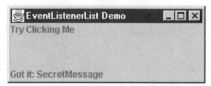

Figure 27-3. A JLabel that uses an EventListenerList to facilitate dispatching events

We set up the standard `addActionListener()` and `removeActionListener()` methods, which delegate to the listener list, and pass in the type of listener we're attaching. (Recall that `EventListenerList` can store any type of listener.) When we actually fire an event, we search the listener list array, checking the even-numbered indices for a particular type of listener. If we find the right type (`ActionListener`, in this case) we use the next entry in the list as an event recipient. You can find other such examples throughout the Swing package in such models as `DefaultTreeModel`, `DefaultTableModel`, and `DefaultButtonModel`.

The `EventListenerList` provides a generic dispatcher that works in just about every situation. However, it is not the only way to dispatch events. For a particular application you may find a more efficient means.

```
// SecretLabel.java
// An extension of the JLabel class that listens to mouse clicks and converts
// them to ActionEvents, in turn are reported via an EventListenersList object.
//
import java.awt.*;
import java.awt.event.*;
import javax.swing.*;

public class SecretLabel extends JLabel implements MouseListener {

  public SecretLabel(String msg) {
    super(msg);
    addMouseListener(this);
  }

  public void addActionListener(ActionListener l) {
    // We'll just use the listenerList we inherit from JComponent
    listenerList.add(ActionListener.class, l);
  }
```

```
  public void removeActionListener(ActionListener l) {
    listenerList.remove(ActionListener.class, l);
  }

  public void mouseClicked(MouseEvent me) {
    fireActionPerformed(new ActionEvent(this, ActionEvent.ACTION_PERFORMED,
                                "SecretMessage"));
  }

  public void mousePressed(MouseEvent me) {}
  public void mouseReleased(MouseEvent me) {}
  public void mouseEntered(MouseEvent me) {}
  public void mouseExited(MouseEvent me) {}

  protected void fireActionPerformed(ActionEvent ae) {
    Object[] listeners = listenerList.getListenerList();
    for (int i = listeners.length - 2; i >= 0; i--) {
      if (listeners[i] == ActionListener.class) {
        ((ActionListener)listeners[i+1]).actionPerformed(ae);
      }
    }
  }
}
```

Our addActionListener() and removeActionListener() methods just defer to a listener list to register and unregister listeners. We don't have to do anything special to get an EventListenerList; we're extending JLabel, and therefore inherit a listenerList field from JComponent. fireActionPerformed() does the actual work; it calls the actionPerformed() method of every action listener stored in the listener list. Note that we walk through the array of listeners two at a time; as we'll see below, the elements in this array alternate between Class objects that tell us what kind of listener we have, and the actual listener objects themselves. Figure 27-4 shows how the array is set up.

And here's the application that creates the SecretLabel and hooks it up to the reporting label. We use the same addActionListener() that we would for things like buttons or lists:

```
// SecretTest.java
// A demonstration framework for the EventListenerList-enabled SecretLabel class.
//
import javax.swing.*;
import java.awt.event.*;
import java.awt.*;

public class SecretTest extends JFrame {
```

```
    public SecretTest() {
      super("EventListenerList Demo");
      setSize(200, 100);
      addWindowListener(new BasicWindowMonitor());

      SecretLabel secret = new SecretLabel("Try Clicking Me");
      final JLabel reporter = new JLabel("Event reports will show here...");
      secret.addActionListener(new ActionListener() {
        public void actionPerformed(ActionEvent ae) {
          reporter.setText("Got it: " + ae.getActionCommand());
        }
      } );
      getContentPane().add(secret, BorderLayout.NORTH);
      getContentPane().add(reporter, BorderLayout.SOUTH);
    }

    public static void main(String args[]) {
      SecretTest st = new SecretTest();
      st.setVisible(true);
    }
}
```

If you have set up your own event source components before, the EventListenerList class may not seem to provide much improvement. But, as the documentation points out, it provides a single access point for serializing your list of listeners.

Field

protected transient java.lang.Object[] listenerList

This field holds the list of class types and listeners.

Constructor

public EventListenerList()

Creates a new listener list.

Listener Methods

public synchronized void add(Class t, EventListener l)

Adds a new listener to the list of listeners. It is synchronized, in an effort to make this class as thread-safe as possible.

public int getListenerCount()
public int getListenerCount(Class t)

Return a count of how many listeners are contained in the list. If a Class argument is provided, you get the number of listeners of that type in the list.

public Object[] getListenerList()

> Returns an array of objects organized as in Figure 27-4. The listener type entry is always a `Class` object. You typically work through this array in increments (or decrements) of 2.

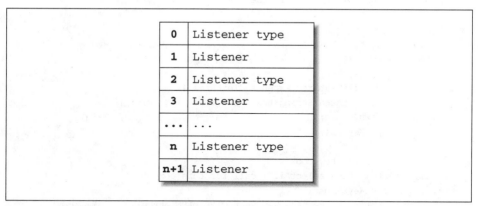

0	Listener type
1	Listener
2	Listener type
3	Listener
...	...
n	Listener type
n+1	Listener

Figure 27-4. The EventListenerList object array structure

public synchronized remove(Class t, EventListener l)

> Removes a listener from the list of listeners. It is synchronized, in an effort to make this class as thread-safe as possible.

The KeyStroke Class

Another convenient class for dealing with events is the `KeyStroke` class. This class allows you to associate actions with particular events through the `KeyMap` class. Figure 27-5 shows an example of a `JTextArea` with support for the "CTRL-A" select-all action, using a `KeyStroke`.

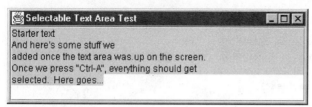

Figure 27-5. A text area with support for a "Select All" keyboard shortcut

Here's the code that created the selectable text area. With the help of the `AbstractAction` class and the `selectAll()` method in `JTextComponent`, the code is very simple. We get the `KeyMap` for the text area and add in an association between the CTRL-A keystroke and the `selectAll()` method using the `addActionForKeyStroke()` method. The `getKeyStroke()` call gives us the correct key-stroke, and the call to the `selectAll()` is encapsulated in the `Action` object. It doesn't take much code:

```
// SelectableTextArea
// A class that extends JTextArea and supports the common Ctrl-A shortcut
// for selecting all of the text in the field.
//
import java.awt.event.*;
import javax.swing.*;
import javax.swing.text.*;

public class SelectableTextArea extends JTextArea {
  public SelectableTextArea(String text, int rows, int cols) {
    super(text, rows, cols);
    Keymap km = getKeymap();

    // get the "Ctrl-A" key code
    // and attach it to a selectAll() call for this component
    km.addActionForKeyStroke(
      KeyStroke.getKeyStroke('A', KeyEvent.CTRL_MASK, true),
      new AbstractAction() {
        public void actionPerformed(ActionEvent ae) {
          SelectableTextArea.this.selectAll();
        }
      }
    );
  }
}
```

And the application that puts this text area to use is also straightforward:

```
// SelectableTest.java
// A test of the SelectableTextArea class.
//
import javax.swing.*;
import java.awt.BorderLayout;

public class SelectableTest extends JFrame {

  public SelectableTest() {
    super("Selectable Text Area Test");
    setSize(400, 300);
    addWindowListener(new BasicWindowMonitor());

    SelectableTextArea sta = new SelectableTextArea("Starter text", 8, 40);
    getContentPane().add(sta, BorderLayout.CENTER);
  }

  public static void main(String args[]) {
    SelectableTest st = new SelectableTest();
```

```
    st.setVisible(true);
  }
}
```

Properties

The KeyStroke class contains the properties shown in Table 27-7. The keyChar property is the character this keystroke represents, such as A or $. The keyCode property is the int value associated with a particular key on your keyboard. This might be the ASCII value of a letter, or some other value associated with a function key. The modifiers property contains information on whether or not any of the modifier keys (Control, Alt, Meta, Shift) are attached to this keystroke. The acceptable key codes come from the java.awt.event. KeyEvent class and are shown in Table 27-8. The onKeyRelease property determines when events associated with this keystroke should be triggered. A true value treats the keystroke as a keyTyped() event, while a false value behaves like keyPressed() event.

Table 27-7. KeyStroke Properties

Property	Data Type	get	is	set	bound	Default Value
keyChar	char	•				"\0"
keyCode	int	•				0
modifiers	int	•				0
onKeyRelease	boolean			•		false

Key Codes

Just for your reference, here's a table of the valid key codes from the java.awt.event.KeyEvent class. You'll notice that many of the key code values correspond to the ASCII value of the character associated with the key. This facilitates coding for the common keys, because you can use shortcuts like 'R' instead of KeyEvent.VK_R wherever a key code is expected. Of course, as a good programmer, you always use the constant, right? (We left out character equivalents that were not related to the VK key.)

Instantiation Methods

The KeyStroke class does not have a constructor. All keystrokes are cached for you. You can use any of the following static methods (listed after the table) to retrieve the appropriate instance you're looking for.

Table 27-8. Valid Key Codes for Use with KeyStroke

KeyEvent Constant	Decimal Value	Hexadecimal Value	char equivalent	KeyEvent Constant	Decimal Value	Hexadecimal Value	char equivalent
VK_0	48	0x30	"0"	VK_X	88	0x58	"X"
VK_1	49	0x31	"1"	VK_Y	89	0x59	"Y"
VK_2	50	0x32	"2"	VK_Z	90	0x5a	"Z"
VK_3	51	0x33	"3"	VK_ACCEPT	30	0x1e	
VK_4	52	0x34	"4"	VK_ADD	107	0x6b	
VK_5	53	0x35	"5"	VK_ALT	18	0x12	
VK_6	54	0x36	"6"	VK_BACK_QUOTE	192	0xc0	
VK_7	55	0x37	"7"	VK_BACK_SLASH	92	0x5c	"\\"
VK_8	56	0x38	"8"	VK_BACK_SPACE	8	0x08	"\b"
VK_9	57	0x39	"9"	VK_CANCEL	3	0x03	
VK_A	65	0x41	"A"	VK_CAPS_LOCK	20	0x14	
VK_B	66	0x42	"B"	VK_CLEAR	12	0x0c	
VK_C	67	0x43	"C"	VK_CLOSE_BRACKET	93	0x5d	"]"
VK_D	68	0x44	"D"	VK_COMMA	44	0x2c	","
VK_E	69	0x45	"E"	VK_CONTROL	17	0x11	
VK_F	70	0x46	"F"	VK_CONVERT	28	0x1c	
VK_G	71	0x47	"G"	VK_DECIMAL	110	0x6e	
VK_H	72	0x48	"H"	VK_DELETE	127	0x7f	
VK_I	73	0x49	"I"	VK_DIVIDE	111	0x6f	
VK_J	74	0x4a	"J"	VK_DOWN	40	0x28	
VK_K	75	0x4b	"K"	VK_END	35	0x23	
VK_L	76	0x4c	"L"	VK_ENTER	10	0x0a	"\n"
VK_M	77	0x4d	"M"	VK_EQUALS	61	0x3d	"="
VK_N	78	0x4e	"N"	VK_ESCAPE	27	0x1b	
VK_O	79	0x4f	"O"	VK_F1	112	0x70	
VK_P	80	0x50	"P"	VK_F2	113	0x71	
VK_Q	81	0x51	"Q"	VK_F3	114	0x72	
VK_R	82	0x52	"R"	VK_F4	115	0x73	
VK_S	83	0x53	"S"	VK_F5	116	0x74	
VK_T	84	0x54	"T"	VK_F6	117	0x75	
VK_U	85	0x55	"U"	VK_F7	118	0x76	
VK_V	86	0x56	"V"	VK_F8	119	0x77	
VK_W	87	0x57	"W"	VK_F9	120	0x78	

Table 27-8. Valid Key Codes for Use with KeyStroke (continued)

KeyEvent Constant	Decimal Value	Hexadecimal Value	char equivalent	KeyEvent Constant	Decimal Value	Hexadecimal Value	char equivalent
VK_F10	121	0x79		VK_NUMPAD7	103	0x67	
VK_F11	122	0x7a		VK_NUMPAD8	104	0x68	
VK_F12	123	0x7b		VK_NUMPAD9	105	0x69	
VK_FINAL	24	0x18		VK_OPEN_BRACKET	91	0x5b	"["
VK_HELP	156	0x9c		VK_PAGE_DOWN	34	0x22	
VK_HOME	36	0x24		VK_PAGE_UP	33	0x21	
VK_INSERT	155	0x9b		VK_PAUSE	19	0x13	
VK_KANA	21	0x15		VK_PERIOD	46	0x2e	"."
VK_KANJI	25	0x19		VK_PRINTSCREEN	154	0x9a	
VK_LEFT	37	0x25		VK_QUOTE	222	0xde	
VK_META	157	0x9d		VK_RIGHT	39	0x27	
VK_MODECHANGE	31	0x1f		VK_SCROLL_LOCK	145	0x91	
VK_MULTIPLY	106	0x6a		VK_SEMICOLON	59	0x3b	";"
VK_NONCONVERT	29	0x1d		VK_SEPARATER	108	0x6c	
VK_NUM_LOCK	144	0x90		VK_SHIFT	16	0x10	
VK_NUMPAD0	96	0x60		VK_SLASH	47	0x2f	"/"
VK_NUMPAD1	97	0x61		VK_SPACE	32	0x20	" "
VK_NUMPAD2	98	0x62		VK_SUBTRACT	109	0x6d	
VK_NUMPAD3	99	0x63		VK_TAB	9	0x09	"\t"
VK_NUMPAD4	100	0x64		VK_UNDEFINED	0	0x00	
VK_NUMPAD5	101	0x65		VK_UP	38	0x26	
VK_NUMPAD6	102	0x66					

public static KeyStroke getKeyStroke(char keyChar)

public static KeyStroke getKeyStroke(char keyChar, boolean onKeyRelease)

Return the `KeyStroke` that represents a character, such as `'A'`. The `onKeyRelease` argument determines whether actions associated with this keystroke are triggered when the key is pressed (`false`) or when it is released (`true`).

public static KeyStroke getKeyStroke(int keyCode, int modifiers)

public static KeyStroke getKeyStroke(int keyCode, int modifiers,
*   boolean onKeyRelease)*

Return the `KeyStroke` that represents a given key code and modifier combination. As with the previous `getKeyStroke()` methods, the `onKeyRelease` argument determines when to fire associated actions.

public static KeyStroke getKeyStroke(String representation)

>   Returns a `KeyStroke` from the given representation of the keystroke. This has not been implemented as of the JDK 1.2 beta 4 release.

public static KeyStroke getKeyStrokeForEvent(KeyEvent anEvent)

>   Extracts a `KeyStroke` from `anEvent`.

Overriden Object Methods

`KeyStroke` overrides the following methods from `Object` to make them more suitable to the `KeyStroke` class:

public int hashCode()

>   This method provides, as the documentation puts it, a "reasonably unique" hash code for putting `KeyStroke` objects into hash tables.

public boolean equals(Object anObject)

>   Compares all of the `KeyStroke` properties to determine if two keystrokes are equivalent.

public String toString()

>   Produces a string equivalent of the `KeyStroke` object. The `modifiers` and `onKeyRelease` properties are represented as appropriate.

The MouseInputAdapter Class

This simple implementation of the `MouseInputListener` interface (which is itself just a conglomeration of the `MouseListener` and `MouseMotionListener` interfaces) provides empty methods for each of the mouse event handlers. You can use this abstract convenience class like any other adapter, extending it and overriding only the methods that interest you. This one simply has the benefit of handling both mouse and mouse motion events.

Methods

public void mouseClicked(MouseEvent e)
public void mousePressed(MouseEvent e)
public void mouseReleased(MouseEvent e)
public void mouseEntered(MouseEvent e)
public void mouseExited(MouseEvent e)

>   These methods come from the `MouseListener` interface. All have empty implementations.

public void mouseDragged(MouseEvent e)
public void mouseMoved(MouseEvent e)

> These methods come from the `MouseMotionListener` interface. Both have empty implementations.

The SwingPropertyChangeSupport Class

Many Swing components support bound properties as defined by the JavaBeans specification. In the `java.beans` package, a utility class called `PropertyChange-Support` is defined to help you register property change listeners and fire property change events. The `PropertyChangeSupport` class does this work in a thread-safe manner that consumes a good bit of memory. The `SwingProperty-ChangeSupport` class provides exactly the same set of features, but does so without thread-safety to reduce memory usage and increase performance. If you're building your own components, you can use this class instead of `Property-ChangeSupport`. (For more information on JavaBeans and bound properties, check out O'Reilly's Developing Java Beans, by Robert Englander.)

Constructor

public SwingPropertyChangeSupport(Object sourceBean)

> This constructor creates a new `SwingPropertyChangeSupport` object with a reference to `sourceBean` kept for use in reporting events. The `sourceBean` will be listed as the source for all property change events coming from this support object.

Methods

public void addPropertyChangeListener(PropertyChangeListener listener)
public void addPropertyChangeListener(String propertyName, PropertyChangeListener
> *listener)*

public void removePropertyChangeListener(PropertyChangeListener listener)
public void removePropertyChangeListener(String propertyName, PropertyChangeListener
> *listener)*

> Add and remove `PropertyChangeListener` objects interested in receiving property change events. If you give a `propertyName`, only changes to the specified property will be reported.

public void firePropertyChange(String propertyName, Object oldValue, Object newValue)

> Creates a new `PropertyChangeEvent` object from `propertyName`, `oldValue` and `newValue`, then it fires it to any registered listeners.

public void firePropertyChange(PropertyChangeEvent evt)

> Fires an existing `PropertyChangeEvent`, evt, to any registered listeners.

public boolean hasListeners(String propertyName)

> Returns true if there are any listeners registered for the given proper-tyName. If a generic listener is present, this method returns true, regardless of whether or not any specific property listeners exist.

Image Utilities

The last category of utility classes to look at is image utilities. The Swing package contains a class that can come in handy for generating images.

The GrayFilter Class

The GrayFilter class is an extension of the java.awt.image.RGBImageFilter class. This class contains a static method that returns a "disabled" version of an image passed in. The image is converted to a grayscale version, and some lighter parts of the image are amplified to ensure the image is recognizable. All of the components that can display images use this class to present a default disabled version of the image if an explicit disabled image was not provided.

Constructors

public GrayFilter(boolean brighter, int percent)

> Creates an instance of the GrayFilter class that you can use to do your own filtering. (Normally you don't call this, but use createDisabledImage() instead.) Both the brighter and percent arguments are used to convert color pixels to appropriately shaded gray pixels.

Image Methods

public static Image createDisabledImage(Image i)

> Use this method to retrieve a grayed-out version of the image i. This method creates an instance of the GrayFilter class with brighter turned on and a gray percent of 50.

public int filterRGB(int x, int y, int rgb)

> Overrides the filterRGB() method in RGBImageFilter, converts the rgb pixel to a gray pixel, and returns that.

The Renderer Interface

The Swing package includes a Renderer interface with the following methods:

public Component getComponent()

> Returns a Component you can use with something like the SwingUtili-ties.paintComponent() method to draw the component.

public void setValue(Object aValue, boolean isSelected)
>   This method can initialize the rendering component to reflect the state of the
>   object aValue.

This interface could be useful if you were to create a library of renderers for use
with your own applications; however, it is not implemented anywhere in the Swing
package as of the JDK1.2 beta4 release.

28

• **Creating Your Own Component**
• **Working with Focus**
• **Lightweight vs. Heavyweight Components**
• **Multithreading Issues with Swing**
• **Painting and Repainting**

Swing Under the Hood

Roughly halfway through writing this book, we sent mail to several Java newsgroups asking what sort of topics you, the Swing developers, would really like to see explained in more detail. We received a tidal wave of responses, many about a variety of arcane Swing topics. Of those that were not covered elsewhere in the book, most of the replies revolved around the same five areas:

- Creating your own Swing component

- Dealing with the Swing focus manager, and writing your own focus manager

- Mixing lightweight and heavyweight (Swing and AWT) components in Swing

- Multithreading issues in Swing

- The Swing `RepaintManager`

So, in response to your requests, we offer this loose collection of tips, tricks, and things that made us cry "Eureka!" at about two in the morning. Since many of these topics had little or no documentation when Swing was created, the three of us had to dig through the Swing source code much more than normal to answer these questions. Hence, we call this chapter *Swing Under the Hood*.

Creating Your Own Component

So you've been bitten by the bug. There isn't a component anywhere in the Swing library that fits your needs, and you've decided that it's time to write your own. Unfortunately, you're dreading the prospect of creating one, because either you've heard somewhere that it is a complex task, or your jaw is still bouncing on the floor after browsing through some of the Swing component source code.

This section helps to dispel those fears. Creating your own component isn't hard—just extend the `JComponent` class with one of your own and away you go!

On the other hand, getting it to behave or even display itself correctly can take a bit of patience and fine tuning. As such, we've provided a step-by-step guide below as an aid to wary programmers that keep running into those hidden "gotchas" when creating their own components.

Remember that when creating Swing components, it's always preferable to create one that adheres to the JavaBeans standards. Not only can your component be used programmatically, but it can also be inserted into one of a variety of GUI-builder tools that are prevalent in the market. Therefore, whenever possible, we try to highlight areas that you can work on to make your components more Java-Beans friendly.

Creating the Component

First things first. If you haven't already, you should read through the JComponent section of Chapter 3, *Swing Component Basics*. This will help you get a feel of what sort of features you can expect in a Swing component, and which ones you might want to use (or even disable) in your own component. If you are creating a component that is intended as a container, be sure to glance at the overview sections on focus managers and layout managers as well.* Remember that you can use any layout manager with a Swing component, including those from AWT as well as a few new layout managers exclusively in Swing.

After you've done that, you're ready to start. Let's go through some steps that will help you pound out that component idea into workable Swing code.

You Should Have a Model and a UI Delegate

If you really want to develop your idea into a true Swing component, you should adhere to the MVC-based architecture of Swing. This means defining models and UI delegates for each component. Recall that the model is in charge of storing the state information for the component. Models typically implement their own model interface, which outlines the accessors and methods that the model must support. The UI delegate is responsible for painting the component and handling any input events that are generated. The UI-delegate object always extends the Compo- nentUI class, which is the base class for all UI-delegate objects. Finally, the component class itself extends the abstract JComponent, and ties together the model and the delegate.

Figure 28-1 shows the key classes and interfaces that are involved in creating a Swing component. The shaded boxes indicate items that the programmer must

---

* This is sort of confusing. Because of the class hierarchy of JComponent, all classes that extend it are capable of acting as containers. For example, it is legal to add a JProgressBar to a JSlider. Clearly, the slider is not meant to act as a container, but Swing will allow it nevertheless . . . with undefined results.

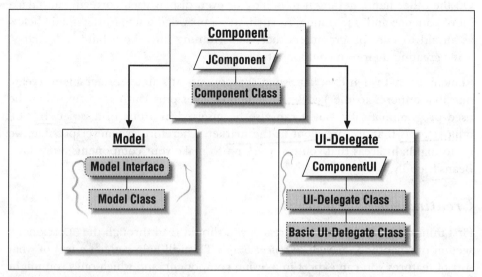

Figure 28-1. The three parts of a Swing component

provide. This includes the model, the basic UI delegate and its type class, and an implementation of the component to bundle the model and UI delegate pieces together. Finally, you may need to create your own model interface if one does not exist that is suitable to your needs.

If you wish to support multiple look-and-feels with your component, you may consider breaking your UI-delegate class down into an abstract implementation of functionality that is independent of look-and-feel (such as those classes found in `javax.swing.plaf.basic`), as well as functionality specific to each look-and-feel (such as those in the `javax.swing.plaf.metal` package or the `com.sun.java.swing.plaf.motif` package). Some common functionality that you might find in the former is the ability to handle various mouse or keyboard events, while painting and sizing the component is typically the domain of the latter. See Chapter 26, *Look & Feel*, for more details on look-and-feels.

So now that we know what we have to build, let's continue our discussion with a look at each one, starting with the model.

Creating a Model

The model of the object is responsible for storing the state data of the component. Models are not hard to build, but they are not necessarily easy either. Here are some important tips to think about when working with models.

Reuse or Extend Existing Models Whenever Possible

This is sound advice. Creating a data model from scratch looks trivial, but it typically takes more time and effort than most people think. Remember that good models are abstractions of component state, and are often capable of representing more than one type of component. For example, the BoundedRangeModel serves the JSlider, JProgressBar, and JScrollBar components. In addition, models are responsible for storing event listeners, handling synchronization issues, and firing property change events to the components that use them.

A great deal of time was spent in creating the individual models for the Swing components. And because they are central to the functionality of the Swing components, you can be assured that they're well tested. For example, with the jog shuttle example that we've created, shown later, we decided to reuse the BoundedRangeModel. This model does an excellent job with any component that contains a value within a closed range. Chances are that there might already be a model that will suit your needs, and you can either reuse or extend it to your liking.

Table 28-1 summarizes the Swing component models that we cover in this book. This should give you a good feel for whether a certain data model can be reused or extended in your own component. For an example of a component built with an existing model, take a look at Chapter 16, *Advanced Table Examples*.

Table 28-1. Swing Models

Model	Chapter	Description
ButtonModel	5	Holds the state of a button (like JButton), including its value, whether or not it is enabled, armed, selected, or pressed, and supports "rollover" images
BoundedRangeModel	6	Holds a value that can vary between fixed maximum and minimum limits; used for JSlider, JProgressBar, JScrollBar, and their relatives
ComboBoxModel	7	Holds the elements of a list, and a single selected element; used for JComboBox
ListModel	7	Holds the elements of a list (as in a JList)
ListSelectionModel	7	Holds one or more elements selected from a list
SingleSelection-Model	14	Holds an index into an array of possible selections; used by JMenuBar and JPopupMenu
TableModel	15	Holds a two-dimensional array of data; the basis for JTable
TableColumnModel	15	Controls the manipulation of columns in a table
TreeModel	17	Holds items that can be displayed with branches; used by JTree

Table 28-1. Swing Models (continued)

Model	Chapter	Description
TreeSelectionModel	17	Holds one or more elements selected from a tree
Document	20	Holds the content (i.e., text) of a document that might be displayed in an editor; used by the text components

Decide on Properties and Create the Model Interface

This is the fun part. You should decide which properties will be located in the model and how to access them. Properties can be read-write, read-only, or write-only. They can be any type of object or primitive data type. Also, according to the JavaBeans standard, properties can be indexed, as well as bound or constrained. For an explanation of these qualifiers, see Table 28-2.

Table 28-2. Property Types

Property Type	Description
Bound	The property must send a PropertyChangeEvent to all registered listeners when it changes state
Indexed	The property is an array of objects or values. Accessors must provide an index to determine which element they want to set or retrieve
Constrained	The property must fire a VetoableChangeEvent to all registered listeners before it changes state. Any one listener is allowed to veto the state change, at which point the original property state is preserved

As you are probably aware, there are three types of accessors that you will commonly use for object properties: "get," "set," and "is." You can use the "get" accessor to retrieve an object or primitive property, the "set" accessor to reset the value of an object or primitive property, and the "is" accessor to retrieve a boolean property from a component. (For boolean properties, developers tend to provide an "is" accessor and omit the "get," but it's not necessary to follow that convention.) The JavaBeans standard states that property accessors should adhere to the method signatures shown in Table 28-3. The italicized *PropertyType* in the table should reflect the object or primitive type of the property.

Table 28-3. Method Signatures for Property Accessors

Type	"get" Accessor	"set" Accessor	"is" Accessor
Standard	*PropertyType* getProperty()	void setProperty(*PropertyType*)	boolean isProperty()
Indexed	*PropertyType* getProperty(int)	void setProperty(int, *PropertyType*)	boolean isProperty(int)

The interface for the model should contain the accessor methods for each of the properties you decide on. This ensures that the access levels are enforced in whatever implementation of the model is provided. You should also include methods to add and remove various `ChangeEvent` or `PropertyChangeEvent` listeners from your model. It is *not* necessary to include a method to actually fire off a change event.

Here is the interface for the `SimpleModel` class we develop later:

```
//  SimpleModelInteface.java
//
import javax.swing.*;
import javax.swing.event.*;

public interface SimpleModelInterface
{
    public int getValue();
    public void setValue(int v);

    public boolean isActivated();
    public void setActivated(boolean b);

    public void addChangeListener(ChangeListener l);
    public void removeChangeListener(ChangeListener l);
}
```

Send Events When Bound Properties Change

This is critical. Components and UI-delegate objects are intrinsically linked and must know immediately when any bound or constrained property in the model has changed state. For example, with the `ButtonModel`, if a button is disabled, the component needs to know immediately that the button cannot be pressed. In addition, the UI delegate needs to know immediately that the button should be grayed on the screen. Both objects can be notified by firing an event that describes the change in state of the bound model property.

Depending on how many changes you intend to send at any given time, you can use either a `PropertyChangeEvent` or a `ChangeEvent` to signal a change to a model property. `PropertyChangeEvent` is the more robust event that is common with JavaBeans components; it describes the source object of the change, as well as the name of the property and its old and new state. `ChangeEvent`, on the other hand, only flags that a change has taken place. The only data bundled with a `ChangeEvent` object is the source object. The former is more descriptive, and does not require the listener to request the current property state from the model. The latter is more useful in situations where there are many change events that can be fired in a short amount of time, and you want to conserve resources.

As we mentioned above, this means that you must also have addPropertyChange-
Listener() and removePropertyChangeListener() methods or addChange-
Listener() and removeChangeListener() methods to maintain a list of event
subscribers, depending on the type of change event you intend to support. These
method signatures are typically given in the model interface. You'll also need a
protected method that fires the change events to all registered listeners; this is
provided in the model.

Reuse the EventListenerList Class

If you look closely through the otherwise mundane javax.swing.event package,
you might find a surprise waiting for you: the EventListenerList class. This
handy class allows you to maintain a list of generic event listeners that you can
retrieve at any time. In order to use it, simply declare an EventListenerList
object in your model, and have each of your event subscription methods turn
around and call associated methods with the EventListenerList:

```
EventListenerList theList = new EventListnerList();

public void addChangeListener(ChangeListener l) {
    theList.add(ChangeListener.class, l);
}

public void removeChangeListener(ChangeListener l) {
    theList.remove(ChangeListener.class, l);
}
```

When you need to retrieve the listener list to fire a ChangeEvent, you can do so
with the following code:

```
ChangeEvent theEvent;

protected void fireStateChanged() {

    Object[] list = theList.getListenerList();
    for (int index = list.length-2; index >= 0; index -= 2) {
        if (list[index]==ChangeListener.class) {
            if (theEvent == null)
                theEvent = new ChangeEvent(this);
            ((ChangeListener)list[index+1]).stateChanged(theEvent);
        }
    }
}
```

Changing this method to handle the more robust PropertyChangeEvent is
simply a matter of adding three passed-in parameters to the method signature,
which are used in instantiating the event object. If you need more information

about change events and listeners and how they relate to JavaBeans, we encourage you to pick up a copy of Rob Englander's *Developing Java Beans* (O'Reilly).

Don't Put Component Properties in the Model

Model properties define the state data of a component type; component properties typically define unique characteristics of a specific component—including the display. Be sure not to confuse the two. While accessors for model properties are located at the component level, they typically map down to identical methods inside the model. Where possible, it's best for outside oobjects to call the component's accessors for model properties rather than working with the model itself. Display properties, on the other hand, are contained at the component level. Hence, it is important that component properties remain in the component and do not creep down into the model.

An example might better explain the difference between the two. The `minimum`, `maximum`, and `value` properties exist in all bounded range components, including `JScrollBar` and `JProgressBar`. Therefore, they make sense as properties of the data model that all bounded range components use. However, major and minor tick marks, as well as labels, are specific to the `JSlider` object and how it displays itself. They serve better as component properties.

Implement the Model

Finally, complete the model by implementing the model interface. The example below shows a model that can be used as a reference. (We don't use this model for the `JogShuttle` component we develop later.)

```
//  SimpleModel.java
//
import javax.swing.*;
import javax.swing.event.*;

public class SimpleModel implements SimpleModelInterface
{
    protected transient ChangeEvent changeEvent = null;
    protected EventListenerList listenerList = new EventListenerList();

    private int value = 0;
    private boolean activated = false;

    public SimpleModel() { }
    public SimpleModel(int v) { value = v; }
    public SimpleModel(boolean b) { activated = b; }
    public SimpleModel(int v, boolean b) {
        value = v;
        activated = b;
```

```java
    }

    public int getValue() { return value; }

    public synchronized void setValue(int v) {
        if (v != value) {
            int oldValue = value;
            value = v;
            fireChange();
        }
    }

    public boolean isActivated() { return activated; }

    public synchronized void setActivated(boolean b) {
        if (b != activated) {
            boolean oldValue = activated;
            activated = b;
            fireChange();
        }
    }

    public void addChangeListener(ChangeListener l) {
        listenerList.add(ChangeListener.class, l);
    }

    public void removeChangeListener(ChangeListener l) {
        listenerList.remove(ChangeListener.class, l);
    }

    protected void fireChange()
    {
        Object[] listeners = listenerList.getListenerList();
        for (int i = listeners.length - 2; i >= 0; i -=2 ) {
            if (listeners[i] == ChangeListener.class) {
                if (changeEvent == null) {
                    changeEvent = new ChangeEvent(this);
                }
                ((ChangeListener)listeners[i+1]).stateChanged(changeEvent);
            }
        }
    }

    public String toString()  {
        String modelString = "value=" + getValue() + ", " +
            "activated=" + isActivated();
        return getClass().getName() + "[" + modelString + "]";
    }
}
```

The UI Delegate

Now that you have the model, you need to create a UI delegate for your component. This means creating an empty class used for type comparison, and a class that extends the abstract `javax.swing.plaf.ComponentUI` class.

Create an Abstract Type Class

This is somewhat of a Swing convention when working with multiple look-and-feels and the `UIManager`. Essentially, it consists of creating a simple abstract class that can be used as the most elementary type of the UI delegate. The class is almost always empty.

```
//  JogShuttleUI.java
//
import javax.swing.plaf.*;

public abstract class JogShuttleUI extends ComponentUI { }
```

In our example, the remaining code will be placed in a file called *BasicJogShuttleUI.java*.

You Must Implement a Paint Method

In the UI-delegate object (`BasicJogShuttleUI` in our example), the `paint()` method is responsible for performing the actual rendering of the component. The `paint()` method takes two parameters: a reference to the component that it belongs to, and a `Graphics` context with which it can draw the component:

```
public void paint(Graphics g, JComponent c)
```

You can use the `Graphics` object to access any drawing utilities needed to render the component. In addition, the reference to the `JComponent` object is necessary to obtain the current model and display properties, as well as any other utility methods that `JComponent` can provide for you.

Remember that in the `paint()` method, you are working in component coordinate space and not the container coordinate space. This means that you will be interested in the `c.getHeight()` and `c.getWidth()` values, which are the maximum width and height of space that has been allocated to you by the container's layout manager. You will *not* be interested in the `c.getX()` or `c.getY()` values. The latter values give the position of the component in the *container's* coordinate space, not the component's. Within the component coordinate space, the upper-left corner of the drawing area that you will use is (0,0).

One more caveat: remember that Swing components can take borders or insets. The size of these, however, is included in the width and height reported by the component. It's always a good idea to subtract the border or insets from the total space before drawing a component. You can adjust your perspective by implementing the following code:

```
public void paint(Graphics g, JComponent c) {

    //  We don't want to paint inside of the insets or
    //  borders, so subtract them out.
    Insets insets = c.getInsets();
    g.translate(insets.left, insets.top);
    int width = c.getWidth()-insets.left-insets.right;
    int height = c.getHeight()-insets.top-insets.bottom;

    // Do the rest of the painting
    g.translate(-insets.left, -insets.top);
}
```

Be Able To Resize Yourself

Your component should always be able to draw itself correctly, based on its current size as dictated by the layout manager minus any insets. Recall that when the component is validated in the container's layout manager, the manager will attempt to retrieve the preferred or minimum size of the component. If nothing has been set with a call to getMinimumSize() or getPreferredSize(), the layout manager will assign the component an arbitrary size, based on the constraints of the layout.

Drawing a component (or parts of it) using a static size is asking for trouble. You should not hardcode specific widths of shapes, unless they are always one or two pixels when the component is resized. Remember that the "left" size of the insets may be different than the "right," and the "top" different from the "bottom." Above all, you should be aware that components can sometimes be called upon to come up with seemingly impossible sizes, especially during application development. While the programmer will quickly understand that this is not what's intended, the more gracefully the component can handle this, the better.

As you are creating your component, place it in various layout managers and try resizing it. Try giving the component ridiculously low (or high) widths and heights. It may not look pretty, but it's much better than throwing an unhandled exception and grinding your user's application to a halt!

Creating the Component Itself

Decide on Properties

Finally, when creating the component, you need to decide which data properties you want to export to the programmer, and which ones you don't. Exported properties usually include several from the data model, and properties that can be used to configure the component's display. All of these properties should have one or more public accessors that programmers can use to obtain or reset their values accordingly. (See our earlier discussion on model properties for more information on creating properties.)

Of course, there are several properties that you will probably want to export, either as read-only, write-only, or read-write. These properties are designed to work better with the Swing MVC architecture. They are shown in Table 28-4.

Table 28-4. Commonly Exported Properties

Property	Description
model	Data model for the component
UI	User-interface (UI) property
UIClassID	Read-only class ID string of the UI delegate, used by the UIManager

Unless there is a really good reason, you should always try to keep the properties of your components private and encourage the use of accessors—even with subclasses. To see why, we should take a look at Swing buttons and the Abstract-Button class. With this class, there are a few restrictions that we should mention:

- You can only arm a button that is first enabled. In this case, the accessor labeled setArmed() first checks the button's enabled property to see if it is true. If it isn't, the button cannot be armed.

- You can't press the button with the setPressed() method unless it is armed. Therefore, the setPressed() method will check the isArmed() method to see if it returns true. If not, the button cannot be pressed.

Both of these cases demonstrate examples of a conditional accessor. In other words, if you call an accessor to set a property, there are isolated cases in which it might not succeed. It also demonstrates why you should try to avoid properties that are protected. In this case, there were prerequisites that were needed in order for the accessor method to succeed and the property to be set to a specific state. If a subclass is allowed override the accessors and ignore any prerequisites on that property, the component state could get unsynchronized, and the results could be unpredictable. Even if you know right now that there are no such cases in your own component, you should buy some insurance and plan for the future with this more JavaBeans friendly approach.

Listen to Your Models

The model is an essential part of any component. If it is sending events to your component, you need to listen. Essentially, this means that you should add your component as a listener for any events that the model fires (typically Change-Event or PropertyChangeEvent objects). This can be done through the addChangeListener() or the addPropertyChangeListener() methods inside the model.

It's always a good idea to add your component class as a listener to the model in the setModel() method. While doing so, be sure to unregister yourself with the previous model that you were listening to in this method as well. Finally, make a call to setModel() during the initialization phase of your component to make sure that everything is set up correctly.

When a change in the model occurs, you will typically want to repaint your component. Hence, if you are not interested in performing extra tasks when a change event is sent to you or in propagating model change events to outside objects, you can probably just get away with calling repaint(). In these cases, you may also choose not to listen to the event at all and let the UI delegate handle it for you.

Send Events When Bound Properties Change

Other components in the outside world will be interested in knowing when properties inside your component have changed. Therefore, you should decide which properties are bound or constrained inside of your component.

You can use the firePropertyChangeEvent() method of JComponent to fire off PropertyChangeEvent objects to all registered listeners. The JComponent class contains overloaded versions of these methods for all primitive data types (int, long, boolean, etc.), as well as for the Object class, which pretty much covers everything else. JComponent also contains addPropertyChangeListener() and removePropertyChangeListener() methods, so you don't have to worry about maintaining an event listener list in the component either. Everything is taken care of for you.

Some Final Questions

Finally, before writing that component and placing it out in the Swing libraries, here are some questions that you can ask yourself while customizing your component. If the answer to any of these is "Yes," then include the following code in your own component.

Q: *Do you want the component to avoid getting the focus through traversal?*

A: Focus traversal refers to the action of pressing TAB or SHIFT-TAB to cycle the focus onto a component. If you want your component to avoid accepting the focus when traversed, then place the following method somewhere in the code for your component:

```
public boolean isFocusTraversable() {return false;}
```

Q: *Do you want the component to avoid getting the focus through explicit settings?*

A: On the other hand, if you don't want any component to be able to call requestFocus() to explicitly set the focus on your component, you can override the isRequestFocusEnabled() method to return false.

```
public boolean isRequestFocusEnabled() {return false;}
```

Q: *Do you want your component to maintain its own focus cycle?*

A: In order to do this, override the isFocusCycleRoot() method of JComponent and return true. This specifies that the component will traverse repeatedly through itself and each of its children, but will not leave the component tree unless programmatically reset to another component outside the cycle.

```
public boolean isFocusCycleRoot() {return true;}
```

Q: *Do you want your component to handle the processing of its own focus keyboard events?*

A: No problem. Override the isManagingFocus() method and return the boolean true. By doing so, you are telling Swing that the default focus manager should send to you any keyboard events that may normally be used to handle adjustment of focus, with the exception of those containing a CTRL modifier.

```
public boolean isManagingFocus() {return true;}
```

Q: *Do you need to send notification of constrained properties?*

A: Changes to constrained properties can be vetoed by any registered listeners. If just one listener vetoes a property change, the property maintains its original value. JComponent has a fireVetoableChange() method which you can use to fire off such an event to registered listeners. JComponent also contains the addVetoableChangeListener() and removeVetoableChangeListener() methods for listener registration.

Q: *Do you want to prevent a border from being placed around your component?*

A: You can override the getBorder() method to return null:

```
public Border getBorder() {return null;}
```

Q: *Are you always opaque?*

A: Whether you are or not, the JComponent portion of your component should correctly report its opaqueness with the isOpaque() method. If you wish to

have a component that is always opaque, override this method and return
true, as follows:

```
public boolean isOpaque() {return true;}
```

The Jog Shuttle: A Simple Swing Component

Here is an example of a component that mimics a *jog shuttle*, a common control
found on many VCRs and television remote controls. It's a dial that can be turned
through multiple revolutions; turning clockwise increases the dial's value, turning
counterclockwise decreases it. The shuttle has a fixed minimum and maximum
value; the range (the difference between the minimum and maximum) may be
more than a single turn of the dial. This sounds like a job for the BoundedRange-
Model, and indeed, we reuse this model rather than develop our own. However,
we have created our own delegate that handles mouse events and is capable of
moving the job-shuttle when the mouse is dragged over it.

The Component

Shown below is the code for the component portion, JogShuttle. This class
extends JComponent, relying on another class, JogShuttleUI, to display itself.
JogShuttle implements ChangeListener so it can receive ChangeEvent notifications from the model.

```java
//   JogShuttle.java
//
import java.awt.*;
import java.awt.event.*;

import javax.swing.*;
import javax.swing.event.*;
import javax.swing.border.*;

public class JogShuttle extends JComponent implements ChangeListener {

    private BoundedRangeModel model;

    //   The dialInsets property tells how far the dial is inset
    //   from the sunken border.
    private Insets dialInsets = new Insets(3, 3, 3, 3);

    //   The valuePerRevolution property tells how many units the dial
    //   takes to make a complete revolution.
    private int valuePerRevolution;

    //   Constructors
    public JogShuttle() {
```

```
        init(new DefaultBoundedRangeModel());
    }

    public JogShuttle(BoundedRangeModel m) {
        init(m);
    }

    public JogShuttle(int min, int max, int value) {
        init(new DefaultBoundedRangeModel(value, 1, min, max));
    }

    protected void init(BoundedRangeModel m) {
        model = m;
        valuePerRevolution = m.getMaximum() - m.getMinimum();
        model.addChangeListener(this);
        setMinimumSize(new Dimension(80, 80));
        setPreferredSize(new Dimension(80, 80));
        updateUI();
    }

    public void setUI(JogShuttleUI ui) {super.setUI(ui);}

    public void updateUI() {
        setUI((JogShuttleUI)UIManager.getUI(this));
        invalidate();
    }

    public String getUIClassID() {return "JogShuttleUI";}

    public void setModel(BoundedRangeModel m) {
        BoundedRangeModel old = model;

        if (m == null)
            model = new DefaultBoundedRangeModel();
        else
            model = m;

        firePropertyChange("model", old, model);
    }

    protected BoundedRangeModel getModel() {
        return model;
    }

    // Methods
    public void resetToMinimum() {model.setValue(model.getMinimum());}

    public void resetToMaximum() {model.setValue(model.getMaximum());}
```

```
    public void stateChanged(ChangeEvent e) {repaint();}

    // Accessors
    public int getMinimum() {return model.getMinimum();}

    public void setMinimum(int m) {
        int old = getMinimum();
        if (m != old) {
            model.setMinimum(m);
            firePropertyChange("minimum", old, m);
        }
    }

    public int getMaximum() {return model.getMaximum();}

    public void setMaximum(int m) {
        int old = getMaximum();
        if (m != old) {
            model.setMaximum(m);
            firePropertyChange("maximum", old, m);
        }
    }

    public int getValue() {return model.getValue();}

    public void setValue(int v) {
        int old = getValue();
        if (v != old) {
            model.setValue(v);
            firePropertyChange("value", old, v);
        }
    }


    // Display-specific properties
    public int getValuePerRevolution() {return valuePerRevolution;}

    public void setValuePerRevolution(int v) {
        int old = getValuePerRevolution();
        if (v != old) {
            valuePerRevolution = v;
            firePropertyChange("valuePerRevolution", old, v);
        }
        repaint();
    }

    public void setDialInsets(Insets i) {dialInsets = i;}
```

```
    public void setDialInsets(int top, int left, int bottom, int right) {
        dialInsets = new Insets(top, left, bottom, right);
    }

    public Insets getDialInsets() {return dialInsets;}
}
```

The component itself is very simple. It provides several constructors, offering the programmer different ways to set up the data model, an instance of Bounded-RangeModel. You can set the minimum, maximum, and initial values for the jog shuttle in the constructor, or provide them afterwards using the accessor methods setMinimum(), setMaximum(), and setValue(). Regardless of which constructor you call, most of the work is done by the init() method, which registers the JogShuttle as a listener for the model's ChangeEvent notifications, sets its minimum and preferred sizes, and calls updateUI() to install the appropriate user interface.

Most of the JogShuttle code consists of accessor methods for various properties. Accessors for the model properties, like getMinimum(), simply call the equivalent accessor in the model itself. Other properties, like valuePerRevolution, are display-specific and maintained directly by the JogShuttle class. (The amount the value changes when the shuttle turns through one revolution has a lot to do with how you display the shuttle and how you interpret mouse events, but nothing to do with the actual data that the component represents.) The user interface object, which we'll discuss below, queries these properties to find out how to paint itself.

Of course, the JogShuttle needs to inform the outside world of changes to its state—a component that never tells anyone that something has changed isn't very useful. To keep the outside world informed, we have made several of our properties bound properties. The bound properties include minimum, maximum, and value, plus a few of the others. JComponent handles event-listener registration for us. The "set" accessor methods for the bound properties fire PropertyChange-Event notifications to any event listeners. This means that any external object that wants to modify the JogShuttle's properties must do so through the JogShuttle itself. It cannot call getModel() and change the properties in the model because the getModel() method is protected. (Admittedly, making getModel() protected is uncommon. We thought it was simpler to force other classes to make changes through the component, which then becomes the single source for property change events.)

One other method worth looking at is stateChanged(). This method is called whenever the model issues a ChangeEvent, meaning that one of the model properties has changed. All we do upon receiving this notification is call repaint(), which lets the repaint manager schedule a call to the user interface's paint()

method, redrawing the shuttle. This may seem roundabout: the UI delegate handles some mouse events, figures out how to change the shuttle's value, and informs the model of the change; in turn, the model generates a change event, the component receives the event, and calls the repaint manager to tell the component's UI delegate to redraw itself. It is important to notice that this round-about path guarantees that everyone is properly informed of the component's state, that everyone can perform their assigned task, and furthermore, that the relatively slow repaint operation is scheduled by the repaint manager, where it won't interfere with other event processing.

The UI Delegate

BasicJogShuttleUI is our "delegate" or "user interface" class, and therefore extends JogShuttleUI and consequently ComponentUI. It is responsible for painting the shuttle and interpreting the user's mouse actions, and so implements the MouseListener and MouseMotionListener interfaces. Although this requires a fair amount of code, it is a fundamentally simple class:

```
//   BasicJogShuttleUI.java
//
import java.awt.*;
import java.awt.event.*;

import javax.swing.*;
import javax.swing.plaf.*;
import javax.swing.border.*;

public class BasicJogShuttleUI extends JogShuttleUI
    implements MouseListener, MouseMotionListener {

    private int KNOB_DISPLACEMENT = 3;
    private int FINGER_SLOT_DISPLACEMENT = 15;

    private Point lastPoint = new Point();

    public BasicJogShuttleUI() {
        lastPoint = new Point();
    }

    public static ComponentUI createUI(JComponent c) {
        return new BasicJogShuttleUI();
    }

    public void installUI(JComponent c) {
        JogShuttle shuttle = (JogShuttle)c;
        shuttle.addMouseListener(this);
        shuttle.addMouseMotionListener(this);
    }
```

```
    public void uninstallUI(JComponent c) {
        JogShuttle shuttle = (JogShuttle)c;
        shuttle.removeMouseListener(this);
        shuttle.removeMouseMotionListener(this);
    }

    public void paint(Graphics g, JComponent c) {

        //  We don't want to paint inside of the insets or borders
        Insets insets = c.getInsets();
        g.translate(insets.left, insets.top);
        int width = c.getWidth()-insets.left-insets.right;
        int height = c.getHeight()-insets.top-insets.bottom;

        //  Draw the outside circle
        g.setColor(c.getForeground());
        g.fillOval(0, 0, width, height);

        Insets d = ((JogShuttle)c).getDialInsets();
        int value = ((JogShuttle)c).getValue();
        int valuePerRevolution = ((JogShuttle)c).getValuePerRevolution();

        //  Draw the edge of the dial
        g.setColor(Color.darkGray);
        g.fillOval(d.left, d.top, width-(d.right*2),height-(d.bottom*2));

        //  Draw the inside of the dial
        g.setColor(Color.gray);
        g.fillOval(d.left+KNOB_DISPLACEMENT,
                d.top+KNOB_DISPLACEMENT,
                width-(d.right+d.left)-(KNOB_DISPLACEMENT*2),
                height-(d.bottom+d.top)-(KNOB_DISPLACEMENT*2));

        //  Draw the "finger slot"
        drawFingerSlot(g, c, value, width, height, valuePerRevolution,
                FINGER_SLOT_DISPLACEMENT-1,
                (double)(width/2)-d.right-FINGER_SLOT_DISPLACEMENT,
                (double)(height/2)-d.bottom-FINGER_SLOT_DISPLACEMENT);

        g.translate(-insets.left, -insets.top);
    }

    private void drawFingerSlot(Graphics g, JComponent c, int value,
        int width, int height, int valuePerRevolution, int size,
        double xradius, double yradius) {

        int currentPosition = value % valuePerRevolution;
```

```
        // Obtain the current degrees in radians
        double degrees = ((double)currentPosition /
                                    100)*java.lang.Math.PI*2;
        degrees -= (java.lang.Math.PI/2);

        // Obtain the X and Y coordinates of the finger slot. Assume that
        // the origin mimics a unit circle (i.e., the right side of the circle)
        int xPosition = (int) (xradius * java.lang.Math.sin(degrees));
        int yPosition = (int) (yradius * java.lang.Math.cos(degrees));
        xPosition = (width/2) - xPosition;
        yPosition = (height/2) + yPosition;

        // Draw the finger slot with a cresent shadow on the top left
        g.setColor(Color.darkGray);
        g.fillOval(xPosition-(size/2), yPosition-(size/2), size, size);
        g.setColor(Color.lightGray);
        g.fillOval(xPosition-(size/2)+1, yPosition-(size/2)+1,
                   size-1, size-1);

    }

    public void mousePressed(MouseEvent e) {lastPoint = e.getPoint();}
    public void mouseReleased(MouseEvent e) { }
    public void mouseClicked(MouseEvent e) { }
    public void mouseEntered(MouseEvent e) { }
    public void mouseExited(MouseEvent e) { }

    public void mouseDragged(MouseEvent e) {

        // This interface is lousy. I encourage you to search for a better one.
        Point thisPoint = e.getPoint();
        JogShuttle theShuttle = (JogShuttle)e.getComponent();
        int difference = thisPoint.x - lastPoint.x;
        if (difference < 0)
            theShuttle.setValue(theShuttle.getValue() - 1);
        else if (difference > 0)
            theShuttle.setValue(theShuttle.getValue() + 1);
    }

    public void mouseMoved(MouseEvent e) { }
}
```

BasicJogShuttleUI starts by overriding several methods of ComponentUI. createUI() is a simple static method that returns a new instance of our UI object. installUI() registers our UI object as a listener for mouse events from its component (the JogShuttle). uninstallUI() does the opposite: it unresigters the UI as a listener for mouse events.

Most of the code is in the `paint()` method and its helper, `drawFingerSlot()`. `paint()` draws the jog shuttle on the screen. Its second argument, c, is the component that we're drawing—in this case, an instance of `JogShuttle`. The `paint()` method is careful to ask the shuttle for all the information it needs, without making any assumptions about what it might find. (In return, `JogShuttle` relays many of these requests to the model.)

The other methods implement the two mouse listener interfaces. We need `mousePressed()` to store the point at which a drag starts. `mouseDragged()` itself figures out the new value of the mouse position, determines which direction to move the jog shuttle, and calls `setValue()` to inform the shuttle (and hence, the model) of its new value. When you play with the shuttle, you'll see that the way we process mouse events is fairly primitive. Improving this aspect of the shuttle is up to you. There's nothing fundamentally complex involved, just more trigonometry for interpreting the mouse position.

A Toy Using the Shuttle

Here is a short application that demonstrates the `JogShuttle` component. We've mimicked a simple toy that lets you doodle on the screen by manipulating two dials. This example also demonstrates how easy it is to work with `JComponent`.

```java
//   Sketch.java
//
import java.awt.*;
import java.awt.event.*;
import java.beans.*;
import java.util.*;

import javax.swing.*;
import javax.swing.border.*;

public class Sketch extends JPanel implements PropertyChangeListener,
    ActionListener {

    JogShuttle shuttle1;
    JogShuttle shuttle2;
    JPanel board;
    JButton clear;

    public Sketch() {
        super(true);

        setLayout(new BorderLayout());
        board = new JPanel(true);
        board.setPreferredSize(new Dimension(300, 300));
        board.setBorder(new LineBorder(Color.black, 5));
```

```
        clear = new JButton("Clear Drawing Area");
        clear.addActionListener(this);

        shuttle1 = new JogShuttle(0, 300, 150);
        shuttle2 = new JogShuttle(0, 300, 150);

        shuttle1.setValuePerRevolution(100);
        shuttle2.setValuePerRevolution(100);

        shuttle1.addPropertyChangeListener(this);
        shuttle2.addPropertyChangeListener(this);

        shuttle1.setBorder(new BevelBorder(BevelBorder.RAISED));
        shuttle2.setBorder(new BevelBorder(BevelBorder.RAISED));

        add(board, BorderLayout.NORTH);
        add(shuttle1, BorderLayout.WEST);
        add(clear, BorderLayout.CENTER);
        add(shuttle2, BorderLayout.EAST);
    }

    public void propertyChange(PropertyChangeEvent e) {

        if (e.getPropertyName() == "value") {
            Graphics g = board.getGraphics();
            g.setColor(getForeground());
            g.drawLine(shuttle1.getValue(), shuttle2.getValue(),
                    shuttle1.getValue(), shuttle2.getValue());
        }
    }

    public void actionPerformed(ActionEvent e) {

        //  The button must have been pressed.
        Insets insets = board.getInsets();
        Graphics g = board.getGraphics();
        g.setColor(board.getBackground());
        g.fillRect(insets.left, insets.top,
                board.getWidth()-insets.left-insets.right,
                board.getHeight()-insets.top-insets.bottom);
    }

    public static void main(String[] args) {

        UIManager.put("JogShuttleUI", "BasicJogShuttleUI");
        Sketch s = new Sketch();
        JFrame frame = new JFrame("Sample Sketch Application");
        frame.addWindowListener(new BasicWindowMonitor());
        frame.setContentPane(s);
```

```
        frame.pack();
        frame.setVisible(true);
    }
}
```

There's really nothing surprising. The main() method calls UIManager.put() to tell the interface manager about the existence of our new user interface. Whenever a component asks for a UI with a class ID "JogShuttleID", the UI manager will look for a class named BasicJogShuttleUI, create an instance of that class, and use that class to provide the user interface. Having registered the JogShuttleUI, we can then create our shuttles, register ourself as a property change listener, and place the shuttles in a JPanel with a BorderLayout. Our property change method simply checks which property changed; if the value property changed, we read the current value of both shuttles, interpret them as a pair of coordinates, and draw a point from the previous location to the new point. Figure 28-2 shows what our toy looks like.

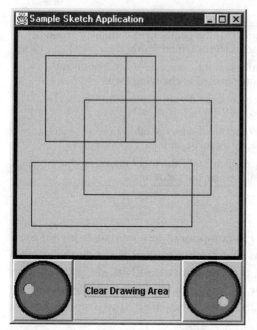

Figure 28-2. The Sketch application with two jog shuttles

Working with Focus

And now for something completely different. In Chapter 3 we offered a terse discussion of various properties of JComponent that can be used to control how a component handles focus. Here, we look at each of those properties more indepth, and discuss some of the peculiarities of using focus in Swing.

You're probably aware that you can shift the focus around in Swing using the TAB key and the SHIFT-TAB key. The path that the focus follows from one component to the next is called the *focus cycle*. The focus cycle is determined by the focus manager. By default, the focus cycle is dictated by the position of the components in the container: those components with a smaller x,y position always get the focus first. Consequently, with the help of the Swing focus manager, the default focus will cycle from left to right and top to bottom—much like reading a book. The TAB key moves the focus one step ahead in its current focus cycle. SHIFT-TAB moves it one step back.

Five properties in JComponent deal with focus. It is important to note that they are used only in conjunction with the Swing focus manager class, DefaultFocusManager. The properties are summarized in Table 28-5. Let's go over each of these properties and discuss how they impact the focus in Swing.

Table 28-5. Focus-Related Properties in JComponent

Property	Description
focusCycleRoot	If true, indicates that the component contains a group of child components all contained within their own focus cycle
managingFocus	If true, indicates that the component will handle any keyboard events directed at changing focus
focusTraversable	If false, the component does not allow the focus to be traversed onto it
requestFocusEnabled	If false, the component does not allow outside objects to programmatically set focus on it
nextFocusableComponent	This property explicitly tells the focus manager which component will receive the focus next

Focus Cycle Root

The focusCycleRoot property says that a component or a container is the "root" of a focus cycle. Essentially, this means that once the focus is inside the component, it will continually loop around the component and its children (if they accept focus traversal) until the user or the program explicitly sets the focus on a component outside the cycle. Figure 28-3 shows the effect this property has on focus traversal.

If you wish to set a component as the root of its own focus cycle, you should override the isFocusCycleRoot() method in the component and return true. If this method returns false, the focus will cycle through each of the components and then move on. Note that there are no "get" or "set" accessors for this property. For example, you cannot instantiate your own JPanel and "set" its focusCycleRoot property to true from outside the class at runtime. The property must be set by subclassing JPanel with your own class and overriding the isFocusCycleRoot() method to return the appropriate boolean.

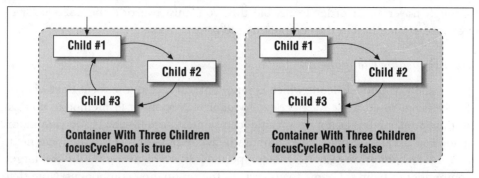

Figure 28-3. Working with the focus cycle root

Managing Focus

The managingFocus property can only be modified by subclassing and overriding the isManagingFocus() method. By doing so, you're telling DefaultFocusManager not to consume any keyboard events that could potentially be used to shift focus on this component. Instead, it should let the events fall through to JComponent's processComponentKeyEvent() method, or more accurately, to the overridden processComponentKeyEvent() method inside your own component. The default focus manager will ignore TAB and SHIFT-TAB keys. However, it will still consume keystrokes that use the CTRL modifier key. The CtrlIFocus-Manager that we developed at the end of Chapter 22 shows one way around this.

Focus Traversable

Again, this property can only be modified by subclassing and overriding the isFocusTraversable() method. If you override this method and return false, the focus manager will skip over this component when it is traversing focus and move on to the next component that is accepting a traversal focus, as determined by the current focus manager. Note that this does not prevent the program from setting focus on the component with the requestFocus() method, such as when the user presses a JButton.

Request Focus Enabled

The programmer can explicitly request that focus be set on a particular component using the requestFocus() method. With a JButton, for example, this method is called whenever the button is pressed. If you want the component to refuse the focus, set the property to false with the setRequestFocusEnabled()

method. Unlike the previous three focus properties, this property can be accessed using a standard "get" and "set" accessor pair. Note, however, that setting this property to false does not prevent the component from receiving the focus through traversal. In order to disable this, you must override the isFocusTraversable() method in the component and return false.

Next Focusable Component

Swing allows you to hardcode which component will receive the focus next when it is traversing. You can use the setNextFocusableComponent() method to do this. If this property is set for a specific component, the DefaultFocusManager ignores its usual method of determining which component receives the focus next, and instead jumps directly to that component. It is not necessary for the target component to be in the same focus cycle as the originating component. Note that there is no setPreviousFocusableComponent() property; you can only specify the one ahead.

Using the Focus Properties

Here is an example that demonstrates each of the focus properties:

```
// FocusExample.java
//
import java.awt.*;
import java.awt.event.*;

import javax.swing.*;
import javax.swing.FocusManager;
import javax.swing.border.*;

public class FocusExample extends JFrame {

    public FocusExample() {

        super("Focus Example");
        addWindowListener(new BasicWindowMonitor());
        MyPanel mypanel = new MyPanel();

        JButton  button1 = new JButton("One");
        JButton  button2 = new JButton("Two");
        JButton  button3 = new JButton("Three");
        MyButton button4 = new MyButton("Four");
        MyButton button5 = new MyButton("Five");
        JButton  button6 = new JButton("Six");
        JButton  button7 = new JButton("Seven");

        mypanel.add(button1);
```

```
        mypanel.add(button2);

        button4.setRequestFocusEnabled(false);
        button6.setNextFocusableComponent(button3);

        JInternalFrame frame1 = new JInternalFrame("Internal Frame 1",
                                            true, true, true, true);

        frame1.setBackground(Color.lightGray);
        frame1.getContentPane().setLayout(new GridLayout(2, 3));
        frame1.setSize(200, 200);

        frame1.getContentPane().add(button3);
        frame1.getContentPane().add(mypanel);
        frame1.getContentPane().add(button4);
        frame1.getContentPane().add(button5);
        frame1.getContentPane().add(button6);
        frame1.getContentPane().add(button7);

        JDesktopPane desktop = new JDesktopPane();
        desktop.add(frame1, new Integer(1));
        desktop.setOpaque(true);

        // Now set up the user interface window.
        Container contentPane = getContentPane();
        contentPane.add(desktop, BorderLayout.CENTER);
        setSize(new Dimension(600, 400));
        setVisible(true);
    }

    public static void main(String[] args) {
        new FocusExample();
    }

    class MyButton extends JButton {
        public MyButton(String s) { super(s); }
        public boolean isFocusTraversable() { return false; }
        public boolean isManagingFocus() { return true; }
        public void processComponentKeyEvent(KeyEvent e) {
            System.out.println("Key event is " + e);
            e.consume();
        }
    }

    class MyPanel extends JPanel {
        public MyPanel() { super(true); }
        public boolean isFocusCycleRoot() { return true; }
    }
}
```

This program creates the seven buttons in the internal frame shown in Figure 28-4. When looking at the source, there are several things that probably jump out at you. First, buttons "One" and "Two" are contained in a special panel, called `MyPanel`, that has declared itself as the root of its own focus cycle. Hence, if you click on either of the two buttons and continually press TAB, you'll see that the focus simply bounces back and forth between the two buttons.

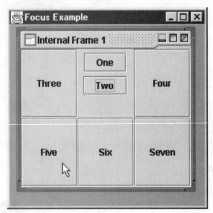

Figure 28-4. FocusExample output

Buttons "Four" and "Five" each claim to be maintaining focus. However, button "Four" has also set the `requestFocusEnabled` property to `false`, so you cannot programmatically set the focus on the button by clicking on it. (Clicking obviously makes the button do what it's supposed to do, but does not cause the button to receive focus.) If the focus is set to button "Five," you can press any key and see the results of a key event sent to standard output. Again, we had to consume the key event in order to keep it from propagating to the next interested party. Also, buttons "Four" and "Five" are both of type `MyButton`, which sets the `focusTraversable` property to `false`. (This leaves button "Four" without any focus capability.) Hence, focus cannot be traversed onto these components.

Finally, button "Seven" has its `nextFocusableComponent` property set to button "Six." Hence, if you try to traverse the focus past button "Seven," it will return to button "Six."

The FocusManager Class

The Swing focus manager is responsible for determining how the focus is transferred from one component to the next. The typical focus manager listens for keyboard events on any Swing object, reacting to various ones that might indicate that the focus should shift. The focus manager does not determine the beginning or end of the focus cycle within a container; that's the responsibility of the container itself. In Swing, there is only one focus manager per thread group. This is necessary to keep competing focus managers from shifting the focus on a number of components. It is important to note the distinction between the Swing focus manager and AWT focus manager. The Swing focus manager deals specifically with Swing components, while the AWT focus manager deals with the heavyweight components of AWT 1.1.

The FocusManager class is an abstract class that handles much of the functionality of the Swing focus manager. The only methods that are not implemented are those that decide how the focus is transferred: processKeyEvent(), focusNextComponent(), and focusPreviousComponent(). You can use these methods to dictate how the focus should be shifted in your own focus manager.

Constant

public static final String FOCUS_MANAGER_CLASS_PROPERTY

This constant is a static String used internally. The string serves as the key to locate the current Swing focus manager class within the UIManager for the current look-and-feel. You typically won't use this constant.

Constructor

public FocusManager()

The default constructor for the FocusManager class.

Methods

public static FocusManager getCurrentFocusManager()

Retrieves the current focus manager for the calling thread group.

public static void setCurrentFocusManager(FocusManager f)

Resets the current focus manager for the thread group.

public boolean isFocusManagerEnabled()

Returns a boolean indicating whether or not the Swing focus manager is enabled or disabled. If the Swing focus manager is disabled, the AWT focus manager is used. The AWT focus manager is typically used in applications that mix lightweight and heavyweight components.

public static void disableSwingFocusManager()

Disables the Swing focus manager and instead allows the components to use the AWT focus manager. This is a prudent action if your application mixes lightweight and heavyweight components.

public abstract void processKeyEvent(Component focusedComponent, KeyEvent anEvent)

This abstract method is called by each JComponent with a keyboard event to process. This method in the focus manager is always consulted before the component searches itself for any registered keyboard actions. This method intercepts and consumes the KeyEvent object passed in, if it can be used to shift the focus. The focusedComponent variable represents the component with which the KeyEvent was directed. If the method should switch the focus, the focusNextComponent() method and the focusPreviousComponent() methods can be called to determine which component gets the focus next. Note that the processKeyEvent() method receives both key-pressed and key-released events—be sure to consume both for the specific keystroke that you're monitoring.

public abstract void focusNextComponent(Component aComponent)

Causes the focus manager to shift the focus to the next component in the focus cycle.

public abstract void focusPreviousComponent(Component aComponent)

Causes the focus manager to shift the focus to the previous component in the focus cycle.

The DefaultFocusManager Class

The DefaultFocusManager class extends the abstract FocusManager class to provide implementations of the three key methods: processKeyEvent(), focus-NextComponent(), focusPreviousComponent(). In addition, it provides several helpful methods of its own. At the heart of the DefaultFocusManager is a special method that helps to determine which components should come first in the focus cycle—compareTabOrder(). This method determines the focus cycle in a very basic way: the cycle traverses from left-to-right and top-to-bottom across a container. If you wish to create a new focus cycle, you can override the compare-TabOrder() method and incorporate new logic of your own.

Constructor

public DefaultFocusManager()

The default constructor for this class.

Methods

public boolean compareTabOrder(Component a, Component b)

Returns a boolean indicating whether the first component passed in should come before the second component in the current focus cycle. This method determines the outcome of the comparison by calculating which component is closer to the top of the container, followed by which component is closer to the left side of the container. The resulting approach yields a focus cycle that goes from left-to-right, top-to-bottom across a container. This method can be overridden by a subclass if a different focus cycle is necessary.

public void focusNextComponent(Component aComponent)

Causes the focus manager to shift the focus to the next component in the focus cycle.

public void focusPreviousComponent(Component aComponent)

Causes the focus manager to shift the focus to the previous component in the focus cycle.

public Component getComponentAfter(Container aContainer, Component aComponent)

Returns the component that is just after `aComponent` in the focus cycle of `aContainer`.

public Component getComponentBefore(Container aContainer, Component aComponent)

Returns the component that is just before `aComponent` in the focus cycle of `aContainer`.

public void processKeyEvent(Component focusedComponent, KeyEvent anEvent)

Called by each `JComponent` with a keyboard event to process. This is always done before the component searches itself for any registered keyboard actions. The method listens for TAB and SHIFT-TAB as well as CTRL-TAB and SHIFT-CTRL-TAB keystrokes, and uses the `focusNextComponent()` and `focusPreviousComponent()` methods to shift the focus as necessary.

public Component getFirstComponent(Container aContainer)

Returns the component at the beginning of the container's focus cycle.

public Component getLastComponent(Container aContainer)

Returns the component at the end of the container's focus cycle.

Writing Your Own Focus Manager

Here's a new focus manager with distinctly different behavior than the default focus manager. Our focus manager moves the focus through a series of buttons in alphabetical order, according to the button labels. For this example, we decided to implement our focus manager by extending `FocusManager` rather than `Default-FocusManager`. You could use either approach for writing your own; if you extend `DefaultFocusManager`, you might be able to get away with overriding the single method `compareTabOrder()`.

```
//   AlphaButtonFocusManager.java
//
import javax.swing.*;
import javax.swing.FocusManager;
import javax.swing.event.*;
```

```java
import java.util.*;
import java.awt.*;
import java.text.*;
import java.awt.event.*;

public class AlphaButtonFocusManager extends FocusManager {

    public void processKeyEvent(Component focusedComponent, KeyEvent event)
    {
        if (event.getKeyCode() == KeyEvent.VK_TAB) {
            // We are only interested in key presses, not key releases
            if (event.getID() != KeyEvent.KEY_PRESSED) {
                event.consume();
            } else {
                // If the user pressed SHIFT, then go to the previous
                // component. Otherwise, go to the next component.
                if ((event.getModifiers() & ActionEvent.SHIFT_MASK) ==
                    ActionEvent.SHIFT_MASK)
                    focusPreviousComponent(focusedComponent);
                else
                    focusNextComponent(focusedComponent);
                event.consume();
            }
        }
    }

    public void focusNextComponent(Component c) {

        Vector v = new Vector();
        Hashtable list = getAllComponentsAtThisLevel(c, v);
        String buttonText;

        if (list != null) {
            if (c instanceof JButton) {
                JButton button = (JButton)c;
                int currentIndex = v.indexOf(button.getText()) + 1;
                if (currentIndex >= v.size())
                    buttonText = (String)v.firstElement();
                else
                    buttonText = (String)v.elementAt(currentIndex);
                JButton b = (JButton)list.get(buttonText);
                b.grabFocus();
            }
        }
    }

    public void focusPreviousComponent(Component c) {

        Vector v = new Vector();
```

```
        Hashtable list = getAllComponentsAtThisLevel(c, v);
        String buttonText;

        if (list != null) {
            if (c instanceof JButton) {
                JButton button = (JButton)c;
                int currentIndex = v.indexOf(button.getText()) - 1;
                if (currentIndex < 0)
                    buttonText = (String)v.lastElement();
                else
                    buttonText = (String)v.elementAt(currentIndex);

                JButton b = (JButton)list.get(buttonText);
                b.grabFocus();

            }
        }
    }

    public Hashtable getAllComponentsAtThisLevel(Component c, Vector v)
    {
        Container cont = c.getParent();

        if (cont == null)
            return null;
        Hashtable h = new Hashtable();
        Component[] components = cont.getComponents();
        v.removeAllElements();

        for (int i = 0; i < components.length; i++) {
            if (components[i] instanceof JButton) {
                JButton button = (JButton)components[i];
                v.addElement(button.getText());
                h.put(button.getText(), button);
            }
        }
        sortVector(v);
        return h;
    }

    private void sortVector(Vector v) {

        Collator c = Collator.getInstance();
        int length = v.size();

        // Sort the vector of strings using a standard bubble sort
        for (int i = 0; i < length; i++) {
            for (int j = length-1; j >= i+1; j--) {
                if (c.compare((String)v.elementAt(j-1),
```

```
                                    (String)v.elementAt(j)) == 1) {
                String temp = (String)v.elementAt(j);
                v.setElementAt(v.elementAt(j-1), j);
                v.setElementAt(temp, j-1);
            }
        }
    }
}
}
```

The most important method in this class is `processKeyEvent()`. This method is responsible for transferring focus to the next (or previous) component if the user types TAB (or SHIFT-TAB). It tests the incoming event against the `VK_TAB` constant (defined in `java.awt.event.KeyEvent`), ignoring any events that don't include a tab. Ignoring these events lets them propagate back to the component, which may use them for keyboard actions, or may handle them in their own `processComponentKeyEvent()` classes. The focus manager consumes all key events that contain a TAB, preventing them from passing to other listeners.

`focusNextComponent()` and `focusPreviousComponent()` are very similar. They both call the helper method, `getAllComponentsAtThisLevel()`, to get a Hashtable containing all the `JButton` objects in the focus cycle and an alphabetically sorted `Vector` containing all the labels, which we use as keys into the hash table. (Another helper method, `sortVector()`, performs a textbook bubble sort.) With these, it's a simple matter to find the label of the current button in the `Vector v`, then find the next (or previous) label, and use the hash table to retrieve the matching buttons.

As we've implemented it, this approach has some shortcomings. The sorting algorithm is slow, but a bubble sort requires less code than anything faster. More to the point, our focus manager retrieves all the components in the focus cycle and sorts them whenever the focus changes. This is necessary—a new component can be added at any time, even between focus shifts. However, if you're working with a lot of components, you might want to cache the hash table and sorted vector. (You'd then want to listen for container events to figure out when to invalidate the cache.) The biggest shortcoming is that our focus manager only deals with `JButton` objects.

Here is a program that takes advantage of the new focus manager:

```
import java.awt.*;
import java.awt.event.*;

import javax.swing.FocusManager;
import javax.swing.*;
import javax.swing.border.*;
```

```
public class FocusManagerExample extends JPanel {

    public FocusManagerExample() {
        super();

        setLayout(new GridLayout(6, 1));

        JButton button1 = new JButton("Texas");
        JButton button2 = new JButton("Vermont");
        JButton button3 = new JButton("Florida");
        JButton button4 = new JButton("Alabama");
        JButton button5 = new JButton("Minnesota");
        JButton button6 = new JButton("California");

        FocusManager.setCurrentManager(new AlphaButtonFocusManager());

        button1.requestFocus();
        setBackground(Color.lightGray);

        add(button1);
        add(button2);
        add(button3);
        add(button4);
        add(button5);
        add(button6);
    }

    public static void main(String[] args)
    {
        JFrame frame = new JFrame("Alphabetized Button Focus Manager");
        frame.addWindowListener(new BasicWindowMonitor());
        frame.setContentPane(new FocusManagerExample());
        frame.setSize(200, 300);
        frame.setVisible(true);
    }
}
```

The only thing interesting in this example is the call to the static method setCur-
rentManager(), which installs our new focus manager. Figure 28-5 shows what
the program looks like.

Lightweight vs. Heavyweight Components

The issue of lightweight and heavyweight components has plagued Swing since its
early days. What has confused the majority of programmers from the start is the
idea of *z-order*, or layering, among the Swing lightweight components and the AWT
heavyweight components.

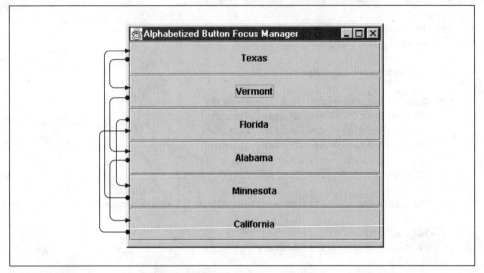

Figure 28-5. JButtons using the alphabetized button focus manager

Understanding the Z-Order

In Swing, it might help to think of a heavyweight component as an artist's easel. Recall that top-level components in Swing (JWindow, JDialog, JApplet, and JFrame) are heavyweight, everything else isn't. Lightweight components that are added to those top-level heavyweights can be thought of as drawings on the canvas of each easel. Therefore, if another heavyweight component (another easel) is moved in front of the original easel, or even attached to it, the lightweight paintings on the original easel are obscured; Figure 28-6 demonstrates this analogy.

The same is true for how Swing interprets the z-order of lightweight and heavyweight components, even in a container. If a heavyweight component is added to a container that has lightweight components, the heavyweight will always be on top; the lightweight components must share the same z-order as the parent container. In addition, lightweight components cannot draw themselves outside the container (easel) they reside in, or they will be clipped.

Mixing Swing and AWT

Our first bit of advice is: *don't do it.* If you can get around mixing the two solely with lightweight components, then you'll save yourself a mountain of testing grief. Okay, that being said, let's discuss some of the common problems that you're likely to run into if you decide to make the attempt.

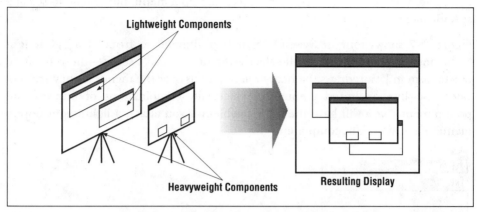

Figure 28-6. Consider heavyweight components as easels and lightweight components as drawings

Overlapping Heavyweight and Lightweight Components

As we mentioned above, the heavyweight component will always display itself on top, no matter what the intended z-order is. The basic strategy is to ensure that lightweight components and heavyweight components in the same container do not overlap. On that note, Table 28-6 shows a list of layout managers and panes that can and cannot be used to mix lightweight and heavyweight components.

Table 28-6. Heavyweight-Friendly Swing Layout Managers and Panes

Layout Manager	Can Be Used to Mix Heavyweight and Lightweight?
BoxLayout	Yes
OverlayLayout	No
BorderLayout	Yes
GridLayout	Yes
GridBagLayout	Yes
FlowLayout	Yes
CardLayout	Yes
JLayeredPane	No
JScrollPane	No
JSplitPane	Yes
JTabbedPane	Yes

Heavyweight Components in Front of Lightweight Menus

This is another (somewhat comical) Swing and AWT problem. Heavyweight components are always drawn in front of lightweight menus. While the menu bar is usually not disturbed, any menus that are drawn are placed *behind* the component. Hence, a user may be able to bring up a menu, but unable to select a specific menu item.

Figure 28-7 shows four heavyweight panels positioned in front of a lightweight "Edit" menu. While you can still select a menu, you can't see it—the repainting mechanism in Java redraws the heavyweight panels over the menus as they are activated. Because anchored menus are essentially combinations of buttons and popup menus, you will have the same problem if you attach a lightweight popup menu to a heavyweight component.

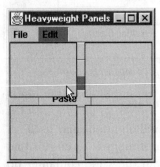

Figure 28-7. Lightweight menus obscured by heavyweight panels

Popups

Popup components are easy targets for these problems. Popup components include elements found in Swing menus, popup menus, and combo boxes. These components get into trouble because they may be called upon to display themselves outside the confines of their heavyweight top-level container. For example, if you activate a popup menu in a component near the bottom of a JFrame, the popup might extend beyond the bottom of the frame when it is raised. If this is the case, then it cannot be rendered using a lightweight component; if it is, it will be clipped against the container boundary.

Swing knows that if this is the case, it can use a heavyweight AWT Window to display the popup instead. However, what if you need to include a heavyweight component inside a container in which popups will be used? Fortunately, popup components in Swing contain a property that allows them to switch from lightweight to heavyweight to display themselves. Incidentally, this is a type of behavior that you may wish to mimic if you create your own popup components.

This single boolean property is called lightWeightPopupEnabled. It can be set to true or false, depending on how you want Swing to display the component. If lightWeightPopupEnabled is true, the component uses a lightweight component to display itself if it is wholly contained inside of a top-level component, and uses a Panel otherwise. If lightWeightPopupEnabled is false, the component uses either a heavyweight AWT `Panel` or a `Window` to display itself, depending on where the component will be displayed. Table 28-7 shows what type of component Swing will use in various scenarios.

Table 28-7. The lightWeightPopupEnabled Property

lightWeightPopupEnabled	Drawn Inside the Top-Level Container	Drawn Outside the Top-Level Container
true	Lightweight `Popup`	Heavyweight `Window`
false	Heavyweight `Panel`	Heavyweight `Window`

For example, you can get around the lightweight menu problem discussed earlier by setting the `lightWeightPopupEnabled` property to `false` on each of the popup portions of the menus:

```
JMenu menu = new JMenu("Edit");
menu.getPopupMenu().setLightWeightPopupEnabled(false);
```

Although there will be a noticeable flicker as the components struggle to repaint themselves, the menu should end up on the right side of the heavyweight component included in the container. If you plan to mix lightweight components and heavyweight components together, you should always set the `lightWeightPopup-Enabled` property for any popups in the application to `false`, including menus.

Heavyweight Components in JScrollPane

This is a common problem in Swing. What invariably happens is that the component inside the `JScrollPane` object fails to clip properly when it is placed inside the pane, and visible artifacts are easy to pick up. Stay as far away from this as you possibly can. Figure 28-8 shows the problem of placing heavyweight components in a `JScrollPane` object.

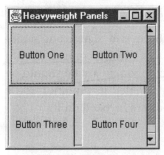

Figure 28-8. Placing a heavyweight component in a JScrollPane object

Heavyweight Components Inside of Internal Frames

This is also an inherently bad idea. The problem here is that internal frames can, by design, overlap. If an overlap occurs, and the internal frame with the heavyweight component is on bottom, the component will still be drawn on top of the overlapping internal frame. Figure 28-9 shows what happens when a heavyweight component in one internal frame overlaps an internal frame in another. Again, stay away from this type of scenario.

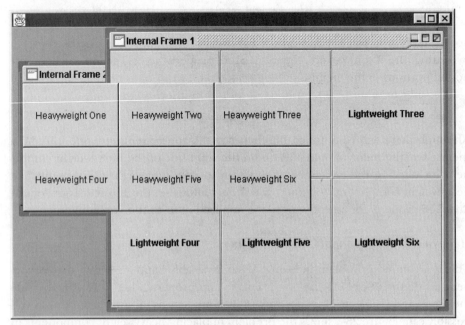

Figure 28-9. Using heavyweight components inside of an internal frame

Multithreading Issues with Swing

As we mentioned at the beginning of the book, there is a significant multithreading issue with Swing. The fundamental rule is this: once a component has signaled its intent to be repainted, all updates to the component's state should be done in the event dispatch thread. A component has signaled its intention to be painted or repainted when any of the following methods are invoked on it:

- `paint()`
- `setVisible(true)`
- `pack()`

While the last method, `pack()`, does not perform a repaint, it does invalidate a component, recalculating its size and modifying its dimensions accordingly.

By confining updates of the component state to the event dispatch thread, you keep changes in sync with the repainting requests of the `RepaintManager`, and avoid potential race conditions.

When Is Thread Safety an Issue?

It's important to understand when you need to worry about this and when you do not. In most situations, you'll be updating the state of your user interface in response to various user events. If this is the case, you can freely update your components, since your event-handling methods (in your listeners) will automatically be invoked in the event dispatch thread.

The only time you have to worry about updating the state of a Swing component is when the request for the update comes from some other thread. An example of such a situation would be events driven by some outside process responsible for notifying your application when something changes. For example, say you had a sports score ticker that showed the scores of a collection of games as they were being played. A separate server process might push new scores out to your client program. This program would have some sort of socket (or higher-level protocol) listener thread to handle the input from the server. This new data would need to be reflected in the user interface. At this point, you'd need to ensure that the updates were made in the event dispatch thread.

Another common scenario involves responding to a user request that may take a long period of time. Such requests might need to access a database, invoke a remote method on an RMI or CORBA object, load new Java classes, etc. In situations like these, the event-handling thread should not be held up while the lengthy processing takes place. If it was, the user interface would become completely unresponsive until the call completed. The preferred strategy is to execute the lengthy call in a separate thread and update the user interface when the call eventually returns.[*] Once again, this update will no longer be happening in the event dispatch thread, so we need to do something special to make this work.

Don't Be Fooled

You might think you'd be safe calling the various `fireXX()` methods defined by certain Swing components and models. However, it's important to remember that

---

[*] One strategy for implementing this type of call is to use a special "worker" thread responsible for executing the lengthy call and then updating the user interface. The Swing team provides a sample implementation of this idea in a class called `SwingWorker`. This class, as well as a discussion of its purpose, can be found on the Swing Connection at *http://java.sun.com/products/jfc/tsc*. We include a slightly simpler (but less reusable) example of the worker concept at the end of the chapter.

while these classes do create Event objects and send them to registered listeners, this does not imply that these events will automatically be executed in the event dispatch thread. In fact, the methods called on the listeners are invoked just like all other Java method calls; the argument just happens to be an event object. So, even if you're updating the user interface from another thread by firing some sort of event (perhaps to indicate that the model's state has changed), you still need to use the methods described below to ensure that the processing takes place in the event dispatch thread.)

Updating Components in the Event Dispatch Thread

Swing provides two methods that allow you to execute code in the event-dispatch thread. These are static methods, defined by SwingUtilities, called invoke-AndWait() and invokeLater(). Both of these methods allow you to execute an arbitrary block of code in the event dispatch thread. The invokeAndWait() method blocks until the code has completed executing, while invokeLater() just adds your code to the event queue and returns immediately.

You're probably wondering how Swing manages to add arbitrary code to the event queue. Here's how it works. Both of the methods we just mentioned take a single Runnable as a parameter. This Runnable may be defined to do whatever you want.* Typically, the Runnable's run() method performs some sort of update to the state of one or more components. When SwingUtilities receives the Runnable, it passes it on to a class called SystemEventQueueUtilities, which wraps it in an instance of a special AWTEvent subclass (a private inner class called SystemEventQueueUtilities.RunnableEvent) and adds the new event to the system event queue. When the event thread gets around to running the special event, the processing of the event results in the Runnable's run() method being executed.

Figure 28-10 shows a more detailed breakdown of what's going on under the hood. Once the event is posted to the system event queue, the call to invoke-Later() returns immediately. If this were an invokeAndWait() call, the calling thread would wait() until the event was executed, and then the processRunna-bleEvent() method would notify() the waiting thread that the Runnable had been executed. Only then would invokeAndWait() return. Note that System-EventQueueUtilities and its inner classes RunnableEvent and RunnableTarget are non-public. We show them here only to give you an understanding of what's going on behind the scenes. The EventQueue class is part of java.awt.

---

* Note that this Runnable is not going to be passed to a new Thread object. The Runnable interface is used here because it defines a single convenient run() method. The common association between Runnable and Thread does not apply here.

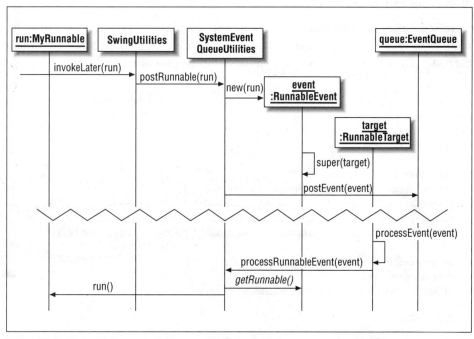

Figure 28-10. SwingUtilities.invokeLater() (under the hood)[a]

[a] The RunableTarget is a static field in the RunableEvent class, serving as an event source when processEvent() is called.

Methods

Here are the method signatures for the SwingUtilities methods we just described. The rest of the SwingUtilities class was described in the previous chapter.

public static void invokeAndWait(Runnable doRun)
   throws InterruptedException, InvocationTargetException
   Places a special event onto the system event queue. When processed, this event simply executes doRun's run() method. The invokeAndWait() call will not return until the run() method finishes. If the run() method throws an exception, it will be caught, and an InvocationTargetException will be thrown by invokeAndWait(). An InterruptedException is thrown if the execution of the Runnable's run() method is interrupted for any reason.

public static void invokeLater(Runnable doRun)
   Places a special event onto the system event queue. When processed, this event simply executes doRun's run() method. The invokeLater() call returns immediately after the event has been added to the queue. Note that any exceptions thrown by the Runnable's run() method will be caught and ignored.

Managing Synchronization Properly

Here is an example that shows three ways you might try to invoke a long-running method in response to a user-generated event. Only one of these strategies works correctly. The other two show the types of things you should avoid.

```java
// InvokeExample.java
//
import javax.swing.*;
import java.awt.*;
import java.awt.event.*;

public class InvokeExample {
  private static JButton good = new JButton("Good");
  private static JButton bad = new JButton("Bad");
  private static JButton bad2 = new JButton("Bad2");
  private static JLabel resultLabel = new JLabel("Ready", JLabel.CENTER);

  public static void main(String[] args) {
    JFrame f = new JFrame();
    f.addWindowListener(new BasicWindowMonitor());

    // Layout . . .
    JPanel p = new JPanel();
    p.setOpaque(true);
    p.setLayout(new FlowLayout());
    p.add(good);
    p.add(bad);
    p.add(bad2);

    Container c = f.getContentPane();
    c.setLayout(new BorderLayout());
    c.add(p, BorderLayout.CENTER);
    c.add(resultLabel, BorderLayout.SOUTH);

    // Listeners
    good.addActionListener(new ActionListener() {
      public void actionPerformed(ActionEvent ev) {
        resultLabel.setText("Working . . .");
        setEnabled(false);

        // We're going to do something that takes a long time, so we will
        // spin off a thread and update the display when we're done.
        Thread worker = new Thread() {
          public void run() {
            // something that takes a long time . . . in real life, this
            // might be a DB query, remote method invocation, etc.
            try {
              Thread.sleep(5000);
```

```
            }
            catch (InterruptedException ex) {}

            // report the result using invokeLater()
            SwingUtilities.invokeLater(new Runnable() {
              public void run() {
                resultLabel.setText("Ready");
                setEnabled(true);
              }
            });
          }
        };

      worker.start(); // so we don't hold up the dispatch thread
      }
    });

  bad.addActionListener(new ActionListener() {
    public void actionPerformed(ActionEvent ev) {
      resultLabel.setText("Working . . .");
      setEnabled(false);

      // We're going to do the same thing, but not in a separate thread.
      try {
        Thread.sleep(5000); // dispatch thread is starving!
      }
      catch (InterruptedException ex) {}

      // report the result
      resultLabel.setText("Ready");
      setEnabled(true);
    }
  });

  bad2.addActionListener(new ActionListener() {
    public void actionPerformed(ActionEvent ev) {
      resultLabel.setText("Working . . . ");
      setEnabled(false);

      // The wrong way to use invokeLater(). The runnable() shouldn't
      // starve the dispatch thread.
      SwingUtilities.invokeLater(new Runnable() {
        public void run() {
          try {
            Thread.sleep(5000); // dispatch thread is starving!
          }
          catch (InterruptedException ex) {}
```

```
                resultLabel.setText("Ready");
                setEnabled(true);
            }
        });
      }
    });

    f.setSize(300, 100);
    f.setVisible(true);
  }


  // allows us to turn the buttons on or off while we work.
  static void setEnabled(boolean b) {
    good.setEnabled(b);
    bad.setEnabled(b);
    bad2.setEnabled(b);
  }
}
```

In the first listener ("good"), we use a worker thread to execute our long-running process. In this new thread's run() method, we execute our code (in this case, just a sleep() call) and then use invokeLater() to update the display. This is the proper strategy.

In the next listener ("bad"), we show what happens if we run this code directly in the event listener. As you'd expect, any attempt to resize or repaint the display will fail while we have taken over the dispatch thread.

Finally, we show another incorrect attempt ("bad2"). In this case, we use invoke-Later(), but we use it incorrectly. The problem here is that our run() method takes a long time to execute. It's just as bad to have a long-running method in an invokeLater() call as it is to do it directly in your event listener code.

Figure 28-11 shows the display after clicking each of the three buttons and then covering part of the display with another window. In the first bad case, our label update and the disabling of the buttons doesn't even occur, since we never got back into the event queue to let those updates happen. In the second bad case, those things are able to occur before we put the dispatch thread to sleep, but we have still made a big mess of things by holding up the event queue.

When you run this example, try resizing the frame (or covering it with another window) to see how the different strategies perform. The key lesson here is that the system event queue uses a single thread to execute events, so any sort of long-running processing should always be kept out of the event queue.

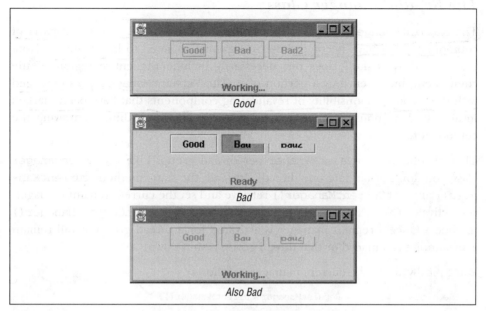

Figure 28-11. Correct and incorrect management of the event dispatch thread

Painting and Repainting

Our last topic in this chapter deals with repainting in Swing. Repainting is a somewhat arcane topic that most people don't really feel the need to talk about. This section is orchestrated to give you a better feel for how painting and repainting via the repaint manager and JComponent works. You typically do not need to get involved with the RepaintManager class, and only the extremely brave will override it. However, there are some instances where a firm understanding of the repaint manager can avoid confusion.

Swing Responsibilities

Recall that Swing uses lightweight components, which are drawn inside heavyweight top-level containers. Hence, the operating system will not deal with the repainting of those components. To continue the analogy first presented in the lightweight and heavyweight discussion earlier, Swing is responsible for painting and repainting everything inside of its own easels. Consequently, Swing delegates this duty to a RepaintManager class to organize and schedule repainting when told to do so.

The RepaintManager Class

The RepaintManager class is responsible for painting and repainting parts of components that have become *dirty*, or regions that need to be repainted. Note that the "dirty region" does not necessarily include the entire region of the component, but often only a portion of it. The RepaintManager is also charged with the second responsibility of revalidating components that have been marked invalid. Both responsibilities ultimately result in the same thing: redrawing the component.

There is only one RepaintManager per thread group. Like the FocusManager class, you don't instantiate one directly. Instead, the static methods currentManager() and setCurrentManager() retrieve and set the current repaint manager, respectively. (Note that there is no RepaintManager.getCurrentManager() method.) Once a repaint manager is activated for a thread group, it will remain active until it is replaced or that thread group is shut down.

You typically access the current manager as follows:

```
RepaintManager rm = RepaintManager.currentManager();
```

At the heart of the RepaintManager are two data structures: a Hashtable of component references and their rectangular regions that need to be repainted, and a Vector of invalidated components. You can add component regions to the hash table of dirty regions with the addDirtyRegion() method. Likewise, you can add a component to the invalidation vector with a call to addInvalidComponent(). If you wish to remove a component from the invalidation vector, you can remove it with a call to removeInvalidComponent().

Here are some important rules for working with the repaint manager:

- If a component has a dirty region on the repaint queue and another region from the same component is added, the repaint manager takes the rectangular union of the two sections. As a result, there is never more than one dirty region per component on the queue at any time.

- If a component has been invalidated with the addInvalidComponent() method, the RepaintManager invalidates the first ancestor of this component to return true for the isValidateRoot() method (typically a container). This has the desirable side effect of invalidating all the components below it.

- Repainting and revalidating are handled via *work requests*, which are Runnable objects sent to the system event queue. Only one work request is sent by the repaint manager at any time. Until it is completed, the repaint manager will wait before sending any more. This prevents the starvation of other tasks (such as event processing) on the system event queue.

You can get the current dirty region for each component by using the getDirty-Region() method. If you want to mark the entire component as "dirty," forcing a complete redraw on its next paint, use the markCompletelyDirty() method. You can check to see if an entire component's region is marked as dirty with the isCompletelyDirty() method. To remove a component's dirty region from the list, use the markCompletelyClean() method.

The RepaintManager class is equipped with a double-buffering mechanism, which it provides as a service to all JComponent objects. By default, it is enabled for all components that wish to take advantage of it. You can deactivate it at any time using the setDoubleBufferingEnabled() method. The maximum size of this double buffer is, by default, the size of the entire screen. However, you can reset the maximum size to less by calling the setDoubleBufferMaximumSize() method. To find out it's current setting, use the getDoubleBufferMaximum-Size() accessor.

Key Methods

The Swing repaint manager works closely with a few key methods in JComponent: paint(), repaint(), revalidate(), and paintImmediately(). A call to repaint() at the component level results in a region being added to the dirty list queue, and consequently, scheduled for repainting. This sets up a work request that is placed in the system event queue. Once the work request is processed, the current RepaintManager calls back to the paintImmediately() method of the component. This method finally renders the dirty portion of the component (without delay).

The revalidate() method in JComponent adds the component to the Repaint-Manager invalidation queue. At that point, the revalidation of the component and its ancestors, if necessary, is sent as a work request to the system event queue. Once the request has been processed, the method calls the validate() method of the original component (from java.awt.Container), which marks the component as valid again. Figure 28-12 shows the RepaintManager at work for both repainting dirty regions and revalidating invalid components.

Methods

public static RepaintManager currentManager(JComponent comp)
> Returns the current RepaintManager. If there isn't one available, Swing initializes one and sets it in use for this thread group.

public static void setCurrentManager(RepaintManager aRepaintManager)
> Sets the current RepaintManager for the invoker's thread group.

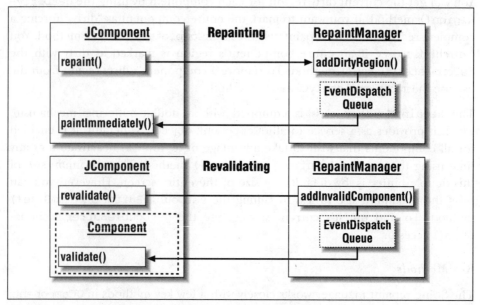

Figure 28-12. Repainting and revalidating with JComponent and RepaintManager

public void addInvalidComponent(JComponent invalidComponent)

Adds a component to the invalidation vector. The method searches for the first ancestor component that returns `true` for `isValidateRoot()` and queues a validation and repaint for that component, and consequently all components below it.

public void removeInvalidComponent(JComponent component)

Removes a component from the invalidation vector.

public synchronized void addDirtyRegion(JComponent c, int x, int y, int w, int h)

Adds a rectangular region for a specific component to the hash table of dirty regions that need to be repainted. If a rectangular region for that component already exists in the hash table, a rectangle that encompasses both regions is calculated and placed on this list to represent that component. There is always only one rectangular region for each component on the dirty-region list at any time.

public Rectangle getDirtyRegion(JComponent aComponent)

Returns the current dirty region for the component specified, or an empty `Rectangle` object if there is none.

public void markCompletelyDirty(JComponent aComponent)

Marks the component's entire width and height as dirty and adds it to the dirty region hash table.

public void markCompletelyClean(JComponent aComponent)

Removes any references to the component in the dirty-region hash table.

public boolean isCompletelyDirty(JComponent aComponent)

Indicates whether the entire component has been placed on the dirty list. If the method returns true, the entire component will be repainted on the next call to paintDirtyRegions().

public void validateInvalidComponents()

Marks all components that have been placed on the invalidation vector as valid.

public void paintDirtyRegions()

Forces each of the dirty regions to immediately repaint themselves. A call to this method is typically placed within a Runnable section of code and inserted into the system event queue.

public String toString()

Dumps a string-based state of the current RepaintManager to the system output.

public Image getOffscreenBuffer(Component c, int proposedWidth, int proposedHeight)

Returns an offscreen Image that can be used as a double buffer. The size of the double buffer is typically set to the proposed width and height passed in, unless it violates a preset maximum buffer size.

public void setDoubleBufferMaximumSize(java.awt.Dimension d)

Sets the maximum size of the RepaintManager object's offscreen drawing buffer.

public Dimension getDoubleBufferMaximumSize()

Retrieves the maximum size of the RepaintManager object's offscreen drawing buffer.

public void setDoubleBufferingEnabled(boolean aFlag)

Activates or deactivates the double buffering mechanism for the objects.

public boolean isDoubleBufferingEnabled()

Returns a boolean indicating whether the double buffering mechanism is enabled for this RepaintManager object.

A

Look & Feel Resources

Table A-1 shows a complete list of the component UI resources (showing the resource name and its expected value type) defined by the `BasicLookAndFeel`. Application-wide changes can be made to these properties using `UIManager.put()`. For example, the following line would cause all `JButtons` instantiated after this call to be created with a background color of black:

```
UIManager.put("Button.background", Color.black);
```

Alternately, a custom look-and-feel typically defines values for many of these properties in its `initComponentDefaults()` method. In this case, most resource values should be tagged as `UIResources`. For more information, see Chapter 26, *Look & Feel*.

Table A-1. Swing PLAF Resources

ResourceName	Type
Button.background	Color
Button.border	Border
Button.font	Font
Button.foreground	Color
Button.margin	Insets
Button.textIconGap	Integer
Button.textShiftOffset	Integer
CheckBox.background	Color
CheckBox.border	Border
CheckBox.font	Font
CheckBox.foreground	Color
CheckBox.icon	Icon
CheckBox.margin	Insets

Table A-1. Swing PLAF Resources (continued)

ResourceName	Type
CheckBox.textIconGap	Integer
CheckBox.textShiftOffset	Integer
CheckBoxMenuItem.acceleratorFont	Font
CheckBoxMenuItem.acceleratorForeground	Color
CheckBoxMenuItem.acceleratorSelectionForeground	Color
CheckBoxMenuItem.arrowIcon	Icon
CheckBoxMenuItem.background	Color
CheckBoxMenuItem.border	Border
CheckBoxMenuItem.borderPainted	Boolean
CheckBoxMenuItem.checkIcon	Icon
CheckBoxMenuItem.disabledForeground	Color
CheckBoxMenuItem.font	Font
CheckBoxMenuItem.foreground	Color
CheckBoxMenuItem.margin	Insets
CheckBoxMenuItem.selectionBackground	Color
CheckBoxMenuItem.selectionForeground	Color
ColorChooser.background	Color
ColorChooser.font	Font
ColorChooser.foreground	Color
ColorChooser.selectedColorBorder	Border
ComboBox.background	Color
ComboBox.disabledBackground	Color
ComboBox.disabledForeground	Color
ComboBox.font	Font
ComboBox.foreground	Color
ComboBox.selectedBackground	Color
ComboBox.selectedForeground	Color
Desktop.background	Color
DesktopIcon.border	internalFrameBorder
EditorPane.background	Color
EditorPane.border	Border
EditorPane.caretForeground	Color
EditorPane.font	Font
EditorPane.foreground	Color
EditorPane.inactiveForeground	Color
EditorPane.keyBindings	JTextComponent.KeyBinding[]
EditorPane.margin	Insets
EditorPane.selectionBackground	Color
EditorPane.selectionForeground	Color

Table A-1. Swing PLAF Resources (continued)

ResourceName	Type
FileChooser.acceptAllFileFilterText	String
FileChooser.cancelButtonText	String
FileChooser.cancelButtonToolTipText	String
FileChooser.detailsViewIcon	Icon
FileChooser.helpButtonText	String
FileChooser.helpButtonToolTipText	String
FileChooser.homeFolderIcon	Icon
FileChooser.listViewIcon	Icon
FileChooser.newFolderIcon	Icon
FileChooser.openButtonText	String
FileChooser.openButtonToolTipText	String
FileChooser.saveButtonText	String
FileChooser.saveButtonToolTipText	String
FileChooser.upFolderIcon	Icon
FileChooser.updateButtonText	String
FileChooser.updateButtonToolTipText	String
FileView.computerIcon	Icon
FileView.directoryIcon	Icon
FileView.fileIcon	Icon
FileView.floppyDriveIcon	Icon
FileView.hardDriveIcon	Icon
InternalFrame.activeTitleBackground	Color
InternalFrame.activeTitleForeground	Color
InternalFrame.border	Border
InternalFrame.closeIcon	Icon
InternalFrame.icon	Icon
InternalFrame.iconifyIcon	Icon
InternalFrame.inactiveTitleBackground	Color
InternalFrame.inactiveTitleForeground	Color
InternalFrame.maximizeIcon	Icon
InternalFrame.minimizeIcon	Icon
InternalFrame.titleFont	Font
Label.background	Color
Label.border	Border
Label.disabledForeground	Color
Label.disabledShadow	Color
Label.font	Font
Label.foreground	Color
List.background	Color

Table A-1. Swing PLAF Resources (continued)

ResourceName	Type
List.border	Border
List.cellRenderer	ListCellRenderer
List.focusCellHighlightBorder	Border
List.font	Font
List.foreground	Color
List.selectionBackground	Color
List.selectionForeground	Color
Menu.acceleratorFont	Font
Menu.acceleratorForeground	Color
Menu.acceleratorSelectionForeground	Color
Menu.arrowIcon	Icon
Menu.background	Color
Menu.border	Border
Menu.borderPainted	Boolean
Menu.checkIcon	Icon
Menu.disabledForeground	Color
Menu.font	Font
Menu.foreground	Color
Menu.margin	Insets
Menu.selectionBackground	Color
Menu.selectionForeground	Color
MenuBar.background	Color
MenuBar.border	Border
MenuBar.font	Font
MenuBar.foreground	Color
MenuItem.acceleratorFont	Font
MenuItem.acceleratorForeground	Color
MenuItem.acceleratorSelectionForeground	Color
MenuItem.arrowIcon	Icon
MenuItem.background	Color
MenuItem.border	Border
MenuItem.borderPainted	Boolean
MenuItem.checkIcon	Icon
MenuItem.disabledForeground	Color
MenuItem.font	Font
MenuItem.foreground	Color
MenuItem.margin	Insets
MenuItem.selectionBackground	Color
MenuItem.selectionForeground	Color

Table A-1. Swing PLAF Resources (continued)

ResourceName	Type
OptionPane.background	Color
OptionPane.border	Border
OptionPane.buttonAreaBorder	Border
OptionPane.errorIcon	Icon
OptionPane.font	Font
OptionPane.foreground	Color
OptionPane.informationIcon	Icon
OptionPane.messageAreaBorder	Border
OptionPane.messageForeground	Color
OptionPane.minimumSize	Dimension
OptionPane.questionIcon	Icon
OptionPane.warningIcon	Icon
Panel.background	Color
Panel.font	Font
Panel.foreground	Color
PasswordField.background	Color
PasswordField.border	Border
PasswordField.caretBlinkRate	Integer
PasswordField.caretForeground	Color
PasswordField.font	Font
PasswordField.foreground	Color
PasswordField.inactiveForeground	Color
PasswordField.keyBindings	JTextComponent.KeyBinding[]
PasswordField.margin	Insets
PasswordField.selectionBackground	Color
PasswordField.selectionForeground	Color
PopupMenu.background	Color
PopupMenu.border	Border
PopupMenu.font	Font
PopupMenu.foreground	Color
ProgressBar.background	Color
ProgressBar.border	Border
ProgressBar.cellLength	Integer
ProgressBar.cellSpacing	Integer
ProgressBar.font	Font
ProgressBar.foreground	Color
ProgressBar.selectionBackground	Color
ProgressBar.selectionForeground	Color
RadioButton.background	Color

Table A-1. Swing PLAF Resources (continued)

ResourceName	Type
RadioButton.border	Border
RadioButton.font	Font
RadioButton.foreground	Color
RadioButton.icon	Icon
RadioButton.margin	Insets
RadioButton.textIconGap	Integer
RadioButton.textShiftOffset	Integer
RadioButtonMenuItem.acceleratorFont	Font
RadioButtonMenuItem.acceleratorForeground	Color
RadioButtonMenuItem.acceleratorSelectionForeground	Color
RadioButtonMenuItem.arrowIcon	Icon
RadioButtonMenuItem.background	Color
RadioButtonMenuItem.border	Border
RadioButtonMenuItem.borderPainted	Boolean
RadioButtonMenuItem.checkIcon	Icon
RadioButtonMenuItem.disabledForeground	Color
RadioButtonMenuItem.font	Font
RadioButtonMenuItem.foreground	Color
RadioButtonMenuItem.margin	Insets
RadioButtonMenuItem.selectionBackground	Color
RadioButtonMenuItem.selectionForeground	Color
ScrollBar.background	Color
ScrollBar.border	Border
ScrollBar.foreground	Color
ScrollBar.maximumThumbSize	Dimension
ScrollBar.minimumThumbSize	Dimension
ScrollBar.thumb	Color
ScrollBar.thumbDarkShadow	Color
ScrollBar.thumbHighlight	Color
ScrollBar.thumbLightShadow	Color
ScrollBar.track	Color
ScrollBar.trackHighlight	Color
ScrollPane.background	Color
ScrollPane.border	Border
ScrollPane.font	Font
ScrollPane.foreground	Color
ScrollPane.viewportBorder	Border
Separator.highlight	Color
Separator.shadow	Color

Table A-1. Swing PLAF Resources (continued)

ResourceName	Type
Slider.background	Color
Slider.border	Border
Slider.focus	Color
Slider.focusInsets	Insets
Slider.foreground	Color
Slider.highlight	Color
Slider.shadow	Color
SplitPane.background	Color
SplitPane.border	Border
SplitPane.dividerSize	Integer
SplitPane.highlight	Color
SplitPane.shadow	Color
TabbedPane.background	Color
TabbedPane.contentBorderInsets	Insets
TabbedPane.darkShadow	Color
TabbedPane.focus	Color
TabbedPane.font	Font
TabbedPane.foreground	Color
TabbedPane.highlight	Color
TabbedPane.iconSpacing	Integer
TabbedPane.lightHighlight	Color
TabbedPane.selectedTabPadInsets	Insets
TabbedPane.tabAreaInsets	Insets
TabbedPane.tabInsets	Insets
TabbedPane.tabRunOverlay	Integer
TabbedPane.tabShadow	Color
Table.focusCellBackground	Color
Table.focusCellForeground	Color
Table.focusCellHighlightBorder	Border
Table.font	Font
Table.foreground	Color
Table.gridColor	Color
Table.scrollPaneBorder	Border
Table.selectionBackground	Color
Table.selectionForeground	Color
Table.shadow	Color
TableHeader.background	Color
TableHeader.cellBorder	Border
TableHeader.font	Font

Table A-1. Swing PLAF Resources (continued)

ResourceName	Type
TableHeader.foreground	Color
TextArea.background	Color
TextArea.border	Border
TextArea.caretBlinkRate	Integer
TextArea.caretForeground	Color
TextArea.font	Font
TextArea.foreground	Color
TextArea.inactiveForeground	Color
TextArea.keyBindings	JTextComponent.KeyBinding[]
TextArea.margin	Insets
TextArea.selectionBackground	Color
TextArea.selectionForeground	Color
TextField.background	Color
TextField.border	Border
TextField.caretBlinkRate	Integer
TextField.caretForeground	Color
TextField.font	Font
TextField.foreground	Color
TextField.inactiveForeground	Color
TextField.keyBindings	JTextComponent.KeyBinding[]
TextField.margin	Insets
TextField.selectionBackground	Color
TextField.selectionForeground	Color
TextPane.background	Color
TextPane.border	Border
TextPane.caretForeground	Color
TextPane.font	Font
TextPane.foreground	Color
TextPane.inactiveForeground	Color
TextPane.keyBindings	JTextComponent.KeyBinding[]
TextPane.margin	Insets
TextPane.selectionBackground	Color
TextPane.selectionForeground	Color
TitledBorder.border	Border
TitledBorder.font	Font
TitledBorder.titleColor	Color
ToggleButton.background	Color
ToggleButton.border	Border
ToggleButton.font	Font

Table A-1. Swing PLAF Resources (continued)

ResourceName	Type
ToggleButton.foreground	Color
ToggleButton.margin	Insets
ToggleButton.textIconGap	Integer
ToggleButton.textShiftOffset	Integer
ToolBar.background	Color
ToolBar.border	Border
ToolBar.dockingBackground	Color
ToolBar.dockingForeground	Color
ToolBar.floatingBackground	Color
ToolBar.floatingForeground	Color
ToolBar.font	Font
ToolBar.foreground	Color
ToolBar.separatorSize	Dimension
ToolTip.background	Color
ToolTip.border	Border
ToolTip.font	Font
ToolTip.foreground	Color
Tree.background	Color
Tree.closedIcon	Icon
Tree.collapsedIcon	Icon
Tree.editorBorder	Border
Tree.expandedIcon	Icon
Tree.font	Font
Tree.foreground	Color
Tree.hash	Color
Tree.leafIcon	Icon
Tree.leftChildIndent	Integer
Tree.openIcon	Icon
Tree.rightChildIndent	Integer
Tree.rowHeight	Integer
Tree.scrollsOnExpand	Boolean
Tree.selectionBackground	Color
Tree.selectionBorderColor	Color
Tree.selectionForeground	Color
Tree.textForeground	Color
Tree.textBackground	Color
Viewport.background	Color
Viewport.font	Font
Viewport.foreground	Color

Index

About the Authors

Robert Eckstein enjoys dabbling with just about anything related to computers. Most of his friends agree, from rendering to electronic commerce to compiler construction to fuzzy logic, that Robert spends far too much time in front of a computer screen.

Unknowingly dubbed "JavaBob" by his managers, Robert strives to learn as much about Java as possible. This makes him the world's largest consumer of caffeine. He is currently working on a book about Java Commerce for O'Reilly & Associates, and in his spare time he has been known to provide online coverage for popular conferences.

Robert holds bachelor's degrees in computer science and communications from Trinity University. In the past, he has worked for the USAA insurance company and more recently spent four years with Motorola's cellular software division. He now lives in Austin, Texas, with his new wife, Michelle. They hope to adopt a talking puppy soon.

Marc Loy is a senior programmer at Galileo Systems, LLC, but his day job seems to be teaching Java and Perl to various companies—including Sun Microsystems. He has played with Java since the alpha days and can't find his way back to C. He is developing an interactive learning application at Galileo written entirely in Java. He received his master's degree in computer science at the University of Wisconsin–Madison, and still lives in Madison with his partner, Ron Becker. He does find time to relax by playing the piano and/or throwing darts, depending on how successful the day of teaching or programming was.

Dave Wood is a Java architect with the Sun Java Center in Denver, Colorado, where he has helped design and implement Java solutions for customers around the world. His B.S. and M.S. degrees are in computer science from the University of Colorado. He has been involved in object-oriented design and development his entire career, and has been obsessed with Java since its early days. When he's not in front of a keyboard, Dave enjoys taking advantage of the beautiful Colorado scenery by camping, kayaking (just lakes, not whitewater), or hiking the Colorado 14ers (the 54 mountains over 14,000 feet, for all you flatlanders). He also enjoys playing chess and spending time with his wife, Shannon (the "real" architect of the family), and two cats, Pussin and Toast.

Colophon

Our look is the result of reader comments, our own experimentation, and feedback from distribution channels. Distinctive covers complement our distinctive approach to technical topics, breathing personality and life into potentially dry subjects.

The image on the cover of *Java Swing* is a 1949 Seeburg, Wall-O-Matic 110A, Table Top Jukebox.

The cover was designed by Hanna Dyer using a series design by Edie Freedman. The cover layout was produced with QuarkXPress 3.3 using the Bodoni Black font from URW Software and Bodoni BT Bold Italic from Bitstream. The inside layout was designed by Nancy Priest. Text was produced in FrameMaker 5.5 using a template implemented by Mike Sierra. The heading font is Bodoni BT; the text font is New Baskerville. The illustrations that appear in the book were created in Macromedia Freehand 7 and Adobe Photoshop 4 by Robert Romano.

Whenever possible, our books use a durable and flexible lay-flat binding, either RepKover™ or Otabind™. If the pagecount exceeds this type of binding's limit, perfect binding is used.

 # More Titles from O'Reilly

Java

Java in a Nutshell, DELUXE EDITION

By David Flanagan, et al.
1st Edition June 1997
628 pages, includes CD-ROM & book
ISBN 1-56592-304-9

Java in a Nutshell, Deluxe Edition, brings together on CD-ROM five volumes for Java developers and programmers, linking related info across books. *Exploring Java, 2nd Edition*, covers Java basics. *Java Language Reference, 2nd Edition, Java Fundamental Classes Reference*, and *Java AWT Reference* provide a definitive set of documentation on the Java language and the Java 1.1 core API. *Java in a Nutshell, 2nd Edition*, our bestselling quick reference, is included both on the CD-ROM and in a companion desktop edition. This deluxe library is an indispensable resource for anyone doing serious programming with Java 1.1.

Java Cryptography

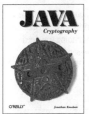

By Jonathan B. Knudsen
1st Edition May 1998
362 pages, ISBN 1-56592-402-9

Java Cryptography teaches you how to write secure programs using Java's cryptographic tools. It includes thorough discussions of the java.security package and the Java Cryptography Extensions (JCE), showing you how to use security providers and even implement your own provider. It discusses authentication, key management, public and private key encryption, and includes a secure talk application that encrypts all data sent over the network. If you work with sensitive data, you'll find this book indispensable.

Java in a Nutshell, Second Edition

By David Flanagan
2nd Edition May 1997
628 pages, ISBN 1-56592-262-X

This second edition of the bestselling Java book describes all the classes in the Java 1.1 API, with the exception of the still-evolving Enterprise APIs. And it still has all the great features that have made this the Java book most often recommended on the Internet: practical real-world examples and compact reference information. It's the only quick reference you'll need.

Java Security

By Scott Oaks
1st Edition May 1998
474 pages, ISBN 1-56592-403-7

This essential Java 1.2 book covers Java's security mechanisms and teaches you how to work with them. It discusses class loaders, security managers, access lists, digital signatures, and authentication and shows how to use these to create and enforce your own security policy.

Java Virtual Machine

By Jon Meyer & Troy Downing
1st Edition March 1997
452 pages, includes diskette
ISBN 1-56592-194-1

This book is a comprehensive programming guide for the Java Virtual Machine (JVM). It gives readers a strong overview and reference of the JVM so that they may create their own implementations of the JVM or write their own compilers that create Java object code. A Java assembler is provided with the book, so the examples can all be compiled and executed.

Java Network Programming

By Elliotte Rusty Harold
1st Edition February 1997
442 pages, ISBN 1-56592-227-1

The network is the soul of Java. Most of what is new and exciting about Java centers around the potential for new kinds of dynamic, networked applications. *Java Network Programming* teaches you to work with Sockets, write network clients and servers, and gives you an advanced look at the new areas like multicasting, using the server API, and RMI. Covers Java 1.1.

O'REILLY®

TO ORDER: **800-998-9938** • *order@oreilly.com* • *http://www.oreilly.com/*

OUR PRODUCTS ARE AVAILABLE AT A BOOKSTORE OR SOFTWARE STORE NEAR YOU.

FOR INFORMATION: **800-998-9938** • **707-829-0515** • *info@oreilly.com*

Java

How to stay in touch with O'Reilly

1. Visit Our Award-Winning Web Site

http://www.oreilly.com/

★ "Top 100 Sites on the Web" —*PC Magazine*
★ "Top 5% Web sites" —*Point Communications*
★ "3-Star site" —*The McKinley Group*

Our web site contains a library of comprehensive product information (including book excerpts and tables of contents), downloadable software, background articles, interviews with technology leaders, links to relevant sites, book cover art, and more. File us in your Bookmarks or Hotlist!

2. Join Our Email Mailing Lists

New Product Releases

To receive automatic email with brief descriptions of all new O'Reilly products as they are released, send email to:
listproc@online.oreilly.com
Put the following information in the first line of your message (*not* in the Subject field):
subscribe oreilly-news

O'Reilly Events

If you'd also like us to send information about trade show events, special promotions, and other O'Reilly events, send email to:
listproc@online.oreilly.com
Put the following information in the first line of your message (*not* in the Subject field):
subscribe oreilly-events

3. Get Examples from Our Books via FTP

There are two ways to access an archive of example files from our books:

Regular FTP

- ftp to:
  ftp.oreilly.com
  (login: anonymous
  password: your email address)
- Point your web browser to:
  ftp://ftp.oreilly.com/

FTPMAIL

- Send an email message to:
  ftpmail@online.oreilly.com
  (Write "help" in the message body)

4. Contact Us via Email

order@oreilly.com
To place a book or software order online. Good for North American and international customers.

subscriptions@oreilly.com
To place an order for any of our newsletters or periodicals.

books@oreilly.com
General questions about any of our books.

software@oreilly.com
For general questions and product information about our software. Check out O'Reilly Software Online at **http://software.oreilly.com/** for software and technical support information. Registered O'Reilly software users send your questions to: **website-support@oreilly.com**

cs@oreilly.com
For answers to problems regarding your order or our products.

booktech@oreilly.com
For book content technical questions or corrections.

proposals@oreilly.com
To submit new book or software proposals to our editors and product managers.

international@oreilly.com
For information about our international distributors or translation queries. For a list of our distributors outside of North America check out:
http://www.oreilly.com/www/order/country.html

O'Reilly & Associates, Inc.
101 Morris Street, Sebastopol, CA 95472 USA
TEL   707-829-0515 or 800-998-9938
        (6am to 5pm PST)
FAX   707-829-0104

International Distributors

UK, EUROPE, MIDDLE EAST AND AFRICA (EXCEPT FRANCE, GERMANY, AUSTRIA, SWITZERLAND, LUXEMBOURG, LIECHTENSTEIN, AND EASTERN EUROPE)

INQUIRIES
O'Reilly UK Limited
4 Castle Street
Farnham
Surrey, GU9 7HS
United Kingdom
Telephone: 44-1252-711776
Fax: 44-1252-734211
Email: josette@oreilly.com

ORDERS
Wiley Distribution Services Ltd.
1 Oldlands Way
Bognor Regis
West Sussex PO22 9SA
United Kingdom
Telephone: 44-1243-779777
Fax: 44-1243-820250
Email: cs-books@wiley.co.uk

FRANCE

ORDERS
GEODIF
61, Bd Saint-Germain
75240 Paris Cedex 05, France
Tel: 33-1-44-41-46-16 (French books)
Tel: 33-1-44-41-11-87 (English books)
Fax: 33-1-44-41-11-44
Email: distribution@eyrolles.com

INQUIRIES
Éditions O'Reilly
18 rue Séguier
75006 Paris, France
Tel: 33-1-40-51-52-30
Fax: 33-1-40-51-52-31
Email: france@editions-oreilly.fr

GERMANY, SWITZERLAND, AUSTRIA, EASTERN EUROPE, LUXEMBOURG, AND LIECHTENSTEIN

INQUIRIES & ORDERS
O'Reilly Verlag
Balthasarstr. 81
D-50670 Köln
Germany
Telephone: 49-221-973160-91
Fax: 49-221-973160-8
Email: anfragen@oreilly.de (inquiries)
Email: order@oreilly.de (orders)

CANADA (FRENCH LANGUAGE BOOKS)

Les Éditions Flammarion ltée
375, Avenue Laurier Ouest
Montréal (Québec) H2V 2K3
Tel: 00-1-514-277-8807
Fax: 00-1-514-278-2085
Email: info@flammarion.qc.ca

HONG KONG

City Discount Subscription Service, Ltd.
Unit D, 3rd Floor, Yan's Tower
27 Wong Chuk Hang Road
Aberdeen, Hong Kong
Tel: 852-2580-3539
Fax: 852-2580-6463
Email: citydis@ppn.com.hk

KOREA

Hanbit Media, Inc.
Sonyoung Bldg. 202
Yeksam-dong 736-36
Kangnam-ku
Seoul, Korea
Tel: 822-554-9610
Fax: 822-556-0363
Email: hant93@chollian.dacom.co.kr

PHILIPPINES

Mutual Books, Inc.
429-D Shaw Boulevard
Mandaluyong City, Metro
Manila, Philippines
Tel: 632-725-7538
Fax: 632-721-3056
Email: mbikikog@mnl.sequel.net

TAIWAN

O'Reilly Taiwan
No. 3, Lane 131
Hang-Chow South Road
Section 1, Taipei, Taiwan
Tel: 886-2-23968990
Fax: 886-2-23968916
Email: benh@oreilly.com

CHINA

O'Reilly Beijing
Room 2410
160, FuXingMenNeiDaJie
XiCheng District
Beijing, China PR 100031
Tel: 86-10-86631006
Fax: 86-10-86631007
Email: frederic@oreilly.com

INDIA

Computer Bookshop (India) Pvt. Ltd.
190 Dr. D.N. Road, Fort
Bombay 400 001 India
Tel: 91-22-207-0989
Fax: 91-22-262-3551
Email: cbsbom@giasbm01.vsnl.net.in

JAPAN

O'Reilly Japan, Inc.
Kiyoshige Building 2F
12-Bancho, Sanei-cho
Shinjuku-ku
Tokyo 160-0008 Japan
Tel: 81-3-3356-5227
Fax: 81-3-3356-5261
Email: japan@oreilly.com

ALL OTHER ASIAN COUNTRIES

O'Reilly & Associates, Inc.
101 Morris Street
Sebastopol, CA 95472 USA
Tel: 707-829-0515
Fax: 707-829-0104
Email: order@oreilly.com

AUSTRALIA

WoodsLane Pty., Ltd.
7/5 Vuko Place
Warriewood NSW 2102
Australia
Tel: 61-2-9970-5111
Fax: 61-2-9970-5002
Email: info@woodslane.com.au

NEW ZEALAND

Woodslane New Zealand, Ltd.
21 Cooks Street (P.O. Box 575)
Waganui, New Zealand
Tel: 64-6-347-6543
Fax: 64-6-345-4840
Email: info@woodslane.com.au

LATIN AMERICA

McGraw-Hill Interamericana
Editores, S.A. de C.V.
Cedro No. 512
Col. Atlampa
06450, Mexico, D.F.
Tel: 52-5-547-6777
Fax: 52-5-547-3336
Email: mcgraw-hill@infosel.net.mx

O'REILLY®